CW00923759

The Songwriting Secrets *Of* The Beatles

Dominic Pedler

OMNIBUS PRESS

LONDON / NEW YORK / PARIS / SYDNEY / COPENHAGEN / BERLIN / MADRID / TOKYO

To Jane and Milo

Commissioning and Project Editor: James Sleigh
Music typesetting: Digital Music Art
Cover design: Phil Gambrill
Proof-reader: Sarah Lavelle
Rights clearance: Michelle Hills/Sarah Holcroft
Picture research: Nikki Lloyd

Exclusive Distributors
Music Sales Limited,
14/15 Berners Street,
London W1T 3LJ.

Music Sales Corporation,
180 Madison Avenue, 24th Floor,
New York, NY 10016, USA.

Macmillan Distribution Services,
56 Parkwest Drive,
Derrimut, Vic 3030,
Australia.

Typeset by Phoenix Photosetting, Chatham, Kent.

Printed in the EU

A catalogue record for this book is available from the British Library.

Contents

Copyright details

All songs:
Words & music by John Lennon & Paul McCartney

Except:

A Taste Of Honey
Words by Ric Marlow
Music by Bobby Scott

A Whiter Shade Of Pale
Words by Keith Reid
Music by Gary Brooker

Ain't She Sweet
Words by Jack Yellen
Music by Milton Ager

All Around The World
Words & Music by Noel Gallagher

Copyright details

All My Trials
Traditional, arranged by Joan Baez
© Copyright 1960 Chandos Music Company, USA.
Carlin Music Corporation, Iron Bridge House, 3 Bridge Approach, London NW1.
All Rights Reserved. International Copyright Secured.

Anna (Go To Him)
Words & Music by Arthur Alexander
© Copyright 1962 Painted Desert Music Corporation, USA.
Shapiro Bernstein & Company Limited, 8/9 Frith Street, London W1 for the British Commonwealth (excluding Canada and Australia) and the Republic of Ireland.
All Rights Reserved. International Copyright Secured.

Answer Me (Mutterlein)
Music by Gerhard Winkler
Original Words by Fred Rauch
English Words by Carl Sigman
© Copyright 1952 Papageno Verlag Hans Sikorski, Germany.
© Copyright 1953 Bourne Incorporated, USA.
Bourne Music Limited.
All Rights Reserved. International Copyright Secured.

Baby, It's You
Words & Music by Hal David, Burt Bacharach & Barney Williams
© Copyright 1961 New Hidden Valley Music Company/Harry Von Tilzer Music Publishing Company/EMI Unart Catalog Incorporated, USA.
Windswept Pacific Music Limited, Hope House, 40 St. Peter's Road, London W6 (33.33%)/Universal Music Publishing Limited, 77 Fulham Palace Road, London W6 (33.34%)/EMI United Partnership Limited, print rights controlled by Warner Bros. Publications Incorporated/IMP Limited (33.33%).
All Rights Reserved. International Copyright Secured.

Bésame Mucho
Original Words & Music by Consuelo Velazquez
English Words by Sunny Skylar
© Copyright 1941 & 1943 Promotora Hispano Americana de Musica S.A., Mexico.
Latin-American Music Publishing Company Limited, 8-14 Verulam Street, London WC1.
All Rights Reserved. International Copyright Secured.

Blue Jay Way
Words & Music by George Harrison
© Copyright 1967 Northern Songs.
All Rights Reserved. International Copyright Secured.

Cayenne
By Paul McCartney
© Copyright 1960 & 1995 MPL Communications Limited, 1 Soho Square, London W1.
All Rights Reserved. International Copyright Secured.

Copyright details

I Want To Tell You
Words & Music by George Harrison
© Copyright 1966 Northern Songs.
All Rights Reserved. International Copyright Secured.

I'd Like To Teach The World To Sing
Words & Music by Roger Cook, Roger Greenaway, Bill Backer & Billy Davis
© Copyright 1971 The Coca Cola Company. © Copyright assigned to Shada Music Incorporated, USA.
Universal/Dick James Music Limited, 77 Fulham Palace Road, London W6 for the United Kingdom and the Republic of Ireland.
All Rights Reserved. International Copyright Secured.

If You Gotta Make A Fool Of Somebody
Words & Music by Rudy Clark
© Copyright 1962 Good Songs Incorporated, USA.
B. Feldman & Company Limited, 127 Charing Cross Road, London WC2.
All Rights Reserved. International Copyright Secured.

In Spite Of All The Danger
Words & Music by Paul McCartney & George Harrison
© Copyright 1958 & 1995 MPL Communications Limited, 1 Soho Square, London W1.
All Rights Reserved. International Copyright Secured.

Life On Mars?
Words & Music by David Bowie
© Copyright 1971 Tintoretto Music/RZO Music Limited (37.5%)/EMI Music Publishing Limited, 127 Charing Cross Road, London WC2 (37.5%)/Chrysalis Music Limited, The Chrysalis Building, Bramley Road, London W10 (25%).
All Rights Reserved. International Copyright Secured.

Live Forever
Words & Music by Noel Gallagher
© Copyright 1994 Oasis Music, Creation Songs Limited & Sony/ATV Music Publishing (UK) Limited, 10 Great Marlborough Street, London W1.
All Rights Reserved. International Copyright Secured.

Love Me Do
Words & Music by John Lennon & Paul McCartney
© Copyright 1962 MPL Communications Limited, 1 Soho Square, London W1.
All Rights Reserved. International Copyright Secured.

Money, Money, Money
Words & Music by Benny Andersson & Björn Ulvaeus
© Copyright 1976 Union Songs AB, Stockholm, Sweden for the world.
Bocu Music Limited, 1 Wyndham Yard, Wyndham Place, London W1 for Great Britain and the Republic of Ireland.
All Rights Reserved. International Copyright Secured.

Moonglow
Words & Music by Will Hudson, Eddie de Lange & Irving Mills
© Copyright 1934 Exclusive Publications Incorporated, USA. © Copyright assigned 1934 to Mills Music Incorporated, USA.
Boosey & Hawkes Music Publishers Limited, 295 Regent Street, London W1 for the United Kingdom and the Republic of Ireland.
All Rights Reserved. International Copyright Secured.

Copyright details

Moon River
Words by Johnny Mercer
Music by Henry Mancini
© Copyright 1961 Famous Music Corporation, USA.
All Rights Reserved. International Copyright Secured.

Mr. Moonlight
Words & Music by Roy Lee Johnson
© Copyright 1964 Sony/ATV Songs LLC, USA.
Sony/ATV Music Publishing (UK) Limited, 10 Great Marlborough Street, London W1.
All Rights Reserved. International Copyright Secured.

My Sweet Lord
Words & Music by George Harrison
© Copyright 1970 Harrisongs Limited.
All Rights Reserved. International Copyright Secured.

Night And Day
Words & Music by Cole Porter
© Copyright 1932 T.B. Harms Incorporated, USA.
Warner Chappell Music Limited, Griffin House, 161 Hammersmith Road, London W6.
All Rights Reserved. International Copyright Secured.

Octopus's Garden
Words & Music by Ringo Starr
© Copyright 1969 Startling Music Limited/Warner Chappell Music Limited, Griffin House, 161 Hammersmith Road, London W6.
All Rights Reserved. International Copyright Secured.

Oh, Pretty Woman
Words & Music by Roy Orbison & Bill Dees
© Copyright 1964 (renewed 1992) Roy Orbison Music Company/Barbara Orbison Music Company/Acuff-Rose Music Incorporated, USA.
Warner Chappell Music Limited, Griffin House, 161 Hammersmith Road, London W6 (50%)/Acuff-Rose Music Limited, 25 James Street, London W1 (50%).
All Rights Reserved. International Copyright Secured.

Old Brown Shoe
Words & Music by George Harrison
© Copyright 1969 Harrisongs Limited.
All Rights Reserved. International Copyright Secured.

Only A Northern Song
Words & Music by George Harrison
© Copyright 1968 Northern Songs.
All Rights Reserved. International Copyright Secured.

Peggy Sue
Words & Music by Buddy Holly, Norman Petty & Jerry Allison
© Copyright 1957 MPL Communications Incorporated, USA.
Peermusic (UK) Limited, 8-14 Verulam Street, London WC1.
All Rights Reserved. International Copyright Secured.

Please Please Me
Words & Music by John Lennon & Paul McCartney

P.S. I Love You
Words & Music by John Lennon & Paul McCartney

Pure And Simple
Words & Music by Tim Hawes, Pete Kirtley & Alison Clarkson

Raining In My Heart
Words & Music by Boudleaux & Felice Bryant

Real Love
Words & Music by John Lennon

Runaway
Words & Music by Del Shannon & Max Crook

Shakermaker
Words & Music by Noel Gallagher
(this work includes elements of "I'd Like To Teach The World To Sing", Words & Music by Roger Cook, Roger Greenaway, Bill Backer & Billy Davis)

Smoke Gets In Your Eyes
Words by Otto Harbach
Music by Jerome Kern

Copyright details

So How Come (No One Loves Me)
Words & Music by Boudleaux & Felice Bryant

Soldier Of Love
Words & Music by Buzz Cason & Tony Moon

Something
Words & Music by George Harrison

S.O.S.
Words & Music by Benny Andersson, Björn Ulvaeus & Stig Anderson

Taxman
Words & Music by George Harrison

The Honeymoon Song
Words & Music by Mikis Theodorakis & William Sansom

The Inner Light
Words & Music by George Harrison

The James Bond Theme
By Monty Norman

The Sheik Of Araby
Words by Harry B. Smith & Francis Wheeler
Music by Ted Snyder

About the Author

Dominic Pedler received an Honours Diploma from the Guitar Institute Of Technology at the Musicians Institute, California, in 1988.

As a freelance writer specializing in rock, pop, jazz and blues, his guitar transcriptions, lessons, articles and album reviews have appeared in specialist music titles such as *Total Guitar*, *Guitarist* and *Guitar Techniques*, as well as various US guitar magazines; with more conventional contributions to *Record Collector* and *The Times*.

His interest in songwriting appreciation developed from playing guitar in his longtime covers band, Contraband, and continues with his freelance music copyright consultancy and postings to the muso website www.aeoliancadence.co.uk (named in honour of the Beatles trivia covered in Chapter 5).

As a blues fan, he compiled the *Century Of The Blues* project for Chrome Dreams in 2003, a 4-CD compilation with an accompanying booklet appreciating 100 early blues classics and their influence on later rock and blues musicians.

When not playing guitar and writing about music he can be found on the golf course or contributing articles to various golf titles, including *Golf International*.

Like Alan Partridge, his favourite Beatles album is *The Best Of The Beatles*.

Acknowledgements

This book developed from a *Total Guitar* magazine Beatles songwriting special, back in 1999. I'm therefore indebted to the then-editor, the late Harry Wylie, for believing in my initial pitch, and to techniques maestro, Jason Sidwell, for bringing that feature to life.

This rather broader project wouldn't have got off the ground without the vision, scrutiny and patience of commissioning editor, James Sleigh, not to mention his ability in securing the most essential element of all – the copyrights to the musical extracts - which, in turn, have been skilfully set by music engraver *extraordinaire*, Simon Troup. Thanks to all at Omnibus Press and Music Sales, including Chris Charlesworth, Arthur Dick, Chris Butler and George Goble; to proof reader Sarah Lavelle, and especially Susan Currie who patiently helped with the final tortuous changes.

A team of music authorities were consulted over the mysteries of the Aeolian cadence, including Peter Franklin (St. Catherine's College, Oxford), Adrian Jack (formerly of the London College of Music), Stephen Hefling, Dr John Williamson (Liverpool University), Mike Brocken (Institute Of Popular Music) and, especially, Aeolian harmony expert, Dr Allan Moore (University of Surrey).

Elsewhere, thanks to guitar magazine gurus, Neville Marten and Phil Hilborne, for encouraging my quest for the precise structure of the 'A Hard Day's Night' intro chord; to Jason at Townhouse Studios who manned the samplers and spectrum analysers; to Gary Spicer and Anthony Spicer for their supplementary electronic wizardry and expert aural interpretation; and to Gary Moore for recounting his George Harrison anecdote. André Barreau ('George' in The Bootleg Beatles) also threw his hat into the ring and shared his favourite songwriting and performing techniques from a catalogue with which he is rather familiar.

'Moonlight' Sonata expert, Timothy Jones (University of Exeter), answered obtuse questions regarding 'Because', as did Ian Hammond (a.k.a. 'Beathoven') on this and other fine points of Beatles tonality. Cyberspace allowed me to meet a range of Beatles fans, especially Tom Hartman at rec.music.beatles (*that* chord again!), and Boris Vanjicki at www.beatlelinks.net.

Meanwhile, a select group of writers graciously responded to various requests, including Terence O'Grady, Walter Everett, Yrjö Heinonen and Spencer Leigh. Gordon Williams, of Lee & Thompson, Paddy Grafton-Green, of Theodore Goddard, and expert music witness Guy Protheroe, also provided some much needed guidance in the murky world of copyright law.

I'm grateful to contemporary tunesmiths Pete Waterman, Guy Chambers, Matt Rowe and Richard Stannard, whose own bracketed names on a haul of No. 1 hits didn't prevent them from graciously sharing their debt to The Beatles.

Thanks also to Beatles authorities Andy Davis (*Record Collector)* and Peter Nash ('Something Precious And Rare'), who both helped to source many of the rare recordings (Beatles and beyond) that helped re-define the scope of this book.

Elsewhere, encouragement was graciously provided by Jock and Judy Howard, Robert Green, and Siân Llewellyn of *Classic Rock*; while technical advice was thankfully on-hand from various quarters including former *Classic CD* writer Roger Mills, Jason (again) at *Total Guitar*; and the magazine's former editor, Tim Tucker, whose perceptive insight and uncanny agreement over the finest Beatles manoeuvres were a joy to share.

Thanks to my maverick covers band, Contraband – not to mention the 'selective audiences' (as Ian Faith would say) who have seen us murder our share of Beatles tunes over the years.

Ultimately, the research for this book dates from my year at California's Musicians Institute, where my teachers Keith Wyatt, Norman Brown, Paul Gilbert, David Oakes, Steve Trovato, Carl Schroeder, theory king Charlie Fechter, and fellow student Harriss Lauderdale, all helped to shape the musical framework on which this book is structured. As did master rock writer, Dave Whitehill, whose unparalleled music analysis in *Guitar World* over the years – and constructive criticism of my own first floundering transcriptions – set a standard to which I will always aspire.

Thanks also to readers of the first edition of this book and visitors to the songwriting appreciation website www.aeoliancadence.co.uk who have contacted me with their constructive feedback over the last few years. As also shown by the growing number of academic courses in popular music, interest in the finer points of Beatles musicology continues unabated, while the remastered catalogue, iTunes availability and even The Beatles-approved *Rock Band* game are just some of the recent developments that have reinforced the musical legacy and introduced it to a new generation.

Similarly, the level of forensics continues to hit new heights with Arthur Dick's definitive new transcriptions and painstakingly recreated backing tracks for his *Play Guitar With… The Beatles* anthologies of 2009; while Jason Brown's fascinating – if controversial – mathematical analysis of the frequencies in the opening chord of A Hard Day's Night make for an essential addition to this 2011 edition.

Finally, I owe my main musical inspiration to my mother who sadly did not live to see the results of this particular misspent youth. Special thanks to my sister for exceptional support over the years ever since her record collection first opened a new world for me; to my father; to Jane for her patience, love and friendship; and to Milo, whose first year on the planet has been defined almost exclusively by Beatles music and strange sounds from a battered Eko Ranger.

There *is* more to life …

Dominic Pedler, 27 July 2011

Introduction

'All music is rehash. There are only a few notes. Just variations on a theme'.
John Lennon[1]

'What's your favourite Beatles album?'

So goes the code of introduction that is now dictated when any two or three Fab Four fans are gathered together – cueing a predictable ritual as John, Paul, George and Ringo go under the microscope for the zillionth time since the sixties. You know the routine. Endless chin-scratching analysis of the backwards recording techniques of *Revolver*, the psychedelic concept of *Sgt. Pepper*, the minimalist artwork of *The White Album* and the seamless blending of the medley on *Abbey Road*. Not forgetting a trawl through the convoluted clues to the real identity of 'The Walrus', and an inventory of those 'Paul is Dead' references (now the subject of a dedicated tome).[2]

For no stone is left unturned in Beatles culture except, too often, the only thing that really matters. The music itself.

We all know that the group changed society in far-reaching ways with everything from their haircuts to their politics. But it's the ultimate irony that the one aspect of their global-dominating legacy that is taken for granted is, well, the melodies and chord changes that *really* changed the world. That's not to suggest that other elements, especially a volume of lyrics now challenging Shakespeare for posterity, don't matter. Far from it. But a look at them in their rightful musical context can surely transform

1 *The Playboy Interviews With John Lennon And Yoko Ono*, conducted by David Scheff. Edited by G. Barry Golson. Playboy Press, New York. September 1980, p. 78.

2 R. Gary Patterson, *The Great Beatle Death Clues,* Robson Books, London. 1996.

our appreciation, while also going some way towards explaining why the songs have become so imprinted on our consciousness.

For one of the highlights of The Beatles' songwriting was their ability to apply a certain musical technique to reinforce the lyrical imagery.

It was an instinctive element of their art and one that is evident at all stages of their career. No need to be a muso to join Paul on his meanderings down 'The Long And Winding Road'; to sense the girl leading us up the garden path in 'Day Tripper'; or to watch the 'sun going down' on the disconsolate 'Fool On The Hill'. The lyrics set the scene but, courtesy of The Beatles' uncanny grasp of musical emphasis, we instinctively *feel* it. Even when the 'Threetles' resumed with 'Free As A Bird' in 1995, the magic hadn't deserted them. With our eyes closed we can still *see* the creature taking flight at certain points in the song as the mood lifts.[3]

In all these cases, and many others we'll be exploring, there is a very specific reason for the effect we enjoy. For while, ultimately, the full beauty of music is down to an intangible element that can never quite be captured, there is nevertheless a way in which we can discover why a song 'works'.

To get to the heart of the songwriting phenomenon, we must take a step back from The Beatles as cultural icons and the groundbreaking instrumentation and electronic wizardry that undeniably also played a part. For the essence of The Beatles' genius is to be found in their simply sublime harmony and melody, and the ability of a single chord-change or deft note to create pop history.

For all their disdain for music theory, The Beatles knew this implicitly. At the simplest level, take John Lennon's memories of writing 'I Want To Hold Your Hand' with Paul McCartney:

> 'I remember when we got the chord that "made" the song. We were in Jane Asher's house, downstairs in the cellar playing on the piano at the same time. And we had, "Oh you-u-u . . . got that something . . ." And Paul hits this chord and I turn to him and say "That's it. That's *it*!" I said, "Do that again!"'[4]

Why *musically* did it work so effectively (after all, the 11 million buyers of this testament to Beatlemania certainly seemed to like it)? And why, for

[3] Listen to these moments in the verses at the following CD timings: 0.48, 1.15, 2.09, 2.35; and especially as Harrison starts his guitar solo at 2.54.

[4] *The Playboy Interviews,* p. 124.

that matter, has there been so much debate among experts as to what the chord actually is?

What we can affectionately call John's 'That's it!' chord is just one of the many musical riddles, myths and mysteries that, down the years, have passed into the burgeoning catalogue of Beatles folklore. We explore this particular one in Chapter 4 but, as a taster for what is to come, here are another ten musical 'gauntlets' thrown down over the years which we'll be attempting to pick up:

1) Why does Paul say the opening chord in the bridge of 'From Me To You' transformed The Beatles' songwriting by going to a 'surprising place', as he demonstrates on the *Anthology* video?
2) What pioneering songwriting principle did John see in a particular Del Shannon song that inspired him to make 'I'll Be Back' 'my variation on the chords'?
3) What was the mysterious 'Gretty chord' that Paul claims he used in 'Michelle' but which prompted a website to devise a challenging riddle for Beatles fans?
4) Does 'Because' really consist of the chords to Beethoven's 'Moonlight' Sonata played backwards, as John and Yoko's comments have led us to believe?
5) Why does McCartney hit the nail on the head when he says 'to go to the B flat was quite good' while reminiscing about his 'sophisticated little tune', 'Things We Said Today'?
6) Just what *is* the construction of *that* opening chord in 'A Hard Day's Night', described as 'one of the great unsolved mysteries in the history of popular music' by the editor of *Guitarist* magazine? We add one more to the dozens of theories already on offer in published Beatles literature.
7) The Beatles' rendition of 'Besame Mucho' may have failed the Decca audition in 1962, but how did its 'big moment musically', as Paul describes it, find its way into some of the greatest Beatles songs?
8) 'You Never Give Me Your Money' is said to kick-off the seamless 'side 2 medley' on *Abbey Road*. But why, subconsciously, do we feel the medley begin one track earlier?
9) Why was McCartney so 'fascinated' by a very specific chord change in a Joan Baez song that, as he admits, he 'nicked it' for 'I'll Get You'?
10) And, most legendary of all, just what was the 'Aeolian cadence' in 'Not A Second Time' which, according to the classical critic of *The Times* in 1963, connected The Beatles directly to Gustav Mahler?

This last puzzle famously non-plussed The Beatles themselves – not to mention a string of interviewers, writers and even academics over four decades – and we duly embark on a search for that particular Holy Grail in Chapter 5.

These puzzles are just the tip of the iceberg and merely seek to make the most of the tantalisingly few musical quotes volunteered by the band themselves over the years. Meanwhile, elsewhere, there is a goldmine of musical nuggets lurking in every corner of the catalogue, just waiting to be unearthed and appreciated. This book attempts to do just that by relating some of the most memorable highlights to the musical principles that John, Paul, George and Ringo mastered so effortlessly in their global domination of pop.

Spanning the spectrum of musical complexity from the humble Three-Chord Trick to the most intricate of multi-key Beatles masterpieces, we construct a framework that introduces each new scale and chord one-by-one, identifying its appearance and explaining its function while also touching on its origins and legacy within pop music. With musical extracts from the entire Beatles catalogue at our disposal, we deconstruct those winning cycles, sequences, intros, outros, and middle eights, by delving into extensions, moving lines, slick key-changes and a whole host of colourful processes – 'tricks', even – that hide behind the veil of a pop song.

In *A Brief History Of Time*, Professor Stephen Hawking relates his fears that for every mathematical equation he included in his book, sales would halve. This author feels a similar apprehension, for there is indeed theory along the way, including the fundamental principles of tonality, root movement, harmonisation, substitution and voice-leading. But there really is no other way. Basic theory and the willingness to see even the most complicated chord sequences as variations on very specific musical formulae is the only route to understanding not just the structure of Beatles songs – but also the effect.

In an early posting on rec.music.beatles, the newsgroup's pioneer, 'Saki', captured the analytical dilemma for the non-musicologically inclined. 'If there's any part of The Beatles' output we're likely to be competent to describe, it's the lyrics … But music requires a road-map if we are to understand what's happening.'[5] Ultimately, this book is intended as just such a companion guide to the rocky terrain of pop music, with *appreciation* the main goal and any tips that future songwriters might glean just a bonus.

[5] 'Saki Reviews The Book Reviews', www.recmusicbeatles.com.

Accordingly, very little prior musical knowledge has been assumed on the part of the reader (the opening chapter dwells almost exclusively on a single chord, before moving on to the Three-Chord Trick in Chapter 2). Those readers who are not familiar with the basic concepts of chords and scales should refer to Appendix 1, which provides important background to the basic major and minor scales and the construction of their respective families of chords. An understanding of these fundamental elements of music is essential to everything that follows. Appendix 3 gives a simple introduction to harmonisation (the way in which melodies relate to an underlying chord progression), a subject vital to appreciating these songwriting elements in context.

We will not be taking a strict classical approach to Beatles music, and while brief references are made to certain high-brow terms and their origins, this is only to enhance our appreciation of a device as it appears within the song itself. This book is written by a practising rock guitarist – *for* guitarists, musicians, and fans of pop music – and acknowledges the fact that many traditional musical concepts are ill-equipped to capture The Beatles' essentially guitar-based compositional approach. In this sense, no apology is made for reworking and twisting certain conventional terminology, in most cases with the intention of better reflecting the contemporary thinking of the modern rock musician.

And if the earlier term 'formula' sounds like anathema to The Beatles, suggesting sterile, contrived, mechanistic devices to which inferior songwriters resort as a substitute for inspiration, then just check out Paul McCartney's own memories of writing 'I'm Happy Just To Dance With You' for *A Hard Day's Night*:

> **'. . . It was a bit of a formula song. We knew that if you went from E to G♯ minor, you could always make a song with those chords, that change pretty much always excited you. This was one of those. Certainly "Do You Want To Know A Secret" was. The nice thing about it was to actually pull off a song on a slim little premise like that . . .'[6]**

At a stroke McCartney succeeds in torpedoing another myth. For the fact that The Beatles famously couldn't read music misses

[6] Barry Miles, *Many Years From Now*, p. 163.

the point. They clearly knew enough about the rudiments of music: the power of root movement and voice-leading within chord changes, to incorporate premeditated ideas into their songs – not to mention repeating the process by transporting them, 'lock, stock and barrel', to another song. In disguise, of course, but then that is one of the hallmarks of the canny songwriter. And we'll be discussing the versatility of this particular McCartney 'formula', which can be spotted equally in the very earliest Beatles excursions, like 'You'll Be Mine', right through to 'Real Love'.

Of course, it's not just Beatles songs that can be understood as a blend of formulaic devices – they form the very language of pop. Many of the same musical principles recur across generations, proving them to be transportable tools for songwriters of all eras. In this sense, The Beatles did not just inherit a legacy of Three-Chord Tricks from fifties' rock'n'roll as is so often assumed. Far from it. Certainly, they pioneered many ground-breaking principles – like the ambitious 'borrowing' of chords that led so directly to the sound of rock. But the idea that the group somehow 'came out of nowhere', with an entirely new, untried-and-untested arsenal of musical devices is another myth – and one that, paradoxically, doesn't do justice to their creativity. The Beatles developed a wide range of ideas from immediate heroes such as Chuck Berry, Buddy Holly and Little Richard, and other fifties giants, not forgetting the great songsmiths of Tin Pan Alley – right back, in fact, to the Delta blues masters. This isn't just speculation or biographical filler – courtesy of *Anthology 1*, *Live At The BBC* and the famous Hamburg 'Star-Club' bootleg, references to which appear throughout, we have the proof.

Remember Lennon's comment: 'variations on a theme'. But what variations.

So while The Beatles form the focus, brief references to songs from all eras of the 20th Century – indeed from Cole Porter to Oasis – will appear at regular intervals to demonstrate the versatility of the principles at work, and how the traditions of songwriting have been passed down through the generations. Similarly, the supposed differences between Lennon and McCartney are explored – usually to question accepted wisdom and illustrate each writer's mastery of a strikingly similar repertoire of songwriting devices.

As The Beatles' legacy is continually reappraised it has become fashionable for critics and fans alike to draw an imaginary dividing line between 'early' and 'late' Beatles periods. So much so that, with today's revisionists nailing their colours to the mast of the *Revolver* and *Sgt. Pepper* period, we'd be forgiven for forgetting that the songwriting revolution of the early sixties ever happened. But were the songs that originally fuelled Beatlemania really so naïve compared with what came later? Of course, The Beatles matured as songwriters in a myriad of respects, as would naturally be expected from any artist over the course of a decade of development. But a preoccupation with the group's pioneering recording practices threatens to obscure the extensive array of musical principles evident in their writing as early as the debut album, *Please Please Me*. Similarly, there is the trap of assuming that innocent pop songs, lyrically long on youthful exuberance, must necessarily be short on musical substance. And *vice versa*, that hip themes of counterculture, rebellion, philosophy and cynicism automatically make for 'superior' music. Aesthetic judgements aside, it can certainly be argued (as eminent music experts already have) that many latter-day Beatles 'classics' actually represent a musical retrenchment from the dozens of early gems which, in the absence of post-modern effects, had to rely exclusively on inspired novelty in harmony and melody to make their statement. The fact that every chapter in this book (without fail) draws repeatedly on their early legacy (indeed, often from the debut album) either to showcase a fully formed musical principle or to suggest an idea 'in development', is testimony that the critical balance needs redressing.

Finally, readers may well not accept the quasi-scientific premise that there is a physiological basis underlying the power of many of the musical principles we'll be exploring. But surely no one would deny that great pop and rock music is characterised by musical highlights of varying subtlety that unashamedly fuel the emotions. We can all identify with the listener who, finger poised on the rewind button of the CD player, swoons: 'Just listen to this bit ... that bit ... that bit *there*!' It's a scene that's been

[7] *The Playboy Interviews*, p. 79.

re-enacted in some form or other since pop began – and probably most often with a Beatles song as the subject.

This book is dedicated to you.

Admittedly it was John Lennon himself who once remarked impatiently, 'Listen, writing about music is like talking about fucking. Who wants to talk about it?'

But then his very next words are never mentioned.

'You know, maybe some people do want to talk about it . . .'

ONE

Tension, Resolution and the Power of V

Like good sex, good songs build to a climax, a moment of truth when music and lyrics combine to reach a peak of emotional intensity with which the listener can instinctively identify. Even humble nursery rhymes tend to feature a natural focus of energy – whether at the end of a verse, bridge or chorus – that defines their structure as our brains subconsciously process the natural ebb and flow of sounds that we call music.[1]

Certainly, 1963 audiences didn't have too much trouble locating the euphoric highpoints of early Beatles live sets, with the offstage mayhem often peaking uncannily with the musical zenith within the respective songs.

Let's start with a handful of numbers whose musical and lyrical punchlines form instantly memorable watersheds within their structures. It's no surprise that many feature those hysteria-inducing 'oohs', 'ahs' and 'yeahs' as John, Paul and George tighten the screw with their heavenly harmonies at the pivotal moment, defining the very essence of Beatlemania. The following table should jog the memory.

In musical terms, it's no coincidence that each of these rousing Beatles peaks (and many others throughout the catalogue) hinge on one essential harmonic prop – the dominant, the chord built on the fifth degree of the scale of the prevailing key, hence the V (the 'five'), or V7, where the triad is joined by its diatonic (flattened) seventh.

[1] Take 'Jingle Bells', where the line 'in a one-horse open *sleigh*' inevitably prompts a resounding 'hey!' – especially when adopted as the eponymous football terrace chant. Musically, this peak coincides with the dominant of the key, the focus of this chapter.

'Dramatic dominants' – a selection from early Beatles hits

Song	Time	Lyric	V[2]
'Twist And Shout'	1.24	'ah, ah, ah, ah [etc]'	A
'From Me To You'	0.46	'and keep you satisfied, ooh'	G [aug]
'She Loves You'	1.01	'you know you should be glad, ooh'	D7
'I'll Get You'	1.21	'you might as well resign yourself to me, oh yeah'	A
'I Want To Hold Your Hand'	1.04	'I can't hide, I can't hide, I can't hide'	D
'This Boy'	1.21	'till he's seen you cry-y-y-y'	A
'Can't Buy Me Love'	0.52	'no, no, no, no!'	G6
'A Hard Day's Night'	0.56	'feeling you holding me tight, tight, yeah'	D7

While the tonic, the I chord in a key, acts as a stable, peaceful sense of musical 'home', the V is an inherently unstable beast used deliberately to create essential musical tension – without which there is no song.

For an instant lesson in both theory and practice, let's return to those heady days and dissect the frenzied anticipation generated at the relevant moment in the Fab Four's cover of 'Twist And Shout'. As every budding muso knows, the vocal arrangement here obligingly spells out, very precisely, the notes of an A7 chord, the dominant in the song's key of D.

'Twist And Shout'

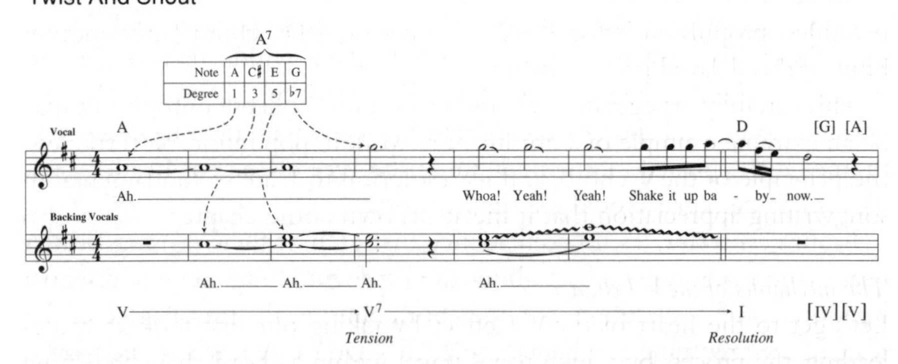

The A in the guitars set the scene but The Beatles reinforce the sound and power of the dominant with an ear-grating statement in the vocals. There's really no need to refer back to Appendix 1 for the formal process of

[2] The V chords are shown here as basic *instrumental* chords, at this stage, with the quality of the *overall* sonority implied by the vocals the subject of several examples, starting with the ♭7th-enhanced A chord of 'Twist And Shout'.

building a dominant seventh chord by harmonizing the major scale. The Beatles do it for us, in textbook fashion, as John's A note (at 1.24), George's C♯ (at 1.27) and Paul's E (at 1.29) stack up, respectively, the root, major 3rd and 5th degrees of an A triad, before John extends the chord with a ♭7th by jumping to the high G (at 1.31).[3]

The result is an orgy of delicious dissonance almost guaranteed to send an audience into a frenzy. But why?

Even this humble episode of Beatlemania demonstrates the fundamental musical truth that, by virtue of its intrinsic instability, we hear the V chord as a tense sonority that *demands resolution.*

This can be achieved, to a greater or lesser extent, depending on the chord it moves to – with the change to the 'I' providing a particularly satisfying resolution.

Having coiled their harmonic spring, The Beatles finally release it when the V7 eventually moves to I (at 1.36), the 'home' D chord our ears had been craving. Beatles expert Chris Ingham sums it up neatly:

> 'The ascending arpeggio moment in 'Twist And Shout' perfectly conveys the dominant's wants-to-go-somewhere quality … it lands on D with quasi-orgasmic relief …'[4]

Admittedly, we then barely have time to rest on the D before we resume the song's basic I-IV-V cycle in which the dominant more subtly fuels the breathless propulsion before finally closing on a D9 chord (after another bout of this delayed gratification).

This carefully arpeggiated A7, and its eventual collapse onto the D, may be an extreme example of a dominant at work in pop music. Nevertheless, the principle of the V chord, and its resolution to I, are so fundamental to songwriting appreciation that it merits its own entire chapter.

The mechanics of the V-I change

Let's get to the heart of the V-I effect by taking our first look at voice-leading, the process by which tones travel within a chord change creating smooth, inexorable motion. Here's what happens as the Lennon larynx finally leads the band home to D on '*baby* now' (at 1.36).

[3] The sequence is clearly shown on the *Ready Steady Go!* footage, recorded live in 1964, available on video as *The Beatles Live*, DCI/EMI (1985).

[4] Chris Ingham, 'Doctor Rock Dissects The Hits; No.12: V, The Dominant Seventh', *MOJO*, Issue 36 (November 1996), p. 30.

A7: V7 'tension'			D : I 'resolution'	
Formula	Note	Voice leading	Note	Formula
♭7th	G	Down a semitone	F♯	3rd
3rd	C♯	Up a semitone	D	Root
Root	A	Down a perfect fifth	D	Root

Central to the understanding of most musical moves is the notion of dissonance in relation to consonance, the generation of tension and its release through resolution. The V7-I change epitomises this as it unwinds the dominant's inherent tension in three specific ways:-

a) By resolving the leading note tension[5]
b) By resolving the 'tritone' tension through 'close' voice-leading[6]
c) By the natural tendency for 'perfect fifth' root-movement

a) The leading note effect
In the same way that the leading note of a major scale takes a simple melody 'home' to its tonic, '7-to-8' (or, Julie Andrews-style, '*ti-do*'), so the presence of that same unstable 7th degree – *now recast as the defining major 3rd of the basic V triad* – is central to the power of the dominant. In 'Twist And Shout' the leading note within the A triad is the C♯ note which duly slides up that effortless semitone to its home target of D, thereby helping to restore our sense of musical 'order'.

The leading note effect is an essential form of musical propulsion that occurs in any V triad as it moves home to its I chord. Sometimes it may be masked within the musical mayhem, while at other times it may be the focus of attention especially when reinforced by the melody, as captured so clearly in 'In My Life'.

Here the G♯ leading note found at the end of the pretty, six-note 'theme' guitar riff repeatedly drives the song by wanting to move upwards to the tonic. The tension is only released at the very end when the melody finally slides up that satisfying semitone, delivering a textbook *Perfect cadence* where a song (or a discrete section within it) comes to rest with a feeling of V-I finality. We elaborate on this type of Perfect 'closure' in Chapter 3.

[5] A recap of the leading note principle, as discussed in Appendix 1, is recommended here.
[6] The sounds of the various intervals in music, illustrated with reference to particular Beatles melodies, is discussed at the end of Appendix 3.

'In My Life'

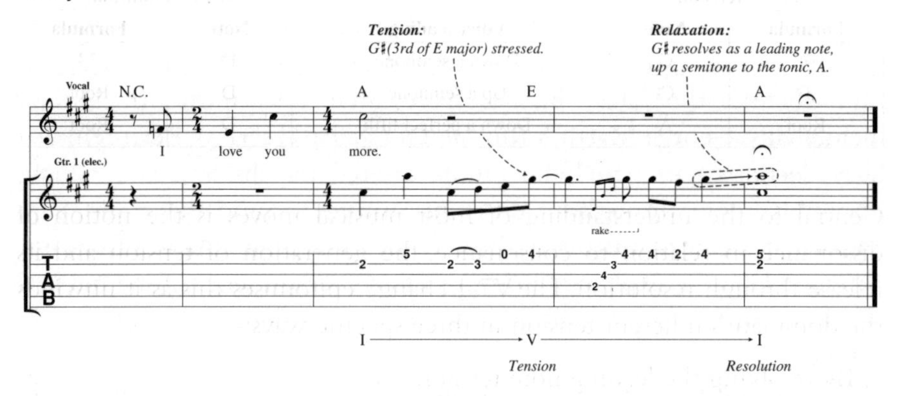

The role of V as the penultimate chord in a Perfect cadence contrasts with those song sections that end with a 'hanging' V, denying us an immediate, flowing resolution and thereby creating such watershed moments as the 'From Me To You', 'I'll Get You' and 'This Boy' references in our opening table. Precisely because of this delaying tactic, the ploy is deemed an *Imperfect cadence*, as we explore in Chapter 4.

b) The tritone and tension

Beyond the basic triad, the more colourful dominant 7th construction (V7) introduces an additional dimension to the concept of tension and resolution.

The highly dissonant tritone, intrinsic to a dominant 7th, is named after the distance (or 'interval') of three whole tones between the 3rd and ♭7th degrees of the chord.[7]

It is this interval that prompts adjectives such as 'dark', 'grating', 'haunting' and 'unstable', for which there is scientific justification. For the tritone registers, in terms of The Laws Of Physics, as the most dissonant of all the intervals in music.[8]

[7] In our A7 chord, the tritone is the interval between C♯ and G.

[8] Pythagoras' Theory Of Proportions is a simple way of ordering the intervals in music according to sonorous considerations. It states that the simpler the vibration ratio is between two tones, the more consonant is their interval. With a ratio of 32:45 , the tritone is the most complex of the entire list of 13 intervals that exist between unison (1:1) and octave (2:1). The perfect fifth and major third are 2:3 and 4:5 respectively. See Frank Haunschild, *The New Harmony Book*, Chapter 2.

The great composer, Leonard Bernstein, even goes so far as to claim that humans are not just conditioned – but 'programmed' – to appreciate tonality and to register such tension and resolution almost from birth. Long before the latest high-tech research into music (including, incidentally, George Martin's *Rhythm Of Life* BBC series), Bernstein was busy deconstructing melodic motifs uttered by children and which, uncannily, recur throughout different cultures around the globe. Sure enough, it seems that many of those reviled playground taunts from our childhood can be explained in terms of an ever-present tritone interval – but one that is rarely resolved in a way that even a young child would appreciate.[9]

In resolving the tritone tension, our table shows how voice-leading in the V7-I change involves 'contrary' motion', with the outer ends of the tritone each moving in by a semitone. This compresses it from a tense six semitones (C♯-G) to a relaxed four (D-F♯) that now represents a consonant, major third interval within the major tonic triad. The result again is musical interest through tension and resolution.

c) 'Perfect fifth' root movement

V-I motion isn't just about the leading note and tritone – the move is essentially named after the root movement that follows one of the most natural moves in music: the descent of a perfect fifth. After all, chord progressions are so called because they do just that – they progress to a destination – with this forward motion usually provided by a strong bass line that creates a *root* progression.

V-I is the strongest of all the many root movements that we will be covering. In Chapter 3 we will introduce a musical phenomenon known as the Cycle Of Fifths, where chords move exclusively in a chain of descending fifths; while Appendix 5 refers to quasi-scientific research that suggests it is a winning formula to which humans seem almost hard-wired to appreciate.

[9] Leonard Bernstein, *The Unanswered Question: Six Harvard Lectures*. Bernstein argues that tonal relationships are built into nature and understood instinctively. Those dissonant playground chants typically juxtapose two of the first three new notes that occur in the partial tone series above the fundamental note. For example, the first three new notes above a fundamental C, are E, G and B♭, with the E-B♭ representing the tritone. Tritones in melody will be revisited in several Beatles songs, especially in the discussion of the diminished scale in 'Blue Jay Way'.

Paul McCartney instinctively describes the power of V-I root action, albeit from a very interesting angle:

> 'If you're in C and you put it on G – something that's not the root note . . . it's great . . . By the time you go to C it's like 'Thank God he went to C!' . . . you can create tension with it. I didn't know that's what I was doing. It just sounded nice.'[10]

McCartney is actually referring to the trick he picked up from The Beach Boys (and also Motown bass ace, James Jamerson) of playing the fifth degree of the chord in question as the bass note. This has the effect of creating an *inversion* of the triad, a more unstable sound than if the root had formed the foundation. While such inversions are a subject for Chapters 9 and 12, the point here is to show how McCartney confirms the strong 'pull' which the root of V exerts towards the I chord. If this natural tendency is not satisfied, the listener is left with a feeling of suspense.

In a bizarre sense, The Beatles have left us hanging in mid-air for decades with a rogue variation on the fifth-in-the-bass that McCartney describes. For the very last sound on *Abbey Road* is a nonchalantly plucked A note that ends 'Her Majesty' (at 0.22). And yet, we are in the key of D and, really, we could do with a D root note for 'closure'.[11]

'Her Majesty'

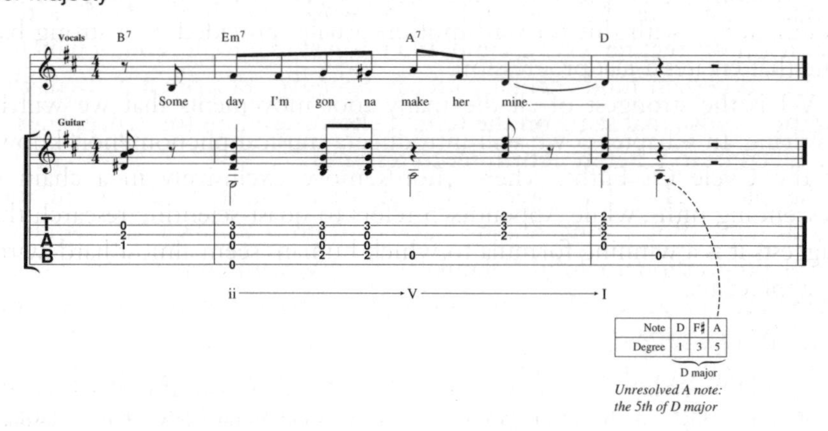

[10] Paul McCartney interview, *Guitar Player*, July 1990, p. 20.

[11] Sir Paul thoughtfully 'corrected' the anomaly (caused famously when editing the *Abbey Road* medley) with a solid closing tonic when playing the song for Her Majesty herself at the Queen's 2002 Jubilee concert at Buckingham Palace!

As a brief summary at this stage, the structure of a dominant chord and the V-I chord change shows us how music 'works', and why we need tension and resolution to drive a song forward through localised climaxes.

Indeed, the self-contained I-V-I theme riff of 'In My Life' demonstrates in a nutshell how we only really need the tonic and dominant to create an entire songwriting premise.

Not too ambitious, admittedly, but The Beatles used simple I-V-I alternations on several occasions, both as a band and in their solo careers. Just listen to the nursery rhyme verse of 'All Together Now' (G-D-G); the chorus of 'Yellow Submarine' (again, G-D-G); and the anti-war-mantra-turned-football-chant of 'Give Peace A Chance' (D♭-A♭-D♭).

The V-I principle in its many guises will reappear regularly in every chapter of the book. In fact, so fundamental is the relationship between the two chords that we must briefly outline one classical theory that virtually states that it is the only move of any substance in all music. . . .

Schenker and the power of V-I

The significance of V-I was never better expressed than by German analyst Heinrich Schenker whose theories have influenced not merely generations of classical scholars but also various Beatles musicologists.[12]

Having studied a vast range of musical works, Schenker concluded that the presence of V-I is intrinsic to every piece of what he defined loosely as 'good' music. His definition related to works widely accepted as tonal music (music that revolves around, and resolves to, a tonic) and in which he observed certain fundamental patterns. Schenker described particularly a 'vertical' move that starts on the tonic I chord, develops (or 'arpeggiates', as he called it) to V, before returning to rest on I.[13]

Simple I-V-I cycles, as referred to above, demonstrate this in the most literal sense. But a song doesn't have to feature an obviously sequential I-V-I progression to fulfil Schenker's theory, with songs often winding their way to a peaking V in mid-song (just as we saw with those euphoric early Beatles singles).

Schenker would indeed have been proud of how The Beatles bore out his theory with those raucous V chords that form such a pinnacle of power,

[12] Refer to the works of Walter Everett, Steven Clark Porter and Allan F. Moore.

[13] For an introduction to the basics of Schenker, see Richard Middleton, *Studying Popular Music*, p.193.

helping to achieve an 'underlying correctness' within the music from both a theoretical and, more importantly, emotional perspective. And while a V chord doesn't need to make its mark as brazenly as on the early Beatles singles in order to define a song's structure in this way, Schenker would have been the first to spot similarly showcased V chords throughout The Beatles' catalogue.

To make the point, let's extend our earlier exercise and pick a dramatic V chord for a song on each of The Beatles' albums (including, for good measure, *Magical Mystery Tour* and *Yellow Submarine*). Starting with *Please Please Me* where we've picked another cover, 'Anna (Go To Him)' by Arthur Alexander, to show that (as with The Isley Brothers' 'Twist And Shout') The Beatles didn't have a monopoly on this particular songwriting secret.

'Dramatic dominants' – a selection from each Beatles album

Song	Time	Lyric	V
'Anna (Go To Him)'	1.27	'what am I supposed to do? Oh, oh, oh, oh, oh, oh'	A
'It Won't Be Long'	0.55	'you're coming home'	B
'You Can't Do That'	0.22	'because I told you before'	D7
'What You're Doing'	0.57	'a love that's true it's me-eeeee'	A
'The Night Before'	1.05	'it makes me wanna cry'	A7
'Drive My Car'	1.23	'you can do something in between'	A7
'And Your Bird Can Sing'	0.49	'I'll be round, I'll be round'	B
'Sgt. Pepper's Lonely Hearts Club Band'	1.31	'we'd love to take you home'	D7
'I Am The Walrus'	1.01	'I am the walrus, goo, goo, g'joob!'	E
'Birthday'	1.24	'Daaaaance!'	E
'All You Need Is Love'	0.39	'It's easy'	D
'Oh! Darling'	1.37	'I nearly broke down and died'	E
'One After 909'	1.09	'I got the number wrong, well'	F♯7

Notice again how, in so many of these cases, the dominant occurs at the end of a section – usually a bridge, where it is often spotlighted by a 'stop' as the instruments drop out, leaving the vocals to deliver the most important line of the song.

And while our opening example of 'Twist And Shout' is an extreme example of a prolonged dominant – one that builds the tension over several bars, The Beatles adapted the same smouldering V-chord concept in a variety of songs.

The bridge to 'Day Tripper' features a stretch on V that lasts for a full 12 bars, during which the harmony vocals again spell out the pitches of the dominant B7, creating a climax before returning to consonance with the song's signature guitar riff, in E.

As late as 'Here Comes The Sun', Harrison was tantalisingly delaying the inevitable with his embellished flat-picking lines that dress up the song's E7 (from 2.03-2.11), making the eventual collapse onto the A tonic (for the next 'Little darlin') all the more powerful.

The 5-4-3-2-1 return to base

Schenker's notion was that this type of 'deep structure' involving the V is a principle that connects all tonal music, with the originality of individual pieces (the specific features that set them apart from each other) appreciated with reference to their differing melodies and harmonies in the 'foreground' and 'middleground'.[14]

In particular, Schenker elaborated on his basic premise to suggest that this harmonic movement is typically reinforced in a 'horizontal' sense by moving lines that descend through the major scale to the tonic. Hence we regularly see melodic patterns that follow structural pitch descents like '3-2-1', '5-4-3-2-1' and '8-7-6-5-4-3-2-1'. Also common are similarly inevitable lines that work their way to the 3rd or 5th of the tonic triad.[15]

The 'Three Blind Mice' nursery rhyme – and it's Beatles counterpart, 'All You Need Is Love' – demonstrate most clearly how a V-I change is often accompanied by a 3-2-1 melodic descent (see Appendix 3).

Such directional melodic lines are rarely so obvious – being typically 'disguised' within the big picture. For example, Appendix 3 also mentions how 'I Will' accords to such principles by falling through a pitch descent in which the tones lead us, as predicted, through an overall 5-4-3-2-1 descent – albeit through an embellished (rather than an unbroken) sequence.[16]

[14] Admittedly Schenker was basing his observations on classical music and certain pop and rock songs would appear to put a spanner in the works. After all, songs like 'Paperback Writer' never make it to the V chord at all; while the pedal-tone stability of 'Tomorrow Never Knows' represents the very antithesis of harmonic movement. Nevertheless, the basic Schenkerian concepts are mentioned in passing as they clearly apply to much – if not all – Beatles music.

[15] For further detail, again, see Middleton, *Studying Popular Music*, p.193.

[16] Hence, even though the ultimate melodic cadence of the verse of 'I Will' is 7-1 (as the leading note rises to the tonic), this fundamental descent can still be found 'hidden' within its melodic structure.

While this type of Schenkerian *melodic* voice leading analysis is an advanced concept only briefly touched on in this book, the basic principle of directional horizontal lines are a fundamental concept which we will be exploring with regard to simple *harmony*. And the basic principle can perhaps best be grasped with reference to some easy-to-spot instrumental examples that clearly 'unfold' the V-I relationship *in the lower harmony*.

Cue up the following songs to hear, in each case, a powerful dominant that, rather than collapsing directly onto the tonic as the next verse resumes, deliberately 'walks' 5-4-3-2-1 down the major scale 'ladder':

'All Together Now' (at 0.52, as the bass drops from D-C-B-A-G)
'You've Got To Hide Your Love Away' (at 0.35, as the bass drops from D-C-B-A-G)
'I Will' (0.57, as the bass drops and the guitar slides C-B♭-A-G-F)

The Beatles themselves would have heard this very same sound, the most signposted of V-I end-of-bridge-returns, in various songs of the fifties – starting with 'Come Go With Me' by The Del-Vikings, the very first song Paul McCartney ever heard John Lennon singing.[17]

Closer to home, dig out The Beatles' cover of 'Don't Ever Change', on *Live At The BBC* where (starting at 1.16) the harmony returns slowly home through 5-4-3-2-1 in the key of E, while the melody complements it with a chromatic drop through the scale pitches 7-6-5-4-3.[18]

The same principle of a dominant homing-in on its target like a guided missile can be seen in a rather more interesting manifestation in the link from 'Polythene Pam' to 'She Came In Through The Bathroom Window', on the *Abbey Road* medley. But notice that, this time, the sequential 5-4-3-2-1 serves to take us from one song in the key of E, to another in the key of A. It's a clever twist that exploits the fact that E is the dominant of A and can therefore lead us to a new key centre, a perfect fifth below.

[17] Listen to how the instruments drop out (at 1.12 on the Del-Vikings original) to highlight the defining dominant, leaving the bass to descend E♭-D♭-C-B♭-A♭, in the key of A♭.

[18] Of course, 5-4-3-2-1 bass descents that link V to I appear throughout the history of pop, and in contexts ranging from the simple folk of Peter Sarstedt's 'Where Do You Go To My Lovely?' (where it's heard throughout, in the key of G); to the Brit-Pop of Oasis' 'Married With Children' (end of bridge, at 2.38, key of E).

'She Came In Through The Bathroom Window'

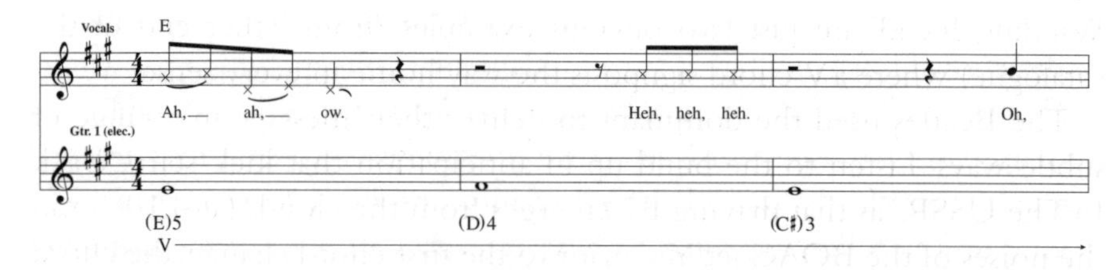

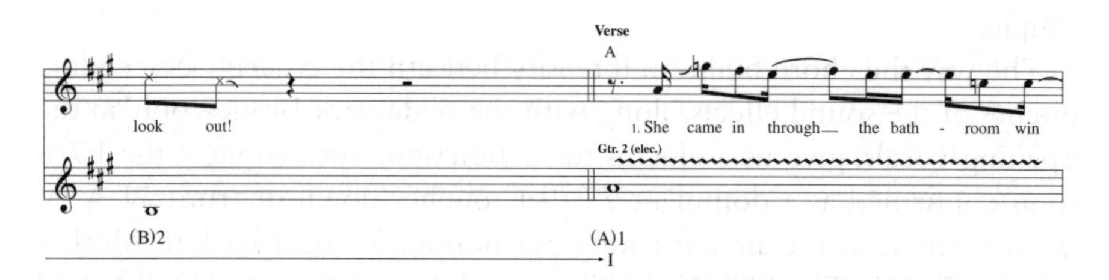

While a detailed look at key switching is beyond the scope of this chapter, it is well worth previewing, even at this early stage, the often pivotal role of the V chord in this process.

'She Came In Through The Bathroom Window' is an obvious example of how The Beatles often followed the simplest guideline for moving to a new tonality: *preceding the 'new' tonic with its own dominant chord.*

This device will be seen in countless cases, and never more clearly than in 'Penny Lane' where McCartney shifts key centres to achieve a striking contrast of mood between verse and chorus. A complete dissection appears in Chapter 10. But, for now, just appreciate how McCartney so clearly uses V7 chords to achieve each modulation. There's even another sublime marrying of lyrics and music to draw our attention to his muse:

a) '. . . very strange' sees a 'stolen' E7 take us V-I to the rousing chorus in the key of A (at 0.33). Then, to *return* to the verse:-
b) 'Meanwhile back . . .' sees F♯7 take us *back* – V-I again – to a verse in B major (at 0.50), the key in which we started.

The very lyrics 'meanwhile back' remind us once again that the dominant is all about setting up a return 'home', both musically and often lyrically.

We will see countless examples of The Beatles exploiting the semantic potential of the dominant V to reinforce a lyrical theme in this way.

Although their contexts may be very different, the lines 'You're coming home' in 'It Won't Be Long', and 'lead me to your door' in 'The Long And Winding Road' are just two obvious examples (from either end of the catalogue) where a V chord signposts the way home in every sense.

The Beatles used the dominant to deliver their message in a range of subtle ways. Listen to the build up in anticipation that kick-starts 'Back In The USSR' as that driving E7 emerges from the clouds (at 0.10) amid the noises of the BOAC jet. Yes, prior to the first chord change, the chord could be just a bluesy tonic, similar to many I7 Beatles chords dating back to 'I Saw Her Standing There'. But that would have been too simple.

The way the chord builds in intensity beneath the crucially descending pitches of the sound effects, along with the trademark Beatles 'ooh' in the opening vocals, give us a clue as to its function. Sure enough, the E7 is soon confirmed as a dominant V7 that touches down on 'runway' A (at 0.16) as surely as the aircraft taking our homesick singer back to Mother Russia. 'Back In The USSR' also illustrates how a songwriter doesn't need to wait until the end of a song section to create a local highlight with a V chord.

As far back as 'Hold Me Tight' The Beatles were priming us for an early peak when, after a modest one-bar vamp on the F tonic, we jump suddenly to the C7 for an early hearing of the punchline: 'It feels so right'.

Then again, some of John Lennon's favourite early songs featured verses starting with the V. Like Johnny Burnette's 'Lonesome Tears In My Eyes', as covered on *Live At The BBC*, which The Beatles played with a B7-E7 move. Meanwhile, the intro to 'She's A Woman' can be seen as an extension of the old blues tradition of cueing the band 'from the V', moving back to I via an intervening IV chord.

Using V as a first port-of-call from the tonic is in fact a defining feature of the 8-bar blues form, with the I7-V7 in bar 2 distinguishing it from the 12-bar variety. Big Bill Broonzy's 'Key To The Highway' is a great example – as is another standard, 'How Long, How Long Blues', popularised by Leroy Carr back in 1928.

Rock 'n' roll would incorporate the 'early V' formula in hundreds of songs by the time The Beatles covered 'I Got A Woman' on *Live At The BBC* (which opens with E to B7 in bar 2 of the verse).

And so 'tonic-to-dominant' can be seen as an opening gambit in many Beatles originals in different styles, including 'Baby's In Black', 'Hey Jude',

'Let It Be' and 'Oh! Darling', even if in such cases the V acts not as a defining peak in the song's structure but as a stepping-stone for further movement in an ongoing progression.

Whatever its various incarnations, the V chord is clearly fundamental in helping to explain how a song 'works' and why we often instinctively respond emotionally to its appearance.

Beyond the V7 – extensions, additions and alterations

So far we have assumed the dominant to be merely a simple construction of root, major 3rd and perfect 5th, with perhaps a ♭7th to add some tritone spice. In a great many cases the V is indeed delivered with just these notes, whether contained in the instrumental chord, the vocal melody or the harmony backing.

But the V can be also 'dressed up' by incorporating a variety of other notes that vary the flavour, or *quality*, of the overall sonority.

For example, the triad can be 'extended' beyond the ♭7th (e.g. with the 9th degree); 'added to' (e.g. with a 6th); or 'altered' (e.g. 'augmenting' the 5th by a semitone).[19]

The remainder of this chapter focuses on just some of the ways The Beatles embellished the V chord – whether with their guitar chords, and/or vocal melodies and harmonies – to create a variety of colourful textures.

1. 'Extension' to a V chord – The dominant 9th chord

'If I Fell' sees the D major chord turned to a 9th chord (at 0.58) courtesy of both a jazzy guitar shape and the E and C natural notes in the vocals.

'If I Fell'

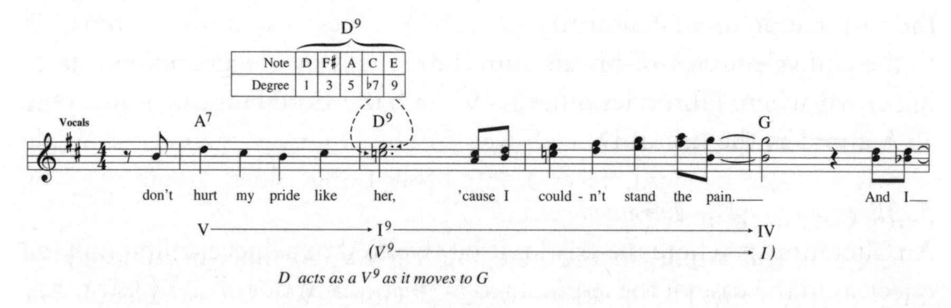

19 Refer to Appendix 2 for a summary of how these additions, extensions and alterations are constructed across a range of chords (beyond just the V), together with some specific Beatles examples.

In another sneak preview of the concept of modulation, this embellishment also signals a change in the function of the D chord within the song. While clearly heard as a home tonic in the verse, it acts here as a 'local' dominant V9 in terms of the following G chord that some would say *feels* like a temporary tonic as we move to the bridge section.

Watch how this extra 9th note falls appropriately on the stressed lyric 'her', as Lennon reminds himself poignantly of some past anguish.

2. 'Addition' to a V – The major sixth chord

The term 'addition' is used to describe a note added to a simple triad – without the appearance of the seventh of the chord. The added 6th chord is perhaps most famous as the tumultuous G6 that closes 'She Loves You' – though there it acts as a *tonic* sonority.[20]

For a poignant V6 sound implied briefly by a vocal melody note, cue up the climax of the bridge of 'What You're Doing'.

'What You're Doing'

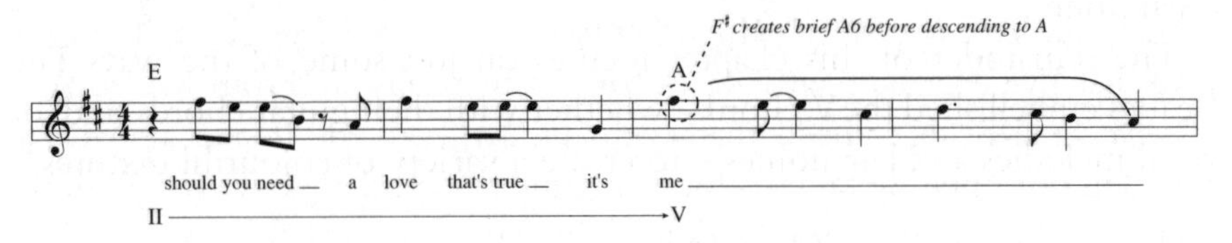

McCartney could happily have hit a triad tone in his melody (perhaps the high A) for this peaking V moment, but opted instead for the F♯ that sits deliciously against the chord, creating a brief A6 in the key of D. Appreciate the fleeting tension beyond the basic triad before the melody skips down the major scale to an A note ahead of the V-I return-to-verse. Compare it to the equivalent end-of-bridge climax in 'This Boy' (logged in our opening chart) where John cries his eyes out with the same F♯ melody note over an A chord in the key of D.

3. Alteration to a V – The augmented 5th

An 'alteration' is where the triad is itself tweaked to achieve an intensifying effect, as in the case of the augmented 5th that jumps out of 'It's Only Love' almost in slow motion.

[20] Guitarists can best appreciate the Vadd6th sound in the slick G6 shapes of 'Can't Buy Me Love' that resolve V-I in the key of C major. Check the 'no, no, no, *no*!' moment referred to earlier, and also the penultimate chord (at 2.04).

'It's Only Love'

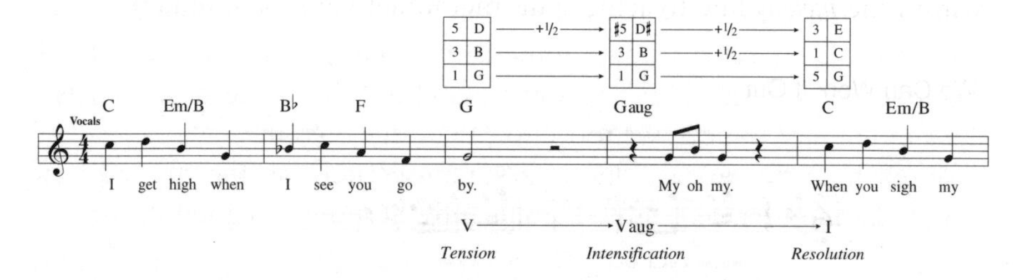

Not satisfied with the plain G chord as a V, Lennon could have turned it into G7 at the critical moment (0.15). But instead he sharpens, or 'augments', the 5th degree by a semitone which acts cheekily as a subliminal 'wolf whistle' in the context of the singer's 'My oh my'. Next time around we share John's 'butterflies' courtesy of that same D♯, with the pulse only slowing as the note resolves up a semitone into the 3rd of the C tonic chord.

A traditionally jazzy effect, the augmented 5th is another device that spans The Beatles career from *Please Please Me* to *Abbey Road* and *Let It Be.* Check out 'Ask Me Why' where Lennon uses it to tell us about 'the only love that I've ever had' (at 0.48). More dramatically, in 'From Me To You' it's *that* final bridge chord that keeps us 'satisfied *ooh*' (Gaug at 0.47, as noted in our opening table). Not forgetting the similarly tweaked V chords that yield the Eaug of 'Oh! Darling' (intro, and again at 1.39) and the F♯aug of 'One After 909' (courtesy of the vocal harmony at 1.11).[21]

4. The 4:3 suspension

Another way to toy with the triad is to temporarily usurp the defining major 3rd of the chord with the note a semitone above it. This creates an ambiguous feeling of suspension as the 4th 'wants' to resolve to the 3rd within the V chord itself (quite apart from the subsequent V-I resolution).

As a purely instrumental ploy we hear this sus4-3 effect in our favourite end-of-bridge setting in songs like 'If I Needed Someone' (E7sus4-E7, at 0.51), 'For No One' (F♯sus4-F♯, at 0.37) and 'Lady Madonna' (E7sus4-E7, at 0.42). Listen in particular to how the famous fireman's bell in 'Penny Lane' ingeniously mirrors the matching sus4 chord's characteristic 3rd-less twang (F♯7sus4-F♯7, at 1.07).

[21] Check the 'aug' chord as an opening device in the blues of T-Bone Walker's '(They Call It) Stormy Monday'; the rock 'n' roll of Chuck Berry's 'No Particular Place To Go'; and the New Wave power pop of The Undertones' 'You've Got My Number (Why Don't You Use It!)'.

In 'We Can Work It Out', McCartney incorporates the same 4:3 effect within the *melody* line to achieve his memorably dissonant refrain.

'We Can Work It Out'

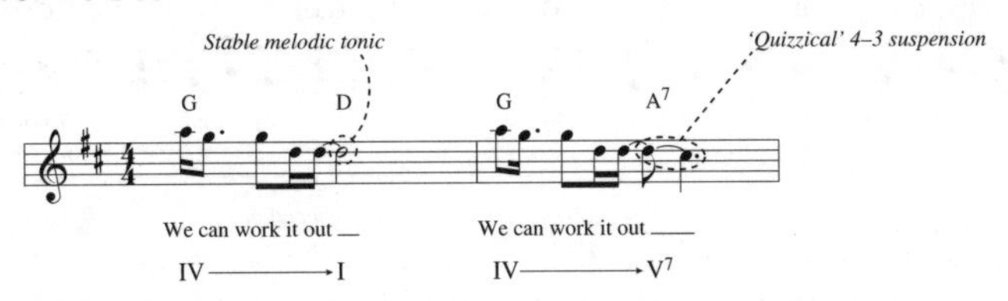

5. 'Exotic intensifiers' – the sharpened 9th, and flattened 9th

These two chords also bring their own distinctively dissonant action to the proceedings. To appreciate the effect, take the same dominant 9th chord of 'If I Fell' and first raise the 9th note a semitone to create a dominant 7♯9. We can hear it in action in the refrain of 'You Can't Do That' (at 0.22).[22]

'You Can't Do That'

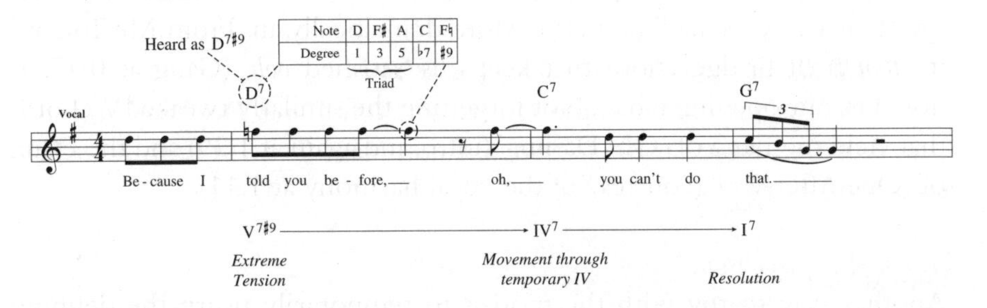

Here John Lennon delivers his reprimand most appropriately above the mayhem caused by a clash of the F natural note over D7 – *a chord which already contains an F♯.* These major and flattened 3rds fight it out, only finally resolving on the word 'that'.[23]

[22] When asked for his memories of 'You Can't Do That', Lennon volunteered: 'That's me doing a Wilson Pickett song. You know, a cowbell going four in the bar, and that chord going *chatoong*.' *The Playboy Interviews*, p.172. He must have meant this D7, vocally enchanced with ♯9.

[23] The F note is the same pitch as E♯ which is, technically, the correct way to describe the ♯9 note in the key of D. But F helps us appreciate more easily that both the major and flattened 3rds are present and why we therefore hear the chord as heavily altered. E♯ and F are therefore said to be 'enharmonic equivalents'.

Then there's the V7 with a *flattened* 9th that George Harrison gives us in 'I Me Mine'. And if we hear George 'coming on strong' at this point, it's surely because of that haunting F note that he sings at 0.27.

'I Me Mine'

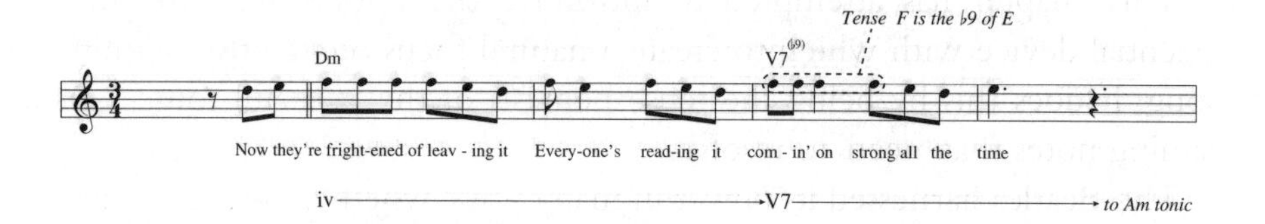

The vital note is the ♭9th, a semitone above the root of E (or a semitone down from the natural 9th we saw in 'If I Fell'). The resulting E7♭9, in the key of Am, creates dark drama in what is our first minor-key example.

To round off this chapter, we've chosen the dramatic moment in 'Drive My Car' where The Beatles deliver one of their most elaborate vocal arrangements to dress-up a V chord.

6. 'Double' alteration to a V – the dominant 7♯5♯9

Here The Beatles combine the effects of 'You Can't Do That' and 'It's Only Love' to build an ultra-dissonant dominant 7th with both ♯9 *and* ♯5 alterations.

'Drive My Car'

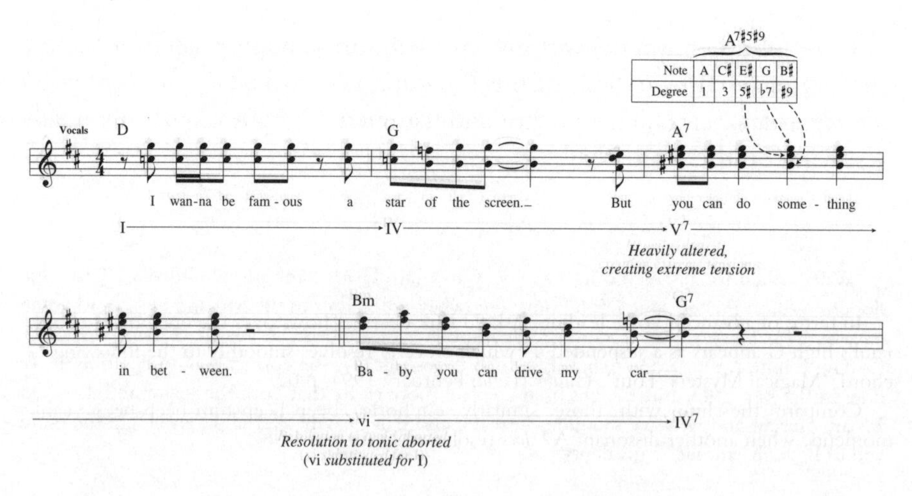

The C and G notes (sung by John and Paul, respectively) have already created some early colour over the I and IV chords by the time George slips 'in between' them with a deliciously grating E♯ that cheekily reinforces the double entendre of this climactic lyric.[24] Then again, as with so many of these examples, we hardly need any fancy technical or semantic analysis to feel the inherent power of a dominant V chord at work.

This chapter has attempted to introduce the dominant as the most essential device with which to create a natural focus of attention within a song. It does this by being the tense nemesis of the peaceful tonic, containing notes that 'need' to resolve.

The Beatles harnessed its power in many ways, whether creating simple, comprehensive V-I 'closure' (as we saw in 'In My Life'), or sign-posting further movement by leaving the V 'hanging' at the end of the line – as with this outrageous 'Drive My Car' cluster.

In this last case, while some of the pressure-cooker dissonances of the monster A7♯5♯9 chord are resolved eventually with the following chord change, we do *not* move predictably 'home' to our tonic of D (as we have done for most of this chapter). The Beatles deliberately drive us down a different road for the chorus – landing on an unexpected B minor that we will later describe as the 'relative minor' of the expected D major.[25]

But, for now, appreciate how, once again, a V chord creates a *crescendo* in the song's structure and a powerful expectation of further movement – a sense that we are 'going somewhere'. And, with The Beatles at the wheel, we certainly are.

[24] In terms of advanced voice leading, Askold Buk decribes how, over the opening D chord, Paul's high G appears as a suspended 4th which cleverly resolves smoothly to the following G chord. 'Magical Mystery Tour', *Guitar World*, February 1994, p.62.

[25] Compare the line with those similarly euphoric 'beep-beep-mm-beep-beep-yeah!' moments, when another dissonant A7 *does* resolve to D (first at 1.06).

TWO

The Three-Chord Trick and the Blues

'We used to travel miles for a new chord in Liverpool. We'd take bus rides for hours to visit the guy who knew B7!', Paul McCartney remembers. 'None of us knew how to finger it and he was the guru. We sat there and he played it a few times; then we all said: "Brilliant, thanks!" We already had E and A. The B7 chord was the final piece in the jigsaw.'[1]

The B7 chord was, of course, just the V7 we've been exploring while the 'jigsaw' itself was the infamous 'Three-Chord Trick': the very foundation of Western popular music from blues and rock 'n' roll to punk and heavy metal.

Despite the seemingly limited musical boundaries of three major triads, the I, IV and V chords allow songwriters a full range of permutations for the very strongest of voice-leading as well as the most powerful root movements in music – fourths and fifths.

And to make the point, this chapter looks at those songs (or clear sections of songs) that draw exclusively on these chords.

Let's define our terms. Some musicians and writers define the Three-Chord Trick as a very specific, prescribed sequence of these three chords, namely: I-IV-V-IV-I. Certainly, this move neatly covers any number of songs from Eddie Cochran's 'C'mon Everybody' to The Troggs' 'Wild Thing'. But it is helpful to widen the net. History relates that a close variation on the same cycle would have been the first thing that the young John Lennon heard Paul McCartney play. For I, IV and V also define the the structure of another Eddie Cochran song, 'Twenty Flight Rock', the

[1] *Guitar Player,* July 1990, p. 18.

subject of Paul's impromptu backstage rendition at the Woolton Village Fête in July 1957.

In fact, the whole point of 'the trick' is that knowledge of just these three chords enables the novice musician to play thousands of songs in dozens of genres. Whether it's blues, early jazz, folk, skiffle, R'n'B, rock 'n' roll or pop, popular music is founded on a catalogue of compositions that each use these three chords – exclusively – albeit in a variety of permutations.

We have already seen the pivotal role of the V chord in the previous chapter, so we will be focusing mainly on I and IV. We will look particularly at the establishment of the tonic, and the role of IV in both cadencing to the tonic (as an alternative to the Perfect cadence) and as a destination to 'visit' from the I chord.

This chapter is, therefore, not merely about the Three-Chord Trick. It is about the pillars of pop music and how The Beatles incorporated the principles heard in the most basic of early covers into some of their most sophisticated songwriting.

Back in the 1950s (and indeed probably still today) the Three-Chord Trick represented the first hurdle for any budding rock and pop musician's early forays into songwriting. And The Beatles were no different. With their famed love of Chuck Berry, Little Richard and Carl Perkins, The Beatles – like their contemporaries – first cut their teeth on sets full of songs that hinged on the I, IV and V chords. Many of these would appear as recorded covers across a range of albums, most famously 'Twist And Shout', 'Roll Over Beethoven', 'Money', 'Rock'n'Roll Music', 'Kansas City', 'Words Of Love' and 'Everybody's Trying To Be My Baby'.

Although The Beatles would become known for their adventurousness beyond this formula, it is nevertheless worth demonstrating how the Three-Chord Trick would appear throughout their career in a whole variety of settings. Such simplicity was not only the domain of the early period, as might be assumed. I, IV and V may have accounted for the first single 'Love Me Do' – but so they would for later songs like 'I'm Down' and 'Don't Pass Me By' right through to 'Dig It' on *Let It Be* – The Beatles' answer to the 'Wild Thing' formula mentioned earlier. Even the elaborate instrumental, 'Flying', on *Magical Mystery Tour* (which Noel Gallagher apparently found so inspirational for Oasis's 'Shakermaker') can be seen as a thinly disguised 12-bar blues.

We will be exploring the 12-bar format below, showing how The Beatles would use it in songs ranging from the obviously bluesy 'For You

Blue' to the cleverly disguised 'Can't Buy Me Love'. But a quick look at the Three-Chord Trick in the even more primitive 8-bar context makes for an appropriate starting point. Not least because The Quarry Men's debut recording (which uses this structure) is ironically thought to be the single most valuable pop record of all time.

'In Spite Of All The Danger'

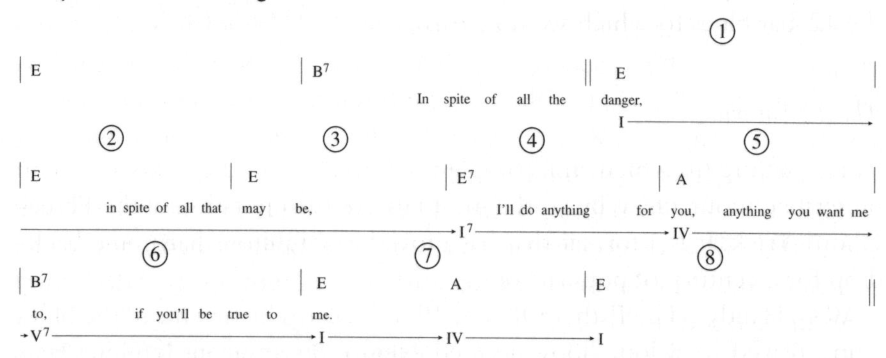

A rare joint composition by Paul McCartney and George Harrison, 'In Spite Of All The Danger' illustrates how the band began composing within the confines of I, IV and V, grasping the simple functions of each of these elements. Conveniently, this 1958 song (which resurfaced on *Anthology 1*) uses these three chords in the key of E, just as mentioned by McCartney in this chapter's opening quote – E is the I chord, A is the IV and (the no-longer-elusive) B7 is the V7 chord.

It may not have been quite up to the standards of Beatles heroes like Little Richard or Chuck Berry but, at a very basic compositional level, the song illustrates the premise of the Three-Chord Trick as it fulfils some of the important principles of most tonal music.

First, the need for movement away from the tonic I chord to create a sense of harmonic development. The IV chord, or *subdominant*, is built on the fourth degree of the major scale and represents a typical destination for the song to progress to before making its way back to I. The progress to the IV chord can be direct from the tonic, as in the case of bar 5 here – or indeed any typical blues. In more sophisticated songs the move will be indirect, with the I-chord typically passing through a range of other chords that can often be thought of as effectively prolonging the tonic harmony while still essentially homing in on IV.

Second, the blues creates a climax, a point of maximum tension which is then resolved, or 'un-wound', by means of a resolution back to the tonic, completing a sense of returning home after the journey. As we know this is a role typically played by the V chord (as here), with the B7 in bar 8 being followed by E. But as well as the 'perfect' V-I move, we can also see an alternative resolution, IV-I (albeit only as a brief turnaround gesture in bar 7), an important move found in many different contexts, including in the 12-bar blues to which we now turn.

The 12-bar blues

This structure (in which, in its simplest form, each chord appears at certain prescribed moments) is by far the most famous manifestation of the Three-Chord-Trick. It is a format that has proved a ubiquitous harmonic backdrop for a century of popular song.

W. C. Handy ('The Father Of The Blues') claims he first heard the blues being played by a lone 'loose-jointed Negro' on an acoustic guitar in a deserted railway station in Tutweiler, Mississippi, sometime around 1903. The chances are that he was playing the 12-bar variety that first defined Handy's own 'Memphis Blues', in 1912, though music historians have suggested that the form actually evolved from 19th Century hymns.[2]

Whatever its origins, it is a format that The Beatles would adopt in many instances in their songwriting, far beyond the obvious '12-Bar Original' (an instrumental in the key of A on *Anthology 2*), or 'For You Blue', where George Harrison even reminds us (in his vocal at 1.18) that this is 'the 12-bar blues'.

Let's use this structure to explore some of the important roles of the chords. The first thing to notice is the presence of a flattened seventh on *all* the triads – not just the V as we would expect from major scale theory. This is characteristic of the blues (and many other Three-Chord Tricks, even if they do necessarily have an intrinsically bluesy flavour). This practice evolved from the blues tradition of the early part of the century, which

[2] Richard Middleton, *Studying Popular Music*, p. 117. Middleton quotes the musicologist P. Van Der Merwe as suggesting that the roots of the 12-bar blues lie in the very specific I-IV-V dance structures of the Renaissance period – which can even be spotted in The Beatles 'I Saw Her Standing There'. However, while many of the chords and cadences are shared, this structure does not follow the most common 'standard' 12-bar format we are discussing with 'For You Blue'.

'For You Blue'

①	②	③	④
D^7	G^7	D^7	D^7
Be-cause you're sweet and love - ly	girl, I	love you.	Be -
I^7 →	IV^7 →	I^7 →	→

⑤	⑥	⑦	⑧
G^7	G^7	D^7	D^7
cause you're sweet and love -	ly girl, it's true.		I
IV^7 →	→	I^7 →	→

⑨	⑩	⑪	⑫
A^7	G^7	D^7	A^7
love you more than ev -	er girl I do.		
V^7 →	IV^7 →	I^7 →	V^7 →

carried over into post-war R'n'B, fifties rock'n'roll and sixties rock. The purpose of the ♭7 in each chord here is to complement the blues-based melodies whose chief source is the minor pentatonic scale that consists of the tones 1-♭3-4-5-♭7.

It is mainly as a result of the influence of Afro-American blues, which adopts this scale wholeheartedly, that popular music is so difficult to pigeonhole in terms of Western diatonic theory. The presence of the ♭7 in the I and IV chords is the first such exception to 'the rules' of major scale harmony. Watch how, in 'For You Blue' the tonic minor pentatonic scale can also be seen to contain the ♭7 of *each* of the I, IV and V chords, thereby explaining their presence in terms of a self-contained 'blues theory'.

Creating the D7, G7 and A7 chords in a blues: key of D

Minor pentatonic scale formula	1	♭3	4	5	♭7
D minor pentatonic	D	F	G	A	C
Chord tones in a bluesey I - IV - V		♭7 of G^7 (IV^7)	♭7 of A^7 (V^7)		♭7 of D^7 (I^7)

The 12-bar blues is a versatile framework within which to explore a range of Beatles devices that may at first seem far removed from the pop genre. Frequent references will be made to specific locations in the 12 bars and therefore the bar numbers and the typical harmonic activity associated with them should be memorised. We will see how entire songs can be fashioned merely from creating a turnaround sequence in bars 11 and 12, while the same format will even help us to understand seemingly complex chord substitutions and modulations.

The overriding importance of the Three-Chord Trick and its origins as the cornerstone of blues and R'n'B right through to fifties and early sixties rock 'n' roll is also worth reinforcing. Certainly, the rules of the 12-bar format where I, IV and V appear in certain prescribed sequences have always been broken. Songs of 8-, 11-, 13-, 16- and 24-bar sequences were regularly being explored by Delta bluesman as far back as Robert Johnson, Charlie Patton and Son House. More important than the bar counts (which are typically a reflection of the metric scanning of a lyrical phrase) is the varying emphasis on the role and appearance of each of the chords themselves.

The preponderance of three-chord covers on the early Beatles albums (and particularly on *Live At The BBC* and *Anthology 1*) confirms just how familiar The Beatles had become with the versatility of this songwriting format.

It is perhaps unnecessary to speculate on the possible influences of the standard structures of these covers in the way that we will be attempting to do with other musical devices. But a quick look at Little Richard's 'Lucille' makes for some interesting observations, as it can be argued that it became a powerful blueprint for the verse of 'Can't Buy Me Love'. After all, The Beatles tackled very few such R'n'B covers in the key of C and it is perhaps no coincidence that 'Lucille' and 'Can't Buy Me Love' – both in C and featuring a similar tempo, format and melody – appear side-by-side on *Live At The BBC* (tracks 31 and 32). Of course, both *Live At The BBC* and *Anthology I* contain legions of other 12-bars, or similar simple three-chord variations – 'Rock'n'Roll Music', 'Dizzy Miss Lizzy', 'Kansas City', 'Long Tall Sally' and 'Ooh My Soul' are just some that operate within this basic structure.

Although the format doesn't provide particular insight into The Beatles' harmonic development, it's worth noting a few nuances of the Three-Chord Trick, to showcase the variety of songwriting possibilities. For example, The Beatles cover of 'Johnny B. Goode' – like the Chuck Berry original – varies the texture of its resolutions by sometimes hanging on the V chord for two bars (and cadencing directly V-I) while, at other points, unwinding more gradually from V through the IV chord.

Elsewhere, there's the busy movement between all three chords, as heard on 'Crying, Waiting And Hoping', showing how the Three-Chord

Trick can be used for rhythmic as well as harmonic interest. This was a trademark of Buddy Holly (who wrote this 1959 release), along with the similarly structured verse of 'Peggy Sue' (another Beatles live staple between 1957 and 1962). Meanwhile, certain other early Beatles covers like 'Nothin' Shakin' (But The Leaves On The Trees)', 'Some Other Guy' and 'I'm Gonna Sit Right Down (And Cry Over You)' have 'stock' three-chord verses but may contain a bridge, coda, or even a single chord that expands the harmonic boundaries and is therefore beyond the scope of this chapter.

In summary, all such Three-Chord sequences are tried-and-tested, formulaic methods of generating harmonic interest. Their success is the result of listener expectations built up over centuries of dance music and, more recently, blues, rock 'n' roll and R'n'B songs.

The power of I – the one-chord trick

Songs do not necessarily have to revolve around even as many as three chords to create interest. 'Tomorrow Never Knows', the closing track on *Revolver* and sometimes regarded as The Beatles' most progressive outing, is paradoxically structured around a single, simply embellished G chord, around which hypnotic modal melodies work their textural magic. And while harmonic stability is a strong tradition of Indian music, the same is also true of blues and rock 'n' roll. Indeed, the effect of a single chord throughout a song is an old blues tradition dating back at least as far as Charlie Patton's 1929 recordings; while such droning blues harmony can still be heard in the 'crossover' blues sounds of R.L. Burnside.

The British rock scene of the sixties was perhaps most directly introduced to this harmonically static sound through bands like the Yardbirds, with their renditions of songs like Willie Dixon's 'Smokestack Lightning', featuring a repeated riff in E. And while one-chord songs are exceptions in pop music, many three-chord songs also make the important premise of establishing a prolonged tonic.

As McCartney remembers,[3] one of the perennial Cavern crowd-pleasers was The Beatles' cover of 'Searchin'', a Three-Chord Trick, but one that hangs on the I chord for what seems like an eternity, as if stubbornly intent on going nowhere. Just listen to The Beatles' version on *Anthology 1* which,

[3] *Paul McCartney's Rock & Roll Roots*, BBC Radio 2, Christmas Day 1999.

like the Coasters' original, hangs on the tonic A chord for 16 bars before finally giving way to a IV chord.[4]

That's not to say that such 'harmonically challenged' songs have no ability to arouse interest. Indeed, such a device can be used effectively to create precisely this false sense of security. Take such influential early skiffle numbers as 'Rock Island Line', one of John Lennon's earliest influences. Originally popularised by Louisiana bluesman Huddie Ledbetter (Leadbelly), the revolutionary sixties version saw Lonnie Donegan strumming a lone G chord – unaccompanied for over a minute – before picking up steam and exploding into life with D and C chords. Such songs were perhaps unusual influences for The Beatles, whose original song-writing would soon be defined by relentless harmonic movement. Yet, as a principle to exploit in a pop song, an extended I chord would even find its way into several Beatles songs. The Eastern-type drone songs on *Revolver* and *Sgt. Pepper*, whose very premise is a stationary 'pedal tone', form a whole category discussed in Chapter 8. Meanwhile, in the context of a more conventional pop song, 'Paperback Writer' can clearly be seen to be built essentially around a similarly prolonged, scene-setting I chord that only makes a brief excursion to IV after a full 8 bars.

Several other Beatles songs in a harder, blues-rock vein display this same, similarly stubborn, opening emphasis. 'Everybody's Got Something To Hide Except For Me And My Monkey', for example, features a ten-bar, driving E tonality for both a four-bar intro and the first six bars of the verse. 'Ticket To Ride' is most certainly not a Three Chord Trick, but this same ten-bar establishment of the tonic occurs here too. This time a four-bar intro on A major is followed by another six bars in the verse before the first harmonic change. In terms of subtle semantics, it's no accident that the lyrics "going away" prompts the shift from our stable tonic 'home'.

The above examples are intended to familiarise the reader with the idea of establishing a tonal centre in a pop song and showing how a sense of anticipation is built up for the first impending chord change.

The Beatles' sense of harmony may, for once, be taking a back seat here, but the static premise nevertheless provides a backdrop for other musical highlights – in the case of 'Ticket To Ride', the guitar motif that lends interest by adding a 9th 'colour' tone, not forgetting the song's famous lilting, syncopated drum beat.

[4] With no turnaround to V at the end of the previous chorus, the I chord is actually sounded for 20 bars without respite (0.39–1.11).

'Paperback Writer'

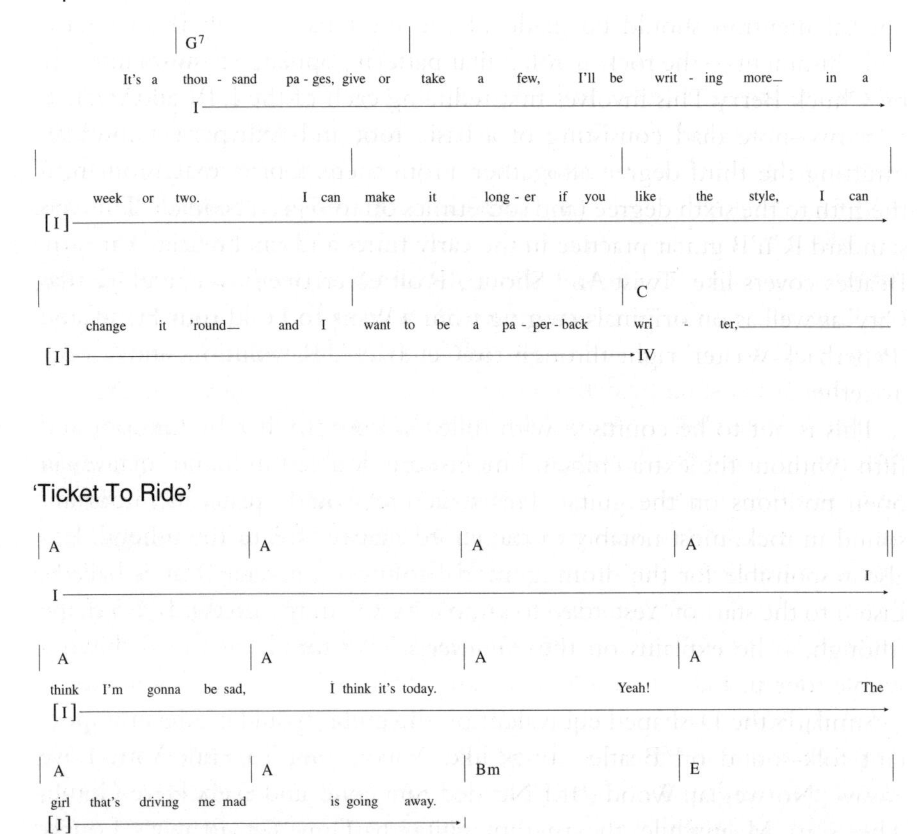

On the subject of 'colour' tones, the I triad, just like the V chord in the last chapter) can be dressed up in a variety of ways beyond the extension of the flattened 7th in a blues context. And The Beatles experimented liberally with everything from major 6ths, 7ths and 9ths, through to 6/9s, 7♯9s, '11ths' as well as 'sus' and 'add' chords, to vary the quality of the major I chord. The various charts in Appendix 3 summarise the full spectrum of these chords, and categorises them once again in terms of 'additions', 'extensions' and 'alterations'.

The Chuck Berry rhythm

Special mention should be made of the most basic of all Beatles triad embellishments – the rock 'n' roll guitar pattern popularised most famously by Chuck Berry. This involves first reducing each of the I, IV and V triads to a two-note diad consisting of a basic root-and-fifth perfect interval, omitting the third degree altogether. From there, a brief extension from the fifth to the sixth degree (and sometimes on to ♭7) can be made. This was standard R'n'B guitar practice in the early fifties and can be heard on early Beatles covers like 'Twist And Shout', 'Roll Over Beethoven' and 'Kansas City' as well as on originals ranging from 'I Want To Hold Your Hand' and 'Paperback Writer' right through to 'Get Back', 'Revolution' and 'Come Together'.

This is not to be confused with fuller '5' chords whereby the root and fifth (without the extra embellishments) are doubled in higher octaves in open positions on the guitar. This structure would create an important sound in rock, most notably in the chord shapes of Pete Townshend. It is also responsible for the droning, modal sounds in several Beatles ballads. Listen to the start of 'Yesterday' to sample McCartney's 'no thirds' G5 shape (though, as he explains on the *Anthology 2* version, he is tuned down a whole tone to F).

Similarly the D-shaped equivalent on the guitar would create an important folk-sound on Beatles songs like 'You've Got To Hide Your Love Away', 'Norwegian Wood', 'If I Needed Someone' and even 'Here Comes The Sun'. Meanwhile, the rhythm guitar part on 'Sgt. Pepper's Lonely Hearts Club Band' shows how voicing the I chord with 'root-fifth[-root]' on the lower strings creates the distinctive sonic foundation, and *timbre*, of a hard rock progression. These guidelines apply equally to our other diatonic major triad: the IV chord.

The IV chord

As we have already established with I and V, chords make their appearance according to different functions. The IV chord (known as the *subdominant* as it is the chord a whole step below the dominant in a harmonised scale) is no different. The IV may be almost omnipresent in pop songs but has varying roles, each of which can be well illustrated in The Beatles' music. These include:

1) The Plagal cadence from IV–I:
 (a) IV–I (b) the IV–iv–I variation
2) As a pivotal destination from the I chord:
 (a) the I–IV 'quick' change
 (b) the 'bridge' modulation from I7–to–IV.
3) Preparing the V chord: the IV–to–V move.

1) IV-I and the Plagal cadence

For all the power of root movement in fifths, and the inexorable pull of the dominant chord's leading note into the tonic, The Beatles appreciated that the predictable 'Perfect' V-I cadence was not the only way to achieve a satisfactory resolution for their chord progressions. Right from the early days they used the more relaxed IV chord to ring the changes. Compare the chorus and ending resolutions in both 'I Saw Her Standing There' and 'I Want To Hold Your Hand' to see how an intervening IV chord can create a memorable twist on the V-I cadence.

These early experiments were perhaps a euphoric development of the 12-bar blues convention of unwinding the V-I tension through a passing IV chord (as with, say, the G7 we saw in bar 10 of 'For You Blue').[5]

But soon The Beatles were using the IV-I resolution in settings that showcased the distinctive voice leading inherent in the 'Plagal' cadence, while also exploiting the potential it provides for melodic novelty.

But first let's look more closely at the mechanics of a IV-I move in isolation, just as we did with the V-I cadence.

As well as root movement that descends by a perfect fourth, the Plagal cadence features '6-5' and '4-3' inner voice movement, formulae that merely reflect the whole- and half-step descents into the 5th and the 3rd of the tonic, respectively, as the chords shift.

While references to 'IV-I' and 'descending fourths' will often be used for practical purposes to describe this type of chord change, the Plagal effect doesn't necessarily hinge on root movement, as shown clearly by the languid intro vamp of 'I've Got A Feeling'. Listen to how a tonic A major chord (I) gets 'Plagalised' by a partial D shape (IV) *but over an unchanging A*

[5] And as we also saw in 'You Can't Do That', in Chapter 1, where the V7♯9 chord created such a peak before resolving to I *via IV*, in what is another thinly-disguised 12-bar blues structure.

bass. The harmonic focus is thus on the '4-3' and '6-5' effect, without the root descent of a fourth.[6]

'I Want To Hold Your Hand'

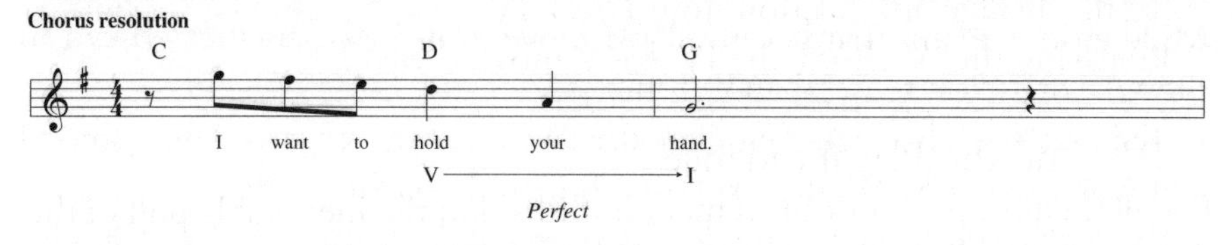

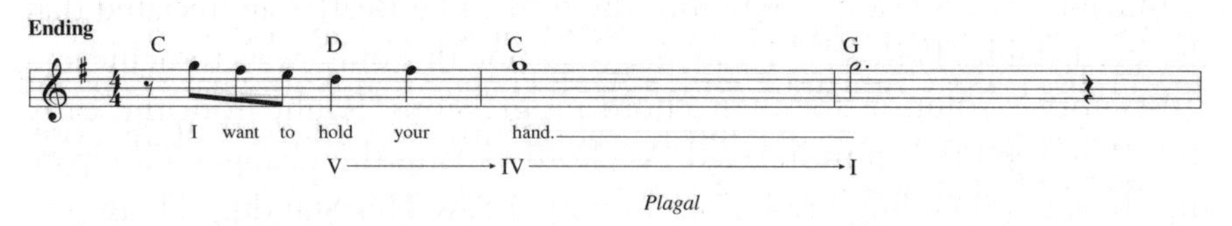

'I Saw Her Standing There'

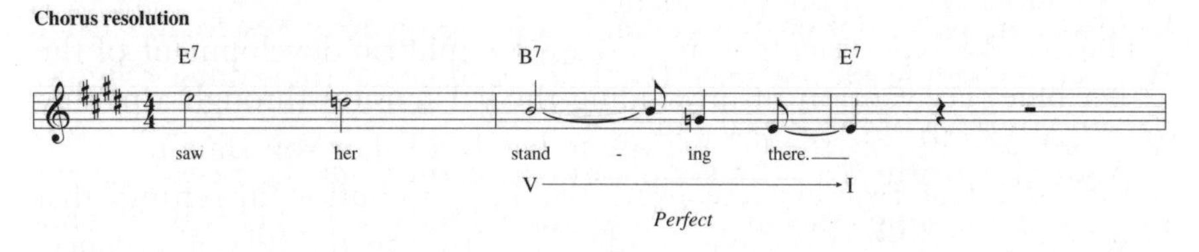

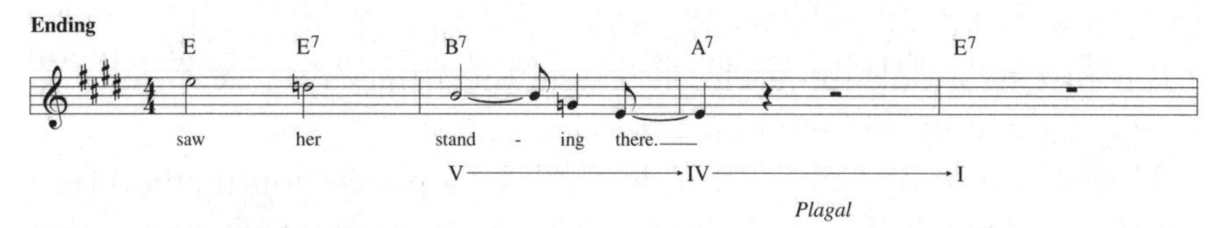

Voice leading in the Plagal cadence

Here is a summary of the action in a IV-I change (in the key of C), highlighting the important 'inner' voice leading.

F (IV) 'tension'			**C (I) 'resolution'**	
Formula	**Note**	**Voice leading**	**Note**	**Formula**
Root	*F*	*Down a semitone*	*E*	*3rd*
5th	C	Common tone	C	Root
3rd	*A*	*Down a whole tone*	*G*	*5th*
Root	F	Down a perfect fourth	C	Root

[6] Guitarists will appreciate how this '4-3' and '6-5' Plagal effect is a signature sound of The Rolling Stones, courtesy of Keith Richard's two-finger, hammer-on (and off) embellishments on songs like 'Brown Sugar' and 'Honky Tonk Woman'.

Notice how the root movement of a descending fourth (from F down to C) creates a more discreet resolution than the wider fifth, while the presence of the unchanging tonic C note (already within the IV chord itself) establishes a sense of security by acting as a constant 'internal pedal'. Middleton explains that because IV–I moves travel less 'distance', they can thought of as 'less tense' than V–I moves.[7]

This feature also helps explain the IV–I move's characteristic soulful ambiguity that The Beatles exploited for subtle semantic effect as far back as the early ballads. For example, the repeated A-E moves in 'All I've Got To Do' gently convey John's open-ended pleading: 'you just got to call on me' (1.36–1.48). Compare it with a B7-E change that would have depicted the singer's greater sense of control over the situation, courtesy of the dominant's 'confident' leading note.

The roots of the Plagal cadence in blues, gospel and pop appear to have been in church hymns where the familiar 'Amen' sound almost single-handedly helps to define the genre. Beatles songs like 'Yesterday', 'Let It Be', 'She's Leaving Home' and 'The End' each evoke their quasi-religious flavour courtesy of the Plagal cadence.

'Yesterday' features a V-I a couple of bars earlier, but the Plagal move is intrinsic to the song's melancholy resolution. Meanwhile, 'Let It Be' – while featuring the V chord within the song, never actually cadences V–I at any time, making the Plagal cadence entirely responsible for its hymnlike mood.

'Let It Be'

In each of these examples, the melody resolves from a variety of different chord tones within the IV chord as it gives way to the tonic. 'The End' is

[7] Richard Middleton, *Studying Popular Music*, p. 200.

perhaps the best example to use, as the 'Plagal-defining' voice leading into the 3rd of the tonic is so clearly heard in the upper harmony.

'The End'

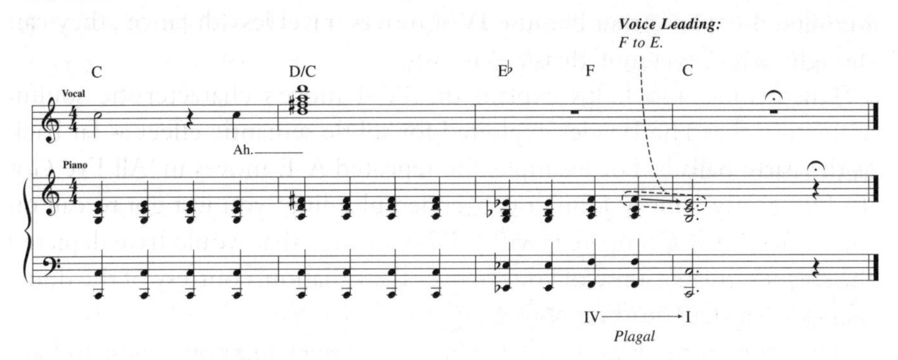

As we discuss in Chapter 8, The Beatles later extended the Plagal cadence by approaching the IV chord *from its IV*, creating the rocky sounding ♭VII-IV-I sequence found in several late sixties classics. Here the roots imply *two* successive descents of a fourth while there is similarly double the action in terms of the distinctive 'inner' Plagal voice-leading.

The IV major-to-iv minor Plagal variation

A favourite Beatles manoeuvre gleaned from a strong songwriting tradition was to play a IV chord – *but switch it from a major to a minor triad before returning to I.* The same root movement applies but now the progression is F-*Fm*-C. This idea dates back most famously to Cole Porter's classic 'Everytime We Say Goodbye', where this hybrid cadence is even cued by the immortal line: 'How strange the change from major to minor . . .'

'Everytime We Say Goodbye'

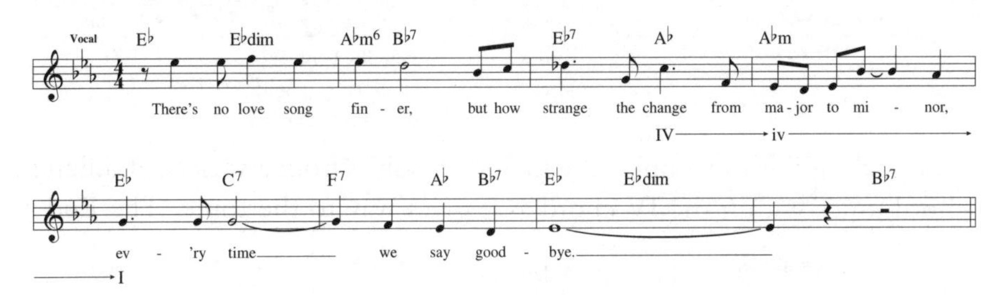

Again, the beauty of this move is in the voice-leading that creates a consecutive three-semitone descent as the major 3rd of Porter's IV chord drops to a minor 3rd and, from there, to the 5th of the I chord.

The ultimate example in which to hear the mechanics of this move is undoubtedly The Beatles' cover of 'Devil In Her Heart', by Richard B. Drapkin, where the melody spectacularly mirrors the harmonic activity (at 0.25-0.31).

'Devil In Her Heart'

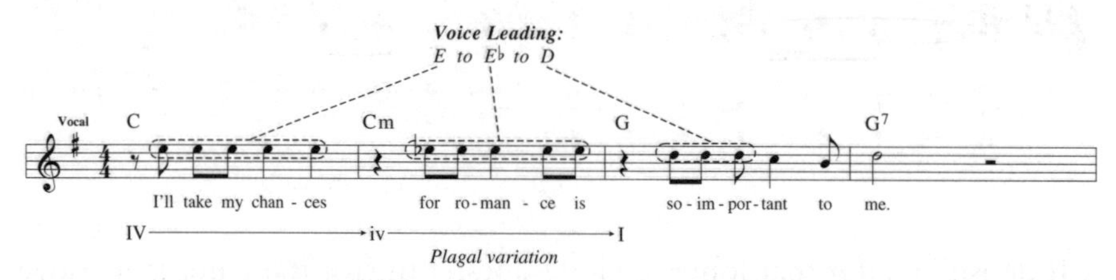

	'chances'	'romance'	'so impor[tant]'
Formula	IV	iv	I
Chords in G	C	Cm	G
Melodic/harmonic voice leading	E (3rd of C)	E♭ (♭3rd of Cm)	D (5th of G)
Scale descent in G	6	♭6	5

While the ballad tradition of the fifties usually reserved this idea for the bridge, The Beatles showed how it could spice up a IV-I move. Whether it was the pure pop of 'Hold Me Tight' or the 'power ballad' meanderings of 'Lucy In The Sky With Diamonds', here is another formula that appears on virtually every Beatles album.

Here is just a selection – again from different eras:

The IV-iv minor 'miracle' move

Song	Section	Lyric	IV - iv change
'I Call Your Name'	Verse	'I *can't* go on'	A - *Am*
'If I Fell'	Bridge	'stand the pain and *I* '	G- *Gm*
'In My Life'	Verse	'all my li-*ife* though some have changed'	D - *Dm*
'You Won't See Me'	Verse	'time ... that *was so hard*'	D - *Dm*
'Lucy In The Sky With Diamonds'	Verse	'boat on a *river*'	D - *Dm*
'Mother Nature's Sun'	Verse	'songs for everyone ... / ...'	D - *Dm*7
'Blackbird'	Verse	'all your life... / ...'	C - *Cm*

Of these, 'In My Life' makes particularly good early use of this idea in establishing a reflective feel consistent with the theme of the song.

'In My Life'

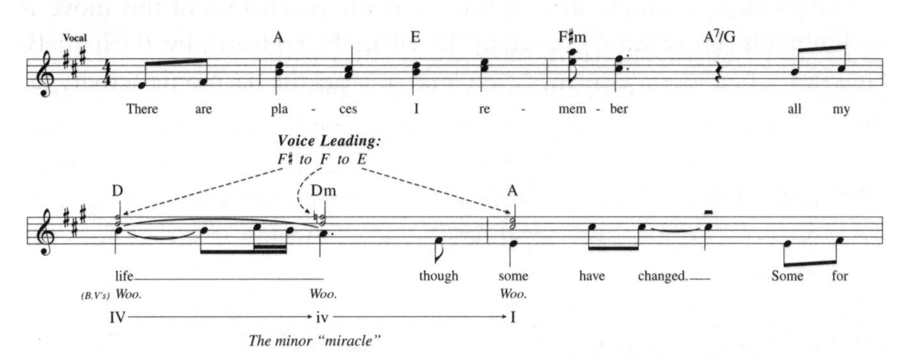

It doesn't matter that John's melody doesn't mirror the chromatic move – although the harmony vocal does happen to do so as the F♯ drops to F natural reflecting the D-D minor change.

While Cole Porter will probably always be associated with this move, it's more likely that The Beatles became familiar with it through a particular pair of favourite early covers that predate 'Devil In Her Heart':

'Till There Was You' (bridge): 'music../..and wonderful..' (B♭-B♭m-F)
'Ain't She Sweet' (bridge): 'cast an eye./..in her direction' (A-Am-E)[8]

What a coincidence that, 30 years after 'Till There Was You', Noel Gallagher should choose to play the song at his wedding ceremony. Only a few weeks earlier, his song 'Don't Look Back In Anger' – containing a textbook use of the same device – was at the top of the UK charts (hear it both in the 'gonna start a revolution from my bed' bridge, and in the final coda where it makes for a melancholy repeat of the title phrase – both times: F-Fm in the key of C).

For while it is often regarded as a dated ballad cliché, IV-iv has proved a winning move that has enjoyed success in several smash hits down the

[8] McCartney also mentions his great love of the Pat Boone ballad 'I'll Be Home' which he says 'swept Britain' (*Rock & Roll Roots*, Radio 2, 25 December 1999). That song, too, features the IV-iv move, delicately at 0.19, with the line 'we'll stroll *along* together . . .' [D♭-D♭m-Ab].

years. You can hear it in the 'progressive' pop of David Bowie's 'Starman', and equally on nineties ballads like Extreme's 'More Than Words'. It was perhaps most cleverly adopted by 10 CC on the classic 'I'm Not In Love' where IV-iv disarmingly opens the verse.[9]

2) IV as a first destination away from the tonic

Having looked at the cadential role of IV as it moves *towards* I, let's explore this chord as a point of harmonic departure *from* the tonic. There are two main areas to discuss: IV as a 'quick change' from I; and the more substantial 'bridge move' where IV – *primed by a tonic seventh chord acting as a temporary V7* – creates a powerful new sense of tonality removed from the original key centre.

a) I-IV – the 'quick' change

Only one step more elaborate than the harmonically static 'extended I chord' songs like 'Paperback Writer' are those many Beatles structures that alternate between I and IV. Indeed the first Beatles single, 'Love Me Do', hinged on this exclusively for the verse and refrain, with only the very briefest of nods to the V-chord in the bridge and solo. Nevertheless, it was sufficient to set the songwriting revolution on its way.

'Love Me Do'

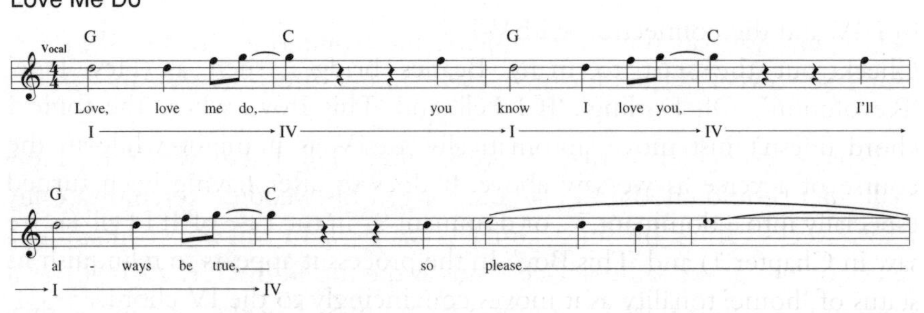

This is indeed a standard method of breaking up the monotony of the tonic and The Beatles used it in a range of songs, often as an opening premise before introducing more harmonically sophisticated material. Once again, we can see it clearly as a principal idea in songs of all eras, including 'There's A Place', 'She's A Woman', 'I'm Looking Through You',

[9] Admittedly, here the trick is adapted slightly as the resolution is not directly to the tonic but to the iii7 – a *substitute* for the I chord.

'Lady Madonna' and 'Revolution', to pick just a few spread across the catalogue.

From a songwriting perspective, this simple, yet driving, rock sound builds on the bluesy notion of the 'quick change' in a 12-bar blues, where the IV chord appears in bar 2 to break up a four-bar run on the I chord. Look back to 'For You Blue' to see precisely this most basic of embellishments, and the extra interest it creates in comparison to, say, 'In Spite Of All The Danger', where there is no 'quick change' and the E chord prevails for the full four bars. The quick change would have been heard by The Beatles in a whole range of three-chord contexts – a staple of such recorded covers as 'Roll Over Beethoven' (the line 'I'm gonna write a little letter, gonna *mail* it to my local DJ', coincides with I-IV-I.) While this can create a hypnotic diversion from the tonic harmony, IV can be a harmonic destination targeted in more subtle ways. The following chapters will illustrate how many 'intermediate' chords that may appear to cloud the picture often have the sole intention of leading the listener – eventually – to the IV chord.

However, we must first examine a more fundamental move which sees the I chord acquire dominant status before changing more emphatically to the IV chord.

b) I-IV and the connection with V-I

Check out the start to many Beatles bridges, such as 'Hey Jude' 'Revolution', 'Oh Darling', 'If I Fell' and 'This Boy', where the tonic I chord doesn't just move 'automatically' to IV as it might while in the course of a verse as we saw above. It does so after having been turned especially into a dominant 7th, or dominant 9th in the case of 'If I Fell' (as we saw in Chapter 1) and 'This Boy'. In the process it appears to relinquish its status of 'home' tonality as it moves convincingly to the IV chord.

Isn't this just the same as the V7-I move we saw throughout the last chapter? In a way, yes. After all, the basic mechanism again involves the same voice-leading of the 3rd and $\flat 7^{th}$, as they lead into the root and 3rd of the new chord, respectively. Meanwhile, the root movement 'up a fourth' can be seen to be just an inversion (or 'mirror image') of the descent of a perfect fifth. For example, ascending five semitones from C and descending seven semitones from C takes us in each case to the F. This is an important phenomenon as it demonstrates how the two moves are related and how the chord change from C to F is not merely a I-IV in the key of

C. It can equally be dressed up as a V7-I – by making C a C7 – thereby allowing F to take on *in some cases* the new mantle of 'tonic' after having been primed by its V7.

3) Priming the V chord: IV-to-V

The role of IV in preparing for the powerful V chord has already been seen in a variety of examples, but it's worth looking more closely at the relationship between these two chords, separated by the interval of a tone.

The IV-V move can in fact be seen as an integral part of not just blues and rock 'n' roll, but all Western pop. It appears not only in the Three-Chord Trick but also the I-vi-IV-V 'Four-Chord Turnaround', which we will describe in the next chapter as another of the most popular harmonic manoeuvres of the 20th Century.

However fleetingly, The Beatles used the IV-V move throughout their songwriting career. It appears equally in John Lennon's very first song, 'Hello Little Girl', as in the very last, 'Real Love'.

In most cases no particular novelty is suggested. But look closely at the intro and the end of the bridge in 'I Want To Hold Your Hand'.

'I Want To Hold Your Hand'

Dm	G	C	D	C	D	C	D
It's such a	feel - ing that my	love	I can't hide,	I	can't hide,	I	can't hide.
		IV ⟶	V	IV ⟶	V	IV ⟶	V

Here the return to the I chord (G) is delayed by a driving, reiterated move between the IV and V (C and D) in a move that showcased how two major triads, a whole step apart, could be exploited and turned into the sound of rock. It is ironic that this simple major second interval between two such common chords should have been so overlooked as a particular source of interest in the fifties before The Beatles. Even though it is, of course, just part of the potential of the Three-Chord Trick!

From a songwriting point of view it is useful to keep all these varying roles of the IV in mind, as the chord will constantly reappear in all genres of Beatles music. Indeed, some kind of initial I-to-IV change appears, without fail, on songs on every Beatles album – starting with the opening track on *Please Please Me*, 'I Saw Her Standing There' (which shifts from E7 to A7), right through to 'The End' on *Abbey Road* which consists almost exclusively of an extended vamp between A7 and D7.

Before we leave the IV chord we should highlight the incarnations in which the chord can appear in terms of the chord *quality*. Technically, the guidelines for 'additions', 'extensions' and 'alterations' are the same as for the I chord (refer again to Appendix 3 for the constructions). In practice, however, the major IV chord is most often heard as a simple triad, a bluesy dominant 7th or 9th, occasionally with an added 6th or a diatonic (major) 7th, such as the 'IV major 7' chords of 'No Reply', 'Yesterday' and 'Sexy Sadie'.

The Three-Chord Trick – revisited

Certainly the extent to which The Beatles moved away from the limitations and predictability of structures using just I, IV and V is the subject of every other chapter in this book.

As explained earlier, our framework attempts to demystify songwriting by breaking up sections of even apparently complex songs into digestible sequences. And, in this sense, it's revealing to see how The Beatles would often spice up all types of songs with a quick nod to these three triads. If not for a whole song, then for a complete verse, chorus or bridge. This is in no way to suggest a lack of songwriting inspiration in these cases. Indeed one of The Beatles' greatest contributions to pop songwriting was their skill in combining the familiarity of simple I, IV and V sequences with dramatically new harmonic material apparently so far beyond the Three-Chord Trick.

The result in many cases was a blues-pop hybrid where verses of unashamedly blues sequences were spectacularly juxtaposed against bridges or choruses containing slick minor chords. Most famous in this category is 'Can't Buy Me Love' whose verse is a pure 12-bar blues, cunningly disguised by being set against a striking chorus which, as we will see, follows a sophisticated, jazzy Cycle Of Fifths pattern. Similarly, songs like 'She's A Woman', 'You Can't Do That', 'I Feel Fine', 'I'll Cry Instead' and 'A Hard Day's Night' all have clearly blues-based sections that give way to deliciously upbeat minor chords, which we will introduce in the next chapter.

These early classics alone should dispel another myth that, as songwriters, The Beatles did not come from a blues foundation in the way that other British bands of the sixties are said to have done. Clearly they did, even if – using precisely such subtle song structures – they were able to disguise it. For it is the *contrast* of the various sections in these songs which provides the key to their success, with the three chords of the blues providing a vital ingredient.

The verse of 'Drive My Car' is another case in point. For all the elaborate jazz qualities of the chords that we visited in the last chapter, the root movement is all I, IV and V. The same goes for sections of many songs ranging from George's 'You Know What To Do' to John's 'Lucy In The Sky With Diamonds'. Indeed 'Lucy' is rightly thought of as one of The Beatles' most sophisticated songs in terms of its *overall* harmonic structure. But don't let's forget that the psychedelic verse meanderings and modulations are nevertheless disarmingly punctuated by a 'sing-along' chorus that cycles exclusively around a I-IV-V pattern.

'Lucy In The Sky With Diamonds'

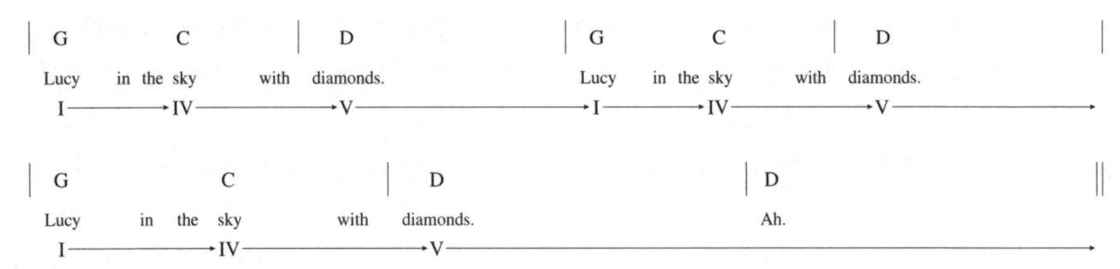

Again The Beatles are playing here on the predictability of I, IV and V specifically for contrast from the more elaborate verse activity that would have overly challenged the listener if continued indefinitely. And the same goes for the equally liberating, rock 'n' roll choruses of 'I'm So Tired' after the intricate ballad-style verses, another example of Lennon using the Three-Chord Trick as an effective tension-breaker, a vital tool for any songwriter.

Having sampled some of the sounds and functions of these three major pillars, it's only a step to appreciating in more detail how the astute song-writer can manipulate them to reinforce his lyrical imagery.

Beatles expert, Ger Tillekens, has developed an intricate theory on how The Beatles' uncanny ability to match harmony to their lyrical contexts (typically 'conversational' themes) was integral to their cultural appeal among the new generation of sixties youth.

While this mastery of semantics is most apparent in those songs filled with 'clever' pop chords that we'll soon be encountering. Tillekens reminds us that the same principle can apply with just I, IV and V. Take a look at how the pivotal line of 'Hey Jude' helps depict the very process underlying the construction and delivery of the singer's message.[10]

'Hey Jude' – matching lyrical themes to I, IV and V

Key of F	B♭	F	C	F
Lyric	'*Remember* to let her into your	*heart* then you can	*start* to make it	*better*'
Process	Thinking	Grounding	Acting	Grounding
Chord	IV: subdominant movement	I: tonic stability	V: dominant tension	I: tonic stability

Is it just coincidence that the word "heart", with its connotations of stability, centering and 'home', should fall on the grounded tonic chord? In contrast, the instruction, "remember", is prompted by an easy shift to the nearby subdominant; while the obvious movement implied in "start" is captured with the tense dominant ahead of that final, satisfying resolution (again in both text and music).

McCartney may well have been oblivious to the semantic subtlety on show here, but scan the songbook to see just how often other positive, grounded words (like 'here', 'home', 'yes', 'love', 'I', 'me', 'us', 'today', 'near' and 'belong') coincide with the secure tonic I chord; while verbs and sentiments expressing movement, distance, negativity and insecurity appear in the context of more 'active' harmony.

Just as we suggested with our V chords in Chapter 1, such songcrafting encourages us to find meaning in music as we subliminally *feel* the dynamic ebb-and-flow of a song unfold; while also providing inquisitive Beatles students with a new dimension in songwriting appreciation.

This basic semantic principle will become an ever more intriguing challenge as we explore the myriad of ways in which The Beatles delivered some of their most memorable lyrics against more sophisticated harmonic backdrops, as well as through distinctive melodic and rhythmic strategies.

Starting with the mellow diatonic chords with which The Beatles *really* spread their songwriting wings.

[10] Ger Tillekens, 'Words And Chords: The Semantic Shifts Of The Beatles Chords' (para 6.2). Essay presented at the June 1st 2000 Beatles Conference, Jyväskylä; reproduced at www.icce.rug.nl/~soundscapes, alongside a synopsis of the same writer's Dutch book, *Het Geluid van de Beatles* (Amsterdam, Het Spinhuis, 1998).

THREE

The Minor Pop Chords

'Buddy Holly was the first time I ever heard A to F# minor. Fantastic, he's opening up new worlds there!' – George Harrison[1]

vi, ii, iii and the elusive vii

For all the versatility of the Three-Chord Trick there comes a point when every songwriter needs to expand his harmonic vocabulary. While the great bluesmen, and rock 'n' rollers like Chuck Berry, represent notable exceptions to the rule, their place in history is due more to their reputation as cultural pioneers, gifted instrumentalists, showmen and lyricists rather than to their deft manipulation of the intricacies of harmony. Pete Townshend implicitly made the distinction when he said 'The Beatles brought songwriting to rock 'n' roll'.[2] That's not to say that the legacy of Three-Chord Trick classics, from Chuck's 'Johnny B. Goode' to The Rolling Stones' 'Satisfaction', aren't great songs.[3] But Townshend's point is, surely, that using a complete arsenal of musical resources, The Beatles dramatically broadened the *potential* of the pop song.

And with that elusive B7 chord now tucked under their belt, it's likely that The Beatles' early songwriting experiments involved adding the minor triads (from the harmonised major scale) to mix and match with those same I, IV and V triads. This chapter expands on the role, origins and functions of all the diatonic minor chords, putting them wherever possible into a historical, theoretical and practical context.

[1] *Across The Universe* (Part 2: 'Tell Me Why'), BBC Radio 2, 15th October, 2002. George wasn't specific but 'Maybe Baby', with its A-F♯m verse, was a Beatles stage fave from 1958–61.

[2] *Jimi Hendrix*, BBC documentary, 1982. Television presentation by Michael Appleton, adapted from the Mediamotion US original.

[3] After all 'Satisfaction' itself was voted number 2 in the list of 'The 100 Greatest Songs Of All Time' by *MOJO* magazine, Issue 81, August 2000.

vi minor – the relative minor

First up would no doubt have been the minor chord built on the sixth degree of the scale, known as the vi, or the *relative minor* of the major I chord, for reasons that will become clear. Let's introduce the sound by seeing some of the main ways that The Beatles exploited it in various simple (and recurring) contexts.

The 'I-vi-I-vi' vamp – The Beatles' first formula?

In any round-up of trademark Beatles songwriting ideas, there's really only one place to start. Alongside the Three-Chord Trick itself, the steady alternation between the tonic and its relative minor (which we can abbreviate as 'I-vi-I-vi') was perhaps the single most common premise of the songs of The Beatles' early career, starting as early as the very second track on the debut album, *Please Please Me*. Listen to the extended final vamp of 'Misery', in the fading coda from 1.33–1.45. We're in the key of C, with the I–vi relationship represented here by C major and A minor.

A distinctive and effective change, and a popular one too – for no sooner has 'Misery' drifted away than we're straight back, within seconds, with another 'I-vi-I-vi' as 'Anna (Go To Him)' kicks off. Even at a slower tempo (and in a different key) the sound is unmistakable as The Beatles play the same cycle (now D–Bm) for the intro and much of the verse on one of their favourite Arthur Alexander covers. The song even shares the same coda as 'Misery' – this time three hearings of the two-bar phrase before coming to rest on the D tonic chord.

As well as Buddy Holly, Alexander may have been one of the main inspirations for this type of dreamy treatment, and both he and The Beatles covered the Moon/Cason composition 'Soldier Of Love' (Alexander's cover was a big hit in 1962). On *Live At The BBC,* listen to the close of 'Soldier Of Love' (starting at 1.51) as The Beatles cycle again repeatedly around I and vi (now E and C♯m) – it's clearly the same musical idea.

'Anna (Go To Him)'

Nor were The Beatles finished with the strategy on *Please Please Me* – it's *déjà vu* as track 10 delivers another unmistakable 'I-vi-I-vi' intro and faded outro on the cover of Bacharach/Williams' 'Baby It's You'.

'Baby It's You'

Still in 1963, and The Beatles opened 'From Me To You' with yet another 'I-vi-I-vi' intro:

'From Me To You'

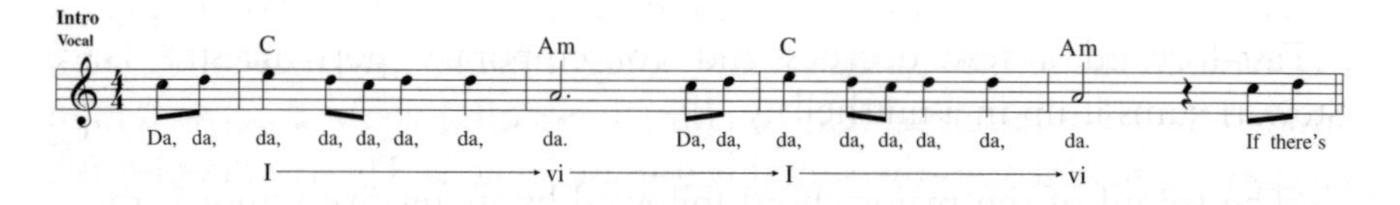

Rest assured that before the year was out, the Fab Four's follow-up album, *With The Beatles,* saw songs as seemingly diverse as 'All I've Got To Do', 'All My Loving' and 'Not A Second Time' all joining the party with a 'I-vi-I-vi' coda.

Just like McCartney, Lennon admits to exploiting good ideas methodically and thoroughly. For when reminiscing about the writing of two other songs, 'Any Time At All' and 'It Won't Be Long' (the latter also on *With The Beatles*), he described them as: 'C to A minor, C to A minor – with me shouting'.[4] Confirmation, once again, that pop music 'formulae' aren't merely in the mind of the indulgent academic.

Surely we need more than 'I-vi-I-vi' (not forgetting the 'shouting') to make a pop song? Apparently not. By coincidence, the very song 'Shout!', by the Isley Brothers, repeats the cycle from start to finish: as we know from The Beatles' version on *Anthology 1* (disc 2, track 16) where they thrash through E and C♯m.

Here, then, is our first songwriting device. Hardly a 'secret', admittedly, but neither should it be seen as just a novice trick in use around 1963. The Beatles regularly composed with this idea in mind. *Anthology I* confirms it in action as early as June 1961, when it opened 'Cry For A Shadow' (the John and George Shadows-style instrumental), while, four years later, the same idea accounts for the entire verse of 'Run For Your Life' on *Rubber Soul*. In the intervening period, the intros and outros of 'It's Only Love', on *Help!*, would also have been in good company back on *Please Please Me*.

'Run For Your Life'

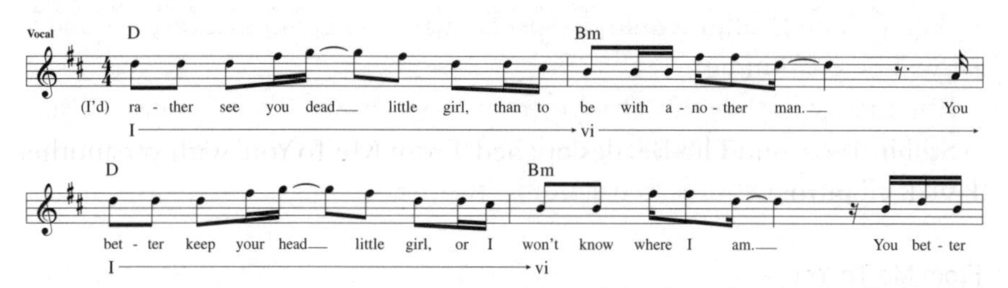

Fast-forward a few decades and contemporary pop maestro Dave Stewart sums it up in a nutshell;

> 'The sound of the major chord followed by its relative minor is the archetypal sound of fifties pop, but musicians never seem to tire of its effect. The theme music of *Twin Peaks* features this major-to-minor, happy-to-sad movement, no doubt with all sorts of post-modern, iconic and ironic intentions – it's still the same old chord change, though!'[5]

[4] *The Playboy Interviews*, p. 173. This quote will be revisited because in these instances (and indeed the intro and verse of 'All I've Got To Do'), Lennon actually reverses the 'I-vi' move to create a subtly different musical effect. The point here is simply to illustrate Lennon's formulaic thinking with regard to basic ideas.

[5] Dave Stewart, *Inside The Music*, p. 11.

It certainly is. Still, there's a danger of nostalgically categorising songwriting principles by eras. After all, the 'I-vi-I-vi' has proved ubiquitous in popular music since rock 'n' roll began. We hear it equally in the bridge to Del Shannon's 1961 classic, 'Runaway'; in the dreamy outro of The Eagles' 'New Kid In Town' on the mega-selling *Hotel California*; and repeatedly in The Jam's 'That's Entertainment' and Oasis's 'Songbird', to pick just four songs from diverse genres, spanning five decades of pop.

Stewart himself used what he describes as this 'classic schmaltzy pop movement' in his song 'As Far As Dreams Can Go', though here he cleverly conjured some novelty by splitting the device in half, following the opening I-vi with another from a different key[6] – rather like The Beach Boys had done back in 1964 on 'The Warmth Of The Sun'.[7]

We've laboured the point to demonstrate that the 'I-vi-I-vi' is a versatile idea that undoubtedly 'works', while its incontestable status as a cliché can be cleverly disguised according to context. In this sense, it's the first of many musical concepts that represent a tradition in pop songwriting, part of a 'virtual manual' of established 'rules'. Of course, rules are made to be broken, as The Beatles would do spectacularly with almost every sequence we will be examining.

But first, why has the change from 'I-vi' proved such a musical 'sure thing' in pop over at least five decades? The answer lies in the relationship between the two chords as harmonic 'relatives'.

Major and relative minor – making the connection

If we look at the construction of the chords themselves we see that the chords I and vi share two common notes. For example, in the key of C, C major and A minor both contain a C note and an E note, making the sound of the two chords related to each other. A minor is said to be the *relative minor* of C major; and vice versa, with C being the *relative major* of A minor.

[6] 'As Far As Dreams Can Go' adopts a B♭-Gm followed by the same move up a third: i.e., D-Bm.

[7] Here a familiar C-Am move is followed, unusually, by E♭-Cm7. This is another I-vi, but one starting a minor third (three semitones) away. The Beach Boys return to the sanctity of the home key of C by means of a ii-V-I (Dm7-G7-C) – a standard move that we will see The Beatles pursuing in many instances when returning to familiar territory after an ambitious harmonic sojourn.

		1	♭3	3	5
C	**Tonic (I)**	**C**		**E**	**G**
Am	**Relative Minor (vi)**	**A**	**C**		**E**

Just to reinforce the point, we can show how an Am7 chord (an Am triad with its appropriate seventh added) actually contains *all* the same notes as C6 (C major with an added 6th). As such, the two chords are said to be *inversions* of each other, containing the same notes but 'stacked' in a different order to yield a subtly different sound.

		1	♭3	3	5	6	♭7
C^6	**Tonic (I^6)**	**C**		**E**	**G**	**A**	
Am^7	**Relative Minor (vi^7)**	**A**	**C**		**E**		**G**

It is through these shared tones that a major chord and its relative minor are heard as different sides of the same musical coin – their individual characters can be explained by a crucial difference. The 'bright' side of the major triad is down to its major 3rd interval (C–E); while the 'dark' side, A minor, is courtesy of that more dissonant minor 3rd (A–C).[8] It is this that explains the effect of the progression: a subtle see-sawing of 'light' and 'shade' as the two chords play out in a hypnotic alternation of gentle tension and resolution.

The Four-Chord Cliché – 'I-vi-IV-V'

Rather than a repeated vamp between I and vi, arguably the single most famous chord sequence of the century features these two chords joined by those other two triads, IV and V, to create a Three-Chord Trick with a difference – a Four-Chord Trick. The original blueprint for this (and various other similar four-chord cycles we'll see in action) is often claimed to be Hoagy Carmichael's 'Heart And Soul', dating from 1938.[9]

Whatever the precise source, here's a sequence that, without question, has become a timeless tradition in pop music. Fast-forward from Tin Pan Alley to the fifties and sixties to find everyone from Danny and the Juniors ('At The Hop') and Chubby Checker ('Let's Twist Again') to The Shadows ('Foot Tapper') and Neil Sedaka ('Stairway To Heaven') all rocking out

[8] Refer to the detailed chart of intervals, with specific Beatles examples, in Appendix 3.

[9] See Jimmy Webb, *Tunesmith: The Art Of Songwriting*, p. 195.

over this progression. The Beatles' beloved Everly Brothers classic, 'All I Have To Do Is Dream', is one of many tracks that uses the same idea in a ballad context, while other big US/UK hits included 'Little Darlin'' by The Diamonds and 'Born Too Late' by The Ponitails.[10]

A look down the list of early Beatles stage favourites throws up a number of classic 'I-vi-IV-V' covers. These include the Bobby Vee hit, 'Take Good Care Of My Baby' (penned by Goffin and King – one of John and Paul's favourite songwriting teams), and Ben E. King's evergreen 'Stand By Me' that Lennon would cover in 1975 (A-F♯m-D-E). Both songs apparently featured as stalwarts in The Beatles' live sets of 1961 and 1962.[11] We need only dip into the recorded archives to hear The Beatles' renditions of several songs based on this classic cliché. Here are three from different sources:

i) 'Keep Your Hands Off My Baby' on *Live At The BBC* (G-Em-C-D);
ii) 'Where Have You Been All My Life' on *Live At The Star Club* (heard as F-Dm-B♭-C);
iii) and, most famously, The Marvelettes' 'Please Mr Postman' on *With The Beatles* (A-F♯m-D-E).

All these progressions feature a sound that we associate with those heady days of early rock 'n' roll, with Chris Ingham confirming the interchangeability of harmonic structures between so many songs of that era:

> 'It is perhaps significant that, with pop music reacting to the rawness and aggression of rock 'n' roll in this period, it often fell back on the sweetest, safest musical sounds; the happy, comforting sound of something familiar, the four chord turnaround was pop's opium for the masses.'[12]

And so it proved to be a handy drug to fall back on for The Beatles in a range of songs during their career. There is no doubt that this was one of

[10] It is interesting to note that these two songs were featured in the 1973 film *That'll Be The Day* (starring Ringo!) which aimed to encapsulate fifties culture. The soundtrack is duly littered with songs that follow I-vi-IV-V, including 'Runaround Sue' (D-Bm-G-A) by Dion and the Belmonts.

[11] Mark Lewisohn, *The Complete Beatles Recording Sessions,* p. 364.

[12] Chris Ingham, 'Doctor Rock Dissects The Hits', *MOJO*, Issue 28, March 1996, p. 24.

the sequences that John Lennon had in mind when he described 'Happiness Is A Warm Gun' as going through the 'whole gamut of rock'n'roll'.[13]

'Happiness Is A Warm Gun'

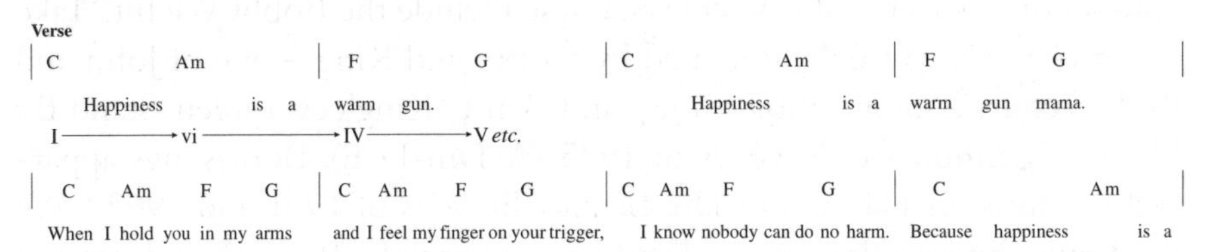

Just as we saw, however, with the Three-Chord Trick chorus of 'Lucy In the Sky', context is everything. The cliché in 'Happiness Is A Warm Gun' has the effect of similarly breaking the tension of the dissonant sections of 'She's not a girl . . .' and 'Mother Superior jump the gun . . .' by using a far more familiar idea.

It has often been suggested that The Beatles were at pains to steer clear of this type of sixties cliché. Nevertheless, the 'I-vi-IV-V' can be seen to resurface on various occasions, *if only for a few bars within a more complex progression.* Whether well disguised ('A Hard Day's Night'), fleeting ('I'll Get You' and 'I'm So Tired'), or accounting for the entire song ('Octopus's Garden'), The Beatles weren't ashamed to fall back on this most clichéd of clichés. Right up to – and including – 'Real Love'.

'Real Love'

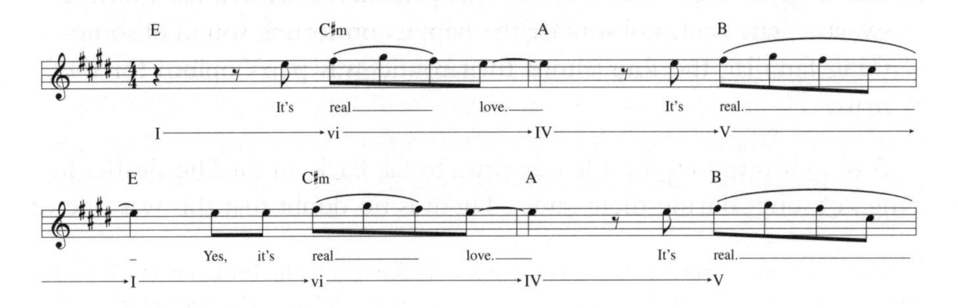

[13] Keith Badman, *The Beatles – Off The Record*, p. 392. The others would have been the minor ballad 'i-iv-v' opening section and the more rocky 'I-♭III-I-♭VII' 'Mother Superior' interlude.

Meanwhile, here is a quick summary of The Beatles' I-vi-IV-V 'Hall Of Fame' (with lyrical references purposely omitted on this occasion to encourage readers to identify the relevant moment for themselves).

The Beatles and the 'I-vi-IV-V' turnaround

Song	Section	I	vi	IV	V
'A Hard Day's Night'	bridge	G	Em	C^7	D^7
'I'll Get You'	verse	D	Bm	G	A
'I'm So Tired'	verse	A	F♯m	D	E^7
'I've Just Seen A Face'	verse	A	F♯m	D	E
'Happiness Is A Warm Gun'	chorus	C	Am	F	G
'Octopus's Garden'	verse	E	C♯m	A	B
'Octopus's Garden'	solo	A	F♯m	D	E
'Real Love'	chorus	E	C♯m	A	B

The celebrated American rock 'n' roll historian Dave Rubin summed it up when he said: 'along with the 12-bar blues, this progression came to define a majority of American music in the 20th century.'[14] Meanwhile, another pop musicologist, Stephen Citron, goes as far as to suggest: 'when the recordings from our time are unearthed a thousand years hence, those people will wonder how our culture was able to spend a century listening to the same four chords'.[15]

And don't think for a minute that these devices are in some way dated, harmonic dinosaurs from the fifties and sixties (or in the case of 'Real Love', the nineties). Far from it. They have remained a songwriting staple ever since Hoagy Carmichael, appearing in hundreds of songs in genres as diverse as pure pop, country, new wave and disco. Across the spectrum, check out (in no particular order): Sting's 'Every Breath You Take', Crystal Gayle's 'Don't It Make My Brown Eyes Blue', Stiff Little Fingers' 'Gate 49', Whitney Houston's 'I Will Always Love You', The Jam's 'Strange Town', Badfinger's 'Without You', The Boomtown Rats' 'I Don't Like Mondays', ELO's 'Telephone Line' and (with only a slight variation) Oasis's 'Some Might Say'.[16]

[14] Dave Rubin, 'Rockin' In The '50s', *Guitar One* magazine, December 1999.

[15] Stephen Citron, *Songwriting*, p. 238.

[16] 'Some Might Say' briefly returns to the tonic in mid sequence: 'I-vi-IV-(I)-V', in the key of D.

Diatonic substitution – the first steps

The principle governing the use of the vi chord in all these progressions is that of chord *substitution*, a songwriting tool that allows us to create new and interesting progressions featuring familiar elements. The basic premise is that, when crafting a song, a writer will look for a chord that is different to the one that might have been expected – but which still enables the progression to *function* as he initially intended. Using the basic guideline that the new chord must have tones that overlap with the original chord, the result can be very subtle – or highly dramatic where *fewer common tones* are involved. At the very simplest level, even the 'I-vi-I-vi' involves 'substitution' as the vi chord is being used to break up what would otherwise be a monotonous run on the tonic chord. Similarly, the 'I-vi-IV-V' instantly takes us beyond the 'Three-Chord Trick' by elaborating on a progression, using diatonic chord substitution.

Of course the very term substitution suggests the complete *replacement* of one chord by another, and it is to this that we now turn. The vi chord itself does replace the tonic in various crucial moments in Beatles songs, including one instance that has inadvertently become perhaps their most celebrated musical move of all time. So much so that we devote the whole of Chapter 5 to the notorious legend of the 'Aeolian cadence'.

Nevertheless, we can now explore another famous pop progression involving the substitution of a relative minor chord for a major triad. But this time it's not the tonic triad that finds its 'dark side' but the subdominant, the IV chord. For as much as I and vi are 'blood brothers', so too are the IV chord and the ii minor. In any key, the *ii minor is the relative minor of the IV chord* and, as a result, the potential for substitution between the two chords exists. This introduces us to the basic roles of the ii chord in pop harmony.

'ii' minor

As with the vi, the ii (or *supertonic*, being the diatonic chord above the tonic) is another of the pop minor chords that appears in scores of Beatles songs – this time usually in three common contexts that we can deal with as follows:

1) the 'ii-for-IV' substitution (the *Doo Wop* cycle)
2) the diatonic 'walk': 'I-ii' and beyond
3) 'ii-V-I': the role of 'ii' as a 'predominant' chord

1) The 'ii-for-IV' substitution in the Doo Wop cycle

Nowhere in pop music is the 'ii for IV' substitution better illustrated than in the legendary Doo Wop sequence, another manifestation of the Four-Chord Cliché – but where the formula is now spelt: I-vi-ii-V. And it's a progression that can be introduced using a suitably historic piece of Beatles trivia: the Woolton Village Fête.

For while Paul McCartney made his impromptu audition for The Quarry Men playing Eddie Cochran's 'Twenty Flight Rock', his earliest encounter with the band was a few hours previously. Indeed, McCartney's first memories of John Lennon are of him busking his way through 'Come Go With Me' by The Del-Vikings, a minor sixties classic now elevated to legend through this piece of pre-Beatles folklore. In songwriting terms it was perhaps appropriate that this historic moment should involve a composition that, though unequivocally simple, nevertheless represented at the time a novel departure from the Three-Chord Trick.[17]

'Come Go With Me'

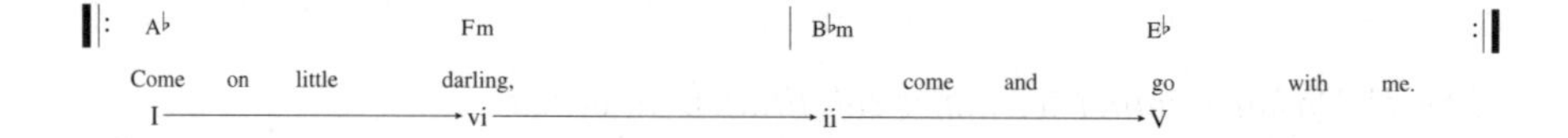

Certainly, 'Come Go With Me' was another 'formula' song, but those crucial extra minor chords do represent an important songwriting step into the deeper, rewarding realms of the harmonised diatonic scale. 'Come Go With Me' was indeed an example of a textbook, harmonic cliché that was highly popular with legions of US groups at the time. Doo Wop itself was a type of R'n'B vocal sound best thought of as 'Barbershop harmonies with a beat'. A whole era of such bands – often with bird names like The Flamingos, Swallows, Ravens, Orioles and Penguins – made almost their entire careers out of recycling this type of progression into a string of popular hits.

While Lennon and McCartney heard the sound of the Doo Wop sequence in the The Del-Vikings' classic, they would also have heard it in an avalanche of diverse songs from their childhood. There were the Tin Pan Alley classics like Gershwin's 'I Got Rhythm', Jack Strachey's 'These

[17] McCartney describes the moment in detail in *The Beatles Anthology*, p. 20.

Foolish Things' and Rodgers and Hart's 'Blue Moon' (probably the blueprint for the whole Doo Wop genre). There were also renowned McCartney favourites like Frankie Lymon's 'Why Do Fools Fall In Love', Johnny Tillotson's 'Poetry In Motion',[18] and various Buddy Holly songs (including 'Last Night') which all used the idea to a greater or lesser extent.

By the turn of the sixties Neil Sedaka had launched his career by taking the device into mainstream American pop. Songs like 'Oh Carol!' (1958) feature the sequence exclusively, while classics like 'Breaking Up Is Hard To Do', 'Happy Birthday Sweet Sixteen', 'I Go Ape', 'Calendar Girl' and 'Stairway To Heaven' (all written between 1959 and 1962) also contain the exact same Four-Chord Trick as a fundamental element of their structure.

In a nutshell, just like the I-vi-IV-V, the predictability of the Doo-Wop cycle makes it a 'sure thing' for listeners. However, now the sound – courtesy of that extra minor chord – is slightly less rocky, making for a more sophisticated texture.

Either way, the sound is merely the result of the substitution process which confirms just how closely the two progressions are related. Ultimately, it's all down to that one extra note – in the key of C, say, the D note:

'ii for IV' 'relative-minor-for-major-substitution' in action

		1	♭3	3	5
F	**Subdominant (IV)**	**F**		**A**	C
Dm	**Supertonic (ii)**	D	**F**		**A**

It was no doubt this 'risk-free' commercial reality that George Martin saw in the now infamous potential Beatles single, Mitch Murray's classic 'How Do You Do It?'. Martin suggested a cover of this uptempo incarnation of the formula as the follow-up to 'Love Me Do', though history relates that the band held out for their own, far more novel, 'Please Please Me'. Nevertheless, The Beatles' September 1962 demo of the song resurfaced on *Anthology 1* and is well worth a listen for what should be seen as a 'pre-Beatles' classic of its kind, a deceptively catchy song of pure simplistic symmetry.

And while The Beatles may have felt the thinly disguised Doo Wop origins of 'How Do You Do It?' to be unambitious, they were by no means

[18] Both these songs also appeared on the *That'll Be The Day* soundtrack.

beyond adopting the same basic formula in several of their own originals over the years. Indeed, in a virtual tribute to the whole Doo Wop genre, the verse of 'This Boy' captures the repeated I-vi-ii-V cycle down to a tee.

'This Boy'

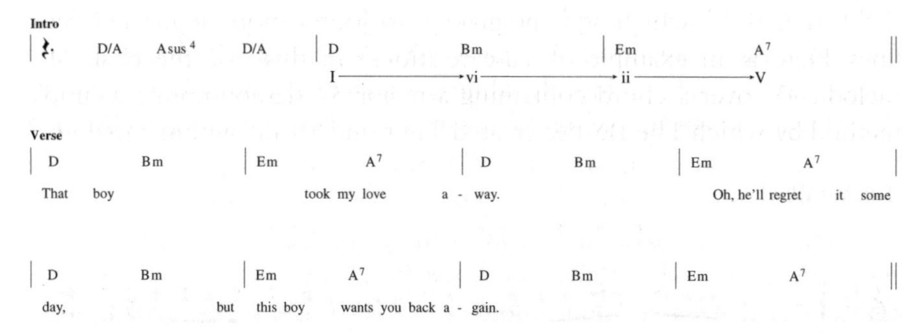

Lennon would say that the song was 'my attempt at writing one of those three-part-harmony Smokey Robinson songs. Nothing in the lyrics; just a sound and a harmony'.[19] We will be revisiting those highly intricate vocals as a detailed case study in Chapter 14. For now, let's just add the progression to the songwriting manual.

The Beatles certainly weren't finished with the idea after 'This Boy' – 'Tell Me Why', for example, which John Lennon 'knocked off' for the soundtrack of *A Hard Day's Night*, also features a pure 'I-vi-ii-V'. As would John's 'Woman', as late as 1980, proving that the lessons of 'Come Go With Me' were rather more than just a distant memory.

'Tell Me Why'

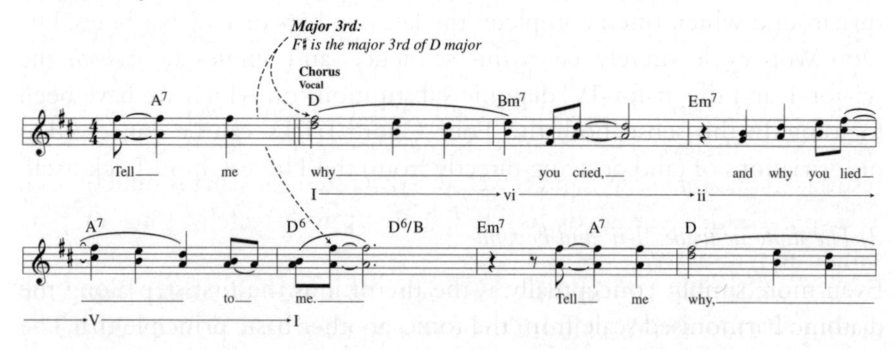

[19] *The Playboy Interviews*, p. 172.

The cyclical feel of the song is guaranteed by the underlying progression that appears similarly in both verse and chorus. But notice how Lennon cleverly detracts from the extreme harmonic predictability by using subtle nuances *in the melody*. Most important is how the F♯, the 'sweeter', major 3rd that appears in the chorus, is contrasted by the F *natural*, the darker, 'bluesey' flattened 3rd, which adds poignancy to John's more anguished verse lines. Here is an example of 'false relations': in this case the clash of a melodic ♭3rd over a chord containing a major 3rd, demonstrating a simple method by which The Beatles created 'light' and 'shade' within a melody.[20]

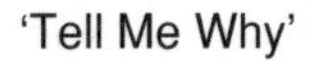

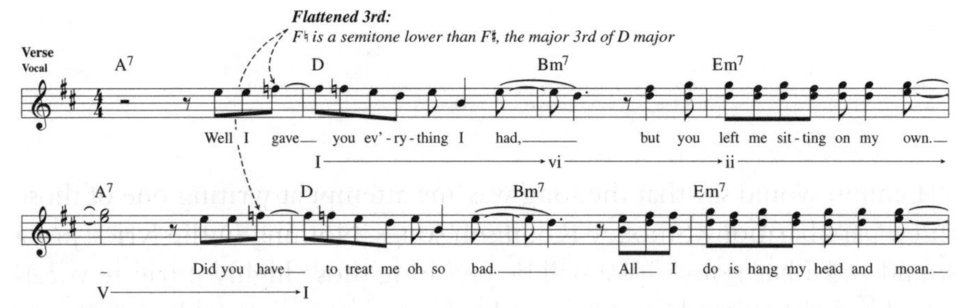

Over the course of their career, some of The Beatles' most intricate songs have featured the very same 'I-vi-ii-V' progression. It kicks off the brilliant verse meanderings of 'You're Going To Lose That Girl', 'I Will' and 'Penny Lane', each time setting the scene with familiar harmonic territory before then moving swiftly to new, unexpected pastures.

In order to appreciate fully the musical origins of the Doo Wop progression one should again refer back to the blues. For the root movement of 1-6-2-5 is nothing more than an embellishment of a simple 'I-IV-I-V' turnaround which often completes the last two bars of a 12-bar blues. The Doo Wop cycle merely takes this sequence, and applies to it *both* the 'vi-for-I' and the 'ii-for-IV' diatonic substitutions on which we have been focusing. In this sense, both the 'Four-Chord Tricks' can be conceived as just variations of (and deriving directly from) the Three-Chord Trick itself.

2) The diatonic walk: 'I-ii' and beyond

Even more simply, conceptually, is the use of ii as the first step along the diatonic harmonised scale from the tonic, another basic principle that The

[20] See Appendix 3 for an introduction to harmonisation and other basic melodic concepts.

Beatles used at various stages of their career. Let's look first at a I-ii-I-ii cycle which we can rationalise in terms of simple substitution. For in the same way that we saw I alternate with IV, so ii minor – *as a substitute for IV* – can take its place. Listen to the sophisticated pop verse of 'Don't Let Me Down', the B-side of 'Get Back' from May 1969:[21]

'Don't Let Me Down'

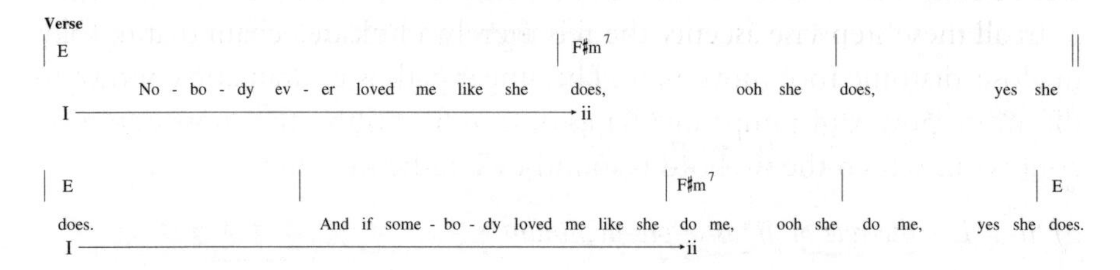

But why stop at ii? We can continue the diatonic walk just by ascending further up the scale in intervals of a second. Songs like 'If I Fell' and 'I'm Only Sleeping' extend the idea to iii; 'Here, There And Everywhere' and the bridge of 'Sexy Sadie' on to IV; while 'Getting Better' takes us effortlessly all the way up the ladder to V (if we include the link between chorus and verse).

'Getting Better'

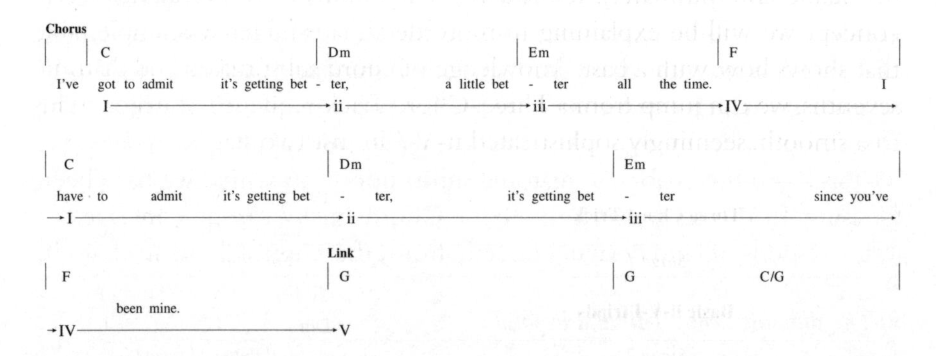

[21] Paul McCartney was well aware of the semantic subtlety he conjured when alternating I and ii (in the key of E) in 'Ebony and Ivory'. '*Sit together in perfect harmony ... side by side*, I thought: "Yes! That's OK! It explains the whole thing about the analogy on the keyboard."'. 'Songwriting', *Making Music* by George Martin, p.62.

The fifties blueprint for this move is probably Johnny Tillotson's 'Poetry In Motion' where the 'motion' in question turns out to be a determined 'I-ii-iii-IV-V' walk that then resolves back to I.[22] But however far you want to take 'the walk', it is undoubtedly another versatile idea, used across the ages of pop. Listen to Jimi Hendrix embellish the 'I-ii-iii-IV-V' on Dylan's 'Like A Rolling Stone' (Live at Monterey). A decade later, Robert Smith was walking-up the 'I-ii-iii-IV' ladder (and back down again) on The Cure's early New Wave outing, 'Boys Don't Cry'.

In all these stepwise ascents, the ii is merely a link in a chain that unfolds in close, diatonic root movement. This linear path is in dramatic contrast to the more powerful jumps involving descending fifths, the most common context in which the ii chord is found in The Beatles' music.

3) 'ii-V-I' – the role of 'ii' as a 'pre-dominant'

If songwriters learn just one concept beyond the Three-Chord Trick from this book it should surely be the ii-V-I progression. Indeed, as we already know from our discussion of substitution, this device *is* a type of IV-V-I move with the ii minor replacing the IV chord as *its* relative minor. A simple variation, maybe, but a fundamental one. For we now have a chord sequence that creates extra momentum through root movement that travels through *two perfect fifths* – instantly doubling the V-I 'journey' whose role in creating inexorable resolution we discussed in Chapter 1.

In just the same way that V-I creates a strong resolution, so reaching V from a chord built on *its* V, plays on that expectation, making it ever more inevitable and, ultimately, reinforcing the sound of the prevailing key (a concept we will be explaining in more detail later). Here's a simple table that shows how, with a basic knowledge of chord substitution and diatonic sevenths, we can jump from a Three-Chord Trick sequence of major triads to a smooth, seemingly sophisticated ii-V-I in just two stages:

Three Chord Trick	IV	V	I
	F	G	C
Stage 1	*Substitute ii for IV*		
Basic ii-V-I triads	ii	V	I
	Dm	G	C
Stage 2	*Add flattened sevenths*		
ii-V-I with diatonic sevenths	ii⁷	V⁷	I
	Dm⁷	G⁷	C

[22] The intro walk is A♭-B♭m-Cm-D♭-E♭ on the original Johnny Tillotson recording.

Voice-leading in a ii-V

Just as we showed the voice-leading in a V-I to be inherently structured for movement, so the ii minor has an in-built mechanism beyond just the 'down-a-fifth' action of the root. Specifically, the 3rd of the ii 'wants' to push upward to the root of the V (even if this is a *whole* tone rather than a semitone); while the seventh of ii (when it appears) is the icing on the cake as it *pulls down by a semitone* into the third of the V.

ii⁷ (Dm⁷)			V⁷ (G⁷)	
Formula	**Note**	**Voice leading**	**Note**	**Formula**
♭7th	C	Down a semitone	B	3rd
♭3rd	F	Up a tone	G	Root
Root	D	Down a perfect fifth	G	Root

This time the 5th degree has been omitted in order to emphasize the importance of the ♭3rd (and the ♭7th if it is present) as the source of the most essential voice-leading in the change.

The Beatles showed how the ii-V movement could be used in three main ways:

a) Ending a section with a prepared *Perfect cadence*

Simply by putting a ii minor chord ahead of the V, we are 'priming' the dominant and thereby encouraging the listener to hear the eventual movement to I from 'further back' in the sequence. Once again this is a formula with which a songwriter can lead us through a chord progression. From dozens of possible Beatles examples, let's take one with a strong accompanying lyrical theme:

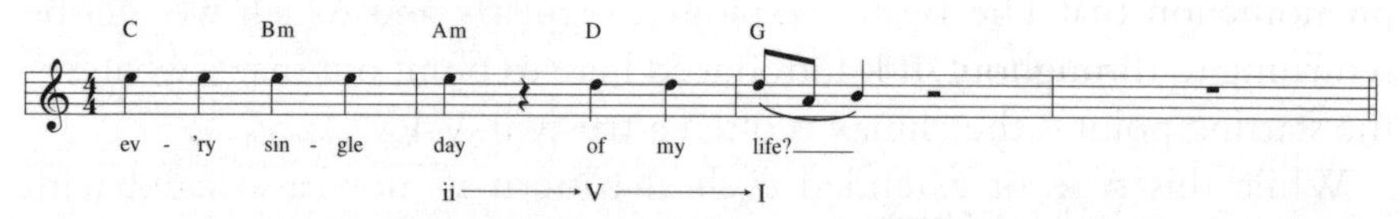

The message is clear, affirming, conclusive and convincing. It doesn't need elaborating on or qualifying in any way – a feeling that's reinforced by both the lyric and the musical context. For here's a progression that represents the inevitabilty of being led home to the tonic –

not just from the V, but with the help of another descent of a fifth preceding it. In 'Got To Get You Into My Life', the descending bass line points the way as we do the IV-iii 'walk', at which point the ii-V-I delivers a mighty musical 'full stop' at the end of the sentence. Notice how the melody also follows a powerful path, with the 5th of the parent scale (supported as the root of the V chord) giving way to the 3rd of the tonic on the final note (though not the tonic itself).

This ii-V-I cadence can be seen to round off, in a similarly conclusive fashion, numerous Beatles progressions – usually in the context of a resolute statement, as above, or sometimes with a suitably fine musical-lyrical metaphor – perhaps with connotations of 'returning home' or some other line that brings out the sense of the tonic as a final destination.

'Golden Slumbers' is a case in point. Listen to how the Dm is pointing the song 'homeward', just as Paul says. Immediately we arrive 'home' on the C chord just as we'd expect. In this case it's too early in the progression for a formal cadence – especially with the melody rising up. But it's only a short delay before we're back home, second time around, finally climaxing with the same ii-V-I on the suitably mellow lyric, 'lullaby', as the melody now also lands on the tonic. Again, musically, it's the end of the paragraph.

This notion of 'going around the block' is important as it demonstrates that we can target the tonic from more than just the two successive descents of perfect fifths that comprise the ii-V-I. In just the same way that we 'tacked on' a ii ahead of the V, we can work backwards again to chain these chords in a longer sequence of fifths. First with vi before the ii, then iii before the vi (as here in 'Golden Slumbers'), and, ultimately, vii before iii in a giant musical conga of descending fifths.

Each of these progressions represents journeys of varying lengths along what is known as *The Cycle Of Fifths*, another fundamental songwriting phenomenon that The Beatles exploited regularly and which we will be returning to throughout. It is introduced here to point out that – whatever the starting point – the climax is often a trusty ii-V-I.

While this type of extended cyclical pattern is more associated with McCartney (and indeed emerges as one notable difference between the two songwriters) John Lennon also had an intuitive understanding of the versatility of the discrete ii-V-I device. The entire verse of 'And Your Bird Can Sing' can be instantly deconstructed as an extended vamp on the tonic followed by a ii-V-I. Think of the lines 'you can't get/see/hear me' in the various verses, with the singer (just like the progression) having the last word to match the finality of the sequence. Let's take the last line of the bridge from 'Tell Me Why' as it provides an important point of comparison with our next discussion.

'Tell Me Why' (end of bridge)

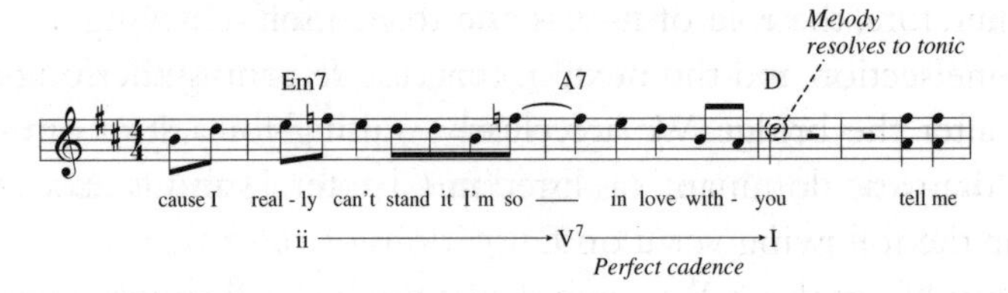

Notice in particular how, once again, the ii-V-I here creates a feeling of a progression being self-contained, with a Perfect cadence taking us to a point of rest (this time with a melody that also homes in on the restful tonic). It creates a point of resolution, both musically, and semantically in terms of John's sobering, soul-baring admission. This is in direct contrast to using the ii-V as a powerful method of creating unreleased tension that drives a song into the next section.

b) Ending a section with an Imperfect *cadence*

Compare the tension-free end of the bridge of 'Tell Me Why' we've just seen (which *isn't* propelling us inexorably into the next verse) with the equivalent point in 'It Won't Be Long'. Here the effect is markedly different – even if 'coming home' is once again a paramount theme in every sense.

'It Won't Be Long' (end of bridge)

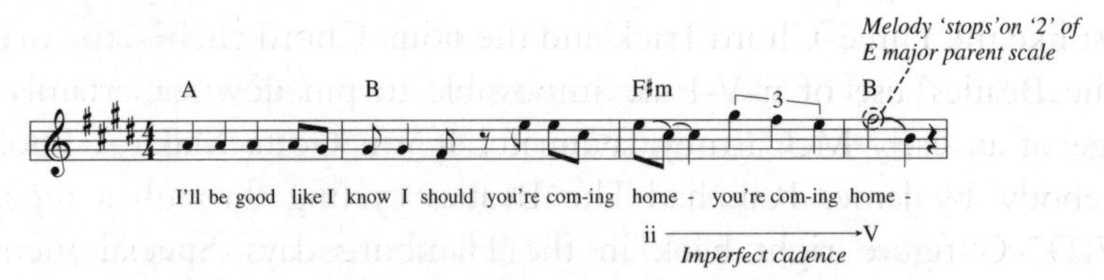

In the key of E now, the F♯m again primes the dominant B chord. This time the sequence of chords that comprises this discrete song section ends not with a ii-V-I resolution *but with the ii-V chords on their own.* The tonic does follow – but only as we start the next verse after a notable delay in which we are left 'hanging on the dominant'. While we are 'coming home', as John Lennon tells us, we aren't doing so quite yet. We have to wait in anticipation just a little bit longer (like John) for the eventual fulfilment.

The cadence is said to be *Imperfect* because of this 'hanging effect', which is typically reinforced by a *melody* that hits a brick wall either on the '5' itself or, as here, on the tense '2' of the key.

Here, therefore, the role of ii–V is as a device for achieving a transition between one section and the next, in this case returning the song back to the verse after the bridge. We are clearly waiting for a strong resolution from this 'dramatic dominant' (as listed in Chapter 1) and it duly comes as we resume the following verse on E.

The versatility of the ii–V is such that it can be used almost anywhere. It is only a slight exaggeration to suggest that many jazz musicians think and play (and talk) almost exclusively in terms of this progression. Even the most complex harmonic jazz structures (like John Coltrane's 'Giant Steps') are often reduced to 'a series of ii–Vs', to use the common jazz language. It is only slightly less common in pop, with the fact that Four-Chord clichés are often preferred in their 'I-vi-IV-V' incarnation (rather than with a 'ii-for-IV sub') showing that minor chords (and certainly minor 7^{ths}) are often regarded as lacking the rocky timbre of their relative majors.

Nevertheless, The Beatles demonstrated that the ii–V sequence could be used in any setting – even in a bluesey number like 'Oh! Darling', which shows how ii and V can alternate on their own, setting up gentle tension by delaying the cadence to I, an idea that would come to be a staple of pop music over the subsequent decades. Check out the verse of George Harrison's 'My Sweet Lord' which features four repeats of ii–V before moving on to I; while Simply Red's 'Holding Back The Years' has been described as 'one interminable Two Five'.[23]

Just like the Three-Chord Trick and the Four-Chord clichés, the origins of The Beatles' use of ii-V-I are impossible to pin down. Certainly the bridge of an early McCartney favourite, 'If You Gotta Make A Fool Of Somebody' by James Ray, had The Beatles cycling through a repeated Am7-D7-G figure right back in the Hamburg days. Special mention should also be made of 'Devil In Her Heart', the Richard Drapkin song covered on *With The Beatles*. This song doesn't wait to use ii-V-I as a 'wrap-up' idea, as we have been stressing, but exploits it from the start, as a cyclical gambit for both the intro and the whole of the verse.

[23] Chris Ingham, 'Doctor Rock Dissects The Hits', *MOJO*, Issue 44, July 1997, p. 22.

Listen also to the start of 'I'm A Loser' where the repeated Am-D theme creates some ambiguity and instability – until, that is, the opening line of the verse confirms that this move is indeed just a key-defining 'ii-V', in G major.

Although there are many other examples, let's dip finally into *Abbey Road* where The Beatles choose a cyclical ii-V-I, this time with psychedelic minor 7th and 6th extensions, for their ethereal vamp on 'Sun King'.

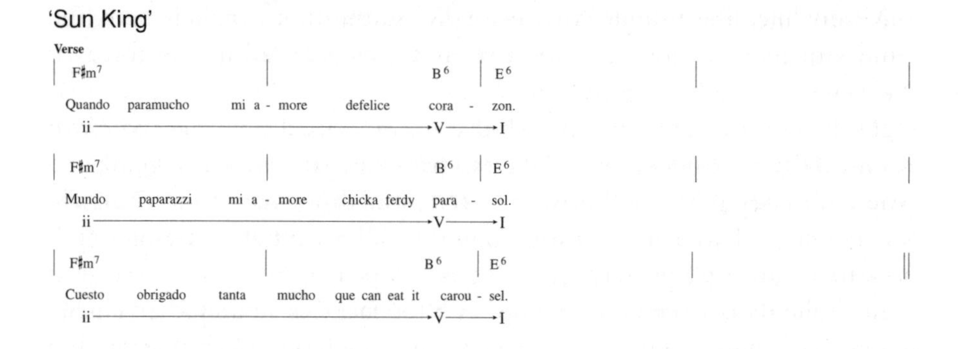

The Four-Chord Cycles revisited – 'ii-V-I-vi'

Now let's return to the Doo Wop sequence, which can also be seen to contain an irresistible ii-V-I movement within its structure. If we now start the sequence a bar late, we arrive at an important variation: 'ii-V-I-vi' – another four-chord pattern that appears throughout pop music. The Tin Pan Alley masters have long since exploited this sequence on such classics as 'All The Things You Are' (Oscar Hammerstein/Jerome Kern) and Cole Porter's 'I Get A Kick Out Of You'. Even as early as 1962, The Beatles can be heard going through the 'ii-V-I-vi' motions on various cover songs, most notably in the neat middle eight of 'How Do You Do It?' (at 0.32 on *Anthology 1*):

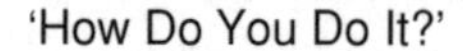

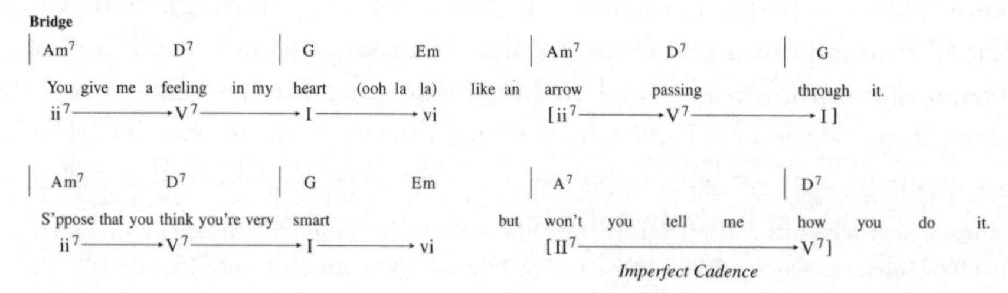

Sure enough, Paul McCartney would feature it across the course of The Beatles' career on songs as seemingly far removed as 'All My Loving' ('Close your eyes and I'll kiss you, tomorrow I'll miss you' – 0.00-0.06, in E major), and 'The Fool On The Hill' ('Nobody wants to know him they can see that he's just a fool' – 0.17-0.23, in D major). The formula was perhaps never more clearly visible than in the middle eight of 'I Want To Hold Your Hand', a discussion that we reserve for later for one crucial reason that will become apparent.[24]

Meanwhile, if we 'undo' the 'ii-for-IV' substitution implicit here, the same sequence can be seen to have a rockier 'cousin' in the form of 'IV-V-I-vi' – another progression that The Beatles used in some surprisingly diverse settings down the years. We can spot it in 'I Should Have Known Better' ('And when I ask you to be mine' – 0.55-1.02, in G major); where it slowly rehashes the same C-D-G-Em sequence of the euphoric title refrain of 'I Wanna Hold Your Hand' (0.22), with both songs winding back to a natural point of rest with a plain IV-V-I.

In all these cases the harmony can be thought of as 'just another Three-Chord Trick' but with the added spice of a vi which specifically creates that turnaround effect.

The ii-V-I and its diatonic variations are hardly advanced technical devices. However, The Beatles transformed their application in modern pop and rock music by using them in a more elaborate role – as a key-switching device that 'relocates' a song to harmonic territory beyond the predictable diatonic world, as we discuss in chapter 10.

Substitution summary – the diatonic 'families'

The 'hand in glove' relationship between major and relative minor is part of a bigger picture that allows us to select chords for simple sequences with almost guaranteed results. For a songwriter can regard chords as not just being constructed from the parent diatonic scale but as *belonging to smaller 'families' of chords within that harmonised scale.* Indeed each of I, IV and V major triads can be seen as being 'assigned' minor chords to which they are related through either a major/relative minor relationship or just the sharing of common tones.

[24] 'ii-V-I-vi' is the correct formula for the bridge of 'I Want To Hold Your Hand' but only when taking into account the key switch from G to C that The Beatles first initiate. This feature, which accounts entirely for the extreme sense of harmonic 'departure', is discussed in Chapter 10.

I	The tonic family:	I, vi and iii
IV	The subdominant family:	IV and ii
V	The dominant family:	V and vii

Moreover, just as we saw with the major triads themselves, each of these extended families of I, IV and V can be seen as representing, respectively: 'stability', 'movement *away* from the tonic', and 'movement *towards* the tonic'. When attempting to fathom even the most complex songs by ear, it is useful to know that these three groups are the most likely minor chords to appear in a song.

And while vi and ii have been neatly explained through their 'relative' relationship, our next chord, the iii, departs from this but nevertheless qualifies for the *tonic family* by virtue of its shared tones.

iii

Let's introduce this new chord very simply by immediately seeing how it makes for welcome variation in that most familiar of songwriting formulas: the Four-Chord 'turnaround'.

Theory tells us that iii minor – being, as we said, part of the tonic family – should be able to substitute for the ubiquitous vi chord within both our 'I-vi-IV-V' and also the Doo Wop version. Sure enough, The Beatles oblige in 'I Feel Fine', whose middle eight neatly demonstrates both variations in the space of its two constituent four-bar cycles.

'I Feel Fine'

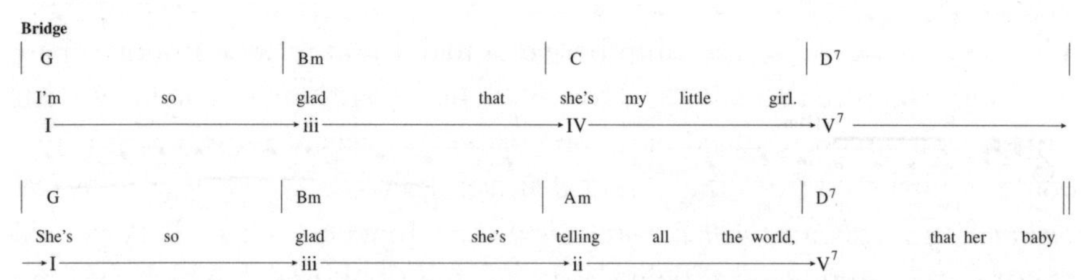

While these cycles can hardly be said to represent songwriting sophistication, in this context they account for the overall success of the song by contrasting minor pop chords with the resolutely bluesy feel of the strictly I-IV-V verses. The Beatles would apply precisely this type of substitute four-chord cycle in songs ranging from 'Girl' and 'You're

Going To Lose That Girl' right through to 'Goodnight'. More importantly, in terms of appreciating The Beatles' development as songwriters, the 'I-iii' move alone should be seen as a dramatic departure from the now numbing predictability of the 'I-vi' that we've seen so far at almost every turn.

This is isn't just academic speculation – Paul McCartney even tells us as much – revealing The Beatles' awareness of this third 'stop' on the harmonised scale (sometimes known as the *mediant*), as a point of emphasis – right from the early days. Let's revisit that quote from the introduction:

> '... ["I'm Happy Just To Dance With You"] was a bit of a formula song. We knew that if you went from E to G♯minor[25] you could always make a song with those chords, that change pretty much always excited you. This was one of those. Certainly "Do You Want To Know A Secret" was. The nice thing about it was to actually pull off a song on a slim little premise like that'[26]

McCartney is actually being far too modest here. For as we will see, these two songs feature a range of other interesting harmonic devices, including major/minor key switching (Chapter 7); a 'borrowed flat submediant' (Chapter 7); and even a highly exotic 'Super-Phrygian' cadence (Chapter 8). But, for now, let's look at the parallels that McCartney draws:

'I'm Happy Just To Dance With You'

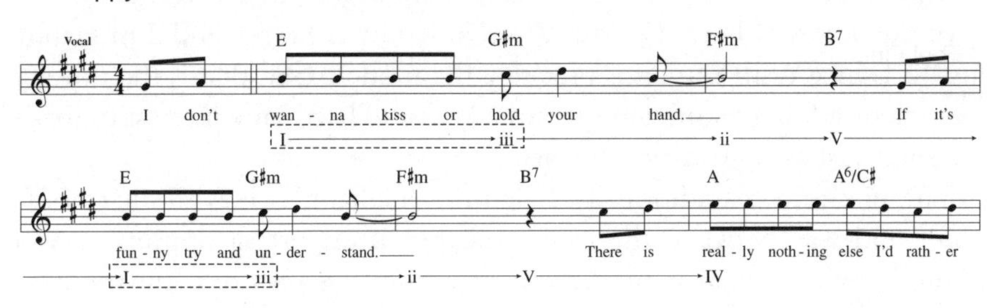

[25] McCartney's actual quote refers to the chord 'A♭ minor' which is the enharmonic equivalent of G♯ minor. But, in the key of E, which he is clearly referring to, the iii minor chord appears as G♯ minor and we have changed it for the sake of simplicity.

[26] Barry Miles, *Many Years From Now*, p. 163.

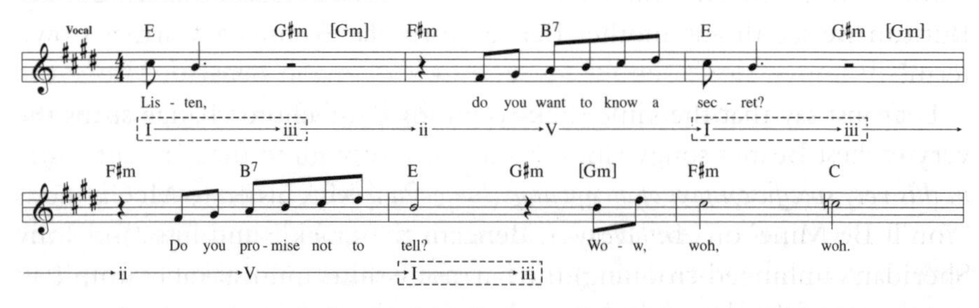

Both songs are in the key of E and, uncannily, the chord sequence in both is virtually identical. McCartney's opening gambit of a major tonic chord (E major) that travels to a minor chord two whole steps away (G♯m) kicks off the verses just as he describes. Both songs even make the return journey back to the tonic through the standard ii-V-I cadence that we have just been exploring. The only difference is the brief Gm chord in 'Do You Want To Know A Secret' which merely acts as a chromatic passing chord that fleetingly links the two minor chords.[27]

As we will see, this was hardly the most sophisticated of Beatles moves, but a novel one, nonetheless, in the context of the early sixties rock 'n' roll scene dominated by Three-Chord Tricks and Four-Chord clichés. It would be wrong to suggest that the iii chord was absent in songs of this era – we will suggest some inspirational Beatles covers later. But on the occasions that other, slicker, pop outings of the era *were* spiced with more colourful harmony, they tended to use the ii and vi chords, as we saw earlier.[28]

In the verses of both 'Do You Want To Know A Secret' and 'I'm Happy Just To Dance With You', it is precisely the modest G♯m that is the novelty ingredient, adding a sufficiently unusual twist of harmonic interest to make the song, just as McCartney confirms.

The iii chord is traditionally called the mediant, as it is the harmonic point mid-way between the tonic and the all important dominant. As a result, it represents root movement of a *third interval* from the tonic, in

[27] This move is adapted from a simple blues embellishment that we can hear The Beatles performing on their version of Chuck Berry's 'I Got To Find My Baby' on *Live At The BBC* (disc 2, track 29).

[28] Dave Rubin, 'Rockin' In The '50s', *Guitar One* magazine, December 1999, p. 190. Rubin also refers to the Doo Wop substitution sequence consisting of C-C6-Dm-G7/D as exemplified by 'Angel Baby' by Rosie And The Originals dating from 1960. Beatles trivia buffs will know that this is the A-side of 'Give Me Love' an early Beatles favourite, as highlighted by Riley (*Tell Me Why*, p. 5) and MacDonald (*Revolution In The Head*, p. 91).

contrast to the fourths, fifths and seconds we have been so far exploring. But can we see this as another Beatles 'formula', to use McCartney's own term?

Let's just say that the same slick-sounding 'I-iii' chord change spans the very earliest Beatles songwriting excursions through to the very last – and *in this very specific context of an opening change in a verse.* Listen to McCartney's 'You'll Be Mine' on *Anthology 1*. Beneath the crackle and hiss (and Tony Sheridan's unhinged crooning) the harmony shifts unmistakably from I-iii in support of the descending melody line as the vocals enter.

Meanwhile, Beatles experts will know that Paul's 'Love Of The Loved', dating from as far back as 1961, and recorded two years later by Cilla Black, is another that opens on the same premise of thirds root movement before wending its way through a myriad of rather more novel changes.

McCartney didn't have a monopoly on this particular songwriting device – just listen to Lennon's verses in 'Help!' or 'A Day In The Life'. And don't let's leave George out of it – having modulated to the key of A in the bridge of 'Something', I-iii is the first change in a sequence that mirrors that of 'Help!' almost chord-for-chord. Just to go full circle, fast forward to 'Real Love', the very last 'Beatles' song of all, as John's 'little plans and schemes' are revealed as (musically at least) just a neat move from, yes, the same 'E major to G♯ minor', albeit subtly disguised by the bass line. Forget the Three-Chord Trick – welcome to the rather more sophisticated 'iii-chord Trick', another of the many Beatles harmonic formulas that each of these songwriters would exploit.

Here's a summary table of memorable moments that in each case can be explained by this single opening chord change of 'I-iii' (italicised lyric falls on the iii).

McCartney's 'formula' – The 'iii-chord Trick'

Song	Lyric	I	iii
'You'll Be Mine'	'When the stars fall at *night*'	A	C♯m
'Love Of The Loved'	'Each time I look *into your eyes*'	E	G♯m
'I'm Happy Just To Dance With You'	'I don't want to kiss or *hold your* hand'	E	G♯m
'Do You Want To Know A Secret'	'Listen *ooh*'	E	G♯m
'Help!'	'When I was younger, so much *younger*'	A	C♯m
'It's Only Love'	'I get *high*'	C	Em
'I Feel Fine'	'I'm so *glad*'	G	Bm
'A Day In The Life'	'I read the *news* today'	G	Bm
'Goodnight'	'Now it's *time*'	G	Bm
'Something'	'You're asking *me*'	A	C♯m
'Real Love'	'All my little plans and *schemes*'	E	G♯m

For such an ostensibly melodic move, and one therefore usually associated with slick 'urbane' pop, it's ironic that this, too, can be understood within the context of a traditional 12-bar blues. And not just in theory, but also in practice.

Let's compare the 'Do You Want To Know A Secret' ladder effect, (involving I, ii and iii) with an elaborate substitution occasionally found within 12-bar blues and R'n'B songs based on this structure. If this sounds like an unlikely source for The Beatles, then listen to their version of Chuck Berry's 'I Gotta Find My Baby', on *Live At The BBC.* Here they use a similar harmonised scale 'walk' from G up to Bm7 and back down to create a specific highlight in the final verse (at 1.42-1.45).[29]

'I Gotta Find My Baby' The 'I-iii scale walk' in the 12-bar blues

Bar no.	**7**		**8**		**9**	**10**	**11**
Formula	I7	ii7	iii7	♭iii7	ii7	V7	I
Key of G	G7	Am7	Bm7	B♭m7	Am7	D7	G

Bars 7 and 8 can be seen as just embellishing two bars of G with the harmonised scale walk, before resolving with a ii-V-I. German guitar teacher Peter Fischer calls this the 'King Bee' blues after jazzy renditions of the Slim Harpo classic.[30] When Fischer refers to this as a way to make the blues 'cheerful' he is implicitly describing the melodic sound of the iii chord. This is because the 5th degree of the chord can be seen to mirror the natural 7th of the *key*, in contrast to the ♭7th, which of course typically sets the bluesy mood. So, in our example, while the G7 chord here stresses the F natural, bar 8 introduces the sweeter sound of the F♯, a feature that we will revisit below.

The most famous blues song that uses this idea is surely Bobby Bland's version of T-Bone Walker's classic 1947 slow blues, '(They Call It) Stormy Monday'. The Allman Brothers would do exactly the same with their later version, while John Mayall and Eric Clapton would similarly walk-up from G to Am and Bm in the solo of 'Little Girl' on the legendary 1966 Bluesbreakers *'Beano'* album.[31]

[29] A feature that does not appear in the Chuck Berry original.

[30] Peter Fischer, *Blues Guitar Rules*, p. 19.

[31] While this type of move can be applied to the blues, it has also become commonplace in ballad pop and soul styles. Stevie Wonder's 'You Are The Sunshine Of My Life', with its 'I-ii-iii-♭iii-ii-V-I' verse structure, is a model.

'Ask Me Why' clearly shows how The Beatles managed to incorporate this 'walk'.

'Ask Me Why'

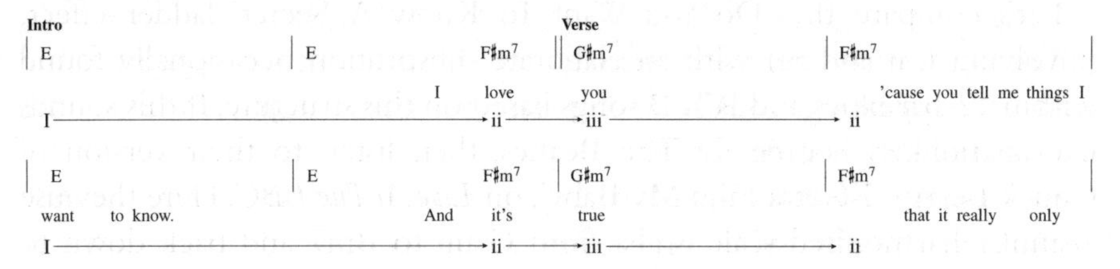

James Ray's 'If You Gotta Make A Fool Of Somebody' must be mentioned again here as an influential favourite covered by The Beatles in their early gigs. 'It was a really good one to have in our act as it got attention from the more discerning people in the audience', McCartney explains on *Rock & Roll Roots*. Paul refers especially to the novelty of the song's 3/4 waltz time in contrast to the 'four-to-the-bar' predictability of most rock 'n' roll of the time. But one listen to the track (on the album that Paul says also prompted George Harrison's later rendition of 'I've Got My Mind Set On You') confirms that it was surely an important influence on all these types of Beatles 'walks' involving the stylish iii chord.

'If You Gotta Make A Fool Of Somebody'

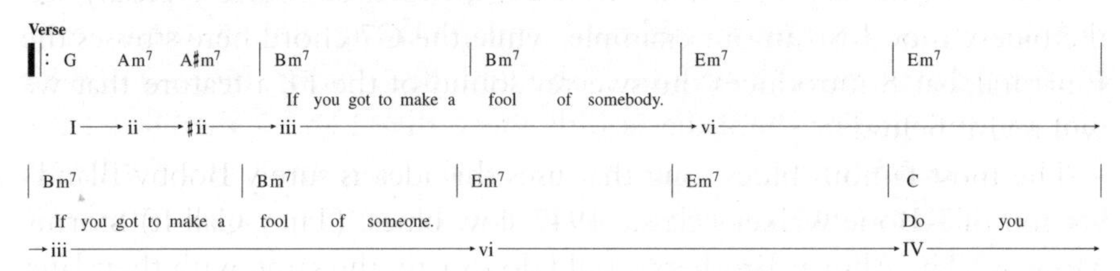

Having climbed up to iii, in similar fashion to 'Ask Me Why', the song (featuring a bizarre 20-bar verse) develops into a sophisticated progression by going on to vi, something that many of The Beatles examples listed in our 'I-iii' chart would go on to do. In songs like 'Help!' and 'A Day In The Life', 'I-iii-vi' is a defining sequence in the verse, while Harrison's 'Something' uses almost the identical sequence as 'Help!' for its bridge.

'Help!'

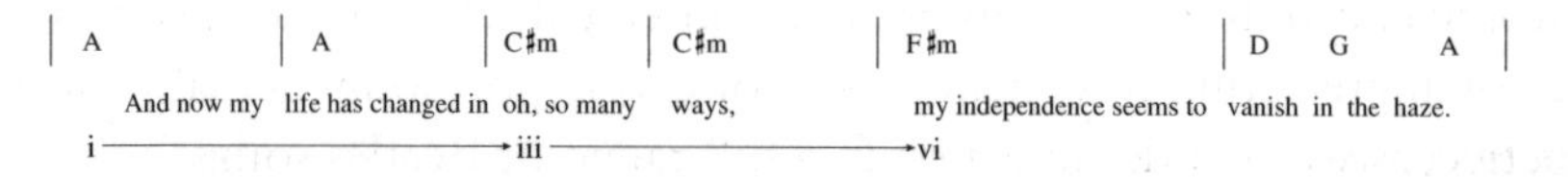

The comparison here demonstrates the versatility of this type of classic sequence, appearing equally appropriate in frantic pop rock as in the tenderest of love ballads.

Even more cleverly, The Beatles recognised that the same chordal relationship 'works' wherever a songwriter chooses to draw arbitary divisions in terms of song 'sections'. For example, you don't need to run the sequence starting on the I chord. From a resolved I chord you can begin directly with 'iii–vi' as the opening gambit for a *new* sequence. This is already evident of course from the *verses* of both 'Ask Me Why' and 'If You Gotta Make A Fool Of Somebody'. But The Beatles' harmonic horizons widened when they began using the ploy as somewhere new (and seemingly novel) to go to when searching for ideas for their famed middle eights. And never more smoothly than in 'A Hard Day's Night'.

'A Hard Day's Night'

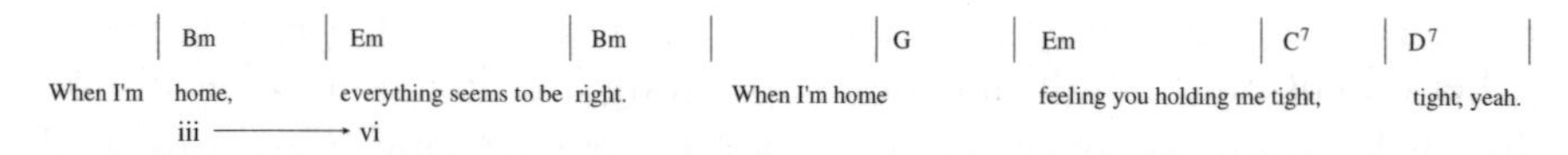

A glance at the guitar fretboard when playing any of these songs confirms that all these 'iii–vi' moves should indeed 'work', because of their root movement. For the iii lies a fifth above the vi and it therefore has a natural tendency to move to it, creating 'stops' along the Cycle Of Fifths, the songwriter's tailor-made 'root map' that we can now explore further.

The mediant and the Cycle Of Fifths

If there is one winning formula at the 'poppy' end of popular music, it is those progressions whose roots follow a predetermined movement descending in intervals of a fifth. If we said as much with the Doo Wop turnaround that's because this, too, is nothing more than a particular excursion along the same cycle.

Applicable to jazz and classical music as well as to pop, the cycle is an unashamedly formulaic system for exploiting the natural tendency of diatonic chords to follow this predetermined path. It provides a very simple way of appreciating how generations of classic pop songs actually work in practice, as we will demonstrate in a full range of Beatles songs.

The Cycle Of Fifths

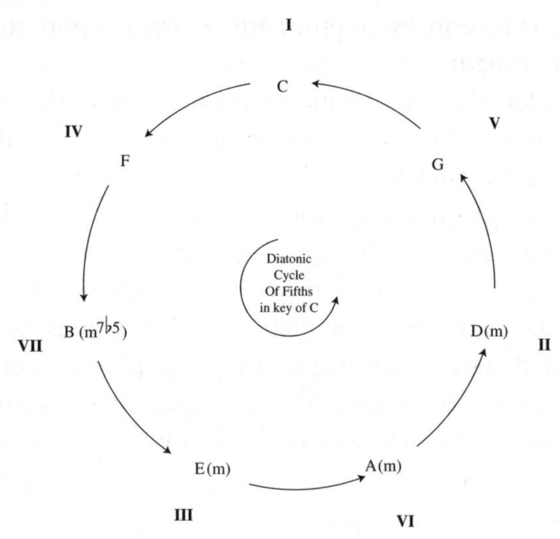

Let's focus on the fifths movement – a song can literally revolve around this cycle continuously or use it as a temporary stepping stone, a musical 'merry-go-round', jumping on and off at will, enjoying its potential for perhaps a few bars before moving on. Complete songs have been built around this idea in such vastly differing contexts, including evergreen jazz standards (Johnny Mercer's 'Autumn Leaves'), definitive rock ballads (Gary Moore's 'Parisienne Walkways'), perennial disco anthems ('I Will Survive'); and even runaway winners at the Eurovision Song Contest (1975 Dutch entry, 'Ding Dingue Dong' by Teach-In). Perhaps the most appropriate use of the circle was 'The Windmills Of Your Mind' (the soundtrack to the film *The Thomas Crown Affair*), whose themes of 'spirals' and 'windmills' mirror the exact same hypnotic path of the music.

The inevitability (and certainly clichéd nature) of the pattern may seem like the very antithesis of The Beatles 'novelty factor' that we have been so keen to stress. But the cycle invariably 'works' because of the ebb-and-flow of tension and resolution that is naturally built into it, with the penultimate dominant V consolidating this flow of fifths as it cadences to the tonic.

Extreme journeys around the cycle (i.e., those starting from at least iii round to I) are mostly associated with standards like 'Moon River' and 'Fly Me To The Moon', and later classic ballads like Peter Skellern's 'You're A Lady' and Marvin Hamlish's 'Nobody Does It Better'. But The Beatles first transformed its use in pop in the chorus of 'Can't Buy Me Love', where it created a stunning contrast alongside the unadulterated 12-bar blues of the verse. Here's the intro, starting (for simplicity) on the second of the two opening Em-Am moves. Follow the arrows anticlockwise (from 7 o'clock!).

'Can't Buy Me Love' (0.04–0.09)

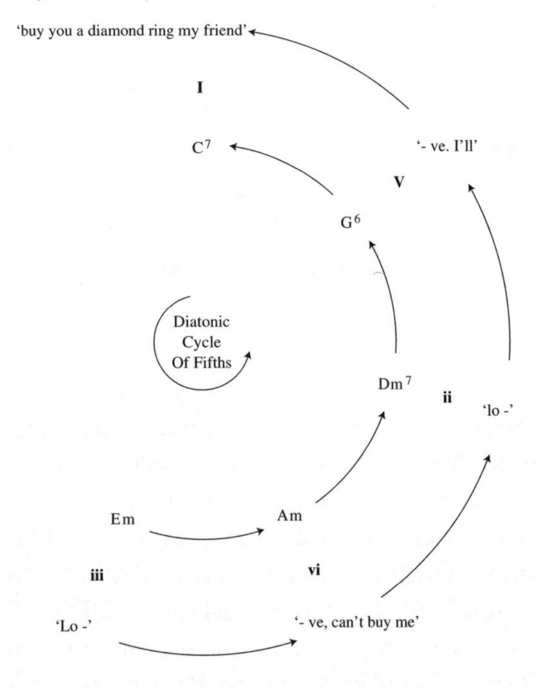

With its underlying almost perpetual motion, this stretch of 'Can't Buy Me Love' is a textbook example of how five of the seven diatonic chords in the harmonised major scale can work their way inexorably towards the final tonic destination in one seamless run. Again, here is a songwriting truth that would resurface throughout The Beatles' career. *Abbey Road*'s 'Golden Slumbers' is another: look at the symmetry of the sequence as the line 'Sleep pretty darling' cues the run E7-Am7-Dm7-G7-C.

'Golden Slumbers'

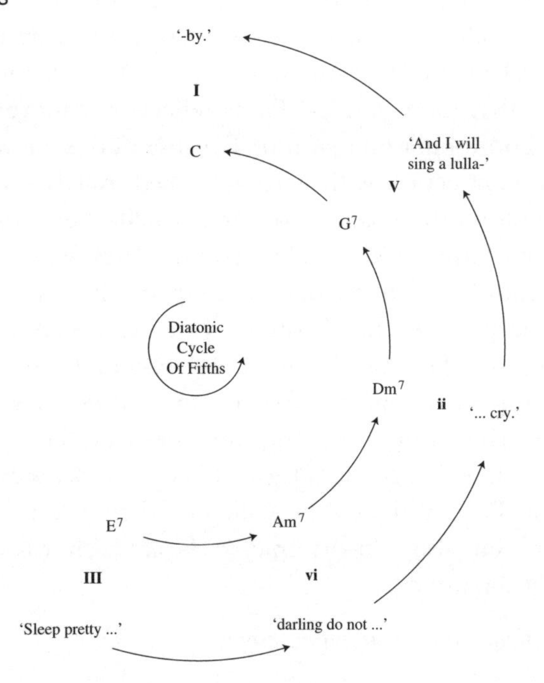

McCartney would top even this (and by a country mile) in the 'The Long And Winding Road', whose very title and theme matches so intuitively his packed musical itinerary around the Cycle Of Fifths. So well, in fact, that a detailed (if at times frivolous) appreciation of this song forms a special case study in Chapter 12.

While all these songs represent extreme examples, many songs will be seen to feature 'sub-sequences' of the cycle, such as 'vi-ii-V-I', 'ii-V-I' and (last but not least) plain old V-I. Each of these cycles and mini-cycles appears in thousands of pop songs and certainly, without fail, on every Beatles album.[32] While The Beatles would no doubt have heard the sound of the cycle on early jazz standards, it's worth mentioning that another of their great early inspirations, Bobby Vee, hit the No. 3 spot in the UK a year before 'Can't Buy Me Love' with 'The Night Has A Thousand Eyes'. That song features a memorable jump of 'iii-vi' before cycling repeatedly around

[32] The Beatles' early influences for these Cycle Of Fifths moves would no doubt have been various. But while we're raving about 'If You Gotta Make A Fool Of Somebody', the bridge here notably heads back to the verse with a cycle of iii-vi-ii-V (at 1.16).

'ii-V-I-vi' for the title refrain (original in the key of E♭). This may well have been an early model for 'Can't Buy Me Love', especially given that three Bobby Vee hits had already featured in early Beatles live sets by that time.[33]

Remember that the Cycle Of Fifths reflects *root* movement – not the *quality* of the chord built on that root. Because of this we will be revisiting it regularly in connection with what are called *secondary dominant* chords: *major* triads built on these same roots, and which often exist almost purely for this purpose. Similarly the cycle accommodates sequences with 'mixed 'n' matched' chords of *both* major and minor quality – just as long as their *roots* follow the predetermined pattern. Later, in a minor key setting, we will also see how The Beatles used the system to revolve through a mesmerising 'super cycle' of all seven diatonic chords. We will also see them use it in pioneering fashion, moving *anti*-clockwise (i.e., down a *fourth*) in settings where it extends the Plagal concept 'backwards' before finally culminating in IV-I. And we'll be widening the cycle to take in not just diatonic chords but also non-diatonic, or *chromatic*, chords as we move into darker, rockier territory.

Reversing direction – the 'vi-iii' minor drop

We briefly mentioned the potential for 'anti-clockwise' movement around the cycle and a quick introduction to the 'descent of a fourth' is useful here. For the notion of the iii now being the target for vi – rather than the other way around, as we expect – can also be seen as an important trademark of Beatles music and another route to harmonic novelty. 'I Will' is a great example of how McCartney avoided being stuck in the Doo Wop rut, by jettisoning the Cycle Of Fifths (after just one hearing) in favour of the mediant, thereby thwarting the potentially clichéd movement.

'I Will'

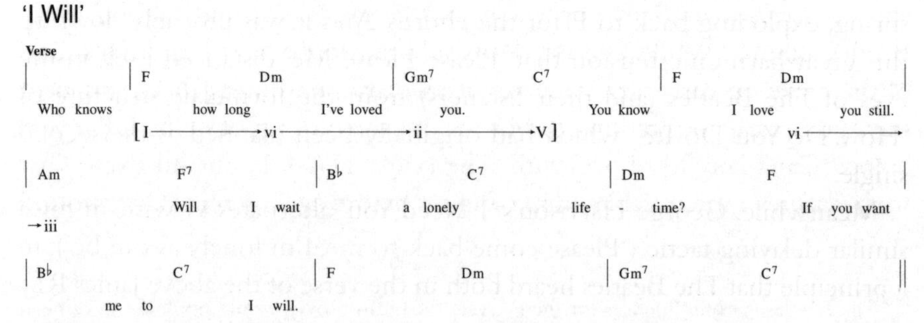

[33] 'More Than I Can Say', 'Take Good Care Of My Baby' and 'Sharing You', according to *The Complete Beatles Recording Sessions* by Mark Lewisohn.

This idea has particular application as a delaying device, with I-vi-iii, keeping us in the tonic family for longer but with a distinctive variation of the earlier I-iii-vi 'prolongation of I'. This was a subtle development back in the early sixties and The Beatles would have encountered it in their cover of Bobby Vee's 'More Than I Can Say', a song that appears to be a four-chord cliché but which unfolds delicately 'I-vi-iii-II7-IV-I' with the drop to iii 'making' the song at the climax of the line 'I'll love you twice as much *tomorrow*'.[34]

Meanwhile, as early as 'Please Please Me', The Beatles were showing their ability to 'unfold' a major chord (in this case IV) by using this same idea. Think back to the dramatic 'pre-chorus' section that builds the pressure cooker effect from 0.21-0.28:

'Please Please Me'

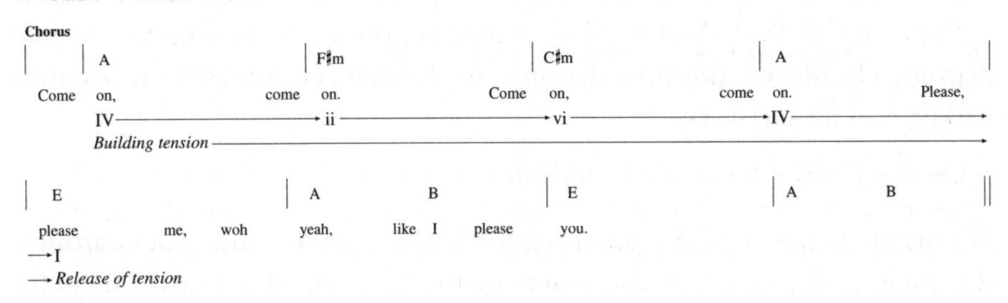

While the song is in E major, this section is all about building tension within the IV chord (A). The F♯m and C♯m chords themselves, which brilliantly help to harmonise the rising line in the backing vocals, can be seen as part of the family of A that's trying to assert itself as a tonality (the vi and iii of A, respectively) – just as Lennon is trying to impress himself on the subject of the song. It's through this that the song winds itself up like a spring, exploding back to E for the chorus. And it was probably down to this great harmonic tension that 'Please Please Me' distanced itself in the eyes of The Beatles (and their listeners) from the formulaic structure of 'How Do You Do It?', which had originally been planned as the second single.

Meanwhile, George Harrison's 'I Need You' alternates vi-with-iii for a similar delaying tactic ('Please come back to me, I'm lonely as can be'), in a principle that The Beatles heard both in the verse of the above James Ray

[34] The chords unwind D♭–B♭m–Fm–E♭7–G♭–D♭ on the original.

song and in the bridge to 'The Honeymoon Song' which alternates C♯m with G♯m (in the key of E), on *Live At The BBC*.

There are many other such 'minor drops' from vi to iii in The Beatles' catalogue, including songs as emotionally diverse as 'She Loves You' and 'Julia', where they appear as sandwiched between I and V, in a 'ready-packed' cycle neatly mixing seconds, fourths and fifths. 'Across The Universe' is a great example, with Lennon prolonging the tonic through I-vi-iii before leading us effortlessly to the second strain with a 'ii-V'.

'Across The Universe'

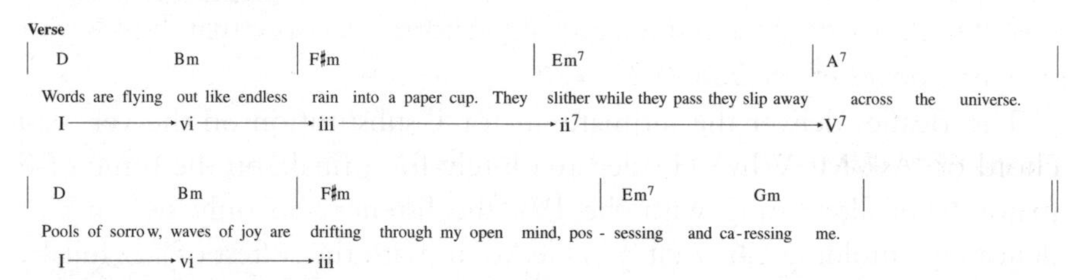

Finally, let's not forget that not only can the mediant extend the tonic in this way, it can also *substitute* for it directly. In this way a song can give the impression of radically changing direction when it is merely exploiting the possibility of substitution within the tonic family. The Beatles had grasped this concept completely as early as 'There's A Place' on *Please Please Me*, where the dominant moves not back to I for a second strain but to an emphatic G♯m (at 0.23).

'There's A Place'

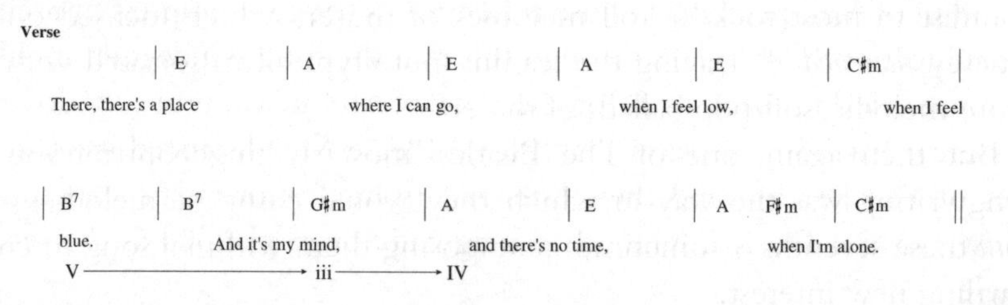

This 'V-iii' is just an alternative to either the standard 'V-I' or the 'V-vi' we previewed in 'Drive My Car'. Yet here the new harmony mirrors perfectly the theme of the singer giving us a fleeting glimpse of that special 'place' – his mind. Meanwhile, this mini-scale 'walk' from iii-IV is a useful idea on which to start a bridge, where it gently prepares for the typical ii-V push to the dominant at the song's climax. As Lennon cleverly constructs on 'Nowhere Man'.

'Nowhere Man'

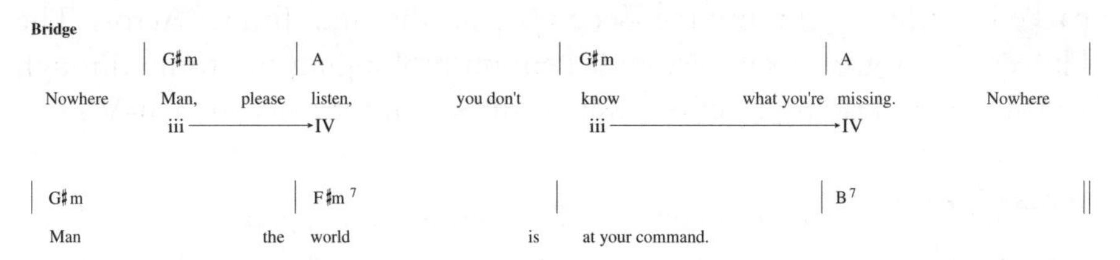

The Beatles deliver the ultimate 'iii-for-I' substitution on the very last chord of 'Ask Me Why'. Headed resolutely for a finale on the tonic of E major (after alternating with the IV), the listener can only swoon as a delicately unfolding G♯m7 (at 2.17) leaves us with the softest of jazz lullaby endings.

The mediant and melody

For all the novel root movement and harmonic texture provided by the iii, it is the scope that the chord provides for the *melody* which The Beatles exploited most cleverly. Specifically, the chord allows a songwriter to highlight the natural 7th of the parent key in contexts beyond a rising leading note (i.e. the 3rd of V7). By supporting the 7th as a chord tone (the 5th) of the more stable mediant, The Beatles achieved melodic colour in ways that few rock 'n' roll acts had attempted. This type of melodic premise was in stark contrast to most rock 'n' roll melodies of the era which focused on the bluesey *flattened* 7th, leaving the leading note typically associated with the more melodic, soft pop ballads of the era.

But then again, one of The Beatles' most striking contributions to songwriting was the way in which they would compose melodies with *both* these sevenths – sometimes juxtaposing them within a song to create startling new interest.

'She's A Woman' is a case in point. The melody starts by making use of the ♭7th in the repeated verse motif, only for the bridge to kick off with a highly rare, ear-catching jump of a major seventh interval to the natural 7th. Here The Beatles were using the mediant to distance themselves conclusively from the familiar strains of R'n'B.

'She's A Woman'

While it might be assumed that The Beatles developed this use of the mediant after years of composing more basic R'n'B melodies, the archives prove that it was really a parallel songwriting development, in keeping with their awareness of the potential for all types of scale tones. The expert Beatles musicologist, Walter Everett, describes in detail how 'You'll Be Mine', on *Anthology 1,* features the natural 7th melody note stressed over the iii minor chord (in a 'I-iii' move that was logged in our earlier chart).[35] Meanwhile, a similar opening melodic semitone drop from '8' to '7' can most famously be heard on George Harrison's 'Something' where the harmony moves from I to I major 7 to accommodate the melody. In this sense, even the ostensibly humble 'You'll Be Mine' can be seen to involve just a 'iii-for-I' chord substitution underneath the identical melodic premise.

And so The Beatles would deliver the 'pop' sound of the 'melodic 7th-over-the-mediant' in songs as diverse as 'Not A Second Time', 'She Loves You', 'A Hard Day's Night', 'Got To Get You Into My Life' and 'Sexy Sadie', with a phenomenal example appearing in 'I Want To Hold Your Hand' which, due to a particular idiosyncrasy, will be discussed in the next chapter.

While the iii may have been under-exploited in pop harmony in the early days, The Beatles were nevertheless familiarising themselves with the chord in other cleverly selected early covers, most notably 'Till There Was You' and 'The Honeymoon Song'. Indeed, we probably need look no further than the opening sequence of the brilliant Buddy Holly song, 'True Love Ways', which exploits the same iii minor twist in the same Four-Chord Turnaround that we saw initially in 'I Feel Fine'.[36]

This simple mediant idea would prove its versatility in pop down the years in the songs of a range of artists, from Elton John (the verse of

[35] Walter Everett, *The Beatles As Musicians: Revolver Through The Anthology*, p.26.

[36] The verse structure ('Just you know why . . .') opens with two hearings of B♭-Dm-E♭-F7.

'Crocodile Rock') to Paul Weller (the chorus of 'Down In The Tube Station At Midnight' and indeed, 'Going Underground'). And while the mediant chord is often regarded as too poppy or melodic for heavier rock, we need only listen to the opening change of Thin Lizzy's 'The Boys Are Back In Town' to hear it add instant substance to a song ('Guess who just got *back* today', I-*iii*). And taking us into the new century with a repeated 'I-iii-I-iii' vamp was Noel Gallagher on Oasis's 'Where Did It All Go Wrong?' (as B♭ alternates with Dm).

Yes, it seems McCartney was spot-on with his 'formula' and, most astutely, the way iii affects the listener: with the key scale's natural 7th dissonance heard as the inoffensive 5th within a mellow minor construction (in subtle contrast to the bolder dominant).[37]

The elusive 'vii' chord

So far we have avoided discussion of the mysterious m7♭5 chord which appears 'naturally' on the seventh degree of the harmonised scale. And for a very specific reason. For with its root, minor third and flattened fifth, this chord features a diminished triad – a particularly dissonant-sounding chord that rarely features in pop. The dark sound of this m7♭5 construction *is* put to regular use in the more appropriate minor-key setting where it appears as part of the equivalent ii-V-I sequence. Still, even in that downbeat context, it is most associated with jazz and classical music, and it's no coincidence that we will be exploring its use mainly in Lennon's minor *opus*, 'Because'. As a result, the leading note as a root for anything more than a passing chord has become rather under-utilised in pop music. However, in a very select group of songs, The Beatles nevertheless show us how to substitute in its place a *regular* minor seventh chord: namely one with a *perfect* fifth rather than a diminished one, creating powerful, ear-catching effects in the process.

In discussing this maverick 'vii7' on the leading note – without question the most stylish and sophisticated chord we have so far encountered – we will make the distinction between two types of Beatles settings. First, those progressions that descend *away* from the root in a cyclical fashion. These are the focus of the remainder of this chapter. Secondly, a category (notably

[37] When discussing the iii, KG Johansson states that the 5th is 'the least important note' when determining the chord's character. 'The Harmonic Language Of The Beatles', STM-Online, Vol.2 (1999), page 4.

taking in Lennon's 'Julia') that creates a different type of tonal ambiguity, where a modal analysis – specifically the *Lydian* mode – can arguably help us better understand the effect on the listener. This is reserved for Chapter 8, which discusses the modes themselves.

The cyclical vii7

One of the most eloquent and perceptive insights into the subliminal effects of Beatles music was made by American music critic Ned Rorem back in 1968. And it concerned just a couple of very specific, delicate chord changes on the *Revolver* album. Let's review one notably colourful extract:

> '"Here, There And Everywhere" would seem at mid-hearing to be no more than a charming show ballad but once concluded it has grown immediately memorable. Why? Because of the minute harmonic shift on the words 'wave of her hand', as surprising and yet as satisfyingly *right* as that in a Monteverdi madrigal . . .'[38]

A close look at the extract confirms that this moment indeed corresponds to a slice of striking McCartney novelty.

After a pleasant, but predictable walk up the diatonic scale, we duly reach Rorem's 'minute harmonic shift' in bar 5. This turns out to involve the not-so-minute root movement of a descending augmented fourth – six semitones from C to F♯m – which then moves neatly down a fifth to B7.

This root movement makes for a striking variation from the simple, 'close seconds' that went before. More importantly, Norem is picking up on the emotional power of the new harmony that is tantalisingly suggesting a shift in the key centre. After the gentle – even bland – opening phrases in bars 1-4, vital musical tension indeed appears fleetingly on the lyric 'wave of her hand', just as Norem describes, in what is one of the finest instances of The Beatles playing on our expectations. The listener is being gently programmed to expect a return to the G tonic chord, or at least a mild variation of it (perhaps in descending seconds, as we hear in 'If I Fell'). But the F♯m7-B7 move stops us in our tracks.

[38] Ned Rorem, *The Music Of The Beatles*, New York Review Of Books, 18 January 1968. Reprinted in *The Lennon Companion* (ed. Thomson and Gutman), p. 105.

'Here There And Everywhere'

The pull to vi

For the first time since the altered dominants of Chapter 1, we have moved beyond our cosy diatonic framework. Not only is the viim7♭5 appearing as a straight m7, thereby introducing a non-diatonic C♯, but the following chord built on the mediant is a dominant 7th, complete with a *major* third rather than a minor third as our G scale would suggest. And this brings in a second 'non-scale' note, the D♯.[39]

[39] Interestingly, on the second hearing, the vii chord here arguably *is* a pure F♯m7♭5. For, over the lyric 'no..bo..dy can deny', the melody rises from B to C, thereby taking the 4th to a ♭5 and briefly creating the full dissonant sonority.

Technically, this is an early encounter with what will emerge as the vital principle of *modulation*: the process of moving to a new key centre. For at the heart of Rorem's 'minute harmonic shift' is precisely the fact that, with the F♯m7 to B7 change, we have jumped on the Cycle Of Fifths and are feeling an inexorable pull towards the darker territory of E minor. More specifically, the aural effect results from the fact that the underpinning of the solid, stable G major tonality is being undermined. Indeed, the emotional intensity develops not just on arrival at E minor but from the *anticipation* created by the minor 7th chord as it alternates with the dominant a fifth below. In this sense, the move can be seen as an isolated, new and fresh 'ii-V-to-tonic' resolution *when viewed from the point of view of the impending E minor.*

This principle of modulation is discussed in more detail in Chapters 5 and 6 when elaborating on what we mean by the whole concept of *tonality*, and also in Chapter 10 on 'mega modulations' where we explore how The Beatles visited scales beyond the single key signature that encompasses both a major key and its relative minor (as in this case).

However, for now, it must be mentioned that the extent to which this formal notion of modulation is useful when analysing The Beatles' music depends on various factors. These include the context of the sequence within the song; how subsequent chords reinforce the establishment of the 'new' key; and the length of time we spend in the new key.

In the case of 'Here, There And Everywhere', clearly the context is a fleeting chord change in the middle of a verse sequence. When we do finally arrive at Em it is only for two brief beats, after which we are immediately headed back to G (from whence we came) by means of a conventional ii-V-I in the parent key. Some would argue that we don't have time to feel *established* in a new key – and hence it's not worth thinking of the chords in terms of a new tonality. It is in such situations that we can adopt a compromise approach recognising the role of what is called a *secondary dominant*.

In previewing this, the subject of the following chapter, we can regard the role of that rogue B7 as being a powerful primer, taking us inevitably to the relative minor. In this sense the appropriate Roman numeral moniker is not just III7 (reflecting the major triad) but, better still, 'V of vi', an abbreviation that attempts to capture the fact that the chord is *the dominant V chord of the vi chord to which it is headed*. This terminology will become clear when we see secondary dominants in a range of applications in Beatles songs. Our reason for introducing it here is to demonstrate how (on its very select appearances) *a vii chord acts in conjunction with a III7 headed for vi.* The secondary dominant itself is therefore a 'partner in crime' in producing this compelling cyclical harmony descending away from the tonic.

McCartney didn't just use this idea in 'Here, There And Everywhere'. A certain ballad entitled 'Yesterday', recorded one year earlier (to the day), also featured a truncated version of this very same vii–'V of vi'–vi idea. Here it constitutes what is arguably the single most famous songwriting move of McCartney's career. For pivotal to the songwriting novelty of 'Yesterday' is this disarming device, which is set in motion when we're only one word into the song! Look at the very second bar of the verse.

'Yesterday'

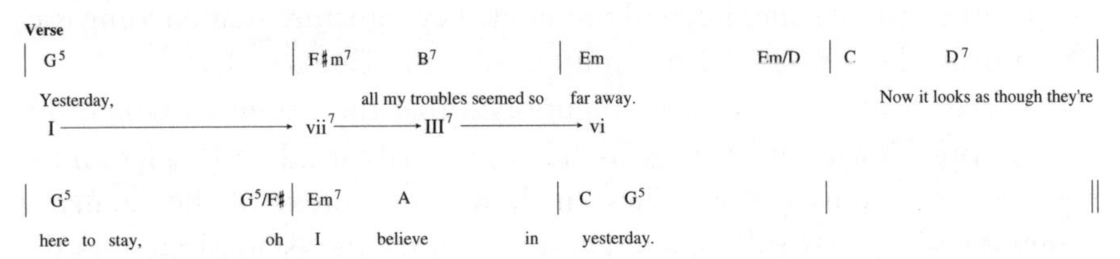

Suffice it to say that this move was exceedingly rare in sixties pop music – though special mention should be given to a couple of songs in very different settings. Firstly, Neil Sedaka's 'Breaking Up Is Hard To Do', from 1962. The verse here begins predictably with a Doo Wop cliché, but the sudden drop to a vii–'V of vi'–vi over the line: 'cause if you go then I'll be blue', is surely a vital element in turning an innocuous ditty into a classic that has notched up 5 million (and counting) airplays.[40] Meanwhile, reminiscing in *The Beatles Anthology,* McCartney himself makes a point of raving about another song that had used the device to capture the imagination the previous year:

'It was great to meet Hank Mancini, because like most people we'd loved 'Moon River'. The line "my huckleberry friend" had done us in: after *Breakfast At Tiffany's* he was a hero.'[41]

[40] The song reached number 7 in UK in July 1962, staying in the charts for 17 weeks.

[41] Paul McCartney, *The Beatles Anthology*, p. 198.

Lyrics aside, Mancini's masterpiece (which charted in the UK in December 1961) also hinges on the same 'minute harmonic shift', which occurs at 0.17 on the original instrumental (or following the word 'someday' on the many vocal renditions). At a stroke, it succeeds in turning a pleasant 'tune' into a timeless classic.

'Moon River'

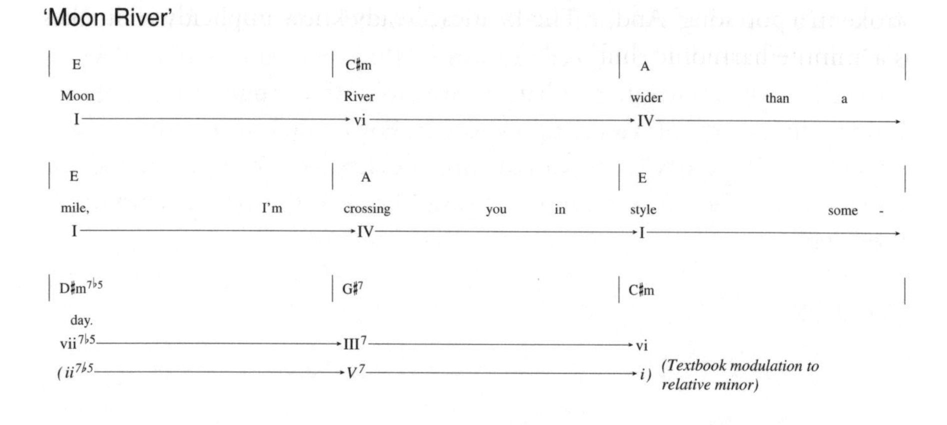

Key Of E	I	vi	IV	I	IV	I	**vii**	**V⁷ of vi**	**vi**
	E	C♯m	A	E	A	E	D♯m^{7}♭^{5}	G♯^{7}	C♯m
Key Of C♯m							**ii**	**V⁷**	**i**

Here the chord is a bona fide vii7♭5, and we have similarly labelled the sequence according to *both* the key of E major and the key of C♯ minor purely to demonstrate that two interpretations can be applied depending on your point of view. This dichotomy – and the ability to view such progressions *in relation to two different tonics* – may appear unduly academic. But it will soon emerge as the secret to appreciating the catalogue of Beatles songs that are compelling for the very sense of tonal ambiguity they create. It will also help in reconciling the seemingly contradictory interpretations offered by Beatles musos down the years over the same extracts of Beatles music.

The message for now is merely that astute songwriters know that the chord built on the vii, followed by a dominant chord down a fifth, takes us to a vi chord in a far stronger way than if we'd just jumped to it directly from the home tonic, or 'walked' to it via a brief bass note on vii. What should be seen as a mini-harmonic 'package' instigates a genuine feeling of movement away from the parent key, however briefly, and as such is ripe for a complementary lyrical treatment. In the case of 'Here, There And Everywhere' the move perfectly matches the 'wave of her hand'. In 'Yesterday', it mirrors precisely the pivotal sense of time distortion invoked by Paul's opening salvo, as he invites us to share his feelings of the previous day.[42]

However you label it, this cyclical move 'from the vii' is a stylish masterstroke in a pop song. And, as The Beatles already knew implicitly, all it takes is a 'minute harmonic shift' . . .[43]

[42] Ironically, that same time distortion also occurs in 'Moon River' with the line 'some day' coinciding identically with the sequence in question.

[43] Beatles expert, Ian Hammond, reminds us how McCartney described the F♯m7 in 'Yesterday' as 'the big waaaahhh', a colourful acknowledgement of how it is 'a feature chord which will drive the song and be instantly recognisable'; 'Same Old Songs', www.beathoven.com.

FOUR

'Supercharging' a Song with Secondary Dominants

The Beatles were familiar, right from the early days, with the 'supercharging' potential of *secondary dominants*, which they used to achieve emphasis within a progression, driving a song forward in ways that couldn't be achieved with the basic harmonised chords.

The primary dominant that we introduced in Chapter 1 appears *only* on the fifth of the major scale (the V7). A secondary dominant, however, can be constructed on other scale degrees – especially the second, third and sixth degrees, which in the harmonised diatonic scale are minor chords. If we change these minor triads to major dominant sevenths, raising the flattened third degree by a semitone and adding the flattened seventh (e.g., iii to III7, vi to VI7, etc.), they can also take on the dominant function.

The III7 (or 'V of vi') of 'Here, There And Everywhere' and 'Yesterday' gave us an early taste of this principle – a device that automatically increases a songwriter's 'master source' of chords by bringing II7, III7, VI7 and VII7 into the equation in addition to ii, iii, vi and vii. In this chapter we'll be exploring various Beatles songs that feature these new chords and explaining their functions and effects.

It should be stressed that while these chords are traditionally termed *dominants* (for reasons that will become apparent), the ♭7 itself may not always be present, as it is in the primary dominant 7th. It is the major incarnation of the chord that is essential (in this sense they could be thought of as secondary *majors*). Nevertheless, the dominant seventh is indeed common and adds a harder, bluesier texture while contributing to what we will see to be effective voice-leading.

But why do these chords even appear if the major 3rd of each triad is so obviously outside the diatonic scale? The answer, once again, is to propel a chord sequence with added impetus while providing scope for a new melody note from outside the parent scale. Just as we have come to expect from the primary dominant, the function of the secondary dominant is usually to intensify the resolution to the next chord in any Cycle Of Fifths movement by effectively creating just another 'V7-I' move.

This familiar voice-leading accounts for the first (and most common) category that we will encounter: *functioning* secondary dominants. These are so called because (by definition) they *always* function as what we can term a 'local V', resolving to a chord down a fifth interval. This is in contrast to the second category: *non-functioning* secondary dominants, which do not follow this path of root movement. They lead a song elsewhere.

Functioning secondary dominants

II7 (the 'V of V')

Think back for a minute to our I-vi-ii-V, Doo Wop cliché. The vi minor chord here happily moved to ii minor courtesy of the tendency of the roots to move down a fifth. However, when ii becomes *II7*, there is an additional driving force as the major 3rd of the chord now acts a leading tone, 'wanting' to resolve upward by that similarly lone semitone to the root of the next chord.

'Like Dreamers Do'

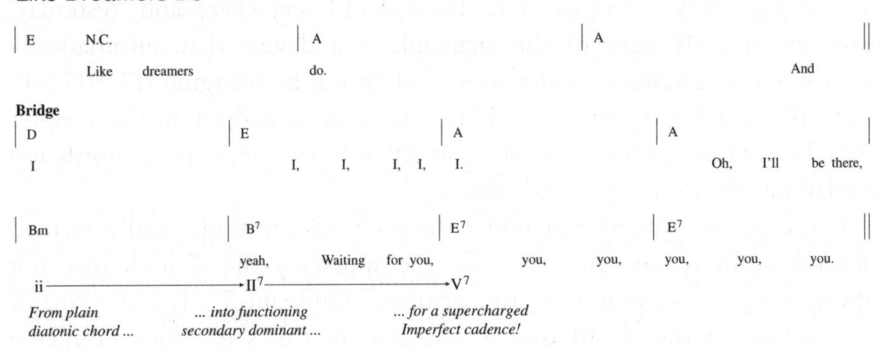

Look at the Bm at the end of the bridge of 'Like Dreamers Do' – it seems that The Beatles are set to end the verse with a familiar ii–V. But, as if at the last minute, they decide to make two changes to the minor chord, adding the major 3rd and the $\flat 7^{th}$ to lead us – now with *B7* – almost mechanically to the E7 chord. We duly feel the shift to this musical and lyrical peak more strongly – as if it were now inevitable.

The B7 is said to be a *functioning secondary dominant* (here a II7). More specifically, as it functions as the V of the primary V chord, it is often referred to in modern muso and session parlance as '*the five of five*'. Reflecting this, it can be even notated as just 'V of V'. While potentially confusing, this merely refers to the fact that the II chord, B7, is *acting as a V chord in relation to the primary V7 of the key*, in this case E7.[1]

VI7 (the 'V of ii' or 'V of II')

In just the same way, a functioning secondary dominant built on the sixth note of the scale would be the major 'VI7' rather than 'vi'. This in turn can be similarly thought of as 'V of II' (or 'V of ii'), as it leads us directly to either the major or minor triad built on the second degree of the scale, with the same root move of a fifth.

Combine the two new chords and we now have the major sequence: I-VI7-II7-V7, a distinctively bluesy version of the otherwise identical Doo-Wop turnaround. Here's a great Beatles example from *Revolver*:

'Good Day Sunshine'

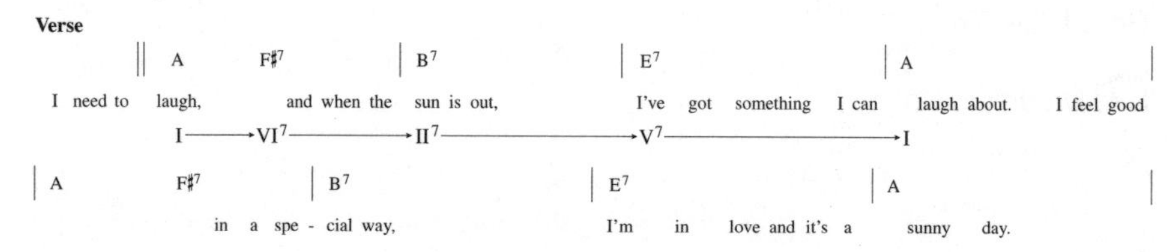

This cycle has a strong blues, R'n'B and jazz heritage which can be traced back at least as far as Delta giant Robert Johnson whose classic 'They're Red Hot' showed the jazzy way his music was headed before his death in 1938. It proved to be a great tool for Tin Pan Alley, powering such jazz classics as the bridge to Gershwin's 'I Got Rhythm' and the main

[1] Eric Taylor refers to this II-V as 'the secondary dominant to the true primary', before explaining: 'Bach sometimes uses this approach to a perfect cadence in his chorales, where it gives a magnificent feeling of solidity and finality.' *The Associated Board Guide To Music Theory, Part II*, p. 151.

structure of 'Sweet Georgia Brown', another influential song in the early Beatles live sets.[2] It's therefore no surprise that long before the days of 'Good Day Sunshine', some of the earliest Beatles songs featured this same idea.

'I Call Your Name'

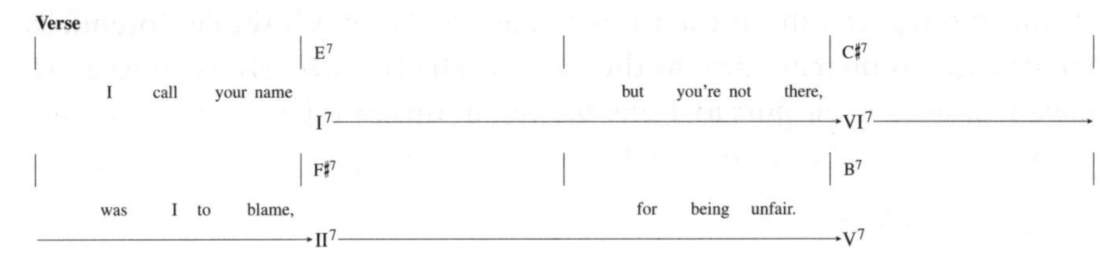

Meanwhile, some writers have cited the similarity between 'Good Day Sunshine' and John Sebastian's 'Daydream', released at much the same time in mid-1967.[3] The verses of both songs open with the same strong I-VI7 move and proceed around the cycle with the same root movement – though 'Daydream' actually retains the 'sweeter' ii minor rather than switching it to II7. This 'hybrid' variation had been used by Lennon years previously, on what he acknowledges as his very first song – while McCartney also exploited it (this time in slow motion) as late as *Abbey Road*.

'Hello Little Girl'

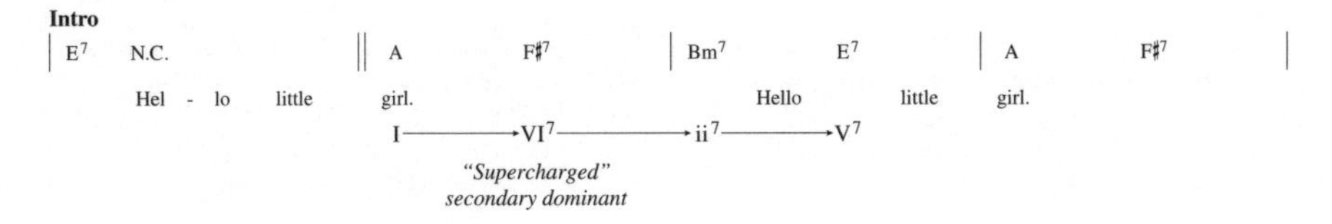

'Maxwell's Silver Hammer'

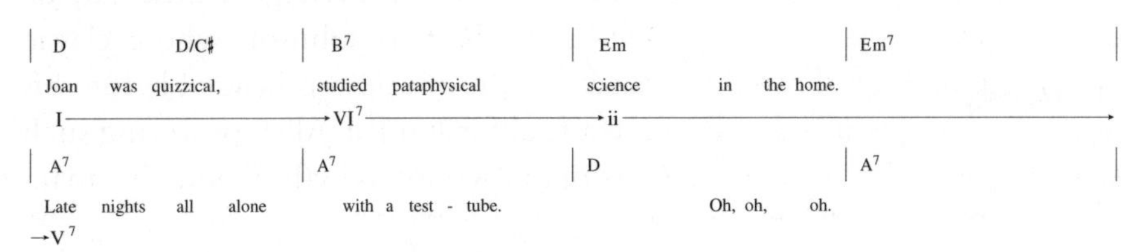

[2] The Beatles can be heard cycling around a modified form of the sequence (starting on the VI: D7-G7-C7-F7, in the key of F) on their infamous early version on *The Beatles' First* (with Tony Sheridan), released as Polydor 236201, in June 1964.

[3] Walter Everett, *The Beatles As Musicians: Revolver Through The Anthology*, p.58.

This I-VI7-ii-V-I structure is part of a great tradition that includes Willie Nelson's 'Crazy' (heard on the definitive Patsy Cline model as B♭-G7-Cm-F7-B♭).

Whatever the quality of the ii chord to which it moves, VI7 is most obvious as a turnaround device at the end of a song. It is frequently used by The Beatles as a repeated tag that takes us 'around the block', with VI7 repeatedly priming the ii (or II)-V-I cadence. Hear it blatantly flagged in this cyclical 'postscript' role at the end of 'Hello Little Girl' over the ad-libbed 'oh yeah' lyric. Just to make the point, here it is joined by two other examples – from both ends of The Beatles' catalogue – all featuring this same, time-honoured lyrical 'filler'.

'Hello Little Girl'

Coda

| A F♯7 Bm7 E | A F♯7 Bm7 E | A F♯7 Bm7 E | A ||

Mmm, you're my little girl, mmm, you're my little girl, oh yeah, you're my little girl.

I → VI7 → ii → V → I → VI7 → ii → V → I → VI7 → ii → V → I

'Little Child'

Coda

| F♯ B7 | E C♯7 | F♯7 B7 | E C♯7 |

Baby take a chance with me, oh yeah. Baby take a chance with me, oh yeah.

I → VI7 → II7 → V7 → I → VI7

'Her Majesty'

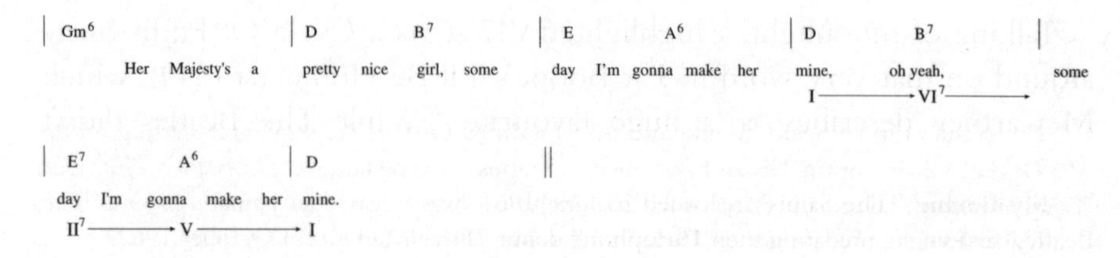

This type of dominant VI chord often appears in the blues as a radical substitute for the V-IV-I move. Another Beatles excursion with Tony Sheridan, 'My Bonnie' shows this in action in a 16-bar structure.[4] Note how the words 'bring back' match the cyclical return home.

'My Bonnie'

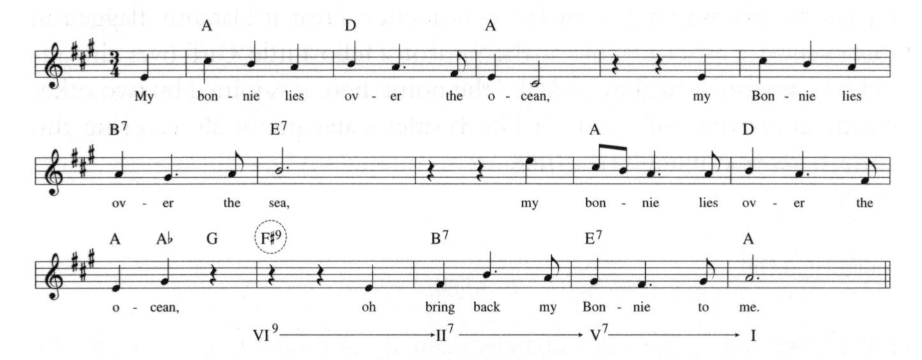

The Beatles' contemporaries were also milking this bluesy cycle for all it was worth. Gene Vincent used it on his fine cover of Hoagy Carmichael's 'Lazy River' (another Beatles live favourite from 1959-1962), while Roy Lee Johnson's 'Mr Moonlight' was even recorded by the Fab Four as late as *Beatles For Sale*.

'Mr Moonlight':

Talking of moonlight, a highlighted VI7 starts a Cycle Of Fifths turnaround on that very word in Pat Boone's 'I'll Be Home' (at 0.49), which McCartney describes as 'a huge favourite'.[5] While The Beatles didn't

[4] 'My Bonnie'/'The Saints', recorded in June 1961, was released in January 1962 as The Beatles' first single, predating their Parlophone debut ('Love Me Do') of October 1962.

record that particular song, they certainly notched up their fair share of dominant VI-II-V-I cycles. Listen to 'I'll Be On My Way' (*Live At The BBC*, track 7) where VI7 is the focus in the bridge (at 0.45) for a move that follows the run: F♯7-B7-E7-A.

While we're on *Live At The BBC*, check out The Beatles' cover of 'I Got A Woman' to hear a perfect example of a secondary dominant. Here The Beatles replace ii with II as John Lennon cues a grand, Las Vegas-style coda (at 2.34), with F♯-B-E appearing now as just a powerful II-V-I.

The 'dominant turnaround cycle' involving VI7 may be commonplace, but the more specific 'II7-V7' move is simply another of the ultimate pop clichés, having being the focus of so many bridges since pop music began.

II7 and the 'Imperfect Cadence' – 'the middle feeling'

Just as we saw Imperfect cadences cued by ii minor (e.g., 'It Won't Be Long'), so we can find a II-V or II7-V7 sequence that *ends* a progression – *again without having resolved satisfactorily to the tonic.* Again the V chord seems to take on a life of its own – as if the key centre had briefly shifted to it – *a feeling to which the II7 contributes more strongly than the ii minor.*

This standard pop feature can be most easily understood with reference to the nursery rhyme 'Jingle Bells'. The line 'in a *one* horse open *sleigh*', defines the II-V Imperfect cadence in the simplest of surroundings. While the tonic certainly reappears after the V, it only does so at the start of the next verse after the all-important delay.

A rather more sophisticated example occurs in 'I Will' on *The White Album*. It is perhaps the ultimate Beatles Imperfect cadence of this type as it simultaneously illustrates the semantic potential provided by the device.

Prior to this point in the song, all the G chords have been *minor* (ii chords). But now the G7 sets up V as we reach the crux of the song. As a bonus, the melody even makes use of the new, non-diatonic B note on the words '*when we're*', taking us in leading-note fashion to the C note, the root of the same V chord. And, of course, *melodically*, this '5' (the C of 'apart') denies us the peaceful tonic and is a simple alternative to the '2' that did so at the equivalent peak in 'It Won't Be Long'.

[5] *Paul McCartney's Rock & Roll Roots*, BBC Radio 2, 25th December 1999. 'I'll Be Home' was a No. 1 hit in the UK in April 1956, staying in the charts for 22 weeks.

'I Will'

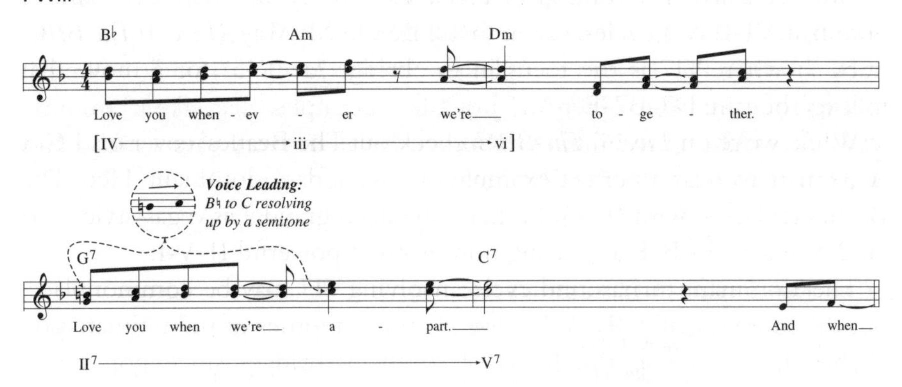

One songwriting expert even re-christens the Imperfect cadence 'the middle feeling' as it tends to occur in the middle of a song (while also avoiding the potential confusion between Imperfect and *Interrupted* cadences we'll discuss in the next chapter).[6] Notice, once again, how this feeling is due to the sense of detachment that the listener experiences as he or she is left hanging in the air (just as with 'It Won't Be Long' and so many of the V chord examples in Chapter 1). The effect on the listener is almost of a brief modulation – actually to the *key* of that V chord (albeit for usually for two brief bars) – with the home tonic appearing tantalisingly out of reach. Trust McCartney to match again, so naturally, the lyric to the chord sequence: the very word 'apart' mirrors precisely the artificial distance between the lovers who are now represented by those musical soulmates, V and I.

And despite its effortless appearance in this type of perfect pop ballad, 'the middle feeling' has venerable roll 'n' roll roots, as confirmed by its appearance in so many clichéd fifties 'middle eights'.[7]

We know that Lennon would have been familiar with the sound as early as the Woolton Village Fête. For 'Come Go With Me' is another song that briefly drops its Doo Wop theme to introduce precisely such an Imperfect cadence. Listen to how, in the key of A♭, the B♭7 takes the glory as a II7 (at 1.10 on the original Del-Vikings version) sparks just the same 5-4-3-2-1 instrumental descent as 'I Will', mentioned earlier, to cue the next verse.

[6] Citron, *Songwriting*, p. 234.

[7] See Chapter 10 for a brief historical tour of the middle eight in pre-Beatles (as well as Beatles) pop.

We don't have a recording of The Quarry Men that night, but *Live At The BBC*, *Anthology 1* and various miscellaneous early releases make up for it by showing The Beatles completing exactly the same 'middle feeling' in a range of cover songs. Here are just a few examples, that take us from the early days right up to Ringo's outing on *Help!*. In every case a strong II–V appears at the climax of the bridge.[8]

'The Middle Feeling': Beatles covers featuring the II^7-V^7 Imperfect cadence

Beatles cover version	Key	II^7- V^7	Time
'Sure To Fall (In Love With You)'	A	B^7 - E^7	0.45
'Nothin' Shakin'	A	B^7 - E^7	1.10
'To Know Her Is To Love Her'	E	$F\sharp^7$- B^7	1.18
'How Do You Do It?	G	A^7 - D^7	0.42
'Besame Mucho'	Gm	A^7 - D^7	1.08
'Lend Me Your Comb'	E	$F\sharp^7$- B^7	0.39
'September In the Rain'	G	A^7 - D^7	0.45
'Beautiful Dreamer'	G	A^7 - D^7	0.34
'Act Naturally'	G	A^7 - D^7	0.42

Given its heritage, it was perhaps no surprise that The Beatles would compose with this idea in a range of rock and pop outings, usually to exit the bridge and make us anticipate the next verse more strongly.

We can spot it in many Lennon/McCartney songs, whether blatantly, as in 'I'll Get You', or fleetingly, as in 'I'll Cry Instead'. Harrison, too, gets in on the act in 'I Need You'. And it's no surprise, given how the device leaves us hanging in suspense, that the Imperfect cadence is usually associated with a suitably poignant lyrical message. It's the crux of the song both lyrically and musically – just as we previewed on 'Like Dreamers Do'.

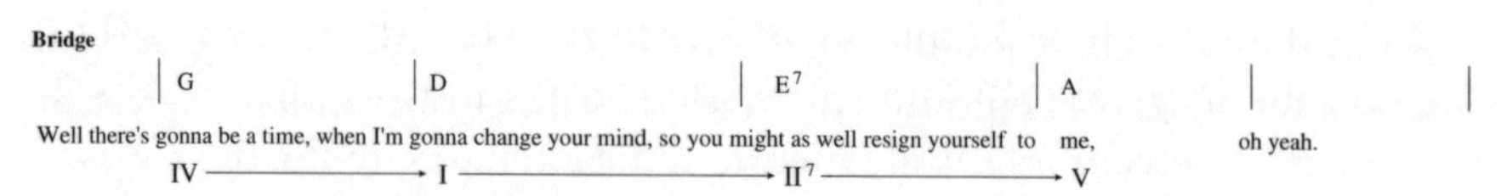

[8] The Beatles would have heard just the same thing in many of their favourite Buddy Holly songs – again in this 'end-of-bridge' context – including the Paul Anka composition 'It Doesn't Matter Any More' ('And wasted all my days over you . . .' A7–D7 in G major).

Here is a summary of just a few examples that demonstrate how The Beatles varied the extent of the effect – from a full bar on the V chord (in most cases) to barely a beat ('I'll Cry Instead').[9]

Song	II - V	Lyrical reference (climax of the bridge)
'Love Of The Loved'	F♯⁷ - B	'that you look at me and say, ah, you love me'
'I'll Cry Instead'	A - D	'but I'll come back again some day'
'I Need You'	B⁷ - E⁷	'I just can't go on anymore'
'I Will'	G⁷ - C⁷	'love you when we're apart'

Why stop at one Imperfect cadence? 'One After 909' features the device *twice* in the space of one, double-length bridge, showing how The Beatles had a twist up their sleeve for even the simplest of rock 'n' roll clichés.

'One After 909'

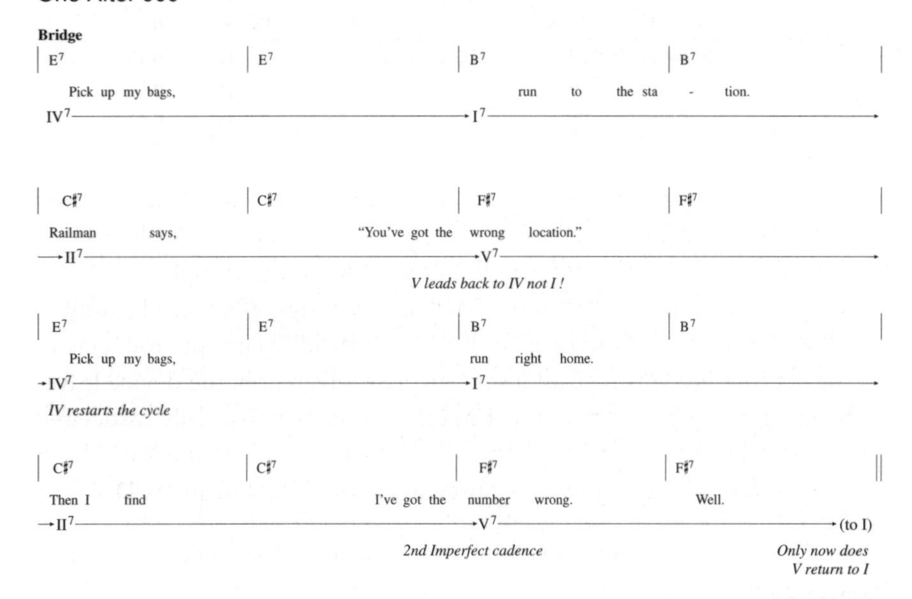

Given the very term 'middle eight', the listener is expecting the verse to resume after eight bars culminating in the first Imperfect cadence – yet we

[9] All these examples are strictly II-V, though the II need not be present to achieve the basic effect of a 'hanging' V. The bridge of the title track on *Sgt. Pepper* can be seen as another type of Imperfect cadence primed, even more primitively, by IV rather than II, as C7 moves to the D7 for the rousing climax 'we'd like to take you home with us' (at 1.33).

are duly thwarted as the progression repeats. The fact this harmonic 'bum steer' coincides sublimely with the lyrics 'wrong location' speaks for itself.

II7 and the Cycle Of Fifths

While most of the ideas so far have been shown to be standard rock 'n' roll fare, the use of II7 in a more prominent Cycle Of Fifths setting helps us make another quantum leap towards an appreciation of more sophisticated Beatles songwriting. McCartney's 'Rocky Racoon' is one song that illustrates this perfectly. The song eventually emerges as clearly in C major; yet it starts on the relative minor (vi) which is soon confirmed as heading for the home tonic via a II-V.

'Rocky Raccoon'

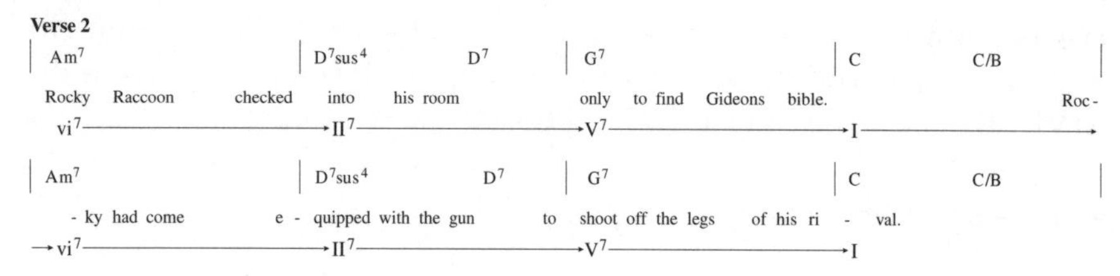

Note how this cycle (virtually the only idea in the whole song) is started by a simple descent from I to vi, via the C/B, a transitionary chord where the bass note is the root of the vii chord. Notice also that, since it isn't part of a ii-V, it doesn't have the power of the 'mini-modulation to vi' that we saw in 'Yesterday' and 'Here, There And Everywhere'. This descending line is nevertheless a standard way of returning to the 'top of the slide' (to borrow a McCartney phrase) as each successive cycle resumes from vi.

'Rocky Raccoon' clearly has an in-built hypnotic mechanism based exclusively on a cyclical fifths idea that is pervasive in all types of pop music. We need only listen to the *Live In Hamburg* recordings to see The Beatles appreciating how entire songs can revolve endlessly 'around the block'. It may seem light years removed from 'Rocky Raccoon', but their rendition of 'I Wish I Could Shimmy Like My Sister Kate' consists entirely of a repeated A-D-G-C root cycle with the apparent key centre of C refusing to settle as it immediately links to the next A major chord.[10]

[10] Note that the A chord in 'Kate' is major (as indeed are all the triads) giving a rocky flavour in comparison with the ballad strains of 'Rocky Raccoon' – but the influence of the Cycle Of Fifths is still apparent.

Rest assured that this cyclical structure will constantly reappear in a range of Beatles songwriting situations. Starting in fact with those sequences that begin from III - one 'bus stop' earlier on the same route- (or rather 'root'-) map.

III7 (the 'V of vi', or 'V of VI')

We have already encountered the III7 chord in the opening of 'Yesterday', where we described it as 'V7 of vi', but this time let's start with a clearer spin around the Cycle Of Fifths, using one of The Beatles' favourite early covers, 'Ain't She Sweet', which travels round the cycle using only dominant 7ths. Originally a 1927 standard by Milton Ager, The Beatles were captivated by the 1956 release by Gene Vincent. Take your pick from The Fabs' version on *Anthology 1* (1961) or *Anthology 3* when they revisited the song in 1969 during a light-hearted break from the *Abbey Road* sessions. In both cases appreciate the symmetry as a jump to III7 starts a run of fifths via VI7, II7 and V7 back to I.

'Ain't She Sweet' (refrain)

I	**III⁷**	**VI⁷**	**II⁷**	**V⁷**	**I**
E	G♯7	C♯7	F♯7	B7	E
'I ask you	very	confidentially	ain't	she	sweet?'

It may seem innocuous in this context, but the use of III7 was evidence of slick songwriting in the early days of rock 'n' roll. II7 was everywhere, but the 'supercharged mediant' – whose task is now to create a sense of anticipation for either the vi or VI7 – was a much rarer, acquired taste. Like the plain iii, it is a chord which The Beatles used in the early days to ensure that their songs stood out from the pack.

Amazingly, as early as 'Ask Me Why' on their debut album, The Beatles were showing us precisely how III7 sounds and functions in comparison to its iii minor 'brother' which, conveniently, is also included in the same composition.

Note how the song takes on a new direction as the G♯7 drives the move to C♯m, thereby taking the listener away from the earlier predictability of the tonic. However in keeping with the whole theme of secondary dominants as a means of lyrical emphasis, the chord serves to elicit the answer to the riddle of the title. What does the singer 'know'? He's about to tell us.

'Ask Me Why'

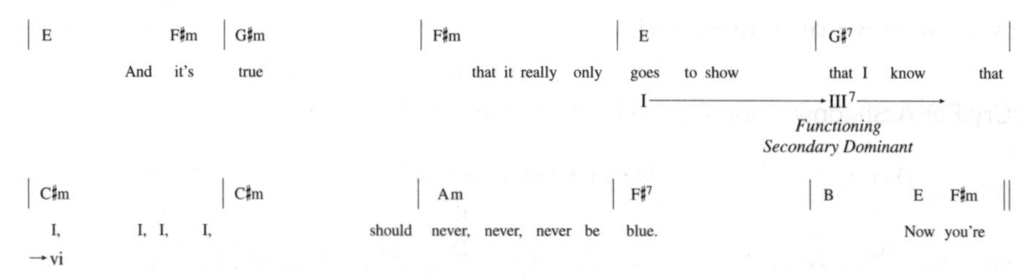

More ambitious was to use the III7 as an opening gambit for a bridge idea. This was brilliantly demonstrated in 'You Can't Do That', where a B7 chord reinforced by it's rogue major 3rd in the melody combine to capture the singer's gloating.

'You Can't Do That'

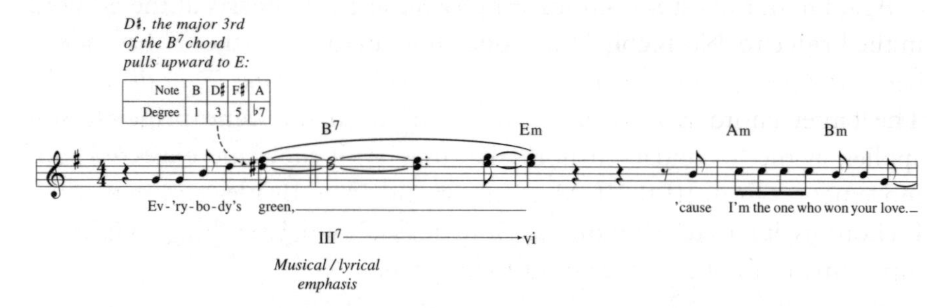

Again, think of III7 as 'V of vi', as the chord is really only destined for one place – the relative minor. This is a principle that we will return to in Chapter 6 when we look at how The Beatles used this same 'III7-vi' move to take us, in a more profound way, to the actual *key* of the relative minor in 'I Should Have Known Better'.

The underlying cyclicality of the move in 'You Can't Do That' should also be highlighted. For while the Bm technically upsets the root movement in fifths, it can be explained as just a nifty relative minor substitute for the D chord that would have led us back, V-I, to G, as it does second time around.

And, talking of bridges with Cycles Of Fifths starting on III, a historical dig into the vaults of both *Anthology 1* and *Live In Hamburg* proves very rewarding at this point. Listen first to The Beatles' 'Cry For A Shadow', the Shadows-style instrumental. Having outgrown the verse's various 'I-vi-I-vi' and Four-Chord Turnaround formulas, the bridge makes a brief bid for freedom by jumping from C to E *major* (at 0.33), and cueing a textbook cyclical move of major triads.

'Cry For A Shadow' – the Cycle Of Fifths bridge (0.33–0.47)

(Verse)	Middle Eight (2 bars each)				(Verse)
(I)	III	VI	II^7	V	(I)
(C)	E	A	D^7	G	(C)

'Cry For A Shadow' was recorded in Hamburg as early as June 1961. So what a coincidence that the variously packaged *Live In Hamburg* recording, the following year, finds The Beatles furrowing the same symmetrical root-path on their cover of the Marlene Dietrich classic, 'Falling In Love Again'. After a verse in the key of E, the bridge (at 0.34) unfolds: G♯7-C♯m-F♯9-B7-E, beneath Paul's famously indecipherable German vocals.[11]

Again in our quest for musical emphasis using III, check out the E chord in the bridge to 'No Reply'. But notice how, in this case, the ♭7th has indeed been dropped, *principally because it clashes with the natural 7th in the melody.* The target chord is now also a major triad, so the same principle still applies, as the 'secondary major' takes us – with the same expected root movement – from III to VI. Most importantly, The Beatles ensure that the E chord itself falls directly on the word 'realise' (and, later, 'lies'), emphasizing dramatically the sentiment of John's gripe.

'No Reply'

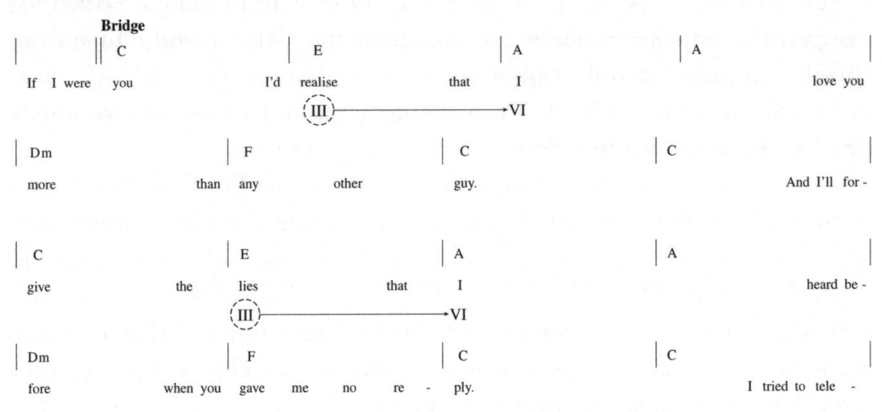

[11] Ignore for the moment the bizarre modulation between intro and verse (the latter starts in earnest at 0.11 in the key of E).

The roots of III7 in 20th Century pop of course date back at least as far as 1930, the year that 'Falling In Love Again' was written (and probably back to ragtime and blues). In terms of its more 'down home' R'n'B heritage, I-III7-VI7 was famously popularised by the piano giant, Leroy Carr, on a host of standards like 'Nobody Knows When You're Down And Out' (which Eric Clapton would later bring into the mainstream). That song features the famous opening line 'Once I lived the life of a *millionaire*', a textbook emphasis of I-III7 that reappears in a select list of intricate blues originals, including The Blues Band's 'Can't Hold On' ('A man just came to call for my *rent*'). As a piece of extreme trivia, Paul McCartney can be seen to use the same theme of financial difficulties over the same harmonic premise when opening his major-key bridge in 'You Never Give Me Your Money', on *Abbey Road*. Look out for the line 'out of college *money spent*' (C-E7).

But then McCartney had been using this harmonic idea as far back as 'World Without Love', one of his earliest songs, recorded by Peter & Gordon in 1964. The opening line 'Please lock me a-*way*' sees E move to a similarly bold G♯7, which develops on to C♯m. And for all its jazz and ballad roots, the 'I-III7-vi' lives on in the pop music of today being a favourite opening verse move of Noel Gallagher, as shown by Oasis songs like 'Stand By Me' and 'Married With Children'.

The Beatles also use I-III as an opening verse gambit, for example on 'You're Going To Lose That Girl'. With customary Beatles novelty, however, the chord *now doesn't resolve down a fifth as we would expect*. It therefore doesn't operate in quite the same way and belongs in another songwriting category: *non-functioning* secondary dominants, which we consider in part 2 of this chapter.

To sum up so far, let's take 'Your Mother Should Know' as a definitive Beatles case study for functioning secondary dominants.

A Secondary Dominant Case Study – 'Your Mother Should Know'

Here's a song where we conveniently find II7, III7 and VI7 all in one neat progression – but now with several Beatles twists which together alter these early pop clichés beyond recognition.

The verse starts on Am which, it could be argued, appears as an opening tonic minor chord; but as we soon wind up in the key of C, can equally be

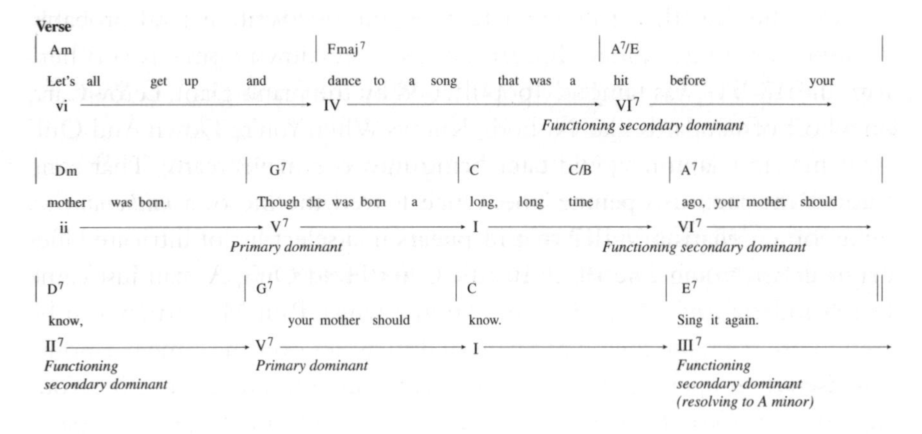

understood retrospectively as 'just' a vi chord.[12] But watch as it is converted into a secondary dominant, A7, that acts as 'V of ii' and 'V of II', resolving naturally first to the Dm (in bar 4) and then to D7 – a chord which is itself a secondary dominant II7 acting as a now-familiar 'V of V'. Finally, there's the E7, the III7 – or 'V of vi' – which acts a 'pick-up', or turnaround chord, that takes us back to the Am at the top. Listen to how the melody notes in bars 7 and 11 land directly on these 'new' major thirds (C♯ for A7; and G♯ for E7), showing just how The Beatles appreciated the melodic opportunities presented by this type of harmonic premise.

VII7 (the 'V of iii')

With those stunning McCartney examples of vii in Chapter 3, we've already seen how the rare appearance of a minor chord built on the leading tone typically leads down a fifth. And again, this same root movement can be accentuated by replacing the chord with a secondary dominant, just as we have done with ii, vi and iii. The same voice-leading and root movement applies, with the target for the manoeuvre being this time a iii or III

[12] Once again, here's a progression that falls under the heading of 'tonal ambiguity' as, technically, it could be regarded as a modulation from Am to C . But, for the purposes of this analysis of dominant chords, we regard it as in C major with the primary V7-I represented by the G7-to-C cadence, in bars 10–11. See the analysis by Tim Tucker, *Total Guitar*, Issue 5 (April 1995), p.76.

chord of some description. In this sense, the VII7 is a slick way of reaching one of The Beatles' favourite targets – the mediant, but by a more sophisticated route than McCartney's now infamous jump-of-a-third 'formula' in 'I'm Happy Just To Dance With You' and Do You Want To Know A Secret'.

Despite its stunning potential, this progression is very rare in Beatles music. But when it is paraded, the result is the ear-catching sequences of 'Sexy Sadie', 'Martha My Dear' and, using an altered 5th chord tone on the VII to generate some added dissonance, 'You Know My Name (Look Up The Number)'.

'Sexy Sadie'

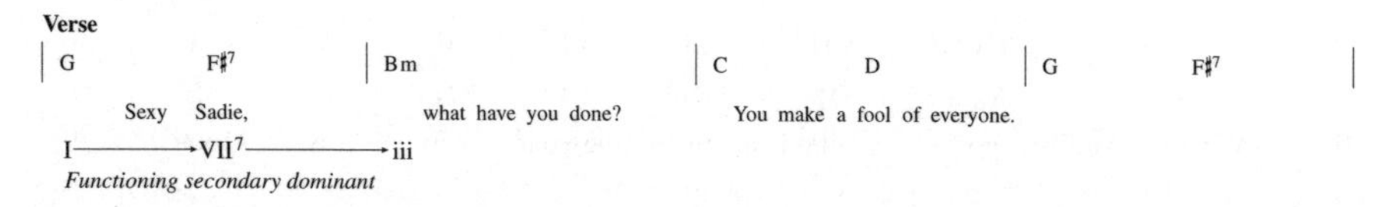

In both theory and practice VII7 is a perfect starting point for an extreme Cycle Of Fifths journey which can proceed inexorably all the way to I. The jazz standard 'Mr Sandman' is perhaps the ultimate blueprint for this, with its beautiful symmetry that runs, in the key C: C-*B*7-E7-A7-D7-G7-C.[13]

'Martha My Dear' itself features a brilliant pastiche of this run, going at least as far as the V chord before opting to 'buy time' with a repeated IV-V embellishment rather than cadencing to the root as we would have expected.

'Martha My Dear'

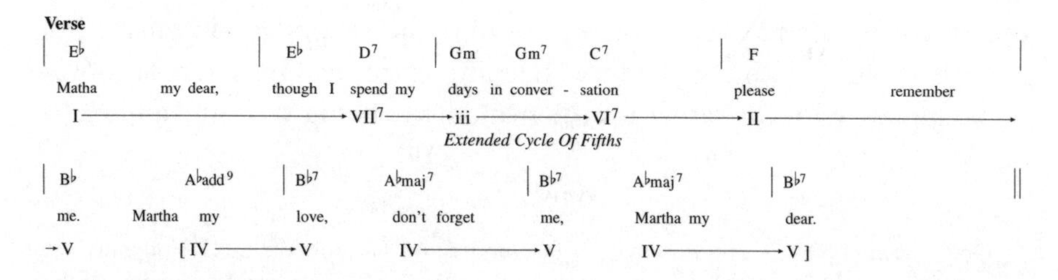

[13] The sophisticated sound of I-VII-iii can also be heard on the bridge of 'Over The Rainbow', which the Beatles covered in their early sets.

Finally, in terms of songwriting traditions we should mention what may have been the original inspirational blueprint for pop's great Cycle Of Fifths songs: McCartney's favourite, 'Moon River'. Mancini's masterpiece even tops 'Mr Sandman' in this regard by engineering the ultimate journey with even VII7 reached from *its* V. Here vi looks all set to move ii–V–I but, instead, Mancini takes us back 'upstream' to the head of the river to begin six successive descents of a fifth (guitarists will particularly enjoy the progression's effortless fretboard root symmetry). Here's a summary of that moment showing also how the secondary dominants fall on VI (after the minor 'vi', of course) and also, crucially, VII.[14]

The Flowing Fifths of 'Moon River'

vi⁷	**♯iv⁷♭⁵**	**VII⁷**	**iii**	**VI⁷**	**ii**	**V⁷**	**I**
C♯m⁷	A♯m⁷♭⁵	D♯⁷	G♯m⁷	C♯⁷	F♯m⁷	B⁷	E
'Wherever you're	go -	ing I'm	go -	ing your	way	- ay,	Moon ...'

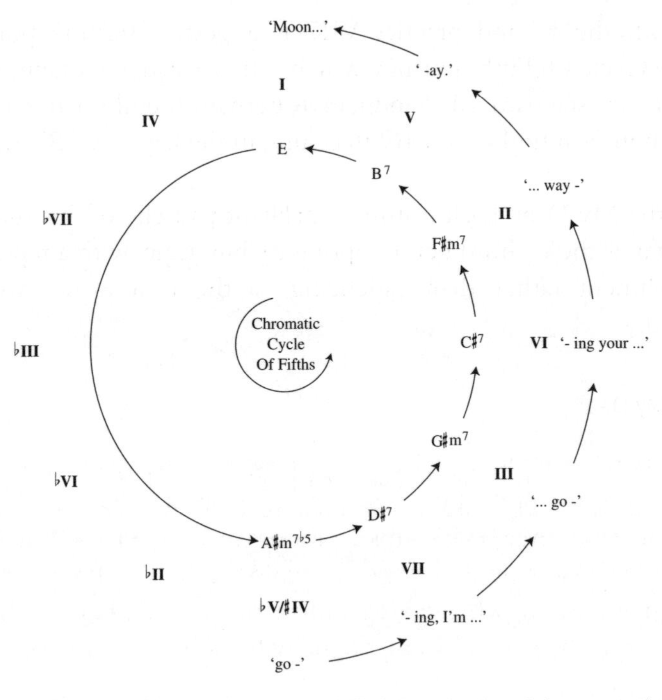

[14] The chorus of Peter Skellern's brilliant 1972 ballad, 'You're A Lady', runs similarly around the cycle, in C, first reaching the anticipation-creating F♯m7 with an opening augmented fourth (similar to 'Here There And Everywhere') before cycling all the way back to the tonic.

The use of the A♯m7♭5 to prime the VII represents a radical departure from our cosy theoretical *diatonic* framework. Suddenly we have introduced not merely notes from elsewhere in the chromatic scale, but also a root: a dissonant ♭V, mid-way between the accepted triads of F and G. While the chord would appear to be the last choice in a tender ballad of this type, it still 'works' precisely because of the power of these very descending fifths. We instinctively *know* that what is coming next will satisfactorily resolve the tension.[15] Just to make the point, we can now introduce a second, rather more elaborate, Cycle Of Fifths formula that accommodates not just the diatonic 'stops' but also all the remaining *chromatic* ones as well.

The Chromatic Cycle Of Fifths

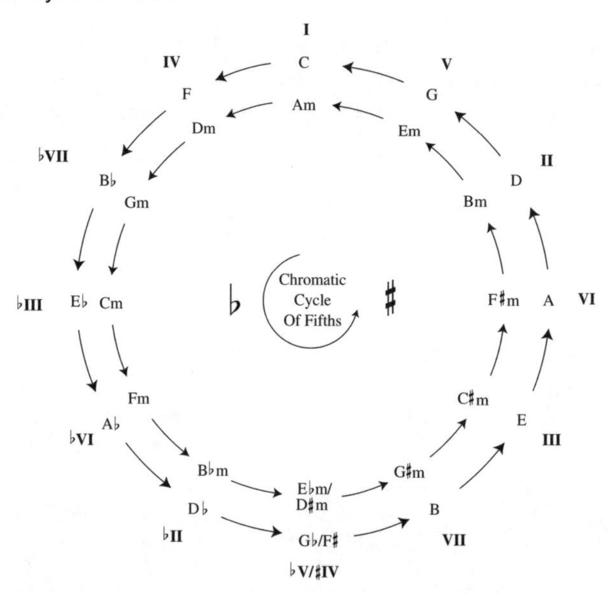

This shows us how the cycle can help take a songwriter 'from anywhere *to* anywhere' in music by means of barely more than thinly disguised sleight-of-hand. Again it's much more than a theoretical tool. The Chromatic Cycle would be expertly exploited by The Beatles themselves, as we'll demonstrate when taking a more formal look beyond the diatonic scale in later chapters. One highlight will be the seven-chord Cycle Of

[15] See Appendix 5 for details of quasi-scientific research that appears to prove that harmony descending through a Cycle Of Fifths in this way actually registers instinctively as a powerful stimulus in humans of all ages.

Fifths that's reserved for Chapter 6 as it unfolds with a few quirks distinct to the diatonic *minor* scale.

The tonic secondary dominant 'V of IV' – The I7-IV change

Secondary dominants aren't necessarily limited to the minor 'slots' in the major scale. For example, while we've seen the tonic I chord appear as a dominant 7th in a blues setting, in certain situations its function is more clearly understood as the V of the subdominant: 'V of IV'. As we saw in 'If I Fell', The Beatles enjoyed moving to the IV through various types of 'prepared' I7 or I9 chords in a variety of different songs. The bridges of 'Revolution', 'Hey Jude' and 'Oh! Darling' all move to the IV in this way; as does 'This Boy', another model case-study for exploring a range of secondary dominants.

'This Boy'

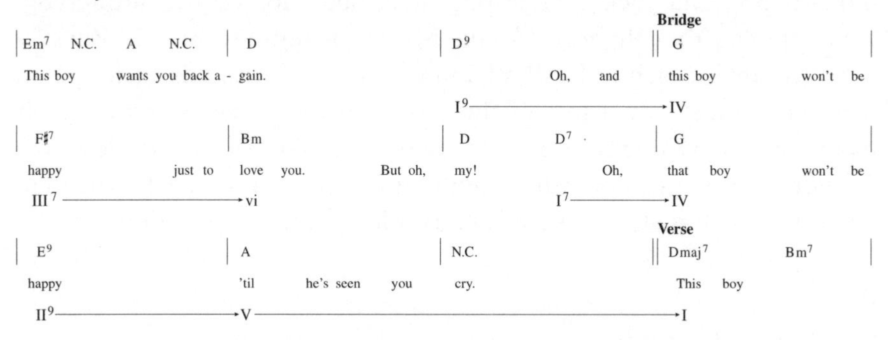

Again, it could be argued that we've successfully meandered away from the key of D, initially to the key of the IV chord, G (a feeling that is reinforced by the all-important re-hearing of the dominant of G, the D7, during the bridge). But we quickly return to the D tonic in midstream, and the overall effect reflects the singer attempting (albeit suitably unsuccessfully) to break free from his frustrations. Particularly slick is John's use of the drop from G to F♯7 and on to Bm, a 'IV-III7-vi' which we'll later find used in the switch to the minor bridge in 'I Should Have Known Better'.

While we are specifically not interpreting any of the moves in this chapter as clear-cut modulations in terms of our Roman numeral system at this stage, this section has shown us that with these non-diatonic notes we can *feel* as if we are straying from the home key in varying degrees, and indeed *to* various scale degrees. We need to keep a similarly open mind as we visit first some *non-functioning* secondary dominants, before plunging deeper into the challenging world of 'tonal ambiguity' in the next chapter.

'Part 2': Non-Functioning Secondary Dominants

In contrast to all the above examples are those secondary dominants built on these same scale degrees but which are now *not* followed by root movements down a fifth (or up a fourth). In a sense, these chords (many of which appear again as just major triads) do *appear* to function in the same way as they set up the same feeling of anticipation for the impending change. But, crucially, the move is thwarted as the song now heads down an alternative avenue. This distinction between the types may appear to be a nicety of classical music but, as an approach to the study of root movement in modern pop and rock songwriting, it is one adopted by cutting-edge contemporary rock theorists like the Musicians Institute, in California.[16]

So let's revisit each of II, III, VI and VII but now with this exciting new slant. For while only a few of the moves in the previous section really represent songwriting novelty (namely some of the III and VII ideas), this category takes us more thoroughly into the 'unexpected' harmonic territory which is at the core of The Beatles' musical explorations.

II7

The first of these is the non-functioning secondary II7 within the four-chord cycle, I-II-IV-I, a sequence that can be seen as an important trademark of several mid-period Beatles songs:

'Eight Days A Week':

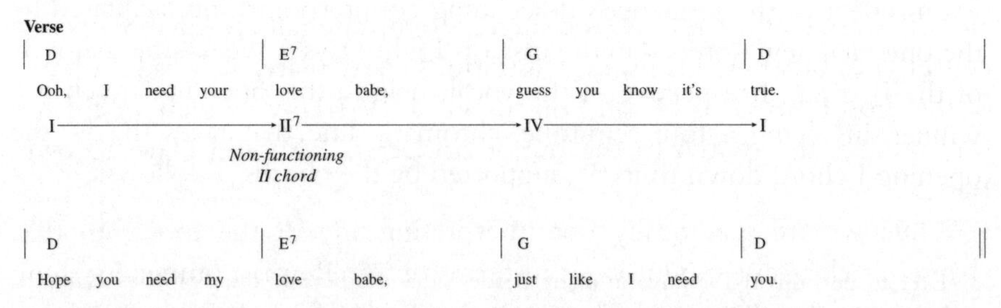

[16] Keith Wyatt and Carl Schroeder, *Harmony & Theory, Musicians Institute Essential Concepts*, pp. 108–12.

'You Won't See Me' and 'Sgt. Pepper's Lonely Hearts Club Band' can be seen to repeat this identical harmonic idea whose novelty in each case is achieved both by the unexpected root movement and the internal voice-leading within the harmony.

'You Won't See Me'

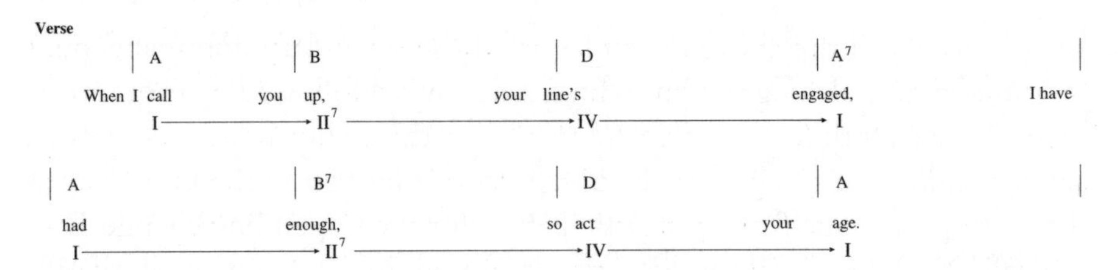

As far as root movement is concerned, the dark, sometimes 'rocky', minor third interval (here between II and IV) created a versatile, modern sound in the mid-sixties. The young Beatles surely heard the II-IV shift when covering 'The Darktown Strutters' Ball', which charted in 1960 for Joe Brown And The Bruvvers. In the key of A, compare the novelty of B7-D (at 0.23), with the more predictable B7-E7 (0.14) in that same song.

Meanwhile, the I-II-IV-I sequence has since become a fixture in pop music down the years, appearing in songs as diverse as The Faces' 'Stay With Me' (key of A), The Beautiful South's 'Closer Than Most' (A♭), Oasis' 'All Around The World' (B) – and, as Noel himself points out, Hear'Say's 'Pure And Simple' (D). Good Charlotte's 'Lifestyles Of The Rich And Famous' (D♭) was still keeping the sequence in the charts in early 2003.

Voice-Leading in I-II-IV-I

Aside from the root movement, Walter Everett highlights the more subconscious effect of the sequence's descending counterpoint line facilitated by the one vital new note: G♯ in the case of 'Eight Days A Week' (the major 3rd of the II triad). Irrespective of the vocal melody, this opening stretch is a winner, involving a four-semitone, chromatic line that takes the 5th the opening I chord down to its 3rd; supported by the chords, as follows:[17]

[17] Everett spots this II-IV move in many Beatles situations beyond these obvious examples, and describes how the voice-leading is manifested variously through both vocals and instrumentation. See both volumes of *The Beatles As Musicians*.

Chord formula	I	II 7	IV	I
Key of D	D	E7	G	D
Chromatic line	**A**	**G♯**	**G**	**F♯**
Chord tone	5th	3rd	Root	3rd
Relative to D major	5th	♭5th	4th	3rd

This is very slick use of II in songwriting, and conceptually far removed from its use in a standard II-V, that we saw earlier. For now the 3rd of the II, as Tillekens also describes, makes for 'an unorthodox but excellent leading tone' – one that now *descends* to the root of the IV.[18]

Meanwhile, in a brilliant twist, The Beatles exploited a delicate variation whereby the first chord in the sequence is replaced by its relative minor in a straightforward 'vi-for-I' substitution, to create 'vi-II-IV-I'. At a stroke, we can now explain the defining cadential progressions in some of the most famous Beatles songs of all time, including 'Yesterday' and 'She's Leaving Home'.

'She's Leaving Home'

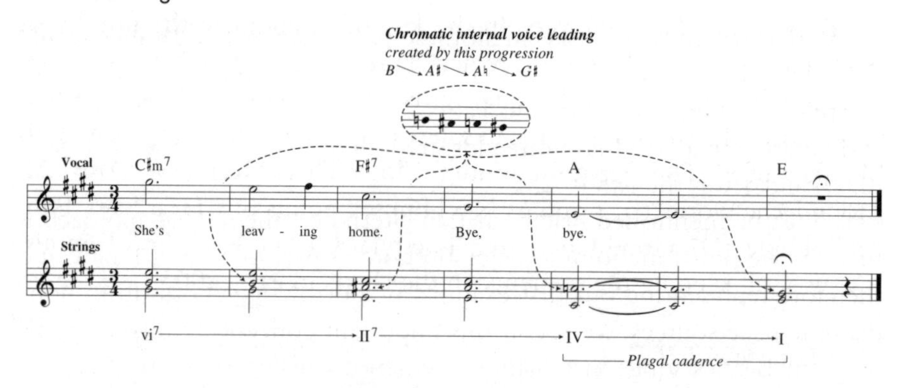

Once again the progressions may seem to appear in unrelated contexts, but playing them will soon confirm to the ear that the effect is of a Cycle Of Fifths movement that is deceptively thwarted by a Plagal cadence which lends a rock or gospel flavour depending on the context. Meanwhile, the four semitone voice-leading is retained exactly as before, though now it is the ♭7th of the vi7 – *the same note as the 5th of I* – that provides the opening tone. Of course, the overall effect is more mellow because of the substitution.

[18] Ger Tillekens, 'Words And Chords: The Semantic Shifts Of The Beatles Chords' (para 4.4); www.icce.rug.nl/~soundscapes.

'Yesterday'

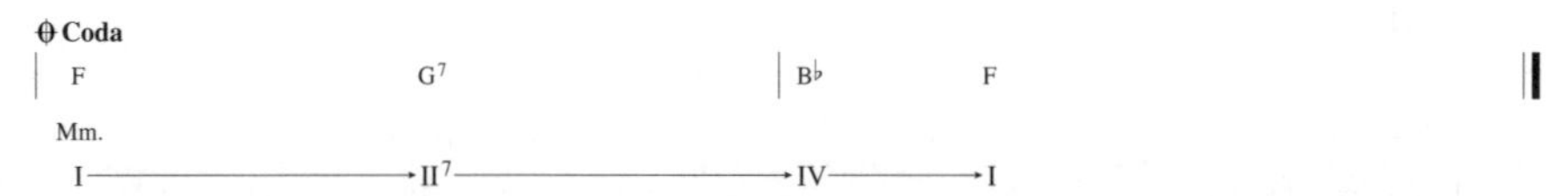

'Yesterday' actually features *both* of these progressions as the final line of the song: 'I believe in yesterday' follows the vi-II7-IV-I. Meanwhile, even songs as seemingly far removed as 'She Loves You' and 'In My Life' can be seen to incorporate the essence of this concept: a II that shuns the expected V tension in favour of the more subtle subdominant.

'In My Life'

Bridge

| F♯m | D | G | A |
All these places had their moments, with lovers and friends I still can recall. Some are

| F♯m | B | Dm7 | A ||
dead and some are living, in my life I've loved them all.
vi → II → iv7 → I

As an alternative to the IV in all these progressions, The Beatles would also take a II chord *directly* back to the root for a disarming resolution after creating a highlight. Just listen to Paul's 'I'll Follow The Sun' where such a II (operating in a I-II-I fashion) adds strength to lines like 'to see I've *gone*' (0.09) and 'I was the *one*' (0.23).

It must be mentioned briefly that an alternative theoretical approach is to view the non-functioning major II chord as part of a 'modal' ploy, and therefore representing our first example of 'borrowing' chords from non-diatonic scale sources. We revisit this important concept of 'mixed mode' usage in Beatles songs in Chapter 8, when discussing other II chords in exotic contexts such as 'I Am The Walrus'.

III7

It was testimony to The Beatles' early songwriting brilliance that one of their oldest known compositions, 'Like Dreamers Do', features a novel thwarting of the expected Cycle Of Fifths movement by means of non-functioning secondary dominant III7.

Notice how a 'I-vi' move here would have copied the verse in a thinly disguised take on the Doo Wop cycle. But the III7 at the start of the bridge is a successful attempt to avoid the cliché – not to mention bringing

'Like Dreamers Do'

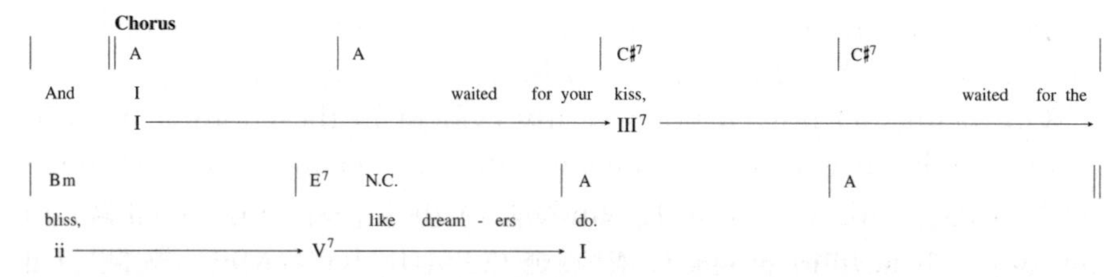

poignancy to the word 'bliss' – by sliding down a second interval to prompt a ii-V-I cadence.

But undoubtedly the most inspired use of this type of III7 in The Beatles' songbook (maybe in the history of pop) occurs in 'I Want To Hold Your Hand'. Here is a pivotal moment in Beatlemania which, for various reasons, has been the subject of almost mythical confusion.

Flashback first to our introduction where we saw John Lennon's own recollections of writing the song 'eyeball to eyeball' with Paul at the piano in the basement of the Asher family residence, sometime in 1963:

> 'I remember when we got the chord that made the song … we had "Oh you-u-u … got that something …" And Paul hits this chord and I turn to him and say, "That's *it*!" I say, "Do that again!"'[19]

But what chord was Lennon actually referring to?! If it's such an obvious songwriting landmark it should hardly be open to debate, but it certainly has been down the years. Technically, the very next chord after this lyric is an Em (the third chord in the sequence after G and D7) which, sure enough, various music experts have nominated as the chord in question.[20] This V-vi change is another early example of subtle Beatles substitution, with Harrison's ladder-like lead guitar lick taking the girl by the hand (and the listener by the ear) to the mellow territory of the relative minor to begin his secret revelation.

But others argue that, even more striking, is the following chord built on the mediant, which supports a boldly sustained natural 7th (F♯ in the key of G) to which the melody has plunged, on the last syllable of 'under*stand*' (at 0.13).[21]

[19] *The Playboy Interviews*, pp. 124–5.

[20] Including Wolf Marshall, *Guitar One*, Volume 6, 1996, p. 16; and Walter Everett, who makes the subtle connection between the Em chord and Lennon's opening E pitches [on 'Oh yeah']; *The Beatles As Musicians: The Quarry Men Through Rubber Soul*, p. 201.

[21] The Beatles had previously used the V-vi move to great effect for the striking cadential shifts of 'P.S. I Love You' (A-Bm at 0.20), and 'Not A Second Time' (the subject of Chapter 5).

Ironically, there is also much debate among Beatles experts as to whether the chord is a conventional iii (namely a diatonic Bm); a B *major* or B7; or a B5 power chord with no major- or minor-defining third.[22]

With neither D nor D♯ notes clearly evident in the chord, it demonstrates how listeners can have different subjective feelings as to how notes are 'implied' within a sonority, guiding them to a particular *quality* of chord. As far as musical appreciation is concerned, one could argue that the cosy semantic setting created by Lennon's low, poignant F♯ melody note (that is not yet driving us euphorically up to the tonic of G), helps us to *feel* a mellow Bm, of the type mentioned in Chapter 3.

On the other hand, others are justifiably swayed by the D♯ clearly contained in George's earlier chromatic lick, and also in his twangy lick on the repeat of verse 1 (at 1.17). They could argue equally that, quite apart from footage of Lennon fingering an open B7 shape (suggesting that he, at

'I Want To Hold Your Hand'

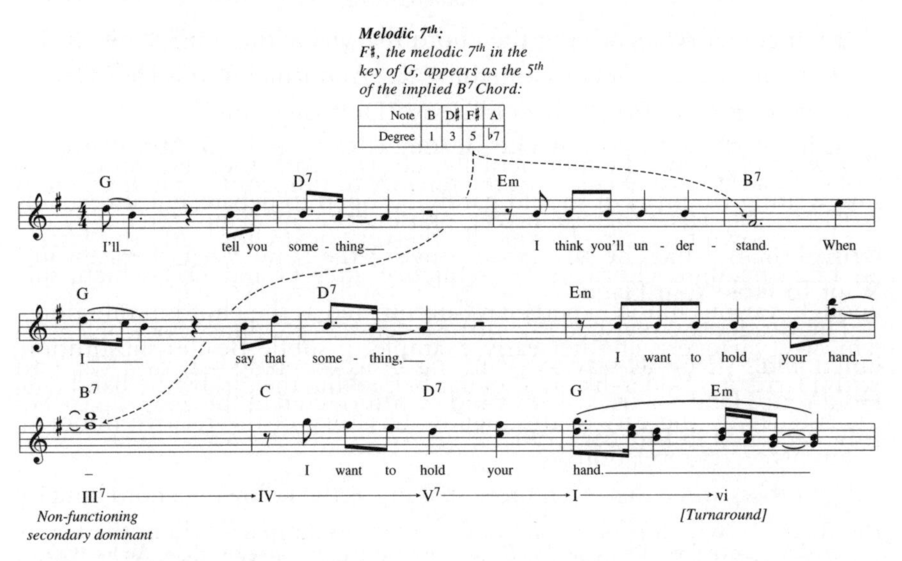

[22] The experts are split down the middle. Those that hear a Bm include MacDonald, *Revolution In The Head*, p. 88; Tillekens, 'Words And Chords', p. 2; and Everett who suggests 'The ear supplies the diatonic D [natural] that is not actually played', p. 393. *The Beatles As Musicians: The Quarry Men Through Rubber Soul*, p.393. In the secondary dominant corner are Rooksby, *The Beatles Complete Chord Songbook*, p. 150; O'Grady, 'a major mediant', *A Musical Evolution*, p.42; Pollack, B major as 'V-of-vi', 'Notes on…Series' no. 43, 1991, www.recmusicbeatles.com; and Tim Riley who writes: 'The chord is major and corresponds to the implied dominant harmony in the verse on under*stand*.'; *Tell Me Why*, p.87.

least, does not conceive the chord as minor), the rocky flavour of the partial chord voicing heard on the record, does not imply it either.[23]

With these various caveats in mind, we have notated the extract with a B7, not least because, four bars later, the same controversial major third would help us explain the power with which the mediant now seems to cue the chorus.

Notice how the *melodic* tension in the soaring vocals is enhanced *harmonically* ahead of the move to an emphatic C chord (at 0.22), cueing the 'IV-V-I-vi' cycle of the chorus that we are now aching to hear. While a diatonic iii-IV would have done the trick through the semitone voice-leading of the root alone, we surely feel that propulsion all the more strongly with the implied D♯ in the B7 chord also gliding up a half-step.

How the B7 chord propels 'I Want To Hold Your Hand'

Lyrical Reference	Leads the song into	Chord change		Semitone voice leading
		Formula	Key of G	
'Hand ... I want to hold'	chorus (at 0.22)	III^7 - IV	B^7 - C	D♯ up to E
				F♯ up to G

Again, high novelty from The Beatles as early as 1963. And it was no wonder that William Mann referred directly to this sequence in his famous article in *The Times* that same year, praising the 'mediant switches', as he termed them, which he saw accompanying 'the famous octave ascent in I Want To Hold Your Hand'.[24]

The Beatles also revisited the intrinsic tension-building device of a non-functioning III on its way to IV in the heart-stopping *coda* of 'I Want To Hold Your Hand' – a trick that would be resurrected in the wrap-up to 'Yes It Is', recorded in February 1965.

[23] See the 'lip-sync' rendition on *The Beatles Anthology*, video 2. Meanwhile, André Barreau ('George') of The Bootleg Beatles agrees that a 2nd position, B7[no 3rd] (B-F♯-A) is the best way to recreate the sound on the record. In conversation with the author, March 2001.

[24] William Mann, 'What Songs The Beatles Sang', *The Times*, 27th December 1963. For a detailed background to this important article in Beatles folklore, see Chapter 5. By 'octave ascent', Mann probably meant that the F♯ note is an octave higher on the word 'hand' than at the equivalent point four bars earlier (on 'under-*stand*'). Not to be confused with the climaxing-inducing B-F♯ interval (on the words 'your *hand*') which is actually an ascent of a perfect fifth.

'Yes It Is'

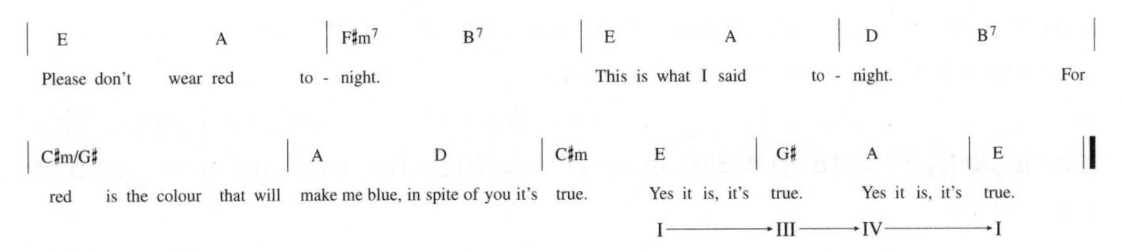

Here a major III appears for the first time in the song especially to create a final highlight before the final Plagal drop to I. And as we now know (courtesy of *Live At The BBC*) The Beatles received an early masterclass in III-IV from the intricate pre-chorus/bridge of 'Soldier Of Love', the fine Cason-Moon composition that we visited earlier.

'Soldier Of Love'

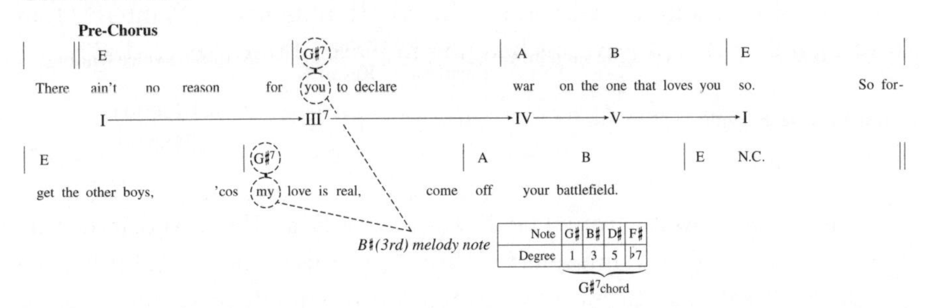

The neat E-G♯7-A-B cycle (at 0.35-0.50) may have been a model for such a rare songwriting treat for the time, though The Beatles' version is more elaborate as the sequence spans verse and chorus making for a powerful link between the sections. Meanwhile, the more standard I-III7-IV-V7 sequence of 'Soldier Of Love' has proved a winner in pop from Bobby Vee's 'The Night Has A Thousand Eyes' ('They say that you're a runaround lover' – possibly another inspiration for The Beatles), right through to Oasis's 'Digsy's Dinner' ('What a life it would be if you would come to mine for tea') and 'Stay Young' ('Hey, stay young and invincible').[25]

Back with Beatles originals, we can see how a variation of this sequence

[25] McCartney also enjoyed this type of progression on the Ricky Nelson hit, 'Lonesome Town', which was also one of Linda's favourites as Paul explained when performing it at the Royal Albert Hall concert in her memory. Hear it covered on the 1999 *Run Devil Run* album, with the sequence E-G♯7-A-B (the Ricky Nelson original is in the key of B: B-D♯7-E-F♯).

in 'You're Going To Lose That Girl' merely involves a 'ii-for-IV' substitution, keeping intact the voice-leading of the 3rd of III into a strong chord tone (this time the 5th of the ii minor).

'You're Going To Lose That Girl'

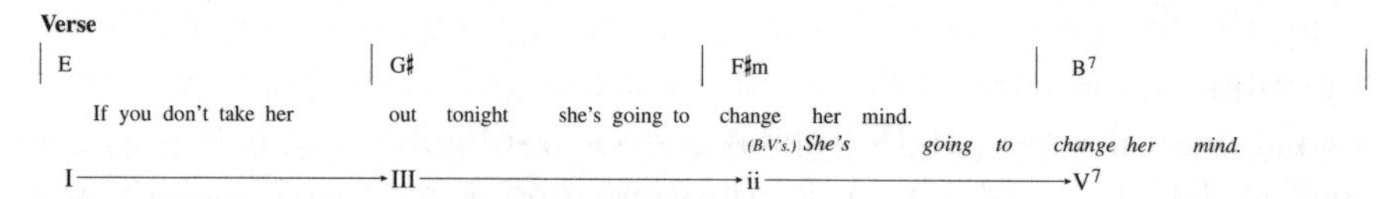

Not only could The Beatles use a non-functioning III to charge the proceedings, so they could also use it to deflate them subtly. Take the bridge of 'That Means A Lot' – in the first strain, a *functioning* III takes us predictably to the relative minor in the key of E. But the end of the bridge delivers a slow-motion variation on the 'vi-III' plunge of 'I Want To Hold Your Hand', as the G♯ leaves us hanging in place of the 'expected' B7.

'That Means A Lot'

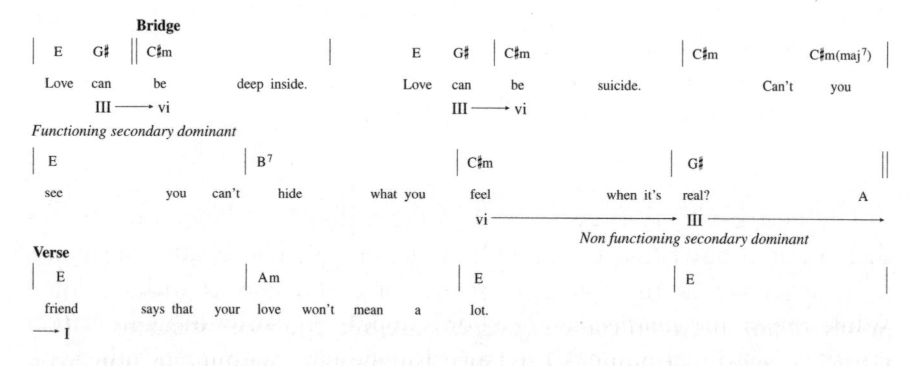

A closer look at the combination of melody and harmony shows us that we have another poignant Beatles blend of consonance and dissonance. The melody features a G♯ note that is happily waiting to 'become' the 3rd of the E chord, while the prominent 3rd of the G♯ *chord* resolves the tension by falling a semitone onto the 5th of E. An arguably lazy – but nevertheless highly effective – way of engineering a re-transition from bridge back to verse.[26]

[26] REM's Peter Buck rates this composition among his Top Beatles songs and regards it as 'the one revelation on *Anthology*', *UNCUT*, July 2001, p. 38. At the other extreme, MacDonald says of the bridge: 'the structure sounds wrong and at worst, seems completely arbitrary'.

Finally the Harrisong, 'Piggies', emerges as a bit of a case study for the non-functioning III chord. In the bridge it appears first as a III-IV-I and then in a not dissimilar context to the same legendary III-IV-V of 'I Want To Hold Your Hand'. Though now providing a 'whacking' good run-up to an Imperfect cadence over the same lyric. 'Piggies' also demonstrates how, really, the 'non-functioning' term is a bit of misnomer. For all chords 'function' in one sense of the word – just to a greater or lesser extent in a formal musical sense. 'III-IV' merely powers a song in a different way to a cyclical 'III-vi' – and it's hardly disorientating in comparison with the other III7 of 'Piggies'. For this maverick C7 enjoys its first appearance in what is a left-field 'bolt from the blue' (at 0.46), instantly revealing a new 'suburb' in George's commuter land by moving neither to Fm nor C♯ but, this time, awkwardly down a tone to B♭ minor.

'Piggies'

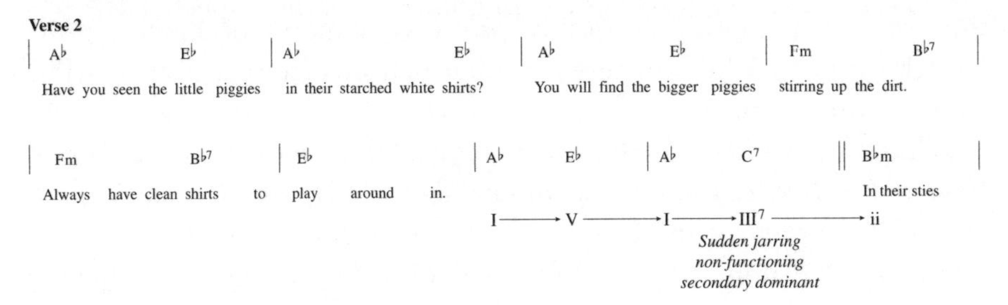

VI7

While the vi and *functioning* VI7 chords appear regularly throughout pop music, a *non*-functioning VI is surprisingly rare within an otherwise diatonic tonal pop sequence. This is essentially because the one 'rogue' note in the chord (the major 3rd) can also be interpreted as *♭2 in relation to the parent key.* For example, in the key of C, an A7 chord introduces the C♯ (or D♭) note – a highly dissonant tone if heard outside of a 'functioning' context where it would be *resolved upwards* to the root of either ii minor or II7.

But listen to the dramatic appearance of the chord in John Lennon's 'Revolution' which (initially at least) features paradoxically unthreatening musical ideas in the key of A, until that striking moment at the end of each verse (first at 0.41) where the song refuses to settle on the tonic.

'Revolution'

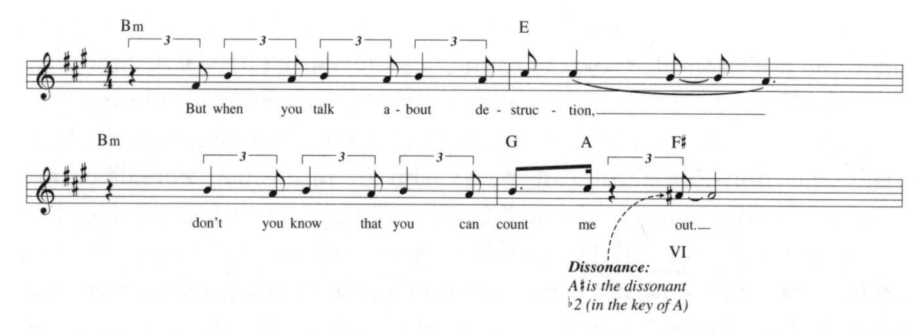

Instead of maintaining A major, Lennon outrageously delivers an F♯, a chord whose major 3rd, A♯, clashes with the A natural we seemed to be guaranteed. Even more spectacularly, that same 'outside' A♯ is the chosen melody note for the very word 'out' in the line 'count me out', making the music intuitively mirror Lennon's independence as a dissenting free thinker[27]. Even in this ostensibly primitive context of brazen, post-Chuck Berry rock 'n' roll, here's another deft nuance that distances The Beatles from the pack.

Lennon had earlier gone for a very similar effect in the verse of 'Doctor Robert' on *Revolver*. Just listen as another A♯ melody note over an F♯ chord effectively introduces us to the medicine man himself at (first at 0.17) upsetting the diatonic security of the key of A we seemed to be enjoying without question.[28]

These two songs alone give a brief flavour of not so much 'non-functioning' as 'truly dysfunctional' VI chords. We'll be seeing a similarly 'revelatory VI' in the special case study of 'Day Tripper' below. And while VI appears to be a favourite ploy of John Lennon (there's another in 'Strawberry Fields Forever'), it's George Harrison who we'll suggest takes the prize for left-field use of the harmony in the suitably maverick strains of 'Only A Northern Song', when we analyse that song in Chapter 12.

[27] While the A♯ eventually resolves to the B in the following E7 chord, it operates in a very different context to a cyclical VI7 that returns home smoothly via II7.

[28] But contrast this with the second hearing of the F♯ when it reappears – now as a *functioning* VI7 – taking us more satisfactorily to B (at 0.29). And also to the *key* of B major thereby succeeding in relieving the clash of notes. Here is our first example of a formal 'V-I modulation' a full discussion of which is reserved for Chapter 10.

'Doctor Robert'

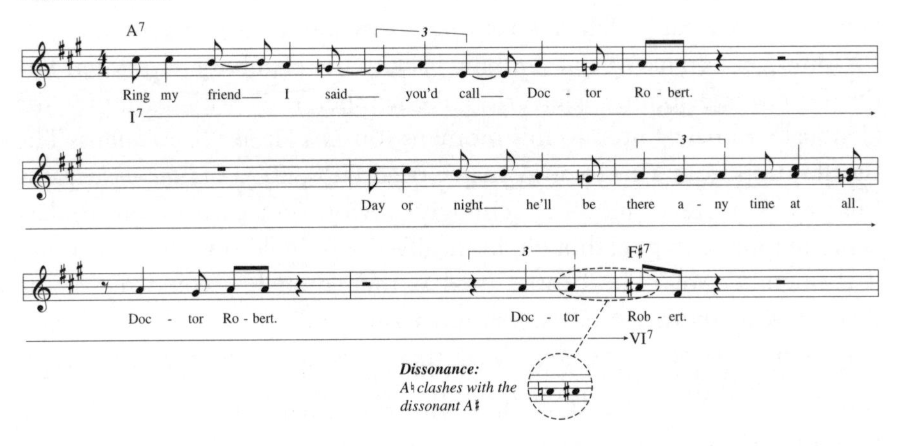

VII7

Even rarer than functioning secondary dominants built on the leading note are the non-functioning ones. And yet Lennon makes it sound so simple as he conjures a Four-Chord cliché with a difference in 'I'm So Tired'. Here, preceding his favourite Doo Wop variation, is a rather more novel one which sees the tonic drop down to precisely this 'VII major' before completing the sequence conventionally through IV and V.

'I'm So Tired' (verse):

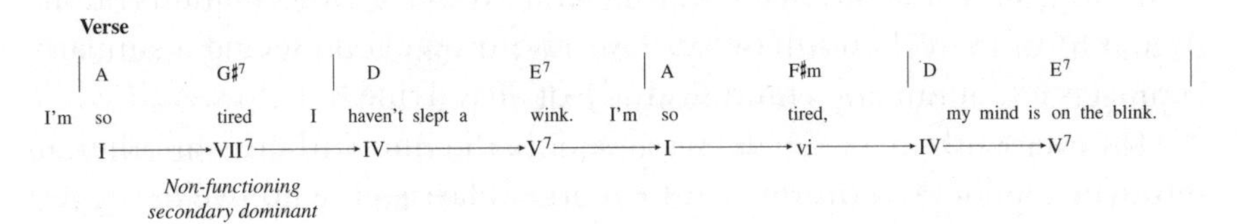

The G♯7 could be seen as a straight (if exotic) swap for the expected F♯m by means of a 'common tone substitution' *as both chords contain the F♯ note.* And check out, too, the voice-leading for two neat, semitone resolutions into the D chord. But the melody is clearly the giveaway here, if we put ourselves in the songwriter's shoes. For Lennon was no doubt looking for a chord that would provide support for the G♯ *note* (the natural 7th) after its drop from A. He could have done this by just moving from A to, say, A major 7th – just as George Harrison would do when using the same pitches in 'Something'. But perhaps the major triad on VII provided Lennon with what he felt was a stronger, less 'lounge ballad' sound.

Could Lennon have been thinking back to the Hamburg days when The Beatles covered Johnny Mercer's 'I Remember You', which features the identical rationale. Listen to this moment (on *Live At The Star Club*) as The Beatles drop from a B♭ to an A major triad (at 0.22) – *and the melody, too, lands on A*. Here is another seemingly obvious but surprisingly under-exploited move in pop, though, ironically, Frank Ifield – whose version of 'I Remember You' The Beatles used as their model – would repeat the same trick in another No. 1 smash hit, 'Confessin''.[29]

Rather more elaborate is the VII7 that leads up a half-step to the root. Take a look at the bold introduction to 'P.S. I Love You':

'P.S. I Love You'

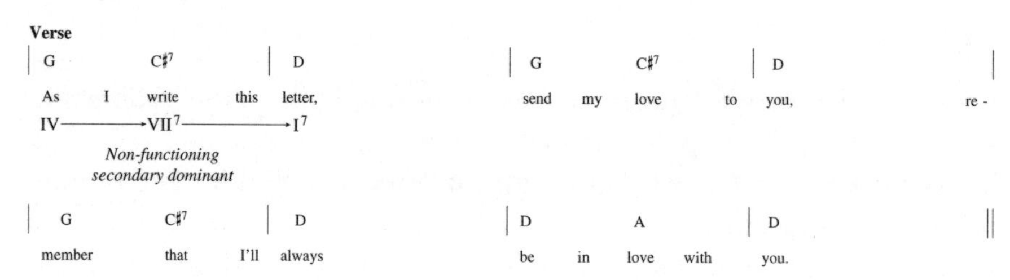

Why is this so unexpected? After all, we know that the root of the leading tone will find resolution on the tonic. And, of course there is, by definition, all that additional semitone voice-leading to be enjoyed by the 3rd and 5th of the VII chord. In any case, isn't it standard musical practice to approach just about any chord from a half-step below?

However, with most half-step approaches the duration that the extreme dissonance prevails is fleeting, and the resolution highly anticipated. Take, for example the ultra-swift 'I-VII-I' cliché that ends 'Octopus's Garden' (C-B-C) after the closing guitar lick. This is very different to 'P.S. I Love You', where McCartney bravely prolongs the chord (over the words 'write this . . .') long enough for a highly disorientating effect, with stability only restored on the tonic over the word 'letter'. Essentially, this is an unexpected resolution because prior to the eventual sounding of the D chord, the ear would have heard a resolution to (believe it or not) an F♯ major, as

[29] 'Confessin'' was No. 1 in June 1963, staying in the charts for 16 weeks. As with 'I Remember You', the opening gambit is A-G♯.

this is the expected I chord a fifth below. Play the sequence, dwell on the C♯7 and confirm it for yourself.

A secondary dominant case study – 'Day Tripper'

To summarise many of the principles we've been covering, let's take a look at 'Day Tripper' in which The Beatles experimented with a full range of dominant chords of all descriptions. In particular we can now differentiate between functioning and non-functioning secondary dominants – neither of which are to be confused with the 'primary dominant' and the blues dominant 7ths on I and IV.

'Day Tripper'

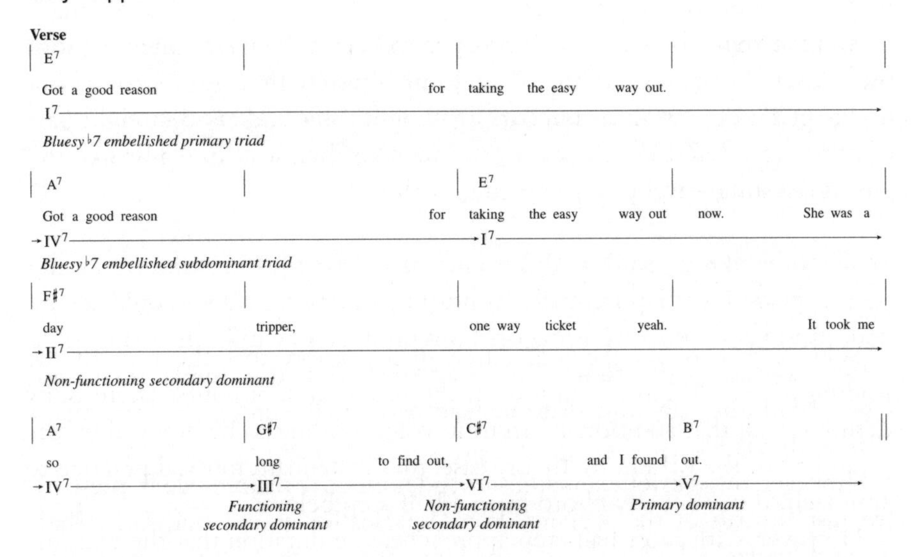

The opening two chords are easily identifiable within the blues context as major triads embellished with flattened sevenths – just like any other blues-based song. However, just when a standard 12-bar blues looks on the cards, the surprises pile up. F♯7 is the first non-functioning secondary dominant, as it doesn't move II7-V7 as we'd expect but ascends up that rocky minor third interval to IV in the style of 'Eight Days A Week' and 'You Won't See Me'.

Then, in a reverse of 'I Want To Hold Your Hand', IV take us *back* to III7, with the latter now a *functioning* 'sec dom' as it homes in dramatically on C♯7(at 0.44). While the root movement is familiar, The Beatles achieve extreme emphasis as this is not 'vi' but a *major* VI chord, with that striking E♯ note making the singer's act of 'finding out' the deception under discussion a musical revelation. Just as with 'Revolution', in fact, as we jumped to VI7 to count Lennon 'out'. In the case of 'Day Tripper', that E♯ (a ♭2 in relation to the home key of E) means that the listener – just like the subject of the song – is certainly a long way from 'first base'.[30]

Similarly, from here the Cycle Of Fifths is *not* maintained as VI7 doesn't function in the expected way, reflecting Lennon's change of tack with regard to the relationship. Instead, the chord moves directly 'down-a-whole-step' to the dominant, creating a type of Imperfect cadence. Here VI7 represents an unusual preparation of the V in comparison to the II7 or ii that we've encountered so far.

All in all, what better musical premise to depict the lyrical theme. From the outset the listener thinks (like John himself) that he's onto 'a sure thing', given how we hear ten bars of straight tonic and another eight bars of just bluesy I and IV. Only for the music to then lead us – just like the girl in the song – right up the garden path.

While some of the chords in this chapter may have looked exotic and some have appeared with potentially confusing functions, they should all be understood as dominants or majors built on degrees within the major scale – they appear on the tones 2, 3, 6 and 7 within the simple 'do-re-mi' system, with the only non-diatonic feature being the presence of the major 3rd in each triad.

However, these brief excursions outside our cosy major scale framework are just the tip of the iceberg. For The Beatles would transform their musical horizons by bringing into their songs a whole variety of chords built *on scale degrees not associated with the major scale we have so far dwelt on exclusively*. Soon we will be encountering chords with numerals such as '♭III', '♭VI' and '♭VII' that reflect the tones 'in between' the familiar scale degrees.

[30] In praising the harmonic craftsmanship of this wandering bridge, Everett refers to the C♯ as being 'tonicized' (*The Beatles As Musicians: The Quarry Men Through Rubber Soul*, p. 117), in effect a temporary tonic, a concept which we will introduce further over the next two chapters and especially in Chapter 10.

It was with precisely such chords that The Beatles moved beyond the realms of pop and R'n'B and pioneered the territory of rock music. This new harmony (which fills much of the remainder of the book) will soon be understood in terms of 'borrowing from the parallel minor', the subject of Chapter 7. And the origins of this phrase will become clear as, in Chapter 6, we introduce a range of Beatles progressions composed and conceived in the 'natural minor' tonality itself.

To introduce the sound and flavour of minor – and indeed to question what we mean by the whole concept of 'tonality' itself – we continue first with an interlude exploring what is surely the single most famous piece of musical trivia in the entire Beatles phenomenon. And certainly the most elusive.

The legend of the Aeolian cadence.

FIVE

'Exotic birds' . . . and the Great Aeolian Cadence Mystery

Of all the defining landmarks in the career of The Beatles, perhaps the most unlikely was a rambling article that appeared in *The Times* on Friday 27th December 1963. Although intended as an indulgent take on the brave new form of pop music then sweeping Europe (if not, quite yet, the globe), it would eventually be blamed by John Lennon for having 'started the whole intellectual bit about The Beatles'.[1] Unattributed at the time, the culprit soon emerged as the newspaper's classical critic, William Mann, who became the first 'establishment' figure to suggest (daringly) that there might actually be some musical justification for the Fab Four phenomenon.

Mann immediately had his peers – not to mention The Beatles themselves – aghast with both his glowing endorsement of their talents and, more specifically, his grandiose observations on their technical songwriting manoeuvres. In stark contrast to most of the media outpourings of the day, which dissected the cultural significance of Beatlemania, Mann controversially proclaimed John Lennon and Paul McCartney as 'the outstanding English composers of 1963'. He then proceeded to pierce through the veil of hysteria with the following extract, now indelibly etched in the annals of Beatles folklore:

> '. . . the slow sad song about "This Boy", which figures prominently in Beatles programmes, is expressively unusual for its lugubrious music, but harmonically it is one of their most intriguing with its chains of pandiatonic clusters and the sentiment acceptable because it is voiced

[1] *The Playboy Interviews With John Lennon & Yoko Ono, conducted by Barry Sheff, ed. G. Barry Golson*, p. 78.

> cleanly and crisply. But harmonic interest is typical of their quicker songs too, and one gets the impression that they think simultaneously of harmony and melody, so firmly are the major tonic sevenths and ninths built into their tunes, and the flat-submediant key-switches, so natural is the Aeolian cadence at the end of "Not A Second Time" (the chord progression which ends Mahler's "Song Of The Earth") . . .'[2]

And so it continued, with references to the mysterious 'mediant' switches in 'I Want To Hold Your Hand', the 'melismas' of 'She Loves You' and even the 'Magyar metre' of 'Baby It's You'.

Just as a later piece in *The Times*, the famous *Butterfly On A Wheel* leader (in the wake of the notorious Rolling Stones drug bust of 1967), would prompt a quantum shift in social attitudes, so Mann's muse would forever change the landscape of pop music. The critical perception of The Beatles' ostensibly 'simple' pop songs changed almost overnight, with Lennon even suggesting that it was directly as a result of the article 'that the middle classes started listening to it [Beatles music] – because somebody put a tag on it'[3].

Mann's 'tags' have duly been immortalised down the decades, and now enjoy *de rigueur* inclusions in all corners of Beatles culture. No need to dig into *The Times'* archives in the vaults of Wapping to relive the exact words – at the time of writing the extract appears, verbatim (and for no apparent reason) on the homepage of TheBeatlesSite.com, one of the many dedicated Beatles destinations on the World Wide Web. Mann in cyberspace? You couldn't make it up.

But quite apart from the formal validation it gave The Beatles (as if any were needed),[4] the extract was guaranteed immortality by the subsequent fall-out from the mysterious reference to the 'Aeolian cadence' and its supposed link with Gustav Mahler. It was a line that would amuse and baffle, in equal proportions, John Lennon himself. 'To this day I don't have *any* idea what they are. They sound like exotic birds', was his legendary reaction, in 1980, when asked specifically about his use of Aeolian cadences on *With The Beatles*, some 17 years previously.

And in a case of the blind leading the blind, even Lennon and his interviewers would confuse which Beatles songs contained the various

[2] 'What Songs The Beatles Sang', *The Times*, 27th December 1963.

[3] *The Playboy Interviews*, p. 78.

[4] 'It worked and we were flattered', said John Lennon, *The Beatles Anthology*, p. 96.

concepts Mann identified so colourfully. 'That was the one where the guy in the *London Times* wrote about the Aeolian cadences of the chords,' answered Lennon when asked about his memories of 'It Won't Be Long' (rather than 'Not A Second Time') which paradoxically contained one of the other villains of the *Times* piece![5] On another occasion Lennon commented, 'It was just chords like any other chords. That was the first time anyone had ever written anything about us like that', without elaborating on just what those chords might have been.[6]

Surely, for all his notorious disdain of music theory, John Lennon would see the irony. Today's average Beatles fan can spot the 82 references to Beatles trivia in the 'Free As A Bird' video, and yet ignores the most tantalising of all Beatles conundrums. Dozens of books among the 400-plus (and growing) list of Beatles titles pay tribute to *The Times* passage yet few define the musical techniques at work or attempt to explain why they 'work' – much less question the high-falutin' connections made.

Mann even gets his very own entry in *The Beatles Encyclopedia*, which quotes the same lines from what it acknowledges 'was a prestigious feature which did much to enhance The Beatles' reputation as serious musicians'.[7]

And as late as 1995, Barry Miles, in his definitive collaboration with Paul McCartney, confirms that 'Aeolian cadences became part of Beatles legend' yet, incredibly, passes up the opportunity to finally put us out of our misery.[8]

Equally surprising is the stream of musically literate critics who have steadfastly refused to be drawn on this one, despite their collective *penchant* for tackling other intricate Beatles niceties with admirable forensics. Take Tim Riley in his affectionate tour of The Beatles' catalogue in 1988. '[Mann] dubs the cadences at the end of "Not A Second Time" "aeolian", a quote that is still batted about with derision, even though what he says is true'. With no further elaboration, we just have to take his word for it.[9]

[5] *The Playboy Interviews,* p. 152.

[6] *The Beatles In Their Own Words*, compiled by Barry Miles via *Beatlesongs*, William J. Dowlding, p. 57.

[7] Bill Harry, *The Beatles Encyclopedia*, pp. 713–4. References to Mann and his article have now become *de rigueur* for Beatles critics. See, for example, Martin O'Gorman's review of *The Beatles: Popular Music And Society* by Ian Inglis (ed.); *Record Collector* No. 255, November 2000, p. 159. Also, Paul Du Noyer's *With The Beatles* retrospective in '1000 Days Of Beatlemania', *MOJO* Special Limited Edition, 2002. 'Valid or not, [Mann's] comments opened a generation of well-stocked minds to the possibility of real art arising in pop music in disguise'; p. 66.

[8] Barry Miles, *Many Years From Now*, 1997, p. 163.

[9] Tim Riley, *Tell Me Why*, p. 102.

The same goes for classical critic Deryck Cooke, who wrote a learned piece on The Beatles in *The Listener*, back in 1968 – even poking fun at Mann and his 'original dovecot-fluttering *Times* article of 1963'. Yet despite being an authority on Mahler, he too left the reference untouched.[10]

A quarter of a century later, in his compelling Beatles retrospective, *Revolution In The Head*, Ian MacDonald mysteriously suggests that Mann's reference to the Aeolian cadence in 'Not A Second Time' was a result of the classical critic being 'struck by the song's self-taught unorthodoxies'. And yet the only ones volunteered are the 'irregular fourteen-bar verse joined to a ten-bar chorus' which, frustratingly, don't qualify in any harmonic sense (given the very nature of a 'cadence' and a 'chord progression' that the extract specifies so clearly).

And following the surviving Beatles' 'official' recollections for their definitive *Anthology* tome, the beast is still with us in the new millennium – though according to Paul McCartney it has metamorphosed over the years into a 'descending Aeolian cadence'.[11]

So what on earth is this sleight-of-hand that supposedly connects The Beatles with Mahler? For too long, it seems, Beatles fans have had to settle for Riley's unquestioned assertion – mirrored, incidentally, by Deryck Cooke who concluded: 'Still, Mann was accurate . . .'

But was he really? Or was he perhaps merely trying to impress *Times* readers still bloated from their 1963 Christmas lunch?

The remainder of this chapter is an attempt to crack this, the Beatle equivalent of Fermat's Last Theorem, even if to lay the ghost to rest requires a journey that may seem at times like a musical shaggy dog story. It is in fact the very gentlest of jumps into the abyss as the entire discussion centres mainly around just two chords. Nor is this just a 'trivia interlude' for the self-indulgent highbrow muso, but rather one that forms essential groundwork for much of what follows. For the concepts it raises, such as 'harmonic deception', 'tonal ambiguity', 'modulation to minor' and 'borrowing', will go on to dominate the remainder of this book.

In beginning our search let's look at the passage again:

[10] Deryck Cooke, 'The Lennon-McCartney Songs', *The Listener*, 1st February 1968.

[11] *The Beatles Anthology*, p. 96. Meanwhile, as we refer to later, Beatles expert Walter Everett helped unlock the mystery for advanced students in his 2001 tome, *The Beatles As Musicians: The Quarry Men Through Rubber Soul*, pp. 192–193 and 392.

> '. . . so natural is the Aeolian cadence at the end of "Not A Second Time" (the chord progression which ends Mahler's "Song Of The Earth") . . .'

It seems a simple enough statement but, amazingly, we will encounter difficulties with reconciling almost every word in this sentence.

Starting with the very term *Aeolian cadence* itself (not to be confused, of course, with another Beatles cultural landmark, the former Aeolian Hall in London).[12] Mann seems to have started the confusion by choosing a term that wouldn't appear in the music dictionary of even the most obsessive Beatles fan. But that's the least of it – for among most of the classical music fraternity (some of them former Mann acquaintances) consulted during research for this project, mention of the term drew a complete blank, except in respect of fond memories of *that* very article.

But then who needs the academics when we can simply dig out track 13 of *With The Beatles*, cue up 'the end of "Not A Second Time"' and check out 'the chord progression' just as it unfolds?

On our first attempt we wouldn't be any the wiser – for the end of the song consists of a two-chord coda that actually fades out. There is no 'cadence' at all, in the conventional sense of completing or resolving a sequence, as we go on to discuss later.

More to the point, the G-Em-G-Em progression that takes us out of the song is, of course, nothing other than the familiar 'I-vi-I-vi' alternation – the very same sequence that, as we discussed in Chapter 3, was already proving to be a ubiquitous pop idea (having already been paraded in at least half-a-dozen recordings by The Fab Four themselves prior to *With The Beatles*). It is therefore surely the least likely musical device for a critic to jump on with such enthusiasm.

The only distinguishing mark here is that a close listen reveals that George Martin's piano part alternates not between G and E minor but, bizarrely, G and E *major*. The presence of that extra G♯ (the *major* 3rd of the E chord) creates a grating, tense colouring in comparison to a G natural. Admittedly, in doing so it sets 'Not A Second Time' apart from all its many 1963 counterparts and is certainly most suitable in the context of the restless, dissatisfied theme of the lyric. So just what *did* Mann mean?

[12] The Beatles recorded various songs that would reappear on *Live At The BBC* at the Aeolian Hall Studios, London, in July 1963, including covers like 'A Taste Of Honey', 'Sweet Little Sixteen', 'Lonesome Tears In My Eyes' and 'Nothin' Shakin''.

Surprise and the search for 'Mann's Moment'

The answer must lie within the fundamental principle that compelled Mann to put pen to paper in the first place – the vital element of 'surprise' in The Beatles' songwriting. It is this theme that flows through almost every reference in Mann's *Times* article, including the 'flat-submediants' that we will be tracking down – thankfully with rather less difficulty – in later chapters. In this case, one would have thought that The Moment (whatever it is) could be spotted by any Beatles fan with an ear for a subtle musical twist. For isn't that the whole reason, as Lennon says, for putting 'a tag on it' in the first place?

Let's try it. Ignore the following transcription for now. Listen instead to the whole of 'Not A Second Time', with your eyes closed or, better still, noting down any ear-catching moments that appear to (as John would say) 'make' the song.

A summary 'aural logbook' could include the following highlights:

1) George Martin's E major piano chords (as mentioned above), which stand out as early as the opening verse (on 'why' and 'cry'), and which continue throughout, except in his solo where he resorts to single notes and we can hear the originally conceived E minor guitar chord rather more clearly.
2) the first appearance of the A minor chord at (0.23), which prepares neatly for the more interesting bridge harmony.
3) the delicate – if barely audible – Am6 shape (at 0.36), which helps us to share John's 'hurt' (even though it might be missed on a cursory listen).[13]

But these three on the checklist are nothing in comparison to:

4) the plunging feeling on each of the three occasions that we exit the bridge.[14] First at 0.42, then at 1.01 (at the end of the piano solo). And, finally, at 1.47 immediately preceding that coda.

[13] Created by adding an F♯ note (on the top E string) to the basic fifth-string-root Am chord in open position.
[14] Some might regard this bridge as the 'refrain'. Either way, it is the 10-bar section that contrasts with the verse structure.

This last instance must surely be Mann's Moment. It has to be.

For, in stark contrast to the 'I-vi-I-vi', we now have something to write home about. Something that clearly falls into the category of 'surprise' as we feel the 'rug being pulled from under our feet', leaving us hanging for two bars before 'order' is restored. This was surely what Mann meant by the 'end' of the song as it completes its structural cycle, with that final coda now confirmed as just a red herring in our search.

Here's what the extract looks like when annotated in the usual manner.

'Not A Second Time'

So just what is happening at this brief, but nevertheless poignantly plunging moment?

Playing 'tag' – The Interrupted/Deceptive cadence

Specifically, the effect is down to the sudden appearance of Em, a chord we've heard before in the verse and bridge – but not in this particular context at what can be seen is a point of climax in the song, both in terms of the form and the lyrical theme. For here we are expecting the D7 chord, the dominant in the key of G, to return us to the G major tonic just as it does at the end of every seven-bar verse (first at 0.13).

However, in replacing it with E minor, which supports that authoritative, isolated E note, John Lennon has dealt us a card from the bottom of the deck. That G major has gone AWOL, only reporting for duty to re-establish stability two bars later, when the song either repeats from the top or, in this final instance, when it is 'saved' by the G chords that reappear in the coda.[15]

It may have been overlooked down the years, buried deep in an early Beatles album, but this is a very neat little musical trick. And one that seems to fall comfortably within manoeuvres widely accepted by the classical fraternity.

For looking through the list of cadences in the music dictionary we stumble across something called the *Interrupted* cadence, defined variously as 'dominant-to-relative minor' or 'dominant-to-submediant', both formal descriptions of precisely this type of 'V7-vi' move. Sometimes it appears as a *Deceptive* cadence, with a variety of 'catch-all' definitions like 'dominant-to-a-chord-other-than-the-tonic' or, more simply, where the 'relative minor appears in place of the tonic'. And that's certainly what we seem to have here.

Whatever the wording, the central principle is the same, and one so important to any study of Beatles songwriting that it will appear constantly in a variety of forms throughout the remainder of the book – deception.

Musical deception takes many forms. Indeed, we've already seen some other incarnations, including those non-functioning secondary dominants that didn't behave as we were led to expect. But the Deceptive cadence itself is perhaps the flagship example of the 'Violation Of Expectations', which covers all such moves and is neatly defined by the great songwriter Jimmy Webb as:

> 'taking advantage of the ear's propensity to expect a certain result by substituting an unexpected one.'[16]

The Interrupted, or Deceptive cadence, in all its forms, deceives us at this very point by not fulfilling an idea that has been planted. Having arrived at the D7 we are looking to 'settle' at the end of the bridge with the ear expecting to be 're-grounded' in the tonic key. After all we've already heard a Perfect cadence (D7-G) previously, in the verse. But here we are literally 'deceived by the vi', which now acts a disorientating *substitute* for the tonic, completely replacing it.

[15] Not only are we expecting the G harmonically but also, it can be argued, *melodically*, with the F♯ note of 'No' (supported as the 5th of Bm) appearing to point the way 'home' as the leading note of G (even before the D7 that contains it within its chord structure as its 3rd).
[16] Jimmy Webb, *Tunesmith – Inside The Art Of Songwriting*, p. 195.

The Deceptive cadence was certainly novel for pop music of the early sixties – but by no means unheard of before The Beatles. Indeed, judging from their very select choice of early covers, it's safe to assume that Lennon and McCartney had been encountering the ploy for some years. The rendition of 'The Sheik Of Araby' on *Anthology 1* subtly thwarts the Cycle Of Fifths as, in the key of C, G moves to Am for another V-vi conclusion (at 0.44). A neat variation of the same trick is found on The Beatles' version of 'The Honeymoon Song', repackaged on *Live At The BBC*.

'The Honeymoon Song'

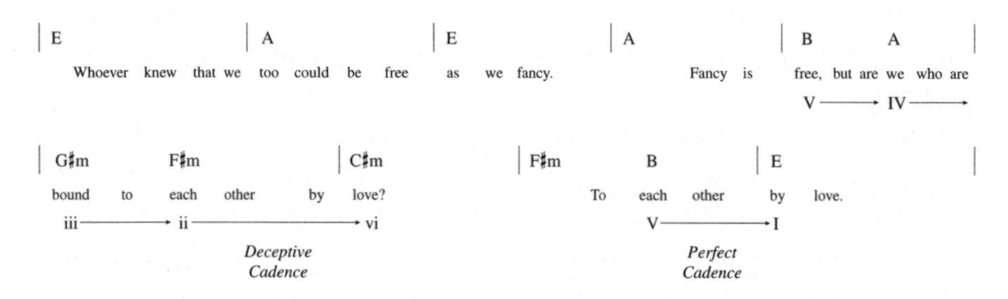

As with 'Not A Second Time' it's all innocuous stuff until that moment (first at 0.52 and again at 1.21) when the tonic major chord is again 'thwarted' by vi. Notice the scalar walk-down that falls V-IV-iii-ii (B-A-G♯m-F♯m), and which seems destined for the tonic chord of E. However, our expectations are denied by the appearance of the vi chord (C♯m), before the chorus obligingly cadences perfectly, 'V-I', as we originally 'wanted'. A pure musical manifestation of delayed gratification because – *unlike 'Not A Second Time'* – the Deception is immediately 'covered up' by an immediate 'rehearing' which now *does* succeed in 'properly' closing the sequence with the expected V-I. This is an important distinction to which we will return later.

By coincidence, The Beatles recorded 'The Honeymoon Song' for the BBC in July 1963 – just two months before 'Not A Second Time'. But then – as with many slick Beatles manoeuvres – this effect certainly wasn't reserved exclusively for just the one song. Sure enough, with a bit of careful listening, it's another device that can be found, in some form, just as clearly on *Please Please Me* as on *Abbey Road*.

More clearly, in fact – for one of the best Beatles examples of a Deceptive cadence appears in 'Do You Want To Know A Secret' – way back on that debut album – where The Beatles diligently go about setting up our hopes only to dash them by using another 'V7-vi'.

'Do You Want To Know A Secret'

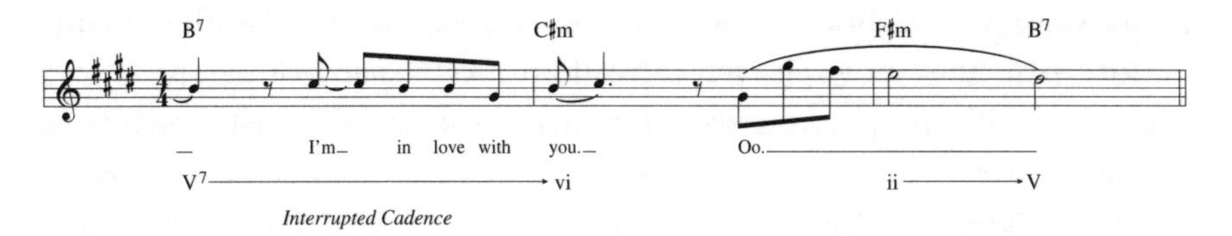

In the key of E again, the first few times that the dominant B7 appears in the song it 'behaves' as the listener expects, resolving directly to the tonic, V-I. But, after alternating with the IV chord, the Perfect cadence we expect at 0.38 is abandoned and replaced by B7-C♯m, providing the perfect sense of mellow deflation for the line 'I'm in love with you'. Just as in 'Not A Second Time' the moment is ear-catching; we sit up and listen as if jolted from our slumbers.

Jumping forward to *Abbey Road*, let's give Ringo the credit (albeit with a little help from George) for the simple but devious little twist at the climax of 'Octopus's Garden', clearly another Deceptive cadence – though again one that (like 'The Honeymoon Song') *is immediately succeeded by a conventional close.*[17]

'Octopus's Garden'

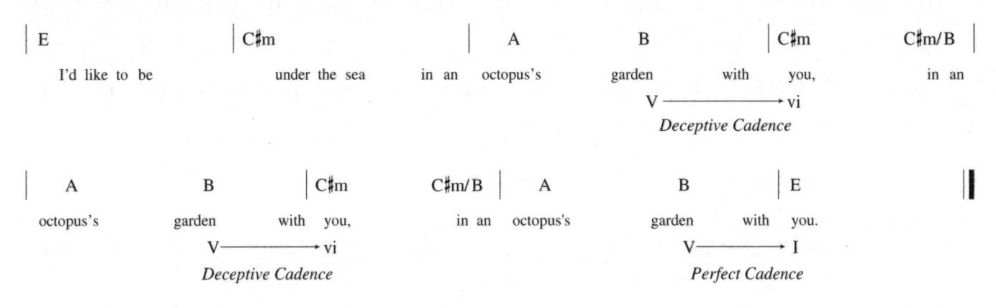

[17] Ringo gets a rare lone credit, famously originating the song while holidaying in Sardinia on Peter Sellers' yacht. 'A couple of tokes later on the guitar and we had "Octopus's Garden",' he explains in *The Beatles Anthology*, p. 312.

Once again the listener has been primed for the V-I Perfect cadence. But, rather than a return to E major at 2.34, the B is followed by C♯m – the vi – for the Interruption. In fact, we hear it twice in what is a 'three-times-around-the-block' exit, before the curtain finally falls with George's pretty guitar lick and a resolution to the E major tonic – proof that such a seemingly 'classical' move can add interest to even the very simplest of Four-chord pop clichés.[18]

But then the move itself is hardly rocket science, merely a deft application of the 'relative minor-for-major' substitution that we've been seeing regularly ever since the Doo Wop sequence of Chapter 3. Now we are merely seeing it applied in its *pure 'vi-for-I'* incarnation as a complete replacement for the tonic.[19]

So is *this*, finally, the Aeolian Cadence that William Mann was raving about all those years ago?

Almost. But not quite, for we surely have to account for the very word 'Aeolian'.

The Aeolian cadence – the search continues

After all, if the terms 'Interrupted' and 'Deceptive' cadences are so widely accepted in the classical community – and describe *precisely* this manoeuvre – then why didn't Mann just use one of them? Why bring 'Aeolian' into the equation, other than for perhaps journalistic embellishment? The dictionary is already full to the brim with all types of cadences, many of which we've seen in action in a Beatles context. Why confuse the issue with what appears to be just an alternative definition of an existing term? But there *is* a solution to the puzzle. And to find it we must introduce a concept that is central to appreciating the effect of a whole catalogue of the very finest Beatles songs. This is the principle of 'tonality', and what we mean by 'being in a key'.

[18] The even more primitive 'Ob-La-Di, Ob-La-Da' enjoyed similar redemption at the equivalent point in the song. Listen to how a Gm chord substitutes for the 'expected' B♭ tonic chord (for two bars at 2.58).

[19] The 'V-vi' move is seen in dozens of Beatles songs – *not necessarily in this Deceptive cadence setting* – but equally *within* a progression (e.g., in the verses of 'I Want To Hold Your Hand' and 'Ticket To Ride'); or as a point of transition *between* sections where it serves more directly to propel a song forward (e.g., to start the chorus of 'Drive My Car'). In each case the 'formula' can be abbreviated as 'V-vi'.

So far we have assumed implicitly that 'Not A Second Time' is in the key of G major – *and that it remains so, throughout.* But the answer to the enigma can only lie in the way that Mann perceives *a change in the tonality, or key centre, as the bridge unfolds.*

The assumption of a continuous key of G is simply inconsistent with the very term 'Aeolian', which in music has direct associations with what we can now introduce as *the minor tonality.* To have been at pains to refer to it in this context, Mann must implicitly have regarded Lennon's striking change as being not just to an E minor *chord – but also to the key of E minor itself, however fleetingly* – indeed, for just those two bars before the key of G major is re-established in subsequent verses and the coda.

This may be a controversial explanation, but it seems the only likely one. Of course, the problem with this – and with tonality in general – is that we can argue the toss until the next Beatles come along. Indeed, as we explore the minor world in more detail in the following chapter, we'll briefly demonstrate how various eminent experts have interpreted a whole string of related Beatles sequences differently over the years. And essentially because, to a very great extent, the concept of tonality is – like beauty itself – in the eye (or rather ear) of the beholder. Are we 'in major' or 'in minor'? At the margin, we can't be sure. Here are some guidelines as we enter the murky world of tonal ambiguity.

What is tonality?

Feeling a song, or indeed a song *section*, to be in a particular key depends on the extent to which we hear the music – both melodies and harmonies – revolving around, 'homing in on', or *resolving to* a central reference point, or tonic, as the song unfolds. This provides our sense of being centered in a key, with the tonic 'one' chord, either 'I major' (or 'i minor' when we are in a minor key) being the base to which the song will return, *or which is at least suggested as a point of resolution.* It is the place where we feel 'at rest', 'stable' or 'satisfied'. Sometimes (particularly with the Cycle Of Fifths) we'll be moving through key centres so quickly that we do not have time to register a sense of stability, merely one of 'homing in' to base.

For most of 'Not A Second Time' few would argue that this reference point is G major. Take the verse – it opens on G, always a very good guide (though by no means a foolproof one) to the tonality. It then progresses through a seven-bar cycle, with the vi taking us inexorably back to G via the dominant of G (the D7) at 0.13. During this time we don't feel as if we could happily come to rest on another chord.[20]

However, do we feel so sure of the tonality at the point of the Aeolian cadences we've identified? Mann himself would surely claim that – *in this context* – the finality of Lennon's E melody note and E minor chord create a new sense of 'home', albeit somewhat menacingly. And that's just the point.

The major/relative minor debate

While the Em came as a surprise, you could argue in retrospect, that the atmosphere of the song was steadily previewing this very twist. We were being 'set up' all along. The bridge lyrics are certainly apprehensive, particularly as each of the first four discrete lines start unsurely on a weak beat of their respective bars. The singer could go either way in both his relationship and his musical conclusion, which we await with trepidation. But the final line seals the mood as the refrain emerges, bathed in negativity, with the first of the three cries of 'No' now falling on an ominous down-beat, encouraging the F♯ melody note to drop to E (rather than rise to G), a fate sealed harmonically with a minor *coup de grâce*.

It is in this context that the plunge to minor occurs, and this sets it apart from, say, the Deceptive cadences of 'The Honeymoon Song', 'Do You Want To Know A Secret' and 'Octopus's Garden' where they appear merely as genuine 'interruptions' in the proceedings. They are therefore, crucially, 'corrected' immediately in the subsequent bars as a more conventional cadence unfolds.

For while the term 'cadence' is often used loosely and incorrectly to describe any old chord change, it typically refers to one that creates a *resolution* at the end of a sequence, where it often creates a 'full stop' at the end of a musical sentence. A point where we metaphorically 'take a breath'.[21] The cadence here is both melodic and harmonic, though Mann's quote

[20] The same goes for the notorious coda – for while we hear a repeated alternation in all these codas, is it really that directionless? For most listeners the 'I-vi-I-vi' means just that. It is tending to the key of the I major, as best illustrated by 'Baby It's You', 'All My Loving' and all the others that don't fade out on this progression but end, satisfyingly, on the I major chord, providing a sense of 'closure'.

[21] The word 'cadence' derives from the Latin *cadere*, to fall. The use of the term in music originally reflected the fact that, in speaking, it is natural to drop the pitch of the voice on the last syllable of the sentence.

directs us very specifically to a 'chord progression'.[22] And while we have been referring to the relevant section in 'Not A Second Time' as a 'bridge', it is more appropriately regarded as a chorus – or rather *refrain* – that concludes the form of the song. You could say that this appearance of the Em as a 'devilish', 'dark' Aeolian punchline closing the proceedings confirms a key switch, for it succeeds in establishing within the listener a new sense of tonality created by a different set of pitch relationships that are distinct from a major key.[23] To explain this further, in the same way that we discussed in Chapter 3 the relationship between major and relative minor *chords*, so we can now extend the concept to their respective scales, and therefore, *keys*.

The Aeolian/Ionian connection

The new pitch relationships that emerge with the closing E minor action are reflected in the E natural minor scale, which corresponds directly to the seven-note Aeolian *mode* of the Ancient Greeks (and whose Ionian mode, incidentally, is directly equivalent to the diatonic major scale).[24]

Just like the natural minor scale, the Aeolian mode starts and ends on the sixth degree of this same major scale in a relationship that can be summarised by the following chart:

	G major (G Ionian)												
Harmonised Scale	I	ii	iii	IV	V	vi	vii dim	I					
G major	*G*	*Am*	*Bm*	*C*	*D*	*Em*	*F♯dim*	*G*					
E minor						*Em*	*F♯dim*	*G*	*Am*	*Bm*	*C*	*D*	*Em*
Harmonised Scale						i	ii dim	♭III	iv	v	♭VI	♭VII	i
						E minor (E Aeolian)							
	I major ...												***... or i minor?***

The fact that both scales are so related, consisting of the same notes and enjoying the same key signature, might appear to confuse the issue. But the

[22] It is in this sense that there is no cadence in the faded outro of the coda of 'Not A Second Time', as briefly suggested earlier.

[23] Context is everything. After all, the 'V7-vi' moves in, say, 'P.S. I Love You' and 'I Want To Hold Your Hand' – while notable in their own way – could never qualify for this kind of interpretation.

[24] Musical modes, of which the Aeolian is just one, can be traced, via Renaissance music theory, back to a Greek theoretical system based on the differing practices of various ethnic divisions. The Aeolians, one division of the Hellenic stock, descend from Aeolus, and founded colonies throughout Greece.

layout of the chart demonstrates that there is clearly scope for a listener to feel as if he is moving between the tonics of G major and E minor-*depending on the emphasis of the music at any particular time.*

We can hear The Beatles appreciating this duality as early as 'The Sheik Of Araby', where the moody A minor guitar intro (starting and ending on an A note) defers immediately to the brighter tonality of C major for the main structure of the song. More subtly, we saw in Chapter 3 how 'Yesterday' and 'Here There and Everywhere' undermined the security of their major tonics by means of a ii–V sequence that pulled us poignantly towards their respective relative minors, within a discrete sequence. The trick to understanding the 'Aeolian cadence' is, first, to appreciate the emergence of the 'superiority of vi' (though, as explained, more fundamentally now in this 'closing' context). Second, to accept that *the cadence itself is not achieved by any of the methods we've previously seen of establishing a tonic.* For the Aeolian cadence is conceptually different from Perfect and Plagal ones that have so far dominated our look at resolution. The D7 in 'Not A Second Time' is neither the V nor the IV in relation to the E minor chord. It is the ♭VII. Viewing it in this way is the conceptual leap we must make in order to solve this riddle.

The Aeolian cadence 'unmasked': the flattened leading note

Ultimately it all comes down to terminology. Mann could have felt this E minor chord as a 'very important vi', as per the Interrupted cadence. But he chose to reconceive it as a new tonic; as a result of a modulation to a new key with a new 'one': *i minor.*

How do we know? Because modal cadences (for which the Aeolian most definitely qualifies) are distinguished by what we call the *flattened leading note.* As we saw in Chapter 1, in G major the leading note is the F♯, which rises by an effortless half-step, a *semitone,* into the root of G whenever a D7 chord (in which it appears as the major 3rd) resolves to G.

In E minor, however, the corresponding seventh note of the scale is a *whole* step – *two* semitones – away from the root. In the D7-to-Em move, it is the D root note that drives the move to the E root by that wider interval. It is because of this – *the essence of the 'Aeolian' part of the Aeolian cadence* – that we can now finally define the rogue as not 'V7–vi' but **♭VII7 – i minor**, *even though both 'formulae' describe the same chord change.*[25]

[25] This therefore elaborates on the author's first published attempt at busting the myth when defining it as the 'V7–vi' in 'Theories, Rants, Etc', *MOJO*, Issue 28, March 1996, p. 8.

Resolution in the Aeolian cadence

♭VII			i minor	
D⁷			Em	
Formula	Note	Voice leading	Note	Formula
♭7th	C	Down a semitone	B	5th
5th	A	Up a whole tone	B	5th
3rd	F♯	Up a semitone	G	♭3rd
Root	**D**	**Up a whole tone**	**E**	**Root**

We can now also re-label the offending extract of 'Not A Second Time' appropriately, stressing the combination of harmony and melody.

'Not A Second Time'

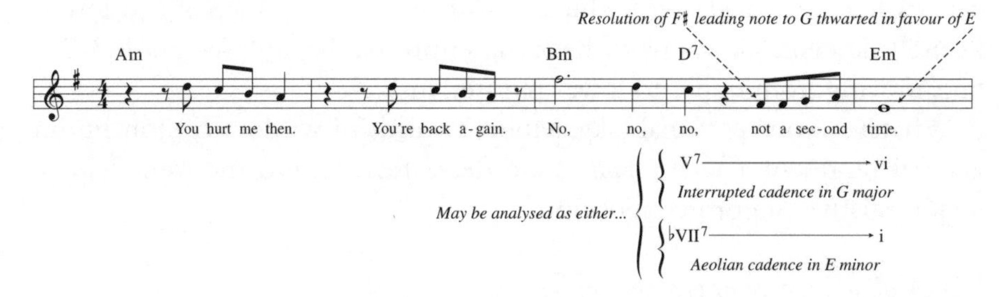

Allan Moore, a classical music expert and leading Beatles authority, helps put the final piece in the jigsaw:

> 'The only way that we can make sense of Mann's use of the word "Aeolian" in "Not A Second Time" is to view that D7-Em as an "Aeolian seven-to-one", with the [♭]VII acting as an "effective V" taking us powerfully to Em as a temporary tonic. In this sense Mann would argue that it is not the same thing as a "V-vi" Interrupted or Deceptive cadence because – at that precise point in the song – the role of the E minor as a "vi" is being questioned and is veering towards tonic status. How you term it depends on whether you feel the G tonic still ultimately in force in the background. And this depends on your own sense of tonality.'[26]

So, in the end it all comes down to the subjective use of musical 'tags' when describing the effect of a device in a pop song. It's therefore no

[26] Dr. Allan F. Moore, University Of Surrey Music Department, in conversation with the author, 27th September 2000.

surprise that music writers have a tradition of applying (and making up) their own terminology to suit their whims – as indeed this author will soon be doing with some even more exotic Beatles cadences than the Aeolian.

But Mann has not been the only Beatles commentator to feel the powerful shifting sands of tonality in 'Not A Second Time' over the years. Take Alan W. Pollack, who astutely matches the music and the theme when concluding that the song takes 'surprising turns toward the mournful, disappointed key of E minor [which] indicate that the hero is not able to follow his own best advice' (yet, ironically, he avoids pinning the effect down to an Aeolian cadence in his careful treatment).[27]

Everett, meanwhile, stresses how the Aeolian cadence is prepared strongly by the path of Lennon's melody as early as the high G pitch six bars earlier (on '*wond*'ring') which, ahead of the final F♯ ('No!') to low E ('time') descent, 'allows us to hear the entire refrain following a [♭]3-2-1 line, moving from upper to lower register, in E'.[28]

Whatever your personal take, Moore's words of wisdom on tonality in general represent a vital *caveat* as we delve further into the minefield of major/relative minor juxtaposition.

The Aeolian cadence in typical context

In order to clarify this principle of 'combining' features of the major key with that of the natural minor key, let's first dig out a rather more *bona fide* example of this modal '♭VII-i' cadence – namely one that exists in its natural habitat: an indisputably *minor-key setting*. To put it in an appropriate historical context, let's select probably the only one that William Mann would have heard on a Beatles recording by the time of his 1963 pronouncements. Admittedly it's on a cover rather than an original, but the refrain of 'A Taste Of Honey' obliges by showcasing the manoeuvre in textbook fashion.

In appreciating the device here we are helped by the fact that there is actually *no primary dominant chord anywhere in the song*, with the defining cadence that establishes the key represented specifically by the E chord that

[27] This is presumably because, as he explains, he regards the cadence as involving not D7 at all but rather a F♯ diminished chord: 'a very reasonable surrogate for the V of the major key ... also one of those chords that enharmonically can also be substituted for the V of the relative minor ... it is this ambiguity that has the effect of smoothing over the deceptive cadence and makes it the more believable when it comes'. Alan W. Pollack's 'Notes on ... Series' no. 041, 1991. Published online at *The 'Official' rec.music.beatles Home Page*, http://www.recmusicbeatles.com.

[28] *The Beatles As Musicians: The Quarry Men Through Rubber Soul*, p.192.

'A Taste Of Honey'

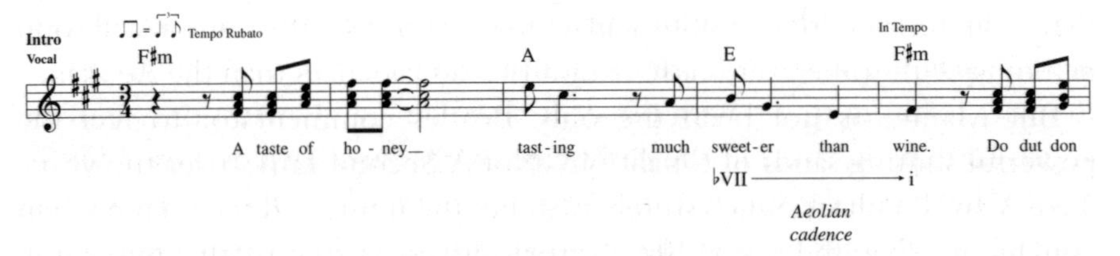

resolves up a whole step to the tonic, F♯m. Notice how the role of the flattened leading note also happens to be reinforced by the melody line at this point as the E and F♯ notes mirror the harmonic cadence. Here, for the first time, we are experiencing a more fundamentally 'minor' mood, while also appreciating how the same device can be worked into a major song to create a minor 'local' tonic, precisely as in 'Not A Second Time'.

'Tonal ambiguity' – an introduction

Despite this explanation, there are many who might question whether Mann is 'right' in identifying a key shift for such a seemingly short and innocuous two-bar stretch. But why not? He was not only accurate (according to this interpretation) but, far more importantly, also uncannily perceptive given how The Beatles' songwriting was rapidly developing. For, by encouraging Beatles listeners to keep an ear out for shifting tonality he was highlighting a concept that should perhaps be regarded as The Beatles' single most important contribution to pop songwriting.

As we'll be soon be exploring, major/relative minor juxtaposition (and with a more prolonged feeling than in 'Not A Second Time') accounts for the success of dozens of songs, from as early as 'There's A Place' (yes, back on the debut), continuing through 'And I Love Her', 'Girl', 'I'm Only Sleeping', 'When I'm Sixty Four', 'Your Mother Should Know', 'Cry Baby Cry' and 'You Never Give Me Your Money', to cover just nine examples from nine different albums. For a token single we can throw in 'We Can Work It Out'.[29]

This duality was not unheard of in mainstream pop of the fifties and

[29] While conceptually different, The Beatles also perfected the sudden deflating drop from I whereby a major song ends on its relative minor. A canny trick on 'Cry Baby Cry' (at 2.31) but which appeared as early as 'From Me To You'. Listen to how, having reached the home tonic on C major (at 1.49), we plunge to Am (at 1.51) in just one of many challenging early Beatles codas. For while pop songs don't have to end on the tonic I chord, certainly back in the early sixties, they normally did.

early sixties but it was nevertheless all too rare. Yet The Beatles had only just begun in terms of their use of a principle that is sometimes referred to as *key dichotomy*, or, as we will refer to it from now on, *tonal ambiguity*. It exists in many forms in music with the drift between 'I and vi' just one of many angles to exploit. Even in the early days, with songs such as 'From Me To You', The Beatles perfected modulations to *unrelated* keys – those that contain 'new' notes beyond the seven already shared between a major key and that of its relative minor.

Some such moments would be subtle and fleeting – and consequently debatable in terms of representing formal modulations. Others were unequivocally full-blooded key switches where the listener has no choice but to be felled as the goalposts of tonality are uprooted and moved to a distant musical landscape. In this sense, the Aeolian cadence can be seen as just one of several musical devices with which The Beatles took their earliest strides into deliciously 'tricking' the listener into a false sense of security.

Much of the remainder of this book is about precisely this effect, with the expression 'tonal ambiguity' cropping up regularly. In most cases it is used to describe a listener's questionable sense of tonic even if – almost by definition – there is debate over the appropriate musical terminology and 'correct' use of Roman numerals. In the next chapter we'll see how critics debate certain Beatles moves in this way, despite the fact that each has presumably only been highlighted precisely because it constitutes an ear-catching moment.

This book maintains that the effect on the listener is the only thing that matters, with the whole saga of the Aeolian cadence surely illustrating this beyond reasonable doubt. So, while theory helps us draw attention to (and hopefully understand) the elements that 'make' the song, we shouldn't get hung up on pigeonholing. Tonality especially exists in degrees, and where we draw the line is a matter of how strongly we feel it *personally*.

How bizarre then that John Lennon (as we were reminded in 2000 by *The Beatles Anthology*), elaborated on the William Mann saga by dismissing him as 'a twit', while adding that: 'Intellectuals have the problem of having to understand it . . . They can't feel anything . . .'[30]

Surely this short-changes Mann's infamous legacy on a grand scale. In what still reads as unbridled excitement over what many regarded as just

[30] *The Beatles Anthology*, p. 96.

fashionable 'pop', Mann (a respected classical critic, remember) put his reputation on the line, boldly going where no one had gone before – and not just in vague, general terms like some tabloid bandwagon jumper, but in ways that spelt out, however cryptically, these very feelings. With the Aeolian cadence alone, it was precisely *because* he felt the power of a single, fleeting chord change so strongly (if anything *too* strongly) that it compelled him to shout about it from the rooftops. The fact that he chose an 'intellectual tag', as Lennon called it, to relay it to the rest of the world surely just confirms how much the earth had moved for him! As long as we can share that feeling, it surely doesn't matter what we call it. Yet the whole point of this discussion (and this book) is that these sometimes grand terms do help us to make connections and enhance our understanding and appreciation of music.

Nevertheless, in what will prove to be a recurring theme from here on in, The Beatles' rewriting of the rules of pop music exposed the limitations of using conventional terms to describe many of their ideas. There simply aren't enough to cover all the bases. Look back briefly at 'Do You Want To Know A Secret'. We termed the moment at 0.38 an Interrupted cadence. But is that still the correct term when the B7-C♯m move reappears in the song's coda?

'Do You Want To Know A Secret' (coda fade)

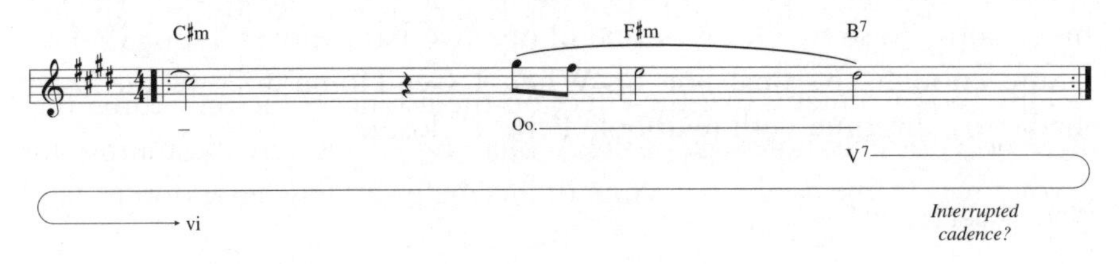

Again we are fed that unsatisfactory relative minor that denies us the resolution to E major we are supposed to crave. But now it is repeated, reinforcing our sense of disorientation on each hearing. At what point does the listener no longer 'require' the resolution to E major and become resigned to regarding C♯m as his new home? After one cycle? Two? Three or more? And what should we call the 'V-vi' now? A 'Permanently Interrupted' cadence? In fact it's hardly a cadence at all now as the perception of rest has been altered irretrievably. How about an 'Aeolian fade out'? It's your call.

This may sound pedantic but let's see immediately how The Beatles built on the concept in 'When I Get Home'. This song from *A Hard Day's Night* effectively summarises the principles of this chapter while introducing another important concept.

Aeolian deception revisited – 'When I Get Home'

Rather than introducing a sly minor twist as in 'Not A Second Time' and 'Do You Want To Know A Secret' the premise of 'When I Get Home' hinges on tonal ambiguity from the off, with our now familiar major/relative minor 'confusion' being just one category. Let's look at it first.

As if to help us in our songwriting studies, The Beatles even ensure that the relevant action all unfolds over the very theme of 'going home', guiding us subliminally to the crux of the matter. Namely, our sense of 'arrival' in a key. But which key? Let's first remind ourselves that we've already seen this musical metaphor as far back as the aircraft noises in 'Back In The USSR', through to the euphoric 'you're coming home' of 'It Won't Be Long' and the cyclical 'homeward' path in 'Golden Slumbers'. To which we can add the similarly destined chorus of 'Two Of Us' ('we're on our way home' over a V-IV-I); and (without straying very far from the analogy) the famous 'lead me to your door' of 'The Long And Winding Road' (a straightforward ii-V-I). The point is that all these sequences succeed in priming – strongly and unquestionably – a major tonic and, equally importantly, do so by means of one of our two basic moves: V-I or IV-I.

Sure enough, the final line of 'When I Get Home' follows the rules obediently, this time with textbook 'Perfect' closure.

'When I Get Home'

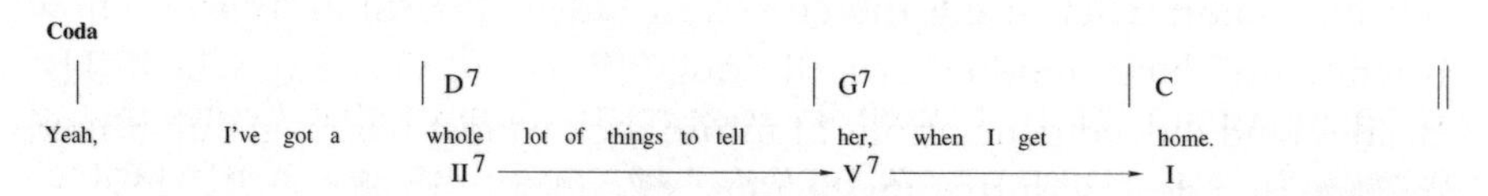

This simple II-V-I 'pay-off' resolution, with a C melody note over a C chord, surely confirms the identity of the key centre we've enjoyed for much of the song: C major. After all, what could be simpler than bluesy, 'Three-Chord Trick' verses set against a thinly disguised Four-Chord cliché bridge?

But while these simple structures make for a catchy enough tune, the song acquires a new dimension from the subtle tonal ambiguity at work in the choruses and at the end of the bridge. Notice how The Beatles manage to deliver not two but *three* different feelings of 'home' as that G chord resolves not just to C major (at the end and at the start of each verse) and the relative minor, A minor – but (even more confusingly) an A *major* chord, A7.

Let's look first at the end of the bridge as this provides us with an instant parallel with 'Not A Second Time'.

'When I Get Home'

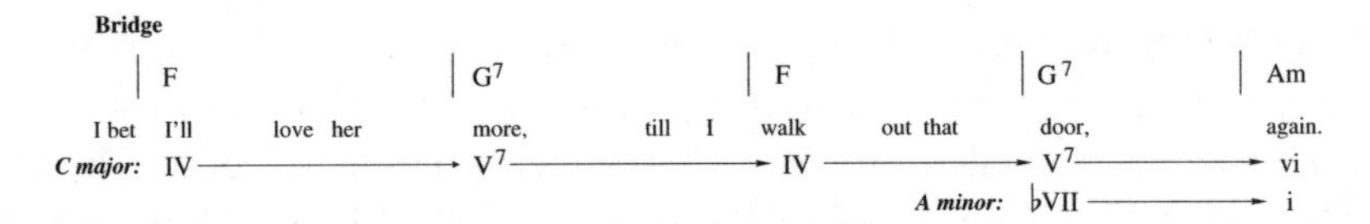

Clearly, in the scheme of this glorified I-vi-IV-V we would seem bound for a V-I move with G moving to C major. But as with 'Not A Second Time', that pay-off cadence at 1.32 delivers 'vi' rather than I – or arguably 'i minor' as, again, it's more 'Aeolian' than Deceptive. For while the A minor gets 'corrected' by the following verse in C, we surely first question its status. Just as we question Lennon's loyalty as 'when I get home' becomes 'till I walk out the door'.

For that minor cadence, whenever it appears in the song, suggests at least some trepidation about getting home. Indeed, the song's very first cadence at 0.12, finds that all-too-ominous Am enjoying supremacy before we've even heard C major for the first time.

So far this discussion has merely extended the principle of 'Not A Second Time', illustrating the powerful relationship between major and relative minor, when using the chords in cadential fashion. But let's now briefly introduce another crucial songwriting secret from which The Beatles (and indeed generations of future rock bands) would get unlimited mileage, and deal with that mysterious *A7* chord.

The Aeolian cadence revisited – '♭VII-I' major

For is this really a VI7 chord in the key of C major? Or could it be a more fundamental point of resolution that raises the musical *ante* of this song even further? After all, the A7 chord is the first sound we hear in the song and it's certainly delivered in a prolonged, pseudo-key-establishing way. We don't feel as if The Beatles are naturally 'pulling us' toward another tonic at this point.

The A7 seems to constitute a discrete tonal platform in its own right, however briefly. Even when we hear it in the penultimate refrain (at 2.02) it is conceptually unlike those turnaround VI7s secondary dominants (of the 'oh yeah' variety from Chapter 4). Just as with the song's Am, this effect derives from the way in which the cadence is achieved from a whole step below the root, i.e., from the G7 chord – *a technique that works irrespective of the quality of the A triad built on that root.*[31]

'When I Get Home'

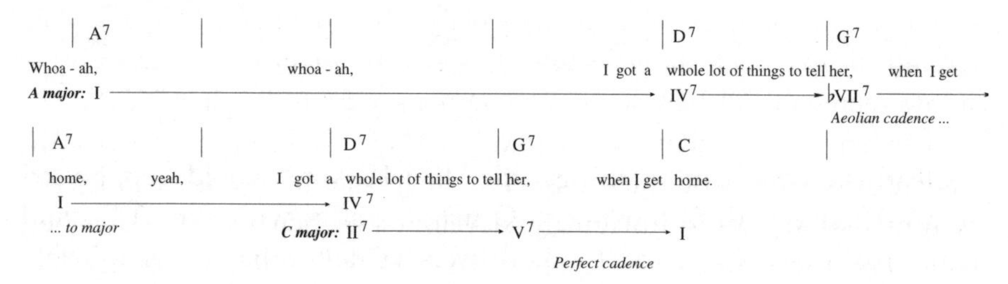

There are three main concepts to take from this discussion, each of which will re-emerge throughout much of our subsequent analysis of modulation and tonal ambiguity.

1) The pivot chord

The first is the concept of a 'pivot' chord as a means to effect a modulation. A pivot chord is simply one that can be seen to have a clear role in two different keys. Clearly, in 'Not A Second Time', this was the D7 chord itself, which acts as the V7 of G major but is reconceived at the 'pivotal' moment as the ♭VII of Em. In 'When I Get Home' the corresponding chord is the G7: now the V7 of C major and again functioning as ♭VII in relation to A. *Indeed, both A minor and A major.*

'When I Get Home' demonstrates that, just as the word 'pivot' suggests, you can use it to 'go both ways' from key to key. We duly both enter *and exit* the territory of C major using G7 pivot (whose dual role can abbreviated 'V=♭VII'). At a stroke we have introduced a concept that

[31] It's for this reason that George Martin's noisy E *major* chord doesn't negate the Aeolian effect of the D-E root movement in 'Not A Second Time'; for as we will see throughout Chapter 7, an Aeolian cadence still applies to a D7-E *major* change, i.e., ♭VII-I.

will emerge as a defining method of modulation in cleverly crafted pop, from The Beatles to Oasis, from 'Something' to 'Slide Away'.

2) Modulation or Tonicisation?

To the extent that the final C chord in 'When I Get Home' delivers the most satisfying sense of closure, it encourages us to view C major as the most fundamental key of the song. Certainly we finally enjoy a sense of having truly *arrived* home, in every sense, when that V-I cadence finally wrap-ups the proceedings (at 2.10).

Prior to that, the 'full stops' on the A chords at the end of certain musical sentences are perhaps written in pencil rather than indelible ink. This reminds us that such ultra-fleeting moves to transient key centres do not always represent full-blooded modulation away from the parent key.

So where do we draw the line? While there is no correct answer, the student of tonality could usefully view such brief harmonic manoeuvres as 'tonicisations', a term originally developed by Schenker to describe a temporary tonic on a scale degree other than that of the parent key. This is in contrast to the unequivocal modulations we will be encountering in Chapter 10, where a song not only targets new tonal territory – but also *develops* within it - often for several bars (or indeed a complete section).

In this way we can describe 'When I Get Home' as tending towards the key of C major but *featuring tonicised A minor and A7 chords by means of the 'V=♭VII' pivot.* We thus acknowledge that these A chords are tonally more important than just run-of-the-mill vi and VI7 chords in the key of C. The wandering tonality they create explains the song's compelling sense of movement, propelling us in ways far more subtle than a single key could manage.[32]

3) The Parallel major/minor relationship – an introduction

Equally important in terms of our emerging songwriting concepts, this A7 chord introduces a vital new musical term. For while the A minor was termed the *relative* minor of C major, that A *major* triad (A7) can now be defined as the *parallel* major of A minor. This reflects the fact that the two

[32] The Schenkerian view is that modulation describes a *permanent* change of tonal centre, whereas a 'tonicisation' (typically achieved with strong V chords rather than this rogue ♭VII) will eventually *return* to the fundamental tonic. While this distinction is more cut and dried, our hybrid approach is deliberate and reflects the reality that viewing modulation as a temporary concept within a song is widespread in contemporary analysis of popular music.

share the same *root* (in contrast to the familiar 'I–vi' relative relationship), *but with the two keys crucially belonging to scales with different interval structures and associated harmonised chords.*

The distinction between relative and parallel major/minor, and the ways in which The Beatles exploited more elaborately the songwriting potential of each device in some of their most famous songs, is the entire theme of the next chapter. 'When I Get Home', a rare case of the two concepts operating side by side in the same song, is a useful taster of things to come while showing again how The Beatles had such slick ideas down pat as early as 1964.

William Mann's Aeolian cadence was indeed more than just a flash in the pan – far from it. In both its minor and major incarnations, it would almost come to eclipse Perfect and Plagal cadences as an entire genre of popular music dubbed 'Aeolian rock harmony' evolved directly from the very types of chord progression that bands like The Beatles were pioneering in the sixties.[33]

John Lennon didn't know it but his 'exotic bird' had barely spread its wings.

The Mahler connection – fact or fiction?

With those 1963 observations, William Mann rightly takes his place as The Father Of Beatles Musicology. But there's just one niggling loose end that we must tie up in that very same sentence we've been deciphering. For as much as Mann's legacy is built on his flowery Aeolian cadence, so it has also hinged for so long on that revered and unquestioned connection with Mahler's 'Song Of The Earth'. But was he equally 'on the money' here? Amazingly, no. Far from it, in fact.

For, in a slice of Beatlology surely up there with any instalment of the 'Paul Is Dead' saga, a comparison between 'Not A Second Time' and Mahler's masterpiece reveals that any connection between the two is at best tenuous and at worst, completely baffling. In closing this chapter, we take a brief detour for ambitious readers to understand why.

When we finally dust off the 'end of Mahler's "Song Of The Earth"' we find, bizarrely, that there is no clear 'chord progression' here at all! After all, it's not too much of a conceptual jump to define a chord progression as

[33] Discussions of the Aeolian mode and the role of the constituent ♭VII crop up regularly in rock music culture. See 'Artful Aeolian', *Guitar Player*, February 2000 ; and 'Exploring Aeolian Changes', *Guitar Player*, October 2000; and 'The so-called "flattened seventh" in rock', Allan F. Moore, *Popular Music*, 14th February 1995, pp. 185–201.

something that does just that – it *progresses* from one chord to another, with movement in the root of the chords as well as some internal voice-leading usually regarded as essential elements.[34] But the coda of Mahler's famous *Farewell* movement – surely the intended point of comparison – is notable for featuring most powerfully the root of just one chord in its legendary dreamy climax. This is a lone, reiterated C note that perpetuates various shades of an exclusive C major chord, in the key of C major.[35]

Far from requiring a convoluted analysis, this concept of the 'pedal tone' – an unfailingly static reference point – paradoxically emerges as the simplest musical concept in the whole saga.[36] By the same token, the entire coda of Mahler's work (involving some 66 bars of music) also arguably involves no *cadence* at all – Aeolian or otherwise – at least in the accepted harmonic sense of one chord *resolving* to another in order to 'round off', 'complete', or 'close' a sequence. This appears to have stopped us dead in our tracks. What can we possibly draw from 'Song Of The Earth' to make a connection with 'Not A Second Time'? The answer is very little. And in searching for clues as to what common ground Mann could have seen between the two works, the classical experts interviewed for this book each admitted that they were left clutching at straws.

Nevertheless, two lines of thinking were raised in attempting to lay the ghost to rest.

When collared for their instant analysis the experts invariably drew attention to the work's stirring final sonority: a celestial C 'added-sixth' chord (C6) that has elicited some of the most colourful eulogies in the history of music criticism.[37]

But while this climactic moment does arguably have an obvious and outrageously famous Beatles parallel, it is unfortunately not one found anywhere in 'Not A Second Time'.

[34] Technically, chords can 'progress' without root movement, relying on voice-leading alone, as we encounter later, but this is not applicable here.

[35] We take 'the end of Mahler's "Song Of The Earth"' to be just that: the 66-bar coda to *Der Abschied* – the sixth and final movement (or 'song') of *Das Lied Von Der Erde* by Gustav Mahler, acknowledged as the composer's finest work and premiered in 1911.

[36] The pedal tone is a principle that The Beatles would later use themselves, most famously in songs like 'Tomorrow Never Knows'.

[37] Take Benjamin Britten: 'It has the beauty of loneliness and of pain: of strength and freedom. The beauty of disappointment and never-satisfied love. The cruel beauty of nature, and everlasting beauty of monotony ... serenity literally supernatural ... that final chord is printed on the atmosphere.' Stephen E. Hefling, *Mahler; Das Lied Von Der Erde*, p. 116.

Taking this a stage further, Mahler's coda can be seen to introduce melodies and upper harmonies above this stubborn C root that can be construed as suggesting elements of A minor, while as we know, the added-6th chord itself can be seen as the fusion of a major tonic and its relative minor.[38] And, of course, any mention of 'I' and 'vi' can be twisted to relate to our directionless alternation between G and Em back in the *coda* of 'Not A Second Time'. However, in the same way that Mahler's major and relative minor hardly constitute a 'progression' over the static bass, so these chords in The Beatles' song do not form a cadence. Neither do they appear particularly 'natural' given that G♯ in George Martin's piano part which surely distances itself from the heavenly – *and purely diatonic* – construction of Mahler's C6 chord.[39]

Meanwhile, leaving no stoned unturned in this mystery, Dr. John Williamson, a renowned Mahler expert and Beatles fan at the University Of Liverpool, draws attention to the melodic elements of an E minor chord (a iii in C major) played by the celesta. And to the flute part which – albeit at a stretch – can be construed as enjoying an Aeolian cadence in so far as its melodic final note is an A note in the key of C. But, as Williamson explains, to do this requires some outrageous mental gymnastics.[40]

> 'Perhaps Mann saw something in this flute passage that suggested an Aeolian cadence. All the notes present in the celesta and flute parts are elements in both the Ionian mode (i.e., C major) and Aeolian mode. Except, that is for an E flat, which is Mahler's favourite minor third in a major context. The flute places its final decline to an A note as part of a complex designed to blur distinctions and reduce the harmonic movement to a final stasis [the C-added-sixth chord itself]. To the extent that the flute's drop from B-A is its 'final', you could call it an Aeolian cadence. But it is not a term in regular use and to view it as

[38] Stephen Hefling (in correspondence with the author, May 2000) explains: 'The C added-sixth chord in the Mahler consists of the notes C, E and G in the trombones and lower strings, with the added A in the oboe and flute. It is seen as derived from the anhemitonic pentatonic Chinese scale, *Gong* (C-D-E-G-A)'.

[39] This might appear to get Mann 'off the hook', by virtue of a fundamental relationship in 'Song Of The Earth' between not just C and A minor, but C and A *major*. But this is not the case. The only important A major sections appear in the 5th movement, 'Der Trunkene im Fruhling'.

[40] Conversation with the author, October 2000.

such in this instance is theoretical fantasy and most likely not what Mann was thinking of at all. But then again, he did like to enjoy himself!'

While the flute's '2-1' melodic descent is a nominal point of comparison, we still lack the harmonic '♭VII-i' that we've have been at pains to identify in 'Not A Second Time'. More to the point, whatever happened to the whole theme of ear-catching surprise and 'deception'? Not only is there no such parallel here but the *essence* of the 'Song Of The Earth' coda is the very antithesis of surprise. The whole premise of the final movement of the work is that it succeeds famously in conjuring a blissful state of relaxed euphoria: the music brilliantly evoking the grand theme of 'omnipotence' and 'natural order' – a mood that is continually *reinforced* rather than undermined. In this sense, nothing could be further from 'Not A Second Time' where John Lennon's apprehension and trepidation is so clearly embodied in both lyrics and music as that moment of truth – the darkness of the minor resolution – unfolds.

In the true spirit of trivia, we'll never know for sure what Mann meant.[41] But both Lennon and Mann would surely have enjoyed the fact that, almost four decades on from *With The Beatles* and *that* article, an even more highbrow dissection of another Beatles album would be included in a learned literary series appreciating the greatest musical works of all time. Allan Moore's companion to *Sgt. Pepper's Lonely Hearts Club Band* duly takes its place proudly alongside guided tours of such classical masterpieces as Beethoven's *'Moonlight'* Sonata, Vivaldi's *Four Seasons*, Verdi's *Requiem* and – neatly taking things full circle – Mahler's 'Song Of The Earth'.[42]

What a shame then that John Lennon didn't live to see this pivotal episode in Beatles mythology unmasked as just that.

A myth.

[41] Indeed, notwithstanding his own astute analysis of the Aeolian cadence in terms of the end-of-refrain plunge, Everett intriguingly suggests: 'Mann compared the I-VI alternation in the "Not A Second Time" coda to the conclusion of Mahler's *Das Lied von der Erde*. Good grief! It's "Mama Said" or "When My Little Girl Is Smiling", not Mahler.'; *The Beatles As Musicians: The Quarry Men Through Rubber Soul*, p.392.

[42] Allan F. Moore, *The Beatles: Sgt. Pepper's Lonely Hearts Club Band*, Cambridge Music Handbooks, Cambridge University Press, 1997. Stephen E. Hefling, *Gustav Mahler: Das Lied von der Erde*, Cambridge Music Handbooks. Cambridge University Press, 2000. Hefling himself confirmed that there is nothing resembling an 'Aeolian cadence' in the Mahler coda, in correspondence with this author, March 2000.

SIX

Relative and Parallel Minor Switches

Ask the average pop listener to describe why, musically, they like or dislike a particular song and they will usually struggle to put their feelings into words. Nevertheless, even small children can appreciate the contrast between 'happy' or 'sad' that we typically associate with major and minor chords, and major and minor *keys*, whose contrasting moods we introduced in the last chapter. Scientific research suggests that humans are 'programmed' at some primal level (not merely conditioned) to respond to certain sounds, and the minor tonality (with its corresponding adjectives of 'dark', 'haunting', and 'mellow') has long been an effective tool with which songwriters play on our emotions.

The legendary Nigel Tufnel, the self-styled Guitar God of the cult rock parody *This Is Spiñal Tap!*, surely speaks for us all when he describes the effect of the minor tonality during his impromptu rendition of the notorious 'Lick My Love Pump', his sensitive fusion of Mozart and Bach ('Mach').

'I don't know why, it just makes me want to weep,' he tells Marti Di Bergi, the 'rockumentary' producer, in a rare moment of melancholy, while specifically pronouncing D minor to be 'the saddest of all keys'.

Tufnel's contention is backed up by the fact that George Harrison's own minor-key masterpiece, 'While My Guitar Gently Weeps', originated in that same heart-rending key of D minor (as The Beatles' *Anthology 3* reveals – though it appears in its final form on the *White Album* in A minor). It is indeed enough to make you weep.

And that's exactly the point – for aside from Tufnel's admirable sensitivity to the specific *timbres* afforded by different minor keys, the minor tonality in general has its own characteristic mood. And, as a result, a strong songwriting tradition has grown up that matches lyrical themes to those same sounds (again, leaving aside Tufnel's delicately titled *opus*).

As important background to this chapter it is worth noting that the minor side of pop music has enjoyed a far more select and discerning legacy than its major counterpart. Take the backdrop to The Beatles' formative years in the fifties and sixties. In stark contrast to the ubiquitous major rock 'n' roll of the day, minor-key hits like Del Shannon's 'Runaway', The Ventures' 'Walk Don't Run', The Shadows' 'Apache', The Animals' 'The House Of The Rising Sun' and Johnny Kidd's 'Shakin' All Over', were relative exceptions. And it's no coincidence that each of these songs, it transpires, was a staple of early Beatles live sets.[1] All appear to have been highly influential on The Beatles' own songwriting development, with John Lennon even admitting that the Del Shannon classic inspired him to write one of his finest songs, 'I'll Be Back'. The highly novel and effective musical connection between the two songs is discussed later.

A quick listen to each of these early pop classics is highly recommended. The reader should also revisit a similarly influential quartet of minor-key covers recorded by The Beatles: 'A Taste Of Honey' (*Please Please Me*), 'I Just Don't Understand' (*Live At The BBC*), 'Three Cool Cats' and 'Besame Mucho' (both *Anthology 1*). Each exploits the minor tonality in various ways using 'signature' progressions and concepts of varying complexity, which we will see resurface in Beatles originals.

The minor tonality – a framework for analysis

It should also be appreciated that the minor tonality covers many moods and contexts in pop music generally – and certainly in Beatles music. At the heart of the sound is invariably the use of a tonic chord featuring a minor triad. This is an instant and practical definition, but from that raw material of a tonic and ♭3, a number of scales can be built – of which our infamous Aeolian mode (a.k.a. the natural minor scale) is merely one option. In Beatles music alone we must also consider the Harmonic minor scale and two other minor modes (the seemingly exotic 'Dorian' and 'Phrygian') when appreciating some very specific and memorable sounds.

[1] As confirmed in the painstaking list of Beatles cover songs that appears in Mark Lewisohn's *The Complete Beatles Recording Sessions*, pp. 361–5.

This chapter looks in detail at the *Aeolian* or *natural minor* scale that we introduced in the last chapter. This is punctuated by a brief excursion to the harmonic minor scale for one overriding practical reason. And, apart from a sneak preview of a major IV chord in a minor setting, we will reserve a formal discussion of the other important minor modes, Dorian and Phrygian, until Chapter 8 when we focus on the 'character notes' that define their identity.

Meanwhile, the fact that this chapter is entitled 'relative and parallel minor switches' should hopefully not confuse the issue if the lessons of the last chapter have been taken on board. For these terms relate to the context in which the natural minor scale is used in Beatles songs. Specifically they help us to describe, in practice, how minor song sections *appear in conjunction with the major sections with which they are typically intertwined.*

The fact is that it is very rare for a Beatles song to stay exclusively in a minor key for its entire duration. Surprising, maybe, but there are perhaps only a handful of exceptions to this rule in the entire catalogue: 'Cayenne', 'Being For The Benefit Of Mr Kite', 'Don't Bother Me' and 'Not Guilty' are a few that are notable for staying exclusively in minor without attempting conclusively to break from the downbeat mood.

Why is this? The answer no doubt lies in the profound effect of the minor tonality itself. For all the power of such songs, most songwriters know that, in minor, a little goes a long way. Take a look at the many covers that The Beatles recorded in their early career. Of the dozens found on readily available albums, perhaps only two songs: 'I Just Don't Understand' and 'A Taste Of Honey' stand out for their exclusive use of the minor tonality.

And with their own extensive repertoire of songs that move judiciously back and forth *between* major and minor keys, John, Paul and George demonstrate another songwriting secret: the success of *contrasting* tonalities. After a major verse and chorus, for example, a minor bridge invariably brings sudden textural poignancy. And *vice versa*: when in minor, a chorus or bridge in *major* often creates a much needed emotional 'lift' that equally can make a song. Ultimately the aim of this chapter is to illustrate how this 'dual key' principle represents another essential Beatles formula.

While we saw these tonal ideas at work in 'Not A Second Time' and 'When I Get Home', we now examine their use in more prolonged, complete song sections; focusing first on *relative* major/minor switches before moving to the *parallel* major/minor world.

Before we look at either, however, there's just one important adjustment we must be aware of when putting our harmonised natural minor-key chords into action. In a minor key the naturally occurring dominant chord is a minor 'v' rather than a major triad. We were conveniently able to ignore this fact in the previous chapter when dwelling exclusively on the role of ♭VII in the Aeolian cadence. But now we must look closely at the function and quality of the dominant in minor.

'v or V'? – the dominant dilemma

Let's delve into the minor world by first thinking in terms of the minor-key equivalent of the Three-Chord Trick. This is no longer I, IV and V, of course, but the minor triads labelled 'i', 'iv' and 'v' as they each consist of a root, minor third and perfect fifth (1, ♭3 and 5).

Among rock 'n' roll's most famous 'minor i-iv-v' hits was 'Shakin' All Over', the 1960 smash which emphasised Em and Am for much of the time while only revealing the B minor 'v' chord at the climax of the guitar solo. The same 'Aeolian Three-Chord Trick' can be found in songs as diverse as Fleetwood Mac's 'Black Magic Woman' and Pink Floyd's 'Money'.[2]

Meanwhile, in a Beatles original, the sound of this 'v' can be heard most clearly in the repeated verse vamp of McCartney's 'Things We Said Today'.[3]

'Things We Said Today'

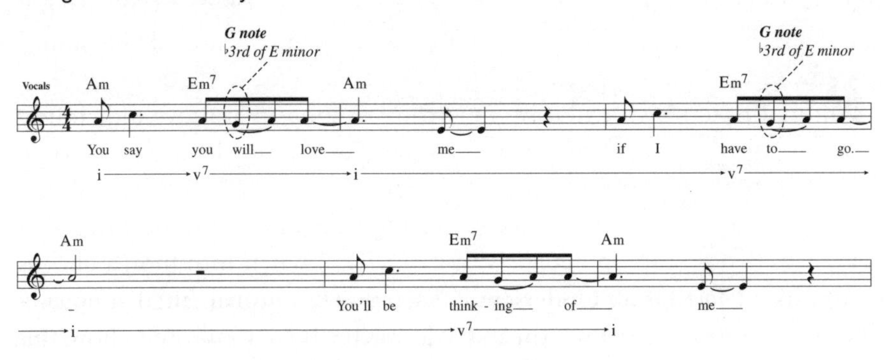

[2] In 'Money', the line: 'new car caviar *four*-star daydream' unfolds over the v minor chord (F♯m in the key of B minor), with the ♭3 appearing in the melody on the word '*four*'.

[3] For a contemporary equivalent of this repeated 'i-v' vamp, listen to R.E.M.'s 'Losing My Religion' (another 'Am-Em' in A Aeolian).

Notice also the particularly appropriate use of the chord – *in a melodic sense* – as the word 'will' appears as the defining ♭3rd.

However, the v minor chord in this context is by no means the most common dominant in minor-key pop music. Aeolian cadences aside, many (indeed, probably *most*) minor-key songs break the diatonic rules in one fundamental respect. They adopt a 'regular' V chord – *a dominant V7* – just as we expect in a major key.

Breaking the diatonic minor rules – the 'borrowed V7'

The purpose of the dominant V7 in minor is to create the same voice-leading that resolves so effortlessly to the tonic in a major key. Chapter 1 established the ubiquitous, fundamental importance of V, and its reappearance here proves the rule once more.

The Beatles understood this distinction between v and V7 as early as what appears be their first minor-key original, 'Cayenne', dating apparently from the summer of 1960 and featured on *Anthology 1*.

'Cayenne'

Just like 'I Just Don't Understand', McCartney's instrumental consists of just these three chords: Em, Am and a dominant B7 – a major V7 chord that can now be rationalised as deriving from the leading tone in a closely related minor scale – the *harmonic minor*.

We already know that, in a *major* scale, the leading tone lies a semitone below the root. And it is this note that, when the scale is harmonised, appears as the 3rd of the V chord, thereby creating the resolution to the tonic as the note moves up a semitone to the root. This doesn't happen in the diatonic natural minor scale because (as we know from the last chapter) the seventh degree is *flattened*. The Aeolian cadence of 'A Taste Of Honey' certainly had a very distinct flavour but classical theorists would say that the whole step between the ♭7 and root simply does not lead the melody (or the harmony) to the tonic with quite the same degree of 'pull'. The characteristic half-step in a major key is a strong factor in establishing tonality, while its *absence* in natural minor often makes tonality less conclusive. And while we don't question tonality in 'A Taste Of Honey', that's because there's no distracting potential major tonic to cloud the picture. But when we move *between* both major and minor tonalities as we will be doing throughout this chapter, a major dominant chord is often needed to reinforce our feeling of a minor tonic.

It is for this reason that this 'flaw' in the natural minor scale is 'corrected' by artificially raising this ♭7 note by a semitone, back to the natural 7th, thereby making it, once again, a leading tone. It is with this new minor scale, *harmonic* minor – with its new interval sequence – that the V7 chord is created.

Here's the harmonic minor scale in the key of A minor.

Creating V7 in minor – the harmonic minor scale

1		2		♭3		4		5		♭6		7		8
A		B		C		D		E		F		G♯		A
	1		0.5		1		1		0.5		1.5		0.5	

0.5 = half step, 1 = whole step, 1.5 = one-and-a-half steps

When harmonised conventionally in thirds, the scale yields some interesting 'new' chords:

i	**ii dim**	**♭iii aug**	**iv**	**V**	**♭VI**	**vii dim**
Am	B dim	C aug	Dm	E	F	G♯dim

And, if we add the sevenths, we can now spot the V7 itself:

i maj^7	**ii$^{7\flat5}$**	**♭iii maj^{7}aug**	**iv^7**	**V^7**	**♭VI maj^7**	**vii dim^7**
Am (maj^7)	Bm$^{7\flat5}$	Cmaj^{7}aug	Dm^7	E^7	F maj^7	G♯dim^7

The important point here is that minor songs tend to be based in *natural* minor using, for the most part, chords that are within that family, and only occasionally 'borrowing' the odd chord from the *harmonic* minor family – the V7 being by far the most common.[4] The two scales can therefore happily co-exist within a song.

What about the melody? Does this also have to feature the raised 7th in a minor progression with V7? It can do. But it doesn't *have* to. Indeed, the example of 'Cayenne' has been chosen specifically because it not only shows the V7 chord in action but also because it compares the sound of *both* these melodic 7th notes over the chord in the space of two bars. Over the V7 appearing at 0.18, listen to the strong, authoritative sounding D♯ that follows in the guitar line at 0.19. However, at 0.21, it's a D *natural* note that now forms a '*melodic* Aeolian cadence' to the E (♭7–1). The D♯ would have sounded stronger, but also more 'classical', or 'Latin'. But stronger doesn't necessarily mean better – as always, it's down to personal preference: the V7 chord provides the *potential* for nailing the chord change with an exotic note, as The Beatles do here on the first occasion.[5]

With this theoretical anomaly under our belt we can now get to the heart of the chapter, looking first at Beatles songs that straddle the tonalities of major and *relative* minor.

Part 1 – relative major/minor switches

1. The relative minor bridge

We can take the presence of V7-i minor for granted in helping to establish and reinforce a feeling of moving to the minor tonic, noting also that this can be used either instead of – or *in conjunction with* – the modal ♭VII-i move from the last chapter. For these two chord changes together prove to be vital landmarks to look out for when navigating between major and minor sections in Beatles songs. Take a look at our first example, 'There's A

[4] It's worth mentioning that we will also find examples of most of these exotic seventh chords in Beatles songs over the course of our travels (in fact all except the ♭IIImaj7aug).

[5] The Latin pop craze of the late nineties demonstrated how the natural 7th can spice up a melody for this type of effect. For example, 'Spice Up Your Life' by the Spice Girls consists mainly of a two-chord vamp between Fm and C7 but where the raised 7th note in question (E natural – the 3rd of C7) occasionally appears as a strong melody note (e.g., on the words 'go round'). Not forgetting the neo-classical rockers of the eighties like guitarist Yngwie Malmsteen, whose sound epitomises the concept of the raised 7th in minor.

Place', a criminally under-appreciated song from *Please Please Me*, which has a special place in the hearts of Beatles musos. For it appears, chronologically, as the group's first convincing flirtation with the dual tonics of major and relative minor on a recorded original.

'There's A Place'

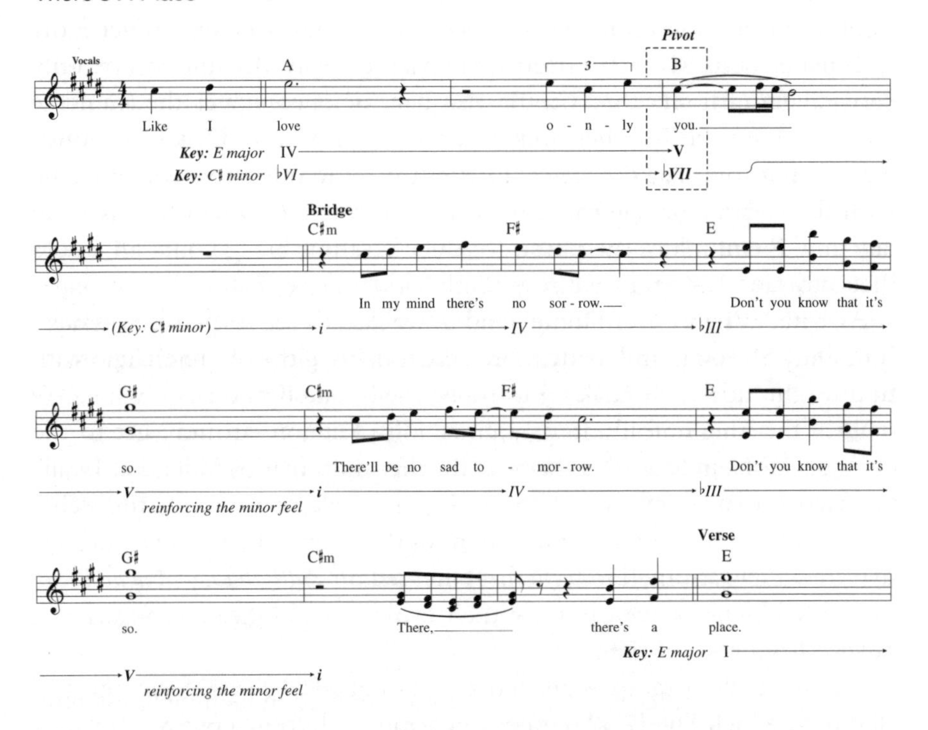

Here, the build-up on the B chord and the C♯ melody note soon makes us feel that we are more than just flirting with the minor tonality. As such, we subliminally reinterpret the entry to the bridge as '♭VII-i'.[6] Meanwhile, we now also enjoy a 'reinforcing' feel from a V-i, as the G♯ chord primes the C♯m at 1.01 and again (at 1.08) before the next verse resumes in E major.

But wait! Isn't this G♯7 just a 'functioning secondary dominant' (III7 in the key of E) just like the ones in 'Ask Me Why' and 'You Can't Do That?'

Well, you could view it this way, and Beatles experts have fallen into

[6] Note that we shouldn't call it an 'Aeolian cadence' here because it is not a cadential setting: far from being a 'place of rest', we're being propelled into the brave new world of the bridge. We'll discuss later how the *major* IV (F♯), in minor, is briefly indicative of the Dorian mode.

both camps in their analyses of this song over the years.[7] However, given that the theme of the song has been described as 'a young man's declaration of independence – an assertion of self-sufficient defiance',[8] it is tempting to see this reflected in the independence of the song's tonality, with a repeatedly tonicised C♯m appearing at all the crucial moments.

Talking of wandering independence, while the relative minor is in the ascendency at these moments, we also flirt with the idea of a ii-V-I move to B major (at 0.58) but, instead we're back on E. And while this chord is certainly familiar territory, The Beatles make it appear novel (i.e. as a ♭III in C♯ minor), especially when followed by the jump to G♯7. It's as though we're being told that the 'place' in question ('my mind') is indeed secret, with the singer only prepared to reveal the briefest glimpse of his inner sanctum. Reinforcing the point, we only hear this bridge once in a song that only lasts 1.46 in its entirety. Blink and it's gone.

As with 'When I Get Home' (and as we'll soon see with 'I'll Be Back', 'I'm Only Sleeping' and many more), the tonality ploys of 'There's A Place' sum up the title itself, making us subliminally question exactly where we stand as the song unfolds. To paraphrase John Lennon – mind games.

Forget William Mann's ultra-brief tonality shift in 'Not A Second Time'; the fact is that alongside all those 'I-vi-I-vi' alternations on the debut album, we can find the humble origins of the many relative minor bridges that are widely assumed to have first emerged on *A Hard Day's Night*. From this early blueprint, we can trace their evolution and glean a songwriting nuance from each of them.

The next two examples are indeed from *A Hard Day's Night*, the first album on which The Beatles used major/minor shifts in a big way. We have already seen traces of this ambiguity in 'When I Get Home' – 'I'm Happy Just To Dance With You' cleverly uses the same versatile pivot premise (remember '♭VII = V'?) but now in mirror image. Look closely.

Having earlier seen how McCartney's 'I-iii' 'formula' accounts for the *verse*, we can now identify the bridge as in the *key* of C♯ minor – the relative minor of E. This time, instead of moving to the minor chord via the pivot as in both 'There's A Place' and 'When I Get Home', The Beatles

[7] Mellers calls it: 'resolutely diatonic, virtually without modulation', *Twilight Of The Gods*, p. 41. While Alan W. Pollack regards the bridge in the key of the relative minor with a modulation to B major aborted. 'Notes on ... Series' no. 31, 2001. *The 'Official' rec.music.beatles Home Page*, www.recmusicbeatles.com.

[8] MacDonald, *Revolution In The Head*, p. 58.

dive straight to the C♯m from E (no problem with that, of course, as it's just 'I-vi'!), with the V7 of the minor key then helping to reinforce the feeling of the minor key.

But note how they emerge from the excursion with those A and B major chords not leading us to the minor tonic but back to the brighter world of E major. The crux is the B chord – it can be interpreted as either the ♭VII of C♯m (the key we are now *leaving*) or as the V of E major (our *destination* key), and duly creates a 'Perfect' V-I move to E major. Indeed, the very same structure starts the song, as follows:

'I'm Happy Just To Dance With You'

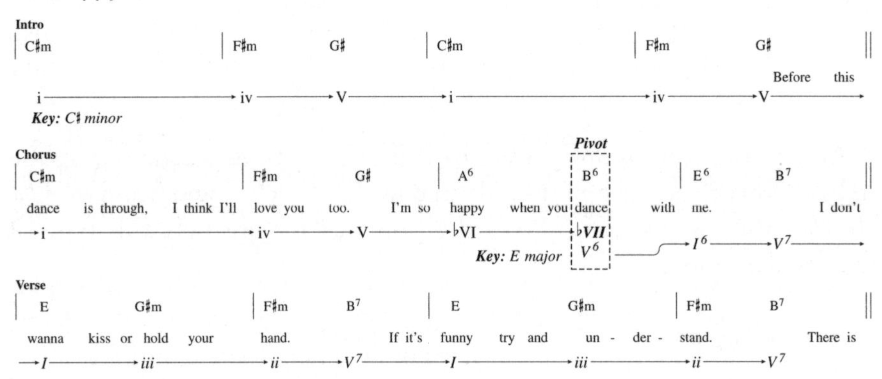

Still on *A Hard Day's Night*, The Beatles dealt us yet another variation of the 'minor middle' in the startling bridge of 'I Should Have Known Better'. On paper, it looks again like all we have here is a secondary dominant III7 that functions as 'V of vi' (certainly it manages to achieve dramatic lyrical emphasis in the song). But the shift to minor is far more fundamental than, say, in 'Ask Me Why' or on the cover of 'Falling In Love Again', that we saw in Chapter 4.

Just listen to the build-up to the bridge as the song dwells ominously on the B7 (at 0.39) and Lennon's frantic cry 'can't you see' heralds another of his famous confessions.

The effect here is of a clear point of *transition*, a harmonic delineation between the primitive major verse and the more intricate bridge in the relative minor. We can view that B7 as 'V of vi', if we like, but we soon get another B7 (like an exclamation mark on 'oh') that reinforces the V-i minor feeling, at least for those first eight bars, before the D chord crucially succeeds in tilting us back to G. As in 'I'm Happy Just To Dance With You', here's the '♭VII=V' pivot being used again for its V chord attributes. Bingo, we are back in major.

'I Should Have Known Better'

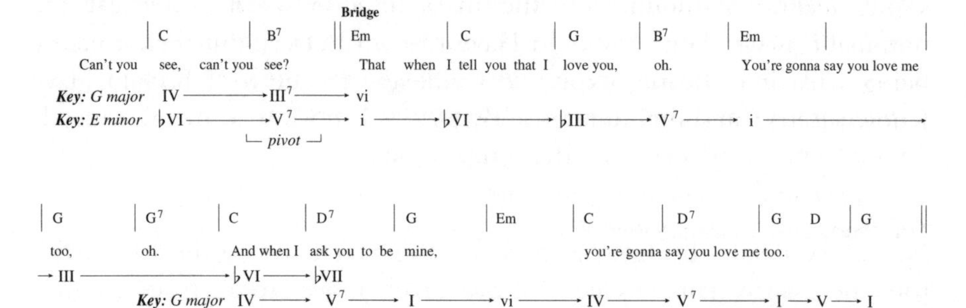

At this point, musos might want to dust off The Beatles' rendition of the stylish 'Don't Ever Change', popularised by The Crickets and heard on *Live At The BBC*, as this song shows the potential for precisely this type of transitionary move.

'Don't Ever Change'

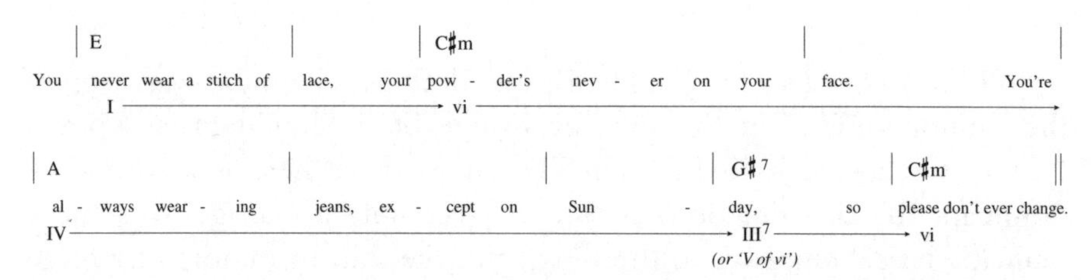

The verse looks headed for a simple I-vi-IV-V, only for the dominant to be shunned as the IV backtracks to III7 (another G♯7, at 0.19). Just like 'I Should Have Known Better', this effective formula is an inspired (and surprisingly rare) 'IV-III7-vi' that leads to a new section (this time a chorus) starting on the relative minor.[9]

'Paul and I wanted to be the Goffin and King of England', John Lennon

[9] Two other interesting examples that use this manoeuvre are Badfinger's 'Without You' and Elvis Costello's 'Oliver's Army'. Like 'Don't Ever Change' they arguably don't establish a new tonality but reach a predictable destination in an unpredictable way.

once admitted, no doubt in reference to this song which would also yield some other brilliant harmonic ideas, as we will see later.[10]

While both songs use the same process to create their most interesting harmonic activity, it's true that in 'Don't Ever Change' we don't feel such a strong feeling of modulation and that's because we don't 'rehear the dominant' as we do in 'I Should Have Known Better'. But then, tonality being what it is, Beatles experts describe the bridge to 'I Should Have Known Better' in subtly different ways.[11]

'vi at the bridge' – move or modulation?

Not every Beatles bridge that starts on the 'vi' relative to the 'old' major tonic necessarily makes us feel as if we've truly moved to the relative minor tonality. This may seem like theoretical hair-splitting, but it's actually important when appreciating a song. To call every opening 'vi at the bridge' a modulation, as some writers are prone to do, doesn't do justice to those Beatles songs that really do enjoy the sustained change in atmosphere that a *convincing*, reinforced key-switch to the relative minor brings.

Once again, the test in any instance is whether the shift to the minor chord is powerful enough to make the listener feel that the song is now revolving around and, more importantly – *resolving to*, a new tonic. This is really a function of the time spent in this tonicised territory and the context in which it occurs – including, obviously, the overall chord sequence. Remember our caveat that tonality shifts exist 'by degrees', which we can elaborate on with the notion of 'weak' and 'strong' modulations.

To illustrate this, compare for example the chorus to 'Drive My Car' with the bridge to 'We Can Work It Out'. For the *transition* in both cases is identical – both see a variation of the Three-Chord Trick that has the V lead to vi to start a new section: in each case on a Bm chord – *and with the*

[10] Jann S. Werner, *Lennon Remembers*, p. 47; referring to the writers of 'Don't Ever Change', Gerry Goffin and Carole King.

[11] Steven Porter sees that B7 as purely the 'secondary dominant of vi', *Rhythm And Harmony In The Music Of The Beatles*, p. 218. In contrast, Riley waxes lyrically over the 'major-verse-with minor bridge layout', *Tell Me Why*, p. 98. MacDonald dubs it a 'bitty minor middle sixteen', *Revolution In The Head*, p. 97. Meanwhile, O'Grady carefully splits the difference saying it 'begins in the relative minor . . . with harmonic leanings back to the original tonic', *The Music Of The Beatles*, p. 172.

same opening D note in the melody. However, we've deliberately labelled one bridge with a minor-key interpretation and left the other in major to draw attention to the differing emotional context.

'Drive My Car'

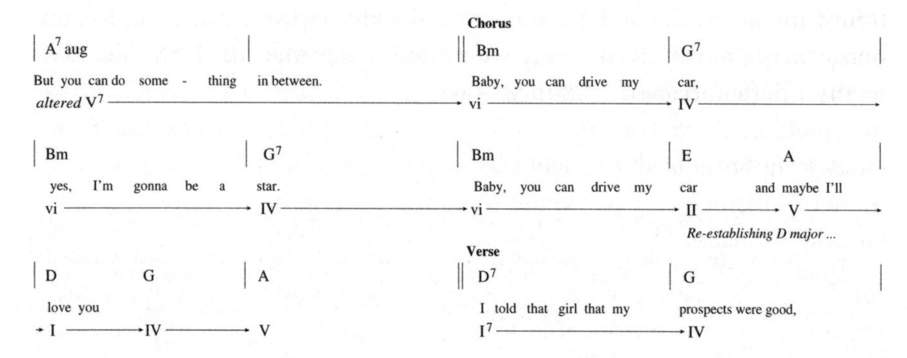

'We Can Work It Out'

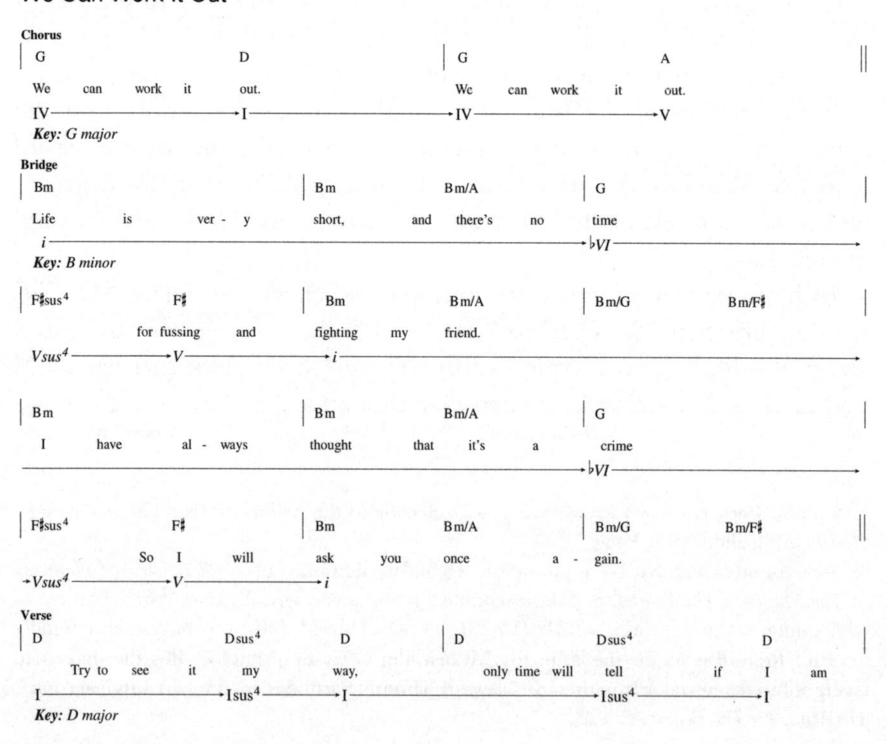

The bridge of 'We Can Work It Out' establishes a minor-key quality far more strongly – with a bassline that drops purposefully to the F♯ chord that acts as the dominant of Bm thereby establishing the minor mood of the new key centre – i minor. Once again, context is everything and, the bridge of 'We Can Work It Out' is assisted in its task by John's downbeat lyrical theme (which itself contrasts so starkly with Paul's famously optimistic, major verse). In this way we can view the A chord as the 'gateway' to the minor territory, a '♭VII-V' pivot that uses the ♭VII element to re-interpret the A to Bm move as ♭VII-i minor. This is in contrast to the cheeky euphoria of 'Drive My Car', where the same move is emotionally more of a major-ish 'V-vi' where we don't feel as if we've really strayed too far from D major. The same goes for the short bridges of 'In My Life', also on *Rubber Soul.* A 'vi' starts each four-bar strain but each time the sequence is headed inexorably for the A major tonic. While the song is reflective and poignant, we don't feel a dark, minor shift and, as with 'Drive My Car', this is partly because the relative minor chord is *not heard subsequently in conjunction with either its V or ♭VII chords.*

Moving forward in time, 'When I'm Sixty Four' saw The Beatles using another major verse/relative minor bridge. While history relates that this song was one of the earliest McCartney originals, it nevertheless features some subtle distinguishing marks that we haven't yet encountered.[12]

'When I'm Sixty Four'

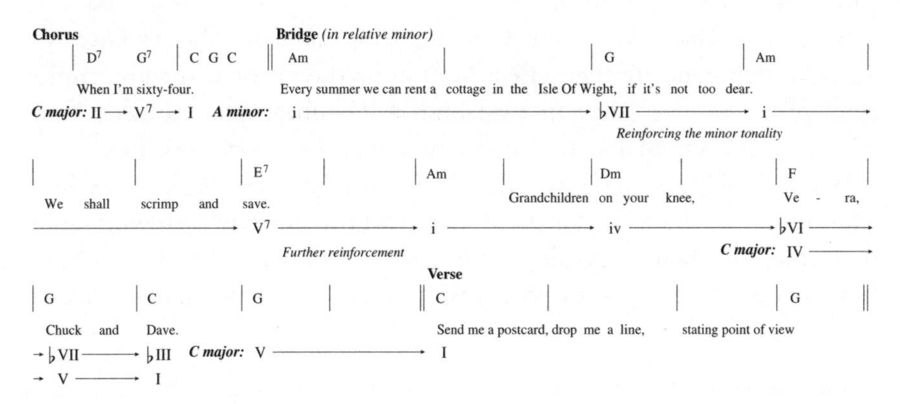

[12] 'Paul originally wrote the tune for "When I'm Sixty-Four" when he was sixteen in Liverpool and revived it for the [*Sgt. Pepper*] album'. Barry Miles, *Many Years From Now*, p. 319.

As with 'I'm Happy Just To Dance With You' there's no priming V or ♭VII chord to 'segue' us into the bridge, we jump straight in from the major tonic. But notice how both these chords do then appear, taking turns to reinforce our sense of the A minor tonality. There's even a Dm chord that gives a feeling of iv, but McCartney brilliantly interprets this as the relative minor of F major, a chord that then helps him to exit the bridge by means of the easiest of all 'retransition' ploys: IV-V-I (again just as we saw in 'I'm Happy Just To Dance With You'). In particular, the G chord really earns its keep here by appearing as *both* ♭VII of A minor and V of C, a dual manifestation for our favourite pivot chord.

It must be said that relative minor bridges were fairly rare in pre-Beatles pop – and that goes for those that just open on a vi chord, much less those that give a sense of formally modulating to it.[13] But even the handful of Beatles examples we've seen so far show how The Fab Four steadily exploited the potential of this ploy – which, of course, still doesn't involve a song leaving its diatonic key signature.[14]

Minor to relative major switches – a caveat

So far all our examples have focused on the 'relative minor bridge' – a phenomenon that appears in a song which has already fundamentally established the major tonality. But this is only one context in which The Beatles exploited the scope for switching between these same tonalities. There's also the mirror image.

Songs like 'Girl', 'Wait', 'I'm Only Sleeping', and 'You Never Give Me Your Money' generate their effect from using the major-to-relative minor principle in reverse. They first establish a downbeat *minor* tonality from which a following major section emerges like a breath of fresh air.

Before looking at some of these, let's first take a step back to see how The Beatles set the scene for these later tonal plays merely by toying subtly with one of their very first songwriting formulas: the 'I-vi' cliché. Immediately we can point out that William Mann was not alone in seeing

[13] Early inspirational 'middle eights on vi' that The Beatles would have heard include Paul Anka's 'It Doesn't Matter Anymore', as popularised by Buddy Holly. After a I-IV-V in the key of G major, the song moves determinedly to Em for the line: 'There's no use in me a-crying'. But even this soon moves back to a major tonic.

[14] Remember that the major scale and its relative minor share the same set of notes – and therefore the same key signature.

some 'Aeolian action' within a simple Beatles chord change that juxtaposed major and relative minor. Here's another pioneering Beatles critic, Wilfrid Mellers, writing about 'Any Time At All' back in 1973:

> 'the tonality wavers between B flat major and an aeolian G minor'[15]

Let's look again at that John Lennon quote we saw briefly in Chapter 3, which covers his memory of writing this very song:

> 'This was an effort at me writing "It Won't Be Long". Same ilk: C to A minor, C to A minor – with me shouting.'[16]

Never mind the key discrepancies ('Any Time At All' is in D major and 'It Won't Be Long' in E major) – both Mellers and Lennon seem to be describing the time-honoured 'I-vi-I-vi' vamp, but there's now an important twist in the tail.

In both these songs Lennon crucially *turns the sequence around* – opening first with the offending *minor* chord.

'Any Time At All'

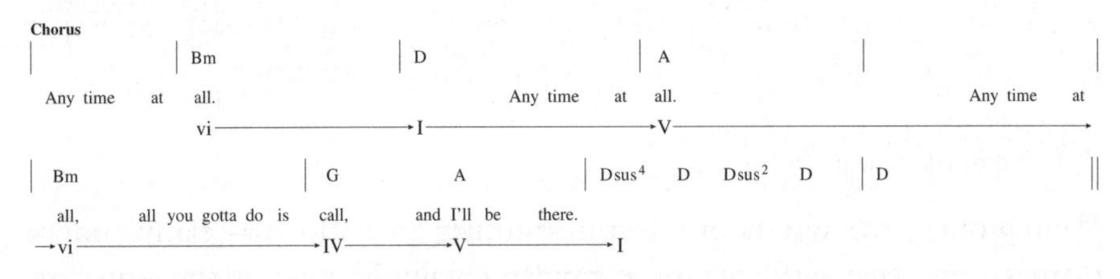

'It Won't Be Long'

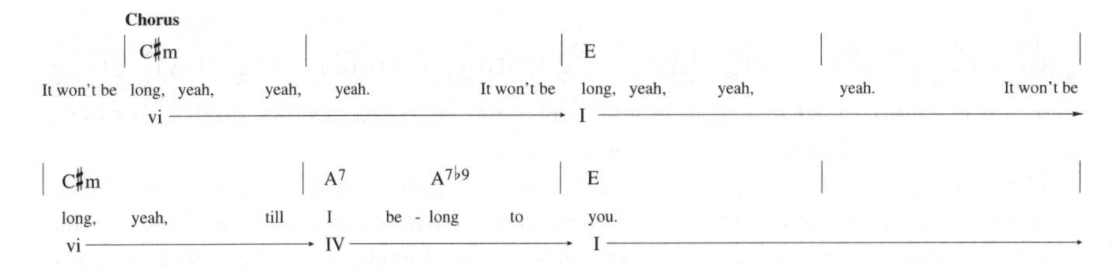

15 Wilfrid Mellers, *Twilight Of The Gods: The Music Of The Beatles*, p. 47.
16 *The Playboy Interviews*, p. 173.

A rather small difference, you might think. But in doing so, Lennon creates a very different effect from the 'I-vi-I-vi' we know so well. Now the listener is dealt a sudden *minor* body-blow before he regains his senses as the tonality gradually confirms the ensuing major chord as the tonic.[17] This type of wavering tonality (which can be also heard as early as 'All I've Got To Do') makes a subtle change from all those intros, verses and codas of 'Misery', 'From Me To You', 'Not A Second Time' through to 'It's Only Love' and 'Run For Your Life'.

An opening minor chord creates a different atmosphere and tonal reference point right from the start. After all, if you stop the song after the first bar, what key are you in – major or minor? That's just the point – for the name of the game even with such a simple two-chord structure is, once again, tonal ambiguity.

Of course, the 'opening vi' is something that we've already seen inherently in far more sophisticated Cycle Of Fifths songs, such as 'Rocky Raccoon', 'Golden Slumbers' and 'Your Mother Should Know', which each start on A minor before wending their way to C major. It's most practical to view these as 'vi chords that home in on their tonic', a view adopted, incidentally, by Guy Chambers from the practical point of view of a leading contemporary songwriter and musician.[18] Nevertheless, it's worth noting that there is healthy divergence among Beatles experts in respect of the ambiguity shown by precisely such structures.[19]

2. The relative major chorus

Having tested the waters of the minor tonality, we can now sample some Beatles songs that start out more fundamentally by establishing a minor-key verse before effecting a transition to relative major. The latter is now, of

[17] The Beatles would have registered this simple but nevertheless slick dichotomy as far back as 'Soldier Of Love' (*Live At The BBC*) which itself features *both* 'I-vi' *and* 'vi-I'. Each verse opens on the C♯m chord that soon yields to E, while the coda cleverly turns the sequence around, thereby establishing the major I more strongly.

[18] Guy Chambers in conversation (and piano demonstration) with the author, March 2000.

[19] Take 'Your Mother Should Know'. Everett, sees the ♭III being 'tonicised' in the key of A minor, *The Beatles As Musicians: Revolver Through The Anthology*, pp. 310–11; after earlier describing how the song's 'applied V7s' [secondary dominants] reveal the key of A minor as 'a pretence', p. 141. Tim Tucker gives a detailed rationalisation of the C major tonality throughout, *Total Guitar*, Issue 5, April 1995, p. 76. MacDonald throws a spanner in the works by seeing the song as exclusively in the key of A minor, *Revolution In The Head*, p. 455.

course, defined as *the key of the major triad built on ♭III* (for example, an A minor verse that moves to a chorus or bridge in C major). This can be seen as the mirror image of the major to relative minor move we've been examining so far this chapter – but note how the *character* of the song is now entirely different as a result.

John Lennon's 'Girl' is a good example, especially as it also encourages us to focus on the role of this very ♭III chord.

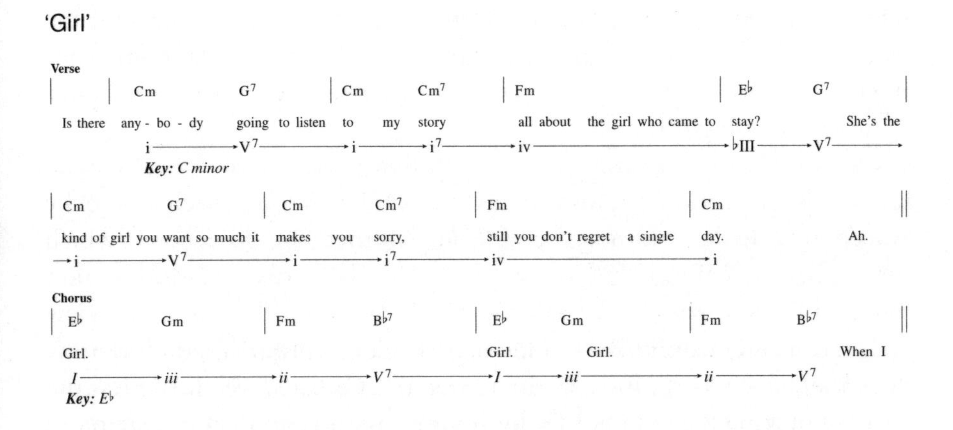

Lennon introduces the sound of the ♭III first on the word 'stay', progressing to V7 and back to the tonic to remain in minor for the repeat. But just as with the vi chord in a major key, so the ♭III is now the point of liberation – and when Lennon needs an upbeat chorus to swoon dreamily over the subject of the song, he knows he can to jump back to E♭ major, and effortlessly begin a familiar I-iii-ii-V7 sequence.

By the time of *Revolver*, Lennon had developed the principle a stage further. From a songwriting point of view, 'I'm Only Sleeping' is similar to 'Girl' in certain respects – but now Lennon cleverly makes use of a new chord from minor – the ♭VI, which lies conveniently up a fourth/down a fifth from the ♭III. Specifically, he exploits it as a 'pivot' chord when targeting the relative major (G♭), which once again represents the desired major harmony with which to generate the song's lyrical contrast. But just watch how Lennon achieves the transition within the whole theme of bleary-eyed sleepwalking:

'I'm Only Sleeping'

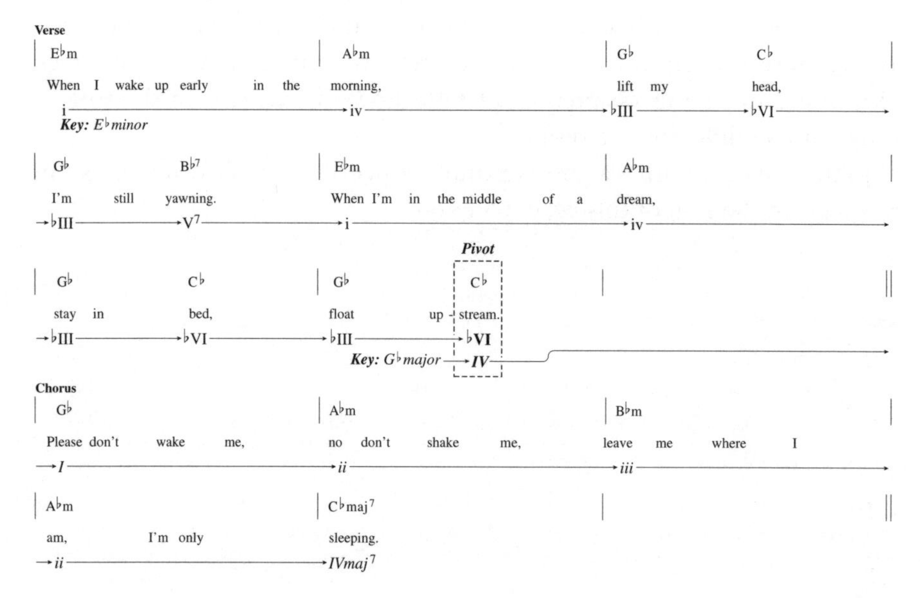

The first time around, the ♭VI just acts as an embellishment as we resume the same i–iv of 'Girl'. But, on the repeat, the G♭–C♭ move almost has the effect of making the ♭VI chord a 'local tonic', with Lennon encouraging us to literally 'float upstream' as that same slide to C♭ major defies the currents. We've labelled it however as a 'pivot' as, from here, a Plagal return to the G♭ now has the effect of making *this* chord the 'new I', duly cueing the chorus action in the relative major as intended.

Some writers view this chorus as maintaining the minor mood, while others even see the whole song in a single key. Again we can only stress that this type of unique Lennon construction naturally encourages a variety of interpretations. Ours is based both on the ease, in practice, of identifying a type of ascending 'diatonic walk' (remember the verses of 'Here, There And Everywhere' and 'If I Fell' and the chorus of 'Getting Better'?). More to the point, the shift in tonality at this point reflects the restlessness of the lyrics, with the singer clearly now pleading against being disturbed from his blissful state. As we'll see later with 'I'm So Tired', here is Lennon brilliantly leading the listener while apparently not quite *compus mentis*.

Other songs that follow this same minor-to-major dichotomy include 'Wait' (which we'll examine in Chapter 8 for its Dorian leanings) and

'You Never Give Me Your Money', explored later in this chapter. And, of course, a stream of great pop songs hinge on this duality between major and relative minor. Spanning a range of genres we can include Roy Wood's wonderful 'Blackberry Way' (Em verse, G chorus); Sting's 'Roxanne' (Gm verse, Bb chorus); Carly Simon's 'You're So Vain' and Elvis Costello's 'Watching The Detectives' (both Am verse, and C chorus). In a rockier vein we can include Bon Jovi's 'Livin' On A Prayer', and Oasis's 'Slide Away' which, incidentally, both use the '♭VII=V' pivot to move between minor and major and in order to match a conceptually similar lyrical premise.[20]

But while all these songs set out very clear points of transition, The Beatles' inspired sense of tonal ambiguity between major and relative minor reached a magical peak with 'And I Love Her' – yet another from the dual-key stable of *A Hard Day's Night.*

The special case of 'And I Love Her'

Here we drift ominously between tonalities, only ever establishing a firm foothold at certain fleeting moments. As a result, the song makes for an essential (if, at times, infuriating) case study against which to pit our understanding of tonality. It is also designed to lay the ground for other tonally ambiguous Beatles excursions that go far beyond this very specific major/relative minor context.

The first complicating factor here is the presence of the E6 chord in the intro, which challenges the listener as to the predominance of major or minor *because it can be regarded as an inversion of C♯m.*[21]

[20] Walser captures the power of the move when he refers to 'Livin' On A Prayer''s 'moment of transcendence' as, after the 'Aeolian grunge' of C-D-Em, we move to the G major chorus 'which symbolically and phenomenologically resolves [Tommy and Gina's hardships]', *Running With The Devil,* p. 122. Compare this to the switch from negative to positive sentiments in 'Slide Away' at the point of 'now that you're mine', as we move from Am to C major [N.B. As well as the G pivot, 'Slide Away' also cleverly uses the V7 of Am (E7) to return to Am for the 'lift' into the guitar solo].

[21] Refer back to Chapter 1, if necessary, where we demonstrated the relationship between (in the key of C) C6 and Am. But note also how the version on *Anthology I* sees the opening E chord as a plain strummed open-string triad, without the 6th in what is an uncomplicated major intro over a single chord. Until, that is, the verse gets underway.

'And I Love Her'

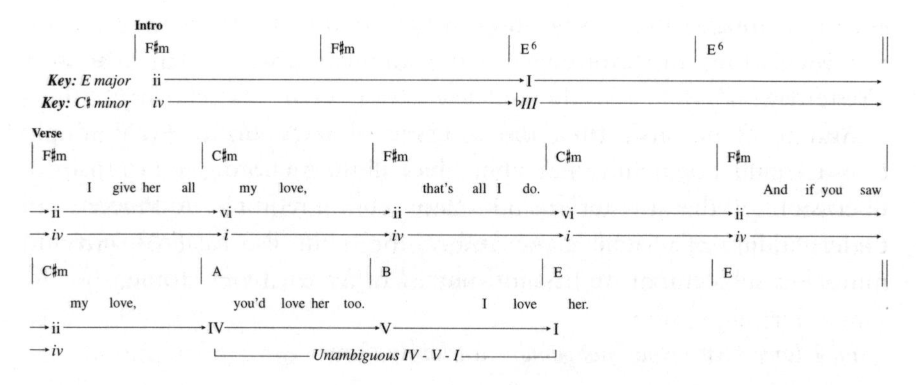

This author hears the intro as major, with the verse opening with a minor 'iv–i' as the F♯m now settles into an alternation with the C♯m itself. Meanwhile, the refrain: 'You'd love her too, I love her', would appear to reflect a clear 'IV–V–I' to at least the temporary tonic of E major. But it seems you can't win, for even this overview is at odds with certain Beatles experts. But that's just the point with genuine tonality ambiguity – it's open to interpretation.[22]

The same goes for the bridge – the harmony now appears to be unequivocally minor, with the C♯m now being even more at the centre of things, alternating against its natural minor dominant and an Aeolian ♭VII.

'And I Love Her'

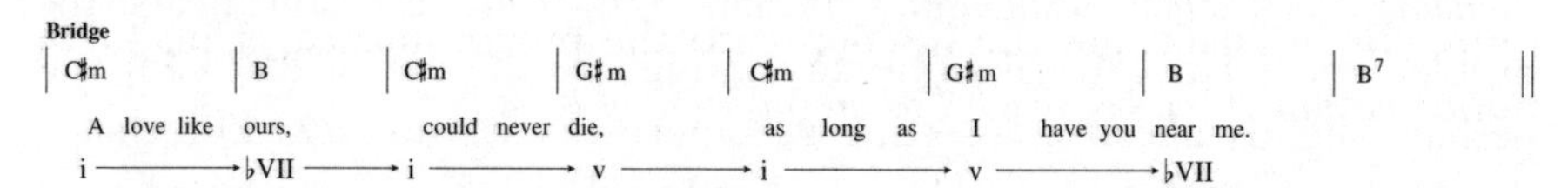

Once again, while on balance this author feels the bridge to be in minor, he accepts that others might analyse it in relation to E major.[23]

Whatever the view, the effect of this song is not just down to the simple pitting of major/minor verses and bridges against each other. For the

[22] For example, O'Grady regards the move to E major in the refrain as 'an embellishing deceptive cadence rather than as an authentic one confirming the major mode'. *The Music Of The Beatles* . . ., p. 182.

[23] Pollack, while acknowledging the ambiguity, treats C♯m as 'i' in the verse but 'vi' in the bridge, 'Notes on ... Series' no. 3, 2000. *The 'Official' rec.music.beatles Home Page*, www.recmusicbeatles.com. Ultimately, Everett confirms the tonal puzzle: 'Any suggestion as to which area [I or vi] should be understood as tonic, results only in ambiguity'; *The Beatles As Musicians: Revolver Through The Anthology*, p. 20.

ambiguity also results from the way the verse and refrain blend seamlessly as a single song section. It's no surprise that John Lennon heaped praise on this McCartney masterpiece with the comment: 'I consider it his first "Yesterday"'.[24]

And that's not forgetting the song's final conundrum – the simply celestial (and potentially indecipherable) closing chord. Conceptually, a discussion of that mysterious D major chord requires not merely an understanding of relative major and minor – but also *parallel* major and minor – a subject that we first introduced in 'When I Get Home'.

'And I Love Her' – the final chord – a Picardy third?

Just to complicate things, the song has now modulated up a half step by the time we reach the coda (starting with George's guitar solo at 1.28).

'And I Love Her'

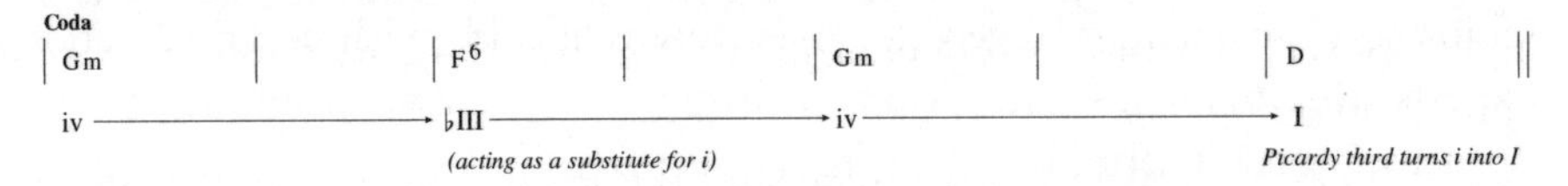

While we haven't yet formally introduced moves to different key signatures, this represents a gentle introduction as the entire song has merely shifted up a semitone, creating a lift for the listener – *but without changing the chordal relationships in any way*. Our ear still hears the problematic 'relative' tonal ambiguity though, to the extent that C♯m was perhaps slightly ahead in asserting its superiority, it's now the Dm that is the strongest tonal draw with the F chord in the closing vamp heard as an inversion of this tonic.

This interpretation means that we can reconcile that closing D major as a classical gambit whereby a minor tonic defers to its parallel 'I major' for a final confident *coup de grâce*. In this sense, the trick is conceptually identical to the final chord in 'A Taste Of Honey'. Listen to the closing chord on The Beatles' cover on *Please Please Me*, as the song ends not on the expected F♯m, but on F♯ *major* (at 1.56).

This is a trick known as a *Tierce De Picardie*, or 'Picardy third', whereby a minor tonic chord gets its ♭3rd tweaked up to a major 3rd to lift a sequence

[24] *The Playboy Interviews*, p. 154.

out of the gloom with all the overtones of 'joy', 'enlightenment' and 'relief' that this implies.[25] A famous example in pop would later appear at the end of Pink Floyd's multi-movement *opus*, 'Shine On You Crazy Diamond'. There, from the anguish and sorrow, a final Picardy third (C major in C minor) lends a glimmer of hope – or at least the prospect of spiritual rebirth – for the acknowledged inspiration behind the piece, the maverick former Floyd member, Syd Barrett.[26]

In much the same way, the effect in 'And I Love Her' is to dramatically re-affirm the immortality of the love between the two parties. 'A love like ours could never die,' we're told in verse 2, and this final gesture seals the bond.

In summarising the song as a whole, one can suggest that the major/minor ambiguity works ingeniously on a deep level in the context of the lyrics. For this is not a tale of yearning, or 'one-way', unrequited love. As much as 'I give her all my love', so 'she gives me everything'. The feelings flow both ways, unconditionally, spontaneously and in ways that cannot be harnessed. Just like the 'bright' stars and 'dark' sky, there is a higher power at work as reflected in the tonality shifts that refuse to be pinned down.

The Picardy third helps us understand the distinction between parallel major/minor and relative major/minor, as the former involves no root switch for the tonic – merely a change in the *quality* of the triad and the implied scale that goes with it. Before examining The Beatles' legacy in this chapter's second category of key switches, a look at four ubiquitous and highly versatile minor-key progressions makes for an essential study. These are:

a) the 'minor two-five-one': 'ii7♭5-V7-i minor'
b) the diatonic minor Cycle Of Fifths
c) the 'VI7-V7-i minor' resolution
d) the minor 'rock runs': '♭VI'-♭VII-i' and 'i-♭VII-♭VI-V7'

[25] MacDonald duly describes the Picardy third effect in 'And I Love Her' as 'celestial', *Revolution In The Head*, p. 97. As regards the tonal ambiguity, Everett suggests, 'At this final cadence, it is difficult – if not impossible – to hear the C♯ minor and D minor areas as [vi] to tonics of E and F, respectively' (*The Quarry Men Through Rubber Soul*, p. 225); while also acknowledging that the closing D major tests the relationship between I and VI *major*, that will later be central to 'Something' (*Revolver Through The Anthology*, p. 354).

[26] Picardy third closing chords feature in songs such as Eric Clapton's version of 'I Shot The Sheriff', Lionel Richie's 'Hello' and The Cure's 'Fire In Cairo' (with Robert Smith acknowledging a Beatles influence, in conversation with the author, November 1997).

a) The 'minor two-five-one': 'ii7♭5-V7-i minor'

Given how we've trumpeted the incessant versatility of the ii-V-I progression and all its variations, it's surprising that the chord built on the second degree in a minor context has so far been conspicuous by its absence. Compared with the major tonality, chords on this degree in minor pop are somewhat rare, partly because of the fact that V can be primed so easily by other chords (including, as we'll see, ♭VI7) while the tonic itself is easily reached directly from other scale members, like ♭III, ♭VI, and ♭VII.

Nevertheless, the second degree does appear on occasions, and The Beatles used it in three main ways: 'ii7♭5', 'ii' and 'II7', the first of which is by far the most interesting.

If we refer back to our theory, this m7♭5 is the official 'supertonic' in the diatonic harmonised natural minor scale. This deliciously dissonant chord is standard fare in classical music and jazz where it appears in the 'ii7♭5-V7-i' progression in dozens of minor-key classics, including 'Autumn Leaves' and 'Blue Bossa'. Its rarity in pop is surprising, however, given that it can create such gut-wrenching poignancy in love songs. One thinks instantly of Elton John's 'Sorry Seems To Be The Hardest Word' and Gilbert O'Sullivan's 'Alone Again Naturally', which both stress the m7♭5 throughout as a melancholy panacea for an inconsolable songwriter.

While most pop writers of the fifties and early sixties couldn't cope with the ultra-dark sound of the m7♭5, The Beatles showed how to use it in a few select examples. It's most easily understood in 'You Never Give Me Your Money', where it appears as part of this same classical/jazzy 'ii7♭5-V7-i minor' at the climax of each compelling verse cycle.[27]

While we're on this extract, notice how (at the end of verse 2) McCartney exits those dark minor strains by means of our favourite pivot chord to take us to that contrasting bright major section. It's that G major again, which leads us V-I to C major (at 1.07–1.09) for the 'out of college, money spent' bridge. The chord also moved V-I within the minor cycle, of course, but now we stay there – as a key centre – and develop a simple, secondary dominant idea that we visited in Chapter 4.

[27] For an early example of Paul's use of the ii7♭5-V7-i check out the ultra sophisticated 'It's For You', as recorded by Cilla Black, in 1964. Dm7♭5-G7 cues the Cm tonic, first at the bridge at 0.35 ('They said . . .').

'You Never Give Me Your Money'

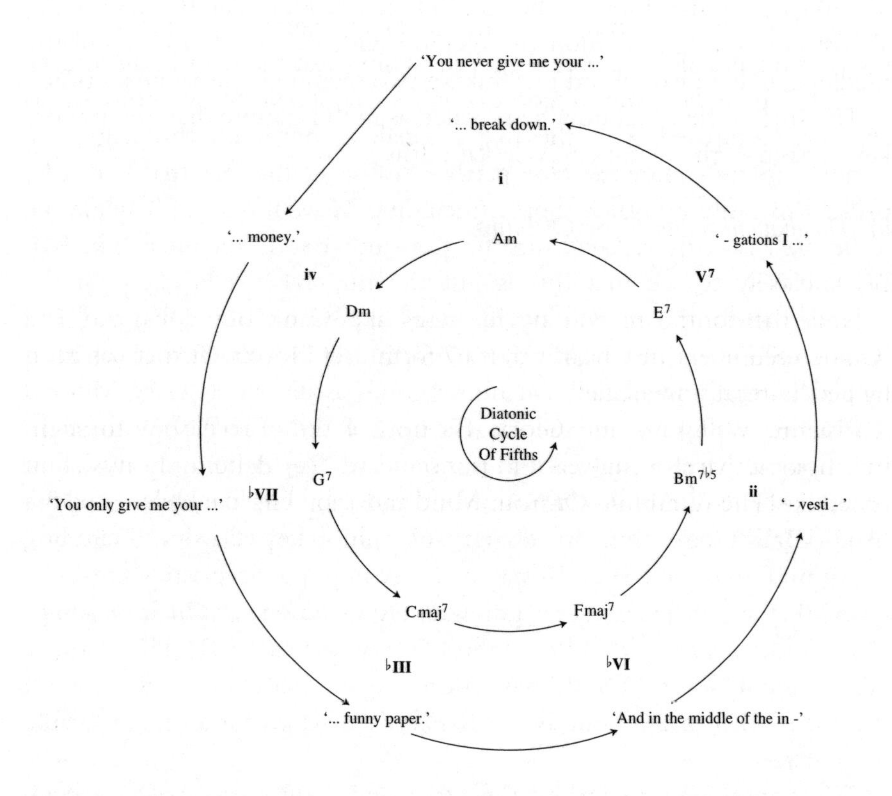

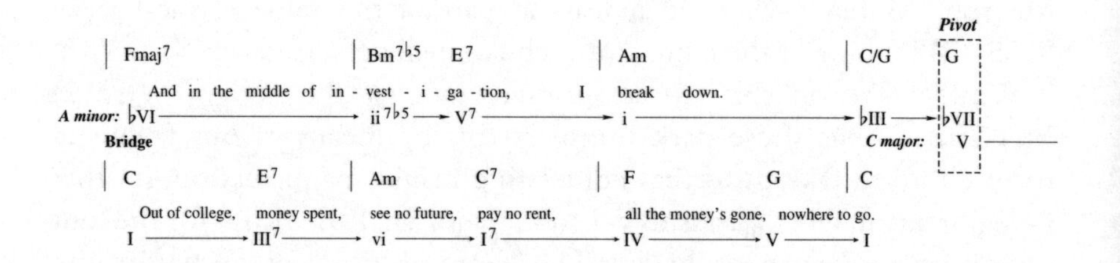

This is a great way of demonstrating to songwriters how unrelated 'chunks' of pop harmony can be pieced together. Here The Beatles do it in almost cut-and-paste fashion (in keeping with the whole history of the medley), with a pivot chord just linking two seemingly disparate sections.

The first of these can now be revealed as nothing more than the minor-key version of the diatonic Cycle Of Fifths.

b) The diatonic minor Cycle Of Fifths

Look closely to see that this is just the minor-key equivalent of the extended diatonic run we saw in songs like 'Can't Buy Me Love' and 'Golden Slumbers' in Chapter 3. It's a formulaic movement that has been tapped (virtually identically) in minor songs as diverse as Gary Moore's 'Parisienne Walkways' and Gloria Gaynor's 'I Will Survive'. With slight variations, we've also enjoyed it in jazz standards like 'Autumn Leaves', film tunes like 'The Windmills Of Your Mind'; and pop hits like Helen Reddy's 'Angie Baby'.

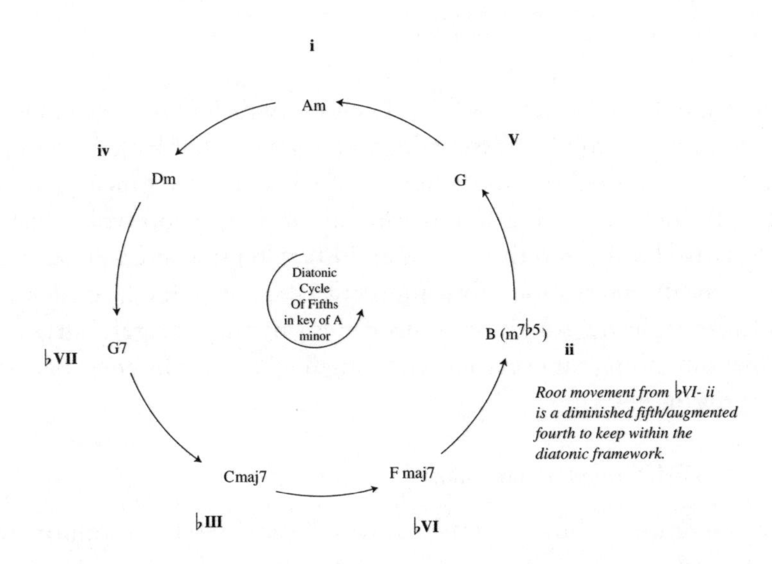

Despite the term 'fifths', we can see that, technically, not each and every one of these chord changes follows the formula quite as religiously as we saw in major. This is a quirk of the cycle in minor, and occurs because the drop between the F and B roots *must be an augmented fourth in order for the roots to remain diatonic to the key.* A further pure descent of a fifth at this point would maintain the visual symmetry but spoil the party by bringing in new notes from beyond the scale. Nevertheless, the ear is successfully fooled, and accepts the tritone root-jump for the very reason that, hot on its heels, our very same 'ii7♭5-V7-i minor' cadence will yield such a perfect resolution of tension.

And how appropriate that McCartney should negotiate this particular quirk of music theory over the very word 'negotiations'.[27]

Of course, the same minor Cycle Of Fifths soon reappears as 'Money' is reprised in the minor-key 'filling' in the 'sandwich' between the two choruses of the upbeat pub sing-a-long, 'Carry That Weight'.

'Carry That Weight'

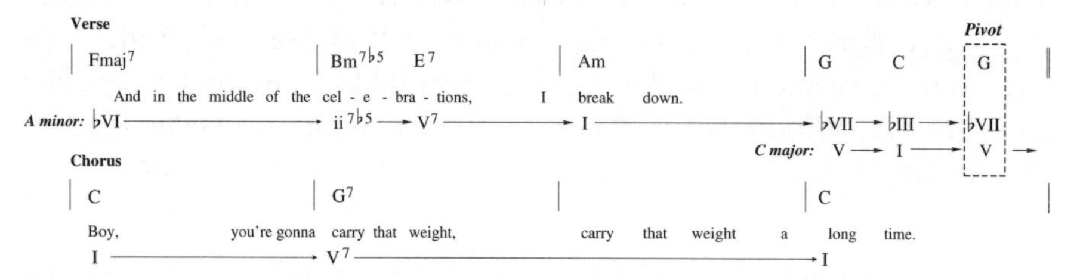

This time the pivot nature of that G chord (which makes the same transition from minor to major) is made even more obvious by just continuing the V-I move throughout the whole major key section. Once again, here are The Beatles contrasting an intricate minor progression with a blatantly simple, two-chord vamp that acts as an instant 'tension-breaker'. As a brief philosophical observation, this moment also provides a clue to the popularity of Beatles songwriting insofar as this type of careful structuring provides something for everyone, covering the bases for listeners of varying sophistication.

c) The '♭VI7-V7-i minor' resolution

A very common but effective way to cadence to a minor tonic involves using a ♭VI7 chord as a 'pre-dominant chord' to prepare the

[27] Look back to Chapter 3 to see how this quirk also occurs in major instances where the Cycle Of Fifths encompasses the vii chord (or movement of a fifth to that vii chord.) Think of the C-F♯m7 move in 'Here, There And Everywhere' in the key of G, or Peter Skellern's extended walk around the cycle in 'You're A Lady', whose chorus, in the key of C, starts with a C-F♯m7 move of an augmented fourth.

V7.[28] In this way the two chords together are just a way of extending the inevitability of the resolution to the tonic, with the semitone drop to V7 being as effortless as the following V7 cadence to the tonic is satisfying. The '♭VI7-V7' is a defining part of the structure of minor classics as varied as Gershwin's 'Summertime'; B.B. King's 'The Thrill Is Gone'; Danny Kirwan's 'Jigsaw Puzzle Blues'; The Eurythmics' 'Sweet Dreams (Are Made Of This)'; and Shirley Bassey's 'Big Spender'.

Whatever we call it, The Beatles would have encountered it on their own Hamburg renditions of Gershwin's 'Summertime', while if we dig into the *Anthology 1* archives we can actually hear them absorbing it on 'Besame Mucho', where it showcases the definitive cadential nature of the progression.

'Besame Mucho'

| Gm | E♭7 D7 | Gm | ||

I'll love you for - ev - er, say that you'll al - ways be mine.

i ⟶ ♭VI7 ⟶ V7 ⟶ i

From these humble origins let's jump grandly to *Abbey Road* to see how Lennon transports the same device majestically to the stirring classical coda of 'I Want You (She's So Heavy)'. In case we're still not sure what it sounds like, we can hear it 14 times – about once every 12.5 seconds, between 4.49 and 7.44 when the rug is pulled from under our feet as the tape was cut.

'I Want You (She's So Heavy)'

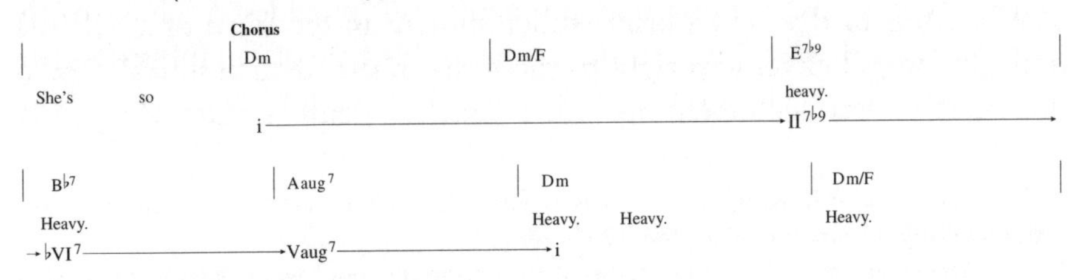

But, notice that we don't hear the cadence when we first hear the ♭VI7-V7 in the intro. It seems like the identical premise, as B♭7 cues an altered V:

[28] We've already seen this pre-dominant concept in action as IV, ii and II7 each also fulfil this function – we will develop it further in the next few chapters: look out in particular for the '♭VII-V7' move.

an A augmented chord that is surely going to only one place (D minor) as it hangs in the air from 0.10–0.14. But no – for Lennon's opening line does not unfold over the D minor tonic that we expect but, disarmingly, over an A minor chord that now dominates this fancy re-write of a standard minor blues sequence.[29]

Once again, The Beatles have thwarted our expectations as we wonder (not for the first time) 'where's the tonic?'. It's a question not answered by the final moment of execution at the end of the song which, according to Sod's Law, just happens to occur on the very V-chord that we know can take us to two different places! Ultimately the song appears to be a brilliant double-edged tribute to both blues and classical music that has attracted some colourful criticism over the years.[30]

d) The minor rock runs: '♭VI-♭VII-i' and 'i-♭VII-♭VI-V7'

We can't discuss the minor tonality without exploring a family of sequences that has become arguably the most famous in the history of minor-key rock and pop.[31] These sequences all exploit the ♭VII and ♭VI, the major triads a whole step and two whole steps below the root, respectively.

'♭VI-♭VII-i'

Once again, The Beatles were at the forefront of the development of each variation in pop. The *White Album*, for example, finds them parading a version of the first type in 'The Continuing Story Of Bungalow Bill', in another relative minor bridge that follows a major verse structure.

While this bridge sees a brief embellishment in the form of a ♭III bass note, the overall effect gets right to the heart of the Aeolian sound. Down the years it has accounted for such timeless gems as Led Zeppelin's

[29] Take a listen to B.B. King's (or rather Roy Hawkins') minor blues, 'The Thrill Is Gone', which similarly features i, iv, ♭VI7 and V7 chords.

[30] Ian MacDonald wrote: 'Sexually addicted to her, he [Lennon] was helplessly addicted, a predicament grindingly explicit in his chord sequence: the sickening plunge from E7 to B flat 7; the augmented A that drags his head up to make him go through it all again. The hammering flat ninth that collapses, spent, on the song's insatiable D minor arpeggio . . . Lennon is literally obsessed . . .', *Revolution In The Head*, p. 301.

[31] 'Minor chord sequences in pop and rock are dominated by I, ♭VII, ♭VI in either direction', sums up Rikky Rooksby, citing songs as varied as 'Achilles Last Stand', 'In The Air Tonight', 'Dreams', 'Because The Night', 'Theme From S-Express' and 'Running Up That Hill'; *How To Write Songs On Guitar*, p. 44.

'The Continuing Story of Bungalow Bill'

Verse

Am Am/C	F G	Am Am/C	F G
He went out tiger hunting with his	elephant and gun.	In case of acc - i - dents, he	always took his mom.
i ⟶	♭VI ⟶ ♭VII ⟶	i ⟶	♭VI ⟶ ♭VII ⟶

'Stairway To Heaven' (coda), Blue Oyster Cult's 'Don't Fear The Reaper', Eric Clapton's 'Layla' (chorus), Free's 'Wishing Well' (verse), 10cc's 'Wall Street Shuffle' and the Hendrix-via-Dylan standard, 'All Along The Watchtower' (all of it!). It's not just 'classic rock' stars who plunder it either – listen to The Cure's '10.15 Saturday Night', Lionel Richie's 'Hello' and Martha & The Muffins 'Echo Beach'. There are dozens from any era you want to pick. In a contemporary setting, it's a move Noel Gallagher favours on 'It's Good To Be Free' and 'The Masterplan'.[32]

'i-♭VII-♭VI-V7'

Rather than retrieving the tonic by a modal ascent, this variation continues the descent, wrapping-up the cycle with the more classical-sounding '♭VI7-V7-i minor' we dwelt on earlier. In fact, a look back at 'We Can Work It Out' shows this definitive minor progression being outlined by the bass line – another reason that we feel the sense of the minor bridge so strongly.

An early Beatles rendition of this historic sequence can be heard on *Anthology 1*, as the suitably politically incorrect middle eight of Leiber & Stoller's 'Three Cool Cats' is revealed as merely two hearings of Em-D-C-B7 (starting at 0.42).

This recording dates from the famous Decca session of New Year's Day 1962, though John Lennon reveals the more likely source for its appearance in various Beatles originals when explaining that his own masterpiece, 'I'll Be Back', was 'my variation of the chords in a Del Shannon song'.[33] John may not have mentioned the specific song but without doubt it is the masterful 'Runaway'. Dating from 1961, here is the defining early blueprint for 'Aeolian harmony' – a term that describes

[32] 'The Masterplan' is another Oasis song that makes use of the '♭VII=V' pivot (G) to take the song between the relative keys of Am and C major.

[33] *The Playboy Interviews*, p. 155.

decades of rock and pop music that plunder the coolest chords from the natural minor scale.[34]

'Runaway'

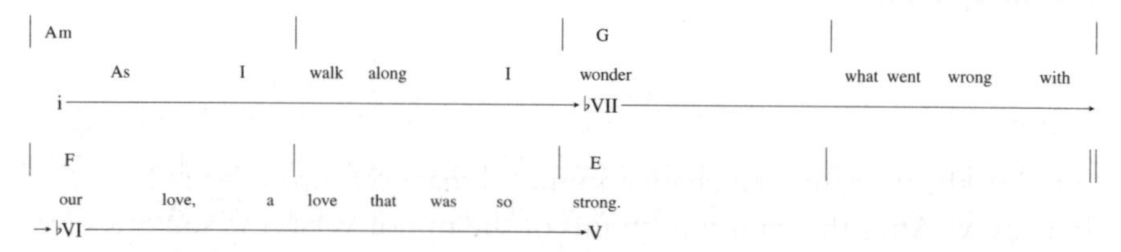

It's no exaggeration to say that this 'i-♭VII-♭VI-V7' progression has become legendary in its own right, a universally understood vehicle for 'jamming' guitarists everywhere. As well as 'Runaway' and The Ventures 'Walk Don't Run', the identical sequence would later spawn such classics as The Animals' 'Don't Let Me Be Misunderstood', The Stray Cats' 'Stray Cat Strut' and Dire Straits' 'Sultans Of Swing'. Each repeatedly cycles around a sequence whose slow-burning minor menace can also be spotted throughout Flamenco and Latin music.[35] Without question, here is a progression that 'works', with that feeling of romantic inevitability as the roots fall down the natural minor scale. If further proof were needed, when *MOJO* magazine nominated their '100 Greatest Singles Of All Time', in August 1997, they settled on The Beach Boys' 'Good Vibrations' as their No. 1, a 1966 song whose verse follows the same formula precisely. The Beach Boy's Tony Asher recalls:

> 'I remember hearing this riff that he [Brian Wilson] liked which is the basis of the song. I wrote an entire lyric to it'.[36]

The Beatles had taken their place in this great tradition with 'I'll Be Back', back in 1964, a song that has (literally) a twist in its tail. And one that

[34] Middleton credits Alf Bjornberg (1985) as the originator of the term that actually covers some other subsets of the mode, including the i-iv-v, not to mention the use of ♭III, ♭VI and ♭VII in a *major* setting – the subject of our next chapter. *Studying Popular Music*, p. 198.

[35] Not forgetting the many great songs based on this sequence but with the briefest of variations. Some of the author's favourites include The Mamas And The Papas' 'California Dreamin'', (which revisits ♭VII before a V7 sus 4); Jimi Hendrix's '(Hey Baby) New Rising Sun' (replaces V with IV); and The Cure's 'Fire In Cairo' (embellishes ♭VII with ♭III during the descent).

[36] *MOJO*, Issue 45, August 1997, p. 86. 'Good Vibrations' features two hearings of 'E♭m-D♭-C♭-B♭' followed by a shift to the relative major for the chorus – through a clever functional V7–I move, i.e., D♭7-G♭ (at 0.24).

ironically stemmed from another fundamental piece of novelty for which Del Shannon's 'Runaway' is also famous. That song featured a bridge not in the relative major – but in the *parallel* major, a concept that we can now develop more fully.

Part 2 – parallel major/minor switches

Listen to the fundamental change in mood that accompanies the bridge of 'Runaway'. After the haunting strains of the minor verse, the song receives a powerful emotional lift for the repeated cries of 'I wonder', with this upbeat feeling confirming that we are indeed back in 'major territory'.

This time the relationship is not one of relative major and minor as defined by 'i-♭III' (our mirror image of 'I-vi') but *i minor* and *I major.* For Shannon's song now unfolds with the commonest of sequences in the key of A major, including an alternation of A and F♯m (yes, our original 'I-vi') – sounds that are light years removed from the earlier strains of Am and F *natural.*[37]

And while 'I'll Be Back' also features a parallel major bridge (in fact three!), the song is most interesting for the way it brings an A *major* chord back into a *minor* verse sequence!

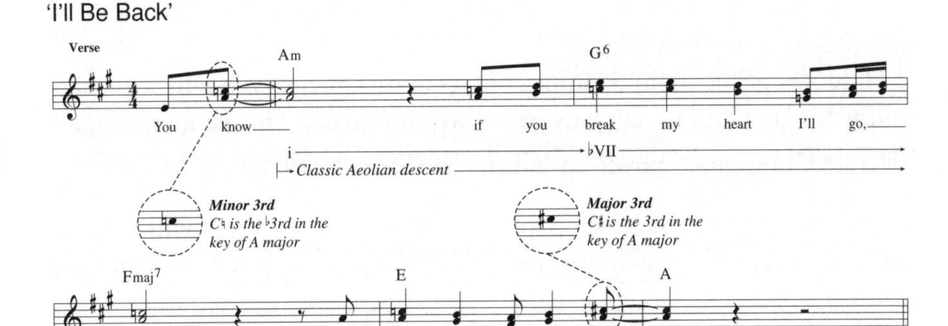

Ultimately Lennon is merely exploiting the basic theory that says that, having 'arrived' at E7, he can *go just as easily to I major as i minor.* But the

[37] Jeff Lynne says of 'Runaway': 'I love the shifts from major to minor – and the frantic atmosphere'. *MOJO*, Issue 45, August 1997, p. 69.

icing on the cake here is the melody line, or, more specifically, the *harmony* part which features *both* the major/minor-defining ♭3rd and natural 3rd of A, in what creates one of the most ingenious of all the many Beatles musical manifestations of lyrical themes. Listen as the 'resigned' C natural moves to 'optimistic' C♯, reflecting the change in sentiment as 'I'll go' becomes 'I'll be back' - and with a hopeful *rising* cadence. Genius at work.

The parallel major/minor relationship defines every aspect of 'I'll Be Back', from the A major intro that gives way to the A minor verse, only to reassert itself in each of the three bridges (with two different constructions). Finally, as if we were still in any doubt that the song is the embodiment of tonal ambiguity, Lennon even goes so far as to alternate A major and A minor repeatedly in the harrowing, two-chord closing vamp.[38] Here are The Beatles once again breaking the rules of tonality. For just as we sometimes struggle to distinguish between *relative* major and minor so, here, we have no chance of separating *parallel* major and minor.

Admittedly, this type of tonal intertwining is an extreme case. Most of The Beatles' parallel switches (which go equally to either major or minor depending on what key the verse starts out in) are clearly delineated in a bridge section. 'Norwegian Wood' is a case in point. It features a simple minor progression that is of most interest for the way that a 'plain' ii triad (in a minor key) leads us back from the bridge to the major verse with, yes, a ii-V-I sequence. This device will reappear in Chapter 10 as *the* modulation mechanism *par excellence*.[39]

Here we get a straight drop from Lennon's major verse to a parallel minor bridge that's usually attributed to McCartney. This is interesting, as the parallel minor bridge of 'Michelle' is famously claimed by Lennon.[40]

[38] The coda of 'Magical Mystery Tour' features a similar idea: a plunge from D major to the darker tones of D minor with the melody abandoning the F♯ note in favour of the defining F natural.

[39] Meanwhile, for a II7 chord in minor, check out the cover of 'Three Cool Cats', on *Anthology I*, which cycles tirelessly around the simple sequence: F♯7-B7-Em. For a subtle comparison with a Beatles example see 'Not Guilty' where, in mid-verse, Harrison uses B7-E7 to prime the Am which helps to temporarily enhance the latter's tonic credentials after the opening E minor had appeared to assert itself as the parent key.

[40] 'Where do I go to now?' Lennon remembers McCartney asking after humming the verse to the song. 'I'd been listening to Nina Simone's "I Put A Spell On You" and I just thought of a similar middle eight. "I love you, I love you, I Love You", I went . . ." ', *The Playboy Interviews*, pp. 122–3. McCartney: 'the original was just the chorus. That sounds like Nina Simone. I'll give him ten points for that', *Many Years From Now*, p. 274.

'Norwegian Wood'

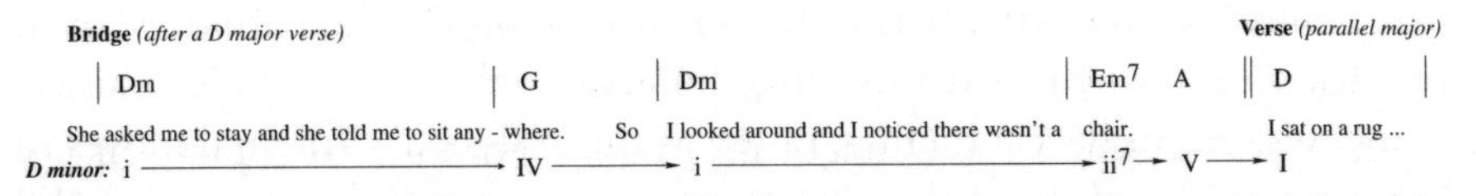

'Michelle'

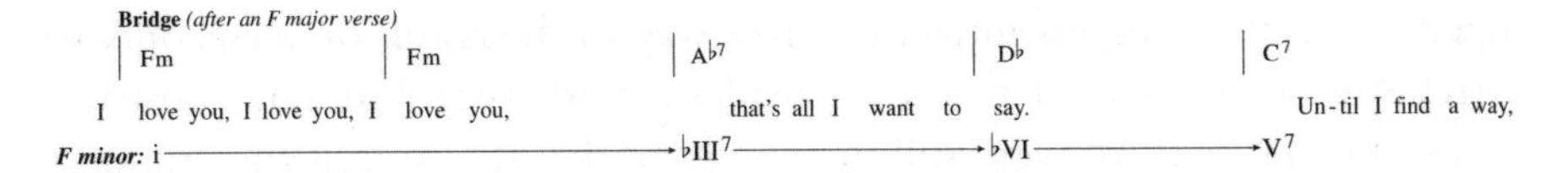

The 'Michelle' sequence is in fact a brilliantly disguised outing for the famous i-♭III-♭VI-V7 progression, which was popularised on the evergreen jazz standard, 'Sunny'. This too can be seen to feature a type of ♭VI-V7-i resolution, but the sequence in this particularly quirky lyrical context gives subtle extra emphasis to that ♭VI chord, over the word 'say' – another great example of The Beatles avoiding predictability in a simple sequence, helped here by altering the rhythmic flow of the tune.

Meanwhile, no discussion of parallel major/minor in popular music would be complete without reference to Cole Porter, the pioneer of such juxtaposition in popular song, who often toyed with the two moods in disorientating fashion. Never more so than in 'Night And Day' where C major and C minor are repeatedly set against each other, teasing the listener with a juggling of the lyrical/musical associations of bright 'day' and dark 'night'.[41]

'Night And Day'

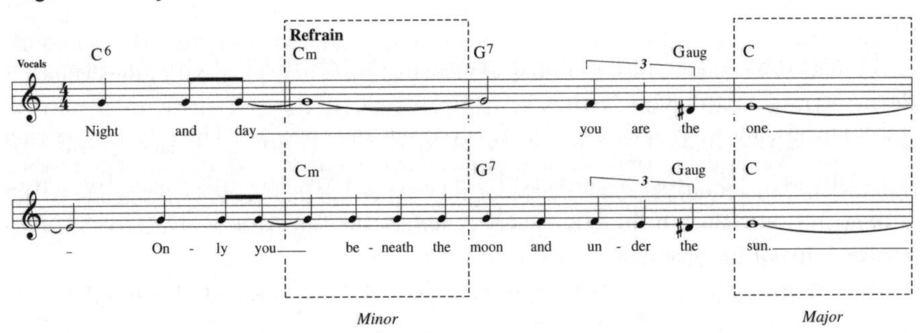

[41] The mismatch of Cm and 'day' is subtly corrected by the C major at the end of each 16-bar refrain.

It is surely testimony to the atmospheric power of this particular device that, decades later, Paul McCartney would resurrect a very similar musical/lyrical premise for 'Fool On The Hill'.

Just watch as the 3rd of D major drops by a semitone to depict – if not quite Porter's 'night' – then certainly the setting sun, as dusk falls on the disconsolate subject at the end of another futile day. The parallel minor here forms a discrete chorus section (first at 0.27) before the D6 chord (at 0.41) lifts the gloom by reflecting McCartney's intuitive sense of musical 'daybreak'.

'The Fool On The Hill'

This extract is particularly important in the context of this chapter as it demonstrates Paul McCartney's inspired use of the ♭6th note in a natural minor melody. In fact we see how both the 9th (here an E note) and this haunting ♭6th (B♭) add a powerful melodic flavour to the basic five-note minor pentatonic 'shell'. The result is the natural minor scale – or Aeolian mode – in all its glory.

For all the obvious sophistication and acquired taste of the parallel key switch, The Beatles managed to use it (and many ingenious variations) in a range of different songs throughout their career. Indeed, alongside Lennon's 'I'll Be Back', McCartney had his very own parallel major/minor ploy back on *A Hard Day's Night*. It can be heard strikingly in 'Things We Said Today' as the A minor verse gives way boldly to an A major bridge (first at 0.59).[42]

Meanwhile, McCartney fascinatingly reveals *his* personal source for this particular songwriting secret as 'Besame Mucho', the much-maligned fifties standard: 'With "Besame Mucho" by the Coasters, it's a minor song and it changes to a major, and where it changes to major is such a big moment musically,' raves Paul, quite rightly (listen out at 0.15 on the *Anthology 1* version).[43] Too bad that, for all the obvious songwriting novelty, The Beatles' rendition of this song famously cut no ice at the legendary failed Decca audition of January 1962.

While we've only a seen a few extracts so far, this parallel major/minor contrast emerges as critical to the structure of several songs from all three Beatles songwriters – dating once again all the way back to the debut album. Here's an at-a-glance reference to their use of the device, albeit in a range of contexts of varying subtlety.

The Beatles and the parallel major/minor switch

Song	Parallel Major		Parallel Minor	
	Section	**Key**	**Section**	**Key**
'Do You Want To Know A Secret'	Verse	E	Intro	Em
'I'll Be Back'	Bridge	A	Verse (bars 1-4)	Am
'Things We Said Today'	Bridge	A	Verse	Am
'Norwegian Wood'	Verse	E	Bridge	Em
'Michelle'	Verse	F	Chorus, Bridge	Fm
'Fixing A Hole'	Chorus	F	Verse	Fm
'While My Guitar Gently Weeps'	Bridge	A	Verse	Am
'I Me Mine'	Chorus	A	Verse	Am
'Savoy Truffle'	Verse	E	Chorus	Em
'The Fool On The Hill'	Verse	D	Chorus	Dm
'Penny Lane'	Verse (bars 1-3)	B	Verse (bars 4-8)	Bm
'Real Love'	Verse	E	Intro/link	Em

No CD reference timings have been included here as this type of switch is surely one of the more dramatic songwriting effects in music and

[42] Advanced students will find more subtle uses of the parallel/major minor principle: including the closing theme motif in 'Piggies', as the harpsichord's C note (the major 3rd of the tonic, A♭) dips to a dark C♭ (at 1.44) briefly creating a classical sounding A♭m.

[43] *Many Years From Now*, p. 81.

therefore (for the most part) 'requires no introduction'. Nevertheless, the parallel action in 'When I Get Home' and 'Come Together' has been purposely left out from the table as they are inherently more ambiguous in their use of the device.

This type of 'parallel trick' would also be exploited in certain notable sixties songs like 'Happy Together' and 'She's Not There' – the latter which, incidentally, we know George Harrison gave the 'thumbs up' to when he appeared as a panelist on *Juke Box Jury*.[44] And in later decades we would hear the same general premise at work in songs ranging from Wings' 'Live And Let Die' and T. Rex's 'Telegram Sam' to The Who's 'Pinball Wizard' right through to Oasis's 'D'You Know What I Mean?'.

And it's perhaps no coincidence that McCartney himself nominates as one of his favourite songs The Who's 'I Can See For Miles', a textbook example of how to use the same shift cleverly *within a song section*, rather than just as, say, a 'bridge shift'.[45] For while we've already seen Lennon do just that in 'I'll Be Back', so Paul's slick use of the same concept in 'Penny Lane' will later be nominated as a defining moment that captures the essence of Beatles musicology.

Finally, as we might have guessed, The Beatles had developed a most novel take on this 'parallel trick' by the time they reached *Abbey Road*. For 'Come Together' is best understood as a very subtle variation of this idea, as a downbeat D minor verse gives way to a very brief parallel major chorus. So where, then, is the D major chord?

Lennon seems to have had his mojo (filter) not just workin' but in overdrive. For instead of the obvious D major that would have completed a Three-Chord Trick chorus, *he substitutes its relative minor, Bm*. Yes, another 'vi for I' which then moves easily to IV and on to the V. Normally, as we have seen so often, such a vi introduces a downbeat twist by appearing as a *relative minor in a major key*. But notice here how it lifts the song.

[44] This excerpt of George's appearance on *Juke Box Jury* can be heard on one of the cult, 11-CD bootlegged compilation, *The Beatles Mythology* (affectionately known as 'The John Barrett Tapes'), Volume Two 1964–66, CD1.

[45] *Guitar World*, January 2000, p. 43 lists Paul's favourites. Listen to the opening line of that song: 'I know you've deceived me now here's a surprise', with the 'surprise' in question being a melody that follows the chords by dropping from major 3rd to ♭3rd. Meanwhile, a stunning variation occurs in Richard Rodgers' 'My Favourite Things', which also juxtaposes verses in minor and parallel major but with a melody that deliberately avoids the defining thirds, thereby neatly avoiding any potential clash.

'Come Together'

The song is clearly in a minor blues setting for the verse itself, and it is the fleeting incarnation of the parallel major tonality that is really responsible for the welcome respite from the moody atmospherics. The more positive refrain: 'Come together, right now' – complete with the introduction of the F♯ note (the major 3rd of D) in the melody – provides another example of The Beatles' matching of music and sentiment before they plunge back into the menacing minor world of 'old flat top' and his disturbing idiosyncrasies.

We are by no means finished with the minor tonality – for these natural minor, 'Aeolian' constructions (with or without that harmonic minor, V7 chord) represent only part of The Beatles' minor-key ideas. They would also tap into the flavours of other exotic modes, notably the 'Dorian' and 'Phrygian' which, while overlapping with Aeolian in certain respects, also adopt certain highly distinctive chords beyond those we've explored so far.[46]

To conclude for now, the natural minor tonality has come to represent a fundamental harmonic territory in rock and pop. William Mann may have made the first reference to Aeolian in a popular music context – but it certainly wasn't the last. The term has littered the pages of guitar magazines over the last 20 years – admittedly usually in connection with artists such as Carlos Santana, Ozzy Osbourne, Iron Maiden, Guns'n'Roses and Metallica. Indeed, over the last three decades no self-respecting Heavy Rock band would leave home without it, knowing full well that their audiences thrive on what one expert rock writer describes as 'the patented quasi-classical, Gothic sound of the Aeolian mode (natural minor) . . . a well known stylistic songwriting device'.[47]

While The Beatles may seem far removed from the era of 'Goth rock', big hair and pointy headstocks, this chapter has hopefully demonstrated that, in terms of the deep heritage of minor-key songwriting, they were among the pioneers.

[46] We've already alluded to one of these already: the IV major chord of 'A Taste Of Honey', and its counterpart in the bridges of 'There's A Place' and 'Norwegian Wood', which will be explained as emanating from the Dorian mode.

[47] Wolf Marshall, *A Music Appreciation Of Iron Maiden, Guitar For The Practicing Musician*, January 1989, p. 113.

SEVEN

'Borrowing' . . . and the Rise of Rock

The diatonic songwriting legacy of the fifties could only take The Beatles so far. They needed new notes and chords in order to build convincingly on their roots and, in the process, take popular music from the American high school rock 'n' roll of 'Johnny B. Goode' to the psychedelic British rock of 'I Am The Walrus'. They did this in what can, conceptually, be seen as a surprisingly logical series of steps using a songwriting technique known as 'chord borrowing'.

We may have left the minor tonality but we haven't left the chords of the minor scale. For it was by 'borrowing' – literally the wholesale importing of chords diatonic to natural minor *back into a whole range of major key settings* – that The Beatles found a new dimension to their songwriting flair and explored their most original musical avenues.

Let's immediately clear up any potential source of confusion that readers could confront. This chapter deals exclusively with sequences that are conceived in a *major* key and which, for the most part, use the familiar chords diatonic to the *major* scale. From this harmonic base, borrowing occurs by mixing and matching chords from the harmonised scale of the *parallel* minor. This may manifest itself in the 'loan' of just one or two chords from this new source, rising at the extreme to the 'full house' effect of 'I Am The Walrus' (where, for 'borrowing', read 'daylight robbery').

It follows that we now have twice the number of chords on which to draw as a master source when putting together a song. For example, the entire family of C *minor* chords is at our disposal when working in C major. Of course, we have seen the two *separate* keys in action within the same song (for example, when a parallel minor bridge sits alongside a major verse), but now we will be intertwining the two sets of chords *within a discrete sequence, with no clearly delineated key switch.*

Let's draw up this enlarged family, which involves recognising minor chords on the scale degrees of 1, 4 and 5 (previously thought of as exclusively major), while 'filling in the gaps' with major chords on the scale degrees of ♭3, ♭6 and ♭7 (sometimes referred to as *chromatic* points when used in a major key).

The 'Parallel' Master Source – C Major and C Minor

Degree	1	2	3	4	5	6	7
Chord	I	ii	iii	IV	V	vi	vii dim
Key of C	C	Dm	Em	F	G	Am	B dim

Degree	1	2	♭3	4	5	♭6	♭7
Chord	i	ii dim	♭III	iv	v	♭VI	♭VII
Key of C	Cm	D dim	E♭	Fm	Gm	A♭	B♭

The Beatles put each of the borrowed triads to work in a range of novel ways throughout their songwriting. This chapter goes through some applications for each chord in this enlarged framework, starting with the new minor chords.

Of course, we have already seen how use of i minor itself necessarily implies a *key* switch to the key of the parallel minor for the relevant extract in which it appears. Hence, by their very nature, such songs effectively straddle these two chapters.

iv minor

This chord is the easiest to accept in our framework because we encountered it as far back as Chapter 2. There it appeared within the Plagal cadence variation that drops IV to iv minor before returning to I, creating in the process a smooth, three-semitone drop to the 5th of the tonic. But in all those examples, iv functioned exclusively as a passing chord – it did not feel like a liberated destination in its own right. The Beatles showed us how to use iv minor as a clear target, without that preparatory IV, in some of their finest moments. But, for our first example let's plunder *Anthology 2* and examine an under-rated gem, 'That Means A Lot', which uses the chord boldly as an opening gambit from the tonic.

'That Means A Lot'

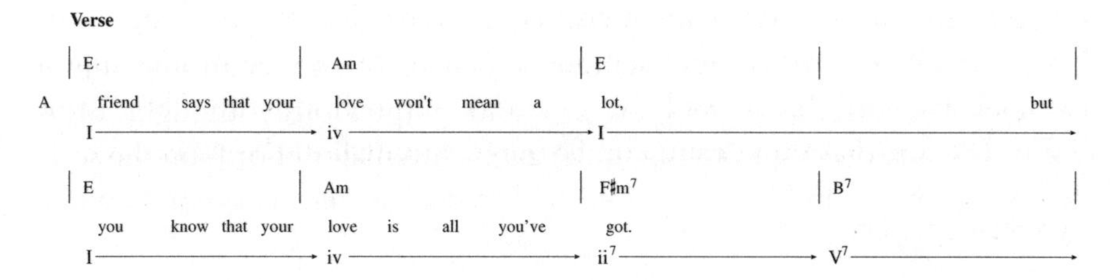

McCartney gets right to the heart of the iv sound by having the melody exploit the only aberrant, non-diatonic note in the chord: the C natural that acts as the ♭3rd of the Am chord. Though now it doesn't drop by that lone semitone to B – as in the 'IV-iv' minor cliché – it lives and breathes in its own right, leaping up to the 5th of the key scale, producing the melancholy effect of the opening line.[1]

Most importantly, the dissonance created by the iv needs resolving and Paul manages to do this in two ways, returning first to I, directly, and then by *suggesting* imminent resolution through a ii-V. The fact that the verse thwarts this set-up, moving instead to new pastures, adds to the sense of meandering that characterises this song.

You don't need the complementary melodic activity to make the iv chord work for you. Take Ringo's simple melody line in 'What Goes On', which has none of the subtle harmonic ramifications of 'That Means A Lot'. The song could easily have been written as just a simple I, IV, V in E major. But by tweaking the IV to iv (and admittedly mirroring the ♭3 of the chord in the *vocal harmony*), the song is suddenly far more effective than if it had been delivered as a 'Three-Chord Trick'.

'What Goes On'

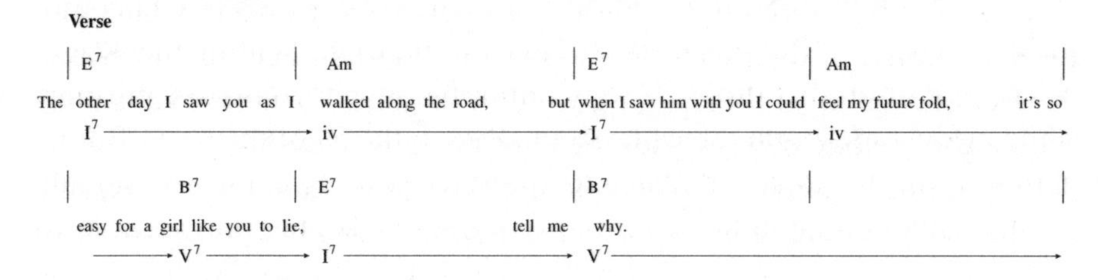

[1] The melodic 9th of E also adds spice as, when harmonised by the iv minor, it implies a tense Am6 sonority.

The principle to take from both these songs is simply that 'iv can substitute directly for IV' – replacing it entirely. Nevertheless, the opening to the bridge in 'I'll Follow The Sun' demonstrates neatly how The Beatles appear to conceive this 'borrowed iv' as originating from the very same 'IV-iv-I' 'trick' that they heard and favoured so much in the early days.

'I'll Follow The Sun'

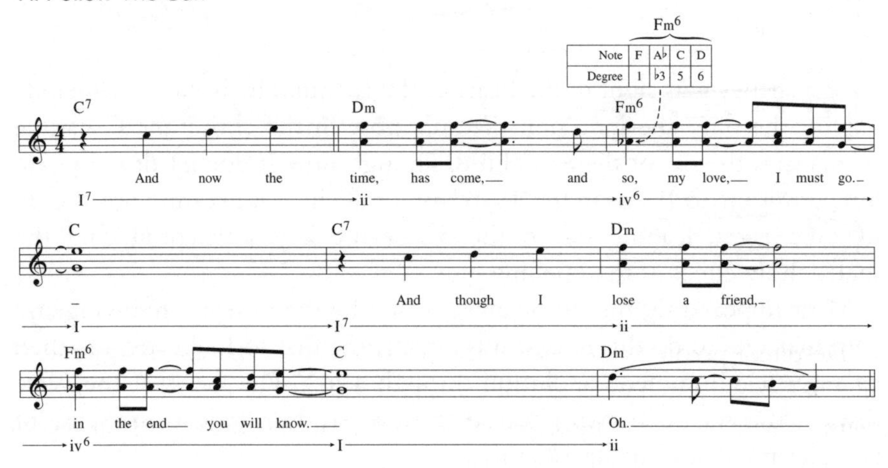

Just think for a minute about this ii-iv-I sequence. Isn't the ii just a relative minor substitution for IV? Replace the IV and we're back where we started! 'Variations on a theme', as John Lennon would say. But it was with precisely such variations that The Beatles distanced themselves so cleverly from cliché.[2]

The iv is another of those stylish chords that might initially be associated with McCartney for the sophisticated ballad feel it creates. Indeed, in terms of early inspiration, The Beatles would have heard the sudden melancholy iv in classics like 'It's Now Or Never', as popularised by Elvis, which The Beatles covered in their early live sets from 1960-62.[3] Feel the power on the second syllable of the opening word in the line 'To*morrow* will be too late', as the melody nails us with the ♭3 of the same chord.

But, again, be wary of pigeonholing. For John Lennon was equally familiar with iv, using it in a wide range of songs. For a Lennon example of

[2] Hear a similarly effective 'ii-iv-I' in Hurricane Smith's 1972 Top 5 UK hit, 'Oh Babe, What Would You Say?' with the line: 'Would there suddenly be sunshine on a cold and rainy day' (leading to an outrageous non-functioning VII7: Dm7-Fm-C-B7).

[3] Lewisohn, *The Complete Beatles Recording Sessions*, p. 363.

a straight 'iv for IV' swap, look no further than the verse of 'Nowhere Man'. The song may start out as a Three-Chord Trick, before the Em adds initial interest, but we soon swoon as Gm replaces G in the final line of the verse.

'Nowhere Man'

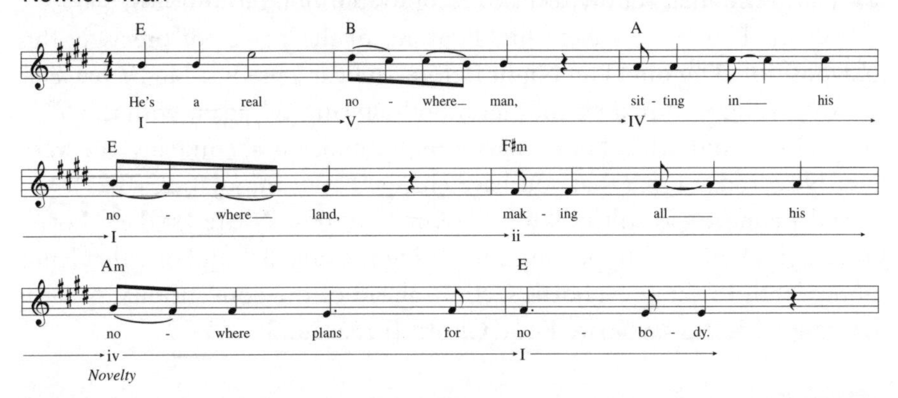

Despite a predictable, 'nursery rhyme' melody - as captured in a radar-like 5-4-3-2-1 pitch descent (follow the staircase from B down to A) - this twist of iv makes the song. Especially as the chord is the support for the G♯ note melody, a simple diatonic major 3rd in the key of E, but which – *over the Am chord* – creates the sudden dissonant sonority of a Am/major7 (a rare but powerful chord that we will explore in Chapter 9). It is this dissonance that ultimately takes the song from bland to beautiful. The same functioning 'iv-I' at the end of a phrase can be spotted instantly in the refrain to 'In My Life' or the 'wrap line' in the coda of 'If I Fell'. Just feel the connection between this pair of famous closing lines: 'In my life I love you more' and 'If I fell in love with you'.

But long before either of these classics, Lennon was using a determined iv-I cadence on *With The Beatles* to reconcile the potential Aeolian ambiguity in the verse of 'All I've Got To Do' (remember the effect of an opening vi chord?):

'All I've Got To Do'

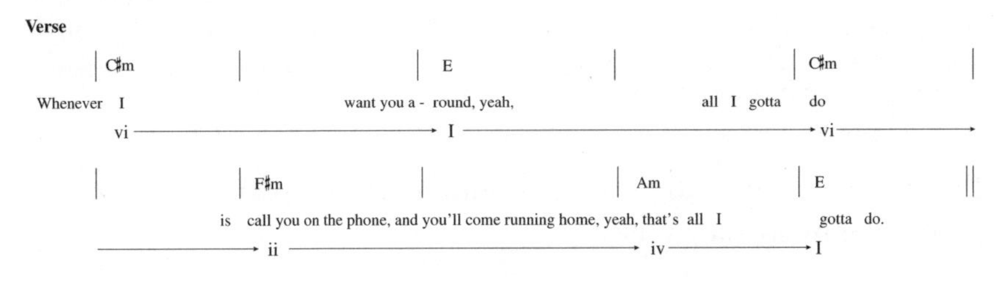

Notice also the preceding ii chord (at 0.16), which gives the effect of the extended ii-iv-I of 'I'll Follow The Sun'. Lennon's use of both the ii and the iv here allows him to avoid the up-beat predictability of the IV (major) until the chorus ('and the same goes for *me*') by which time we are ready for it after the melancholy feel of a long stretch of minor chords.

It seems The Beatles were highly aware of the power of precisely this juxtaposition. Dig out 'The Night Before' to hear a predictable IV (*en route* to a V-I) being trumped by another mood-altering 'iv', again with the 6th in the melody. And what better 'harmonic rethink' to accompany the very line: 'Now today I *find* that you have changed your mind' (0.23-0.27)?

And Lennon was still milking the same contrast as late as 'Real Love'. Once again here's 'iv supporting a touching melodic 6th', and one that lends subtle depth to the pre-chorus section, ahead of the conventional A *major* that follows in his favourite Four-Chord Turnaround.

'Real Love'

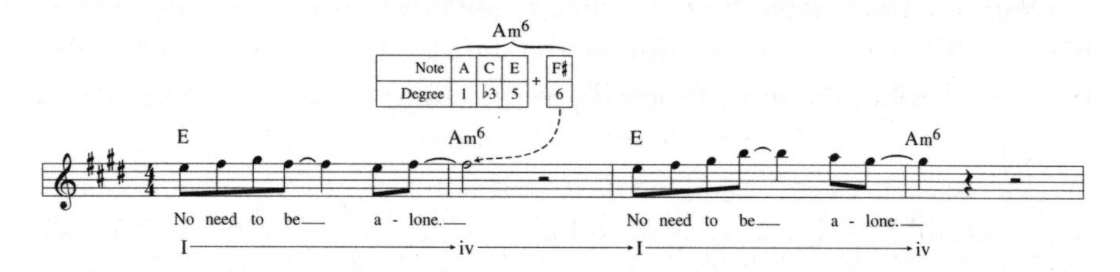

But Lennon's use of the minor subdominant surely reached a peak in 'The Continuing Story Of Bungalow Bill'. It first features proudly in the sing-along chorus – one that's, incidentally, repeated identically in another key three semitones away, and each time with the melody line using the ♭3 of the highlighted chord.

'The Continuing Story Of Bungalow Bill'

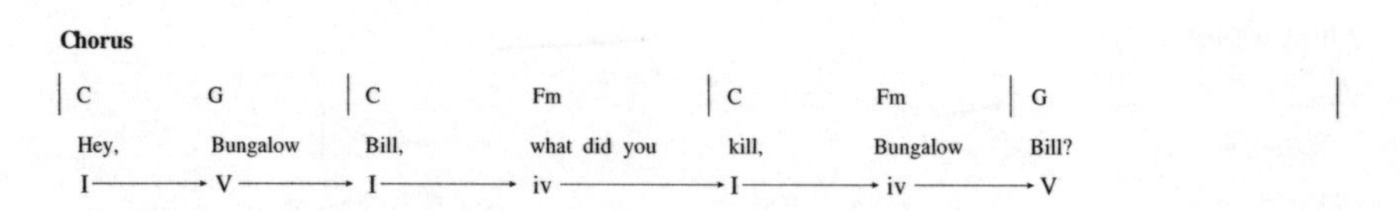

But this use of iv in the chorus is nothing in comparison to Lennon's exit from the minor-key verse:

'The Continuing Story Of Bungalow Bill'

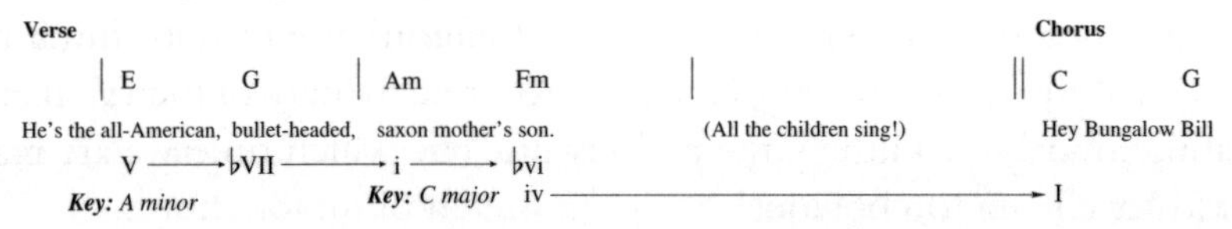

Building on his knowledge of the *cadential* properties of iv-I from his earlier songs, Lennon now exploits the *modulatory* potential of the same change to take him back to the relative major key.[4] Yes, the melody uses the 5th of the chord, and therefore it could equally have been F *major* – but that would have lacked the drama introduced by the A♭ note.

We could think of the chord as a bizarre '♭vi' chord, but with his stunning harmonic vision, Lennon himself conceives it as 'iv of C' (a move that we can add to our list of cadential, or 'tonic affirming', chords that already includes V7, IV, and ♭VII). And just when we think The Beatles have finally bitten off more than they can chew and are lost up a musical *cul-de-sac*, there's John Lennon as Harry Houdini, managing to return instantly back to his nursery rhyme theme in C with this neat 'iv-I' escapology routine. Just as if nothing had happened.

v minor

In his celebrated Beatles' tome, *Revolution In The Head*, Ian MacDonald decries the standard of post-Beatles pop for what he sees as essentially the widespread demise of musical 'surprise'. And, of all the many possible examples from The Beatles catalogue at his disposal, he singles out a certain moment in 'I'll Get You' (originally the B-side to 'She Loves You') to sum it all up.

'I'll Get You'

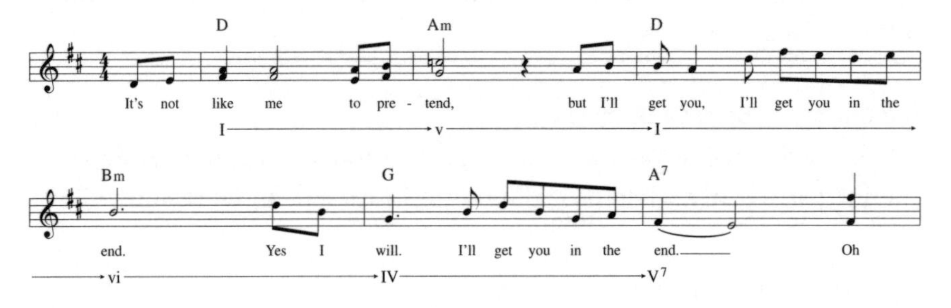

[4] The listener is later 'zapped right between the eyes', most famously at 1.20, by Captain Marvel, with another Fm that appears as if from the jungle itself.

A humble setting, but that's precisely why it makes the point so well. For this moment can be seen purely as a *'borrowed v minor'*, a chord that MacDonald perceptively suggests was used not to 'pique classical ears by creating modal instability in the melody line but because going to A major would have been too obvious'.[5]

McCartney knew this too – and most consciously – as he explains in *Many Years From Now* when reminiscing about this very moment:

'It's got an interesting chord in it: "It's not easy to pre-*tend*". It's like D, which goes to A minor, which is unusual, you'd normally go from D to an A major. It's a change that has always fascinated me . . ."[6]

It is the presence of the Am's ♭3rd (C natural) that creates the drama (first at 0.25) after the rigid diatonicism of the opening bars. The note jumps out at us, also appearing in the melody, where it represents the ♭7th degree of the parent key of D – while making for a stark contrast as it sits against the C♯ heard in the earlier A *major* chord. Once again here is the notion of musical emphasis in action, with The Beatles opting blatantly for a sonority that suddenly highlights the lyrics and their undertones of seduction.[7]

And it's a change that obviously fascinated John Lennon, too. For while it may have been light years removed from this early, hysteria-fuelled Beatlemania context, the same 'I-v' move would later be responsible for some memorable, psychedelic unease in 'Strawberry Fields Forever'. Here it defines the plunging denouement at the end of the line 'Let me take you down 'cause I'm going to . . .'

'Strawberry Fields'

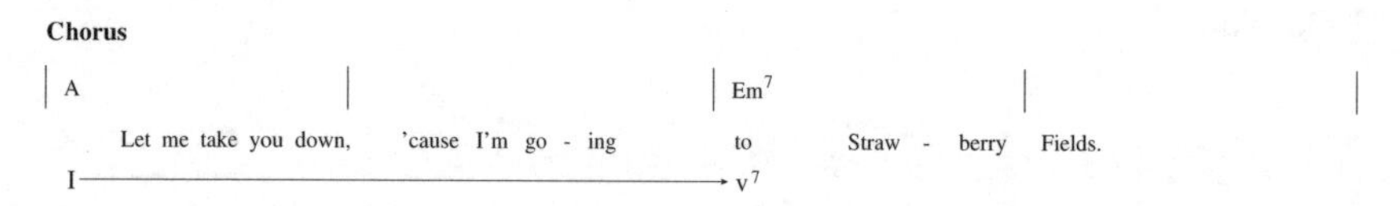

Here again the v proves a sure-fire method of creating tension and interest, particularly when providing support for a ♭7 in the melody. Check

[5] MacDonald, *Revolution In The Head*, p. 340.

[6] Miles, *Many Years From Now*, p. 151.

[7] MacDonald even draws attention to the slice of Beatlemania excitement audible above the chord change (first occurring at 0.29 on the live version on *Anthology 1*) to demonstrate how the audience itself seems to appreciate this ear-catching harmonic shift.

out too, how, in the ballad context of 'She's Leaving Home', a 'I-v' creates a dreamy backdrop for the teenage girl as she tip-toes downstairs on 'Wednesday morning at 5 o'clock'.

'She's Leaving Home'

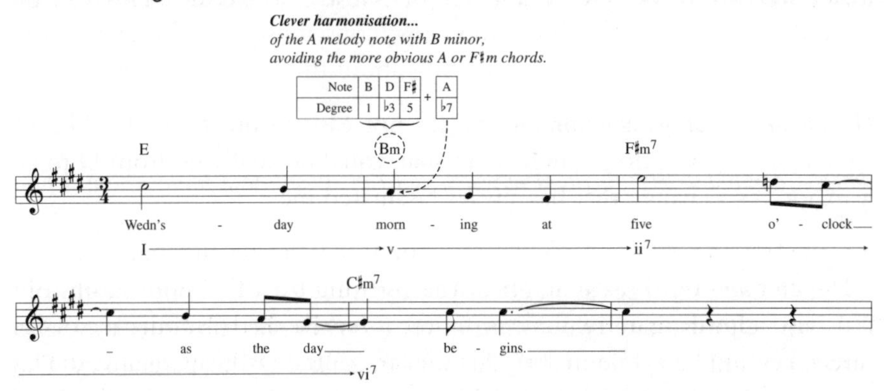

Note how the minor dominant contrasts with the regular, *major* V, which itself resumes at the end of each verse, before the return to E major.

Finally, the appearance of the same chord in two Lennon songs, 'Julia' and 'Sun King', helps us to make some interesting observations in terms of substitution analysis (both songs in the key of C for ease of comparison).

'Julia'

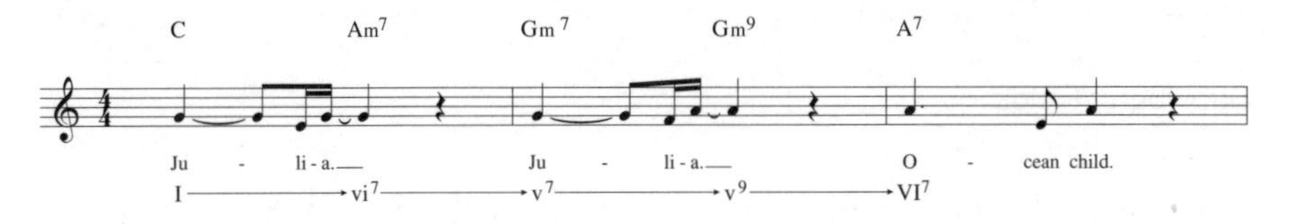

'Sun King'

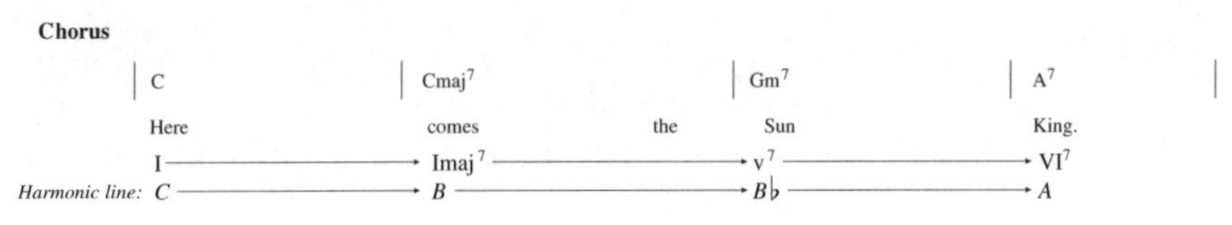

Both extracts are harmonically similar, with the one differing chord easily explained as a simple 'vi-for-I' substitution. Meanwhile, the v minor itself can be seen as a substitute for a tonic dominant seventh chord that would have added flavour directly ahead of another secondary dominant. Play the 'Sun King' sequence as C7–A7 to hear the familiar sound. But, instead, Lennon effectively harmonises the line using a standard jazz device known as the 'Dominant Minor Substitution Rule'. This can be stated as:

The Dominant Minor Substitution Rule

'when a dominant seventh chord appears, you can substitute a minor chord a fifth above'.[8]

Hence Gm7 emerges as an effective substitute for a C dominant chord.[9] The basic chords share two common tones, while the substitute now also introduces implied 9th and 11th flavours in terms of the parent key. The following chart sets out the relationship.

Understanding the 'v-for-I dominant' substitute

Gm 7 ('v' substitute)		**C 7**
Chord tone	**Note**	**Chord tone**
♭7th	F	[11th]
5th	D	[9th]
♭3rd	B♭	♭7th
Root	G	5th
	E	3rd
	C	Root

In 'Julia', the Gm works especially well as the F and A notes in the melody create pretty ♭7th and 9th extensions that reinforce the dreamy theme.

In 'Sun King', the ♭3 of the chord (B♭) acts to extend *in the harmony* the descending chromatic line *begun by the melody* as C drops to B. The latter represents a great example of the way that harmony acts to subtly develop an idea even though the melody may have taken a different path. To

8 The rule here has been adapted from the technical version set out in *The Complete Jazz Guitar*, written and arranged by US guitar instruction guru, Fred Sokolow, p. 22.

9 In fact, later in 'Sun King' this Gm7 is indeed replaced by C7 helping the song move more formally to F, the subdominant.

confirm our understanding of these harmonisation principles, compare 'Sun King' with the famous opening line of George Harrison's 'Something', which features the same three-semitone drop of '1-7-♭7-6', but this time in *both* the melody and the harmony.

'Something'

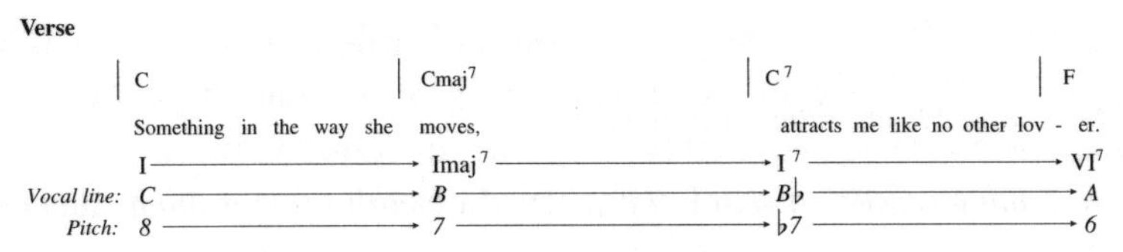

Here George chooses to harmonise that final B♭ more predictably as the ♭7 of the tonic dominant. But a quick bit of experimentation confirms that he could equally have elaborated by playing the v minor 7 – just as in 'Sun King'. But then with both songs appearing on *Abbey Road*, we just might have spotted the connection.

It should be stressed that these examples have aimed to show 'v' at work within a specific section of a song – and *within a single key centre*. For while the chord is non-diatonic to the parent key, we don't feel in these extracts as if we have modulated convincingly to another key. This is in contrast to those v chords that act as a point of departure for a modulation, as we will see so dramatically in Beatles songs as diverse as 'From Me To You', 'I Want To Hold Your Hand', 'The Night Before' and 'Step Inside Love'. In these cases, we will be swiftly re-labelling the chord as a 'ii7' on its way to a new target.[10]

♭VI

At last we have arrived at William Mann's other great whim: those infamous 'flat-submediant key-switches', which we promised to unearth back in Chapter 5. In true Mann fashion we're required to do a modicum of detective work to track down this ultra-slick device as he didn't even specify a song!

[10] Talking of 'the fab v', listen to The Beach Boys' breezy hit, 'California Girls'. It might seem far removed from the dark clouds of 'Strawberry Fields' but the same ♭7 effect appears in the opening line 'I really *dig* those clothes they wear', over the same implied I-v move. Brian Wilson's twist on the word 'dig' creates the sly denouement that makes the verse, cleverly belying the kitsch throwaway sentiment of the song.

Here's the paragraph that followed the extract we've already seen:

'Those [flat] submediant switches from C major into A-flat major . . . are a trademark of Lennon McCartney songs – they do not figure much in other pop repertoires, or in The Beatles' arrangements of borrowed material, and show signs of becoming a mannerism . . .'[11]

In terms of Beatles songwriting 'secrets', this is a nugget well worth mining. For, by the time of his article, Mann could have heard a 'flat submediant chord' – best defined within our framework as *a borrowed ♭VI chord in a major setting* - in only five official Beatles songs. Not many, given that The Beatles had released some 40 songs by then. But perhaps enough, nevertheless, to qualify it as a Beatles 'trademark' given its radical effect in a pop song.[12]

In catalogue order, this elite quintet comprises:

1) 'P.S. I Love You'
2) 'I Saw Her Standing There'
3) 'Do You Want To Know A Secret?'
4) 'It Won't Be Long'
5) 'Till There Was You'

Of these, only two actually feature a move resembling Mann's specific 'C major into A♭ major' quote, describing a move from I to ♭VI. There's no doubt that he would have been felled first by 'It Won't Be Long' where, in the key of E, the tonic E major moves strikingly to C major in the verse, first at 0.17 and again at 0.23.

'It Won't Be Long'

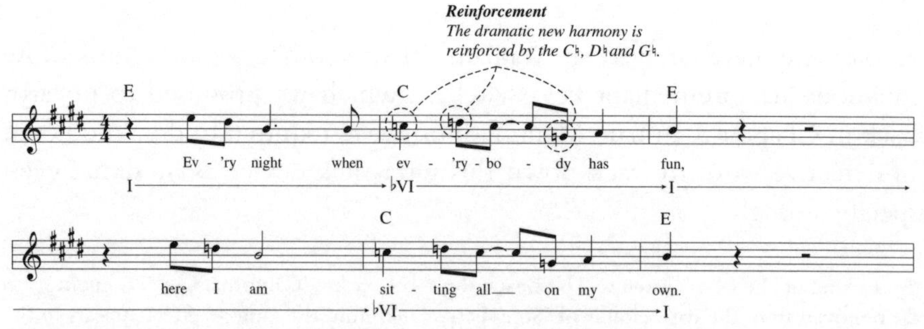

[11] 'What Songs The Beatles Sang', *The Times*, 27th December 1963.

[12] McCartney's 'Nobody I Know' (recorded in 1964 by Peter & Gordon) also features a bold 'flat submediant' of this type. As Paul challenges, 'see if you agree' (A♭ in C, at 0.21).

Notice how the sense of security provided by the opening 8-bar chorus is so poignantly – if fleetingly – questioned as we jump to the rogue chord on the words 'when everybody has gone', reinforcing the lyric perfectly with a tinge of sly knowingness.

It's really no surprise that Mann singled out this precise moment, another that neatly encapsulates The Beatles' novelty just as surely as the 'v' of 'I'll Get You'. Just to confirm this, let's see how that C major chord – the ♭VI from E *minor* – gatecrashes the party in E *major*, in true 'borrowed' style.

Locating the 'borrowed' 'Flat Submediant' – ♭VI

Key of E					***Flat* Submediant**	Submediant	
I	ii	iii	IV	V	**♭VI**	vi	vii dim
E	F♯m	G♯m	A	B	**C**	C♯m	D♯ dim

Many writers have picked up on the play on words between the lyrics 'be long' and 'belong'. But, in a sense, Lennon's title could be twisted for musos: 'It Won't Belong' could equally refer to the C chord that appears to have no place in the key of E, especially as the C♯m – a lone semitone away – has already staked its claim so strongly on our ears as the very first chord we hear in the song. But then The Beatles make it belong.

We can't leave this revelatory chord without questioning Mann's observation that this switch 'does not figure much in other pop repertoires, or in The Beatles' arrangements of borrowed material'.

A borrowed ♭VI in this type of context is a rare bird indeed, but we now know that The Beatles had been exposed to an identical 'I-♭VI-I' in both the verse of Carl Perkins' 'Honey Don't' and also the bridge of Buddy Holly's 'Peggy Sue'. The Beatles performed both these songs in their sets in the early sixties, and even went on to cover 'Honey Don't' on *Beatles For Sale* (listen to the same bold jump, from E to C again, at 0.10).[13]

[13] Similarly dramatic opening I-♭VI moves down the years include John Barry's 'Goldfinger' (E-C); and John Entwistle's 'My Wife' (B-G, conjuring similar trepidation for the line: 'My life's in jeopardy', on *Who's Next*). Meanwhile, the roots of ♭VI in rock and pop date back at least as far as the Pre-War Delta blues. Listen to the opening change on Oscar 'Buddy' Woods' 1936 'Evil Hearted Woman Blues' (A♭ to F♭, at 0.03); or Black Shine Boy's 1937 'Gamblin' Jinx Blues' (where ♭VI embellishes the V, E♭7 in G, at 0.29).

'Honey Don't'

In both Perkins' and Holly's great rock 'n' roll classics the ♭VI appears as the only departure from the Three-Chord Trick.[14] But what a departure! Given the extreme rarity and novelty of such a move there would seem no question that The Beatles were influenced by this pair of songs. Nevertheless, in keeping with our theme of songwriting development, they duly perfected the idea by also featuring the very specific non-diatonic notes that the chord introduces – *in the melody*. It is the C and G *natural* notes in the tune – notes that are *facilitated* by this C chord – that create The Beatles' knock-out punch.

We can also explain the power of this change in terms of an extreme substitution: for theory tells us that *as long as there is at least one common tone between two triads we can substitute one for the other*. E major and C major do share that lone E note, and so ♭VI can substitute for I.[15]

While the 'I-♭VI-I' move was integral to 'It Won't Be Long', the re-emergence of the same chord change as a throw-away gesture at the close of 'Till There Was You', a few tracks later, shows the nonchalant facility with which The Beatles could incorporate exotic harmony at will. Even in 1963, we find a string of elaborate codas confidently featuring dramatic twists and exceptional attention to detail. The closing bars of this cover are a case in point.[16]

[14] Interestingly, Holly's 'Peggy Sue Got Married' is even more ambitious in this regard, opening the bridge on the ♭VI over the line: 'You recall the girl that's been in nearly every song'.

[15] Buddy Holly implicitly knew this given that, in 'Peggy Sue', he opts for the 'safety' of the tonic in his melody ('pretty, pretty, pretty' at 0.48) knowing that it represents common ground with his ambitious ♭VI chord (as A major dips to F major and back).

[16] Listen out too for George's 'add 9' 'flutter' as he plays the D♭ chord in 9th position with the colourful tweak of an E♭ note on the top E string (not forgetting that final 'lounge' major 7th).

'Till There Was You'

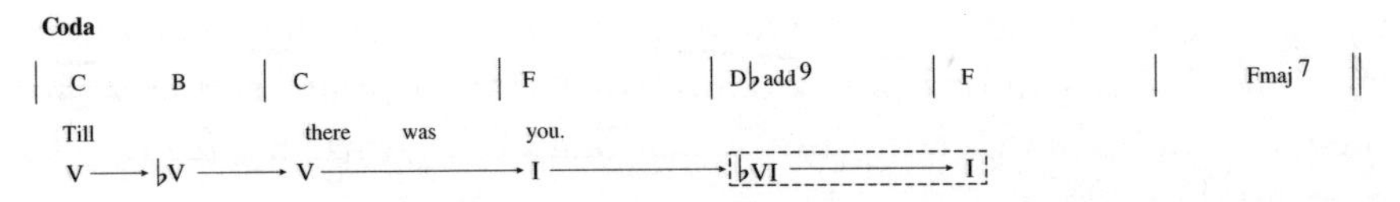

Not content with that brief disorientating slide back from the dominant to the ♭V, the tonic then alternates with ♭VI to give us something far tastier than any of our familiar cadences. In terms of our theoretical framework, we'll soon see how this deceptive wrap-up can actually be rationalised as a super-slick alternative to the Plagal cadence. Regarding this very specific coda ornamentation, Beatles historians could also point to the final stages of Tony Sheridan and Bill Compton's 'Why', on which The Beatles played in May 1961. By far the most intriguing track of the Sheridan sessions, the coda features a sudden move to F in A major just when a continued V7-I tag seems guaranteed.

Meanwhile, despite a few precedents such as these in early sixties pop, Mann was right in suggesting that ♭VI represented extreme novelty in pop music in 1963. Nevertheless, The Beatles had already used it for an earlier landmark in Beatlemania, their very own 'I Saw Her Standing There':

'I Saw Her Standing There'

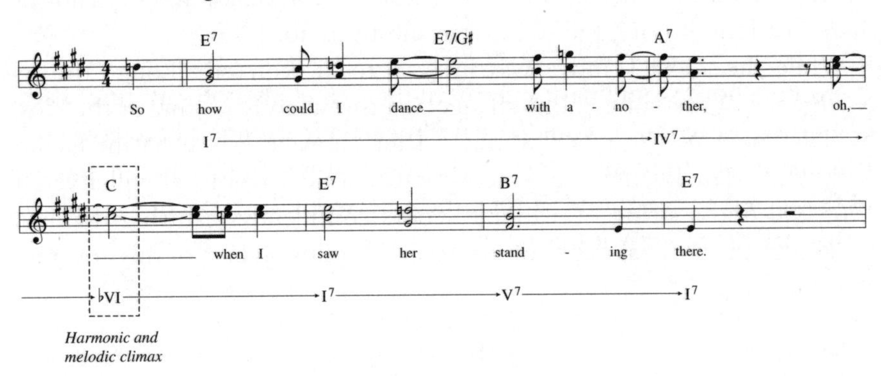

What seems like an innocent rock 'n' roll opener to the debut album, *Please Please Me,* reaches a sudden climax as the ♭VI chord emerges (at 0.25), sending 1963 audiences into convulsions. It's the same devious C chord in the key of E – now a cleverly contrived harmonic backdrop for a resounding vocal highlight – and one that transforms the song from a frivolous R'n'B standard into a pop classic while turning, as one writer, suggests 'implied innocence into sexual bravado'.[17] Amazing, really, what one chord can do.

How strange, then, that many Beatles songbooks have this pivotal moment in 'I Saw Her Standing There' down as not ♭VI at all – but 'iv minor'. But the confusion is understandable and well worth analysing. For these two chords are closely related: emerging as nothing more than relative major and minor. In just the same way that we've encountered 'vi for I' and 'ii for IV', so 'iv and ♭VI' are *direct substitutes* for each other.[18]

This relationship can be seen in action in various essential Beatles moments such as the refrain of 'Hello Goodbye'. Again you could argue that, like 'I Saw Her Standing There', the song looks set to cue a 'IV-iv-I' Plagal-type cadence only to deliver instead a tougher, 'steelier' dimension by means of the ♭VI alternative.

'Hello Goodbye'

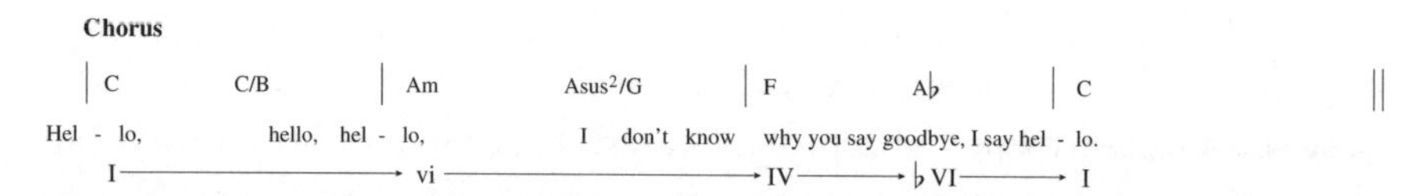

An Fm chord would have supported the C melody note just fine (as the 5th of the chord) but it wouldn't have 'rocked'. It wouldn't have *been* rock. It is that minor third interval – an element that is steadily emerging as one of the secrets to the sound of rock (here between the roots of IV and ♭VI) – that drives the song at this point.

[17] Tim Riley, *Tell Me Why*, p. 50.

[18] Not every instrument in the band therefore *has* to play the ♭VI chord to achieve the effect – we can mix and match the two chords. For example, Lennon's minimal finger movement on the *Anthology* video of 'I Saw Here Standing There' suggests that he is indeed just dropping from IV-vi. It's George who clearly slides a sixth-string-root barre-chord up to the 8th fret to nail the C major that's matched in Paul's bass.

Compare this with McCartney's 'When I'm Sixty Four', which this time *does* deliver an 'F-Fm-C' with no ♭VI chord apparently in sight. This time the recorded version finds McCartney's bass hanging on the F root as the woodwind drops from A to A♭ to make the implied iv chord, before returning to the root.

'When I'm Sixty Four'

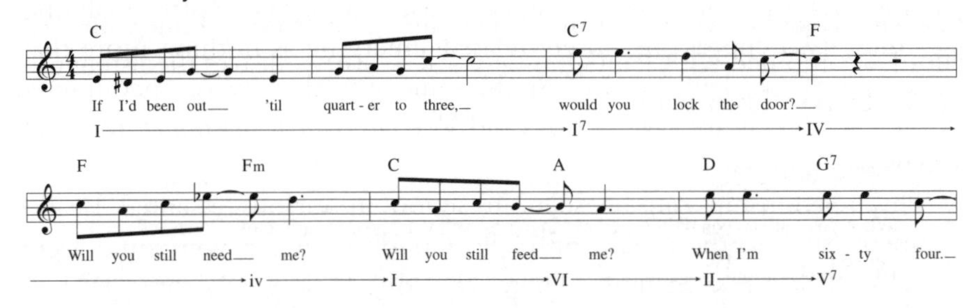

Try the '♭VI for iv' substitution yourself for size, playing an A♭ major in place of the Fm. Suddenly it adds a rock spin to the proceedings. It's just a thought, but if McCartney had gone for substitution here, thereby creating the wicked root movement of IV-♭VI-I (especially ahead of the ensuing VI-II-V-I), would today's trendy critics still have bemoaned the song for its departure from the emerging rock ethic of the *Sgt. Pepper* era?

'When I'm Sixty Four' also provides a great example of how a song can be structured so as to gather pace as it moves towards a local climax. Notice how there are really only three chord changes in the first 12 bars, following which the song bursts into life with six changes in the last four bars as we move into the refrain. This is a songwriting principle known as 'harmonic acceleration to cadence', a useful tool to create interest by stepping up the harmonic activity – almost as if the tempo itself had moved up a gear.

We can't leave the relationship between iv and ♭VI without seeing how The Beatles dealt with it in a bridge context. The middle eights of 'Oh! Darling' and 'Ain't She Sweet' help us again to appreciate the evolution from pop to rock in the sixties.

In the hands of a typical early pop songwriter, the opening D chord of 'Oh! Darling' would have dropped to D minor, leading the song back to the A tonic in the style of a thousand fifties pop bridges. Indeed, just like The Beatles' version of 'Ain't She Sweet', transposed here into the key of 'Oh! Darling' in order to compare the second chord in each sequence.

'Ain't She Sweet' (bridge)

'Let's cast an eye in her di - rec - tion'				
(0.32 - 039)	IV	**iv**	I	I^7
	D	**Dm**	A	A^7

But in the *Abbey Road* song, McCartney delivers the relative *major* of Dm – the F chord (at 1.12–1.15) – instantly avoiding the cliché, in favour of a hard-edged blues-rock sound.[19] The difference is everything as the ♭VI chord – combined with Paul's frantic vocal delivery – leaves the listener in no doubt as to his anguish.[20]

'Oh! Darling' (bridge)

'When you told me you didn't need me anymore, well you know I nearly broke down and cried'				
(1.08)	IV	**♭VI**	I	I^7
	D	**F**	A	A^7

The Beatles were toying with the mirror images of ♭VI and iv as early as 'Do You Want To Know A Secret' Listen closely to the chord change that occurs at 0.25. We're in the key of E, but is it an Am or a C major – or perhaps even an F major that at least one Beatles expert suggests returns us to the tonic at this point?[21]

From our knowledge of harmonisation we know that it could theoretically be any of these three chord options, as each would acceptably support John's ambitious C natural melody note. Specifically, the C would appear as the ♭3rd of Am, the root of C major or the 5th of F major, respectively. On close listening, we suggest that George is playing an Am7 chord at the 5th fret of the guitar – but this is best thought of as an inversion of C6, given that Paul's bass has clearly opted for an ear-catching tritone jump from F♯ to C.[22] All in all, an implied ♭VI at the very least.

[19] Interestingly, when Oasis encountered the same dilemma in their bridge to 'Don't Look Back In Anger' Noel Gallagher opted for the sweeter – and arguably more commercial – IV-iv-I sound.

[20] Riley elaborates: 'In these moments he [Paul] nearly leaves everyone else behind, and his focus dares the others to match his emotional intensity'. *Tell Me Why*, p. 320.

[21] Alan W. Pollack goes for the ♭II-I, F to E move. 'Notes on … Series' no. 32, 2001. *The 'Official' rec.music.beatles Home Page*, www.recmusicbeatles.com.

[22] The A note on the top string is the clue, although this could of course also be the top note of a barred, fifth-string-root, C6 chord in 3rd position.

As late as 'Free As A Bird' John Lennon was milking this same '♭VI/iv' relationship when tinkering slyly with a versatile Four-Chord Turnaround. Listen to how the opening 'A-F♯m-F-E' idea (in the verse at 0.28) develops as, on the third hearing, the F major is replaced by Dm (at 0.41) to engineer a delicate modulation (explored in Chapter 10).

We will be revisiting the rock pedigree of ♭VI when seeing how it conspired with ♭III and ♭VII at the heavier end of The Beatles' sound spectrum.

The '♭VI7' 'pre-dominant'

We can't leave ♭VI without sampling its role as a special type of dominant 7th, which we've already seen in minor songs as diverse as 'Besame Mucho' and 'I Want You (She's So Heavy)'. This effortless descent sees ♭VI7 slide down a half-step to the V7 in order to prepare for a return to the tonic.[23]

The easiest way to appreciate this move *in major* is to consider its origins as a gentle embellishment of the V chord before a perfect cadence. Listen first to George's twangy solo 'What Goes On' to hear (albeit very fleetingly at 1.51) the B7 chord briefly tipping upwards to C7 – the ♭VI7 – before returning for a V-I cadence. In this rockabilly setting, this is purely an extension of Scotty Moore's tricks, dating back to some of The Beatles' favourite Elvis songs. These include 'Baby, Let's Play House', nominated by Paul as one of his early inspirations on his 1999 Christmas radio show. Listen to that ♭VI7-V7-I move (at 0.11) over the refrain: 'Come back baby I *wanna play* house with you'.

No great shakes, but look back to the last chapter to see how its minor-key equivalent spiced 'Besame Mucho' and 'The Thrill Is Gone' rather more substantially. In the same way, it's a small conceptual jump to the verse of 'Ain't She Sweet' on which The Beatles would have absorbed the sound of a definitive '♭VI7-V7' in major. Take your pick from the versions on both *Anthology 1* and *3*:

[23] In classical music theory literature, this chord may be referred to as an *augmented sixth*. Space doesn't allow for an explanation of this confusing and complicated subject here – for a helpful discussion, refer to Eric Taylor's *The Associated Board Guide To Music Theory* Part II, p. 161.

'Ain't She Sweet'

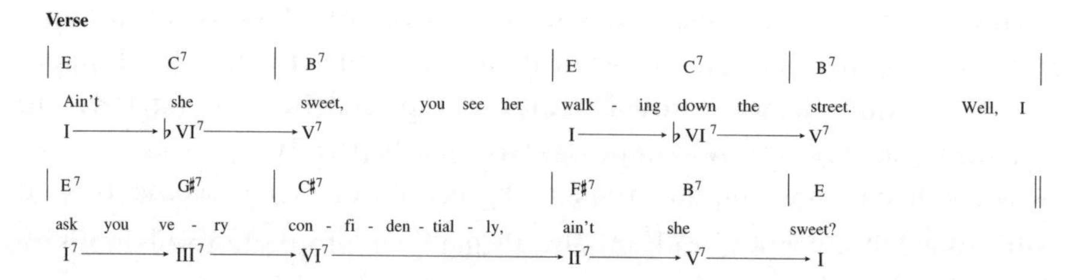

And from here it's only a short step to seeing the principles at work in various Beatles originals. Here are two examples – one early and one late – but each using the same idea of a '♭VI7–V7' to create, this time, an Imperfect cadence when wrapping up a section ahead of the tonic.

'I Call Your Name'

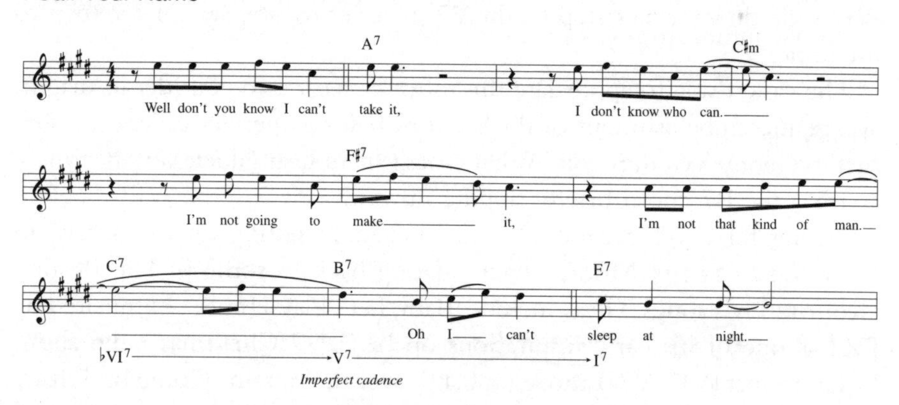

This was one of John Lennon's very earliest compositions, and he was still using the idea as late as *Abbey Road*, for those 'mean old man'/'dirty old man' pay-off phrases that form such a great recycled hook.[24]

'Mean Mr Mustard'

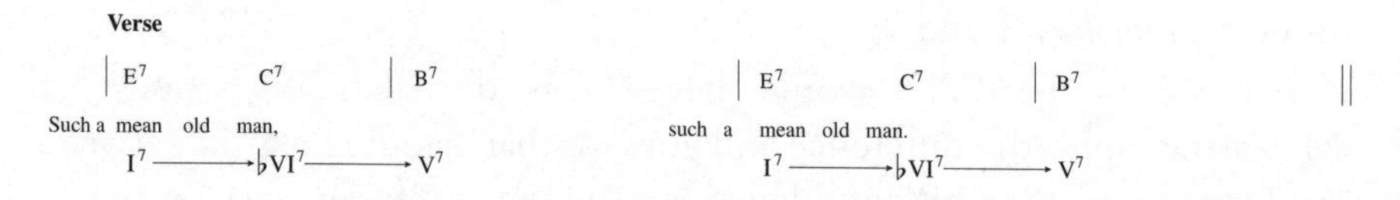

[24] See also the chorus of 'Run For Your Life', where the line 'that's the end' coincides with a G–F♯7 preparation of Bm.

Meanwhile, to hear the distinctive sound of ♭VI7–V7 in a contemporary setting, listen to Noel Gallagher adopt it repeatedly in the verse to Oasis's fine acoustic ballad, 'Married With Children'. Indeed, while doubling up the bar count to drag out the coda, Gallagher uses the finality of this cadence (one that's surprisingly under-exploited in modern pop) as the parting shot for the whole *Definitely Maybe* album – accompanied, in the very finest songwriting tradition, by a suitably appropriate resolving lyric: 'Goodbye, I'm going home'.

♭VI7 and the crazy case of 'Honey Pie'

If there is certainly a formulaic touch to all these ♭VI7s as they head so predictably to the dominant, Paul McCartney's use of the chord in 'Honey Pie' features a slice of novelty that arguably belongs in the list of the top-10 coolest Beatles chord changes. Just listen to the opening move as the verse jumps from G to E♭7 (at 0.42).

'Honey Pie'

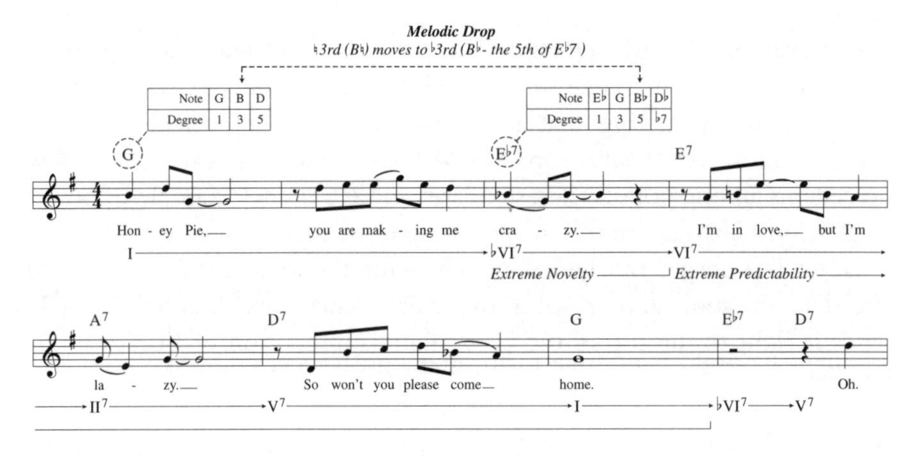

I-to-V7 or I-to-VI7 would have been the 'default' options but McCartney splits the difference and goes for that 'hanging gap' in between. And it's a measure of his confidence as a songwriter that he decides to start the verse with a melody that drops from the 3rd of the parent key to the ♭3rd – but look how the chord he chooses supports it.

Let's think this through for a minute. Yes, we saw John construct the same 3rd to ♭3rd *melodic* premise in 'I'll Be Back' while also mentioning The Who's 'I Can See For Miles'. However, in both these cases, the chord that harmonises the ♭3 melody note is the tonic minor. Meanwhile, another famous '3rd-to-♭3rd' melody is 'What's New Pussycat?' where Burt Bacharach uses the ♭III major chord to support the same note over the phrase '*I've* got flowers'.

All these examples represent standout songwriting but McCartney's idea trumps them in various ways. The crucial melody note is still supported as a strong chord tone, though now as the 5th of the chosen chord (rather than ♭3rd or root). This allows him to achieve the same stunning opening root move as 'It Won't Be Long' though, from here, 'Honey Pie' continues the drama by resolving not downwards to V7, as we might expect, but *upwards* to the (*natural*) VI7. Play this move to see just how slick and unique it is. After this excursion, order is restored and a natural Cycle Of Fifths has no trouble in returning us to the root – but that brilliant twist still lingers.

Once again, The Beatles mix the familiar with the unexpected (only this time in reverse order) on a song that hasn't been fully appreciated over the years.

For example, Ian MacDonald claims that Lennon felt the song to be 'beyond redemption', while short-changing 'Honey Pie's extreme slice of ingenuity' by suggesting that it features 'the correct period harmonic design'.[25] However, this very specific '♭VI7-VI7' move appears to have few precedents among popular jazz standards and is a model example of how a single chord change can transform a song from cliché to classic.[26]

Don't let's forget the lyrical match – for the fact that the unhinged chord in question appears over the words 'crazy' and 'frantic' arguably sends it right to the top of the class in any appreciation of Beatles song-writing.

We have already suggested that the remaining chords from the parallel minor scale, ♭III and ♭VII, were responsible for changing pop and R'n'B into rock, heavy rock and heavy metal. This is not merely because they are

[25] *Revolution In The Head*, p. 281.

[26] Everett suggests Jelly Roll Morton's 1923 song, 'The Pearls', as perhaps the only example, *The Beatles As Musicians: Revolver Through The Anthology*, p. 189.

borrowed from the harmonised natural minor scale, but in a more primitive sense, they can be seen as the pillars of the rawer *minor pentatonic* scale. To appreciate the theory behind this, all we need to do is combine these chords with the IV and V from our major scale to provide a hybrid family of five major chords.

Minor Pentatonic scale:	1	♭3	4	5	♭7
Hybrid rock chord scale:	I	♭III	IV	V	♭VII

This mini 'master source' is all many rock bands ever need. The use of ♭III and ♭VII in simple three- and four-chord cycles (typically with the IV supplementing the tonic) has become a powerful foundation for the legacy of rock, from The Beatles to The Spice Girls, from 'The Word' (I-♭VII-♭III-IV) to 'Wannabe' (I-♭III-IV-♭VII).

We continue with a look at both these remaining borrowed chords, starting with ♭III.

♭III

Let's start at the beginning with one clearly influential early cover on *Anthology 1,* which may well have first demonstrated the rocky potential of ♭III.

Track 27 on CD 1 finds The Fab Four tackling Carl Perkins' version of 'Lend Me Your Comb', a song that appears to have been a fixture in Beatles live sets from as early as 1957 through to 1962.[27]

There's no mistaking the rogue chord that appears in the intro as the opening tonic makes its first move from E-G *natural* (a 'borrowed' ♭III), before moving on to the IV and V.

Although nobody knew it at the time, this was rock music in the making. The Beatles were clearly so taken with the sound that they presumably couldn't resist making a fleeting gesture to 'Lend Me Your Comb' when it came to 'Please Please Me'. Guitarists all know the moment: that seemingly off-the-cuff ascending figure (first at 0.13) that adds some serious 'balls' to the proceedings.

[27] Lewisohn, *The Complete Beatles Recording Sessions*, p. 363.

'Please Please Me'

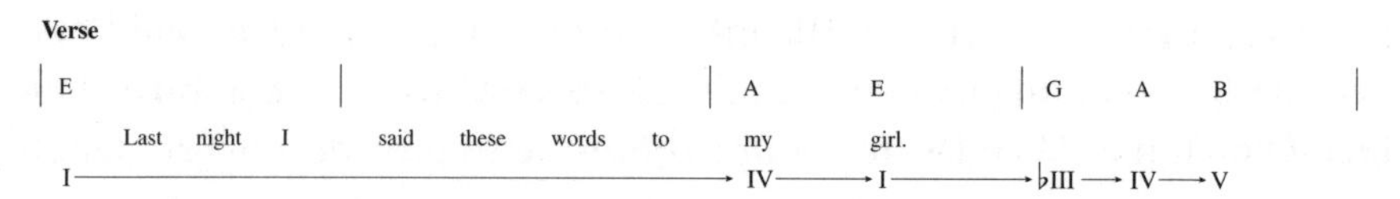

This was the first of several musical factors that distanced 'Please Please Me' from the predictable (if catchy) Four-Chord Cycles of 'How Do You Do It?', the song that was originally earmarked as their second single.[28]

Within a few years The Beatles were building their own simple but powerful sequences using minor third and major second intervals. To devour the sound, cut to late-sixties classics like 'Magical Mystery Tour' and 'Sgt. Pepper's Lonely Hearts Club Band' which both hinge on what every rock band will know as the 'I-♭III-IV-I' formula. Think of it as the 'Eight Days A Week' cycle – but with a difference – for as the ♭III substitutes for II, so 'pop-rock' becomes 'hard rock'.

'Magical Mystery Tour'

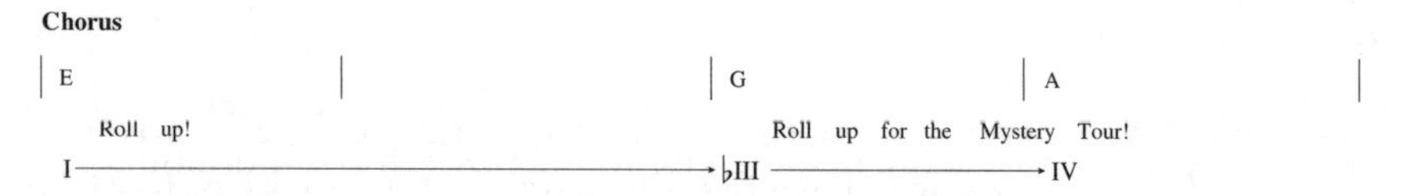

'Sgt. Pepper's Lonely Hearts Club Band'

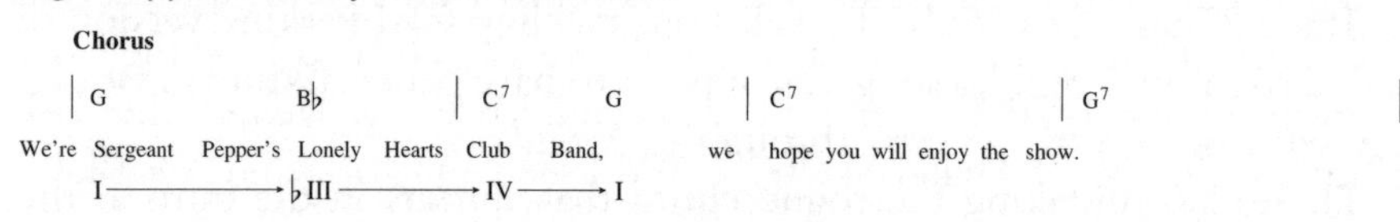

Here is another songwriting ploy that has remained a defining idea in pop music far beyond The Beatles: hear it equally on The Who's 'I Can See For Miles'; in Sam & Dave's soul standard 'Hold On I'm Coming' and on Robbie Williams' driving signature anthem, 'Let Me Entertain You'.[29]

[28] Ironically, barely two weeks after 'Please Please Me' hit the UK chart, in January 1963, the same move could be heard opening Bobby Vee's Top-3 smash 'The Night Has A Thousand Eyes' (original Liberty recording heard in E♭).

[29] In The Who song, the line: 'If you think I don't know about the little things you play' features the sequence with the ♭III now cleverly reharmonising the opening line of the song which featured the I-i minor parallel drop referred to in the last chapter.

The chorus of 'Back In The USSR' also features this same run after a verse sequence in which the ♭III first appears *after* the IV. What could have been a Three-Chord Trick emerges as pure rock as the C chord delivers the line 'Didn't get to bed last night'.

'Back In The USSR'

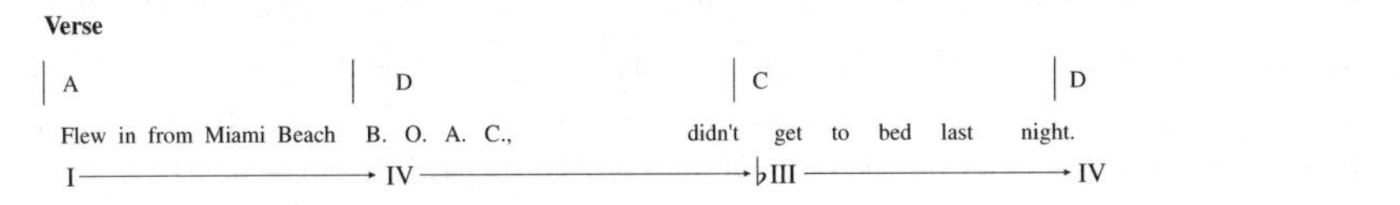

For a George Harrison example, the ♭III creates a vital downbeat reference point in 'Think For Yourself', over the line 'To say about the things that you do'. Again, '♭III-IV' with a return to the tonic is the plan.

Strangely enough, the deeply rocky sound of ♭III-IV was being used by The Everly Brothers as far back as 1957, on classics like 'Bye Bye Love' and 'Wake Up Little Suzie' (if only very specifically and fleetingly on the intros to those songs). It's as if the chord itself, with its dark undertones, represented overly daring, almost forbidden fruit in those early days.[30]

The rocky fill in 'Please Please Me' might only have been a 'tip of the hat' to the I-♭III-IV-V sequence but, by 1965, The Beatles demonstrated confidently how the sequence makes for a powerful stand-alone rock progression in the intro to 'The Night Before'.

The song's instrumental fills elaborate on this sequence, with the ♭III at the heart of the gestures. Listen especially to the coda to hear the even more primitive 'I-♭III-I', a premise that would reappear later in the dark blues-rock strains of 'Helter Skelter' ('And I see you *again*') and 'Yer Blues' ('If I ain't *dead already*').

The idea of a song returning to base with a '♭III to I drop' is another bluesy stalwart that gets reincarnated as a defining idea in standards ranging from 'Voodoo Chile' to 'Midnight Hour' only to be picked up again and again by generations of rock bands in genres from Punk to Britpop.[31]

Still, for all the claims of 'The Night Before', the emergent sound of ♭III

[30] 'Bye Bye Love' opens with I-♭III-IV, in the key of A; while the intro to 'Wake Up Little Suzie' slides back for a I-♭III-IV-♭III, in the key of D.

[31] From the Sex Pistols to Supergrass. Hear it boldly on the sing-along refrain of 'Pretty Vacant' (D-C-A in the key of A). And equally in the refrain of 'I'd Like To Know', 'I'd like to know where all the strange ones go'; after F (the ♭VI) cues the same C-A resolution.

can be seen not only in the fleeting riff of 'Please Please Me' but also in the self-contained instrumental that ends that same song.

'Please Please Me'

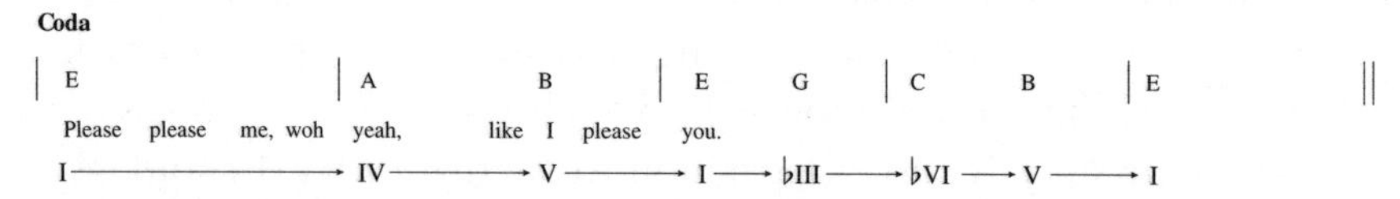

Here The Beatles conjured, out of nowhere, a progression lasting just a few seconds (and unrepeated elsewhere in the song), yet one that succinctly encapsulates a sound that would be built upon by generations of rockers. The permutations of ♭III and ♭VI are particularly interesting when constructing four-chord, rock-based classics.

Think of Traffic's 'Gimme Some Lovin'', which after a lengthy vamp on a bluesy E tonic, finally explodes into life with I-♭III-IV-♭VI. Fast-forward to Nirvana's landmark grunge album, *Nevermind*, as the historic guitar lick of 'Smells Like Teen Spirit' cycles around I-IV-♭III-♭VI, with the latter two chords reminding us once again of the potential for up-a fourth root movement between these two members.[32]

Meanwhile, the sound of ♭III should be seen as a powerful ingredient that can lend instant harmonic toughness to a song. For an evergreen example take Lynyrd Skynyrd's 'Free Bird', which moves from gentle ballad to uncompromising rock as the ♭III enters at 2.44. Talking of evergreen, the ♭III single-handedly fuels the chorus of Slade's 'Merry Xmas Everybody' by driving a clever four-chord cycle (I-iii-♭III-V) over the line: 'Every*body*'s having fun'.[33]

♭VII

Of all the chords we are visiting in this chapter (make that the whole book) the ♭VII will ultimately emerge as the most important, both in terms of its theoretical versatility and in the way in which The Beatles developed it in a complete range of songwriting situations.

[32] You could also view the 'Smells Like Teen Spirit' riff as effectively delivering a pair of I-IV moves a minor third apart.

[33] Noddy Holder cleverly chooses the B♭ to support a bluesy F natural note (a ♭7 in the key of G) as the 5th of the ♭III, in the cycle G-Bm7-B♭-D.

While a select band of fifties and early-sixties pop and rock 'n' roll songwriters deftly plundered the chromatic scale in search of non-diatonic novelty, it's fair to say that the ♭VII was a criminally under-utilised chord before the advent of The Beatles. Generations have been told that the group were 'breaking the rules' of songwriting and 'gave birth to rock' in the sixties, but the musical process by which they achieved this is often shrouded in mystery. It's no exaggeration to say that the ♭VII chord (as we indicated back in Chapter 5) was a very specific device at the heart of the revolution. 'All My Loving', 'Help', 'A Hard Day's Night', 'Norwegian Wood', 'Hey Jude', 'Tomorrow Never Knows', 'Dear Prudence', 'Revolution' and 'Get Back' (to name just a very few) may cover a vast range of styles but, in each case, it's the ♭VII chord that proves to be one of the defining harmonic forces that make the song.

However, the chord displays a myriad of *functions* among these songs, some of which render redundant much classical convention when analysing and appreciating rock and pop music (of The Beatles and beyond). A revolution, indeed. Let's get familiar with the chord by seeing how The Beatles put it to work.

♭VII as a 'pre-dominant' – fuelling the V7

'All My Loving', back on *With The Beatles*, is a useful starting point. Here the chord appears suddenly towards the end of an otherwise strongly diatonic stretch of E major chords that begins, incidentally, with that 'poppy' 'ii-V-I-vi' sequence referred to in Chapter 3. But notice how the second time that the all-important dominant appears it is *not* the 'ii' that primes it as we have come to expect, but the ♭VII.

'All My Loving'

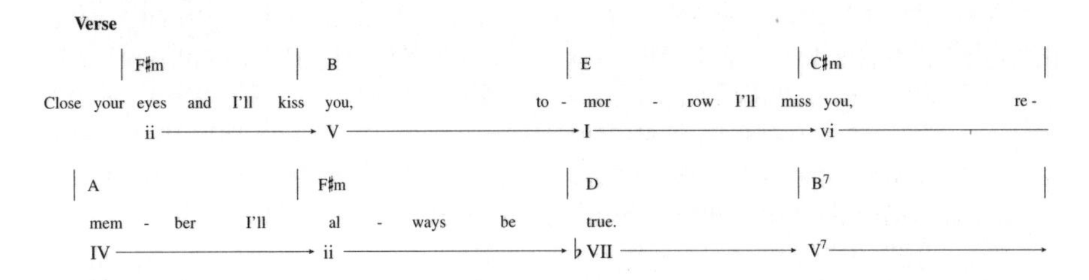

Upstaging the ii minor chord as the designated pre-dominant chord, the ♭VII has the effect of dramatically altering the voice-leading. We now subliminally enjoy a three-semitone ascending harmonic line into the strong major 3rd of the dominant.

Voice-leading in the ♭VII 'Pre-dominant' of 'All My Loving'

Formula	ii	♭VII	V^7
Chord	F♯m	D	B^7
Voice leading	**C♯**	**D**	**D♯**
Relative to chord	5th	Root	3rd

And as much as this internal action is interesting, don't let's forget that, as D changes to B, we now have a root movement of a minor third creating a distinctive rock interval within an otherwise 'pure pop' structure. Suddenly there's a steelier edge to McCartney's otherwise light (if busy) pop song, as a special backdrop is created for the word 'true', as the singer takes the plunge in admitting his loyalty.

Here is a great example of The Beatles getting the chords to 'do the work' in a song. For while that melodic F♯ (on 'true') is supported as the 3rd of the D, so it would have appeared happily as the root of the preceding ii – or indeed as the 5th of the following V7. In this sense, the D chord can be regarded as superfluous to the proceedings. Yet its role as a means of propelling the song forward to this 'hanging' V is confirmed by comparing it with the more conventional 'IV-V-I' that now seems to decelerate the song as it wraps up the 16-bar verse. But then the harmonic ebb and flow at these specific moments is one of the very reasons why the song works so well.

Nor does the idea have to be confined to such a euphoric uptempo category of song. Refer to Appendix 3 to see how The Beatles re-harmonize the melody of 'Yes It Is' specifically to accommodate the '♭VII-V' change. Notice how, in turn, this drives the 'development' section as vi again substitutes for the tonic (in bar 9). A humble love ballad, but featuring some deceptively ingenious songwriting.

Meanwhile, John Lennon takes the same idea to its logical conclusion in the chorus of 'Help!'.

'Help!'

Chorus

Bm				G				
Help me if you can, I'm feeling down,			and I	do ap - pre - ci - ate you be - ing 'round,				
ii ⟶				♭VII ⟶				
E				A				‖
help me get my feet back on the ground,			won't you	please,	please, help me?			
V ⟶				I				

Again, a ♭VII headed for V keeps the song dramatically in motion, but now that inner chromatic climb is *extended* a *further step* into the heart of the key centre, as set out in the following voice-leading chart.[34]

Formula	ii	♭VII	V	I
Chord	Bm	G	E	A
Voice leading	**F♯**	**G**	**G♯**	**A**
Relative to chord	5th	Root	3rd	Root

A look at the crafted intro of 'Help!' – often lauded as a separate section not repeated anywhere in the song – confirms that the identical idea is at work here too.

'Let It Be' sees another development of this principle in the distinctive instrumental interlude that closes the song. While, at first sight, the passage may appear to be rather more elaborate than our earlier examples (and the chordal activity is very busy) we can still pick out the same defining '♭VII-V' move prior to the appropriately hymnal Plagal cadence (now in its distinctive 'church organ' setting).

Guy Chambers makes a point of praising the voice-leading in this very move, while Ian Hammond also highlights the clash of the B♭ in the 'Chromatic Subtonic' (a grander name for the ♭VII) and the B natural and how this dichotomy gives the song 'just that extra little kick'.[35] As with the borrowed ♭III, so the role of the ♭VII has been to give generations of pop songs a 'kick' of varying intensity.

American rock writer Askold Buk points out that this '♭VII-V7' move is integral to the sound of several rock, soul and R'n'B classics, including

[34] 'All My Loving' doesn't do this, both because of the 'Imperfect' way that the dominant ends the first cycle, and because the cycle continues anyway from ii rather than I.

[35] Guy Chambers in conversation with the author, March 2000. Ian Hammond, 'The Chromatic Subtonic' at www.beathoven.com.

'Proud Mary' by Creedence Clearwater Revival, Wilson Pickett's '(In The) Midnight Hour' and Otis Redding's 'Dock Of The Bay'.[36] Meanwhile Citron sees it as prevalent in American Country music, with writers like Glen Campbell and Jim Webb adopting it for what is now colourfully referred to as an 'open prairie feeling'.[37]

Sixties' rock 'n' roll, Brit-pop and even Punk would all adopt the move in settings as varied as The Kinks' 'Where Have All The Good Times Gone' ('Will this depression last too long?'; key of G); The Sex Pistols' 'Pretty Vacant' ('Oh just remember don't decide'; key of A); and The Spice Girls' 'Say You'll Be There' ('Make you understand'). Each sees ♭VII move to V for this very special type of pre-dominant effect, which The Beatles first delivered in 'All My Loving'. The device is perhaps most easily spotted in another song with a Beatles connection: 'No Matter What', a Top 5 hit in 1971 for fellow Apple artists Badfinger. Listen to the end of the meandering 17-bar middle as a dreamy Cycle Of Fifths excursion climaxes out of thin air with a G to E move (first at 1.13) that re-establishes the A major tonality for the following verse. Suddenly a 'sweet' pop song acquires instant street credibility by delivering a taste of rock with this one extra chord.[38]

From a theoretical point of view we can regard this use of the ♭VII as just another type of 'pre-dominant' ploy – a 'primer' or 'preparation' for V; but one rather more novel then the conventional ones, IV, ii or II7 (and indeed ♭VI7). And the *effect*, as the voice-leading charts confirm, is to 'charge', very specifically, that same dominant as the subliminally clocked chromatic line moves into it.

♭VII and the Four-Chord Turnaround

We've already seen the Four-Chord Turnaround accommodate both 'I-*vi*-IV-V' and even 'I-*VII*-IV-V', along with many other variations. It would be a shame if we couldn't 'plug-in' ♭VII into that slot, as the 'X' in the formula 'I-'X'-IV-V'. As we might have guessed, The Beatles weren't going to let such an obvious one slip through their fingers:

[36] Askold Buk, 'Magical Mystery Tour', *Guitar World*, February 1994, p. 59.

[37] Citron, *Songwriting*, p. 254.

[38] This same 'iron hand in the velvet glove' effect can be spotted in the coda of Elvis Costello's 'Alison', where the ♭VII is deftly introduced for the final repeated cycle of E-A-D-B in the key of E major.

'The Night Before'

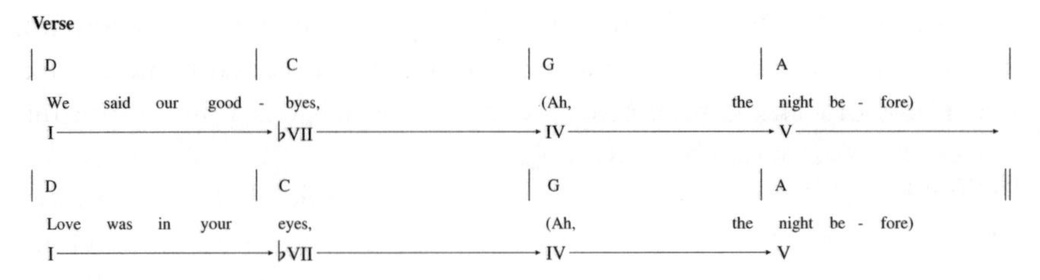

The main lesson of this simple cycle is to see how the dissonant 4th degree of the parent scale is supported not as the root of the IV (which less inspired 'harmonisers' could easily have settled for), but as the 5th of the more novel ♭VII chord.[39]

But, having seen the role of the 3rd and 5th of the ♭VII in supporting the melody, it's fair to say that the 'rocky' flavours of the chord become most apparent when the melody mirrors the root. In other words, in songs where the bluesy ♭7th of the chromatic scale is brought into the proceedings *harmonised by the ♭VII chord itself.*

Here's the verse/chorus structure of 'Another Girl', which appears to be just a variation on the Three-Chord Trick (and it does stress I, IV and V triads in all the conventional roles). But the way in which McCartney incorporates a ♭VII chord to alternate with the tonic succeeds in creating a deeper resonance to the ♭7th note in the bluesy melody.

'Another Girl'

[39] An alternative harmonisation here would have been to use the ♭7th of Am7, the v minor, which lacks the rocky punch of the I-♭VII root movement. Meanwhile the 'I-♭VII-IV-V' would become another popular pop-rock sequence over the years. Listen to Buzzcocks' 'Get On Our Own', the power pop gem from their debut album, *Another Music In A Different Kitchen*.

As we move towards the harder rock flavours of ♭VII, let's take a look at the verse of 'The Word'. Don't be fooled by The Beatles' irresistible pop melody and exacting vocal arrangement; the verse structure here is the very model of a classic rock progression.

'The Word'

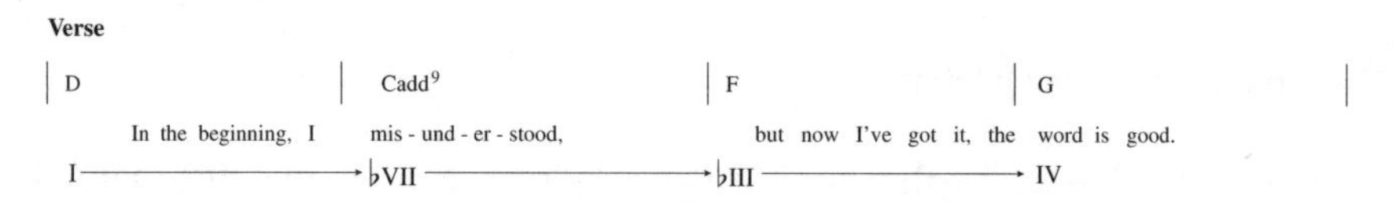

We can instantly hear the bluesy ♭7th of D major in the vocal part, supported again as the root of the C chord. But, beyond this, the power of the sequence can be explained by the fact that it consists of the I-♭VII drop we've just seen – but now followed by the ♭III-IV-I wrap-up that added such heavy-duty credibility to songs like 'Back In The USSR'.

So inherently rocky is this combination of chords that two generic sequences, 'I-♭VII-♭III' and 'I-♭III-IV', both appear (coincidentally adjacent to a photo of John Lennon) among a credible list of the Top-10 most representative pop and rock moves of the last half century.[40]

Let's take this a stage further by noticing that you can't see the join between the parts of the progression, as ♭VII merely moves to ♭III with the stock default move of a descent of a fifth. Nothing new there, except that what we have here is a glimpse of The Cycle Of Fifths in a *chromatic* rather than diatonic context. Here we find The Beatles exploiting the potential for the darker sounds of rock using borrowed chords that take us into uncharted territory.

'Lovely Rita' demonstrates this principle perfectly by contrasting the use of this new territory with the standard cycles that have become so familiar.

The Cycle Of Fifths revisited – the 'sharp' and 'flat' side of 'Lovely Rita'

So far our journeys around the Cycle Of Fifths have been mainly diatonic, only extending the circle briefly when appreciating the mega-descent of

[40] 'Songwriting 101: A Crash Course In Getting Started', *Guitar One* magazine, August 1998, p. 33. Classic examples range from The Who's 'Pinball Wizard' chorus (B-A-D-E, at 0.48) to Blur's 'Song 2' that consists of a repeated I-♭VII-♭III-IV-V crammed into a two-bar power chord riff.

'Moon River'. However, when looking at root movement involving ♭VII, we have to widen the circle further in order to accommodate it (by definition, in fact, as the chord is of course a borrowed one from the chromatic scale). This feature takes us into the left-hand side of the circle, and into the harmonic world sometimes referred to as the 'flat side'.

The Chromatic Cycle Of Fifths

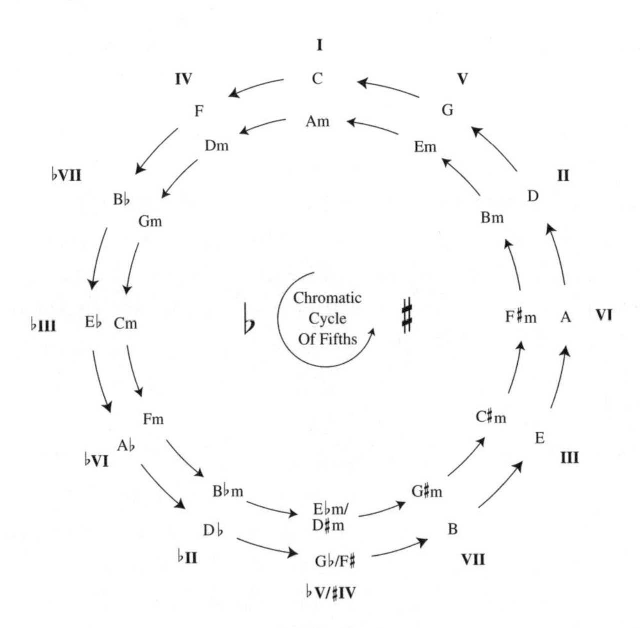

The principle of the cycle is nevertheless the same – we can join this enlarged musical Ferris wheel at any point, and travel along it in fifths for as long as we like. It's just that now the sounds are different ('darker'), as the rocky borrowed chords on the flat side kick in.

'Lovely Rita' represents a great case study as it features runs in fifths using both a 'flat side' *and* a conventional 'sharp side' sequence (on the right-hand side of the circle). Let's look first at the latter, which will help us contrast Paul's (not so) subtle ploys as the differing lyrical themes so expertly tie in with the music. The full cycle lets us literally follow Paul's 'seduction plan' in graphic detail.

'Lovely Rita'

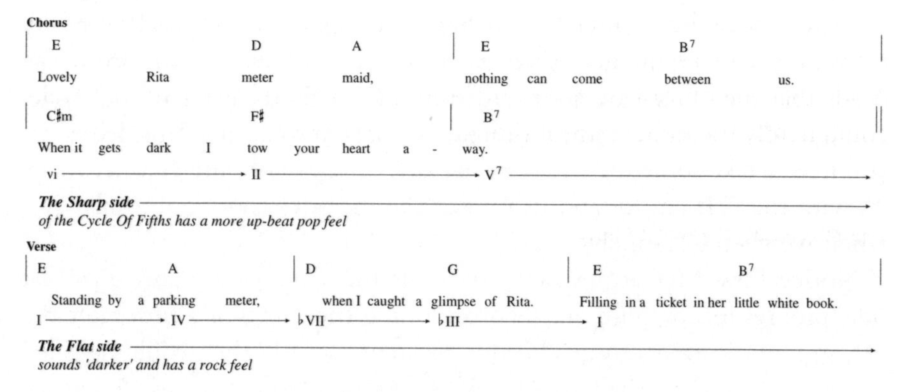

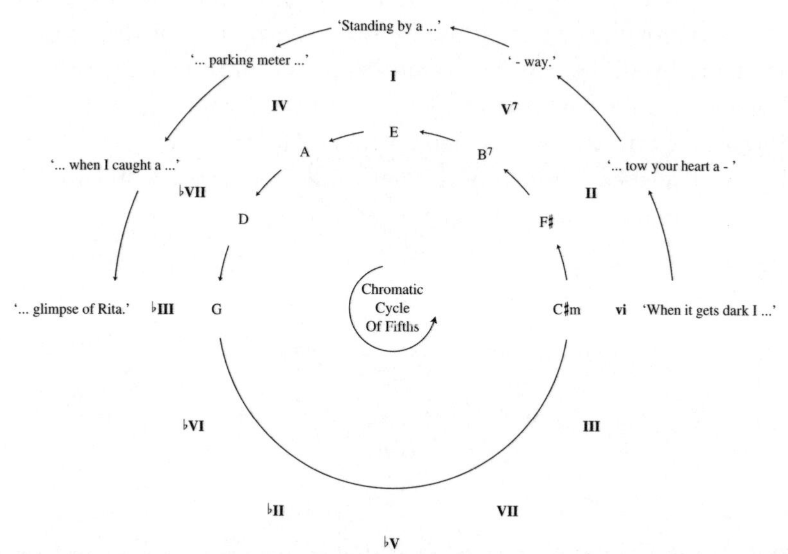

First up then is the familiar 'vi-II-V-I' root movement of the chorus, the most standard of pop sequences used here to effect an innocent introduction to the lady herself.[41] However, these fresh sounding, 'poppy' undertones depicting the singer's fantasy give way to the more 'knowing' sound of the borrowed chords (certainly by the time we get to his true intentions in Verse 4).

[41] Listen also to the link sections to find Paul inserting his favourite I-vi-ii-V Doo Wop ideas that contribute to the strictly 'above board' feel (E-C♯m-F♯m-B at 0.50 after 'military man', and again at 1.39).

The IV chord may be no great shakes as a 'default' opening destination for a new idea, but watch how – *from there* – McCartney runs down in fifths to give us a sequence containing a distinctive pair of borrowed major triads that the chromatic cycle encompasses: ♭VII and ♭III. And the lyrics could hardly track the musical shift any better as, in a later verse, 'When are you free to take some tea with me' becomes 'took her home, I nearly made it', with the ♭VII chord (and its root in the melody) coming into play just when we need its raunchy effect.[42]

Notice how McCartney actually spoils the symmetry of his own 'flat side' progression by temporarily abandoning the move of a fifth after the ♭III, and substituting a tonic chord in place of the ♭VI7 that would have led smoothly down by a half-step to the V7. Had he gone for this alternative harmonisation (the E melody note would have been supported comfortably by the 3rd of the C chord in a 'common tone' substitution) McCartney would have matched the ultimate flat-side Cycle Of Fifths conjured so perfectly by his hero, Buddy Holly. Here is the textbook bridge of 'Everyday', which, not surprisingly, emerges as having been a favourite Beatles live cover between 1957–62.[43]

'Everyday'

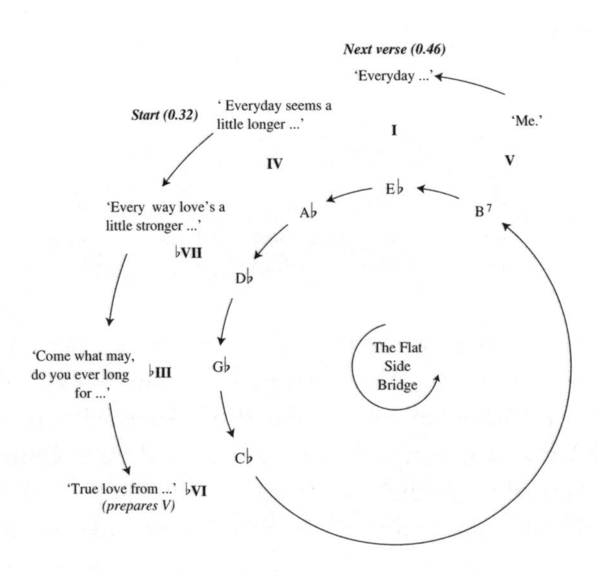

[42] No need to analyse the intentions of 'Lovely Rita's' coda, which kicks in at 2.11 in the low down and dirty tonality of A minor, complete with gratuitous heavy breathing.

[43] Lewisohn, *The Complete Beatles Recording Sessions*, p. 362.

The Power of the ♭VII-I 'major rock' cadence

So far we have seen a variety of situations where the ♭VII chord provides important new colour for harmonisations. Nevertheless, the main cadence to the tonic in all these songs has been a familiar V-I, with that familiar, 'safe' fifth movement taking us back to base (whether delivered 'perfectly' or 'imperfectly'). But rock and pop music would take on a whole new character when songwriters began using ♭VII in a major key to usurp the role of the V chord altogether, cadencing either directly to I, or using it to prime a Plagal cadence. We can follow the evolution of these ground-breaking developments in rock harmony using some very specific Beatles reference points.

The verse of 'A Hard Day's Night' provided an early watershed in this respect. The bluesy melody is hardly groundbreaking stuff, with the ♭7 melody note having been common to generations of 'minor-pentatonic-in-major-key' Three-Chord Tricks from Charlie Patton to Chuck Berry. More to the point, we appear to have regressed, as the first eight bars of the verse use just three chords – but this merely highlights the role of the ♭VII as it alternates with, and cadences directly to, the tonic.

'A Hard Day's Night'

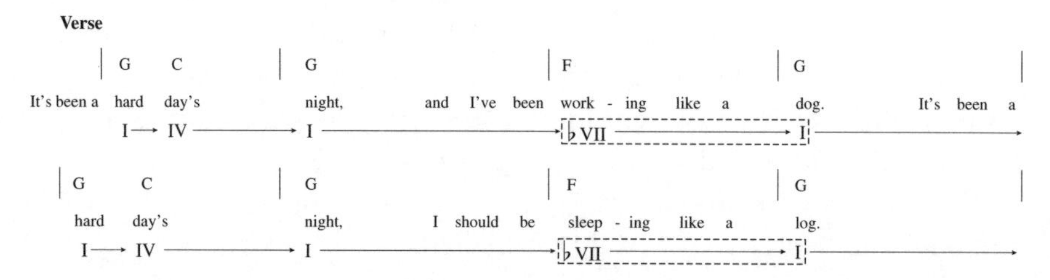

Notice how for each of the first two four-bar phrases, both V-I and IV-I resolutions are shunned in favour of this alternative rocky upstart. This makes for a more primitive touchstone than 'Another Girl' which still relies on both these conventional cadences at important points of rest in the sequence. Here though, the ♭VII chord not only supports the ♭7 note in the melody but its suitably driving, 'parallel' return to base manages to musically symbolise emerging sixties youth – whether he is 'working like a dog' or 'sleeping like a log'.

At a stroke, the resulting sound distanced The Beatles from fifties rock 'n' roll, R'n'B and country, on the one hand, and pure pop on the other. And so the ♭VII-I cadence in various settings would be behind the poignant strains of numerous songs in every later period. Think of the same slide up in the refrain of 'Every Little Thing' ('*She does for* me, yeah'); or the verse cadences in 'For No One' ('Of kindness linger *on, when she no* longer needs you'). Right through to 'Free As A Bird' where the closing refrain subtly distances itself from the opening pop by jettisoning the V chord and closing G-A (on every cycle from 3.34-3.54).

'Help!' provides one of the most clearly identifiable examples as it unfolds on the lines: 'help in *any* way' and 'opened *up the* doors'.

'Help!'

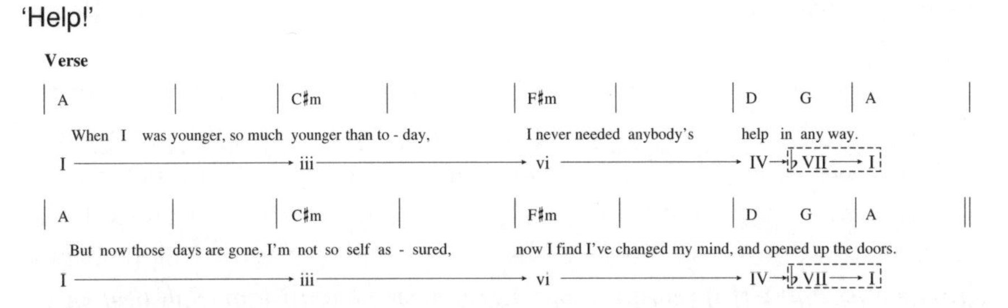

The chord did indeed open up the doors – and not just for The Beatles – for the device within a simple I-♭VII-I alternation would appear in a gobsmacking range of early rock landmarks in the mid-sixties. The Kinks are often cited as the pioneers of this ♭VII 'rock' sound and, as every bar band knows, they milked this interval for all it was worth on classics like 'You Really Got Me', 'Where Have All The Good Times Gone' and 'All Day And All Of The Night'.

This harmony became the stepping-stone to even heavier rock, creating anthems like 'Born To Be Wild' (where those single-strummed E-D-E chords comprise the refrain), the smouldering verse of The Doors' 'Roadhouse Blues' and Alice Cooper's 'Elected'. Not forgetting of course, The Who's 'My Generation' (described by one academic as 'a continuous I-♭VII chord oscillation').[44] And did Punk and New Wave really turn the old order on its head? Several landmark hits from the era, including Siouxsie & The Banshees' 'Hong Kong Garden' and Magazine's 'Shot By Both Sides', were based on the hypnotic effect of the same I-♭VII-I premise – a versatile root movement we first encountered in our discussions of the Aeolian cadence in Chapter 5.

[44] Middleton, *Studying Popular Music*, p. 284. 'My Generation' of course generates much of its interest by modulating – but nevertheless repeats the same I-♭VII-I idea in the new keys.

The Beatles also display their own I-♭VII-I 'oscillations', most obviously in the two-chord vamp (G7-F7-G7) that concludes the experimental 'Wild Honey Pie' (from 0.39) on the *White Album*. And while this particular track is rightly acknowledged as a harmonically challenged throw-away, the fact is that the very same repetitive root sequence defines many of The Beatles' famous mantra-like, modal excursions, which reach a hallucinatory peak on *Revolver* and *Sgt. Pepper*. 'We Can Work It Out' sees them straddling the boundaries of 'pop' and 'modal rock' in what is often regarded as their 'transitionary' period in 1965-66:

'We Can Work It Out'

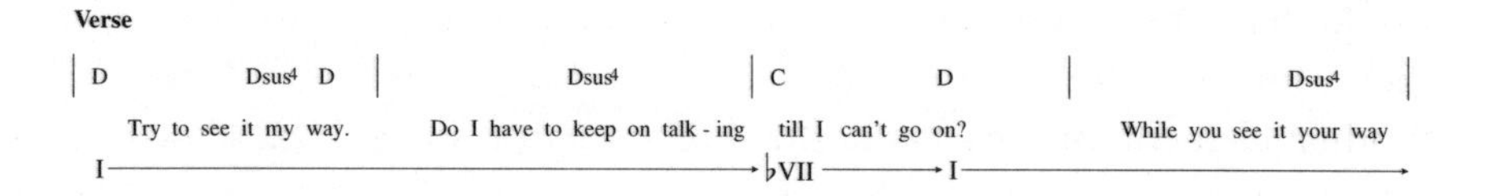

Reconceiving the ♭VII–I cadence – the 'Reverse Dominant Minor Substitution'.

All these simple ♭VII-I moves represent primitive 'bluesy' or 'modal' gambits, but The Beatles' sense of harmonisation suggests that they conceived the cadential properties of the chord in various different ways. It may have been instinctive in many instances, but the breathtakingly subtle reharmonisation displayed in the chorus of 'Hello Goodbye' suggests that it could also be deliberate.

We saw earlier how the first return from IV to I is 'rocked-up' by means of an intervening '♭VI for iv substitution' (at 0.27). But watch how, for the *final cadence* of the chorus (at 0.35) we switch to a B♭9-C close, which now creates a ♭VII-I cadence.

'Hello Goodbye'

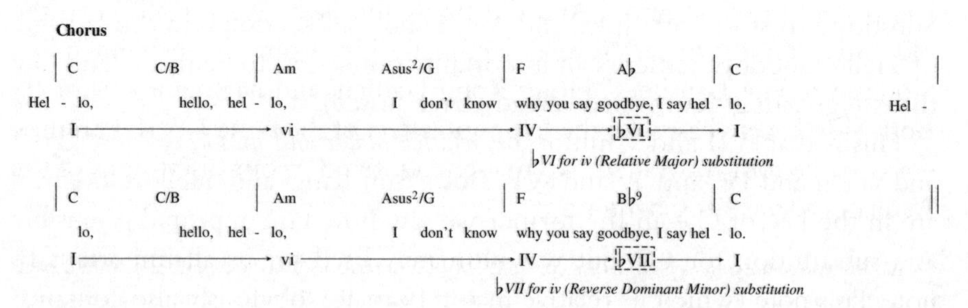

The 9th quality of the ♭VII chord is a stylish touch that cries out for a theoretical justification for its use. Sure enough, we can rationalise this manouevre as the reverse of our 'Dominant Minor Substitution'. We need merely turn our earlier rule on its head, as follows:

'Given a minor chord, we can substitute a dominant seventh chord a fourth higher.'

OK, so we don't appear to have a minor chord to work with here. But this is where we must take a further step in advanced songwriting. For in just the same way that the ♭VI appears as a relative major substitution for a phantom iv minor (as IV returns to the tonic), so ♭VII9 is a *reverse* Dominant Minor Substitution for that very same iv minor chord. Fm-C would have been the simple ploy, but the dominant chord a fourth above Fm, i.e., B♭9, is the substitute that fits the bill and creates yet another element of variety in this highly active song. Here's the same type of chart as we set out in 'Sun King'; but remember, the principle is reversed: it's the dominant that now appears rather than its minor substitute.

Understanding the '♭VII9 for iv' substitute

Fm (the 'phantom' iv)		**B♭9 (substitute for Fm)**
Chord tone	**Note**	**Chord tone**
5th	C	9th
♭3rd	A♭	♭7th
Root	F	5th
	D	3rd
	B♭	Root

Theory interlude

Now that we've seen both mirror images of the Dominant Minor Substitute (first in both 'Julia' and 'Sun King' and, secondly, in this last line of 'Hello Goodbye'), there's an important connection to be made (and one that songwriting sleuths may already have sussed).

This is that ♭VII and v minor are *relative major and minor*. Yes, just like 'I and vi', 'ii and IV' and 'iv and ♭VI'. Both 'Sun King' and 'Hello Goodbye' are in the key of C – in the former we saw how Gm appeared ostensibly as a substitution for C7, but was ultimately used for its all-important B♭ note. This note (which its relative major, B♭ major, obviously also contains) is used to effect the rocky modal cadence (the flattened leading note in the B♭-C close) in 'Hello Goodbye'.

As well as being another mathematical quirk this is very useful for songwriters as it dramatically increases the range of options at their disposal when seeking to harmonise that versatile ♭7th note in a melody. Here's a three-stage approach to applying it:

a) From any tonic chord we can create movement by adding a ♭7th and turning it into a I7 chord, just like any blues on its way to the IV chord.
b) But that same ♭7th effect can be generated either with a v minor in, say, a stylish ballad context, (through the *Dominant Minor Substitution* rule) or,
c) When a more rocky sound is required, by using a ♭VII that represents a *Relative Major Substitution for that same dominant minor*![45]

This may sound complicated but, as we've just explored, it explains the brilliance of certain great Beatles moments.

But never mind the theory – even at this stage we can suggest that the power of the ♭VII-I 'rock' cadence is such that it spans decades of popular music from The Beatles to the Spice Girls. In this sense it is a pivotal point of study, and to truly appreciate The Beatles' development we have to go back to the very early days. All the way back, in fact, to *Please Please Me* to unearth, ironically, the last of the four 'pre-1964 flat-submediants', which eagle-eyed readers will have noticed we failed to tackle earlier in this chapter.

That was because the *function* of the ♭VI chord in 'P.S. I Love You' is so inherently connected to that of another borrowed chord – the ♭VII that also appeared in that song – that we have reserved it for discussion here.

The Beatles origins of the 'major' Aeolian rock run: ♭VI-♭VII-I

Back in 1962 (and, indeed, even now), McCartney's 'P.S. I Love You' was hardly regarded as a defining moment in Beatlemania. Rather, the reverse – this B-side of 'Love Me Do' was even criticised by George Martin as not

[45] Ian Hammond implicitly makes the same point when commenting on 'Sun King': 'The C7 (or B♭) is replaced by Gm7. This replacement occurs a number of times in Lennon songs. v7 is not much more than an inversion of ♭VII, and not much more than a different root of C9.' The Chromatic Subtonic, www.beathoven.com.

being up to scratch. Nevertheless, for modern rock historians, many elements of this song represent landmarks in pop songwriting. And none more so than the novel cadence that sees the tonic retrieved with an ascending resolution that unfolds ♭VI-♭VII-I.

'P.S. I Love You'

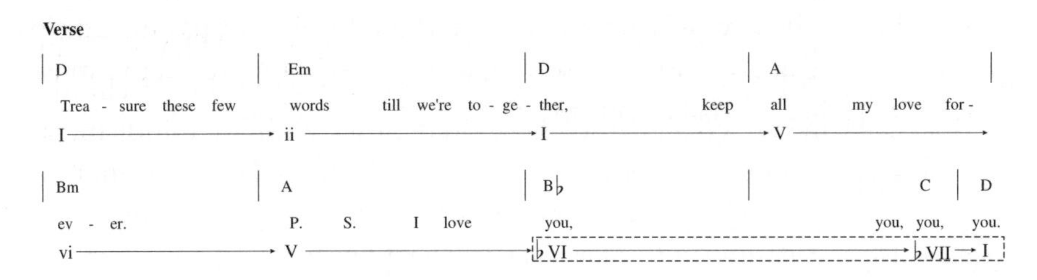

For now at least, we can best think of this as the 'major-key version of the Aeolian rock run (♭VI-♭VII-i minor) that we discussed earlier. As we will see later, however, the term 'Aeolian' is only being maintained here in recognition of the fact that the *♭VI* chord is present.

First, let's see how, in this particular context, the role of both chords was also to *delay* the expected cadence by using a rather special type of deception, a feature with which we are becoming increasingly familiar.

Watch how the song seems headed inexorably from V to I as A appears to set up the expected move to D. Tantalisingly, the D note itself is indeed then heard, but it proves immediately to have been a false dawn. This is because the note appears not as the root of the D major tonic we anticipated but, courtesy of McCartney's inspired approach to harmonisation, as the 3rd of B♭. The cadence to D is thereby delayed, only reaching its intended target two bars later; and turning what seems destined to be an 8-bar section into one of 10 measures.

And with that two-bar *addendum* crafted perfectly as a subliminal musical *postscript* for the very words of the title, here is a lyrical/musical premise of which even Cole Porter would have been proud, and one that certainly matched the famously extended phrasing of 'Love Me Do' back on the A-side of the single. P.P.S. That was subtle, Sir Paul.

But forget the 'delay' factor. More significant for the rock historian is the *nature of the cadence*, namely that the sequence represents The Beatles' earliest example of returning to a major tonic with the novelty of ♭VII. Already McCartney was rebelling against the standard Perfect and Plagal cadences (or, if we were lucky, 'iv-I') that typically prevailed in the simple harmonic framework of fifties rock 'n' roll. Three *major* triads – 'in parallel' – each separated by a whole tone, became a powerful alternative that The Beatles would constantly rework.

Just as ♭VI-♭VII-i *minor* would become a defining rock progression, so would this 'borrowed' version in a major key (or even with third-less power-chords). It may only have constituted the briefest of passing chords in 'P. S. I Love You', but listen closely now to 'Lady Madonna' as the music literally helps her to 'make ends meet' with its novel resolution.

'Lady Madonna'

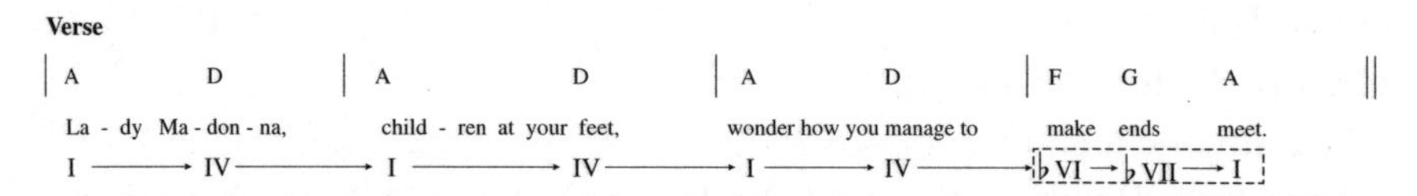

The same goes for the start – and end – of 'With A Little Help From My Friends' as Billy Shears enters – and exits – *Sgt. Pepper*'s Big Top, again with the lyrical theme subliminally matching the cadential drama of C-D-E. And so it continued, right on through to 'Polythene Pam' on *Abbey Road*.

'Polythene Pam'

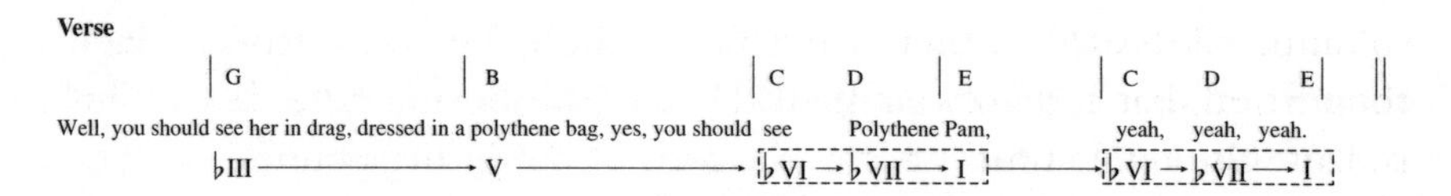

The famous Beatle battle-cry of 'Yeah, yeah, yeah' is back in evidence, but the ballsy sound is now far removed from early Beatlemania as those ascending second intervals work their magic. Here is a sound surely recognisable as having been exploited by every rock band as thoroughly as the Three-Chord Trick itself.

A post-Beatles tour of the major 'Aeolian rock run'

The verse of David Bowie's 'Suffragette City', with its laid-back 'Hey man' lyrics underpinned by the relentless power of the repeated F-G-A ascent, is a landmark that perhaps best links the sixties origins of the sequence with the latest contemporary excursions.

Meanwhile, even a short stretch of this progression can be seen to immediately add rock clout to a diverse range of classics. Listen to the same run-up in The Kinks' 'Lola' (C-D-E); in The Fall's mighty 'Futures & Pasts' (A-B-C♯); or the Pretenders' 'Kid' (F-G-A) (in the latter it makes for a sudden, powerful rock interlude, in contrast to the 'pure pop' Four-Chord Turnaround of the verse). It is also an essential part of any stadium rock band's repertoire: The Rolling Stones would dine out on this sequence in songs like 'Gimme Shelter' – where it accounts for almost the entire song. Van Halen have delivered it on many occasions, most effectively on the mighty 'Unchained', while Scottish rockers Gun rode it to stardom on their cover of 'Word Up'. As a driving cadence it as integral to the classic rock of Jethro Tull's 'Aqualung' (D♭-E♭-F) as to the raw punk of Buzzcocks' 'Orgasm Addict' (F♯-G♯-A♯).

Lest anyone feel this is a *passé cliché*, Brit-pop listeners can find it in songs ranging from Robbie Williams' 'Old Before I Die' (F-G-A), where it again appears as a meaty diversion to the classic pop flavours, to the Oasis single, 'Go Let It Out'. The critics may have dwelt on the famous Beatles influence on Oasis – not least with those 'Strawberry Fields'-style Mellotron fills – but, ironically, by far the most appropriate point of comparison is Abba's 'S.O.S', given that the choruses of both these songs hinge so fundamentally on a move to IV before heading onwards and upwards through ♭VI-♭VI-I. Ironically, The Sex Pistols had previously volunteered 'S.O.S' as their harmonic prototype for 'Pretty Vacant' – a connection that certainly baffles this author. However, the same cannot be said of 'Go Let It Out' which so closely follows the identical harmonic sequence of the ABBA classic (and with similar melodic phrasing).

'S.O.S' (chorus)

'When you're	gone, how can	I even	try to go	on?'
	IV	♭VI	♭VII	I

'Go Let It Out' (chorus)

'Go let it	out, go let it	in,	go let it	out'
	IV	♭VI	♭VII	I

Meanwhile, talking of connections, the minor key origins of this Aeolian rock sequence can be best appreciated in a pair of acknowledged classics that use ♭VI-♭VII to cadence variously to *both a major and a minor tonic.* Eric Clapton's 'Layla' and Van Halen's 'Running With The Devil' are landmarks in the genres of classic rock and Heavy Metal and both deliberately exploit the tonal ambiguity we now know this progression can provide.[46] The title of Robert Walser's definitive deconstruction of Heavy Metal is even derived from the Van Halen song that so epitomises the ambiguities of the whole metal culture. It does this, Walser explains, through its harmonic construction, which pits ♭VI-♭VII-i against ♭VI-♭VII-I as the tonic changes schizophrenically between E major and E minor.[47]

Finally let's suggest a humble piece of trivia regarding The Beatles' early exposure to the ♭VII-I cadence which has so effectively transformed the rock landscape. Buddy Holly surely deserves some credit (once again) for the way in which his 1958 song, 'Well All Right', opens so boldly with the I-♭VII-I pattern (F♯-E-F♯), before alternating with the dominant. There's no record of The Beatles playing this particular Holly song, but Beatles music historians are also encouraged to check out the deceptively sophisticated song 'Why', on which The Beatles backed Tony Sheridan.

In the key of G we hear a clearly cycled I-♭VII-I intro that is dramatically at odds with the 'sweet' pop progression that comprises the verse.[48]

Meanwhile, tucked away on *Live At The BBC* is a Beatles version of Ritchie Barrett's 'Some Other Guy', an early stage favourite that has a special place in the hearts of The Beatles themselves courtesy of some priceless black-and-white footage of the band. Here's Paul McCartney:

> '"Some Other Guy" is a great song . . . It really got us started because that's one of the earliest bits of film of The Beatles. It was a song we sang when Granada Television came to The Cavern. It was also a bit of a muso song . . .'[49]

[46] We've already mentioned the chorus of 'Layla' which runs repeatedly down and back through i-♭VII-♭VI, in D minor. But note how the verse line 'nobody waiting by your side' sees the same C-D-E root move as E major becomes the new tonic.

[47] Robert Walser, *Running with the Devil: Power, Gender and Madness in Heavy Metal Music*, p. 48 describes the 'no thirds', implied E Aeolian move of C-D-E that culminates later in a 'full' E major chord. The author also cites various other heavy duty '♭VI-♭VII-I' formula songs including Bon Jovi's 'Livin' On A Prayer' (p. 122), and Iron Maiden's 'Seventh Son Of A Seventh Son', (p. 156).

[48] In the key of A, the intro of 'Why' wraps up with G-E (an early hearing of the predominant ♭VII) before unfolding its pretty verse with a repeated 'I-iii-ii-V' cycle.

[49] *Paul McCartney's Rock 'n' Roll Roots*, BBC Radio 2, 25th December 1999.

Quite why Paul adds that final 'muso' observation to what is ostensibly a simple, three chord, R'n'B standard, is anybody's guess. But could it be perhaps for the fact that the song is topped and tailed by a highly rare, early example of precisely this type of ♭VII-I rock cadence?

In the key of D, listen to the almost slow-motion A-C-D intro (and outro at 1.52). Not forgetting – in the song proper – those deft, embellishing 'second interval' slides that fleetingly deliver I-♭VII-I on every tonic (and the equivalent for IV and V).

By the end of 1967 The Beatles had recorded what could regarded as the ultimate testament to the power of borrowed chords in rock music . . .

'Borrowing' – the primary text: 'I Am The Walrus'

It's too bad that John Lennon didn't approve of people analysing his songs, for here he unwittingly provided contemporary rock students with a textbook demonstration of how to plunder the parallel minor. While the song has a seemingly sprawling format, where nothing is quite what it seems, the sounds of the ♭III, ♭VI and ♭VII all act as important reference points as they join I, IV, and V chords in the harmonic party. For a start, most of the verse sections can be explained as essentially a collage of two of the sequences we've been exploring in this chapter. Namely:

a) The 'I-♭III-IV-I' rock pattern
b) The '♭VI-♭VII-I' Aeolian ascent[50]

Moreover, variations on the latter sequence appear in other surprisingly symmetrical ways that also capture the essence of rock. But it is the slapdash inconsistency in the way the progressions unfold that makes the song so compelling to listen to as we subconsciously search for tonal footholds.

For example, notice how Lennon keeps his powder dry with the ascending Aeolian rock run. It doesn't appear in the first verse, which consists mainly of the ♭III-IV action in (a) above. It's reserved to jet-propel the phrase 'waiting for the band to come' and its later equivalents: 'dripping from a dead dog's eye' and 'climbing up the Eiffel Tower'. Each of these lines jump out at us as we rise to the tonic.

[50] The Knack's 1979 No. 6 hit 'My Sharona' combines both these sequences to create one seamless run in the key of G.

'I Am The Walrus'

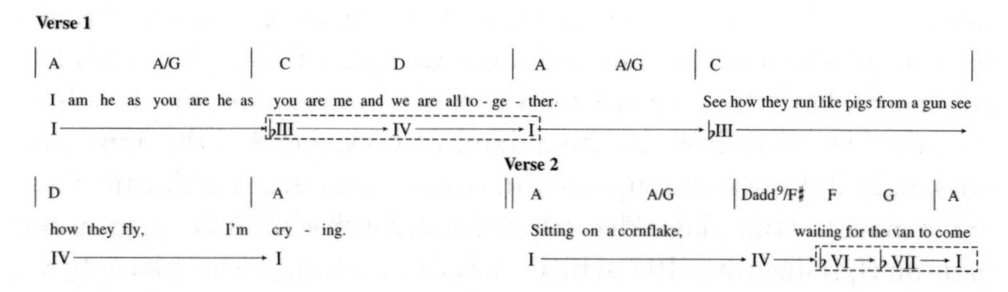

The chorus itself then uses another manifestation of the three-major-triads-in-parallel of (b). But now it's '♭III-IV-V', an uncannily symmetrical-sounding ploy, that delivers an inexorable drive to the dominant for the acid-spiked 'middle feeling' over the infamous 'Goo goo g'joob'.

'I Am The Walrus'

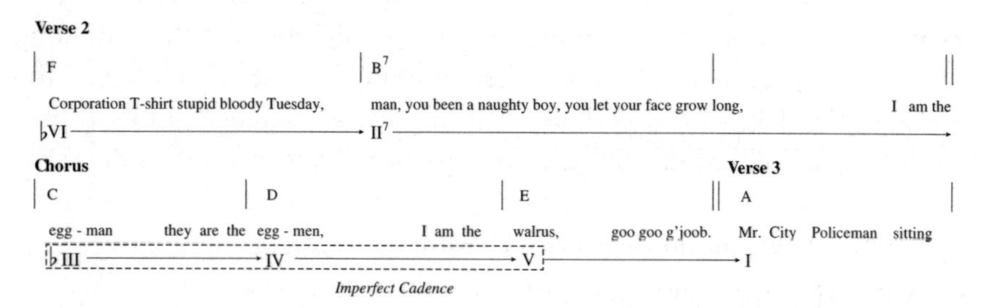

The climactic E chord here creates a type of Imperfect cadence: another 'hanging V' chord that achieves a brief sense of detachment before inevitably retrieving the tonic on the next verse. The only difference now is that it's been 'prepared' in Lennon's own cocksure, psychedelic way: through ♭III and IV, rather than through the more conventional ii, II or 'unprepared IV'.

And if we work back one stage from the chorus we can appreciate the role of the potentially confusing II chord, the B7 in the key of A that we've so far ignored. For the sudden root jump of an augmented fourth, as F moves to B, is a touch of genius. It is a maverick presence and instantly takes 'Walrus' beyond the catalogue of songs that hinge on many of the same basic rock runs.

Nevertheless it is difficult to rationalise this chord. It isn't directly 'preparing the dominant', nor is it part of a non-functioning 'II-IV-I', in the pop-rock style, say, of 'Eight Days A Week' or 'You Won't See Me'. This author believes (perhaps controversially) that the moment can best be appreciated as the rock version of the transition from verse-to-chorus in 'I Want To Hold Your Hand'. In both cases we have an 'A.W.O.L.' secondary dominant whose task is to kick-start a chorus by ascending, first by a half-step, and then to culminate with a standard IV-V move to the dominant. Looking at it this way explains how the listener is pulled along by the force of the move in both songs. The only difference is that, in 'Walrus', the move starts on II7, rather than III7, which allows it to accommodate precisely the desired hard rock flavour of the ♭III chord as it makes that extra 'stop' on the journey to the dominant.[51]

Still, the B7 takes on a quite different function in the 'English garden' interlude.

'I Am The Walrus'

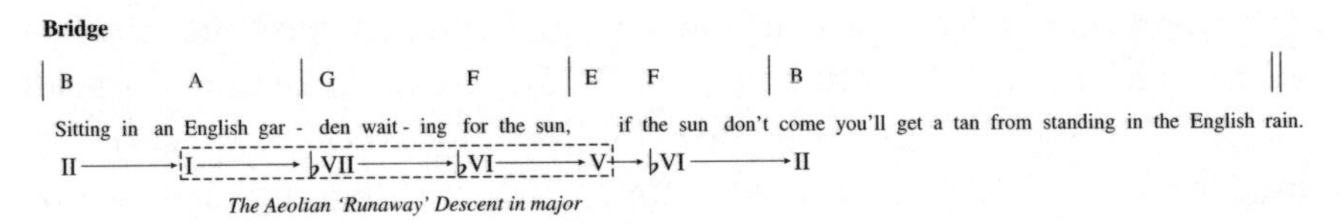

Here it acts to cue another of rock's most famous sequences: 'I-♭VII-♭VI-V', which emerges as nothing more than the major version of the Aeolian 'Runaway' descent. Another versatile musical sure thing, for however you conceive the tonic, the root movement is identical. It's a run that, in major, has appeared in classics from The Ventures 'Walk Don't Run' to The Who's 'Pinball Wizard'.[52]

One of the most effective elements of 'I Am The Walrus' is the way in which this sequence reappears in the final chorus and coda – but now creating a sublime feeling of tonal ambiguity that goes beyond the use of multiple borrowed chords in a single key. Look first at the coda in the following extract.

[51] And, of course, there's no dinky, pop 'I-vi' turnaround (as we find in 'I Want To Hold Your Hand'), with 'Walrus' preferring to hold its power on the V chord, finally collapsing menacingly back on the tonic for the next verse.

[52] 'Walk Don't Run' actually uses both versions: A major in the intro and post-bridge link, and A minor in the verses.

'I Am The Walrus'

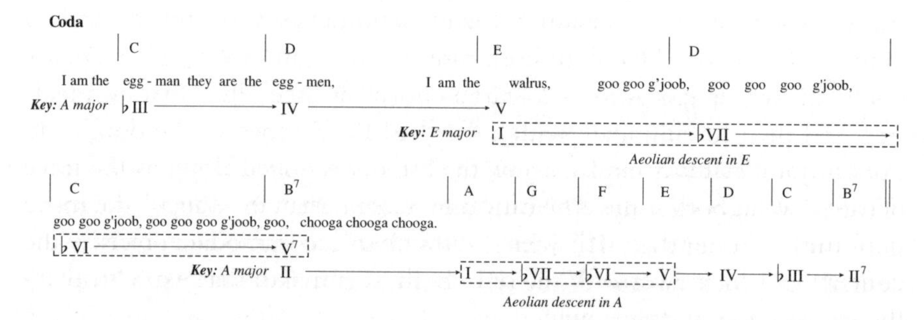

No problem at first. The same Aeolian descent in A is visible even if it now extends 'below' the dominant to pick up the B7 again. However, the fact that it now appears to start on A major itself (at 3.26) represents a fundamental twist.

To appreciate it, look back at how chorus 4 is lengthened after the E is reached on the final V-chord climax at (3.15). This time, Lennon does not return V-I to start a verse (as he does for 'Mr City', verse 3, at 1.04) – he drops back to D. OK, so this also happens when extending chorus 3 (at 2.33), but that was merely because John (as a loose rule) prefers IV-I moves to V-I moves, and therefore wanted to drop *Plagally* into verse 5 ('Expert Texpert') with a D-A move, just as he'd also done when coming out of the 'I'm crying' section and landing in the 'Yellow matter custard'.

This isn't the case in the last chorus where the line is extended even further back from the D chord. Down to C, and on another half step to B7. The result? A re-hearing of the 'Runaway' downward root movement that is so natural in music that – this author at least – subliminally hears it as precisely this I-♭VII-♭VI-V7 – *but now in the key of E.* It's as if the 'middle feeling' climax to E now establishes a new tonality on the V just as any formal Imperfect cadence threatens to do. Of course, it only lasts for one cycle as we are thwarted when the B7 doesn't take us back to E, instead prompting the same downward coda journey, in the key of A, just explained. It's that moment, at 3.26, where we sense we've been duped by a musical sucker-punch complementing the lyrical nonsense on offer, that makes us question the tonality of the song.

In this way 'Walrus' is as harmonically slippery as a seal and represents a landmark in rock music for reasons far beyond its psychedelic themes and unhinged lyrics. Ever since, rock progressions which don't merely 'tip the hat' to Aeolian harmony but cycle restlessly on seemingly unrelated scale degrees, have become standard fare in hard-edged popular music.

Schenker revisited: the ♭VII 'spanner in the works'

We cannot conclude our discussion of ♭VII without briefly mentioning the debate that rages over the application of Schenkerian thinking to rock and pop music in general. Chapter 1 attempted to introduce briefly the concept of 'the power of V' as one of the central themes of Schenker's theory of classical music, which accepts the overriding influence of the dominant (and the sequential voice leading it supports) throughout a comprehensive body of classical music.

But over the last two chapters we have been consistently jettisoning the V-chord altogether, with the subtext that it is precisely by doing so that rock music developed one of its most important characteristics. For while the ♭VII can often complement the V (e.g., as a 'pre-dominant'), so it can happily usurp it by returning a song to the tonic directly with these ♭VII-I cadences. In the process it appears to undermine the conventional Schenkerian notion of a ubiquitous V-chord-supporting-a-melodic-2nd-degree.

Dr. Allan Moore addresses the issue in his landmark 1995 paper entitled 'The so-called "flattened seventh" in rock'.[53] He concludes that far from being 'one-off' gestures in rock, ♭VII chords virtually describe the genre. Using examples from artists as diverse as The Beatles, Led Zeppelin, Jethro Tull, David Bowie, Peter Gabriel, Chesney Hawkes and cult Mod outfit, Secret Affair, he presents the ♭VII chord as almost *the* means of cadencing and modulating. Far from being 'aberrant', Moore regards the chord as quintessentially 'normative'. Other practical overviews come to the same conclusion, seeing cadences of ♭VII-tonic and ♭VI-♭VII-tonic – *in both major and minor keys* – as representative of rock music since the sixties.[54]

While conceding that Schenkerian purists might regard the ♭VII as a technically legitimate rogue *substitute* for V (the two chords do, after all, share a common tone), Moore suggests that to do so downplays one of the

[53] *Popular Music*, May 1995, pp. 185–201.

[54] See the ten generic sequences listed in 'Songwriting 101: A Crash Course In Getting Started', *Guitar One* magazine, August 1998, p. 33.

vital harmonic practices of rock, which 'while sharing many features with classical tonality, are nonetheless distinct'.

Elsewhere Robert Walser succinctly captures the uneasy relationship between classical and rock attitudes to harmony when describing Ozzy Osbourne's and Randy Rhoads' neo-classical rock masterpiece 'Mr Crowley'. The ♭VI-♭VII-i minor sequences in this 1981 landmark are depicted as symbolising the very essence of the rock ethos: a 'frantic scramble' against the fateful inevitability of the predictable (and thus 'fateful') classical traditions, represented by the 'Vivaldian' Cycle Of Fifths into which the song's celestial coda takes flight.[55]

Powerful stuff. And The Beatles paved the way for precisely such a transition in many ways, dating back in various forms to their very earliest excursions. After all, didn't William Mann say as much with his own Aeolian cadence and its modal '♭VII-tonic' action, way back in 1963? By this time, as we've seen, McCartney had already rebelled against Perfect and Plagal cadences and predictable pop structures with his deceptive ♭VI-♭VII-I ascent in 'P.S. I Love You'.

Far from being a theoretical debate exclusive to academia, this touches on a crucial thread in the evolution of rock harmony. Moore even captures the cultural context – the very *attitude* – of the ♭VII-tonic cadence when he says that while it 'does not have the finality of the traditional V-I . . . it seems to me to qualify that certainty with "nevertheless" '.[56]

With ambiguity of various sorts defining the whole rock genre, let's make that a 'maybe'.

[55] Walser, *Running With The Devil: Power, Gender, And Madness In Heavy Metal*, p. 80.

[56] Everett also notes how the rocky ♭VII-I cadence, with its lowered seventh, 'packs a rebellious punch against the major key that the diatonic, polite, and instantly subservient dominant-supported leading tone lacks.'; 'Confessions From Blueberry Hell, or, Pitch Can Be A Sticky Substance', *Expression In Pop-Rock Music, A Collection Of Critical And Analytical Essays*, p. 327–328.

EIGHT

The Modal Connection

Few subjects in music are greeted with more apprehension than the *modes*, a seemingly imponderable mathematical system of scales that appear to have no obvious application to the making of music in the world of pop and rock.

This is the first of many myths surrounding a basic musical framework that not only explains the structure of most genres of popular music but also very effectively helps us to recognise, appreciate and *describe*, the essence of the actual sounds we hear.

The modes help us go far beyond the basic notions of 'happy' and 'sad' that we identified when discussing major and minor scales, and provide us with a standard method for rationalising our instinctive reactions to pieces of music that evoke 'folk', 'Latin', 'Spanish' or 'Indian' flavours. As such, they are a useful tool for analysing a complete spectrum of songs.

Misunderstandings over the role of the modes are due to a combination of factors – their exotic Ancient Greek names (of which Aeolian is one), the impractical dictionary definitions of their construction, and similarly archaic teaching conventions as to their appearance and use in pop. It's really no wonder that when Frank Gambale, the Aussie fusion guitar virtuoso, compiled a video on the subject, he titled it: *Modes – No More Mystery.*[1]

Not that modes are the exclusive domain of the sophisticated jazz guitarist. That is the next myth – for a mode of some description is implied in every song we hear. The major scale is itself equivalent to the *Ionian* mode, as is the natural minor scale to the *Aeolian*. In this sense, all the

[1] Frank Gambale, *Modes: No More Mystery*, DCI Music Productions, 1991.

modes in this chapter (Dorian, Phrygian, Lydian, Mixolydian and Locrian) are similarly just inversions of the major scale, but starting and ending on the remaining scale degrees.

The following chart summarises how each derives from the major scale:

Modal summary chart

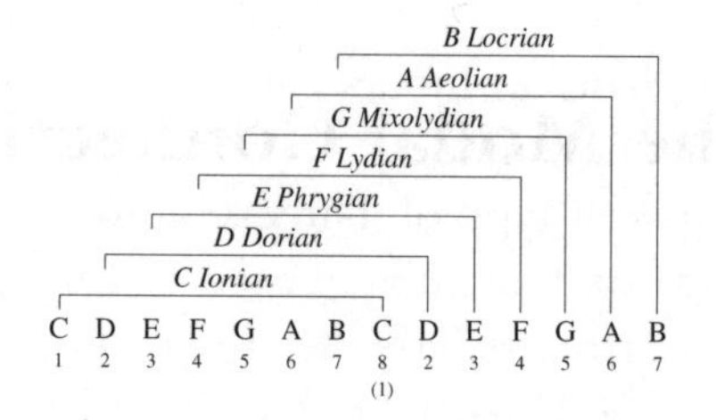

We can create each new mode by simply playing the notes of the major scale, starting on a different note for each mode. It is this 'displacement' that needs qualifying when explaining how modes manifest themselves in pop and rock music. For in attempting to provide a handy reference point for students, conventional teaching practice invariably describes a mode as equivalent to a particular major scale. Hence A Aeolian is described as 'equivalent to C major'. While the two scales share the same notes, this misses the only thing that matters and which Gambale himself captures in one word – emphasis.

As we saw throughout Chapters 5 and 6, the Ionian and Aeolian modes and their chord families appear identical on paper but sound vastly different when revolving around a C major tonic, on the one hand, and A minor, on the other.

John Lennon's 'Girl' does not open in G major, even though the key signature might lead you to believe that it does. That was just one song where a minor verse demonstrated how character is dependent on a *distinct set of interval relationships viewed in relation to a tonic.* Keeping this in mind, here is a concise definition that underlies this entire chapter:

> 'A mode is an inverted scale, where one of the notes from the scale functions as a starting point (tonic or root) and is the focal point of the scale.'[2]

Since we have already covered the basics of the Ionian and Aeolian modes, this chapter introduces the remaining modes, each with their own

[2] Don Latarski, *Practical Theory For Guitar*, p. 28.

structure which emphasizes notes and chords in new relationships. This will prove to be a fascinating way to appreciate a whole spectrum of chord progressions, vocal melodies and other sounds in Beatles songs.

The Mixolydian Mode

The concept of 'emphasis' in modes can be demonstrated very simply as we introduce our first new mode.

Let's consider a special type of Three-Chord Trick that comprises the entire 4-minute coda of 'Hey Jude'. Listen to this 4-bar progression as it repeats relentlessly (starting at 3.09). It's three chords alright – but it's not to be confused with *the* Three-Chord Trick. Why not? After all, a quick look at the progression on paper confirms that these are the I, IV and V chords in the key of B♭. And yet, when we tap into the flavour of the song we do not hear a conventional R'n'B cycle as we do, say, in 'Twist And Shout'. Instead The Beatles depart from the familiar strains of rock 'n' roll with this sequence – delivered no less than 18 times.

'Hey Jude'

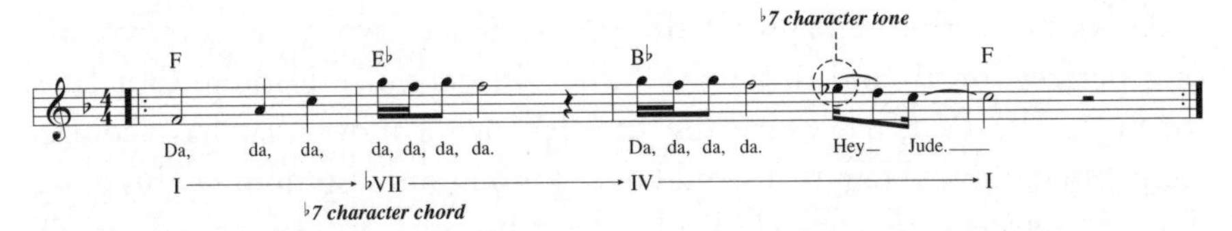

Yes, you can resolve the progression to B♭ major, if you wish, but the ear won't accept that satisfactorily. In any case, it misses the point – for the emphasis here is not on B♭ but on an F tonic. The cycle starts from this focal point by dropping a whole step to E♭ (a rocky ♭VII in relation to F), before two descents of a perfect fourth take us back to base. The three major triads should therefore be viewed as I, IV and ♭VII in F major or, more specifically, F Mixolydian:

F Mixolydian

Scale formula	1	2	3	4	5	6	♭7
Scale tones	F	G	A	B♭	C	D	E♭
Chord formula	**I**	ii	iii dim	**IV**	v	vi	**♭VII**
Chords in F	**F**	G	A dim	**B♭**	Cm	Dm	**E♭**

Some cyclical structures of this type require a degree of theoretical contortionism in order to rationalise them.[3] The confusion is understandable and arises from the fact that these chords occur naturally in *both* B♭ major and F Mixolydian (which we defined, according to our initial chart, as the fifth mode of B♭ major).

The following table confirms that the two scales share the same chords, and that the Mixolydian scale is defined by its major triads on I, IV and ♭VII. The ♭VII, built on that 'subversive' flattened 7th, becomes an intrinsic 'character' chord, which helps us define the sound of the mode.

F Mixolydian	I	ii	iii dim	IV	v	vi	♭VII
Chords	**F**	G	A dim	**B♭**	Cm	Dm	**E♭**
B♭ major (Ionian)	**V**	vi	vi dim	**I**	ii	iii	**IV**

Notice how the Mixolydian mood of 'Hey Jude' only asserts itself in the coda as the ♭7 becomes more prominent in the melody and is joined for the first time by a ♭VII chord. Moreover, it does so in a 'character' *sequence* that uses each of the mode's three major triads in a specific pattern that involves extending the Plagal cadence 'backwards'.

As we know from Chapter 2, the IV-I cadence involves root movement of a perfect fourth and distinctive 'inner' Plagal voice leading. Our latest formula, ♭VII-IV-I, has twice the fun. It's also a move that has acquired some hip highbrow tags that would have John Lennon spinning in his grave. The *Mixolydian Turnaround* neatly describes the modal sound of the progression, although it can be used interchangeably with the terms *Double Fourth* and *Double Plagal* cadence, which reflect the versatility of the idea in a range of settings.

Whether incorporating it into our songwriting manual or following its role in the development of rock, the move encourages us to revisit the Cycle Of Fifths. But now we must take a conceptual leap and reconceive the device as a Cycle Of *Fourths*, which involves following progressions that move in a *clockwise* (rather than anti-clockwise) direction. The Double

[3] Philip Tagg dubs it the Mixolydian Turnaround, *Tagg's Harmony Handout* (2000); while Everett pioneers the 'Double Plagal' term in a Beatles context. Advanced readers are directed to his comments which paradoxically question the modal nature of the progression: '♭VII-IV-I relies on contrapuntal neighbours, not its roots, for its identity.'; *Expression In Pop-Rock Music*, p. 325.

Plagal is the first of an interesting family of 'extended fourths progressions' that work in this way:[4]

The Double Plagal

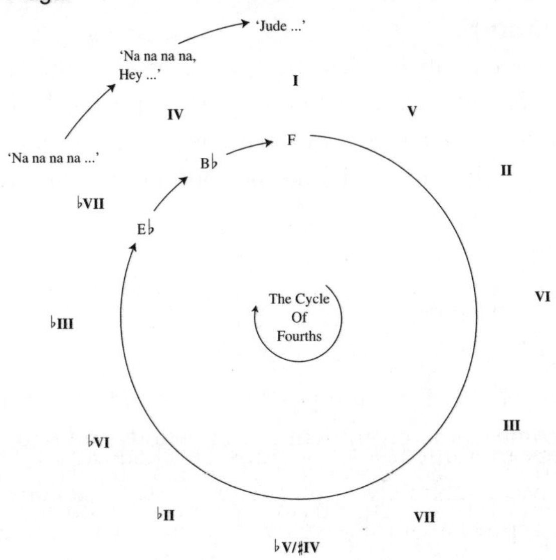

Here's another highly versatile trademark sound of rock, most associated with mid- and late-period Beatles songs. 'You Never Give Me Your Money' sees it showcased as a Mixolydian Turnaround, in a similar circular, 'Hey Jude' fashion (from 1.31-2.09).

'You Never Give Me Your Money'

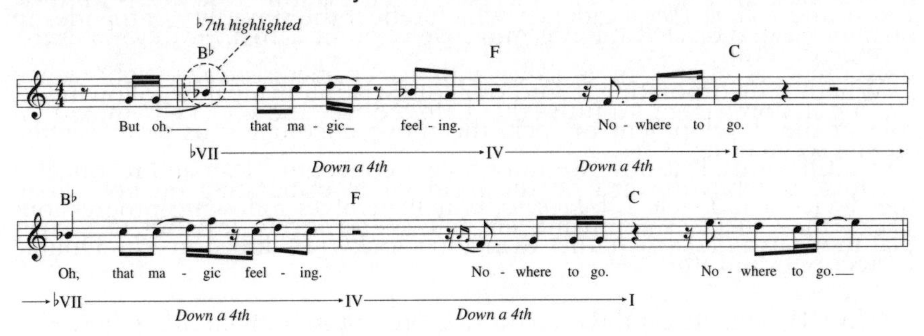

[4] The 'Extended' term has been adopted from Dr. Allan F. Moore's groundbreaking 1995 analysis of both the ♭VII-I and ♭VII-IV-I cadence: 'The so-called "flattened seventh" in rock', *Popular Music*, May 1995, p. 191.

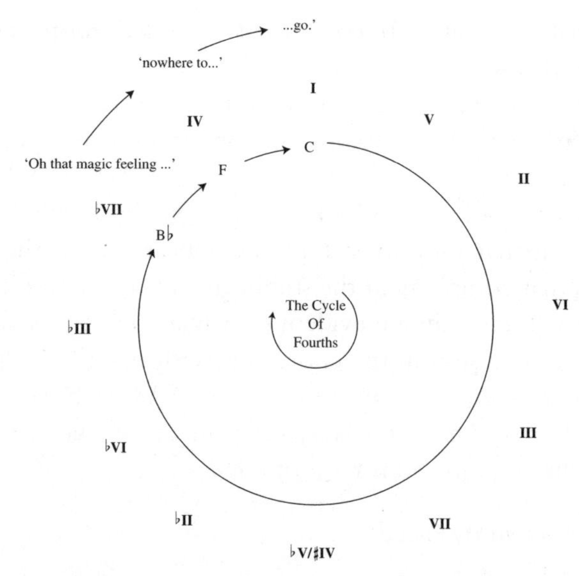

It may not appear immediately obvious but here again The Beatles manage to contrive a sublimely appropriate musical backdrop for their lyrics. In order to appreciate it fully we need to move several stages beyond the simple notions of 'coming home' (e.g., in Perfect cadences), or moving from 'dark' to 'light' (in major/minor shifts).

McCartney's choice of sequence for the 'nowhere to go' lyric is simply another touch of genius in the way that it captures the essence of the chord movement, in particular, and brings out the character of the Mixolydian mode, in general. Obviously, the fact that the chord progression is a cycle from which the singer cannot escape is a start. But then so is a I-VI-II-V, or any repeated Cycle Of Fifths move we've come across. However, it is the movement of chords in fourths, with its characteristically 'tight' voice leading in comparison to fifths, that helps convey the singer's 'hemmed in' feeling so vividly.

Middleton hits the nail on the head when elaborating on how these Plagal movements are intrinsically felt as 'traversing less distance' than Perfect ones in fifths:

> '[In I-IV sequences] the tonic note is present in both chords, whereas [in I-V sequences] only the dominant . . . is common. The result, perhaps, is that I-IV is less tense, more static.'[5]

[5] Middleton also confirms that this is Bjornberg's conclusion about Aeolian rock harmony in general; *Studying Popular Music*, p. 200.

And so it follows that '♭VII-IV-I' is less tense and more static than its mirror image, 'II-V-I'. McCartney must have known this implicitly. After all, he took pains to contrast The Cycle Of Fifths in the minor verse of this very same song with the Mixolydian Turnaround, in fourths, in this development section.[6]

But then, incredibly, a close look at many of The Beatles' Mixolydian excursions reveal that they most typically appear within the context of lyrical themes that complement the stubborn and lazy harmonic character of the mode itself. It's a theme evident over many examples, starting with the very same progression in the chorus of 'With A Little Help From My Friends'. Here a 'poppy', strictly Ionian verse is offset by a more prosaic Mixolydian chorus where the lazy movement of the Double Plagal perfectly matches Ringo's admission of idleness.

'With A Little Help From My Friends'

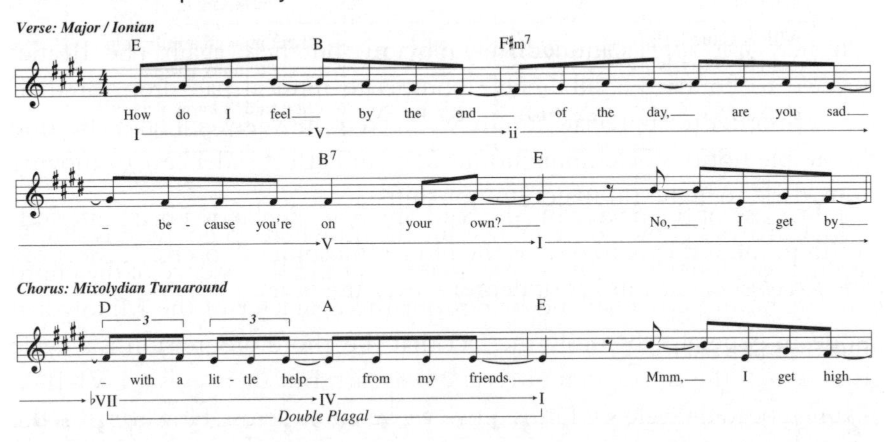

And that's not the end of the Double Plagal cadence. Think of the lazy yearning of the chorus of 'Dig A Pony', or Lennon's similarly ill-disguised frustration as he begs 'Dear Prudence' to join him.

The sequence doesn't have to cycle in this way, or appear as a formal, end-of-phrase, cadence. The following summary chart shows that this same ♭VII-IV-I progression (sometimes with various degrees of 'displacement') makes a distinctive appearance in Beatles intros, verses,

[6] Mention of the Mixolydian mode in the context of this song demands clarification. For by the time we reach this section in Paul's multi-part opus we've already convincingly visited both Aeolian (in the intro/verse) and Ionian (in the bridge 1.10–1.31).

choruses, tags and codas. As with so many of the devices we've been exploring, the table also shows, at a glance, how Lennon and McCartney were matching each other stride for stride, with George also getting in on the act.

The Beatles' '♭VII-IV-I' 'Double Plagal' excursions.

Song	Section	Chords	Lyric
'Dig A Pony'	Chorus (1.00)	G - D - A	'All I want is you ...'
'Dear Prudence'	Verse tag (0.53)	C - G - D	'Won't you come out to play?'
'Taxman'	Chorus (0.23)	C - G - D	'Cause I'm the Taxman'
'Polythene Pam'	Intro (0.01)	D - A - E	'You should see Polythene Pam'
'Magical Mystery Tour'	Intro (0.01)	D - A - E	Opening chords
'Hey Jude'	Coda (3.09)	E♭- B♭- F	'Na, na, na, (etc.)'
'You Never Give Me Your Money'	Bridge (1.31)	B♭- F - C	'Oh that magic feeling, nowhere to go'
'With A Little Help From My Friends'	Chorus (0.26)	D - A - E	'I get by with a little help from my friends'
'She Said She Said'	Verse (0.07)	G♭- D♭- A♭	'She said "I know what it's like to be dead"'

John's use of the device in 'She Said She Said' demands a brief interlude at this point, not least to discuss the ultra-philosophical forensic dissections this *Revolver* excursion has undergone over the years.

'She Said She Said'

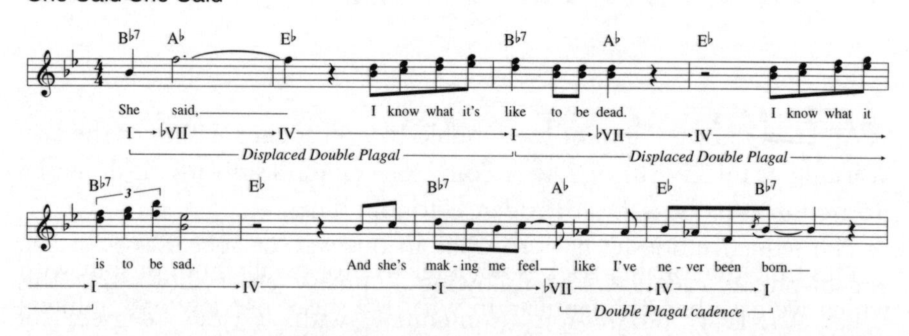

One of the most thought-provoking interpretations was volunteered by David Laing, back in 1969, in a eulogy describing how Beatles songwriting moved adventurously beyond the standard, time-honoured pop theme of love:

'The love-lyric's conventional disregard of the substantive dimensions of time and space (a love song is seldom set anywhere in particular) is transformed under the influence of oriental notions of interior consciousness from being non-dimensional into being supra-dimensional.'[7]

It's only a step from here to matching the inevitability of the human life cycle to Lennon's choice of musical mode and chord pattern. Not only is his sequence itself relentlessly cyclical, in terms of form, but the Double Plagal and the mode's roguish flattened seventh echo the same hemmed-in mantra of 'nowhere to go' as the singer struggles to grasp the concept of life after death, and spirituality in general.

But Lennon wasn't finished with the subtle semantics in 'She Said She Said'. For the brilliance of the song is the way that the bridge breaks free from the harmonic straightjacket of the verse, with a shift in both time signature and tonality that combine expertly to draw attention to the more upbeat lyrical theme of "when I was a boy".

'She Said She Said'

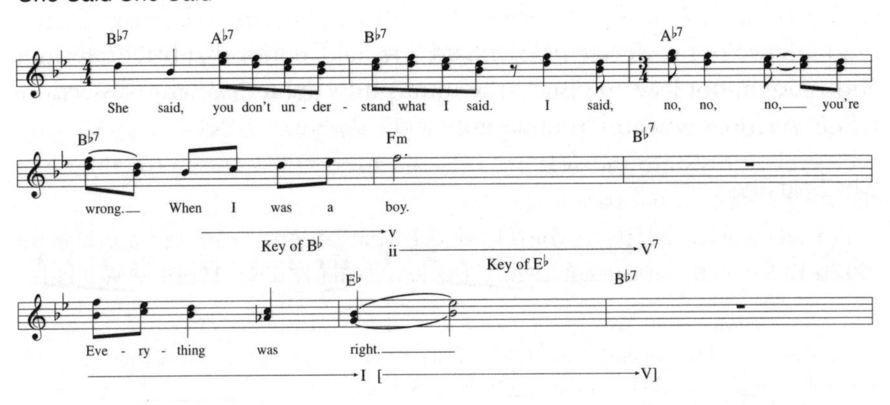

This time the tonality trick is not a relative (or parallel) minor shift with which we have become familiar. In what is a sneak preview of a quintessential Beatles modulation analysed in Chapter 10, we can appreciate how

[7] 'The way in which the song moves from one kind of reality to another is like the way the pieces of a kaleidoscope form a new pattern each time you look at them'; David Laing, *The Sound Of Our Time*, pp. 126–7.

the striking Fm chord functions as rather more than a v minor that is of course indigenous to the Mixolydian mode. Here it serves as the ii that kicks-off a ii-V-I shift not merely to the E♭ *chord* - but to the very *key* of that subdominant that now briefly becomes a new tonal 'home'.

Beatles expert Ger Tillekens explains that The Beatles instinctively understood the semantic potential of the ploy: 'Turning the subdominant into the tonic can be used to signify a retreat into the inner self'.[8]

Meanwhile, the Double Plagal has lived on powerfully down the years in a diverse range of pop and rock settings. Here is a candidate from each of the last five decades of rock; take your pick from endless Mixolydian Turnarounds to hard-hitting, one-off statements:

60s: The Rolling Stones' 'Midnight Rambler' (main structure)
70s: Peter Frampton's 'Do You Feel Like We Do' (title refrain)[9]
80s: Guns 'n' Roses' 'Paradise City' ('. . . please take me home')
90s: Oasis' 'Rock 'n' Roll Star' (chorus)
00s: Oasis' 'Little James' (coda)[10]

Other great Double Plagals include: The Kinks' '20th Century Man', Cheap Trick's 'I Want You To Want Me' (intro and outro), Bachman-Turner Overdrive's 'You Ain't Seen Nothin Yet' (verse), and The Who's 'Won't Get Fooled Again' and 'Magic Bus'. In keeping with the semantics of the move, a fine example is Wire's proto-punk 1977 anthem, '12XU', which again cycles relentlessly around ♭VII-IV-I (E-B-F♯), complementing the theme of claustrophobic sexual paranoia.[11]

For all its rock heritage, the Double Plagal cadence can add a powerful touch to even the most ostensibly mellow ballads. Take Robbie Williams'

[8] 'A Flood Of Flat Sevenths' in '*Every Sound There Is: The Beatles*' Revolver *And The Transformation Of Rock And Roll* [Russell Reising (Ed.)], p.131.

[9] 'It's A Plain Shame' (another from the multi-platinum *Comes Alive* album) also features a refrain with the same I-♭III-♭VII-IV-I premise.

[10] The ♭VII-IV-I is a favourite of Noel Gallagher: listen out for it in a range of songs, including the chorus of 'Shakermaker' (which follows 'Rock 'n' Roll Star' on *Definitely Maybe*, with the same A-E-B cadence); and the chorus of 'Acquiesce' (F-C-G). Liam follows in his brother's footsteps in the extended coda of 'Little James', which follows the 'Hey Jude' formula by cycling repeatedly around the Mixolydian Turnaround (from 2.38 in the key of G) before fading out.

[11] Fatboy Slim took a similarly relentless (if somewhat slower) Double Plagal structure to the UK No.1 spot in 1999 with 'Praise You' (F-C-G).

nineties phenomenon, 'Angels', where the song appears to take a U-turn to deliver ♭VII-IV-I on the crucial punchline.[12]

While The Beatles expanded the potential of the sequence in the mid-sixties, they can be first heard running the idea on their version of 'So How Come (No One Loves Me)', finally released on *Live At The BBC*. Seemingly an innocuous, 'I-IV-V' rock 'n' roll number by The Everly Brothers, each 8-bar verse in the key of G wraps up with a ♭VII-IV-I cadence that was way ahead of its time. Even by July 1963, the pillars of Mixolydian harmony were being established.[13]

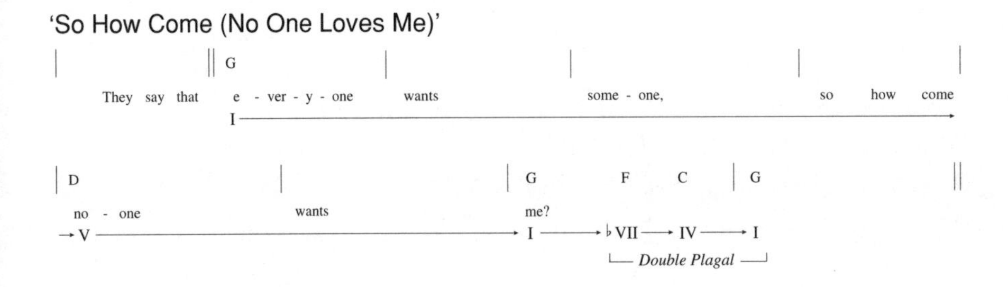

Beyond the Double Plagal: 'Triples' and 'Quads'

But, just as with shots of tequila and bogeys in golf, so Plagal cadences exist not merely as 'singles' and 'doubles', but also as 'triples' and 'quadruples'. Using the Cycle Of Fourths, just count back the requisite number of stops, extending the progression so that each successive chord is reached by means of a descent of a fourth.

A 'Triple Fourth' or 'Tri-Plagal' (Everett's term) cadence can be heard in 'Here Comes The Sun' – in the hypnotic bridge it is disguised with a V7 chord tagged-on for good measure (creating another fourth in the process!), while, in the coda, the sequence makes for a definitive wrap-up:[14]

[12] Over the line: 'I'm lovin' angels instead', a Double Plagal cadence thwarts the expected ii-V-I resolution, as explained by Robbie's co-writer, Guy Chambers, in conversation with the author, March 2000.

[13] The *Live At The BBC* liner notes confirm The Beatles 'sourced' this Bryant track from *A Date With The Everly Brothers:* 'a Top-3 album in 1961'.

[14] Technically, the roots of this particular progression fail to follow the expected Cycle Of Fourths, but the internal harmony is still defined by a sequence of 'inner' Plagal voice leading.

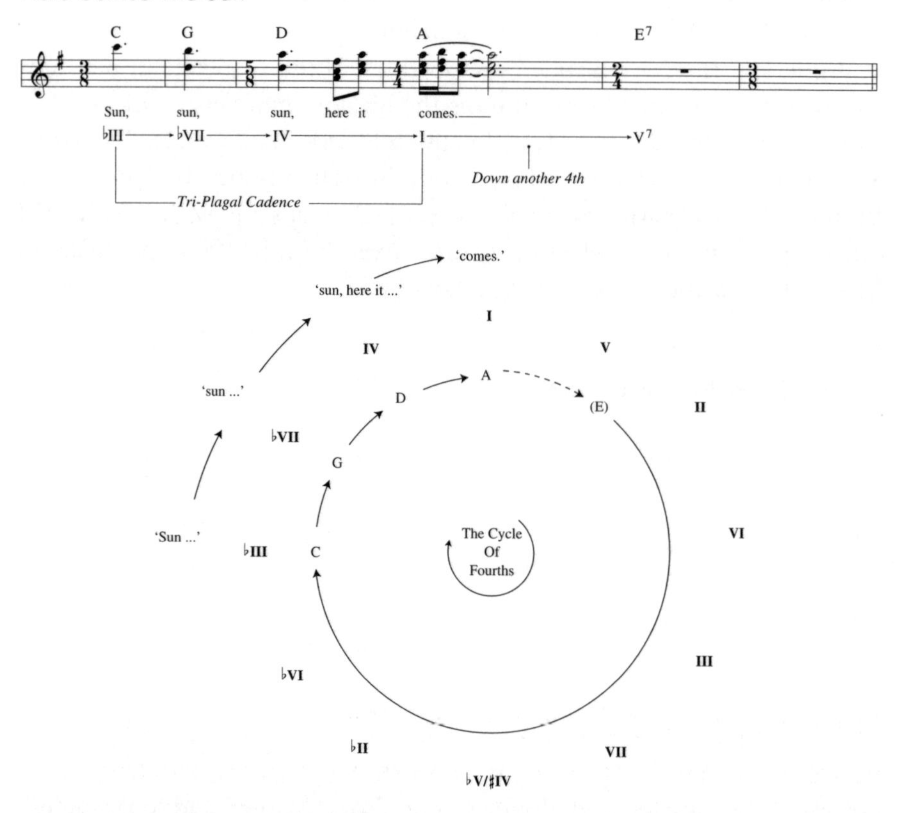

True to form, the repeated mantra 'sun, sun, sun' doesn't rise much above the 'na, na, na' that we saw in the 'Hey Jude' coda.

The Beatles deliver their ultimate string of sequential Plagal runs in the transcendental dream interlude in 'A Day In The Life' (2.49–3.15). Just as we saw with the 'super-cycles' in Fifths, that followed III-VI-II-V-I, so the equivalent five-chord progression in reverse becomes ♭VI-♭III-♭VII-IV-I, creating, for guitarists, an easy extended barre-chord pattern on the fretboard.

This sequence is particularly effective within the context of this song as a whole. For the Plagal moves here contrast from, on the one hand, Lennon's 'reflective' opening verses (which stress thirds and fifths movement) and, on the other, McCartney's 'reality check' (at 2.20) which happily embraces the dominant with standard I-V-I moves.[15]

[15] Not to mention the song's legendary piece of mega-chromaticism as the orchestra makes its heavenly ascent, 'turning us on' in religiously climbing semitones (first at 1.41 and again at 3.46).

'A Day In The Life'

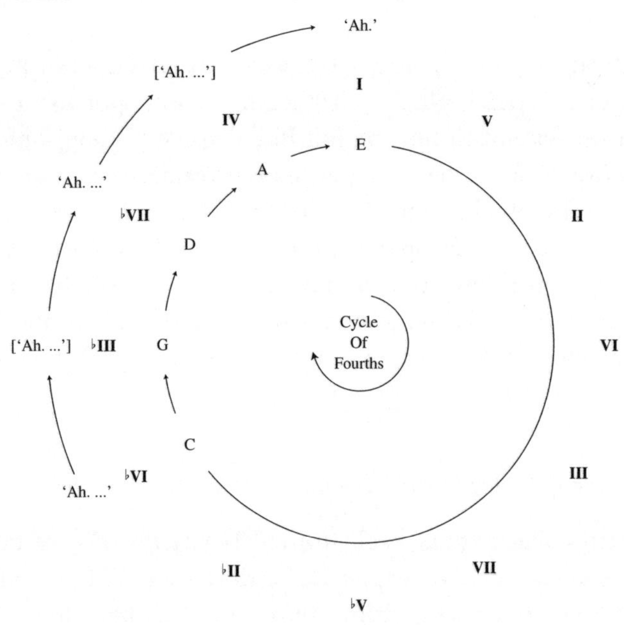

As every bar-band guitarist will know (and as every musicologist including Tagg, Middleton and Everett also points out), Jimi Hendrix's cover of 'Hey Joe' is the definitive 'multi-Plagal' rock song, with its single structure that cycles exclusively around this Quadri-Plagal harmony.[16] The sound of the 'Quad' was back in the charts in the nineties, in Kula Shaker's rendition of Joe South's 'Hush' (made famous by Deep Purple) with the 'na, na, na'

[16] 'Hey Joe', conceived in E (though heard in E♭ due to detuning), works its way to the tonic with the run: C-G-D-A-E. See, in particular, the 'tree diagrams' devised by Middleton to show 'structures of equivalence' in harmony using this song as a model for 'subdominant branching'; *Studying Popular Music*, p. 199.

chant once again maintaining the great tradition of 'lazy lyrics over chained Plagals'.

While 'Quads' are rare in rock, variations on 'Triples' can be found in songs of all eras. Indeed, Noel Gallagher has a soft spot for it – a Triple Fourth root movement (if not the full Plagal voice leading) unfolds on its way to a minor tonic in his mega-anthem 'Wonderwall', a ploy wheeled out identically (by Noel's own admission) for the later Oasis single 'D'You Know What I Mean' (the opening track on *Be Here Now*). Was it pure coincidence that in nominating his favourite all-time singles for a *MOJO* poll, Noel selected The Rolling Stones' 'Jumpin' Jack Flash' and The Small Faces' 'Tin Soldier', two songs that just happen also to feature Triple and Double Fourth root moves, respectively?[17]

Rationalising the ♭VII chord: Mixolydian or 'borrowed'?

Cyclical fourths that extend back from ♭VII strictly take us beyond the Mixolydian mode, with the reappearance of ♭III and ♭VI evoking notions of straightforward 'borrowing from minor'. But just like clockwise moves in Fifths, so these longer, anti-clockwise journeys are exempt from straightforward notions of tonality. After all, taken to their logical conclusion, such progressions result in 360-degree cycles that, by definition, visit all 12 keys (as sometimes created by jazz students as a teaching tool for improvising).

Certainly there is a grey area where the use of ♭VII can perhaps be seen as leaning towards either Aeolian or Mixolydian. After all, songs like 'Polythene Pam' and 'With A Little Help From My Friends' appear to use *both* the 'Mixolydian Turnaround' and also the '♭VI-♭VII-I' run previously described as *the* defining run of Aeolian harmony. So what modes do these songs really imply?

The crux of the debate is: at what point do we cease viewing the ♭VII as 'borrowed' from parallel minor and belonging intrinsically to the

[17] Gallagher quoted in *The 100 Greatest Singles Of All Time*, *MOJO*, Issue 45, August 1997, p. 51. Two other famous Triple Fourth *root* moves that work to minor tonics (now via minor subdominants) include The Kinks' 'Dead End Street' (C-G-Dm-Am) and Irene Cara's 'Flashdance . . . What A Feeling' (Bb-F-Cm-Gm), *Tagg's Harmony Handout*, Institute Of Popular Music, Liverpool University.

Mixolydian mode? Cynics would argue that this is splitting hairs, as the thing being borrowed – the ♭VII – is the same chord whatever its source.

And does it matter? After all, Miles Davis fought against the idea of pigeonholing music into genres, famously claiming that 'there is only good music and bad music'. This is an understandable stance for a jazz master whose musical vision was not constrained by simple modality, and whose improvisations often defied categorisation due to an ever-shifting tonality created by liberal use of all 12 notes of the chromatic scale. But pop music isn't like that. And while there are overlapping terms of reference, at the margin, when describing certain songs, modes remain a highly useful term of reference. Similarly, they can help us speculate on the evolution of genres to which we implicitly relate every time we look in the racks in a record shop.

For example, some regard the Mixolydian rock sound as emerging from *both* the Blues, which stresses the ♭7th in its minor pentatonic and six-note scales, *and* Country, whose major pentatonic delivers the major 3rd and 6th. Hence songs like 'A Hard Day's Night' contain a ♭VII chord but betray their bluesy origins with a melodic ♭3rd. Contrast this with the folk and Eastern-influenced Mixolydian outings that we shall explore later where the ♭3rd is relegated in importance, the tritone clash of ♭7th and major 3rd becomes more prominent and melodic 4^{ths} and 6^{ths} abound.

In many cases the presence of I-♭VII-I sequences, or powerful ♭VII-I cadences *in the absence of the Aeolian bVI chord*, is a clue that a song's harmony is not so much 'borrowed' as intrinsically Mixolydian. Indeed our earlier discussion of 'A Hard Day's Night' could be regarded as a preview of The Beatles' early modal leanings.

We've mentioned how Mixolydian identity is often characterised by limited musical movement both in terms of melody, harmony and the lyrical theme. The remainder of our discussion reinforces this point by showing how The Beatles used the mode to achieve ever-greater harmonic 'downsizing', gradually reducing the number of chords until they were finally left with a single, lone pedal point over which their Mixolydian melodies, with their rebellious ♭7^{ths}, wafted evocatively.

As far back as *Beatles For Sale* the modal-folk-rock strains of 'I'm A Loser' were suggesting a hybrid development of the group's sound. While the ♭7th melody note may only be fleeting here, the strong 3rd and 4th are powerfully in attendance – as is, of course, the ♭VII character chord.

'I'm A Loser'

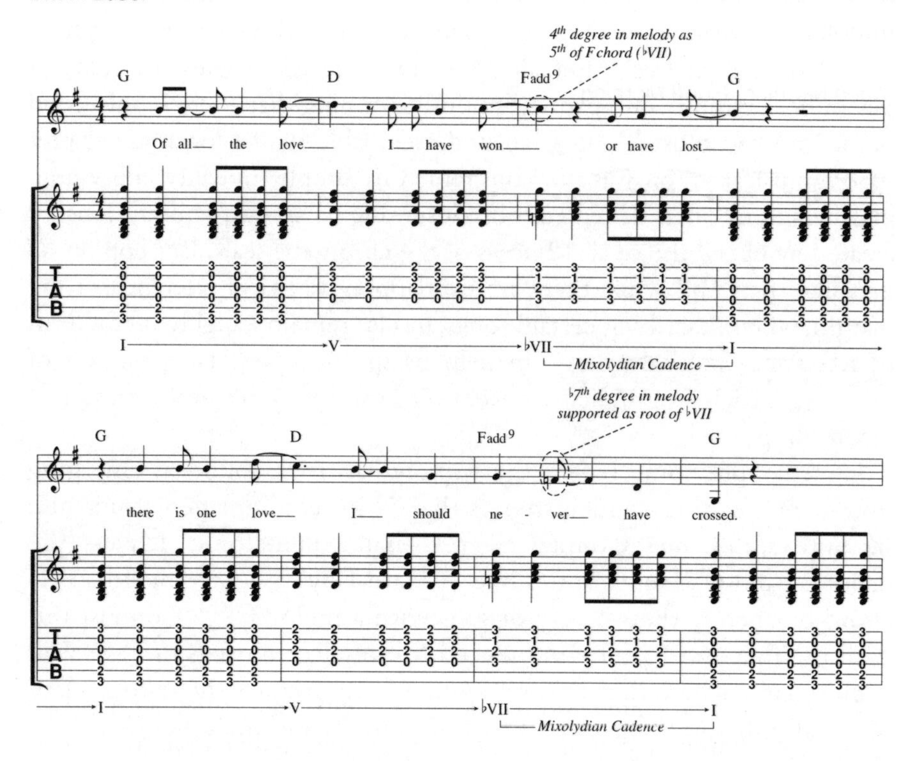

Notice that, unlike the 'pre-dominant' of 'All My Loving', the ♭VII is now switched to appear *after* the V. Indeed at the risk of nit-picking over the precise application of technical tags, the ♭VII–I cadence should really now be best thought of as a *Mixolydian*, rather than an Aeolian-derived, cadence.[18]

This harmony now becomes paramount as we appreciate the sound of a whole string of Beatles songs which have become regarded as some of the finest from their catalogue.

Among them, 'Good Morning, Good Morning', another Lennon contribution to the 'songwriter's manual', demonstrates a truly textbook application of the Mixolydian mode. Here the melody hangs heavily on the ♭7th while the harmony features *both* the ♭VII and the mode's intrinsically weak dominant - the v minor chord, with Lennon again taking

[18] While both these modes feature the ♭VII chord, the latter conjures notions of either ♭VII–*i minor* or, in a major key, a sequence also involving ♭VI. In these songs neither is appropriate.

advantage of the fact that the two chords (G and Em) are relative major and minor.[19]

'Good Morning, Good Morning'

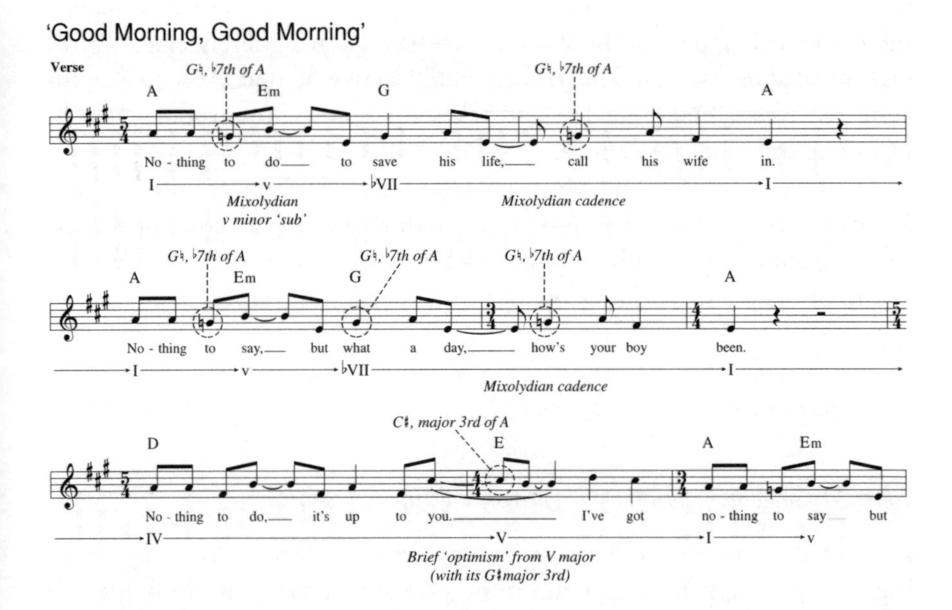

The ♭VII-I is presented as a harmonic straightjacket, involving that lazy interval of a whole step and, of course, no complicated voice-leading as all the notes move *identically in parallel*. Similarly, we don't need to make a leap of faith to see the inherently static feeling of the mode matched brilliantly once more by the very theme of the song. Lennon has 'nothing to do' and 'nothing to say' – even when he leaves the house he's only 'going to work', and he's soon 'headed for home again'. 'Spatially challenged' would be the politically correct way of describing the scant harmonic activity. Just as Lennon munches his corn flakes and dwells on the mundanity of his predicament, so the music of 'Good Morning, Good Morning' is going nowhere.[20]

[19] With regard to this relationship, Ian Hammond suggests that Lennon may have conceived the v minor in 'Strawberry Fields' in this way. See *The Chromatic Subtonic*, www.beathoven.com. And if we accept that 'Fields' was written in A major, then the 'ringing' open guitar string that yields the G natural note is equally present in both open G (♭VII) and open Em (v minor) thereby flagging the substitution potential between these two chords better in this key than any other for the guitar-based songwriter.

[20] Laing sees the song as 'a nightmarish confusion of time and emotion . . . whose only fixed points are the four pillars of modern life, Home, Work, School and Organised Leisure'; *The Sound Of Our Time*, p. 136.

But it's not all doom and gloom – for when the singer briefly gets a grip ('it's up to you'), a major dominant triad (E) *does* appear, bringing with it a glimmer of hope with its G♯ leading note. Once again the fact that the two different triads appear in the space of a short sequence merely confirms the culture of contrast that The Beatles could evoke at will. At a stroke, the song receives a breath of life and takes on a new dimension – just by changing one note in a chord.

The first strain of 'Good Morning, Good Morning' epitomises the character of Mixolydian and so provides a useful opportunity for comparison with the Ionian mode. The following table highlights how the darker, folky sound of the Mixolydian is down to those contrasting sevenths.

Mixolydian	1	2	3	4	5	6	♭7	
Major/Ionian	1	2	3	4	5	6		7

More Mixolydian – folk flavours, pedals and 'Indian-esque drones'

One of the greatest of The Beatles' achievements was the songwriting juggling act they managed for most of their career. Far from moving sequentially from one genre to another (as is sometimes conveniently suggested) the group maintained *in parallel* their mastery of the traditional, catchy chart hit while simultaneously forging rock and dabbling with a wide range of peripheral influences from Country to vaudeville.

One of these threads was their take on folk music, which would form such essential groundwork for their later collisions with Indian music and philosophy. The connections may not be instantly obvious but both these genres are characterised by Mixolydian melodies with a ♭7 bias and broadly static harmony. Often reinforcing the lackadaisical sound of the mode are 'pedals', 'drones' and 'slash chords', musical concepts that we now introduce.

The term 'pedal' can be defined as a sustained common tone in either the upper, middle or lower (bass) harmonies. In this sense The Beatles can actually be heard exploring ringing, folk-like common tones as far back as 'Cry For A Shadow' (*Anthology I*). Listen to John's rhythm figure as it alternates between G/F and Fadd9 (first in the intro) with voicings that keep the top-string G-note ringing out.

To further appreciate the evolution of this technique, listen to the outro guitar figure of 'A Hard Day's Night', from 1964, and the pioneering faded intro of 'Eight Days A Week'. The latter, on *Beatles For Sale*, finds Harrison's upper inversions of D, E, and G chords ascending over Lennon's triplet drone figure (an open D with a D note an octave higher).[21]

By August 1965, *Help!* found The Beatles' droning activity evolving subtly in both inner and upper harmony.[22] 'You've Got To Hide Your Love Away', Lennon's folky ballad (often regarded as being inspired by Bob Dylan), is particularly important as the effect is maintained in a more sustained fashion over a formal verse section of a song. Here a subtle upper drone is achieved by the held G 'pedal' note that appears as a common tone on top of every chord yielding Dsus4 and Fadd9 (as well as G itself) as the chords shift in first position on the guitar fretboard.[23]

'You've Got To Hide Your Love Away'

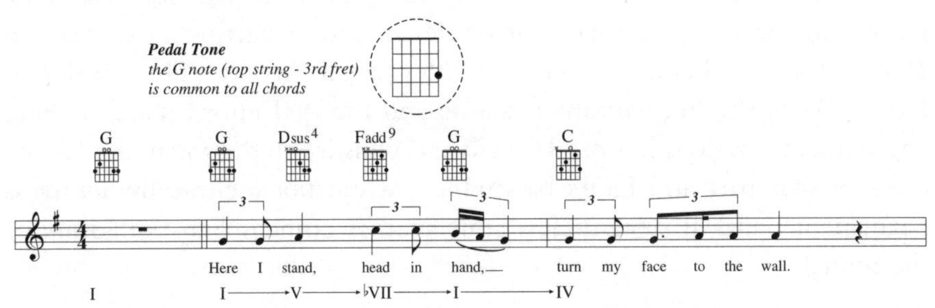

While it could be argued that the chord family here is common to those in 'A Hard Day's Night', this pedal effect is one feature of the song that distances itself from blues and R'n'B traditions.[24] The melody consistently highlights a major 3rd rather than a ♭3rd degree while also emphasising the suspended modal sound of the 4th (another important Mixolydian scale

[21] *Guitar World* regards this as 'one of the first truly signature Beatle riffs', referring also to the added 6th notes with which George embellishes his triads; 'Magical Mystery Tour', by Askold Buk, *Guitar World*, February 1994, pp. 60–2. Drones and common tones exist in all shapes and sizes – listen to the intro to 'Helter Skelter' on the *White Album* to hear a late-Beatles droning intro that is part of a tradition in pop that takes in songs as diverse as Brian Hyland's 'Sealed With A Kiss' and The Rolling Stones' 'Paint It Black'.

[22] Starting on the title track itself, where George's slick descending guitar run links the intro and verse with a deceptively tricky chromatic pattern using droning G and B strings as 'anchors' (at 0.08, 1.26 and 2.07).

[23] A favourite ploy of Noel Gallagher and the *Unplugged* culture generally: listen especially to Oasis's 'Whatever' as the chords shift: G-G/F♯-Em-D-C-D-G, with the same G note acting as a pedal on the top E string throughout.

[24] Others include the lilting 12/8 metre and the delicate flute instrumentation.

degree). However, this tone acts not as a conventional 'sus 4' over a tonic I (as, say, in 'We Can Work It Out'), because Lennon has 'nominated' the ♭VII itself to provide the strong support (C is the 5th of the F chord). It is presumably this distinctive interaction between harmony and melody that Wilfrid Mellers has in mind when he says of the song: 'the modal false relations are more like Vaughan Williams (or his sixteenth-century forebears) than the blues,' before concluding with his own colourful lyrical interpretation: 'John hides his love away, becoming a holy fool or clown, because the world destroys truth'.[25]

OK, so there was no Mixolydian ♭7th note in the *melody* but the F chord, the subtle ♭VII-I movement, and the common tone activity in general, makes up for this, contributing to the modal flavour of the song.

Soon The Beatles were building on this concept of harmonic stasis by reining in the inner and bass harmonies, a feature starting in earnest on *Rubber Soul*. In Lennon's verse to 'Norwegian Wood (This Bird Has Flown)' both the full Mixolydian scale and the ♭VII chord make starring appearances – as do other modal 'bells and whistles' in the form of both the droning sitar part and Paul's bass which, while not technically acting as permanent pedal, is nevertheless conceived as emphasizing the sound of the tonic.[26]

'Norwegian Wood'

The melody helps us to appreciate again the distinct flavour of the mode, though our modal *caveat* with regard to the parent major scale is worth reviewing. While Lennon's top line does indeed visit all the notes of an A major scale, any analysis using this reference point misses the tonal

[25] Mellers, *Twilight Of The Gods*, p. 54.

[26] Technically, Paul embellishes the pedal with the 5th and some brief flurries but the effect is essentially one of static harmony.

emphasis championed throughout this chapter. Again, the relationship between E Mixolydian and A major (A Ionian) is apparent here: the former is equivalent to starting on the fifth degree of the latter, as follows:

A Major (Ionian)	1	2	3	4	5	6	7
Notes	A	B	C♯	D	E	F♯	G♯
E Mixolydian	4	5	6	♭7	1	2	3

Again we must reconfigure our intervals starting with the new tonic, for the song hinges on the feeling of a modal tonic, E, above which the defining 4th and ♭7th revolve.[27]

	E	F♯	G♯	A	B	C♯	D
E Mixolydian	1	2	3	4	5	6	♭7

Despite the distinctive melody that descends the octave, 'Norwegian Wood' ultimately elicits the favoured Mixolydian theme of 'going nowhere', perhaps suitably mirroring the plight of the singer. It's a scene conveyed by both sitar, bass and reinforced by an early workout for the Double Plagal cadence as heard in the rhythm guitar. For while Lennon could easily have wrapped up the sequence with an effortless slide of C-to-D, he actually flirts with an intervening G chord that (surely not coincidentally) neatly brings out the *double entendre* of the word 'had'.

The Beatles developed the principle of the bass pedal even further on George's 'If I Needed Someone', a song that first paraded an interesting modal 'slash' chord that would soon become a fundamental feature of the harmony of several mid-period Beatles songs.[28]

'If I Needed Someone'

[27] The song is heard in E but was clearly conceived in D (as confirmed by *Anthology 2*) using the familiar D open-string shapes, but with a capo to take it up a whole tone.

[28] One-off modal poly-chords had been used for sudden effect in earlier Beatles songs (e.g., the opener to 'A Hard Day's Night') but not in such a sustained context.

This chord is often thought of as an '11th', named after the 4th degree (which appears, along with the 9th, in the octave above the root). The result is an ambiguous, spacey sound that is simultaneously jazz and folk (and even New Age). Today, guitarists like Robben Ford often play the 12-bar blues using 11th chords on each of the I, IV and V roots to achieve a fusionistic slant on contemporary blues.

But in 'If I Needed Someone' the effect is quite different – the chord functions as an *embellishment* of a stubborn tonic, and the song allows some inner harmonic action when the moment of change arrives. But there *is no change to the root of the tonic that continues to dominate our perception of tonality.* Hence the tag '♭VII/I' (a ♭VII triad over a I root) best reflects a sonority that pulls in two directions, drifting while still shackled by the tonic of the key centre.

This chord creates an effect that The Beatles would repeat on 'Got To Get You Into My Life' on *Revolver*, and later 'Baby You're A Rich Man' (remastered on the expanded 1999 reissue of the *Yellow Submarine* soundtrack).

'Got To Get You Into My Life'

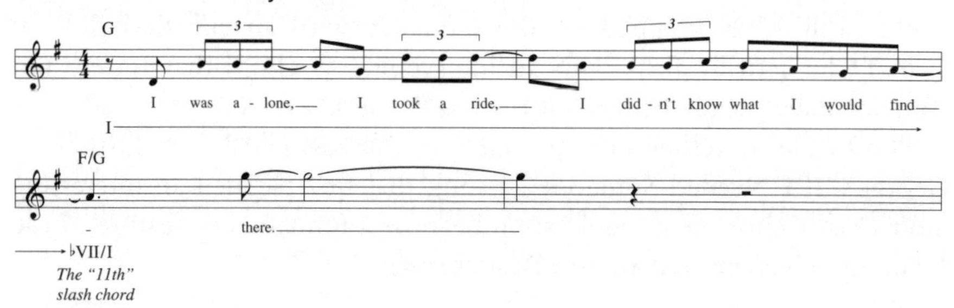

'Baby You're A Rich Man'

Notice how 'Baby You're A Rich Man' eventually arrives in the key of C major,[29] but only after the intro and opening bars of the verse have created a pseudo G Mixolydian flavour by virtue of the slash chord, over which the C notes initially sound as melodic 4^{ths}.

It's no exaggeration to suggest that with such modal melodies and pedals, The Beatles fundamentally reconfigured the traditional relationship between tension and resolution in a pop song. No longer would the listener rely on those busy Beatle chord changes to 'take a song somewhere' with their brilliant mix of familiar and unfamiliar root movement. Pedals imply a new conception of tension, as harmonies and melodies now float with differing degrees of freedom above their tethered 'anchor'. In this sense The Beatles' move toward such harmonic stasis was a logical extension of their growing penchant for Plagal movement in their mid- and late-period songwriting.

Revolver made quantum leaps in this respect though, before that, the 'Paperback Writer'/'Rain' single of June 1966 represents an important watershed. For all their similarities (both feature extended tonic action, in verse and chorus, respectively) the two tracks can be seen as being evolutionary landmarks for two quite different branches of Beatles songwriting. For while both songs are in G major and nominally deliver elements of droning modality, this author sees, on the one hand, 'Paperback Writer', with its hard driving rock riff, as part of a blues heritage building on the guitar meanderings of 'Day Tripper' and paving the way for the hard rock riffs of 'Yer Blues', 'Helter Skelter' and 'Everybody's Got Something To Hide Except For Me And My Monkey'.[30] For a guitarist, the song's minor

[29] An interesting comparison can be made with 10CC's 'I'm Not In Love', which opens with a droning B11-B alternation with B retrospectively seen as an embellished dominant. In this case, the E major tonic is not confirmed until the very end of the verse which starts on an expertly-disguised 'IV-iv-iii' move.

[30] Certainly one can also interpret the song in terms of a modal flavour: '"Paperback Writer" is quite Mixolydian,' says Alan W. Pollack, referring to the emphasis of the ♭7 in the melody and the lack of a V chord; 'Notes on ... Series' no. 91, 1993. *The 'Official' rec.music.beatles Home Page*, www.recmusicbeatles.com. But is it always appropriate to term all songs that use the $♭7^{\text{th}}$ 'Mixolydian', with all the modal connotations the term is intended to evoke? For example, MacDonald regards 'Love Me Do' in this mode (*Revolution In The Head*, p. 451), as does Milton Okun when commenting on 'I Feel Fine' in *The Compleat Beatles*. Both have prominent $♭3^{\text{rds}}$ as well as $♭7^{\text{ths}}$ which clearly betray their blues roots (a distinction taken up Riley, *Tell Me Why*, p. 396). Nevertheless, the distinction between Mixolydian and blues has become blurred, and it is now an accepted convention of guitar magazines to award the Mixolydian tag even to generic blues playing that juxtaposes major 3^{rds}, 4^{ths} and $♭7^{\text{ths}}$ merely as a result of mixing the standard major and minor pentatonic scales.

pentatonic riffing – which can be directly related to Chicago blues – is ultimately the enduring legacy, beyond the intricate vocals explored in Chapter 15.

Meanwhile, the chorus of 'Rain' takes the attention firmly away from the lead guitar and onto the bass, specifically forcing us to focus on a highlighted pedal that contrasts starkly with the busy lines of the verses.

This evocative 12-bar section certainly helps us appreciate profoundly the emergence of what is affectionately know as The Beatles' 'Indian period' where pedals, ♭VII chords and Mixolydian melodies dominate. In the case of 'Tomorrow Never Knows', The Beatles created an entire structure in which the two triads, I and ♭VII, fight it out as 'slash' chords over a single tonic pedal, as we first saw in 'If I Needed Someone'.

'Tomorrow Never Knows'

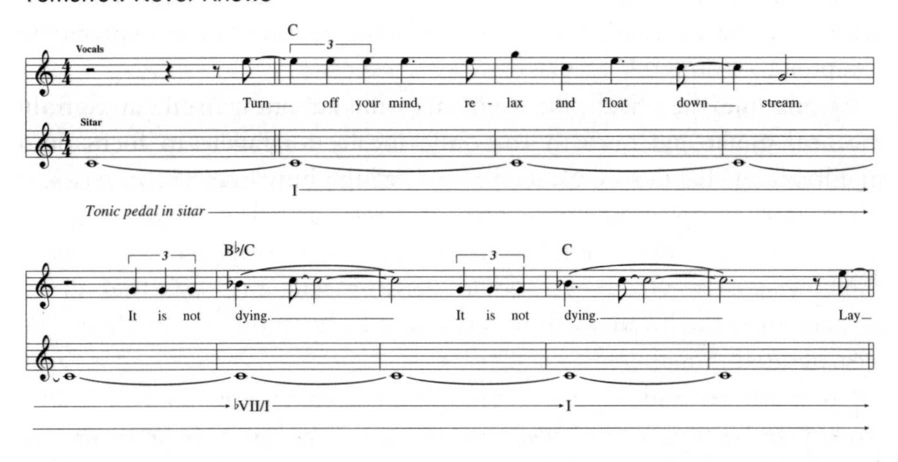

Revolver's heavyweight closer demonstrates that pedal drones do not have to imply a total absence of harmonic ingenuity. They provide the opportunity for not just moving lines of single notes in the upper harmonies but also double-stops and triads that drift over the hypnotic drone.

The Beatles would develop this principle in two main ways: firstly with those songs in which moving inner harmony lines develop over a drone. Listen to 'Dear Prudence', notably written when The Beatles had decamped to India to seek enlightenment from the Maharishi at his Rishikesh HQ.

Secondly, in songs where the harmony gets truncated even further. On 'Within You Without You', for example, Harrison dispenses with even the brief ♭VII harmony of 'Tomorrow Never Knows'. Here the entire song rests on rhythm, texture and an exotic Mixolydian-type melody over a rigidly unchanging pedal – in this case a C 'root-fifth' drone that is neither major nor minor.

For all their acquired taste, these quasi-Indian songs, which broadly include 'Love You To', 'The Inner Light' and 'It's All Too Much', are useful vehicles for deconstructing the mechanics of exotic Beatles melody. This is precisely because the droning pedals mean that we can appreciate the effect of 'pure' top line intervals without the complications posed by changing harmony.

Not surprisingly, The Beatles' use of exotic drones in such songs has attracted colourful criticism when interpreting the psychedelic lyrics invariably on view. Recurring themes include the Eastern fixation with mantras, meditation and, most importantly, the notion of escaping from the constraints of time that so shackle Western society.

In 'She Said She Said', the cyclical Double Plagal movement cleverly mirrored the life cycle, and at least one writer sees a parallel in the random tape loops of 'Tomorrow Never Knows', which instill the idea of death as a transition, complementing the lyrics that see the end as a beginning.[31] So too the static pedal symbolises a sacred, unwavering plane of higher consciousness to which we should strive; a state that (whether drug-induced or naturally attained) transcends rationalisation, or any other type of structured thought.[32]

Laing also reminds us that Pepperland, the paradise island The Beatles created in the film *Yellow Submarine*, is a privileged place 'where laws are abolished and time stands still'. Long before that particular animated film, The Beatles were embodying the concept, musically, with lazy $\flat 7^{\text{ths}}$ floating above a drone creating the very void into which Lennon invites us to surrender ourselves.[33]

The degree to which The Beatles succeed in communicating their newly acquired Eastern ideals in such songs has been philosophically analysed to the 'nth' degree. Laing himself reminds us of the central paradox that, as mortals strive to tap into their spiritual beings, so language – and musical communication itself – become inherently precluded. The Zen Buddhist dictum captures the dilemma: 'he who speaks does not know; he who knows does not speak'.

Meanwhile, for a historical perspective on The Beatles' landmark use of the pedal, Ian MacDonald suggests that, outside folk music (where bagpipes and hurdy gurdy have traditionally provided an omnipresent pedal), the extended drones of 'Tomorrow Never Knows' had been 'absent from Western music since the passing of the religious "organum" style in the 12th century.'[34]

Nor can we forget how the mystical pseudo-Eastern connotations of many pioneering sixties songs were famously satirised by Spinal Tap on

[31] Riley, *Tell Me Why*, p. 201.

[32] The song's lyrics were famously inspired by a version *of The Tibetan Book Of The Dead* prepared by the maverick Timothy Leary as a manual for hippies seeking a quick-fix to spiritual enlightenment via the mind-expanding properties of LSD. See Riley, *Tell Me Why*, p. 199.

[33] Laing, *The Sound Of Our Time*, pp. 129–130.

[34] MacDonald, *Revolution In The Head*, p. 169.

their psychedelic '(Listen To The) Flower People', complete with 'authentic' droning sitars and kaleidoscopic footage.[35]

'Pedal power' continued to be a potent force in pop over the years, with Ingham seeing the principle underpin rock classics like The Who's 'Pinball Wizard' and Deep Purple's 'Smoke On the Water'.[36] While these songs each see the effect used 'locally', constant pedal bass in songs like Sly Stone's 1970 single, 'Thank You (Fallettinme Be Mice Elf Agin)', added to The Beatles' legacy and threatened, once again, the applicability of Schenkerian thinking to certain branches of rock music.[37]

It should also be stressed that the identification of any mode does not depend on the sound asserting itself throughout a song. This is important, as soon we will be exploring mixed-mode songs that imply perhaps two or three different modes in the space of a few bars as a song unfolds.

Just as The Beatles adopted a flexible attitude to tonality, so they did with modality, shifting between character tones to suit the mood (a term that best describes the purpose of all these scales). This is evident not only in terms of broad harmonic structures but right down to the level of certain Mixolydian phrases in various guitar solos. Here's one example from each of the three guitarists:

Harrison: evokes the mode in the solo to 'Something', targeting a B♭ in the key of C, as the tonic major 7th harmony dips to a bar of C (flattened) 7th, at 1.49.

Lennon: has a stock 'Mixo' pattern down pat in 'Get Back', homing in on the major 3rd, 6th and ♭7th notes of the D chord that acts a IV chord in the key of A (first heard at 0.43).

McCartney: famously inserted some Eastern-sounding activity to amuse Harrison in the frantic off-the-cuff solo to 'Taxman' (often assumed to have been played by George himself). The solo starts at 1.13, with bar 4 soon featuring distinctive C natural and B notes (♭7th and 6th of D Mixolydian).

35 See also The Kinks' 'See My Friend' and The Yardbirds' 'Heart Full Of Soul'.

36 Chris Ingham, 'Doctor Rock Dissects The Hits', No. 14, *MOJO*, Issue 40, March 1997, p. 24.

37 'Schenkerian tonalism could not be satisfactorily applied . . . where harmonic structure in any case plays a comparatively small role (for example, songs with a drone chord, but with a richly inflected melodic structure)'; Middleton, *Studying Pop Music*, p. 195. 'Thank You (Fallettinme Be Mice Elf Agin)' was resurrected in the New Wave era by Howard Devoto's Magazine. Listen to the prominence of the G pedal throughout the sparse live version on the album *Play*.

Finally, one famous Mixolydian moment from 'Strawberry Fields Forever' illustrates this point most exotically. Tune in and drop out as the swordmandel makes its grand entrance at 1.19 and again at 2.04.[38]

'Strawberry Fields Forever'

The song arguably 'tipped its hat' to the mode as early as the first v minor chord, which introduces the required G natural note into the key of A.[39] But with the cascading notes: D-C♯-A-G-E (4-3-1-♭7-5) it now strongly creates the modal flavour, complete with Indian overtones courtesy of the swordmandel.[40]

From a cultural point of view, it is interesting how the Mixolydian mode has made such an impact over the years. The songs presented so far in this chapter have, as a group, tended to attract particularly great praise among the self-styled Beatles *cognoscenti*. Admittedly the lyrical themes of such songs find The Beatles at their most philosophical, cynical – and therefore, (presumably) trendiest. Musically, meanwhile, the stressing of the 4th and ♭7th in the mode clearly added a new dimension. And in so far as this succeeded in departing effectively from the legacy of mainstream Ionian pop, the Mixolydian character can implicitly be seen as a hip musical rationale for this alleged 'creative peak'.

The Lydian Mode

The idea of subliminally identifying with modal fashion in music is nothing new; it is evident globally throughout different cultures, and dates

[38] The swordmandel is an Indian instrument similar to a table harp, or the Appalachian hammered dulcimer. Meanwhile, for the most accurate (and practical transcription in the key of A) guitarists are referred to *Guitar For The Practicing Musician*, May 1993, pp. 55–61.

[39] We initially conceived the Em as being 'borrowed from parallel minor' as a 'reverse dominant minor' substitute for the ♭VII (G).

[40] In 1982, the group Monsoon reached the UK Top 20 with 'Ever So Lonely', a pseudo-Indian pop pastiche whose title refrain unfolded along an almost identical Mixolydian scale fragment, complete with a droning modal pedal.

back at least as far as the Ancient Greeks who developed the modal system in the first place. After all, each of the seven modes originated broadly from the popular tonal practices of tribes and regions in Greece and Asia Minor.

Next up is the Lydian mode, a sequence of notes whose interval structure differs again in only one respect from that of the major scale: the fourth note is sharpened by a semitone.

A potential area of confusion is that of reconciling the Lydian mode with the diatonic major scale. But Lydian is now the fourth mode of the major scale, which means that its chords and intervals are those of a major scale starting on its fourth degree.

The Lydian mode

Formula	1		2		3		♯4		5		6		7		1
C Lydian	C		D		E		F♯		G		A		B		C
Intervals		1		1		1		0.5		1		1		0.5	

Like the Ionian mode the Lydian retains the natural 7th, but now the sharpened fourth (or '♯11th' as it is often called) provides a striking element of dissonance.

Lydian	1	2	3		♯4	5	6	7
Major/Ionian	1	2	3	4		5	6	7

To appreciate the flavour, let's first spell out the pitches in a classic Ionian 'pop' melody, as exemplified by McCartney's 'I Will' before comparing it with the most convincing Beatles excursion into the highly acquired taste of Lydian: 'Blue Jay Way'.

'I Will'

Contrast McCartney's relaxing Ionian flow with Harrison's song, which delivers the F♯ note in the key of C along with all the other notes that together make up a complete C Lydian tonality.

'Blue Jay Way'

Both melodies are highly representative examples as they each contain all the members of their respective modes. The ♯11th is the main character tone of the Lydian mode although the prevalence of the 7th is also distinctive. Notice how the latter is used more freely in 'Blue Jay Way' than in 'I Will', though not necessarily tending upwards to the tonic as a leading note. This itself conjures a modal flavour and is partly responsible for the 'floating' feel as that 'independent' 7th refuses to be drawn to base.

Even more effective, though, is the ♯11th itself. We first encounter it in the song (at 0.19), as a lone cello breaks the Ionian mood, instantly warning the listener to expect something far more challenging. The note duly features in the truly haunting verse melody along with, intermittently, some disturbing flattened 3rds.[41] Meanwhile, in the chorus, the ♯11th evokes an Eastern feel in the mantra-like counter-melody while also leading the formal top line to a closing major 3rd.

In this way it is hardly stretching the point to see the music of 'Blue Jay Way' as imaginatively reflecting Harrison's friends losing their way in the LA fog en route to their rendezvous in the Hollywood Hills.[42]

[41] The resulting implied diminished arpeggio is discussed in Chapter 11.

[42] 'Blue Jay Way' was apparently written by George on 1st August 1967, while he and Patti waited for Derek Taylor in the rented LA house of the same name; William J. Dowlding, *Beatlesongs*, p. 196.

Owners of *Magical Mystery Tour* are encouraged to review the closing moments of the previous track on the album, 'Flying'. The Beatles are famous for leaving little musical clues in various corners of their catalogue, and musos will appreciate the Lydian signpost that the Fabs create, ever-so-briefly, in the closing, freetime coda.

'Flying'

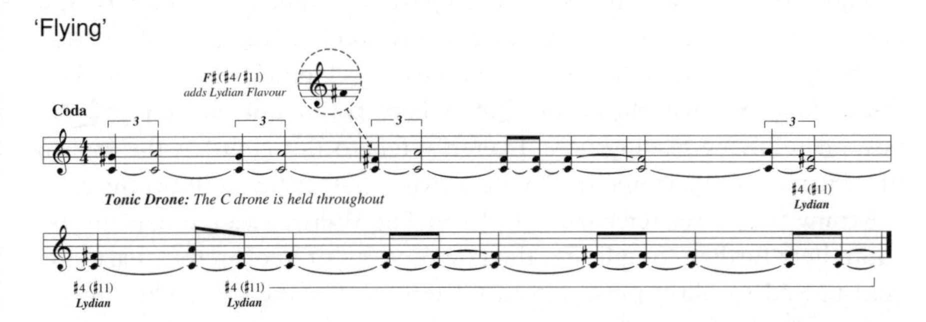

The song is essentially a 12-bar blues structure in which a C major melody unfolds in a repeating one-bar motive using the major 3rd, 4th and 6th degrees; while the occasional B♭ in the keyboard briefly lends a bluesy, Mixolydian angle. But the mood changes as the droning harmony introduces first a ♭3 (at 1.48) and then an F♯, the ♯11th of the key, which we hear alternate in the drone over the remaining few bars. By the time we get to 'Blue Way Jay' the Lydian fog is already descending.

While 'Blue Jay Way' represents The Beatles' Lydian showcase, elements of the mode can be spotted in some other select moments in the catalogue, according to one's musical interpretation. Before briefly visiting some of these, it is useful first to derive the chords of the harmonised Lydian scale in the usual way, and highlight the mode's 'character' chords.

Lydian scale formula	1	2	3	♯4	5	6	7
C Lydian notes	C	D	E	F♯	G	A	B
Chord formula	I	II	iii	♯iv dim	V	vi	vii
C Lydian triads	C	D	Em	F♯ dim	G	Am	Bm

One effect of the ♯11th is to create a striking F♯major7♯11th sound against the tonic triad – a favourite of jazz fusion guitarists seeking a richer alternative to the major scale. More relevant to pop music are the first two chord members that appear side by side as *major* triads (I and II). In C Lydian, therefore, the F♯ note appears as the defining major 3rd in the II chord, turning the D minor of C Ionian into D *major.*

In this sense, one might argue that any II chord in a major sequence gives us a clue that there might be some Lydian activity at work. But note that this is only effectively the case where the II chord *does not move to V*, as it normally does (most commonly when a secondary dominant primes a harmonic move in fifths to the dominant V).

The Lydian flavour is best seen when we have a 'non-functioning II': just as we saw in Chapter 4 in 'Eight Days A Week', 'You Won't See Me', 'Yesterday', 'In My Life' and 'She's Leaving Home', each with their descending, internal chromatic lines where ♯11 is not conceived as an upward-resolving leading note. Everett refers to this chord as the Lydian ♯II, reflecting a supertonic triad with a major (rather than minor) third.

Meanwhile, if we refer back to 'I Am The Walrus', we see that the B7 chord here further complicates the cosy notions of Aeolian rock harmony (and indeed tonality) presented in Chapter 7. For the descending major triad on II (the B chord) arguably introduces a Lydian flavour.

'I Am The Walrus' (intro)

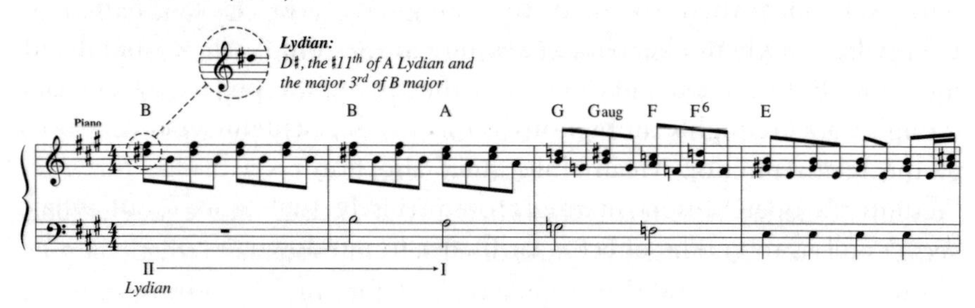

The tell-tale ♯11th (D♯) soon re-appears in Lennon's ranting verse melody though now it could be happily dismissed as essentially an ornamenting neighbour note to the 5th degree. However, by the time of the bridge interlude, it has now been transformed in stature. We now definitely hear that D♯ not merely in the chord but as a powerful, contrasting melodic destination in its own right, with Lennon succeeding in visually transporting us to the 'English Garden' itself.

The other important Lydian character *chord* is the vii7. Unlike in Ionian, this triad has no complicating ♭5, just a straight minor triad that brings out the sound of the Lydian ♯11 as this note now appears as the 5th of the chord. Ian Hammond provides food for thought by suggesting that 'Yesterday' may

'I Am The Walrus'

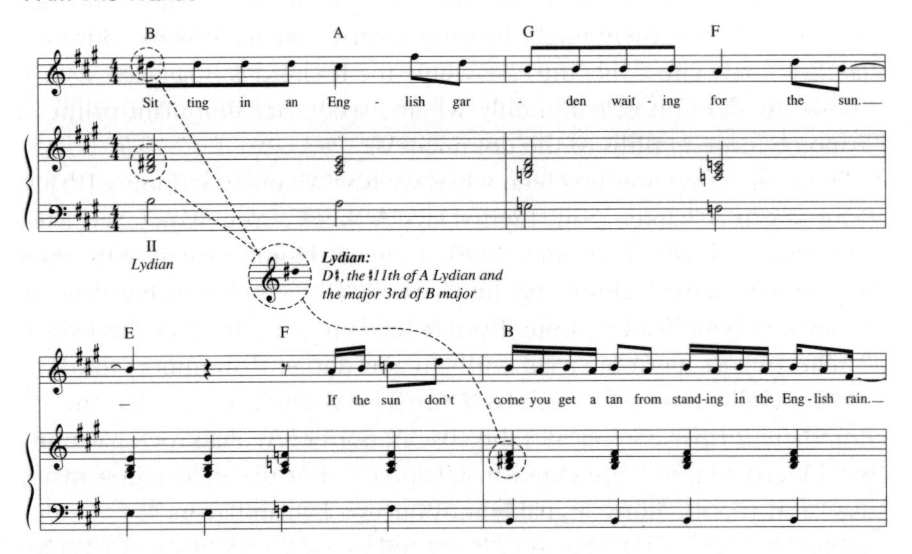

even have some claims to Lydian status.[43] And we have already seen how 'vii7' was so pivotal to both this song and also 'Here There And Everywhere' (where the chord was integral to the 'wave of her hand' moment). Both these contexts could be fleetingly interpreted in this mode though both are highly ambiguous as the vii7 is essentially cueing a move to the relative minor. Meanwhile, 'Julia' also features a bridge that (like 'Yesterday') opens disorientatingly on precisely such a vii7 but which *doesn't* pull us to vi. The effect is far harder to pin down.[44]

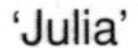
'Julia'

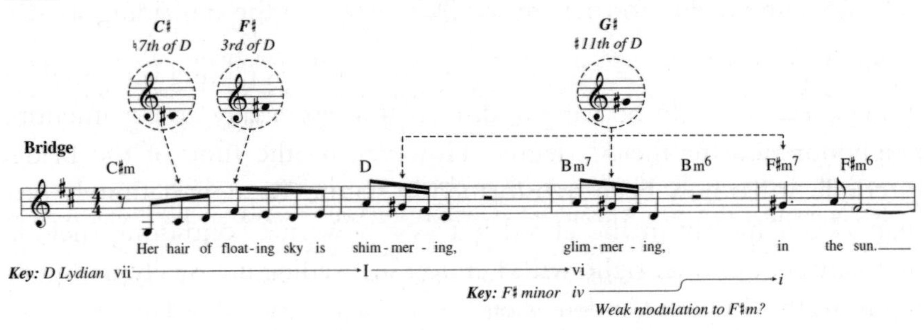

[43] Hammond refers to the I-vii change as being a 'distinctive feature' of the Lydian mode; '"Because" (3): Puzzles', www.beathoven.com.

[44] 'Martha My Dear' also has a bridge that opens on vii7 but the song soon develops into a brilliantly conceived modulation (see Chapter 12).

Even more than the verse itself (see Chapter 7), the bridge tune has a floating quality to it, a feature familiar to most Lydian structures. The fact that the C♯m chord immediately moves back to D major is also an interesting ploy that makes us feel that we haven't drifted convincingly to another key. The G♯ notes in the melody over the D major chord now hang with an air of Lydian modality as they represent pure ♯11ths over a tonic major. Nevertheless, the shifting sands beneath the dreamy 'Julia' (the song is a tribute to John's late mother) can be interpreted in various ways, with Lydian merely one option suggested for the purposes of this particular exercise. As the F♯m chord unfolds, a modulation to the relative minor is another way of looking at this bridge (with the opening C♯m now seen retrospectively as the 'iv' of this temporary key centre).[45]

Whether or not you agree with the Lydian flavour suggested here, the mode is rare in pop music. Everett cites The Left Banke's 'Pretty Ballerina' (from December 1966) as perhaps the only pre-'Blue Jay Way' Lydian example in pop.[46] Later, Lydian scales would become a favourite of virtuoso rock guitarists like Steve Vai and Joe Satriani.[47] And more recently a striking Lydian theme riff defined 'Come Original', the 1999 song by the US group, 311.[48] Nor can we forget Leonard Bernstein's 'Maria', from *West Side Story*, whose opening interval is a melodic ♯11th acting as a tense leading tone to the 5th. Steve Vai himself describes this moment as the very epitome of the sound of his favourite mode.[49]

The Dorian Mode

While the Ionian, Mixolydian and Lydian can be usefully bundled together as 'major modes' due to their major 3rd interval, so the remaining modes,

[45] Alan W. Pollack is one who sees it as such a type of weak modulation. 'Weak because of the continued usage here of the minor v chord and the plagal cadence', he explains (referring to the Bm-F♯m move); 'Notes on … Series' no. 145, 1998. *The 'Official' rec.music.beatles Home Page*, www.recmusicbeatles.com.

[46] Everett, *The Beatles As Musicians: Revolver Through The Anthology*, p. 340.

[47] It's interesting that Joe Satriani's most distinctive Lydian workout just happens to be entitled, 'Flying In A Blue Dream' – possibly a subconscious pun on 'Flying' and 'Blue Jay Way'?! See also Steve Vai's 'Headcuttin' Duel', from the film *Crossroads: The Movie.*

[48] Written by Nick Hexum, the descending lick, features prominent C♯ and G♯ notes (7th and ♯11th in the key of D) over a Dsus4/A chord.

[49] In conversation with the author, August 1995. 'I'm a big fan of the Lydian mode but I don't think of it as a major scale with a sharp fourth. I just think of "Maria". Bernstein often wrote in Lydian and that's a perfect example for me', Dominic Pedler, 'Steve Vai: Into The Ultra Zone', *Total Guitar*, Issue 23, October 1995, p. 42.

Dorian, Phrygian and Locrian, feature a ♭3rd that creates an underlying minor mood in which distinct character tones work their magic. In this sense, the remainder of this chapter is intended as a colourful extension to Chapter 6.

The Aeolian mode is still a most helpful reference point, to which we can now make incremental changes which create some subtle new sounds. In the case of Dorian, the centre of attention is the natural 6th degree that appears in the scale, and the *major* IV chord that results from harmonisation in thirds.

Formula	1		2		♭3		4		5		6		♭7		1
C Dorian	C		D		E♭		F		G		A		B♭		C
Intervals		1		0.5		1		1		1		0.5		1	

A comparison with Aeolian confirms that Dorian differs by only one note:

Dorian	1	2	♭3	4	5		6	♭7
Aeolian	1	2	♭3	4	5	♭6		♭7

The C Dorian Mode – harmonised

Dorian scale formula	1	2	♭3	4	5	6	♭7
C Dorian notes	C	D	E♭	F	G	A	B♭
Chord formula	i^7	ii^7	♭IIImaj^7	IV^7	v^7	vi$^{7\flat5}$	♭VIImaj^7
C Dorian chords	Cm^7	Dm^7	E♭maj^7	F^7	Gm^7	Am$^{7\flat5}$	B♭maj^7

This mode can be seen to consist of all the notes of the B♭ major scale, starting on C, before going 'around-the-clock'. However, once again, this is not a practical way of viewing it. The interval structure is unique and the important *aural* reference points, namely 1, ♭3 and 6, are far removed from any *visual* perception of B♭ major.

A typical workout in Dorian would involve a repeated vamp around this 'i-IV7' change. The Beatles kindly oblige with their impromptu jam, 'Los Paranoias' which follows John's interruption of Paul's phenomenal acoustic fragment of 'Step Inside Love', on *Anthology 3*; (track 23 at 1.32).

'Los Paranoias'

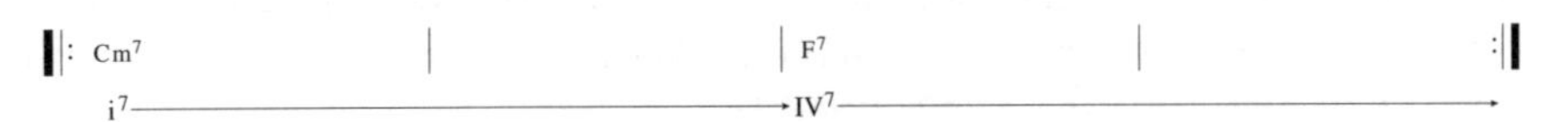

Here the Cm7-to-F7 vamp can be thought of as in the key of C minor but, more specifically, in *C Dorian*. This 'labelling' is again important, as the ♭6 in the C Aeolian scale would be an inappropriate choice of note for a soloist to use over the F major.[50] Long before 'Los Paranoias' (September 1968), the i-IV-i Dorian alternation would feature in George's 'Don't Bother Me', on *With The Beatles*.

'Don't Bother Me'

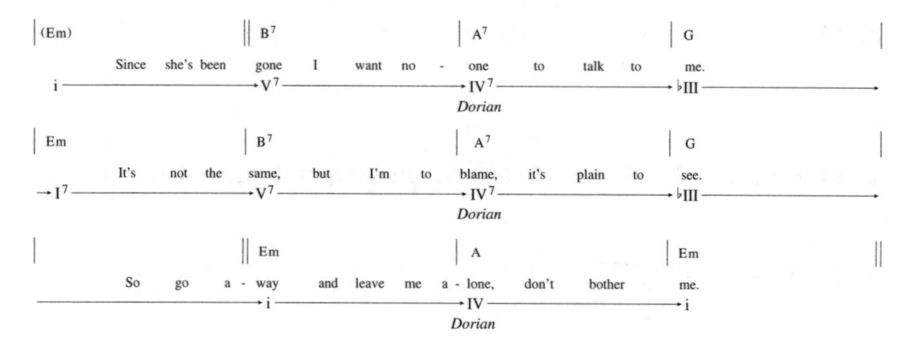

The IV chord in a minor setting is enough to evoke the sound of Dorian: look back to the parallel minor middle eight in 'Norwegian Wood', and the relative minor bridge of 'There's A Place'. See also the Bm-E-Bm-E bridge vamp in 'Run For Your Life'; while two Harrisongs, 'While My Guitar Gently Weeps' and 'Savoy Truffle', also feature minor sections that go for the confident IV chord in a minor setting.

None of these songs clearly features an intrinsically Dorian-esque melody – they lack the brave natural 6ths that identify the character of the mode in the top line. To sample the sound, let's return to 'A Taste Of Honey', right back on *Please Please Me*. While we earlier identified an *Aeolian* cadence in the song's harmonic structure, the melody displays a textbook Dorian character, with The Beatles' version faithfully showcasing

[50] Listen for example, to this same Dorian sequence in the hands of one of its most famous proponents, Carlos Santana, on Tito Puente's 'Oye Como Va'. The guitar lines prominently feature the natural 6th of the scale over the IV chord (F♯ over a D9 in A Dorian), thereby strongly reinforcing the sound of the mode. The i-IV-i Dorian vamp is a popular sound heard on many songs, including 'Spooky', the cult sixties song by Classics IV (recently resurrected by Bill Wyman And His Rhythm Kings). The song was nominated by Brian Wilson as one of his favourite singles: 'I love the mood,' he says, (and presumably the mode too); 'The 100 Greatest Singles Of All Time', *MOJO*, Issue 45, August 1997, p. 66.

the natural 6th degree (D♯ in the key of F♯ minor), in addition to the sound of the IV chord.[51]

'A Taste Of Honey'

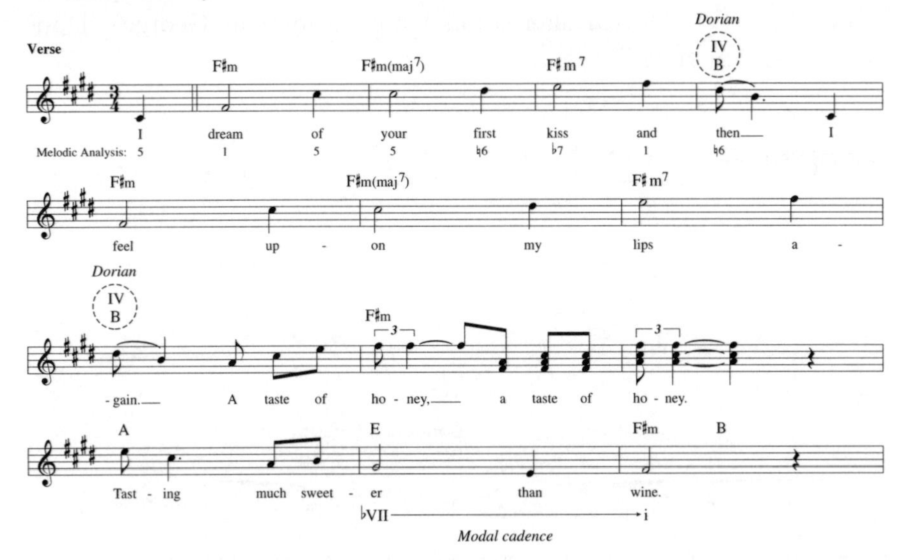

'A Taste Of Honey' arguably represents the most emphatic Dorian example in the catalogue, though, for a Beatles original, 'Fixing A Hole' finds a McCartney melody outlining F Dorian, flirting with the D natural in his top line as well as in the B♭9 chord.

The complicating F major and C 'aug' chords in that song are revisited in the following chapter, where they will bear out the theme of The Beatles' liberal approach to tonality and modality. Some of their finest songs hinge on the drifting flavours that are evoked when modes shift from bar to bar – a feature mastered equally by John, Paul and George. Here is an example from each:

First up is Paul's 'Eleanor Rigby', sometimes referred to as being 'in Dorian'. But beware of hard and fast labels – the following extract shows that the E minor melody features both natural and flattened 6ths. The natural 6th (C♯) in the verse certainly conjures a Dorian flavour. But so the *flattened* 6th note (C natural) – not to mention the ♭VI *chord* (C major is the

[51] No confusion is intended after the deliberations of Chapter 5, but both the harmonised Aeolian and Dorian modes offer the potential for the modal ♭VII–i minor cadence.

only other chord in the song) is equally indicative of E Aeolian, or E *natural* minor.

'Eleanor Rigby'

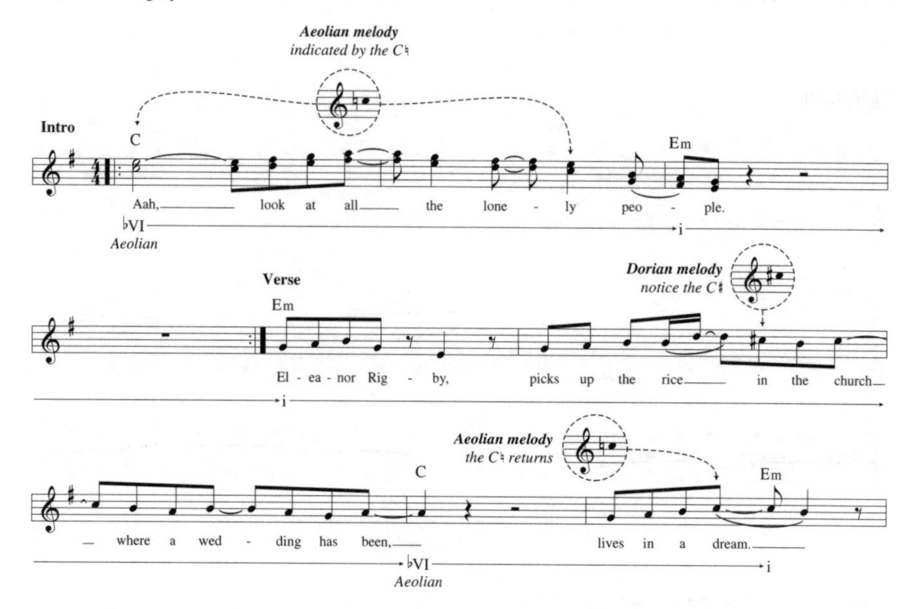

The song duly reminds us that modes are not to be confused with key centres. It is more helpful to regard the song in E minor – as a 'generic' minor tonality – with the ♭3 of Em (G natural) defining the overall mood. But within this minor tonality, suggestions of Dorian and Aeolian are emphasized at different points. There are, of course, no rules with regard to melody construction and all these scales are merely guidelines from which excursions to new character tones, implying new modes, can be made – as Lennon demonstrates in the first section of 'Happiness Is A Warm Gun'.

'Happiness Is A Warm Gun'

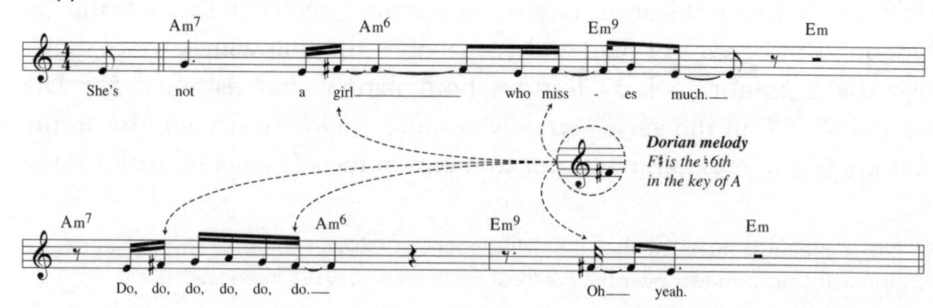

We are clearly in a minor key here. This time A minor, with F♯ notes in the melody suggestive of A Dorian. However, by bar 5, those F *natural* notes present in the D minor chord now belong to the more mellow Aeolian.

For a Harrison 'mixed-mode' foray switching between the same two character tones, check out 'I Me Mine'.

'I Me Mine'

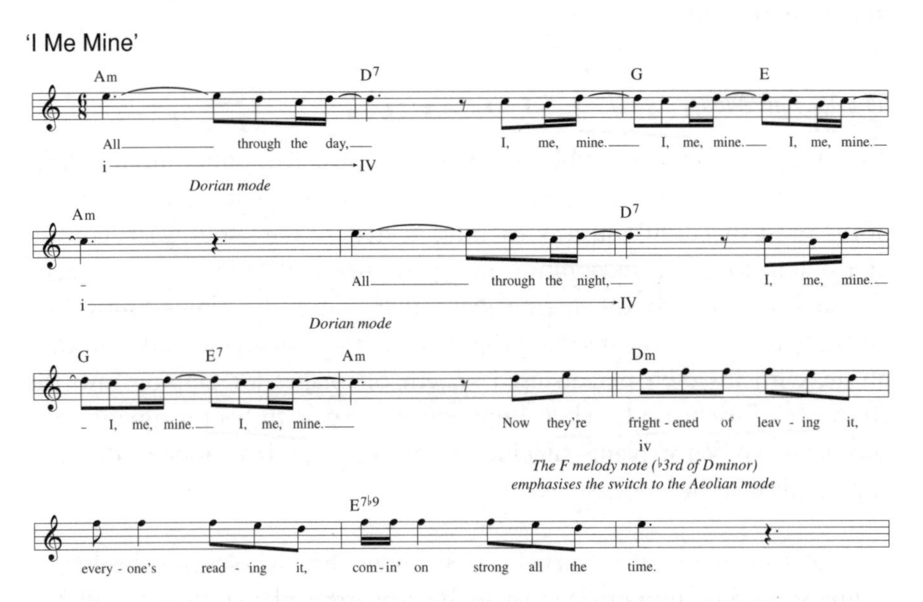

The sound of the strong D dominant chord in the key of A minor sets the Dorian backdrop in the opening bars, only for the melody to plunge to F natural – now the Aeolian-esque ♭3rd of the D *minor* (at 0.23). In terms of lyrical matching, it's no coincidence that the darker Aeolian mode is evoked on the very word 'frightened'. Once again we have a Beatles juxtaposition of modes within a key as the songwriters draw selectively on the chromatic scale at will. Back on *Rubber Soul*, 'Wait' represents a humble example with which to make the point.

'Wait'

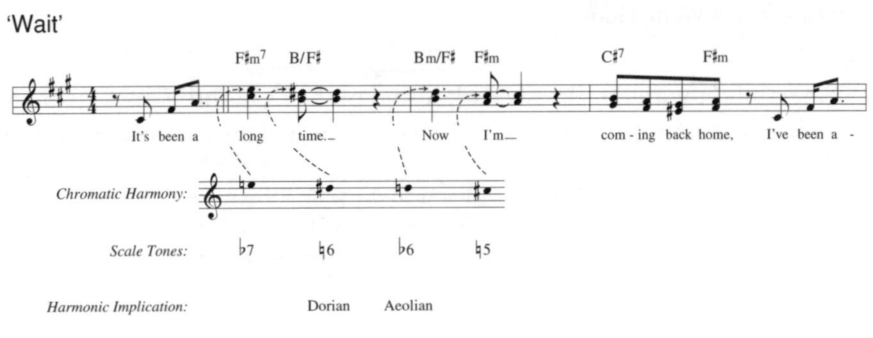

Look closely at how the strong vocal harmony line descends purposefully from ♭7 to 5 via both natural 6 and ♭6, suggesting the presence of both IV and iv minor chords. The IV-to-iv minor drop has already been seen in a major setting as a way of cadencing back to the tonic, and because the voice-leading here is directed 'into the 5th degree', so it can occur equally in a *minor* tonality.[52]

The Locrian Mode

To make the modes accessible and practical, musicians often find it helpful to associate the sound of a scale with a particular *visual* image. Indeed, one of the most successful musical teaching devices of the last 20 years consists of a system for pitch recognition using colours, with students encouraged to match intervals to a recurring *timbre* that crosses the senses. Steve Vai is probably the most high-profile proponent of the visualisation ethic in rock music, with his own personalised system of images for tapping into the character of each mode when improvising. And with his imaginative and eccentric wit, Vai explains succinctly why the Locrian mode is the least exploited of all the modes.

> 'The Ionian mode is very Julie Andrews, her wholesome healthy image is very Ionian. She could be from the planet Ionia . . . but Locrian? That mode is a world apart. It's like a diseased island. I think of Molokai, in Hawaii, with its leper colony. Scary and strange . . .'[53]

Hence the singular dirth of Locrian action in The Beatles' catalogue and pop music generally. A quick look at the construction of the mode confirms why.

Formula	1		♭2		♭3		4		♭5		♭6		♭7		1
C Locrian	C		D♭		E♭		F		G♭		A♭		B♭		C
Intervals		0.5		1		1		0.5		1		1		1	

Not content with the already dark sound of the ♭3, ♭6 and ♭7 (as were their neighbours the Aeolians), the Locrians compounded the dissonance by also

[52] In a contemporary setting, Noel Gallagher used the same 'IV-iv-minor tonic' ploy rather more clearly throughout the Oasis song '(It's Good) To Be Free' (A-Am-Em).

[53] Dominic Pedler, 'Steve Vai: Into The Ultra Zone', *Total Guitar*, Issue 23, October 1995, p. 42.

flattening the 2nd and the 5th degrees. With a tritone creating unbearable unresolved tension between the tonic and a makeshift dominant, the Locrian mode is the very antithesis of pop: the aural equivalent of Milton's *Paradise Lost*, or a Hieronymous Bosch vision of Hell.[54]

The sound of the Locrian mode has been largely confined to the heaviest of Thrash or Death Metal bands, a representative example being Metallica's 'Blackened', whose signature riff inhabits this nightmare world with a tonic that trades frantically with both ♭2 and ♭5.

As Vai says, we're far removed from the *Sound Of Music*, with the ♭5 character tone being the main culprit. For suddenly we have a note that forms a direct tritone with the tonic, magnifying manyfold the principle of dissonance we explored in the dominant chords of Chapter 1. Playing just '1' and '♭5', as root notes in close proximity, is simply *the* Heavy Metal secret to evoking a Satanic atmosphere, and dates from the 'Diabolus In Musica' warnings of the Middle Ages,[55] as Metallica's James Hetfield confirms when talking about his band's disturbing modal excursions:

> 'It's definitely evil. They used to hang you for stuff like this. [Black] Sabbath was a major influence earlier on my life, and those sounds were the most evil things I heard in their songs.'[56]

No piece of music sums up the entire tritone phenomenon in rock better than Tony Iommi's deliberate three-note riff on the title track of Black Sabbath eponymous debut.[57]

The Beatles very occasionally used chords on the ♭5 though rarely in a prolonged sense, or in ways that evoked the flavour of the Locrian mode.[58] However, they did occasionally – and spectacularly – use the ♭II major chord - but in instances where it is arguably reconciled as the character chord of our final mode: Phrygian.

[54] In a jazz setting, the Locrian mode is most commonly used for soloing over the m7♭5, a chord that we have already seen is a highly acquired taste in songwriting. Even in jazz such chords are rarely – if ever – established as a tonic. However, the B Locrian mode (for example) most commonly appears over a Bm7♭5 chord that acts as a ii-chord in a minor 'ii-V-i' in the key of A minor.

[55] It was no coincidence that Slayer's 1998 album was entitled *Diabolus In Musica.*

[56] Wolf Marshall, 'The Heaviest Riffs Known To Man: A Lesson With James Hetfield', *Guitar World*, August 1991, pp. 56–7.

[57] The riff juxtaposes G (octaves) with D♭. For a cool contemporary Locrian line check Brand Violet's 2003 'Alien Hive Theme' riff which features F (♭2) and B♭ (♭5) notes in E minor.

[58] See especially the special ♭vm7♭5 of Honey Pie (Chapter 12); and various melodic ♭5s: 'I Want You (She's So Heavy)', 'Glass Onion' and 'Catswalk'.

The Phrygian Mode

Whereas the Dorian mode was defined as starting on the second degree of the parent major scale, and Aeolian on the sixth, so Phrygian starts and ends on the third degree. This time, though, this exotic mode is more practically thought of as a natural minor scale with a flattened second degree.

Formula	1		♭2		♭3		4		5		♭6		♭7		1
C Phrygian	C		D♭		E♭		F		G		A♭		B♭		C
Intervals		0.5		1		1		1		0.5		1		1	

A comparison with Aeolian confirms that Phrygian differs by just this one note:

Phrygian	1	♭2		♭3	4	5	♭6	♭7
Aeolian	1		2	♭3	4	5	♭6	♭7

When harmonised, Phrygian yields a defining major triad just above the root on this same ♭2 degree known as the 'flat-supertonic'.

Phrygian scale formula	1	♭2	♭3	4	5	♭6	♭7
C Phrygian notes	C	D♭	E♭	F	G	A♭	B♭
Chord formula	i	♭II	♭III	iv	v dim	♭VI	♭vii
C Phrygian triads	Cm	D♭	E♭	Fm	G dim	A♭	B♭m

The Phrygian sound is most associated with Spanish and Latin songs, with the instant, 'mode-defining vamp' of i-♭II, and its variations (particularly Em-F, or Am-B♭ on a nylon-string guitar).

Amazingly, The Beatles' catalogue also contains the sound of the ♭2 note in its traditional setting of a flamenco-flavoured Phrygian *melody*. Step forward the controversial Spanish guitar solo that opens 'The Continuing Story Of Bungalow Bill'. 'Controversial' because, for many years, it was assumed that either George Harrison had played it himself or, alternatively, some authentic (if uncredited) Flamenco giant had been flown in for the session. However, it would be many years before the true source of the sounds – a Mellotron – was widely known. This elusive instrument was originally marketed as a home keyboard for the novice musician. Its main novelty was in being able to play seven-second tape loops featuring a range of pre-recorded sounds. Beatles fans have long known that this was the source of the flute effect on 'Strawberry Fields Forever', but the game was up in 1995 when *Electronic Musician* reviewed the Chamberlin, a custom-built US version of the Mellotron, which incorporates some of those original sixties sounds. Among them was a strangely familiar piece of virtuoso Spanish guitar playing – with the patch itself now even renamed 'Bungalo [sic] Bill'.[59]

'The Continuing Story of Bungalow Bill'

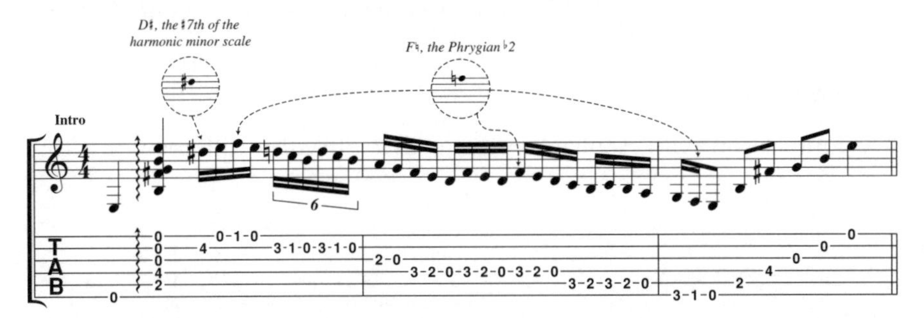

But whether man or machine, this exotic single-note line still spells out all seven notes of the Phrygian mode, complete with the Spanish-sounding ♭2 (here an F natural in the key of E minor) which gives the scale its flavour, alongside the ♭3, ♭6 and ♭7 tones. However, this lick demonstrates again that modality is not a fixed concept. After all, the *natural* seventh from the *harmonic* minor scale is also present, while the bluesy ♭5 also puts in an appearance.

The flattened 2nd degree is highly rare as a featured melodic premise in pop music. Die-hard fans may have spotted one in a Beatles context when The Bootleg Beatles descended on The Royal Albert Hall in December 2000. Rather than 'Bungalow Bill', however, it was played briefly by 'George' (a.k.a. André Barreau) as part of a fleeting reference to 'Misirlou', the Dick Dale surf instrumental famously revived for the film, *Pulp Fiction*.[60]

[59] Meanwhile, another Mellotron owner, Noel Gallagher, came to the same conclusion while experimenting with various patches on his own model (as used for his own 'Strawberry Fields'-type flute sounds on 'Go Let It Out', on the Oasis album *Standing On The Shoulder Of Giants*).

[60] The riff was played by 'George' in the lull between 'Get Back' and 'The Ballad Of John & Yoko' at the 4th December 2000 concert. 'Misirlou' actually combines the Phrygian ♭2 with a *major* 3rd to evoke the exotic Byzantine scale: 1, ♭2, 3, 4, 5, ♭6, 7. Meanwhile, Barreau, in a rare departure from the authenticity of this tribute band, also uses the natural 7th from harmonic minor for added spice in his solo acoustic renditions of 'While My Guitar Gently Weeps'.

♭II and the search for 'Phrygian' and 'Neapolitan' cadences

It was with a highly select batch of excursions with the ♭II *chord*, however, that The Beatles made some of their most breathtaking musical moves. And never more expertly than in 'Things We Said Today'. For if 'the unexpected' is one element that defines greatness in a pop song, then take a look at the piece of left-field novelty that Paul McCartney crafted on this gem, back on *A Hard Day's Night*.

'Things We Said Today'

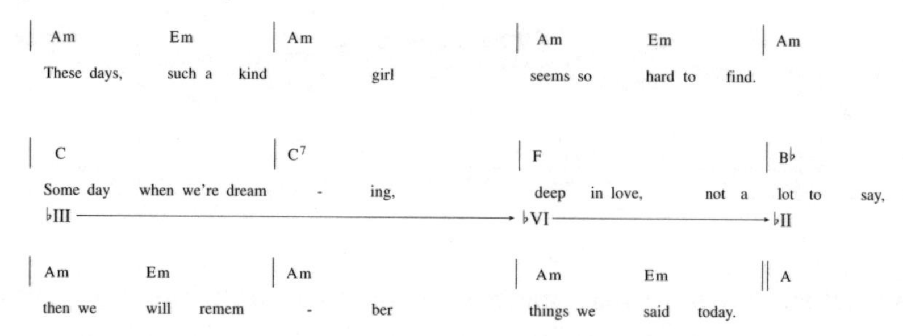

While The Beatles are notorious for their characteristic modesty in the face of their phenomenal talents, it's nice to see Paul finally blow his own trumpet concerning that very special B♭, which fells the listener at 0.23. Here he is reminiscing about the song in *Many Years From Now*:

> 'It has interesting chords. It goes C, F which is all normal, then the normal thing might be to go to F minor, but to go to the *B flat* was quite good . . . It was a sophisticated little tune'[61]

Credit where credit is due. For we can illustrate, visually, just what he means with another expanded Cycle Of Fifths which brings in chromatic destinations along our familiar diatonic path. Here we are going even deeper into the 'jungle country' on the left-hand side, proving that McCartney was intuitively pushing the harmonic envelope as far back as 1964.

Look closely at the root movement which starts on the ♭III and progresses to ♭VI – in the familiar *anti-clockwise* path of fifths, continuing ever further into the 'flat-side'. If we proceed further round the cycle from F major, McCartney's subsequent B♭ is revealed as precisely this highly unusual ♭II chord.

[61] Miles, *Many Years From Now*, p. 122.

Paul's 'quite good' B♭ of 'Things We Said Today'

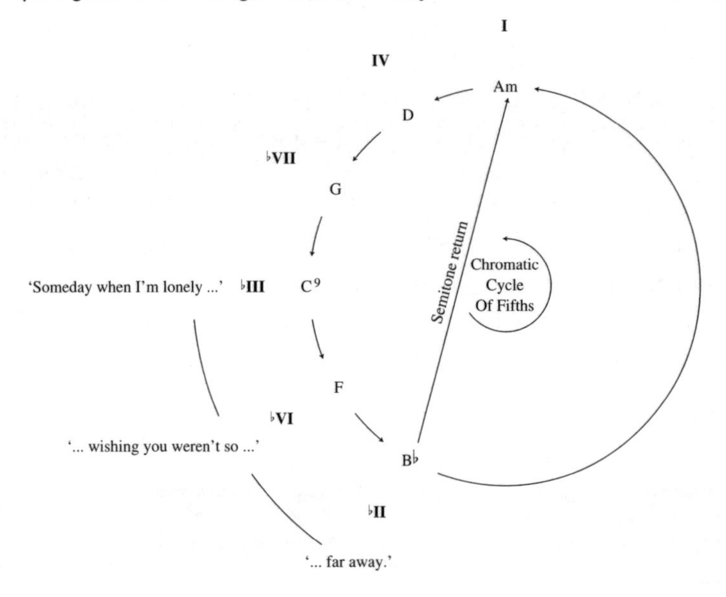

Degrees	1	♭2	♭3	4	5	♭6	♭7
Scale	A	**B♭**	C	D	E	F	G
Formula	i	**♭II**	♭III	iv	v dim	♭VI	♭vii
Chords	Am	**B♭**	C	D	E dim	F	Gm

Again we can think of the song as being in the key of A minor – *but implying the Phrygian mode* briefly during this extract.

The B♭ now only has to drop by a smooth, single semitone to retrieve the tonic of A minor for the brief refrain section that follows. The fact that the chord occurs on the phrase 'so far away' (further highlighted by a change in texture on the McCartney live versions) is just the icing on the cake.[62] For while a semitone from the root is *physically* not too distant, it seems a long way from home *musically,* hanging precariously in oblivion and awaiting that fulfilling resolution. 'Quite good'? Sir Paul, you are too modest.

[62] Listen to McCartney's *Tripping The Live Fantastic* version as the song stops on the B♭ chord, at 2.13 in the guitar solo, especially to highlight Robbie McIntosh's celestial climb up an extended B♭ arpeggio (in 6th position).

Meanwhile, a similar 'half-step downward shift' would also be used by John Lennon, notably in the humble, but disarmingly subtle, 'Cry Baby Cry'. Confirmation, once again, of how the two songwriters were matching each other, stride-for-stride, when it came to incorporating some seriously fancy songwriting principles.[63] The song can be seen broadly as one of those Beatles 'double tonic', 'major-to-*relative* minor' excursions, as a G chorus (that also acts as the intro) moves to an E minor verse. But with a difference. In two instances at either end of the song John approaches the E minor – not from its dominant or subdominant – but with a ♭II-i minor in what we can regard as a brilliant reworking of McCartney's B♭-Am in 'Things We Said Today'.

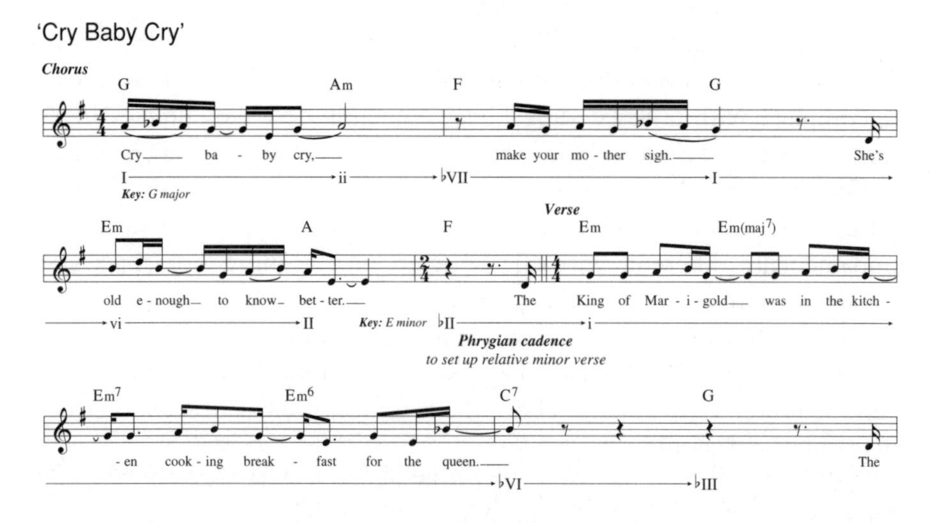

What makes it extra special is the way in which John conceives the role of the F as a 'pivot' chord for the key switch. Being common to sequences in both keys, pivot chords work by definition, by stealth, priming and delivering a key change with seamless effect. Typically a pivot chord moves conventionally, V-I or IV-I, or up a whole tone for an Aeolian cadence.

[63] The ♭II chord is a rare, acquired taste in rock and pop songwriting but appears in some memorable contexts. These include the ascending I-♭II in The Clash's 'London Calling' (Em-F), Sherbet's 'Howzat' (Gm-A♭, also featuring an ambitious ♭2 melody note); and an inspired, classically contrived ♭II-♭VI in Abba's 'Money Money Money'. The Fall show how to employ it in a New Wave rock riff (combined with borrowed ♭VI and ♭VII) in 'Futures And Pasts'.

Hence the '♭VII=V' label describes a chord's functions with respect to the two keys at play.

In 'Cry Baby Cry', however, the F chord acts as both ♭VII in the opening tonality of G and a retrospective ♭II in the new key of Em. The whole manoeuvre is made even more effortless by the way that the F chord (first heard in bar 2) is subsequently delivered for action (two bars later) as a tonality establishing mechanism. For having moved conventionally from Em to A7, the listener is subconsciously preparing for movement to a D root. But with his instinctive understanding of 'I for vi' substitutions, John gives us something better – the relative major of the D minor that could have been built on that chord. Bingo! He has his ♭II-i minor to lead us to the court of 'The King Of Marigold'.

Once again we can't leave this song without a tonal ambiguity *caveat.* Some writers see this entire unfolding Em as just a 'vi chord' in the key of G, complete with a descending linear embellishment not unlike the A minor chord in Harrison's 'Something' (after all, even the melody is similar to 'I don't want to leave her now').[64]

But this author believes the classic Phrygian approach makes this fundamentally different, with the targeted minor chord not appearing *within* a section (as in 'Something'). Rather it now starts a verse for which Lennon has specifically earmarked a melancholy minor atmosphere for his images of a séance 'in the dark with voices out of nowhere'. Mellers, too, feels the power as he describes how 'the flattened (phrygian) second grows increasingly threatening'.[65]

Sure enough, when the song eventually closes at 2.31, leaving us hanging on an Em (with a treacherous A note in the melody implying Em11) it is really no surprise, as we have become accustomed to this root as one of the song's two tonics.[66]

[64] Pollack sees 'vascillating ambiguity' between G major and E minor but plumps for an unfolding vi chord in his analysis: 'Notes on … Series' no. 154, 1998. *The 'Official' rec.music.beatles Home Page*, www.recmusicbeatles.com.

[65] Mellers, *Twilight Of The Gods*, p. 134.

[66] Of course, track 11 on the *White Album* doesn't end there. Within a few seconds a filler ditty ('can you take me back') emerges in the unlikely key of Fm, a modulation far removed from the clichéd 'gear shift' key change that repeats a previous idea up a semitone (see Chapter 10).

'Cry Baby Cry'

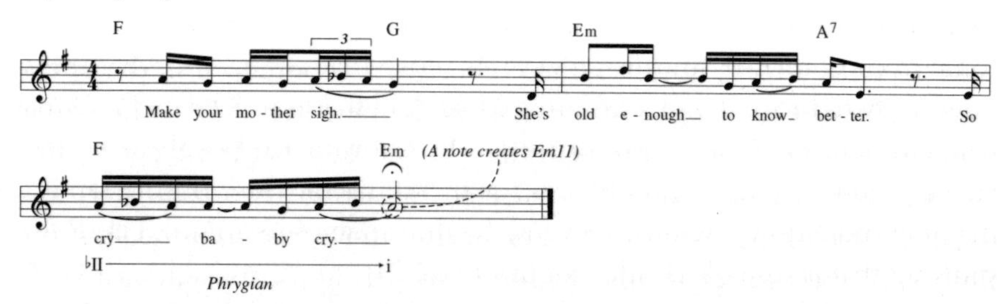

Once again, ambiguity rules throughout 'Cry Baby Cry', with the song's rogue B♭ note (the ♭7th of the C7) spoiling the cosy notion of either G Mixolydian (B♭ being the ♭3rd of G) or, indeed, pure E Aeolian (where the same note is the ♭5th). Far from being a subtle nuance, the C7-G change emerges as the most striking thing in the whole song. And analysing it (or attempting to) helps us to appreciate a rather more famous Lennon sequence but one surely conceived in a harmonically similar way: the verse in the mighty 'A Day In The Life'.

For, with that C7 chord, was Lennon perhaps setting up a ♭VI–V–i move – only to tease the listener by thwarting the expected 'down a semitone drop' (to B7, the V7 of Em) and heading back to his G major base?

Turn now to the closer on *Sgt. Pepper*, in the key of G again, and check out the similarities:

'A Day In The Life'

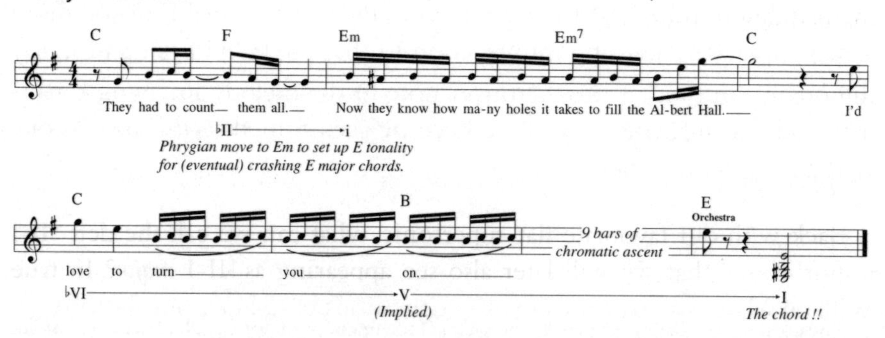

The same unusual F-Em drop is visible, though now Lennon does deliver it within a verse sequence, so that the relative minor effect is not as marked as 'Cry Baby Cry'.[67]

[67] Compare with David Bowie's haunting intro to 'Space Oddity' with its repeated F/E – Em.

Notice however that, this time, the following C chord *does* drop a semitone to B major. So what? Well, in doing so it subtly shifts our sense of tonic from G to E by means of a ♭VI-V move that we instinctively feel is now ready to move down a fifth to a tonic. And that is indeed exactly what happens here. First when modulating to E major for Paul's upbeat, reality-check 'middle'; and ultimately also for the climactic close on the same E major chord – now fatefully delivered by three pianos in unison. Tim Riley sums up that landmark Beatles sonority at 4.21:

> 'The aural image couldn't be more stark; it has a sense of tragic inevitability that haunts long after the record is played'.[68]

Although it's true that, in both these modulations, the orchestra cues the key change with those infamous multi-instrumental chromatic ascents, the change to E is powerful because the B chord is heard retrospectively as a strong V chord. And this, in turn, is facilitated by the last Phrygian drop, from F-Em (at 3.39), which subliminally previews the tonal shift to an E root. In doing so, it prepares us for that final moment of impending doom.

Part of the enduring fascination (not to mention critical obsession) with 'A Day In The Life' is perhaps that it represents a rare example of a Beatles song in which the music switches disarmingly between matching the lyrical themes and contradicting them. While McCartney's 'middle', and the Quadriplagal dream sequence, capture the mood, Ned Rorem has a point when he describes Lennon's verse as 'crushing poetry . . . intoned to the blandest of tunes'.[69] Moreover, how ironic that the final E major chord achieves precisely the opposite reaction to that predicted from its Picardy third.[70]

Phrygian trivia

Back with our favourite flat-supertonic, what can we call the deft '♭II-i minor' move, that we will later also see appearing as ♭II-I *major*? In true William Mann style, various exotic suggestions have been put forward.

[68] Riley, *Tell Me Why*, p. 229.

[69] Ned Rorem, *The Music Of The Beatles*, New York Review of Books, 18th January 1968.

[70] The alternative interpretation of a modulation to VI (from the home key of G major) should bring similar uplift : as with the bridge in 'Something', or the guitar solo in 'Free As A Bird', where in each case, VI conveys images of 'hope', 'love' and 'freedom', rather than ominous, fatalistic inevitability.

With regard to the B♭ in 'Things We Said Today', MacDonald ambitiously volunteers the 'Neapolitan Sixth' tag, which prompts a search for a true Beatles example of what is one of the very slickest devices in classical music.[71]

For while the 'Neapolitan' is sometimes used to describe a major chord on the flat supertonic, the 'Sixth' suffix very specifically describes the triad in first inversion, and invariably on its way to a grand cadence – but via another chord, the V7.[72] Mellers too alludes to this elaborate manoeuvre in his own description of the B♭-Am move in 'Things We Said Today': 'a kind of Neapolitan cadence drooping back (without the linking dominant) . . .'[73]

If we add back that 'linking dominant' we emerge with a highly rare '♭II-V7-I' move which consists of a dramatic and disorientating root jump of a tritone, deliciously comforted by the following descent of a fifth. Here is an even more refined musical device and yet one that, incredibly, we can also find in The Beatles catalogue. Indeed, it accounts for one of the most underrated musical moments in their entire career. And far from appearing on a 'sophisticated' Beatles album in their 'mature' period, this gem of a songwriting secret lurks sublimely in the ballad-style, 'thirties' intro to 'Do You Want To Know A Secret' (right back on *Please Please Me*), where it provides a breathtaking context for the minor-to-parallel-major switch as we enter the verse.

'Do You Want To Know A Secret'

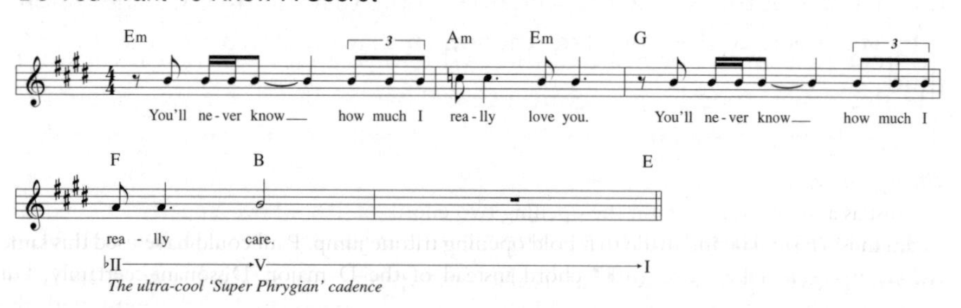

[71] Macdonald, *Revolution In The Head*, p. 108.

[72] In the key of A minor, for example, a Neapolitan Sixth would see a B♭ major chord voiced (low to high) D-F-B♭ (3rd, 5th, root), with the 'Sixth' element referring to the interval between high and low notes. Note: the 8-semitone interval from D-to-B♭ is not described as a *flattened* sixth in classical convention as the ♭6 in a minor key is the (only) sixth note of the scale. See Taylor, *The Associated Board Guide To Music Theory* Part II, p. 153.

[73] Mellers, *Twilight Of The Gods*, p. 47.

Played on its own, the F-B7 change does indeed suggest to the ear that an E (major or minor) tonic will follow, courtesy of a beautifully symmetrical piece of semitone voice-leading – albeit one tinged with the suitable disquiet of the tritone jump captured in the following table:[74]

♭II			**V^7**	
F			**B^7**	
Formula	Note	Voice leading	Note	Formula
5th	C	Down a semitone	B	Root
3rd	A	Common tone	A	♭7th
Root	F	Up a semitone	F♯	5th
Root	**F**	**Up a tritone**	**B**	**Root**

One must surely christen both these highly rare cadences (♭II-I and ♭II-V7-I), if only in tribute to Lennon and McCartney's inspired excursions with the flat supertonic.

Moreover, other songwriters have used the ♭II-tonic cadence to brilliant effect down the years. Think of Roberta Flack's classic 'Killing Me Softly With His Song' which sees the very same ♭III-♭VI-♭II move as 'Things We Said Today', before also cadencing down a semitone. Justin Hayward also used the ♭II-i minor cadence sublimely in The Moody Blues' 'Nights In White Satin' when providing a sudden contrast from the dreamy Aeolian cadence that previously dominates.[75]

It is certainly widespread practice to term both these moves 'a kind of Neapolitan cadence', just as Mellers suggests. However, the shadow of the exotic 'Sixth' looms so large when using this term that rockers are advised to steer clear of it. For none of these ♭II chords appears in first inversion in Beatles songs, merely as a conventional barre-chords on the guitar fret-board. In this sense it is crucial to do justice to the way guitar-based

[74] Just as a fun exercise, revisit the opening two chords of 'P.S. I Love You' (G-C♯7) and play them in isolation. Having made that bold opening tritone jump, Paul could have used this same exotic move to take us to an F♯ chord instead of the D major. Dissonant, certainly, but dramatic. The point being that the tritone gives us the choice to go either way, with the relationship between D and F♯ roots (within the same tonic family, i.e., tonic and mediant), confirming the potential for substitution.

[75] In the key of Fm, 'Killing Me Softly' cadences G♭-F major (a parallel major tonic for effect) at 1.36 on the famous 'false' mid-song ending, while 'Nights In White Satin' moves F-Em on the line 'never meaning to send'. Slade managed to take the haunting strains of a B♭-Am Phrygian cadence to the very top of the charts with 'Coz I Luv You' (No.1 in October 1971), on the line 'I just like the things you do' at 0.28. In a slightly different context check out the ♭II return at the end of each title refrain in Deep Purple's 'Smoke On The Water': A♭-G5.

songwriters conceive such moves. It is the very fact that the instrument allows such an effortless, one-fret slide between parallel-voiced ♭II and tonic chords – that helps us appreciate how such seemingly elaborate Beatles ploys evolved in practice.[76]

The '♭II-tonic' drop should surely be dubbed a *Phrygian cadence*. The latest on-line edition of *The Grove Dictionary Of Music* defines the move as:

> 'a cadence in which the lowest part descends to the final, or tonic, by a semitone.[77]

This definition, which evolved from close harmony practices over the ages, is certainly logical, given that the character tone of the mode (♭2) is retrieving its tonic.

However, it's also worth noting that, just as with a certain other problematic modal cadence, 'the Phrygian' has the potential to cause extreme confusion for music students. For many other definitions have evolved that seem to bear precious little relevance to the mode itself. For example, *The Oxford Dictionary Of Music* first defined a Phrygian cadence as:

> 'a sequence in a major key that is brought to a close on the dominant of the relative minor . . . an acquired (and highly rare) effect that leaves the listener with a "musical question mark"'.

In the key of C, this involves ending on a disorientating E major chord (III), creating a celestial effect, due to the Picardy effect on the mediant. For a rare example in pop listen to the end of The Carpenters' 'We've Only Just Begun' which leaves us with an inspired manifestation of precisely this 'musical question mark'.[78] Other definitions of the Phrygian cadence are even less helpful.[79]

[76] MacDonald describes the move as 'derived from a Lennon-like chromatic descent' that we'll later see in 'You're Going To Lose That Girl', though 'Things We Said Today' confirms that the move was equally McCartney-like.

[77] The *New Grove Dictionary Of Music And Musicians* [2001], ed. Stanley Sadie; on-line edition.

[78] The song ends on a C♯ major chord relative to the prevailing key of A major.

[79] *The Oxford Dictionary Of Music* later defined the cadence as: 'any sort of Imperfect cadence in a minor mode', and 'the first inversion of a subdominant chord followed by a dominant chord'. This could widen the field to include other non-tonic closing chords, perhaps including Harrison's 'I Me Mine', which ends on a ♭VI (Fmaj7 in A minor). Elsewhere in rock, Alice Cooper's 'School's Out' closes on a Dorian IV (C in G minor) while Mark Knopfler ends 'What It Is' on a hanging ♭VII (E in F♯ minor).

However, if we accept the simple definition of the Phrygian cadence as ♭II-tonic, then it also seems appropriate to extend the term to describe The Beatles' use of the '♭II-V-tonic' change in 'Do You Want To Know A Secret', which we therefore christen the *Super-Phrygian* cadence.[80] The alternative – the Neapolitan cadence – is even more elusive and misunderstood than its Phrygian cousin.[81]

As one classical expert explained to *BBC* listeners a few years ago: 'No one knows how the Neapolitan Sixth got its name, nor did Rudyard Kipling write a *Just So Story* to fill the gap. It remains a mystery'.[82]

[80] The bold ploy of the ♭II-V-i move may be rare in pop but it has a strong jazz heritage dating back to the stirring Gypsy jazz compositions of Django Reinhardt (e.g. 'Manoir De Mes Rêves': E♭9-A13-D6/9, in the key of D).

[81] Rock critics have long been making up their own rules, with the Phrygian cadence even being used loosely to describe the *ascent* from a tonic to ♭II. For example, Wolf Marshall refers to the 'ethnic impression [of] the Phrygian cadence from E-F' in Dick Dale's 'Misirlou'; *Guitar*, December 1995, p. 73.

[82] Adrian Jack, *The Harmonic Series*, BBC Radio 3, New Year's Eve, 1998. Jack continues: 'Neapolitan composers of the Baroque period didn't use it any more than composers from other parts of Italy'. As far back as 1947 *The Oxford Companion Of Music* was itself at a loss: 'But why Neapolitan? It is surely no special characteristic of what is called the Neapolitan school . . . and it was in use long before', (p. 608. 7th edition). The mystery continues in the latest *Oxford Dictionary Of Music*, with the riddle now distilled: 'Reason for its name is unknown'.

NINE

Descending Bass, Inversions and 'Aug' Chords

'Everyone wants to write a hit tune but when we talk with our peers, we're proudest of our bottom line.'[1] – Stephen Citron

So much for the idea that melody is the ultimate test of greatness. Of course, our own discussion has been heavily weighted towards harmony rather than melody, with much emphasis on this very 'bottom line', at least as defined by the root movement of a chord sequence. And deliberately so, for while not denying the allure of the perfect tune (there are two chapters devoted to melody to follow) the study of Beatles harmony has proved essential to appreciating their songs on a deeper level.

This chapter, however, focuses on a category of Beatles songs where a 'moving line' in the harmony manifests itself as an instantly identifiable, *strongly directional* pattern on which the song hinges. While we have seen various directional ascents of the harmonised diatonic scale (like the 'I-ii-iii-IV' of 'Getting Better', 'Sexy Sadie' and 'Here, There And Everywhere'), it's The Beatles' skill in structuring powerful *descents from a tonic* that dominates this chapter.

Descending bass lines are typically described by music writers as 'romantic' (Citron) for their 'sweet inevitable collapse' and their 'yearning, strangely satisfying sound' (Ingham).[2] We will therefore be building on the principle of 'inevitable collapse' seen in the '5-4-3-2-1' bass run which occasionally accompanies a fundamental V-I shift. We will often be using numbers rather than Roman numerals to describe a range of single-note

[1] Citron, *Songwriting*, p. 248.

[2] Citron, *Songwriting*, p. 249. Chris Ingham, *Doctor Rock Dissects The Hits*: No. 1, *MOJO*, Issue 14, January 1995, p. 28.

lines (usually, but not exclusively, in the bass) which now define the harmony, and above which a variety of interesting chords appear.

And while the essence of The Beatles' magic is emerging as songwriting novelty, the success of their songs also depends on the way they blended these twists and turns within familiar structures that give listeners an overall sense of security. The Three-Chord Trick is one such structure, as is the Cycle Of Fifths, while some of the following descending scalar patterns have formed the bedrock of songwriting since pop began.

1) The Diatonic Major Descent (8-7-6-5)

Never mind 'pop' – the first of these descending patterns has been in use in classical music for over two centuries, as we are reminded whenever Procol Harum's sixties classic, 'A Whiter Shade Of Pale', is discussed.

For no analysis of this 1967 hit is complete without a reference to Johann Sebastian Bach's 'Air On A G String' which – via a certain 1967 Hamlet cigar TV commercial – inspired the Gary Brooker and Keith Reid composition.[3] Matthew Fisher's swirling organ figure, played so majestically on a Hammond organ, is invariably described as the connection between the two pieces. However, the shared, two-bar opening bass descent also encapsulates another timeless formula as appropriate to pop songwriters as it was to the classical masters.[4]

Both pieces enjoy a leisurely opening walk down the diatonic major scale: starting on the root, falling gracefully to the major seventh, on to the sixth and then inexorably to the dominant. Just listen to the *Hamlet* cigar ad to hear Bach's steady drop through D-C♯-B-A, while Procol Harum's version unfolds a whole tone lower (C-B-A-G). In each case this descent can be represented as '8-7-6-5', a sure-fire formula that has underpinned

[3] *Smash* (Programme 1, 'Rock and Pop Anthems'), ITV, November 2000 and *100 Greatest Number One Singles*, Channel 4, January 2001, both stressed the Hamlet connection, while *MOJO* also refers to 'Air On A G String' when ranking the song No. 22 in *The 100 Greatest Singles Of All Time*; *MOJO*, Issue 45, August 1997, p. 75. Though Brooker explains (in an unreleased documentary by Henry Scott-Irvine) that 'A Whiter Shade Of Pale' was equally inspired by another Bach piece, 'Sleepers Awake', and Jacques Loussier's popular sixties classical album, *Play Bach*.

[4] 'Even though the organ figure is from Bach, the words and the melody are original,' explained Paul Gambacini, when introducing the song ranked as No. 20 in *The Songs Of The Century*, BBC Radio 2, 31st December 1999. Both pieces have strikingly similar (though by no means identical) melodies, which open on the major 3rd and embellish the root with the leading note, before making a leap of a major 6th interval.

chart-toppers from 1730 through to the 1990s.[5] In the tradition of rock 'n' roll medleys that switch between classic covers over the same Three-Chord progression, so Procol Harum's later live renditions of 'Whiter Shade' would segue into a heritage of similar Diatonic Major descents, ranging from Percy Sledge's 'When A Man Loves A Woman' to Bob Marley's 'No Woman, No Cry'.

'A Whiter Shade Of Pale'

The Beatles themselves used this same initial four-stop descent to lead the listener through a variety of songs. It has been integral to two 'final' Beatles outings; for we enjoy a '8-7-6-5' both on 'Her Majesty', the *Abbey Road* swansong, and on 'Real Love' (presumably now definitely the *very* last Beatles hit). Both these songs form particularly useful studies as they demonstrate a crucial principle of this chapter – namely, that while such a harmonic line is ubiquitous in pop, the versatility of the device in songwriting is due to its potential for harmonisation with a variety of accompanying chords. A few examples from The Beatles' catalogue will illustrate just how an accomplished songwriter can exploit this basic principle.

At the very simplest level, 'Her Majesty' shows that you can use this bass sequence without changing the chord at all.

'Her Majesty'

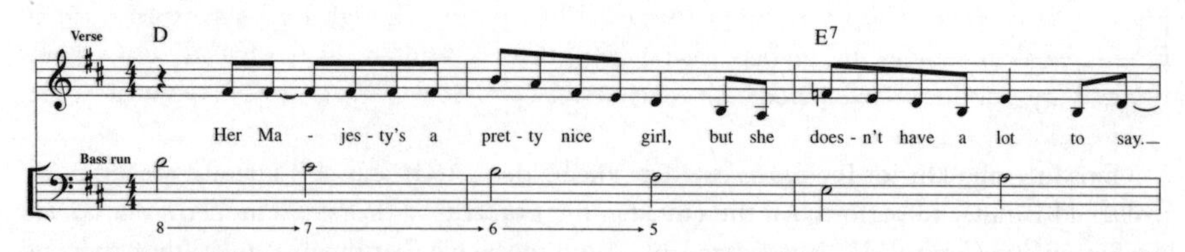

5 '8' is used to denote the tonic, rather than '1', in order to help visualise the effect of a sequence that descends.

So common is this idea in pop that Chris Ingham awards it the tag: 'Descending Elaboration of Static Harmony' ('DESH') which reflects the fact that the chord is kept constant while the bottom line drops down the major diatonic scale from the root down to the 5th.[6] The bass line carries the song on its own and is not reliant on activity in either the chords or the tune.

The simplest chord that can form the static harmony of a 'DESH' is a major triad. However, in practice, some liberties can be taken according to the key the song is written in, particularly given the inherent quirks of the guitar. With an open-position D chord, for example (as in 'Her Majesty'), it requires a contortionist to ring out each of the chord tones, 1-3-5, while also playing the bass descent. Never mind, the fleeting droning open strings add spice even if, technically, they take us away from *truly* static harmony.[7]

In any case, simple simultaneous movements in chords add interest to the progression, as we can hear with the few extra fills that McCartney adds in 'For No One', another blatant manifestation of the Diatonic Major descent, heard earlier on *Revolver*.

6 Chris Ingham, 'Doctor Rock Dissects The Hits: No. 1', *MOJO*, Issue 14, January 1995, p. 28.

7 DESH is easier to perform on the guitar in the key of C, as heard on modern folk classics like Simon and Garfunkel's 'Mrs Robinson' (listen to the fill after the line 'more than you will know'). This song also suggests that the 8-7-6-5 entered pop through folk traditions, rather than via a classical connection.

'Inversions': implied chords for the '8-7-6-5' descent

Guitarists playing this song in B major (using a 5th string root in second position on the fretboard) will appreciate how the scope for elaborating the chordal harmony emerges naturally when using this run. By the time we reach the 6th degree in the bass, the B triad above it means that the B/G♯ slash chord we are fingering identifies itself as nothing more than a G♯m7 chord. In this way we are immediately reminded of the relationship between I6 and vi7 as *inversions* of each other, a realisation that is integral to appreciating and exploiting the concept of descending basslines in song-writing.

Now look more closely at the second chord in the sequence. For the whole point of the '7' in the bass is to create a link between the major and its relative minor. One of the oldest tricks in the songwriting book is to go from I to vi with a straight jump, as we explored for most of Chapter 3. But the descent of the bass to '7' colours what is essentially the very same move with a touch of harmonic class. The Beatles exploited a variety of such embellishments, demonstrating their intuitive understanding of this implied harmony.

Major scale theory tells us that the 'correct' chord on the 7th degree of the scale should be a diminished triad, or perhaps a m7♭5 if we add a seventh to the stack. But we have long since ruled this chord too dissonant for pop or, as Rooksby puts it succinctly, 'horrible to sing over'.[8] The chord is therefore typically substituted in various ways, with The Beatles showing us the three most important options when using this specific line.

Each merely involves using another diatonic triad that appears on a root other than this leading tone.[9] Crucially, however, the bass note that forms part of this unmistakable sequence does not have to be the *root* note of the chord being played above it – chords of this type are called *inversions.*

Depending on the choice of chord, we can create 1st inversion chords (with the 3rd of the chord in the bass); 2nd inversion (with the 5th in the bass); and 3rd inversion (with the 7th in the bass). The following table summarises these inversions which will soon emerge as an essential Beatles songwriting

[8] Rikky Rooksby, *How To Write Songs On Guitar*, p. 113.

[9] A m7 chord built on the 7th degree would appear to be an obvious replacement for the m7♭5, but (as we know from 'Yesterday' and 'Here, There And Everywhere') this chord tends to pull us down a fifth to the mediant (specifically III7). The aim here is to use a chord that pulls us *directly* from '7' to '6' in the bass descent.

tool. Note that while the chart shows the conventional, 'theoretical' constructions for the complete chord, the important thing in practice is the location of the *bass note.*[10]

Inversions: 're-stacking' a major chord – a summary

	Root position		1st inversion		2nd inversion		3rd inversion	
	D		D/F♯		D/A		Dmaj ^{7}/C♯	
							5 th	A
	5 th	A	Root	D	3 rd	F♯	3 rd	F♯
	3 rd	F♯	5 th	A	Root	D	Root	D
Bass	**Root**	**D**	**3 rd**	**F♯**	**5 th**	**A**	**7 th**	**C♯**

This simple concept is the secret to understanding a wide variety of these seemingly complicated 'slash' chords,which merely capture the fact that a chord appears above a bass note other than its root.

Let's look first at examples of how The Beatles used chords in 1st, 2nd and 3rd inversions when harmonising the bass notes in The Diatonic Major Descent. With the first note in the sequence ('8') invariably taken care of by the tonic triad in root position, we only have to find chords for the '7', '6' and '5'.

The next table sets out the three most common options for harmonising the '7' (for a run in the key of C). It also indicates in each case the simple root position triad before confirming the implied inversion in the context of the run. For tracking the bass note *in relation to the chord* is essential to understanding advanced chord substitution in pop sequences.

Harmonising the '7' (B) in the Diatonic Major Descent

Basic chord options	Key of C	Slash chord needed	Inversion	Function of B note
I	C	Cmaj ^{7}/B	3 rd	7 th
V	G	G/B	1 st	3 rd
iii	Em	Em/B	2 nd	5 th

We've just seen how 'Her Majesty' and 'For No One' adopt the first of these options: a I major 7 triad in 3rd inversion, so called because the 7th of

[10] The order that the major 3rd and root appear in a 2nd inversion chord (for example) is of secondary importance to the role of the 5th in the root. This ambivalence to 'subsidiary' voice-leading is a reality of pop and rock and is another vital feature that distinguishes it (in terms of strict voice-leading analysis) from classical music.

the chord (rather than the root) appears as its lowest note. This creates tension as the structure is inherently unstable and 'wants' to resolve, thereby encouraging the bass to descend further. 'Hello Goodbye' and 'Penny Lane' also feature the same ploy, in their chorus and verse, respectively.

For an example of the next option, the V chord, take a look at 'All You Need Is Love'.

'All You Need Is Love'

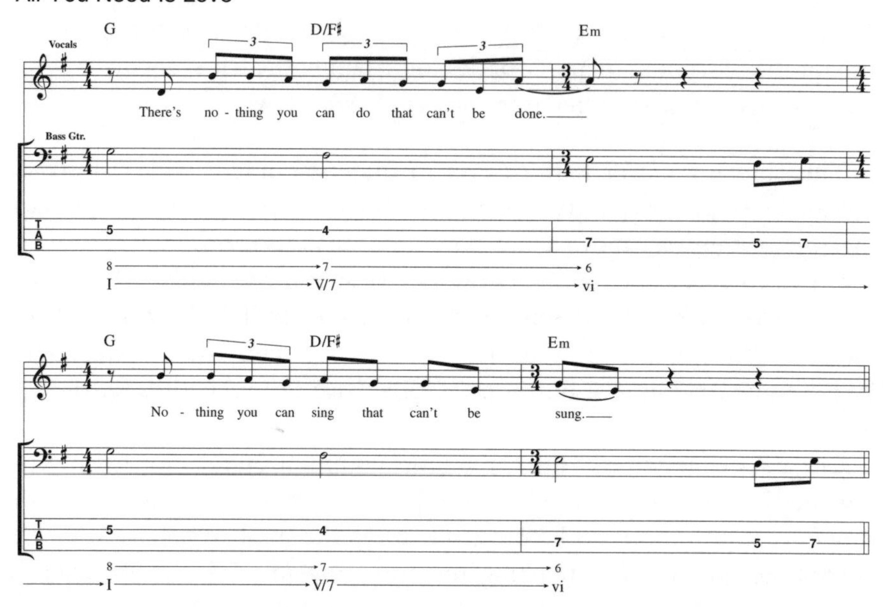

Again the bass descends from the tonic to the relative minor, but now the linking '7' is harmonised by the simple dominant triad of the key which must now appear in 1st inversion to keep the required F♯ in the bass. The basic chord sequence can be thought of as just 'I-V-vi' and, in a band setting, the guitar player might well just play a basic root position D chord. But for solo acoustic renditions, the 'slash chord' D/F is the secret to maintaining the voice leading.[11]

This V chord harmonisation has been used regularly down the years – and never more famously than in Lynyrd Skynyrd's mighty 'Free Bird':

[11] This type of truncated '1-7-6' run does not have to feature a harmonised chord on the '7'. Look back to songs like 'Your Mother Should Know', 'Golden Slumbers' and 'Rocky Raccoon' which link I and vi just by a passing bass note.

another organ intro, and another '8-7-6' descent that could also be seen as 'Son of Air On A G-String'.

TV advertisers obviously love the romance of the full Diatonic Major Descent – after Hamlet, Levi's 501 jeans were marketed to the strains of Percy Sledge's 'When A Man Loves A Woman', which uses the '8-7-6-5' descent again, with this same implied 1st inversion V as the second chord.

Although I and V are the most popular chords used above the 7th degree in this run, 'Real Love' found Lennon cannily employing his knowledge of substitution. With I and vi already at work in the sequence, John found a use for the remaining member of the tonic family, the trusty mediant. With its measured, two-beats-per-note descent, 'Real Love' is a great showcase for the diatonic bass run.

'Real Love'

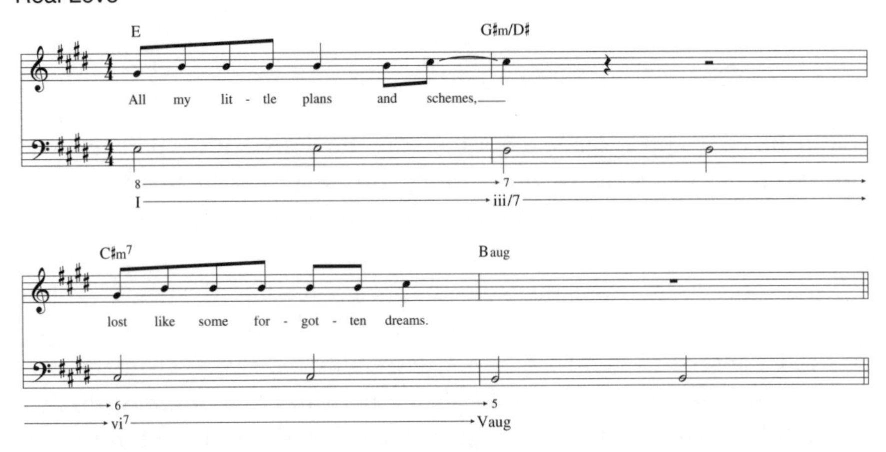

Here, therefore, is another outing for Paul's I-iii 'formula'. Though now, in the context of the '7' (the D♯ bass note), we find the chord as a 2nd inversion 'slash' chord.

Having seen some alternatives for harmonising the '7', understanding the options for the next two destinations, '6' and '5', should be straightforward.

Harmonising the '6' (A) in the Diatonic Major Descent

Basic chord options	Key of C	Slash chord needed	Inversion	Function of A note
I	C	C/A	I/6	6th
vi	Am	Am	Root	Root
vi7	Am7	Am7	Root	Root
IV	F	F/A	1st	3rd

The Beatles usually use the '6' as an opportunity to move to the relative minor (either as a straight vi or an *implied* vi7). While this would appear to be the obvious option, there is in fact an even simpler alternative that allows the whole descending run to operate within the context of a Three-Chord Trick. Just check out the verse of The Kinks' 'Waterloo Sunset', where the guitar plays a plain IV chord over the '6', in the run E-B/D♯-A/C♯.[12]

That just leaves the chord choices for the '5'.

Harmonising the '5' (G) in the Diatonic Major Descent

Basic chord options	Key of C	Slash chord needed	Inversion	Function of G note
I	C	C/G	2 nd	5 th
V	G	G	Root	Root
vi	Am	Am^7/G	3 rd	7 th
iii	Em	Em/G	1 st	3 rd

A plain, root-position V chord is the obvious route, perhaps with 'alterations' to the triad to spice things up (as just seen in 'Real Love' where a raised 5th creates an 'augmented' chord to which we will soon be returning).

But a tonic in 2nd inversion is also popular with The Beatles, as seen in the 'DESH' structures of 'Her Majesty' and 'For No One' (refer all the way back to Chapter 1 to find McCartney describing his use of '5th-in-the-bass' voicings and the gentle tension the structure brings to a progression).

A stylish alternative is to use the iii at this point. While 'Real Love' shows how it can provide great harmony over the '7', (in 2nd inversion), it also fits the bill perfectly over the '5', this time in 1st inversion. A fine example is 'When A Man Loves A Woman' which features Fm (in the key of D♭) at this point in the very same descending run.

But whatever chord you plump for over the '5', the underlying song-writing message to the listener is the same: 'Expect more movement'. For V propels you back to the tonic, either directly or, if you want to delay it, then via IV (which effortlessly extends the moving line by another

[12] Part of the swooning effect of 'Waterloo Sunset' is precisely that the intro consists of a '5-4-3-2-1' 'Schenkerian' bass descent, which is then merely extended down the diatonic scale as '7-6-5' begins the verse. Meanwhile, to hear the 'churchy' Gospel sound of these inversions check 'Answer Me', Frankie Laine's massive 1953 No.1 hit, which harmonises a textbook 8-7-6-5 with E♭-B♭/D-A♭/C-E♭/B♭ (at 0.10-0.19).

diatonic stop).[13] Either way, the songwriter will be looking to get back to his starting point within the next few bars in order to wrap up what is typically either a 4- or 8-bar idea, depending on the speed at which the bassline unfolds.[14]

The following chart demonstrates the variety of ways in which The Beatles 'returned to base' after a '8-7-6-5'. In every case they do so by means of a standard cadential formula that we have come across before – a simple Perfect cadence, perhaps preceded by a 'pre-dominant' II, a rocky ♭VII-I, or in the case of 'Hello Goodbye' both this modal ploy *and* the '♭VI–for-iv' substitution that adds balls to the pretty 'IV-iv' Plagal drop. Both chords *and* Roman numerals have been used here to help identify the actual keys and bass runs while allowing the cadences themselves to be identified immediately through their familiar formulae.

Song	Section	Root movement				Cadence
		8	7	6	5	
'Her Majesty'	Verse	D	D/C♯	D/B	D/A	II - V - I
'For No One'	Verse	B	B/A♯	B/G♯	B/F♯	IV - ♭VII - I
'Real Love'	Verse	E	G♯m/D♯	C♯m^7	B aug	IV - II - V - I
'Penny Lane'	Verse	B	B/A♯	B/G♯	B/F♯	I - (V - I)
'Hello Goodbye'	Chorus	C	C/B	Am	Asus^2/G	♭VI - I, ♭VII - I
'Martha My Dear'	Coda	E♭	E♭/D	E♭/C	E♭/B♭	(V - I)
'Hey Jude'*	Bridge (on IV)	B♭	B♭/A	B♭/G	B♭/F	II - V - V^7 - I
'Something'*	Bridge (on VI)	A	C♯m/G♯	F♯m^7	A/E	IV - ♭VII - I

The last two examples in the table require qualification as, unlike all the others, the run does not unfold from the song's main tonic. They are included to demonstrate that while the diatonic bass descent is undoubtedly a cliché, inspired songwriters can take it a stage further by using it on other scale degrees. In each case the pattern still works, as we can temporarily regard these degrees as the new tonic and therefore the new starting point for the '8'.

[13] Note that Percy Sledge's complete run is a brilliant '8-7-6-5-4-5-1' (using the chords D♭-A♭-B♭m-Fm-G♭-A♭-D♭). Once at the iii, of course, we can just think in terms of a half-step harmonic shift to IV to spark a IV-V-I cadence. Check out, too, the way our other two blueprints develop beyond the '5': 'A Whiter Shade Of Pale' also continues its bass descent all the way to the C tonic an octave below; while Bach, having reached '4' on 'Air On A G String', immediately ascends a semitone to lend a tense ♭5 flavour.

[14] As well as 'Her Majesty', which descends '8-7-6-5' in two bars, 'Penny Lane' stands out for the 'double-time' feel of the bass line that completes the run in a single bar.

The IV chord is an obvious example. After all, the interval structure in the run (half step, whole step, whole step) is the same from both these starting points within the diatonic structure of the major scale. So, while the table uses the formula 8-7-6-5 in relation to the IV chord (B♭), equally a songwriter could conceive it as 4-3-2-1 in relation to the original I chord (F major).

Either way, McCartney was hip to this symmetry by the time of 'Hey Jude'.[15]

'Hey Jude'

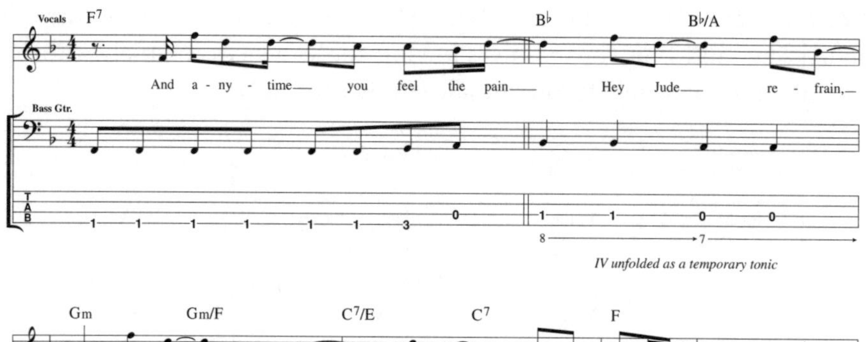

While the IV chord may be an obvious destination on which to start the bridge, the way that this descending run embellishes the chord exaggerates the feeling of movement. In doing so, we feel that we are moving more comprehensively away from the verse tonic as the spotlighted subdominant fights to take on the mantle of tonic. It is helped in its attempts by the C7 chord which now appears 'displaced', rather like a II7 chord on its way to

[15] Listen also to Harrison's 'Long, Long, Long' (*The White Album*) where the bass descends in a '4-3-2-1' pattern, as the chords drop IV-iii-ii-I, from B♭ to F. The song makes for an essential study as this descent is the main way that the tonic is established. The song's floating feel is precisely because Perfect cadences are avoided, with the stubborn dominant C7 refusing to be drawn home. Even the Plagal moves in the chorus are fleeting and the song soon heads away from the tonic, with the tonal ambiguity reflecting the restless lyrical theme.

V. It is only at the end of the bridge that this chord reasserts itself as an effective V7 as it cues an Imperfect cadence that awaits a return to an F verse.[16]

Just as we 'truncated' the original descent in 'All You Need Is Love' to take us only as far as the relative minor, so The Beatles often used what can be seen as '4-3-2' to take us to the relative minor of the IV. In the verse of 'Two Of Us', this idea provides the only embellishment to the basic tonic-to-subdominant structure seen back in Chapter 2.

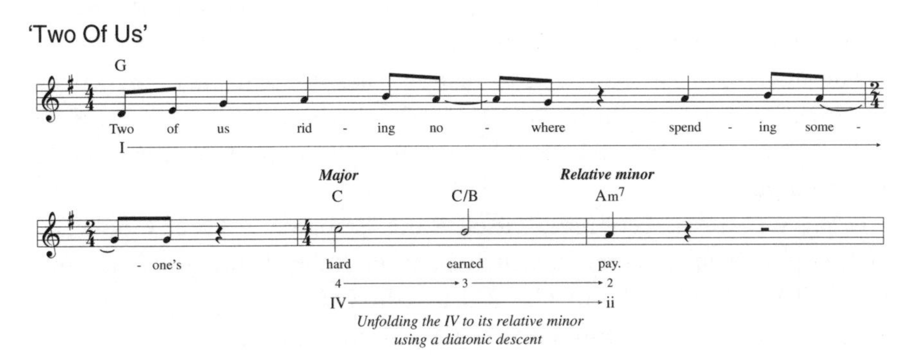

In this way the IV-ii move is merely a ploy to extend the subdominant harmony. The moving line here neatly reflects the lyrical theme of 'returning home' – in deft contrast to the static images of 'riding nowhere' and 'not arriving' that fall on the initial bars of the extended tonic.

The 8-7-6-5 formula has stood the test of time in rock and pop, as Chris Ingham points out, mentioning a range of songs including a trio from the 'DESH-*meister*' himself, David Bowie: 'Changes', 'All The Young Dudes' and 'Oh, You Pretty Things'.[17] To that diverse list must be added the 1994 Oasis smash hit, 'Whatever', in which Noel Gallagher delivers another '8-7-6-5' (followed by a textbook IV-V-I cadence) as the repeated intro and verse motif (see Chapter 8, footnote 23).

Finally, a special mention must be made of one of the most original uses of the '8-7-6-5' descent in post-Beatles pop: Slade's 'Merry Xmas Everybody'. The intro unfolds over a B♭ triad only for the verse to emerge

[16] Meanwhile, Harrison's 'Something' uses the device in the A major bridge after an ambitious key switch from the C major verse (hence the 'VI').

[17] Ingham's other examples of 'DESH' include: XTC's 'The Loving', Tears For Fears' 'Sowing The Seeds Of Love', and Echobelly's 'Insomnia'. 'Doctor Rock Dissects The Hits: No. 1', *MOJO*, Issue 14, January 1995, p. 28.

in G major. Holder does this expertly by making his next stop '♭3', harmonising a D major chord that acts as a big V chord for G itself. Most cleverly, that opening B♭ is being previewed for its later use as a rocky ♭III, in G major itself.[18]

2) The Diatonic Minor Descent (8-♭7-♭6-5)

Not surprisingly, The Diatonic Major Descent has a minor counterpart. Equally predictably, it involves falling sequentially through scale degrees of the natural minor scale, and building a chord on each note.

The '8-♭7-♭6-5' descent is now happily harmonised with the corresponding harmonised chords: 'i-♭VII-♭VI-V', with no inversions necessary as the awkward diminished triad that we needed to avoid in a major key is out of range.

In this way the descent reveals itself as the 'Runaway'/'Three Cool Cats' trick explored in Chapter 6, which Lennon worked into songs ranging from 'I'll Be Back' to 'I Am The Walrus' (the latter in major, and with its coda using the descent from two different starting points).[19]

In all these cases the bass run is heard complete with the expected root-position chords, while a true minor 'DESH' can be heard powerfully in 'We Can Work It Out'.[20]

Having previously focused on the chords, let's look again at this extract to see how the descending bass buys time on the Bm chord, while the triad stays *in situ* as the bass drops through the scale tones, providing further reinforcement to the tonic status of the relative minor in this middle eight.[21]

[18] Ingham also points to Slade's use of the run here, and in 'Skweeze Me Pleeze Me' (which opens with an electrifying 8-7-6-5, in the key of E, returning to base via ♭7-7-8.)

[19] A look through the list of early Beatles stage favourites suggests that they would also have been absorbing this same descending run in their renditions of 'Hit The Road Jack', a Top 10 hit for Ray Charles in October 1961 and in the Fab's live repertoire over the next year; see Lewisohn, *The Complete Beatles Recording Sessions*, p. 362.

[20] For a powerful variation on the Diatonic Minor 'DESH', see Joy Division's haunting 'New Dawn Fades' (*Unknown Pleasures*), based entirely on '8-♭7-♭6-4', for a Plagal return, in the key of Em.

[21] Note how The Beatles painstakingly highlight this effect by switching the rhythm to a melancholy 3:4 waltz (at 0.46 and 0.59) which combines with the harmony to evoke neatly the world-weary mood of the moment.

'We Can Work It Out'

3) The Dorian/Aeolian hybrid descent (8-♭7-6-♭6)

Just as The Beatles broke free from diatonic boundaries with their basic chord shapes, so 'borrowed' and modal harmony would find its way into some of the most distinctive descending lines in their catalogue.

'Chromaticism' is the key to understanding a select group of lines that 'fill in' the gaps in the diatonic runs detailed above, while keeping the overall principle of a line effortlessly heading 'south' from the tonic. Tweaking these major and minor runs in subtle ways helps bring dozens of Beatles songs into our songwriting framework.

For the first of these, we can take the Diatonic Minor Descent itself and give it a Dorian flavour by incorporating the 'character' sounds of that mode – a natural 6th scale tone and a major IV chord. In 'While My Guitar Gently Weeps' George Harrison shows us exactly how these two elements combine to create a IV chord in 1st inversion. For here, in the key of A minor, his D major chord's major 3rd (F♯) acts to 'fill in' one of the gaps in the minor descent. This deftly changes '8-♭7-♭6' into a more leisurely '8-♭7-6-♭6', with two successive semitone drops following the opening whole-tone descent.

'While My Guitar Gently Weeps'

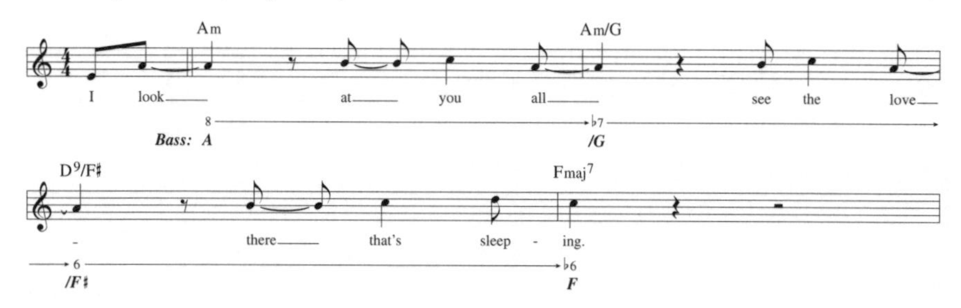

With F♯ now joining the F natural in the sequence, we are back in the mixed-mode territory of songs like 'Wait', which feature both the natural and flattened 6th notes in their structures. In the same way we can think of this hybrid line as a 'Dorian embellishment' of a standard natural minor line. The following chart summarises the run, focusing again on the relationship between the basic chords and the bass notes and inversions implied.

Aeolian/Dorian hybrid	**8**	**♭7**	**6**	**♭6**
Moving line in A minor	A	G	F♯	F
Basic chords	Am	Am	D9	F
Slash chord with bass note	Am	Am/G	D9/F♯	F
Inversion	Root	3rd	1st	Root

This hybrid bass run would emerge as a highly popular and successful line in both rock and pop. Jimmy Page exploited its folky possibilities in 'Babe, I'm Gonna Leave You', the acoustic mega-ballad on Led Zeppelin's seminal 1969 debut, which cycles hypnotically around this descent (continuing on to '5', E in the key of A minor). In a similar genre, Aerosmith's haunting 'Dream On' features intricate harmony that suggests the run in the Fm verse, before opting for a 'regular' Aeolian run in the chorus. It also surfaces distinctly in a pair of cult songs – 'In A Broken Dream' by Python Lee

Jackson (a.k.a. Rod Stewart), in G minor, and Chicago's '25 Or 6 To 4' (A minor). More recently Rooksby points to Mark Knopfler's use of the idea in the main theme of the soundtrack to *Wag The Dog*.[22]

Back in the sixties, The Kinks' 'Sunny Afternoon' found Ray Davies descending the same line in 'DESH' fashion, with a D minor chord holding the fort while the line continued its descent down the natural minor scale all the way to the tonic.[23]

4) The Rock Descent (8-♭7-6-♭6 – in major)

While this Aeolian/Dorian hybrid may sound like a bastardised creation, at least it appears in the 'correct' minor-key setting, with that crucial first ♭7 destination familiar to that tonality in just the same way that the natural 7th was the defining element of the major run.

But The Beatles weren't going to let such classical rules stand in the way of their redefinition of harmonic goalposts. For perhaps the most famous and pioneering of all their descending lines involved taking this very same minor run and transplanting it to a *major* setting.

We now start with a whole-step descent from a major tonic triad, with ♭7 the first port-of-call from the root, before then continuing with a semitone descent. The following chart confirms that the blatant undermining of the delicate, 'classical', natural 7th results in a rogue harmonic backdrop, perfect for conveying some of The Beatles' most psychedelic, post-1967 excursions.

The '♭7' and the rise of 'The Rock Descent'

	8	♭7	6	♭6	5*
'Lucy In The Sky With Diamonds'	A	G	F♯	F	E
'Dear Prudence'	D	C	B	B♭	A
'I Am The Walrus'	A	G	F♯	F	
'Magical Mystery Tour'	D	C	B	B♭	

[22] Rikky Rooksby, *How To Write Songs On Guitar*, p. 112. While Knopfler is more famous for the strict Aeolian runs that drop directly from ♭VII to ♭VI (e.g., 'Sultans Of Swing' and 'What It Is'), Rooksby explains how, in the key of A minor, a D major chord in 1st inversion embellishes the line with a ♮6 (F♯) in the bass.

[23] In this way, 'Sunny Afternoon' descends a complete octave: 8-♭7-6-♭6-5-4-♭3-2-1 in the key of D minor.

No mention of psychedelia would be complete without a look at 'Lucy' herself and her rather special harmonic personality (to which the asterisk in the above table is intended to draw attention).

'Lucy In The Sky With Diamonds'

McCartney's famous bassline opens (at 0.06) with a perfect demonstration of the drop from tonic to ♭6 in a two-bar phrase. The line then continues on to '5' (at 0.12) but this note now acts as a replacement for the tonic with subsequent two-bar phrases now re-emerging as: '5-♭7-6-♭6'.

This '5' under the tonic chord is merely another manifestation of McCartney's tension trick, namely a tonic chord in 2nd inversion. Either way, the cyclicality of the line complements the repeated instrumental melody and reflects the hypnotic premise of the song. The ♭7 adds a maverick flavour while the subtle displacement of the line through '5' contributes a subliminal effect that is at once relaxing and disturbing.

There are various possible interpretations of the implied chords of 'Lucy', given the beautiful, sparse theme melody which, as a verse counter-melody, is our only guide. The third chord, in particular, could be seen as an A6, or its relative minor equivalent, F♯m7. However, we have chosen to label it D/F♯ for the purposes of creating handy reference points within our overall framework. For not only are the 3rd and 5th of D major easily identifiable, but the inversion is identical to the one we pointed out on this same scale degree in 'While My Guitar Gently Weeps'. Finally (and perhaps most usefully) it helps us make the connection with that early Beatles favourite device: the IV-iv minor drop; as that is, effectively, exactly what we have here – *except that D and Dm are now both in 1st inversion.* Given Lennon's history with this move ('If I Fell', 'In My Life', etc.) we could speculate that these were the 'original chords' that George Martin refers to in his memories of the *Summer Of Love.*[24]

Irrespective of the precise chords, the song was clearly an inspirational template for many line-based outings of the late sixties, with one writer even dubbing this very bassline 'The Lucy' in tribute.[25] By the time of 'Dear Prudence' on the *White Album*, the hanging, droning effect meant that the different starting points of '8' and '5' effectively operate at the same time. Solo guitarists may instinctively hear (and play) the line starting with the droning D note, but listen to McCartney's lovely bass figure (played in a notably high register) to appreciate how, for him, the cycle begins on the '5' (A in the key of D).[26]

In a sense, we have already seen one potential inspiration for this Rock Descent way back in our discussion of 'The Power Of V'. Look again at 'You've Got To Hide Your Love Away' and its inevitable '5-4-3-2-1' descent, which accompanies D in the key of G.

So what is the connection? In relation to the V chord, this basic run starts with a whole-step-half-step descent. Given the ease of experimenting with moving lines around the open D-shape on the guitar, Lennon only had to reconceive D as the I chord and he was away.[27]

But whatever the original Lennon inspiration, here is the 'borrowing' ethic as applied to descending harmony, with the darker strains of that ♭7 (the root of the all-important ♭VII chord) helping to shape the sound of rock. This quartet of Beatles songs (and others, like 'Wild Honey Pie',

[24] George Martin reveals that the line was 'not formally composed' but evolved by means of McCartney improvising arpeggios of Lennon's original chords; *Summer Of Love: The Making Of Sgt. Pepper,* p. 102.

[25] In his challenging discussion of its '5-♭7-6-♭6' incarnation, Ian Hammond suggests that 'The Lucy' derives broadly from 'Norwegian Wood' while being identifiable in songs as late as Lennon's 'Isolation'; www.beathoven.com.

[26] For a recommended solo guitar transcription see Askold Buk's effective attempt in *Guitar World Acoustic*, Issue 21, 1997.

[27] To make the same connection in a contemporary setting, listen to the Oasis song 'Sunday Morning Call' (at 1.26), as the moving line cycles around D-C-B beneath a D chord in the key of G (before thwarting the cadence to G and returning abruptly to the verse key of B♭, at 1.38.)

'Dear Prudence'

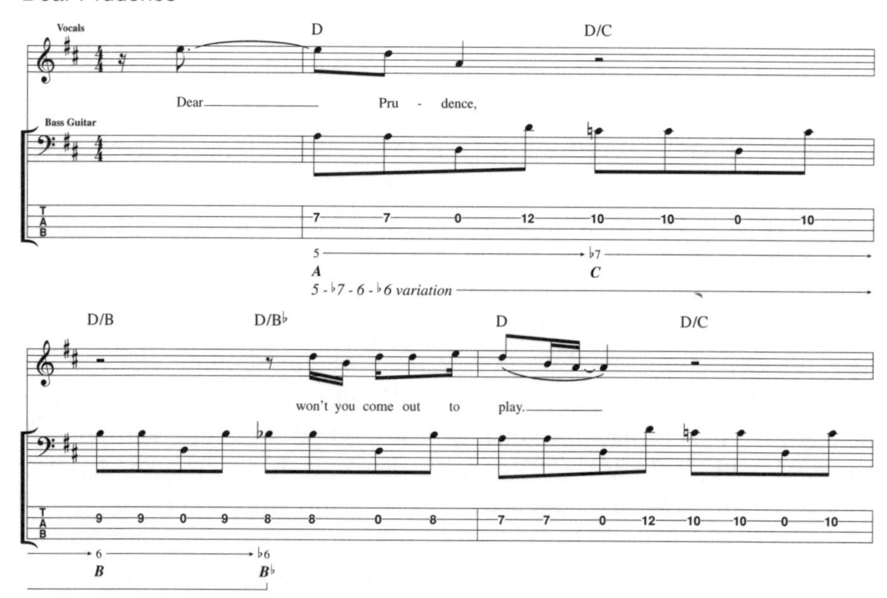

which also use the move)[28] were joined in the sixties by a pair of Cream songs ('White Room' and 'Tales Of Brave Ulysses'), which each similarly structured complete song sections around the idea.[29]

And the legacy of the Rock Descent didn't end with the sixties. Down the years it has been pivotal to songs like Neil Young's 'Needle And The Damage Done', which opens with a 'Dear Prudence'-style descent (again around an open D-chord); and Paul Weller's 'The Changingman', where the run (in C this time) neatly captures the lyrical theme of 'shifting sands'. The device also lives on in quasi-psychedelic songs of the new century like Oasis's 'Who Feels Love?'. Listen how the '8-♭7-6-5' descent (from a G root, at 2.47) contrasts with the pedal-tone structure of the

[28] After 'Lucy' and 'Prudence', honorary mentions should also go to 'What's The New Mary Jane?' – even if this song acquires some of its quirkiness by omitting the ♭7 from the 'Rock run'. In the key of D, a novel opening move to a subdominant in 1st inversion means that the bass drops boldly from '1' to '6' (to match the melody) before continuing a semitone descent to 5.

[29] As Everett mentions, by the end of the decade the line would be tapped equally by a trio of 1969 songs: Led Zeppelin's 'Babe, I'm Gonna Leave You', The Doors' 'Soft Parade' and King Crimson's 'The Epitaph'; *The Beatles As Musicians*, p. 349. Steve Winwood's 'Can't Find My Way Home' continued the tradition a year later.

verse, thereby neatly encapsulating two of these pioneering sixties ploys in one song.

And what a coincidence that for their Millennium TV advert, British Airways should feature the music of 'Something In The Air', Thunderclap Newman's 1969 classic, featuring another unmistakable '8-♭7-6-♭6'.[30] Musos may spot the gentle irony, for joining the cast of travelling spoof celebrities on the TV footage, was the pioneer of this Rock Descent, John Lennon, in his trademark white suit.

5) The Chromatic Descent (8-7-♭7-6) – in Minor

While all the moving lines so far have seen the bass itself drive the song, a number of common chord sequences derive from moving lines *within* the harmony. The distinction can be seen clearly in 'Michelle', McCartney's gem from *Rubber Soul* variously described as 'archetypal love song', 'French film music' and 'lounge ballad'. True to Citron's opening quote in this chapter, Paul himself prefers to talk about his delicate counterpoint bass line that adds '5'-tension beneath the tonic chord. However, it is the instantly memorable descending guitar figure (which unfolds beneath a static minor chord) that most Beatles fans forever associate with the song.

'Michelle'

Here we have, visually at least, the simplest moving line formula so far. Descending down a diatonic scale is hardly rocket science, but 'Michelle' glides romantically in *consecutive semitones down the chromatic scale.*

This creates one of the most soothing of structural descents and one that, understandably, has proved irresistible to listeners and songwriters. Rarely does a year go by in pop without this run imprinting itself on our

[30] Over an E chord, after the line '. . . and you know it's right'.

subconscious. Vying with 'Michelle' for immortality is none other than Led Zeppelin's 'Stairway To Heaven', followed not far behind by gems like Leon Russell's 'This Masquerade', Jim Croce's 'Time In A Bottle', Morris Albert's evergreen standard, 'Feelings' and Tom Petty's 'Into The Great Wide Open'.

TV advertisers like this run too, with Fiat's use of 'Music To Watch Girls By', complete with its signature '8-7-♭7-6' run in G minor, fuelling an Andy Williams revival.

So just how does this run work its magic?

Harmonising the '7' – The major/minor seventh chord

In most cases, the songwriting interest is down to the subtle tension that arises from the chord that is implied when harmonising the '7'. Unlike the other three members of the run, this note is not diatonic to either natural minor (Aeolian), or any other of the minor modes (Dorian, Phrygian or Locrian), for in each of these, the seventh degree is always *flattened*.

To appreciate the implied chord on the natural (or 'raised') 7th, we have to look beyond our basic framework and recall the Harmonic minor scale that we introduced in Chapter 6.

Harmonic minor revisited – F harmonic minor

i maj^7	**ii**$^{7\flat5}$	♭**iii** maj^{7}aug	**iv**^{7}	**V**^{7}	♭**VI** maj^7	**vii** dim^7
Fm (maj^7)	Gm$^{7\flat5}$	A♭maj^7 aug	B♭m^7	C^7	D♭maj^7	E dim^7

This time we don't require the V, but another chord that contains the scale's 7th: the tonic triad itself. As its bulky name suggests this is merely a minor triad joined by a seventh, but one that is a *major* seventh interval from the root. Here is the full chord in more detail.

'Michelle's Fm/maj7 chord

Formula	**1**	**♭3**	**5**	**7**
Fm (maj^7)	F	A♭	C	E

The dissonant sound of the chord acts to propel the moving line along to the next 'stop', ♭7, which now implies a more familiar Fm7 chord.

While 'Michelle' is usually assumed to be The Beatles' first use of this idea, a quick listen to their cover of 'A Taste Of Honey' confirms that the idea was in action many years previously. We've also seen it in 'Cry Baby Cry' where the run was extended by a further semitone to the root of a C7 chord (8-7-♭7-6-♭6).

Whether you regard the latter song's unfolding E minor as a tonic or a 'vi' in G major makes little difference to how the pattern works. Indeed it demonstrates its versatility, for a quick scan of the catalogue reveals the identical descending idea not merely on a minor tonic but also on the conventional minor chords of the *major* scale: ii, iii and vi. Sometimes this involves truncating the line (confining the descent to, say, '8-7-♭7'), or perhaps reharmonising the '6' with a different chord, a concept that should now be familiar.

Here's an example of iii minor unfolding with the Chromatic Minor Run:

'Got To Get You Into My Life'

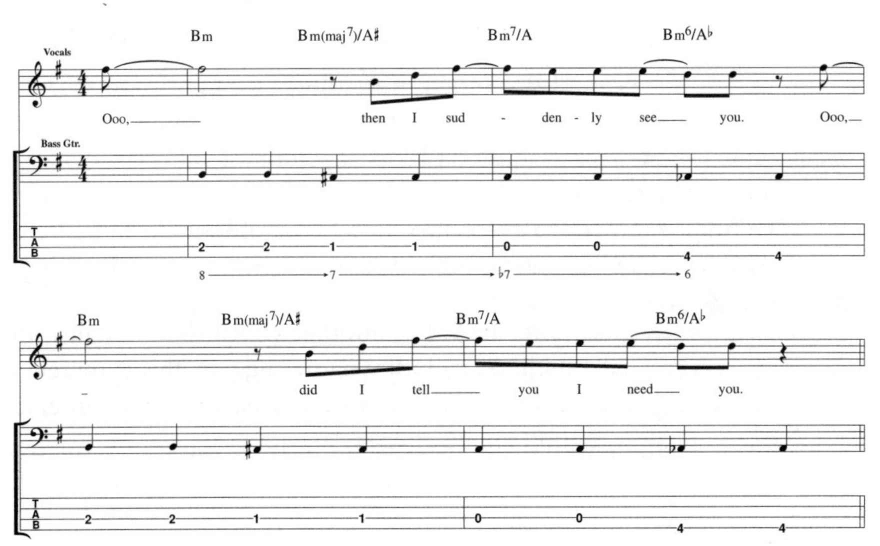

Notice that the essential chromatic line is identical (although, because of the more static bass on B on this occasion, the final chord now remains as a Bm6). In 'And Your Bird Can Sing', a dominant chord, whose root is a fifth lower, appears in place of the minor 6th:

'And Your Bird Can Sing'

Bridge

G♯m	G♯m (maj^7)	G♯m^7	C♯^{7}
When your prized pos - ses -	sions,	start to weigh you	down,
iii →			VI^7

E	F♯m		B
look in my di - rec -	tion, I'll be 'round,	I'll be	'round.
I →	ii →		V

Sometimes the '8-7-♭7-6' run can be heard briefly in various truncated permutations to add fleeting interest to a minor chord. For example, listen out for the '8-7' drop (complete with the dissonant m/major 7th chord), in the following Beatles moments:

– the intro to 'Mother Nature's Son' (unfolding as a vi)[31]
– the verse of 'Blackbird' (as a vi)
– the second bridge of 'I'll Be Back' (as a ii)
– the bridge of George's 'You Know What To Do' (as a ii)[32]

6) The Chromatic Descent (8-7-♭7-6) – in major

While the '8-7-♭7-6' descent can usefully be dubbed the 'Michelle' trick, it has possibilities far beyond the simple unfolding of a minor chord. Folk artists have frequently used the run to structure complete songs starting on a *major* tonic.[33] As far back as 'It Won't Be Long', John Lennon was demonstrating how to use the four-semitone chromatic descent in major, creating one of his finest moments. The combination of chords, melody, bass and vocal harmony yield an intriguing implied progression in the song's delicious bridge (starting at 0.42).

Here again, harmonising the line is the key to appreciating this sound. After the opening E major, listen to the harmony over the D♯, the '7' in the chromatic descent. A iii minor (G♯m) in 2nd inversion would have done nicely, just as Lennon would do later in 'Real Love'. However, on this

[31] In relation to the song's impending key centre of D major.

[32] Among the myriad of non-Beatles examples featuring a brief m/maj7th embellishment, listen to 'Oye Como Va' to hear Santana prolong the tonic A minor chord; Bread's 'Guitar Man' (on the ii); and the minor-key blues standard, 'I'll Play The Blues For You' (where it unfolds the iv chord).

[33] Simon and Garfunkel's 'Homeward Bound' provides a good example of the folk legacy, adopting a chromatic guitar line that moves through G-F♯-F-E for the verse ('Sitting at a railway station . . .'), in conjunction with a droning D-string as an 'inner-pedal'.

'It Won't Be Long'

occasion the implied chord must capture not only the bass, but also the B note in John's melody – and the G note in the beautiful descending chromatic counter-melody sung by Paul and George in the backing vocals.

OK, so a iii minor chord spelt: 'G♯m/major7/D♯' (G-sharp-minor-major-seventh in second inversion) technically takes in this single, stunning sonority. But rather more concise is 'D♯ aug', a major triad with a raised (or 'augmented') 5th built on the very root we want and containing all the necessary notes.

To appreciate the fact that these two chords are inversions of each other we can compare them in the following table. But in order to understand the construction of the augmented chord it helps to be aware of certain notes as *enharmonic equivalents*. For it is the augmented chord's raised 5th, (technically A##, or A *double sharp*) that represents the correct enharmonic equivalent of the B note; while *its major 3rd, F## ('F double sharp')* is the 'official' identity of the pitch notated as G.[34]

Reconciling the 'aug' chord in 'It Won't Be Long'

Notes	A× = B* (melody)	F× = G (backing)	D♯(major 7 in moving line)
D♯ aug	♯5 th	3 rd	Root
G♯m (maj 7)	♭3 rd	5 th	5 th

*NB: × = ##

With the bass line now on its way, a further drop to '♭7' sees a D major chord with an implied added 6th reflecting neatly the B note in the melody (the F♯ in the counter-melody matches the major 3rd of D).

Similarly the '6' is now a major triad due to the E♯ counter-melody which creates a major 3rd in relation to the root of C♯. Indeed, the counter-melody tracks the descending bass precisely, using this same interval, thereby enjoying its own chromatic drop which can be captured as '3-♭3-2-♭2' against the bass line of 8-7-♭7-6.[35]

The bridge then continues not with a Cycle Of Fifths move to the expected F♯m, but to its relative major, A major and up to the dominant.[36] The final ii-V cadence provides the simplest of foils to a four-bar stretch of

[34] The ## (sometimes written as ×) is used when raising the pitch of a note already containing a ♯ by a semitone. While it is simpler to call F## by its enharmonic equivalent of G, it doesn't help us to construct and visualise the 'aug' chord. For the 3rd of any D♯ chord must use the letter F from the alphabet. F♯ is the ♭3rd and therefore F## is the required major 3rd interval. Similarly, A♯ is merely a perfect 5th above the tonic and must be raised a semitone to get the required tension-inducing augmented effect.

[35] Refer to 'Do You Want To Know A Secret' to see an earlier example of a Beatles countermelody unfolding similarly as a chromatic descent in parallel with descending harmony. The repeated line 'do-da-do' (first heard at 0.42 after 'Listen') features thirds that fall in tandem with the G♯m-Gm-F♯m drop (iii-♭iii-ii, in the key of E) and consists of the ♭3rd and 5th of each minor chord.

[36] Note how the countermelody continues its descent by further semitones to the root and on to '7'.

pure Beatles magic which – despite its 1963 date – ranks among their finest-ever harmonisations.

Mark Herstgaard rightly raves about precisely this moment with some appropriate heavyweight name-dropping:

> 'When Dylan said The Beatles' chords were "outrageous, just outrageous," it's songs like "It Won't Be Long", he was talking about. Its chords go places they "shouldn't", according to conventional musical theory, but never having learned musical theory, The Beatles were free to disregard it in favor of what their ears told them worked. The middle eight of 'It Won't' Be Long' is a brilliant example . . . giving the melody a whole new texture and direction . . .'[37]

This chromatic run in major is surprisingly rare in pop, especially considering how its scope for interesting harmonisation makes it far harder to spot as a cliché in comparison, say, to its minor-key counterpart. Nevertheless, songwriting students are particularly encouraged to check out The Move's 'Fire Brigade' in which Roy Wood managed to pack *both* this descending run *and* a chromatic unfolding of a minor chord all into one action-packed 8-bar sequence.[38]

As with many of the other powerful descents of this chapter, The Beatles kept an inspired ear open for other contexts in which to use this type of seamless, four-note chromatic run by starting from other scale degrees.

One of the most novel can be found at the end of 'Hello Goodbye', just before the coda vamp on the tonic. Starting at 2.36, McCartney initiates a brilliant wrap-up as the bass collapses deliciously from the rocky ♭VI down to IV, making the run no longer '8-7-♭7-6' but '♭6-5-♭5-4', before finally prompting a Plagal cadence.

[37] Mark Herstgaard, *A Day In The Life: The Music And Artistry Of The Beatles,* pp. 56–7. Bob Dylan is quoted from Anthony Scaduto's biography, *Bob Dylan*, p. 203, in which the Zim also says: 'and their harmonies made it all valid'. Perhaps he was indeed thinking of this stretch of 'It Won't Be Long'.

[38] A No. 3 hit in February 1968, 'Fire Brigade' descends 8-7-♭7-6 (in the key of G) but instead of moving to IV, unwinds the 'Michelle' descent on Am, the relative minor substitute of Lennon's IV chord. Elsewhere, The New Seekers reached No. 2 in March 1972 with 'Beg, Steal, Or Borrow', using another Chromatic Major Descent in the key of G. Note: both songs use a 'Real Love'-style 'iii minor in 2nd inversion' to harmonise the '7', rather than the 'aug' alternative. Keeping the progression going (in every way), The Osmonds hit No. 1 in August 1974 with 'Love Me For A Reason', whose verse featured the same unmistakable, chromatic descent.

'Hello Goodbye'

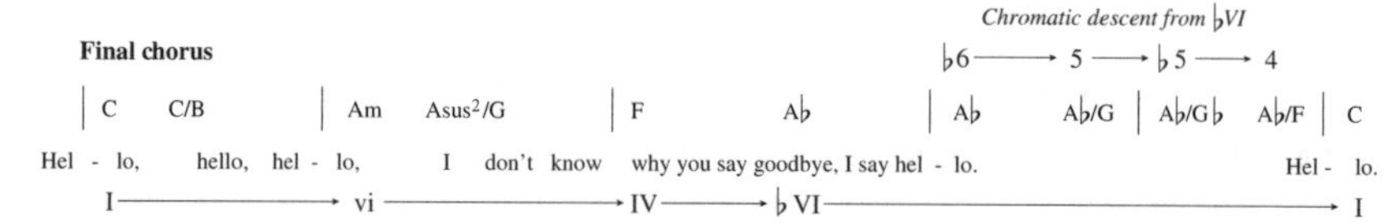

For another variation, look back to the corresponding moment at the very end of 'It Won't Be Long' (at 2.04). Here the guitar and bass both fall '3-2-♭2-1' to the tonic *in parallel,* with the closing E major 7th creating what is now thought of as a common Lounge cliché.

'Mr Kite's Circus Tricks'

Part 1: The Chromatic Minor Descent revisited

No discussion of descending lines in Beatles songs would be complete without reference to John Lennon's inspired novelty number on *Sgt. Pepper*, which begs us to revisit the 8-7-♭7-6 run in a minor context.

This will widen our understanding of chord substitution and harmonisation, but also our appreciation of perhaps one of the finest examples of matching music to a lyrical theme in the history of pop. It may seem at first like a simple reworking of the 'Michelle' formula, but 'Mr Kite' requires us to view each of the harmonised chords in the sequence with even greater care. This is specifically due to the complicated three-way relationship between, firstly, the descending line itself (which is heard in the organ

'Being For The Benefit Of Mr Kite'

part), secondly, the implied chords in the harmony above it; and thirdly, the *lowest harmony* as heard in the conventional bass line. The juggling of these three elements is not the only circus metaphor, although the sound affects us in a similarly disorientating way. Let the show begin . . .

After the opening C minor, let's start by appreciating the chord on the '7', which appears as an augmented chord rather than a 'm/major 7' as we might expect in a minor setting. A close look at the construction of the 'G aug' shows that it is indeed an effective inversion of the Cm/major7 – and, therefore, a substitute.

Harmonising the '7': Mr Kite's 'G aug'

Notes	C	D♯ = E♭	B (organ)	G (bass)
G aug	11th	♯5th	3rd	Root
Cm (maj7)	Root	♭3rd	7th	5th

The reason the chord emerges with a G, rather than a B, root is precisely because McCartney's bass is adding interest at this point by not doubling the '7' in the organ part but, instead, playing his now familiar 5th-in-the-bass trick. In this way, 'G aug' can be rationalised as 'Cm/major 7-in-2nd-inversion'. The C note is still present in the organ chord but can be seen as an 11th in relation to the G bass where it now 'defers' to both this root and the important B note in the moving line.

As we continue the sequence we can see that 'Mr Kite' delivers some further interesting departures from the 'Michelle' formula (which couched all the chords in terms of the tonic). This is crucial to the effect of the song in the context of the lyrical theme. Look first at the mechanics on the remaining stops in the moving line:

Over the '♭7', a B♭ major appears as a clever substitute for the obvious Cm7 by virtue of The Common Tone Substitution Rule, which is satisfied as both chords contain the required B♭ note.

Harmonising the '♭7': reconciling Mr Kite's B♭

Notes	F	D	B♭ (bass and organ)
B♭	5th	3rd	Root
Cm 7			♭7th

Similarly when looking at the '6', we find the organ playing not a C minor 6th as the source of the A note (as in 'Michelle'), but a D minor chord in 1st inversion. However, with the bass now playing an D note itself, we can still happily view the overall chord as being in root position. Again, The Common Tone Substitution Rule means that we hear Dm as an acceptable alternative to Cm6.

Harmonising the '6': reconciling Mr Kite's Dm

Notes	A (organ)	F	D (bass)
Dm	5th	♭3rd	Root
Cm 6	6th		

These tables are not merely for academic show. The fact that there are so few common tones in some of these substitutions is the secret to understanding the quirky character of the song. Unlike the effortless romantic glide of 'Michelle', or 'It Won't Be Long', with its complementary swooning counter-melody, 'Mr Kite' appears to jump around on his harmonic trampoline, perfectly capturing the atmosphere of the circus. Yet amid the eccentricity, the whole show is expertly held together by the moving line that runs through each chord with all the precision of the high wire act.

This forms 'part 1' of the analysis of this outrageously constructed song, offering a first insight into how the combination of music and lyrics works on our imagination.

Mr Kite will return for a later performance in Chapter 10 . . .

The augmented chord – anatomy of a secret weapon

The augmented chord deserves a closer look for its use in a select range of Beatles contexts. To appreciate it further we need to look briefly at the scale source from which the chord derives, which explains a particular quirk that allows the identical chord to exist on different roots – and therefore to be named in three different ways.

To demonstrate this, the following chart shows how both B augmented and D♯ augmented would have made equally effective substitutions for the G augmented in 'Mr Kite'. For all three of these augmented chords contain exactly the same notes, despite their apparent enharmonic complexities.

The triple identity of the G augmented chord

	1	3	5♯
G aug	G	B	D♯
B aug	B	D♯	F𝄪 = G*
D♯aug	D♯	F𝄪 = G*	A𝄪 = B*

*NB: 𝄪 = ♯♯

We can immediately reconcile the second option, B augmented, with the augmented chord in 'It Won't Be Long', for this is the 'correct' name for the chord in situations where the low harmony drops by a semitone to the '7'.

All three augmented chords are just inversions of each other, for reasons that can be best understood with reference to its ultimate source: the Whole Tone scale. This spacey-sounding sequence is an example of a *symmetrical* scale, so called because the distance between every note is identical (in this case, a whole tone or 'second' interval).

The G Whole Tone scale – the source of the 'G aug' chord

Formula	1		2		3		♯4		♯5		♯6/♭7		1
Notes	G		A		B		C♯		D♯		E♯/F		G
Intervals		1		1		1		1		1		1	

Because of this symmetry, whichever note in the scale you use to start 'stacking' alternate notes on (using our customary harmonisation in thirds) will yield a chord with the defining augmented formula of 1, 3, ♯5. It is straightforward to confirm that the B and D♯ augmented scales themselves contain the very same notes and, consequently, all the chords are indeed substitutes for each other.

And not just in theory, but also in practice – listen to the intro to Stevie Wonder's 'You Are The Sunshine Of My Life' to hear an augmented line ascend in second intervals, seemingly covering all the notes on the keyboard. In effect, this creates a sound that implies nothing other than an altered V chord, which will move to the tonic when the verse starts.[39]

A natural consequence of the internal symmetry of this scale is that there are only two whole tone scales in existence. The one we constructed above, which can be named by any one of its constituent tones, and the other, which automatically encompasses the remaining members of the chromatic scale: A♯, C, D, E, F♯ and G♯, or their enharmonic equivalents.[40]

While this theory hopefully explains the background to the chord, in

[39] In the key of B major, Stevie Wonder's intro alternates B with F♯ aug (the latter heard as an F♯ bass pedal over which root and ♯5 move through various inversions as they ascend the octave in six consecutive steps of a whole tone).

[40] The Whole Tone scale, and its relationship to the augmented chords, is not to be confused with the Augmented Scale, another symmetrical scale defined as 1-♯2-3-5-♭6-7-1. It is deemed symmetrical through its pattern of alternating augmented second intervals and half-steps.

practice, as we have already seen, the augmented chord can in many cases be seen as effectively identical to the minor/major 7th with which it enjoys such a close structural relationship. The chorus of 'All My Loving', which neatly uses the device as a spicy link between a minor chord and its relative major, bears this out.

'All My Loving'

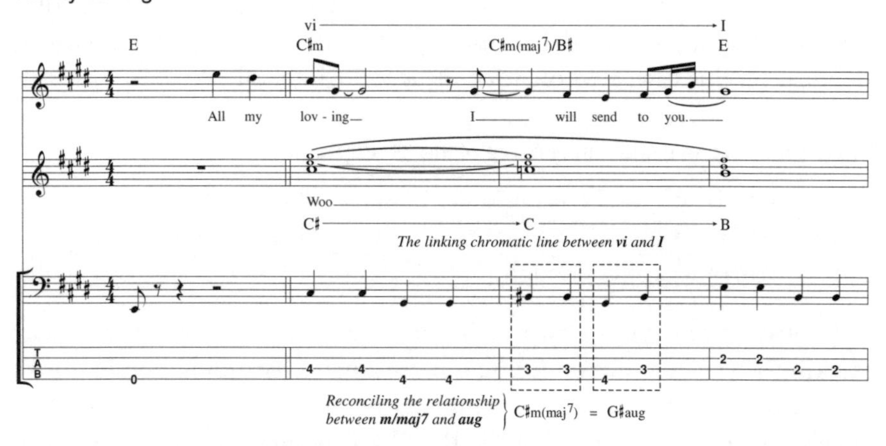

Here is another example of skill that made early Beatles songs stand out from their contemporaries, and left guitarists struggling to decipher the all-important linking chord that set the sequence apart from just another vi-I.

The fact that McCartney's bass plays both a C natural and G♯ means that, technically, the chord appears *both* in its C♯m/maj7th and G♯ aug incarnations, while guitarists may actually find it easier to think of it as E augmented (given that we are in the key of E). Each are effective substitutes for each other, though in this case the first option best captures the role of the major 7th as a link note that achieves the smooth chromatic voice-leading, allowing the root of the relative minor to fall chromatically into the 5th of the relative major (C♯-C *natural*-B, in the key of E).

Voice-leading in the 'All My Loving' 'link' chord

Chord	C♯m (vi)	C♯m (maj7)	E (I)
Moving line	C♯	C (= B♯)	B
Degree	Root	Major 7th	5th

This linking device was another idea that The Beatles were clearly absorbing from the favourite covers of their formative years. It's a move that can be heard most clearly on their *Live At The BBC* version of the Goffin & King classic, 'Don't Ever Change'. Here's the chorus (0.20-0.33):

'Don't Ever Change'

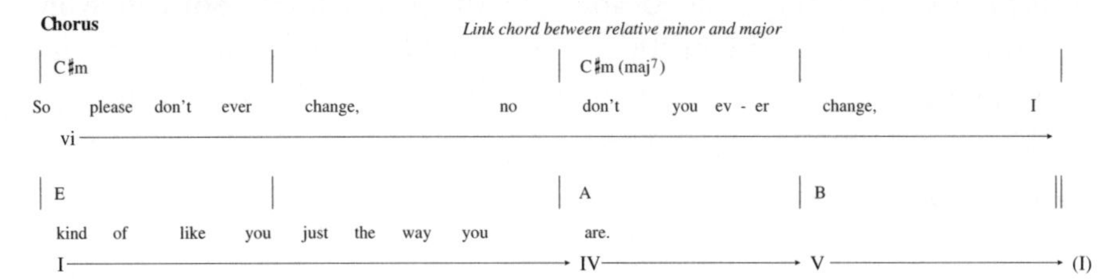

Soon The Beatles were using their new-found trick in the most stylish of contexts, such as the cool coda of 'From Me To You'. It's the same linking principle again, though, not content with the major tonic they arrive at, The Beatles fool us all by plunging back to the relative minor, leaving us hanging 'in the dark' many years before the Em close of 'Cry Baby Cry'.

'From Me To You'

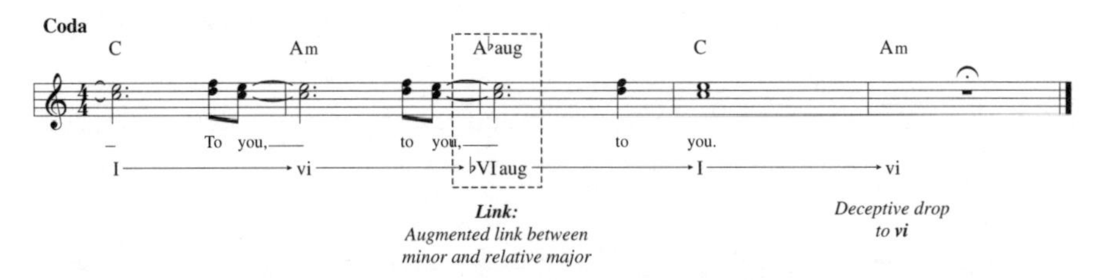

The Beatles resurrected this linking principle on 'That Means A Lot' (as heard on *Anthology 2*), in a coda that cycles around the same three-chord sequence as 'All My Loving'.

'That Means A Lot'

Coda

| C♯m *Link chord* C♯m (maj7) | E C♯m | C♯m *Link chord* C♯m (maj) | E C♯m ||

Can't you see, yeah. Can't you see, yeah.

vi → I → vi → I → vi

The Augmented Masterclass: 'Fixing A Hole', 'I'm So Tired' and 'Old Brown Shoe'.

While classical buffs may dismiss the start of 'All I've Got To Do' as just a fancy sound gesture, there's no getting away from some of the other brilliant ways in which The Beatles put the augmented chord to work within the main structure of their songs. A look at a textbook trio – one each, appropriately, from Paul, John and George – finds them at the very height of their songwriting powers.

'Fixing A Hole'.

Here we see that chromatic '8-7-♭7-6' descent again, with 'C aug' the appropriate name for the second chord because (like 'Mr Kite') we hear a strong V in the bass, leaving the line to unfold within the inner harmony.

But are we in a major or minor key this time?

In the last chapter we defined this song's melody as the embodiment of the Dorian mode, so surely we are in minor (with its defining ♭3)? But with F *major* opening the verse before giving way almost immediately to the dark moods of F minor, we seem to be facing some serious tonal ambiguity. For here are parallel major and minor fighting it out almost simultaneously, in a way conceptually similar to John's 'I'll Be Back' or, indeed, Cole Porter's 'Night And Day'.

As in those pieces, McCartney knows he can pull off the contradiction through a deft choice of melody notes. Crucially, he allows a Dorian interpretation by ensuring that his melody focuses purely on the root and 5th degree over the rogue F major chord, steering clear of its major 3rd.[41] In this way the melody avoids a defining 3rd of any kind until the third bar, when the A♭ helps to paint a minor picture.

However, the essence of the song's brilliance lies not in the switch *per se*, but in the role of the augmented chord in effecting it. For by that time we have already heard the A♭ note (or its enharmonic incarnation, G♯) within the C augmented itself, prior to the remaining sequence which establishes F minor without question.

This is important, because it demonstrates a pivotal songwriting function of the augmented chord that each of the Beatles songwriters intuitively mastered in this trio of songs. The chord serves to lead the listener from an upbeat, major tonality towards darker, minor territory by 'previewing' a note that will soon be subconsciously interpreted as the minor 3rd of the parallel minor. The following chart attempts to depict this 'half-way house' as F gives way to F minor.[42]

Borrowing between parallel major and minor – 'Fixing A Hole'

F major		**C aug**		**F minor**	
		3	E		
1	F			1	F
3	A	♯5	G♯ = A♭	♭3	A♭
5	C	1	C	5	C

[41] In this way 'Fixing A Hole' joins a Hall Of Fame that also includes Richard Rodgers' 'My Favourite Things'. This classic also allows free switching between between parallel major and minor roots, by emphasising roots and 5ths. Think of the verse 'Girls in white dresses,' which switches to E major, from previous verses of E minor.

[42] With this sly twist, 'Fixing A Hole' joins those Beatles songs that make us question our harmonic surroundings when we've barely established our opening tonal foothold. While 'Yesterday' flagged a drift to the key of the relative minor within the first two bars, this 'aug' undermines our sense of mode on the *parallel* root when we're just two *beats* into the song.

The matching of music and lyrics that this achieves is similarly inspired, at a stroke conveying the change in mood not just from 'light' to 'dark' but, more specifically, from optimism to pessimism. The words expressing achievement ('fixing', 'filling' and 'painting') all fall in major before immediately giving way to the singer's inclinations of wandering self-doubt. While the song's parallel major chorus delineates the structure more obviously, this ultra-subtle take on the switch is in a class of its own.

Or almost on its own – for Lennon fans can rightly point to the conceptually identical effect in 'I'm So Tired', and within arguably an even more subtle harmonic framework.

'I'm So Tired'

Key: *A Major*
A G♯7 D E
I'm so tired, I have - n't slept a wink. I'm
C♮ *Major third*
Implied: *A minor*
A F♯m D E A Eaug
so tired, my mind is on the blink. I won - der should I get up and
Implied: *A minor*
C♮ *Minor third [of A]*
F♯m Dm
fix my - self a drink. No, no, no. I'm

Beatles expert, Tim Tucker, sums it up:

> 'The music provides a perfect evocation of Lennon's insomniac state of mind. His half-sleeping, half-waking demeanour is subtly depicted through the use of chords which create an ambiguous A major–A minor tonality'.[43]

We open in A major, alright, but just where is the elusive A minor? This time we need to look even more closely to appreciate the ploy. For just as 'Come Together' didn't 'need' a D major chord for us to feel a switch from D minor to its parallel major, so the reverse is the case in 'I'm So Tired'.

[43] Discussion with the author, summer 2000.

Lennon's switch between A major and A minor here works on an even deeper level than either 'Fixing A Hole' or his own 'I'll Be Back', with the indecision that he sings about uncannily reflected in the harmony of bars 5-7. After an obvious A major opening stretch, the augmented chord acts like a sleeping tablet, introducing C natural to sedate the key's major 3rd (C♯), only for the following chord, F♯m, to restore it. The song continues to slip in and out of consciousness as the F natural in the Dm introduces an Aeolian ♭6 note that, together with the C natural now in the melody, is now at odds with the F♯m in the previous bar! Hence both the 'E aug' and Dm chords are heard as delicately borrowed from the parallel key of A minor, which directly explains the sleepwalking effect of the progression.[44]

Meanwhile, George Harrison had yet another take on the same overall principle as 'Fixing A Hole' and 'I'm So Tired' in 'Old Brown Shoe'. Though this time the ambiguity is with *relative* – rather than parallel – minor.

'Old Brown Shoe'

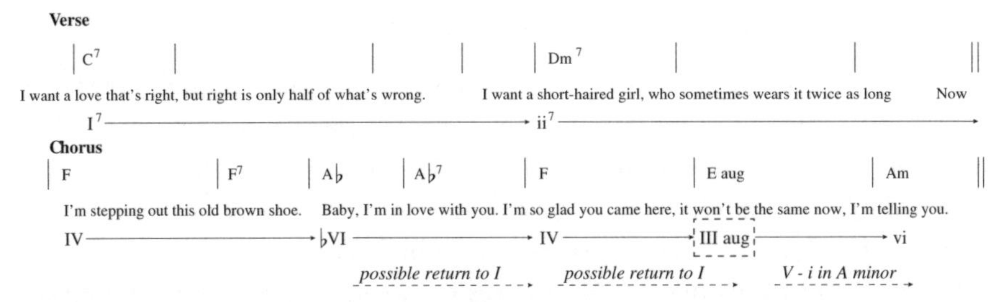

Having wrestled with Lennon's harmonic handiwork, deciphering George's manoeuvre is somewhat less involved. Nevertheless, this highly underrated song features some typically inspired Harrison-esque sleight-of-hand, courtesy again of the augmented chord.

With the song essentially in the key of C, we expect a cadence back to this bluesy I7 chord after the development on IV. In fact, George has two opportunities to return us to the tonic. First, with his A♭7 (which could have formed a rocky 'IV-♭VI-I' cadence, as in 'Hello Goodbye') or, having then back-tracked to the subdominant, via a Plagal IV-I cadence. But he ignores both these possibilities, preferring instead to drop gracefully by a

[44] With its C natural (B♯) and G♯ notes, E aug is effectively a combination of Am and E7 (i and V7, in A minor) while the Dm is a straight iv.

semitone to the E aug that serves as the dominant of the impending A minor.

We can reconcile this with those earlier inspired 'IV-III7-vi' gambits that we reinterpreted as a tonicisation of the relative minor, i.e., '♭VI-V-i minor'. This in itself is a great ploy which we saw, for example, in the transition into the bridge of 'I Should Have Known Better'. But here the augmented chord adds a new dimension to the V-I voice leading. For, in addition to the leading note-effect that moves powerfully into the root of A minor, so that chord's defining ♭3 (C) is previewed as the B♯ within the augmented E chord.

As with 'Fixing A Hole' and 'I'm So Tired', 'Old Brown Shoe' creates a perfect match between music and lyrics. Cadencing on the relative minor (rather than the tonic) at the end of the line 'it won't be the same now' is already clever enough. But 'warning' the listener ahead of the punchline 'I'm telling you', by means of this C note in the augmented chord, is another touch of Beatle genius.

The Augmented Ascent (5-♯5-6-♯5) – James Bond and beyond

For all the great subtlety of these advanced uses of the augmented chord, the sound of the defining raised 5th in its most simple role as an embellishment to a major or minor chord has become one of the most easily recognisable sounds in music – due partly to the exploits of James Bond. For Monty Norman's classic 007 theme, which has featured in some form in every Bond film since *Dr No,* hinges on a special chromatic embellishment of a minor chord. Not a descent from the tonic, this time, but a *chromatic ascent from the 5th*.

The James Bond Theme (intro chords)

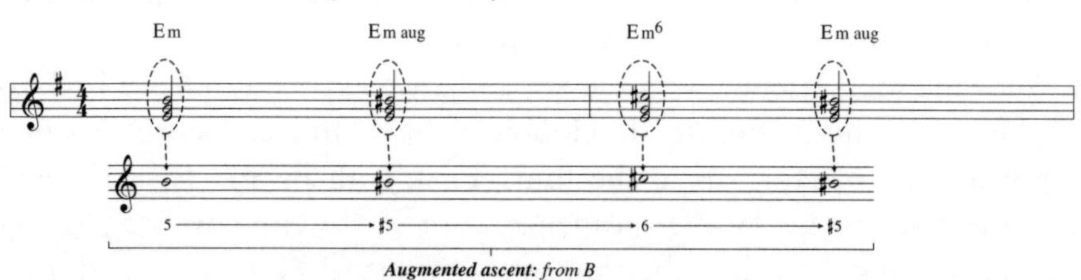

The result is the very opposite of the romantic collapse of 'Michelle'. For even before Vic Flick's legendary single-note guitar riff kicks off the opening theme, the air of menace associated with the climb up to the tense ♯5

and natural 6th succeeds in dramatically evoking the impending battle of wits between hero and villain. As a result this type of line – and augmented and m/major 7th chords, in general – have become a trademark of spy themes, film soundtracks, and TV programmes in the whole gangster genre.[45]

Meanwhile, 007's main competition as a sixties icon, The Beatles, would absorb and develop this trick in various ways over the decade, starting with their early covers. In fact a few months before *Dr No* hit the silver screen, The Beatles were recording their version of 'Besame Mucho', complete with the rhythm guitar's deft unfolding of the minor iv chord over the very same '5-♯5-6-♯5' chromatic colour.

Because the term 'augmented' centres around the 5th degree of the chord, the major 3rd remains untouched, meaning that the alteration can equally be applied to a major chord. Again, The Beatles demonstrate the sound on two songs on *Live At The BBC*. Dig out 'Don't Ever Change' once more (CD 2, track 32), and refer now to the intro (and the bridge, which sees the same idea transferred to the subdominant). Exactly a year after The Crickets reached No. 5 in the UK charts (June 1962), The Beatles were recording 'I'll Be On My Way' (CD 1, track 7), a Lennon-McCartney original that opens boldly with the same augmented run.[46]

With the action taking place in all these cases from the 5th (rather than from the root), this line can be difficult to visualise at first. The following chart focuses purely on the relevant notes 'in play' in these various songs as they rise up two semitones before dropping back one.

The Augmented '007' line (5-♯5-6-♯5) and early Beatles covers

Song	Time	Chord	Ascent			Descent
			5	♯5	6	♯5
'007 Theme'	0.01	Em	B	B♯	C♯	B♯
'Besame Mucho'	0.06	Cm	G	G♯	A♯	G♯
'Don't Ever Change'	0.01	E	B	B♯	C♯	B♯
'Don't Ever Change (Bridge)'	1.06	A	E	E♯	F♯	E♯
'I'll Be On My Way'	1.01	A	E	E♯	F♯	E♯

[45] For further study see Jesse Gress, 'Goldfingers: A Criminally Cool Lesson In '60s Spy Guitar', *Guitar Player*, July 1995, pp. 107–116; and Jesse Gress and Joe Gore, *Technicolour Twang: A Guide To The Great Guitar Scores, Guitar Player*, April 1997, pp. 99–115.

[46] The song was later released by Billy J. Kramer And The Dakotas. Travis use the same '007 run over a major chord' to prolong the dreamy closing vamp of 'As You Are' (starting at 3.30, in the key of E♭, with the effective line B♭-B-C-B).

The Augmented ascent and its variations are another useful songwriting trick for 'buying time' – especially on the tonic – and have a tradition dating back to Tin Pan Alley.[47]

By the time of the *White Album*, George was using the same harmony for the chorus of 'Savoy Truffle' as the switch to parallel minor unfolds over an E minor chord.

'Savoy Truffle'

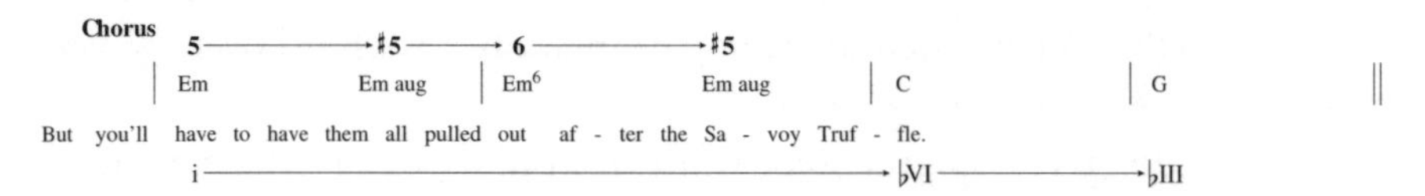

Lennon was still taken with the sound of the augmented chord in this context as late as 1980, in the opening line of '(Just Like) Starting Over'.[48]

Song	Time	Chord	Ascent			Descent
			5	♯5	6	♯5
'Savoy Truffle' (Bridge)	0.28	Em	B	B♯	C♯	B♯
'(Just Like) Starting Over'	0.06	A	E	E♯	F♯	E♯

This '007' run has been a popular device over the years in pop and has cropped up distinctively in songs by artists ranging from The Move in the sixties through to The Seahorses in the nineties.[49]

But with the augmented line underway, why stop at the 6th? After all, The Beatles had also been enjoying a four-step variation that takes the Augmented Ascent up to ♭7 on their early live renditions of 'Raining In

[47] Citron cites great showtunes like Kander and Ebb's 'Maybe This Time', Stephen Sondheim's 'Losing My Mind' and Harold Arlen/Johnny Mercer's '(You've Got To) Accentuate The Positive'; *Songwriting*, p. 249.

[48] For another augmented Beatles inspiration, listen also to their cover of Bobby Vee's 'Take Good Care Of My Baby'. The slow intro features the turnaround: G-Gaug-Am7-D7 (harmonising the first three members of the run: 5-♯5-6, in the key of G) over Lennon's line 'And though it really hurts me so there's something that I've got to say' (coincidentally, at 0.07).

[49] Never better than in Roy Wood's 'Blackberry Way', a No. 1 hit for The Move in December 1968, where an E minor augmented ascent is the very first sound we hear. Thirty years later, The Seahorses' 'Love Me And Leave Me', found John Squire using it to similarly stylish effect in the haunting Bm intro. Ingham also spots the same run in Ben Folds Five's intricate 'Underground', where it makes for another distinctive Bond-like opening theme (here over a B pedal): 'Doctor Rock Dissects The Hits: No. 14', *MOJO*, Issue 40, March 1997, p. 24.

My Heart', popularised by Buddy Holly.[50] The song is a surely the ultimate blueprint for the line with harmony and melody working symbiotically, ascending hand in hand.

'Raining In My Heart' (verse)

Formula	I	I aug	I6	I7
Chords in the key of G	G	G aug	G6	G7
Moving line	5	♯5	6	♭7
Notes in the key of G	D	D♯	E	F
Lyrics	'... *sun* is out, the *sky* is blue, there's *not* a cloud to *spoil* the view'			

It is this variation of the Augmented Ascent that would be developed by The Beatles in two particularly powerful instances. The chorus of 'Hey Bulldog' finds Lennon doing the same climb on B minor (at 0.52), before immediately raising the stakes and repeating the idea a fourth higher on Em.

'Hey Bulldog'

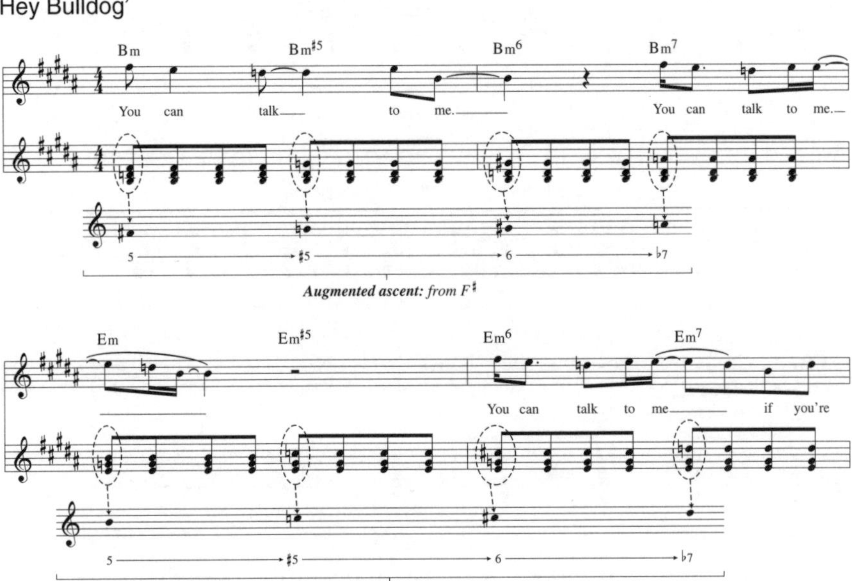

[50] The song was a regular in Beatles live sets from 1959–62; Lewisohn, *The Complete Beatles Recording Sessions*, p. 364. It remained a McCartney favourite during Wings tours, with Denny Laine on vocal duties on live recordings – note how the '007' resurfaces for the guitar intro. In the key of A, F♯ drops back to E♯ rather than going on to G, showing the interchangeability of the two augmented ascents.

As in all these cases the moving line occurs within the internal harmony rather than in the bass. But 'Hey Bulldog' works particularly well as the 'coiled spring' effect of the line appears to get ever tauter, the jump of a fourth giving the illusion of drifting further from the anchor.

Contrast this with the instrumental bridge link in 'Glass Onion' (1.01–1.16).

'Glass Onion'

The same internal harmony is clearly in operation over the bass pedal as Lennon's already disturbing atmosphere becomes ever moodier, but now it is being harmonised within a song structure that implies chords beyond the straight minor tonic. The following chart shows how the middle two members of the run find support within F and D7 chords, that contribute to the song's thicker harmonic texture.

Harmonising the Ascending Augmented Run in 'Glass Onion'

	Ascent			
	5	♯5	6	♭7
Moving line	E	F	F♯	G
Chords (over A pedal)	Am	F	D7	Am7
Degree relative to chords	5th	Root	3rd	♭7th
Time reference	1.01	1.05	1.09	1.13

As with the 007 line in '(Just Like) Starting Over', so Lennon would use the same four-note climb in his solo years, this time on 'Isolation', on the *Plastic Ono Band* album.[51]

Whether you go for the straight '007', or the extra step to ♭7, both these Augmented Ascents create a highly distinctive form of harmonic tension, in contrast to the easy flow of the descending lines that have been the main focus of this chapter.[52] The line is inherently tense given the lack of imminent resolution it faces as it develops. Heading 'north' from the 5th involves a long journey before arriving at the next strong chord tone. And with the very word 'cadence' having strong connotations of 'falling' towards a point of rest, the fact that we are ascending makes it all the harder.

To prove the point, simply reverse the '5-♯5-6-♭7' ascent and head back down – just like Lennon does in the bridge to 'Julia'[53] and McCartney does in the chorus of 'Eleanor Rigby'.

'Eleanor Rigby'

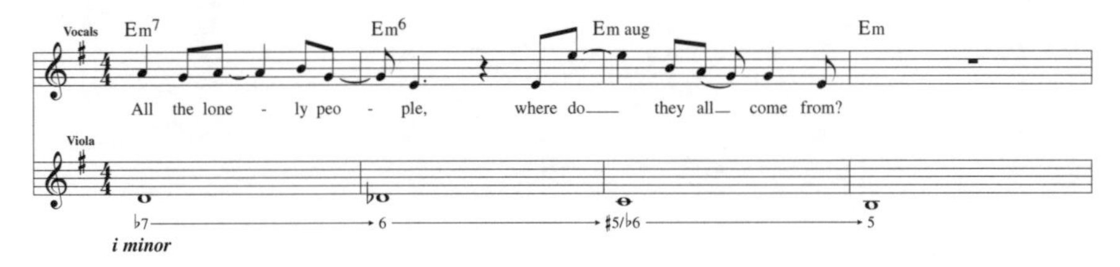

[51] In the key of D, the chromatic line to listen for in 'Isolation' is: A-A♯-B-C. Ian Hammond makes the connection with the Bond theme; www.beathoven.com; while Chris Ingham refers to the 'major to augmented 5th' as 'a familiar Lennon chord shift'; *John Lennon Special Edition*, *MOJO*, Issue 9, Winter 2000, p. 139.

[52] For other great '5-♯5-6-♭7' ascents, check out: Julie London's 'Cry Me A River' (and great covers by John Martyn and Aerosmith), over the opening line 'And now you say you're lonely' (on the opening Em in the key of G). Also, Robbie Williams' 'Old Before I Die' (written with Desmond Child) resurrects it for the suitably disturbing backdrop to 'these are strange days'. Note the great harmonisation for the ♭7 tone as the tonic pedal gives way to a striking ♭VII chord, on '*c'est la vie* I say' (G in A major).

[53] On the line: 'In the sun' (F♯m7-F♯m6-F♯maug-F♯m).

The colour of the ♯5 is still there, with Paul taking a melodic jump to add poignancy to his question. But the harmony no longer appears to be fighting that upward current, and the descent now adds a familiar air of inevitability to the flow of the music (and perhaps also to the plight of the characters in the song).

Talking of which, it's too bad that James Bond himself wouldn't have appreciated the subtle ways in which The Beatles developed his augmented theme tune during the sixties. For as Sean Connery says to Shirley Eaton in *Goldfinger*:

'My dear girl, there are some things that just aren't done. Such as drinking Dom Perignon '53 above a temperature of 38 degrees Fahrenheit. That's as bad as listening to The Beatles without ear muffs . . .'

TEN

Middle Eights and Mega Modulations

'Well here's another place you can go' – John Lennon ('Glass Onion')

'Where do I go to now?', John Lennon remembers Paul McCartney asking him after humming the verse to 'Michelle'.[1] It's a question that faces every songwriter who ponders the path of a song once their initial inspiration has been exhausted. A verse progression, or perhaps a chorus, may be 'in the bag' but just where *do* you go from there to create interest in a song? This may seem like the most elusive of all songwriting principles but it's a question that can be answered emphatically with select references to The Beatles' catalogue.

Of course, John and Paul tell us that certain masterpieces like 'Yesterday', 'Nowhere Man' and 'In My Life' arrived – almost fully formed – as if by divine inspiration.[2] But (as we know from the many half-finished, experimental demos alone) the majority of Beatles songs required a conventional compositional process: a stage-by-stage evolution no doubt involving painstaking trial and error.

This chapter attempts to provide an insight into one of the most crucial elements of the songwriting phenomenon – the way in which Beatles songs lead the listener by *developing* through the various sections, building

[1] *The Playboy Interviews*, p. 122.

[2] Musically at least, the lyrics to 'Yesterday' were famously first conceived in the 'scrambled eggs' format after McCartney 'woke up one morning with the tune in my head', *Anthology*, p. 175. John also remembers plucking ideas out of the ether as he lay down in frustration after a night trying to write a song. '"Nowhere Man" came, words and music, the whole damn thing. The same with "In My Life"'; *Anthology*, p. 196.

tension by creating vital contrast between verse, chorus and bridge (or, as The Beatles invariably called it, the 'middle eight').[3]

Here, therefore, we return to the concept of shifting tonality, but broaden our horizons considerably beyond the confines of Chapter 6 as we delve deeper into The Beatles' outrageously rich legacy of key-switching.

Modulation – the ultimate songwriting secret?

Singalong hooks are often touted as the secret to instant chart success – and The Beatles had plenty of those. But when trying to account for the group's musical longevity, it is the harmonic twists and turns engineered through formal modulation that emerge as a recurring feature – and so they do in most acknowledged pop classics, from Cole Porter to Oasis. The principle of modulation goes a long way towards explaining the ability of a song to withstand repeated listening.

When explaining why modulation is so important in music, writers often use a geographical metaphor. Rikky Rooksby compares chords in a given key to districts within a home town, each with their different associations of character and mood.

> 'Changing a chord *within* a key is like making a short journey . . . A key *change* is like a visit to another county or state, which could be nearby and therefore have similar terrain, or distant and have a very different landscape.'[4]

The notion of journeys of varying distances is crucial to appreciating the sheer depth of The Beatles' songwriting catalogue. For their songs take us across the complete spectrum of the chromatic scale, from short trips around the block to long-haul flights to brave new worlds.

Paul McCartney himself effectively confirms The Beatles' recognition of this emphatic songwriting secret in a revealing comment in *Many Years From Now*:

> 'The thing I liked about "From Me To You" was it had a very complete middle. It went to a surprising place. The opening chord of the middle

[3] This book uses the terms 'bridge' and 'middle eight' interchangeably. While some writers regard a bridge as being a short (perhaps two- or four-bar) 'link' between, say, a chorus and the ensuing verse, the overriding convention in practice is to regard a bridge as a substantial section of new material that contrasts from the verse and chorus.

[4] Rikky Rooksby, *How To Write Songs On Guitar*, p. 124.

section of that song heralded a new batch for me. That was a pivotal song. Our songwriting lifted.'[5]

By the time of the *Anthology* tome Paul was still singling out this moment, describing it now as 'a very big step'.[6]

So just what *is* happening (first at 0.35), in this pivotal third Parlophone single?

In a nutshell, McCartney is describing a crucial stage in The Beatles' development, when one of their seemingly innocent songs modulated to a new key, taking the listener to a new tonal destination.

In order to appreciate the mechanics of this device, and to see why McCartney describes it as 'a surprising place' in the context of 1963 pop, let's set the scene with a whirlwind tour of some typical middle eight traditions of the time.

Early rock 'n' roll 'Middle Eight' clichés

Back in the pop and rock scene of the fifties and early sixties, key-switching of all types was surprisingly rare, while middle eights (with a few spectacular exceptions) were mundane affairs in comparison to what The Beatles had up their sleeve. Listening to some of the early Beatles covers is the easiest way to confirm the formulaic, single-key traditions of the period.

The convention was invariably to start the bridge with a direct move to the IV chord, and after some innocuous filler, end with an Imperfect cadence on V before resuming the verse on I. 'I'm Gonna Sit Right Down And Cry (Over You)', from *Live At The BBC*, shows the most primitive of such bridges in action, with the eight bars divided into the following format:

'I'm Gonna Sit Right Down And Cry (Over You)' – Middle Eight

Bars	1 - 2	3 - 4	5 - 6	7 - 8
Chord	IV	I	IV	V

[5] Barry Miles, *Many Years From Now*, p. 149.

[6] 'I remember being very pleased with the middle because there was a strange chord in it, and it went into a minor [sic]: "I've got arms that long . . .". We thought that was a very big step…'; *Anthology*, p. 94.

'Nothin' Shakin'' develops this a stage further by adding a II to prime the Imperfect cadence on the final V: further anticipating the return to the verse but hardly raising the roof in terms of novelty.

'Nothin' Shakin'' – Middle Eight

Bars	1 - 2	3 - 4	5 - 6	7	8
Chord	IV	I	IV	II	V

It's no surprise that some of The Beatles' own early bridges, such as Paul's 'You'll Be Mine', would follow this structure. Here, beneath Tony Sheridan's ramblings about 'toast in the morning', the only other addition is a tonic I7 to 'smooth the change' to IV in bar 5, just as the blues would do:

'You'll Be Mine' – Middle Eight

Bars	1 - 2	3	4	5 - 6	7	8
Chord	IV^7	I	I^7	IV^7	II^7	V^7

While typically used within an 8-bar structure, the move to the IV chord can be seen to derive from the conventional 12-bar blues format where the switch to the subdominant in bars 5 and 6 is a defining feature of the whole genre.

Meanwhile, the middle eight of what became known as the 'commercial bridge' would delay the IV chord by a bar in order to stress this same move.[7] We know that The Beatles would have tackled this variation of the 'subdominant bridge' on occasions, most notably on their live renditions of Elvis's 'Are You Lonesome Tonight?'

The Commercial Bridge – 'Are You Lonesome Tonight?'

Bars	1 - 2	3 - 4	5 - 6	7 - 8
Chord	I^7	IV^7	II^7	V^7

This variation, heard on Tin Pan Alley classics as far back as 'Satin Doll' and 'Pennies From Heaven', was so called because it was the preferred

[7] See Citron, *Songwriting*, p. 241.

structure to fall back on for professional songwriters churning out Broadway hits in the twenties, thirties and forties. It fitted into a standard 32-bar song structure, consisting of an AABA structure (where 'A' is a verse and 'B' an eight-bar variation). It is from this format that the term 'middle eight' is derived.

Even in terms of bar-counts, The Beatles showed that the bridge section of a song could be far removed from any of these standard, 8-bar formats. They brought great *structural* novelty to the form of the pop bridge: the bridge of 'Yesterday' has seven bars, for example, while that of 'I Want To Hold Your Hand' has eleven. McCartney explains how an endearing slice of Beatles confusion was probably responsible for some of these pioneering experiments in form.

> 'We used to call everything a middle eight even if it had thirty-two bars or sixteen bars . . . we didn't get the significance of the word 'eight'.'[8]

Nevertheless, while experiments in form add greatly to The Beatles' songwriting legacy, form is rarely a substitute for harmonic substance – as the bridge to 'Please Please Me' demonstrates. Although the subtle verse and pre-chorus devices put this rousing single into a different league from 'Love Me Do', its novel 10-bar format doesn't compensate for the harmonic reliance on the clichéd direct jump to IV.

A harsh verdict but an inescapable one given the quantum leap The Beatles would make with their very next outing.

IV ... and the search for McCartney's 'surprising place'

With 'From Me To You', The Beatles suddenly appreciated the need to depart from the conventional move to the subdominant, despite its tried-and-tested formula. Moreover, this appears to have been the result of a conscious awakening, as illustrated by McCartney's brief but tantalising songwriting workshop during the interviews for the *Anthology* video series. It's perhaps the only formal lesson we're treated to in the entire 11-hour project, yet it takes us to the cutting edge of 1963 songwriting by bringing to life the earlier description of the same moment.

[8] Barry Miles, *Many Years From Now*, p. 177.

> 'We'd listen to something that somebody else had done and try and beat it . . . By the time we got to 'From Me To You' I remember being very pleased with the chord in the middle, which was different: "I got arms". Going to that minor chord there [plays a G minor chord on the piano]. It was like "oooh", this was something we hadn't done before'[9]

Let's look closely at Paul's wheeze. Shunning that customary direct move to the IV, The Beatles decided to venture to the 5th degree of the scale. But here they built not a dominant chord (or major V triad as they'd done in the bridge of 'Love Me Do') but a minor one – complete with its minor 3rd degree, alien to the C major key of the verse. The result was an instant coming of age for The Beatles as songwriters, as the *Anthology* footage reminds us by ignoring the verse preamble and cutting straight to The Moment.

'From Me To You' – Middle Eight modulation (0.35)

	Key of C				Key of F				Key of C	
Old key	I	V	I	I^7	v			II^7	V aug	I
Sequence	C	G	C	C^7	Gm	C	F	D^7	G aug	C
New key					ii	V	I	VI^7		
	'With love from me to you. I got...'				*'arms that long to hold you, and keep you satisfied...'*				*'If there's anything...'*	

The secret of this magical move is that it takes the song comprehensively away from the main key centre, thereby achieving a musical effect rarely created by bridges that start on one of the familiar diatonic chords.

To illustrate this vital point, and explain why McCartney views this Gm chord as 'surprising', the following table lists some Beatles song sections (all bridges except for the chorus of 'Can't Buy Me Love'), each opening on a different chord in the harmonised diatonic major scale.

The point here is that none of these songs implies a formal modulation beyond the song's initial key centre. Stop any of these sequences in full flow and the most comfortable point of resolution, or 'resting point', is still the original tonic of the verse. To revert to our geographical analogy, we are merely moving between the 'districts within the town'.

[9] Paul at the piano before the 'From Me To You' footage on *The Beatles Anthology* video series: at 12.50 on Tape 2 (March '63–February '64).

Diatonic Beatles bridges – starting chord relative to the verse tonic

Starting point	Song	Lyrical reference	Key	Starting chord
I	'I Feel Fine'	'I'm so glad'	G	G
ii	'I'll Be Back'	'I ... thought that you'	A	Bm
iii	'Can't Buy Me Love'	'Can't buy me love'	C	Em
IV	'Please Please Me'	'I don't want to sound'	A	D
V	'Love Me Do'	'Someone to love'	G	D
vi	'I'll Be Back'	'I love you so'	A	F♯m
vii dim	N/A			

We have of course seen more formal tonicised shifts to vi (the relative minor switches of Chapter 6). But these still only relocate us 'across town' – albeit more than fleetingly – for they operate within a given key signature and thereby introduce no 'new' notes of particular interest.[10]

With 'From Me To You' The Beatles intuitively grasped the fact that there are options beyond these seven chords when making that all important opening gambit. Hence the first addition to our middle eight chart could look like this:

Starting point	Song	Lyrical reference	Key	Starting chord
v	'From Me To You'	'I've got arms that long'	C	Gm

However, the Gm minor chord is heard as far more fundamental than a simple 'borrowed v minor' in C major. It is integral to the *process* of modulation. For it now has a new role, functioning as a ii chord in a ii-V-I, a familiar move, but one that we now revisit as one of the most effective key-switching devices in music. Here it is the mechanism by which we move to F major.

OK, so the bridge moves again to the clichéd IV – but this is only the *eventual* target. For by virtue of the 'preparatory' Gm, and the following C chord now reinterpreted as a temporary V, the song takes on a new dimension.[11]

[10] Of course we do hear the *parallel* major/minor shifts of Chapter 6 as more fundamental. This is because we now trade at least major and minor 3rds (by definition), with scope for two other chromatic notes between the keys of, say, A minor (no sharps) and A major (three sharps).

[11] Because the modulation is so fleeting, some musicians might regard the sequence as some kind of 'v-I-IV-ii' in the parent key of C, with this alien chord, the 'v', being a borrowed chord just as we saw in 'I'll Get You'. But there the chord acts *within an existing key centre* helped by the fact that it unfolds within an existing progression. In 'From Me To You', the function is to relocate the tonality more convincingly.

Let's briefly review this with some basic theory that will help to set the scene for later, more complicated, modulations.

Using our familiar major scale framework, now for F major, we arrive at the following family of chords which can be understood as the source of these bridge chords in 'From Me To You'. The Gm, C and F chords duly stand out in their new roles.

The F major tonality – the bridge harmony of 'From Me To You'

Scale Degree	1	2	3	4	5	6	7
Notes in F	F	G	A	B♭	C	D	E
Formula	**I**	**ii**	iii	IV	**V**	vi	vii
Chords in F	**F**	**Gm**	Am	B♭	**C**	Dm	E dim

Admittedly, in terms of our geographical analysis, it's not a distant journey, as there is only one note different between F major and the verse key of C major: the B natural note is replaced by B♭. Nevertheless, it's a trip 'out of town'.[12] We feel the change compellingly, even if we are soon back in the key of C as the verse resumes, cued by means of a familiar Imperfect cadence with an augmented 'enhancer' on the V (G aug).

The modulation to IV and the blues connection

While the modulation in 'From Me To You' did much to distance The Beatles from rock 'n' roll songwriting, the irony is that the whole manoeuvre is entirely consistent with a simple substitution within the framework of the 12-bar blues. Here, instead of just switching to the IV chord in bars 5 and 6, jazz-blues practitioners typically lend deeper emphasis to the tonality of the IV by approaching it via this very same ii-V movement.

The basic 12-bar blues (bars 1-6)

Bar	1	2	3	4	5	6
Formula	I	I	I	I^7	IV^7	IV^7
Chord	C	C	C	C^7	F^7	F^7

[12] It is enough to hear the B♭ in the chord – but notice how the note is also stressed in the melody (on 'arms') to reinforce this brave new world.

Substitution for bar 4: the jazz-blues switch from I-IV

	Key of C			Transition		Key of F	
Bar	1	2	3	4		5	6
Formula	I	I	I	ii	V	I^7	I^7
Chord	C	C	C	Gm^7	C^7	F^7	F^7

The Gm (with its B♭ note) is again the crucial difference, creating a move to a temporary key centre on IV. In this way the bridge of 'From Me To You' is a bolt from the blue compared with the direct move to IV chord which can still be seen opening many other Beatles bridges in the time-honoured rock 'n' roll tradition.[13]

Amid the technicalities, we mustn't lose sight of the very *purpose* of the modulation in songwriting, not merely to alleviate harmonic boredom but as a means of complementing the lyrical theme. In 'From Me To You' the middle eight mood-shift coincides deftly with the singer revealing his true intentions, as the lighthearted verse pleasantries give way to a glimpse of his inner desires.

All in all, another example of how The Beatles' fully formed vision of songwriting was in action as early as 1963 – a point appreciated by songwriters as eminent as Richard Carpenter who nominates 'From Me To You' as his favourite Beatles composition.[14]

So radical was this bridge that both John and Paul feared the song might be *too* novel for pop fans in 1963.[15] They shouldn't have had too many sleepless nights as 'From Me To You' shot to the No. 1 slot. Moreover, so emphatic was the reaction, that John and Paul obviously decided to repeat the very same middle eight harmony a few months later on 'I Want To Hold Your Hand'. Paul's corresponding swooning moment is now first heard with the rogue, non-diatonic, Dm at 0.51.

[13] And throughout their career – see the direct-to-IV bridges of 'You'll Be Mine', 'Please Please Me', 'Tell Me Why', 'What You're Doing', 'Ticket To Ride', 'I Need You', 'The Ballad Of John And Yoko, 'One After 909', 'Sgt. Pepper', 'Back In the USSR', 'Oh! Darling' and many others.

[14] Describing his favourite 'miss' of all time', Carpenter expresses his disbelief that Capitol had turned down the US rights to the song. 'I was delighted to learn subsequently that my ear had not let me down and that the recording had gone to Number 1 in Britain'; *MOJO*, Issue 9, John Lennon Special Edition, Winter 2000, p. 19.

[15] John: 'We thought "From Me To You" was too way out . . . although we always thought it would make it somewhere!'; Paul: 'I played it on the piano and thought: No. No one's going to like this!'; 'How To Write A Hit', *Melody Maker*, 1st February 1964, p. 11.

'I Want To Hold Your Hand' – bridge modulation

	Key of G			Key of C						**Pivot**	Key of G		
Old key	IV	II	I	v						**IV**	V	I	V
Sequence	C	D	G	Dm	G	C	Am	Dm	G	**C**	D	G	D
New key				ii	V	I	vi	ii	V	**I**			
	'I wanna hold your hand'			*'And when I touch you I feel happy inside...'*						*'I can't hide...'*		*'Yeah, you got that something'*	

The secret of Beatlemania? It was certainly one of them. We're in a different key this time but it's the identical jump to a minor chord built on the 5th degree, prompting a ii-V-I to the 'old' IV chord. And if we step back to see the big picture of the bridge we can see it consists of a similar four-chord sequence – 'ii-V-I-vi' – the same progression found in songs ranging from 'All My Loving' to 'The Fool On The Hill'. Meanwhile, in terms of songwriting history this bridge is obviously related to the middle eight of the much maligned 'How Do You Do It?'. It's the identical ii-V-I-vi sequence – though, as we now know, The Beatles crucially deliver it in a different key to the verse.

This last point is important as it confirms that, once in the new key, all the standard harmonic ideas are back up for grabs. As well as several more 'ii-V-I-vi' moves, we'll be seeing old chestnuts like I-V alternations, I-vi developments, Cycles Of Fifths, Four-Chord turnarounds, etc. To make the point using the very simplest possible modulation, let's fast forward to *Abbey Road* to find 'Octopus's Garden' blending a pair of I-vi-IV-V cycles in two different keys: one for the verse/chorus sections and another for George's guitar solo.

'Octopus's Garden' – solo modulation (entry)

	Key of E					**Pivot**	Key of A		
Old key	I	vi	IV	V	I	**IV**			
Sequence	E	C♯m	A	B	E	**A**	F♯m	D	E
New key						**I**	vi	IV	V
	'I'd like to be, under the sea, in an octopus's garden in the shade.'					*Guitar solo*			

For all the superficial associations of this song, the result is a deceptively effective interlude, forcing us (with a little help from the sub-aqua bubbles) to subliminally visualise Ringo taking a dive from Peter Sellers' yacht to join the creatures themselves. Compare this modulation with the pair from the early days. It's another switch to the key of the IV, but whereas the two from 1963 hit us with a priming ii chord, the 'Octopus' creeps up on us by stealth.

The solo starts with a direct jump to the IV chord, and we don't immediately feel that the tonality has shifted. That's because the chord that contains the one 'new' note (in this case the D in D major) has been withheld for the first two bars of the bridge, thereby delaying, and diluting, the effect we enjoy in 'From Me To You'. For a key switch can only be implied when a progression features a chord that is *in the new key but not in the old.*[16] The secret is therefore the A chord which acts as the pivot taking us both towards the new key (at 1.34) and away from it (at 1.52) as it reverts to its IV chord status for a IV-V-I return to verse.

'Octopus's Garden' – solo modulation (exit)

	Key of A				**Pivot**	Key of E			
Old key	I	vi	IV	V	I				
Sequence	A	F♯m	D	E	A	B^7	E	C♯m	A
New key					IV	V^7	I	vi	IV
	Guitar solo						*'We would shout, and swim about...'*		

In this way, for all its apparent predictability, the 'Octopus' solo still works as a formal key switch and is conceptually different from all those bridges that use the IV within the existing parent tonality.

And the 'From Me To You' trick wasn't just a 1963 fad. The middle to 'The Night Before' is clearly rooted in the exact same concept, in a sequence that confirms The Beatles' intuitive skill at journeying around the Cycle Of Fifths.

'The Night Before' – bridge modulation

	Key of D			Key of G			Key of D		
Old key	I	IV^7	I	v			vi	II^7	V^7
Sequence	D	G^7	D	Am	D^7	G	Bm	E^7	A^7
New key				ii	V^7	I	iii		
	'Treat me like you did the night before.'			*'Last night is the night I will remember you by'*			*'When I think of things we did, it makes me wanna cry'*		

[16] The D major chord of 'Octopus' is equivalent to the Gm in 'From Me To You'. They act as IV and ii in terms of their respective bridge keys and are therefore direct substitutes that each contain the important chromatic note in their triads (as root and ♭3, respectively).

Once again, a 'cut and paste' view of the action enhances the beauty of the ploy, especially in the context of these particular lyrics. For the whole bridge can be reduced to two main elements: a 'From Me To You' switch that takes us briefly to IV, followed by another journey around the cycle that retargets the original tonic. In this way the listener blatantly hears the 'there and back' premise that matches the past and present lyrical theme – just as it did in the "when I was a boy" bridge of 'She Said She Said' with which we previewed this manoeuvre in Chapter 8 (p. 247).

While each of these modulations to IV represents an important development from the standard bridges of the fifties, they are the tip of the iceberg in terms of the variety of other 'surprising places' that The Beatles had in store for us. For wherever you decide to go in the harmonic universe, as one writer sums up: 'what better way to create freshness than by choosing a totally new tonal centre?'[17]

'Destination Anywhere': the Cycle Of Fifths revisited

An imaginary four-point key-switching blueprint might look like this:

1) Pick a target key centre
2) Decide on a means of entry to the new key
3) Choose a progression that establishes the new key centre
4) Find a means of exit back to the original key

So where else can we go? The answer is anywhere. Not just in theory but, as The Beatles showed us, in practice. We can refer back to our versatile Cycle Of Fifths to appreciate some of the other exotic destinations visited within the chromatic universe. The cycle in fact represents a perfect 'map' for this very purpose, as it is founded on the concept of harmonic distance. The immediate neighbours of any chord are musically closer than those physically further afield on the chart. Hence the IV and V chords are typically easy to switch between in comparison to, say, the ♭VI.

The same goes for key switching. This is because the cycle also reflects the progression of key signatures – the incremental appearance of chromatic notes that defines each new key through the creation of sharps (as we move clockwise), or flats (as we move anti-clockwise). For example,

[17] Citron, *Songwriting*, p. 242.

we saw how the switch 'to the key of the IV' in 'From Me To You' involved the creation of one flat, B♭. But depending on what other keys we target we need to get musically more ambitious, depending on the distance from home.

The following cycle shows at a glance how the 'From Me To You' switch was just the tip of the iceberg as The Beatles visited almost every corner of this particular musical globe. With one example from nearly every port-of-call, it provides a sneak preview of our own journey as we attempt to follow in their footsteps.

The Beatles' Modulation 'Map' – a guide to tonal destinations

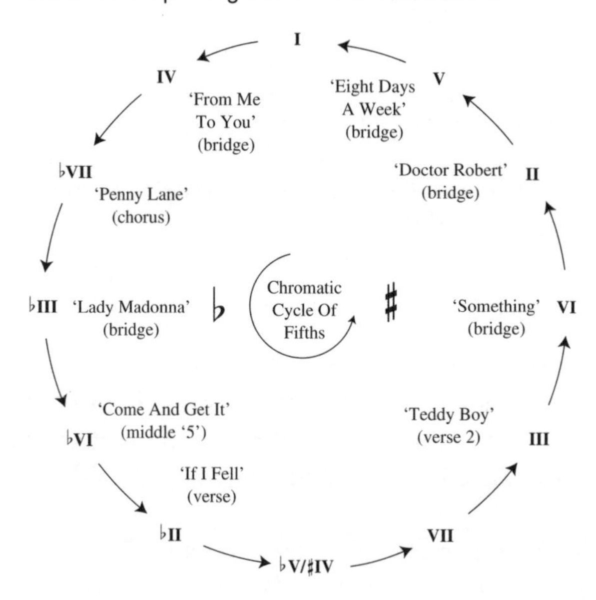

♭VII

Moving anti-clockwise from IV, the next key centre in the chain, ♭VII, now has two notes different from the key of the I chord, providing a point of modulation with an even greater sense of relocation.

The I-♭VII key shift in 'Penny Lane' is a perfect example. In this instance the transition takes place with a chorus rather than a middle eight, but the principle of creating movement is no different. The song enters a new dimension as Paul's detached, 'third party' verse commentary (in the key of

B) famously gives way to a rousing chorus participation, a whole step down (in A).

'Penny Lane' – entry to chorus

	Key of B		**Pivot**	Key of A		
Old key	V^{7}sus^4	V^7	**IV**	♭VII		
Sequence	F♯^{7}sus^4	F♯^{7}	**E**	A	A/C♯	D
New key			**V**	I	I (1st inv.)	IV
	'In the pouring rain – very strange.'			*'Penny Lane is in my ears, and in my eyes'*		

'Penny Lane' – exit from chorus

	Key of A			**Pivot**	Key of B			
Old key	I	I (1st inv.)	IV	**VI**	II			
Sequence	A	A/C♯	D	**F♯^{7}**	B	G♯m^7	C♯m^7	F♯^{7}
New key				**V**	I	vi^7	ii^7	V^7
	'There beneath the blue suburban skies I sit, and meanwhile back ...'				*'In Penny Lane there is a fireman with an hourglass'*			

Pivot chord modulation – dual roles revisited

Having chosen this particular chorus target, how does Paul navigate the waters? The answer lies again in 'the Power of V' with the lyrical themes of 'very strange' and 'meanwhile back' providing perfect visual counterparts for both the V-I entry to the new key and the V-I exit back to the verse.

What could be simpler? Here we don't even need the priming ii chord of 'From Me To You', with The Beatles recognising that a plain, 'unprepared' dominant is usually enough to take them anywhere they fancy.

Notice how the smooth transition in McCartney's modulation in 'Penny Lane' is aided again by a *pivot chord* – a common chord shared by both keys and which therefore enables the 'baton of tonality' to be passed from one section to another with the minimum of fuss.[18]

[18] Note that pivot chords can appear *after* a non-diatonic chord as well as before it in order to facilitate our perception of a key change. Hence in the Gm-C-F move of 'From Me To You' the C chord acts as a pivot, helping us to 'accept' the dramatic opening appearance of v minor.

'Very strange' – the pivot entry to the 'Penny Lane' chorus

We identified the dual roles of the '♭VII=V' chord when switching between I and vi in Chapter 6. The '=' symbol is used again here to convey the idea of 'equivalence' between the old and the new keys. Hence, the E chord in 'Penny Lane' can be dubbed 'IV=V', meaning it functions as IV in the departing key of B, and V in the new key of A.

The terminology may appear complicated but this is a versatile way of capturing the mechanics at play, helping us to literally 'unlock the key' to the key change.

Rather than returning to B major, the tonal centre of the verse, McCartney instead slides down a whole tone from dominant to this pivot, the secret gateway to those brave new chorus sounds. It hardly matters that the chorus progression emerges as merely the humblest of I-IV alternations – the modulation alone guarantees a captive audience.

	Key of B	**Pivot**	Key of A		
Old key	V⁷	**IV**	♭VII		
Sequence	F♯⁷	**E**	A	A/C♯	D
New key		**V**	I	I (1st inversion)	IV
	Verse	*'very strange'*	Chorus		

'Meanwhile back' – returning to the verse key

The return to the verse key in 'Penny Lane' merely proves again the number one rule of modulation: if in doubt, tonicise the chord you want with its dominant: i.e., *target it from its V*. Hence, to move from A major back to B major, McCartney duly finds the V of B. As it happens, the resulting A-F♯7 jump turns out to be the most standard of 'I-VI7' turnaround ploys (see the 'oh yeah' trick of Chapter 4). Of course, in this case McCartney doesn't want to return all the way back to A and therefore takes the first exit off the Penny Lane roundabout, moving from F♯ to B and the familiar territory of his original home. As with so many textbook Beatles ploys, the lyrics alone say it all.

	Key of A		**Pivot**	Key of B			
Old key	I	IV	**VI⁷**	II			
Sequence	A	D	**F♯⁷**	B	G♯m⁷	C♯m⁷	F♯⁷
New key			**V⁷**	I	vi⁷	ii⁷	V⁷
	Chorus		*'meanwhile back'*	Verse			

McCartney had in fact already used a similar B-A key scheme for 'Good Day Sunshine' on *Revolver*, while later conjuring a subtle variation when crafting the tonal contrast between the two main sections of 'Magical Mystery Tour'. Although the latter uses more rocky 'borrowed' chords (in contrast to the pop cycles of the earlier pair), its structure still hinges on a dual-tonic premise of I and ♭VII which underlies the basic themes of the songs.

'Magical Mystery Tour' – bridge modulation

	Key of E		**Pivot**	Key of D					**Pivot**	Key of E
Old key	I	♭III	**IV**	♭VII					**IV**	I
Sequence	E	G	**A**	D	D/C	G/B	Gm/B♭	D/A	**A**	E
New key			**V**	I	I^7	IV	iv	I	**V**	
	'Roll up, to make a reservation...'			*'The Magical Mystery Tour is waiting to take you away...'*						*'Roll up'*

Whether you regard the transition here as verse-to-chorus or chorus-to-bridge, the means of entry is identical, as the same 'IV=V' pivot primes the key change. Once in the new key, The Beatles again relied on a familiar idea, this time unfolding the new tonic with an '8-♭7-6-♭6' Rock Descent (from Chapter 9). This approach is intended to demonstrate the overriding principle of this book, namely that an appreciation of songwriting can be enhanced by breaking up the structures and seeing them as bite-sized chunks that are spliced together.

Of course, joining the dots is the fun part, a task at which The Beatles excelled by constantly mixing and matching their palette of cadences.

For example, listen to the exit from the D major section of 'Magical Mystery Tour'. This time the return to the 'old' key heralds a departure from the ubiquitous V-I mechanism. For the E chord of the main theme is now retrieved *Plagally* from the last A chord in the bridge. Here therefore is the IV–I pivot trick with which we saw Lennon 'float upstream' in 'I'm Only Sleeping'.

As with all Plagal moves, the movement is smaller than a V-I and (partly through this 'laziness') the effect in 'Mystery Tour' is more subtle than the emphatic 'meanwhile back' of 'Penny Lane'. But however the modulation is achieved (and the original tonic *retrieved*) the crux is that this key-switch again allows the song to live up to its title.

♭III

It should be no surprise that the key-switching devices that unlock the magic of new tonalities are rapidly emerging as the very same select group of cadences that we have been using throughout when closing a sequence or making transitions between diatonic sections.

A deeply useful principle of modulation is to view these methods of entry and exit in terms of the main tags of Perfect (V-I) and perhaps 'Extra' Perfect (ii-V-I), Plagal (IV-I), Aeolian (♭VII-I) and even Phrygian (♭II-I) cadences. We'll be seeing Beatles key-switches that hinge on each of these as we make our way around the Cycle Of Fifths.

These mechanistic modulations are in stark contrast to *direct modulations,* where the new key centre is plucked from the air without warning. Their whole effect is precisely down to the fact that *no* such smooth connection exists. Some destinations are obviously more acceptable than others for this ruse, and ♭III, the next stop on the Cycle Of Fifths was a great Beatles favourite.

Watch how McCartney manages it in 'Two Of Us', a song that might appear to be just an innocuous hippy folk-rock tribute – until the bridge.

'Two Of Us' – bridge modulation

	Key of G		Key of B♭			Key of G		
Old key	IV	I	♭III			ii	V^7	I
Sequence	C	G	B♭	Dm	Gm^7	Am	D^7	G
New key			I	iii	vi^7	[vii]		
	'We're going home.'		*'You and I have memories, longer than the road that stretches out ahead'*					*'Two of us...'*

The B♭ chord suddenly takes the song out of its slumbers with an ambitious choice of opening chord. And yet the sound is acceptable to our ears – essentially through the subtle feature that the new and old tonics share a common tone between them. In this case the D note that is both the 5th of G and the major 3rd of B♭. By targeting this note in the melody, Paul deftly eases us into the new territory, creating a melodic pivot for what, *harmonically*, is a *direct* modulation.

Don't let's forget the effect of the music in a lyrical context. Just as we saw in 'Yesterday', here is modulation as a time-distorting device, with the songwriter taking the listener to another point in time. After the cosy 'here and now' banter of the verse we don't even need to be told exactly what those 'memories' are in order to be transported nostalgically back in time.

The B♭ is soon confirmed as much more than a borrowed ♭III, given its context and the way that the bridge progression unfolds. The chords in the new key (B♭, Dm, and Gm) are obviously totally incompatible with a tonal centre of G major, until McCartney orientates us by flagging his return to G with a now functional ii-V.

Meanwhile, the fact that we do so via an Imperfect cadence on the line 'the road that stretches out ahead', is just the icing on the cake. For we aren't going home just yet. As with the 'love you when we're apart' of 'I Will', the corresponding moment in 'Two Of Us' reinforces the temporary detachment from the stabilizing tonic that is inherent in all such 'middle feelings'.

The Beatles first mastered the modulation to a ♭III bridge in 1965, on a pair of songs on *Help!*: 'Another Girl' and 'You're Going To Lose That Girl'. Despite the fact that they appear 'back-to-back' on the album, The Beatles cleverly disguise their use of the device by varying their opening melody note in each case. While the latter goes for the major 3rd (as in 'Two Of Us'), the former nails the root of the chord thereby making the change even more sudden.

'Another Girl' – bridge modulation

	Key of A				Key of C					**Connector**	Key of A
Old key	I^7	IV^7	I^7	IV^7	♭III					**V^7**	I
Sequence	A^7	D^7	A^7	D^7	C	G^7	C	G^7	C	**E**	A
New key					I	V^7	I	V^7	I	**III^7**	
	'For I have got an - other girl. Another'				*'girl who will love me till the end. through thick and thin she will always be my friend.'*						*'For I have got'*

Note the exit 'connector' this time: a III7 chord in relation to C major but which we hear expertly taking us back V-I to A major on the word 'always'.[19]

But direct modulation is only one way in which The Beatles exploited the ♭III target as a new tonal destination. They also did so using the

[19] The distinction between a connector and a pivot is that the former doesn't have a formal role in both keys. The E7 is included here purely to act as the V of A and is unrelated to the departing key of C.

functional ii-V-I entrance mechanism that worked such a treat in 'From Me To You'. However, if we now work backwards from our new target of ♭III, we can see that the starting bridge chord must provide a rather unusual workout for not the v minor, but the iv minor chord. Formulaic thinkers may like to visualise it as Paul's 'surprising place' trick of 'From Me To You' – but starting a whole step down before working in fifths towards the new tonic, C major – just as McCartney himself does in 'Lady Madonna'.

'Lady Madonna' – entry to middle eight

	Key of A					**Pivot**	Key of C			
Old key	IV	♭VI	♭VII	I	iv^7	**♭VII^7**	♭III			
Sequence	D	F	G	A	Dm^7	**G^7**	C	Am	Dm	G^7
New key					ii^7	**V^7**	I	vi	ii	V^7
	'Did you think that money was heaven sent?'				*'Friday night arrives without a suitcase ...'*					

Here too, a modulation proves the perfect time-distorting ploy for the lyrics as McCartney takes us through Lady Madonna's mundane weekly schedule. Even the choice of bridge progression (another outing for 'ii-V-I-vi') conveys appropriately the idea of going through the motions.

But there's nothing pedestrian about the way in which McCartney returns to the original key of C for the next verse (1.15-1.20). For on the second circuit, Paul extricates himself with all the cunning of Houdini from what looks to be a musical *cul-de-sac.*

'Lady Madonna' – exit from middle eight

	Key of C		**Connector**		Key of A			
Old key	I	vii^7	**III^{7}sus^4**	**III^7**				
Sequence	C	Bm^7	**E^{7}sus^4**	**E^7**	A	D	A	D
New key		ii^7	**V^{7}sus^4**	**V^7**	I	IV	I	IV
	'See how they run...'				*'Lady Madonna, baby at your breast...'*			

The deft semitone slide from C to Bm7 cries out to be compared with the signature I-vii move of 'Yesterday' (no less), complete with the ensuing descent in fifths that now takes the song directly to its target, the A major verse. The euphoric 'see how they run' has been famously analysed for its *double entendres* of stockings, but it can equally be seen as a reaction to this musical Great Escape.

In the circumstances it seems incredible that John Lennon once moaned that the song 'never really went anywhere'.[20] Either he somehow overlooked the deceptive subtlety of this modulation to (and return from) the key of the ♭III, or it was disingenuity on a grand scale. For what it's worth, this author has previously nominated 'Lady Madonna' as The Beatles' Most Perfect Bridge. While there are arguably dozens of candidates for that title, the thinking was that, with the intricate mechanics of its modulation, which mixes simple textbook theory with breathtaking novelty, it neatly encapsulates exactly what a middle should be in a three-minute pop song.

And did Lady Madonna's diary jog Paul's memory when conceiving a modulation for 'She Came In Through The Bathroom Window'? For here again McCartney indulges in the same calendar effect ('Sunday', 'Monday' and 'Tuesday', this time) backed by the very same formula of iv minor cueing effectively another 'ii-V-I-vi' cycle in the key of the ♭III.

'She Came In Through The Bathroom Window' – mid-bridge modulation

	Key of A			**Pivot**	Key of C						Key of A
Old key	I	iv	I	**iv**		♭III					I
Sequence	A	Dm	A	**Dm**	G^7	C	G/B	Am	G^7	C	A
New key				**ii**	V^7	I	V	vi	V^7	I	
	'Didn't anybody tell her, didn't anybody see?'				*'Sunday's on the phone to Monday, Tuesday's on the phone to me.'*						

But for all the similarities with 'Lady Madonna', there is now a crucial difference that represents another giant leap forward in The Beatles' songwriting maturity. For rather than opening the bridge with an unexpected chord that will flag the modulation, McCartney opens on the tonic, lulling the listener into a false sense of diatonic security. The Dm on 'tell' is a gentle tug to the new territory and it only pulls us helplessly along towards C major following the second hearing (on 'see')[21]

With the listener now at his mercy McCartney can do what he likes and, sure enough, soon teases us with the complete antithesis of this ploy – an abrupt return to the original key of the verse through a direct – utterly non-functional – jump to A. Like the chord, the 'Oh yeah' exclamation comes as a suitable two-fingered salute from the master. With these few

[20] *The Playboy Interviews*; p. 179.

[21] The 'iv' now works as a pivot as, having heard it already alternate with the A tonic, Dm now smooths the way for a move to C as a ii chord in the ii-V-I.

bars, McCartney demonstrates admirably that while slick, functional modulations may prove his technical prowess it is the *blending* of the textbook and the outrageous that makes for compelling, timeless music.

Meanwhile, the same type of mature, disguised modulation to ♭III resurfaced expertly in Lennon's 'Free As A Bird'. A close listen to the song reveals it as much more than a posthumous marketing exercise. Here again John Lennon deftly blends the key-switch *within* a progression rather than unveiling it more predictably at the start of a new section. More profoundly, he camouflages the move still further by means of an elaborate substitution effect that bears the mark of genius.

'Free As A Bird' – mid-verse modulation

	Key of A		**Pivot**	Key of C			**Connector**	Key of A	
Old key	I	vi	**iv^7**		♭III		V	I	vi
Sequence	A	F♯m	**Dm^7**	G^7	C	Am	E	A	F♯m
New key			**ii^7**	V^7	I	vi			
	'... next best thing to be'		*'Free as a bird.'*					*'Free...'*	

Unlike 'Lady Madonna' where the opening iv chord automatically flagged the key change with its non-diatonic note, we don't feel the modulation in 'Free As A Bird' until the V-I arrival on the new tonic that formally consummates the key switch. This is because the Dm7 chord has already appeared in the verse as a 'borrowed iv' in the key of A, in what is a subtle variation on the I-vi-IV-V Four-Chord Turnaround. By virtue of its role in both keys, the iv chord acts as a highly subtle pivot. So natural is the move from Dm7 down a 5th to G that the whole manoeuvre goes by almost undetected until subliminally we feel the bird spread its wings at those select moments. Here is a summary of what was one of Lennon's most delicate songwriting gambits.

'Free As A Bird' – Dm^7's dual status

	Key of A						**Pivot**	Key of C		
Old key	I	vi	**iv^7**	V	I	vi	**iv^7**	(♭VII)	♭III	
Sequence	A	F♯m	**Dm^7**	E	A	F♯m	**Dm^7**	G	C	Am
New key							**ii^7**	V	I	vi

'Free As A Bird' proves that there are no hard and fast rules about viewing a pivot chord in a modulation. For now the chord that ultimately leads us V-I into the new key is the ♭VII of A, which now makes its first appearance in the song as a non-diatonic 'connector' chord.[22]

And wait a minute, John! Isn't this just exactly the bridge formula of 'Lady Madonna' – a song that didn't really go anywhere?

But when it comes to functional modulations of any sort, few Beatles moves have attracted more acclaim than the bridge to 'Here, There And Everywhere', another that hinges on a move to ♭III. For while the 'wave of the hand' moment of the verse flirts delicately with a relative minor shift, the emphatic tonics on 'Here' and 'There' keep us firmly in the original key at the start of each verse section. However, McCartney's middle takes us, literally, to the 'everywhere' in question.

'Here, There And Everywhere' – bridge modulations

	Key of G		**Conn-ector**	Key of B♭			**Conn-ector**	Key of Gm		**Pivot**	Key of G
Old key	ii	V^7	**♭VII**	♭III			$\mathbf{V^7}$	i	iv	$\mathbf{V^7}$	
Sequence	Am	D^7	$\mathbf{F^7}$	B♭	Gm	Cm	$\mathbf{D^7}$	Gm	Cm	$\mathbf{D^7}$	G
New key			$\mathbf{V^7}$	I	vi	ii	$\mathbf{III^7}$			$\mathbf{V^7}$	I
	'She doesn't know he's there'		*'I want her everywhere, and if she's beside me I know I need never care...'*								*'Every - where'*

The relationship to the other functional modulations to ♭III we've been exploring should be evident. No opening minor chord this time, just a straight slide down to the ♭VII that acts as the connector chord into the key centre like all the others. There's no real pivot this time and the F7 appears for barely a beat. But then lyrically, of course, perhaps it's important that we are guided through this transition.

Cleverer still is the way that 'everywhere' indeed means more than one key centre. For the key of B♭ is arguably not the only tonality featured in this meandering bridge. The subsequent visits to Gm are soon reinforced by a visit to its own dominant D7 in a way that briefly makes us feel that we have now progressed to the poignant parallel minor of the verse key. And this naturally makes McCartney's retransition plain sailing, for just as

[22] Once again, the term 'connector' is used here to distinguish it from the iv chord 'pivot' and demonstrates how a V chord (even built on a degree outside the original key) is the first choice of gateway into any key. The term is also used by Jimmy Webb, see *Tunesmith*, p. 243.

Lennon had shown us back on 'I'll Be Back', that D7 chord can take us just as easily to G major as G minor.

♭VI

Here is our chance to tackle a 'flat-submediant key-switch' head on. For William Mann's famous terminology is best applied not to the sudden borrowed ♭VI chords that spice progressions *within a given key*, as in 'It Won't Be Long', 'Honey Don't' and 'Peggy Sue', but rather to compositions where a new section formally establishes a new progression in relation to a new key centre on ♭VI.

We had to wait until *Anthology III* to hear The Beatles deliver the most sublime example on an original composition, as the Three-Chord predictability of 'Come And Get It' is transformed by its short but simply breathtaking 'Middle Five' – blink and you miss it.

'Come And Get It' – bridge modulation

	Key of E			Key of C		**Pivot**	Key of E	
Old key	I	IV	V	♭VI		**♭II**	I	V^7
Sequence	E	A	B	C	Em	**F**	E	B^7
New key				I	iii	**IV**		
	'I can give it, but you better hurry, 'cos it may not last'			*'Did I hear you say...'*		*'Would you walk away from a fool and his money?'*		

Why bother with bridges of 8, 10, 11 or 12 bars when you can say everything and more in five of the sweetest ever conceived? Never was the cliché 'less is more' more appropriate than in this criminally overlooked Beatles song (nonchalantly tossed to Apple label-mates Badfinger) which can be seen as a work of minimalist genius.[23]

The verse consists of nothing more than a Three-Chord Trick, but note how the cyclical pattern is cleverly displaced to settle on the dominant rather than the tonic as we move to the bridge. It's a ploy that allows McCartney to make his switch to ♭VI not directly from the tonic but by means of an effortless, half-step root ascent.[24] A whole step would have given him Aeolian entry to the relative minor on natural vi, but why go two steps when one delivers a far more interesting musical destination?

[23] Badfinger's version, released in January 1970, reached number 4 in the UK charts.

[24] More conventional would have been to use a V connector, as we'll see in 'Smoke Gets In Your Eyes'.

Simplicity prevails as the chosen progression in the new key appears to be nothing more than a familiar four-chord cycle in the new tonality. But Paul never makes it to the V that would have completed the 'I-iii-IV-V' – though he would surely have done if the middle eight had actually been eight bars long.[25] Instead, during the first cycle he seems to spot the home tonic of E just a semitone down from the F chord – why bother to go up to G (as convention dictates) when you can drop out now and save yourself the effort?

In fact, in keeping with the slothful theme of the lyrics, the harmony takes the line of least resistance throughout, going both into and out of the bridge key with the smallest of half-step chromatic movements. In doing so, 'Come And Get It' subliminally delivers the subtext: 'if you want it, come and get it'-*yourself.*

The final jump back to the dominant results in a bastardised Super Phrygian cadence with the lingering tritone interval between the F and B7 chords hanging in the air. The icing on the cake is the Imperfect cadence this creates in the context of the lyrics, separating the fool from his money with the hanging V again proving the perfect musical symbol of separation as we await the return to the E tonic. But, better still, the fact that we have already glimpsed the E chord for a split second before being pulled to V evokes, breathtakingly, the sense of the cup being dashed from the lips as the fool tantalisingly fails to grasp the nettle.[26]

This is pop music as the acceptable face of sheer delicious compositional laziness. Talking of which, just check out this extract from one glossary of technical terms:

> 'The *key* of the flat submediant tends to produce a feeling of passive, even luxurious relaxation: especially in the music of Schubert, who was partial to it.'[27]

In this way the not-so-humble 'Come And Get It' illustrates another rarely appreciated Beatles songwriting truth. Not only did The Beatles appreciate the need for a song to modulate beyond the diatonic world but, moreover, appear to have intuitively recognised precisely *which* destinations in the chromatic spectrum were most appropriate to convey a particular theme.

[25] Try it for yourself to see how the move from F cries out for a G-C resolution.

[26] Compare this to its precedent in the intro to 'Do You Want To Know A Secret' where the move sounds more classical due to the direct jump from F-B7 without the intervening E chord.

[27] Mellers, *Twilight Of The Gods*, p. 205.

'Come And Get It' later revisits the ♭VI in this way with an even more dreamy feel at 1.43. Though, as MacDonald points out, Paul fluffs the bass line at this point on the *Anthology 3* demo, moving to the E tonic against the C major in the piano as if caught out by his own brilliance.[28]

Meanwhile, to demonstrate just how expertly nonchalant the modulation to ♭VI is in 'Come And Get It', let's compare it with a more formal, functional key switch to this 'flat submediant' target. Given the distance between the two keys there aren't too many songs that establish ♭VI convincingly.[29] But let's pick one from a song that McCartney tells us was on The Beatles' favourite jukebox in Hamburg.

> 'On this jukebox there were two songs that I really used to like: The Platters' "Smoke Gets In Your Eyes" and Little Richard singing "Shake A Hand" . . . it stuck in my brain so much as being a really interesting, off-the-wall Little Richard track.'[30]

Really interesting? Surely, Sir Paul, you've got them the wrong way round! 'Shake A Hand' cycles monotonously through a single, repetitive Three-Chord Trick with not so much as a contrasting chorus or bridge.[31]

But 'Smoke Gets In Your Eyes', a massive No. 1 hit in 1960, is a different kettle of fish. There's surely no way that The Beatles as budding songwriters, could have failed to have been impressed by the breathtaking 16-bar bridge which, from a simple E major verse, targets C major with the most cunningly conceived of dominant 'connectors'.

'Smoke Gets In Your Eyes' – bridge modulation

	Key of E				**Connector**	Key of C	
Old key	V^7	I	ii	iii	**♭III**	♭VI	
Sequence	B^7	E	F♯m	G♯m	$\mathbf{G^7}$	C	G
New key					$\mathbf{V^7}$	I	V
	'Smoke gets in your eyes'					*'So I chaffed them and I gayly laughed'*	

[28] MacDonald, *Revolution In The Head*; p. 317.

[29] Compare this with songs that open with a direct modulation to ♭VI from the tonic for the bridge but which then don't subsequently establish the new key convincingly. 'I Only Want To Be With You' (Dusty Springfield/The Tourists: 'You stopped and smiled at me'); and 'Every Breath You Take' (The Police: 'Since you've gone I've been lost' – F from A).

[30] *Paul McCartney's Rock & Roll Roots*, BBC Radio 2, 25th December 1999.

[31] Hear McCartney go through the G-C-D cycle on *Run Devil Run*. Perhaps he was taken with the form: a slightly hypnotic 8-bar structure.

A simple walk-up from the root unfolds the tonic before iii turns back to ♭III for the V-I entry. It's the boldest of modulations and a nice take on IV-III7-vi ('I Should Have Know Better') or IV-III^7-VI ('Day Tripper') moves which use the same root relationship *a whole step higher.*[32]

Finally in this section we visit 'Glass Onion', complete with the chapter's opening Lennon lyric that so well captures the vital role of modulation in pop songwriting. So here's that other place you can go . . .

'Glass Onion' – mid-verse modulation

	Key of A minor?					Key of F?				
Old key	i	♭VI^7	i	♭VI^7	i^7	**♭vii^7**				
Sequence	Am	F^7	Am	F^7	Am	**Gm^7**	C^7	Gm^7	C^7	F^7
New key						**ii^7**	V^7	ii^7	V^7	I^7
	'I told you 'bout Strawberry Fields... well, here's another '					*'place you can go, where everything flows. Looking through...'*				

After the traumatic dissonance of the Am-F7 alternation (a sequence that is best thought of as centered somewhat awkwardly in the key of A minor), we badly need 'another place' for tonal contrast. John duly puts us out of our misery with an implied change, not merely to the F chord that we've already heard, but to the *key* of F major. It doesn't matter that the eventual resolution to F is so fleeting for, as with 'Yesterday', the fact that we pluck a 'ii-V' out of the air is enough to take us away in every sense. While 'Yesterday' built that ii-V on vii, here John builds it on ♭vii, with Gm being an even more unlikely choice of chord having come from A minor.[33]

Nevertheless, after that disturbing tritone activity, the familiar diatonic swooning of a conventional ii-V means that, just as John says, we've been transported to a place 'where everything flows.'

Talk about 'luxurious relaxation'. . .

♭II

We aren't even halfway around the Cycle Of Fifths and yet the role that modulation can play in transforming and appreciating some of the cleverest touches in Beatles music should already be evident. So how can

[32] Elsewhere this bridge deserves further praise. Most notably for the C to Am relative minor switch that captures the love that has 'flown away', in a thematic ploy right up there with The Beatles' best.

[33] Notice how the return to A minor from F requires only a ♭VI-♭VII-i Aeolian ascent.

the great Jimmy Webb write the following paragraph apparently criticising the concept?

> 'Modulation is in disrepute. Suggest modulation to a contemporary musician and you are likely to be sneered at if not banished in perpetuity to the boneyard of the un-hip. Your invitations may begin to wander mysteriously in the mail . . .'[34]

Webb's put-down is a perceptive comment in response to a gradual but fundamental sea-change in songwriting practice over the last few decades. His objection is not to the *transitory* modulations that move away from – *and then back to* – a given key centre, as we've seen Beatles songs pull off with such panache. No, the target of derision here is what has become known as the *final* modulation, which Webb defines as 'modulating without returning to the original key, usually for suspect, overly dramatic reasons'.

The Semitone Shift/'Truck Driver's' Modulation and 'Gear-Box' Effect

The most famous example of a final modulation is the 'up-a-semitone shift' that effectively takes a song to the destination of ♯I, or ♭II in terms of our musical 'map'. Why is this so sneered at by musos?[35] After all, we are now in the nether regions of the Cycle Of Fifths, suggesting that we have reached one of the most ambitious key targets in music – and one that, theoretically at least, should also be highly impenetrable given that there are no pivot chords to help us make a smooth transition.[36]

The reason is that songs that 'resort' to the semitone shift do so by merely *repeating a previous harmonic idea* (almost always the chorus) *identically* a half step higher, i.e., with no new interval relationship between the chords. To the extent that there is no other harmonic, melodic or rhythmic development, the trick is seen as a cheap, tacky way of generating momentum. That's not to say that it doesn't work. Pop history is littered with hits that use the trick for a sudden burst of energy.

Stevie Wonder's 'You Are The Sunshine Of My Life', Abba's 'Money Money Money' and Lionel Richie's 'Easy' are just three whose last choruses take us to ♭II territory in this way. That's not to say that these aren't all great songs, but the formulaic effect of the closing chorus is

[34] *Tunesmith: The Art Of Songwriting*, p. 241.

[35] Webb is by no means on his own – other pop commentators feel the same way: Rooksby describes the semitone shift as 'slightly vulgar'; *How To Write Songs On Guitar*, p. 131.

[36] C major has no sharps or flats, but the key of the ♯I, C♯, has seven sharps.

instantly apparent. Whatever the gripes of the purists, audiences and song-writers have been lapping it up since pop began.[37]

As The Beatles knew, right from the early days – listen to them go through the motions on 'Beautiful Dreamer', as the song takes flight with a shift from G to G♯ for the last chorus. The same goes for 'Take Good Care Of My Baby', though here in remaining faithful to Bobby Vee's original they at least make the effort of entering the new key functionally rather than directly. In doing so a D♯7 connector adds a modicum of interest by taking the song from G to G♯ by means of a V-I.[38]

However, it was testimony to The Beatles' sense of originality that they rarely exploited this type of modulation in their own compositions, and when they did it was hardly a throwaway gesture.[39] Compare John's blatant use of it in 'Woman', in 1980, with Paul's 'And I Love Her' where, far from hyping a final chorus, the device lifts George's guitar solo into our consciousness, while adding yet another dimension to the delicate play between relative minor and major that we have already investigated. In keeping with all these semi-tone shifts we remain in the higher key for the remainder of the song.

The American slang for this type of shift is *The Truck Driver's modulation* because the effect is one of changing harmonic gears.[40] You can either go directly to the new key as an automatic or, like 'Take Good Care Of My Baby', use the new dominant as a clutch.

But that's not the end of this particular modulation trick. After all, if you're going to move the entire progression, lock stock and barrel, why stop at a semitone? How about a whole tone? Just as The Beatles do in the reprise of 'Sgt. Pepper', climbing from F to G (via the D7 at 0.42).

Ultimately, the same 'gear-box effect' can take the song to any destina-

[37] Our love-hate relationship with this device is captured at www.gearchange.org, a website dedicated affectionately to the dubious heritage of the Truck Driver's modulation, in all genres ranging from Peggy Lee's 'Fever' (1958) to a handful of post-2000 songs by serial offenders, Westlife.

[38] Bobby Vee's original is in the key of F♯, with the D7 'connector' making its appearance at 1.40. But Vee didn't bother with the niceties in 'The Night Has A Thousand Eyes', taking us directly from D♯ to E at 1.33.

[39] George Michael describes how Atlantic Records supremo, Jerry Wexler, berated him for his use of the semitone key shift, calling it 'the worst cliché in the book'; *Bare*, p. 107.

[40] Everett pioneers the term, describing it as 'an odious time-killer in much commercial music' while acknowledging its subtlety in 'And I Love Her'; *The Beatles As Musicians*: The Quarry Men Through Rubber Soul, p. 366.

tion with sequences ranging from the simplest of 12-bar blues through to a more complex Cycle Of Fifths.

It was a principle that The Beatles used as far back as Hamburg when switching between the distant key centres of E and C on their highly personalised rendition of Marlene Dietrich's 'Falling In Love Again'.[41] While it would be pushing it to call this an original approach to modulation, the completely off-beam arrangement is in its own way revealing, perhaps indicative of a rebellious or, at the very least, highly inquisitive attitude to the whole concept of tonality.

The following table attempts to extend the basic principle of The Truck Driver's modulation by listing various Beatles (including solo) excursions where a 'gear-box' effect is clearly apparent. In each case the essential harmony and melody clearly resurfaces identically within the song but in a different key. While the various target keys represent different distances in terms of modulating from home base, it seems sensible to treat them as a group.[42]

The Beatles and the 'Gear-Box' Effect

Target	Song	Progression	1st key	2nd key
♯I	'Beautiful Dreamer'	I - II^7 - V	G (verse)	G♯ (verse)
♯I	'Take Good Care Of My Baby'	I - vi - IV - V	G (verse)	G♯ (verse)
♯I	'And I Love Her'	iv - i - iv - i	C♯m (verse)	Dm (verse)
♯I	'Woman'	I - ii - iii - ii	E♭ (verse)	E (verse)
II	'Sgt. Pepper (Reprise)'	I - ♭III - IV - I	F (chorus)	G (chorus)
II[43]	'Penny Lane'	I - IV	A (chorus)	B (chorus)
II	'My Sweet Lord'	ii - V	E (chorus)	F♯ (chorus)
III	'Teddy Boy'	I - V - v - ii - IV - V	D (verse 1)	F♯ (verse 2)
IV	'Octopus's Garden'	I - vi - IV - V	E (chorus)	A (solo)
IV	'Happy Xmas (War Is Over)'	I - ii - V - I	A (verse 1)	D (verse 2)
♭VI	'Falling In Love Again'	I - IV - I - vi - ii - V - I	E (verse)	C (solo)
VI	'The Continuing Story of Bungalow Bill'	I - V - I - iv - I	C (chorus)	A (chorus)

[41] After an intro in the key of C, The Beatles move to E at 0.11 to unfold a Cycle Of Fifths verse and bridge at 0.34. But at 0.56 the verse/bridge format is repeated for the solo in the key of C; before returning back to the key of E at 1.31.

[42] Advanced readers should check the close of 'Good Day Sunshine' where the IV-I chorus in B seems to be recycled a key higher (at 1.58). But we don't make it to C, fading out on the F that feels like a tonal No Man's Land a disturbing ♭V away from B.

[43] The I-II final chorus effect (at 2.33) should be reconciled as ♭VII-I within the clever twin-key scheme.

The Far Side – true key switching to ♭II, ♭V and VII

While 'The Semitone Shift' dominates pop music's excursions from I to ♭II, very occasionally a song will manage a more 'respected' key-switch to this destination – i.e., one that does genuinely introduce new material and thereby succeeds in altering our sense of tonality in a far more subtle, less identifiable way.[44]

Incredibly John Lennon would manage to do just this – and with the precision of a surgeon – as early as *A Hard Day's Night*. But so intricate is the relevant modulation in 'If I Fell', that it is being kept under wraps until Chapter 12 as it hinges on a device known as *Tritone Substitution*.

♭V

The same goes for modulations to the key of ♭V – the furthest point from our home tonic. This is harmonic Indian country, as we already know that chords are rarely built on this scale degree in pop.[45] Certainly, bridges that start on ♭V in relation to the previous tonic are highly rare. Nevertheless, here is an opportunity to dust off McCartney's brilliant forgotten instrumental, 'Catswalk', which features a piece of structural and harmonic novelty unknown in 'official' Beatles music.

As an immediate caveat it should be stressed that the bridge does not involve a modulation to ♭V but it *is* heard deceptively as the first chord of the bridge and is integral to the modulation that follows. The following chord chart confirms that the verse is in G minor, while the bridge is a whole step down in F minor. The table homes in on the point of transition, which sees the bridge proper preceded by an extra bar of 2/4 that houses the secret to one of McCartney's most unusual functional modulations. Having ended the verse with a 'Besame Mucho'-style wrap-up (the same E♭7-D7 return to Gm), Paul then decides to find the new tonal centre of F using the very same device.

This is where the ♭V comes in – for, in sliding into the dominant of F from a semitone above, he delivers briefly the extreme dissonance of D♭, reached by an augmented fourth jump from our last resolved G. Like its

[44] One of the most famous is Antonio Carlos Jobim's 'The Girl From Ipanema' whose bridge opens powerfully in G♭ major after an F verse.

[45] While the ♭V in the 'Till There Was You' coda (C-C♭-C, at 1.59) was just a chromatic gesture to spice the dominant, check out McCartney's 'It's For You' (for Cilla) which extends the 'Far Side Cycle' of 'Things We Said Today' boldly from ♭II on to ♭V (G♭ in key of Cm, at 0.14).

'Catswalk' – McCartney's dissonant ♭V transition

	Key of G minor			**Transition**		Key of F minor			
Old key	♭VI⁷	V⁷	i	♭**V**					
Sequence	E♭⁷	D⁷	Gm	**D♭**	**C**	Fm	B♭m	A♭	C⁷
New key				♭**VI**	**V**	i	iv	♭III	V⁷

feline cousin, 'The Theme From The Pink Panther', you never quite know where this particular animal is going to take you next.

Leaving aside this striking quirk, formal modulations to ♭V (progressions that reinforce this destination as a tonal centre in its own right) are highly rare. Tonality anoraks are directed to the bold bridges of 'Ding Dingue Dong' by 1975 Eurovision winners, Teach-In, and 'Ghost Town' by The Specials' (as we'll see later).

Having rounded this musical Cape Horn on the southern tip of the cycle, we turn from the 'flat side' to the 'sharp side' and continue our harmonic world tour by visiting keys built on roots that can now be reconciled with the major scale: VII-III-VI-II-V.

Our first stop should be VII. Yet in the same way that it is rare for a pop song to build any kind of chord on the leading note, so it is even more unusual to establish this degree as a key centre in its own right through modulation. Arguably 'Martha My Dear' manages briefly to do precisely this – not merely because both parts of her jazz-flavoured, two-part bridge start on an elusive vii chord. Chapter 12 looks at the complicated, wandering bridge tonality when introducing the subject of 'polychords'.

III

The mediant was a popular modulation target in the Golden Era of Tin Pan Alley and Broadway. Listen to Gershwin's 'They Can't Take That Away From Me' which formally tonicises the minor mediant in the fine bridge by alternating it with its dominant.[46]

Certainly The Beatles got great mileage from opening a new section on either a minor iii or major III, but rarely did they convincingly reinforce or maintain the tonality on this third degree.[47] Perhaps they were

[46] Listen to the line: 'Well we may never ever meet again' where the E♭ gives way to the Gm-D7-Gm bridge.

[47] John Lennon, however, did do this on his solo track 'Love', which, after an intro in D major, alternates F♯m and C♯7 ('Love is real, real is love') before returning to D.

influenced by the bridge of 'Falling In Love Again' which demonstrates how chords on this degree cry out to return to base by back-cycling around the Cycle Of Fifths – just as we see in Beatles originals like the chorus of 'Can't Buy Me Love' and the middle eight of 'Cry For A Shadow'.

Nevertheless, a fine example can be heard on 'Teddy Boy', formally released on McCartney's debut, but considered as an official Beatles release following its inclusion on *Anthology 3*.

Paul's choice of new key (at the end of the second verse) is novel enough, but the bold way in which he engineers a potentially awkward transition shows his confidence as a songwriter. The switch starts at 0.23, moving from the key of D to the new tonic of F♯ at 0.27.

A single V7 connector would have done the job, but McCartney chooses instead to prime this C♯7 with a B7, and we therefore hear two dangerously non-diatonic chords before tonal stability is established.

However, having already heard a similar G-A move as an essential riff-like gesture (first at 0.11 on 'alright') the listener now understands the complementary symmetry of this otherwise alarming move. We expect this pattern to move down a fifth to secure the tonality – and so it does. Only now the IV-V-I takes us to F♯. Brilliant.

VI

During interviews for this book Robbie Williams' musical partner, Guy Chambers, contributed a fascinating few hours' insight into his favourite Beatles moments. To set the ball rolling, Chambers instinctively played the transition from George Harrison's 'Something', where the song 'lifts' courtesy of a tonal shift from C to A. Unlike the standard denouement to the relative minor, the bridge to 'Something' targets VI *major* as its new key centre and in doing so takes the song to an emotionally higher plane.

'Something' – entry to bridge

		Key of C		**Pivot**	Key of A		
Old key		IV	♭III	**V**			
Sequence	*from C major verse...*	F	E♭	**G**	A	C♯m/G♯	F♯m
New key				**♭VII**	I	iii	vi
		Instrumental link			*'You're asking me will my love grow'*		

Our grounding in I-vi key switches will nevertheless help us to understand the mechanics of this exquisite modulation. With the same *roots* in operation, here is another outing for the most versatile of pivot chords of Chapter 6: the V=♭VII. For, when moving between A and C, Harrison knows that G major is the perfect gateway. In its incarnation of ♭VII it can take him to the bridge in A by sliding up a whole tone, invoking our favourite Aeolian cadence.

And the G-A move reappears within the first strain of the bridge as one means of reinforcing the new tonality. But notice also the reinforcement of A from the gentle chromatic bass descent to E which subtly provides a V-I 're-start' for the second half, at 1.28. As the singer suggests, so the tonality of A major does indeed 'stick around'.

'Something' – exit from bridge

	Key of A					**Pivot**	Key of C	
Old key	I	iii	vi	I	IV	**♭VII**		
Sequence	A	C♯m/G♯	F♯m	A/E	D	**G**	C	Cmaj^7
New key						**V**	I	Imaj^7
	'You stick around now, it may show, I don't know, I don't know'						*Guitar solo*	

So how do we exit back to C major to enjoy one of George's most melodic solos? No problem. The same G pivot – no longer required as ♭VII of A – is recast as the V of C, just as it was when entering the previous verse structures.[48]

The voice-leading chart below attempts to show that the drama of the modulation in 'Something' is down to the introduction of the rogue ♭2 note in relation to the parent key. Compare the effect as that distinctive opening theme progression establishes first the verse tonality, and then that of the bridge. In stark contrast to the stability on C, the bridge delivers a C♯ that is smuggled into the proceedings as the major 3rd of A: a sound heard both in the chord and the vocal melody. With the help of a formal progression unfolding in the new tonality, the result is a compelling key switch.[49]

[48] Hence we can view it as now functioning like the ♭VII=V pivots that took us from i-to-♭III (Am-to-C via G) in 'You Never Give Me Your Money'.

[49] A simple sequence, almost identical to the verse of 'Help!', as noted earlier.

Voice-leading in the 'Something "theme' melody

Verse entry (0.01-0.05)

	End of 'Something' 'theme'			**Interval**	Verse in C
Chord	F	E♭	G/D		C
Melody note	A	B♭	B	**semitone**	C
Chord tone	3rd	5th	3rd		Root

Bridge entry (1.07-1.11)

	End of 'Something' 'theme'			**Interval**	Bridge in A
Chord	F	E♭	G/D		A
Melody note	A	B♭	B	**tone**	C♯
Chord tone	3rd	5th	3rd		3rd

To capture the contrast instantly, listen to the final coda as George briefly modulates to A once again (this time for just a bar at 2.46); before the final cadence unquestionably restores 'order' on C major (at 2.54).

It's worth mentioning the unusual theme sequence itself, as it appears in almost every transition in the song.[50] Technically a bizarre 'IV–♭III–V' in relation to the impending verse key, this unusual progression is merely an embellished IV–V headed for a tonic. However, it also provides a novel way of harmonizing the second note of the four-semitone chromatic melody that ascends magically into the root of the I chord. If the E♭ chord is still difficult to conceptualize, think of it as a common tone substitution for a B♭, the ♭VII in the key of C, that would have prepared the V chord, as we saw in Chapter 7 (B♭–G–C).

For all the mileage that can be obtained from switching between major and relative minor (vi), VI represents a particularly stylish destination in music, with Harrison's deft manoeuvre representing another songwriting rite of passage for The Beatles.[51]

[50] If this sequence sounds unnatural to guitarists (attempting it in any of the basic fretboard positions) – and George himself agrees – that's because he wrote it on the piano.

[51] Notable pre-Beatles shifts to VI include 'As Time Goes By' and Frank Ifield's 'I Remember You'. More recently Oasis's 'Sunday Morning Call' turns its iii chord in B♭ major (Dm) into III major (D at 0.31) which then acts as the V of the new tonic, G major. A textbook I-VI key switch from Noel.

II

As we move closer to home the transitions become less ambitious but are nevertheless worthy of discussion. Once again, bridges that start on the second degree of the scale are not necessarily the stuff of modulations as this target can be conceived as just the first diatonic step away from any tonic, with a V-I return to base always a possibility. We saw Mitch Murray doing just that on 'How Do You Do It?', while James Ray fashioned a similar bridge to his fine 'If You Got To Make A Fool Of Somebody', complete with its Cycle Of Fifths wrap-up.

'If You Gotta Make A Fool Of Somebody' (bridge)

ii	V	I	ii	V	I	ii	V	iii	vi	ii	V
Am^7	D^7	G	Am^7	D^7	G	Am^7	D^7	Bm^7	Em^7	Am^7	D^7

Both Ray's and Murray's bridges formed welcome departures from standard rock 'n' roll bridges, though not really from their song's primary key centres.[52]

But The Beatles were adept at tonicising any degree. Contrast these modest offerings with McCartney's 'For No One', where our sense of moving to a tonality a whole step up is now formally enforced through the use of a dominant chord. The result is a deeper sense of departure and a different backdrop. Nevertheless, the principle (if not the target key) is lyrically related to many other Beatles songs, given how it switches from the trivialities of the day to looking into the eyes of the subject and searching for clues to deeper feelings.

'For No One'

	Key of A			Key of Bm				**Pivot**	Key of A		
Old key	IV	♭VII	I	ii				**ii**	$Vsus^4$	V	I
Sequence	D	G	A	Bm	$F\sharp^7$	Bm	$F\sharp^7$	**Bm**	$Esus^4$	E	A
New key				i	V^7	i	V^7	**i**			
	'She no longer needs you. And in her...'			*'eyes you see nothing...'*				*'A love that should have lasted years.'*			

[52] Listen also to the bridge of 'I'll Be On My Way' on *Live At The BBC*, to hear The Beatles first experimenting with II major in a similar context. The formula here truncates the James Ray 'model' with II-V-II-VI7-II-V-I, again with an initial move up a whole step before back-cycling to the tonic in fifths.

Hopefully, this chapter has demonstrated that when aspiring to a particular harmonic destination there is more than one way of skinning a cat. While the ii in the bridge of 'For No One' is the opening gambit and has to 'find' its dominant Plagally when reinforcing the tonality, 'If I Needed Someone', back on *Rubber Soul*, takes a rather different route to the same target.

'If I Needed Someone' – bridge modulation

	Key of A	Key of Bm					**Pivot**	Key of A		
Old key	I	v					**ii**	V^7sus^4	V^7	I
Sequence	A	Em	F$\sharp^7$	Bm	Em	F$\sharp^7$	**Bm**	E^7sus^4	E^7	A
New key		iv	V^7	i	iv	V^7	**i**			
	'If I needed someone'	*'Had you come some other day, then it might not have been like this...'*								*'Carve your number ...'*

Here George throws us delightfully off the scent of his bridge target by making the now familiar v minor his first port of call. Yet unlike 'From Me To You', this is not a precursor to a key centre on IV but an inspired alternative that demonstrates his innate vision of the structure of any key.

While Em creates a dramatic change of harmony in its own right, George has his eye ultimately on ii, B minor. Yet rather than a ii–V entry, he recognises that iv–V provides an equally effective method of modulation. While IV-V-I is an obvious move in a major key, switching the principle from major to minor is the masterstroke of a confident songwriter. All the more so, since this particular destination necessitates the introduction of a disorientating Em after a verse founded on an unflinching A major tonic.

As with 'Glass Onion', purists might feel that the key-switch to ii in both 'For No One' and 'If I Needed Someone' should perhaps not be discussed under this location on the Cycle Of Fifths. For in terms of 'distance from the home key' as measured by the new implied key signature, it is technically equivalent to a move to IV (since ii is the relative minor of IV). This is true, and key centres can indeed be ranked using this criterion.[53]

[53] Rooksby adapts the Cycle Of Fifths to devise a system of concentric circles around a given key centre to represent near and distant keys. He concludes succinctly: 'From C major, the closest keys are F, G, Am, Dm and Em – chords IV, V, VI, II and III of the key. Next would come C minor the tonic [parallel] minor. *How To Write Songs On Guitar*, p. 126. This can be reconciled with the chromatic cycle, which sees each stop in terms of a major and (relative) minor destination.

However, we are using the cycle here as an analytical guide that is visually helpful in targeting the *root* of a new tonal centre from any given tonic – if not necessarily the major/minor quality of that new key. After all, from any V chord we can modulate just as easily to a minor key as a major one. Hence from A major we can use F♯7 to take us not just to B minor, as George does in 'If I Needed Someone', but also B major. Just as John does in 'Doctor Robert'.

'Doctor Robert' – bridge modulation

	Key of A		**Pivot**	Key of B			**Pivot**	Key of A
Old key	VI^7	V^7	$\mathbf{VI^7}$				**V**	I
Sequence	$F\sharp^7$	E^7	$\mathbf{F\sharp^7}$	B	E	B	**E**	A
New key		IV^7	$\mathbf{V^7}$	I	IV	I	**IV**	
	'No-one can succeed like'			*'Doctor Robert. Well, well, well, you're feeling fine...'*				*'Doctor Robert'*

Once again it is a brilliantly conceived pivot chord that helps us make sense of a seemingly awkward progression. The opening change to a non-functioning VI7 (with its clashing A♯ in the wake of A natural) was mentioned in Chapter 4. But, in true pivot fashion, this F♯7 has a dual role, combining with the preceding E7 (now jettisoned as V of A) to take us to the new home of B, quite conventionally, IV-V-I. More Lennon magic.

Everett contrasts the 'normal workaday world portrayed by dull motives' in the verse, with the 'blissful state' of the bridge. The modulation 'illustrates transcendence' he says, presumably a euphemism for the good doctor's bag of pharmaceutical tricks, which lifts Lennon along with his key switch.[54]

And yet, was the tonal structure all a harmonic hallucination? No less an expert than Alan Pollack suggests that 'Doctor Robert' should be turned on his head, so to speak. While the song opens in A, it is B that acts as the song's main key centre, with A ultimately the ♭VII in the grand scheme of things.[55] It's an interesting theory, and this concept of 'bi- (and indeed 'tri-) tonality' also features in most of our remaining excursions.

[54] Everett, *The Beatles As Musicians: Revolver Through The Anthology*, p. 46. Compare this with another 'II bridge', The Who's 'Won't Get Fooled Again' ('I move myself and my family and child'), described as 'hopeful' by Chris Ingham, 'Doctor Rock Dissects The Hits, No. 4', *MOJO*, Issue 20, July 1995, p. 39.

[55] 'Notes on…Series' no. 100, 1995. *The 'Official' rec.music.beatles Home Page*, www.recmusicbeatles.com)

We start with the mental gymnastics of the harmonically triple-jointed 'Mr Kite'.

Circus tricks in minor – the tonal magic of 'Mr Kite'

If Lennon took the easy way out with his primitive (if deceptive) structure in 'Doctor Robert', the same cannot be said about this *tour de force*. Having already swooned over the way the chromatic descent runs through the main theme, we can now tackle the second instalment of this case study which focuses more specifically on the tonal ambiguity that makes the song. And while the whole framework is in minor, Lennon again toys with tonics a whole step apart.

The concept of the pivot chord is again the secret to solving the intrigue behind a rare multi-key modulation within an exclusively minor-based song. 'Mr Kite' is sophisticated stuff (even by Beatles standards) as, technically, the song moves through three key centres: C minor, D minor and E minor, in an ascending theme appropriate to the circus spectacular unfolding beneath the Big Top itself.

Similarly uncanny is the way in which these tonalities are not 'sectionalized' in a predictable way, with rarely an obvious transition between say, verse, chorus and bridge. It is this effortless gliding between the tonalities, as the audience subliminally follows the progress of the different acts on the bill that represents a highpoint in John Lennon's career.

Ultimately it is the way that Lennon conceives the dual tonality of the verse that is so unique. And to help us appreciate Mr Kite's magic we need to take a peek at the three harmonic props up his sleeve:

1) The popular natural minor reference points of i-♭VII-♭VI;
2) The V chord principle that leads to (and reinforces) a tonality.
3) A pivot chord to reinforce the sleight-of-hand – in fact a pair.

Mr Kite's first trick – the Cm to Dm verse switch

The first three chords establish the C minor tonality with basic V, ♭VII and i chords, including our previously mentioned augmented chord. Meanwhile, the ii minor we are also showcasing here, D minor (with its 5th, A, also in the melody), has the effect of suggesting C Dorian while happily functioning as we would expect, as a primer for the V again, in bar 2.[56]

[56] Dorian is the only mode that features minor triads on both first and second scale degrees. Hence, Cm and Dm are indicative of a C Dorian play at this point.

'Being For The Benefit Of Mr Kite'

	Key of C minor			**Pivot**	**Connector**	Key of D minor			
Old key	i	Vaug	♭VII	**ii**					
Sequence	Cm	Gaug	B♭	**Dm**	**A**	Dm	B♭	A	Dm
New key				**i**	**V**	i	♭VI	V	i
	'The Hendersons will all be there, late of Pablo Fanque's fair, what a scene!'					*'Over men and horses, hoops and garters...'*			

The cycle then resumes for what appears to be a second hearing of these same four bars. But when the Dm is next heard, in bar 6, it acts as a pivot chord for the modulation. For now the ii chord in C Dorian is about to be redefined as the new i chord, just as soon as it bounces back off its V chord (that sudden A major) as surely as the trampoline in the ring. In true Beatles fashion, the new territory is heralded with a complementary lyric: 'What a scene'. At which point the transition brilliantly introduces the C♯ note in the chord, in contrast to the C natural of the original key.

The effect is a perfect harmonic backdrop for Lennon, The Master Of Ceremonies, to turn our attention to the 'men', 'hoops', 'garters' and 'hogsheads of real fire'.[57]

But that's not the end of the show, for now in D minor, the B♭ chord reveals its identity as another important pivot in the proceedings. Previously heard as ♭VII of Cm, the B♭ chord (which now supports the B♭ note in the melody) is reinterpreted as ♭VI in D minor. The combination of pivots is the musical equivalent of the multi-talented Mr Kite himself.[58] The following table shows how a theoretically minded John Lennon could have neatly conceived the Dm and B♭ – *chords common to both C minor and D minor* – as operating in two different keys in just this way.

Mr Kite's pirouette: The changing roles of Dm and B♭

Key of C minor	Chord	Key of D minor
ii	Dm	i
i	Cm	
♭VII	B♭	♭VI

[57] For other sudden appearances of ♭2 refer back to those stirring I-VI major jumps in 'Revolution', 'Doctor Robert' and 'Day Tripper'.

[58] In this way the D tonality can be reconciled as D *Aeolian*, with the B♭ (the ♭VI chord in D *natural* minor) unfolding a defining ♭VI-V-i move.

From then on – right through to the end of the link – it's plain sailing to see ourselves in D minor, with easily digestible i-iv and V chords. Note how the Gm-A-Dm first reinforces the key centre (like the iv-V-I of 'If I Needed Someone'), while taunting us in the link as we immediately U-turn to G major to restart the next verse on C minor.

	Key of D minor						**Connector**	Key of Cm	
Old key	iv	V	i	iv	V	i	**IV**		
Sequence	Gm	A	Dm	Gm	A	Dm	**G**	Cm	Gaug
New key							**V**	i	Vaug
	'In this way Mr K. will challenge the world!'			*Instrumental link*				*'The celebrated Mr K.'*	

Mr Kite's grand entrance

In this way the intro can be understood, retrospectively, as a brilliant preview of the link's high-wire act. For we open with the same ♭VI-V-i in D minor but which chooses to continue around the Cycle Of Fifths until, with G major as a standard V chord, it cues the first act on the bill: verse 1 in C minor (at 0.07).

Mr Kite's bridge too far out: the Em key centre

The third key centre, E minor, is reached midway through the solo, and this time it is sprung upon us without a pivot chord.

Not content with alternating i-V, Lennon jumps directly to B at (1.14). Like the A major that went to Dm in the verse, the B chord acts as the same connector, conceived purely as the V of E minor.

But forget the mechanics and listen instead to how the new tonality completes the musical/circus connection by climbing the rickety ladder to the top of the tent, reaching a key now perched four semitones above the circus floor.

And how does Lennon – now the musical trapeze artist *extraordinaire* – get back to earth? Simple. By flying through the ring from this E minor to its relative major, G, from where the original V-i move of the intro can announce the next performance on Cm. Bravo!

'Ten summersets he'll undertake'? Certainly few Beatles songs require quite such acrobatics to appreciate their musical construction and few have been subjected to such differing interpretations.[59]

Still, given such quirky harmony in the context of the circus theme, it is nothing short of spellbinding that such a confirmed muso-phobe as John Lennon could have conceived the work while blissfully unaware of the mechanics.

V

Here we reach the last port-of-call in our circumnavigation of the musical globe as represented metaphorically by the Cycle Of Fifths.

In a sense we have been repeatedly flirting with modulations to the key of the V throughout this book. Take those Imperfect cadences where a II7-V7 leads to a 'hanging V' effect at the end of so many bridges. To the extent that the 'V-of-V' is involved in all these, we are indeed feeling a tonicisation of this key, however briefly. However, the expectation that we 'should return to I' is almost always there. And so it is in bridges like 'Love Me Do' where an opening V chord immediately returns to the tonic of the verse.[60] Compare this with the middle of 'Eight Days A Week', which finds The Beatles putting an unusual spin on the dominant. Like 'Love Me Do' it's the first time we're treated to the V chord in the whole song, with the D tonic of the verse having been established purely through Plagal cadences. More importantly the feeling of a more autonomous A tonality is reinforced by the subsequent progression with B minor being not so much a deceptive cadence, but more of a ii chord in A. The following E chord could square the circle directly (as it would do similarly in 'Happy Xmas (War Is Over)'),[61] but instead the move back through G now drives us back to the original tonic through a IV–V-I.

We could view this bridge as a self-contained dominant tonality –

[59] Take your pick from Pollack who sees the third key centre, E minor (with which we are ultimately left following the last switch at 2.12) as the ultimate tonality of the piece ('Notes on ... Series' no. 13, 2000. *The 'Official' rec.music.beatles Home Page*, www.recmusicbeatles.com); and Everett who says 'neither C, D, or E can claim traditional authority as a single tonal centre, especially with the same melodic/harmonic material appearing in each key.'; *The Beatles As Musicians: Revolver Through The Anthology*, p. 110.

[60] The middle: 'Someone to love . . .' opens with a D chord before returning to the G tonic.

[61] Note here that the 'I-ii-V-I' is reheard in the key of the IV rather than the V (see the earlier 'Truck Driver's' Table).

conceptually similar to (if rather more innocent than) the coda twist of 'I Am The Walrus'.

'Eight Days A Week' – bridge modulation

	Key of D				**Pivot**	Key of A			**Pivot**	Key of D	
Old key	I	II^7	IV	I	**V**				**V**	I	II^7
Sequence	D	E^7	G	D	**A**	Bm	E	G	**A**	D	E^7
New key					**I**	ii	V	♭VII	**I**		
	'I ain't got nothin' but love babe...'				*'Eight days a week, I love you...'*					*'Ooh, I need your love, babe'*	

Either way it's a far more sophisticated play on the unflinching B chord in 'Day Tripper' that forms a complete 12-bar bridge starting at 1.21.[62] And as we preview some final thoughts on a song's 'grand design', both of these bridges can be seen as giant V chords within the overall structure, reinforcing the emphatic return to the parent tonality by building tension that we feel 'must' move V-I.

Though not necessarily immediately, for in the same way that The Beatles recognised the potential for Deceptive and Interrupted cadences as diversions from the expected resolution, so songs like 'Birthday' took this a stage further with a disorientating modulation on the heels of a prolonged V chord.

'Birthday' is a humble but helpful example of The Beatles using musical licence in this way. For all its apparent frivolity the song works hand-in-glove with the lyrics, this time by engineering an ambitious key switch that takes us to the celebrations. In keeping with our framework for this chapter the play is ultimately a move from A to C and back again, which could therefore have been dealt with under the category of ♭III above. But that would have ignored the role of the prolonged V chord in what is (literally) a two-stage process taking us ever further from the home key.

Having metaphorically received the invitation in our key centre of A, the extended link on E finds us in transit – in rather the same way that the lengthy spell on the V in 'Day Tripper' matched at least one of the interpretations of the title. But unlike that earlier song we don't climax V-I but move instead to the distant territory of C major where the party itself is already under way.

[62] See also the bridge to 'I'll Cry Instead' which opens on iii in the key of G, like 'A Hard Day's Night', then moves to tonicise V from *its* dominant in the *middle* of the bridge rather than by means of an Imperfect cadence at the end.

To round things off, an upbeat V-I in the context of this song does actually occur but, suitably, not until the brazen climax to the proceedings (at 1.24) a kind of musical 'last orders' as we return home to A.

In this way the stunted harmonic flow of 'Birthday' can be seen to match most effectively the evening's entertainment, as the following distillation of the main tonal movements attempts to capture.

After all, you can't come home from the party until you've got there in the first place.

'Birthday' – summary of tonalities

Section	Verse	Link/Bridge	Middle	Instrumental
Time	0.23	0.56	1.10	1.28
Lyric	'You say it's your birthday'	'Yes, we're going to a party'	'I would like you to dance'	*(Solo back in home key)*
Chords	A^7 - D^7 - E^7	E	C - G - E	A^7 - D^7 - E^7
Key	A	(E)	C	A
Formula	I	V	♭III	I
Transition		Extended V	Direct	V - I

Multi-key modulations and The Big Picture

The notion of a Grand Design is crucial to appreciating the structure of various other Beatles songs that take the listener on a more elaborate journey than just a one-dimensional 'there and back' key-switch. Indeed, if we return to 'Magical Mystery Tour' and take a snapshot of the entire song harmony we can also see signs of a prolonged V in the dreamy instrumental interlude.

The result is neither squarely in the verse key of E or the bridge key of ♭VII that we saw earlier, thereby evoking the whole mystery of the tour even more effectively.

'Magical Mystery Tour' – The tonal itinerary

Section	Verse	Link/Bridge	Interlude	Verse	Coda	
Time	0.09	0.33	1.13	1.27	2.24	2.28
Lyric	'Roll up'	'The Magical Mystery Tour'	*Instrumental*	'Roll up'	'Today'	*Piano*
Key	E	D	(B)	E	D	Dm
Formula	I	♭VII	V	I	♭VII	♭vii
Transition		IV = V pivot (A chord)	V = ♭VII pivot (A chord)	V^7 - I	V^7 - I	Parallel Switch

Meanwhile, if we accept that the 'Truck Driver's' modulation is a special case, here is an example of a Beatles song ending in a key bearing no relation to the one in which it started. Which begs the question, what is the 'home' key of the song? Is there one? We have analysed the various moves here in relation to E major, which felt like the obvious base – especially with what sounded like a definitive Double Plagal rock entrance. It also formed a practical reference point for a sequential dissection of the song.

But, ultimately, are we so sure of the tonality? Perhaps D major should be seen as the true destination to which the 'tour' was always headed? This type of complex key scheme clearly takes The Beatles' tonality tricks to a new level. To appreciate further how different levels of ambiguity can make a song so intriguing, we need to step back and look in more detail at The Big Picture.

Schenker Revisited

Any discussion of multi-key modulations inevitably leads us back to Heinrich Schenker whose theories remind us not only of the various definitions of the term *modulation*, but also question this whole chapter's very approach to the analysis. For, as Steven Porter summarises succinctly, the Schenkerian view is that 'a work which begins and ends in the same key is said to prolong that key throughout,' thereby reducing most of our exotic and elaborate moves to what his disciples would see as just 'disturbances' within a single grand design.

Indeed, when discussing many multi-key songs that do *not* return to their initial starting point (as we just saw in 'Magical Mystery Tour'), the notion of a single key-centre exerting such control over an entire piece is questioned by rock theorists. Here's Beatles expert, Allan Moore:

> 'Modulations are seen, therefore [in Schenkerian theory], to be simply local departures. This is by no means so in rock where an initial mode can be no more than a convenient starting point carrying no necessary implication of return. Modulation, therefore, at the moment of the change of modal focus, has a far higher priority.'[63]

[63] Dr. Allan F. Moore, 'The so-called 'flattened seventh' in rock', *Popular Music* 14/2, May 1995, p. 193. Building on his earlier comments about the widespread role of ♭VII, Moore analyses various rock songs: Peter Gabriel's 'Here Comes The Flood', Jethro Tull's 'This Is Not Love' and Led Zeppelin's 'Out On The Tiles' which each use the ♭VII chord to effect a modulation.

Hence the big deal we've been making of it. Moore's comment was made in relation to some elaborate multi-mode rock songs, whose development through various keys questions both the role of the opening key; as well as the omnipotence of the V and Schenkerian doctrine as it might be formally applied to rock music. Take 'Mr Kite' for example, which starts in D minor, moves through C minor, eventually ending in E minor.

Ultimately the point of this discussion is that, when appreciating certain select, multi-tonal Beatles masterworks, we can enhance our enjoyment of them by analysing them on a number of harmonic levels, deferring to various schools of thought. In particular, 'Lucy In The Sky With Diamonds' and the mouthwatering medley on side 2 of *Abbey Road* cry out to have their intricate modulations dissected for their mechanical precision, before then prompting us to step back in awe and admire their grand structural design.

As the chapter's final case study, 'Lucy' provides a detailed insight into John Lennon's genius in blending seemingly disparate sections into a complete work. In doing so it forms essential groundwork for an appreciation of the *Abbey Road* medley which, as it relies on concepts from later chapters, is reserved for Appendix 4 where we provide an instant guide for readers prepared to take the trip. Talking of trips . . .

'Lucy In The Sky With Diamonds' – triple key heaven

After the hypnotic cyclicality of the opening progression, created by the descending rock figure in A that we saw in Chapter 9, Lennon's first ploy is to lift the song out of its slumbers by transporting us to the distant territory of ♭II.

Step 1: The psychedelic verse switch (A to B♭)

	Key of A		**Pivot**		Key of B♭			
Old key	I	I^7	**iv**	$\mathbf{iv^7}$	♭II			
Sequence	A	A^7	**Dm**	**Dm/C**	B♭	C	F	B♭
New key			**iii**	$\mathbf{iii^7}$	I	II	V	I
	'A girl with kaleidoscope eyes'				*'Cellophane flowers of yellow and green, towering over your head'*			

But this is no direct Truck Driver's modulation with the new key reached lethargically up-a-semitone. Instead, Lennon adopts the very slickest of pivot ploys, with the Dm magically smoothing the way for this captivating development section. Topping even the intricacies of 'Mr Kite', Lennon recognises that, as well as Dm appearing as part of the IV-iv Plagal drop within the opening A major sequence, the same chord can have another identity as the iii chord in B♭ major.

It's a truly brilliant vision, for while most of our minor chord pivots take us predictably to the new key with a ii–V–I (e.g., 'Free As A Bird'), here we treat it as iii and walk back to the new I in a suitably lackadaisical *diatonic descent.*

The C-in-the-bass is the icing on the cake that achieves this. For while technically putting the Dm in 3rd inversion, it also leads sublimely to B♭ in the most textbook of 3-2-1 scalar drops to B♭. The die is cast and we're on our way.[64]

Once in the new key, John's simple climbing sequence is the perfect foil for the earlier drop, and it cleverly matches the imagery of the flowers that tower 'over our heads' and 'grow so incredibly high'. It also provides us with a gentle warning that the pace of activity (both harmonic, melodic and rhythmic) is about to hot up.[65]

Step 2: Real 'gone' – the chorus transition (B♭-G)

Given his penchant for Plagal transitions in multi-part modulations, John now chooses the C chord (acting as a secondary major triad II in B♭) as the pivot to lead IV-to-I into the next key in the chain: G major.

	Key of B♭				**Pivot**	Key of G				
Old key	I	II	V	I	**II**					
Sequence	B♭	C	F	B♭	**C**	G	D	G	C	D
New key					**IV**	I	V	I	IV	V
	'Cellophane flowers of yellow and green, towering over your head'				*'Look for the girl with the sun in her eyes, and she's gone'*			*'Lucy in the sky with diamonds'*		

[64] This movement of a minor chord to a major chord two steps below via root midway constitutes the same relationship seen in many situations. Think back, in particular, to the intricate ballad workings of 'Yesterday', where (conceived in the key of G) the Em-Em/D smoothed the way to the Cmajor7 chord (effectively a vi-IV switch via '5').

[65] Moore refers to the 'metric modulation' that sees the 46 b.p.m. tempo of the 12/8 verse doubling to 93 b.p.m., for the refrain. *The Beatles: Sgt. Pepper's Lonely Hearts Club Band*, p.32.

We hear the germ of a transition on the words 'look' and 'sun' while reaching an appropriate sense of inevitability on 'gone'. By this time Lennon has already taken us into the new key centre with this stealthy C pivot which smuggles us in, being common to both B♭ and G.

The brilliance of this delicate execution is that it provides an early glimpse of the new tonic (the G at 0.42) some eight seconds before the refrain. In this way we are indeed drifting helplessly on that 'boat on the river' beyond the obviously descending bassline of the A section. By the time we reach the V chord that sets up that nursery rhyme and its Three-Chord Trick, there's no turning back. Just like Lucy herself, we are 'gone'.

Step 3 – Coming down to earth – the verse return (G-A)

The last piece in Lucy's puzzle is the retransition to the verse which again confirms Lennon as the master of the Plagal pivot shift. Here he reconceives V of G as IV of A which returns to base with the swooning 'aahhh'.

	Key of G			**Pivot**	Key of A			
Old key	I	IV	V	**V**				
Sequence	G	C	D	**D**	A	A^7	D	Dm
New key				**IV**	I	I^7	IV	iv
	'Lucy in the sky with diamonds'			*'Ah...'*	*'Follow her down to a bridge by a river'*			

The various modulations and transition mechanisms are clever enough. But like Julian's drawing of his friend Lucy, there's a bigger picture here, with classical theory suggesting that Lucy is much greater than the sum of her parts[66]. Moore himself calls the meanderings 'the very model of illusory movement', and homes in on the crucial pitches that lend an underlying correctness to the proceedings through the 5-1 descent into the chorus tonic of G.[67]

[66] John Lennon explains the full story behind the inspiration for the song in *The Playboy Interviews*, p. 16.

[67] Allan F. Moore, *The Beatles: Sgt. Pepper's Lonely Hearts Club Band*, p. 33.

Section	Verse	Verse (development)		Chorus
Time	0.06	0.32	0.47	0.50
Lyric	'Picture yourself...'	'Cellophane flowers...'	'... and she's gone'	'Lucy in the sky with diamonds'
Pitch in G		D	A	G
Structural Pitch		5	2	1
Key	A	B♭	G	
Structural Chord	A	(B♭)	D	G
Grand Design	**II**	**♭III**	**V**	**I**

Meanwhile, Everett's analytical *coup de grâce* is that if we step back from Lucy's hallucinatory minutiae and appreciate the Grand Design, the opening verse in A is now seen in relation to the fundamental key of G, yielding a giant II-V-I structure that demonstrates John's uncanny tonal craftmanship.

> 'Through the verse, transition, and chorus, counterpoint and harmony seem to cooperate at deep levels to unify the superficially unrelated keys of A, B♭ and G.'[68]

Most intriguingly, however, Everett consequently relabels the B♭ and C within the 'Cellophane flowers' development section as ♭III and IV in this masterplan, where they now represent an 'expanded version of the cadence in 'Please Please Me'.[69]

Not only does this put a whole new spin on Lennon's 'variations on a theme' dictum but confirms the extent of the uncanny method that somehow underpinned The Beatles' composing madness.

[68] Everett, *The Beatles As Musicians: Revolver Through The Anthology*, p. 105.

[69] Namely, the brief 'I-♭III-IV-V' riff which links the two four-bar strains of the verse and which introduced us to the borrowed ♭III chord in Beatles music (see Chapter 7).

ELEVEN

Diminished: Songwriting Sleight-of-Hand

'Major, minor, augmented and diminished – everything comes out of those four chord forms.' – George Benson[1]

If, as George Benson claims, the foundations of harmony can indeed be reduced to these four pillars, it must be an oversight that so far in our discussion, one of them – the diminished – has been conspicuous by its absence.

A close look at the unusual construction of this chord (and a listen to its sound in isolation) will go some way towards explaining the relative dirth of diminished chords in pop music. Diminished harmony epitomises the concept of dissonance. You may recall that we said the same of the m7♭5 chord when explaining why it is rarely used in practice despite its theoretical diatonic eligibility. But the diminished seventh raises the stakes further, making it the ultimate 'handle-with-care' chord, and while its application is often assumed to be reserved for specialist jazz use, the inherent properties of the diminished chord make it one of the most interesting and versatile weapons in the armoury of the pop songwriter.

Tin Pan Alley and Broadway show tunes certainly made good use of the chord earlier in the century, though its role in the golden era of fifties rock 'n' roll was strictly limited. However, by the end of the sixties, The Beatles had built emphatically on its legacy with a select group of songs that demonstrated both the potential of the chord and the scale from which it derives.

This chapter introduces the diminished sound and looks at how The

[1] Interview in *Guitar Player* magazine, July 1979.

Beatles exploited it in situations ranging from Beatlemania pop and outright rock, to quasi-classical structures and modal-inflected experiments.

While the whole concept of the diminished chord requires some careful thinking to rationalise and appreciate, the fact is that The Beatles were using it in a variety of ways from the early days. From 'Like Dreamers Do' right through to 'Because', examples from John, Paul, and George will be used to illustrate the essence of the chord, which is to create novel voice-leading by appearing in one of two roles: as a *passing chord* or a *substitute for a dominant chord.* The distinction between the two contexts will become clear as we expand on the following pair of rules:[2]

1. Diminished as a passing chord
A diminished chord functions as a passing chord when *none* of its four notes are the leading note of the following chord.

2. Diminished as a dominant substitute
A diminished chord functions as a dominant substitute when *any* of its four notes are the leading note of the following chord.

Part 1 – Diminished as a passing chord

Before tackling the necessary theory that will help us chart our course, dust off *Anthology 1* and sample the basic sound of the diminished chord on one of Lennon's earliest songs, 'Like Dreamers Do'. This provides a useful point of departure both chronologically and musically for here, (starting in the coda at 2.17) a diminished chord (normally abbreviated as *dim*) appears unannounced, and alternates disarmingly with a tonic major triad built on the same root.

'Like Dreamers Do'

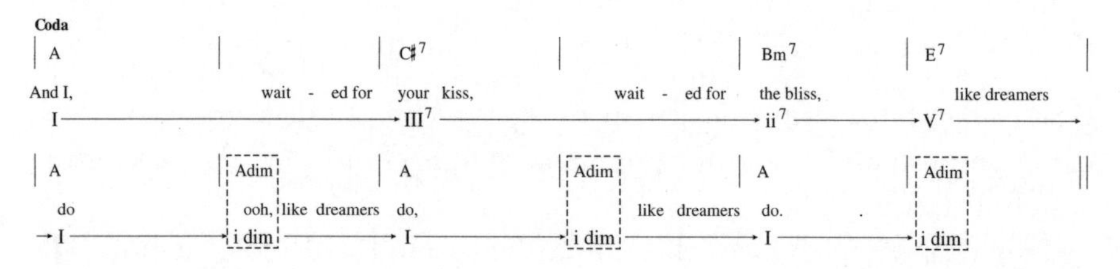

[2] Adapted from *Harmony & Theory* by Musicians Institute teachers, Keith Wyatt and Carl Schroeder, p. 123.

We are definitely in the key of A major and yet Harrison's lightly cascading arpeggio neatly delivers the sound of the ♭5th, ♭3rd and 6th in relation to the tonic, before resolving back to the major triad. The result is some novel textural dissonance that actually goes far beyond the supposedly artistically groundbreaking fade out of 'I'll Be Back', which it predates by several years.[3]

For in that later song, the parallel major/minor vamp was merely a play on major and minor 3rds with no implications for the 5th degree of the key. But here we enjoy a more elaborate colouring from the different tones in the diminished chord, which compares to the major triad as follows:

	Root	Third		Fifth		Seventh
	1	**♭3**	**3**	**♭5**	**5**	**♭♭7**
A major triad	A		C♯		E	
A diminished 7th	A	C		E♭		G♭

The table also shows that, far from necessarily being a dated, 'jazz dinosaur' (as the diminished and its augmented cousin are often regarded), the diminished chord actually offers great scope within the genres of blues and R'n'B. For in addition to the basic chordal tension, it can also help to harmonise the dissonant ♭5th melodic 'blue' note – or indeed the 'micro-tones' between the 4th and ♭5th degrees that the best bluesy singers strive for – just as McCartney does here as he varies the pitch of the first word of the title refrain – especially on the second repeat before the final closing run.[4]

Theory interlude – the structure of the diminished seventh

Let's firstly explain the appearance of the '♭♭7' hieroglyphic, the 'double flattened seventh', in the dim chord. In the same way that we previously encountered 'double sharps' so we have this equivalent on the flat side. For while the note F♯ makes ample sense as the 6th of A major, it doesn't reflect the way that this new chord has been built. But then nor does the convention of terming the chord 'dim' or even 'diminished' adequately reflect the full role of the chord at work. For we have already encountered a *type* of diminished chord back in Chapter 3, namely the diminished *triad* within

[3] The *Anthology 1* version of 'Like Dreamers Do' was part of the Decca session of New Year's Day 1962, while 'I'll Be Back' was recorded in June 1964.

[4] The song ends with a dramatic example of an early Beatles chromatic line: a five-semitone ascent from ♭VI to I (F-to-A, alternating with the respective V7 chords).

the m7♭5 chord, a structure that occurs naturally within the diatonic scale. The diminished *seventh*, however (even if we will be guilty of the same shorthand oversight throughout) is a different animal by virtue of the note that appears as its seventh.

When looking at the construction of the diminished it's worth noting that the m7♭5 chord itself is sometimes referred to as *half-diminished*. This is because part of it is diminished – the triad 1, ♭3, ♭5. But the other 'half' (or rather quarter) is not. The seventh appears there as a ♭7 which occurs naturally in the natural minor scale. The *full* diminished chord arises when that same already flattened ♭7 is flattened again. This creates the ♭♭7, 'double flattened', or the diminished seventh, the dissonant interval from the root that gives the chord its name.

Nevertheless, that G♭ pitch is enharmonic to (i.e., the same note as) the 6th (F♯), as we can see from the following diminished scale which, when harmonised in the usual manner, gives rise to the chord in the first place.

The Whole-Half diminished scale

Formula	1	2	♭3	4	♭5	♯5	6 /♭♭7	7
Scale of A diminished	A	B	C	D	E♭	E♯	F♯/G♭	G♯
Chord tones of Adim^7	A		C		E♭		G♭	

The Half-Whole diminished scale

Formula	1	♭2	♭3	3	♭5	5	6 /♭♭7	♭7
Scale of A diminished	A	B♭	C	D♯	E♭	E	F♯/G♭	G
Chord tones of Adim^7	A		C		E♭		G♭	

Notice that the diminished scale is a symmetrical one, with a repeating interval structure that divides the octave into eight (rather than seven) notes. There are two full diminished scales, as we can achieve this symmetry in two ways: either by following a half-step/whole-step formula, or a whole-step/half-step.[5]

While a jazz soloist will choose his scale depending on the alterations in the *chords* in a progression, the important thing when conceiving the origins of the chord is to appreciate that *both scales give rise to the same diminished seventh chord when harmonised* in thirds:

[5] The scales can be seen to be related as modes of each other. The 'half-whole' version arises from starting on the second degree of the 'whole-half' scale. Given this symmetrical structure there are indeed only these two possible modes of the diminished scale.

A closer look reveals that the diminished chord is composed of three minor thirds stacked on top of each other, creating in the process two dissonant tritone intervals, in addition to the defining 'dim seventh'. And if we double up by repeating the tonic on top, yet another minor third is formed, thereby dividing the octave into four intervals of a minor third.

The diminished seventh – stacked minor 3rd intervals

Formula	Root		♭3		♭5		♭♭7		Root
Chord tones of Adim7	A		C		E♭		G♭		A
Interval		Minor 3rd		Minor 3rd		Minor 3rd		Minor 3rd	

It is this bizarre symmetry that results in the chord's 'spacey', ambiguous sound, and which renders it much more versatile than the m7♭5 chord. For, in practice, the dim chord doesn't sound as if it formally belongs anywhere, and this allows us to accept its presence as a drifting nomadic sound almost anywhere that a skilful songwriter chooses to place it. Theory goes so far as to tell us that the diminished chord can actually be used between *any* two chords (albeit with varying success) such are its magical properties of dissonance and resolution.

We can test this by using it as an ambitious substitute within our stock unit: a Four-Chord Turnaround. The Beatles oblige with their maligned – but harmonically rich – rendition of 'The Sheik Of Araby' on *Anthology 1,* which shows The Fabs absorbing the legacy of Tin Pan Alley down to the smallest detail. While the verse could happily open with a pure Doo Wop cliché of C-Am-Dm7-G7, George Harrison throws in some cool dissonance by replacing that second chord with a diminished seventh (at 0.07) built on the same root of the relative minor.[6]

'The Sheik Of Araby' : verse (0.05)

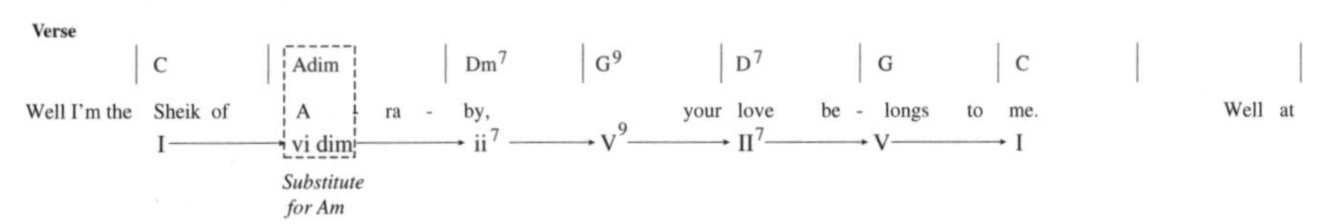

[6] George's chord is a familiar-shaped dim played in 7th position on the top four strings, voiced (low-to-high) A-E♭-G♭-C. The C note, on the top string at the 8th fret, is an important reference point for, as we discuss later, the dim chord can be named after *any* of the notes in its structure and therefore this chord is, in practice, best thought of as C diminished in this overtly C major context.

Why does this work so effectively?

The simple answer is that A dim obviously qualifies as a common-tone substitute for the 'missing' Am that would have been the obvious choice, by virtue of their common A roots. But notice also how one of pop's most famous clichés takes on a new dimension by being harmonised in this more exotic manner.[7] We now have voice-leading within the harmony that sees the G note (the 5th of the tonic) walk down a semitone to G♭ and then to F, the 3rd of the Dm7 chord. Here's a summary of the action based on George's guitar part (irrespective of the precise passing bass motion):

How A dim 'subs for vi' in a Four-Chord Turnaround

Original Formula	**I**	**vi (Am)**	**ii**	**V**
Substitute sequence	C	A dim	Dm^7	G^9
Lyric	'Sheik of	A - ra	- by'	
Voice leading	G	G♭	F	
Scale tone descent	5th	♭5th	4th	

In this way Harrison's use of the diminished chord creates a new dimension for the simple 'I-vi-ii-V' formula, engineering internal harmonic lines that would not be present in the basic sequence. The versatility of this simple substitution in such a common progression should already be obvious.

Technically, the diminished chords in both 'The Sheik Of Araby' and 'Like Dreamers Do' have each acted in a 'passing' capacity. The same principle underlies what is undoubtedly the most popular passing dim in pop and rock: the ♯iv dim that colours a return from the subdominant to the tonic.

To appreciate this slick move refer briefly to 'P.S. I Love You' and its bizarre G-C♯7-D intro. The premise here is essentially to embellish the Plagal return from IV to I with a chord that makes sense as a colourful link, while supporting the line: 'write this (letter)'.

McCartney's C♯7certainly succeeds in harmonising (with its root) the melody while also delivering a smooth, semitone chromatic climb into the 5th of the D tonic. However, there's no getting away from the intrinsic dissonance of a chord built on the leading note of the key – especially when reached by the jarring jump of a tritone (G-C♯).

[7] Notice how McCartney reinforces the diminished harmony with his E♭ and G♭ notes, between standard C major and D minor arpeggios.

Paul may well have been intrigued by the same IV-VII7-I on Joe Brown's version of the old 'Darktown Strutters' Ball' standard (another Fab 1962 stage favourite). Check that version to hear how, in the key of A, we get a startling D-G♯7-A (on the lyric 'blue suede *shoes*', at 0.25).

Most would agree that this effect is disorientating, and it's no surprise that it is extremely rare in pop. However, the cunning songwriter can achieve a similar effect while at the same time 'correcting' for that maverick tritonal root movement, by using the passing ♯iv dim.

The #iv dim and the 12-bar blues

Far from being a sophisticated jazz idea, this passing diminished trick can be found in the most primitive of blues structures. Having moved to the IV chord (in bar 5 of a typical 12-bar) the ♯iv dim can substitute for this chord in the next bar, before the progression returns home in bar 7.[8]

Bar	1	2	3	4	5	6	7
Formula	I	IV	I	I	**IV**	**♯iv dim**	**I**

The effect is again a three-semitone ascending line that 'walks' from the root of the subdominant into the 5th of the tonic but now via the root of the passing diminished chord. In doing so it creates a colourful line within the internal harmony that can be understood immediately as a cool variation on the voice leading in the IV-iv Plagal drop of Chapter 3, which of course *descended* into the 5th of the I chord.[9]

Voice-leading in the #iv dim blues substitution

Formula	**IV**	**♯iv dim**	**I**
Substitute sequence	F	F♯dim	C
Voice leading	F	F♯	G
Scale tone ascent	4th	♯4th	5th

[8] In this way you could adapt the 'quick change' in bar 2 to accommodate two beats of IV and two beats of ♯iv dim before returning to the tonic in bar 3.

[9] Moving into the 5th of the chord creates the potential for viewing the tonic chord in second inversion with the 5th-in-the-bass. In this case, a G note under the C chord would yield the progression: F-F♯dim-C/G. Listen to Eric Clapton's 'Snake Lake Blues' to hear a fine example; in the key of E: A-A♯dim-E/B.

Here is one departure from the Three-Chord Trick that bluesmen have been adopting since the Pre-War era. The recordings of guitarists like Blind Blake and Scrapper Blackwell suggest that this embellishment was also being absorbed into the blues from Ragtime, and piano standards such as 'Nobody Knows You When You're Down And Out'.[10]

The IV-♯iv-I move became a favourite of songwriters of all genres during the 20th century, earning cliché status in the hands of Tin Pan Alley writers before drifting into rock 'n' roll, probably via Gospel music. The move could perhaps have entered The Beatles' orbit through songs like Ray Charles's 'Hallelujah, I Love Her So', with the 1960 Eddie Cochran version being a particular favourite of McCartney's.[11] Beneath the celestial string parts on Cochran's version (in the key of G), the ascending bass line defines the move as D♯ appears in a chromatic run in which the major 3rd of the I chord can also be seen to imply a 1st inversion tonic (G/B).[12]

'Hallelujah, I Love Her So'

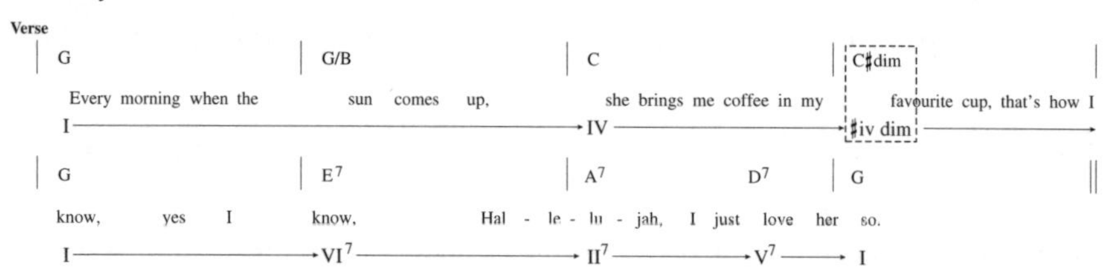

The Cochran version is shown here, as the *Anthology 1* outing is seriously rough and ready. But the corresponding extract begins there at 0.10, in the key of B♭, with the diminished action occurring at 0.15 when (after the E♭ IV chord) an E natural note emerges through the mayhem.

Relating a diminished chord to a dominant 7♭9

Even when incorporating the ♯iv dim into their originals, The Beatles had a particularly novel take – listen to 'It Won't Be Long' where the all-important passing tone is heard as dissonant inner hamony rather than

[10] Listen to solo recordings like Blind Blake's 'Diddie Wa Diddie' which clearly uses the ♯iv dim substitution as far back as 1929.

[11] With regard to The Beatles' version, the *Anthology I* liner notes state: '. . . the clear influence here is Eddie Cochran's cover version. This had been a minor hit on the British singles chart in February 1960, helped there by Paul who bought the record . . .'; p. 8.

[12] The bass here is just elaborating on the opening I chord by playing it in 1st inversion.

rooted in McCartney's bass. Here we have the A♯ (or B♭) note in the the guitar's A♯ dim chord and the vocal harmony creating the very same link between the A and E chords and yet *over a bass note that has remained on IV.*[13]

This raises an interesting point about the relationship of the diminished chord to the harmony for which it typically substitutes. For if the bass note stays on IV before returning to the tonic, leaving the ♯IV note to appear elsewhere in the harmony, what chord do we really have?

'It Won't Be Long'

McCartney's A note in the bass means that the *overall* sonority is not a formal ♯iv diminished chord, but rather a dominant 7th chord built a semitone below (i.e. on IV) and now coloured with a flattened 9th. It is this chord that provides a vital reference point when it comes to using the diminished seventh substitute. The following chart demonstrates the relationship between the two chords, reconceiving the ♭9 of A (B♭) as enharmonic to the root of the diminished chord a semitone above (A♯).

Understanding the '♭9 dim' substitute

A♯ dim^7	Root	♭3	♭5	♭♭7
Notes	A♯	C♯	E	G
A$^{7♭9}$	♭9	3	5	♭7

[13] Guitarists can best capture the relevant sound (at 0.11) with a 2nd-position A♯ dim inversion built on E, using the notes E-A♯-C♯-G (low-to-high).

A cover band playing 'It Won't Be Long' could save themselves the intricacies of the backing arrangement by playing the B♭ in the bass. In doing so they would be following an important rule that will resurface to help us through this chapter:

'The ♭9 rule'

When a dominant seventh ♭9 chord appears, you can enhance the voice-leading by substituting a diminished chord built on a root a semitone higher.

Hence for A7♭9, we can play the A♯dim that will take us back to E major yielding us the very IV-♯ivdim-I blues run of 'Hallelujah, I Love Her So' that we started with.

The heritage of this move is indeed well established. Cole Porter used it most distinctively in his melody to 'True Love', a song that George Harrison would himself cover.[14] Meanwhile, the ♯iv dim chord became a stalwart of blues in the sixties through Freddy King instrumentals like 'The Stumble', adopted by British artists like John Mayall, and 'I Need Your Love So Bad', the Little Willie John number turned pub standard (Fleetwood Mac).[15]

For readers unsure of the pure sound of the diminished chord (especially given the potentially confusing relationship between chords, bass and backing vocals that we have been exploring), check out John Lennon's humble solo acoustic rendition of 'Dear John', one of his very last demos. Heard in the key of B♭, John goes for the E♭ to E dim move (first at 0.58), with an affectionate chuckle.

Meanwhile, at 'The End' of The Beatles' own recording career, we find them adopting a rather novel spin on the 'IV-♯iv dim-I', which kicks off the final leg of the *Abbey Road* medley. Here by way of an introduction to Ringo's drum solo and the famous three-way headcuttin' guitar duel, we find a repeated figure that culminates in an interesting cadence.

After the basic block chords that begin the track as it segues from 'Carry That Weight', the harmony defers to ascending counterpoint guitar runs

[14] Harrison's version is in the key of D – listen out for the G♯ in the melody on the second hearing of 'give' in the opening line of the verse: 'I give to you and you *give* to me'.

[15] Listen to the bridge – 'Won't you give it up, and come on *home* to me' (D-D♯dim-A). In a contemporary blues-rock setting it can be heard in Gwyn Ashton's 'Someone Like You', which tips its hat to Hoagy Carmichael's 'Georgia'.

that walk up to a dissonant hanging sonority (first at 0.06) and, after a euphoric 'oh yeah' vocal entry, again on the word 'dreams' at 0.17.

'The End' – intro 'theme' (0.11)

A quick inventory of sounds shows that:

1) having left their home of A, the bass and one guitar walk chromatically from B to their temporary resting place of D♯; meanwhile,

2) the second guitar harmonises the line a minor third higher, peaking this time on F♯.

For all its apparent intricacy the idea can be reconciled very simply with the very same IV-♯iv dim-I passing run. Admittedly it's not so much a 'walk' through the ascending tones as a 100-yard dash but, just as in 'Hallelujah, I Love Her So', we've got some chromatic action that takes us to a point of local dissonance on the ♯iv degree ('dreams') before an emphatic resolution back to the home tonic ('tonight').

Perhaps more than any other example this moment demonstrates how the whole concept of the IV-♯iv dim-I should be seen as a way of supercharging a basic Plagal cadence, with this precarious ascent being the intense mirror image of the more mellow 'sister' move that makes the return from IV to the tonic through a IV-iv minor descent.

'The End' also shows that you don't need the full chord to imply the presence of diminished. Here we have just the skeleton of that minor third interval, but its role is unmistakable. In this same way we can also appreciate various diminished 'doublestops' that crop up sometimes in the most subtle of passing contexts but which still lend distinctive dissonance and serious style to a song.

Before we move on to 'Part 2', we should remember the common principle governing all these 'type 1' diminished chords, namely that *none of the four notes in the diminished chord operates as the leading note of the target chord*. This is important, for while we have seen some interesting voice-leading, the dim chords so far have not 'driven' the progression in the way that we will see in our second category. These 'dominants' enjoy a more powerful role in a song by 'functioning' in the sense with which we have become familiar.

Part 2 – 'Dim For Dom' substitutions

With its double tritone structure, the diminished chord is well qualified for its most important role as a special kind of supercharged dominant chord. So versatile is the dim sound, that it does not merely substitute for the obvious dominant V chord – but also for a full range of secondary dominants. It is vital to demonstrate that whatever the apparent disguise of the dim chord in this discussion (and there are many) its appearance can nevertheless always be traced to this underlying function.

The easiest way to begin our tour is to review the exotic structure of the harmonic minor scale, as this is *the only setting in music where the diminished seventh appears as a diatonic chord*. Here it is not necessarily substituting for anything. It is just appears as itself, as in this D harmonic minor scale:

i maj⁷	**ii⁷♭5**	**♭iii maj⁷aug**	**iv⁷**	**V⁷**	**♭VI maj⁷**	**vii dim⁷**
Dm (maj⁷)	Em⁷♭5	Fmaj ⁷aug	Gm⁷	A⁷	B♭maj⁷	C♯dim⁷

The first step is to see the diminished chord's potential for resolution with respect to this scale. For while we have become used to seeing the V7 to i minor cadence that this scale also allows, so we can also accept that 'vii dim 7' provides an interesting alternative. The sound is one of dark, haunting subtlety due to the very particular voice-leading, with the root of the tonic reached from a semitone below, in contrast to the wider V-i root movement.

The Beatles don't go *directly* for this Harmonic minor context in their songs, but we can examine it in one highly distinctive pop context: Abba's 'S.O.S'.

'S.O.S' (verse)

In stark contrast to our earlier discussion of passing chords, notice here the luscious effect that results from resolving all the constituent dissonances of the diminished seventh in one fell swoop. The following table captures each of those three, slick semitone moves:

C♯dim ⁷			**D minor**	
Formula	Note	Voice leading	Note	Formula
♭♭7th	B♭	Down a semitone	A	5th
♭5th	G	Up a whole tone	A	5th
3rd	E	Up a semitone	F	3rd
Root	**C♯**	**Up a semitone**	**D**	**Root**

The C♯ to D resolution here constitutes the *leading note effect* – a feature with which we are familiar. The term arises from the semitone movement into the root of the new chord, though unlike a conventional dominant (which achieves this through its major 3rd moving up), *the diminished chord achieves it with its root.*

The following table shows this by setting out the close relationship between 'vii dim 7' and the dominant V7 chord within the harmonic minor scale minor scale we built back in Chapter 6.

The relationship between viidim7 and V7 (key of D minor)

C♯dim⁷ (vii dim⁷)	Root	♭3	♭5	𝄫7
Notes	C♯	E	G	B♭
A7♭9 (V7)	3	5	♭7	♭9

The diminished chord on the leading note has three notes in common with the dominant seventh of the same key, with *both* chords containing the leading note, which guarantees a strong pull towards the tonic (in this case D minor).[16] It's a powerful relationship with the only effective difference between the two chords being the chord tone which effects the resolution into the root of the tonic: the 3rd in the case of V, *and the root in the case of vii dim.*

In this way, the C♯dim can be seen to be a tense reincarnation of an *A7♭9 without a root* (as we no longer need it); and therefore an effective *substitute* for any dominant V7 chord.[17]

A glance back at 'S.O.S' helps us appreciate the substitution potential between vii dim 7 and V7 in a song context. For clearly we would not have questioned a basic progression that unfolded Dm-A7-Dm, with any ♭9 dissonance merely adding some poignancy (especially given the lyrical theme of the song).

With even this much theory under our belt we can now view the diminished chord as a 'surrogate' dominant, even when taking it out of its harmonic minor habitat. For we will be finding it employed by The Beatles in many *major* key settings, in places where either a primary, or a secondary, dominant seventh might otherwise have prevailed. In every case, we will be able to understand it as a chord whose main function is to resolve just like the vii dim chord in 'S.O.S'.

[16] For a rare contemporary example of a textbook vii dim 7-to-i cadence listen to Kelly Osbourne's 'More Than Life Itself' (2002), where the melody of the opening line 'but you *always are to me*' reinforces the harmony as a spine-tingling B♯ dim 7 rises to the C♯m tonic (at 0.31).

[17] It does not matter that we no longer have our favourite root movement of V-I (or V-i). The C♯ note (the root of vii dim which crucially equates to the 3rd of the 'phantom' V) is now the driving force behind the resolution.

The symmetry of Diminished and its inversions

The only remaining essential piece of theory which The Beatles force us to face relates back to the symmetry of the diminished chord. For this feature directly explains the mysterious, chameleon-like way that *the chord can be named after any one of the four notes in its structure*. This is the final concept that prepares us for every eventuality.

Because of the location of its root a semitone away from its target, the C♯ dim was easy to conceive as a chord resolving to D minor. However, the fact is that *a diminished chord rooted on any of the other notes in its structure would have functioned in just the same way*. Hence when substituting for the virtual A7 in 'S.O.S', Abba could have happily used E dim, G dim, or B♭ dim instead of (or as well as) the C♯ dim that we find in this song. While each of them have their own timbre, texture and indeed bass note movement, they would each achieve the same resolution as the formal vii dim 7 because of our earlier rule: *a diminished chord is acting as substitute dominant when (any) one of its four constituent notes is the leading note of the target chord.*

This feature is due, in turn, to the symmetry of the structure, which ensures that each of them is an *inversion of the same chord*. The fact that a diminished chord is comprised of ascending minor thirds means that whichever note in the chord you chose to call the root (and build your ♭3, ♭5, ♭♭7 tones with reference to) means that you end up with the same collection of notes. Try it in practice. Slide a C♯dim chord up three frets on the guitar and you have, by definition, E diminished, consisting of E, G, B♭, D♭. Rename the D♭ as its enharmonic equivalent, C♯, and you're back with the same notes of the C♯dim chord you started with!

The following chart confirms that the same four notes are present in each of these four diminished chords, with the staggered configuration showing that they are all part of a giant chain of repeating minor third intervals.[18]

	C♯	E	G	B♭
C♯dim^7	Root	♭3	♭5	♭♭7
E♮dim^7	♭♭7	Root	♭3	♭5
G♮dim^7	♭5	♭♭7	Root	♭3
B♭dim^7	♭3	♭5	♭♭7	Root

[18] The enharmonic notes that technically apply for each individual chord have not been included here.

This table should confirm that, when finding substitutes for any dominant chord, we can chose one of four diminished alternatives. When cadencing to the D minor tonic, *each of these dim chords would be functioning as a primary dominant substitute by acting as 'vii dim7 of i minor'*.

This last sentence summarises the entire discussion so far. It also encourages us to view the locations of these roots in relation to the tonic so that we can identify diminished chords that are *acting* in this way whatever their 'name'. The next table does this by showing how diminished chords built on ii, iv and ♭vi in relation to a target chord (here D) are equivalent to the 'pure' one built on vii.

Basic Formula	**ii**	**V⁷**				**I**
Basic chords in D	Em	A⁷				D
Dim substitute		'vii dim⁷ of I'				
Chord options		C♯dim	E dim	G dim	B♭dim	
Degree built on		vii	ii	iv	♭vi	

We will soon find Beatles examples of diminished chords that act as vii dim7, but built on 'ii', 'iv' and '♭vi' (in 'I Want To Tell You', 'You Won't See Me' and 'Because', respectively).

Before we look at these in detail, one early moment in The Beatles' career demonstrates how George Harrison understood implicitly the scope for exploiting this relationship between a dominant chord and its diminished substitutes.

Subbing for a I7 that cues a bridge on IV

Listen closely to the very end of Harrison's guitar solo in 'Till There Was You', at the point where the verse structure over which he has been playing moves to a bridge on the IV chord. To smooth the transition, the rhythm guitar turns the F tonic into a I dominant (just as happens in Beatles originals ranging from 'This Boy' and 'If I Fell' through to 'Hey Jude' and 'Oh! Darling'). But now, as the harmony in the rhythm guitar intensifies the F7 into an F9, George recognises the scope for some diminished activity.

Had the ♭9 appeared, F7♭9 would have equated to a *bona fide* G♭ diminished chord. But this is not a prerequisite for exploiting the scope for substitution, with George duly playing a G♭ diminished seventh chord, including all the notes of that same chord in an ascending diminished arpeggio.

'Till There Was You' : solo-to-bridge transition (1.22)

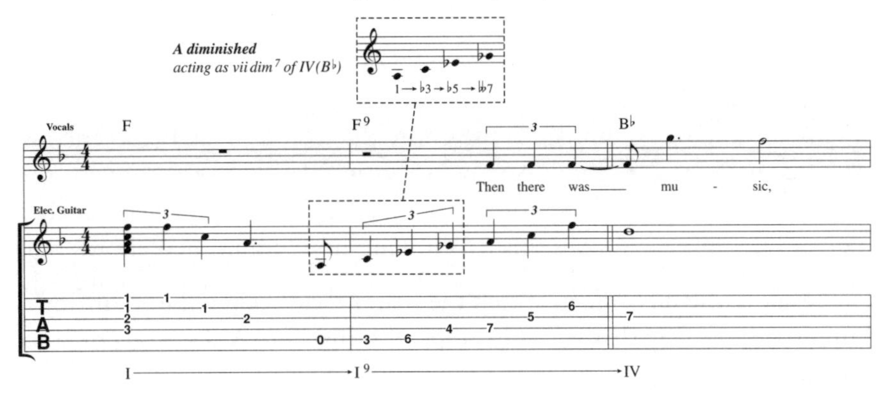

So where is the leading note effect?

George actually starts his run on an A note, before running up to C, E♭ and G♭ – and even on to the A and C in the next octave - leading us effortlessly to the bridge with the precision of a jazz master. For our theory tells us that whichever of these notes we nominate as the root of the implied diminished chord, the effect is of a substitute for the V of the impending B♭. Specifically, Harrison's diminished arpeggio functions as 'vii dim7 of IV', with that A note fulfilling the role of leading tone with respect to the next chord.

Despite being conceived well before its 1963 appearance on *With The Beatles*, this is one of George's most enlightening solos, which gives the impression of having been studiously worked out, given the deliberate chord tone targeting at every turn.[19] That final diminished run may not quite match Yngwie Malmsteen's neo-classical exploits with the same scale in the eighties, but it represents an important stylistic precursor to The Beatles' (and Harrison's in particular) later exploits in the diminished world.

One needs only look at the opening melody of 'Blue Jay Way' to see a repeat of the diminished ascent of two consecutive minor third intervals which helps to make 'there's a fog up on L.A.' the single most left-field opening Beatles melody in the catalogue. The phrase is disorientating precisely because of this climb from the root to ♭3 and on to ♭5.

[19] The solo unfolds almost identically on the various versions available – compare those on *With The Beatles*, *Live At The BBC* and the Royal Variety Performance rendition on *Anthology 1*.

'Blue Jay Way' – verse (0.21)

Notice how this melody unfolds over a C chord that includes a *major* 3rd. The result is a static tonic in which the major triad is altered from major to diminished in a way that we can compare to that A to A dim coda of 'Like Dreamers Do'.

Nevertheless, the majority of diminished Beatles activity centred not so much on creating atmospherics, but on functionally driving a song. We now return to this concept, making the distinction between a diminished chord that substitutes for the *primary* dominant and one that does so in respect of a *secondary* dominant.

Diminished for Primary dominant – the 'vii dim 7 of I'

The relationship between a diminished chord and a dominant 7♭9 was never more clearly exploited than by George Harrison on his ambitious *Revolver* outing, 'I Want To Tell You'. Here, after using E7♭9 as a striking, altered dominant V chord in the key of A, the bridge then unfolds with a B diminished chord. A look at both chords helps to appreciate the conceptual unity, starting with the E7♭9 (heard here in verse 2 at 0.46–0.53) which has itself become one of the most legendary in the entire Beatles catalogue.

Here's George Harrison's revealing take on this matching musical and emotional dissonance, when quizzed by Vic Garbarini about the 'weird, jarring chord at the end of every line that mirrors the disturbed feeling of the song'.[20]

> 'I'm really pleased that you noticed that. That's an E7th with an F on top, played on the piano. I'm really proud of that as I literally invented that chord. The song was about the frustration we all feel about trying to communicate certain things with just words. I realised that the

[20] Vic Garbarini, 'When We Was Fab', *Guitar World*, January 2001, p. 200.

chords I knew at the time just didn't capture that feeling. I came up with this dissonant chord that really echoed that sense of frustration. John later borrowed it on "I Want You (She's So Heavy)": . . . "It's driving me mad"'.[21]

George succinctly confirms the eloquent interpretations proffered by writers like Laing and Riley, while reminding us that technical connections between musical and lyrical themes are not just the stuff of self-indulgent academics.[22]

As we move to the bridge, we can immediately understand the chord on the second degree of the key ahead of the A major tonic. For here B dim

[21] George goes on to say: 'To my knowledge there's only been one other song where somebody's copped that chord – "Back On The Chain Gang" by The Pretenders.' A close listen to that song reveals only the novel dissonance of an E♯ in an A7 chord (yielding A7aug) in what is a textbook altered V-I move to D minor. A standard V-chord dissonance in Latin jazz (see 'Manha De Carnaval'), E7♭9 is indeed rare in pop. Aside from Harrison's own later use in 'I Me Mine' (see Chapter 1), the author's favourite appears in the chromatic coda descent of Rick Emmett's 'Suitcase Blues', where the ♭9 in the melody reinforces the sound.

[22] Laing talks of the song's 'serene desperation' in its 'attempt at real total contact in any interpersonal context'; *The Sound Of Our Time*, pp. 128–130. Riley points out that 'the tension surrounding the exchange in the song need not rely on any rigid measurements of time'; *Tell Me Why*, p. 197.

is clearly masquerading as a virtual 'vii dim 7' on its way to I. In terms of our earlier table it is built on 'ii' in relation to the target chord.[23]

'I Want To Tell You' : bridge (0.59)

Most interesting in the overall context of the song is how the B dim reharmonises the E7♭9 that by this time has already emerged as so essential to the proceedings. The 'guts' of the B dim chord can seen as very similar, and yet the pedal effect from the B in the bass helps us focus on the flowing voice-leading in the inner harmony. Here the B dim chord supplies George's same, all-important F note within the chromatic line that descends delicately from F♯ to E.

[23] While the G♯ leading tone (to prime A) is not readily apparent, it is strongly implied, having been heard earlier in the E7♭9.

Suddenly the music now appears to reflect the bridge lyrics, pointing a way to the communication that proved so elusive to the singer in the verse. While both chords are technically highly dissonant, George makes them work for him in the context of the song by intuitively playing on the reduction of tension provided by the temporary B pedal.

Indeed, even with this brief use of the pedal tone, 'I Want To Tell You' illustrates exactly how a diminished chord can emerge without being necessarily formally planned. For unlike the pre-conceived E7♭9, the B dim here is essentially an 'accident of bass'.

The same goes for the dissonant sonority we hear in the bridge of 'You Won't See Me'.

'You Won't See Me' : Bridge (1.18)

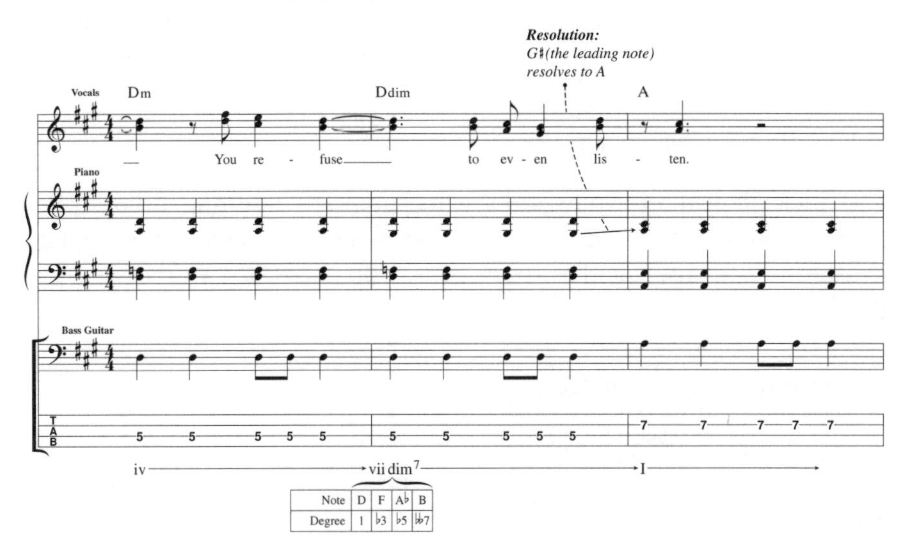

Here we have what could have been a conventional V7-I return, with E7 taking us back to the A tonic on the mid-bridge cadence (on the word 'listen'). Harrison's partial E7 shape suggests that this is indeed *his* line of thinking. And yet, just like the lyrical theme itself, McCartney's bass refuses to toe the line, hanging resolutely on the D note, awaiting a Plagal root-move back to the A tonic. It's not a straight Plagal cadence, though, as a dissection of the sonority at 1.22 reveals a B note in the vocals, which together with the G♯ in the guitar and an F in the piano creates a stack of minor third intervals above that D bass. The result is an implied D diminished chord, rooted now on iv, and yet still functioning as 'vii dim 7 of I' as the G♯ slides into the subsequent A chord.

Diminished for Secondary Dom: 'vii dim 7 of ii, iii and vi'

It's not just primary dominants that diminished chords can substitute for. Wherever a leading note is in action a diminished chord can function as a dominant substitute – hence secondary dominants can also come in for this slick treatment. 'Till There Was You' gave us an early taste of I7 which qualifies as a 'sec dom', though more familiar within our framework are the II7, III7 and VI7 that we encountered in their basic incarnations in Chapter 4.

The Beatles engineered diminished substitutes for each of these, too, with the underlying intention in each case being to create a smooth ascending chromatic line between two diatonic chords.

♯i dim – or the 'vii dim 7 of ii'

Let's kick off at the most logical starting point, by inserting a diminished chord in the 'gap' between I and ii. Conveniently, we need only refer back to the opening bars of the early cover 'Till There Was You' to see The Beatles delivering precisely this:

'Till There Was You' : verse (0.07).

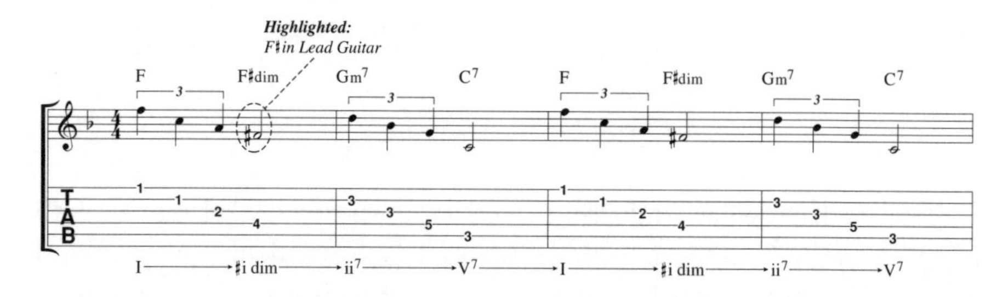

We can immediately reveal this four-chord sequence to be nothing more than a thinly disguised variation on one of the most popular of all Four-Chord Turnarounds. The I-ii and V are evident enough, leaving our spotlighted F♯ dim (at 0.10) to be unmasked as a deputy for a simple VI7 chord. The leading note? Fairly obviously, it's the F♯ itself that moves up a semitone directly into the root of the next chord, confirming the function as now: 'vii dim 7 of ii' ('seven diminished of two').[24]

To tie up any loose ends the following table confirms the substitution in action, showing us again how the diminished chord functions as a virtual altered dominant 7th chord without its root.

How #i dim7 substitutes for VI7♭9

F♯dim	Root	♭3	♭5	♭♭7
Notes	F♯	A	C	E♭
D7♭9	3	5	♭7	♭9

This same ♯i dim7 has proved a popular linking tool, dating from the Tin Pan Alley era, with such Four-Chord Turnaround progressions fundamental to the verses of 'Stormy Weather' and 'It's Only A Paper Moon', and also to the turnarounds of songs ranging from 'White Christmas' to 'I'm Going To Sit Write Down And Write Myself A Letter'.[25] Indeed, one could speculate that, given its distinctive jazz and show tune heritage, The Beatles deliberately avoided repeating this run in their originals.[26]

Nevertheless, check out Harrison's 'My Sweet Lord' for an alternative

'My Sweet Lord' (verse development)

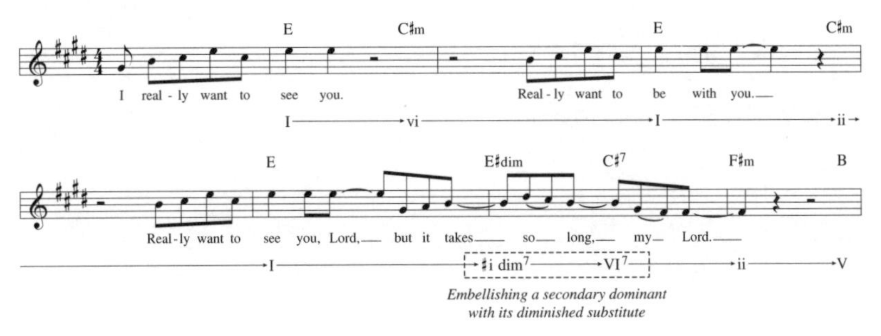

Embellishing a secondary dominant with its diminished substitute

[24] As with the 'plain' secondary dominants, contemporary theory regularly labels these diminished substitutes according to their function with respect to the chord to which they resolve. See *Harmony & Theory* by Musicians Institute teachers, Keith Wyatt and Carl Schroeder, p. 122.

[25] Citron goes so far as to term both this 'I-♯idim-ii-V7' and the 'I-idim-ii-V' 'passing' alternative (that we saw in 'Sheik Of Araby') as 'The Diminished Cliché', adding: 'These four chords work so strongly together that they make the strongest dissonance seem right'; *Songwriting*, p. 246.

[26] Perhaps as a result of its nostalgic legacy this is one musical move that has come to be regarded as 'dated' in pop. Or was it a complete coincidence that when The New Seekers adopted it in their April 1973 song, 'Nevertheless' (E-F dim-F♯m-B7), they failed to repeat the Top 20 success of their previous six singles?

look at a ♯i dim substitution for VI7 on its way to ii. Though, rather than a straight replacement, here is an example of embellishing a secondary dominant with its diminished substitute.

Here George wants to return from this E major tonic to the song's signature ii-V move, to start the next verse. But rather than a predictable *direct* jump to VI7 to cue F♯m, he goes via E♯ dim, greatly enhancing the harmonic interest and appropriately delaying the arrival on VI7 over the line, 'it takes so long my Lord'.

'Blackbird' – Paul's diminished flight of fancy

The Beatles certainly fashioned a whole range of diminished links between diatonic members using the same principle of substitution. And never more effectively than on the *White Album*, with McCartney's delicately fingerpicked 'Blackbird', a song that represents a great case study of the potential of the diminished chord in modest folky surroundings.

Here two intervening diminished chords act to turn what is basically a simple IV-V-vi diatonic run into an inexorable five-semitone ascent that beautifully represents the flight of the blackbird itself.

'Blackbird': verse (0.04)

Having moved to the subdominant this bird keeps on going, ignoring the chance to return to the tonic 'nest' from both IV and V. The driving force behind this tension-inducing ascent can be seen to be the diminished substitutes that stand in for the two other secondary dominants II7 and III7, as follows:

1) C♯ dim substitutes for A7 on its way to the D major by acting as 'vii dim7 of V'.
2) D♯ dim substitutes for B7 on its way to the Em chord by acting as 'vii dim7 of vi'.

Again we don't need a full chord to feel the power of diminished, the root movement – harmonised with some serious tritone action - says it all.

To appreciate the delicacy of the chromatic line at work here, play the same progression instead with the basic secondary dominants (i.e., C-A7-D-B7-Em). The sequence still works, but sounds comparatively clumsy, demonstrating the sublime effect of diminished voice-leading in the hands of a skilful songwriter.

If that wasn't enough, a diminished chord reappears on ♯iv dim – but now as a *passing* chord during the descent from the skies, over the line 'all your life'. It's so simple to slide between V and IV *directly*, that pop and rock songs typically don't bother with an elaborate two-stage process, but McCartney fully captures this classical sound as an embellishment to the progression.[27]

While such extended, diminished runs provide for a jazzy or quasi-classical sound, they can nevertheless be seen in a variety of diverse settings. Famous examples in pop and rock include David Bowie's 'Life On Mars', which is worth a look for the way it starts a 'Blackbird'-style run, but this time from the tonic. In doing so it takes in both ♯i dim and ♯ii dim – the latter substituting for VII7 on its way to iii.[28] It's no surprise (especially in the context of the lyrical theme!) that the listener again enjoys a feeling of inexorable ascent as Mick Ronson's guitar melody heads for the stars in the memorable instrumental 'link'.

It's also worth mentioning that while using a straight III7 to prime a relative minor is standard enough, the ♯v diminished alternative is surprisingly rare. Nevertheless, the subtle power of the leading note in the bass on this scale degree has been exploited in various ways in pop over the

[27] There is no leading note effect this time, only a chromatic descent of the roots from V through what is best seen as a '♭v dim' passing sonority into IV.

[28] Chromatically rising roots can support a variety of harmonised chords beyond the diminished 'filler'. Take Van Halen's outrageous seven-semitone line from tonic-to-fifth in the 'Panama' bridge interlude, which unfolds: E5-F-D/F♯-G-E/G♯-A-Gm/B♭, before climaxing (suitably on 'no stoppin' now') on B ahead of a V-I chorus return to E (at 3.09).

'Life On Mars': instrumental 'link'

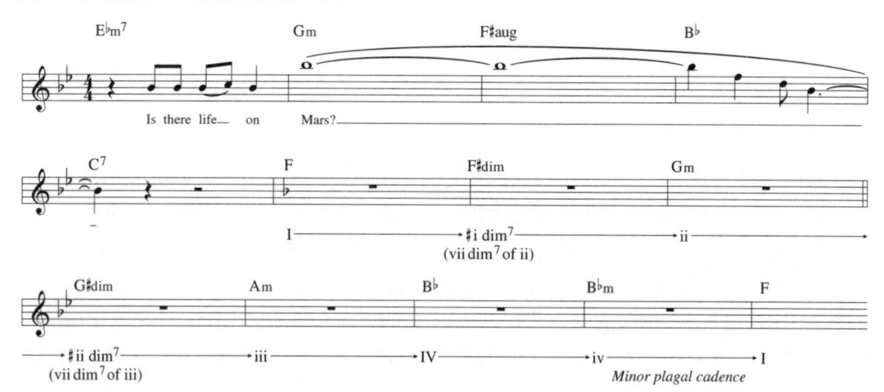

years. Right through in fact to Oasis's 'Don't Look Back In Anger'. Here (after three hearings of the delicate IV-iv minor Plagal bridge trick) Noel Gallagher's own 'V-♯v dim-vi' creates a defining moment of harmonic tension (at 0.56 in the pre-chorus).[29]

'Don't Look Back In Anger': pre-chorus (0.35)

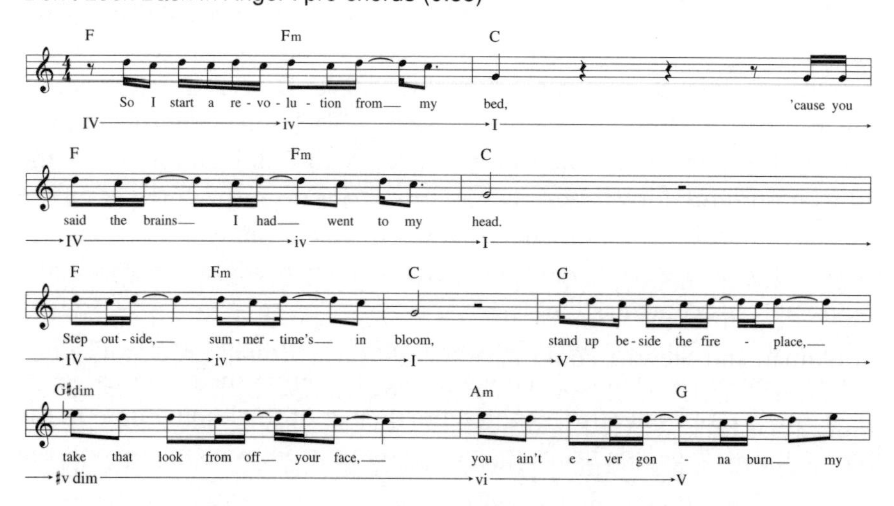

And don't let's forget a slick 'third way' of engineering a functioning move to vi which involves combining the essence of *both* a III7 (or 'V of vi') and 'vii dim7 of vi', at the same time. The secret, as Smokey

[29] Noel also highlights the same moment in the guitar solo where it brings a touch of pseudo-classical grace (3.25–3.28).

Robinson and Stevie Wonder showed us at the pivotal moment in 'The Tears Of A Clown', is to fill this same gap between V and vi with a III chord *in 1st inversion.*[30]

'The Tears Of A Clown' (pre-chorus – key of D♭)

	V	III/♯V	vi
Lyric	'..sad things known to	man but ain't	too much sadder..'
Chords	A♭	F/A	B♭m
Voice leading	5 (A♭)	♯5 (A)	6 (B♭)

The vital A bass note almost gives the feel of a diminished chord on ♯v, while the harmony benefits from an extra bit of counterpoint tension from the 5th of the impending minor chord arriving a bar early. The table also shows how the melody's voice leading (of 5-♯5-6) neatly matches the chromatic ascent in the bass line.

Meanwhile, the relationship between a secondary dominant III7 and its diminished substitute on ♯v was never better illustrated than in 10CC's classic ballad, 'I'm Not In Love', where iii seems headed for vi in standard fashion, before a ♯v dim helps it deftly on its way.

'I'm Not In Love' (verse – key of E)

	iii	♯v dim	vi
Lyric	'..It's just a	silly phase I'm	going through'
Chords	G♯m	B♯ dim	C♯m
Voice leading	5 (B)	♯5 (B♯)	6 (C♯)

The melody here rises from B to B♯, creating an intensifying leading note effect into the root of the C♯ minor chord. To harmonise this, Gouldman and Stewart could have merely turned their G♯m7 into a G♯7 and created a III7 move to the relative minor, just as John Lennon was doing as far back as 'Ask Me Why'.

But the B♯ dim substitute proves a far more delicate alternative in the context of the song, complete with a root movement that reinforces the melodic action courtesy of its role as 'vii dim of vi'.[31]

[30] When referring to 'In My Life', McCartney explains that Smokey Robinson songs like 'You Really Got A Hold On Me' and 'Tears Of A Clown' 'had really been a big influence'; Barry Miles, *Many Years From Now*, p. 277.

[31] Again we have a '5-♯5-6' ascent in terms of the essential melodic voice leading, though now the '5' (the B note on 'just') is harmonised as the ♭3rd of G♯m, rather than its root.

♯iv dim-to-V: the Imperfect cadence revisited

It is no coincidence that of all the diminished chords, ♯iv dim is the most popular in practice. For this chord both returns us from IV to I, in a passing capacity, while its *functioning* role is as a replacement for that famous II on its way to V.

Its relationship with the Cycle Of Fifths is therefore apparent in this latter role, providing us with a quick connection to the dominant and therefore also appearing in many Imperfect cadences as an alternative to the predictable II7–V7.

George Harrison used the ♯iv dim in precisely this way when setting up the hanging V in 'Old Brown Shoe'.

'Old Brown Shoe' (1.04)

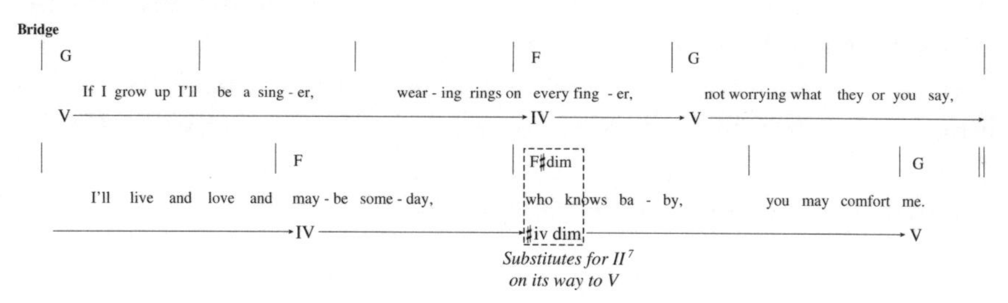

The whole bridge can be seen as deeply rooted in the clichéd rock 'n' roll bridges of the early sixties. There isn't much action beyond a direct move to IV and a re-transition to the next verse through a disguised Imperfect cadence – but what a disguise. It only takes that fleeting dark dissonance of the dim chord at 1.18 to add a touch of class. Using the same approach as before we can see how this F♯ dim stands in for the 'obvious' D7 that would have delivered the functioning F♯ note in the traditional Cycle Of Fifths framework:

How #iv dim7 substitutes for II7

F♯dim7	1	♭3	♭5	♭♭7
Notes	F♯	A	C	E♭
D7♭9	3	5	♭7	♭9

Look for the same idea among the off-the-cuff frivolity of 'You Know My Name (Look Up The Number)'. Here the vaudevillian setting and piano texture spotlights the 'old timey' roots of the move.

'You Know My Name' (Look Up The Number)': (2.42)

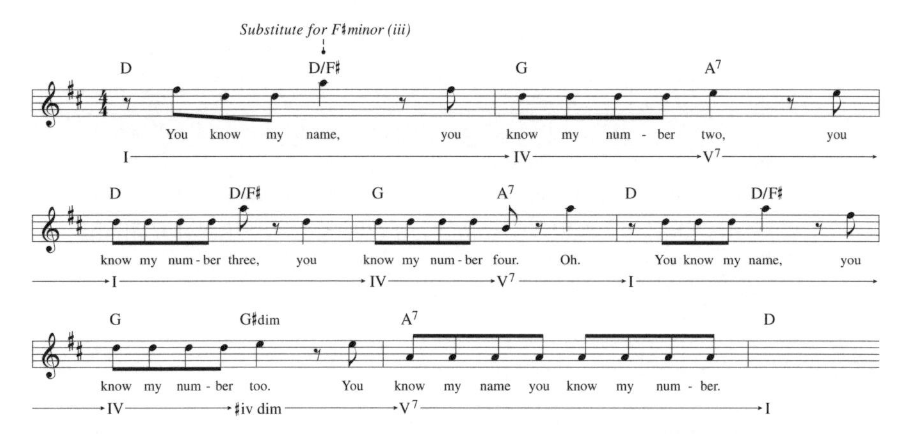

By this time the song has degenerated into a cycle that reworks the familiar Four-Chord turnaround bridge structure of 'I Feel Fine' ('I'm so glad . . .').[31] Notice how the diminished chord helps to apply the brakes: just when the cycle seems to be out of control an effortless semitone slide to G♯ (at 2.54) means that we have our substitute for II7, which can take us to the 'middle feeling'.

Given its obvious application as a replacement for II7, it's perhaps surprising that The Beatles didn't use this particular dim ploy more often in the early days. After all, their hero Buddy Holly had used ♯iv dim on its way to V by 1958, when it appeared distinctively in 'Early In The Morning'. And despite its jazzy tension, this has been a songwriting device heard periodically in pop since then – right through to The Foo Fighters' 'Next Year', in 2001.[32]

At this point we can summarise some of these 'dim for dom' substitutions (including the Bowie one) noting that they each nominally replace a primary or secondary dominant; and also that two dim chords built on the same scale degree can resolve to a different target. The important point is that, in every case, the diminished chord functions as 'vii dim 7' of the target chord *even if the leading note involved is not the root note.*

[31] The implied harmony is the same I-iii-IV-V which we hear as D-F♯m-G-A earlier in the song, though now the piano reharmonises the second chord as a D chord in 1st inversion, using the F♯ note in the bass.

[32] 'Early In The Morning' (key of F) sees B♭-B dim-C7, at 0.12. The bridge to 'Next Year' (key of G) climaxes with C-C♯ dim-D at 1.14.

'Dim for Dom' substitutions – a quick summary

Dim degree	Subs for	Song	Reference	Chords
♯i dim	VI^7	'Till There Was You'	'On a hill'	F-F♯dim-Gm
♭ii dim	I^7	'Because'	'Love is new'	D dim-F♯
ii dim	V^7	'I Want To Tell You'	'If I seem to act unkind'	Bm-B dim-A
♯ii dim	VII^7	'Life On Mars'	*Instrumental*	Gm-G♯ dim-A
iii dim	I^7	'Till There Was You'	*Solo to bridge transition*	A dim-B♭
iv dim	V^7	'You Won't See Me'	'You refuse to even listen'	Dm-D dim-A
♯iv dim	II^7	'Old Brown Shoe'	'Who knows baby'	F-F♯dim-G^7
♯v dim	III^7	'Blackbird'	'Learn to fly'	D♯dim-Em

'Michelle's dim': these are chords that go together well

Long before the brilliance of 'Blackbird' McCartney had demonstrated his intuitive understanding of both diminished substitution and the symmetrical construction of the chord itself.

By way of introduction to the following dissection, the delicious dissonance in the verse of 'Michelle' was repeatedly cited as a highlight by interviewees during the research for this book. Even several non-theoretically-minded Beatles fans felt that there was 'something going on' over these elusive few bars even if they were unable to elaborate too much on their gut reaction. Sure enough, this moment on *Rubber Soul* represents another songwriting landmark for McCartney as he puts a rather special spin on the exploitation of diminished harmony.

Notice how the song heads for the dominant (the C in bar 6) by way of a couple of diminished chords starting on D.

'Michelle': (0.08)

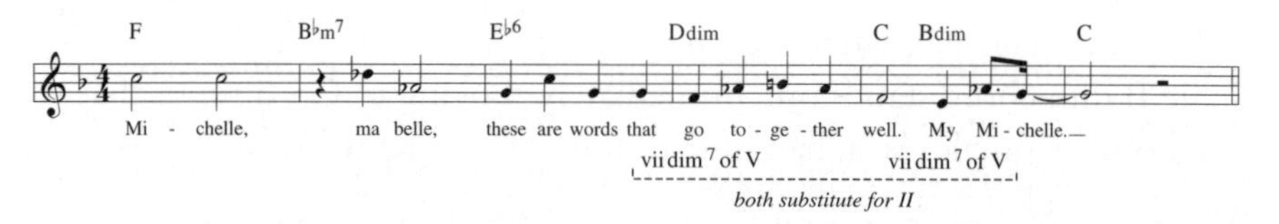

Reduced to its bare bones, Paul is merely finding an alternative device for a II7 on its way to a V. Rather than priming the primary dominant *with its own dominant*, as in a conventional Cycle Of Fifths movement, McCartney uses diminished harmony *as a 'sub for the V-of-V'*.

But this technical summary seriously short-changes the beauty of the move – not least in the context of the lyrics. For a start, the use of the chord here, in mid-verse, distances itself from 'Old Brown Shoe' and 'You Know My Name' where it appeared as an obvious cue for a simple Imperfect cadence within the song's structure.

But that's only the beginning. Better still, with the melody notes at this point unfolding in minor third intervals (two ascents and one descent on 'go to-ge-ther'), McCartney realises he can slide *different inversions of the same diminished chord* around the fretboard in tandem with these intervals, thereby *harmonising* the melodic line like a chord-melody jazz master.

The following table attempts to capture the intricacy of the move while showing how the whole manoeuvre can be appreciated as just a highly dressed-up B diminished chord that resolves with its root as a leading note (i.e., up a semitone to the primary V chord, C).

Reconciling Michelle's diminished harmony and melody

Lyric	'... go...'	'... to ...'	'... ge...'	'... ther...'	'... well...'
Guitar chord	A♭dim	B (C♭) dim	D dim	B dim	C
Melody	F (G♭♭)	A♭	B (C♭)	A♭	G
Chord tone	♭♭7th	♭♭7th	♭♭7th	♭♭7th	5th
Bass note	D		B		C
Chord name	D dim^7		B dim^7		C
Function	vii diminished 7th of V				V

The fact that the chord is first notated as D dim is purely a reflection of the D note in the bass which makes us feel that the diminished chord is built on this root. In reiterating the most important rule of this chapter: each of the diminished chords here is an inversion of the same chord and therefore *functions in the same way irrespective of which note appears in the bass.*

The little tag, 'Ma Michelle', helps to confirm this function, as here a single B dim chord stands out, immediately moving to C – a move that we can now reconcile as a hanging dominant conceptually related to the Imperfect cadence in the bridge of 'Old Brown Shoe'.

One of the most revealing Beatles rarities is McCartney's solo acoustic demo of 'Michelle'. It shows how Paul conceives the song in the key of C, using many of the same shapes that would later reappear in the *Rubber Soul* version (in the key of F with a capo at the fifth fret). It also shows us far more clearly how he actually plays the run in question using partial diminished shapes on the inner strings (D, G and B) without sounding the top note. Starting in first position he slides a three-note chord (built first on E♭) up in minor third intervals. The following table shows the implied diminished chord (now in the key of C) with the 'missing' implied note included.

'Michelle's humble origins: McCartney's solo demo in C

		F♯	**A**	**C**	**E♭**
'... go ...'	E♭dim^7	♭3	♭5	♭♭7	Root
'... to ...'	F♯dim^7	Root	♭3	♭5	♭♭7
'... geth ...'	A dim^7	♭♭7	Root	♭3	♭5
'... er ...'	F♯dim^7	Root	♭3	♭5	♭♭7

Once again, by the time he's ready to move to the V chord (here G) he's delivered all the notes of a F♯ dim chord (which acts as vii dim7 of the dominant) – the point being that, this time, there are no bass notes to confuse the labelling of the chords.

Lyric	'... go...'	'... to ...'	'... ge...'	'... ther...'	'... well...'
Guitar chord	E♭dim	F♯dim	A dim	F♯dim	G
Melody	C♯	E♭	F♯	E♭	D
Chord tone	♭♭7th	♭♭7th	♭♭7th	♭♭7th	5th
Function	vii diminished 7th of V				V

However you name 'Michelle's dim chords, or whatever key you play the song in, the diminished run works sublimely in the context of the lyrics. For, surely, the flowing dissonance of these unusual shapes brilliantly conjures the image of McCartney practising his joined-up writing as he ponders some impromptu poetry in a foreign language.

While it appeared as a bolt from the blue in 'Michelle', this type of ascending diminished chord run was by no means alien to The Beatles prior to *Rubber Soul*. In yet another revealing example of the group's sophistication in the early days, their rarely heard cover of 'September In The Rain' finds them showing off stylishly in the coda with another ear-catching diminished ascent.

Here it appears as a passing 'dim' gesture that elaborates on the 'Like Dreamers Do' coda by taking I diminished in the key of G♯ and, rather than alternating it directly with I major, sliding the same shape through all its inversions.[33]

[33] The moment comes after the final refrain. The song has modulated from G natural by this point, using a Truck Driver's 'up-a-semitone' shift.

'September In The Rain': The Beatles' first 'dim run'? (coda at 1.44)

Chord	G♯ dim	B dim	D dim	F dim	G♯
Function	i dim 7th as a passing embellishment of I				I

Far from being mere trivia, this not-so-humble moment is historically intriguing – not merely as an early variation on the 'Michelle trick', but also to what, a full decade later, would prove to be unquestionably The Beatles' most accomplished use of the diminished run in any setting: namely, as a means of modulating to another key.

Key switching with advanced 'dim' runs: 'One sweet dream'

The glittering showcase appears on *Abbey Road*, as 'You Never Give Me Your Money' rises majestically out of its drifting instrumental passage, in C

'You Never Give Me Your Money': (2.17)

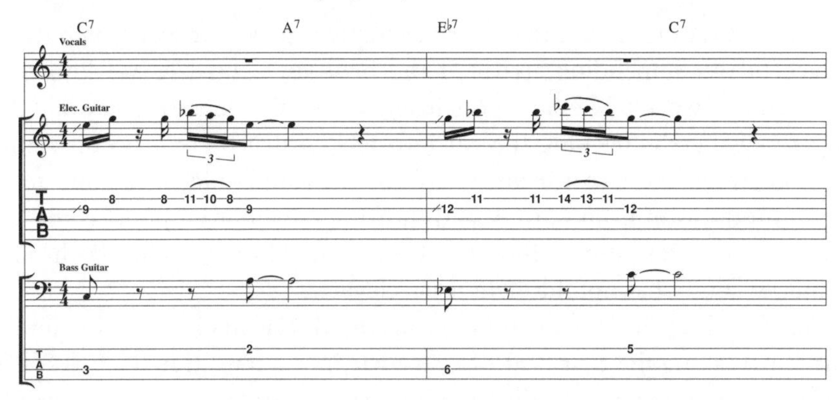

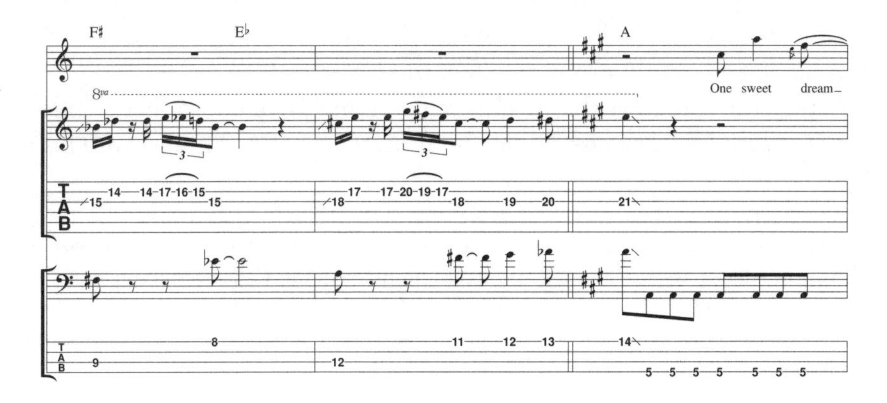

major, to deliver that uplifting 'one sweet dream' passage in A major.

Having just bemoaned that he had 'nowhere to go', McCartney set about conjuring what is arguably the most technically adept of all Beatles modulations. And, as we know from Chapter 10, that's saying something.

Here we need to combine our knowledge of modulation, diminished substitution and unfolding diminished symmetry to appreciate fully what is one of McCartney's most accomplished musical moments.

At first sight the magic is undetectable, with just some nifty root movement and dissonant guitar licks culminating in a four-step chromatic walk into A major. But look (very) closely at the following summary:

McCartney's mystery modulation from C to A major

CD timing	2.17	2.20	2.22	2.25	2.28
Bass run	C A	E♭ C	G♭ E♭	A G♭ [G G♯]	A
C dim^7	C	E♭	G♭	A	

These bass notes reveal that a powerful pivot ploy is at work, helping us to accept our impending arrival at the new key centre. As we know, all pivot chords work by being reconcilable to *both* the departing key *and* the target key, thereby tricking the ear into feeling that there is no unseemly 'join' between the two tonalities. Of course, Paul could have gone for a direct modulation from C to A with just the same brazen jump as the 'oh yeah' verse retransitions in 'She Came In Through The Bathroom Window', but what unfolds here is far cleverer.

For if we look at the bass run once again, McCartney's pivot ploy jumps out at us. Taking the first beat of every bar in the transition, C-E♭-G♭-B𝄫, the ear hears a slowly unfolding C diminished chord which can be seen as the perfect pivot chord by which to effect the key-switch.[34] For the B𝄫 is of course enharmonically equivalent to A natural, which succeeds in deftly introducing a common tone to effect the key switch.

Better still, it follows that C dim is a genuine pivot chord that is indeed *related to both keys*, because C dim is an inversion of A diminished. This in

[34] A point appreciated by academics such as Everett (*The Beatles As Musicians: Revolver Through The Anthology*, p. 262) and practising guitarists like Wolf Marshall: 'Here the two guitars join together in an aggressive unison riff that climbs in minor thirds: C-E♭-G♭-A. Notice that this riff implies a diminished scale in its melody and ascends as if climbing the degrees of a diminished arpeggio. That's conceptual unity.' *The Beatles Favourites*, Guitar Signature Licks Series, Hal Leonard, p. 77.

turn (as we know from 'Like Dreamers Do' and 'September In The Rain') is a chord that an A tonic can defer to as a dissonant embellishment *or cadence from*, given the voice leading into the crucial major 3rd and 5th.

But there's more.

The *coup de grâce* is that the other element of McCartney's bass run (i.e., the note on beat 3 of every bar) can now be seen to spell out this very A diminished chord *in root position*, delivering a harmonic vehicle that we can instantly see as qualified to take us to the key of A using the same passing mechanism. The final walk-up through the leading note (G-G♯-A) just makes doubly sure.

Destination A ... or C?: McCartney's 'double' pivot

CD timing	2.17		2.20		2.22		2.25	
Dim formula	Root		♭3		♭5		♭♭7	
C dim^7	C		E♭		G♭		A	
A dim^7		A		C		E♭		G♭

Nor should we forget the role of the lead guitar in the proceedings, for this effectively creates a third 'pivotal' element by harmonising the bass line in thirds in the course of its own diminished ascent. As the bass plays C-E♭-G♭ and A, the guitar targets the major 3^{rds} (E-G-B♭ and C♯) on the opening note of each lick, which simply slides up the neck in minor third intervals.

Dividing the run into these distinct elements helps to explain the sense of excitement as we await the formal result of this tonality jousting. With both C and A in the frame throughout, the fate is not sealed until that arrival on 'one sweet dream'.[35]

It would be a long time before pop delivered a key-switch based on a diminished premise quite as clever as this (in fact, one struggles to find something that's worthy to put alongside it). Though perhaps McCartney himself would have admired the way The Specials engineered their rather special key-switch in 'Ghost Town' – another brilliantly conceived ascending diminished run.

The chromatic diminished chords in this 1981 UK chart-topper instantly conjure the image of silent Westerns and Gold Rush fever, but

[35] Criminally overlooked by many writers, Pollack is one who raves about this move, comparing it to Gershwin's 'Rhapsody In Blue' and tracing it back to composers like Liszt: 'What prompted Macca to think of it is beyond me,' he concludes; 'Notes on ... Series' no. 13, 2000. *The 'Official' rec.music.beatles Home Page*, www.recmusicbeatles.com.

their purpose is rather more than just nostalgic effect. As with all the best diminished modulations, the final chord in the chain here proves its versatility by acting in two very distinct ways.

'Ghost Town' (dim run at 0.06 – to the verse)

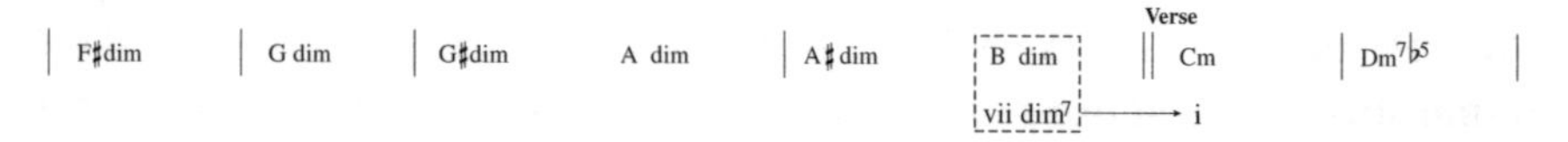

At 0.12 a B diminished chord cues the main structure of the song – a verse in C minor – by acting as 'vii dim 7 of i minor' (just as in 'S.O.S'). But when the run reappears at 1.30, The Specials expertly use this same chord in a spectacular modulation to the most remote root possible from C – the ♭V. And with this G♭ major middle eight tonality, 'Ghost Town' takes us to a location that not even The Beatles visited. Watch how the key switch is achieved:

'Ghost Town' (dim run at 1.30 – to the bridge)

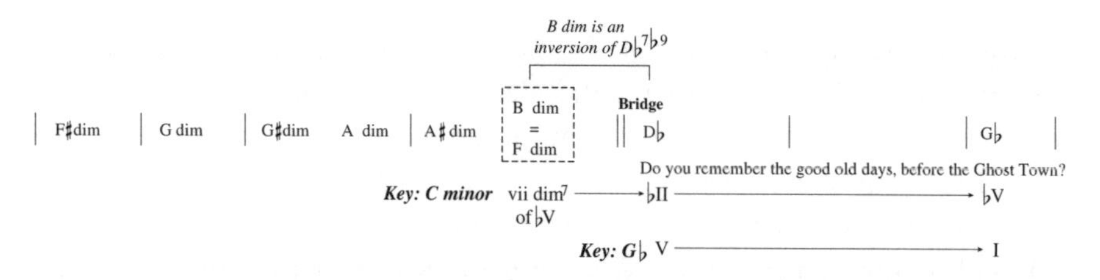

Given the 'four-way' capabilities of diminished, Jerry Dammers knows that the B dim chord can take him to not just the verse's C root, but also to either of A, E♭ and G♭, as each chord tone can work as a 'leading note vii' into these targets. He duly earmarks G♭ – but has a serious trump card to play in his ghost town gambling saloon.

Rather than resolving the F note in the B dim directly to G♭, he reconceives it as the 3rd of D♭ major – the dominant of G♭. And why not? For B dim is nothing more than an inversion of D♭7♭9. In this way he buys time, starting the bridge on the V of G♭, thereby subtly taking some of the heat out of the cadence, allowing him to depict happier times before finally landing on the new tonic on the title phrase in bar 3 of the bridge.

Having done the hard work, the retransition to C minor is child's play (and yet still utterly inspirational) as G♭ rises a semitone to spark not a clichéd Truck Driver's modulation, but the simplest of V-I cadences to take us back from that nostalgic interlude in another time zone to the harsh, modern-day reality of the Ghost Town itself.

Back with The Beatles, McCartney had to pull out all the stops with 'You Never Give Me Your Money'. For in the finest traditions of Beatles songwriting politics, the track has the unenviable task of directly following John Lennon's own magical use of the diminished chord as a tool for modulation – and more.

Let's clear the decks for the masterpiece that is 'Because'.

'Because' – Lennon's diminished showpiece

If forced to pick one Beatles track as a case study for the use of the diminished chord it would have to be Lennon's pseudo-classical composition on *Abbey Road*. Notwithstanding the subtle twists of 'Michelle' and the high drama of 'You Never Give Me Your Money', 'Because' scores for the way that its lone diminished chord, sitting proudly on the song's flat supertonic, functions compellingly in three very different ways: firstly, as an extraordinary cadential chord, and later in some rather special key-switching contexts.

Task 1 for D dim – embellishing the Phrygian cadence

Here is yet another Beatles song in which the music and lyrics are inexorably intertwined. Indeed, 'Because' arguably represents the ultimate conundrum, as the lyrical theme of bowing to the relentless power of nature and the eternal spirit is simultaneously matched and questioned by the music in equal measure. Consider the verse:

'Because'

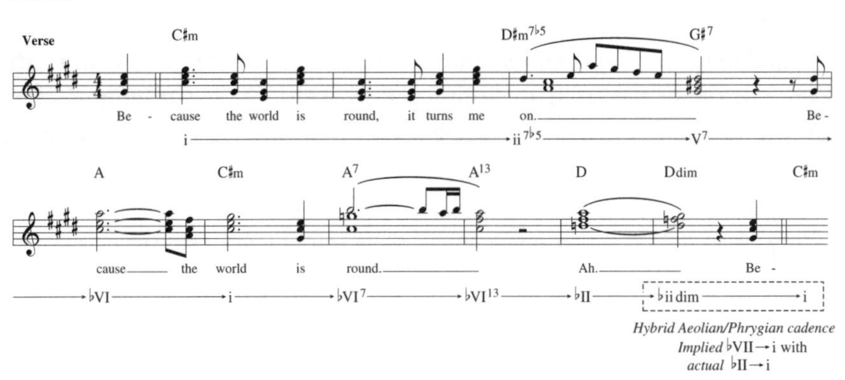

It would have been all too easy, given theses images of 'circularity', for Lennon to have based the song on an extended minor key Cycle Of Fifths structure, perhaps in the style of 'The Windmills Of Your Mind' (to use an obvious parallel) or indeed the first strains of 'You Never Give Me Your Money'.

But to Lennon's credit, 'Because' doesn't follow this predictable path. For while it does include fifth movements that mirror the slow spinning motion of the globe, so it thwarts them too, as if metaphorically throwing the song to the four winds. A detailed analysis of the build-up to the D diminished chord is demanded.

From the start, Lennon sets out his tonic before developing the most textbook of ii7♭5-V7 moves, which should return him to base in the manner of minor key cadences favoured in classical music and jazz standards. But he chooses not to return to i minor, as we'd expect and instead substitutes an A major chord (♭VI in the key of C♯ minor). As we know from 'Eleanor Rigby' and 'Glass Onion', the ♭VI chord can be alternated with i minor on its own, but it can also replace it entirely using the common tone substitution.[36]

Sure enough, the E note shared between C♯m and A forms a prominent reference point in the vocal harmony. Indeed it forms the most accessible melody line within the three-part, triple-tracked vocals, and therefore the song finds perfect, consonant support from the A chord, despite this odd tilting of the musical axis. After an alternation with the tonic the ♭VI takes on a dominant incarnation as it is now asked to support the G natural melody note that now corresponds to the ♭7th of the A7. And so it does when the melody now drops a semitone to the 6th of A, making the chord A13.[37]

At this point, a look back to 'Things We Said Today' will act as a useful reference point, because Paul's 'quite good' F to B♭ move in that song is comparable to the A to D move here. Both constitute a ♭VI to ♭II move that takes us to the outer reaches of the flat side of the Cycle Of Fifths. In both cases it's more than just a lazy way back to the tonic: rather it's a masterful

[36] The 5th degree of ♭VI corresponds to the ♭3rd of the tonic i chord. Here the E natural note is the common tone.

[37] The chord is A13 (sometimes written as 'A7 add 13'), rather than straight A6, because the ♭7 is already present. This is in contrast to the V chord of 'Can't Buy Me Love', a G6 chord where there is no ♭7 present (1,3,5,6).

chord change that allows the dissonant 4th note of the parent scale to be harmonised as the major 3rd of ♭II.[38]

At this point 'Because' departs intriguingly from 'Things We Said Today' with what we can rationalise as a stunning twist to the expected Phrygian cadence. For the next chord in the sequence at last delivers the heralded diminished chord, built mysteriously on the same ♭II degree a precarious semitone above the tonic. Including the implied 𝄫7, it consists of:

Formula	1	♭3	♭5	𝄫7
D dim7	D	F	A♭	C♭ (B)

The appearance of D dim at this point can perhaps be best understood in the context of the melody. For Lennon wants to find a way of dropping the root of the chord that deft semitone from ♭II to tonic, and also easing that F♯ melody a whole tone down into the E note – a resolution to the ♭3rd of the tonic. To do this smoothly he needs to drop the melody in two stages, i.e., via F natural, *providing of course he can find a chord that will harmonise it.*

He had two real choices. Firstly, he could have created a Super-Phrygian cadence, as we saw in 'Do You Want To Know A Secret' (i.e., following ♭II with a V chord before returning to I). A G♯7 would indeed have done the trick, with the F note creating a jazzy 13th. But (presumably to retain the close harmony of a semitone drop in the root, rather than a predictable fifth) Lennon plumps for a D dim, which fits the bill so much more satisfyingly.

Perhaps more ambitious was the decision to highlight the F natural note in this way. After all, it is the *major* 3rd of the parent key of C♯ minor, and therefore probably the last note you'd choose to stress in a delicate melody. But, in this chromatic context, and with the imminent resolution clearly signposted, our ears never question it.

We could indeed conceive this chord as an exotic altered V with no root. But this misses the point – not only does it require a degree of contortionism to view this functioning as a dominant, but it can also be appreciated as something far more subtle. The following chart shows that, far from being an implied V-i move, the essence of the voice-leading in the

[38] In 'Things We Said Today' it was the D note in the key of A minor ('so *far away*') that appeared as the major 3rd of B♭. In 'Because' it's the sustained F♯ melody note which was already harmonised as the 13th of A, now reconceived as the 3rd of D by virtue of this cool chord change.

cadence is a tonic root approached by *both* a ♭II-to-i descent *and* a flattened leading note ascent from the D dim chord's implied seventh (C♭). With all due respect to William Mann, here one could argue that The Beatles are conjuring a Phrygian and an Aeolian cadence *at the same time.*

Lennon's Aeolian/Phrygian 'hybrid' cadence?

D dim⁷ (♭ii dim)			**C♯minor (i)**	
Formula	Note	Voice leading	Note	Formula
♭♭7th	C♭	Up a whole tone **(Aeolian cadence)**	C♯	Root
♭5th	A♭	Common tone	G♯	5th
3rd	F	Down a semitone	E	♭3rd
Root	D	Down a semitone **(Phrygian cadence)**	C♯	Root

Task 2 for D Dim: the bridge modulation

While task 1 admittedly requires a degree of mental agility to appreciate its extreme novelty, the reappearance of D dim as we reconvene for the bridge can be seen as a far more familiar substitution for a dominant chord, though one that now builds on our earlier examples by prompting a delightful key switch. In contrast to 'You Never Give Me Your Money', we're now talking about a 'functional' (rather than 'passing chord') modulation.

Here's an extract that captures the transition from verse to bridge, starting with this unusual 'tag' sequence from the ♭II.

'Because' (verse 2 to bridge transition)

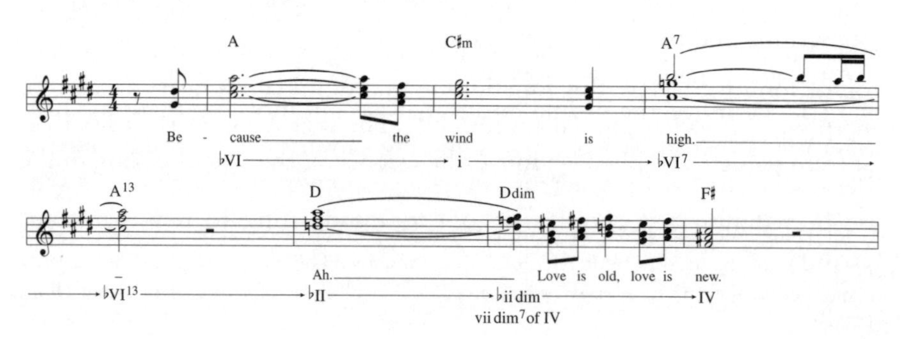

This time we're not returning to C♯ minor, yet the same D dim chord still makes perfect sense in cueing the bridge modulation. For the listener now experiences an effortless, tension-releasing functional cadence, which we can relate to our theoretical framework without too much trouble. Indeed, ironically, we need only refer back to George's Harrison's diminished vision in the solo-to-bridge transition of 'Till There Was You' to understand this move in its entirety.

Both songs ultimately feature a structural bridge on IV, where the move to the subdominant is enhanced by its leading note. This can either be achieved by turning the tonic into a dominant and going for a I7-IV move, or through a diminished substitution acting as 'vii dim7 of IV'. As Harrison's arpeggio in 'Till There Was You' demonstrates, when conceiving the diminished chord that will take you to your target, you have a choice of any inversion of 'vii dim of IV' – for they all contain the required 'active ingredient' of a leading note.

Hence, when homing in on F♯, Lennon has a choice of four diminished chords and their enharmonic equivalents: F dim, B dim, A♭ dim and, yes, his original D dim.

The 'dim for dom' in practice : the ♭9 rule

Rather than merely confirming this with theory, let's consider how Lennon may have conceived the bridge modulation here, and try to come up with a set of songwriting guidelines that will allow diminished chords to be used in a practical setting.

The most helpful of these is surely the ♭9 rule that effectively allows us to replace any dominant chord headed down a fifth (or up a fourth) with a diminished chord built on that same dominant's ♭9th degree. This may sound contorted but it is the short-cut to bringing diminished chords into songwriting and performing situations.

After all, so many songs move naturally to IV at the bridge. But instead of a I-I7-IV move, the ♭9 rule means that we can move up that lone half-step to find a effective and classy-sounding substitute. Using the bridge of 'Because' as the example, here is a quick five-point plan that rationalises the use of a diminished chord as a tool for modulating to new harmonic territory:

The ♭9 'dim for dom' substitution – step-by-step

With the aim of always relating each manoeuvre back to the simplest of principles, the stages are set out to help songwriters regard the whole process as just an exotic variation on that most standard of cadences:V7-I.

a) Choose your target chord for the bridge (F♯ major)
b) Find the dominant V7 chord that will take you there: (C♯7)
c) Intensify that same V-I move by adding a ♭9 to the V7: (C♯7♭9)
d) Substitute a 'dim' chord whose root is on that same ♭9: (D dim)
e) Resolve D diminished *directly* to F♯ to effect the modulation.

The following confirms how Lennon does just that as D dim substitutes for that virtual C♯7♭9:

D dim^7	Root	♭3	♭5	♭♭7
Notes	D	F = E♯	A♭= G♯	C♭= B
C♯$^{7♭9}$	♭9	3	5	♭7

Of course, in the case of 'Because', Lennon – having already made it to D major with that imported Phrygian ♭II – was already halfway to the ♭9 substitution. While we've already seen this type of 'dim for dom' in action, we should appreciate once again the voice-leading that takes three of the four notes in the diminished chord directly into the chord tones of the F♯ by means of a shift of a single semitone.

While the 'vii dim' mechanism is still evident through the F-F♯ root move, the bonus in this context is that we move not merely to the diatonic F♯ minor, but far more upliftingly to F♯ *major*. The sense of almost celestial rebirth is akin to a Picardy cadence, though now it's the major 3rd of F♯ (the A♯) that works its magic and reminds us that it's a powerful Beatle tradition to modulate to major at some point in the structure of a minor key song.[39]

In true Beatles style, how better to match the pivotal line of the song: 'love is old, love is new', than with this transition from an introspective minor to a fresh, optimistic major tonality?

Having taken us ethereally away in this manner, John soon returns us to the next verse in the parent minor key through G♯ for what is indeed the only conventional V-i return in the whole song.

[39] Hammond points out that the contrast is powerful for, up to that point, we have been so used to hearing the A *natural* note in each of the D♯m7♭5, A7 and D chords (where it appears as the ♭5th, root and 5th, respectively); www.beathoven.com.

The Bridge modulation – 'love is old, love is new'

D dim⁷ 'Love is old'			**F♯major** 'Love is new'	
Formula	Note	Voice leading	Note	Formula
♭♭7th	C♭	Down a semitone	A♯	3rd
♭5th	A♭	Down a whole tone	F♯	Root
3rd	**F**	**Up a semitone**	**F♯**	**Root**
Root	D	Down a semitone	C♯	5th

These two functions might seem like quite enough work for one diminished chord in a song. And perhaps even the way John Lennon saw it, it was. But is that the end of it?

Task 3 for D Dim: The secret start of the Abbey Road *medley?*

For anyone interested in the glorious descriptions and interpretations of Beatles music, Wilfrid Mellers' *Twilight Of The Gods*, with its wonderfully evocative style of music criticism, is thoroughly recommended. One of the most intriguing lines describes the sudden 'silence' that follows that final climactic vocal cluster in 'Because', a feature with which, Mellers suggests, The Beatles 'betray something like genius'. He continues:

> 'Causality is released and there is no before and no after: *because* that flat supertonic is a moment of revelation, it needs no resolution.'[40]

We have indeed been left hanging in almost excruciating suspense as the expected home of C♯ minor, which we feel should follow D Dim for a final time, fails to come to our rescue. The result is a pivotal moment of unfulfilled yearning that tears at the soul, begging for emotional closure.

Mellers was not the last to attempt to capture the moment.

'It's like finishing a story with a question', says Hammond, 'Because' 'is not always an answer', he suggests, perfectly capturing the tonal conundrum at play. And later, more cryptically but equally appropriately: '"Because" needs no why'.[41]

How indeed can we resolve (literally) The Beatles' thinking here?

[40] *Twilight Of The Gods*, p. 118.

[41] Hammond himself makes an interesting case for viewing the coda as distinct from the previous verse 'tags', identifying a formal modulation to D major as the emphasis of tonality shifts to this chord.

Certainly it was not the first time they'd left their listeners hanging awkwardly in mid-air. Nor would it be the last.[42]

Bearing in mind the track's original location on *Abbey Road* ahead of that legendary medley, could 'Because' be seen as part of a bigger picture, perhaps another of The Beatles' Grand Designs? For in an intellectual puzzle that has occupied the minds of the deepest Beatles thinkers, does that D dim chord (and melodic F natural) really linger so precariously? Or does it actually resolve satisfyingly to our ears – in the next song.

Listen again to *Abbey Road* and see how, after the celestial heights of 'Because' have been snatched from our grasp, the opening strains of 'You Never Give Me Your Money' find us miraculously, humbly, back on *terra firma*. Underlying this feeling of gentle fulfilment is our need to hear those hanging F and G♯ notes in the final bar resolve. And so they do – though not in the form of the expected C♯ minor but rather by means of the mellow A minor piano chord that follows.

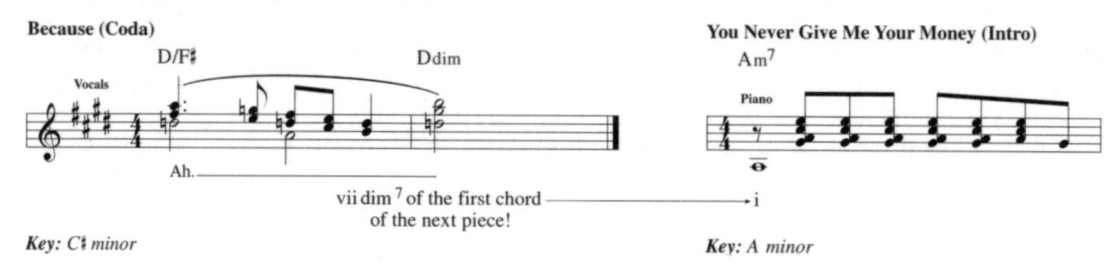

In this way, the D diminished chord can now be seen retrospectively to have conspired in another modulation by now acting as 'vii dim 7 of A minor', with the A♭ note (now enharmonically a G♯) becoming the leading note of the new tonal centre.[43]

Most intriguingly, using this 'cloak and dagger' approach to harmonic design, the famous medley on side 2 of *Abbey Road* surely begins not with 'You Never Give Me Your Money', as every Beatles fan has been led to believe, but one track earlier with 'Because'. This prompts the question whether the location of 'Because' in the final running order, ahead of that

[42] Indeed, it's part of a tradition of Beatles songs dating from at least 'Do You Want To Know A Secret' and 'Not A Second Time', through to 'And Your Bird Can Sing' and 'For No One'. Meanwhile, we saw the hanging '5th-in-the-bass' that ends 'Her Majesty' in Chapter 1.

[43] Steven Porter suggested the sonority as a pivot operating in both C♯ minor and A minor, back in 1979; *Rhythm And Harmony In The Music Of The Beatles*, p. 355. Meanwhile, Everett refers to the song's 'unresolved circular harmony' while also pointing to the closing chord as being vii dim 'of what follows'; *The Beatles As Musicians: Revolver Through The Anthology*, p. 259.

The 'Because' transition – Abbey Road's hidden key switch?

D dim⁷ (vii dim of i)			**A minor** (i minor)	
Formula	Note	Voice leading	Note	Formula
♭♭7th	C♭	Up a semitone	C	♭3rd
♭5th	*A♭*	*Up a semitone*	*A*	*Root*
3rd	F	Down a semitone	E	5th
Root	D	Down a fourth	A	Root

A minor key centre, was conceived as a true stroke of genius as a precursor to the medley itself. Or was it just stumbled upon as a musical fluke?

Then again, the haunting, vocal-only *Anthology 3* presentation, takes the song out of its album context, leaving the only resolution in the form of the studio banter ahead of 'Let It Be', with John Lennon inquiring: 'Are we supposed to giddle in the solo?'.

This interpretation of the close of 'Because' may seem unduly intricate but, at the very least, it demonstrates the versatility of any given diminished chord, which is the whole premise of this chapter. For while music history relates that the diminished chord was originally used to extend the properties of resolution that were a feature of leading note sevenths, its potential in modulation subsequently proved an eye-opener.[44]

In his famous Harvard Lecture Series, the great Leonard Bernstein explains that, because 'dim' can be viewed as any one of four different chords, so it occupies four different tonalities; which in turn means it is interchangeable between four different keys (or indeed eight given the scope for a major or minor tonality on any given tonic). If we accept the slick segue to the next track on *Abbey Road*, then 'Because' exploits two of them.[45]

'It blows my mind' sings Lennon at 1.05 in 'Because'. With its labyrinthine twists and turns, all topped off by a combination of diminished-fuelled resolutions and modulations, that's really no surprise.

[44] See Ralph Denyer, *The Guitar Handbook*, p. 128; and especially p. 139 for practical tips on modulating using the diminished chord.

[45] Jimmy Webb also quotes Bernstein's 'minimum four-way ambiguity' (*The Harvard Lectures*, p. 232, ex. 68); *Tunesmith*, p. 242. As a songwriting experiment, try out some of the other 'surprising places' that the D dim chord could have taken us to in 'Because'. Using our 'four-way' formula, a vii dim 7 built on D could take us to new tonics built on F♯ and A, D♯ and C; with the D root itself appearing as 'vi', 'iv', 'vii' and 'ii' in relation to each of these new tonics respectively.

'Because' and Beethoven – the 'Moonlight' myth

Finally, we can't leave 'Because' without briefly delving into a piece of Beatles trivia that has occupied the minds of the *intelligentsia* like none other. John Lennon may have been flummoxed by the Aeolian cadence, but he's certainly had the last laugh. For in a final twist that continues to linger long after his death, he managed to turn the tables on the musos and academics with his references to Beethoven's 'Moonlight Sonata' as an inspiration for the chord progression of 'Because'.

It's nothing new for Beatles fans and critics to take every word uttered by any of the group as gospel – and understandable when it comes to the near-void of meaty songwriting quotes. Nevertheless, a virtual pantomime has unfolded with regard to the provenance of 'Because' as, one by one, a succession of writers down the years began taking literally off-the-cuff Lennon comments such as:

> 'Yoko was playing some classical music one day. I don't know whether it was Beethoven or something, and I said "Give me those chords. Play that backwards" and I wrote "Because" on top of it. It was "Moonlight Sonata" backwards.'[46]

In the finest traditions of Beatlology, this and other such suitably vague references from both John and Yoko tied the academics up in knots.

The speculation began in earnest in 1973 with Wilfrid Mellers:

> 'He [Lennon] says it's the Moonlight Sonata backwards though I don't hear that.'[47]

It continued through Lewisohn:

> 'John in clearly inspirational mood, reversed the chords, added some simple but eloquent lyrics and the song was written.'[48]

And on through to Ian MacDonald:

> 'Lennon erroneously claimed that "Because" is based on playing Beethoven's chords in reverse.'[49]

[46] Keith Badman, *The Beatles – Off The Record*, p. 471.
[47] *Twilight Of The Gods*, p. 116.
[48] *The Complete Beatles Recording Sessions*, p. 184.
[49] *Revolution In The Head*, p. 320.

The idea that John and Yoko had really gone to the end of the sheet music and made their way to the front like a Japanese book certainly 'makes good copy', to paraphrase O'Grady, who also picked up the gauntlet in 1983 and concluded that the progression 'bears only a small resemblance'.[50]

Nevertheless, with Pete Waterman still making the connection in 2002, the similarities are worth mentioning if only to help settle the odd pub debate.[51]

Mellers himself highlights how 'the sudden shift to the flat supertonic, is, in the Lennon and Beethoven examples, unmistakable'; while O'Grady also refers to 'especially the use of the Neapolitan or ♭II chord', while noting 'the second phrase moves to the major submediant (a comparable event occurring in Beethoven's work as well) . . .'

Meanwhile, Everett goes further in his analysis, and includes a reference to the diminished chord, whose hieroglyphic label and function should be familiar.

> 'The song is Lennon's recomposition of the first movement of Beethoven's "Moonlight" Sonata and there are a few points of similarity between the song and its model. Both arpeggiate triads and seventh chords in C♯ minor in the baritone range of a keyboard instrument at a slow tempo, move through the submediant to ♭II and approach vii dim7/IV via a common tone.'[52]

Still, these observations on the Beethoven/'Because' riddle pale in comparison to the wonderful, self-styled 'rambling four-part examination' conducted by 'Beathoven' in cyberspace. No stone is left unturned as visitors to the site are treated to a dissection of everything from the title, lyrics and arpeggio sequence to an appreciation of the subtle tonality ploys at work and an idiosyncratic look at how they compare to other Beatles works.

The highlight is a patient exercise in reversing the 'Moonlight' sequence, picking out the common chords. Without giving the game away for inquisitive readers in need of some serious further reading, we can focus on Hammond's own counter-argument, which concedes that many of the chord changes (e.g., ii7♭5–V7), and shifts from subdominant to dominant, are, of course, standard fare for any diatonic progression in the minor tonality.

[50] *The Beatles: A Musical Evolution*, p. 161.

[51] '"Because" was taken from Beethoven's *Moonlight* Sonata'; Waterman quoted in 'Pop Go The Great Composers', *BBC Music*, Vol. 12 No.3, p.35.

[52] Everett, *The Beatles As Musicians: Revolver Through The Anthology*, pp. 259–260.

It seems that because 'Because' is in the same key as the 'Moonlight' (the only Beatles song in C♯ minor) and instantly exudes clichéd classical imagery for pop listeners from the use of the harpsichord, the comparisons are inevitable.

But are they musically that close? Even the vagaries of the distinctive triplet line in both pieces represents an important point of difference rather than one of similarity. Ultimately, by far the most important piece of shared novelty is that ultra-smooth ♭VI-♭II move that we first saw The Beatles use back on 'Things We Said Today'. As Pollack points out, this occurs as early as the third measure of the 'Moonlight'. Here's a transcription and chord chart that confirms this:

Beethoven's 'Moonlight Sonata': Op.27, No. 2

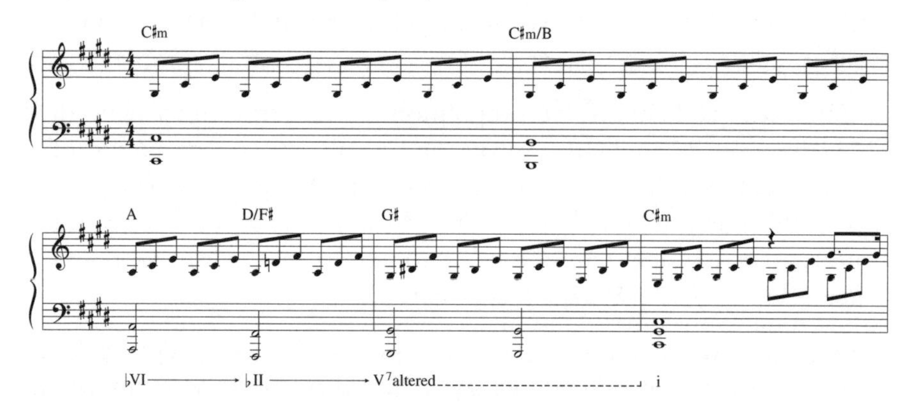

Adagio sostenuto – summary of bars 1–5

Bar	1	2	3		4	5
Chord	C♯m	C♯m	A	D	G♯7♭9	C♯m
Formula	i	i	♭VI	♭II	V7♭9	i
Bass	C♯	B	A	F♯	G♯	C♯
Bass run	1	♭7	♭6	4	5	1

And that's about as close as we can get. There's the move alright, but remember that all this is looking at things *forwards* rather than backwards, with the ♭VI-♭II manoeuvre matching rather than reversing Beethoven's harmony. To turn it on its head requires us even more exotically to back-track the same Phrygian-esque harmony and return in fourths from ♭II to ♭VI.

Not a Beatles move for sure, but with tongue firmly in cheek we can put forward one special candidate from the annals of pop, with Abba's 'Money Money Money' confirming their classical European influences in a rather special moment. No harpsichords or haunting arpeggios this time, but the Swedish popsters nevertheless use the single most important backwards chord change that Lennon 'should' have nicked from Beethoven.

'Money Money Money' (pre-chorus)

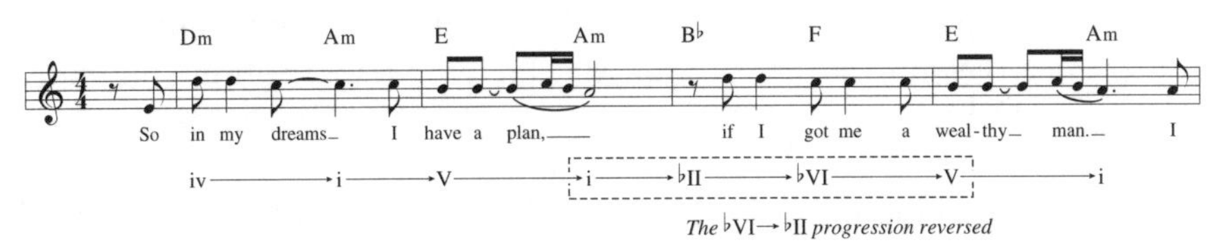

Meanwhile, as much as Lennon's (and Beethoven's) ♭VI-♭II move emerges as a point of similarity, so other fundamental features stand out as essentially different. Clearly the descending bass run of 'The Moonlight', which falls romantically from the tonic in formulaic diatonic fashion, is in stark contrast to Lennon's opening gambit of *ascending* to the second degree.

Then there's the marked discrepancy in the way the two pieces cadence to the tonic with John's diminished chord – so often a Beethoven trademark – emerging here as another point of contrast. For all the elaborate arpeggios in bar 4 of 'The Moonlight', which embellish the harmony with some slick alterations and suspensions, Beethoven's ploy is a conventional V-i return to base through an altered G♯7.[53]

The final arpeggio on beat 4 of bar 4 could, at a stretch, be viewed as F♯ dim whose B♯ note implies 'vii dim 7' of the following C♯ minor tonic. However, in the context of an unyielding and emphatic G♯ in the bass, it is effectively a dominant G♯7 sonority taking us home.[54]

Yet the great novelty of the verse cadence of 'Because' is precisely that it doesn't do this, with John's Aeolian/Phrygian 'combo cadence' eschewing the V-i root movement in favour of that 'crushed diminished' semitone slide.

[53] The A note in bar 4 creates a fleeting G♯7♭9 alteration, while the C♯ appears as a 'sus 4' in place of the major 3rd, B♯.

[54] The notes spell out 1-3-5-♭7 of the G♯7, albeit in the sequence: 1-♭7-3-5.

Finally, at the risk of falling into precisely the same trap that Lennon laid so glaringly for us, let's summarise, in a nutshell, the entire 69-bar 'Moonlight'.[55]

Part 1	Bar numbers	No. of bars	Main Harmony
Introduction	1 - 5	5	C♯ minor
Phrase 1	5 - 10	5	C♯minor, E major, E minor
Phrase 2	10 - 15	5	E minor, B minor
Phrase 3	15 - 23	8	B major (V of E minor) , F♯minor
Phrase 4	23 - 28	5	F♯minor, G♯(V of C♯minor)
V - pedal	28 - 41	14	G♯(V of C♯minor)
Part 2	42 - 69	28	C♯ minor (extended i minor)

For those looking to go further, the table reveals that there are indeed strikingly few other points of harmonic common ground between the two works – whichever way up you hold up the manuscript paper. As Beethoven expert Tim Jones describes, the 'Moonlight' modulates freely throughout part 1, progressing inexorably through the Cycle Of Fifths from E major and E minor to G♯ (the dominant of C♯ minor).[55] Moreover, further resolutions through Perfect cadences in these tonalities can be seen in bars 5, 9, 15 and 23.

Perhaps most interesting is Phrase 4, which stands out for its root movement from subdominant to dominant, and begs comparison with the bridge of 'Because'.[57] Yet surely the reason that this is a defining moment in Lennon's work is that we modulate to the cool air of F♯ *major* rather than its parallel minor.[58]

But enough, already. For with every comment, we musos just dig ourselves into a deeper hole. We can almost hear Lennon laughing. For as Ian Hammond himself astutely remarks when restoring some sanity to the whole Beatles 'Moonlight Myth':

[55] Adapted from *Beethoven: The 'Moonlight' And Other Sonatas, Op.27 and Op.31* by Timothy Jones.

[56] In conversation with the author, summer 2000.

[57] See Beathoven as he describes how: 'Ludwig repeats his tattoo theme in F sharp minor followed by a 14-bar peroration over a G sharp bass (bar 28). Both pieces use the same game plan' (www.beathoven.com).

[58] Further anorak observations could include: Bar 12: a 'local ♭II', namely a C major that resolves Phrygian cadence-style down to Bm. Bar 20-21: the A (the submediant relative to C♯ minor) which moves to the G natural, itself representing a Neapolitan ♭II in relation to the F♯ minor to which it then resolves.

'"Backwards" was a code word Lennon used when saying he had adapted someone else's music – just as he described any assistance on a song as "helping out with the middle eight".'

That just leaves the last word to Beethoven himself who, history relates, is known to have exclaimed in moments of exasperation: 'Everyone always talks about the C♯ minor Sonata!'.[59]

Especially, Ludwig, when they're talking about The Beatles.

[59] Timothy Jones, *Beethoven: The 'Moonlight' And Other Sonatas, Op.27 and Op.31*; Preface ix.

TWELVE

Tritone Substitution and Other Mystery Chords

'If I found a new chord, I'd write a song around it . . . sometimes the chords got to be an obsession.' – John Lennon[1]

Long before George Harrison strummed his way to immortality with the opening crash of 'A Hard Day's Night', The Beatles appreciated the power of a carefully chosen chord. Far from gradually stumbling across new sounds as part of their widely believed 'musical maturation' in the mid-sixties, The Beatles' impressive early facility with a range of exotic chords is a fascinating area of study.

A cursory listen to the first batch of primitive recordings confirms that even by 1963, The Beatles were well acquainted with a whole spectrum of harmonic colours – the added 6th of 'Can't Buy Me Love', the dominant 9th of 'This Boy', the augmented thrill of 'Please Please Me', the slick diminished of 'It Won't Be Long', and the jazzy major 7th of 'Till There Was You', are just for starters.

Even the dodgy sound quality of the previous rough demos can't hide the ear-catching sophistication of the added 9th in the intro to 'Cry For A Shadow', the ultra-jazzy dominant 7♯5 that George uses in 'The Sheik Of Araby', the diminished ornamentation in 'Like Dreamers Do' and the all-purpose rock 'n' roll 6/9 closer delivered in 'Hello Little Girl'.

While a summary is given in Appendix 2 for readers interested in broadening their own repertoire, this chapter probes deeper into the wonderful world of Beatles chords. In particular we will visit a select range

1 'How To Write A Hit', *Melody Maker*, 1st February 1964, p. 11.

of highlights from the catalogue where either an exotic chord is involved or, equally, where a familiar construction manages to hit the spot through *acting* in an unusual way.

There's no better place to start than with 'The Mystery Of The Gretty Chord', a latter-day piece of Beatles trivia that has intrigued musos in the nineties despite its origins, which date back to the pre-Beatle Liverpool scene of the late fifties.

The Gretty Chord Mystery – from Whitechapel to the World Wide Web

John, Paul and George would no doubt have measured their progress as budding guitarists with the ritual passing of every new shape, with that now infamous trek across Liverpool in search of the B7 chord just one landmark in a wide-eyed quest for new sounds.

The painstaking process of the formative years is well illustrated by images of Harrison doodling chord shapes on his school exercise book, and McCartney's father Jim encouraging the young Paul to copy his impromptu sounds at the living room piano on a £15 cello guitar with violin holes. 'Come on, Paul. Now try this one!' was how the McCartneys' family friend, Olive Johnson, captured the scene at Forthlin Road in Philip Norman's definitive biography.[2]

We're told it was slow going at first, but when Paul re-strung the guitar as a left-hander the penny dropped and he was 'lost' in his new world as 'the guitar became a passion overruling all else in his life'.[3]

It was the same story in nearby Menlove Avenue as John Lennon, nurturing his Elvis Presley fixation from early 1956, absorbed every musical titbit from his mother. Friends would drop round only to find 'John oblivious to time or the soreness of finger-ends split by the steel strings'. One of them, Nigel Whalley remembers: 'He'd sit on his bed, just strumming . . . strumming the banjo chords Julia had shown him and singing any words that came into his head.'[4]

As well as their parents, and an assortment of 'Play In A Day' tutors, the youngsters had another valuable musical source that would fire their imagination – a certain Jim Gretty, the showroom manager at Hessy's, the

[2] Philip Norman, *Shout! The True Story Of The Beatles*, p. 28.

[3] 'He played the guitar in his bath, even while sitting on the lavatory,' Norman assures us (p. 28).

[4] *Ibid.*, p. 22.

music shop in Whitechapel, central Liverpool. Norman describes how Gretty was selling guitars at a rate of one a minute, just as quick as the van ferrying them up from the Soho markets in London could deliver them. More importantly as far as the young Lennon, McCartney and Harrison were concerned, Gretty was a guitarist 'western style', and each week held a beginners class in an upstairs room, chalking huge elementary chord-shapes on the wall.[5]

Little did he know that the precise construction of one of those shapes, would – 40 years later – create such confusion and intrigue, sparking a lengthy debate on The Beatles Internet newsgroup and prompting one website to devote a special page requesting solutions to 'The Riddle Of The Gretty Chord'.[6]

As with Mann's Aeolian cadence and John's 'backwards' Moonlight Sonata, the story stems from an innocuous comment that could have been nipped in the bud with just a few words of elaboration. This time it was McCartney's turn to taunt us with a musical mindbender as he sat down to reminisce with Barry Miles about his crafting of 'Michelle':

> 'There's a very jazzy chord in it – "Michelle ma *belle"*. That second chord. That was a chord we used twice in The Beatles: once to end George's solo in "Till There Was You" and again when I used it in this. It was a chord shown to us by Jim Gretty who worked behind the counter at Frank Hessey's where we used to buy our instruments on the "never never" in Liverpool. So Jim Gretty showed us this one great ham-fisted jazz chord, bloody hell! George and I learned it off him . . .'[7]

So just what was 'The Gretty Chord' that Paul dangles so tantalisingly before our eyes? For a start, the chord in question is actually first heard *before* the words 'ma belle' (not on the second word as Paul makes a point of emphasizing). Far more importantly, delve into virtually any transcription of 'Michelle' to see the second chord of the verse described as a fairly routine B♭ minor 7th. Hardly the 'great ham-fisted jazz chord' we'd been led to expect.

[5] *Ibid.*, p. 22.

[6] See Ian Hammond's 1999 challenge to the cyberspace guitar community at www.beathoven.com.

[7] McCartney quoted in Miles, *Many Years From Now*, p. 274. Note that the spelling of the name of the shop is different to that suggested by Norman.

Moreover, if we turn to 'Till There Was You' we find that 'the chord that ends George's solo' creates its own confusion. Without being too pedantic the final chord of the solo is a 5th-string-root F dominant 9th (from Lennon's rhythm guitar – strummed three times in half-note triplets at 1.24-1.25), over which George plays the intricate ascending A diminished arpeggio that we dissected in the last chapter. Even *George*'s last chord is the immediately preceding F major (which he strums and briefly arpeggiates downwards at 1.23) that acts as the resolving tonic before this exotic preparation for the bridge.

However, it doesn't require too much initiative to backtrack one further bar to find the highlight of the solo: George's *penultimate* chord. Here we find a strikingly lush, dissonant G♭7♯9 that hangs in splendid isolation (at 1.21). Meanwhile, on the *Live At The BBC* version the chord gets the full treatment, fluttering in and out of tune (at 1.22) courtesy of George's tasteful use of the vibrato bar. Whether on the studio recordings or the live *Anthology* footage, the novelty of this chord is unmistakable.[8]

'Till There Was You' (solo at 1.10)

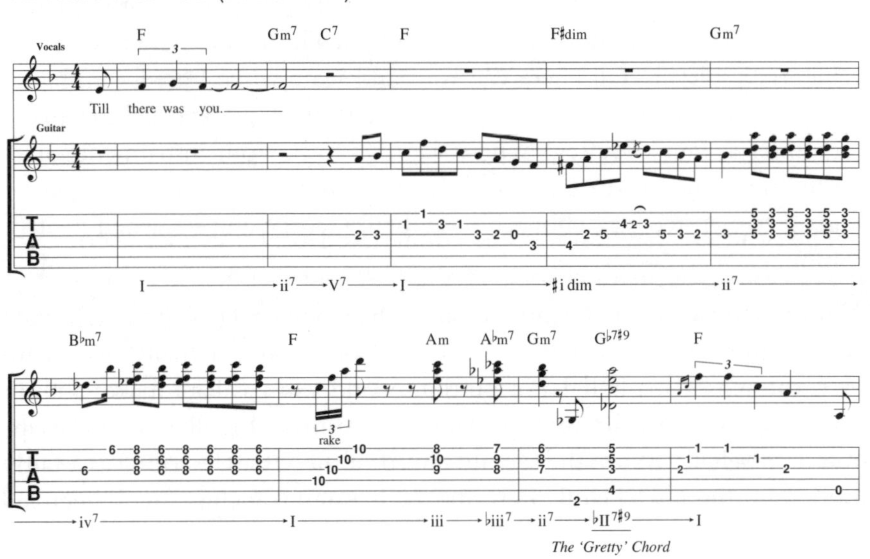

This was indeed a highly rare chord for pop music of the time. Its 'ham-fisted' nature arises not merely from the full barre-chord fingering

[8] See footage of the complete song on *Anthology*, video 2.

(across six strings and four frets), but because of its range (spanning a minor third interval above the standard two octaves for this type of position on the guitar).

More to the point, McCartney's description surely relates to its inherent *sound*, created by the clash of the basic major third of the chord against the ♯9 (A, enharmonically equivalent to B double flat). Put another way, the single defining characteristic of the chord is the presence of both the major and minor thirds (B flat and B double flat, respectively).

But if this is The Gretty Chord, then where is it in 'Michelle'? The answer is the second chord of the verse, just as McCartney says. The guitar chord on the *Rubber Soul* version is a B♭7♯9, which follows the verse's opening F major chord, with the root of the B♭ chord now up at the 6th fret of the guitar.

The Gretty chord – unmasked

		'Till There Was You'		'Michelle'	
String	**Formula**	**Notes**	**Fret**	**Notes**	**Fret**
1st	♯9th	A	5	C♯	9
2nd	♭7th	F♭	5	A♭	9
3rd	3rd	B♭	3	D	7
4th	x[9]	x	x	x	x
5th	5th	D♭	4	F	8
6th	Root	G♭	2	B♭	6

The confusion has however been understandable for various reasons, not least because the melody note of the first word of 'ma belle' is a D♭, a delicate ♭3 relative to the prevailing B♭ root which *in itself* does indeed imply a B♭ *minor* chord (B♭, D♭, E♭). However, this is not inconsistent with McCartney's description. It is merely another example of the false relations that are a feature of the *Rubber Soul* album, namely a clash of a *melodic* ♭3rd over a *harmonic* natural 3rd. It's a slice of stylistic tension that (melodically) dates from the blues, while here the juxtaposition occurs *within the chord itself*.

Appreciation of the chord is not aided by the rhythm guitar being so low in the mix, making the offending D natural easy to miss. But it can nevertheless be heard on close inspection, especially in the last verse after

[9] The 4th string is traditionally muted in this shape, hence the 'x'.

'Michelle' : verse (at 0.08)

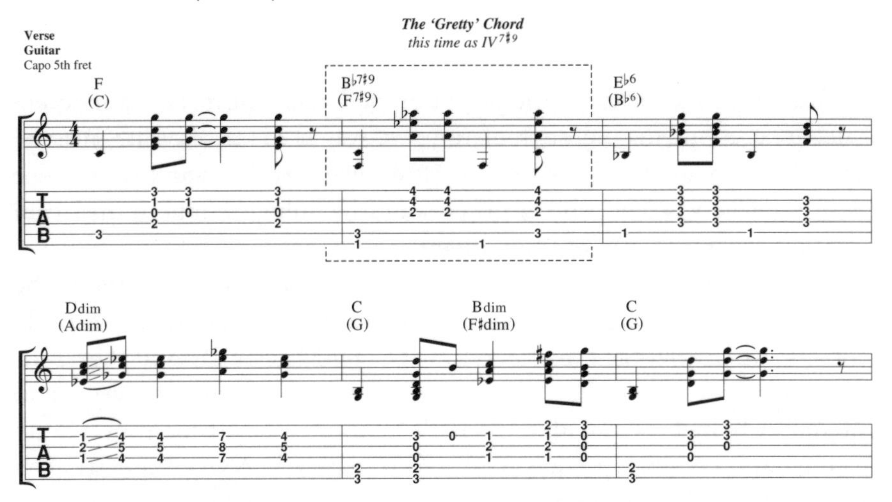

'ma belle' (at 2.02) and also in the closing solo in the same progression (at 2.22). Once again don't be put off by the resounding clash of false relations, with the D♭ now prominent as a target note in the guitar solo – that's the whole point of the chord.

The Beatles have a tradition of fooling us with major chords that are assumed to be minor chords – indeed it is a very specific element of their charm as songwriters. Refer back to the mediant in 'I Want To Hold Your Hand' and the debate between B7 and Bm. Or 'Not A Second Time' where George Martin's E *major* piano heavily discolours what is always assumed to be just another 'G–Em–G-Em' vamp.

Here in 'Michelle' it is a rarely appreciated point of detail that, in many ways, 'makes' the song. For those still unconvinced, track down McCartney's demo of the song, in the key of C. In this version, by the time we reach that diminished run, Paul has already made the change from C major to a resounding F7♯9 in a move that confirms without question how he conceived the song – delicacy tempered with judiciously placed dissonance.[10]

In this sense the mixing on the *Rubber Soul* version perhaps doesn't do justice to the song. For 'Michelle' is not quite the gentle ballad it is always

[10] Listeners to the demo will also hear another striking Gretty chord later in the wandering 'development' section: this time A♭7♯9 on its way to G7sus4 as McCartney effects a striking return from an early attempt at a bridge.

assumed to be. Play that second chord as a minor 7th and, yes, one can hear the associations with languid French film music. But substitute the Gretty chord, and suddenly it's Françoise Hardy-meets-Jimi Hendrix.

If Paul was spot-on about the power of the Gretty chord, he wasn't quite as accurate about the number of times it was used during The Beatles' career. One doesn't need to look too far to hear that distinctive dissonance being used very selectively in other songs by John, George – and Paul himself. Let's hunt some of them down.

The most famous instance must surely be in Harrison's 'Taxman', the *Revolver* opener, where the jarring dissonance of the dominant 7♯9 sonority evokes George's disaffection with Her Majesty's Inland Revenue. In this particular song, however, guitarists can distinguish between two different voicings of the dominant 7♯9 chord: a 6th-string root Gretty version, and a 5th-string equivalent affectionately known simply as 'The Hendrix Chord' by generations of guitarists, due to its use in a range of rock classics (most famously 'Purple Haze'). The latter is not quite such a ham-fisted beast and can happily be played on the inner four strings, a shape that omits the 5th degree of the chord but retains the defining element of the clashing thirds.

Hendrix actually used both 6th- and 5th-string voicings – and so did The Beatles. In 'Taxman', as in 'Purple Haze', it is the latter shape that acts as a disturbing altered tonic embellishing the basic D7 chord at the end of each two-line verse (e.g., at 0.12 and 0.19).[11] The Gretty only makes a fleeting appearance, stage left, as the subdominant chord in the refrain gets super-charged on two occasions: first at 1.29 after the solo, and again at 2.16.

'Taxman' (refrain at 1.25)

A comparison of all these moments reminds us that our discussion of the Gretty chord is not merely a trainspotting exercise. For beyond providing

[11] Compare with Stevie Ray Vaughan's cover of 'Taxman' which goes for the ♯9 dissonance all the way through. For more recent uses of the chord, check out Blur's 'Stereotypes' and Kula Shaker's cover of Joe South's 'Hush', built around B7♯9 and C7♯9, respectively.

a song with a suitably rich jazz colour, the Gretty chord – like any other chord in music – *functions* within its chord progression. This has been the overriding principle of this book so far and one that continues in this chapter as we introduce new concepts in chord movement that explain some of the most interesting of all Beatles moments.

In both 'Taxman' and 'Michelle' we are re-treading familiar territory, for the chord appears as a IV7♯9 – though in each case it is acting in different ways. In the former it is resolving a progression through a ♭VII-IV-I, Double Plagal wrap-up in fourths. While, in 'Michelle', it is the complete mirror image: functioning within a slick Cycle Of Fifths movement with the root movement of F-B♭-E♭ recognisable as a 'flat side' progression of I-IV-♭VII.[12]

However, when it comes to appreciating the same chord in 'Till There Was You', the picture is rather different. In stark contrast, the Gretty chord here fulfils a most unusual function and one that we have yet to encounter in our theoretical framework.

Tritone or 'Flat Five' substitution

With his casual remark McCartney has led us inadvertently to a perfect example of one the slickest of all textbook jazz manoeuvres – one that is all too rare in pop music. This is the Tritone or 'Flat Five' substitution, which, in most cases, sees a dominant chord replaced by a chord a flattened fifth or 'tritone' away. As with so many substitutions, the object of this harmonic switch is to create a more interesting resolution within a chord progression than the one that the listener would have expected.

This is exactly what Harrison does in his solo. For up to this point, the song is characterised by predictable ii-V-I cycles, with Gm moving to a C dominant chord and then down a fifth to the tonic – a path that we hear as early as the intro and subsequently in the verses.

But having reached the last Gm of his solo, George jettisons the V chord, and substitutes that G♭ monster. This is another example of how the idiosyncratic structure of the guitar encourages songwriting manoeuvres that are theoretically advanced. For a Gretty chord on G♭ is sandwiched

[12] Note that, in Michelle, this Cycle Of Fifths root movement persists whether or not that controversial chord on B♭ is played with a minor *or* major 3rd. However, when we play it as the latter, there is indeed a familiar leading tone effect, with IV7 (rather than iv) now functioning as a secondary dominant as D natural rises into the root of the following E♭.

midway between Gm and F and requires only a small change in fingering to execute.

The resulting Gm7-to-G♭7♯9-to-F might have been standard fare for Joe Pass in 1963, but in a Beatlemania context it was, frankly, outrageous.

The G♭ chord itself represents a Flat Five Substitute because its *root is a flattened fifth interval away from the C7 chord it is replacing*. The alternative 'tritone' description describes how the two chords are an augmented fourth, *or three whole steps* away from each other in either direction, dividing the octave in two symmetrically:

Tritone substitution : 'G♭ for C'

Tritone (6 semitones)							Tritone (6 semitones)					
G♭	G	A♭	A	B♭	B	C	D♭	D	E♭	E	F	G♭

In terms of voice-leading, the Flat Five substitution 'works' because the two important tones in the original dominant chord, the 3rd and the ♭7th, are also found in the substitute. Indeed these tones appear as mirror images within the two chords: the 3rd of the C7 becomes the ♭7th of the G♭7, while the ♭7th of the C7 becomes the 3rd of the G♭7.

'Till There Was You' – Common Tones in the Flat Five Substitute

Basic dominant V^{7} (C^{7})			**Flat Five Substitute** (G♭$^{7♯9}$)	
Formula	Note		Note	Formula
♭7th	B♭	Common Tone	B♭	3rd
3rd	E	Common Tone	E = F♭	♭7th

The connection with the secondary dominants of Chapter 4 should also be made. For Tritone substitutes can also be viewed as dominants built on degrees other than the primary V, though now the appropriate shorthand terminology is not 'V of' the target chord but '♭II of' it. Hence the function of George's G♭7♯9 can be abbreviated as '♭II of I'.

John Lennon was using exactly the same technique five years later, in 1968. The demo of 'Sexy Sadie' (*Anthology 3*, CD 1, Track 15) features a resounding Gretty chord functioning in just this capacity. In the key of G, listen out for the A♭7♯9 that appears at 0.05–0.06 in the gently falling intro, and again for the bridge climax at 1.17. In both cases the crucial cadence to the tonic is through a Flat Five substitution.

'Sexy Sadie' (*Anthology 3* version) (bridge)

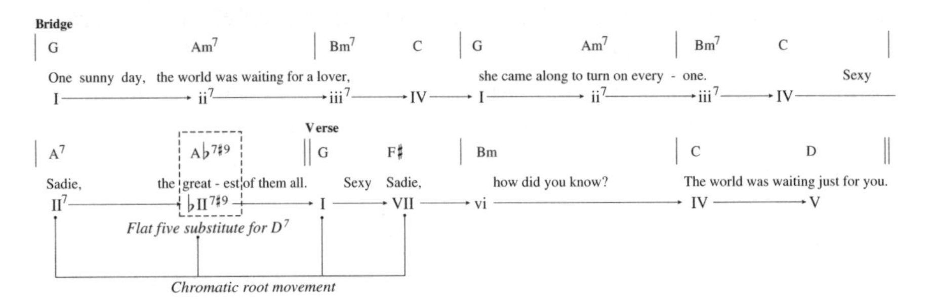

Lennon's use of the Flat Five sub here is particularly inspired, for the song is already characterised by an unusually high complement of second intervals – both major (two semitones) and minor (one semitone) – and both ascending and descending. The A♭ that replaces the conventional D root (which would normally take Am back to G in time-honoured ii-V-I fashion) means that Lennon's chromatic descent now extends beyond just the two half-steps. For the run immediately becomes three, consecutive, slithery semitones as G gives way immediately to F♯ as the verse resumes. All in all, the perfect tonal ploy for Lennon's disenchanted depiction of the subject of the song, the slippery Maharishi Mahesh Yogi himself.

Without even changing CD we can hear The Beatles deliver another couple of Gretty chords in a similar Flat Five context. Jump forward to track 23 to find Paul himself skipping through the stunning demo of 'Step Inside Love'. One of them involves the very same chord – and in the same sequence – as 'Till There Was You', linking Gm and F major with a G♭7♯9 standing in for an invisible C dominant. Hear it first after the lyric 'smile on your face' (at 0.36), and unmistakably at 1.20–1.21 just as John rudely interrupts.[13]

Beyond the Gretty chord – more Beatles tritone subs

Having detailed the essential qualities and fingering of The Gretty Chord, we should of course point out that the precise alterations of this dominant

[13] And could this Gretty shape have inspired the ultra-dissonant guitar intro of The Beatles' early cover of 'September In The Rain'? The F-B-E notes (low-to-high) that yield ♭7th, 3rd and 13th tones against a G tonality match the top-three strings of a 9th-position C♯7♯9.

construction are not the crucial determinant of how the chord functions in a progression. As well as dominant 7♯9, the chord could equally have been another type of dominant, perhaps a 7♯5 or even the supercharged jazz chord of 'Drive My Car' (7♯5♯9).

Perhaps the most common Flat Five substitution involves a dominant 7th with a *flattened* 5th built on the ♭II. This is because, in addition to the common tones already highlighted, the ♭5 of the new chord can be seen to mirror the root of the chord it replaces. A number of Latin standards such as 'The Girl From Ipanema' and 'Manha De Carnival' feature this move as a matter of course.

In the key of A minor for example, a Flat Five sub for E7 built on B♭ would find the ♭5 'bit' of a B♭7♭5 chord (the F♭ or E note) as an additional common tone with the chord it replaces.[14]

Common tones in a dominant 7♭5 Tritone Substitute

Basic dominant V⁷ (E⁷)			**Tritone Substitute on ♭II** (B♭⁷♭⁵)	
Formula	Note		Note	Formula
♭7th	D	Common Tone	D	3rd
3rd	G♯	Common Tone	G♯ = A♭	♭7th
Root	E	Common Tone	E = F♭	♭5th

But while three common tones make for an obvious substitution, ultimately we do not need even a complete dominant chord on ♭II to effect a perfectly adequate tritone substitution. Any type of major triad will do as at least the major 3rd still equates to the ♭7th of the dominant it replaces. Hence the A♭ *major* 7th that we hear in place of the Gretty chord on *The White Album* version of 'Sexy Sadie' does not alter its function. The C note is present in both these substitute chords and the D7 they replace, while the ultimate effect of the chromatic root movement via A♭ is unaffected.

As we delve into The Beatles' repertoire of similar chromaticism we should remember that this type of semitone moving line is usually a clue that a Tritone Sub is in operation.

[14] Jazz and blues crossover king, Robben Ford, demonstrated how to incorporate the move into a pop standard most clearly in his cover of the minor-key standard 'Don't Let Me Be Misunderstood', on the 1995 album *Handful Of Blues* (Cm11-C♭7♭5-B♭m7 at 1.42–1.45).

♭II: Tritone substitution and the Phrygian cadence

All this discussion of root movement resolving from ♭II down to a tonic should remind us of the Phrygian cadence of Chapter 8 – especially McCartney's 'quite good' B♭ in the verse of 'Things We Said Today', which resolved down to the A minor.

Another look at that 1964 song is now essential as, fascinatingly, the reappearance of the B♭ chord in the bridge prompts a slightly different interpretation, while suggesting that McCartney himself might have conceived the chord in two different ways.

The B♭ of the verse, following on from C and F in the key of A minor has already been explained as a flat side Cycle Of Fifths sequence that takes ♭III to ♭VI and on to ♭II.

But now take a look at the Middle Eight. At first sight, this progression appears to consist of two textbook loops of I-IV7-II7-V7. But, on the second circuit, the E7 dramatically metamorphoses into B♭.

'Things We Said Today'

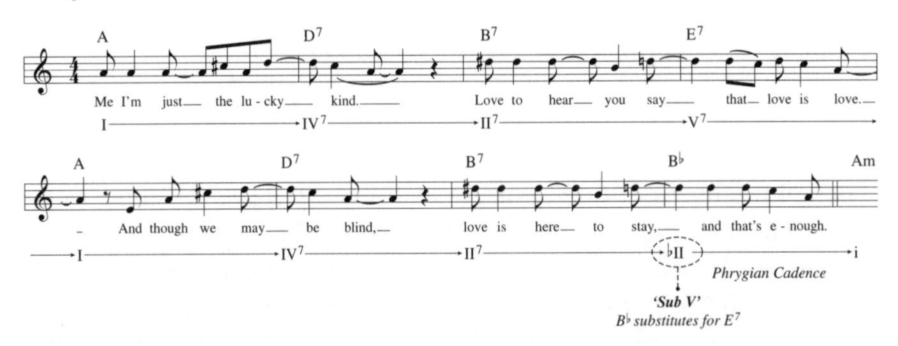

Having already delivered the II-V-I in the first strain, Paul seems now to be envisaging a Tritone Substitution on the second circuit, with the tell-tale three-semitone drop of B-B♭-A creating another local highlight in the song. McCartney uses this harmonic mechanism to conjure a climax to a Beatles bridge which emphatically distances itself from the rut of early sixties Imperfect cadences.

The differences and similarities between verse and the bridge uses of B♭ should now be apparent. In the former there is no three-semitone voice-leading and it only partially thwarts the expected Cycle Of Fifths movement – unlike the II-♭II-i of the bridge which drives a straight line through the cycle, with a root movement that returns to base 'as the crow flies'. The ultimate resolution in both cases is a Phrygian cadence, as ♭II moves to the tonic. And yet ♭VI-♭II-i can also be construed as a tritone sub for a V7 *only now in the context of a ♭VI-V7-i resolution.*

Here it's a minor tonic as McCartney reverts from parallel major bridge to parallel minor verse, but he could equally have stayed in major as in the startling re-transition from bridge-to-verse in 'You're Going To Lose That Girl'. Here is an example of just such a Tritone substitution, which now concludes with a Phrygian cadence in major.[15]

The context is a verse and chorus firmly in E major that John and Paul take boldly to G major for a contrasting bridge.

'You're Going To Lose That Girl'

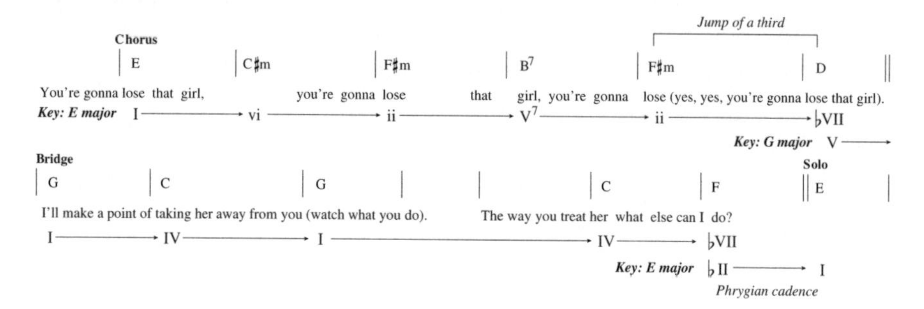

For all the novelty of this exit, we can also appreciate the entry to the bridge. There is a parallel here with 'Here, There And Everywhere' in that the opening bridge destination of ♭III is reached functionally through its dominant, although the way that the D chord connector is deftly introduced is arguably even smoother. For, compositionally, this song illustrates brilliantly the way The Beatles exploited mediant relationships in harmony: making root jumps of a third – either down (E-C♯m) or up (E-G♯m). And it is this feature that helps us to explain, and accept, the introduction of the D chord. For having landed on F♯m (as a familiar ii chord), The Beatles abandon the obvious V and move to D major. This is not merely acceptable as a common tone substitute for B7, but doubly slick in the context of the song by being *itself a third away from F♯m.*

[15] We already saw a ♭II-I 'major' Phrygian cadence in 'Come And Get It'; but that particular F-E move was not primed by either II or ♭VI to imply a tritone substitution, as is our present focus.

The D chord now not only brings a rocky ♭VII tinge to the key of E but expertly represents *the required V chord of the G major bridge.* Having done the hard work with this super-cool transition, the actual bridge harmony itself need be no great shakes, emerging as a simple I-IV-I-IV alternation (as 'Penny Lane' would do later). However, unlike 'Penny Lane' and many others, the return to the original key for the next verse is not through the obvious route of a V7 'connector'. It could so easily have been, of course, with that final C chord begging to be slid down to B for the simplest of ♭VI-V-I returns to E major. Try it, perhaps with a melody line that follows the roots of C and B – it works.

So 'what else can I do'? How about a Tritone substitute for the missing V of E, allowing the harmonisation of a more poignant, darker A note in the melody (as the 3rd of F major)? That's exactly what The Beatles do, taking us just a semitone away from the E major target they need for their re-transition.

Another sublime piece of songcrafting which, even 30 years on, has few parallels in pop. Again, it's especially noteworthy for the fact that it appears as early as the *Help!* album, and has also been singled out by pre-eminent classical writer, Joshua Rifkin, in his eloquent whirlwind appraisal of Beatles music.[16]

Meanwhile, the reappearance of the same D major chord at the end of the song creates another moment of true songwriting subtlety. The final chorus ends with a Double Plagal cadence, which brings in a rocky sounding fourth movement that adds some 'balls' after the poppy thirds and fifths. It also reminds us that one of the cleverest (and least appreciated) concepts in Beatles songwriting is the way in which they 'reincarnate' certain musical elements in new ways during the course of a song.

The B♭ of 'Things We Said Today' and the D chord of 'You're Going To Lose That Girl' both creep up on us in different ways and yet in both cases our ear becomes more disposed to the second function by virtue of its earlier appearance. And while these are modest examples, both Lennon and McCartney used the same principle to breathtaking effect in two of their very finest moments: the thirties-style intros in both 'If I Fell' and 'Here, There And Everywhere'.

[16] Joshua Rifkin, *On the Music of The Beatles*, originally written for Edward E. Davis's anthology, *The Beatles Book* (New York, 1968) but withdrawn and later reprinted in *The Lennon Companion*, p. 117.

Better still, in both cases, the chord with the 'dual role' obligingly makes its first appearance as a Tritone substitute, before being reconceived as a target for a modulation. While a technically demanding analysis is required for the next pair of extracts, rest assured that the complexity of the mechanics is directly proportional to the beauty of the songwriting premise.

'If I Fell' (intro-to-verse transition)

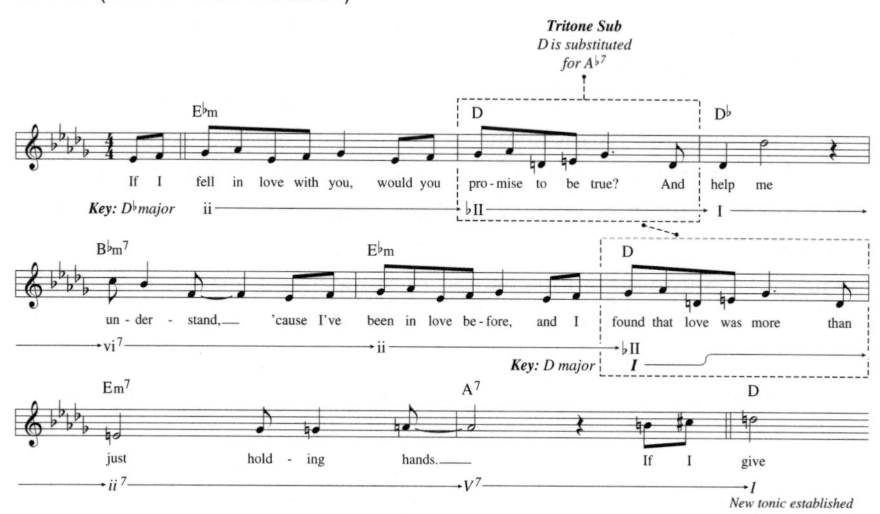

Just what is Lennon up to in this delightful but meandering Tin Pan Alley intro? Again, the three-semitone chromatic root action provides incriminating forensic evidence, with the ultimate clue found in the mysterious D major chord in bar 2. For whatever the harmonic riddle at this point, we soon find the song emerging unequivocally in a D major tonality as the verse gets underway.

Sure enough, that first D major links a ii chord with its tonic by functioning as a Tritone substitute for what should have been the V chord in the home key of D♭. Viewed this way, all we have is a gentle, ultra-familiar 'ii-V-I-vi' pattern, but with a crucial difference: ♭II replaces V.

So why didn't Lennon just play the A♭7 like a normal pop songwriter? The answer surely lies in the ingenious method by which he chooses to give the song a lift – modulating to a key a semitone higher so that the mellow intro can give way to a spirited verse. But switching from D♭ major to D major can be a tall order for a pop song given the distance between the two keys on the Cycle Of Fifths. After all, these two keys have no common diatonic chords with which to facilitate a smooth switch (ignoring the possibility of the Truck Driver's modulation). Using the Tritone substitution, however, Lennon effectively fashions an unlikely *pivot chord*, introducing us to the *sound* of D major and helping us makes sense of a modulation to harmony that is, nominally, distant and inaccessible.

His strategy unfolds according to plan on the second circuit, as he sets about tonicising that same D chord as a new I chord through that unfailing modulatory manoeuvre, a ii-V of the new target. The requisite Em7 initially sounds grand and dramatic as we search for a tonal foothold, but we soon find one as the re-emergence – or rather 'reincarnation' – of D major explains the harmonic teasing.

This is spectacularly elaborate songwriting of which Cole Porter would have been proud. Yet, as ever, Lennon and McCartney match each other stride for stride, and even this ultra-subtle sneak preview of a later key centre has an uncanny counterpart in a McCartney song.

More Tritone substitution – beyond the V replacement

In the case of 'Here, There And Everywhere' Paul provides us with a perfect example of how songwriters can develop the principle of Tritone substitution beyond its most obvious role as stand-in for the primary dominant.

'Here, There And Everywhere' (Intro)

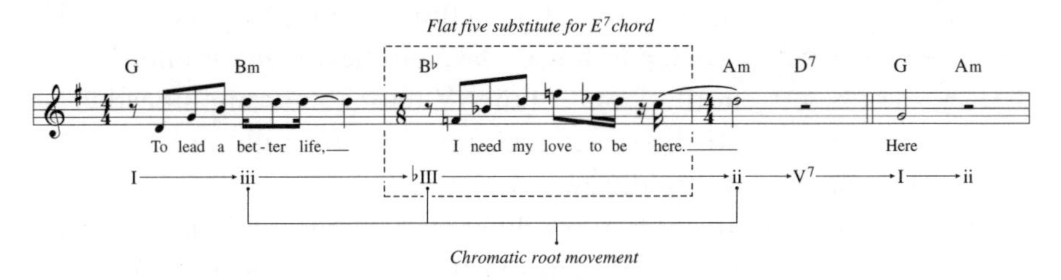

It's the same principle, but instead of ♭II replacing V, here ♭III stands in for VI. Again, the object of the exercise is a gentle semitone descent that links two diatonic members, thereby ringing the changes from the predictable Cycle Of Fifths merry-go-round. So instead of the expected E7 that would have taken us to Am, Paul delivers a jarring B♭ major chord that makes us sit up and listen. Of course B♭ doesn't occur naturally in the key of G, but its presence here is not as a 'rocky' borrowed chord in the manner of Chapter 7. Note how the melody deftly arpeggiates the B♭ triad.

To use our terminology, B♭ acts as '♭II of ii' as it descends from iii. Surely, with the use of the Flat Five device in a specially constructed intro, McCartney is tipping his hat to the premise of 'If I Fell' and giving the listener a sneak preview of a later tonality to be targeted. Not the verse on this occasion, but the bridge that we analysed in Chapter 10. It may take half the song for the B♭ chord to reappear, but we nevertheless subliminally reconcile its use and make sense of the chosen destination of the modulation. It's the songwriting equivalent of movie thrillers where a seemingly irrelevant object is given some early exposure only to re-emerge as the murder weapon in the final scene!

Partly because it is less dramatic than a ♭II that hangs tensely above the tonic, the ♭III-for-VI7 sub is perhaps the most popular of 'Flat Fives' in rock and pop. Listen for it in contexts ranging from Jimi Hendrix's 'Little Wing' ('. . . and moonbeams') to Tom Jones's 'It's Not Unusual' (on the melisma of 'miiiiine'). In both cases it manifests itself as a chromatic line of Bm-B♭-Am in the key of G, as in 'Here, There And Everywhere'.[17]

Theory Nazis will baulk at the liberties taken when making some of our Flat Five interpretations but the intention is to draw attention to slick, chromatic root-drops in places where predictable 'backcycling' in fifths might have been expected. And while the mechanism has strong jazz connotations from its use in standards such as 'Georgia', 'Misty' and 'Autumn Leaves', how about 'Back In The USSR', where the rhythm guitar exploits the unique symmetry of the fretboard just like a good rocker should – by driving a coach and horses through the Cycle Of Fifths?

From the obvious starting point of the IV chord, the song is headed for II, so why not just go straight there, dropping that power chord chromatically via III *and ♭III*, making the latter function as a '♭II of II'?[18]

And there's one more obvious instance in a major key where a Flat Five substitute can link two diatonic chords: ♭VI. Of course, we can understand a dominant chord here, in its own right, as part of a sequence on its way to

[17] In a contemporary context, Supergrass have emerged as Brit-Pop masters of the Tritone sub. Check the challenging 'iii-♭III-ii' in the bridge to 'Alright' ('Are we like you? I can't be sure': F♯m-F-Em7 at 0.32). The same run continues stylishly on to the tonic via ♭II in the instrumental link of 'Strange Ones', and with even greater Phrygian flavour as A major moves to its parallel minor.

[18] Note how the line almost reverses the most basic of chromatic ascending ideas – a four step approach to your target – which starts the bridge as I heads for IV.

'Back In The USSR'

V7. Nevertheless, in the wonderful coda of 'Tell Me Why', The Beatles show us how to arrive at this chord as a genuine substitution, replacing a previously heard chord a tritone away and creating that semitone root drop.

It may be a brief coda gesture but it's still one of the most interesting moments in the entire song, as Lennon looks to wrap up his relentless Four-Chord Turnaround. He finds a slick exit route, first by means of a deceptive vi, as V7 heads for the relative minor rather than the major tonic (as in 'Not A Second Time', 'Do You Want To Know A Secret', 'The Sheik Of Araby' and later 'Ob-La-Di Ob-La-Da' and 'Octopus's Garden'). However, to resolve the tension John doesn't just return to the original cycle – the Em7 that would have closed the song (simply and predictably with a ii-V-I) gets binned in favour of something far tastier.

'Tell Me Why' (ending)

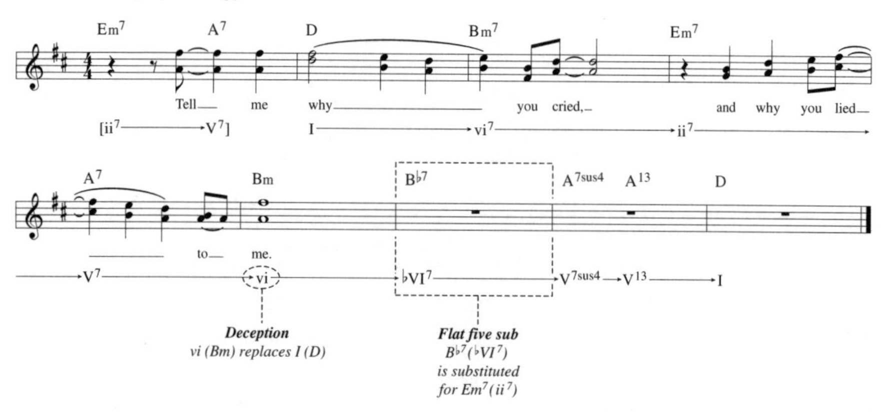

The B♭7, a tritone away from the E root. Now he's home and dry with what, *from here*, does become a ♭VI-V run to I, albeit with some delicious 'sus 4' and 13th action in the guitar to embellish the V before finally cadencing on D. Another brilliant coda delivered by 1964.

Incredibly, The Beatles' understanding of the basic principles of Tritone substitution can be traced back even earlier – right back to the historic showcase of New Year's Day 1962.

The cascading coda of 'Hello Little Girl' on *Anthology 1* may seem like another nonchalant, off-the-cuff wrap-up. But, on close inspection, it can be seen to feature some highly intricate voice-leading that illustrates The Beatles' forensic attention to detail in all areas of song construction.

This cool collapse (at 1.29) is highly novel for the way in which the bass and guitar combine almost telepathically, while apparently viewing the manoeuvre completely independently. If this sounds like a contradiction in terms, look closely at the following chart that shows how:

a) the bass targets the 5th degree of the scale (i.e., ahead of a V-I finish) in a run that descends from the tonic; while,
b) superimposed above it, the guitar opts for an embellished diatonic descent from the iii chord to the tonic.

The crucial harmony is of course the B♭ chord played by the guitar, which deftly achieves a chromatic 'ii-♭II-I' run comparable to the more famous Gretty-fied moment in 'Till There Was You'. Most impressive is the way in which this Tritone-conceived device complements the bass run. For the B♭ is an astute alternative to the obvious V7 chord that would have

'Hello Little Girl' (coda) (1.29)

		Main descending sequence					Final Cadence
Bass	Bass sequence	8	7	6	♭6	5	1
	Key of A	A	G♯	F♯	F	E	A
Guitar	Chord Sequence	I	iii	ii	♭II	I	$I^{6/9}$
	Key of A	A	C♯m	Bm	B♭	A	$A^{6/9}$
	Implied inversion	Root	2nd	2nd	2nd	2nd	Root

'stolen the thunder' from the bass run, which itself will only reach the '5' two beats later.[19] But played together the combined sonority is B♭/F, basically a ♭II with the 5th in the bass. Not bad for those innocent Beatles of 1962 – but not good enough for Decca!

Meanwhile, for some '4-3-2-1' root movement as part of a formal song structure seek out recordings of McCartney's renditions of 'Don't Let The Sun Catch You Crying', a highly ambitious inclusion in Beatles live sets in 1960, the year that Ray Charles released his version of this subtle blues standard.[20]

Given the highly rare and undeniably dramatic sound of the Phrygian drop from ♭II-to-I, The Beatles' treatment of the equally intricate coda of 'I Remember You' also deserves a mention. It proves that as far back as the Hamburg days they were aware of the value of semitone root movements in occasionally punctuating the diet of fourths and fifths that was gorging mainstream rock 'n' roll.

Take a close look – for The Beatles did just that when delivering the exact intricacies of the Frank Ifield original, right down to that very last half-step cadence.

'I Remember You'

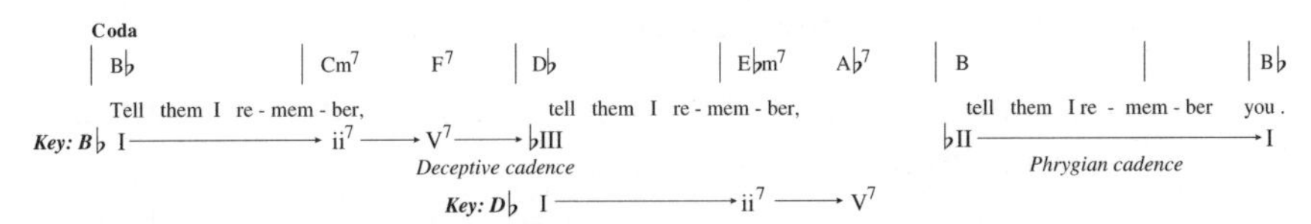

[19] This run is much more subtle than the corresponding moment at the end of 'It Won't Be Long'. There (at 2.04) the guitar and bass both fall '4-3-2-1' to the tonic *in parallel,* with the closing E major 7th now thought of as a common Lounge cliché.

[20] Lewisohn, *The Complete Beatles Recording Sessions*, p. 362. Here, in the key of F, the 'bright' opening walk up the harmonised major scale (F-Gm7-Am7-B♭-C) gives way to the darker strains of A♭-G-G♭-F. This bold chromatic descent to the root from ♭III would later feature in heavier rock contexts ranging from The Spencer Davis Group's 'I'm A Man' to Oasis's 'Fuckin' In The Bushes', where the organ descends G-G♭-F-E in the key of E (first at 0.49).

Here is the clearest example of an Interrupted cadence that we've encountered so far, with the expected V-I move completely thwarted. Not this time in favour of the relative minor, but through a delaying modulation – *complete with another ii-V which is itself interrupted* – finally returning unexpectedly to the tonic via ♭II. No three-semitone sequence here, as in conventional Tritone substitutions, but clearly that awkward B natural chord appears in place of the F7 that should have taken us back to the B♭ before this delightfully flowery finish.[21]

It's worth highlighting that the delaying tactics here take place in the temporary key of D♭, thereby effectively recycling the immediately preceding melody (and lyric) up a minor third in what can be seen as a mini, self-contained 'Truck Driver's' modulation. This is a useful trick and one that The Beatles would use later, for example in 'Mean Mr Mustard'.[22]

And lest we forget, when appreciating the power of the Phrygian cadence in major there is no need for any complicated voice-leading table to explain what's going on, as *every note in a ♭II major triad moves blissfully down a semitone.*[23]

Polychords: more inversions, slash chords and cool cadences

The Gretty chord aside, the simple major triads and dominants that we have seen so far may have fulfilled some interesting roles but they hardly fit the bill as constructions that would have become 'an obsession', as Lennon put it.

However, the same cannot be said of the resonant jazz chord at the start of 'All I've Got To Do'. This is the first stop on our remaining tour of Beatles chords which we will find functioning in even more unusual ways in terms of the resolutions they create.

[21] As with so many of our ♭IIs, notice how it harmonizes the prevailing melody note as the major 3rd of the chord. On a deeper level, the ♭II-I finish here sublimely complements the opening move of the song, which we saw was an equally unusual I-VII semitone drop *from* the root (B♭-A).

[22] There the melody of 'sleeps in a hole in the road', over a B7 chord, is shifted up, lock stock and barrel, to D7 for the next line 'Saving up to buy some clothes', before returning to the original key.

[23] This type of cadence is a favourite closing device of many standards – its use in 'Spanish Eyes' cleverly mirroring the Latin associations of the chord built on the ♭II 'Phrygian' degree itself.

The 'All I've Got To Do' chord: E augmented 11th

'All I've Got To Do'

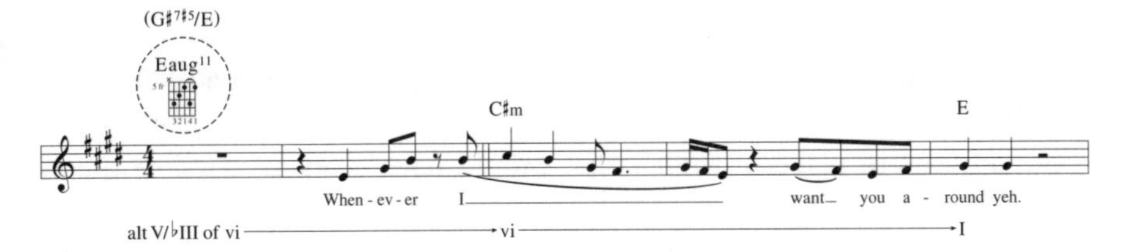

This grand, one-off opening gesture, which basks in such splendid isolation ahead of Lennon's ballad, is indeed one of the most distinctive of all Beatles chords and represented a challenge to guitarists in the early sixties – at least until the earth-shattering opener to 'A Hard Day's Night'.

And it's almost as complicated to rationalise. Here are the notes, fingering and chord tones – the latter viewed in relation to the lowest note of E, implying a colourfully extended augmented chord.

String	Fret	Notes	Chord tone
1st (high E)	5	A	11th
2nd	7	F♯	9th
3rd	5	B♯	♯5th
4th	6	G♯	3rd
5th	7	E	Root
6th (low E)	x	x	x

The tell-tale 4th above the 9th gives us effectively an 11th chord above an altered triad. 'E augmented 11th' is one way to view it – though it is of course the *triad* that is 'augmented', not the 11th suffix. E11 (♯5) is another alternative, though in each case it should be noted that the 7th that 11th chords conventionally assume is missing.

With that out of the way, just what is the point of this chord? Does it function in any way – or were The Beatles just determined to show it off?

Again, there *is* method in the madness, with the relative relationship between C♯m and E major (the two chords that dominate the verse) helping us to understand its function in context. It may not be linking these two chords *directly*, as we saw in Chapter 9 (with 'All My Loving' and 'That Means A Lot'). But the semitone voice-leading, combined with two 'anchoring' common tones, again confirms the tendency for the 'aug' built on a major chord to resolve to act as a link chord between I and vi, or as here, just as a cue directly for vi.

Voice leading in the 'All I've Got To Do' opening 'aug'

E aug^{11}			**C♯minor**	
Formula	Note	Voice leading	Note	Formula
11th	A	Down a semitone	G♯	5th
9th	F♯	Up a whole tone	G♯	5th
♯5th	B♯ (C)	Up a semitone	C♯	Root
3rd	G♯	Common tone	G♯	5th
Root	E	Common tone	E	♭3rd

The addition of the F♯ note (the 9th of E) was a clever Beatles touch, adding a Tin Pan Alley-esque colour to the sound. This is in contrast to the stripped-down augmented inversions of Chapter 9, which were confined to the 1, 3, ♯5 formula.[24]

Meanwhile, the fact that chord resolutions can be appreciated from more than one perspective is a principle that dominates the remainder of this chapter. For this augmented chord can also be seen as acting like a glorified version of a tangible dominant V7 chord. Are we really that far removed from the basic, wide-eyed Beatles 'V aug' that fuels the bridge/verse retransition in 'From Me To You'? Not only is 'E aug' enharmonic to the augmented chord built on the V of C♯m (G♯), but the structure used here contains all the elements of a G♯7♯5♭9, a supercharged altered jazz sonority highly reminiscent of the one built by the vocals in 'Drive My Car'.

If in doubt go for the simplest explanation. And 'the power of V' would appear to be just that.

E aug^{11}		**G♯7♯5♯9**
Chord Tone	Note	Chord Tone
11th	A	♭9th
9th	F♯	♭7th
♯5th	B♯ (C)	3rd
3rd	G♯	Root
Root	E	5th

And yet, given the extreme ambiguity of the sound, it's no surprise that there's a healthy range of both technical and emotional descriptions among Beatles writers.

Everett refers to the same collection of notes as a 'mixture-colored V minor ninth with root omitted, sounding over anticipatory 1 and 3 pedals'; MacDonald focuses on 'the loneliness evoked in the stark suspended 4th'; while Pollack hears a C♯ augmented triad (C♯-F *natural*-A) 'suspended over an E bass' which works as 'a surprising IV-like antecedent to the C♯m chord'.[24] Take your pick.

Whatever the answer, this early brain-teaser takes us deeper into the world of inversions, slash chords and, indeed, *polychords*.

What is a polychord?

As the Greek prefix suggests, a polychord is defined as harmony in which the sounds of more than one chord are combined. Technically, a true polychord must therefore be able to be broken down into the basic elements of at least two constituent chords. Of course many extended chords can be re-ordered to imply the presence of more than one chord. Take C major 9th, which contains the notes C, E, G, B and D, and which therefore can be viewed as a combination of a C major triad (C-E-G) and a G major triad (G-B-D).

But such a definition is too limited for the rock and pop student. As *The Guitar Handbook* points out, polychords in contemporary usage take many forms, encompassing a range of slash chords that *may merely feature a bass note that is not the normal root of the chord rather than suggesting the presence of an additional triad.*[25]

We have already used the 'slash' chord to denote *basic* inversions, where a triad is played with its 3rd or 5th in the bass. But the principle is also used for bass notes that represent any of the following:

1) inversions implied by extensions beyond the 5th degree (e.g., where the 7th, 9th, 11th or 13th appears in the bass),
2) alterations to the basic triad (e.g. ♭5th or ♯5th)
3) other chromatic colour (mainly ♭7th)[26]

[24] See *The Beatles As Musicians: The Quarry Men Through Rubber Soul*, pp. 190–191; *Revolution In The Head*, p. 86; and 'Notes on…Series' no. 36, 1991. *The 'Official' rec.music.beatles Home Page*, www.recmusicbeatles.com.

[25] Ralph Denyer, *The Guitar Handbook,* p. 136.

[26] Look out for other interesting chromatic colours, like ♭2nd-in-the-bass, B/C, a favourite of Andy Summers; see 'Harmonic Divergence', *Guitar Player*, January 2001, p. 91. Or 6th –in-the-bass, one interpretation of the most famous of all chords, the final 'chaang' of Monty Norman's James Bond Theme: G major 7♯5/E. Or, if you prefer, Em9 (major 7th) see *Total Guitar*, February 2001, p. 7.

With these basic guidelines in mind we can tackle a whole variety of complex sounds. For example, for those that appreciate the 'altered V' interpretation of the 'All I've Got To Do' chord, the slash construction G♯7♭9/E can be instantly appreciated as belonging to category 2. While this type of bass alteration is rare (and more common in the realm of highly dissonant jazz harmony), Beatles chords do fall regularly into the other two categories to create some distinctive tension.

Take 'Only A Northern Song', where George Harrison even warns listeners that the chords are going wrong – but they're not, he just wrote it like that. Check how the E in the bass riff (at 0.19) spices the supertonic.

'Only A Northern Song': verse

Our ears would never have questioned the Bm7 in a simple diatonic I-ii walk, without the deliciously offending E note within the lower harmony. But rather than write Bm7-with-11th-in-the-bass, the slash chord, Bm7/E, tells us all we need to know while warning us in print to expect some whacky, fusion-esque harmony.

While George's 'wrong' chord, like most slash chords, can be played by a solo guitarist, such sounds – *in terms of their composition* – are usually the result of a band setting, where an independent bass line creates an overall sonority that implies the slash treatment. 'All You Need Is Love' is a perfect showcase as McCartney's busy bass walks all over the song implying a string of interesting chords over and above the basic buskers shapes. If in doubt just play the chord on the left-hand side of the 'slash' and leave the other bit to the bass player.

As well as 1st and 2nd inversions, there's now a dominant V chord with the 9th in the bass, and our first look at the cool jazz sound of D/C (category 3 above) a sound that resurfaces powerfully at various Beatles moments, notably the very climax to 'The End'.

Meanwhile, readers may have made a connection with a major chord

'All You Need Is Love'

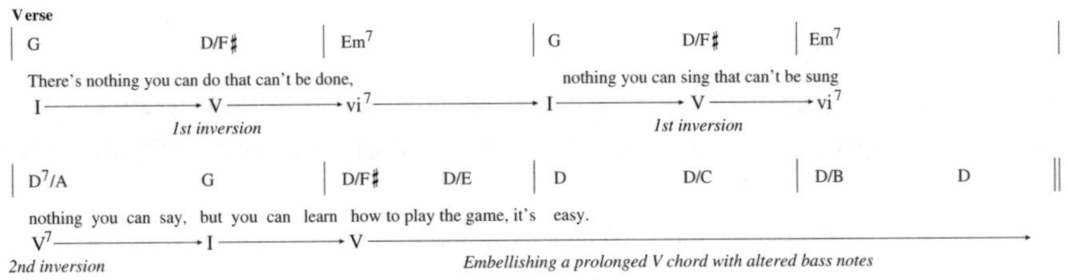

with a 9th-in-the-bass, and those floating ♭VII chords tethered to a tonic bass that we also variously described as 11th chords in Chapter 7. Are all these the same construction?

They are indeed, but the way we name them depends on the context. In 'Tomorrow Never Knows', the B♭/C (or C11) is clearly just embellishing an otherwise highly static C tonic with a B♭ triad. As is the equivalent G/A in 'If I Needed Someone'. Contrast with the D/E in 'All You Need Is Love' which adds passing colour to a prolonged dominant.

While these all make for some interesting sounds, none of them depend on their slash status to drive the progression in a structurally important way – unlike the same chord that reappears in the examples that follow.

Slash Chords and Combination Cadences

In the same way that the D dim of 'Because' resolved to its tonic in a way that combined elements of *both* a Phrygian and Aeolian cadence, so The Beatles found a select batch of slash chords that also appear to act in two ways at once, blurring the lines between the familiar cadences of Perfect, Plagal, Aeolian and Phrygian which we normally find operating individually.

Take the B♭/C slash chord above – McCartney showed us impressively in 'The Long And Winding Road' how this same structure can be used to work its magic by acting as a highly unusual 'combination cadence' that blends elements of the Perfect and Plagal at the same time.

Here two appearances of the chord unfold within a larger framework of a giant Cycle Of Fifths structure which, in another stroke of McCartney genius, itself delivers musically the lyrical theme of the song. Indeed, the very title of the song can be seen as a metaphor for the Cycle Of Fifths as a compositional tool, showcasing the potential of the device as well as any song in the history of popular music.

To follow and appreciate the masterpiece, let's start by accepting that the premise is (as the title tells us) one of movement. An obvious point, but by no means one that is applicable to every Beatles song. More specifically, movement that both frustrates as well as satisfies, as The Beatles take the listener through a series of carefully planned twists and turns *en route* to that final destination.

Let's use the stripped-back *Anthology 3* version as our reference (if only to avoid the notorious Phil Spector production on *Let It Be*) and a transcription in the key of D (rather than E♭ as heard on the recording) in order to simplify the analysis of certain complex chords. (To play along with the original, guitarists can just capo at the first fret.) Here's the verse:

'The Long And Winding Road'

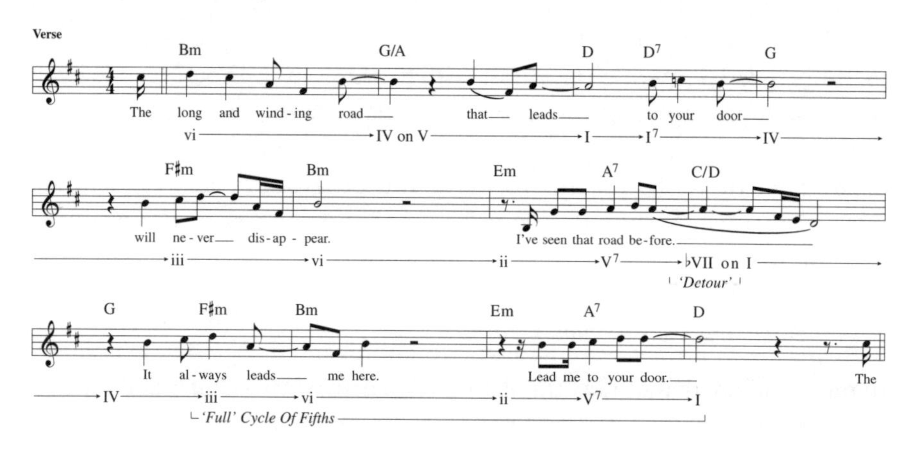

A quick peak at the final cadence reveals a simple 'ii–V–I' that leads us right to the knocker on the front door, reassuring us that there is indeed a way out of McCartney's maze. Moreover, with the preceding 'iii' and 'vi' also in evidence, the whole final stretch can be seen simply as plain sailing around the Cycle Of Fifths – all the way back to the tonic, just as in 'Can't Buy Me Love' or the 'homeward' jaunt in 'Golden Slumbers'.

But that's cheating. For we must first negotiate the various obstacles that Paul puts in our path: special musical landmarks that question our sense of direction before we see that final signpost up the drive. The 'travelling' analogy may appear trite, but that's *exactly* what is happening here.

Specifically, these hurdles are the G/A chord, in the second bar, and the C/D chord that provides another bum steer, a few bars later. Both exhibit

'The Long And Winding Road' – Cycle Of Fifths

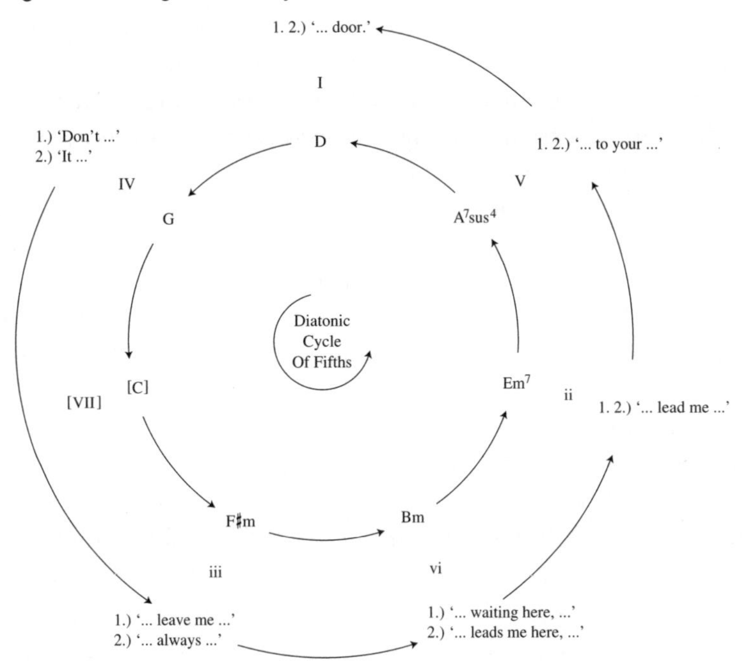

the same basic construction as the 11th or slash chords of 'Tomorrow Never Knows' and 'If I Needed Someone'. But here they act more specifically as a *polychord* – as if they were indeed two chords fused together. Let's tackle them in the order that they appear on McCartney's musical 'map'.

The G/A 'U-Turn' (0.03)

The A11 or A/9/11 monikers are technically accurate, but ones that don't do justice to the *function* of the chords in the song. 'G/A' here means just that: a G major triad over an A bass note, and it is best thought of in this way for the particular effect it creates in this context.

As with various Beatles songs (ranging from 'It Won't Be Long' right through to 'Your Mother Should Know'), the opening Bm chord immediately disorientates us. This is because after its downbeat opening effect it is to be understood retrospectively as the relative minor of D major. Indeed the seeds of doubt about the permanence of the minor key are instantly planted as the melody opens with a D note reached from the leading note a semitone below.

But it's a long time before we know for sure quite where we stand, as that first polychord soon questions the way we feel about any D tonality struggling to assert itself. For the two elements of the G/A chord soon emerge, with the A element leading us 'Perfectly' down a fifth, to that D base; while the G part moves Plagally, making this polychord effectively resolve to D major *by means of a IV-I and V-I at the same time*!

'Cadence' is perhaps not the right term to use, because far from this double whammy making for a convincing resolution, the listener questions the potential role of the G chord. We certainly expect to hear it again. And so we do – rather more convincingly this time after the D chord turns to D dominant. Of course, being now within an unfolding verse progression, we've hardly started on our travels – and yet we feel as if we've already had to make a U-turn.[27]

After this first example of cleverly shoddy map reading, we're soon cruising in overdrive – even if we are taking the long way back to the tonic around the Cycle Of Fifths. McCartney could have taken a direct 'rat run' from his now 'pure' IV back to I – but that would have been too obvious. Instead, he makes us travel the 'full fare' (skipping just one stop *en route*) around the Cycle, as an effortless 'iii-vi-ii-V' jaunt takes us in sight of the gravel drive at our destination – or so we think.

The C/D 'Detour' (0.25)

Instead of the tonic, McCartney now delivers his second polychord, again pulling us Plagally and Perfectly at once. This time, though, the root is D, our home tonic. And yet we haven't quite truly arrived at a point of rest, for the C triad that sits above it *wants to continue to move in fifths, taking us back again to G.*

This C triad is technically outside the parent key (it is the ♭VII of D major) but, by virtue of also being the IV of G, it succeeds in establishing another Plagal pull, this time *towards* G. We know that G isn't 'home' and yet we can't stop ourselves going there, as if for a temporary pit-stop. In the context of the song we don't feel 'lost', as the lyrics tell us that we've 'seen

[27] To harmonise the crucial B melody note (on the word 'road') Paul could have easily used as alternatives a straight G major chord (with B as the 3rd); or an A major (with B as the 9th). Try them for size. But it's the *combination* of the two that is just the ticket here in order to create that feeling of being in limbo. Allan Moore captures the sound of this construction when dubbing it the 'soul cadence'; *Rock: The Primary Text*, p.74.

that road before'. It's as though the C/D chord constitutes a special landmark giving us our bearings and pointing out a secret path that will lead us to our target – just as soon as we can turn the bend on to the final Cycle Of Fifths we ear-marked earlier.

Arriving home to D major (0.40)

This time we genuinely do feel as if we've arrived home. The D chord is now a 'proper' one, a triad with a root, 3rd and 5th. Meanwhile, the melody walks gently from the leading note '7' to the tonic '1', reinforcing the closure. The result is a clear sense of home tonic, which we didn't feel over the previous D root when the melody appeared as the 5th. Indeed, with the D note now anticipating the tonic ahead of time, creating a brief 'sus4' over the last V chord, it's as though we can't wait, tripping over the suitcases as we run up the steps.

The wandering bridge and its inversions (1.27)

While the verse alone covers the main features of the cycle, it's worth mentioning how McCartney elaborates on the theme of movement so expertly in the bridge.

This time he uses a different musical premise, for while 'fifths action' is plainly evident in the triads (Em-A7-D-G is a straight, four-stop 'trip around the block'), it's the movement in the roots themselves that now threatens our stability.

'The Long And Winding Road'

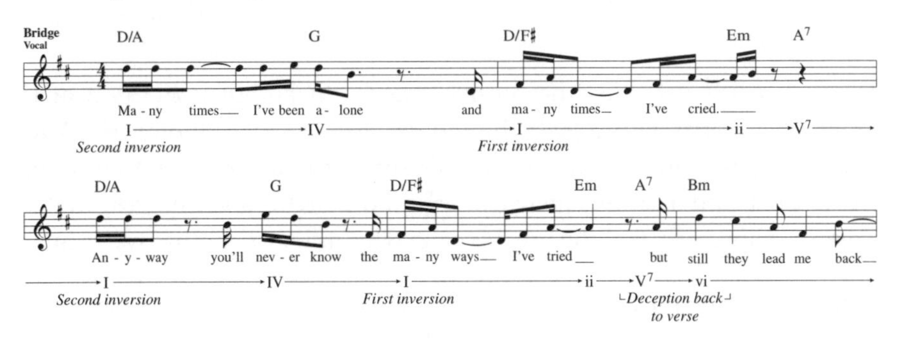

The two 'slash' chords here now do represent familiar inversions of the tonic triad, as we saw back in Chapter 9. Here we find examples of both 1st and 2nd inversion D major chords. Compare the stinging 5th-in-the-bass, A note (at 1.27) with the more fragile 3rd-in-the-bass, F♯, that follows on behind (at 1.30).[28]

Certainly a lone guitarist can busk the bridge to 'The Long And Winding Road' using just the basic root-position chords. But the subtle nuance for a Beatles *connoisseur* is precisely the contrast from the fifths created by the bass as it drops in *seconds* (A-G-F-E) on its fleeting excursion to the Em chord. And while we're soon right back with a 'ii-V' to D (at 1.34 on the word 'anyway'), it's another unstable D/A that appears, demanding a second cycle of the progression.

Overall, and with the lyrics at the end of verse 2 having already questioned his 'arrival', the bridge expertly complements the verse, putting a new harmonic spin on the singer's restless quest.

Losing the way: the deceptive A7-Bm move (1.41)

When the line 'many times I've cried' leads us back into the verse, not with V-I but rather V-*vi*, we have the direct substitution of 'vi-for-I' which now explains that very opening gambit of the song. The singer is admitting he's now lost as we repeat the verse with that same tonality-threatening Bm chord. The traveller's initial success now appears the result of fantasy, for when he has to do it 'for real', in verses 3 and 4, he now pleads with the object of his affections to lead him (literally or metaphorically depending on your interpretation) to whatever is waiting for him at the end of the Cycle Of Fifths. Was there ever a more appropriately titled song?

The G/A punchline (3.23)

The kicker is the reappearance of the same G/A combination, this time in a formal cadential setting, even though we already arrived 'home' on D. It's really a superfluous gesture but consistent with the theme of revisiting previously heard harmony in a new way. And when you've got a chord that works as supremely stylishly as this one, why not, as Lennon says, write a

[28] While inversions are used to create movement (as here, and in much of the *Sgt. Pepper* era, including 'Penny Lane'), they can also be used for the very opposite effect – to create stability. Listen, for example, to 'I've Got A Feeling', where alternating I and IV triads, over an A bass pedal, create a D/A chord – just as we have here – but this time setting up a hypnotic tonic groove rather than embarking on a distinct progression.

song around it? It's as though McCartney can't resist one last hearing of his prize polychord, and so creates this mini-coda especially to accommodate it.

Martha's adventures in rambling harmony

Having tackled this A-level case study, it's time to face McCartney's advanced version for PhD students, indeed one that had already set a stiff musical examination back on *The White Album*. 'Martha My Dear' bears many similarities to 'The Long And Winding Road': it is dominated by Cycle Of Fifths movements, though fights against them at times with the help of both deceptive cadences and the very same slash chord of a major triad-with-9th-in-the-bass.

But if the journey along 'The Long And Winding Road' was not without its diversions, then 'Martha My Dear' is a musical rollercoaster at the mercy of McCartney's free spirit, and in this respect is like no other song in The Beatles catalogue. No neat harmonic hedgerows on this particular suburban path, just wild countryside where Martha herself – Macca's sheepdog that is – can roam free.

The Cycle Of Fifths action in the verse has already been discussed in Chapter 4: a highly conventional 'Mr Sandman'-style mega-Cycle (set up by that great 'V7 of iii' 'sec dom') that dates from twenties Tin Pan Alley. In stark contrast, however, are the utterly novel meanderings of the elaborate 'double bridge' structure, which appear as follows:

'Martha My Dear' (part 1)

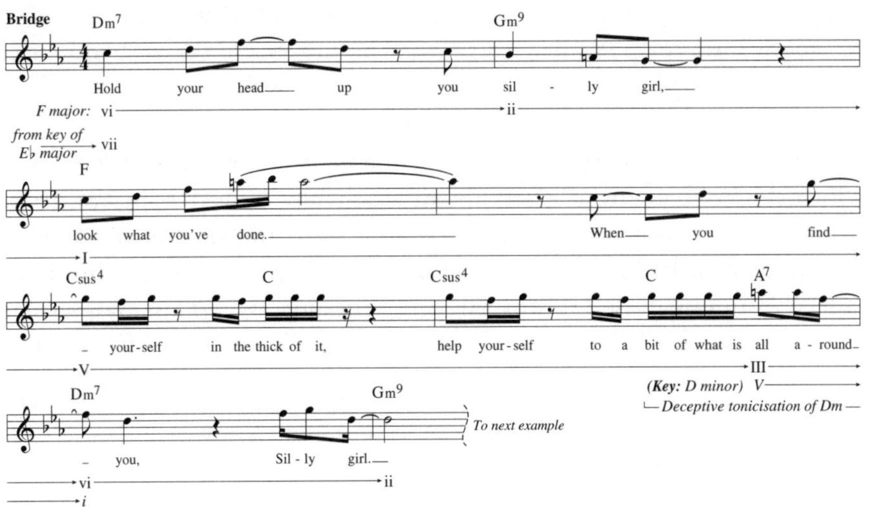

From the word go we're faced with one of the very few Beatles middles that starts on vii minor. As we know, this doesn't automatically confirm a modulation to a key centre on this root – a 'ii–V' that pulls to the relative minor is the most likely explanation (as we find in, say, 'Yesterday'). Alternatively we've seen how this chord can lead to an eventual modulation to iii, or to a modal (Lydian) ploy in the original key (as in the various theories on the 'Julia' bridge).

But Martha does none of these, for as we follow the thread, the Dm7 is eventually best seen (uniquely in The Beatles catalogue) as a new vi chord that is gravitating towards the main bridge tonality of F major. The Cycle Of Fifths is again our best guide as we follow McCartney's muse, but, in keeping with the uncontrollable subject, nothing quite goes according to plan – or certainly musical convention. For a start, the new tonic is reached initially 'from the ii' (unusual but still just a slide down the harmonised scale). Having missed out on the dominant in those opening bars, McCartney immediately teases us with an obvious V, as the C chord gets into the action with some repeated sus 4s that, for all the world, *must* resolve to F.

Yet they don't, as we enjoy yet another type of Deceptive cadence, which takes us right back to the opening Dm7 as a vi chord. With shades of the Aeolian cadence, the relative minor is arguably briefly targeted *as a key centre* in its own right, though the mechanism for the tonicisation is not through a dreamy, flattened leading tone, as in 'Not A Second Time'. For that intervening A7 – plucked out of thin air as a priming dominant – almost catapults the song to this distant destination. Indeed, if we glance back to our modulation map of Chapter 10, we can understand this as a very brief move to 'the key of the vii' in relation to our parent key of E♭. What better musical representation of Martha's adventures in pastures new?

As if that weren't enough, we have the second act of the middle section where McCartney now expertly ups the ante in terms of the tonal ambiguity. The Gm is now replaced by a G7 that makes our sense of key as hard to read as the new landscape in the song.[29] This author then feels the pull to B minor gently reinforced, before graduating back towards F via our long-awaited slash chord, which teases us in a similar fashion to 'The

[29] One interpretation would be that ii of F is being replaced by II7 of F (or 'V of V'). This mixing of minor and dominant is another stylish Tin Pan Alley convention that has the effect of changing the emphasis in a Cycle Of Fifths resolution. See especially Jack Strachey's 'These Foolish Things' whose verse mixes Em7 and E9 en route to D.

'Martha My Dear' – (part 2)

Long And Winding Road'. As in that song, the B♭/C should take us to F major, homing in on it from both sides in a IV-I and V-I pincer movement. Even when McCartney eases off the tension to give us a straight B♭ major, we expect the underlying progression to unfold in a familiar sequential V-IV-I blues resolution. But again the principle of *The Violation Of Expectations* is working overtime as F is thwarted again by the relative minor, though now with 'IV-vi' – yet another Beatles method of achieving a Deceptive cadence.

In the first strain our brief sojourn to Dm introduced the 'silly girl' in the form of that tonally ambiguous Gm9. The same chord now prompts the retransition from the second section by neatly acting as a pivot common to both F major (if you accept this as a temporary tonality) and the parent key of E♭ major to which we head for the solo.

It's often said that while The Beatles touched on styles ranging from R'n'B, blues, pop, rock 'n' roll, country, vaudeville, hard rock and even heavy metal, they didn't experiment with jazz. 'Martha My Dear' surely disproves that. With a verse rooted in the traditions of pure trad jazz and this double bridge bordering on free-form fusion, the song is, as the muso quip goes, 'close enough for jazz'. For what it's worth, this author finds it one of the most harmonically, and analytically, challenging pieces of music in the entire Beatles catalogue.

But then some revisionists claim the song isn't about a sheepdog at all but is rather some friendly advice to a former McCartney girlfriend. Or perhaps a bit of both, with Ian MacDonald suggesting the sheepdog itself somehow gets mixed up in a recent love affair.[30] 'Scintillatingly gifted as this song is, it's also totally devoid of meaning,' is his verdict. But whatever the true inspiration, this affectionately rambling harmony weaves a magical spell that ultimately defies analysis.

Meanwhile, refocusing on this same special slash chord, we can jump forward to *Abbey Road* to find The Beatles using it to prompt a rather more easily appreciable modulation within the side 2 medley. Not such a frantic setting this time, as that ethereal sonority leads us gloriously into the verse of 'Sun King'. Having seen the chord played by both piano and guitar, here it is fashioned by means of vocal harmony.

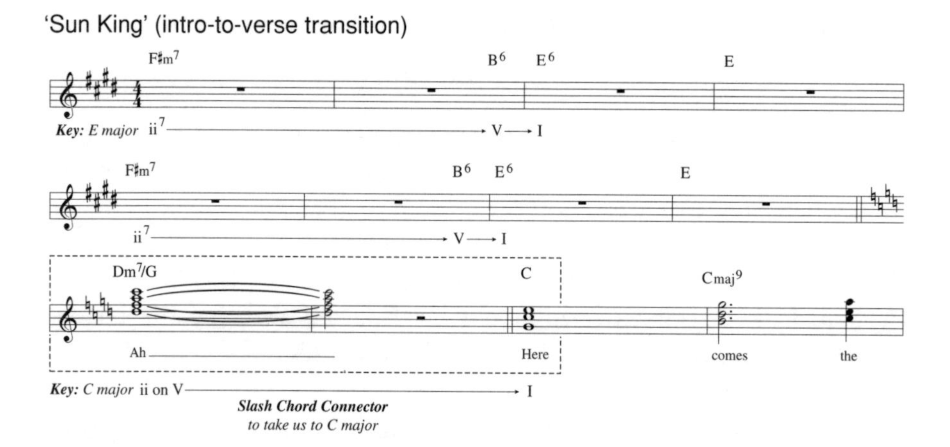

If the name of the chord doesn't appear quite the same as our earlier constructions it can be understood through the most basic of substitutions. Indeed many transcriptions notate the chord as an F/G on its way to C, and that is a perfectly practical way of looking at it. Others, however, hear the prominence of a D note which adds a rather sweeter, lush flavour to the chord, effectively turning the F major triad (on the left-hand side of the 'slash') into its relative minor, Dm7. Technically, therefore, while the bass still moves V-I, the voice-leading in the upper harmony sees a variation on a formal IV-I Plagal move through a simple step-wise diatonic descent

[30] *Revolution In The Head*, p. 282.

from ii-I in terms of the targeted C chord.[31] As Dm7/G, this chord represents another combination cadence to go with the Aeolian/Phrygian of 'Because' and the more formal 'soul cadence' of 'The Long And Winding Road'.[32]

Indeed slash chords help us to identify other hybrid permutations. For example, look back at the famous C to A bridge modulation of 'Something' to find that, while the basic mechanism is a ♭VII-I cadence, the bass adds a delicate twist. The G chord that prompts the A major is in second inversion (G/D), with the D bass adding some Plagal 'down-a-fourth' action (D to A) to the whole step ascent from G to A.

The D note is already a member of the G triad – which is one reason why these ♭VII-to-I moves work so well in the first place.

The same move appears further into the 'one sweet dream' section of 'You Never Give Me Your Money', though here the harmony is not as clear-cut as a straight modulation from C major to A major, with McCartney again toying expertly with tonal ambiguity in tandem with the lyrics.

'You Never Give Me Your Money' – F section (at 2.38)

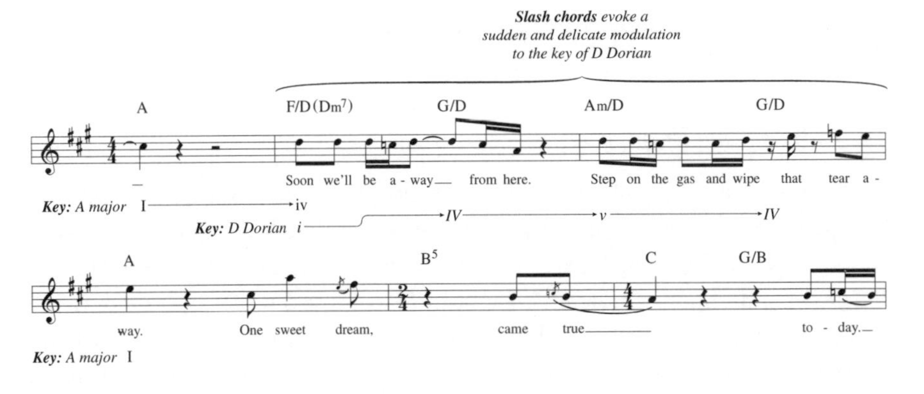

Having reached A major so resoundingly, McCartney immediately takes a U-Turn, with the euphoric major tonality giving way just as quickly as it

[31] Either way, the chord's function is without question to effect colourfully the modulation from E major to C major. No fancy pivots here, just a dominant-rooted connector that The Beatles pull out of the bag as a first choice when making any key switch.

[32] Citron specifically describes the fashion 'since 1960' among piano-based songwriters of using this slash chord as a 'lead-in chord by putting V in the bass, and the ii in the right hand (right hand D,F,A,C; left hand G)'; *Songwriting*, p. 241.

arrived. The D root section looks initially to be just a run-of-the-mill development of the subdominant but now the harmony is minor. And not merely a 'borrowed iv' which will quickly take us back to a major footing (as in 'That Means A Lot'), but one which, followed by a G triad, teases us with a ii–V to C major. This is then thwarted by the A minor that confirms we have left A major, but all the while we are dealing with slash chords courtesy of that resolute D bass which acts as a pedal for all these floating harmonies.

The only satisfactory explanation is a deft interlude in D Dorian that expertly represents a new tonality to match the line 'soon we'll be away from here'.

Just how much cleverer can this song get? Remember, this is yet another in a long line of spectacular musical devices crammed into this multi-part masterpiece that works all by itself as a mini-medley, setting a standard that the rest of side 2 of *Abbey Road* can hardly hope to match.

The special case of the 'added 6th' and 'minor 6th'

We cannot leave any discussion of slash chords and inversions without referring to two chords that can also masquerade under different names due to their rather special constructions.

The added 6th and its inversion

First up is a favourite chord of The Beatles in a whole range of contexts. It appears as a colouring for a V chord in songs like 'Can't Buy Me Love' (as we saw in Chapter 1), though it can be heard long before *With The Beatles* in 'The Sheik Of Araby'. Even in Hamburg, The Beatles were using it as a clichéd jazzy closer on the tonic in their cover of 'I Remember You'. Later they would use it to colour triads in songs ranging from 'No Reply' right through to 'Sun King'. Look again at 'Sun King' to find a perfect Beatles example of the 'somnambulistic' properties of the added 6th chord as Jimmy Webb describes them, explaining:

'The sixth tone in the scale is thought by some to have a mesmerising effect on the human psyche … the impressionists (Ravel, Debussy, etc.) used it to good effect in creating dreamlike textures.'[33]

[33] Jimmy Webb, *Tunesmith: Inside The Art Of Songwriting*; p. 202.

The lush arpeggios of 'Sun King' are surely as dreamlike a texture as one could hope to find in pop, though the description is surely valid for some of The Beatles' early R'n'B faves, like Chuck Berry's 'Havana Moon' and Bo Diddley's 'Crackin' Up', both founded on the premise of hypnotic, dreamy 6ths.[34]

The quirk of the added 6th is that it is an extended chord *that is not constructed in straight harmonised thirds.* Normally an added chord is built by piling up diatonic thirds above the 5th degree. Hence the 6th note of, say, G major (E) should only appear as a 13th, i.e., after the 7th, 9th and 11th notes have been added to the stack. This makes it officially the last possible extension before the double octave.

But the added 6th short-cuts this mega-pandiatonic cluster by being, as its name suggests, just added to a simple major triad. The upshot of this is that the chord's constituent tones can be juggled to reconstruct another chord genuinely built in conventional thirds.

This is a roundabout way of elaborating on the relationship between G added 6th and Em7 that we introduced in Chapter 3 (the two chords are just inversions of each other). But this more detailed background helps us tackle a rather more involved construction involving the *minor* 6th.

The minor 6th and its incarnations

Again the relationship is between roots that are a diatonic third apart, though the m6 is equivalent to a dissonant m7♭5 chord a third lower, a structure we've had trouble using in a pop song. For example, Em6 contains *exactly* the same notes as C♯m7♭5 – the point being that both chords must therefore feature a disturbing tritone in their make-up, creating some serious tension for discerning songwriters to exploit. In Em6 we can spot it between the ♭3rd and 6th notes (G and C♯), transposing the root-♭5 disquiet of its 'cousin', C♯m7♭5.

But that's not the end of this special harmonic relationship, for both these chords can also be thought of as equivalent to a dominant chord a fourth higher – in this case, A9 without its root.[35]

[34] Hence the added 6th can blur the line between major and relative minor ('And I Love Her'); and makes a neat closing gesture when juxtaposing the two ('I'm Happy Just To Dance With You').

[35] The fact that there is no A root demonstrates how, when playing and naming chords, seemingly vital notes can in fact be omitted. The essence of a chord is captured far more by the 3rd and 7th of the structure than by the easily discarded 5th and even the root.

The following table shows how each of these chords share the same collection of notes.

		← Tritone →		
	E	**G**	**B**	**C♯**
Em^{6}	Root	♭3	5	6
C♯m$^{7♭5}$	♭3	♭5	♭7	Root
A^{9}	5	♭7	9	3

The result is that the three chords often exchange names depending on context. The Beatles demonstrate how this relationship increases a songwriter's opportunities for root movement and texture, with a highly unusual chord change in the bridge to 'Honey Pie'.[36]

'Honey Pie' (bridge)

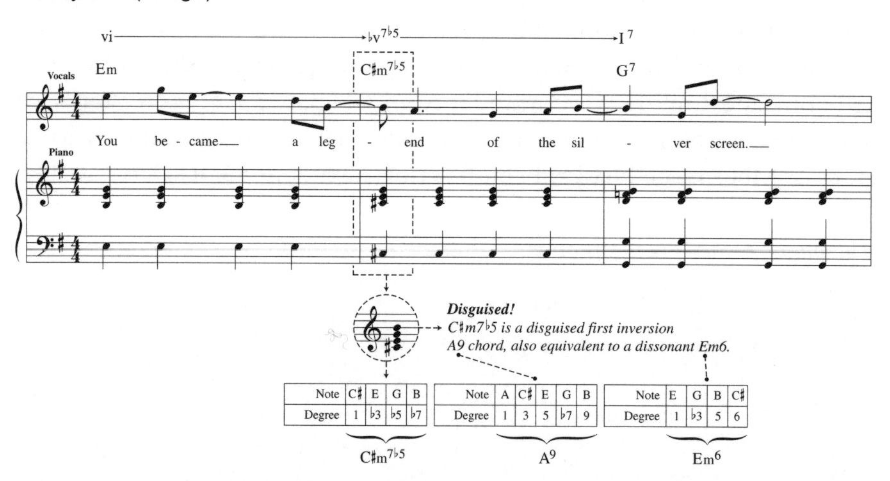

The table above will help us to follow McCartney's thinking, as well as transcriptions that term the chord a seemingly interloping C♯m7♭5. For the song's chief tonal centre is G major, and therefore any chord built on this ♭5 degree should be unthinkable (given the reputation of *Diabolus in Musica*). Even more so for what might be mistaken for an innocent, rigidly diatonic pop song.

[36] See Sokolow, *The Complete Jazz Guitar*, p. 24, for practical application of the substitution rules arising from this special relationship.

Having moved predictably to Em, the relative minor, to start the bridge, McCartney looks set to begin a Cycle Of Fifths move to an A7.This would be in keeping with the Pre-War style of the song, while providing the perfect harmonisation for the A and G notes in the melody, Indeed, playing the song in precisely this manner works almost as well.

Almost – for, being McCartney, he had to include a signature touch of brilliance. Rather than a root-position bass (or even a 2nd inversion, which would have been so familiar from the earlier *Sgt. Pepper* album), Paul effectively delivers this phantom A chord in 1st inversion.The result is a C♯ in the bass which lends a brilliant touch of sophistication, due to the fleeting tritone created between C♯ and the G (the latter note being in the melody at this point as well as being the tonic to which we return in the next bar).

The heart of the legendary 'Honey Pie' chord is therefore a simple A7, with a B note in the melody, but this takes on a new dimension when seen in terms of the bass note (the vital clue to the nature of the manoeuvre). In summary therefore, McCartney is employing a *C♯m7♭5 substitute* for an A dominant 9th in 1st inversion'.[37] While many such inversions are the result of McCartney's bass runs on his electric bass, it was highly revealing to find him playing this run interspersed with chords – *on guitar* – on the *Anthology 3* out-take, suggesting that he was thinking of bass and upper harmony simultaneously.

However you view it, the air of surprise and uncertainty created by the ambiguous m7♭5 chord plays on our emotions far more than the straight A dominant and forces us to evoke subliminally the image of the 'legend of the silver screen'.[38]

We've already seen the beautifully bizarre G-E♭7-E7 change in the verse of 'Honey Pie' (see Chapter 7), and this moment almost tops that for novelty. Given that the song contains two of The Beatles' most interesting (and unique) chord changes, it seems bizarre that it has been the target of such vitriolic attack – from John ('beyond redemption') Lennon downwards.

[37] Em6 with the 6th in the bass would be another way to see the relationship.

[38] Tagg refers to the role of the m7♭5 as 'a sign denoting that a key change may or may not occur', and that it is this 'uncertainty of direction, with all that such modulation might (or might not) entail in terms of heightened musical drama and rhetoric' which provides a 'dramatic charge' relevant to the semiotics of 'tritonal crime'; *Tritone Crime*, p. 8. The C♯m7♭5 of 'Honey Pie' could itself take us to various places, most obviously to B minor via F♯7; and from there back to G major via D7.

Still, while this particular three-headed 'Cerberus' requires a head-scratching interpretation, it is nothing compared to the ultimate piece of harmonic schizophrenia in The Beatles' repertoire of unusual chords. Make way for a rather distinctive jolt to the system, courtesy of a single magical onslaught of sound, which requires its own entire chapter to appreciate fully.

THIRTEEN

The 'A Hard Day's Night' Chord – Rock's Holy Grail

'*Chaaaang!* . . . It's been a hard day's night'

No single sound in the history of music is as instantly recognisable as the throat-grabbing tones that herald the start of 'A Hard Day's Night'.

'The most famous chord in all of rock & roll,' claimed *Rolling Stone* when revisiting the introduction that needs no introduction, a sound that continues to reverberate five decades after kick-starting the 1964 film and soundtrack of the same name.[1]

'The chord is quirky, arresting, unmistakably original – the musical equivalent of the song's title,' says Mark Hertsgaard, neatly summing up the scores of eulogies that pre-date his own 1995 Beatles retrospective. 'A hijacked church bell announcing the party of the year'.[2] *Guitarist* magazine also acknowledges that George Harrison 'pretty much defined the sound of an era,' with one strum of his legendary Rickenbacker 360/12 – a 12-string guitar immortalised, as a result, among *The 10 Greatest Electric Guitars In The World . . . Ever!!*[3]

The adjectives and accolades keep piling up for this three-second commotion which seems to unite Beatles fans across all walks of life:

'The opening chord of the song was like an amazing wake-up call,' said Joey Ramone, when choosing the song in his list of all-time favourite

[1] 'The Stories Behind The Making Of The 27 Number One Songs'; *Rolling Stone*, Issue 863, 1st March 2001, p. 33.

[2] Hertsgaard, *A Day In The Life: The Music And Artistry Of The Beatles*; p. 74.

[3] See list chosen by *Guitarist*, December 2000, p. 70.

tracks.[4] It's not just rock stars and bedroom guitarists for whom the chord has become so symbolic. Long-time Beatles authority, Ray Connolly, picked it for its sheer 'bravura' when asked for his stand-out sound-bites from the entire catalogue.[5] Similarly, of all the *embarras de riches* on *1*, the 20 million-selling compilation of US and UK chart-toppers, the review in the *Daily Mail* singled out this same 'invincible' moment as its first highlight.[6]

Among the litany of adjectives used to describe the chord, Adrian Thrills' 'invincible' says it all. Certainly, in terms of heated debate over its constituent notes and precise construction (not to mention 'correct' name), there's nothing to touch it anywhere in rock. With apologies to Wagner's 'Tristan' chord (which has been responsible for armies of classical critics destroying small forests), no sound since The Big Bang has attracted so much analysis and interpretation.

'So what *is* that damned chord?' challenge the experts at *Guitarist* magazine, mirroring the frustrations of their readers and anyone who has ever searched in vain for the magic voicing.[7] It is testimony to the chord's enduring charm and mystique that the magazine's editor describes it as 'a genuine Holy Grail . . . one of popular music's great unsolved mysteries . . . a chord that I've still not heard anyone play convincingly'.[8]

This is despite a stupefying range of theories put forward over the years, which incredibly – without exception – serve to bamboozle the hardened muso and bedroom guitarist alike. Take the following table, which summarises just some of over 30 suggestions collected down the years (all assume the song is in the correct key of G major unless otherwise specified).

The search for The Gretty Chord may have kept Beatles musos busy in the nineties, but it was merely a quaint diversion from the main event.

Some of the suggestions can be binned immediately. Any that aren't in the intended recorded key of G are obviously wide of the mark, for start. As are those that throw a G *major* 7th into the ring, for there is surely no

[4] '60 minutes with Joey Ramone', *Guitar World*, August 2000, p. 40.

[5] Ray Connolly in correspondence with the author, December 2000.

[6] Adrian Thrills' review of *1* in the *Daily Mail*, November 10th 2000.

[7] 'Fab Gear, Beatles Tracks and Guitars', *Guitarist*, Live 2001 issue, p. 81.

[8] Neville Marten, in conversation with the author, elaborating on his column from *Guitarist*, March 2000, p. 9.

That chord – the nominations are . . .

Author	Date	Publication	Description
Wilfrid Mellers	1973	*Twilight Of The Gods: The Music Of The Beatles* (p. 43)	'A dominant 9th of F' (in the key of C)
Terence O'Grady	1975	*The Music Of The Beatles* (p. 178)	'G-C-F-B♭-D-G ... an open strum at the 3rd fret'
Songbook	1970s	*Beatles Songbook* (p. 90)	'C-B♭-D-F-G-C' (Key of C)
Steven Porter	1979	*Rhythm & Harmony...* (p. 216)	'A polytriad ii^7/V in A♭major'
Terence O'Grady	1983	*The Beatles: A Musical Evolution* (p. 48)	'A polychord which juxtaposes the tonic and subtonic'
Alexander Villinger	1983	*Die Beatles Songs...* (p. 165)	'G-D-F-C-D-G' (G^7sus^4)
Milton Okun (ed.)	1984	*The Beatles Guitar* (p. 112)	G^7sus^4(open position)
Songbook	1986	*The Beatles Rock Score* (p. 24)	D^7sus^4(open position)
Tim Riley	1988	*Tell Me Why* (p. 99)	G^7 with added ninth and suspended fourth
Alan Pollack	1992	'Notes on ... Series' (no. 49)	'A superimposition of Dm, F and G'
Fujita, Hagino, Kubo, Sato	1993	*The Beatles Complete Scores* (p. 359)	'$Gsus^4$/D' – 6 string: D-G-C-G 12-string: $Gsus^4$ (3rd fret)
Ian MacDonald	1994	*Revolution In The Head* (p. 102)	$G^{11}sus^4$
Mark Herstgaard	1995	*A Day In The Life* (p. 74)	'A variant of F major or of G major^7'
Allan Kozinn	1995	*The Beatles* (p. 96)	'Different voicings of $Gsus^4$'
Wolf Marshall	1997	*Guitar Signature Licks series* (p. 61)	G^7sus^4(on 6- & 12-string)
Rikky Rooksby	1999	*Complete Beatles Chord Songbook* (p. 8)	G^7sus^4(barre chord at 3rd fret)
Joe Bennett	2000	*Guitar On Tap!* (p. 43)	'G^7sus^4/A'
Pandel Collaros	2001	The Music Of The Beatles *(Beatlestudies III)*	Dm^{11} with no 9th
Walter Everett	2001	*The Beatles As Musicians: The Quarry Men Through Rubber Soul* (p.237)	12-string: F-A-C-G [matched in piano], above D bass
Charles Shaar Murray	2002	*MOJO: The Beatlemania Special Edition* (p.116)	'Gm7add11'
Arthur Dick	2009	*Play Guitar With . . . The Beatles 1962–1966* p. 56 (with recreated CD audio tracks)	G9sus4/D

F♯ note anywhere within earshot. The same goes for the 'open strum at the 3rd fret' which implies a rogue B♭, a sound that is also absent.

By the time we kick into touch The People's Choice, 'G7sus4', guilty, as we'll explain, of a sin of both omission and position, we're left with barely a handful of realistic descriptions from our panel of experts, and most of those fall frustratingly shy of a name and shape.

This might seem like nit-picking, but surely this definitive Beatles mystery needs solving. However, as we may have guessed, this is easier said than done. The dedication of a complete chapter to barely three seconds of music may smack of self-indulgence, but these complex textures genuinely require the most intricate of jigsaw puzzle approaches to piece together.

Setting the scene – gathering the evidence

Accompanying us on our adventure are at least a dozen different versions of the intro chord. Ironically they both help and hinder us in almost equal measure as we attempt to speculate on just what The Beatles were up to on 16th April 1964. As well as the finished stereo soundtrack version there's the impromptu 'Crinsk Dee Night' rendition on *Live At The BBC*, whose sparser sound will prove important to our analysis. Different again is the *Anthology 1* out-take, which emerges as 'Take 1' of the nine listed takes that took place that historic day in Abbey Road.

It was certainly a hard week for John, Paul, George and Ringo as they filmed sequences for the film itself, running amok through pubs and makeshift 'police stations', in Holland Park, and charging down fire escapes at the old Hammersmith Odeon. However, their main appointment on the Thursday was a three-hour stint in Studio 2. As the bootlegs reveal, it was a session that saw The Beatles deliver several strikes of The Chord, both on the various takes (some of which were aborted because they fluffed the chord itself!) and, in a few helpful instances, *in-between* takes. We will be summarising the sounds from a bootleg of the surviving session reel and devising a theory of how The Chord might have developed that night.[9]

The Harrison chord – revealed!

But why make life difficult for ourselves when George Harrison himself has come to our rescue to reveal not only his incontestably vital contribution – but also what is a disarmingly simple guitar chord?

George finally spilled the beans during an online chat in early 2001. Here is a transcript of that magic moment:[10]

[9] Our discussions of the original unreleased backing tracks refer to those available on *Abbey Road Studio Sessions Volume 3* and also *The John Barrett Tapes* of the Abbey Road years, Box Two 1964–1966, CD 1.

[10] *Yahoo!* online chat, 15th February 2001 – see transcript at hollywoodandvine.com.

Q: Mr Harrison, what is the opening chord you used for 'A Hard Day's Night'?
A: It is F with a G on top (on the 12-string), but you'll have to ask Paul about the bass note to get the proper story.[11]

With these priceless words, George not only shatters the illusions of generations of buskers who swear by a trusty G7sus4 as the correct chord, he also confirms what many a Beatles fan has long suspected – that this is not just about a single twang from a lone guitar.

George's shape emerges – perhaps surprisingly – as a not-so-dramatic, easily-fingered F major triad with added 9th, played in first position on the guitar (however, for many this alone constitutes a piece of controversy – to which we shall be returning).

The next revelation is that this chord only contains four notes: the F, A, and C that reflect the root, 3rd and 5th of F major, together with the G that is the added ninth. This is a long way from the mega-cluster of *at least* six different notes that we will eventually be suggesting. More to the point, while there is scope for 'doubling' the F note by 'thumbing' the first fret of the bottom string, the evidence all points to the fact that George is only playing the top four strings of the guitar. Here is how the fingering looks on paper:

Harrison's F added 9th

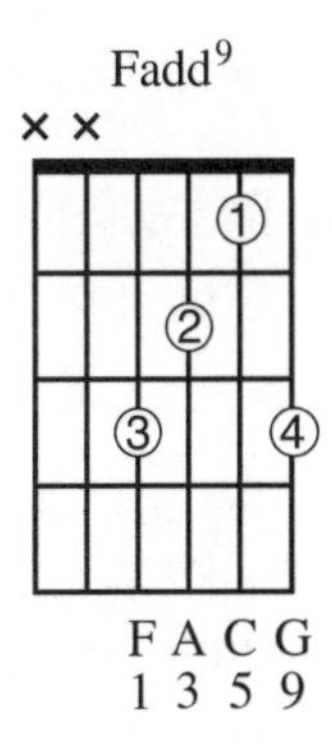

[11] This in fact mirrors George's reply to a rather more select audience in Auckland, New Zealand, at a press conference to support the launch of 'Fifty Years Adrift' by Beatle press officer, Derek Taylor. 'F, with a G on the first string,' were the words that day, captured on videotape by *Eyewitness News*, on 28th November 1984 (as unearthed by Walter Everett).

At this point some readers may be sceptical as to the validity of this chord. Certainly if you expect it to match the sound you hear pounding through your speakers on the original single, or soundtrack album, you're going to be disappointed.

This is for many, many reasons, starting with the fact that, in the case of a 12-string guitar, the 'top four strings' actually means the top four *pairs* of strings.[12] This combination of octave and unison tunings has vital sonic ramifications, and means that we will struggle to duplicate the sound on any 6-string instrument. Here is tablature and music notation that shows why those 'doubled' notes are so vital to the texture of the chord.

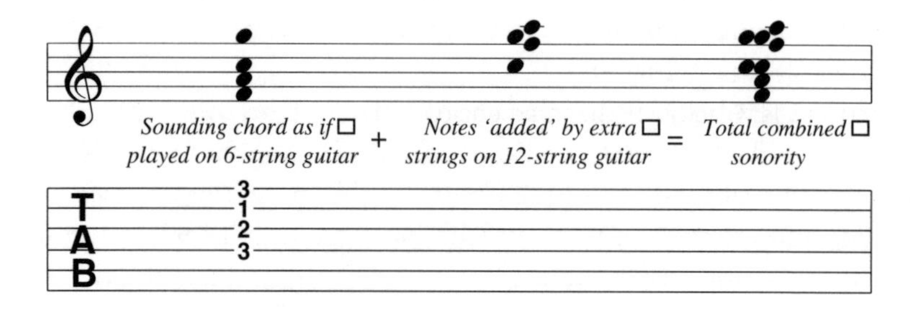

The Coda Clue

As a brief interlude let's jump from the beginning of the song to that famous jangly passage at the end (2.21–2.27). This nifty bit of picking has attracted almost as much attention as the intro itself:

> 'A swirling fade-out that foreshadows the druggy electronics that will play such an important role in the group's music a few years hence,' suggests Hertsgaard.[13]

More importantly for our purposes, this coda chord happens to be another Fadd9 in 1st position, albeit one now heard far more clearly since it is arpeggiated in isolation. Could it in some way confirm the essence of the opening chord of which many will still be unconvinced?

It doesn't seem too far-fetched to suggest that Harrison is, in effect,

[12] The six pairs of strings on the 12-string Rickenbacker are tuned as follows (from low to high): E, A, D and G in octaves; B and E in unison.

[13] Hertsgaard, *A Day In The Life: The Music And Artistry Of The Beatles*; p. 74.

symmetrically 'book-ending' the whole song with a single chord. Everett is one of several Beatles experts who thinks so. 'It was a common Beatle effect to end a piece with a dissonant sonority that relates to the work's opening,' he explained when dissecting 'You Never Give Me Your Money', before referring back to 'A Hard Day's Night' and citing the 'coda's "frozen" subtonic element that is related to the introduction'.[14]

Of course we don't *have* to accept this theory – it's perfectly conceivable that George is playing two different chords. But before we examine the intro in more detail it is essential to listen very carefully to the various notes of the 12-string as the picking unfolds – and, in particular, *their registers*. This will help us in the identification parade we need to undertake within the opening texture.

The jangly coda: F added 9th as an arpeggio (2.21)

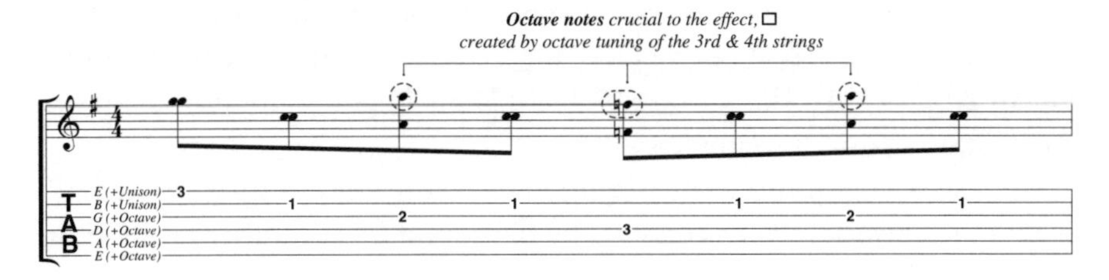

This transcription explodes the established myth that the line is played by alternating the G and F notes by lifting the little finger on and off the top E string.[15] As George himself once explained to Gary Moore, the authentic sound is achieved by holding down a single *stationary* shape throughout, allowing the right-hand picking and the idiosyncrasies of the 12-string octave/unison tuning to create the moving line.[16]

One of the defining elements of the sound is a high A note – *an octave above* the A fingered at the 2nd fret of the G string. For despite the fact that the highest note being *nominally* fingered is George's top G at the 3rd fret, an A pitch a whole-step higher appears as the peak of a delicate ascending

[14] Walter Everett, *Concert Music, Rock And Jazz Since 1945*, p. 222 (and footnote 37).

[15] The transcription here relates to the second of the repeated two-bar figures, to avoid the slight confusion caused by George playing a brief upstroke across the top strings of the chord (on the final word 'right') before starting the pattern.

[16] Gary Moore in conversation with the author, 21st February 2001.

line. It is that shimmering presence *back in the intro* that helps us not only to identify the Rickenbacker's Fadd9 chord, but also to distinguish it from by far the most common attempt at this chord, G7sus4. A chord that, rather fundamentally, lacks an A note.

Building the Polychord – the Live At The BBC *intro*

Meanwhile, the version heard on *Live At The BBC*, recorded three months later on 14th July 1964, represents essential listening.

In this sparse setting we get the ideal chance to hear an Fadd9 from George's 12-string chiming away in the mix. There's that giveaway 'high A' note, now easily distinguished both on the initial attack, and when later resonating above the G during the decay. The C note is also in evidence in the cluster, as is – though rather less obviously – the F itself.

While this excursion at the Beeb seems to confirm the composition and shape of George's 'F with a G on top', it also reminds us (if we didn't already suspect) that the intro to 'A Hard Day's Night' is not just about one cataclysmic strum on a single guitar.

For a start, the shimmer of a Ringo ride cymbal is clearly in evidence – even if the crash at attack is masked by the sound from another rather more fundamental source.

Just as Harrison himself pointed out, we don't get the whole story without McCartney's bass contribution, a resounding D note with which he opens the whole saga. This vital punch is heard clearly on the *BBC* version as a *low* D (at the 73Hz frequency, as we must crucially specify at this point) on Paul's Hofner electric bass, and puts another spanner in the works.[17]

D represents an additional note to the original cluster of four, and also scuppers any chance we have of viewing this *combined* guitar and bass sonority as a conventional chord. We now have a sound that takes on a whole new dimension, with F, A, C, G and D best understood as the slash chord: F added 9th/D.[18]

Guitarists wanting to capture the overall effect of the *Live At The BBC* intro might want give the following hybrid shape a whirl. This is the first

[17] It is suggested that this low D is played at the 5th fret of the A string.

[18] Notice that on *Live At The BBC* the low D is also heard prominently under the closing Fadd9. As we'll discuss later, the same notes in relation to D spell Dm7 [add 11] (though not Dm11, as there is no 9th).

of several strategies with which we will be attempting to replicate the overall sound of The Chord, first taking the Harrison shape and blending it with a D bass note, cheekily accommodated here through dropped-D tuning:

The 'Virtual *BBC*' Dropped-D clanger: 'F added 9th /D'

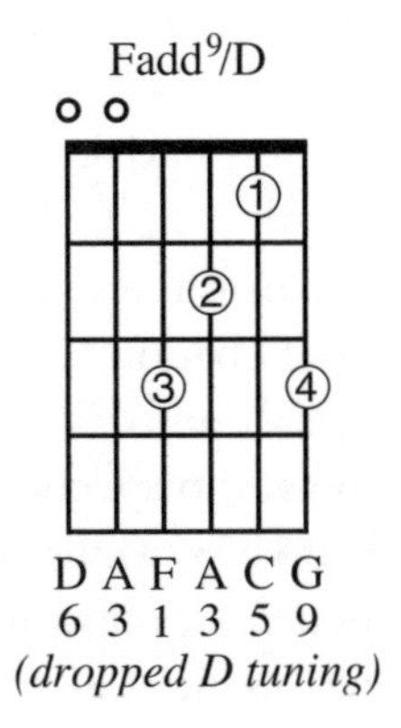

Admittedly it will be difficult to progress much further into the song with the bottom string detuned, but it might be enough to impress your friends at a showcase consisting of a single strum.[19] Certainly if *Live At The BBC* had been the only version of 'A Hard Day's Night' that The Beatles had ever recorded, this simple slash formula – easily recreated by any cover band with a 12-string guitar and bass (and cymbal!) – would have spelt the end of our obsession. But it wasn't, and it doesn't!

After all, why is it that among the many nominations from our panel of experts, an Fadd9/D, clearly split between guitar and bass, is conspicuous by its absence?[20] This rather novel combination, which may have eluded some commentators, surely accurately reflects the concept and sound of the chord as we've explored it so far.

The answer is, of course, that the *BBC* intro is different in many fundamental respects to its soundtrack counterpart, which we all implicitly take as the definitive version. *BBC* is but a mellow twang in comparison to the crashing chord from hell that greeted listeners to the

[19] You could of course re-finger the basic F and G chords in the song as F/G and G/A to stay in tune!

[20] Walter Everett and Arthur Dick are among the few to describe this relationship.

album and single. Here we have something far more exotic – a huge, threatening 'pan-chromatic cluster' that casts a giant shadow over the rest of the song.

That's not to say that Fadd9/D is not relevant to the soundtrack chord – it is absolutely fundamental to the structure. But there are other elements in the overall sound that distort – sometimes seriously, sometimes subtly – the way we perceive this complex sonority in its entirety.

Splitting the difference – the right and left channels

Early Beatles recordings are famous for their extreme positioning of sounds between the left and right channels. Pan certain songs hard right or left and you will find that vocals and guitars will magically drop out, sometimes completely, from the audio spectrum.

The stereo version of 'A Hard Day's Night' is a case in point – and a comparison of our opening nemesis as it emerges from the two different channels is a recommended ear-opening exercise for any Beatles fan.

What follows is an analysis based on many hours of teeth-clenching listening, involving not merely splitting the channels, but sampling them independently into a computer, and tracking each of the waves on the screen as it unfolds over those 3 seconds, searching for clues – *any* clues. Further research involved manipulating the wave so as to both *extend* it (doubling the time period at the same pitch) and *vary its pitch.*

When all this proved inconclusive, certain sections of sound were divided up into split-second, bite-size chunks, and then looped continuously on a CD player and 'walked through' in fractions of seconds, 'freezing' each increment with various sampler-based devices designed to home-in on rogue sounds.

Apart from reviewing at least 30 published theories, literally dozens of 'accomplices', including musicians, sound engineers, guitar teachers, music transcribers and cyberspace geeks – were consulted intermittently over many weeks. Even Beatles tribute bands (whose search for the 'A Hard Day's Night' chord is an essential part of the job description) were petitioned in an attempt to solve a riddle that makes the search for the Aeolian cadence look like a stroll in the park.

While this author would not stake his life on the accuracy of what follows, he feels honour bound, especially given the long tradition of experts at the front line of Beatles trivia, at least to throw his hat into the ring. At the very least we'll be finally emerging with a radically different theory to add to the growing mountain already out there – and one that Beatles enthusiasts are welcome to demolish along with all the others.

The left-hand channel – Paul's high D note

Our first port-of-call might seem, initially, not to add anything to what we already know. For the left-hand channel, reassuringly, seems broadly identical in concept to the sound we hear as the total chord on the *BBC* version. Once again a resounding D bass note is heard from McCartney's Hofner above which floats George's Rickenbacker and its ringing Fadd9. Again, each of the constituent notes of D, F, A, C and G can be heard (with varying degrees of clarity as the chord unfolds), both in real-time listening and certainly with a slow-motion 'walk through' with the sampler.

However, as well as a subtle twist in Ringo's drum strategy (to which we will return later), there is a vital difference in the *register* of the D bass note. On *Live At The BBC*, it sat darkly underneath the guitar chord, well out of the way – a deep, sustained boom in the bottom end. We will later be referring to another such low D (at 73Hz , as stated earlier, and termed D2 in the standard system where C4 corresponds to middle C) but, crucially, only on the *right-hand* channel. On this left-hand side, it is a D3 (equivalent to the open D of a conventional six-string guitar) that now dominates.

It's a punchy, penetrating sound that intertwines with the F note in the guitar, making the notes at times difficult to distinguish from each other. There's even what can be described as a slight oscillating 'wave' effect as the F, most prominent at attack, seems to defer to this D three semitones below, almost like a 'virtual pull off', giving the illusion that the former is dropping out of the audio spectrum.

The effect indeed seems to be down to the register of this D which clashes with the F guitar note a minor third above. Meanwhile, in our (admittedly foolhardy) attempt to address every detail, it is also suggested that Paul is playing the D in question at the 12th fret of the Hofner's D string (rather than the 7th fret of the G string). We are swayed here by Arthur Dick who tracked down (almost) authentic Beatle instruments when painstakingly recreating the chord in 2003 for the CD accompanying his latest *Play Guitar With... The Beatles* project.

This 'high D' is a crucial stylistic quirk that we will later see has serious sonic ramifications for our entire analysis. George's suggestion that we question Paul about the bass note should now be seen in a whole new light. If it was the case that we were dealing with an obvious low bass note (as we hear, say, on *Live At The BBC*) we wouldn't really need to ask him – it would stand out like a sore thumb. But this deft voicing, *which fools us into thinking that the D is coming from the guitar rather than the bass*, is more complex, and some McCartney guidance would indeed have helped!

If this seems like totally superfluous *minutiae* it will soon emerge as an utterly pivotal part of the mechanics of the sound, creating a most bizarre effect, ironically, on the *other* side of the mix, where both sound and plot thicken considerably . . .

The right channel – the crashing piano

A radically contrasting landscape greets us as we make the switch from left to right channels. The previously familiar jangle in the upper register is noticeably less pronounced, replaced by a myriad of sounds dominated by the crash of something rather more cataclysmic than a 12-string guitar.

Guitarist magazines speaks diplomatically for all novice strummers when it proclaims:

> 'A lot of people don't notice George Martin's piano chord that sits behind the 12-string Rickenbacker of Harrison on that infamous opening "chaaang".'

George Martin's attempts over the years gently to distance himself from his role in the chord have certainly helped to perpetuate the mystery. As late as 1995, he talked in terms of a 'big clanging guitar beginning' when reminiscing about the intro.[21] But as we know from even a cursory listen to this right-hand channel (not to mention the piano-less out-takes and the modest *BBC* intro), this isn't the whole story.[22]

Apart from doubling the notes of Harrison's guitar *solo* later in the song, the overdubbed presence of the piano in the *intro* is pivotal. If Paul's bass

[21] *In My Life*, BBC TV documentary, 27th December 2000.

[22] *The Live At The BBC* liner notes explain that Martin was expected to join the proceedings at Broadcasting House on 16th July 1964, but never made it: 'The piano solo from the record was rather obviously cut into the session tape as no-one could reproduce what George Martin had played on the single'. That certainly goes for the intro chord!

adds some serious *oomph*, the Steinway Grand now looms just as large and is certainly the next factor that manages to distort our perception of the overall sonority.

Tom Hartman, pianist and guitarist and a long-time Beatles expert at the Internet newsgroup rec.music.beatles, sets the scene:

> 'The piano plays an *enormous* role in the attack and sustain of the chord on the original soundtrack version. It is heavily compressed – as is the entire chord – and would ring-out forever if allowed. It fills in all the mid- and lower- frequencies on the recording, while the 12-string guitar really only supplies the shimmer on top. But guitarists are trying to feel and match that big 'punch', which is coming from the piano, so they can't accept this simple solution and Harrison's minimal four-note chord on just four-strings'.[23]

Just when we think we've cracked it, another twist in this enduring mystery emerges. So what are the notes and fingering of the piano chord? With a bit of detective work we can come up with at least a passable suggestion . . .

In search of the piano voicing

For his 1995 'swansong' album, *In My Life*, George Martin invited Goldie Hawn to record a jazzy version of 'A Hard Day's Night'. Not surprisingly a 'clanging guitar beginning' was deemed inappropriate for this particular 'lounge' rendition, but it didn't stop Sir George from reminiscing about that great moment 31 years previously when interviewed on camera. This is what he said:

> 'We were looking for something big to open it with, an introduction. It needed a strong chord, a dramatic thing. And John hit a chord which I still, to this day, don't know exactly what the notes were – but it was *almost* the open strings.'[24]

[23] In correspondence with the author, January 2001. On the issue of compression, notice how the overall sound is far more powerful on the soundtrack version, due to this effect, than on both the Abbey Road out-takes and *Live At The BBC* where (notwithstanding the absence of piano) the sound of both guitar and bass decays rapidly.

[24] *In My Life*, BBC TV documentary, 27th December 2000.

Sir George immediately followed this comment by plonking out a single dissonant cluster on the piano at which he was sitting. But, just when we think we've been handed the final piece of the jigsaw . . .

> 'That wasn't it!' Martin taunted us, infuriatingly. 'But it was something *like* that!'

Thanks a lot, Sir George!

Martin made no reference to his own contribution, and even seems to have got 'John' mixed up with 'George' (a point to which we return later). Nevertheless, the words 'almost the open strings' – despite being a reference to the guitar – paradoxically provide a vital clue as to the mystery chord played by the *piano*!

Here's why. We already know that Harrison's guitar chord was most definitely not the complete set of un-fretted strings, E-A-D-G-B-E, even though, to this day, this is often the first choice of many a beginner guitarist having a crack at it. Nevertheless, there is an interesting connection between this guitar shape and both Martin's impromptu chord for the TV cameras *and* the one that is sometimes said to feature on the 'A Hard Day's Night' original.

To make that link, let's not forget that this seemingly nondescript, open-string sound has a name. Several, in fact, depending on which note you view as the root. Martin's *In My Life* piano chord was a cluster of these very same notes, reminding us that – *from an E root* – that particular mystery sound emerges as an Em7 (add 11) chord: the notes re-stacked as E-G-A-B-D to reflect the formula: Root-♭3-11-5-♭7.

How does this help us? Play this chord on the piano (or even on the guitar)[25] and you create a dissonant cluster that, while not totally convincing on its own, is good enough, after some lingering dissonance, to kick-start a rough rendition of 'A Hard Day's Night'. Here the effect is created by the root of E moving down a fifth to cue the first chord of the verse in A major. The original is, of course, in the key of G so we need to transpose the chord down a whole step – where we find a rather familiar collection of notes.

With this intricate Dm7 (add 11) now poised a fifth above G major, we're getting somewhere. Sure enough, D-F-G-A-C-D, *effectively doubling the collection of notes played by George and Paul*, is a popular suggestion for

[25] For guitarists, even the primitive open strings will do for this experiment, but to capture rather better Sir George's sound on the *In My Life* mini-masterclass, re-voice the Em7 (add 11) as follows (low to high): E-B-D-A-D-G (frets: 0-2-0-2-3-3) on its way to an A major chord.

George Martin's 'open strings' clue to the piano chord

Key of A			Key of G
□ Em⁷ (add ¹¹)		Formula	Dm⁷ (add ¹¹)
Top string	E	Root	D
↑	B	5th	A
	G	3rd	F
	D	♭7th	C
	A	4th	G
Bottom string	E	Root	D

Martin's mystery piano chord.[26] However, while the A note in Harrison's guitar is certainly a point of detail for the AHDN *connoisseur*, many piano theories specifically omit it from their voicing, presumably regarding its 'sweet' flavour (in this context) as detracting from the instrument's dark, ominous onslaught.

The majority of suggestions we tracked down define the piano chord in terms of the remaining notes, D-F-G-C, with some game Beatlologists helpfully speculating on the fingering and register of the voicing.

Most interesting are the D2-F3-G3-C4-D4 strategy discussed by regulars at rec.music.beatles, and the D2-G2-F3-C4-D4 alternative put forward by bassist and sound analyst, Gary Spicer, after many hours of tortuous frequency analysis and piano noodling.[27]

Both these ploys pricked up the fickle ears of this author, who initially considered a compromise of the two, namely G2-D3-F3-C4-D4. A structure which, though we will later (crucially) discard, we now briefly elaborate on – if only to illustrate the most common misconception surrounding the chord.

This first tentative attempt, whose fingering is set out below, acknowledges that, above an insistent G2, D3 sustains proudly during decay (as

[26] Everett describes: 'Martin's piano doubling Harrison's twelve-string above McCartney's bass'; *The Beatles As Musicians: The Quarry Men Through Rubber Soul*, p. 236. See also Hans Gunter-Neumann's (albeit 5th-less) piano voicing (transposed from the key of C): G-F (Left hand); A-C-F-G (Right); *The Very Best Of The Beatles, Vol.1* (Bosworth, 1999), p. 10.

[27] Sourced from rec.music.beatles 'threads' in 2000 between Ian Hammond and Tom Hartman (who later speculated on a possible A3 within this voicing, in correspondence with the author in 2001). Gary Spicer, bassist with covers outfit, Contraband, in protracted discussions 2001–2003.

illustrated by strong frequency activity around the 147Hz level on a spectrum analyser) suggesting that the piano is indeed matching Paul's high D 'Hz-for-Hz'. Meanwhile, the right-hand takes care of both the middle C and neighbouring D that most theories seem to acknowledge on this side of the mix.

The piano chord . . . possibly!

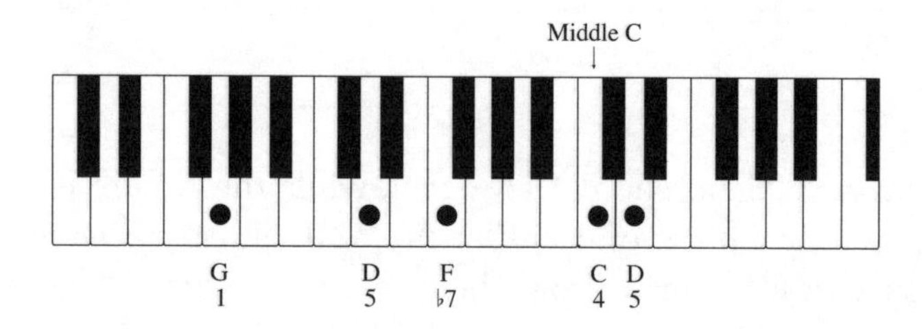

Meanwhile, even if the piano is an intriguing piece in the jigsaw, why does its presence matter so much – apart from, obviously, its dramatic (if heavily produced) texture? After all, it doesn't add any new notes to those already found in the guitar and bass.

The answer is perhaps in the way that it *reshuffles* certain notes in the Harrison guitar chord, changing some essential musical relationships and making us question the very nature of the overall chord. Not to mention confusing generations of guitarists into thinking that, yes, the piano chord is the *guitar* chord itself!

The origins of the G7sus4 confusion

Compare the shapes we have arrived at for both piano and guitar. In the former, the C note is no longer below the G, as in George's chord, it is *above* it – moreover in the *octave* above, reinforcing the powerful 'sus 4' effect between these notes.[28]

So distinctive is this 'suspended' relationship that, to many ears, it dominates the sound of this cluster and encourages us to regard the piano chord as G7 suspended 4th (or G7sus4 for short). The fact that such a strong

[28] The 3rd in a typical major chord is more clearly defined when heard in the octave above the root, rather than merely two whole tones above where it can sound 'muddy'. Similarly, a 'sus 4' that obliterates the 3rd often sounds more prominent in the higher octave.

D (the D3 in both bass and piano) is now *above* the G also encourages us to view D as the 5th of a G-rooted sonority.

Indeed, irrespective of their precise fingering, the other [A-less] piano strategies just mentioned correspond to different inversions of G7sus4, a chord which just happens to be by far the most popular description of the *overall* AHDN sonority.

G7sus4 – that suspended feeling

Notes	G	C	D	F
G7sus4	Root	sus 4th	5th	♭7th

The buskers' choice: G7sus4

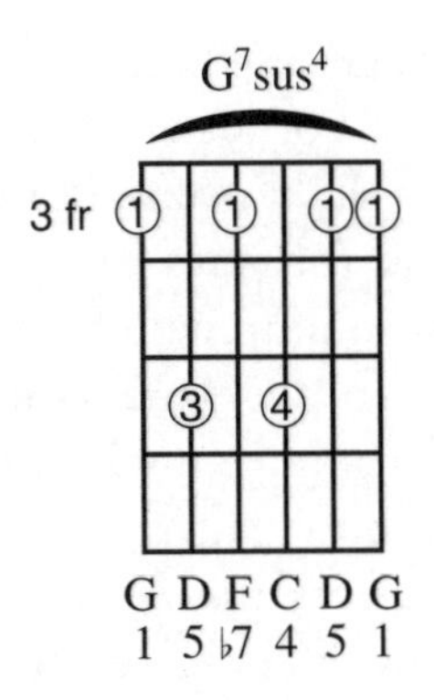

But why is this favoured even by highly revered Beatles tribute bands (some of whom who have played more gigs than The Beatles themselves ever did) when they can just use George's authentic Fadd9? Here is The Bootleg Beatles' André 'Harrison' Barreau:

> 'For years, we used the G7sus4 barre shape when playing "A Hard Day's Night" live – even though we knew it was the wrong chord! But it seemed the simplest way of capturing the most essential elements of the total sound.'[29]

This shape certainly hits the spot, by featuring two things that Fadd9 on its own lacks. Firstly, it contains the resounding D note that is so essential

[29] In conversation with the author, March 2001.

to the sound, especially for the lone guitarist who lacks the luxury of a bass player alongside him. Better still, this fingering captures *both* the C-G relationships present. C *below* G as in George's guitar chord, and *above* it, as in the piano. In this way G7sus4, The People's Choice for the entire chord, reflects perfectly the way that the piano turns the Harrison chord on its head, while also explaining why the 'correct' Fadd9 chord is a damp squib as a voicing for a single guitar.

That's not to say that G7sus4 is the only practical solution adopted by guitarists in their unending quest to recreate that famous sound. Here is a selection of the best suggestions, including, believe it or not, one more from George Harrison himself.

The quest continues . . . more strategies for guitarists

For all its enviable simplicity, G7sus4 lacks a certain authenticity for the 'A Hard Day's Night' *connoisseur*. For a start, Harrison's A note is altogether absent from the structure – a slight oversight to say the least.

We should therefore look for ways to include this integral element of the ringing 12-string sound, which sharp-eared guitarists have long regarded as essential to the true colour of the overall chord. But just how do you incorporate it without losing any of the other notes? Guitar experts on both sides of the Atlantic recommend a novel arrangement that delivers the A note on the 6th string of the instrument. This shape now includes each of Harrison's four notes, plus the D.

The musos' choice: G7sus4/A

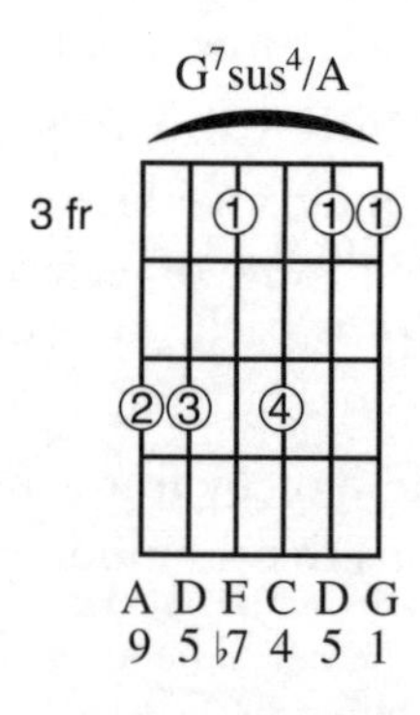

Here's a fifth-fret shape that, while sadly losing the F note, provides 6-string guitarists with a way to cheat on another distinctive (if highly subtle) element of the original Rickenbacker sound – collaring the chiming, upper octave A-note.

The 'virtual' 12-string sound: 'D7sus4/A'

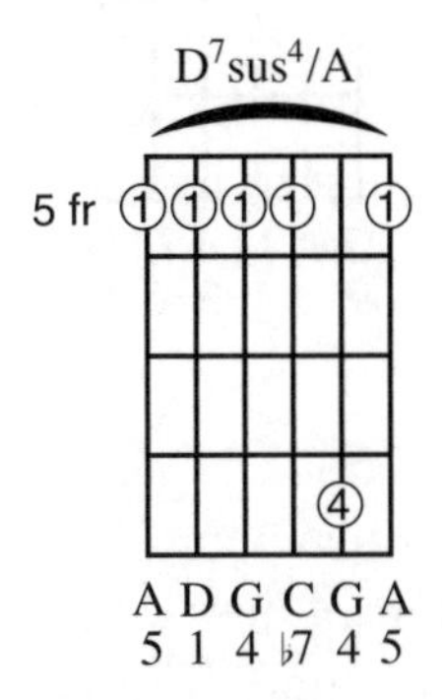

Of course, this effort may capture many of the sweeter, jangly upper *timbres* of the left-hand channel, but it distances itself from the darker looming presence of the piano at the other end of the spectrum – especially as both these suggestions now scupper the low-G strategy.

It looks like we can't have our cake and eat it. Adding a further twist to this ultimately unsolvable mystery is rock guitar virtuoso, Gary Moore, who suggests another shape for us to grasp – one that Gary explains, originated from a certain George Harrison:

> 'I always thought that the chord was a G7sus4 barre chord at the third fret. I'd been playing it like that since I was about 10 years old. But one day I was discussing it with George and he said: "No! That's not it! Give me that guitar! I'll show you how you *should* play it." '[30]

At a stroke, with the thumb hooked over the top of the neck to fret the low G, our earlier 'sus' strategy is back on course. And it's certainly some consolation to know that even Harrison himself has devised a way to reflect better the original intro.

[30] Gary Moore in conversation with the author, 21st February 2001. He later elaborated: 'We had an argument about that brilliant chord. I said, "Are you sure? It doesn't sound like that!". He sort of looked at me – "Yes, I'm sure, actually, Gary."'; *UNCUT*, July 2001, p. 32.

The Harrison Hybrid: F added 9th/G

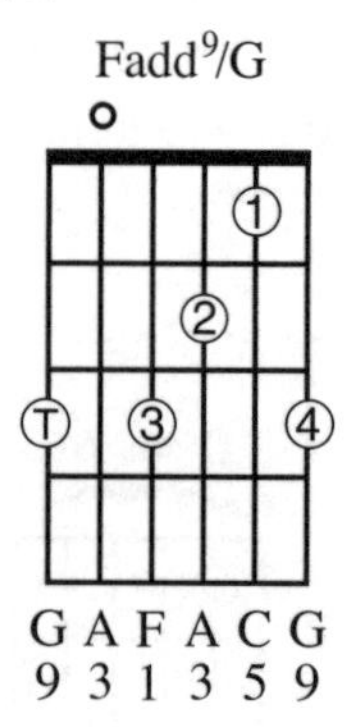

The Holy Grail – confirmed!

By now the reality should be dawning on guitarists – the nature of the overall sonority means that lone guitarists, by definition, will never be able to deliver with one strum the sound that they hear on the record. There is no single Perfect Guitar Voicing that covers all the bases – whether on 6- or 12-string guitar. Indeed, the fact that we have several notes of the same alphabetical denomination in different registers, guarantees that it is impossible to recreate the sound on a single guitar.

Nevertheless, let's briefly look at a final pair of voicings designed for guitarists intent on copping the essence of this jarring piano sound.

The first of these requires whole-tone detuning of the low E and A strings to mimic the droning low D and G, while a simple bar shape at the 3rd fret busks the rest.

The second, recommended by André Barreau (and, independently, guitar teacher Anthony Spicer), delivers an alternative body blow in rather more practical standard tuning. Indeed, given that The Bootleg Beatles endorse a combination of this latter G7sus4/F and the thumb-over-the-top Harrison Hybrid (Fadd9/G, as above) it looks like we've reached the end of the road for even the sternest of AHDN *cognoscenti*.[31]

[31] See also 'Phil Hilborne's A-Z of Great Riffs', *Guitar Techniques*, April 1994, p.59, where Neville Marten describes the Harrison/Moore hybrid as 'G11/No 3rd' [with optional low C thumbed on the 5th string]; alongside the alternative strategies of G7sus4 and G7sus4/A. Contortionists should check out a novel classical guitar voicing for G7sus4/D (fingered X-5-3-0-1-3), attributed to Bob Wysong on Donald Sauter's website, although this lacks an A note. See 'Best-Yet Hard Day's Night Chord' at www.geocities.com/CapitolHill/Lobby/7049/hdncd.

Virtual piano shapes for guitar

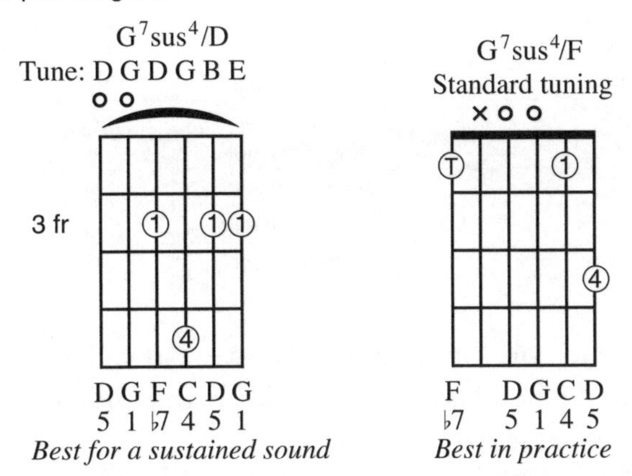

And if it's good enough for an Albert Hall-full of baying Beatles fans, then this is surely, in practice, *the* way to deliver *that* chord.

The Number of the Beast – the naming dilemma

How should we christen this three-dimensional monster sonority consisting, so far, of Fadd9 (guitar), D (bass) and G7sus4 (piano)?

The problems in naming the sound stem from its polychord status. For, as Pollack and O'Grady point out, we now have formal triads of both F major (F-A-C) and D minor (D-F-A) as well as a configuration that can be seen as G with a suspended 4th (G-C-D).

To cover pedantically every possible option, the chord could theoretically be named with reference to any of its five constituent notes:

The notes	**The basic chord options**				
	Dm^7(add^{11})	F$^{6/9}$	Am$^{11\sharp5}$	C$^{6/9/11}$	G^{9}sus^4
G	11th	9th	♭7th	5th	Root
C	♭7th	5th	♭3rd	Root	4th
A	5th	3rd	Root	6th	9th
F	♭3rd	Root	♭6th = ♯5th	11th	♭7th
D	Root	6th	11th	9th	5th

As always, however, the correct name should reflect the essence of the sound we hear and the important voice-leading involved as the juggernaut finally resolves after those timeless three seconds onto the plain G major triad that starts the verse. Here's roughly what happens:

Resolving the polychord – the basic voice-leading

The intro chord		**G major**	
Note	Voice leading	Note	Formula
G	Common tone	G	Root
C	Down a semitone	B	3rd
A	Down a whole tone	G	Root
F	Up a whole tone	G	Root
D	Down a fifth	G	Root

Looking at the role of certain notes we can quickly see that three candidates have the best harmonic credentials, both in terms of theory and the effect on our senses.

So, could it be some kind of F, as suggested by George's shape? Some kind of D, after Paul's contribution? Or does the piano trump them all, dictating some kind of G chord?

Ironically our earlier, open-string-derived Dm7 (add 11) itself reflects not only all the notes but captures the V-I movement as D descends to G, surely the most fundamental element of the harmony. The D camp would argue that the overall feeling is D, a point confirmed both by frequency analysis (which sees the D dominating in physical terms) and by classical theory.

'Hullabaloo aside, this chord functions as a surrogate dominant (i.e., V) with respect to the chord on G,' says Alan Pollack, who nevertheless quaintly acknowledges his own "cop-out" when refusing to be drawn on a single name for the sound.[32]

Meanwhile, Everett also alludes to the classical reticence towards naming the chord when he refers to the 'thirdless V7 function coloured by an anticipation of tonic'.[33] This illustrates an interesting philosophical issue as to how different schools of academia view the concept of a third in a dominant chord. After all, jazzers would happily regard F as the third of D – albeit the *minor* third. Everett kindly elaborates on his earlier comment as follows:

[32] Alan W. Pollack, 'Notes on ... Series' no. 49, 1992, *The 'Official' rec.music.beatles Home Page*, www.recmusicbeatles.com.

[33] Everett, *Concert Music, Rock And Jazz Since 1945*, p. 222, footnote 37. Everett elaborates on this in his 2001 book: 'Because the tonal center of G will eventually become clear, McCartney's bass imparts dominant function to a chord that otherwise sounds as if it includes both neighbors to, and anticipation of, I.'

> 'The chord is "thirdless" to the extent that there is no conventional *major* third of a functioning D dominant, an F♯ note that would act as a leading tone on its way to the root of the following G chord. In this way you could view the chord as a functioning D – with all the other notes just counterpoint in an unrelated chord.'[34]

While this explains why Everett (like Pollack) sensibly avoids christening the complete chord, those swayed by the dominant argument will no doubt favour the 'D-something' theory. However, while we might therefore want to think in terms of Dm7 (add 11), this chord instinctively *feels* wrong in this instance. The minor status just doesn't do justice to the chord's intrinsic ambiguity, which Riley, for one, puts down to a feeling that in fact the chord is 'neither major, nor minor'.[35]

Alternatively, we could really break the rules with a true musical oxymoron that acknowledges the lack of a third by reconceiving the F as its enharmonic equivalent – a sharpened 9th. A first outing in rock history, perhaps, for D7♯9sus4, a chord previously thought not to exist. While it defies convention it also captures another element of the chord to which Pollack refers when he says: 'Even if you don't know a thing about harmony or musical dictation, you can at least hear the G as a suspended fourth over the D on the bottom'.[36]

Meanwhile, we can't forget the overriding popularity of the 'G camp' given the strength of the other suspension in the sonority: the 'C-over-G'. In this way there is a justifiable case to be made for naming the chord G9sus4 – or better still, G9sus4/D.

At a stroke this chunky moniker succeeds in describing four elements of the actual sound. We get the big suspension, the V-I movement, the notion of the A as a less essential, upper embellishment, as well as the 'anticipation of tonic' that Everett refers to (this is the G note, which acts as a common tone between chord and target).[37]

Still, there is one powerful factor that might encourage some theorists to discard all these and go full circle.

[34] Everett in conversation with the author, April 2001.

[35] Riley, *Tell Me Why*, p. 98.

[36] Alan W. Pollack, 'Notes On … Series' no. 49, 1992, *The 'Official' rec.music.beatles Home Page*, www.recmusicbeatles.com.

[37] As in, say, a Plagal cadence where IV contains the root of I.

The combination cadence – the case for Fadd9/D

For all the credentials of these fancy chords, we should not forget that the Fadd9/D 'solution' is the term that best reflects how The Beatles themselves, left to their own devices, originally conceived the chord – Harrison's chord above Paul's bass. While this may hide the piano chord, the notes are already taken care of within the formula.

This slash chord also fits The Big Picture: namely, the context of the subsequent chord progressions that comprise the song itself, not to mention the coda concept that can be seen as starting, as well as ending, the song.

In this sense 'A Hard Day's Night' represents The Beatles' first experiment with the cool combination cadences that we dipped into in Chapters 11 and 12. This time, the magic hybrid is a standard V-I bass move that joins forces with a ♭VII-I elsewhere in the harmony. Here is another manifestation of the Aeolian cadence, as a flattened leading tone leads into the root of the tonic – though here, of course, it is in its Mixolydian incarnation as ♭VII is found in the context of primary *major* triads.[38]

Moreover, on a deeper level, it is this ♭VII/V alchemy that explains why the chord (with or without the piano) 'pretty much defined the sound of an era,' as *Guitarist* suggested, by symbolically representing a key element in the dichotomy between rock and pop that The Beatles themselves helped to create.

Remember Robert Walser's eulogy on the metaphorical struggle of rock music's guitar-based protagonists, armed with their flattened leading tone cadences, against the inevitability of classically descending fifths?[39] The mystery polychord from 'A Hard Day's Night' is effectively a snapshot of that very same highbrow doctrine, but condensed into a single, rousing sonority. In the circumstances, we should surely try to incorporate this ♭VII into the ultimate rock 'n' roll formula.

One that many would capture as: 'F added 9th/D, in the key of G'.

But will we really ever have a satisfactory solution to the mystery – *whatever we choose to call the chord*?

The fact is that any attempts to recreate the chord with the guitar, bass and piano elements we have identified just don't cut it, and not in some

[38] Everett also points to the Mixolydian nature of this F note.

[39] Refer to the closing discussion of Chapter 7.

microscopic, pedantic sense that relates to tuning differences, string-gauge or even the barometric air pressure that evening in Studio 2. No, these reservations are far more fundamental.

However painful it is to admit it, when you listen to the soundtrack chord closely, there is something else going on, over and above (or perhaps underneath) what we have already accounted for. Something essential that must be unlocked before we can claim to have cracked *that* Chord.

The right-hand channel revisited – the piano's harmonic maelstrom

It is the strange melting pot of shifting sounds in the right-hand channel that causes us to question all our earlier judgements of the chord – both in terms of the final line-up of instruments and the collection of notes present.

Let's look again at the notes we have on this side. As well as the G2-D3-F3-C4-D4 notes already reflected in our earlier piano voicing, is that a G3 we hear? And traces of A notes as well? And would you believe – gasp – even a B?

How else can we explain the drifting feeling, *over the duration of the opening chord itself*, which almost feels like a temporary resolution of the crashing dissonance, before we even get to the first G of the verse?

Listen to how the sound appears to drift after about 1 second following attack – somewhere on the right-hand side the sonority seems *briefly to lose the suspended feeling that defines the sound at attack and towards the latter stages of the decay*. It is as though these G and B notes momentarily assert themselves as the different frequencies fight for supremacy. In the process, they appear to drag the A and C notes that resonate above back down towards them. C feels like it is falling a semitone to B, while the A sounds as if it is dropping a whole tone down to G. And the G and B notes appear to be joined even more noticeably by the F moving down to D. This was mentioned with respect to the left-hand channel, but on this side it is far more marked. The feeling may be almost subliminal, and while there is no formal chord change going on, the following table attempts to capture this effect by depicting it as if it was the result of some genuine inner harmony voice-leading.

If these three moving elements are difficult to appreciate on paper, guitarists are encouraged as an exercise, to isolate and loop the offending channel on a sampler, and play along using a delicate pull-off followed by hammer-on that effectively links the two guitar shapes in question.

Subliminal harmony – the chord change within a chord!

F□			G/D	
□	Note	Quasi voice leading	Note	Formula
	C	Down a semitone	B	3rd
	A	Down a whole tone	G	Root
	F	Down three semitones	D	5th

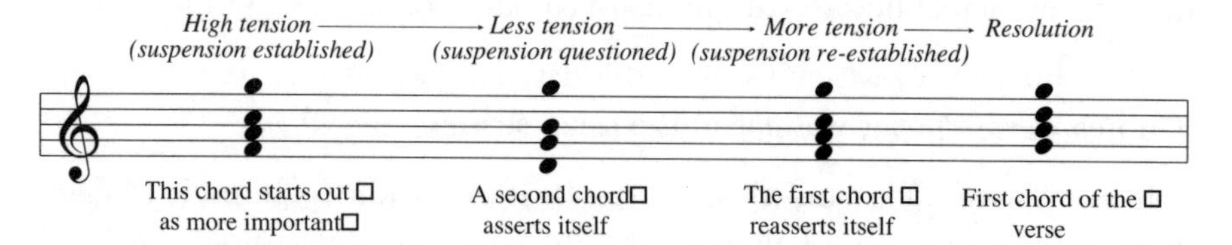

Played on its own this exercise sounds like a pseudo-Hawaiian pedal steel lick – but it reflects the sound we hear in respect of this very specific element of the chord and alters our perception of the musical activity at work.

The F triad element of the chord is anyway headed for a move up a whole step to G, and this complex effect is therefore, in effect, a preview of that same move. After all, the G, B and D are nothing more than a G major triad, though, with the D in the bass, this 'halfway harmony' still retains a suitable degree of tension by appearing in second inversion.

While all this would appear to be utterly irreconcilable with our earlier conclusions, music expert Arthur Dick, in an inspired piece of 'outside-the-box' thinking, offers a convincing explanation for generations of frustrated Beatles fans.

'The secret is in a far more sparse piano voicing of just D2-G2-D3 which, when played on a mic'ed up real piano, naturally produces powerful G, B [and D] harmonics. Especially when laced with vintage 1964 reverb, it's this that makes us feel that a G major triad is interacting with the Fadd9 in the guitars,' he suggested while carefully cloning the chord in his studio in 2003.

With this *eureka*! moment (right up there with Archimedes and the guys who cracked the code for DNA) we have surely, finally, solved the mystery.

Still, after ditching our electric pianos (and the right-hand notes that also inhibit the effect) let's just tidy up a few loose ends. Starting with the very last word of Arthur's quote: 'guitars' – *plural*!

At this point, readers should appreciate another previously unmentioned sound on this right-hand channel. Chiming above the crashing piano at attack is an elusive strum from what must surely be a second guitar. It may be more 'percussive' than truly 'harmonic', thereby rendering the constituent notes more difficult to grasp, but this must be the final piece of evidence we've been looking for.

Partners in chime – the second guitar

Any attempt to solve this part of the puzzle should begin with a reference to that earlier recollection of George Martin. Look at that last line again:

> 'John hit a chord which I still, to this day, don't know exactly what the notes were – but it was *almost* the open strings.'

It goes without saying that if The Beatles' producer himself remains flummoxed by the chord, then what hope have we mere mortals got?

But wait a minute! *'John'*?!!!

For all the debate about the guitar chord, it seems the very identity of the original perpetrator is also at issue. While we've so far assumed that it was Harrison (and Harrison alone) who was responsible for The Strum, George Martin makes us question this carefully.

And he isn't the only one who goes for the Lennon option. Take *Rolling Stone* which suggests: 'a radiant burst from John Lennon's guitar evoking the chaos and euphoria of Beatlemania at its height'.[40]

So, was it John, or George, or John *and* George? On the evidence of the right channel sounds (on which we can now elaborate further) the answer must be: the two together.

The theory of two guitars on the soundtrack intro (if not the BBC version) will hardly come as a revelation. Several authoritative Beatles writers and transcribers have acknowledged the presence of John on a 6-string complementing George on 'the 12'.

Still, these fall into two camps – those who see a single chord shape doubled by the two guitars (e.g., Wolf Marshall's G7sus4 at the 3rd fret, and Arthur Dick's Fadd9), and those who, more fundamentally, hear the presence of *two different shapes*. For example, the *Complete Scores* matches a giant Gsus4 (not G7sus4) barre-chord at the 3rd fret, with a more minimal open-position voicing: D-G-C-G on the top four strings of a 6-string.[41]

Things hot up considerably as Kozinn refers to: 'an intriguingly ambitious configuration' involving 'two different voicings of a Gsus4 – G major with

[40] *Rolling Stone*, Issue 863, March 2001, p. 33. Martin confirms Lennon's role in his interview for the 2002 *A Hard Day's Night* DVD (complete with Sir George's air guitar gestures!).

[41] *Complete Beatles Scores*, p. 359.

an added C'. Frustratingly we're not told what those two voicings are (nor is the vital A note accounted for), but it certainly suggests that we are not alone in looking for Lennon's guitar.

Swayed by the 'solution' of the piano's B harmonic, this author agrees that it is indeed a *pair* of Fadd9s from George and John, along with Paul's D3 and the inspired D2-G2-D3 piano punch, which ultimately accounts for rock's most elusive harmony.

However, in order to indulge one rather romantic whim considered during research, let's cheekily speculate on how, rather than the piano, these rogue, right-channel G and B sounds just could have been have the result of an equally rogue strategy – *from John Lennon's guitar*!

It must be stressed that what follows is deliberately fanciful, but designed to amuse Beatles fans who (like this author) think they subliminally feel (and, if the wind's blowing in the right direction, actually *hear*) these same rogue open G and B notes on some of the *piano-less* out-takes from the 1964 session.

A twist of Lennon – John's hidden voicing: G/F

Video footage would have saved us all a lot of time and aggravation, but Sod's Law dictates that the title track itself is the only song on the *A Hard Day's Night* rockumentary that The Beatles did not perform on camera.

And yet, ironically, of the few shots of the band playing this song, the only remotely helpful frames of the intro find, yes, *John Lennon* fingering what looks suspiciously like the very same Fadd9 usually credited to George![42] While it's a helpful guide, perhaps John is not merely doubling George's shape. In contrast to what we can call 'The Harrison chord', it could be that (the almost inaudible) John kept his first and second fingers above the two inner strings of the shape, allowing them to resonate *unfretted*. This would explain the quiet (but nevertheless distinct) open G note, as well as that rogue open B (the presence of which this author fully expects Beatles fans to contest furiously).[43]

[42] This footage is probably of the session of Friday 17th July 1964 at the BBC's Paris Studio, in London. The Beatles were recording tracks for their Bank Holiday radio special, *From Me To You*, which was broadcast on 3rd August.

[43] Not least because experts as eminent as Pollack have made a point of suggesting: 'to my ears only the B is missing', when referring to the elements of the tonic G triad present in the opening chord. 'Notes on … Series' no. 49, 1992, *The 'Official' rec.music.beatles Home Page*, www.recmusicbeatles.com.

The essence of the soundtrack chord, and its contrast from the *BBC* rendition is due to several factors – but one of them could be the extra dissonance created by the juxtaposition of George's Fadd9 and John's G/F.

The Harrison Chord (Fadd9) . . . and the Lennon Chord (G/F)

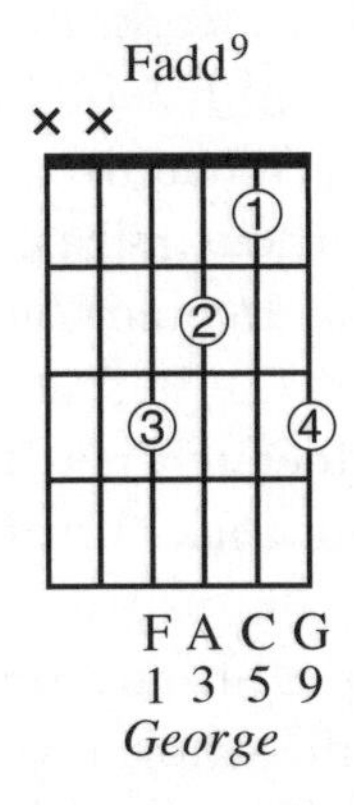

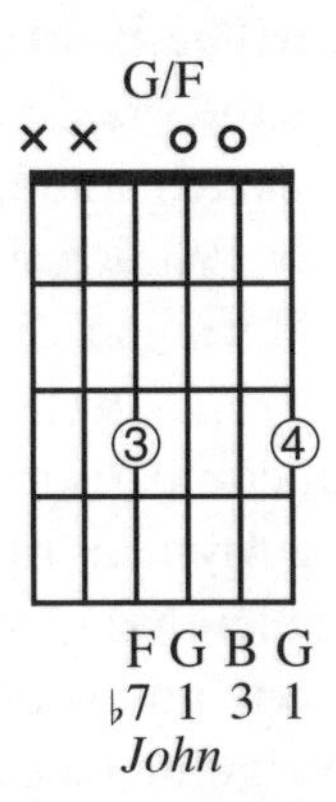

What was it that George Martin said - 'almost the open strings'? That's certainly what we instinctively feel, and G/F gives us two open strings – which is two more than George's Fadd9. John's open G note now rings out in the *octave below* the G on the 12-string, which means that, when *combined* with George's chord, it creates the G-below-C suspended structure that we've so far assumed is only featured in the piano chord. The B note sits awkwardly, if fleetingly, below the held C in Harrison's shape (and the piano) and causes us to question the permanent status of that same suspension over the life of the sonority.

Let's now speculate on the origins of these guitar shapes, since both appear to have been part of The Fabs lexicon long before they walked into Abbey Road that evening.

The Banjo heritage and the 'Cry For A Shadow' connection

Far from being the result of a 'visitation from above' in April 1964, The Beatles had long been familiar with both the 'add 9' and the G/F.

Indeed, it's likely that John Lennon himself would have been particularly familiar with these very specific shapes from the very first time he picked up the guitar. This type of four-string voicing of a major chord with either 'add 6' or 'add 9' embellishments is a standard 'work-horse' shape for banjo, and so would surely have been handed down to John from his banjo-playing mother, Julia.[44]

Then there is a rock 'n' roll legacy of similar guitar shapes that dates back to fifties classics like Chuck Berry's 'Havana Moon' and Bo Diddley's 'Crackin' Up', to name but two of McCartney's favourites.[45]

And we can hear The Beatles using them in a range of settings prior to April 1964. There's the brazen add 6th-enhanced F and G triads that open 'One After 909' (March 1963), the deft Dadd9 in 10th position in 'Till There Was You' (July 1963), and the twangy finishing shape of 'Where Have You Been All My Life?' on the 1962 *Live In Hamburg* Star-Club recording.[46]

All these pale in comparison to the sounds of another Beatles recording from the Hamburg days; this time dating right back to that historic session with Tony Sheridan, in May 1961.

A listen to the opening bars of 'Cry For A Shadow' uncovers perhaps the single most intriguing piece of trivia in the whole mystery of 'A Hard Day's Night'.

Dig out your copy on *Anthology 1*, track 12. Not only is Fadd9 the second chord that greets us in this highly novel rhythm guitar intro, but the opening sound is John Lennon playing none other than the exact four-string, droning G/F that can arguably be extracted from the right-hand channel of the soundtrack version of 'A Hard Day's Night'. Interestingly, MacDonald even makes a point of singling out Lennon's rhythm guitar figure in 'Cry For A Shadow' as the song's 'only musical point of interest'.[47]

And what a coincidence that this instrumental is credited as a unique joint composition by John Lennon and George Harrison!

Is it possible that the origins of the 'A Hard Day's Night' intro date back to the very earliest excursions in Hamburg?

[44] The banjo provenance of these four-string shapes was raised by André Barreau [a.k.a 'George' in The Bootleg Beatles] in discussion with the author, March 2001. Meanwhile Paul McCartney remembers: 'I had to wean John off ukulele chords, 'coz he played his guitar with ukulele chords.....we had to give him *The Bert Weedon Songbook*,'; *Across The Universe* (Part 2: *Tell Me Why*), BBC Radio 2, 15th October 2002.

[45] *Paul McCartney's Rock 'n' Roll Roots*, BBC Radio 2, 25th December 1999. The 'Havana Moon' riff hinges on the familiar add 6th shape slid between I and ♭VII positions (but acting more as tonic add 6th and *dominant* 9th over the A♭ bass). The solo of 'Crackin' Up' showcases Eadd9 as a delicately embellished tonic (at 1.05).

[46] The latter features a chiming Fadd9 in all its glory (heard at 1.43).

[47] MacDonald, *Revolution In The Head*, p. 43.

'Cry For A Shadow' (rhythm guitar intro)

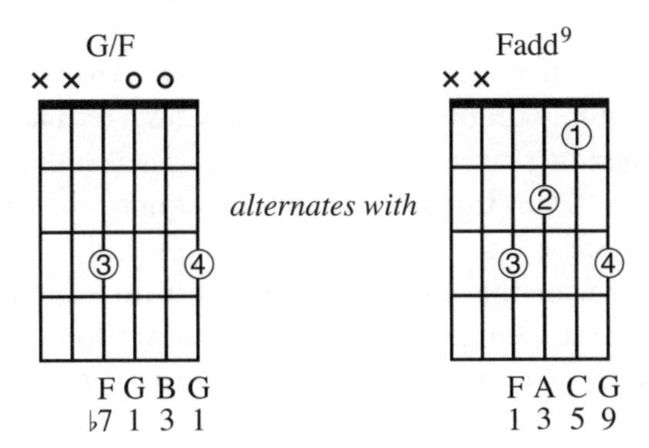

Superimpose, rather than alternate, these two shapes, and add in McCartney's D note (delivered, remember, in that upper – *intrinsically guitar* – octave) and you have the essence of the sound that would wreak such havoc three years later.

If 'Cry For A Shadow' is really a red herring and was no inspiration for the 'A Hard Day's Night' intro, it's all a hell of a coincidence!

Finally we should mention that Fadd9 itself is not some sort of harmonic freak, but a common stalwart for folk and rock progressions, especially those that see the little finger anchored on the top G throughout a mix of 1st position and open-string shapes. It can be heard most prominently in Beatles songs like 'You've Got To Hide Your Love Away' (G, Dsus4, Fadd9, C); and also 'I'm A Loser' and 'I Don't Want To Spoil The Party'. Meanwhile, contrast all these with The Beatles' most distinctive Fadd9 of all: the opening bars of 'Getting Better', formed by G octaves at the 12th fret over a regular F triad.[48]

Tying up the loose ends – The Bleeding Acoustic Guitar

Eagle-eyed readers – whether or not they believe the chords and notes suggested – might feel they have spotted a flaw in this Right Channel Theory.

[48] Of course, The Beatles do not have a monopoly on the Fadd9. For a shining multi-platinum example, take Peter Frampton's 'Do You Feel Like We Do?', where Fadd9 resonates as a deceptively coloured ♭III (with matching 9th in the melody), cueing a rocky Tri-Plagal cadence in the key of D on the euphoric repeated 'You' of the refrain.

For even if the controversial G and B sounds did come from a John G/F shape – what about the A and C notes in the same right-hand channel? It doesn't make sense. If neither John nor George Martin are responsible, these notes must surely originate from the 12-string. Yet Harrison is on the *other side of the mix*!

Of all the many details that the mystery forces us to confront, this is one of the most interesting.

The explanation for this essential quirk lies in the difference between the guitars John and George were playing that day. John may be widely credited with both acoustic and electric guitars in this song, and it is usually assumed that he played *electric* guitar on the *backing* track and overdubbed an acoustic contribution later. This view is reinforced by the *Anthology* version which finds two electric guitars discernible on Take 1. But is a Lennon electric contribution really audible on the finished recording? More than anything it's the bongos that drive the song, and a second electric guitar is surely absent.[49]

Sure enough, the out-takes confirm that John switched guitars during the course of the evening – certainly by the time The Beatles delivered the take chosen as the backing track. Those harsh early takes (1, 2 and especially the crunching second attempt at take 3) are transformed by the time we reach Take 4, with John now appearing to have ditched his Rickenbacker 325 in favour of his Gibson J-160E, which accounts for his far more mellow acoustic contribution for the remainder of the evening.[50]

The very nature of the acoustic guitar means that other sounds in the studio – namely from both Paul's bass and George's 12-string – would have leaked into the wooden sound-box and been captured by the pick-up along with the strings of the Gibson itself. And so we duly appear to have traces of Harrison's C and A notes (both A3 and A4 octaves are evident), as well as what instinctively feels like a McCartney D3. While we've suggested that the piano also plays this note, the fall-out from Paul's bass

[49] The two electric guitars on Take 1 are best discerned in the bridge on the line 'tight, all through the night' (at 0.58-0.60) as a brief arpeggio contrasts with a grungy electric strum.

[50] Two electric guitars can still be heard on the final version, but only on the lead break as George's overdub (again on 12-string and doubled on piano) joins his original rhythm part. Meanwhile, out-takes of various other Beatles songs confirm Lennon's flexibility in switching instruments between takes, e.g., 'I'm A Loser' where he starts out on J-160E, only to switch to 12-string acoustic for the chosen version (thanks to Tom Hartman at rec.music.beatles).

through John's soundbox would help explain the bizarre way that, after a split-second delay, we feel what is surely (initially) John's F3 deferring to a texturally different D3, thereby unwittingly amplifying the latter's 147Hz frequency.[51]

It's a feature that also characterises the vital Take 9 of the out-takes.

The evolution of a sound: takes 1–9 in focus

All this may sound far-fetched and it is certainly much simpler to believe that there is just a single, simple Harrison chord involved here. But then what of those descriptions of the studio deliberations that describe the conscious evolution of the chord in the minds of The Beatles themselves? They can't just be journalistic licence – take Kozinn's colourful account:

> 'It took several tries to find the right chord, and the right coloration, they tried it distorted and plain, more dissonant and less, and even with tremolo. The bright, open sound they settled on was perfect for the gesture.'[52]

Meanwhile *Rolling Stone* magazine makes a similar point when recounting how 'Lennon toyed with the tuning and tone of the opening chord', further quoting George Martin as remembering: 'It was by chance that he struck the right one – we knew it when we heard it.'

These suggestions that The Beatles 'toyed' with the sound question the cosy notion that the band decided on a single chord at the start of the evening, and stuck with it throughout all nine takes. Admittedly, one favourite scenario is that, before the session started, Lennon brought that closing Fadd9 coda chord back to the 'top of the form' in response to George Martin's request for, as he says, a 'dramatic thing'.[53] Moreover,

[51] This amplification of the D note is confirmed by frequency analysis, with the note feeding back rather than decaying as we would expect.

[52] Kozinn, *The Beatles*, p. 96.

[53] 'In those days, the beginnings and endings of songs were things I tended to organise', says Martin, reminiscing on the chord in *Rolling Stone*, Issue 863, 1st March 2001, p. 33. Though MacDonald (who carefully avoids the question of the personnel on the intro and outro) suggests the ending was envisaged by Lennon as a transition from the film's main titles to the first scene; *Revolution In The Head*, p. 103.

questioning this version of events forces us to dispute the description of Take 1 in the authoritative *Anthology I* liner notes:

> 'The crashing guitar chord that distinguished the master is already in place.'[54]

It most certainly isn't – this author strongly believes that the structure of the chord(s) in the 'A Hard Day's Night' intro evolved over the course of the session. The final leg of our adventure, a whirlwind summary of the nine takes recorded by The Beatles at Abbey Road that historic night, is an attempt to explain why.

Take 1. References in our discussion to this, one of the few readily available alternative hearings of the intro, have so far been surprisingly brief. That's because they would have confused our perception of the finished chord even more. For this strum is very much a case of 'work in progress'. It may be a confidently struck chord – and suitably resonant with a tremolo enhancement effect – but compare it even to *Live At The BBC* to find a subtly different sound – not only in texture but also *composition.*

D7sus4 – the 'F-less' first attempt[55]

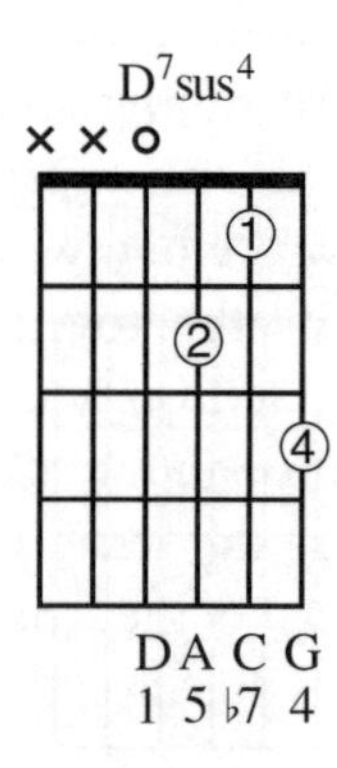

[54] According to *The Usenet Guide To Beatles Recording Variations*: 'The heavy reverb on the opening chord and at the end were added for *Anthology 1* without comment. A clean stereo mix has been bootlegged'. See 'Recording Variations' at www.recmusicbeatles.com.

[55] For another hearing of this shape, refer to the brief impromptu practice strum immediately following the aborted Take 2. It is now heard with the volume control turned down for rehearsal purposes, and with the A strummed lightly in the bass making a chord best thought of as D7sus4/A.

The F note itself, hardly prominent on *BBC*, is nevertheless conspicuous by its absence – in both of the expected guitar octaves – and is replaced instead by a droning open D giving us yet another slightly different guitar chord to add to our collection.

Before leaving Take 1, notice that this D note sustains long after McCartney's muddy bass attacks so unsatisfactorily the octave below. Given the serious lack of penetration from this *low* D bass, here surely are the origins of McCartney's D3 ploy that we first hear a few takes later.

Take 2. Here we get our first taste of John and George playing *different* shapes in the guitars – if only by virtue of a musical Freudian slip. For no sooner has John delivered his '1-2-3-4' count off, than the song is immediately aborted as a rogue chord thunders into the air in studio 2.

'That's not it,' we hear John exclaim. 'Wrong chord,' says Paul, somewhere in the distance. 'You're playing "This Boy"!' John teases the perpetrator, George, who has just created an ear-grating sound by delivering a startling open B-string (yes, definitely!) within what seems to be the following shape.[56]

George's 'wrong chord'? – F♭5[add9]

Not only is this a defining moment in Beatles 'bootleg' culture but perhaps, in this one seemingly innocuous moment, the seeds of our speculative 'combination dissonance' were planted.

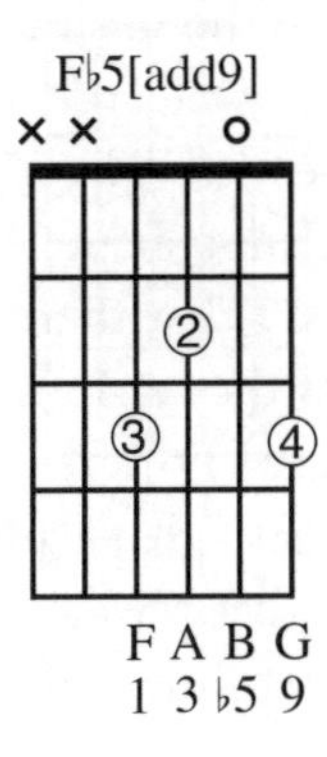

Yet was this chord a total mistake? It may seem so from a quick listen to the surviving session reel – but then we are not party to any discussion

[56] Again, refer to 'The John Barrett Tapes', and also the reference to this incident in 'The Mythology Of The Beatles' by Bernard Webb, *Record Collector*, June 2000, No. 250, p. 45.

between The Beatles that took place after Take 1. After all, delivering one different note from the shape played in Take 1 (the B) is unfortunate, but *two* (the F that also does not feature in D7sus4) seems so careless that it is, frankly, unlikely. Not least because this same F note survived the very next take, and many of the later ones – including the one that matters.

Is it possible that, following Take 1, John, still in the quest for George Martin's 'dramatic thing', suggested ways of spicing up the intro with two different guitar chords? He himself would continue to play D7sus4 but George was now to experiment with the Fadd9 that he would anyway be playing at the end of the song. Then, when George first attempted it on Take 2, he accidentally forgot to finger the C and left the open-B ringing by mistake! And *that* gave John an idea.

Take 3. Sure enough it is this D7sus4 and Fadd9 combination that we suggest now crashes out, though Lennon now fluffs the first attempt ('I missed the beat!' he says). Given that John himself counted them in, could it be that his mind was not in gear, perhaps reflecting on George's dissonant B and filing it away for use on a later take?

A second Take 3, with the same chord combination, duly makes it to the verse itself. Notice, once again, how the F note is instantly in evidence, in stark contrast to Take 1.

Take 4. It's all change again. We're back with what seems like a pair of distinctively smooth-sounding D7sus4s, with the F note now AWOL.

Take 5. There is no Take 5 on the session reel – at least not the one used by this writer and referred to by collectors petitioned for this project.

Take 6. Once again The Beatles deliver an 'F-free' zone with those D notes ringing out from the D7sus4 shape. A retrogressive step in terms of the guitars – but that's not to say that there's no experimentation here. In another soundbite that survives the session, McCartney is heard – seconds before the take – playing a *pair* of D notes in octaves. In the true spirit of the mystery, Tom Hartman suggests that Paul also plays octaves on the final take, while Gary Spicer agrees that a weakly struck D2 (beneath the bold D3) might help explain the brief flurry of activity at 73Hz on a spectrum analyser at attack.

This is the last take on which The Beatles appear to deliver a single, uncluttered guitar shape – though it is difficult to be sure if George and Paul are alone, or whether John's acoustic is indeed somewhere in there 'doubling up'.

Take 7. The Sound takes shape. Immediately prior to this take John plays a lone, impromptu open G chord – complete with a B note. Of course, this could just be subconscious noodling in respect of the first chord of the verse. Or was he getting into position for the G/F with which (our counter-theory suggests) he experiments on this take for the first time?

The crucial culprits – a ringing open G, the elusive B and that strange F-to-D 'drop-out' heard on the finished version – now also occur for the first time, lending credence to the theory of the clash between the D bass and the F from the acoustic guitar. Those still convinced that there is really only one crashing guitar chord on the intro to the finished soundtrack are encouraged to compare this take with, say, Take 4.

Take 8. We're getting close. But there's still time for one more mistake. This time it's Paul's turn, as he delivers, of all things, an A bass note under the guitar stack causing the take to be aborted immediately. The Beatles have now decided on their final strategy.

Take 9. The preamble finds Paul brushing up on the notes of the song's bridge with which he is still unsure. After a quick practice bass run (B-low E-B-G-low E and on to C) he's ready to start on D for the intro. 'Go!' he shouts.

The elements of Take 7 are now repeated, but now louder, in terms of absolute level, and far more confidently. History is captured, and the backing track is now complete, leaving just the overdubs (one of them George Martin's piano, of course) before the engineers can prepare the thundering tones of the final mix that still reverberates today.[57]

Once again we stress that this G/F fantasy is just a fun red herring to spice things up. Nevertheless, readers are challenged to account for the subtle harmonic drift on Take 9. Could John be quietly releasing two fingers thereby momentarily turning Fadd9 into G/F? Are these out-takes 'bounces' rather than virgin backing takes (as the double-tracked vocals on the Abbey Road session reel suggest), complete with leakage from untraceable sources?

And, hey, don't let's forget Ringo, who we earlier teased is heard in a subtly different way to the (later) *Live At The BBC* cut. For these out-takes also reveal a discrete snare drum strike (from Take 4 onwards), with both attack and decay also audible on the left-hand channel of the finished mix.

Enough already. The following table summarises our final theory on the harmonic feast we love to hate.

[57] In the *Anthology 1* liner notes Lewisohn refers to 'take 9, the last and most satisfying of the basic track[s]', p. 37.

'A Hard Day's Night': *that* chord . . . (probably!)

Note	Nominal Frequency (Hz)[58]	Left Channel		Right Channel		
		Paul McCartney	**George Harrison**	**John Lennon**	**George Martin**	
		Bass	Guitar	Guitar	Piano	
		Hofner 500/1	*Rickenbacker 360/12*	*Gibson J160E Acoustic*	*Steinway Grand*	
A4	440		G-string, fret 2, 8va			
G4	392		E-string, fret 3	E-string, fret 3		
F4	349		D-string, fret 3, 8va			
D4	294				Harmonic	
C4	261		B-string, fret 1	B-string, fret 1		
B3	247				Harmonic	
A3	220		G-string, fret 2	G-string, fret 2		
G3	196				Harmonic	
F3	175		D-string, fret 3	D-string, fret 3		
D3	147	D-string, fret 12			Thumb	*Left hand*
G2	98				3rd finger	*Left hand*
F2	87					*Left hand*
D2	73				5th finger	*Left hand*

Paul McCartney:

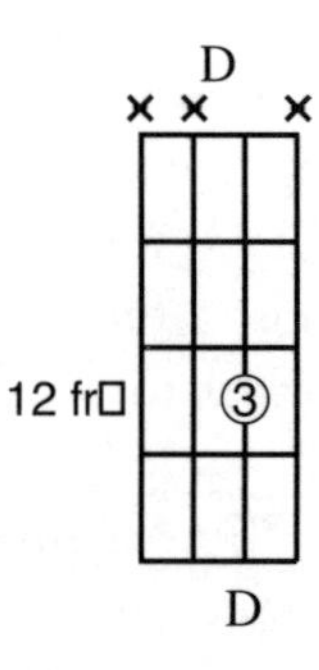

John Lennon:

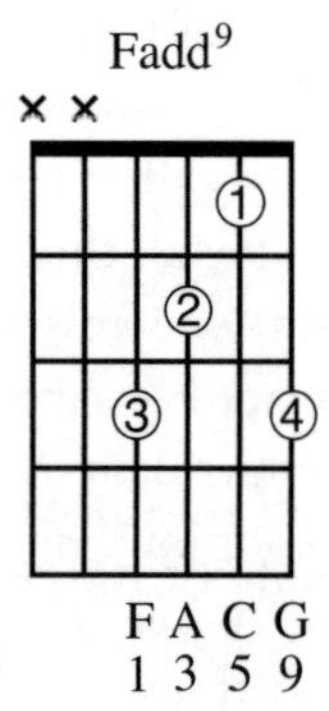

[58] These frequencies have been set out to ensure there is no confusion with the relative register of the notes being suggested (with 'Harmonic' noted where we *feel* we hear them!). However, in absolute terms, some of the instruments appear to be slightly sharp, at least as interpreted from the frequency analysis devices specified below. Certainly there is some tuning inconsistency suggested by the oscillation between the supposedly matching D notes in the bass and piano. On this subject *Guitarist* magazine draws our attention to the solo later in the song where 'a definite out-of-tuneness is apparent between bass and guitar'. It is thus possible that even small tuning inconsistencies between the instruments may also have contributed in certain incalculable ways to the dissonance of the overall opening chord. Meanwhile, Paul's bass fingering is shown right-handed by convention!

George Harrison:[59]

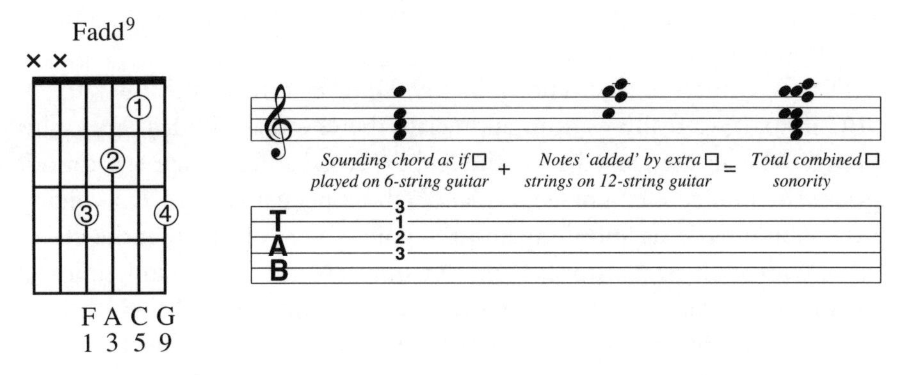

George Martin:

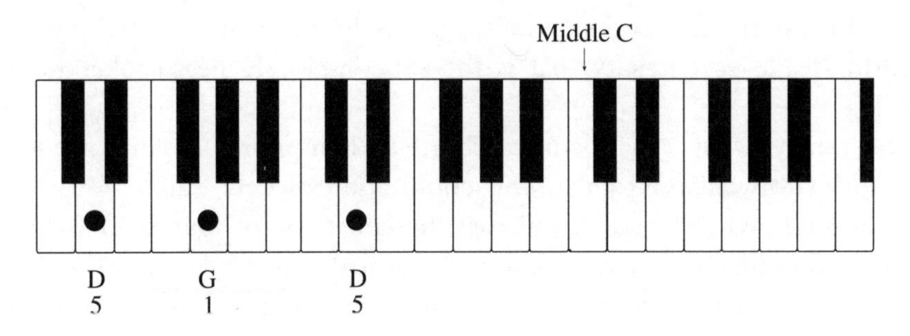

The Final Formula – revealed

In the spirit of this mystery, this author acknowledges that these ideas may indeed be wide of the mark in various respects, and he duly invites other Beatles fans to shoot down in flames every last detail as they attempt to find The Truth.[60]

Maybe we will never know for sure – and no doubt the very magic of The Beatles is that certain nuances could never be replicated even if The

[59] Note that guitar notation sounds an octave lower than written. This means that McCartney's highest D is the same note as George Martin's lowest D.

[60] For example, sharp ears may hear the sound of an open G string in the *left-hand* channel. Could this also have come from a bleeding pick-up?

Fabs themselves were beamed back to 1964. Ultimately, it is hoped that this theory will both enlighten and intrigue Beatles fans by drawing attention to at least one critical element.

That is, while the slash chord 'Fadd9/D' takes care of the *Live At The BBC* intro, if we really want to appreciate the chord as The Fab Four plus George Martin conceived it in the Abbey Road studio, then we cannot ignore the hidden element – the piano, whose primal D2-G2-D3 voicing pits a subliminal B harmonic against the guitars' C to ensure that the chord fights with itself over its duration. Not only do the various instrumental voicings mean that no single guitar can ever capture the sound with a lone shape, but also that there will never be agreement over even the 'best' *static* strategy as it all depends on which of the *shifting* elements you want to emphasize at any one moment.

The B harmonic may be the most microscopic nuance in the equation; nevertheless, this author believes it is precisely this unappreciated piece of (Fifth) Beatle eccentricity that is the subconsciously heard joker in the pack.

So, finally, 'what *is* that damned chord?' When pressed at gunpoint for a name for this enlarged beast, you could affectionately dub it 'G9-with-dodgy-sus4', while pointing out that the collection of sounds, G-B-D-F-A-C, spells out a formal, complete G11 construction. One where – in both theory and practice – the 11th co-exists begrudgingly with the major 3rd. NB. The asterisks highlight the B as a harmonic rather than a formal note.

That chord – the final formula?

Formula	**Root**	**3rd***	**5th**	**♭7th**	**9th**	**11th**
G11*	G	B*	D	F	A	C

You should then refine it to G11*/D to highlight the bass vision, even though the formula already accommodates a D alongside this unsettling intermingling of B and C sounds that is surely the secret ingredient in The Beatles' lethal cocktail – and yet one necessarily denied by the 'suspended' tag typically adopted.[61]

[61] Chords in which the 3rd and 11th co-exist are rare due to this intrinsic dissonance. Examples include the opening chord of Oasis's 'All Around The World' where the notes D♯ and open E (in the electric guitar) create an intriguing clash in the context of B major harmony.

For it is in this way that the chord is indeed 'the musical equivalent of the song's title,' just as Hertsgaard says, with the consonant B struggling for respite beneath the tense suspension as surely as the singer craves a break from his labours.

Despite all these attempts at collaring the chord on paper, it must be said that any transcription can only be a guide given the sheer novelty and nature of the sound. Certain things in music just can't be put on paper, and we are reminded of the eccentric antics of master rock transcriber, Steve Vai, in whose *magnus opus* on the works of Frank Zappa we occasionally find bizarre hand-drawn sketches substituting for exceptionally intricate conventional music notation.

> 'I often think in abstract terms, and "seeing" music as images is part of my vocabulary. I am a *king* at transcription. I know how to notate weird stuff. But [sometimes I think] . . . what good is that? To me it sounds like a picture!'[62]

Which leaves just one final loose end to tie up . . .

Harrison's Rickenbacker 360/12 was acquired in New York on 8th February 1964, courtesy of an astute piece of self-promotion by company president Francis C. Hall. It is famous not merely for George's patronage (which sparked the electric 12-string craze), but also for its unique construction which helped shape every last *timbre*.

There's the laminated maple and mahogany neck that travels right through the body, the single coil-pickups and the hollow wings created by a thin maple top, back and rims.

But it is the unusual stringing, where the thinner octave strings sit *above* (or *behind*) the bottom four – rather than *below* (or *in front of*) them, as on most other 12-string guitars – that leaves one vital detail still at large.[63]

Your never told us, George, was it a downstroke or an upstroke?

[62] Steve Vai in discussion with the author; see *Total Guitar*, Issue 23, October 1995, p. 42.

[63] According to *Guitar Player* this guitar (made in December 1963) was the second ever Rickenbacker 12-string – but the first to be strung in this way. See 'Fab Gear! The Guitars Of The Beatles' by Bob Mytkowicz, November 1987 issue, p. 103. Also *Guitarist*, December 2000, p. 70.

Our collective obsession with the AHDN chord shows no sign of abating, as illustrated by the fascinating frequency analysis attempted by Jason Brown, Professor of Computer Science at Dalhousie University in Halifax, Nova Scotia, in 2004.[1] This involved taking a digital sample of the opening chord and forensically dissecting it into its constituent frequencies and implied notes using a mathematical operation known as Fourier Transform.

The research raised some interesting – if highly controversial points, notably the apparent absence of a frequency for G2 – in any instrument – a note central to almost all previous theories of the overall sound.

The analysis also suggested F4 was missing, leading Brown to claim that the F present in the octave below (F3) could not be attributed to Harrison's guitar as these two notes would have been paired on his 12-string.

In striking contrast to earlier suggestions, Brown deduces Harrison's chord to contain A2, A3, D3, D4, G3, G4 and C4, played on the inner four strings (tabbed X-0-0-0-1-X, low to high). George Martin's piano chord is now deemed to be a busy D3, F3, D5, G5 with a contentious E6 on top; with Lennon playing a single C5 at the 8th fret of his top string. Paul's D3 bass is about the only constant with our own analysis.

But clearly, some Beatles experts remain unmoved – most notably, Arthur Dick who, in 2009, delivered the most convincing recreation of the chord (so far) on his *Play Guitar With.... The Beatles* multi-media project, complete with authentic Beatle-era instruments. "The G2 is audible in the piano and is integral to the overall composition of the chord we hear," he says. "The question is, if the ear can hear it, why can't the science?"

Sticking with his earlier G9sus4/D assessment, Dick also points out that the maelstrom of rogue harmonics inevitably generated by The Beatles during the original recording (not to mention the piano overdub), along with the typical imperfections associated with strumming pairs of strings on George's narrow-necked Rickenbacker, would render any type of digital frequency analysis a highly inexact science.[2]

Still, the quest continues and we await with interest the next hypothesis on rock's most elusive sound.[3]

[1] *Mathematics, Physics and A Hard Day's Night* by Jason I. Brown, Dalhousie University; www.mscs.dal.ca/~brown/n-oct04-harddayjib.pdf

[2] In conversation with the author, July 2011. Checkout Arthur's chord on the CD for the *Play Guitar With... The Beatles 1962–1966* songbook, Wise Publications/Music Sales (2009).

[3] Send them to info@aeoliancadence.co.uk. In the meantime, see also the manipulation of the chord using Celemony's Melodyne Editor. As reported in *Melodyne Makes Easy Work of 'Hard Day's Night'* at www.wired.com.

FOURTEEN

Melody – Intervals, Motifs and Phrasing

'It doesn't really matter what chords I play,' sings George Harrison in 'Only A Northern Song' – a tongue-in-cheek tribute to the facile nature of the record business.

But many a true word is spoken in jest – change the context and you could indeed argue that, so far on our travels, the unashamed bias towards harmony has been at the expense of arguably the most important element of a pop song – melody.

Have we focused too much on groundbreaking progressions at the expense of those catchy Beatles tunes? After all, for all John Lennon's self-confessed 'obsession' with chords (which we've indulged to extremes on occasions), it was his own songwriting partner who suggested:

> 'Musically, I don't think the stuff you do chord-wise is quite as important as the tune . . .'[1]

A powerful songwriting philosophy – and McCartney is in good company as, 35 years later, The Beatles' No. 1 fan, Noel Gallagher, independently mirrored the sentiment: 'A good single? It's all down to the melody,' says the Oasis tunemeister. 'Basically, "D'Yer Know What I Mean" is the same chords as "Wonderwall", but it's got a different tune. That's the thing.'[2]

[1] Paul McCartney, 'How To Write A Hit', *Melody Maker*, 1st February 1964, p. 11.

[2] *MOJO*, Issue 45, August 1997, p. 51. The verses of both songs indeed broadly follow the Em-G-C-D 'Tri-Plagal' formula mentioned in Chapter 7.

A controversial view, but one lent further weight by various Beatles writers who have bemoaned the dearth of melodic scrutiny afforded to The Fab Four down the years. Take Deryck Cooke, who stressed that 'a purely harmonic analysis is misleading' when critiquing William Mann's 1963 *Times* article.[3]

Perhaps even the average non-musical Beatles fan (i.e., most of the world) would argue that it is melody, if only we could bottle its elusive essence, that ultimately deserves to be the focus in any analysis of Beatles songs (or, indeed, any pop song). For isn't it the 'tune' that we whistle *unaccompanied* when walking down the street or sitting in the bath? As such, the harmony that we have attempted to deconstruct so painstakingly could conceivably be regarded as secondary to the proceedings.

We all talk instinctively of 'a nice tune' or 'a beautiful melody' and nobody ever questions it. Rather the reverse, a whole sub-culture of pop terminology has developed among fans, critics and artists, that refers to the generic concept of 'a Beatle-esque tune'. We've all heard that phrase and its variations used to describe hordes of pop songs apparently reminiscent of the Fab Four. The Oasis/Beatles comparison may be a favourite game for trainspotters, but Noel Gallagher himself volunteers that his own nineties masterpiece 'Live Forever' was 'vaguely Beatle-esque in its melody'.[4] Even Oasis's manager suggested that the success of one of the band's later singles, 'Wonderwall' was helped by its 'strongly Beatle-esque tune' in the tough-to-crack US market.[5]

At first sight this hardly appears too controversial given the variety of Beatles associations we take for granted when discussing Oasis. We all know instinctively what they mean – or do we? Think about it – is there *really* a particular type of melody that is truly identifiable as a Beatles songwriting trademark?

As an analytical challenge we can certainly attempt to search for one as we shift the emphasis of our discussion to the various mysteries of melody.

Helping us out is the dictionary definition, which confirms that – just as

[3] Deryck Cooke, 'The Lennon-McCartney Songs', *The Listener*, 1st February 1968 (Reprinted in *The Lennon Companion*, p. 110). Though with his references to 'pandiatonic clusters', 'octave leaps', 'melismas' and 'metre' Mann encompassed more than just the chord progressions.

[4] *Uncut*, March 2000, p. 54.

[5] 'Mouth And Money', by Robert Sandall, The Business magazine, *Financial Times*, 26th February 2000.

we suspected – melody not only has its own identity but can exist *independently* of harmony. The fact that harmony is a collection of notes gathered *vertically* (and therefore played simultaneously) while melody consists of notes played *horizontally* (in a sequence) appears to make a fundamental difference, and certainly allows them to be analysed independently.

There are indeed particular ways in which we can focus on single-note lines to help us appreciate certain characteristics of Beatles melody. Our framework will cover:[6]

1. **Intervals** – the power of pitch recognition
2. **Patterns** – the structure and contour of motifs and phrases
3. **Rhythm** – how phrasing affects bar counts, form and metre

While this will form an unusual interlude, we should point out now that 'the case for the defence' will soon force us to refocus on melody *in context* – namely over the instrumental chords themselves and in conjunction with The Beatles' infamous catalogue of crafted vocal arrangements. Hence the following chapter focuses in more detail on the mechanics of *harmonisation* – how melody is supported by, and creates colourful extensions to, the chords.

1. Memorable intervals – the power of pitch recognition

The obvious starting point in analysing and appreciating melody is the study of intervals between successive notes. While this can be a laborious task when trawling through a complete song, we instinctively identify many great pop songs from all eras through the *opening* interval of their tune.

Harold Arlen's '(Somewhere) Over The Rainbow' (with its soaring octave leap on the opening word), and Leonard Bernstein's 'Maria' from *West Side Story* (with its enigmatic rise of an augmented fourth), are traditionally the first to be wheeled out to music students to illustrate this principle. As with this pair, the opening interval involved usually corresponds to the first two

[6] For an advanced look at the theory and practice of melody structure, refer to Philip Tagg's article 'Melody And Accompaniment' for the *Encyclopedia of Popular Music Of The World*. Tagg uses a five-part plan that covers 1. Pitch contour; 2. Tonal vocabulary; 3. Dynamics and mode of articulation; 4. Rhythmic profile; and 5. Metric and periodic articulation.

syllables in the lyrics, and is particularly effective where this coincides with the song title.

Numerous candidates from The Beatles catalogue that feature this type of isolated pair of pitches come to mind instantly, including: 'Hey *Jude*', 'She *Said* She Said', 'Be-*cause*', 'Good *Day* Sun-*shine'*. Or it could be some close variation of this, where a specific early interval provides an instant reference point. Think of the opening interval of 'Yes-*ter-day'* 'Dear *Pru*-dence' or 'Oh! *Dar*-ling'. Equally, the memorable interval might be in the next word or further into the phrase, but nevertheless still defines the opening impact, as in 'Michelle' ('ma-*belle*') or 'Blackbird' ('dead *of night*').

Despite the theoretical potential within the chromatic scale there are, in practice, only a limited number of accepted opening intervals. The Harold Arlen and Leonard Bernstein examples above are relative rarities. Vast numbers of songs tend to cluster into the category of thirds, fourth and fifths – either descending or ascending.

Let's look at 'Hey Jude', simply because the interval in question is a descending minor third, which can be heard in many famous popular melodies (think of 'The Theme From *Rocky*' – 'Gonna *fly now*.)[7] With the 5th falling to the major 3rd of a tonic major, it just happens to be the same interval that starts the melody of 'Live Forever'. Noel might just have a point, for 'Live Forever' also follows 'Hey Jude' with the *next* important pitch change:

The opening intervals of 'Hey Jude' and 'Live Forever'

'Hey Jude'

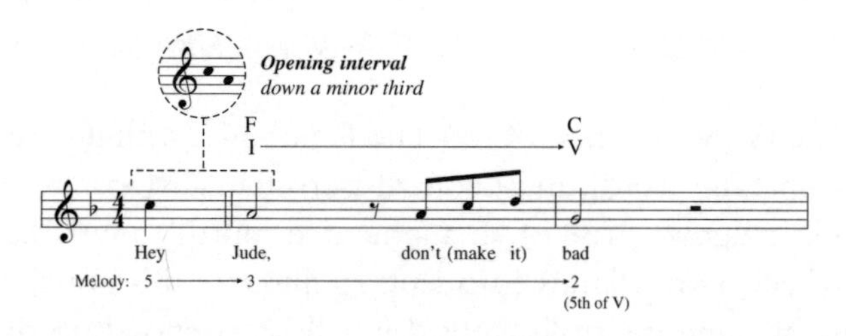

[7] For more famous intervals refer to Citron, who includes various Tin Pan Alley classics and showtunes, showing, say, the minor third descent to be the opening feature of various songs that also include: 'Don't Rain On My Parade'; 'Honey' and 'Bewitched, Bothered And Bewildered'; *Songwriting*, pp. 176–9.

'Live Forever'

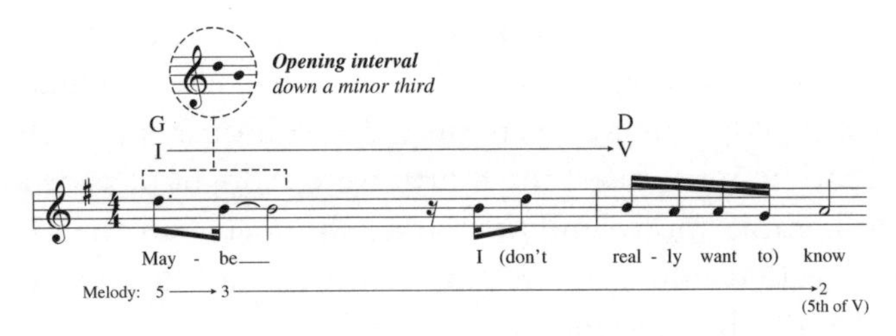

The lyrics in brackets have their own pitches and place within the melody but we should remember that fundamental to the study of intervals, is the *emphasis* of the pitches. Those that are isolated (or which fall on the strong downbeats) are especially important in determining how we perceive the path of the line, with others often heard as 'pick-up' notes, 'grace' notes or other embellishments. In this sense, both tunes can be seen to open with a distinctive '5-3-2' structural descent over (don't let's totally ignore the harmony) a I-V chord change.

Of course, it's too early to talk of 'Beatle-esque' melodies, as a minor third descent is just one example of a memorable Beatles opening. In fact we can find others that use almost every interval in the chromatic spectrum – from 'unison' to 'octave', and in both ascending and descending directions.

As an exercise that will help us learn to recognise instantly the common intervals in music, Appendix 3 provides Beatles examples of (almost) all of the 24 possible intervals in music. Associating the sound of an interval with a memorable phrase from a favourite song is the easiest way to understand how melodies flow in practice. In most examples we've chosen either the opening interval or a simple variation that should be instantly recognisable. In a few cases we've had to look elsewhere within a song to find the more awkward leaps which are therefore less common starting ploys.

While only one example is given in each case, the important thing is to tap into the identity and effect of such intervals as they recur in a variety of songs. Compare the perfect fourth of 'Nowhere Man' with the one that starts 'I'll Follow The Sun' ('One *day*'), or 'Ticket To Ride' ('I *think*'), or, beyond The Beatles, in various tunes embedded in our consciousness like, say, 'Here Comes The Bride' ('Here *comes* . . .'). All use the identical opening premise as the pitch on the 5th degree of the scale rises by a perfect fourth to the tonic, over a I chord (i.e. '5-8').

It's an interesting quirk of music that, while interval dissonance is something that can be mathematically measured and ranked, it has nevertheless been subject to fashion.[8] Historically, diatonic intervals like the unison, octave, third, fifth and sixth were treated as consonances; while the second, seventh, and (in most cases) the fourth were thought of as dissonances. But as music became more ambitious (i.e., chromatic) in the late 1800s, the sound of second intervals (creating ninth chords) and sevenths (creating major sevenths) became more accepted.

While most people today would still regard an opening major seventh interval as disorientating, we don't flinch at songs that end on a major seventh *chord* (e.g., 'It Won't Be Long', 'Julia' or Billy Joel's 'Just The Way You Are'). Even though the chord contains the same interval, we don't feel as if it *needs* to resolve. Similarly, it has become highly fashionable for dozens of minor-key rock songs to close on a minor 9th chord.

Ultimately, the interval tables confirm that Beatles melodies have no 'trademark', on the basis of this first simple (but distinctive) melodic criterion. Clearly, these melodies set out ambitiously across both the diatonic and chromatic spectrum to experiment with virtually all the intervals in music (not forgetting the unison starts of 'This Boy' or 'Michelle').

Rather than labouring through all the various intervals, let's look in particular at the use of the tritone. For while at first sight we might assume that The Beatles confined their melodic exploits (especially their opening intervals) to the consonant or at least 'the mildly dissonant', a whole selection of songs find them taking up the challenge of extreme tension.

'Blue Jay Way', 'Within You Without You' and 'The Inner Light' are cases in point. Their respective uses of the tritone are the very antithesis of the 'catchy pop melody' with which many associate The Beatles – but that's a vital part of their fascination. This dark interval represents an acquired taste to be savoured as a foil to Beatlemania – with McCartney himself captivated by the tune of 'The Inner Light', Harrison's 1968 B-side to 'Lady Madonna'.

> 'Forget the Indian music and listen to the melody. Don't you think it's a beautiful melody? It's really lovely.'[9]

[8] For a full discussion of interval theory and Pythagoras' Theory Of Proportions, refer to Haunschild, *The New Harmony Book*, pp. 38–42.

[9] *Beatlesongs*, William J. Dowlding, p. 202; referring to *The Beatles in Their Own Words*, compiled by Barry Miles, and *The Beatles Forever* by Nicholas Schaffner.

It is the 'Indian' elements (drones, pedals, etc.) that create a static harmony, while allowing us to focus cleanly on the highly unusual intervals of Harrison's Eastern-sounding modal melodies. Admittedly, we have cheated slightly by suggesting these are opening augmented fourths as, technically, the tritone does not appear as a single discrete interval. Nevertheless, a look at each of these songs confirms that the disorientating tritone, created either between the root and ♭5th or the 3rd and ♭7th on the all-important opening downbeats *within the opening phrase,* clearly defines the haunting modal nature of the melody.[10]

'Blue Jay Way'

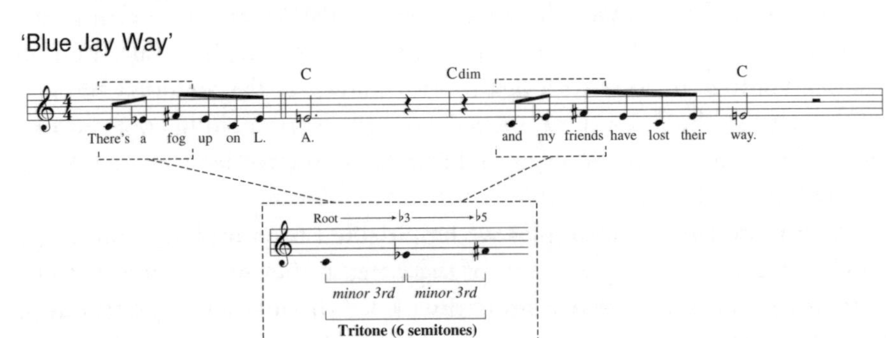

'The Inner Light'

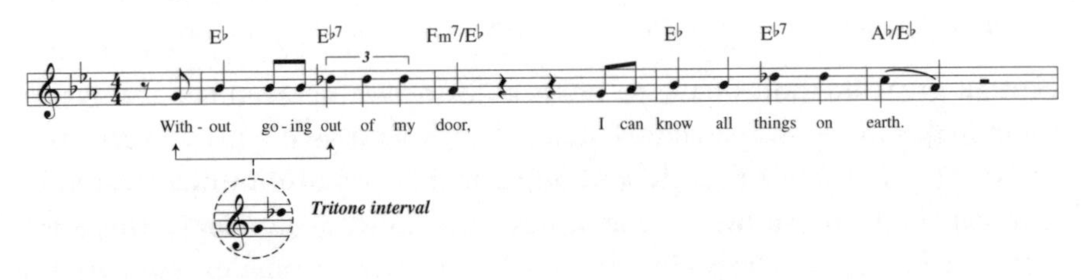

'Within You Without You'

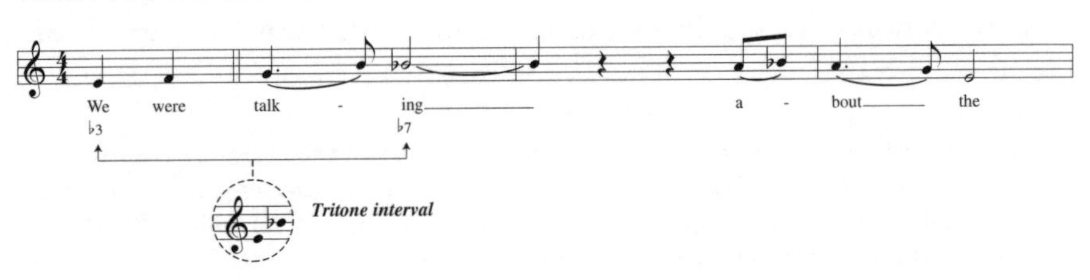

[10] Pitches on upbeats are usually far less important to a melody. In this sense we could have taken 'Penny Lane' as the 'ascending major third interval' as we don't hear the intervening second in the 1-2-3 walk-up (on the second syllable of 'Penny') as strongly as the root and third that 'book-end' the phrase.

We have already described the Lydian flavour of 'Blue Jay Way', while these other two songs emerge as essentially Mixolydian in terms of their overall collection of notes. As we prepare to delve deeper into our exploration of the structure of Beatles 'tunes', the real songwriting lesson here is that it is not the scale itself that matters – it's what you do with it.[11]

As we know, critical to the use of dissonance in pop is resolution, something that the tritones of 'Blue Jay Way' and 'Within You Without You' lack, leaving these songs to meander through prolonged dissonance – thereby distancing themselves from conventional notions of pop music.[12]

Perhaps Paul feels that 'The Inner Light' is particularly beautiful as the tritone effect (created as the 3rd heads for the ♭7th) is a challenging sound, an acquired taste in melody – though most would agree that precisely because of the tritone, the line is far removed from the 'very melodic' notions of a pop 'tune' which most people would probably use to describe, say, 'From Me To You' or 'I Will'.

With these last few examples we have drifted from looking purely at a single interval to an appreciation of the notes as they are constructed *in a particular phrase*. This is useful groundwork for the following discussion of melodic phrasing.

2. Melodic patterns – the structure and contour of motifs and phrases

Not all great melodies have to boast a distinctive, spotlighted interval in their make-up – and certainly many Beatles songs do not. Every tune works on a number of levels, and quite apart from the sounds created by intervals and the moods of the scales they collectively imply, there is a whole approach to 'top line analysis' that looks at the *patterns* of the notes.

This section forms a brief introduction to the way that notes of a

[11] For a fascinating discussion of the Indian characteristics of various Beatles excursions, see Porter, who introduces The Raga System with terms such as the *saptak* (scale) whose variants form mode-like *thatas* consisting of *swaras* (fundamental tones) from which fragments of melody (*ragas*) are crafted. The *Khamaj thata* is equivalent to our Mixolydian, while the *kafi thata* is our Dorian; *Rhythm And Harmony In The Music Of The Beatles*, pp. 83–91. See also Everett's discussion of 'Love You To', *The Beatles As Musicians: Revolver Through The Anthology*, p. 41.

[12] Compare the theme at 1.51 of 'Within You Without You' to the swordmandel riff of 'Strawberry Fields Forever'.

melody are joined together to make musical 'words', 'phrases' and 'sentences', perhaps developing a simple two-note interval into a complete 8-bar verse.

Motifs

Most successful pop songs are characterised by 'hooks' that instantly draw in the listener. These can take a variety of forms and everyone has their own idea of what is an 'ear-catching' hook. It could be a simple instrumental 'riff' – like the guitar figure of 'Day Tripper', or the bass line to 'Taxman'. It could even be the drum pattern of 'Ticket To Ride', or perhaps the stabbing strings in 'Eleanor Rigby'.

In a formal *melody* line, these hooks typically appear as 'motifs', a word that we have already used but which can now be defined as *a string of notes organised into a memorable unit of varying length.* A motif can be as short as one or two notes (as in the case of some of those opening intervals e.g., 'Good Day Sunshine'); or it can run to a whole breathless four-bar phrase, as in the verse of 'Across The Universe'.

The versatility of the melodic motif throughout The Beatles' catalogue can be explored in a variety of ways:

a) Repeated motifs
b) Motifs as melodic sequences
c) Disguising and developing motifs
d) 'Call and response' and complementary motifs
e) 'Story' type melodies

a) Repeated motifs

For chord-crazed guitarists whose melodic inspiration normally develops from strumming through a variety of progressions, Citron provides a simple but revealing insight into the workings of the more melody-conscious, piano-based songwriters.

> 'Some get their musical kernels by fooling around with a group of pitches, not by being arbitrary, but by picking and repeating a string of pitches until they arrive at a series that takes their fancy'.[13]

[13] Citron, *Songwriting*, p. 180.

Easier said than done, perhaps, but the emphasis here should be on the word 'repeating'. For a look at certain Beatles melodies confirms that repeating motifs are indeed what so many of them ultimately consist of. Indeed, in its most basic incarnation, a motif is usually thought of as a repeated figure that has an irresistible sing-a-long quality.

Most common is a motif that unfolds over one or two bars *and which is then either repeated and/or developed.* The long fade-out coda of 'Hey Jude' and the chorus of 'Lucy In The Sky With Diamonds' are obvious candidates. In both cases, a discrete melodic motif is first presented as the 'hook', then repeated, either verbatim or with very small changes. In this way, we can break down a melody that covers a complete song section into manageable bite-size chunks. Think, too, of the choruses of 'Don't Let Me Down', 'Yellow Submarine', 'With A Little Help From My Friends', 'I Wanna Be Your Man', or the theme of 'Birthday'.

'With A Little Help From My Friends'

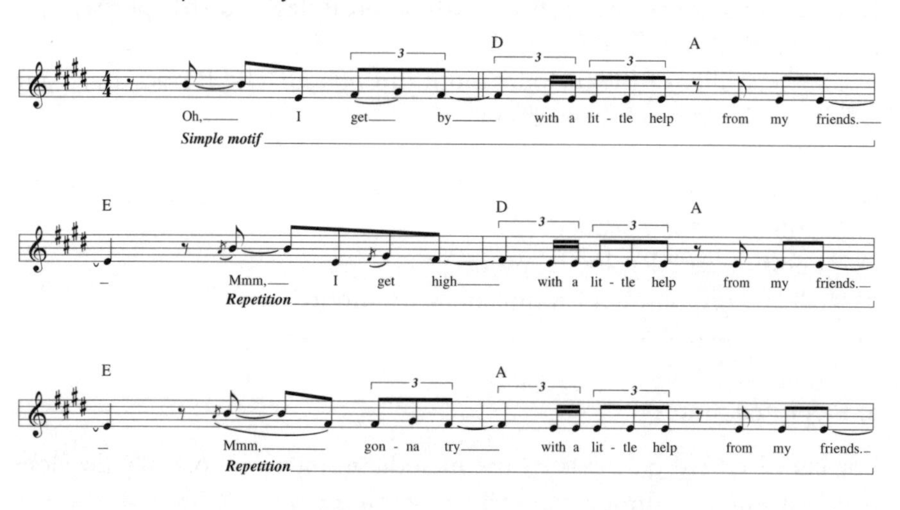

A crucial point here relates to the harmony. Compare these blatantly 'flagged' phrases, which *repeat over the same chord progression*, with those motifs whose repetition is *disguised by a shift in the underlying harmony*.

In the 'last' Beatles song, 'Real Love', the very first line is a motif, which is then repeated almost exactly – *and at the same pitch*. However, we hear it as subtly changed because of the changing harmony beneath it, which almost gives the illusion that other *melody* notes have been introduced. But as John Lennon knows, why waste energy on a new *melodic* idea when you can just change the chord?

'Real Love'

b) Melodic sequences

Of particular songwriting interest in this category is a motif that repeats identically – *but starting on a different note.* This idea is known as a *melodic sequence* – a motif that is successively repeated at higher or lower pitches.

The blues is an obvious example here, with much of the genre defined by opening motifs that are repeated with identical lyrics up an interval of a fourth (as the I chord moves to IV in bar 5 of a 12-bar). The Beatles followed this melodic formula faithfully in blues-based sections, such as the verse of 'I Want You (She's So Heavy)'. In this case it's a minor blues, where the opening phrase over Am is repeated almost identically as the harmony shifts to Dm.[14]

But apart from this obvious use in the blues, the ultimate Beatles example in this category is found unquestionably in 'The Continuing Story Of Bungalow Bill', where John Lennon employs a radical key change to engineer this very precise effect. The two phrases are identical – apart from the fact that they begin and end three semitones apart.

'The Continuing Story Of Bungalow Bill'

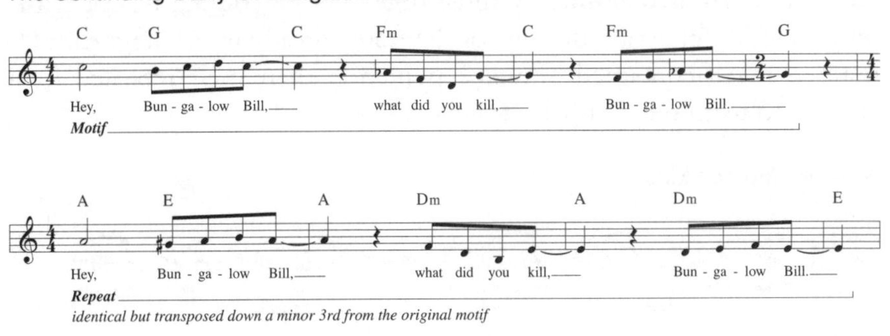

[14] *Almost* identically, as the wavering between the 4th and 5th interval which taps into the dissonant ♭5 on the repeat, creates subtle contrast (as we discuss under harmonisation in Chapter 15).

Listen too to 'Mean Mr Mustard'. The lyrics may have changed, but the bite-size motif appears three times, with the first repeat appearing a minor third higher, creating a 'sandwich' effect. As in 'Bungalow Bill' this has the profound effect of highlighting the motif as a definite hook with its own momentum.

'Mean Mr Mustard'

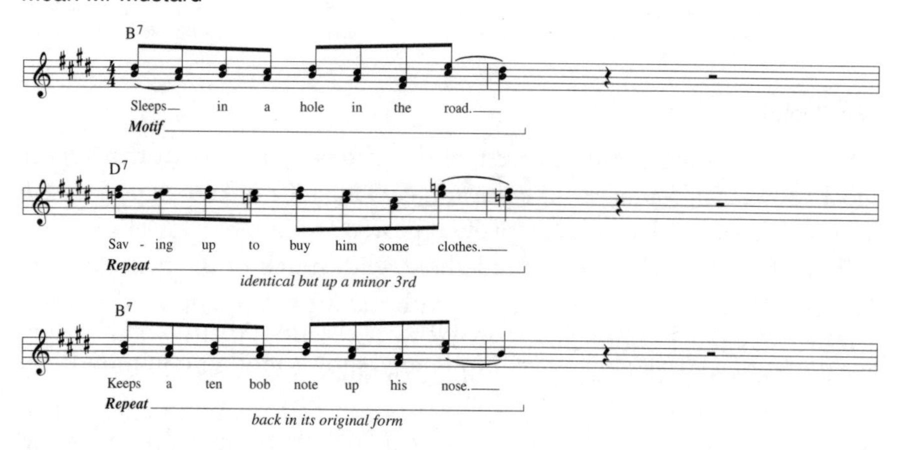

c) Developing motifs

Repeating a motif, perhaps once, twice – or even three times – is a great way of establishing a melodic foothold, but at some point the idea must be developed or resolved. Dozens of Beatles melodies demonstrate how this can be achieved by briefly tweaking the initial fragment.

At the simplest level, take 'You Like Me Too Much', a primitive, four-note motif repeated seamlessly three times, before coming to rest with a simple closing interval onto one of the notes already in the fragment. The result is a self-contained sentence (which is then itself repeated in its entirety to form the first half of the verse).

'You Like Me Too Much'

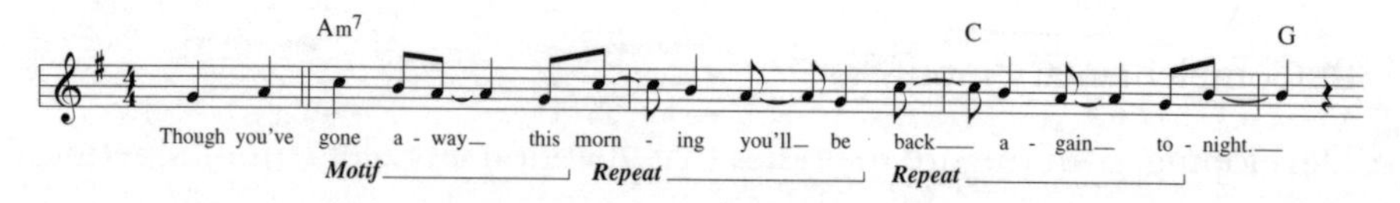

The repeated unit could be anything from a three-note figure ('Little Child') to one- and two-bar motifs ('No Reply'). In both these cases the motifs are developed to form a complete sentence with this 'tailing' approach.

'Little Child'

'No Reply'

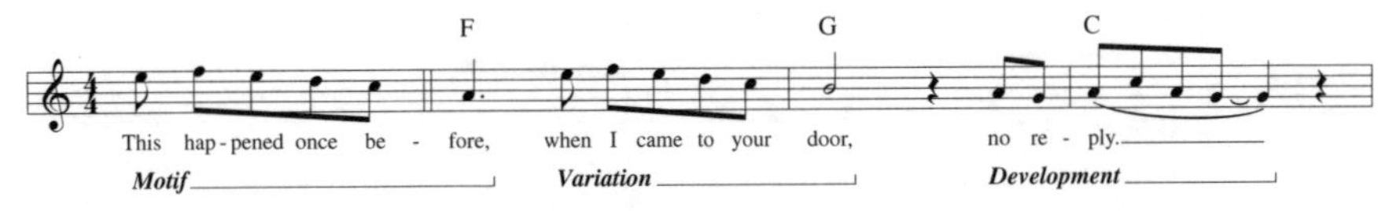

In each of these cases the isolated motif is followed by new material *not directly based on what went before.* 'No Reply' shows another common Beatle approach – the thematic development of a given motif where, on its second (or even third) appearance *it is restated with subtle variations.* You can see it in songs of all eras, including 'From Me To You', 'I Wanna Be Your Man', 'And I Love Her', 'Glass Onion' and 'Her Majesty'.

'Her Majesty'

d) Complementary motifs

Developing from this are melodies that abandon any element of repetition in favour of new material, but which still *complement* the original motif (perhaps being based on a similar rhythmic pattern). This approach to melody in pop originates from the blues concept of 'call and response', whereby an opening 'cry' is answered by new melodic idea. Middleton highlights The Who's 'My Generation' as a classic example in rock where an opening cry is answered by the masses (as represented by a two-part backing).[15] Many variations on this have developed, with 'Hey Bulldog' seeing a twin vocal 'call' phrase, answered by an elaborating 'response' from a single party.

'Hey Bulldog'

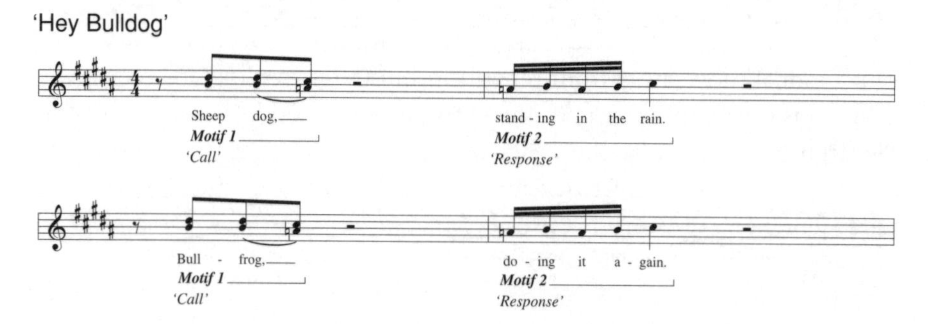

But the general principle of two, complementary melodic ideas can be seen in settings as varied as the hard rock of 'Back In The USSR' and the gentle ballad of 'A Day In The Life'. Both open with melodies that consist of an initial 2-bar motif that is turned into a 4-bar phrase in precisely this way.

'Back In The USSR'

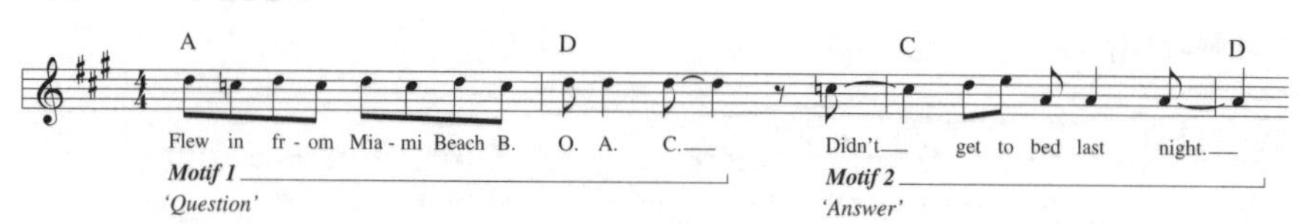

'A Day In The Life'

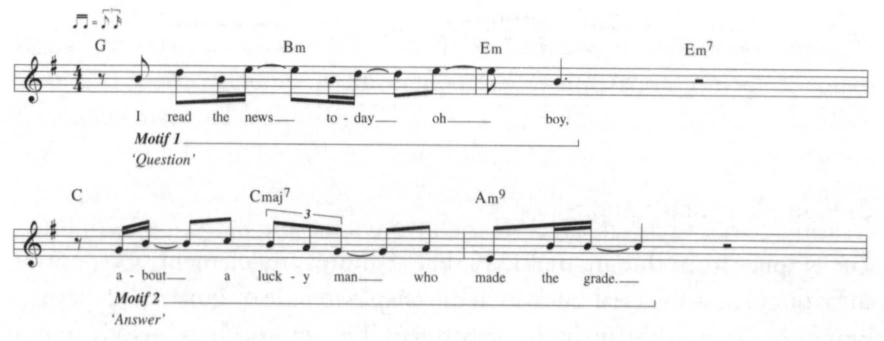

[15] Middleton, *Studying Popular Music*, p. 49.

Even George Harrison's 'Something', which might appear to be merely repeating its opening motif at a higher pitch (given the reappearance of the title lyric), in fact introduces new intervallic relationships which complement the original motif with similar rhythmic phrasing.

e) 'Story' type melodies

Our gradual move away from repetition illustrates that melodic construction exists on a continuum. At one extreme are 'Good Day Sunshine'-style repeated phrases and at the other are those melodies that dispense with both repetition and direct development of a motif and display more of a pure 'sentence', or 'story', construction, *with new directions in every phrase.* These are melodies involving more of a 'stream of consciousness' as seen in another vast category of songs including 'Yesterday', 'Here There And Everywhere', 'Sexy Sadie', 'Penny Lane' and 'Hey Jude' (excepting the coda, obviously!). Each of these verses unfolds far less predictably than those structured on repeated motifs, bringing in new material that leads the listener in the antithesis of a sing-a-long melody.

Melodic contour or 'shape'

> 'There was a period when I thought I didn't write melody . . . Paul wrote those and I just wrote straight, shouting rock 'n' roll.'[16]

John Lennon's famous quote raises interesting questions as to our perception of the very term 'melody', which, as we already know, we cannot take for granted.

The word 'melodic' is itself highly subjective but it can perhaps be seen to imply a number of features, one them being the 'full' use of the 7-note major scale, in comparison to, say, pentatonic fragments or less. But, then even the 'straight, shouting rock 'n' roll' to which Lennon refers still involves 'melody' – however few notes are belted out of the Lennon larynx. Nevertheless, the fewer notes in your motif, the less scope for creating a stereotypical 'shapely' melody with a pitch path, or 'contour', that is specifically designed to make the most of a particular scale.

[16] *The Playboy Interviews*, p. 123.

Once again we are on a continuum that makes it impossible to generalise. Certainly the vast majority of tunes rise and fall naturally, with no discernible pattern, even if subtle, unpredictable changes of direction are responsible for their effect. However, for the sake of analysis we can identify various categories of melodic shape. The three types suggested by US magazine *Guitar One* are a useful starting point:[17]

a) **Linear** – based on, or around, a single note
b) **Circular** – rising up, or falling down, a scale
c) **Square** – characterised by wide interval jumps

These headings are only an analytical tool as, in practice, most songs tend to be a combination of all three. But it is nevertheless useful to demonstrate the songwriting effect of the various options – and memorable Beatles melodies clearly demonstrate each principle.

Obvious examples of **linear** melodies include 'Help' (based around one famous C♯ note that we will be examining later), 'I Am The Walrus' (E alternating only with a neighbouring E♭), and 'Lucy In The Sky With Diamonds' (C♯ again, with just a few 'neighbour' tones).

But, particularly in this category, let's not forget the relationship between melodic shape and *harmony*. For example, a songwriter may require his melody to be fairly static or otherwise unadventurous *specifically to draw attention to a descending harmonic line* such as we saw in Chapter 9. Take 'Lucy In The Sky With Diamonds' – John's linear melody may be 'hypnotic' in its own way, but the overall effect of the song hinges on the way this static melody is complemented by the harmonic interest generated by the blissful collapse in the bass.

'Circular' melodies (which create a definite flow away from their starting point) are the most common category, especially those that display that clichéd 'sense of 'innate melodicism' that we might associate with the Tin Pan Alley era. John Lennon's ultra-smooth line in 'Don't Let Me Down' surely qualifies, floating up and easing back down the scale, all within the space of a short, one-bar motif.

[17] *Guitar One*, August 1998, p. 20.

'Don't Let Me Down'

Sometimes called 'vertical', circular melodies are perhaps most commonly found in pop in the form of structured *ascents* or *descents* that are then repeated to achieve a cyclical effect.[18] As well as their geometric shape, such tunes encourage us to focus on the grand scheme of their voice-leading. The most common category is, of course, those Schenkerian descents through 5-4-3-2-1, which we first saw hidden in 'I Will' (Appendix 1) and blatantly flagged in 'Nowhere Man' (Chapter 7).

More challenging are those tunes that thwart such a direct flow to the tonic in favour of other closing pitches. We will later see how 'Yesterday' closes quizzically on the 3rd of the key; while, in the context of circular contour, watch how 'Norwegian Wood' targets the 5th of the key (B) with a carefully plotted octave drop that contrasts cleverly with the more static harmony.

'Norwegian Wood'

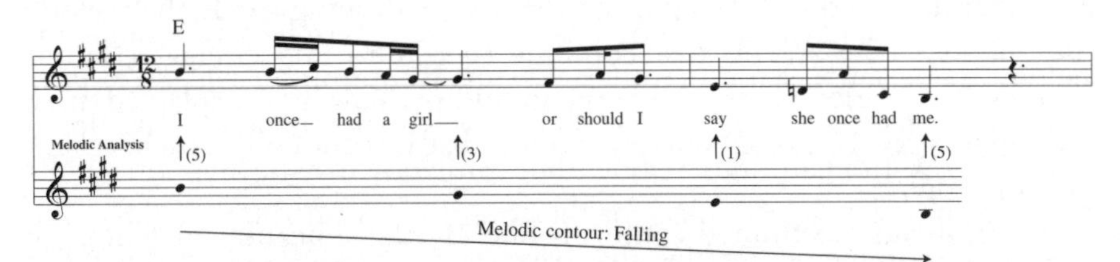

Mention of harmony should, once again, encourage us to graduate from strict 'top-line' analysis to looking at complementary vocal or bass lines in the backing, which form a counterpoint effect that adds new dimensions to a song. (This is not to be confused with backing vocals that track a given melody *in harmony*, which we will discuss later.) *Counter melodies* display their own independent movement – most effectively in songs like 'Help!', 'Sexy Sadie' and, in the context of 'circularity', 'Hello Goodbye', which sees an unrelated countermelody in action, along with a textbook example of a counterpoint *descending* bass line against a *rising* melody:

[18] Rooksby refers to this category as 'vertical', and makes the comparison between 'Bali Hai' and the opening Viking cry on Led Zep's 'Immigrant Song' as both also feature an octave leap followed by an exotic down-a-semitone drop; *How To Write Songs On Guitar*, p. 86.

'Hello Goodbye'

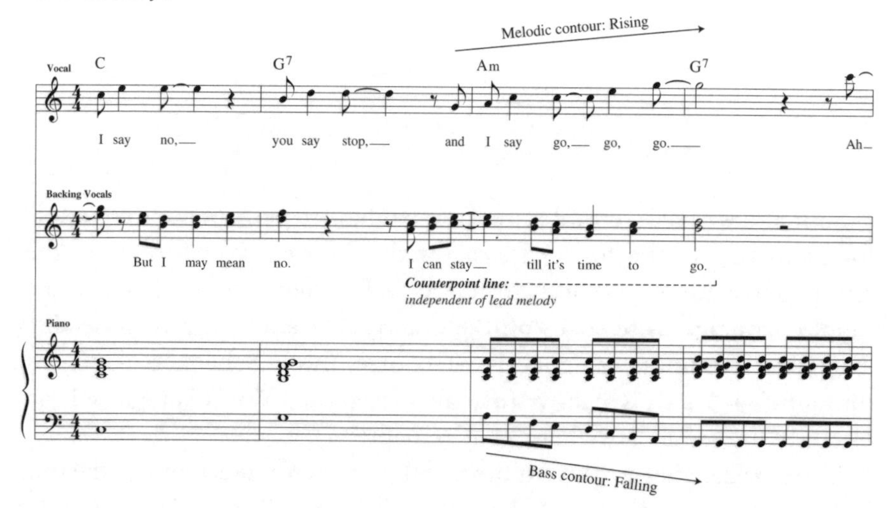

Here is an extreme example of counterpoint, as various elements move in opposite directions in a manner that dates back to Bach and his famous 'Bourrée'. Fast-forward to *The White Album* to find McCartney using the same principle, but in the ultra-primitive setting of 'Helter Skelter'. While the guitar line on the B-string drops against the droning top E, the melody rises, in step-wise ascents that combine *both* linear and circular contour features. As Charles Manson's lawyer should perhaps have explained, it all adds up to a raw blend of contrary motion that was enough to tip his client over the edge.[19]

We've already examined some of The Beatles' uncanny matching of lyrical and *harmonic* concepts; now we can see how they extended the principle to *melody*. The jagged melody of 'Helter Skelter', combined with this disorientating counterpoint, brilliantly mirrors the title itself and the whole lyrical theme of climbing to the top of the slide after each ride.

The final '**square**' category is less popular with songwriters, who are perhaps instinctively aware of the 'textbook' notion of melody as a 'gradual' melodic contour that precludes too many sudden jumps and changes of direction. But The Beatles proved that there are no such rules, with tunes like 'Because', for all its gentle ambience, featuring intervals that

[19] See also the descending line against static tones on the title phrase of 'Mother Nature's Son', and the famous backing vocal lines in 'Do You Want To Know A Secret', where a three-note semitone scalar descent complements the chromatic drop of the chords.

'Helter Skelter' – contrary motion

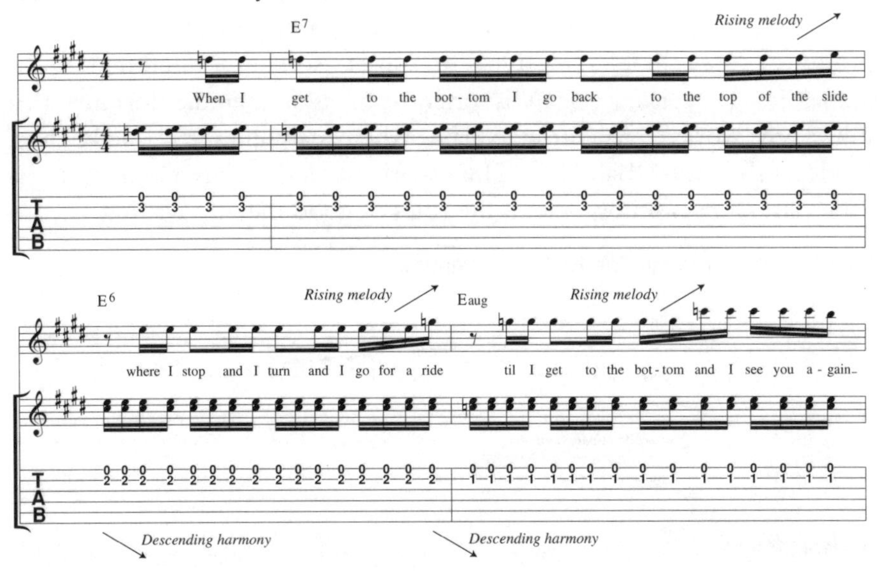

leap up and down as if on a trampoline (although admittedly the slick harmony and sustained notes smooth out the rough edges). In 'You Won't See Me', a clearly 'square shape' melody with awkward, wide-interval changes in direction is highlighted by the clipped edges from the *staccato* delivery.

'You Won't See Me'

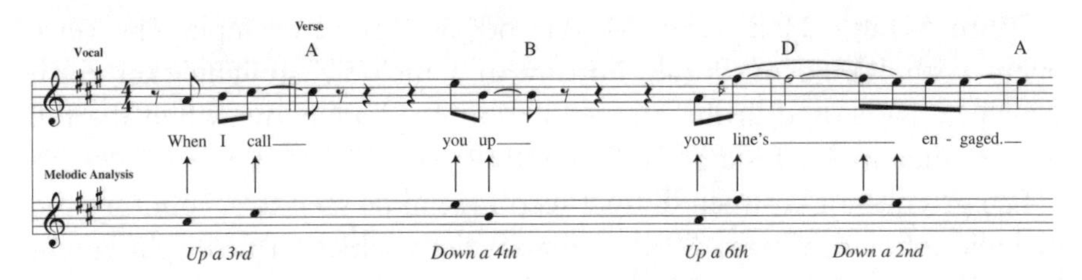

This might be an obvious case, but even the most mellow ballad settings of 'In My Life', 'I'll Follow The Sun' and 'Sexy Sadie' also feature a series of unusual jumps that could be seen as falling into the 'square' category.

They demonstrate that, in practice, most melodies combine elements of the 'linear', 'circular' and 'square' categories. One of the most popular hybrid ploys is to open a tune with an initial striking interval jump, before beginning a more delicate structural descent, as in, say, the verses of 'Can't Buy Me Love', 'She Came In Through The Bathroom Window' and the bridge of 'Hey Jude'. This type of subset (sometimes referred to by academics as *tumbling strain*) is often seen as a melodic formula that inherently 'works'.[20] As Citron explains when analysing the classic Richard Rodgers showtune 'Bali Hai': 'The way the melody turns and goes in the other direction is simply one of the rules of good melody writing.'[21]

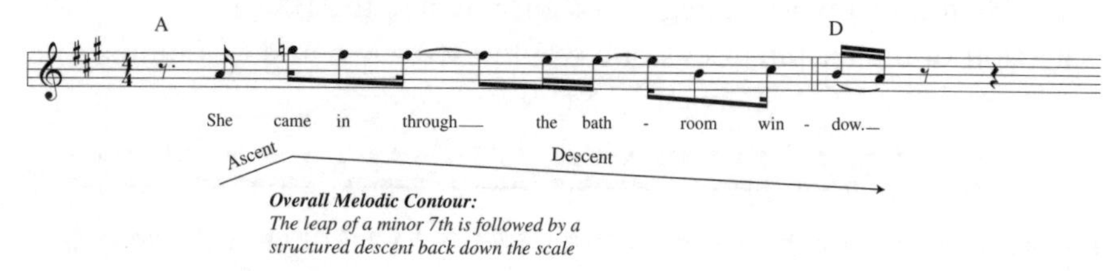

Melodic Range

Related to contour is the notion of *range*. Now we aren't looking at the *relative* movement between the notes – merely the *absolute* 'field' or 'extremes' of the collection of notes used in the melody. For practical singing purposes, most pop melodies tend to operate within a relatively narrow range, typically one octave. More common are songs of contrasting sections where a verse may be held within an interval of a fifth (i.e., seven half-steps between highest and lowest note) before markedly widening in the chorus or bridge section.

'With A Little Help From My Friends' is a good example. The verse opens with Ringo on vocals, initially in a melodic 'straightjacket' from which he is released in the phrase 'do you need anybody', when the full octave range makes for a powerful contrast.

Range contrast between distinct sections can be seen to account for the melodic interest in many Beatles compositions which, at first sight, might be assumed to operate within narrow bounds.

'Help!', 'Come Together' and 'Good Morning, Good Morning' all explore a much wider range in their respective choruses in contrast to their

[20] 'Tumbling strain' is one of Philip Tagg's subdivisions of contour profile that go far beyond our three categories, with such exotic titles as 'oscillating', 'centric', 'V-shaped', 'wavy' and 'terraced'. See *Melody and Accompaniment*, pp. 4–5.

[21] Citron, *Songwriting*, p. 182.

ponderous, mantra-like verses. Meanwhile, 'Sgt. Pepper' turns the principle around with (the hardly grand) range of a sixth for the verse, being effectively halved for the almost monotone chorus.

Again, if we're looking for some kind of Beatle trademark in this area we're going to be disappointed – the group's real secret was to create contrast both within songs and *between* songs.

Jon Fitzgerald's study of early Beatles songs homes in on the contrast between melodic pitch placement in different sections of The Beatles' early songs. He found a whole category of songs where the B section moves to a collection of higher pitches, as one would expect when developing a song for the euphoria of Beatlemania: 'I Saw Her Standing There', 'A Hard Day's Night', 'Can't Buy Me Love', and even 'We Can Work It Out'. Nevertheless, he found an equal number that started the B section on what one might have thought would be an anti-climactic set of lower pitches – understandable, for the mellow, reflective bridges of ballads like 'And I Love Her', but perhaps surprising in the context of early singles like 'Love Me Do', 'Please Please Me', 'From Me To You' and 'I Want To Hold Your Hand'.[22]

3. Melodic Rhythm – phrasing, form and metre

Another theoretical notion of 'textbook melody' that is often bandied about is the idea that the rhythmic flow of a tune should mirror the natural phrasing of conversation. There is a perception that melodies should feature words and phrases of different lengths, all punctuated by suitable pauses (or 'rests'), just as in (supposedly) natural, everyday speech.

Certainly songs like 'Yesterday', 'Let It Be' and 'In My Life' have this type of narrative flow. 'Golden Slumbers' perhaps best illustrates this principle by featuring all the basic rhythmic subdivisions of whole, half, quarter, eighth and sixteenth notes (complete with some ties for natural syncopation) together with examples of most of their respective rests – all in the first few bars.

Here is a mature, 'speech-like' melody if ever there was one. But if this type of structure was ever a songwriting rule, The Beatles were there to break it. Take the stressed whole notes of 'Sun King' on the very same album, or the hypnotic half notes of 'If I Fell' and 'Within You Without You', none of

[22] 'Lennon-McCartney and the Early British Invasion, 1964–1966' by Jon Fitzgerald; published in *The Beatles, Popular Music And Society: A Thousand Voices*, Edited by Ian Inglis; p. 63.

'Golden Slumbers'

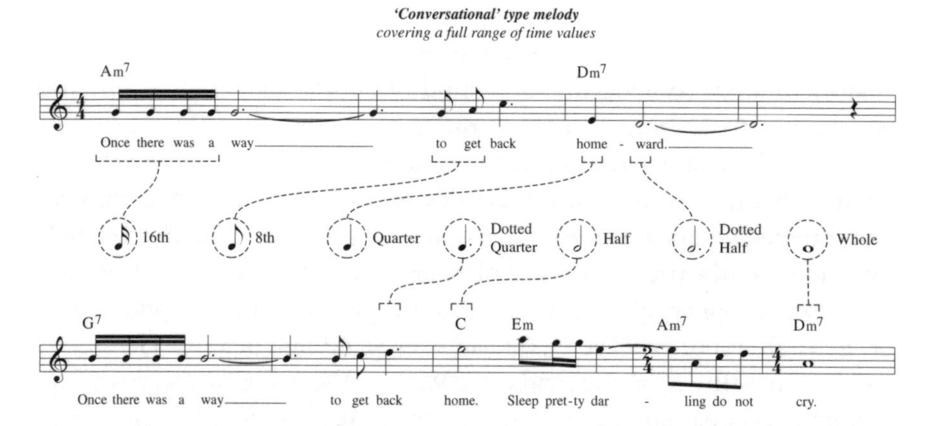

which can be seen to accord with any notion of 'speech rhythm'. Yet these songs clearly 'work' in their contexts, with the 'Sun King' delivery in particular evoking beautifully the procession of the lyrical theme just as the emphasis in 'A Hard Day's Night' reflects the singer's labour. Similarly, tunes like 'Cry Baby Cry' work precisely *because of* the hypnotic metric monotony provided by the relentlessly repeated rhythm, rather than despite it.

'Cry Baby Cry'

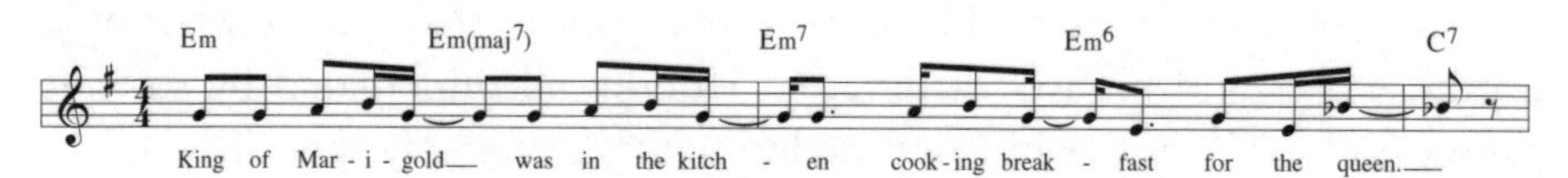

Meanwhile, at the other extreme are those Beatle melodies that literally 'pour out', as in 'Across The Universe' and 'I've Just Seen A Face', creating virtually 'rest-free' zones that fly in the face of melodic convention.

'Across The Universe'

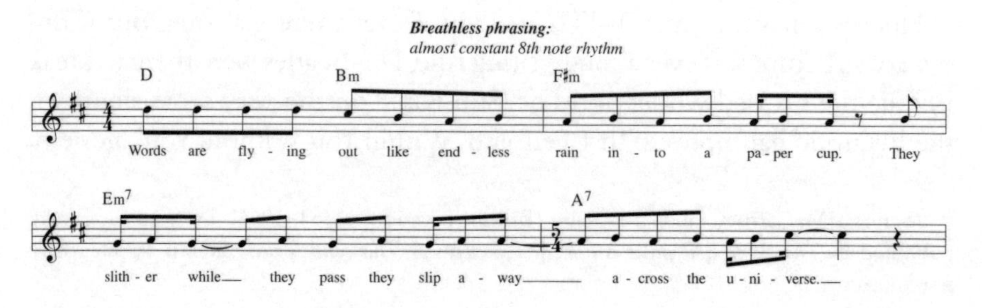

The intensity of the melody (in terms of note *values*) is also related to the level of *syncopation*. The extent to which the phrasing feels secure and predictable is related to whether words fall on or off the beat.

The grouping of stressed and unstressed syllables is called *metric feet*, a term that helps us capture the degree of 'grounding' we feel as we sing the melody while tapping our feet. Most melodies will naturally mix strong downbeats with weaker upbeats as they unfold, but the *balance* between them can be an important element in the way a song works. As music publisher and songwriting expert John Braheny points out:

> 'In songwriting, you need to repeat the metric feet in a way that not only makes them fit comfortably with the musical pulse, but *emphasises the intended meaning of the lyric.*[23]

Let's pick two Beatles songs to illustrate the principle. At one extreme is 'She's Leaving Home' where the first syllables of almost all the important lyrics fall relentlessly on the downbeats, with just a few upbeats in evidence. Sure enough, this highly *unsyncopated* delivery couldn't be more appropriate for the theme of the song, where cold, hard 'facts' (here a definite sequence of historical events), are being recounted, very precisely, and without equivocation.[24]

'She's Leaving Home'

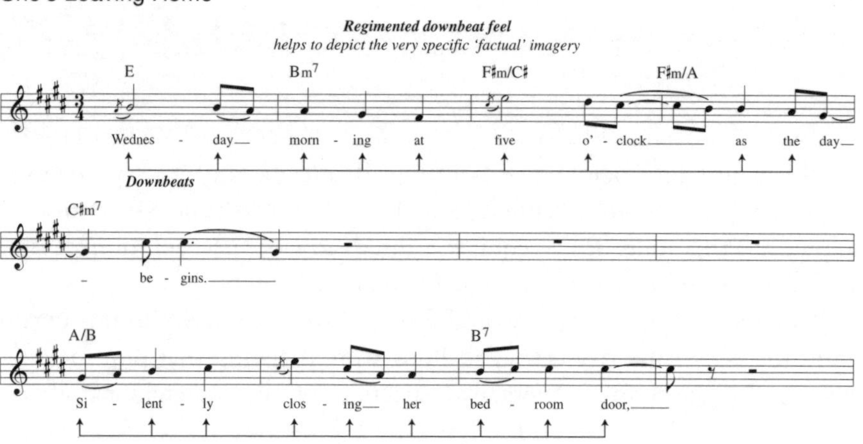

[23] John Braheny, *The Craft And Business Of Songwriting*, p. 63.

[24] While the song is in 3/4 time, the principle of up and down beats is the same whatever the time signature (a term we look at in more detail below).

At the opposite extreme, George Harrison's 'If I Needed Someone' is a rare example of a melody where the rhythm is almost exclusively *syncopated*. Try singing the line while tapping your foot to hear how the tune shuns almost every downbeat, preferring to go against the grain (in typical Harrison style), by favouring off-beats (i.e., the 'and' within the eighth-note count of '1 and 2 and 3 and 4 and').

The result is a far more rhythmically challenging melody that lacks the obvious hooky footholds that tunes are also 'supposed' to have. But then the lyrical theme of the song is far removed from 'She's Leaving Home' whose present tense reality is replaced here by future speculation, with the 'If' of the title symbolising equivocation.

'If I Needed Someone'

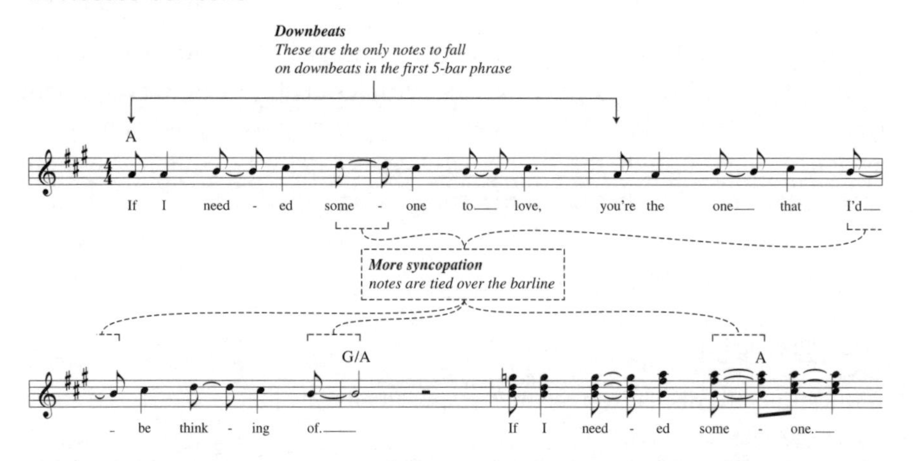

This is just one example of how The Beatles became true pioneers of melody in the way they refused to be bound by rhythmic convention. To appreciate this more fully requires a discussion of the evolution of their idiosyncratic approach to phrasing, form and metre.

While later compositions would feature extreme novelty in this regard, from the very early days The Fab Four were dictating that pop melodies need no longer be so regimentally restricted to four- and eight-bar phrases within a strict 4/4 metre. If the lyric and the melody suggested adding or dropping beats then The Beatles would make the bar structure adapt as necessary – a point well captured by Deryck Cooke when summarising The Beatles' appeal in his 1968 article:

> 'Popular song has long been confined to an appalling eight bar monotony. An eight bar section, repeated; a 'middle eight' and the first eight again: only the finest songs have overcome this crippling restriction . . . But Lennon and McCartney have broken completely free: sections of five, seven, nine, 11 and 13 bars are nothing to them.'[25]

Of course, long before The Beatles, Delta bluesmen were freely playing around with irregular phrase-lengths and rests in the early part of the 20th Century – hence the 11- or 13-bar blues structures of Robert Johnson and John Lee Hooker. But the Tin Pan Alley era, for all its harmonic originality and sophisticated sense of melodic contour, had indeed established a widespread convention in terms of this *form* in popular song.[26]

But The Beatles shook up these conventions for good, unafraid of the ramifications their idiosyncratic metric phrasing would have on the precise form of their songs, whatever the broad chosen structure. In this regard, it's only a slight exaggeration to suggest that if it wasn't a 12-bar or 16-bar blues-based rock 'n' roll format, the standard vehicle for a pre-Beatles pop song was indeed this 8-bar 'unit', often delivered in an AABA blueprint, or close variations of it.[27] Of course, The Beatles themselves followed this square 8-bar formula – *and rigidly* – on several occasions.

For example, let's examine the structure of 'From Me To You'. OK, so *harmonically* the bridge featured a groundbreaking modulation that we raved about in Chapter 10, thereby contributing quite enough novelty for one song. Nevertheless, in terms of the actual *phrasing* of the melody, it unquestionably displays great metric predictability, falling squarely into a highly conventional 8-bar unit. The result is that the whole song can be distilled into a simple symmetrical pair of A and B sections as follows:

Section	Lyric	Bars	Phrase length
A (verse)	'If there's anything...'	8	2 + 2 + 2 + 2
B (bridge)	'I've got arms...'	8	2 + 2 + 2 + 2

[25] Deryck Cooke, *The Listener*, 1st February 1968. Reprinted in *The Lennon Companion*, p. 111. The notion of a 32-bar 'rule' is somewhat of an exaggeration with classics like 'I Got Rhythm' (36 bars: 8+8+8+12) and 'Moonlight In Vermont' (28 bars, 6+6+8+8) being two of many exceptions, as noted by E. Lee, *Music Of The People* (1970).

[26] Cooke even describes how a classic like 'Stormy Weather' had the novelty of its 7-bar A section 'spoiled by Harold Arlen's mechanical addition of an unnecessary instrumental bar to make up the eight', though the song later departs from from 32-bar predictability with its '8+10+8+10' form.

[27] AABA describes a typical pop structure where A represents a verse and B a chorus. Less specifically, A and B can represent any two contrasting sections of a composition.

The reference to '2+2+2+2' is only a guide, of course, as 'pick-up' notes and rests and other elements of phrasing obviously vary, but the formula helps to capture the overall nature of the phrasing. Indeed the very predictability of the phrasing ensures we are never 'lost' – we know instinctively where we are in the song – unlike many that specifically work their magic by taking the listener on a mystery tour.

Many early Beatles songs can *broadly speaking* be shoehorned into this AABA category, as one fascinating songwriting study demonstrated when comparing various Beatles songwriting features with those of three other leading British Invasion bands: The Rolling Stones, The Kinks and The Dave Clark Five.[28] Of the pre-1966 Lennon/McCartney songs analysed, almost three-quarters were found to follow the basic AABA premise (with others mainly in the alternating ABAB 'verse-chorus' format), while not a single example was found of, say, the simpler AAA form found in many of the Rolling Stones and Kinks songs.[29]

However, an appreciation of the way that each of Lennon, McCartney and Harrison bent the basic blueprint completely out of shape is crucial to understanding another fundamental element of their songwriting skills.

If we take the AABA structure alone, they did this on two levels:

1) Moving away from square phrasing and 8-bar predictability
2) 'Re-stacking' or 'reordering' the basic song sections.

The latter refers to a more mechanistic approach – juggling the sections once the music has been written. For example, having opened with AABA, the song may not then repeat that same overall form as was conventional in Tin Pan Alley times. This evolution was partly due to the realities of radio play in the early sixties, demanding as it did sub 3-minute (sometimes sub 2-minute) songs. This, combined with a 'modern' approach to soloing (if there was a solo) over only part of the form (usually a single A section) meant that, though the AABA structure might be the basic premise, it became a moveable feast.

[28] 'Lennon-McCartney And The Early British Invasion, 1964–1966' by Jon Fitzgerald; published in *The Beatles, Popular Music And Society: A Thousand Voices*, edited by Ian Inglis, p. 72.

[29] Examples of AAA form include Stones songs like 'Lady Jane', 'Paint It Black' and 'As Tears Go By'.

'This Boy' is a very rare example of a Beatles song that consists of a 'pure' AABA, with just an intro and coda tacked on. Even with 'From Me To You' we find that, after being initially faithful to this form, the song completes with solo-bridge-verse, making the total form: AABA + ABA.

As we shall see, this represents miminal development of the form, compared with what The Beatles would do with both AABA and their other most favoured song format – ABAB. Variations on the latter would go far beyond the ploy used by George Martin when he took the choruses of 'Can't Buy Me Love' and 'She Loves You' to the top of the song, and, with them, The Beatles to the top of the charts.

The construction of Beatles songs and their (often seemingly haphazard) stacking of song sections is fascinating. In Appendix 4 we set out the radically different ways in which they combined the main elements of intro, verse, chorus, bridge and solo. A great number of these structures can indeed be seen as variations on the basic stalwarts of pop form, namely AABA and ABAB. Yet the sheer variety of bar counts *within* each of these sections, the range of *development* sections, and the sometimes disorientatingly arbitrary way in which these units are cut and pasted together, means that we will again be struggling to identify a Beatle 'trademark' in respect of form.

Ultimately, it is far more important to appreciate the way in which The Beatles graduated to a whole range of bizarre song forms, as the result of the first process suggested above: novel melodic *phrasing*.

Breaking away from the 8-bar rut through phrasing

The AABA model certainly forms an important reference point. For it was through the constant manipulation of the 8-bar units *within the actual A and B sections themselves*, in order to accommodate the idiosyncratic phrase lengths of their melodies, that The Beatles threw the conventions of song structure to the four winds.

It is vital to appreciate that it is the irregular phrase length of melodies that determines novel bar periods, not the other way around. And the essence of the novelty can be found in the 'conversation-type' phrases with which The Beatles took pop melody beyond a straightforward diet of predictable motifs. A look at 'Not A Second Time' demonstrates a melodic revolution in the making.

'Not A Second Time'

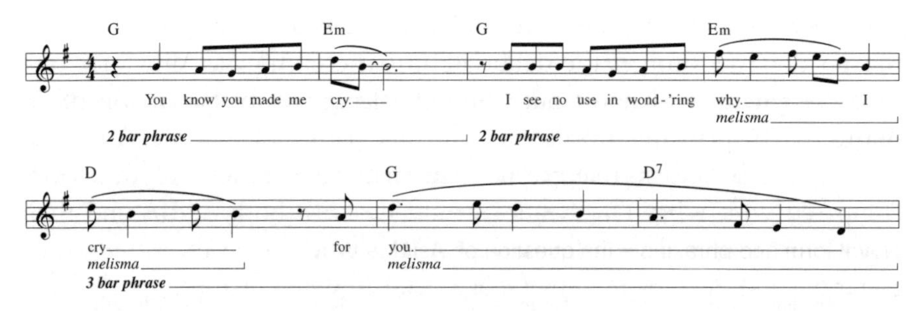

Here is another song that, in broad terms, follows the AABA structure, but now with the 8-bar formula abandoned to suit John Lennon's eccentric phrasing. The simple 2-bar opening motif appears to get repeated with a slight variation before cueing an extraordinary three-bar stretch characterised by even more extreme *melismas* (on '*criiiied*' and '*youououou*').[30] If we feel totally disorientated in terms of our instinctive sense of the song's form that's because the symmetrical structure suggested by the predictable first 2-bar phrase is soon undermined by Lennon's inspired rambling. This is confirmed by a bar-count that shows the verse to consist of (two cycles of) seven bars – whether we view them as split into phrases of 2+2+3 or, using an alternative interpretation, 3+4.[31]

After the repeat John goes on to follow this A section with a 10-bar B, with similarly unusual phrasing that you could perhaps subdivide into melodic fragments of 2+2+1+1+3 with a 1-bar rest.

'Not A Second Time' was by no means an isolated case of what Pollack calls 'a free-verse feel to the music that is very typical of John Lennon even in this relatively early period'.[32] Check out various others, including 'All

[30] A *melisma* is a single *syllable* in the lyric that is extended within the phrase over a series of *different* pitches. They are usually isolated ideas, as in 'All I've Got To Do' ('whenever I-I-I-I-I') or 'In My Life' ('in myyyyy life'). The multiple *melismas* (or correctly '*melismatas'*) of 'Not A Second Time' are an extreme example of this useful melodic principle.

[31] While Pollack describes the former, Everett sees the second phrase starting at bar 4; *The Beatles As Musicians: The Quarry Men Through Rubber Soul*, p. 192. While we're on *With The Beatles*, compare this with the rather clearer 3+4 verse scheme of 'It Won't Be Long' [as noted by both experts], where Lennon re-enters hastily (at 0.21) after only half the 2-bar guitar lick heard at 0.12.

[32] Alan W. Pollack, 'Notes on ... Series' no. 41, 1991. *The 'Official' rec.music.beatles Home Page*, www.recmusicbeatles.com.

I've Got To Do' (for its 11-bar A section), 'Little Child' (6-bar B section); and Harrison's 'Don't Bother Me' (12-bar A against 8-bar 'B').[33]

And don't let's forget the debut album where 'Ask Me Why' not only broke out of the 8-bar rut but featured a landmark bastardisation of the entire AABA principle by altering the very nature of the final A section, creating a hybrid form that can be summarised as follows:

Novel form and phrasing – the question of 'Ask Me Why'

Section	Lyric	Bars	Phrase length
A (verse)	'I love you...'	8	3 + 1 bar rest + 4
B (verse)	'That I, I, I, I...'	5	4 + 1 bar rest
C (bridge)	'I can't believe...'	8	4 + 4
D (chorus)	'Ask me why...'	6	5 + 1 bar rest

What we've labelled here as D is clearly a reworking of the original A section, but it is nevertheless different enough in terms of phrasing and bar-count to warrant its own moniker. In terms of *overall* form, however, the distinct identity of these four sections and their phrasing is compounded by the way that these building blocks are juggled together to create a bizarre sequence of ABAB/CDABDCD, which was as radical for a pop song in 1963 as it would be today. Here is an example of Beatles *form* working its magic, with a jigsaw structure that causes us to question our whereabouts in a sublimely clever take on the title itself.

The structural novelty of 'Ask Me Why' (and indeed others on *Please Please Me* like 'P.S. I Love You') can be seen as lighting the blue touch-paper for later, more exotic, Beatles adventures in phrasing and form.

This area of melodic phrasing has indeed remained vastly under-appreciated in comparison to the basic pitches and contour of tunes, and the underlying harmony on which (albeit understandably) we tend to focus. Yet classical writers have picked up on The Beatles' novelty in this regard, with Joshua Rifkin marvelling at the 10- and 15-bar phrases of 'If I Fell', the subtle variation of the 12-bar form between verse and bridge of 'We Can Work It Out', and on to 'Good Day Sunshine' where he describes

[33] While 'Don't Bother Me' is still AABA, it provides a link to the form of 'I Want To Hold Your Hand' and 'Thank You Girl' whose three distinct sections pitch a verse-chorus structure (*totalling* 12 bars) against a formal 'middle eight'; as emphasized by O'Grady, *The Music Of The Beatles From 1962 to Sgt. Pepper*, p. 230.

'a six-bar chorus consisting of three two-bar groups with an internal beat pattern of 3,3,2' that we will later decipher.[34]

The last reference confirms that The Beatles experimented with phrasing and form, which not only had ramifications for *bar* counts and form – but also occasionally for *beat* counts, as their melodic ideas began to imply changes in the *metre* or 'time signature' itself.

Before looking at the mechanics of this in practice, an introduction to rhythmic concepts is essential.

Rhythm primer: time signatures and the beat

Rhythm as a whole has indeed been underplayed throughout our travels, partly because, as George Martin himself points out, the very nature of rhythm, in terms of following a beat or pulse, is instinctive in humans.[35] Natural rhythm is a common denominator in music that enables musicians from radically different cultures and styles to come together and 'jam' with reference to a sense of pulse with which we are all born. On the BBC documentary *Rhythm Of Life,* Martin's guest, former Police drummer Stewart Copeland, describes a simple '2 and 4' rock 'backbeat' (where the snare emphasizes the second and fourth beats in a bar of 4/4) as the single most important rhythmic feature in virtually all pop and rock styles.[36]

Nevertheless, many Beatles songs demonstrate the scope for rhythmic embellishment – specifically the ways in which the beat is *subdivided* and *accented* to create variations in *feel*.

Most early rock 'n' roll (and Beatles) songs are in 4/4 time, subdivided into eighth notes (hence 1-2-3-4 becomes '1 *and* 2 *and* 3 *and* 4 *and*), with the eighth notes played 'even' or with a 'swing feel'. Listen to 'I Call Her Name' to hear the shift between the two feels.[37]

Syncopation (subversion of the expected beat) started in earnest with the lilting drums of 'Ticket To Ride', as the accented snare on beat 4 is

[34] Joshua Rifkin, 'On The Music Of The Beatles', Reprinted in *The Lennon Companion*, p. 119.

[35] *George Martin's Rhythm Of Life*, BBC TV documentary.

[36] Copeland explained that the notable exception was reggae which 'turns the beat around' to highlight the first and third beats.

[37] 'Swing feel' divides each beat into three: each beat consists of triplets with the first note tied to (i.e., held over for the duration of) the second. Listen to the transition to swing feel for George's solo on 'I Call Your Name' (at 1.10).

anticipated (although the tambourine maintains the conventional back-beat).

Meanwhile, 'Lady Madonna's layered beat subdivisions from different instruments create subtle rhythmic intrigue. Listen to Ringo's laid-back drum groove, which appears to be out of step with the busy piano and overdubbed brushes. Either he's bizarrely accenting the *third* beat of the bar; or operating conventionally on 2 and 4 – but in half-time. It all makes sense when the lyrics 'see how they run' finally match Ringo's sedate underlying beat.

In his essential paper on Beatles rhythm, L.J.K. McCarthy argues that the late-period Beatles changed rhythmic convention by emphasizing sixteenth-note rather than eighth-note subdivisions of the beat – *especially in songs with a nominally slow tempo.* He cites 'Come Together', 'She Came In Through The Bathroom Window' and 'Everybody's Got Something To Hide Except For Me And My Monkey' as songs which, despite their moderate tempi, 'still maintain the energy and feel of faster-tempo rock music'.[38]

It should be stressed that all these are 'adventures in common time', with the pulse of the music instinctively grouped into bars of four beats. But 4/4 wasn't the only time signature being explored.

As early as 'My Bonnie' The Beatles were playing in 3/4 time, a feel with which they became enamoured (very specifically) from the lilting waltz of James Ray's 'If You Got To Make A Fool Of Somebody'. The 'three' rather than 'four feel' would reappear on various songs like 'This Boy', 'Baby's In Black', 'Norwegian Wood', 'She's Leaving Home', 'You've Got To Hide Your Love Away' and 'Oh! Darling' – where in some cases the triplet feel is maintained as subdivisions of a basic two- or four-beat bar (time signatures given the names 6/8 and 12/8, respectively).[39]

The table below lays out some of the most common time signatures in

[38] L.J.K. McCarthy, 'Slow Down! – How The Beatles Changed The Rhythmic Paradigm Of Rock', advance paper from *Beatlestudies III*. Such slow tempo/fast feel was not unheard of in pre-Beatles pop (see Buddy Holly's 'Not Fade Away' from 1957).

[39] *Anthology 2* gives us a great insight into the way that The Beatles experimented with how a given song would feel in a different time signature. The out-take of 'I'll Be Back' finds Lennon dictating the first run-through with his waltzy: '1-2-3, 2-2-3', count (track 17), before switching to 4/4 (track 18) – which duly emerges as better choice to accommodate the phrasing of the bridge melody in particular.

use, together with the subdivisions of the beat in so called *compound* time signatures such as 6/8 and 12/8:

<table>
<tr><th>Time signature</th><th colspan="12">Metric pattern</th></tr>
<tr><td>2/4</td><td colspan="6">1</td><td colspan="6">2</td></tr>
<tr><td>6/8</td><td colspan="2">1</td><td colspan="2">2</td><td colspan="2">3</td><td colspan="2">2</td><td colspan="2">2</td><td colspan="2">3</td></tr>
<tr><td>3/4</td><td colspan="4">1</td><td colspan="4">2</td><td colspan="4">3</td></tr>
<tr><td>4/4</td><td colspan="3">1</td><td colspan="3">2</td><td colspan="3">3</td><td colspan="3">4</td></tr>
<tr><td>12/8</td><td>1</td><td>2</td><td>3</td><td>2</td><td>2</td><td>3</td><td>3</td><td>2</td><td>3</td><td>4</td><td>2</td><td>3</td></tr>
</table>

The next stage is to appreciate how a songwriter can move between these basic time signatures *within* a song to create 'mixed metre'. On *Revolver*, for example, listen to 'She Said She Said' as John takes time out (literally) to describe life 'when I was a boy', using 3/4 for contrast (0.59-1.11) against the verse of 4/4. Still in 3/4, but now on *Sgt Pepper*, we can't leave out the most distinctive Beatles waltz of all, as Henry The Horse gives us a twirl in 'Mr Kite' (right on cue with the very word 'waltz' at 1.00). And, talking of The Beatles' cast of characters, how about *Abbey Road* where 'Mean Mr. Mustard', after idling by in 4/4, gets exposed as 'a dirty old man' in 6/8 (at 0.59) on his way to 'Polythene Pam'.

So far this diversion into rhythm has made no reference to melody or melodic phrasing – which are, essentially, the subjects of this chapter. Certainly these examples of metric embellishment seem independent of any 'top line' considerations – the choice of rhythmic feel can obviously create interest in isolation to other factors. The remainder of this chapter examines mixed metre as *a direct function of melodic phrasing creating a varied beat count within bars*. It is the result of accommodating what the songwriter wants to say, and for how long (and, equally, for how long he wants to pause).

We need only try to count Little Richard's 'Good Golly Miss Molly', McCartney's 'great favourite from the fifties' and another early Beatles live staple, to appreciate the subtle effect of adding or dropping beats.[40] While

[40] Paul raves about the song, the lyrics and the influence of Richard himself on *Rock & Roll Roots*. Lewisohn confirms that this 1958 Blackwell/Marascalco composition appeared in Beatles live sets (sung by Paul) during 1960 and 1961; *The Complete Recording Sessions*, p. 362.

the song appears to be exclusively in 4/4 time, Richard's phrasing has the effect of subtly turning the beat around when the opening title refrain in the A section (chorus) reappears in the B section (the syncopated verse).

'Good Golly Miss Molly' – beat count of title refrain in the A section

4/4	1	2	3	4	1
		Good	Golly	Miss	Molly

'Good Golly Miss Molly' – beat count of title refrain line in the B section

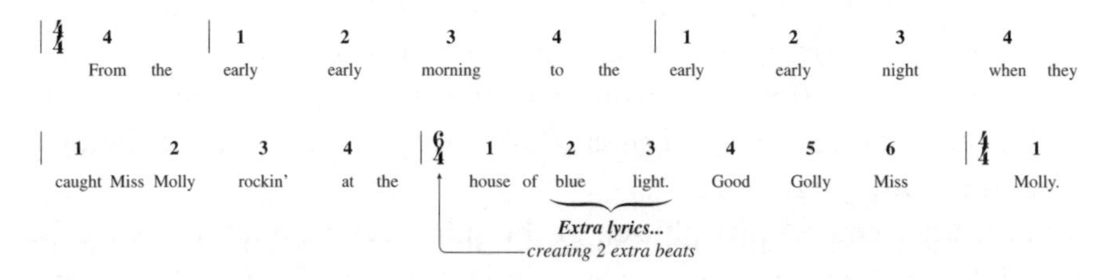

It is important to trace the source of these extra two beats. Richard doesn't appear to hang about with his delivery even though the band stops to create a 'hole' effect. The culprit, as we might expect, is the singer's idiosyncratic free-form phrasing which extends the previous line with the words 'of blue light' (which, ironically, McCartney himself volunteers as his favourite line in the song).

The result is that we are already on the third beat of the bar by the time the next 'Good Golly' is cued. The song could just carry on with a 4/4 time signature – but then Molly herself would no longer be able to make her grand entrance on the all-important first downbeat of the next bar when the band returns. Hence the song effectively enjoys – *automatically as a result of the lyrics* – two extra beats that must be reflected in the time signature by treating this as one, long bar of six beats: hence 6/4 (or alternatively a bar of 4/4 with one of 2/4 tacked on).

Looking at it the other way, Richard needn't have gone to the trouble. He could merely have truncated his phrase by leaving out McCartney's favourite words, ensuring that he ended that second line on the downbeat of 1 thereby restoring the original rhythm for the refrain. With major apologies to Little Richard (and McCartney) for the artistic licence, this would have seen the song home and dry in 4/4 time throughout.

'Good Golly Miss Molly' – Cueing the chorus in straight 4/4 time

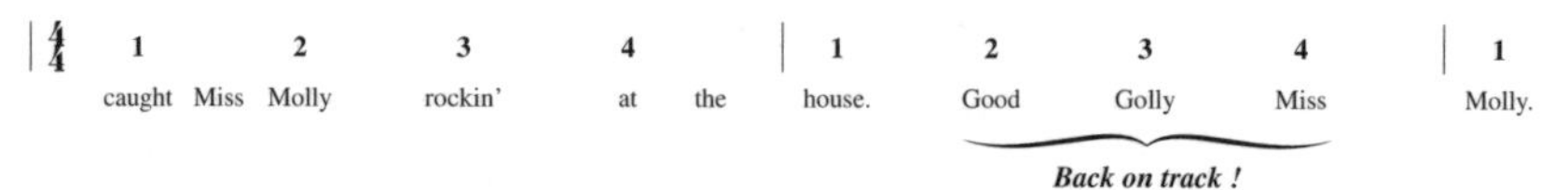

Notwithstanding the rhyming deficiency, the phrase is now distinctly inferior – lacking the very rhythmic originality that had dancers in the fifties briefly, deliciously disorientated. For the whole point of tweaking the time signature in this way is to get listeners subconsciously thinking 'where's one?' (as musicians like to say) before the metric *status quo* is restored, either in the following bar (as with Molly), or soon after.

This may be a simple example from the annals of rock 'n' roll, but it is with reference to this same basic principle that we can appreciate the mixed-metre phrases of *Sgt. Pepper* that ushered in a new era of rhythmically ambitious songwriting.

From the strange 5-bar phrases of the title track through to 'A Day In The Life' (where Lennon's verses alone run to 10, 9 and 9½ bars), almost every track here features unusual phrase lengths delivered in odd time signatures while, in some cases, even the tempo itself is altered for effect.[41] 'Lucy In The Sky With Diamonds' is the most obvious example, with different signatures operating discretely in different song sections, as Lennon juxtaposes a dreamy 3/4 verse with a sing-a-long chorus in 4/4.

Rhythmically more subtle are those songs that shift *within* a section, thereby disorientating us in full flow. Even the apparently simple nursery-rhyme chant of 'All You Need Is Love' features a deceptive metre change courtesy of a dropped beat in the second bar.[42]

[41] The issue of actual tempo changes within a song should be kept separate; but listen out for contrasting speeds in various *Pepper* songs like 'Lucy', 'Mr Kite' and, especially, 'A Day In The Life', where McCartney's 'woke up' section is twice the speed of Lennon's verse ballad.

[42] As George Harrison himself points out:'John has an amazing thing with his timing, he comes across with very different time signatures, you know. For example, on 'All You Need Is Love', it just sort of skips a beat here and there and changes time. But you question him as to what he's actually doing and he doesn't know. He just does what comes naturally.'; Geoffrey Giuliano, *Two of Us: John Lennon & Paul McCartney Behind The Myth*, p. 103.

'All You Need Is Love'

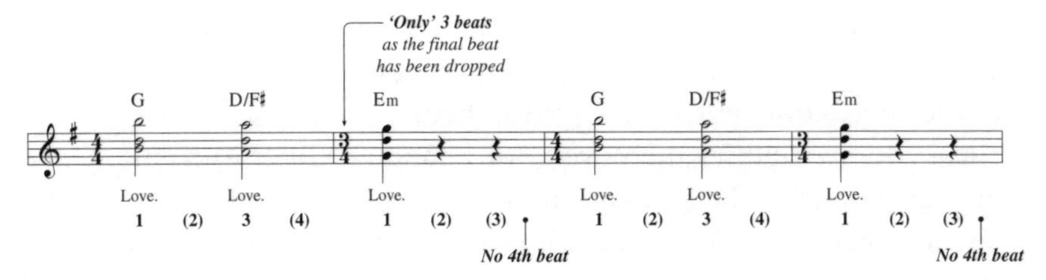

Again we can take the mystery out of the cold calculations by suggesting that The Beatles could easily have rested for that extra beat to maintain a 4/4 rhythm. Meanwhile, the quirky chorus of 'Good Day Sunshine' demonstrates how mixed metre can be dictated not merely by beat *counts* but by the rhythmic *emphasis* of a particular lyric. Certainly we could notate the famous refrain in straight 4/4 time – some songbooks do just that, with the eight beats of the basic refrain split equally between two bars. But to do so requires awkward treatment of the word 'sunshine': it is forced to unfold 'over the bar-line' rather than starting a new bar on the first strong downbeat, as we instinctively feel.

'Good Day Sunshine'

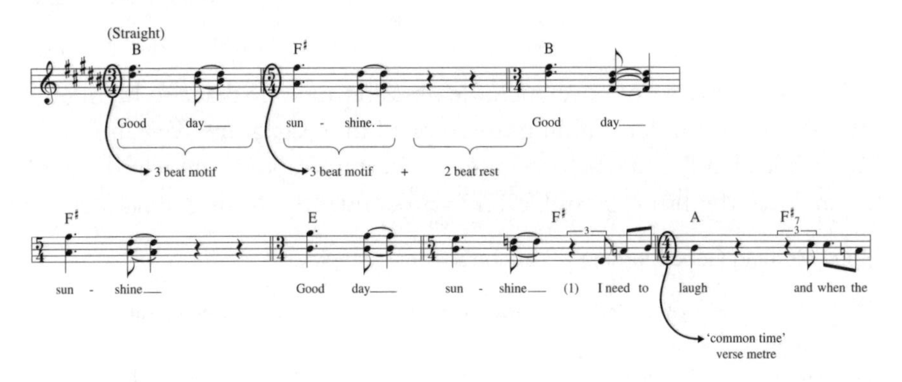

This metric juxtaposition of 3/4 and 5/4 now helps us to make sense of Joshua Rifkin's description of the refrain's 'internal beat pattern of 3,3,2', that reflects the melodic rhythm with its two, syncopated three-beat phrases followed by two beats of rest. These same two-beats of course neatly accommodate the 'pick-up' as we move into the verse – which, with The Beatles' brilliant sense of contrast, now *does* unfold regimentally in 4/4 time.

But while many would argue that these temporal ploys are incidental rhythmic embellishments, one particular song on *Sgt. Pepper*, above all others, uses mixed metre compellingly throughout its form and in a way that uncannily complements the lyrical theme.

Allan Moore captures the novelty of Lennon's 'Good Morning, Good Morning' perfectly when he says the song does 'violence to the very idea of the four bar beat'.[43] Yup, try finding 'one' in this verse after a couple of pints . . .

'Good Morning, Good Morning'

This is a showcase of novel melodic phrasing and one that also highlights the role of rests in determining the implied time signature. We can follow Moore's lead and extract the phrases, by beat, to capture the weirdness of the melodic rhythm responsible for these constantly shifting signatures.

'Good Morning Good Morning' – Lennon's lonely timeplay

	CD timing	Beat count	Lyric on downbeat
Verse			
Phrase 1	0.11	3 + 3 + 4	'Noth-' 'save' 'call'
Phrase 2	0.16	3 + 5 + 4	'Noth-' 'what' 'been'
Phrase 3	0.22	5 + 4	'Noth-' 'you'
Phrase 3	0.27	3 + 3	'Noth-' 'it's'
Chorus	0.30	4 + 4	'Morn-'

[43] Allan F. Moore, *The Beatles: Sgt. Pepper's Lonely Hearts Club Band*, Cambridge Handbooks, p. 50.

Moore himself makes the splendid connection between the phrasing and the whole lyrical theme of alienation: 'The strangeness is used to reinforce the notion of this as an outsider's song: everybody else in the singer's world is comfortable,' he says, pointing out that the normality of 4/4 time is only retrieved on each chorus with the greeting that symbolises Lennon's forced interaction with the outside world.

By the time of the *White Album*, The Beatles truly overdosed on multimetre machinations – most famously in the sprawling structure of 'Happiness Is A Warm Gun', which captured Lennon's collage approach to songwriting in all its glory.

The simple observation that the song consists essentially of four sections, each based on a different basic metre, is just the tip of the iceberg. It is the highly complex variations – within the C and D sections especially – that turns this particular flexible Lennon frolic into a transcriber's nightmare.

One of the most incisive of all technical studies undertaken on Beatles rhythms finds Jouni Koskimäki attempting to harness this particular song's unique rhythmic character.

Here is a summary snapshot based on his approach, which he appropriately entitles *Happiness Is ... A Good Transcription:*[44]

Section	CD timing	Lyric	Metre
A	0.00	'She's not a girl who misses much...'	**4/4**
B	0.44	'I need a fix...'	**3/8**
C1	1.13	'Mother Superior jump the gun...'	**6/16**
C2	1.15	*One bar*	**3/8**
C3	1.16	'Mother Superior jump the gun...'	**6/16**
C4	1.18	*One bar*	**4/8**
D1	1.34	'Happiness is a warm gun...'	**4/4**
D2	1.47	'When I...'	**3/8**
D3	2.02	'Because, happiness is a warm gun...'	**4/4**

Most fascinating is Koskimäki's focus on section C, where he says, 'the Beatles go Balkan', as Mother Superior jumps the gun against a highly unusual backdrop of 'complex polyrhythms and frequent changes of pulse'. As demonstrated in the following extract of his transcription.

[44] Adapted from *Happiness Is . . . A Good Transcription, Shortcomings in Sheet Music Publications of 'Happiness Is A Warm Gun'*; reprinted in *Beatlestudies 2* (2000), University of Jyväskylä, Department of Music, Finland, p. 183.

This highly unusual 'additive rhythm' matches 6/16 time with both 3/8 and 4/8, a ploy more characteristic of Bulgarian folk musicians and progressive composers like Béla Bartók, than sixties popular music.[45]

6/16 means that each bar features six 16th notes, generating a flowing triplet rhythm for the lyric 'Mother Superior jumped the gun'. However, no sooner have we grasped the first two bars than, in the very next bar, the beat itself changes from 16th notes to 8th notes.

As if that's not confusing enough, you'll notice that the *count* of the beat in this bar changes between the first and second endings of that same Mother Superior line! This in effect gives us two different endings to that lyric – with 3/8 becoming 4/8 the second time around.

'Happiness Is A Warm Gun' (section C) – Decoding Lennon's Balkan beat

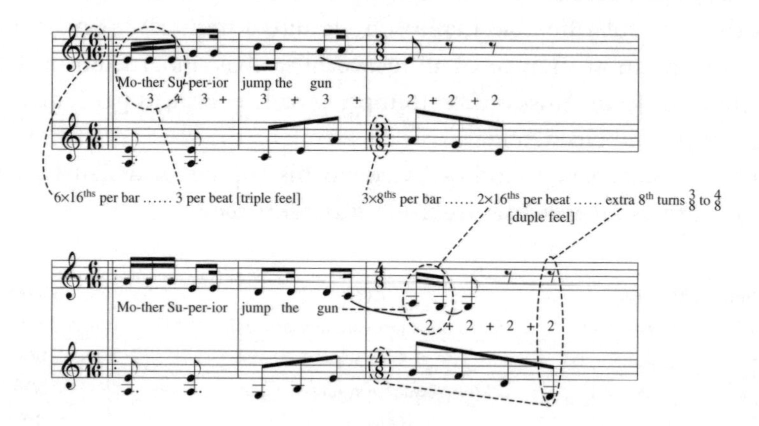

Koskimäki concludes that this section is:

> 'genuinely Balkan in the sense that its phrases are naturally written in the same manner as the additive Balkan rhythms are taught by local musicians: the first phrase goes as 3+3+3+3 + 2+2+2, and the second one as 3+3+3+3 + 2+2+2+2.'

'Happiness Is A Warm Gun' is quite a benchmark against which to pit your understanding of beat, metre, rhythm and phrasing, so don't worry if

[45] Allan Moore describes how additive rhythms (showcased in the music of Jethro Tull) derive not from dividing a bar into equal portions, but from adding together unspecified numbers of "the smallest possible unit" (here 16th notes) to produce "uneven length beats". *Rock: The Primary Text*, p. 104.

at first you don't get it – neither did Ringo! As Chris Ingham says, it's really no wonder that the rhythm track for this, the 'perplexing peak of John Lennon's rhythmic originality', needed 70 takes.[46]

Phew! But, as we know, more important than the cold numbers is the extra dimension the whole principle of exotic phrasing brings to song-writing, with Ingham himself perceptively nominating 'Lennon's Timeplay', particularly his "instinctive subversion of even metre", as one of the four quintessential elements that define the Beatles phenomenon.

Nor should we forget that McCartney and Harrison were also vital contributors to The Beatles' metric minefield. Among the many highlights is the way Paul throws listeners delightfully off the scent in 'Martha My Dear' (not to mention Martha herself), with an opening ramble through 3/4, 2/4 and 4/4 in the first three bars alone. And how about George's extreme 2/4, 3/8, 5/8, 4/4 interludes in 'Here Comes The Sun', which give guitarists so much more than just a finger-twisting arpeggio workout?

In summarising our melodic journey so far, we can suggest that while there are few obvious trademarks in terms of their use of intervals and motifs, The Beatles most obviously pioneered the use of unusual phrasing, creating rhythmic interest through shifting bar counts and beat counts implying mixed metre. From the 9-beat '*pleeeease*' on 'Love Me Do', to the Balkan-beat bonanza of 'Happiness' (and beyond), the Fabs once again re-wrote the rulebook.

But then, even in a case like 'Good Morning, Good Morning', how aware is the average listener of the dramatic shifts in bar lines, as long as he can still tap his foot adequately to the underlying 'pulse' throughout?

And that's the point – the apparent complexities of metric phrasing do add subtle nuance – and are certainly a way for a songwriter to tax his drummer disproportionately. But Lennon *need* not have rested after the phrase '. . . let your wife in . . .'. Come to that, he could have rewritten the lyric to leave out the word 'in', and reconstructed the whole song in 4/4 time.[47] Sure, musos would lose their cerebral connection between rhythm and meaning. But, played casually on the pub jukebox, would the average Beatles fan really notice?

[46] Chris Ingham, 'The Quintessence Of Beatleosity', Doctor Rock Dissects The Hits, No. 6, *MOJO*, Issue 24, November 1995; p. 35.

[47] Alternatively, the opening 3/4 time could have been extended by maintaining the phrasing of the first bar. Think of this three-bar experiment: 'Nothing to do to/save his life/nothing to say but/it's OK'.

FIFTEEN

Harmonisation in Focus

Our discussion of intervals, motifs and phrasing confirms that McCartney, Gallagher and critics like Deryck Cooke do indeed have a point. The complex and elusive world of Beatles melody *has* been underplayed, and our attempts to redress the balance have so far only scratched the surface.

And yet we cannot *really* make sense of melody independently from the harmony. To appreciate the powerful effect of even some of the simplest Beatles tunes we need to revisit the relationship between melody and the underlying *chords*, while also taking into account the role of vocal harmony that is such a beloved element of many of these songs. While, texturally, these create different effects in a song, in terms of the study of music they are bound by the same musical principle of *harmonisation*, the way in which melodies are 'supported' by other notes within a sonority.

This chapter looks at some of the important characteristics of these two areas, starting with an introduction to The Fabs' magical world of vocal harmony.

Part 1. Vertical intervals – the tools of two-part harmony

Having examined *horizontal* intervals in melodies in the last chapter, we now take a look at *vertical* intervals, and discover some of the ways in which The Beatles stacked melodic lines on top of each other to form a layering of melody.

The secret here is to accept that, when a second vocal part joins a lead line, as John and Paul would do when combining, it can use a variety of intervals. Different effects arise from close, consonant harmony or more distant, dissonant flavours. In the simplest sense, a second line can join in to match the pitches of a melody *exactly*, truly 'doubling' the lead and thickening the sound. This is singing in unison, as we hear on songs like 'A Hard Day's Night', 'I Should Have Known Better', 'She's A Woman', 'And I Love Her' and 'Any Time At All'.[1]

But the vocal interest is multiplied when the two parts still track each other in terms of the contour and rhythm of the phrase – but now *above* or *below* the original line, i.e., *at a higher or lower series of pitches*. This may be an obvious, primitive description of how to 'harmonise a tune', but it is one that raises an interesting point. McCartney himself describes how the presence of more than one vocal part creates a paradox as to the very nature of melody and harmony:

> 'Sometimes the harmony I was writing in sympathy to John's melody would take over and become a stronger melody. Sometimes a piebald rabbit came out of the hat! When people wrote out the music score they would ask, "Which one is the melody?" because it was so co-written that you could actually take either.'[2]

Paul was actually referring to 'Baby's In Black', a song whose various sections demonstrate that, in practice, the songwriter has a choice of intervals to create the specific colour and vocal *timbre* that he wants.

The most obvious option is to start the lead melody with one of the three strong chord tones: the root, 3rd or 5th, leaving the other two triad notes as guaranteed winners for the harmony part. Combining the major 3rd with either the root or the 5th creates a *harmony in diatonic thirds*, which confirms that, for all the apparent mystique of vocal harmony, we are merely once again harmonising a major scale in conventional, 'stacked' thirds.

'Baby's In Black' is just one of many Beatles songs that demonstrates this principle as, over the opening A chord, John and Paul each pick a chord tone, with the E note (5th) harmonising an interval of a third above the C♯ (3rd) – the latter being perhaps the slightly stronger lead melody.

[1] Tony Barrow's original cover notes on *A Hard Day's Night* describes how Lennon's double-tracked voice on the title track achieves a 'duet effect'; see sleeve of Parlophone PCS 3058 (stereo).

[2] Miles, *Many Years From Now*, p. 175.

'Baby's In Black' – A section (0.04)

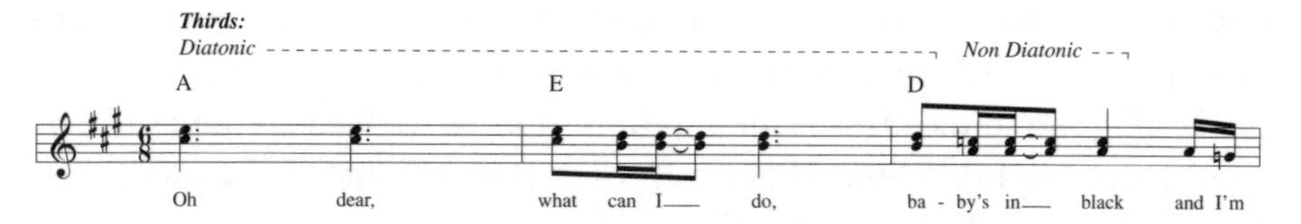

In this way we can immediately understand George Martin's comment on The Beatles' approach to harmony in the early days:

> 'We established the working format that whoever wrote the song generally sang it, and the others would join in. If it were John's song, he would sing it . . . Paul would sing thirds above or below . . . It was a very simple formula'.[3]

It is important to remember that, as a line unfolds in harmonised thirds, the interval at any given point might consist of either a major or a minor third (i.e., distances of both 3 and 4 semitones will be involved over the course of a line in order to keep the harmony *diatonic*, or to accommodate a non-diatonic effect in one of the lines). 'Baby's In Black' demonstrates both situations particularly clearly in the second part of the verse:

'Baby's In Black' – B section (0.14)

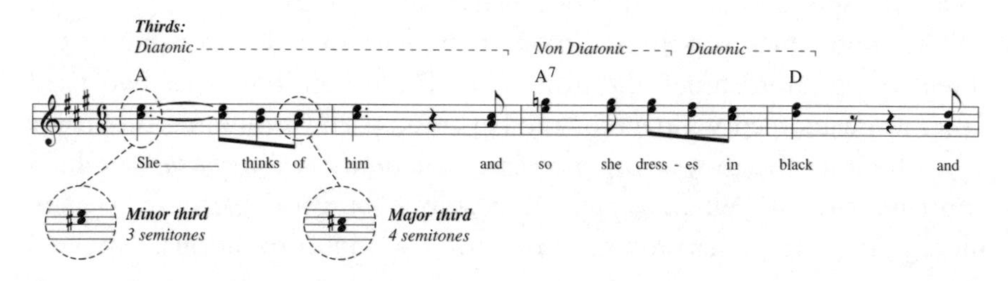

Here we have thirds harmony throughout, though the opening interval between C♯ and E is a *minor* third while, on the word 'of', it's a *major* third between A and C♯. Similarly, in bar 2, Paul's G natural (which matches the

[3] George Martin with Jeremy Hornsby, *All You Need Is Ears,* p. 132. Martin was referring more specifically to adding a harmony in the middle eight as a contrast to a single-part verse, but even in the early days, many Beatles songs featured close harmony intermittently throughout their structure.

bluesy ♭7th that helps take the A chord to D as an A7) means that we now have a *minor* third, instead of the major third that would have ensured that both parts were *strictly* diatonic to A major.

Beyond the 'thirds formula' – fourths, fifths and sixths

However, a close look at the two-part verse lines of 'Baby's In Black' reveals some vital details that are essential to appreciating The Beatles' approach to harmony. For while 'harmonisation in thirds' characterises most of the melody in these two sections, the interval between the two lines *does not remain rigidly in thirds throughout*. The two voices can be heard to diverge in various ways as each motif develops. A close listen to 'feeling blue', for example, reveals one part going *up* to the 5th (B) while the other goes *down* to the root. This of course results in the interval of a *perfect fifth,* while the bold leap on 'Tell me . . .' (at 0.10) briefly finds even wider intervals of a sixth and seventh before the voices reconverge.

It may be only a brief departure from thirds in these two cases, but by the time we get to the song's bridge we can see that the neat reliance on thirds has been ditched in favour of fourth and fifth intervals. These now create a radical alternative to the smoother, more lush harmony that the song starts out with. 'It's got a good middle,' says McCartney of 'Baby's In Black', and while it may only last four bars, it scores highly precisely for this textural contrast.

'Baby's In Black' – C section (0.50)

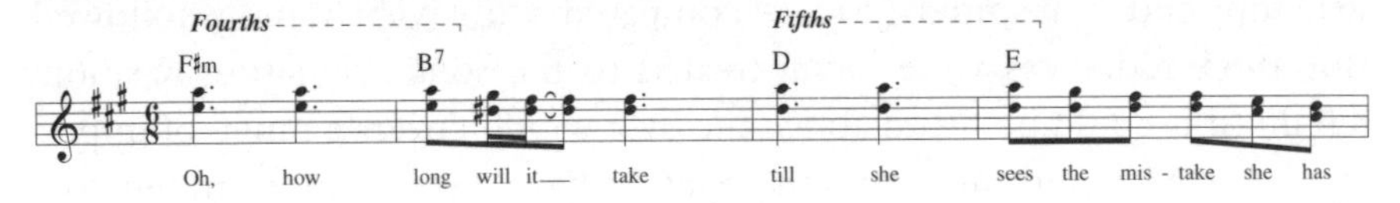

Again the two single-note lines – while still bound by a common rhythm – develop their own sense of independence in terms of pitch, confirming The Beatles' understanding of the very essence of contemporary harmony. Namely, that interest is created when companion lines move during the course of a single phrase between a range of the different intervals in music: seconds, thirds, fourths, fifths, sixths, sevenths and octaves.

A brief bit of history may be useful here. The basic principle of harmonisation in Western music developed around 900 AD when another vocal line was added either above or below a plain chant (initially as a way of accommodating the different registers of men and woman – or of sopranos, altos, tenors and baritones in general). However, in this technique of *organum* the voices moved in *parallel* throughout, usually in perfect intervals of octaves, fourths or fifths, with each line remaining tethered to the melody, forming an unflinching parallel movement of lines.

But over the following centuries singers found more adventurous ways of combining voices so that they had more individuality without clashing. As classical expert Adrian Jack explains, another paradox in music is that 'to move in parallel, at a fixed interval, is to *deny* harmony'.[4] Modern harmony evolved out of the concept of *polyphony,* which requires each part to have a different shape so that the intervals between them change constantly. Hence the free interchange during the course of a tune between a variety of intervals.[5]

The Beatles' legacy of vocal harmonies is based on their flexible approach to harmonisation in terms of this *category* of intervals themselves. While excellent examples can be found throughout the catalogue, particularly rewarding is an appreciation of the early days, when vocal harmony was *the* main way in which interest was added to a Beatles arrangement, before exotic instrumentation and studio effects were to bring their own distractions.

The Beatles' intuitive understanding of the textures afforded by varying the intervals of harmonisation in two-part harmony was evident as far back as 'Love Me Do'. The Parlophone debut, with its tentative No. 17 UK chart peak, is rightly seen as an inferior Beatles song in terms of its chord structure and uninspired lyrics – compared with what rapidly followed. But 1963 audiences were being treated to the song's signature harmony refrain (if it could be heard above the din) which covers a range of important bases. Most prominent are the open fifths that stood out from the usual pop diet of straight thirds, and which contributed to an arrangement that Pollack describes as 'stylistically prophetic'.[6]

[4] Adrian Jack, *The Harmonic Series*, Part 7, BBC Radio 3, 30th December 1999.

[5] Jack explains how the perfect intervals fell out practice for many centuries – to the extent that 'consecutives' (e.g., 'parallel fifths') became regarded as bad practice until the 1900s, even though great composers like Bach still used them on occasions.

[6] Alan W. Pollack, 'Notes on … Series' no. 21, 2000. *The 'Official' rec.music.beatles Home Page*, www.recmusicbeatles.com.

'Love Me Do'

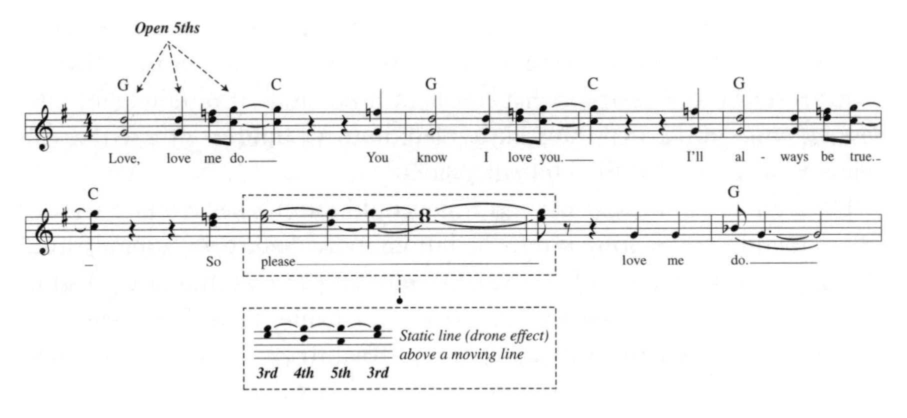

One element of that style was The Beatles' practice of juxtaposing an 'active' melody in one part against a different line that reiterates a single note across several beats. In 'Love Me Do' this technique is heard on the climactic line that unfolds the word 'please' with various degrees of dissonance, as John's lower *melisma* and Paul's upper pedal combine in bars 7 and 8 to create intervals of thirds, fourths and fifths.[7]

This last effect was never better heard than on the opening line of the follow-up single, 'Please Please Me'. Listen closely to hear an onslaught of consonance and dissonance depending on the flavour of the interval in play at any one time.[8]

'Please Please Me'

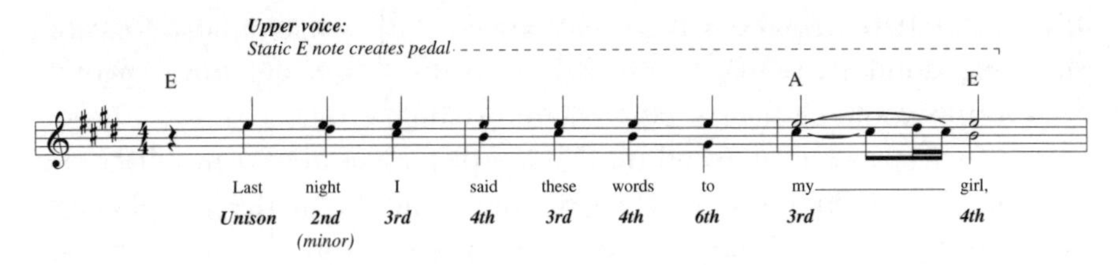

[7] While the Everly Brothers are often seen as a prime influence on Beatles harmony, the use of fourth and fifth intervals is a point of contrast between the artists. See Stephen Valdez, 'Vocal Harmony As A Structural Device In The Commercial Recordings Of The Beatles 1962-1970', *Beatlestudies 3*.

[8] Fitzgerald singles out this moment as epitomising the technique; 'Lennon-McCartney and the Early British Invasion, 1964–1966' by Jon Fitzgerald; published in *The Beatles, Popular Music And Society: A Thousand Voices*, edited by Ian Inglis, p. 75.

Starting with a unison sound where both John and Paul, for once, sing the same opening note ('Last . . .'), the moving line drops against the upper E, moving first to a jarring minor second ('night'). This is created by the major-seventh-against-tonic that rings out dissonantly, if briefly, before the descent continues down the scale, widening to an interval of a sixth ('to') before settling on that final fourth ('girl').[9]

These more exotic fourths and fifths could also be heard on the *Please Please Me* opener, creating the rousing (make that positively ecstatic) vocal highlights in the refrain of 'I Saw Her Standing There'. But if we had to pick one moment to illustrate the way The Beatles took harmony away from the predictability of thirds, it would have to be the bridge of 'Eight Days A Week':

'Eight Days A Week'

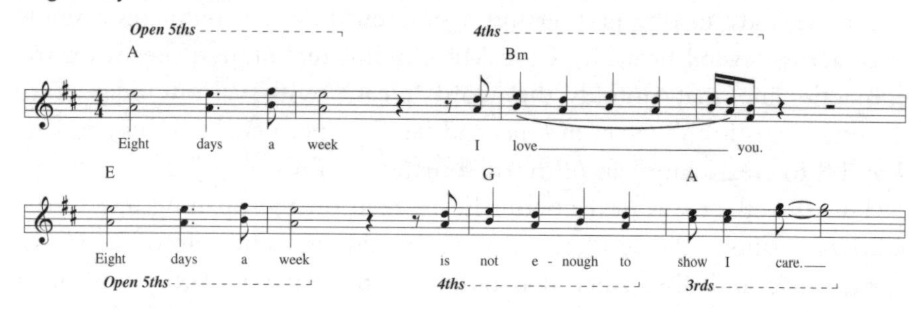

Here is a sound at odds with the Doo Wop conventions of early pop which, with a few exceptions, favoured diatonic thirds as their chosen interval for harmony. Fourths in particular exude an angular dissonance that can sound particularly oriental – try playing these vocal parts as doublestops on the guitar to tap into the flavour.[10]

Such an experiment reminds us that the principles of two-part harmony are in no way confined to vocal parts. The Beatles knew they would work just as well instrumentally, as they demonstrated early on in seemingly

[9] Even the simple 'Love, love, love' chant on 'All You Need Is Love' takes on a new dimension as a reiterated D drone in the vocal harmony matches the triad tones of the G and D chord while adding a 6th flavour to the Em that completes this particular three-chord sequence.

[10] Think of 'Western' pop songs that have attempted to evoke the sound of the East through fourth intervals in guitar parts, including David Bowie's 'China Girl', Siouxsie And The Banshees' 'Hong Kong Garden' and The Vapors' 'Turning Japanese'. Similarly, grating perfect fourth vocal harmonies were perfect for conveying Harrison's displeasure with the 'Taxman'.

humble settings such as the intro to 'I Want To Hold Your Hand'.[11] Within a few years this approach would develop into the sophisticated harmony parts of 'And Your Bird Can Sing'.[12]

In what George describes as 'quite a complicated little line', the guitars weave between each other, conjuring a shifting tapestry of thirds, fourths, fifths and sixths.[13] The four-bar intro (which provides the signature theme repeated in the other instrumental passages) captures the principle in a nutshell, as The Beatles' harmony figure (starting in bar 2) moves from a third to a fourth to a sixth to a fifth and back to a third.

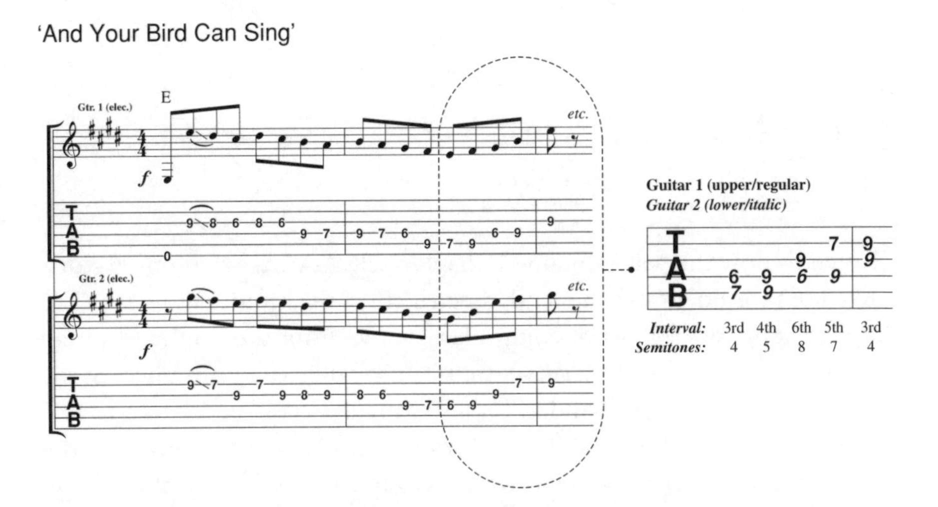

The principle of multi-part weaving of harmony reached an awesome peak on 'Because', the ultimate case study for further dissection by ambitious readers. But the principle of extreme independence of vocal lines can also be appreciated in Beatles songs from many years earlier. Take

[11] Here a simple riff over Lennon's primitive C-D chord alternation takes on a new dimension when it is harmonised by Harrison – starting on the 3rd of C and playing a repeated, three-note figure (E-G-D), with McCartney starting on the root of C before joining the guitars on D.

[12] With these cult instrumental parts alone, The Beatles almost single-handedly paved the way for a generation of twin- (and triple-) lead guitar bands such as The Eagles, The Allmans, Boston, Thin Lizzy (and, talking of 'lines intertwining', Spinal Tap).

[13] 'Listening to some of the CDs, there are some really good things, like "And Your Bird Can Sing", where I think it was Paul and me, or maybe John and me, playing in harmony – quite a complicated little line that goes right through the middle eight. We had to work those things out you know'; *Guitar One*, Volume VI, 1996, p. 20.

the intro to the 1965 single, 'Paperback Writer', where an uplifting multi-layered vocal, delivered as a sinewy, carefully plotted prologue, creates a subtle take on the title theme. Here's a rough resumé:

'Paperback Writer'

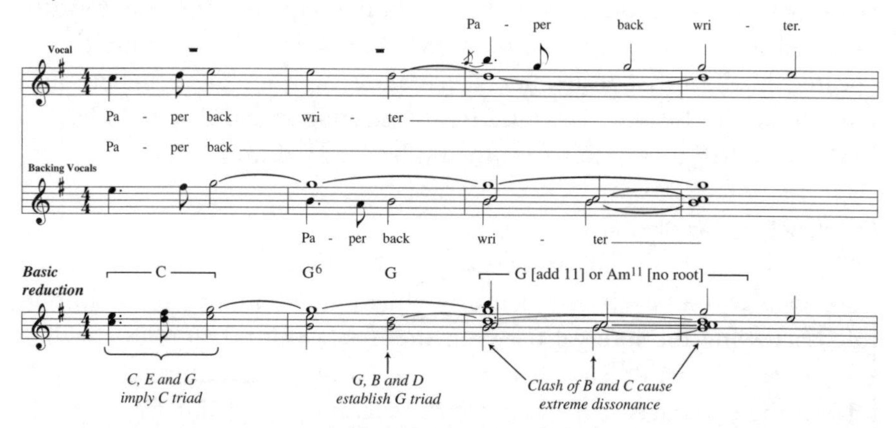

Listen to how this self-contained 'chapter' tells its own harmonised story. While the prominent G note lends a pedal effect that guides us to the G of the main song, we feel an opening Plagal move from the implied C triad to the G established in bar 2. But extreme dissonance rules from here as the overdubs in bar 3 juggle B and C for a serious '4:3 clash' in relation to G.[14] Arguably the ear rationalises the maelstrom as a type of supertonic chord – after all, the notes B, C, D, G (and the closing E) are all members of an Am11 chord without the root! Try the chord on a guitar for size!

The entrance of the B note in bar 2, a *sixth* below G, reminds us of the direct relationship between this interval and simple thirds. To make the connection, let's use the two-part harmony of 'If I Fell' which itself makes an excellent study of two-part harmony since the slow, measured phrasing (in half notes) dwells so clearly on each relevant interval.

If we take Paul's arguably more effective upper line as the melody, then John's part, which moves in parallel a sixth below, is the harmony. But the reality of sixths as inverted thirds should now be evident, because if those F♯ and G notes had been *an octave higher* they would have created a harmony a 3rd *above* Paul's melody.

[14] Refer back to the 'A Hard Day's Night' chord which we suggested was down to the uneasy clash of B and C notes in a G11. If the vocal texture here feels more palatable, then 'freeze-frame' the track on a sampler after precisely 3.5 seconds. That's dissonance for you (especially with the high B slightly flat!).

'If I Fell': verse (0.19)

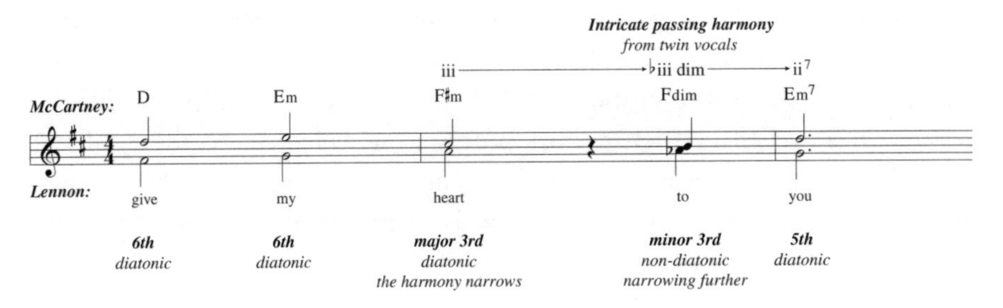

True to form, the parallel movement is abandoned as soon as the second bar as Paul *descends* to the word 'heart' while John continues his *rise* into it, duly narrowing the interval between them to a third. The roles are then reversed at the start of bar 3 as they move out to a perfect fifth.

Both these extracts prepare us for the second part of this discussion of harmonisation by reminding us that harmony vocals do not exist in the vacuum in which we have been describing them. The notes of a melody and its harmony vocal have novel implications for the *underlying* harmony of the song, by colouring it through extensions and alterations.

The G triads of 'Paperback Writer' (which effectively determined the key of the song) are an obvious example. But consider also the rather special sound on the last beat of bar 2 in the verse of 'If I Fell' – it's a two-note vocal sound labelled as F diminished, and yet a listen to the song confirms that there is no diminished chord in the *instrumental* harmony, despite George's healthy knowledge of such shapes by this time.

It is the vocal arrangement *in the context of the chord sequence* that implies the diminished gesture here. The progression features diatonic seconds, as 'iii' is headed for 'ii' in a descending line. As we know from Chapter 10 these two adjacent chords can be linked by a diminished chord (i.e., ♭iii dim) to 'fill the gap' in a passing, chromatic capacity.

Incredibly, The Beatles achieve this through the harmonised *melody* which delivers a minor third interval (A♭–B) that, with reference to the F natural bass note *implied* as the passing root between F♯ and E, creates a complete F diminished triad. It doesn't matter that Paul doesn't actually play the passing F natural note in the bass! The sonority – especially on that isolated final beat of the bar – has the effect of deliciously anticipating the following Em chord.

This isn't the first time that minor third intervals resulting from chromatic excursions in one of the vocal lines have implied non-diatonic chords. The A7 of 'Baby's In Black' is an obvious example, even if it was just a standard, bluesy tonic embellishment on its way to IV. The diminished gesture in 'If I Fell', which occurs purely as a welcome accident of two independent melody lines passing like 'ships in the night', marks a degree of sophistication in a pop song that is light years removed from the standard ♭7th blues effect.

Part 2. Triad tones, scale tones and chromatic colour

With these last few comments we have shifted our exploration of harmonisation away from the intervals between individual single-note lines towards the sound created by a melody note as it appears above a root. This still involves the same stacking principles of harmonisation but focuses on the way in which a given note in a melody can result – either fleetingly or dramatically – in a more interesting chord than might be played by the instrumental harmony alone. Paul's G note in 'Baby's In Black' is the simplest of examples, as he shows that singing a ♭7 above a major triad makes a dominant seventh, whether or not the guitars themselves bother to play the extra note.

Of course, that ♭7th note itself is just one of the 12 notes in music, and The Beatles used all 12 in their melodies to create novel, varied and powerful harmonisations. Using a few hand-picked Beatles examples, this final (and perhaps most important) leg of our discussion of melody attempts to show the character of each of the various notes, in terms of the varied levels of tension they create.

This background immediately helps us to unlock a rather legendary piece of Beatles trivia on the subject.

Melodic colour: Mann's 'Pandiatonic clusters' in focus

There's no better place to start than with the first (and still the most famous) comment on The Beatles' approach to harmonisation. William Mann's original 1963 article inadvertently provided *Times* readers with a potted lesson on a subject crucial to the beauty of so many Beatles songs.

Let's look again at the relevant line from the passage we quoted at the start of Chapter 5.

'One gets the impression that they think simultaneously of harmony and melody, so firmly are the major tonic sevenths and ninths built into their tunes.'[15]

While Mann wasn't citing any particular song, he had of course just been swooning over 'This Boy' with its mysterious 'chains of pandiatonic clusters'. As we will see, this grand concept demonstrates perfectly how The Beatles exploited the relationship between harmony and melody to create interest in even the most standard of chord progressions.

In elaborating on 'This Boy', Mann might have explained that despite the clichéd Doo Wop sequence, the melody – and, equally, *the carefully chosen 'extra' notes provided by the vocal harmony* – transform the *quality* of the underlying chords. The harmonisation is in thirds, with George joining in to create a continuous, lavish, three-part harmony, an idea The Beatles would later repeat in 'Yes It Is' and 'Because'.[16]

'This Boy' (verse)

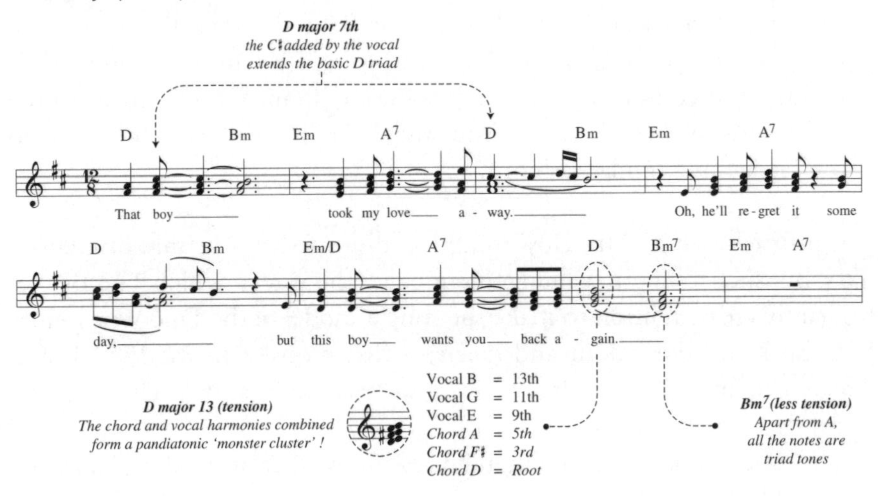

Mann's focus is not the three-part vocal – *per se* – but the harmonic *extensions* that are added to the basic triads in the instrumental harmony. He's drawing our attention to the fact the *overall* chords we hear are not

[15] 'What Songs The Beatles Sang', *The Times*, 27th December 1963, p. 4.

[16] George Harrison refers to the influence of Frankie Lymon And The Teenagers and The Platters when talking about the three-part harmony of 'This Boy'; *The Beatles Anthology*, p. 96.

just the basic major and minor *triads* played by the guitars, but more elaborate extensions of *sevenths* and *ninths*.[17] Here are some of the highlights:

1. The tonic D major 7ths created as a C♯ is added to the D chord. (e.g., in bar 1, at 0.10.)
2. The 9th effect as the D triad is joined by the E note (in bar 7, at 0.29-0.30).
3. The presence of the B and G notes in this same 'cluster' which effectively makes this sonority an extremely colourful 'D major 13th' for the first two beats of bar 7 (on 'ag-*ai*-n').
4. It's not just the tonic that enjoys such seventh extensions as the vocals float over the various chords in the progression. In bars 1 and 7, the Bm chord is combined with an A note in the cluster to yield a jazzier Bm7 (now, of course, a ♭7th – rather than a *major* 7th – in relation to the prevailing chord).
5. Then, as the tonic becomes a D *dominant* chord to accentuate the move to the IV chord at the bridge (in bar 8 of the repeat), the E note reappears. It's now an octave higher in John's (briefly unaccompanied) melody and conspires to yield a jazzy tonic dominant 9th (similar to the 'I9' chords in 'Till There Was You' and, later, 'If I Fell' which take us to the bridge in a similar fashion).

On first hearing, 'This Boy' might be dismissed as a quaint, innocuous ditty. But such a superficial judgement belies the way in which The Beatles brilliantly create tension to make the song a model of the Doo Wop genre. Just check out the colour and *timbre* of that monster major 13th 'cluster' referred to in (3) – which isn't even an elaborate jazzy V chord, just a seriously embellished tonic.

The vocal notes are highlighted to show that it is these that are responsible for creating the extensions to the chord. By targeting these ninths and sevenths, whose dissonance cleverly detracts from the predictable progression, they 'make' the song in comparison to, say, a simple melody that might merely have chosen the 'obvious' triad tones of root, 3rd and 5th.

[17] Hence the point that while The Beatles actually play the D chord as a D major *triad*, songbooks often notate it as D *major* 7 – specifically in order to help the solo guitarist recreate the overall intended flavour of the song.

The mega D major 13th 'Pandiatonic cluster' in 'This Boy'[18]

Scale tones	1	3	5	[7]	9	11	13
Notes	D	F♯	A	[C♯]	E	G	B
Location	Guitar			Bass	Vocal harmony		

But rather than a clear-cut build-up and release of tension, listen to how these dissonant harmonies subtly *perpetuate* the tension by maintaining the extensions as the cycle progresses. Look closely at the mechanics of the D-Bm move on 'again' (at 0.29-0.31), that Pollack cites as a case in point.[19] The tense melodic B that creates the D13th 'wants' to shift down to the 'grounded' triad tone of A. Yet when it arrives there, it now paradoxically creates a delicately tense 7th extension above the Bm to which the rest of the harmony has now shifted!

Here's a voice-leading chart for the three-part harmony at this point:

'Back again' – 'Resolving' the vocal harmonies in 'This Boy'

D maj 13 (I)			**Bm7 (vi)**	
tension			**'resolution'**	
Formula	Note	Voice leading	Note	Formula
13th	B	Down a whole tone	A	♭7th
11th	G	Down a semitone	F♯	5th
9th	E	Down a whole tone	D	♭3rd

In this way we can see that Mann's 'pandiatonic clusters' (another truly cult term among Beatles musos)[20] are merely the implied chords resulting from the layered harmony involving a collection of pitches *spread across the full diatonic spectrum.* It's surely down to the delicious flow of variable tension that 'This Boy' can withstand repeated listening and remains such a favourite among hardcore Beatles fans.

[18] The D major 13th chord rarely appears with this 'full' '1-3-5-[7]-9-11-13' construction in any form of music because of the extreme dissonance created by the clash of the 11th (G) with the major 3rd, F♯. Far more common is to find the 11th sharpened or, alternatively, to omit the 3rd, which has the effect of re-labelling the chord a D major 13th sus 4. However, close listening suggests that The Beatles are not concerned with 'masking' the F♯ in the D major chord heard in the acoustic rhythm guitar part.

[19] Alan W. Pollack, 'Notes on ... Series' no. 44, 1991. *The 'Official' rec.music.beatles Home Page*, www.recmusicbeatles.com.

[20] Mann's 'Pandiatonic clusters' have become almost as legendary as his Aeolian cadence. Listen to Malcolm McDowell's reference (complete with highly dodgy pronunciation) in his celebrated voice-over for the documentary *The Compleat Beatles*.

The Beatles continued to deliver such cool clusters intermittently throughout their career, right up to the carefully crafted, continuous three-part harmonies of *Abbey Road*. Here's another example of major 9th harmony in 'Sun King' where, above the tonic C major triad, both B (seventh) and D (ninth) combine boldly in the vocals to form a suitably lush fanfare for the monarch himself.

'Sun King'

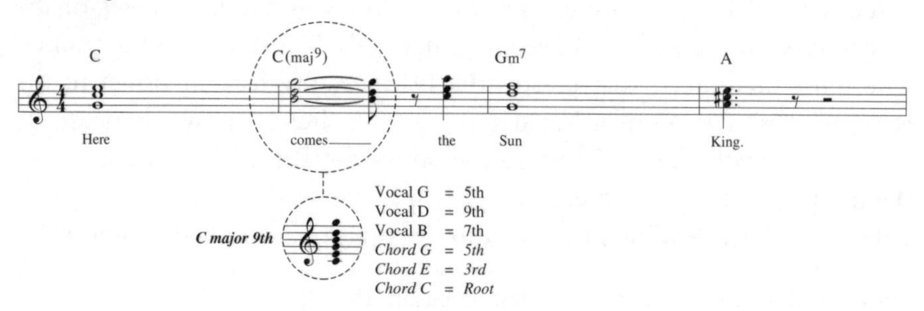

Melodic tension across the 12-note spectrum

Mann's 'major tonic sevenths and ninths' are just two colours in The Beatles' harmonic rainbow. Let's split the 12 notes of music into three categories to help us to appreciate the strength and flavour of a melody that results from stressing each one.

Here's how the notes in a melody heard above, say, a given major chord might be captured:

1) **Triad** tones: 1 (root), 3rd, 5th
2) **Scale** tones: 2nd, 4th, 6th, 7th
3) **Chromatic** tones: ♭9th/♭2nd, ♯9th/♭3rd, ♯11th/♭5th, ♯5th/♭6th, ♭7th

We must be careful with our definitions here. Obviously 'scale tones' normally include the 'triad tones' themselves, while 'chromatic tones' in one sense covers the lot. To help make the distinction, we can refer to Rooksby who uses the same subdivision but refers to triad tones as notes in a melody that sit 'inside' the chord concerned. The other diatonic scale tones sit 'outside', while the remaining chromatic tones sit 'against' the harmony.[21] The labels are indeed helpful as they describe *the relative tension between the three categories*.

[21] Rooksby, *How To Write Songs On Guitar*, p. 84.

Once again emphasis is the secret as, in practice of course, a given melody features a variety of different notes suggesting different degrees of tension as the line develops. Nevertheless, the point of this exercise is to demonstrate that certain types of tunes draw more regularly from one category of tones than others, depending on the effect and level of sophistication that the songwriter wants to achieve.

For a discussion of triad tones, please refer to the *Introduction to Harmonisation* in Appendix 2, before we up the tension with a quick tour of the 'outside' reaches of Beatles melody.

'Outside' – the non-triad scale tones: 7th, 9th, 4th, 6th

While 'This Boy' demonstrated the principle of creating 7ths and 9ths through multi-part harmony, The Beatles were happily tapping into the tension potential of these same notes in less elaborate melodic surroundings.

There is no need for multi-part harmony to cloud the picture – a single melody note is enough to create the same colour (if not the *texture*) if judiciously chosen. From the hundreds of examples that could be used to describe the same sevenths and ninths in a discrete top line, the following pair of extracts have been chosen specifically because they feature a lyric that is immediately repeated over the same chord, *but with a different melody note*. This allows us to contrast 'inside' and 'outside' tones directly while everything else stays the same.

In the coda of 'Not A Second Time', the last word of the title is heard first as a D note, the 5th of the G chord – a strong, 'inside' triad tone. That's fine, of course, but just compare the effect as the line is repeated (at 1.51) and the F♯ note takes its place, creating G major 7th and making us share in John's pain as he rues his luck in love, with a far more poignant, *extended* sonority.

'Not A Second Time'

Lennon expertly reversed the roles many years later in 'I'm So Tired', now with the 9th and the major 3rd as the subject of the contrast over a repeated A major chord. This time the song opens with the 'outside' note, a tender 9th on the word 'so', delivering a sound that is not as harmonically stable as the C♯ we hear on the repeat. We're barely into the song but already the harmonisation succeeds in depicting the singer bemoaning his insomnia with varying degrees of frustration.

'I'm So Tired'

This example also reminds us that the memorable opening intervals of the previous chapter don't exist in isolation – they are all heard in relation to the underlying harmony. Here, after all, is an example of a perfect fifth ('I'm *so*') – but this seven half-step jump starts on the 5th of the scale and takes us to that 9th in the octave above (hence '5-9'). This is clearly different from the perfect fifth of 'She Said She Said', or other famous Beatles fifths like 'The End' ('And *in the end*'), or indeed an evergreen rhyme like 'Twinkle Twinkle, Little Star'. The same interval is involved in each case, but these last three examples are easier to sing in context than 'I'm So Tired' as they each employ a 'root-5' jump over a tonic I chord, thereby landing on consonant chord tones.

Already we can see that the nature of these 'outside' scale notes is to change the character of a melody from the secure, 'grounded' feeling we get with the plain triad tones. It confirms what we suggest in Appendix 2, that while there is a whole tradition of sing-along-tunes with melodies that rigidly track the root, 3rd and 5th of each passing triad, ultimately such melodies lack the subtlety and ebb and flow that such 'outside' tension can bring.[22]

The secret is, of course, in the *contrast*. To make the point, let's revisit 'Lucy In the Sky With Diamonds', one of the songs from that Appendix whose simple triad-tone melodies – *at least in one particular section of its structure* – we used to illustrate 'lesson 1' of harmonisation.

However, if we look at the other sections of the song we begin to see The Big Picture, the genius of the composition as a whole. The contrast between the verse and chorus provides a classic example of how to construct a melody with reference to tones that *complement* each other. While the chorus homes in on the tones of the primary triads, it does so as a welcome antidote to the virtual flood of 'colour' notes that spiced the earlier 'Cellophane flowers' development section.

'Lucy In The Sky With Diamonds'

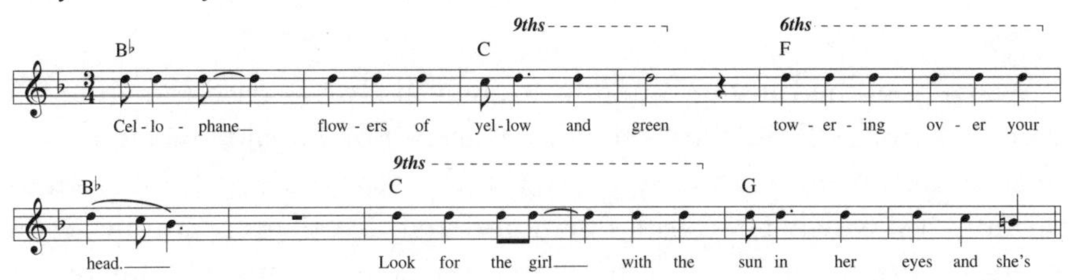

Don't be fooled by Lennon's linear tune, the secret's not 'all in the melody', but in the harmonisation, with the added 9th and 6th tones, *relative to the novel chords beneath,* accounting for this section's notoriously spacey, dreamy and (let's face it) hallucinogenic reputation.

'Lucy' is the classic example of how such 'outside' notes shouldn't be overused or the listener will lose his sense of tonal reference and the dissonance will be perceived, paradoxically, as 'un-melodic'. Lennon knows that the song can't tolerate his outside melodic displacement indefinitely. And *that's* why he duly restores the balance with the complete opposite – the nursery rhyme chorus of tension-free triad tones. What might therefore be seen in isolation as a naïve melody proves to be a masterful juxtaposition of tonal contrasts when we take a step back.

[22] Of course, where the chord family itself moves far beyond the primary triads, the harmony brings its own compensating interest, e.g., 'All My Loving', where an analysis of the harmonisation reveals a preponderance of triad tones, but over a busy sequence that spans not only the diatonic scale but also introduces that famous borrowed ♭VII.

The Beatles' masterfully judicious approach to 'outside' and 'inside' notes in their melodies can be seen brilliantly in 'No Reply' where the Lennon-McCartney lesson for the day is not merely harmonisation but *reharmonisation*. This is an important songwriting skill where a given melody previously heard in relation to one particular chord (or sequence of chords) takes on a whole new character when supported by another.

'No Reply'

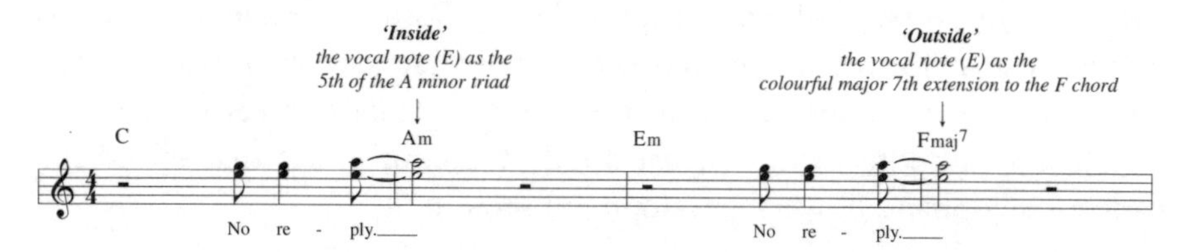

Watch how the rousing E note is stressed firstly as a triad tone (the 5th) over an A minor chord, but is then *reharmonised* by F major, where it now creates a lush major seventh sonority. It is this type of flexible approach to harmony by which The Beatles demonstrated that there is no one set of 'correct' chords with which to harmonise a given melody. There are various ways of harmonising a tune, and reharmonisation shows that we can add dramatic interest by switching between different options.

The special case of the melodic fourth

While sixths, sevenths and ninths are standard tools for adding interest to a melody, the 4th is a rather maverick note among the category of outside tones. Its particular character is down to its precarious location a semitone above the major third, to which it often feels as if it should be resolving. The 4th degree does not appear in the major pentatonic scale and, as such, it represented a source of novelty for folk-based pop songwriting in the early sixties. Trust The Beatles to show us how to exploit the note's intrinsic tension in what should consequently be seen as some of their most pioneering pop melodies.

Songs like 'I Feel Fine' proved a watershed in this regard, with the famous guitar riff yielding not only added 9th colour but also creating lively unease between the 4th and 3rd in relation to each of the I, IV and V chords.[23] The same distinctive flavour reappears in the verse melody where John Lennon gave the whole tune a healthy dose of The Fourth Degree.

'I Feel Fine'

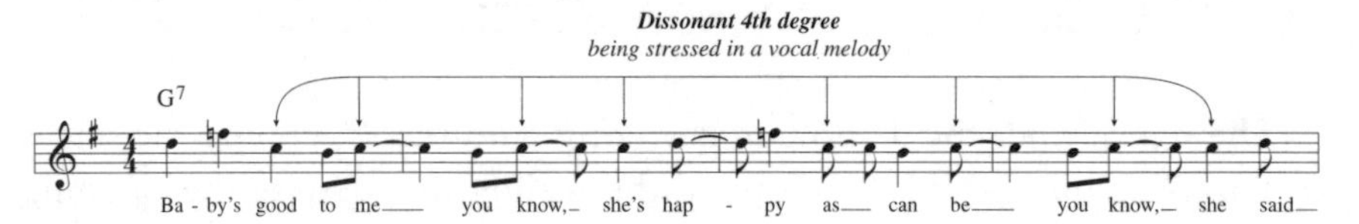

Of all the 12 notes in music it seems that the fourth degree is one that The Beatles consciously strove to incorporate into their playing. This may sound trite, and the image of John, Paul and George comparing the tension qualities of different notes seems rightly absurd. But the relative dirth of prominent fourths in so much folk, pop, and even blues, prior to The Beatles is significant, while the appearance of the note in so many songs of the *Rubber Soul* era is more than just a coincidence.

The opening line of 'Day Tripper' surely seals it. Faced with the task of finding a descending melody line for a five-syllable motif over an E7 chord, most songwriters would head for the chord tones for their opening gambit.[24] But The Beatles just *had* to be different and managed to write a classic that would force generations of cover band frontmen to flail wildly as they attempt to pluck that dissonant 4th out of the air as their very first note. A cult test for singers at auditions, not to mention *karoake.*[25]

[23] Lennon's riff features the added 9th degree in a series of distinctive sounds and shapes that would later become a trademark of Andy Summers in various songs with The Police. 'Message In A Bottle' and 'Every Breath You Take' are the prime examples, with the latter transforming the four chord cliché of A-F♯m-D-E by adding the 9th to each of the triads in a finger-twisting arpeggio workout.

[24] A more obvious descending line for the lyric 'Got a good reason' might be 8-♭7-6-5-5, or 5-3-2-1-1, or 3-2-1-♭7-5 or, at the outside, ♭7-6-5-3-3; try them for size.

[25] David Williams of covers outfit Contraband, sums up the plight of the journeyman singer: 'It's the one note of the whole set that I have to consciously think about every time I sing it'. Meanwhile Pollack also eludes to the same deceptively challenging novelty: 'Have you tried singing this song in the shower lately?'; 'Notes on. . .Series' no. 4, 2000. *The 'Official' rec.music.beatles Home Page* (rmb.simplenet.com).

'Day Tripper'

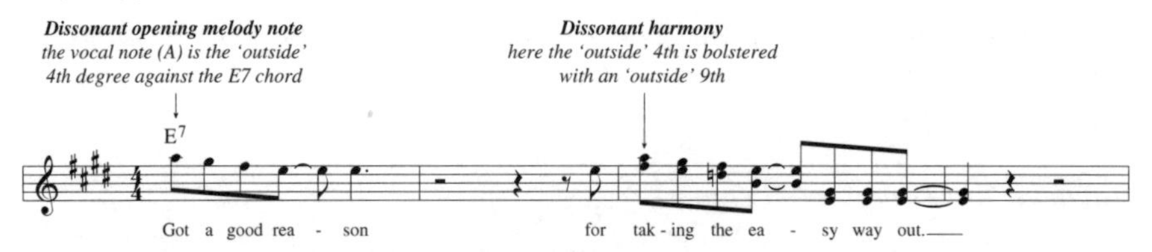

The repeat finds the 4th now in harmony with the 9th, upping the stakes in tension while notably reinforcing the feeling that despite the opening blues-based harmony (as I7 moves to IV7), the very specific choice and emphasis of melody notes instils a great originality that distances the song from the blues genre.

As a brief aside to our earlier discussion, this extract also shows the varied way that The Beatles would approach their vocal harmonies in terms of *structure* rather than just the interval, – in 'Baby's In Black' the harmonies are *continuous*; in 'Hey Bulldog', the opening harmony is answered by a single voice; here the single voice is answered by the harmony; while George Martin's favoured early formula was for a single-part verse to be joined by harmony in the middle eight, e.g., 'A Hard Day's Night'.

One of The Beatles' most instantly recognisable 4th degrees is the isolated peak in the verse of 'Hey Jude'. As we saw in the last chapter, the song starts with a predictable, consonant chord tone. But this is rudely disturbed by the introduction of the 4th degree on the word 'song', prompting us all to rise to the occasion.

'Hey Jude'

It is in this distinctively 'outside' way that the 4th degree creates suspensions – a 'sus 4' chord is created when the 3rd is usurped. As well as supercharging a hanging V at the end of a bridge, the most common Beatles context for this is at the end of a phrase when it embellishes a Perfect cadence with a 'V7 sus 4' on its way to a tonic – as seen most famously in 'The Long And Winding Road' where the 4th effectively resolves 'into' the tonic triad before the other notes ('*your* door').[26]

Giving it the 4th degree – Lennon's cry for 'Help!'

While the 4th scale degree creates effective tension against a major chord, it took on a monumental role in Beatles melodies when appearing over a *minor* chord. And never more effectively than in 'Help!' where it represents precisely the cry for attention of the lyrical theme, in a moment of compositional brilliance that captures the whole concept of melodic tension through harmonisation better than any other Beatles song.

As with 'Lucy', the genius of 'Help!' lies in the contrast between the triad-tone-rich, 'inside' section – here a verse – and the tension-fuelled, 'outside' chorus, which emerges as a masterpiece of harmonisation. Lennon creates this blend with very simple top lines, surely refuting once and for all the idea that melodies *per se* are the overriding element of a song.

Viewed in isolation, the famous one-note linear premise that dominates much of the song (Lennon's top line) is inauspicious – whichever way you look at it. Ignore the countermelody for now. The verse dwells almost relentlessly on a single, static C♯ note for most of the 8-bar phrase, with only the most fleeting excursion to another note, or 'neighbour' tone.

Using our earlier criteria for gauging melodic appeal, this tune leaves a lot to be desired in terms of opening intervals, motifs, melodic contour, thematic development, range, rhythmic interest, etc. Hum it as a stretch of single notes and it compares unfavourably even to 'Three Blind Mice' for ingenuity. But when you add in the chords it's a different story, with the beauty of the harmonisation steadily becoming apparent.

Take the verse first:

[26] The sus 4 note doesn't have to appear in the melody to spice a chord progression. Think of 'We Can Work It Out' with its 'sus 4-embellished' tonic D chord; or 'Happy Xmas (War Is Over)' where the harmony is defined by both 'sus 4' and 'sus 2' chords throughout. In 'Penny Lane' the famous fireman's bell cleverly complements the sus4 chord's distinctive third-less resonance (at 1.07, over a 4:3 suspension on F♯7). Meanwhile, refer back to Chapter 1 to see how Beatles bridge-to-verse retransitions go through the 'V7sus4' motions, whether with a matching melody or without, e.g., 'If I Needed Someone', 'For No One', etc.

'Help!' (verse)

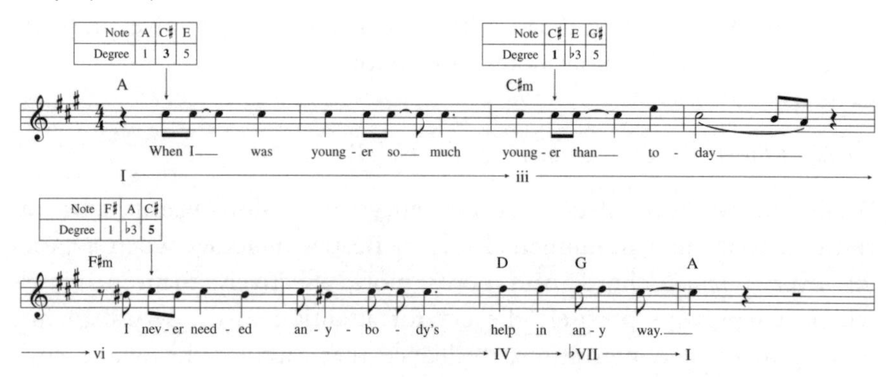

That stubborn C♯ note doesn't really *feel* as though it is static. And, really, it isn't – the function of the note is constantly changing according to the chords. Initially it appears as the 3rd of the A chord, then as the root of the C♯ minor chord, followed by the 5th of F♯ minor. A subtle melodic flow has effectively been created despite that notoriously 'unmelodic' top line.

The changing role of the C♯ note in the 'Help!' verse

Melody	C♯	C♯	C♯
Harmony	A	C♯m	F♯m
Function of melody note	3rd	Root	5th

These predictable triad tones may, by definition, lack tension but this is precisely why they create such a clever effect in the context of the song *as a whole*. For Lennon is delivering them specifically to reflect his previous untroubled state of mine, harking back to a time everything was in order, and using music that reflects that *status quo*.

This 'inside' melody only magnifies the false sense of security that hits us in the chorus as Lennon begs to be heard. It's another broadly static linear line – but one that now delivers crucial outside tones that instantly explain the rise in excitement in the chorus, which we can all relate to.

The first thing that we hear in the chorus is the disturbing E note against the Bm. Of all the notes in the minor pentatonic scale that one might choose to pitch against a minor chord, the 4th is the toughest for a singer (or indeed an instrumentalist) to use. Lean on it at the start of a line and you have instant dissonance, just as Lennon manages here, disorientating us after the cosy, non-threatening triad tones of the verse.

'Help!' (chorus)

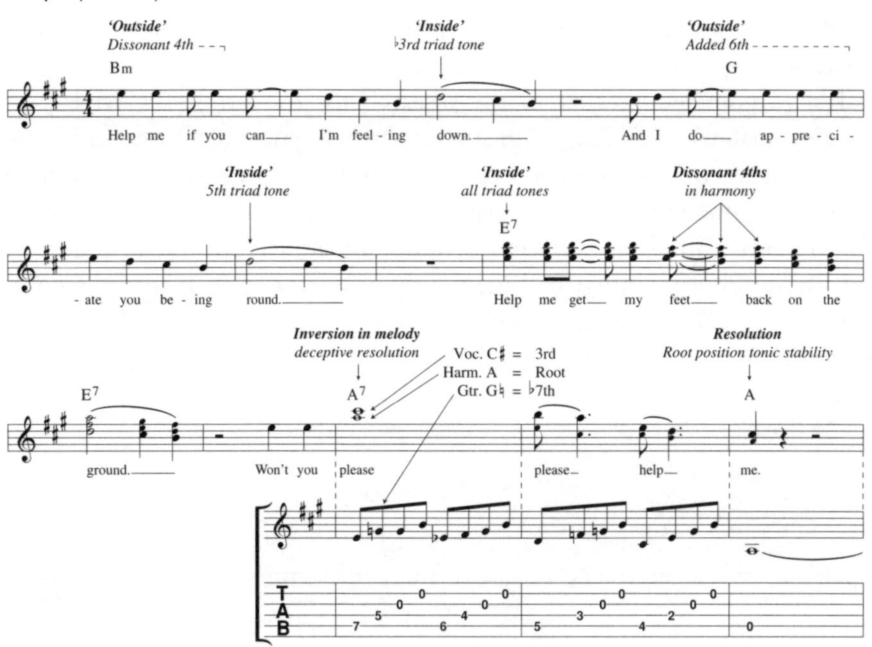

The outside feel is maintained as a ♭VII G chord (which we know is itself deftly borrowed from the parallel minor) emerges with an added 6th note in the melody, which brings its own dreamy tension, keeping our feet off 'the ground'. The sense of departure from order and sanity now continues though the E chord. For while the melody hits the root, the chord is itself the V chord and, by definition, unstable, keeping us from the home we crave.[27]

The *coup de grâce* (and final irony) is that even as we cadence from V to I, the distraught singer still doesn't automatically find the relief he seeks. The melody and vocal harmony hit the chord tones of the tonic but now George's great guitar run gives us a line that starts on the same 5th we thought we'd left behind, fashioning a descending line that only reaches the safety of a stable root position tonic chord two bars (and two 'pleases'!) later.

Forget the mystique of Beatles psychedelia with all its exotic instrumentation, here was Lennon songwriting at its finest with John himself

[27] Moreover, the harmony vocal duly adds an A note – another dissonant 4th in relation to the chord – just to make the point.

claiming it as one of his two favourite, most 'honest', compositions. And while John would scoff, the crafting of the melodic tension within the lyrical theme is surely the essence of the charm.

It's no coincidence that in the research for this book, several expert Beatles analysts, including Tim Tucker and Terence O'Grady, independently picked out this moment, very specifically, for precisely this evocative musical manifestation of insecurity and the resolution of that tension.[28] Tucker also reminds us that John Lennon's innate feel for the 4th degree in this minor chord context had previously jumped out at us in the second bridge of 'I'll Be Back', again with the same prolonged, unsettled emphasis that created a whole new chapter within the song.

'I'll Be Back'

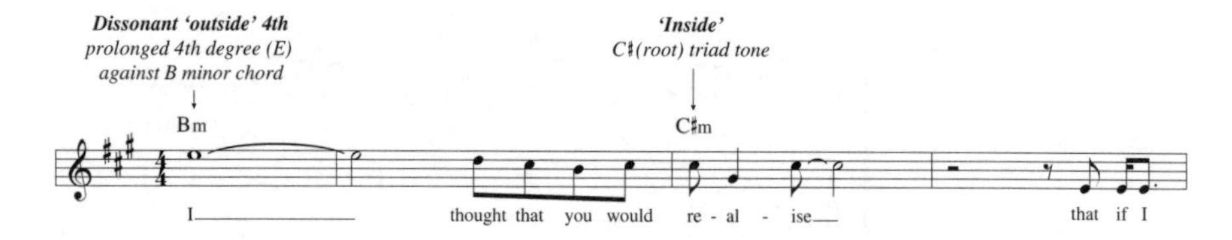

'Against' – the bluesy chromatics of ♭3rd, ♭7th and ♭5th

Any discussion of the melodic sounds available in our third category – the remaining notes in the chromatic scale that can sit poignantly 'against' a chord – must start with the blues. Integral to the blues sound are the uneasy strains of a ♭3rd sounded against a triad with a major 3rd. This tradition of *false relations*, while part of the heritage of deep blues, is also an essential feature of the sound of rock and R'n'B.[29]

It was certainly a melodic principle that The Beatles exploited despite the assumption that their pop pretensions might have involved almost exclusive focus on the brighter major 3rd. There's nothing bright about 'Yer Blues', where John leans unerringly on the ♭3rd with the very darkest of dark blue associations.

[28] Tucker and O'Grady in discussion with the author, September and December 2000, respectively.

[29] False relations refers to the fact that a sound features two notes with same 'number', i.e., two types of 3rd: a flattened *and* a major 3rd; and, similarly, two notes with the same alphabetical spelling. In 'Yer Blues' it's a G♯ in the chord and a G *natural* in the melody.

'Yer Blues'

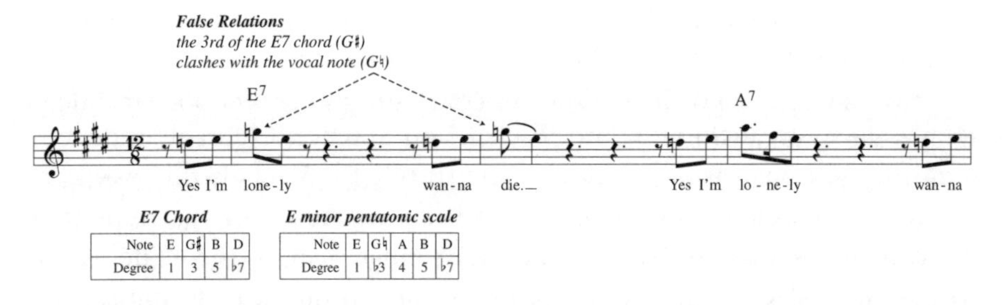

E7 Chord

Note	E	G♯	B	D
Degree	1	3	5	♭7

E minor pentatonic scale

Note	E	G♮	A	B	D
Degree	1	♭3	4	5	♭7

We all struggle to define the magic and essence of 'the blues'. But, from a technical point of view, it is this juxtaposition of 'false relations' that gets to the heart of the sound. Some writers even imply that the principle is the musical manifestation of the black and white power struggle at the heart of blues culture.[30] The musical rationale for this is essentially that the pioneers of the genre strived for earthy, 'tense' pitches with which to communicate a special type of cultural emotion. The notes of the diatonic major scale contain tension but not *enough*. Hence the borrowing of deeply affecting chromatics of which the ♭3rd is only one.

Another trademark of much blues melody is the ♭7th that turns a major triad into those tonic dominant sevenths of Chapter 2. It's no coincidence that 'I Wanna Be Your Man', a song highlighting the bluesy nature of this ♭7th degree, should end up in The Rolling Stones' repertoire of songs, which, collectively, highlights the links between the deep blues of Robert Johnson and Muddy Waters with rock 'n' roll and rock in general.

'I Wanna Be Your Man'

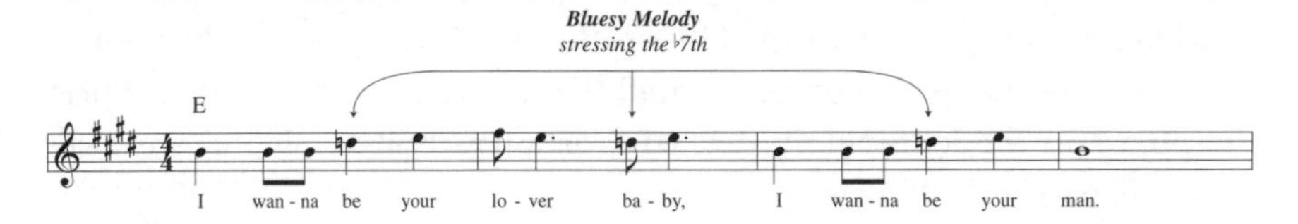

While we can find many Beatles songs that feature both the ♭3rd and ♭7th, the widespread notion that The Beatles were more 'pop' and 'less bluesy' than The Stones' is understandable when taking a snapshot of their catalogues as a whole. After all, we've already discussed, in Chapter 3, how

[30] Wilfrid Mellers, *Twilight Of The Gods*, p. 42.

major sevenths defined a whole category of Beatles repertoire as an antidote to the blues legacy of the ♭7th. In the same way, when the ♭3rd does appear in a Beatles melody, the blues effect is often tempered by combining it with the more upbeat major 3rd – either in contrasting song sections, or indeed within the same motif.

In this sense, 'Yer Blues' is somewhat of a Beatles rarity – more common are hybrid melodies with one foot in the blues and the other in pop. 'She's A Woman', whose melody mixes notes from both major and minor pentatonic scales in this way, makes for an interesting study of tension in a blues-based pop tune.

'She's A Woman'

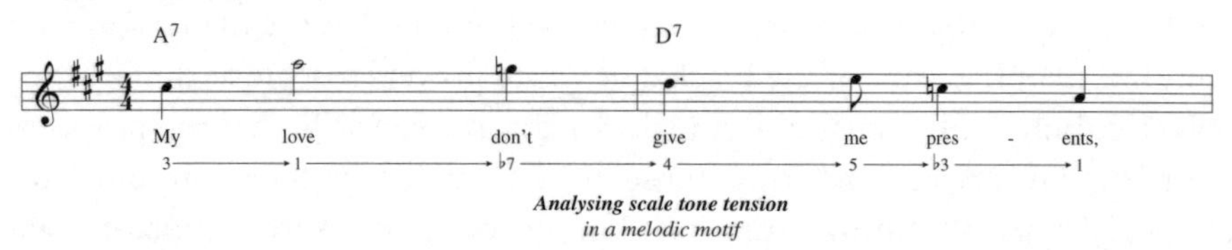

Analysing scale tone tension
in a melodic motif

Let's try to appreciate the nature of the melody using our understanding of both horizontal and vertical intervals. The first note of the motif is a consonant major 3rd that 'sits inside' the triad and automatically implies an 'upbeat', major sound. This feeling is then reinforced by the first horizontal interval in the melody – a distinctive leap of a sixth as we head upwards to another triad sound – the root. (Notice that we're far away from the blues anguish of 'Yer Blues' at this point.)

From there, however, the presence of two 'blue notes' ensures that the motif develops a darker side with the 4th putting us in a melodic No-Man's Land before the ♭3rd leaves a final bluesy twist as it descends to the root. To put this analysis in perspective, we might rank the six pitches that comprise the phrase in the following order, with dissonance increasing as we move from left-to-right.

Table of tension in a blues melody[31]

Less tense ←			'Average' tension	More tense →	
Root	5th	3rd	4th	♭7th	♭3rd

[31] Adapted from 'The Blues I Chord Tension Chart', *Music Theory Made Easy* by David Harp, p. 60.

Viewing the scale tones in a melody in this way might appear overly analytical, but it helps us to appreciate that tension exists along a continuum, with the ♭3rd emerging as a powerful tool (as every blues-based rocker knows).

And so too is the ultimate blue note, the famous 'flattened fifth'[,] which, due to its tritone relationship with the root of the chord, puts it somewhere on the extreme right-hand side of the chart, beyond even the ♭3rd. The inherent blues tension of this note can be heard most clearly in a Beatles song in the minor blues setting of 'I Want You (She's So Heavy)'.

'I Want You (She's So Heavy)'

Just compare the emphasis on the first 'you' (where the guitar leads the vocal to the 5th), with the repeated phrase. Here Lennon falls short (on E♭) before going on to squeeze out those neighbouring 'microtones', which represent the indeterminate pitches that only true blues artists (and no sheet music) can capture.[32]

'Against' (continued) – ♭9th, ♯9th, ♯11th, ♯5: chromatic tension beyond the blues

While the ♭3rd as a chromatic tension tone against major harmony is forever associated with the false relations of the blues, The Beatles could take the premise of this same clash to create dramatic and disorientating effects in contexts far beyond that particular genre.

Rubber Soul was the watershed in this regard, demonstrating The Beatles' new-found confidence in vocal dissonance. In 'Drive My Car' we saw how

[32] The Kinks' 'You Really Got Me' is sometimes cited as the ultimate rock 'n' roll melody as it contains each of the dissonant tones of ♭3rd, ♭7th and ♭5th in one short phrase; as Ingham reminds us: 'Doctor Rock Dissects The Hits; No.10: Blue notes and the Blues Form', *MOJO*, Issue 32, July 1996, p. 26.

clusters of carefully chosen chromatic ♯5th and ♯9th vocal notes could transform a simple V chord into The Altered Dominant From Hell (A7♯5♯9). This reminds us that the ♯9th and ♭3rd tones are enharmonic to each other, demonstrating how prolonged dissonance involving false relations can (even in this basic Three-Chord Trick setting) deliver a 'jazzy pop rock' effect that is seemingly removed from blues or R 'n' B tradition.

'The Word' and, later, 'Taxman' would arguably go one better by featuring the prolonged dissonance of major thirds and flattened thirds not in their respective V chords (as one might expect from our study of tension) but actually *in their tonics*!

'The Word'

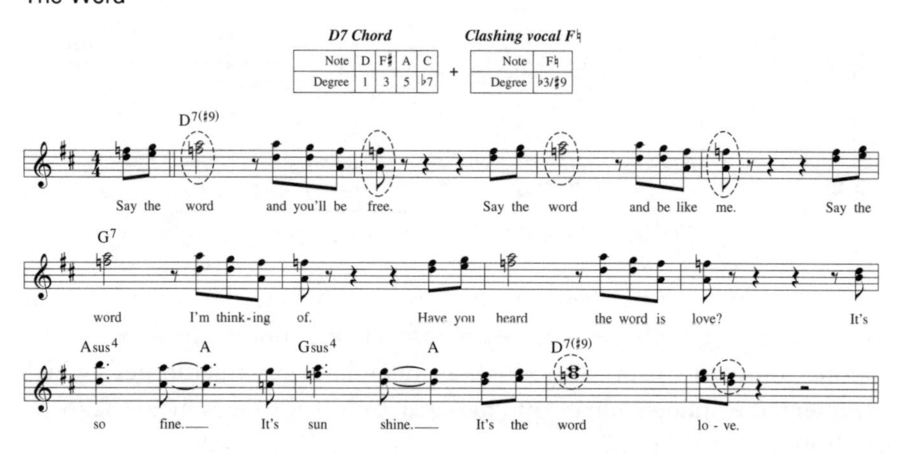

This incredible stretch of melodic drama illustrates that The Beatles were not afraid to spice their songs with jarring dissonance that should – in theory – have been the antithesis of mainstream pop music. The tonic is traditionally a sacred haven of rest and tranquillity – but not the way The Beatles conceive it here, delivering a nightmare of vocal dissonance that was as historically unprecedented then as it remains audibly compelling today.

Any chance that the F♯ in the D7 chord will suggest consonance is rudely scuppered by the ♯9 in the vocal line.[33] When the resolution finally

[33] We have switched to calling the villain ♯9 instead of ♭3 because we now effectively have a dominant 7♯9 sound, a chord that we can relate to The Gretty Chord and The Hendrix Chord – even if the sound here is more down to the vocals than the guitar.

comes, one is reminded of McCartney's sentiment regarding tension and resolution when using his '5th in the bass'. In this case it's: 'Thank God they got off that ♯9!'

Meanwhile, let's revisit the maverick tritone in a context beyond the blues. For the ♭5th is itself enharmonic to the ♯11th, or 'augmented 4th', an interval that John Lennon brings so deftly into 'A Day In The Life'. Here the sound is heard as a result of another borrowed ♭VII chord, which puts a whole new spin on a melody note previously heard quite conventionally in the song.

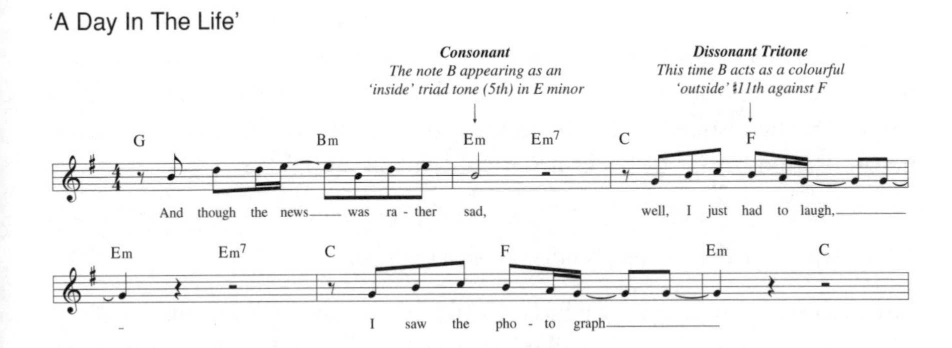

Just like the verse of 'Help!' (which also opened with a chord progression of I-iii-vi), the B note in the melody starts out as 'merely' a note contained within each of the G, Bm and Em chords. However, as the rogue F chord appears, the B note now acts as a ♯11th, creating a poignant moment referred to by MacDonald as 'the sudden chill of F in G major'.[34] As much as the chord, it's the melodic B note that sits so 'against' it that's responsible for the icy blast.

Meanwhile, another special Beatles ♯11th had appeared years earlier in 'Ticket To Ride', which came in for similar praise from O'Grady.[35] The moment (at 0.29) involves another borrowed ♭VII, as in 'A Day In The Life', though now the listener gets a triple whammy as the *melisma* unfolds over *three* notes that each imply either 'outside' or 'chromatic' drama over this single chord.

[34] MacDonald, *Revolution In The Head*, p. 339.

[35] O'Grady, *The Music Of The Beatles from 1962 To Sgt. Pepper*, p. 251. 'Ticket To Ride' was also picked by Noel Gallagher as one of his 10 favourite singles, *MOJO*, Issue 45, August 1997, p. 51.

'Ticket To Ride' (0.23)

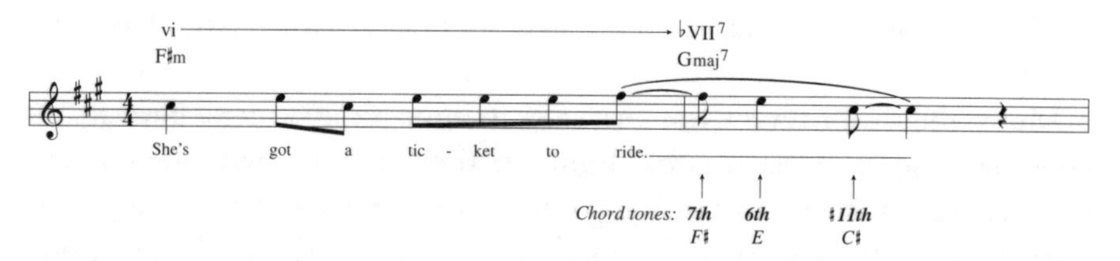

Here the notes F♯, E and C♯ are all diatonic *in relation to the parent key of A*, but they take on new life when heard over the borrowed ♭VII. Again it's all in the harmonisation as they represent the *major* 7th, 6th and ♯11th, respectively, of that G chord (which follows 'vi' in what is a surprisingly rare, but highly effective chord change). As if to showcase this inspired highlight of the song, the drums back off, leaving the chord to sustain in isolation before Ringo brings us back in with a deft roll (at 0.30).

'Yesterday' – the finest – and hardest – melody in pop?

No discussion of Beatles melody would be complete without a look at McCartney's most famous ballad. In the interviews for this book, Guy Chambers singled out 'Yesterday' as the prime example of a 'challenging' Beatles melody. He volunteered that, despite the song being so universally loved (not to mention being the most covered song of all time), its melody is particularly difficult to sing. Even the most tone-deaf Beatles fan can sing the chorus to 'All You Need Is Love', 'Yellow Submarine' or 'Lucy In The Sky', each with their simple repeating motifs that unerringly target 'grounded' triad tones, but 'Yesterday' is a different kettle of fish – even though we've heard the song a thousand times. This is due to a range of subtle melodic features that combine over just a few bars to contribute to what Elton John volunteered as a rare example of 'a perfect song'. Let's dissect the first eight bars and attempt an insight into the character of the tune using all the melodic criteria of the last two chapters.

With that opening title phrase alone we can immediately introduce another melodic concept – the grandly termed *appoggiatura*, or 'leaning note', which uses the non-triad tones that sit 'outside' or 'against' the melody, but in a very specific way.

Melodic 'leaning' notes create a highly delicate tension and resolution effect on the listener due to the way that they are *stressed on a strong beat* (hence they are said to 'lean' on the harmony) before resolving soon after *onto a chord tone on a weak beat*. Typically, they involve sixths, sevenths, ninths and fourths from the relevant diatonic scale source, but *not* in a way that prolongs the dissonance, as might a regular extension or alteration that is held for perhaps a beat or two. The distinction here is very subtle, but it is precisely such subtlety that characterises many of the most revered tunes in history.[36]

'Yesterday' – verse[37]

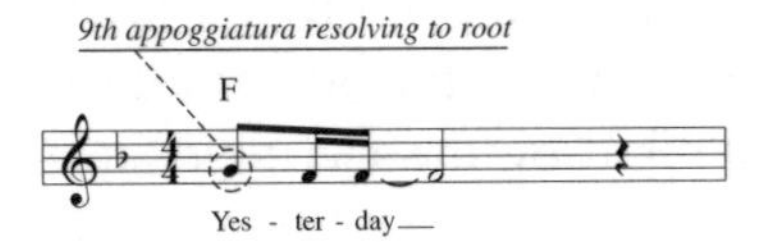

The timeless opening motif captures the essence of the melodic *appoggiatura* in splendid isolation, making the title phrase instantly memorable and poignant before we're even into the second bar. Yes, there's a 'memorable opening interval' at work here (a descending major second), but equally it's the *way* that the interval is harmonised that creates the effect.

The first syllable 'Yes-' sees the G note create a brief 'add 9' as it leans on the prevailing F chord, on the first downbeat of the verse. The delicacy comes from the fact that the tension is barely established before it is immediately relaxed, when that 9th resolves to the root of F on the second and third syllables ('ter-day'). Notice how these now fall on a weak beat: the upbeat (or, technically, the third and fourth sixteenths) of '1'. You don't even need to use dynamics to emphasise the first syllable in relation to the other two – the *appoggiatura*, by its very nature, does it for you.
A self-contained moment of tension and resolution is created, gently paving the way for further melodic development.

It would be misleading to suggest that such leaning notes are a rarity in pop. They appear in most tunes at some point, but the 'ebb and flow' of

[36] 'Yesterday' is thought to be the most covered song in history. It was voted as 'The Song Of The Century' by BBC Radio 2 after a poll involving 3,000 songs. It is also one of only five songs to have notched over 6 million performances by June 2000.

[37] In this analysis please remember that although the song was originally conceived in G, it is heard in F, with the guitar tuned down by a whole tone.

what we think of as 'sophisticated melody' is often down to a healthy prevalence of *appoggiaturas*. In particular, they are often used to start important phrases, as here, rather than falling back on predictable chord tones as a kind of 'default' melody.[38]

But the melodic interest of 'Yesterday' has only just begun, with the highly elaborate second phrase not only immediately reversing the initial descending contour, but also stressing the now revered 4th degree over a minor chord. Here it's an A note, a basic major 3rd in the parent key of F, but transformed in context thanks to Paul's outrageous Em7 (vii7) in the harmony. As we saw in 'Help!' and 'I'll Be Back', this combination of note and chord is not easy to marry at the best of times, though here things are made far more complicated by the fact that the Em7 chord itself is *not diatonic to the key*.

'Yesterday' (verse)

It's no wonder that singers have trouble plucking that 'all' out of the air, on the second beat of bar 2, when their bearings have been so threatened by this harmonic gesture on the previous beat.[39]

[38] 'Yesterday' is certainly special for its opening leaning note but as far back as 'Do You Want To Know A Secret' The Beatles were featuring such *appoggiaturas* within a memorable opening motive. There on 'Lis-ten' the leaning note is a 6th in the key of E, on the syllable 'Lis..', which then resolves to the 5th on the second syllable ('..ten..'), again on the upbeat. *Appoggiaturas* can also resolve upwards, as in the opening line of 'Hello Goodbye' where 'You *say yes*' sees another 'leaning 6th', but one which now resolves to the tonic above.

[39] As we discussed in Chapter 3, the Em7 makes us feel the drift of an implied modulation, which is reinforced by the following A7 which now pulls us to D minor.

The sophisticated unease continues in bar 2 with slick 'passing' notes (like the D that appears as the 4th of A7) and especially the F note, a now dissonant ♯5th in relation to this same A7 and a highly adventurous 'neighbour' tone to the first note of bar 3. Normally such a dissonant chromatic note (which sits so strongly 'against' the chord) would find immediate resolution on a strong chord tone. No such luck here, as Paul puts the listener through the emotional mill by dropping into another 9th *appoggiatura*, which again momentarily delays that stability for another half beat as we await the next triad tone to ground us.[40]

In this way the melody of 'Yesterday' works powerfully, but the (extra) touch of genius is the 'so far away' that accompanies this disturbing E-D in the top line, an inspired marrying of music and lyrics that is soon reinforced by the 'here to stay' of the following phrase which falls (you guessed it) on the now grounded *triad* tones of the *tonic.*[41]

And so the harmonisation of 'Yesterday' continues to weave its spell in the bridge as the modulation to the relative minor opens with that same 4th over the initial Em7, now brought forward to kick things off as we appear to lose the opening bar of F.

Which brings us to another vital element in the construction of McCartney's masterpiece. Quite apart from the *pitch* action (which has us struggling to hit the notes when whistling it in the bath), the secret magic of 'Yesterday' lies in the deep disorientation created by its deceptive *form*.

Don't be fooled by the supposed Tin Pan Alley tradition of the song – this is another example of The Beatles moving away from the 8-bar unit, with the initial bar being not so much 'removed' from the remaining three metrically conventional 2-bar phrases of the verse, as abducted quietly into solitary confinement:

The 'missing bar' of 'Yesterday'

Phrase	Length	Lyric
1	1 bar	'Yesterday...'
2	2 bars	'All my troubles seemed so far away'
3	2 bars	'Now it looks as though they're here to stay'
4	2 bars	'Oh, I believe in yesterday.'
Total	7 bars	

[40] Albeit now on the relative minor of the F major we started out on.

[41] And wasn't 'so far away' the very same lyric used to depict the similarly distant Phrygian ♭II chord of 'Things We Said Today' (see Chapter 8)?

The result is a 7-bar structure in which we constantly feel lost, in search of the extra bar – with the two different treatments of the title refrain also being crucially responsible for this sophisticated musical equivalent of Blind Man's Buff. As well as the mystery of The Missing Bar, the most famous critiques of the song refer to the way that it breaks the rules of conventional *melodic cadence*.[42] Listen closely to the opening refrain that *falls* in pitch, '2-1' to a restful tonic – a principle that we would normally expect to find at the *end* of a section. Yet the 'yesterday' that *closes* the verse, in the seventh bar, *rises* in pitch (and by a hopeful major third interval), a gambit that might typically have started the song.

It all adds up to a hypnotic circularity where we constantly chase our tail, wondering where we are in the structure and, of course, whether it's today or yesterday.

If the lyrical subtlety of 'Yesterday' can be attributed to the representation of distance (in time and physical space), the intricate matching of this 3-way strategy of harmony, melody and form is the secret to appreciating the song's deeply emotional effect on our psyche and its status at the very pinnacle of popular music.

In search of the 'Beatle-esque' melody

Can we tentatively attempt a conclusion with regard to Beatles melody at the end of two chapters of musical forensic science? Only that, ultimately, there are no rules or intrinsically 'Beatle-esque' melodic characteristics that define their songs. While there are several recurring winning ploys, like, say, the 4th over a minor chord and other 'outside' scale and chromatic extensions, the notion of a 'trademark' doesn't do justice to The Beatles' tapping of the complete spectrum of colour tones and structural concepts.

Certainly, 'Yesterday' shows that certain melodies, *per se*, display great character in the contour and development of a 'top line'. But the brilliance of other, 'melodically challenged' Beatles songs (most notably the verse of 'Help!') confirms that the power of a tune undoubtedly depends on the context.

And with The Beatles, that context is, invariably, the chords.

Of course, it is the *combination* of a chord and melody note that is

[42] See Mellers, *Twilight Of The Gods*, p. 55; and Deryck Cooke, 'The Lennon-McCartney Songs' *The Listener*, 1st February 1968 (*The Lennon Companion*, p. 112). Contrast this with Beatles melodies that, more predictably, close a section 2-1 ('All My Loving', 'Nowhere Man'), or 7-8 ('I Should Have Known Better', 'The Long And Winding Road').

responsible for songwriting magic – the popular notion of 'crafting a pop melody' only tells half the story. If you have The Beatles' sense of harmonisation, great songwriting can be about creating very simple melodies – but in conjunction with a highly imaginative approach to chord sequences.

It's a conclusion not surprisingly echoed by legions of Beatles writers down the years. Take the experts at *Guitar Player* magazine:

> 'No wonder those melodies had somewhere to go. Big clear chord maps helped them find their way home along numerous harmonic paths, courtesy of Lennon and Mac's deft voice leading.'[43]

Let's conclude our discussion of melody with perhaps the ultimate example of the importance of harmony to support a tune – courtesy of George.

A short but rather special stretch of 'Only A Northern Song' succinctly encapsulates the whole principle of harmonisation by operating like a glorified version of 'Help!' – an unashamedly blatant linear melody that acquires its interest purely from harmonic movement.

Here the single pitch at work is just a humble B note. Yet, as a hotchpotch collection of both diatonic and borrowed chords shift all around us, we find pop music on the verge of anarchy.

'Only A Northern Song'

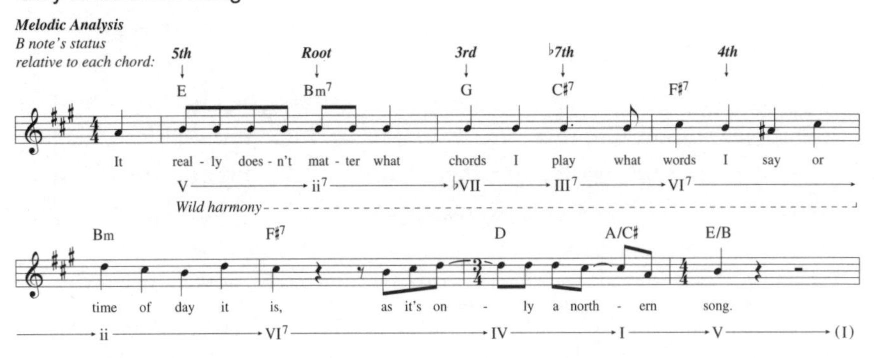

Order is brilliantly maintained (just!) as the first four chords in the progression can be seen to contain that vital B-note, harmonising the static tune in successively different ways – yet mostly with a chord tone that supplies an anchor of stability amid the musical mayhem.

[43] *The Genius Of John Lennon* by James Rotundi and Jas Obrecht, *Guitar Player*, September 1994, p. 66. Meanwhile, advanced students are encouraged to delve deeper into the world of melodic voice leading, covered expertly by Everett in both volumes of *The Beatles As Musicians*.

Specifically, the B note appears – relative to each chord – as follows:

The changing role of the B note in 'Only A Northern Song'

Melody	B	B	B	B	B
Harmony	E	Bm^7	G	C♯^{7}	F♯^{7}
Function of melody note	5th	Root	3rd	♭7th	4th
Lyric	'doesn't'	'matter'	'chords'	'play'	'I'

The result is another fine Beatles showcase, with the purposefully non-chalant, uninspired melody perfectly evoking Harrison's disenchantment with his publishing deal. Meanwhile, in every sense, the real action is happening 'under the table', with the seemingly haphazard harmony cleverly 'pulling the strings'.[44]

'It really doesn't matter what chords I play'? You've just shown us, George, that it most definitely does.

[44] Rooksby refers to another great example of linear melody harmonised in this way: 'I Want You Back' by The Jackson Five where, throughout the chord sequence Fm-Cm-D♭-A♭-B♭m, a single melodic C note appears as the 5th, root, 7th, 3rd and 9th, respectively; *How To Write Songs On Guitar*, p. 85.

SIXTEEN

'I nicked it!' – Derivation, 'Plagiarism' and Pop

'What do they say? "A good artist borrows, a great artist steals" – or something like that. That makes us great artists then, because we stole a lot of stuff.'[1]

Who said that? A commercially astute Tin Pan Alley duo? A derivative Brit-Pop combo, perhaps?

No – it was Paul McCartney, admitting the unwritten rule of songwriting: that talent and genius do not operate in a vacuum. Even the finest tunesmiths regularly derive inspiration by drawing on and re-adapting the existing body of popular music to which they have been exposed. And not always vaguely or subconsciously, but often by deliberately making new and original use of a range of very precise ideas from their heroes.

There is no doubt that The Beatles raised songwriting to new levels by ambitiously manipulating harmony, melody and rhythm with a degree of imagination and variety unmatched in the 20th Century. This book has attempted to explain the mechanics of that very phenomenon.

But, as a parallel theme, we have also attempted to capture the nature of tonal pop music which, for all its apparent complexity, can to a large extent be explained by a simple framework of scales, chords, intervals, sequences and cadences that form recurring reference points – not merely within, but also *between* different pieces of music.

This tradition of 'influence' is regularly acknowledged in blues-based music, no doubt due to the great standardisation of the 12-bar format and the predominance of narrow-range melodic fragments from the major and

[1] *Guitar Player* magazine, July 1990, p. 18.

minor pentatonic scales. Between them they help us to accept the existence of a compositional 'formula' pervading much of the blues and R'n'B genre.

Hence we have no problem in referring to the historic 'legacy of the blues', drawing a straight path from Robert Johnson to Muddy Waters, on to B.B., Albert, Freddy King and Buddy Guy and through to Eric Clapton, Stevie Ray Vaughan and Kenny Wayne Shepherd.

But the traditions of more harmonically complex pop music, especially that which exploits the 7-note major scale, necessarily give rise to song structures and influences that are far harder to trace. This is perhaps one reason why it is convenient to suggest that The Beatles, for all their well-documented love of Chuck Berry, Little Richard and Buddy Holly, Carl Perkins and The Everly Brothers, somehow 'came out of nowhere' and 're-wrote the rules' of songwriting by 'drawing a line under all that went before'.

This is the biggest Beatles myth of all. Firstly, it does a great disservice to the band's own revered influences which, along with the famous quintet of names mentioned above, included writers and artists as diverse as Cole Porter, Gershwin, Goffin & King, Del Shannon, The Platters, Duane Eddy and dozens of others. While this is hardly news to Beatles fans, it's not always appreciated that the evidence is there for all to hear, both on the rough and ready cover recordings of the early days and also in the structure of many Beatles originals.

As we have demonstrated, it is possible to pierce through the heavy veil of Three-Chord Tricks and Doo Wop cycles (on the covers alone) to find a select goldmine of highly intricate songs which provide a powerful bedrock of songwriting ideas.

This chapter looks briefly into the 'sourcing' of a handful of slick musical moves as a way of illustrating and elaborating on the time-honoured theme of 'influence' and 'borrowing' in popular songwriting. This is then used as background to a brief look at the issue of plagiarism in pop, a favourite subject for the pub muso, but one fraught with legal and practical considerations.

As a first step on this particular long and winding road, readers may like to refer to Appendix 6, which details the harmonic points of interest in many of the non-'Three-Chord Trick' songs that were either formally covered by The Beatles or associated with them in some way. It is intended as innocent speculation on how John, Paul, George and Ringo might have been absorbing many of the important sounds with which they would 'change' popular songwriting. Look out for some sweet pop progressions –

borrowed 'rocky' chords from the parallel minor, Interrupted and Double Plagal cadences, parallel major/minor switches and even some distant modulations. All of them are essential elements of the language of pop songwriting and recur regularly in The Beatles' own original compositions.

That's not to suggest in any way that they represent the sum total of The Beatles' musical ideas, merely that they provide a hefty vocabulary for any budding songwriter planning a global onslaught on pop music. Equally, to suggest that The Beatles chanced upon all of these principles in isolation is surely fanciful. Just like the elusive B7 chord that needed to be retrieved from the other side of Liverpool, many (if not all) of these musical ideas would clearly be registering in the psyche of the young Beatles as they developed their own musical awareness.

Many close connections have already been made with these 'tools' – like the augmented chord that links the I and vi chords in both 'Don't Ever Change' and 'All My Loving'. Or the minor chord sequence from the bridge of Leiber & Stoller's supposedly naive 'Three Cool Cats', which neatly embodies the principle of Aeolian rock harmony.

The reappearance of these devices over the years demonstrates a tradition in pop, which great artists such as The Beatles first appreciate, then absorb, and finally rework to great effect. McCartney's acknowledgement of the parallel major switch of 'Besame Mucho' (which we saw in Chapter 6) is just one example of a 'source' being duly identified. In doing so, Paul is confirming that for every 'Yesterday' that appears fully formed, as if by divine intervention, there are dozens of Beatles songs that involved searching far and wide for more earthly sources of inspiration. That source can often be an existing song, especially if it showcases a discrete musical formula that takes your fancy.

Consider that rather striking 'I-v minor' switch in 'I'll Get You' which we saw in Chapter 7 and which, even by Beatles standards, represented such a novel manoeuvre for 1963. Was it plucked out of the blue? Or is there some other explanation as to its origins?

One theory is that the chord was innocently stumbled upon by Lennon and McCartney when 'letting their fingers wander speculatively as they sang'.[2] The truth, it seems, is rather less romantic, as McCartney himself reveals when confessing that this harmonically 'borrowed' chord was just that – borrowed.

[2] MacDonald, *Revolution In The Head*, p. 340.

'That was nicked from a song called "All My Trials" which is on an album I had by Joan Baez. It's a change that has always fascinated me, so I put it in.'[3]

A listen to the Baez original confirms that that a 'I-v' is behind that deft opening change of the song (first at 0.12). Moreover, 'I'll Get You' includes the premise of both harmony and melody – almost identically – for those two bars.

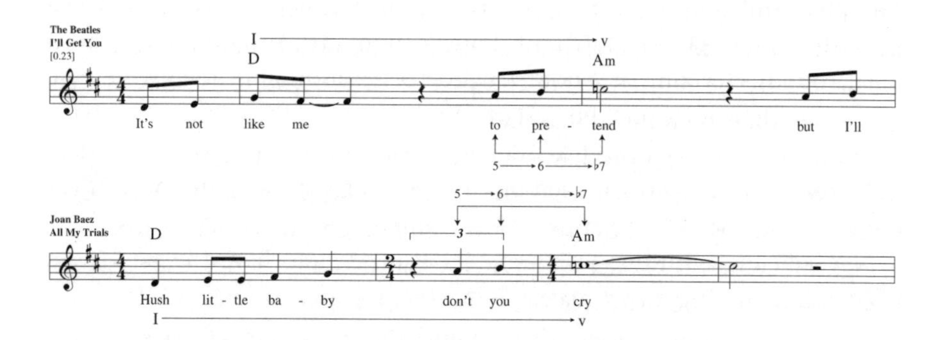

The two settings could hardly be more different: 'innocent, euphoric Beatlemania' against 'introverted philosophical folk'. Yet in each case the very specific device that makes our ears prick up is the tension as the melody hits the ♭7 of the parent major scale. This delivers a chromatic note in a non-bluesy context, a note that is now harmonised as the ♭3rd of that highly unexpected v chord within a major key. In each case it creates a piece of stylistic tension that 'makes' the song.

It is surely this common language of pop music (in which various obvious and not-so-obvious devices are up for grabs at any point in a song) that McCartney has in mind when he acknowledges that 'a great artist steals'.

More specifically, it is the *way* in which he 'steals'. Indeed, the notion that The Beatles were somehow above 'sourcing' ideas from their song-writing ancestors paradoxically detracts from one of the most compelling elements of their genius – the innate skill with which they could rework very specific musical devices while combining them with other threads of inspiration, to emerge with a finished work that was unquestionably all their own.

[3] Miles, *Many Years From Now*, p. 151.

The moment in 'I'll Get You' discussed above is a case in point. Its context is far removed from its 'source', with the melody an octave lower and reserved for a moment of novelty in the 'development section' rather than featuring as the song's opening chord change. Hence it blends, chameleon-like, into the proceedings with only the saddest of trainspotters ever likely to trace its provenance.

Let's make one thing clear at this point. The use of this idea in 'I'll Get You' in no way means that the song lacks originality. Rather the reverse: its very presence ensures it, as it now spices a song whose predictability looked assured by an opening salvo of Three-Chord Tricks and Four-Chord Turnarounds. Certainly, it is not to suggest plagiarism, an issue to which we return later in the chapter. For a start, would anyone have noticed 'the Baez nick' had McCartney not let us in on the secret? Surely not. As Paul himself says: 'You start off with a nicked piece, it gets into the song and you never notice in the end where it was nicked from.'[4]

Nevertheless, with due respect to Sir Paul, we can have the odd guess here and there. For, as Q magazine puts it, spotting similarities between pop songs is 'the music buff's favourite parlour game'.[5] And while invariably the trail *ends* with The Beatles, there seems no harm in extending the fun to the Fabs themselves.

Of course they often help us in that regard, making regular references over the years that go far beyond Joan Baez. As books like *A Hard Day's Write* set out so definitively, Beatles sources encompass everything between the cultural extremes of *Snow White And The Seven Dwarfs* and Beethoven's 'Moonlight Sonata'. Meanwhile, the first *Anthology* video alone saw the surviving Beatles run through a stunning array of influences – right down to Ringo's early penchant for Frankie Laine songs.[6]

This refreshingly broad-minded approach to 'influence' goes a long way towards explaining The Beatles as a songwriting phenomenon. The remainder of this chapter is intended as an interlude, reinforcing many of the principles of this book – namely that making such connections between songs is intended both to demonstrate the *effect* of such devices, and to show that while they can emerge in dramatically different song situations they can still be appreciated as discrete, digestible musical concepts.

[4] *Where There's A Hit There's A Writ*, BBC Radio 1, 21st February 1989.

[5] 'Why Can't Rock Stars Be Original?' Q, Issue 165, June 2000, p. 31.

[6] Check out Tape 1 of the *Anthology* video series to find Ringo introducing us to footage of Frankie Laine singing 'Jezebel'.

Indeed, for all the fascinating songwriting connections within The Beatles' music itself, much of the inspiration for this book came directly from the release of *Live At The BBC* and *Anthology 1,* which provided a deep insight into The Beatles' early songwriting influences.

'Spot the nick' – a lighthearted look at Beatles influences.

There's no better place to start than with that legendary 'flat submediant', and especially the left-field switch of 'It Won't Be Long' which, back in 1963, William Mann suggested 'does not figure much in other pop repertoires, or in The Beatles' arrangements of borrowed material'.

A rare bird certainly, but The Beatles would have been exposed to a rather special 'I-♭VI-I' in the verses of Carl Perkins' 'Honey Don't' – a song that they went on to cover on *Beatles For Sale.* (Listen out for the same bold jump, from E to C – at 0.10.) And while we're at it, we can also throw in the bridge of Buddy Holly's 'Peggy Sue' which opens A-F-A (at 0.45 on the original). George Harrison even demonstrated the novelty of the chord change with some impromptu strumming during one nostalgic interview, explaining: 'A to F.... "Peggy Sue". Buddy Holly was sensational. A little of that rubbed of in as much as I no longer have a fear of changing from A to F.'[7] In both Perkins' and Holly's great rock 'n' roll classics, the ♭VI notably appears as the only departure from the Three-Chord Trick.

[7] *Across The Universe* (Part 2: 'Tell Me Why'), BBC Radio 2, 15th October 2002. The Beatles also performed both 'Honey Don't' and 'Peggy Sue' in their early sets (1962–1965 and 1957–1962, respectively) before writing 'It Won't Be Long' in 1963 (dates from Lewisohn, *The Complete Beatles Recording Sessions*, p. 362 and p. 364).

Once again the trick was for The Beatles to absorb this move into a song, a task perfected in 'It Won't Be Long'. While the progression remains intact, originality is guaranteed by ambitious use – in the melody – of the non-diatonic notes that the chord brings to the song. It is the C, D and G natural notes that create The Beatles' knock-out punch while distancing the song from its likely 'inspiration'.

While we're on the notorious ♭VI, we can't help but speculate on the origins of the great deceptive ending that appears in McCartney's 'I Will'. Now, what could have prompted Macca here?

Here is one of those great I-♭VI-I false endings that we traced back to Tony Sheridan's 'Why'. But take a look now at Frank Ifield's 'Confessin''. Here, after harmonising the tonic F note as the major 3rd of the ♭VI, Ifield, (the king of vocal range in the early sixties) fires the melody up an octave in a prolonged chant over several beats as we cadence ♭VI-I.[8] It's just a couple of notes over a single chord change – but a combination that can be heard clearly at the climax of 'I Will'.

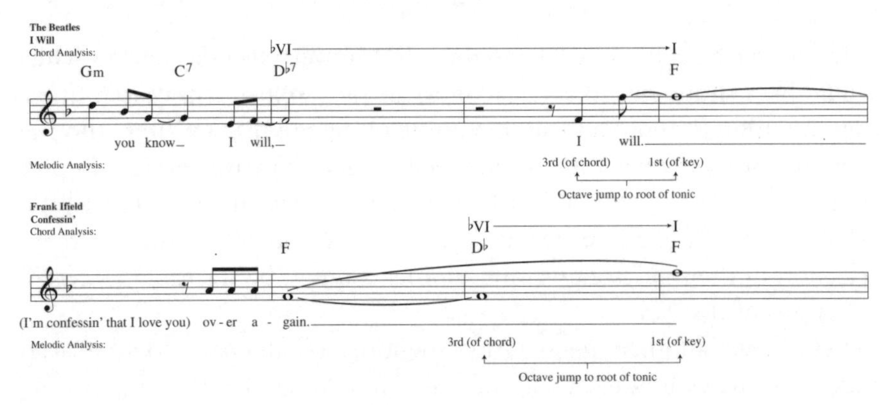

These two pretty songs are clearly in the same genre of melodic pop with a similar tempo and feel. Given the status of 'Confessin'' as a million-selling UK No. 1, sandwiched between 'From Me To You and 'She Loves You' in the summer of 1963, it seems unlikely that The Beatles (or any other top songwriter of the time) were oblivious to its very precise charms.

That rousing octave leap is perhaps the giveaway, though that's not to suggest that distinctive octave leaps on tonics have not always been up for grabs (Harold Arlen's 'Over The Rainbow' and Gerry And The

[8] Example transposed into the same key as 'I Will' for ease of comparison. Its original key is A major.

Pacemakers' 'I Like It' showcase the same leap). But surely McCartney both heard and appreciated the stylistic nuance of the 'Confessin'' coda, with that obtuse ♭VI, in the same way that Lennon would have enjoyed the same song's equally novel I-VII opening chord change, which later appeared on his 'I'm So Tired'.

The White Album, of course (on which both 'I Will' and 'I'm So Tired' appear), wasn't released for another five years and no one could suggest that these later 'moments' could not have been arrived at independently of Ifield's song. Nevertheless, and as Matt Aitken explains so succinctly, the processing of our musical experiences takes place subconsciously as well as consciously:

> 'Everything you perceive musically – every melody that you *think* is coming from you – is really an amalgamation of everything you've ever heard. From The Beatles to Mozart. You're not born with a quartz crystal that invents tunes.'[9]

Moreover, both the I-♭VI-I and the I-VII are very specific devices which would have shone out like a beacon to an early sixties songwriter. In fact they are still rare enough in all pop music to suggest that a writer who uses them in a song probably has some specific – rather than generic – inspirational 'reference points' in mind. Given the passion with which The Beatles refer to their early favourites, it is hardly unreasonable to suggest that a selection of their key songwriting moments might be traceable to certain select hits of that era.

Let's have another guess. Any mention of dramatic octave leaps inevitably draws us back to 'I Want To Hold Your Hand' whose rousing refrain has always represented one of the highlights of Beatlemania. As we saw in Chapter 4, the pivotal moment can be defined, very specifically, as a non-functional III7 that powers on to IV while the melody, harmonising the 3rd and 7th of the key, is held for a full bar. But was it a moment that *really* distanced The Beatles so completely from the old order?

An essential comparison can be made with The Platters' 'Smoke Gets In Your Eyes' – a fixture, remember, on The Beatles' favourite Hamburg jukebox.[10]

[9] Matt Aitken of 'Hit Factory' songwriters, Stock, Aitken and Waterman speaking on *Where There's A Hit There's A Writ*, BBC Radio 1, 21st February 1989.

[10] *Paul McCartney's Rock & Roll Roots*, BBC Radio 1, 25th December 1999 – see Chapter 10.

The Platters may have lacked cute Mop Tops and cool guitars but, as with all these connections, cast aside your non-musical preconceptions for a moment. Forget the artists, the instrumentation and other textural issues and focus on the mechanics of the music. How does the song *work*?

In both cases the secondary dominant harmonises the strong chord tone – not merely for a melodic peak but clearly as *the* moment of musical ecstasy in the song. It forms a watershed that separates the build-up of the opening bars and the winding-down that follows.

In each case that tension is released precisely through harmony that moves chromatically up a half step to the subdominant, before 'releasing' back to the tonic. The Platters go for a familiar 'I-vi-ii-V-I' Cycle Of Fifths, closing with a deft 5-6-8 melodic cadence; while The Beatles opt for the more primitive variation to support a standard 3-2-1 descent.[11] Reduced to their basics, both songs work by creating a highly distinctive moment of euphoria using essentially the same musical premise.

If this connection is too tenuous then let's try something simpler – like the chorus to 'Girl', whose 'I-iii-ii-V7' sequence is precisely the type of sophisticated take on the Four-Chord Turnaround which we associate with The Beatles. It's not rocket science, but by combining the inevitability of the I-vi-ii-V Doo Wop cliché with the novelty of McCartney's 'I-iii formula' the sequence was a stage on from the mainstream legacy of the late fifties. And yet just how groundbreaking *is* the chorus of 'Girl' over which we all swoon?

A listen to the Tony Sheridan song, 'Why', finds the identical progression, complete with a similarly delicate melody that milks a one-syllable title refrain[12]. Watch how the phrasing again stresses the move from the 5th to the 3rd of the major scale, with that latter C♯ in the key of A being neatly re-harmonised as the root of the following chord.

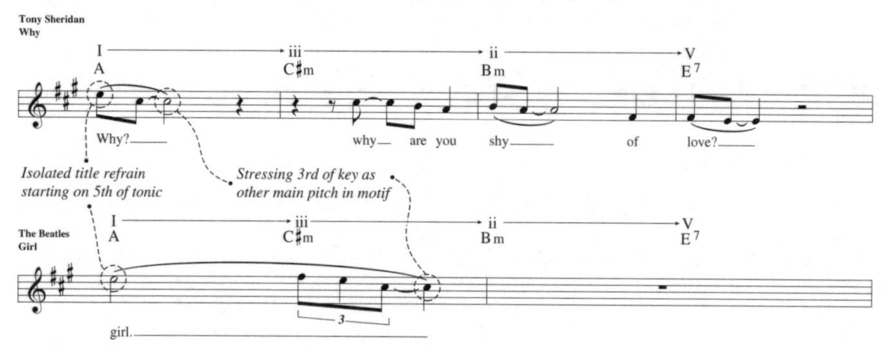

Is there no way that The Beatles could have been influenced by Sheridan's song? After all, they played on it.

Of course, this move is just the jazzier version of I-iii-IV-V as found, say, in the bridge of 'I Feel Fine'. And similarly, that more primitive sequence (but still novel for the times) has an essential pre-Beatles counterpart in the verse of Buddy Holly's 'True Love Ways' from 1958.

Irrespective of one's view of the provenance and inspiration behind these songs, the bottom line is that appreciating the connection between them will, at the very least, drastically reduce a musician's learning time

[11] The delicious diminished chord in The Platters' song merely acts as a 'type 1' passing chord that creates an ascending chromatic line (4-♯4-5) into the 5th of the tonic.

[12] 'Girl' transposed into the same key as 'Why' for ease of comparison.

when building a repertoire. One of the aims of this book has been to encourage an awareness that not all songs are as fundamentally different as the novice musician often assumes. As jazz guitar legend, Howard Roberts, would explain to each new intake of students at the Musicians Institute:

> 'music seems so complicated at first, but that's because nobody tells you that the same doggone sequences recur constantly in songs of so many styles and eras.'[13]

Not that we need any of this anecdotal evidence, the very existence of the Roman Numeral system (which we have been using as a global standard to track the path of chords) proves that formulaic thinking is integral to the writing, performing and understanding of all music. And formulas in pop do not stop at the Three-Chord Tricks and Four-Chord Turnarounds that we already accept as being part of the tradition of pop. They can also feature some obscure ideas whose 'heritage' is confirmed by some notable pre-Beatles examples.

Let's compare the musical peak of 'Day Tripper' with a corresponding moment in 'I Remember You', another song that just happened to feature in The Beatles' early live repertoire. Both reached the UK No. 1 slot, though the connection does not end there. Musically they both enjoy the same ♭VI-V tonicisation of a VI major chord – a premise unheard of in the songs of the average beat group in sixties Liverpool. Let's compare them in the key of E:

Of course, the IV-III7-*vi* move brought great beauty to a select collection of sixties songs, but the same preparation of a non-diatonic VI *major*, with its greater sense of tonal displacement, creates a startling variation.

While most borrowed ideas get 'worked into' a song by switching a few melody notes, here we find the crucial notes of the Ifield melody recurring

[13] Howard Roberts, co-founder of the Guitar Institute of Technology at The Musicians Institute, in Hollywood, California.

in relation to each chord in the sequence. Making us wonder, as with 'I'll Get You', was this another of the 'lifted licks' that McCartney has periodically referred to'?[14]

Everett calls the 'Day Tripper' moment a 'nearly incredible German sixth',[15] which makes it all the more unlikely that The Beatles would have failed to have been intrigued by the basic progression when dissecting the Ifield version covered on the Star-Club recording.

In fact we *know* they were, for The Beatles' version of 'I Remember You' (a song that Lennon once referred to as 'a terrible thing')[16] is identical to the original in every respect except one. Rather than keeping this bridge in its original place, The Beatles start the song on the refrain, in order to introduce this bridge after only four bars, with the result that we hear the modulation *three* times rather than the two times of the model version![17]

Talking of intriguing connections with No. 1 hits, we mentioned back in Chapter 3 how 'Yesterday''s defining ii-V-i modulation to the relative minor had a close counterpart in Paul's favourite 'Moon River' by Henry Mancini, where the ploy occurs over the similarly time-distorting lyric, 'someday'. And yet Ian Hammond cites Ray Charles' 'Georgia' as a possible inspiration for Macca's masterpiece; while songwriting historian, Spencer Leigh, makes an intriguing lyrical comparison with 'Answer Me', a huge 1953 hit for the Ringo-rated Frankie Laine, and recorded later that year by another McCartney hero, Nat King Cole with the line: 'You were mine yesterday, I believed that love was here to stay'.[18]

As well as a handful of shared words, and the multiple rhyming emphasis on '-ay', there are some uncanny similarities in the scanning of the verse lines. Adjusting for the fact that 'Answer Me' is in 3/4 time, it's a fascinating piece of trivia that, starting with the isolated 'yesterday' in both songs, the only phrases that don't broadly overlap in terms of their *rhythmic phrasing* are the last two syllables of Paul's closing 'yesterday'.

[14] *Guitar Player*, July 1990, p. 18.

[15] Everett, *The Beatles As Musicians: Revolver Through The Anthology*, p. 20.

[16] Jann Wenner, *Lennon Remembers*, p. 79.

[17] These bridges start at 0.08, 0.40 and 1.21 on The Beatles' version, compared to 0.40 and 1.13 on the Ifield original.

[18] 'Both the lyrical content and its execution are close to "Yesterday" and the melody is not far away. McCartney's song is not a steal, but if someone had pointed out the similarity to him, would we have even heard "Yesterday"?'; *Brother, Can You Spare A Rhyme? – 100 Years Of Hit Songwriting* by Spencer Leigh, p.109. For Ian Hammond's 'Georgia' case study, see 'Old Sweet Songs' at www.beathoven.com.

The 'Yesterday'/'Answer Me' phrasing puzzle[19]

Phrase	Song	Lyric								
1	'Yesterday'				'Yes-	ter-	day'			
	'Answer Me'	'[You	were	mine]	yes-	ter-	day'			
2	'Yesterday'	'All	my	trou-	bles	seemed	so	far	a-	way'
	'Answer Me'	'I	be-	lieved	that	love	was	here	to	stay'
3	'Yesterday'	'Now	it	looks	as	though	they're	here	to	stay'
	'Answer Me'	'Won't	you	tell	me	where	I've	gone	a-	stray
4	'Yesterday'	'Oh	I	be-	lieve	in	yes-	[ter-	day]'	
	'Answer Me'	'Please	an-	swer	me	my	love'			

The budding muso might also note that both verses are founded on a Diatonic Major Descent that extends down the scale to 4; both boldly build a stylish chord on the leading note; and both feature a cadence that rises quizzically to the major 3rd of the key.

OK, but the expert would counter that 'Answer Me' follows a basic 8-7-6-5-4 drop, harmonises '7' as a 2nd inversion IV for a 'churchy', gospel sound, and 'corrects' its '5-3' mid-verse cadence (earlier on 'sweet*heart*') with an expected closing tonic in an 8-bar structure in 3/4 time. In contrast, Paul exudes novelty with his detour to '3' (and III7) *en route* to '6', his awesome root-position m7th chord on '7', and his famously *uncorrected* '1-3' melodic close to his quirky seven-bar structure in 4/4 time.

And, of course, 'Yesterday' is stunningly original in terms of its unique structure of melodic *pitches*. Six million (and counting) airplays would have turned up a blueprint by now if it wasn't.

But the 'Answer Me' connection is still fascinating – especially given the quintessential Beatles story that Paul woke from *that* dream with the fully-formed tune of 'Yesterday' – to which he only later added lyrics.

As Miles writes when describing the song's evolution: 'Freud suggests that dream formation is determined in part by the previous day's activities and it would be interesting to know what Paul had been listening to the night before'.[20]

[19] The lyrics here are from Nat King Cole's version which slightly altered Frankie Laine's original verse 2 which began 'She was mine', and ended not with 'my love' but 'Oh Lord' – which famously resulted in a *BBC* ban for its supposed blasphemy. For the anoraks, the song originates from the German 'Mutterlein' by Gerhard Winkler and Fred Rauch, with the English lyrics by Carl Sigman. See *The Guinness Book Of Number One Hits*, 1994, p.16.

[20] *Many Years From Now*, p. 203. Miles also describes how, when searching for a possible pre-existing blueprint for 'Yesterday' in June 1965, George Martin drew attention to Peggy Lee's 'Yesterdays', but noted that 'the title was all they had in common'; p. 205.

Sometimes connections seem far more tangible. Following the release of 'Free As A Bird' in the nineties, links were noted between the bridge and The Shangri-las' 1964 classic 'Remember (Walkin' In The Sand)'.[21]

Certainly there is lyrical overlap here – and indeed there is *musical* overlap, too – for while the straight-eighths feel of 'Free As A Bird' differs from the swing-eighths feel of 'Remember', the opening bars of both tunes hinge on a repeated, three-pitch, ascending motive that feels uncannily similar.[22]

And while McDonald refers to the 'Free As A Bird' bridge as being '*subconsciously* borrowed' from The Shangri-las, it would have been a nice touch if Lennon had *deliberately* copied the *lyric* from 'Remember' as a way of drawing attention to the skill with which he turned a simple musical idea into something so much more elaborate.

Everett also points out the similarities between the melody of 'Hey Jude' and The Drifters' classic, 'Save The Last Dance For Me'. This time the focus is essentially on a selection of shared melodic pitches as they unfold over a common primary chord sequence with a similar harmonic and semantic movement ('don't forget' and 'remember').

As well as the build-up of 5-to-6 which occurs on the shift to the subdominant IV chord in both songs, the delicate extensions implied by a mix of '2-1-7-6-5' seem to create a similar melodic contour in both songs. Yet, once again, a close look reveals enough subtle variations in precise pitch placement (and volume of notes) to question the true extent of any direct inspiration.

Interestingly, 'Save The Last Dance For Me' turns out to be another cover that surfaced in The Fabs' live sets of 1961, while they even revisited it during the *Let It Be* sessions.[23]

The finest anecdote with respect to The Beatles and 'Save The Last Dance For Me' comes courtesy of Will Bratton, the son-law of Doc Pomus, who wrote the 1960 classic and who, in the seventies, lived on same street in Manhattan as John Lennon.

[21] 'The upward progression in a chromatically ambiguous A minor for the middle eight may seem striking in this sleepy context, but it's merely a variant of the same doo-wop cycle, subconsciously borrowed from the Dm verse of The Shangri-Las' kitsch 1964 classic'; *Revolution In The Head*, p. 332.

[22] From a common starting point, Lennon's 'whatever happened to' walks up 1-2-♭3 rather than 1-♭3-4 as in the Shangri-las.

[23] See Lewisohn, *The Complete Beatles Recording Sessions*, p. 364. For a full list of the *Let It Be* sessions see Dowlding, *Beatlesongs*, pp. 309–10.

> 'Doc's daughter, Sharyn, and I ran into John and Yoko at the Central Park Deli on West 72nd Street, one afternoon. "I think you know my father," Sharyn said. John asked her whom that might be. When she told him, John said: "Doc Pomus ... Doc Pomus!", and sang the entire 'Save The Last Dance For Me' to Sharyn in the store.'[24]

So far we've just speculated on the origins of a few isolated bars here or there. But, turning back specifically to chords, let's look at how, say, an unusually inspiring 8-bar bridge harmony might reappear when skilfully absorbed and restructured.

There is certainly a most compelling connection to be made between one of McCartney's very earliest songs, 'Love Of The Loved', and 'To Know Her Is To Love Her', a US No. 1 hit for The Teddy Bears way back in 1957, and covered by The Beatles on *Live At The BBC*.

'That was the first three-part harmony we ever did; we learned that in my Dad's house in Liverpool,' McCartney explained to Mark Lewisohn, even singing the slow deliberate refrain to his interviewer.[25]

In which case, the song's middle eight, consisting of *the* most harmonically ambitious chord progression on a No. 1 pop hit of the fifties (or since?!) would not have escaped his attention.

After opening on the ♭III (revolutionary enough for the fifties), other borrowed chords abound in the form of ♭VII and ♭VI chords, with unusual intervals of minor seconds and minor thirds creating an intriguing game of harmonic cat and mouse. With a potential ♭VI–V return to E (i.e., C–B–E) thwarted in favour of a ♭III that re-starts the second four-bar strain, we're practically begging for the bridge's final Imperfect cadence cliché to re-establish our bearings.

If Phil Spector's first success didn't exactly rewrite the rules of music, this whacky sequence was certainly the very antithesis of the formulaic rock 'n' roll bridge. Moreover, the harmonic challenge surely provided inspiration for McCartney's own exotic excursions on 'Love Of The Loved'. Never a formal Beatles release, the song is nevertheless a historically important composition, with its bizarre structure apparently related

[24] Thanks to Will Bratton, and to Spencer Leigh for bringing this story to the author's attention.

[25] Lewisohn, *The Complete Beatles Recording Sessions*, p. 10.

to a batch of efforts from the late fifties. Here's the middle eight, as heard on the bootleg of The Beatles' run-through at the 1969 *Get Back* sessions:

'Love Of The Loved' (0.35)

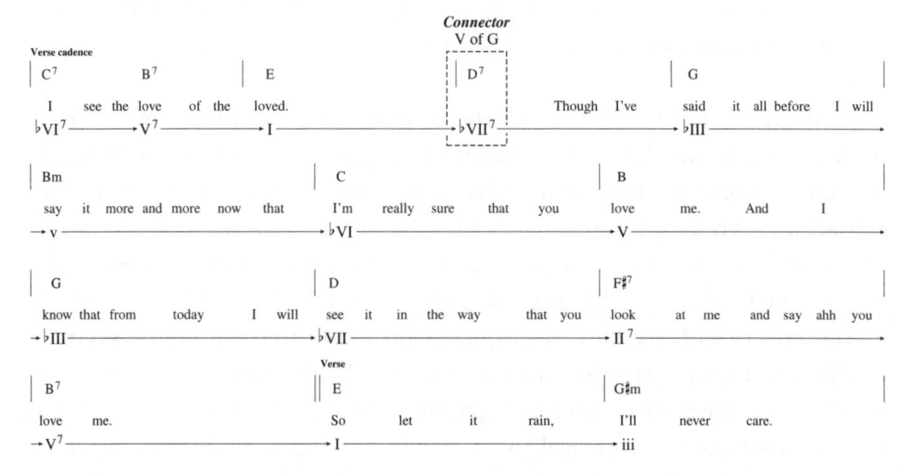

With so many unusual chords being batted about, the connection between the two bridges might not be immediately obvious. The following chart summarises the harmony, and confirms some obvious parallels, as well as some subtle differences. To make things easier, the Roman numerals ignore the implied modulations and are expressed in relation to the verse key of E major throughout.

Summary of middle eight harmony – key of E

Bar	1	2	3	4	5	6	7	8
'To Know Her Is To Love Her'	♭III	♭VII	♭VI	V	♭III I	♭VI V	II	V
	G	D	C	B	G E	C B	F♯	B
'Love Of The Loved'	♭III	v	♭VI	V	♭III	v	II	V
	G	Bm	C	B	G	Bm	F♯	B

The comparisons are inescapable. There's the same feel of tonal ambiguity as I and ♭III wrestle for supremacy, with the teasing, unresolved ♭VI-V move the main culprit as it threatens to take us back to E in bar 5. The main difference is McCartney's Bm – which is of course related to Phil Spector's D major as a straightforward relative minor substitution.[26]

[26] Everett similarly suggests that it is 'very likely' that McCartney's bridge is 'modeled' on that of the Spector. *The Beatles As Musicians: The Quarry Men Through Rubber Soul*, p. 107.

Unlike 'To Know Her Is To Love Her', 'Love Of The Loved' maintains its twisting tonal moves throughout the song, a feature that would no doubt have gone over the heads of early Beatles audiences, who appreciated rather more gentle introductions to life outside the diatonic world. Although the song was diverted to Cilla in 1963, its construction confirms The Beatles' early awareness of the whole concept of 'unexpected harmony', a principle that defines so many Beatles originals.

While we're on the subject of middle eights, it doesn't take too much detective work to find important precedents for some of the most important early Beatles landmarks. How about the groundbreaking middle of 'From Me To You' which, by McCartney's own admission, saw The Beatles make a quantum leap in their songwriting.[27]

Despite having gone to great lengths to praise the novelty of this very specific bridge modulation, the move was not unprecedented in pop music of the time. For a start, Paul's hero, Buddy Holly, had already been a visitor to this same 'surprising place' in the bridge of 'Raining In My Heart', as the verse key of G gives way so powerfully to a sense of C major.

Given how highly we know McCartney regards this move, it is inconceivable that this Boudleaux and Felice Bryant composition was

[27] Refer back to Chapter 10 for the mechanics of this modulation, which has its roots in the bridges of early jazz standards such as 'Sunday Kind Of Love'.

not a powerful influence on John and Paul as they came to write their 1963 gems. The Holly song was a fixture in Beatles live sets from its release in 1959 through to 1962, the year before the success of 'From Me To You'.[28]

And don't let's forget 'I Want To Hold Your Hand', which also features this middle eight premise of a ii-V-I 'from the v minor'. A look at these three songs together demonstrates a method of absorbing any cool sequence into a song by personalising the melody (often by simply varying the crucial opening note at the start of the sequence) or the vocal harmony. In this particular Tale Of Three Bridges we find irreproachable novelty in every case. Yes, they all start ominously on a v minor and modulate to IV in a ii-V-I. But each uses a *different vocal arrangement* over that initial rogue chord.

The 'v' minor bridge: same chord . . . different melody

Song	Lyric	Vocals
'Raining In My Heart'	'*Oh mis* - ery'	5th
'From Me To You'	'I've got *arms* that long to hold you'	♭3rd + 5th
'I Want To Hold Your Hand'	'*And* when I touch you I feel happy inside'	5th + ♭7th

With the stronger 'lead' melody targeting the mellow ♭3rd of the chord, the 'From Me To You' bridge is instantly distanced from 'Raining In My Heart'. And while the opening 5th 'bridge pitch' for 'I Want To Hold Your Hand' briefly evokes the Holly classic, the choice of ♭7th in the harmony (and, of course, the quickly rising melodic phrase) once again ensures its originality.

Whether or not you buy this particular piece of trivia, it's clear that 'ringing the changes' in this way, by experimenting with different tones and harmonisation over any set of cool new chord changes, is another of The Beatles' songwriting secrets.

Though Holly himself didn't pen all his own songs, his catalogue rightly stands at the top of the pile of Beatles influences, with McCartney making his respect ultimately clear by acquiring the copyrights to many of his hero's songs. Among the influential highlights, he'd no doubt appreciate the dark ♭VI-I bridge of 'Peggy Sue Got Married'; the I-♭VII-I of 'Well All

[28] Lewisohn, *The Complete Beatles Recording Sessions*, p. 364.

Right' (a prototype rock move years before 'A Hard Day's Night'); and a selection of other slick bridge moves that depart comprehensively from the predictable 'middle eight on IV'[29]

As well as the 'v' of 'Raining In My Heart', there's the 'opening vi' of the middle eight of 'It Doesn't Matter Anymore', which is perhaps one of several ancestors of The Beatles' own relative minor middles (as featured in 'There's A Place', 'When I'm Sixty Four', 'Drive My Car' and 'We Can Work It Out').

Nor can we leave another Beatles hero, Roy Orbison, out of it. For while Holly had died in a plane crash in 1959, The Big O was befriended by The Beatles themselves and, as McCartney explains, his presence helped to initiate some gentle songwriting rivalry.

> 'I remember we'd be on the tour bus and Roy would be at the back . . . writing something like "Pretty Woman". I remember him playing that to us. We thought: "Phew! Great song". From this, a little bit of competitiveness would come in . . . we thought: we've *got* to write one as good as that.'[30]

You can be sure that The Beatles would have appreciated the essential ingredients of *that* particular classic. It starts with a catchy blues-based riff around E7, which takes on a pop dimension by leaning heavily on the melodic ninth – just as 'Day Tripper' would do not long after.[31] Meanwhile, beyond the catchy tune (and a slick bar of 6/4 in the verse that throws the listener every time) is the swooning bridge section, which features another textbook functional modulation. Not from the 'v' this time, but from the 'iv', heard here as a beautifully distant Dm chord (at 1.07 on the original), which carries the song to the key of the ♭III, with a familiar 'ii-V-I-vi' emerging in the new tonality.

[29] The bridge of 'Peggy Sue Got Married' starts with a plunging move to E (F♭) in the key of A♭ ('You recall the girl . . .', at 0.34) and perhaps even tops the 'I-♭VI-I' of 'Peggy Sue' and Perkins' 'Honey Don't' as an influence on 'It Won't Be Long'. 'Well All Right' opens with a F♯-E-F♯ alternation; 'It Really Doesn't Matter' moves to an Em bridge in the key of G ('There's no use . . .', at 0.37).

[30] *Anthology* video series, Tape 2.

[31] Bobby Parker's 'Watch Your Step' is sometimes suggested as an alternative inspiration for the 'Day Tripper' riff.

'Pretty Woman' bridge (at 1.07)

| E⁷verse riff || Dm | G | C | Am |
Pretty woman stop a while. Pretty woman talk a while.
Key: A major V⁷ → iv
Key: C major ii → V → I → vi →

| Dm | G | C | C |
Pretty woman give your smile to me.
→ ii → V → I

We can't pretend that The Beatles were oblivious to the draw of this other 'surprising place',[32] because this is the same slick key-switch that we raved about when describing bridges as varied as 'Lady Madonna', 'She Came In Through The Bathroom Window' and 'Free As A Bird'.

Looking through the list of early covers favoured by The Beatles in their formative years (diligently compiled by Mark Lewisohn), it is clear that some songs immediately stand out as richer in musical features than others. The vast majority are Three-Chord rock 'n' roll numbers that, while helping the band become the tightest of Beat outfits, probably contributed little in terms of song construction.

However, a select handful would have presented the young tunesmiths with an instant jackpot of songwriting ideas. None more so than 'Till There Was You', written by Meredith Willson for the musical *The Music Man*, and recorded by 'one of our favourite American groups . . . Sophie Tucker!', as McCartney famously teased when introducing The Beatles' rendition at the 1963 Royal Variety Performance.[33]

'Till There Was You' may have been widely dismissed as a novelty throw-away, but its constantly twisting harmonic structure contains a feast of essential devices. The following off-beat exercise is a bar-by-bar break-down of the main sections of the song, making parallels with identical chord changes in a dozen or so later Beatles originals.

Once again, many of the connections may seem tenuous, and, of course, many of these nuggets can be found in hundreds of songs dating back to Tin Pan Alley and on to Brit Pop. However, this is intended as another case

[32] Buddy Holly also opens the bridge of 'True Love Ways' on a distant iv (E♭m in the key of B♭ for 'throughout the days' at 0.48). Interestingly though, he doesn't tonicise it formally in a ii-V-I – the unusual progression E♭m-A♭7-B♭-D♭-F-C7-F finds the expected D♭ (at 1.00 on 'joys') delayed and heard more as a borrowed ♭III ahead of the Imperfect cadence retransition, rather than a tonal centre in its own right.

[33] Lewisohn suggests that the model for The Beatles was probably Peggy Lee's version; *The Complete Recording Sessions*, p. 365.

study of the demystification of a pop song, demonstrating how artists make similar use of the same raw materials whose *functions* are completely transportable between songs.

Anatomy of a Beatles cover: 'Till There Was You'

Analysis and timings relate to the studio version heard on *With The Beatles.*

VERSE (0.08-0.23)

Bars 3-5 Gm7-B♭m7-F

A slick ii-iv-I move, with an interval of a minor third between the two minor chords, which was unusual for the time; followed by a 'minor Plagal' cadence to the tonic.

Beatles example: 'I'll Follow The Sun' (bridge) ('And now the time has come and so my love I must go', Dm-Fm-C).

Bars 5-6: F-Am7-A♭m7-Gm7-C7-F

McCartney's I-iii 'formula', just as described in 'Do You Want To Know A Secret'. Here we find the same sequence unfolding precisely, right down to the chromatic descent to ii via ♭iii, followed by the inevitable V-I return to base.[34]

[34] 'I'm Wishing' from *Snow White* was apparently the musical, as well as the lyrical, inspiration for 'Do You Want To Know A Secret' (see Miles, '*Many Years From Now*, p. 95.). While an analysis reveals some ii-V-I progressions in the key of A (as well as a deft ♭III-V sequence) this section of 'Till There Was You' seems a far better fit! But then Harrison nominates The Stereos' 1961 hit, 'I Really Love You' (also rich in 'ii-Vs'), as the true 'source' for the song.

Bar 8: Gm7-C7

A standard ii-V turnaround to cue up a repeat of previously heard material re-starting on the tonic. A universal songwriting move.

Beatles example: 'Tell Me Why' (Em7-A ahead of each chorus on D major).

VERSE (2nd ending) 0.35-0.39

Bar 15-16: F-F9

The verse closes on a restful F tonic (in both harmony and melody) before the chord turns to a dominant to intensify the move to the subdominant at the start of the bridge, coloured with a 9th degree for jazzy effect.

Beatles example: 'This Boy' (D-D9-G).

BRIDGE (0.39–0.54)

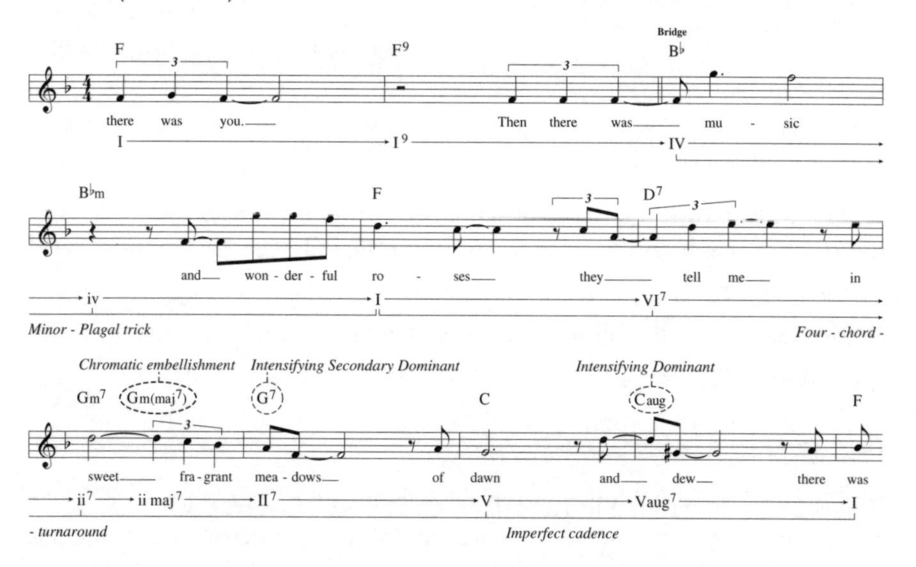

Bars 1-3: B♭-B♭m-F.

The minor Plagal variation IV-iv-I, so common as a starting ploy in early rock 'n' roll bridges (e.g., 'Ain't She Sweet'). While The Beatles would shun that cliché, they cleverly transported the sequence to other areas to create similarly delicate cadences.

Beatles example: 'In My Life' ('All my liiiiife, though some have changed', D-Dm-A).

Bars 3-4: F-D7

I-VI7 cues a Cycle Of Fifths movement, building an extended progression based on a standard two-bar turnaround on the roots of 1-6-2-5.

Beatles example: 'Good Day Sunshine' ('I need to laugh', A-F♯7).

Bar 5-7: Gm7-G7-C

Rather than move directly from ii in bar 5 to V in bar 6, as in a conventional turnaround, Gm is turned into a secondary dominant II7, which primes an Imperfect cadence on V more intensely due to the leading note effect.

Beatles example: the bridge of 'Like Dreamers Do' ('I'll be there [Bm] yeah [B7] waiting for you [E7]', in the key of A).

Bar 5: Gm7-Gm/maj7

An embellishment of the basic move from Gm7-G7, with a falling chromatic line in the inner harmony. The result is the first half of the Chromatic Minor Descent (the 'Michelle' 'Minor Walk'), though unfolding here on the ii chord.

Beatles example: 'I'll Be Back' (2nd bridge) over John's '*melismatic*' 'I-I-I-I-I' (Bm–Bm/maj7).

Bar 7-8: C-C aug

An augmented embellishment of the V chord: the classic method of spicing the dominant with a sharpened 5th to accentuate the change back into the I chord, as the bridge returns to the verse.

Beatles example: 'From Me To You' ('satis-*fied ooh*', G-Gaug-C).

Why stop at the harmony? How about some recurring melodic themes too? The 2-1 verse cadence ("was you") of course has numerous parallels (see 'I Want To Hold *Your Hand*' on p. 601). But then the opening pick-up phrase has a rather familiar three-note motif, as 'There were birds' walks up the parent major scale from the 3rd to the 4th and on to 5th, hanging on the latter for two beats. Sounds familiar? The tune of 'Yellow Submarine' opens identically, as 'In the town' follows the same 3-4-5, duly hanging on the final word of the three-word motif for two beats.

Of course The Beatles had long forgotten about 'Till There Was You' by the time they sat down to pen this *Revolver* ditty. The point again is that pop has traditions of harmony, melody and rhythm that form the bedrock of the culture.

John Lennon's 'All music is rehash, just variations on a theme' quote, which opened this book, should, by now, be emerging as not such a flippant philosophy. These tried-and-tested ideas represent the lexicon of pop – building blocks of songwriting that are constantly being re-synthesised in ever more inventive ways.

Though not necessarily – Lennon himself would surely accept that the long path from 'Please Please Me' to 'Imagine' doesn't necessarily involve the quantum leap in songwriting that we might be forgiven for assuming. Iron out some superficial riff-ology and you have the common premise of an opening section that hinges on a repeating tonic-to-subdominant (both even hit the IV chord on the word 'try'). This is followed in each case by a development section on IV that unfolds with a colourful juxtaposition of the ii and vi chords of the key, before moving to a local climax on the dominant.

The lyrical themes may be far removed from one another – but musically, the compositions themselves are not.

This characterisation of musical ideas as self-contained devices to be transported lock, stock and barrel between songs isn't intended as a theoretical point for the muso. In fact, it is the way that songwriting traditions are passed on through successive generations. To reinforce the point, the following quotes from some massively successful songwriters depict this process of 'influence-enhanced' inspiration in action. Taken together they clearly define the incremental nature of songwriting, evolving with reference to a shared legacy of musical ideas that are constantly being recycled.

Keith Richards:

'I generally go through the Buddy Holly songbook, or Eddie Cochran or The Everly Brothers, or a little Chuck. If there's something that I'm playing of theirs that suggests something else to me, I think, "Hey, there it is," and then I hang onto the end and follow the motherfucker.'[35]

[35] *Guitar Player*, October 1993, p. 61.

Matt Aitken:
'If we're stuck for an idea we'll often toss some chord sequences around, maybe one from a Billy Joel number, and use that to develop a song. It's very nice to have a firm base to start.'[36]

Paul McCartney:
'Anything that gets you into writing a song is good really. It gives you a framework to work in. We used to say "we'll have this bit from here, and this bit from The Marvelettes", and so on. But by the time we've sung it in our Liverpool accent, it's nothing like The Marvelettes who are American girls! So we never worried about any of that.'[37]

'People lift licks. It's part of the fun of being ALIVE. You hear somebody's incredible riff and you go, "Oooh". You hear a new chord somewhere and you go, "Oh my God, that's it!"'[38]

John Lennon
'I'd often carry around someone else's song in my head, and only when I'd put it down on tape ... would I consciously change it to my own melody because I knew somebody would sue me'.[39]

What is plagiarism?

As an introduction to both the legal and practical difficulties of this intruiging subject (for songwriters and pop trivialists alike), here's a comment from Pete Waterman who admits to some lighthearted banter with McCartney himself, over the years, regarding the 'sourcing' of various songwriting ideas:

[36] *Where There's A Hit There's A Writ*, BBC Radio 1, 21st February 1989.

[37] Paul added: 'The beginning of 'Here There And Everywhere' was based on The Beach Boys. It may not sound like The Beach Boys - but in our heads it was a Beach Boys beginning.'

[38] *Guitar Player*, July 1990, p. 18. Paul goes on to discuss the bass line of 'I Saw Her Standing There', famously 'borrowed' from Chuck Berry's 'I'm Talking About You': 'I'm not going to tell you I wrote the bloody thing when Chuck Berry's bass player did'!

[39] *The Playboy Interviews*, p. 134.

> 'When people read that writers "nick" they get the wrong impression. What we do is analyse a piece of music we like and ask ourselves "What is it about it that makes us feel the way we do? How do the chords work?". It's the *inspiration* that you nick, the trigger for your song. The song may feature a similar musical element but that's very different from a verbatim steal of the melody – that's plagiarism.'[40]

But just where is that 'fine line between clever and stupid' as Spinal Tap would say? It's a question that the music industry and the legal profession have wrestled with over decades of alleged plagiarism cases.

Let's make it clear immediately that there is no *clear* test – for example in terms of note- or bar-counts of overlapping notes. Nor can there be, as the following examples will demonstrate. That's not for a minute to suggest that pre-existing songs are a free-for-all, or that a writer's efforts should not be both respected by other artists or protected in a court of law. It's just that the workings of copyright law, the nature of pop music and the subjective way that individuals listen to music means that nothing is certain until the verdict is delivered in court – if you haven't already settled along the way. Given the costs of defending an action (not to mention the freezing of royalties often required), the vast majority of cases are settled out of court, with the result that guidance from case law is all too rare.

Lawyers, as well as listeners, talk in terms of 'striking similarities', and a 'substantial taking from an original work'. But just how similar do two songs have to be before it is deemed legally unacceptable? This is the first of several dilemmas, and one neatly summarised by songwriting expert and music publisher, John Braheny:

> 'A popular myth says that more than four bars need to be copied before it constitutes infringement. Not true! There are probably a lot of songs with four-bar passages that are technically the same, but they sound so much different that one would not remind you of the other. But there are other songs that are instantly recognisable in just four notes, which establish the identity of the song so strongly that using them would constitute a substantial taking.'[41]

[40] In discussion with the author, March 2000.

[41] John Braheny, *The Craft And Business Of Songwriting*, p. 137. Sometimes other guidelines on length are suggested, yet these are also invariably qualified: e.g., Citron: '*seven bars essentially the same is plagiarism* [but] the law is vague. Different judges have different interpretations.' *Songwriting*, p. 303.

The word 'substantial' itself is therefore used in a *qualitative* rather than quantitative sense – the *essence* of an original work.

So far so good, you might think – but our problems are just beginning.

The key to understanding the test for plagiarism (if not some of the verdicts over the years) is the notion that, unlike a patent where your good idea is protected, copyright does not *automatically* protect *even the novelty* of your song. Next time you hear 'your' song on the radio, hijacked by someone else, before you reach for the phone to call your lawyers, ponder the following sentence:

> 'In theory a composer may write a work identical in every way to another pre-existing work and enjoy the same copyright protection as the earlier work.'[42]

While this may indeed apply only 'in theory', it reminds us that plagiarism is an infringement of *copyright,* where an author's *exclusive* rights have been violated. Hence, even if it is demonstrated 'on the balance of probabilities' that a song has been copied, there is still another question to ask: *does that copying violate the songwriter's exclusive rights – or is it 'fair use'*? The notion of 'fair use' acknowledges the vast standardisation of the many principles that we've been discussing in this book. The reality is that vast numbers of songs over the years have made use of clichéd chord progressions.

The problems start when dealing with the single-note elements that should help us distinguish between songs. At one level, as Roger Greenaway explains, a whole range of 'rock boogie basslines and Chuck Berry licks fall into the general library of things that you can openly use' without fear of reprisal.[43]

And yet even the similarities of melody – normally the focus of a case – may not necessarily be deemed to be 'sufficiently striking'.

These principles were never better highlighted than in perhaps the most gripping plagiarism case in pop history, *Selle v. Gibb*, where the origins of The Bee Gees' smash disco hit 'How Deep Is Your Love' were called into question.

Musical analysis submitted in court found that 'Let It End', a song written some years previously by Ronald Selle, a part-time musician and

[42] M. Fletcher Reynolds, '*Selle v. Gibb* And The Forensic Analysis Of Plagiarism'; *College Music Symposium* 32 (1992).

[43] *Where There's A Hit There's A Writ*, BBC Radio 1, 21st February 1989.

antiques dealer from Illinois, featured what many would regard as 'striking similarities' in terms of overlapping notes with the contested song.

The jury was carefully shown that, of the 34 notes in the opening eight bars of 'Let It End' and 40 in the corresponding section of 'How Deep Is Your Love', as many as 24 were identical in pitch while 35 were identical in rhythm.

More poignantly, the defendants themselves weren't oblivious to the extent of the similarities. In an impromptu bout of 'name that tune' that forever epitomises the problems of perception and subjectivity, Maurice Gibb himself was asked to identify a section of music played by the plaintiff's experts. It was a defining moment when he plumped for his 'own' song, 'How Deep Is Your Love', when the extract was in fact taken from 'Theme B' of the Selle song![44]

More dramatically still, the judge controversially nullified the jury's guilty verdict given the very specific circumstances of the case *with respect to the principles of law at issue.*

The Selle song had never been commercially released, and while a demo of the song had been submitted to 14 record companies, it could not be reasonably demonstrated that The Bee Gees had had access to it before they sat down to write 'How Deep Is Your Love'. A rough tape recording of the brothers apparently working on the song at a French chateau was played in court. While not *necessarily* proof of the song's initial creation, here was at least *some* evidence of its independent genesis, whereas the prosecution was unable to provide *any* evidence that the song had, in fact, been copied.[45]

But what of the dozens of overlapping notes and rhythms themselves? Weren't they evidence enough that somehow The Bee Gees must inevitably have had access in some way? Not *in themselves*. This seems tough, especially as even changing notes and the rhythms of a work you've copied could still leave you liable for plagiarism. But again, *copying* is the issue. The burden fell on the Selle team to show that the Bee Gees' song could not have come into being without copying that of their client.

On this subject the defence made much of the fact that Selle's expert musical witness was a classical specialist and admitted to little knowledge of

[44] See 'Lawyers Play "Name That Tune" in The Bee Gees Case,' *Variety*, 23rd February 1983.

[45] Reynolds, '*Selle v. Gibb* And The Forensic Analysis Of Plagiarism'; *College Music Symposium* 32 (1992), p. 69.

pop. But should this matter? Music is music, after all. The Bee Gees' lawyers didn't think so – they claimed that it prevented the jury from being given an effective direction on the notion of 'striking similarities' in the context of this case.

Which takes us full circle, for the implication of that last comment is that the law acknowledges that similarities are part and parcel of pop. And whether they are so 'striking' as to violate exclusive rights depends on the nature of the music under discussion.

Reynolds sums it up when he says:

> 'The question of the striking similarities goes to the heart of the composition process; it asks how the defendant composer could achieve the result he did.'

Central to the issue of plagiarism is the balance of probabilities that the contentious song could not have been crafted without reference – whether consciously or subconsciously – to its prior model.

'Subconscious plagiarism' was certainly the famous verdict against George Harrison when his 1970 smash 'My Sweet Lord' was deemed too close in essence to 'He's So Fine', a 1963 hit for The Chiffons.

'He's So Fine' v. 'My Sweet Lord' – a 'fair cop'... or not?

'If you listen to George Harrison's 'My Sweet Lord' you will understand why he lost the infringement suit by the owners of "He's So Fine"', says John Braheny.[46]

Of course, The Chiffons were one of George's favourite bands from the early days, and 'He's So Fine' was a US No. 1 hit, so 'access' was not an issue in this case. But while many of us would agree, would we all necessarily rule that the striking similarities were legally unacceptable? As well as reviewing the common ground, we can also take a Devil's Advocate approach to show just a few of the complex factors that make that fine line so difficult to judge.

As George Harrison recounted not long before his death, 'the lawsuit [which I had] was all down to these two phrases. One was "Doo Doo

[46] Braheny, *The Craft And Business Of Songwriting*, p. 137. The court ruled: 'His subconscious knew it already had worked in a song his conscious did not remember . . . That is, under the law, infringement of copyright, and is no less so even though subconsciously accomplished.'; *Bright Tunes Music Corp. v. Harrisongs Music, Ltd.* 420 F.Supp. 177 (1976).

Doo", phrase A, and "Doo Doo Doo Doo Doo" was phrase B. And that constituted what they said was an infringement of a copyright.'[47]

Dealing first with Motif A, a cursory dissection of the two songs confirms a shared reliance on this simple three-note phrase restated over a repeated ii-V vamp. Both feature a three-syllable title refrain that forms a hook that follows a descending figure of notes corresponding to 5-3-2 of the major scale in the parent key (G major in the case of 'He's So Fine', and E major for 'My Sweet Lord').

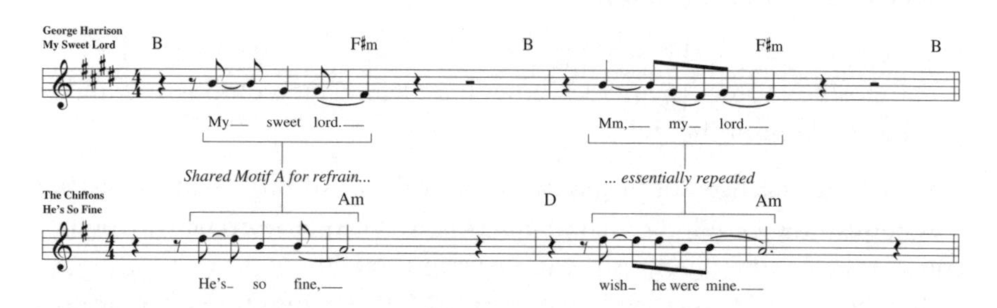

The isolated nature of this catchy phrase and the fact that it is repeated as an obvious theme in both songs stands out as a point of comparison. The broad similarity of metre and tempo (145 and 121 b.p.m., respectively), while not intrinsic to the case, *per se*, nevertheless means that, *rhythmically*, any melodic similarity in terms of pitch will be rendered more conspicuous.

However, even before turning to Phrase B, there are some observations that one can make in defence of Harrison. For a start, look at the harmony – while the test of originality naturally *tends* to focus on melody, a tune doesn't operate in isolation, and the repeated ii–V here is hardly the most novel musical premise – just one level less clichéd than a Four-Chord Turnaround.

When it comes to the melody itself, two of the three notes in the basic motif are not only strong triad tones of the two chords involved in the vamp, but they are the *roots* themselves. The point being that they are not ambitious melodic extensions, nor deft *appoggiaturas,* which one might expect to find when faced with one important element of plagiarism – establishing the 'melodic ingenuity' *of the earlier song itself.*

The only other note in the motif is the 3rd of the key (the 6th of the V chord) which serves to link the two chord tones *perhaps* with a high degree

[47] 'The Quiet One Speaks', interview with Chris Carter, *Record Collector,* No. 262, June 2001, p. 89.

of novelty. But even this note is arguably heard in a passing capacity and, one could also argue, is of less structural significance given its location ahead of the highlighted third words 'fine' and 'Lord'.

This is quite apart from the fact that The Chiffons' original motif introduces another note into the cluster on the third and fourth hearings. An interesting difference – but how significant would *you* regard it?

The issue should also be considered with regard to the context of each song *as a whole*, with all the elements that contribute to the big picture. For example, while the general structural flow of the melodic motif is downwards – so the effect in The Chiffons' song is arguably transformed by its countermelody as the insistent 'Doo-lang-do-lang-do-lang' rises from C to D (from the ♭3rd of the ii to the root of the V). Is this an integral part of the song? Or just a catchy distraction? Either way there is no obvious counterpart in 'My Sweet Lord'.

The plaintiff, of course, maintained that the similarities continued into this development 'B' section. Both tunes now highlight an ascent through 5-6-8, including a distinctive alternation between the last two pitches that forms a 'tension and release effect' as the ii-V now gives way to the tonic.

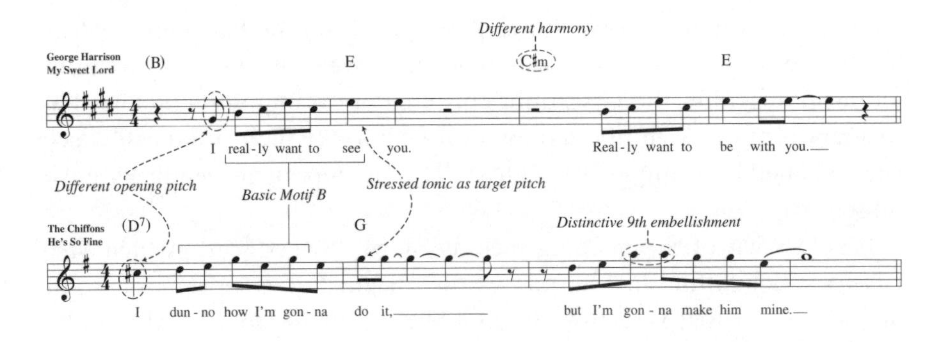

But again there are some notable differences. For a start, The Chiffons stay resolutely on the G tonic for four bars, while Harrison maintains the alternating feel of the harmony by introducing the relative minor for a 'I-vi-I-vi' alternation (a progression that we suggested was the first Beatles formula!). This more colourful harmony distances itself dramatically at the end of the section as the vi is turned into a secondary dominant to lead us back to the verse.

The Chiffons' song does no such thing. It is harmonically far more primitive, with a jump straight back to the ii of the verse after a two-beat stop at the end of the B section where there is no music at all!

As well as this re-harmonisation, the tune itself now has some notable differences. While the opening phrases of both songs ascend, the pick-ups start on different notes. The word 'I' is unfortunately the shared opener lyrically. But melodically, Harrison starts with a more considered minor third interval, as G♯ rises to B in '<u>I</u> *real*-(ly). The Chiffons go for a more impromptu, half-step approach from C♯ to D '<u>I</u> *dun*-(no). Both *target* notes are, however, the 5th of their respective keys. The main difference, however, is on the repeat of the motif, as The Chiffons take the melody up to an A note which creates a 9th *appoggiatura* over the first syllable of 'gonna'.

While this author would cite this *appoggiatura* as one of several important *distinctions* between the two works, at least one expert sees a counterpart to this very note in 'My Sweet Lord' – and therefore concludes: 'It is possible that this grace note is what pushed the court over the edge in determining infringement.'[48]

Melodic motifs aside, one cannot ignore several fundamental differences in terms of form – the number of repetitions of the motifs, the bar counts of the various sections, and the ordering of the sections themselves (intro, verse, chorus, bridge, etc). While no automatic defence against plagiarism, these are important factors. This is quite apart from the harmony – which in 'My Sweet Lord' features commendable novelty in the form of a deft modulation within the C section. This intricate bridging section, leading to a repeat of the A and B sections a tone higher (which could easily have been reached by a simple Truck Driver's cliché) represents genuinely novel substance.

Finally, what of the opening melody of 'My Sweet Lord', which finds George's delightful slide motif, whose originality is not in question, unfolding over that B section! It would be interesting to see if the verdict would have been different had this melody been *vocal* rather than instrumental. One could argue that this equally catchy, repeated motif – the first

[48] 'Particularly telling, however, is that the fourth repetition of Motif B [in 'My Sweet Lord'] includes the grace note.' Benedict Mahoney; see case summary at www.copyrightwebsite.com. Defence could counter that the only time we hear four repetitions of anything resembling Motif B on the original *All Things Must Pass* version of 'My Sweet Lord' is as the song shifts keys (at 1.52). However, the F♯ here that might possibly constitute a 9th grace note with respect to E is now part of a notably different phrase and is heard as the tonic of the new key as the song modulates up a whole step.

that is heard in the song – is a hook almost as fundamental in status as the contentious refrain itself. In that sense, the extent to which 'My Sweet Lord' relies on the 'He's So Fine' motif may still be high – but it is nevertheless reduced *vis-à-vis* the song as a whole. Will the court deny Mr Harrison the originality of arguably an equally 'substantial' portion of 'My Sweet Lord' by failing to take into account the intrinsically repetitive and self-referential nature of twentieth century pop?

If the notorious muso T.W. Adorno had been on George's legal team, he might just have swung it.

Adorno and the 'standardisation' of pop

Long before Lennon's 'rehash' quote, Adorno effectively fleshed out the very same principle of recurring formulas to create an entire theory denouncing what he saw as the 'standardisation' characterising so much popular music.

Peter Middleton summarises Adorno's thinking:

> 'Basically his argument is that all aspects of musical form – overall structure, melodic range, song-types, and harmonic progressions – depend on pre-existing formulae and norms, which have the status virtually of rules, are familiar to listeners and hence are entirely predictable.'[49]

Adorno's ideas were not merely about popular music in isolation. He saw them in a wider context within capitalist society, epitomising 'the power of the banal' that leads to social conditioning and consumer brainwashing.

The musical culprits in this conspiracy included 32-bar form, 8-bar units and the emphasis of primary triads, through to subconsciously identifiable movements in fifths and thirds. However, at the heart of his observations was the principle of *repetition* which, while hardly absent from much of the classical music he regarded as 'superior', is certainly intrinsic to all popular music.

Adorno thought in terms of different levels of recurring concepts. Firstly, repetition *within* songs: verse and chorus structures, right down to reiterating motifs in quick succession within a section ('With A Little Help

[49] Middleton, *Studying Popular Music*, p. 45.

From My Friends'), or even within a single phrase ('Good Day Sunshine'). Secondly, repetition *between* songs in the pop genre, as we have been alluding to. Familiarity, as Adorno saw it, is the essence of all pop – even if stylistic departures make for novelty *at the margin*.

Adorno would no doubt have appreciated the irony implicit in a practical 'test' for plagiarism. In couching 'substantial taking' in terms of the essence of a song, judgements paradoxically favour compositions that feature highly repetitive short, catchy melodic motifs.

'He's So Fine' is a case in point – if you ignore the stock bridge, the whole song is effectively structured around these two motifs, with hypnotic repetition of each ensuring that they do indeed constitute the *essence* of the song.[50] What else is there?

At issue here is not seven, eight or 16 bars of melody, but barely two bars in two different sections. It is only through repetition that a motif succeeds in taking on far greater status in the mind of pop listeners who, Adorno explains, crave familiarity.

This line of thinking merely reinforces the view that, as much as artists strive for (and often achieve) *degrees* of originality, there's no getting away from the principle of pop formulas. As Noel Gallagher put it rather more bluntly when confronted for the umpteenth time in the mid-nineties about the musical 'influences' behind some of his songs:

> 'There's 12 notes in a scale and 36 chords and that's the end of it. All the configurations have been done before.'[51]

What's The Story? – The Beatles, Oasis and beyond

The Oasis phenomenon provides an interesting philosophical angle to the whole debate. As the leading Brit Pop band of the nineties, they have become a favourite target, with trainspotters compiling shopping lists of musical trivia with each passing album. Magazines featuring columns with

[50] The bridge starts at 1.00 on the IV chord and ends on a II-V Imperfect cadence in time-honoured fashion.

[51] Noel Gallagher, 'Through The Past Darkly', *MOJO*, Issue 54, January 1995, p. 58.

titles like 'Noel On The Blag!' have become routine fodder, while even academics have got in on the act, penning learned papers like Derek Scott's 'What's The Copy? The Beatles And Oasis'.[52]

Yet Scott's analysis makes for sobering reading, and eventually finds far more differences than similarities between the two songwriting styles of these British pop phenomena.

'Often there is little more than an indefinable feeling that two songs share family resemblances,' is the surprising bottom line of a diligent analysis.

The whole notion that some bands are 'derivative' while others manage to escape the tag raises some interesting questions as to what we mean by 'originality' in pop. Do we really mean that a song copies another that was itself truly original? Or are we confusing harmony and melody with other elements of sound, such as *texture, instrumentation, and vocal delivery.*

This is a critical distinction – if the Oasis song 'Whatever' sounds 'Beatle-esque' it is surely because we associate the string section on the record with The Beatles in 1967 rather than the appearance of any songwriting features that are truly trademarks of The Beatles. OK, so 'Whatever' shares the same descending bass line as 'Hello Goodbye', but this 8-7-6-5 major diatonic drop dates from Bach's 'Air On A G String' and had been heard everywhere from Percy Sledge and Procol Harum through to Cheap Trick's 'I Want You To Want Me', long before Noel wrote his first song.

Similarly, culture and fashion undeniably cloud the picture. Would we really feel the same way about Oasis as Beatles clones had Noel and Liam not worn their heart on their sleeves about The Fab Four? Before you even hear the music it's tough to avoid the links: the constant soundbites in interviews, the plethora of Beatles connections in lyrics ('the long and winding road' in 'My Big Mouth'), song titles ('Wonderwall'), album titles (*Be Here Now*), and even the names of their progeny (Lennon!).

But Scott is right – the pigeonholing of the band is far more neat and predictable than the *songwriting* ever suggests. The 'Beatle-esque tune' of 'Live Forever' was questioned in the last chapter, while Scott himself

[52] 'Noel On The Blag!', *Total Guitar*, Issue 15, February 1996, pp. 38-40. Derek B. Scott,'What's The Copy? The Beatles And Oasis', School Of Music, Media and Performance, University of Salford (2000).

suggests that the melody of 'Wonderwall' is as much reminiscent of The Lovin' Spoonful's 'Summer In The City' as of any obvious 'square' Beatles melody (such as 'Things We Said Today').

Meanwhile we could suggest that Oasis's 'Go Let It Out', their first No. 1 single of the new millennium, is another case in point. Again a Beatles songwriting influence was the talk of the town – but how much of that was down to instrumentation, with just a couple of notes from the Mellotron taking us back to Strawberry Fields?

Yet, as we have mentioned previously, a more appropriate songwriting comparison would surely be with Abba's 'S.O.S', an earlier UK No. 1 that also hinges powerfully on a repeated motive which builds from IV before heading onwards and upwards through a ♭VI–♭VII–I cadence.

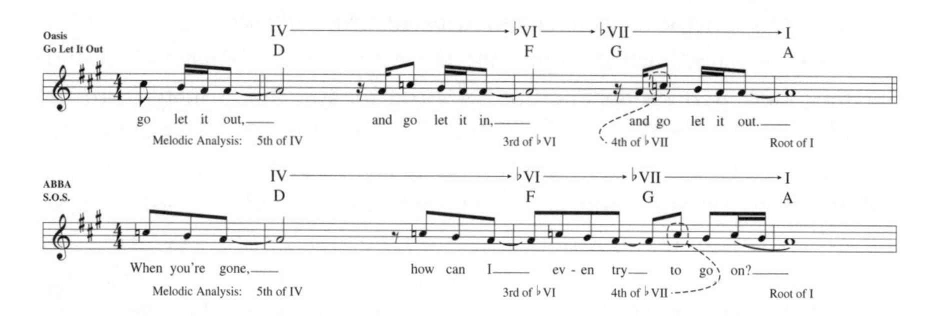

Some of the main overlaps in the melodic phrasing can be summarised as follows:

Abba and Oasis – Summary of shared chords and melody notes

	Pick-up	**Bar 1**	**Bar 2**		**Bars 3 & 4**
Chords	I	IV	♭VI	♭VII	I
Melody	9th	5th	3rd	4th	Root
'S.O.S.'	'When *you're*	*gone*, how can	*I* even try	*to* go	*on*?'
'Go Let It Out'	'Go *let* it	*out*, go let it	*in*,	*go* let it	*out*.'

But then this same smouldering rock progression was used by The Knack, as they shot to superstardom in 1979 with 'My Sharona', another gem that returns to the tonic by means of this Aeolian rock run – a run that The Beatles had used as far back as 'P. S. I Love You'. Which reminds us, weren't The Knack touted back then as 'The New Beatles'?

The tag, of course, crops up with each generation, with legions of bands accused of being 'derivative' merely for daring to venture beyond the Three-Chord Trick. But a look into the Oasis catalogue shows a consistent and impressive degree of originality in many songwriting departments, including harmonic root movement, form, melodic phrasing and ambitious modulation ploys – some of which have no counterpart in The Beatles catalogue. Indeed, The Beatles/Oasis myth is probably due as much to the fact that the Fab Five brought tonal modulation back into fashion, rekindling a fundamental practice that many have long regarded as a dying art in chart pop (certainly in the nineties – and arguably since The Beatles).

In any case, it is ironic that for all the assumed Beatles connections, the most famous allegation of Oasis 'borrowing' came in respect of 'Shakermaker', a song that allegedly copies not The Fab Four but The New Seekers.

Even then, just how guilty is Noel of adapting 'I'd Like To Teach The World To Sing'? While we might initially swear that the melodies of each opening 4-bar stanzas are identical, a close look reveals some important differences.

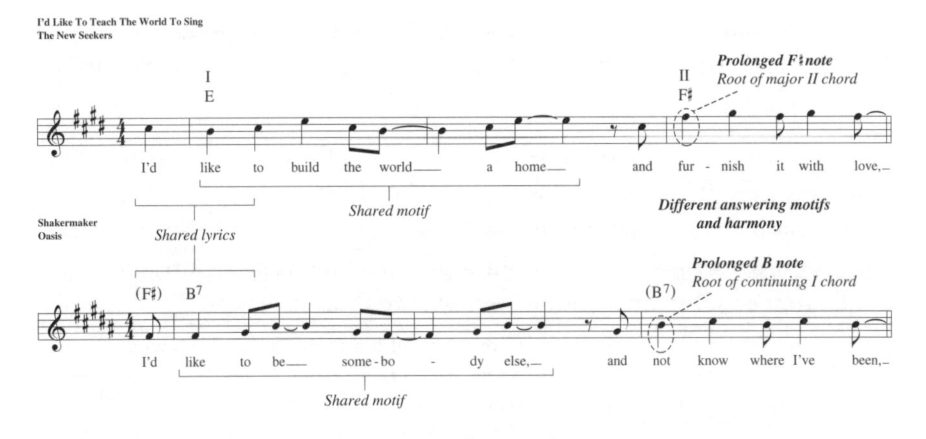

The opening motif is certainly similar – apart from the pickup, which, in 'I'd Like To Teach', works as a 6-5 in terms of the opening chord, rather than reiterating the 5th. But as early as the third bar there is a departure that is surely significant. Roger Greenaway's melody makes a point of following the harmony as the tonic lifts to a major II chord, with the tune homing in on the 3rd of the new chord on the strong first downbeat.

In stark contrast Oasis stay on the tonic, creating a less poppy, harmonically static landscape. While the melodic *rhythm* of this second phrase is identical to its 'blue-print', the tune also switches the emphasis of two of the shared pitches from downbeat to upbeat. Is this enough of a defence for plagiarism?

What plagiarism?:

'I'll just go on record here as saying that it's fuck-all to do with The New Seekers,' Noel told *Melody Maker*, before throwing the cat completely among the pigeons with another reference to his primary songwriting influence. 'Actually it's more of a rip-off of "Flying" by The Beatles than anything else, and anyway it's just twelve-bar blues!'[53]

While this brief similarity between 'Shakermaker' and 'I'd Like To Teach' didn't escape the attention of The New Seekers' lawyers, the episode demonstrates how preconceptions about borrowed music (both melody and harmony) can be hugely distorted by borrowed *lyrics*, a whole subject in its own right.[54] It also confirms a vital principle in the whole debate about plagiarism, namely that the *positioning* of an offending line within a song is crucial.

The similarity between the two opening lines is less convincing than McCartney's lift of 'All My Trials' in 'I'll Get You'. But, due to its location in the first phrase of the song, it arguably takes on the status of a 'hook line', the importance of which is summarised by copyright lawyer, Paddy Grafton-Green:

> 'In practice, the "hook line" effect is usually over-riding. If you immediately think of an existing piece of music when you hear the opening bars of something it may well constitute an infringement. If it's very recognisable, you could argue that it's very significant and therefore a "substantial taking" – however short it may be.'[55]

[53] See story in *Oasis: Supersonic Supernova* by Michael Krugman, p. 32. Meanwhile, beyond the fact that both songs repeat a one-bar motif over a three-chord sequence, the comparisons with 'Flying' are even more tenuous! The latter's distinctive motif walks up the major scale: 3rd-4th-5th-6th, with the 'grounding' of the strong major 3rd providing a very different 'direct' melodic effect than the 'Shakermaker' motive, which notably lacks either a major 3rd or a bluesy ♭3rd, while also following a very different contour.

[54] In fact, so fraught are the problems of trying to agree a test for musical plagiarism that songwriters have become preoccupied with lyrical references. The Beatles managed to upset Chuck Berry's lawyers with the 'old flat-top' lyric in 'Come Together', while Robbie Williams' 'Son Of God' line in 'I Am The Way (New York Town)' eventually fell foul, not of its immediate source, Loudon Wainwright III, but a previous inspiration – Woody Guthrie. See 'Why Can't Stars Be Original?' *Q*, Issue 165, p. 31.

[55] Paddy Grafton-Green, copyright expert at Theodore Goddard was the featured lawyer in the BBC's *Where There's A Hit There's A Writ*. Here in discussion with the author, March 2001.

The hook line effect was enough to cause many people to question the origins of 'Pure And Simple', the unfeasibly mega-selling UK No. 1 single that took the manufactured ITV *Popstars* band, Hear'Say, into the record books in March 2001.[56]

Many listeners were moved to remark that the song was reminiscent of Noel Gallagher's 'All Around The World'.[57] And strangely enough, when comparing the two songs, the major II chord that distinguished 'I'd Like To Teach The World To Sing' from 'Shakermaker' again comes into the spotlight. This time though it is unmistakably present in both songs as they plot their way through identical I-II-IV-I progressions.

There's no escaping the familiarity of the chord sequence, played at a similar tempo (76 and 82 b.p.m. respectively), with the phrasing of the two melodies also showing some notable similarities in terms of overlapping pitches and rhythms. Each uses a short eighth-note pick-up phrase to home in on a stressed tone, with the ploy continued for each chord in the sequence, to create a distinctive, repeating hook. Perhaps the only notable exception is in the third bar of 'Pure And Simple' where, on the first syllable of '*sim*-ple', the extension of a 6th represents a brief departure.

Would this be ruled plagiarism in a court of law? After all, irrespective of the issue of copying we have the notion of two songs that unfold over chord progressions that have become ingrained in pop consciousness, ever

56 The single became the fastest-selling non-charity single in chart history.

57 See 'An Oasis In The Desert Of Pop', *Evening Standard*, 23rd March 2001.

since The Beatles themselves followed the basic premise at least a couple of times in the mid-sixties.

Let's not forget that this repeated I-II-IV-I was the featured device of both 'Eight Days A Week' and 'You Won't See Me', and while such a harmonic structure may have been regarded as original four decades ago, it could understandably be perceived as up-for-grabs in the third millennium.

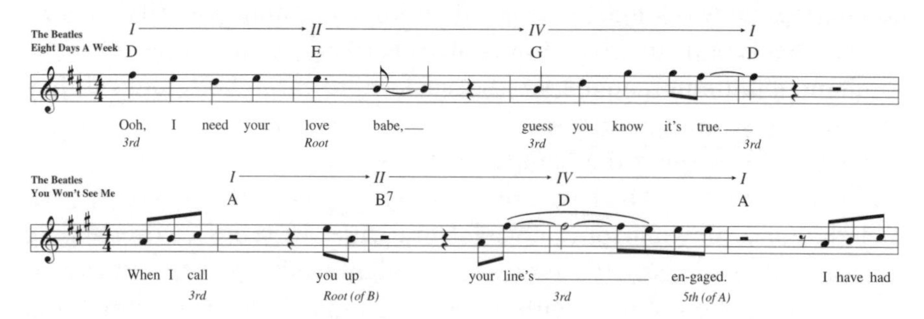

Ever since, the cycle has enjoyed a popular heritage ranging from The Faces' 1972 hit, 'Stay With Me' (another A-B-D-A verse with strong melodic chord tones), to The Beautiful South's coda of 'Closer Than Most', in 2000, and Good Charlotte's 'Lifestyles Of The Rich And Famous' (2003).

Of course melody is one of the defining elements, but remember our earlier principles, as re-stated succinctly by Gordon Williams, Head of Litigation for industry law firm Lee & Thompson:

> 'If what you claim has been ripped off is a completely derivative, formulaic, musical phrase with no real originality or melodic ingenuity, it isn't plagiarism'.[58]

If Adorno himself had been a defence lawyer today, his line would no doubt have been to suggest to the court: to what extent do *any* of these songs display 'melodic ingenuity'? For while they all differ by degrees, it is surely relevant that each of these tunes is dominated by strong 'inside' triad

[58] See 'Why Can't Rock Stars Be Original?' Q, Issue 165, June 2000, p. 32.

tones above each new chord. In fact, all but 'Eight Days A Week' are arguably characterised by short, repeated melodic fragments designed to stress these isolated notes.

Of course, the juggling of strong chord tones in a familiar chord progression is the first consideration for songwriters crafting a pop song. When you consider that there are only three triad tones for each of the three different chords in this particular pop formula, it doesn't take long to see that overlapping of stressed melodic tones is inevitable. Here are those highlighted notes in these five songs:

The Great 'I-II-IV-I' Merry-Go-Round

	Pick-up	**Bar 1**	**Bar 2**	**Bar 3**	**Bar 4**
		I	II	IV	I
'All Around The World'		Root	Root	5th	Root
	'All around the'	*'world'*	*'word'*	*'heard'*	*'day'*
'Pure & Simple'		Root	Root	6th - 5th	Root
	'Wherever you'	*'go'*	*'do'*	*'sim - ple'*	*'you'*
'Closer Than Most'		3rd	3rd	Root	Root
	'Hey'	*'hey'*	*'hey'*	*'hey'*	*'hey'*
'Eight Days A Week'		3rd	Root	3rd	Root
		'Ooh'	*'love'*	*'guess'*	*'true'*
'You Won't See Me'		3rd	3rd	3rd	5th
	'When I'	*'call'*	*'up'*	*'line's'*	*'engaged'*

So this classic songwriting premise remains commercially viable (if not cutting-edge) in the hands of today's chart-toppers. While any of the above can be paired off as more similar than the others, to what extent do we feel that any of them are *really* intrinsically different *at the margin*?

George Harrison confirmed the potential impact of small changes when he described why he took the trouble to re-record 'My Sweet Lord' for the special 2001 edition of *All Things Must Pass*:

> 'I really enjoyed singing the song again and not using those three notes in that order. That was one of the reasons I liked to do it.'[59]

[59] 'The Quiet One Speaks', *Record Collector*, No. 262, June 2001, p. 89. Expert witness Guy Protheroe volunteers: 'Motif A is still essentially the same, but Motif B is now different in terms of melodic pitches and rhythms, and also in harmony. I believe that, on balance, a court today would find that the part of 'He's So Fine' which has been copied in 'My Sweet Lord (2000)' is too brief and unsubstantive to be regarded as a "substantial part"'; in conversation with the author, September 2001.

There are indeed some complications in store when trying to identify the 'essence' of a song - 'All Around The World' may have an obvious catchy chorus (first heard at 1.09), but what about the equally catchy tunes heard subsequently over the same progression as the song builds over the course of nine minutes? We might initially swear it's the same basic melody throughout, but the top line changes in a myriad of different ways, matching the theme of the title.

Is the essence of the song that first hook? Or is it perhaps the one that's left ringing in our ears after the rousing instrumental *reprise* that recycles the same chord sequence but with a different melody!

Hence plagiarism of a melody is intrinsically harder to establish where songs feature harmonic progressions that are imbedded in our consciousness. Along with the 12-Bar Blues, Three-Chord Trick, Doo Wop and other Four Chord Turnarounds and Cycle Of Fifths movements, the I-II-IV-I is one of many familiar, winning formulas that would seem to be standard fare as pop moves into the new century. And where simple chord tones are used in basic motifs, it gets harder by the year to argue that certain melodic similarities are so striking as to suggest that even direct copying is not 'fair use'.

For all the minutiae that might swing any case, Derek Scott's conclusion with regard to The Beatles and Oasis encapsulates the whole debate:

> 'Claiming that Oasis copy The Beatles is not dissimilar to accusing Mozart of copying Haydn. The latter does not *own* the classical style even though he developed a distinctive voice within it. Oasis appear to ask: "What in The Beatles' style is a common musical language and what is The Beatles' individual articulation of that language?".'[60]

Again we are reminded that songwriting and *recording* are not the same thing. Both listening to, and judging the originality of, a piece of music is not just about analysing notes and chords from the sheet music. In practice, it is about appreciating *sounds* on a number of different levels. The demonstration of overlapping notes and chords made throughout this chapter (indeed throughout the book) merely illustrates the repetitive nature of the *mechanics* of music – not the *performance*.

The intention has never been to suggest that these are the only factors that we respond to on a finished recording. And similarly plagiarism does

[60] Scott, 'What's The Copy? The Beatles And Oasis', p. 2.

not – and should not – hinge on the similarity of particular notes but, as The Bee Gees' lawyer reminded us in *Selle v. Gibb*, on the copying of a musical *expression*.[61]

And while it is difficult to argue too vehemently with many of Adorno's observations on *composition*, he was out of touch in terms of how pop artists communicate through *performance*, *sound* and *texture*. Even Beatles expert Allan Moore, who talks in terms of 'a single harmonic language for rock, pop and soul', qualifies this by adding:

> 'That's not to deny stylistic differentiation. Merely to argue that it is chiefly played out in other domains, particularly those of rhythm, texture and production.'[62]

While the whole approach of this book emphasises the mechanics of harmony and melody, and their links to lyrical themes, they are indeed only part of the effect of the finished recording on the listener. A quick look at Philip Tagg's checklist of 'parameters of musical expression' illustrates some of the categories that academics use when exploring the nuances of pop.[63]

1. **Aspects of time**: pulse, metre/motifs
2. **Melodic aspects**: register, range, contour, timbre
3. **Orchestrational aspects**: type and number of voices, instruments and parts
4. **Aspects of tonality and texture**
5. **Dynamic aspects**: levels of sound strength and accentuation
6. **Acoustical aspects**: reverb, microphone placement, etc.
7. **Electromusical and mechanical aspects**: panning, filtering, compression, phasing, distortion, delay and mixing.

[61] Reynolds summarises Robert Osterberg's comments as follows: 'Copyright does not grant a monopoly on a particular musical expression; it only prevents another from copying that expression. Coincidental similarities, attributable to the limited number of notes in the vocabulary of popular music, provided no basis for legal redress'. *College Music Symposium*, p. 60.

[62] Allan F. Moore, 'Patterns Of Harmony', *Popular Music,* 11/1 (1992), p. 81. Moore's comment is made despite his stunningly compiled, mini-encyclopedia of pop chord progressions.

[63] Philip Tagg, 'Analysing Popular Music', *Popular Music,* pp. 47–8.

Bundle all these non-harmonic/melodic aspects into 'texture' (for the sake of argument) and it becomes clear why so many pop songs featuring nominally similar musical devices *on paper*, are so rarely connected when we finally inwardly digest the music in practice.

As The Beatles themselves remarked back in 1964, the *sound* of certain progressions that they heard on some of their favourite Buddy Holly recordings was completely altered when they attempted them with their British Beat combo slant – due principally to the choice of *instrumentation.*[64]

'Raining In My Heart' is a perfect example, with the recording that The Fabs would have encountered being dominated by a distinctly un-rock 'n' roll string arrangement. It's no wonder that the slick bridge modulation sounds very different when delivered by twin electric guitars and bass. Yet despite the instrumentation, these 8 bars represent a precursor to the groundbreaking bridge of The Beatles' 'From Me To You', as we just saw.

The role of such textural factors may be obvious, but it is highlighted again here to stress that they are crucial to our perception of individual identity when comparing any two songs.[65] Nor can we make such comparisons in isolation – would, for example, the *Bright Tunes v. George Harrison* verdict have gone the way it did had 'He's So Fine' not been covered by Jodie Miller ahead of the court case? For that version cheekily featured an arrangement that clearly adopted several stylistic features of 'My Sweet Lord' itself! Right down to a repeated slide guitar lick that sounded, for all the world, as if it had been played by a certain former Beatle!

If that might seem like a red herring, remember that Phil Spector, the producer of 'My Sweet Lord', was not only *the* US 'Girl Groups' expert but also apparently gave Ronnie Mack a hand with the writing of (wait for it) 'He's So Fine'! If the similarities of the two songs were so *objectively* striking then why didn't he, of all people, have a word in George's ear at the 1970 session?[66]

[64] See The Beatles' comments in *How To Write A Hit, Melody Maker*, 1st February 1964, p. 11.

[65] Especially with the rise of sampling, which takes the actual *recorded* music (rather than the notes on the page). Record companies often have established departments to review whether or not there is the possibility of copyright infringement as a result of musicians using other people's material in their own work. Originally taboo, sampling has now become an accepted way of making music – just as long as the artists get to share the spoils.

[66] As remarked by Roger Greenaway, *Where There's A Hit There's A Writ*, BBC Radio 1, 21st February 1989.

For all our attempts to respect artists' copyright, we can't avoid the fact that the sum total of our musical experiences will always help to shape our judgement of a piece of music. And so human perception means that plagiarism verdicts are never a sure thing. Moreover, while forensic musical dissections are typically involved in all such cases, not only are we likely to come to a conclusion by *listening* to the songs in dispute – but the law rightly instructs us to do so.

More specifically, the judge is traditionally expected to put himself into the position of the 'uneducated listener' when considering such cases, which itself raises a potential *Catch 22* situation. Expert witness Guy Protheroe explains: 'For a judge to have musical credentials can be very helpful in explaining and understanding the issues in a case, but there is the danger he might make his judgement on the strength of his own musical opinion rather than on the evidence which the witnesses and experts put before him'.

How ironic then, that the District Court Trial Judge in the 'My Sweet Lord' case, Richard Owen, should turn out to have impeccable musical credentials having composed music (including a three-part opera) and conducted orchestras!

But the final sting in the tail for George Harrison was when the judge showed that he, too, was only human. Chatting to George's lawyer after the verdict he volunteered: 'I actually rather like both songs.' To which the reply came as a *stiletto* of legal precision: 'What do you mean *both* songs? You just ruled that they are one and the same!' Rapidly backpeddling, the judge corrected himself: 'What I mean is, I like the *one* song – but with the two sets of lyrics!'[67]

Now that's more like it – as Keith Richards once said:

'There's only one song in the world – and Adam and Eve wrote it!'[68]

[67] As recounted by George Harrison himself: *Where There's A Hit There's A Writ*, BBC Radio 1, 21st February 1989. While 'My Sweet Lord' remains the ultimate case study, refer also to Harrison's 'If I Needed Someone' whose guitar riff and melody (complete with 'floaty' syncopation analysed in Chapter 14) closely resembles The Byrds' 'The Bells Of Rhymney'. But then The Byrds seem to have been chuffed that George admitted to having been inspired by their song, released in August 1965, some four months before *Rubber Soul*.

[68] *Guitar Player*, October 1993, p. 60. For an entertaining (non-technical) round-up of famous legal battles see 'Silence In Court!' by David Wells, *Record Collector*, No. 284, April 2003, pp. 83–89.

SEVENTEEN

And in The End . . . Lyrical and Tonal Movement

So, just what are the songwriting secrets of The Beatles? Why do we regard their songs as 'superior' and never seem to tire of them? What are the essential differences (if any) between John, Paul and George, as writers?

Tough questions, for sure. The conclusion at its very simplest level is that The Beatles' catalogue is dominated by songs whose lyrics complement the music (or vice versa). Hardly a revelation. But we can be far more specific, and steadily refine that obvious statement to reflect the *way* that lyrics are *highlighted through the use of complementary harmony, melody, rhythm and form.*

From the early V-I 'dominant *harmony* landing' of the BOAC jet in 'Back In The USSR', the staircase *tune* of 'Helter Skelter', the additive Balkan *rhythms* of 'Happiness Is A Warm Gun' to the inquisitive, restless song *structure* of 'Ask Me Why', you can flick to any page of this book to find a connection of some sort and a lyrical theme that encourages us to find meaning within.

A common feature that so many of the songs share at pivotal moments is that of conjuring imagery of *lyrical movement* with complementary *harmonic movement.*

The Beatles achieved this imagery through a complete encyclopaedia of musical devices, and they excelled especially at developing this principle through the use of harmony that represented *surprise.*

Lyrical movement and tonality teases – a brief reminder

It is these 'tales of the unexpected' that seem to bring so many Beatles songs to life, creating a twin effect – first, there's the 'violation of expectations' which generates a natural emotion in the listener; secondly, the corresponding lyrics draw us into the song to appreciate the semantic symbolism of movement.

In many cases the *lyrical* angle of this 'movement' is obvious from the title itself ('Here, There And Everywhere', 'I'll Be Back', 'The Long And Winding Road', 'There's A Place', 'Across The Universe') but such movement has a whole range of differing manifestations beyond physical transportation from A to B (the places not the keys!).

While this effect can occur in many ways it is perhaps most effectively illustrated by identifying *modulations* where extreme harmonic surprise gently upsets our cosy sense of *tonal place.*

Lyrical and tonal movement – a quick recap

Song	Lyrical premise (movement between)	Movement between keys
'Here, There And Everywhere'	Physical actions ('wave of her hand')	G – E minor
'Here, There And Everywhere'	Physical locations ('everywhere')	G -B♭
'Magical Mystery Tour'	Physical/drug-induced locations	E – D [-B]
'There's A Place'	Metaphoric locations	E – C♯ minor
'I'm Only Sleeping'	States of consciousness	E♭ minor – G♭ – A♭ minor
'Girl'	Character features	C minor – E♭ – F minor
'Day Tripper'	Ignorance and knowledge	E – C♯^{7}
'We Can Work It Out'	Points of view	D – B minor

There is a whole subcategory of movement in *time*. Once again, The Beatles cover all the bases: taking us through the complete spectrum of time zones, whether in the past, present or future. Readers are encouraged to explore songs such as 'Yesterday', 'The Fool On The Hill' ('day after day'), 'When I Get Home', 'Two Of Us', and 'When I'm Sixty Four' ('many years from now').

Of course, modulations need not take place only when switching between formal sections – 'Yesterday' and 'Day Tripper' show they can be highly fleeting affairs with the briefest tonicisations within a verse. The essential element is that the song succeeds in 'taking us away'.

The Beatles also showed how we can be effectively transported, or at least deliciously disorientated, by rogue harmony that disturbs our sense of *mode*. Think of the 'so far away' line in 'Things We Said Today', which emphasizes lyrical movement (another change in physical location) through a sublime B♭ in the key of A minor which takes us from the Aeolian mode to the Phrygian.

Similarly, 'Good Morning, Good Morning' paints its work/home dichotomy through lazy Mixolydian harmony that briefly gives a glimpse of a more formal Ionian dominant.

Tonality and a sense of place

When discussing tonality we have invariably referred to a sense of *place*, as if tonal centres were *physical* locations. That's because a sense of place is the key (both literally and metaphorically) to so much great songwriting emotion throughout popular music history.

Let's start with two seemingly diametrically opposed Beatles songs from different eras which nevertheless both 'work' by communicating their respective messages through subtle tonality shifts that gently disturb our sense of place.

How about a place for a secret tryst? 'Do You Want To Know A Secret' finds the innocent Fabs in a simple combo setting, skipping through themes of young love in a song that cynics might initially dismiss as a simple, inconsequential ditty.

However, such a view severely short-changes the gentle tonal novelty. Just listen to how The Beatles make us feel the relationship between the song's two subjects progressing to a logical conclusion in the bridge, thanks to the subtle drift in tonality.

'Do You Want To Know A Secret' (bridge: 1.09-1.20)

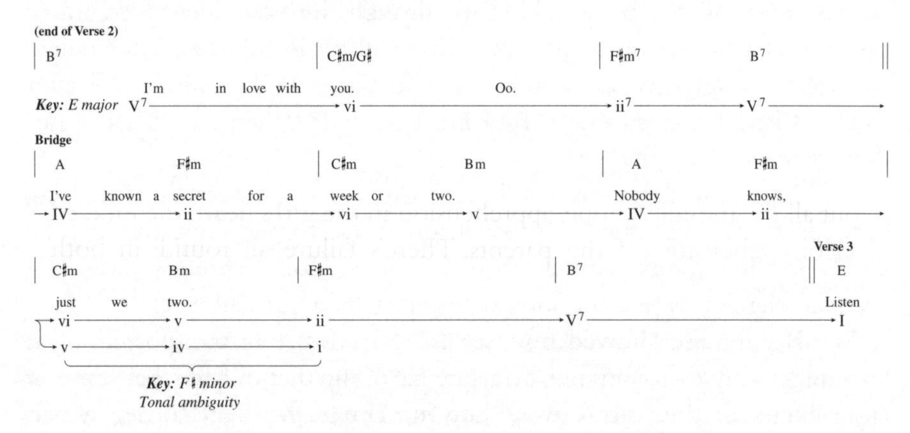

Why does this bridge feel so special in the context of the lyrics? On paper it could pass as a stock middle eight that starts on IV and returns via

V7. But a close look at the way the chords unfold confirms that there is something far more interesting at work.

It is the surreptitious use of the Bm chord – the v *minor* of the parent key of E major – that changes the entire complexion by making us feel as if we have formally moved away from the verse key of E. Yet the chord does not prolong IV harmony in the expected way, or operate as part of an obvious functional modulation to the key of the IV, as we find in those deft middles of both 'From Me To You' and 'I Want To Hold Your Hand'.

It is with this Bm chord, and the subsequent wandering root movement, that the singer leads his friend by the hand (and the listener by the ear) to an even more 'surprising place' than the key of the IV. The target is the F♯m chord, which might have been viewed as either the ii of E, or the vi of A, but which now arguably presents itself as a deliciously brief tonal centre in its own right after having been established – albeit very weakly 'v-iv-i' – with the descent from the C♯m.

We may still be on *Please Please Me*, but this very early Beatles modulation still qualifies as slick semantic movement.

Turn immediately to 'She's Leaving Home' – with a lyrical theme as serious as its elaborate multi-layered string arrangement, these two songs could surely not be farther apart. But the underlying semantic principle remains.

Perhaps of any Beatles song, 'She's Leaving Home' has been the focus of the most eloquent dissections by the most respected classically schooled Beatles masters, for the way its music matches the theme of the song (as captured fairly obviously in the title itself). The accounts of Mellers, Moore and Everett are the most compelling, with the former setting the scene by suggesting how the music:

> '*enacts* the story, conveying not merely the fact of the girl's departure but all the muddled hope, apprehension in the girl's heart, the fuddled incomprehension of the parents. There's failure all round, in both generations.'[1]

This time the music works with the lyrics on a number of levels. A swooping v minor and powerful vi are again central to the sense of disorientation. Note also how that minor dominant eventually gives way to a *major* B dominant which, primed by its own convincing ii-V

[1] *Twilight Of The Gods*, p. 93.

'She's Leaving Home'

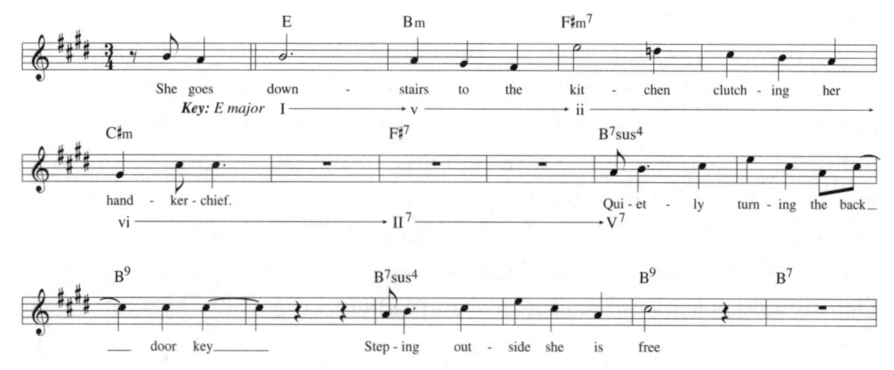

Prolonged dominant reinforces theme of 'departure'

(C♯m-F♯7) depicts the subject turning 'the back door key' and breaking 'free'. More obviously, the falling melody line takes us literally 'downstairs', complimented by the spotlighted string descent (at 0.35).

More subtly, the *harmonisation* itself, with floaty 7th extensions on 'stairs' and 'kit[chen]', later accentuated by layered 9ths in the accompaniment, reinforces the theme of insecurity as we distance ourselves from both tonal and lyrical home.

While 'She's Leaving Home' may be a Beatles masterclass in lyrical and musical meaning, this interdependence is perhaps most easily appreciated in those Beatles songs that move between more clearly defined keys. Especially those that we can genuinely regard as being structured on the premise of a 'double tonic', with all the potential for lyrical interpretation that this implies.

The Double Tonic in focus

Of course we've been encountering this ever since the Aeolian cadence of 'Not A Second Time' undermined our sense of G major – even for just those two meagre bars at the end of the form. The balance between major and relative minor was rather more evenly distributed in 'I'm Happy Just To Dance With You', 'Drive My Car' and 'We Can Work It Out', and also (if far more subtly) in the gently swaying schemes of 'And I Love Her' and 'Cry Baby Cry'.

Then there was 'Penny Lane', 'Good Day Sunshine' and 'Dr Robert', whose double tonics a whole step apart (A and B major in each case) were clearly delineated between verse and chorus. 'Mr Kite' played on the same ploy but in minor as well as, more intricately, intra-verse.

Naphtali Wagner explains why double tonic schemes, in general, work powerfully and subconsciously in a song:

> 'Oscillation between two well-defined key centres is a simple solution to a fundamental compositional problem: how to "stop time" without paralysing movement. Back and forth motion between two alternative tonics neutralises the forward march of notes and thereby stops the hands of the musical clock; the music moves and stands in place, simultaneously.'[2]

Multi-key meanderings and a forgotten McCartney classic

But why stop at two key centres? Some of the very finest Beatles songs portray multiple themes of lyrical movement with multiple tonal movement beyond two clear keys. 'Mr Kite' is one member of this advanced class, while 'Lucy In The Sky With Diamonds' also took us from the 'boat on the river' up to the glittering skies through three keys.

However, the prize for multiple tonal glory must go to what might just be McCartney's most technically accomplished pop composition. It says everything about The Beatles' boundless songwriting depth that the 24-carat gem 'Step Inside Love' was, just like 'Come And Get It', resigned to the Fabs' scrap heap. But thanks to *Anthology 3* we can finally sample this forgotten treasure in the hands of its author.

Effortlessly skipping through a variety of keys by means of a full range of cadences, here is a Beatles' modulation case study *par excellence*. It's one for the music teachers to put up on the blackboard:

'Step Inside Love' (verse 2) 0.23-0.50

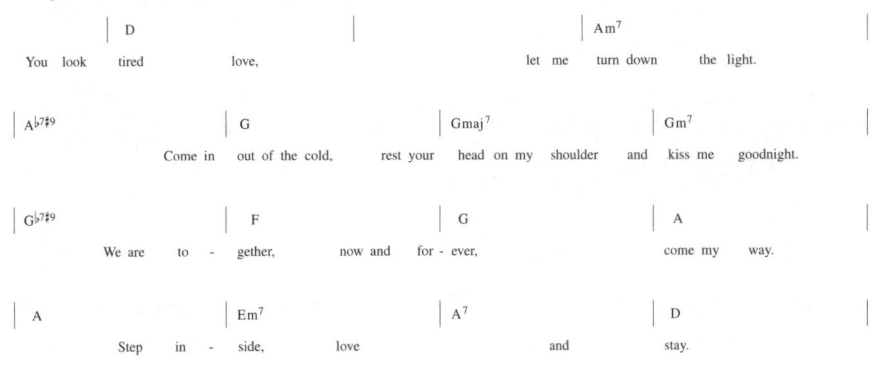

[2] 'Tonal Oscillation in the Beatles' songs', Naphtali Wagner, *Beatlestudies 3*, University of Jyvaskyla, Department of Music, Finland.

It's all over in a flash, but the following chart of the verse summarises the mechanics of McCartney's magical meanderings:

Step inside... Paul's tonal masterplan

Chords	D	Am7	A♭7♯9	G	Gm	G♭7♯9	F	G	A	Em7	A7	D
Key of D	I											
Key of G	V	ii7	♭II7	I								
Key of F					ii	♭II7	I					
Key of A							♭VI	♭VII	I			
Key of D									V	ii7	V7	I

The verse can be seen to modulate from the parent key of D, to the key of IV, on to ♭III and back to I through a driving move to V. Just take a look at the variety of devices that Paul crams into 25 seconds of music:

(0.23) 'You look tired love, let me turn down the light'

A move from D to G major from the v minor using a Tritone substitute for the expected V chord (the D7 that would have appeared in a ii-V-I). Yup, A♭7♯9 signals the return of The Gretty Chord!

(0.33) 'Rest your head on my shoulder and kiss me tonight'

G itself now drops deftly to the parallel minor, which *itself is then conceived as the ii minor of the impending F major.* Another Gretty chord, the G♭7♯9 (at 0.36), again slides down a semitone into its target.

(0.39) 'Now and forever, come my way'

A move that we can reinterpret retrospectively as ♭VI-♭VII-I in A major. The effect overall is of an exotic variation on an Imperfect cadence because A is the V of the parent key.

(0.45) 'Step inside love and stay.'

Stunningly appropriate in terms of the lyrics, the home key is retrieved by a formal ii-V-I that finally sees us back in D major ready for a chorus.

This is serious songwriting movement that sweeps us along helplessly through constantly shifting tonal and lyrical schemes. It's like a giant Cycle Of Fifths, with formal, if brief, tonicisations of various points on the dial.

MacDonald surely hits the nail on the head when he describes the song as having an 'intuitive sophistication neither Lennon nor Harrison could hope to match'.[3]

Could we finally be moving towards identifying some fundamental differences between John and Paul? 'Step Inside Love' certainly provides a glimpse of two features that explain at least some of the *perceived* differences between the two songwriters.

First is Paul's use of the intensely strong *anti-clockwise* movement around the Cycle Of Fifths.

The Cycle Of Fifths revisited – Paul's anti-clockwise tonal progression

Notice especially the *way* in which each key in 'Step Inside Love' is tonicised. The song is dominated by both the 'perfect' ii-V-I movement (as we prime the chorus), and by *substitutions* for this same ii-V-I move, using 'Tritone subs' which still feature a note that acts as a *leading note* into the new target. So while the song's tonal movement is very busy, the perceived *threat* to our emotions through thwarted cadences and other prolonged dissonances is mild.

It is this *formal way* that these *functional* modulations take place, and also the *speed* with which they occur, that gives the song an unshakeable sense of 'correctness'.

In stark contrast, the appeal of many of Lennon's finest songs lies in the very absence of such musical 'order'. 'Strawberry Fields Forever' is an ideal example with which to make the point.

'Strawberry Fields Forever' – the elusive intro

For a start, look at the way the key of the song is established.

Most songs give us our tonal bearings either instantly, with a secure tonic that grounds us, or with at least the *suggestion* of an impending tonic – think of the sudden V chord of 'Hold Me Tight' that soon homes in to I.

To understand how 'Strawberry Fields' differs from this model, let's

[3] MacDonald, *Revolution In The Head*, p. 276. The song rarely enjoys high-profile acclaim, though Teenage Fanclub's Norman Blake gave it the nod in 'The Beatles 50 Greatest Songs – All-Star Vote', *UNCUT*, Issue 50 (July 2001), p. 52.

convert the opening arpeggios to 'block chords' – something which George Martin kindly does for us in his book, *Summer Of Love*.[4]

'Strawberry Fields Forever'

Martin's transcription is actually not in the key of the original record but is consistent with the compelling work-in-progress we hear on the *Anthology 2* out-takes.

Follow the chords from left to right. At what point do we feel that the key of the song has really been established? The following table attempts to capture the way the listener is toyed with.

Taking us 'down' to the tonic – Lennon's harmonic madness

Chords	E	Emaj 7	E7	F♯m	E	D	A
							'Let me take you down...'
Key of E?	I			ii	I	♭VII	IV
Key of F♯m?	♭VII			i	♭VII	♭VI	♭III
Key of A?	V			vi	V	IV	I

The opening phrase features a melodic, chromatic descent of 8-7-♭7 (with respect to E), a ploy that forms an instantly identifiable motif in 'Mother Nature's Son'. But there, of course, the line unfolds with respect to a chord that is unequivocally the *tonic*, moving through a very similar melody which descends chromatically through natural and flattened sevenths, finally retrieving the tonic Plagally. But that's not what happens in 'Strawberry Fields'.

There's no A-Am here that could have taken us back to E major. If E feels like the tonic for the first couple of seconds, it certainly doesn't by the time the following three chords descend through F♯-E-D. What is going on? Is it a type of Aeolian progression in F♯ minor, perhaps ready to slip

[4] 'It did still need an introduction. Paul had been doodling with the chords of the verse, and he turned up a sequence of notes which were really the song's chords, but stretched in an arpeggio style'; George Martin, *Summer Of Love: The Making Of Sgt. Pepper*, p. 18.

'Mother Nature's Son'

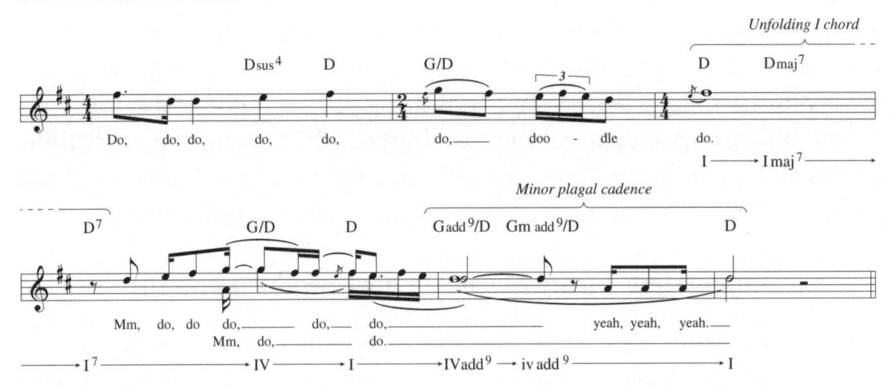

down a semitone to a C♯ dominant in a subtle reworking of John's beloved 'Runaway'?

No, this is pop as progress, with Lennon teasing us, keeping his cards close to his chest. For it is only when that D finally diverts Plagally to A major that we feel we may have found an underlying tonality in this challenging composition.

Retrospectively, this now makes those opening E chords an unfolding *dominant*, with the tonic of A actually established through a wickedly disguised V-IV-I move.

This principle of wandering, insecure tonality is developed even more powerfully throughout the rest of the song. As the intro sequence is brought back in the verse we find the tonal ambiguity reappearing, but now expertly matched by the restless lyrical theme.

'Strawberry Fields Forever' (verse 3) (2.06)

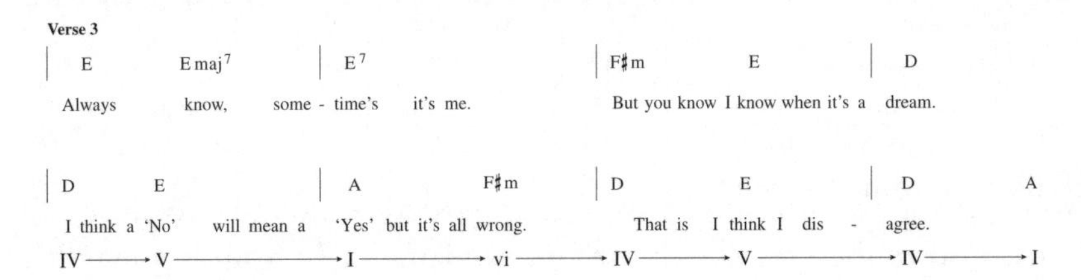

It doesn't take too much imagination to see that the song operates within an elaborate scheme of musical and lyrical meaning. There are the obvious connections of 'no' on the dominant and 'yes' on the tonic, and even a 'wrong' as we shift from an all-too-fleeting tenure on the tonic to its relative minor.

Lennon doesn't need a fancy modulation to create musical 'space' and 'place' – in fact, there is only one note from outside A major in this entire verse. Admittedly that's the D♯ that helps to unfold the E chord, and just as it does in the intro, it's the note that distorts our perception of home.

This 'thwarting of expectations' continues in the chorus, as non-diatonic chords and secondary dominants combine with chromatic melodic tension intensified through outrageous harmonisation and root movement.

'Strawberry Fields Forever' – the wandering chorus

This chorus is the musical equivalent of a Hieronymous Bosch painting, as Lennon skilfully displaces our sense of stability by means of a melody that blends triad tones with scale tones and dark chromatics to create arguably the most extreme dissonance in any Beatles song.

Of course, the lyrics, the tempo, the instrumentation and the production are all responsible for contributing to what one writer describes as the song's 'spectral desolation'.[5] Nevertheless, as the harrowing bare bones out-take of *Anthology* confirms, the song retains its essential power with just lone voice and guitar, with a stretch of pure tension so unsettling that it's worth deconstructing the harmonisation in detail.

The following chart draws attention to the mechanics of the most powerful elements – a highly select collection of notes that sit not merely 'outside' the chords but 'against' them.

'Strawberry Fields Forever' – anatomy of a dissonant melody

Lyrics	'... to	Straw	- ber	- ry	Fields	no -	thing	is	real'
Prevailing chord	Em					F♯7			
Melody note	G		A	A♯	E	G	A	A♯	E
Note relative to chord	♭3		4	♭5	Root	♭9	♭3	3	♭7
Level of dissonance	High		Extreme		Low	Extreme	High	Extreme	High

You are simply guaranteed to feel unsettled – not merely from the dissonant notes themselves – but more fundamentally from the length of time that they are left hanging.[6]

[5] *MOJO*, Issue 45, August 1997, p. 85.

[6] Notice how the second chorus becomes even more intense due to the instrumental arrangement. The F♯7 darkens considerably (at 1.05-1.09) as G is added to the stack, making for a tritone-rich F♯7♭9. However, when heard in *second inversion*, thanks to the plunging C♯ in the cello, the sound is best thought of as a lingering C♯dim7.

With this extreme range of musical surprise it's no wonder that the song has a special place in The Beatles Hall Of Fame. The accolades are hardly in short supply, with master songwriter Jim Vallance being one of many Beatle experts to pick it above all others as epitomising The Beatles' craft:

> 'It's just so "off-the-wall". It's so unstructured; and so unprecedented in its melody. And how it was strung together from two separate takes. I still marvel at that. I never get tired of it. Ever.'[7]

While (as with many Beatles songs) the overall effect is down to a multitude of factors, there's no doubt that the *basis* for the song's disturbance can be traced to a couple of essential chord changes that do not resolve as we expect.

Resolving the v minor ... a clue to John and Paul's tonal philosophies

A comparison between 'Strawberry Fields' and 'Step Inside Love' is not as daft as it might seem. Indeed, it helps to define the very different challenges of both songs. After all, both clearly feature – as their opening premise – a tonic that moves awkwardly to a borrowed v minor. This is unusual songwriting for a kick-off, and demands a closer look.

As a non-key chord in major, the 'v' immediately adds tension to *any* song.[8] The difference is in the way that the different songs *resolve* this tension.

In Paul's, fast and functionally; in John's, slow and dysfunctionally.

It's a distinction that gives us *something* to grab onto when looking for differences in their musical philosophies. Of course, the v chord is just one device, but this chord is perhaps more revealing than most. Pick any other of the harmonised major and minor chords and you can find so many equivalent treatments between John and Paul that they become meaningless as evidence for stylistic differentiation.

However, their respective use of the 'v' appears to be just a little bit different, and encourages us to probe a little further.

Take a look. 'Step Inside Love' and McCartney's earlier songs that feature the v chord, all resolve *immediately*. Either the song returns to base after a

[7] *Beatlology* magazine; Vol. 2. No.1, September/October 1999, p. 13.

[8] 'From Me To You', 'I Want To Hold Your Hand' and 'I'll Get You' remind us that this chord was one that 'always fascinated' McCartney; while 'Strawberry Fields', 'Julia' and 'Sun King' are just a few that remind us that it also interested Lennon.

fleeting dissonant gesture, or the v minor is soon intuitively understood as part of *a fulfilled functional modulation* to the key built on a root a whole step below.

The tension is *resolved* and the modulation is not *aborted*.

On the other hand, the v minor of 'Strawberry Fields Forever' does not operate in this way. Just as with the intro, the essence of the tonal game plan of the chorus is the *thwarting of expected resolutions*.

Hence the Em here does *not* move back from whence it came – or to a substitute that could be felt to be related. It moves *up* a whole step to F♯7, a chord whose 3rd degree (A♯) is the sharply dissonant ♭2 of the parent key scale itself. This, already, is something Lennon-esque.

But there's more. The F♯7 itself might just have been OK had it behaved as we *expect* secondary dominants to do. But from here, where does the song go compared to what we might predict?

This is a VI7 that most definitely does *not* tow the line. We intuitively like to hear VI7 chords resolving in a neat cycle – just as in Paul's 'Good Day Sunshine'. In 'Strawberry Fields' this would have involved moving down a fifth to B7; and from there to E7 and home to A.

Try it – there is a sense in which a gentle move to a B might have eased the harrowing mood. Yet Lennon ignores this, and even when he gets a second chance to stabilise things he persists in denying us the feeling of *tonal directionality* we crave.

In this way, 'Strawberry Fields' is the musical nemesis of 'Step Inside Love' – despite both songs hinging on a dramatic shift to v as a striking early gambit. In stark contrast to McCartney's song, 'Strawberry Fields' leaves a trail of abandoned Perfect cadences in its wake – it is a rogue's manual of maverick songwriting that sticks two fingers in the face of musical convention.

Thus, 'Strawberry Fields' epitomises the many Beatles songs – *Lennon's in particular* – that cast a dark, 'alternative' spell by jettisoning harmonic *pro*gression in favour of *re*gression. It is this sense of relative harmonic disorder that both explains the moody feel of this dysfunctional challenge and *might* explain one prototypical John v. Paul 'theory'.

'Bright' Paul and 'dark' John – origins of a myth

So many theories have been put forward down the years to explain the so-called differences between Lennon and McCartney that it would take another book to list them. They range from sociological character dissections through to analysis of their musical influences and their respective needs for communicating through songwriting. Making distinctions between the two writers has become such a part of Beatles culture that it cannot be ignored.

The following description of the rise of British pop and rock in the sixties from *The Grove Dictionary Of Music* is perhaps representative of the typical distinctions that Beatles fans tend to make:

> 'The Beatles were irrefutably the leaders: bringing together John Lennon's taste for rock 'n' roll simplicity on the one hand, aesthetic experiment on the other, and Paul McCartney's melodic inventiveness and intuitive melodic ear.'[9]

Of course the road to generalisation is paved with potholes. 'Rock 'n' roll simplicity'? Wasn't it McCartney who started his musical career by singing Little Richard songs standing on his school desk? Aesthetic experiment? Wasn't it Paul who had the penchant for Stockhausen and pioneered those seagull loops on *Revolver*?

On the other hand, surely there is no smoke without fire. Is there perhaps some objective musical justification for the stereotypical view of John as the untethered visionary of 'dark' rock 'n' roll, and Paul as the conventional, cultured craftsman of 'bright' pop songs?

The differences in the tonal ploys of 'Strawberry Fields' and 'Step Inside Love' are certainly revealing, but to expect to find them across the whole catalogue is daft. Nevertheless, we can take the essence of those findings to form a hypothesis that does at least focus on perhaps the most important element in the whole Beatles phenomenon – the kaleidoscopic *variety* of harmonic movement within The Beatles' catalogue.

The premise of the chart below is that for every 'bright' sequence in a McCartney song, we can find a related Lennon equivalent that can be heard as a darker, more tense, perhaps more 'challenging' counterpart.

It's important to note that we aren't looking for *identical* sequences from each writer, nor are we just listing 'Lennon rock' songs against 'McCartney pop' songs. That would be similarly unhelpful, and we already know that both writers have many in each category. What we are looking for is an insight into their use of *similar musical devices*, just as we saw with the

[9] *The Grove Dictionary Of Music*, IV, 1 (i): 'The British Isles: From rock & roll to rock', p. 112.

fundamentally different treatment of the borrowed v minor in 'Step Inside Love' and 'Strawberry Fields'. This (admittedly pedantic) exercise is a simple attempt to suggest that, for many of the basic musical concepts we have covered in this book, there is a Lennon *variation* heard as *relatively* more 'tense' – in some cases due to an expected resolution being flagrantly *aborted.*

'Penny Lane' and 'Strawberry Fields' have been especially emphasized as, invariably, it is these two songs that are touted as *the* pair that 'best demonstrate the quintessential differences between Lennon and McCartney'.[10]

'John v Paul' – testing the cliché 'bright v dark' theory

Paul McCartney		**John Lennon**	
More conventional		Less conventional	
More 'pop': brighter		Less 'pop': darker	
More functional		Less functional	
V-I	'Penny Lane'	V-vi	'Not A Second Time'
ii-V-I-vi	'All My Loving'	IV-V-I-vi	'Strawberry Fields'
I-vi-ii-V	'Penny Lane'	I-vi-IV-V	'Happiness Is A Warm Gun'
8-7-6-5	'Penny Lane'	8-♭7-6-5	'Lucy In the Sky With Diamonds'
Melodic leading note (7-8)	'I Will'	Flattened leading note (♭7-8)	'Good Morning, Good Morning'
Melodic 3rd over major triad	'Penny Lane'	Flattened 3rd over major triad	'Yer Blues'
iv-V-i	'Here, There And Everywhere'	iv-V-VI	'The Continuing Story Of Bungalow Bill'
IV-iv-I	'Mother Nature's Son'	ii-iv-I	'Nowhere Man'
I-vii-III7-vi	'Yesterday'	I-VII-iii	'Sexy Sadie'
v-I (=ii-V)	'Step Inside Love'	v-VI7	'Strawberry Fields'
v-ii	'She's Leaving Home'	v-VI	'Sun King'
VI7-II7	'Good Day Sunshine'	VI7-IV	'Strawberry Fields'
I-ii-iii	'Here, There And Everywhere'	i-II7- ♭VI7	'I Want You (She's So Heavy)'
♭VII-I	'For No One'	♭VII-I-VI	'Revolution
Anti-clockwise Cycle Of 5ths	'Golden Slumbers'	Clockwise Cycle Of 4ths	'Polythene Pam'

Most of us would probably agree that the McCartney examples are more satisfying in terms of their resolution, if not *necessarily* their aesthetics. In

[10] Paul Du Noyer, 'McCartney/Lennon', Q, *The Beatles: Band Of The Century* (1999 special publication) p. 96.

many cases this is explained by the use of functional harmonic movement in fifths. As such, these songs are more likely to attract adjectives like 'bright', 'happy', 'fulfilled', 'melodic' and 'pop'.

Of course, in cases where a sequence doesn't move down a fifth (as with the Plagal moves or the Aeolian ♭VII-cadence), the overall feel is darker. But, again, Paul's examples are not *as* dark as those in the Lennon column, which are in most cases obviously tougher, harder, and rockier.

On the basis of this table alone, which covers many essential and recurring moves in popular music, we would indeed be forgiven for feeling that our intuitions are borne out. Here's the theory that we might come up with.

Paul's 'Perfect' Fifths and natural sevenths – tonal 'conformity'

Paul has a more conventional approach to harmony and melody. He favours traditional, '7-8' leading note resolutions, a greater number of Perfect cadences and V-I moves in general, either for *establishing*, or *reinforcing*, a given tonality. Paul represents *functional* harmony.

We could point to his great use of chained sequences around the 'Cycle Of Fifths', specifically those sequences based mainly in the top right quartile of the circle, which has long had particular associations of emotional 'brightness'. This gives us the free-falling harmony of classics such as 'Can't Buy Me Love', 'Golden Slumbers', 'The Long And Winding Road' and, even in the naturally darker minor key, the inherent diatonic order of the verse of 'You Never Give Me Your Money'.

The principle of Paul's 'conformity' applies when making *modulations* – even when switching to a non-adjacent key centre, Paul tends to move into his targeted key centre from the V of the new tonic. 'Penny Lane' is a model example, and even when targeting the ♭III in the bridge of 'Here, There And Everywhere' Paul makes sure he slips in a dominant for just half-a-bar to ease us in. And when he needs to get out of a tight corner (e.g., to *return* to a verse tonic) he does so either with a dominant or, better still, a ii-V. Again, whether intra-verse ('That Means A Lot') or when spectacularly escaping from a bridge ('Lady Madonna').

That's not to say that strong fifths movement can't create dramatic harmonic surprise, as we can see in two classic songs that go out of their way to establish an unexpected ii-V move – 'Yesterday' and 'Here, There And Everywhere'.

This favouring of falling fifths is the single most important feature that accounts for the high degree of tonal 'order' in many of McCartney's songs. That's not to suggest that musical conformity and novel songwriting are mutually exclusive. If tonal conformity has aesthetic connotations of predictability and low emotional content, then refer to Appendix 5 to see that 'harmony descending through a Cycle Of Fifths' is one of the most emotionally effective techniques in music.

John's 'Plagal' Fourths and flattened sevenths – tonal unconformity

In stark contrast to this formal functionality, the same theory states that John Lennon's harmony is characterised by dysfunctional moves that go against the grain, starting with a greater penchant for less direct, less authoritative, and less 'classical', Plagal moves.

We've described the IV-I move as more 'rock' than 'pop' – a harmonic cadence that, despite its religious heritage, has more of an *attitude* due in part to the rocky 4-3 effect and the fact that the subdominant already contains within its triad the root of the tonic to which it is resolving.

This alone makes the move more 'droney' – easier and lazier. The contrast in sound and attitude with fifths is best appreciated in sequences that involve *clockwise* movements around the cycle. The Double Plagal cadence was just one dimension to John's love of lazy Mixolydian harmony – a mode that, of course, avoids the traditional leading note (and therefore a V7 chord) in favour of the 'subversive' flattened seventh. Intuitively, this seems to tally with what we know of John's character.

Such Plagal activity characterises many repeated cyclical progressions of course, but Lennon's finest songs seem to make a particular feature of it. In doing so he challenges the listener by weakening his sense of tonal direction. In a nutshell, it's a more uncertain ride.

This theme of tonal ambiguity is indeed a recurring feature of the Lennon classics, with John steadily building up his attack on pop convention long before the 'Strawberry Fields' peak we've just visited.

Even a seemingly gentle pop ballad like 'Girl', back on *Rubber Soul*, demonstrates his penchant for Plagal action. Here, for all the predictable use of the V chord *within* each sequence, Lennon moves us very subtly *between* sections using IV-I transitions. In doing so, he creates a slightly more ambiguous sense of tonal place, but nevertheless, one that is challenging and poignant.

Notice how Lennon avoids the dominant at each of these four crucial points.

1) A i-♭III direct jump takes him to the relative major chorus
2) An Aeolian cadence returns him to the verse,
3) After the next chorus the bridge is found by dropping the dominant B♭ major down a fourth, into F minor.
4) Finally, and best of all, we get that positively swooning A♭ chord at 1.18, which is the ♭III of F – but again *the IV of the target key* of the E♭ major chorus.

'Girl's key switches: shunning the V-I transitions

	Chorus	**Verse 2**	**Bridge**	**Chorus 3**
Lyric	'Ooh, *girl*'	'When I *think* of all'	'*She's* the kind of girl'	'Ooh *girl*'
Target	E♭ major	C minor	F minor	E♭ major
Relation to opening Cm	♭III	i	iv	♭III
Method of entry into the next key	Direct pivot (i-♭III)	Aeolian cadence (♭VII-i)	Plagal pivot (IV-i)	Plagal pivot (IV-I)
Chord change	Cm - E♭	B♭^{7}- Cm	B♭^{7}- Fm	A♭- E♭
Time	0.21	0.31	1.01	1.20

The triple key structure depicts beautifully the different moods of the subject, while the avoidance of predictable V-I tonicisations reinforces the message that her attraction lies in just such unpredictability.

Plagal shifts and 'thwarted fifths', in general, are an essential way in which The Beatles achieved astute tonality shifts and songwriting atmospherics, beyond the methods already inherent in more conventional, functioning harmony.

On occasions when Lennon did opt for a V-I transition to a new key, he would often generate the surprise 'up front' by preparing the move with a totally unexpected chord.

The bridge to 'I'm Only Sleeping' is a classic example. As with 'Girl', the song's basic double-tonic premise (E♭m verse/G♭ chorus) is supplemented with a third tonality, a bridge in the key of A♭ minor. However, rather than reaching his target directly from the departing E♭m (at 1.10), John jolts us rudely with a truly alien D♭m (at 1.14), a suitably alarming ♭vii that we only later rationalise as iv in a iv-V-i shift to A♭ minor.[11]

[11] Hammond astutely describes how such iv-V moves are a Beatles (especially Lennon) 'signature'; whether they do (as here) or do not (as in 'Strawberry Fields') go on to establish a new key centre. See '"Because" (3): Puzzles', www.beathoven.com.

John's rebellious harmony often reflects his left-field, asymmetrically phrased melodies that shun the natural leading tone in favour of modal '♭7-8' moves ('Good Morning, Good Morning') and embrace bluesy false relations of clashing 3rds ('Yer Blues'). Not for him those formal 7-8 and 2-1 cadences, as he showed as early as 'Not A Second Time' with its legendary plunge to '6'. Or so the theory goes.....

For all the important stylistic differences within these selected songs, we can't ignore the fact that the highly eclectic catalogues of both writers makes any comparison between them fraught with difficulties. And, as we should expect, for every Beatles theory – there's a counter-theory.

The counter-theory – 'bright' John, 'dark' Paul

To a great extent John and Paul – and George, too – seem to have been blessed with virtually equal facility with respect to almost all the essential musical manoeuvres that we have been covering. Whether looking at their use of substitution, secondary dominants, borrowed harmony, descending basslines, key destinations – even the diminished and tritone ploys – a vast number of the musical extracts show them matching each other, stride-for-stride, in terms of technical proficiency.

Not only that, but any of these devices can be used to tilt the song towards either functioning, or non-functioning harmony. This is especially the case when looking at McCartney's Cycle Of Fifths jaunts. OK, so he relies on it far more than Lennon, but his penchant for bum steers that thwart our expectations more than offsets much of his notional functionality. Just think of the blind alleys on 'The Long And Winding Road' and the frustrated resolutions in 'Your Mother Should Know', two songs where lengthy descending fifths define the songs.

There are simply too many exceptions in each category to devise a theory that even begins to stick. Just think of Paul's 'Magical Mystery Tour' with its leading note-free Rock descent and twin-key scheme now re-designed for lazy Plagal tonic retrieval. Paul, equally, could rock out with bluesy ♭7ths and ♭3rds ('I'm Down') and ♭7-8 Mixolydian modality ('Every Little Thing'), just as John could craft predictable ii-V-I cadences ('Tell Me Why'), structural 5-4-3-2-1 melodic pop descents ('Nowhere Man'), and use the leading note for 'local' 7-8 ascents ('I Should Have Known Better').

OK, so Chapter 14 focused more on John's rhythmic adventures - with even George Harrison seeing metric intrigue as an intrinsically Lennon-esque trait (see p. 550). A flick through the *Complete Scores* quickly firms John's love of odd metre and bar counts - but so Paul and George have their own portfolio in this regard.

We can even re-jig our table to turn the theory squarely on its head.

Paul McCartney		**John Lennon**	
Less conventional		More conventional	
Less 'pop': darker		More 'pop': brighter	
Less functional		More functional	
♭VII-I	'For No One'	V-I	'I Should Have Known Better'
IV7-V7-I7	'I'm Down'	ii-V-I	'And Your Bird Can Sing'
I-vi-IV-V	'I've Just Seen A Face'	I-vi-ii-V	'This Boy'
8-♭7-6-5	'Magical Mystery Tour'	8-7-6-5	'Real Love'
Flattened 3rds and 7ths	'Can't Buy Me Love' (verse)	Melodic 3rd and 7th leading note	'If I Fell'
I-iv-I	'That Means A Lot'	I-IV-I	'The Ballad Of John And Yoko'
ii-iv-I	'I'll Follow The Sun'	IV-iv-I	'In My Life'
i-♭VI-i	'Eleanor Rigby'	I-vi-I	'Run For Your Life'
I-♭III-IV-I	'Sgt. Pepper'	I-iii-ii-V	'Girl'
I-II-♭III-IV	'The End'	I-ii-iii-IV	'Sexy Sadie'
I7-II7	'Sgt. Pepper'	I-ii	'Don't Let Me Down'
II-♭II-i	'Things We Said Today'	ii-♭II-I	'Sexy Sadie'
I-III7	'You Never Give Me Your Money '	I-iii	'A Day In the Life'
I-i (verse/chorus)	'The Fool On The Hill'	i-I (intro/verse)	'Real Love'
I-i (mid verse)	'Penny Lane'	i-I (mid-verse)	'I'll Be Back'
Triple Plagal	'Step Inside Love' (chorus)	Double Plagal	'Dear Prudence'
I-IV-♭VII-♭III	'Lovely Rita'	II-V-I-VI	'Hello Little Girl'
Final IV-♭V	'Good Day Sunshine'	Final V-I (with '7-8')	'In My Life'

But wait a minute,'Penny Lane' as an example of the *dark* side of Paul'?! Surely there must be some mistake.After all, isn't this (at least) the one song universally regarded as the antithesis of 'Strawberry Fields', and described as 'bright and breezy as the suburban day it celebrated'?[12]

It is perhaps appropriate that this inseparable pair (which at first sight confirm the stereotypical view of the 'quintessential differences' between the two writers) challenges us to reconsider our prejudices.

Yes,'Penny Lane's double tonic structure of B major verse and A major chorus could not be further removed from the weak, wandering tonality of

[12] Paul Du Noyer, 'McCartney/Lennon', Q, *The Beatles: Band Of The Century* (1999 special publication), p. 97.

'Strawberry Fields'. Furthermore we move between these two tonal poles with military precision, using formal pivoting dominant chords. 'Very strange' and 'meanwhile back' tell us exactly where we are going, brightly illuminating the path of tonality. Moreover, this sense of predictable formality is further reinforced by the basic verse cycles hinging on I-vi-ii-V.

However, any suggestion that 'Penny Lane' in some way demonstrates McCartney's songwriting predictability, or worse, lack of ambition with respect to musical risk, is kicked completely into touch by a secret modulation that represents the dark side of 'Penny Lane'. Of all the song's twists and turns, it is perhaps the single essential element that turns it from simple nursery rhyme into deeply affecting pop masterpiece.

The dark side of 'Penny Lane'

If this author was forced at gunpoint to pick one small extract from The Beatles' catalogue to illustrate the notion of 'Quintessential Beatles surprise', it would have to be the verse harmony of 'Penny Lane'.

After all, there isn't anything much more familiar in pop than a 'I-vi-ii-V' Doo Wop cycle. Nor are there many things more *unexpected* than abandoning it – in mid-cycle – for a totally unprepared plunge to parallel minor:

'Penny Lane' (verse)

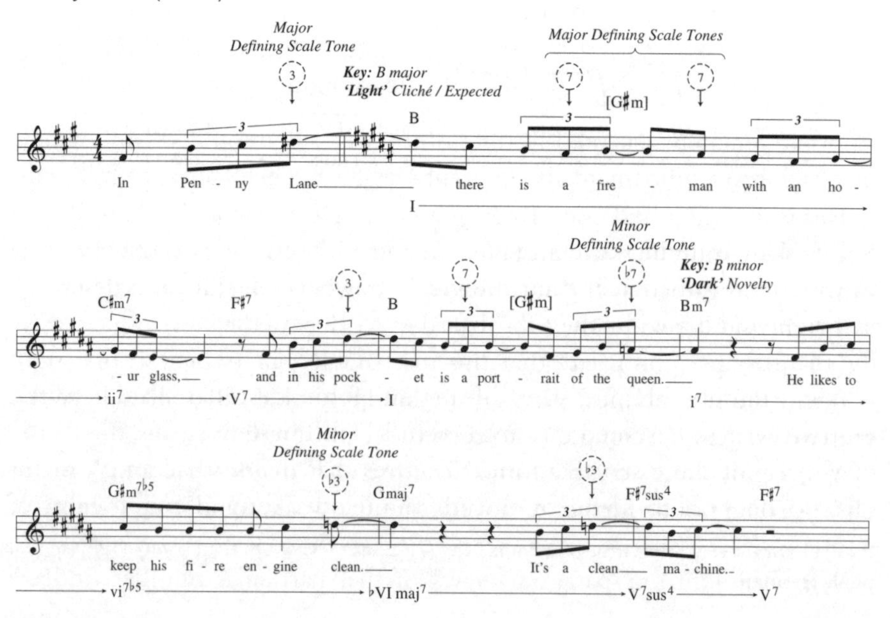

There is certainly nothing formulaic about this move, with a look at the *melodic* content on both sides of this watershed moment confirming the rationale for the harmonic strategy. In the opening bars we find major 3^{rds} and major 7^{ths} depicting the residents of 'Penny Lane' going quietly about their business. McCartney then ensures that the melody switches to both *flattened* 3^{rds} and *flattened* 7^{ths}, making us feel the full force of B minor in both melody and harmony.

To appreciate fully the 'Penny Lane' move, consider that Paul could have easily not bothered to drop to Bm, and continued the initial Doo Wop cycle for the whole eight bars. He would still have conjured a perfectly fine pop song, relying just on the chorus switch for novelty. But it is the sophistication of this highly concise minor progression that makes such a perfect foil for the opening predictability (this author's favourite moment being the G♯m7♭5 chord that glides into the slick ♭VI-V descent to F♯).

The effect is especially profound in that the ploy occurs *within* a song section. McCartney doesn't wait for a bridge or chorus to deal us this deftest *coup de grâce.*

In this crucial respect, 'Penny Lane' and 'Strawberry Fields Forever' are not as diametrically opposed as we might think, sharing the same fundamental premise of creating extreme surprise through the sudden insertion of a (as it happens, the same) non-diatonic ♭7th melody note.

John, Paul, and 'seamless' songwriting

Another generally accepted distinction between Lennon and McCartney, that each had a fundamentally different set of influences, now seems highly spurious.

Far from bringing diverse tastes to The Beatles, the strength of each member was not merely their individual *range* of musical heroes but the vast *overlap*, and a willingness to absorb quickly any disparate influences at the margin.

For example, despite the idea that John despised Paul's ballad influences, as represented by songs such as 'Till There Was You', the fact is that many of the essential musical features that define that song can be seen to be vital to some of the more melodic songs Lennon himself wrote.

Whatever John's disparaging views of that particular number (indeed

McCartney would himself brand it as 'uncool')[13], as we saw in Chapter 16, students of songwriting dismiss it at their peril when appreciating how 'sophisticated pop harmony' helped The Beatles make a fundamental transition away from 'primary triad-obsessed' fifties rock 'n' roll.

The stereotypical views of John as 'authentic rocker' and Paul as 'commercial craftsman' aren't borne out by the musical facts. Even a nominal distinction between Paul's French Chanson, Folk, Tin Pan Alley and classical leanings, on the one hand, and John's raw rock 'n' roll and R'n'B, on the other, is difficult to back up. As Tillekens points out: 'Each individual song of McCartney can be matched by a song of Lennon with almost the same musical characteristics'.[14] He goes on to cite Frith's view that the whole saga is essentially a construction of Beatles fans in the seventies 'when a cultural distinction between commercial and authentic rock music became an important criterion for good taste'.[15]

With fans needing to pigeonhole their cultural icons, and with John's songs confirmed – *lyrically* – as more, cynical, sad and introspective, so the chips fell in his favour. This seems, sociologically at least, understandable.

The conclusion of our travels is twofold. First, that for much of the catalogue it is not the musical differences but the *similarities* between John and Paul that are perhaps most astounding. However, the *way* in which *some* musical devices were *emphasized* does mean that certain pivotal compositions subliminally confirm the stereotypical view of their respective characters.[16]

By far the most interesting and meaningful differences would appear to lie in a differing attitude with respect to musical 'risk', as defined by both the *duration of dissonance* and the *conventions of tonality*.

Both writers use powerful harmonic surprise to create novelty in their songs. But Paul's skill and charm lies in how he *resolves* those dissonances *quickly* within a more *conventional tonal plan*. In contrast, John wears his heart on his sleeve, prolonging dissonances, thereby sailing close to the wind *for longer,* and often within a *highly ambiguous tonal scheme*.

[13] 'We went on from "Love Me Do" to writing deeper, much more intense things. So it was just as well that someone didn't come up to tell us how uncool "Till There Was You" was', *The Beatles Anthology*, p. 68.

[14] Ger Tillekens, 'Baroque And Folk And . . . John Lennon' (1998), www.icce.rug.nl.

[15] Simon Frith, *Performing Rites: On the Value of Popular Music* (1996), Oxford University Press.

[16] MacDonald, for example, suggests: 'The simplest reduction of the differences between Lennon and McCartney would be that the former was basically a pessimist and the latter basically an optimist. There are exceptions to this rule...'. 'A Perfect Match', *MOJO*, 1000 Days Of Beatlemania, Special Limited Edition (2002), p. 66.

McCartney instinctively sums up the whole debate when he says:

> 'If a song is really great you shouldn't really notice what's going on, like key changes or tempo changes. I like a song to be seamless. I like a trick to have happened but then I don't notice it until later, then I go, Jesus Christ! and try and work out how they did it.'[17]

Paul implicitly places a premium on moves whose magic lies in the *speed* with which they unfold and the *smoothness* of their resolution. 'Seamless' is the key word here, depicting dissonance lurking like subliminal advertising – you don't know it's there, but you bow helplessly to its power, nonetheless. Just think of the verse of 'Here, There and Everywhere', where the listener is led from light to dark – and back into the light by an invisible Pied Piper. In this way, Paul's songs tend to follow a secure path towards a tonal resolution that is *intuitively understood*.

Whether or not you share Paul's appreciation of 'seamless' songwriting, it should be becoming obvious that songs with different attitudes to the duration of dissonance work on our emotions in different ways. It is perhaps due to this 'speed factor' that we instinctively regard so many of Paul's songs as technically more musically sophisticated – however we might feel about the emotional complexity of the song as a whole.

Paradoxically, this 'seamless' philosophy might lead us to question the widespread view of McCartney as The Beatles' craftsman. Surely, it is Lennon's songs, intricately pieced together from a collection of harmonically and rhythmically diverse ideas, that bear the hallmark of craftsmanship.

'Happiness Is A Warm Gun' is the most obvious of many John examples. While that song is most expertly fused together, its charm lies in the very fact that it is obviously the product of a human hand. McCartney, on the other hand, appears to have been more blessed with the ability to pluck ready-made masterpieces from the ether, as if by magic.

While not suggesting for a moment that there is never 'toil and trouble' on McCartney's part, he has on occasion described himself as an unwitting channel for a higher power:

> 'Sometimes you don't even know if it's you who's writing it. That's the magic I'm talking about. You can't explain it … and I'm not gonna knock that'.[18]

[17] *MOJO*, Issue 81, August 2000, p. 84. Paul was actually referring to 'Here, There, And Everywhere' which he regards as 'one of my best bits of that type of craftsmanship'.

[18] *Where There's A Hit There's A Writ*, BBC Radio 1, 21st February 1989.

By contrast the magic of 'Strawberry Fields Forever' and many other Lennon songs is precisely that we *don't* intuitively receive them in such an effortless way, perhaps because they are so tonally and metrically challenging. They are more clearly the work of a human, whose flaws are essential to communicating emotion. John's gift from the Gods is perhaps the talent to conjure songs with a touch that starkly reflects his human frailty.

Tonal ambiguity – a final caveat: 'Think For Yourself'

Songs like 'Strawberry Fields' and 'Because' emerge as thought-provoking, acquired tastes, stretching the frontiers precisely *because* of the *extent* of the musical risks taken in thwarting our expectations.

Yet such an approach to songwriting does not come without a health warning, as Naphtali Wagner explains:

> 'The lack of commitment to a single tonality may free the listener from the tyranny of the tonic, However, the suppression of tonality is a dangerous game as the connection to the tonic is what gives meaning to every occurrence, and giving it up may make the music empty or incomprehensible.'[19]

In its own way this statement confirms our underlying conclusion that, in basic terms, we do indeed find meaning in music through relative movements away from, and back to, a tonic.

Perhaps, ultimately, it is the way in which The Beatles catalogue spans the complete spectrum of tonal security that is their greatest, collective, songwriting triumph. From predictable, 'safe' songs like 'All Together Now', where our home is never in doubt, to the wandering tonal teasing of 'Because' where we are ultimately denied that security, the listener is set a wide collection of tonality challenges in which to find musical and semantic meaning.

As Hammond suggests, Lennon doesn't 'need that certainty of tonic' and it is by exploiting such ambiguity that he finds new dimensions of space within which to express himself.

Perhaps most extraordinary is that even when The Beatles crossed what might be seen as acceptable limits of tonality – thereby potentially endangering our interpretation of musical meaning – their songs still

[19] 'Tonal Oscillation in the Beatles' songs', Naphtali Wagner, *Beatlestudies 3*, University of Jyvaskyla, Department of Music, Finland.

manage to captivate us by reinforcing *appropriately ambiguous* thematic images.

'Strawberry Fields' is just one of many, in this regard, with 'I Am The Walrus' being another *tour de force*. There, by cramming the song with borrowed chords, Lennon duly ensures that the line between major and minor is as unclear as the meaning of 'semolina pilchards', or an 'elementary penguin singing Hare Krishna'. It is by matching the *lyrical gobbledegook with its musical equivalent* that Lennon creates a textbook example of just how to suppress tonality without suppressing meaning.

Nor should we ever forget the way George Harrison contributed so powerfully to The Beatles' pioneering vision of challenging tonality. A perfect example is the harmonically outrageous 'Think For Yourself' – a maverick blueprint for left-field pop-rock.

Once again, the musical premise is ambiguity through extensive borrowing from parallel minor. The plundering of ♭III, ♭VI and v minor from G minor is already enough to threaten our sense of G *major*. Beyond that, the song's bizarre root movement, combined with the unusual emphasis on certain chords, ensures that we constantly question not only our perception of *mode*, but also whether G is the correct tonic in the first place.

Where is the music going? Where does it *feel* it should settle? What is the key centre, and the mode? The whole *point* is to think for yourself!

'Think For Yourself'

Intro

| G^7 | G^7 ||
I^7 →

Verse

| Am | Dm | B♭ | C |
I've got a word or two to say about the things that
→ ii → v → ♭III → IV →

| G^7 | G^7 | Am | Dm |
you do. You're telling all those lies
→ I^7 → ii → v →

| B♭ | C | G^7 | Am ||
about the good things that we can have if we close our eyes.
→ ♭III → IV → I^7 → ii →

Chorus

| C^7 | C^7 | G^7 | G^7 |
Do what you want to do, and go where you're going to.
→ IV^7 → I^7 →

| E♭/B♭ | D^7 | G^7 |
Think for yourself 'cause I won't be there with you.
→ ♭VI → V^7 → I^7

Here is a song that, rather than swaying neatly between major and its parallel minor, almost permanently *intertwines* modes and their respective harmonies. There's no neat, 'sectional' parallel key-switch – as in, say, 'Things We Said Today' and 'The Fool On The Hill, or indeed in George's own 'While My Guitar Gently Weeps' and 'I Me Mine'.

Nor is the demarcation clear within a section, as might have been identified by the formal I major and i minor tonic chords that we find in 'I'll Be Back' and 'Penny Lane', or indeed at the very end of George's 'Piggies'. That would have been too obvious.

Here the ambiguity is more unsettling in that it exists almost permanently throughout the song. Even when we get our chief, 'tonic-identifying' V-I cadence at the end of the chorus, not only is V primed by a ♭VI, but that chord is in second inversion, making us question its authority.

While the G7 intro vamp appears to ground us in G major (or G Mixolydian), the verse soon opens on a powerful Am. Are we in A Dorian – or perhaps A Aeolian, with the following move to Dm arguably heard as a stock minor iv? Yet soon the B♭ and C chords seem headed for a driving ♭VI-♭VII rock run in *D* Aeolian! Either way, George leads us around the harmonic houses before returning all too briefly to (presumably) the key centre of G, but which quickly cues another trip up the tonal garden path as if a more satisfactory resolution was being sought.

Because it stretches our sense of tonal boundaries, 'Think For Yourself' makes little sense on its own, *musically*. But, just like 'I Am The Walrus', it is the combination of this musical uncertainty with the lyrical theme that subconsciously makes perfect sense.

When distilling 'The Quintessence Of Beatology' into four musical elements, Chris Ingham nominated 'Harrison's Harmonic Gloom' as one of them, yet immediately points out the interesting paradox behind his choice:

> 'Surprisingly, of the 23 Harrison songs recorded by The Beatles, only three ('Don't Bother Me', 'While My Guitar Gently Weeps' and 'I Me Mine') take the obviously downbeat minor key as its central tonality. Elsewhere, his shadowy vision is otherwise expressed.'[20]

[20] 'Doctor Rock Dissects The Hits; No. 6', *MOJO*, Issue 24, November 1995, p. 35.

This overlapping of major and minor harmony, together with restless root movement that we saw as far back as his debut outing, 'Don't Bother Me', emerges as one of George's many secret recipes.

The tradition of surprise

Of course, tonal ambiguity can only be measured relative to our expectations and experience. We are conditioned, subconsciously, to expect certain levels of dissonance, and for that dissonance to be resolved appropriately. A songwriter can create a variety of musical and emotional effects by either granting the listener the movement that he or she 'expects', or, more interestingly, by generating the expectation of a certain move, only to thwart that expectation by then taking the song in a different direction.

It is perhaps The Beatles' appreciation of this technique of musical 'surprise' that emerges as ultimately the single most important 'secret' of all.

We can trace the heritage of this concept back to the Aeolian cadence of 'Not A Second Time' and the Interrupted cadences of 'Do You Want To Know A Secret'. Right back, in fact (for sharp-eared Beatle historians), to the cheeky ii-V-vi move on The Fabs' cover of 'The Sheik Of Araby'.[21]

Ultimately, The Beatles used the principle of the 'unexpected' to radically redefine the emotional potential of tonality and melodic phrasing within mainstream pop.

A one-word conclusion is perhaps hardly a radical conclusion with which to sum up the brilliance of Beatles songwriting. 'Surprise' has been explicit in the writings of all the leading Beatles writers down the years: from Mann, Mellers, Porter and O'Grady through to Everett, MacDonald, Tillekens and Hammond. In many cases eulogies on the 'unexpected' have provided a springboard with which to decry the dirth of this seemingly essential ingredient in so much pop songwriting in the post-Beatles era.

Certainly one of the great mysteries of popular music is the changing fashions in modulation, and the relative de-emphasis of harmony, in general (and hence – by definition – melody), in favour of more rhythmic elements. A point noted by so many contemporary writers, including Rooksby and MacDonald:

[21] Check out 'The Sheik Of Araby' on *Anthology 1*. At the end of verse 2, D7-G cadences not to the tonic C major but rises instead to Am (at 0.44 - before a brief return to G on the first beat of the following bar). As mentioned in Chapter 5, the resolution to 'home base' is therefore denied until the first bar of the next verse.

> 'Modulation can certainly be found in much popular songwriting, though noticeably less so toward the end of the 20th century, as popular music became increasingly rhythmic and devoid of harmonic colour.'[22]

> 'The dominance of harmonic, rhythmic and melodic cliché during the last decade proves that anything but the manipulation of effects technology is no longer appreciated, let alone missed.'[23]

There is indeed a sense in which there has been a cultural re-evaluation of the pop song, with electronics and rhythm appearing to enjoy a premium in the mass psyche. Ironically, this is even evident in some retrospective evaluations of The Beatles. As *Revolver* and *Sgt Pepper* top the ubiquitous 'All Time' charts, references to the band's pioneering adventures in studio trickery and instrumentation often seem to eclipse celebrations of the craft of basic songwriting.

That's not to deny that these other elements should be appreciated, but the result has been that the flood of surprise harmony that defined so much sixties songwriting has reduced to a trickle in recent decades.

And yet we do miss it, for when it does surface the cream soon rises to the top. It is not without justification that Paul Weller and Noel Gallagher – two writers who wear their Beatle influences proudly on their sleeves – are widely acknowledged as the greatest British songwriters since Lennon and McCartney.

In both cases their reputation hinges on songwriting that grasps the nettle of busy harmonic movement. Weller distanced himself from the Punk pack, almost overnight in 1978, with The Jam's third outing, *All Mod Cons*, an album whose musical charms can ultimately be attributed to the fundamental principles of chord substitution, formal modulation and tonality teasing, complete with strong semantic connections – essentially the most fundamental 'successful' songwriting principles that The Beatles enshrined.

Even a song as ostensibly humble as 'The Place I Love' captures the essence of emotional songwriting – a Three-Chord Trick suddenly, dramatically, thwarted in mid-stream by a v minor chord that takes us fleetingly to the key of the IV by means of an unexpected ii–V–I. The song's

[22] Rooksby, *How To Write Songs On Guitar*, pp. 124–5.
[23] MacDonald, *Revolution In The Head*, p. 341.

title says it all, with the lyrics deftly taking us to and from that special 'place'. Many of The Jam's other songs worked their magic through dynamic relative major/minor shifts ('Mr Clean', 'Eton Rifles', 'The Butterfly Collector') and progressively wandering key schemes ('Going Underground').

In the nineties, Oasis earned their reputation (well the songwriting one anyway) from challenging harmony, leading us by the hand from A to B, from dark to light, with compositions crammed full of supercharging secondary dominants, modulations and lashings of tonal teasing with which to match lyrical themes.

Whether it was 'Don't Look Back In Anger' with its 'I Want To Hold Your Hand'-style 'I-V-vi-III-IV' sequence, or 'Slide Away', which plays between minor and relative major (deliberately switching on the word 'away'), many Oasis songs 'work' in ways that readers should now be able to understand.

These non-Beatles references throughout are essentially designed to illustrate one fundamental point, captured in Ned Rorem's legendary observation:

> 'The unexpected is of itself no virtue but all great works seem to contain it.'[24]

Some final thoughts on genre *bending*

Paradoxically, it seems that if there is anything quintessentially Beatle-esque it is that there is really no way to pigeonhole their composing style, either collectively or as individuals. Despite the recurrence of so many basic harmonic or melodic 'skeletons', there is an extraordinary range of ways in which these were adapted to create novelty.

This variety is seen in every facet of Beatles songwriting: whether in the use of musical principles; the range of lyrical themes; and, perhaps most obviously, the musical *genres* that filled every known category. In fact, it was surely The Beatles' consistently open-minded approach to genres that was not only the secret to their own musical fulfilment, but also to the *extent* of their commercial success.

Unfeasible amounts of intuitive technical talent is only half the battle when tapping into a global psyche. To appeal to virtually every human on

[24] 'The Music Of The Beatles' by Ned Rorem; New York Review of Books, 18th January 1968; reprinted in *The Lennon Companion*, p. 99.

the planet (and, in time, perhaps a few beyond) you have to create music that spans international borders in its emotional scope.

At the simplest level this manifested itself in songs that spanned every genre-rack in the record store, from gentle ballad, folk, country, vaudeville, pop and classical, to blues, rock 'n' roll, rock, pop rock, heavy rock and heavy metal. This alone ensures that their catalogue is the ultimate antidote to musical snobbery. What other artist can span the ultimate extremes of 'All Together Now' and 'Revolution 9'?

Beyond such obvious musical distinctions, individual songs were intrinsically structured for mass appeal. The 'dark side' of 'Penny Lane' is one example of how a single song can deliver 'something for everyone', here moving from jaunty major nursery rhyme to moving minor-key challenge in the space of eight short bars of music.

This sophisticated diversity saw Lennon, McCartney and Harrison exploit the flavour of all 12 notes in ways that went far beyond the already ambitious formal modulation between *diatonic* major and minor song sections. They created songs that redefined our cosy scalar expectations by having major sounds that were not always Ionian, and minor ones that were not always Aeolian. Hence, in addition to the tonally challenged masterpieces, there were the *modally* ambitious ones to marvel at.

The blending of primal blues and sweeter major scales, on songs like 'Can't Buy Me Love', was an early indication of the possibilities that this technique would open up, ultimately leading to elaborate combinations, such as the parallel play of a Mixolydian verse and a Dorian bridge in 'Norwegian Wood'.

In particular, it was this special deception through unexpected modality that saw George take his songs to places we didn't know existed. The Mixolydian Eastern songs, and the Lydian action of 'Blue Jay Way' may stand out as obviously exotic, but we also saw 'Think For Yourself' effectively fuse Mixolydian, Aeolian and fleeting shades of Dorian.

Riley says it all when he talks about the 'odd relief' that 'Think For Yourself' provides on *Rubber Soul*. For that oxymoronic expression quirkily captures the fascination of so many Beatles songs – the unexpected, the tonal teasing, the flow of tension and resolution, the semantic challenge, and the final processing of the synapses which, in the end, delivers the emotion of a song to our souls.

As we reach the end of this particular long and winding road, it seems appropriate to wrap-up our discussions with a look at 'The End' itself.

The *Abbey Road* climax sums up perfectly The Beatles' utterly eclectic combination of the three essential musical themes of genre, mode and tonality.

'The End' – where raw blues meets celestial voice-leading

The emphasis here is on the striking contrast associated with the modulation of the final section of the song, which follows the thrilling electric blues guitar playing of John, Paul and George.

The contrast of tones and phrasing between the three guitarists takes in a spectrum of feels and emotions as they trade in rotation over a stock I7-IV7 change in the key of A. In doing so they draw on the full blues vocabulary, mixing major and minor pentatonic scales with slides, doublestops, repeated notes, low-bass string runs and wailing bends that reach for the sky as surely as the great Albert King.

After this primal emotion, the temporary denouement is palpable as we hear the piano at 1.29, which is about to build to a final *crescendo*, though the harmony that follows could not be further removed from the predictability of a tonic-subdominant alternating blues scheme.

Once again, the sparse texture belies the content of the following few bars which are crammed full of clever voice-leading and tonal disturbance.

'The End' (final modulation)

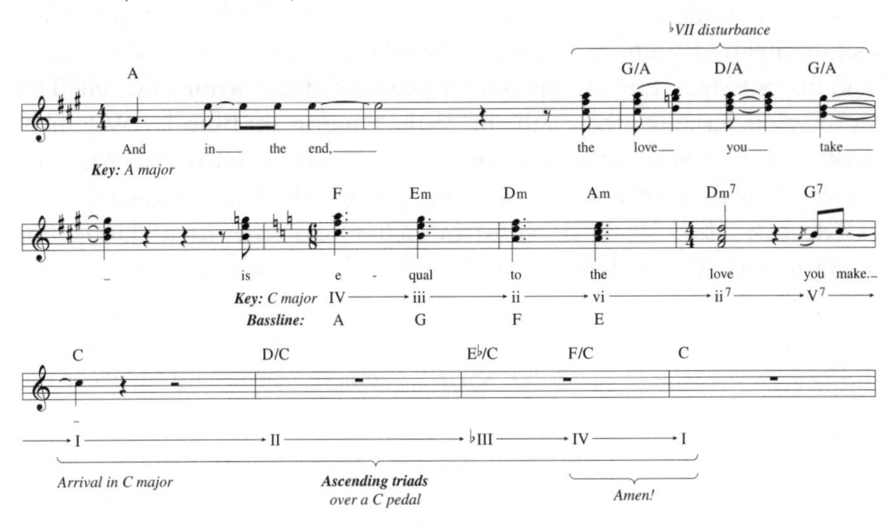

The first twist is the G/A chord that emerges, appropriately on the word 'love', and which gently destabilises our sense of A major by adding a ♭VII chord above a tonic pedal.[25] However, when used in conjunction with the D note in the key of A, the effect is of an implied pull to D major by means of a combination V/IV cadence.

The tonic is stubbornly maintained throughout this brief upper harmony buffeting, but it starts to crumble at 1.40. Here McCartney slips in a musical tranquilliser in the form of an F chord which sets the modulation in train, while a shift from 'straight four' to 'triplet feel' flags the impending highlight with rhythmic novelty.

The intricacy of the harmonic modulation is worth marvelling at. In essence, all we have is a move from A to C major. The F chord 'sows the seeds of tonal doubt' the instant it appears in both harmony and melody (on the first syllable of 'equal'), where it threatens the dominance of the F♯ of the departing key.

The chord could happily have made a direct Plagal connection to C but instead we get almost a complete diatonic unfolding of the harmonised C major scale. So, too, Paul could have descended stepwise all the way to I, but the effective backtracking to vi sets up the tonic with a strong, classical Cycle Of Fifths feeling, with the heavens opening as the new tonality is ushered in on 'make'.

In this way 'The End' achieves the most blissful of resolutions, with various funky theories put forward to explain the symbolism of the words and music. The most elaborate suggest that by switching keys on the word 'equal', the modulation captures the two halves of the A - C tonal riddle that dominates the entire *Abbey Road* medley.[26]

C major may not be the opening key centre of the medley, but the final modulation certainly defuses the dramatic, tense ascent from C to A which took us to the 'sweet dream' section of 'You Never Give Me Your Money'. Reconcile it yourself, with the snapshot in Appendix 4 of the tonal scheme of side 2 of *Abbey Road* which forms such an essential rite of passage for the serious Beatles student.

[25] This chord harks back to those tethered, ♭VII/I 'slash' constructions of *Rubber Soul, Revolver* and *Magical Mystery Tour.*

[26] Everett takes this on several stages to suggest how the song is reconciling 'the self gratifying love' of A major ('the love you take'), with the generous kind ('the love you make') represented by C major; *The Beatles As Musicians: Revolver Through The Anthology*, p. 271.

But that's not the end of 'The End'. We still have that elegant stretch of ascending triads which creates an almost spiritual climax to the entire album.

'The End' – the pedal ascent

The modulation is already complete and the song could easily have been brought to a close without further ado. But the final bars contain powerful ascending harmony that serves to celebrate the technical and emotional quality of the whole move. Here we stay essentially rooted in C, with the tonic grounding us, providing a pedal above which chords create a gentle walk before finally coming to rest.

The comparison with 'one sweet dream' is again inescapable, as we rise with another I-II-♭III progression that lends a mild rock touch to what has now become a grand textural landscape. However, the final IV-I cadence represents a point of difference while subconsciously providing deep thematic unity. For while it seems like a lifetime, the strains of the unrelenting I7-IV7 blues jam have barely drifted away, and the choice of final cadence helps the listener instinctively reconcile two totally different genres of music within the same track.

In the very end, as all Beatles fans already know from the song's title, this quasi-religious Plagal emotion requires no more than a one-word interpretation – Amen.

CODA

'She Loves You' – Anatomy of a Perfect Pop Song

Just as 'Her Majesty' creeps up on 'The End', questioning the grand scheme of *Abbey Road*, so this coda is a reminder that The Beatles' musical legacy is full of twists that challenge our preconceptions.

The assumption that the group's songwriting development can be described as a neat, chronological evolution of technique and musical sophistication has been challenged throughout this book. There is a vast overlap of common ground that exists between songs of different eras, when stripped to their basics, with many deft devices of later years directly traceable to a whole selection of early experiments. Indeed the popular description of the mid to late period as the 'experimental' years threatens to detract from the harmonic and melodic experiments that first set The Beatles apart.

In fact, if this author had to pick one Beatles song above all others, it would be a certain 1963 classic that, so far, has been conspicuous by its absence.

'She Loves You' is a powerful sixties landmark that both sparked and epitomised truly unhinged Beatlemania, and has become universally acknowledged over the years as *the* defining symbol of 'pop music' itself.

The evergreen themes of innocent young love, trepidation and expectancy found in the purest pop of any generation have never been captured so concisely. Meanwhile, the music itself set a new benchmark as The Beatles truly distanced themselves from the pop clichés and three-chord rock 'n' roll that went before.

More than any other in their prodigious catalogue, the song encapsulates John and Paul's trademark talent for injecting tried-and-tested formulas with sudden, striking musical surprise at every turn. 'She Loves You' forms a mini-encyclopaedia of pop devices, and as such, is the only song in this book that we will analyse from beginning to end (all 2.17 of it).

The structure forms a rollercoaster ride that can nominally be split into three sections: A (verse), B (pre-chorus) and C (chorus).

The C section – the intro variation

The song opens with Ringo's distinctive drum roll – the tom-tom delivers a primal, syncopated edge, pitting sixteenth-notes against eighths in a rhythm that, if sampled, slowed down and looped, would form a trance-inducing motif at a Voodoo ritual.

Then immediately a driving chorus hits us between the eyes before we've even started.[1]

These eight bars provide their own instant guide to The Beatles' tools of the trade: novelty in chord substitution, root movement and inner-harmony voice-leading, which all combine to harmonise a perfectly formed, symmetrical motif.

'She Loves You': opening chorus (0.01-0.10)

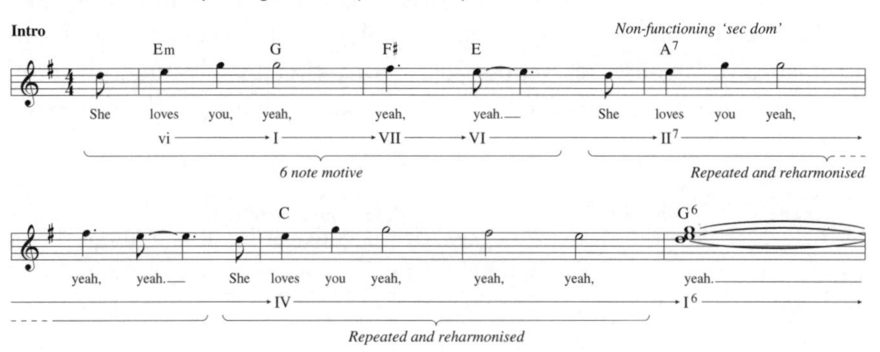

The shape of the six repeated melody notes even looks good on paper while, when matched with the lyrics, the line unfolds with an intuitive 'call-and-response' structure.

The sophistication of the harmony is light years removed from traditional Three-Chord Tricks of blues and rock 'n' roll. The Em chord ensures some gentle tonal ambiguity, creating momentum as it gravitates towards

[1] The principle of moving the chorus to the start of the song was also used in later songs like 'Can't Buy Me Love', 'It Won't Be Long', 'Any Time At All' and 'Help!'.

the brief resting point of G major, which finally emerges as the tonic in bars 7-8.[2]

Note too the unusual II7 chord that moves, not to V7 as we would have expected from the rock 'n' roll era, but on to IV. This non-functioning secondary dominant creates novel inner-harmony voice-leading – the maverick major 3rd of the A7 (the C♯ from outside the key of G) drops chromatically into the IV chord and then onwards into the 3rd of the tonic. At the same time, the *root* movement of A-to-C delivers a rocky minor third interval that brings some steel to the pure pop I-II-IV-I progression soon to feature in songs like 'Eight Days A Week' and 'You Won't See Me'.

'Yeah, Yeah, Yeah!' – reharmonisation of a motif

The deceptive simplicity of the G-F♯-E line in the 'yeah, yeah yeah' refrain can now be appreciated in its harmonic context. In fact, the highly active harmony discourages elaborate melodic development, as this motif is successively re-harmonised over different chord sequences.[3]

Here's a chart of the implied sonorities as the chords shift. Note how the F♯ (the second 'yeah') appears as a colourful non-chord tone. It sits chromatically 'against' its supporting chord thereby creating powerful dissonance that is then resolved as a chord tone resumes (on the following 'yeah').

Time	**Chord**	**Three-note motif (x3)**		
		'Yeah!'	'Yeah!'	'Yeah!'
		G	F♯	E
0.02	Em	♭3	2	1
0.05	A7	♭7	6	5
0.08	C	5	♯4	3
		Chord tones	**'colour'**	Chord tones

[2] As in later classics like 'It Won't Be Long', 'I'm Happy Just To Dance With You' and 'Any Time At All', the trick of starting on a vi, relative to an impending major tonic, almost *guarantees* driving movement.

[3] Everett describes how the reharmonisation of the G-F♯-E line is the musical manifestation of the singer trying 'to get his simple message across in as many ways as possible, by exploring the common-tone functions of G and E'; 'Voice Leading and Harmony as Expressive Devices in the Early Music of The Beatles: "She Loves You"'; *College Music Symposium*, 32, p. 27.

The G added sixth – the first encounter

The exception to this pattern of resolving dissonance is the final 'yeah', where we first find the legendary G added 6th which concludes the song so effectively.

Despite the obvious melodic tension, it's worth appreciating that there *is* an element of resolution here, as the E note in the main motif does lead formally to D, the 5th of the G chord - however, this 'departing' E note is simultaneously *replaced* by another, now left to hang as the floating sixth.[4]

The original controversy between The Beatles and George Martin over the use of the chord is an endearing part of Beatles folklore. 'You can't do the end of course, that sixth, it's too like the Andrews Sisters!', McCartney remembers George Martin saying when he first rehearsed it for him. But soon the producer was on side – 'You're right. It's great'.[5]

It is this mix of intricate reharmonisation and ambitious sound gesture that not only lets The Beatles get away with the mundanity of the 'yeah, yeah, yeah' lyric, but goes some way to explaining how this line has become enshrined as the motto of pop music.[6]

Finally, we must mention George's Chuck Berry-style doublestops in fourths, delivered on the Gretsch Country Gentleman, which take us into the verse. The lick here creates essential variety within the song by undermining the melodic *major* seventh of G with the bluesy false relations of F *natural* and B♭ (respectively, the ♭7th and ♭3rd of G).[7]

Incredibly, the result is that, in the first 12 seconds of the song, The Beatles have managed to use 11 of the 12 notes in music – something that most free-jazzers would be pushed to do.

The verse – A section: 'You think you lost your love'

As we start the verse, The Beatles once again depart subtly from cliché by

[4] McCartney refers to the song's signature sixth as 'that tight little sixth cluster', with the 5th and 6th scale degrees appearing a narrow *second* interval apart.

[5] Mark Lewisohn, 'The Paul McCartney Interview', *The Beatles Complete Recording Sessions*, p. 10. It's worth noting that as an instrumental sound the final 6th chord litters the playing of early rock 'n' roll guitarists like Chuck Berry, Scotty Moore and James Burton, while as a purely vocal gesture, it was a common Doo Wop closer.

[6] According to Schaffner, Beatles music was known as 'yeah, yeah, yeah music' in Southeast Asia by government decree; *The Beatles Forever* (1978) [via Dowlding: *Beatlesongs*, p. 45].

[7] Listen out for the lick at 0.11 and 1.14 where it is heard over a G chord; the same lick is heard once in the song over D7 at 0.37 at the end of the B section.

transforming the standard I-vi-IV-V, Four-Chord Turnaround, replacing the third chord, the subdominant, with iii minor.

As Askold Buk explains: 'Though this may seem like a small change, the Bm chord adds depth and a subtle melancholy quality to what could have been a stock change'.[8]

The A section – the verse (0.13)

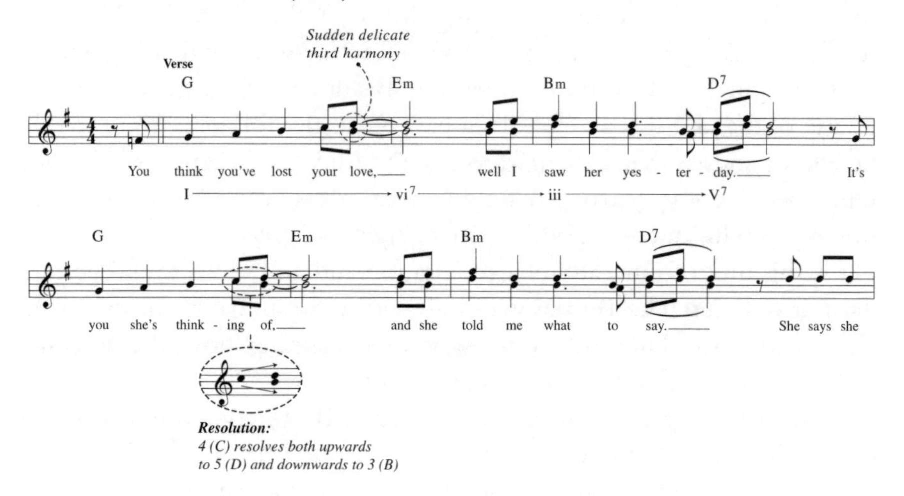

As we know, the iii chord can have huge melodic impact, introducing the sound of the natural 7th of the key (F♯ is the 5th of Bm). The Beatles grab this opportunity with both hands, making F♯ the poignant target for '*saw* her yester-day-*ee*-ay'. The way that this 7th stands alone, without upward resolution to the G tonic, is not the only highlight of this line of melody.

The 'love' harmony – the stylish third

The tune opens by climbing naturally up the scale, but perhaps the neatest touch is in the way the harmony vocal enters at 0.15 to embellish the word 'love', a third above, creating two different – but complementary – points of resolution.[9]

[8] Askold Buk, 'Magical Mystery Tour', *Guitar World*, February 1994, p. 59. Check out the chorus of David Bowie's 'Starman' to hear a classic post-'She Loves You' outing for the I-vi-iii-V progression.

[9] Most cleverly, this combination vocal harmony of G and B retains a strong sense of the opening G triad and dilutes our feeling of Em to which bass and guitars have now moved. In this way The Beatles keep their powder dry for the later gripping plunge to 'bad'.

John's lead comes to a temporary rest by hitting the dissonant 4th (the C note on 'your') and bouncing back *down* a semitone to B. However, the new voice provides contrast by effectively continuing the *ascent* of the tune to D, the 5th of the key and the ♭7th in terms of the Em to which the guitars shift. The combined effect is of rest and momentum at the same time, reasonably appropriate in the context of the lyric.

The effect is all the more memorable because the lead vocal is *not* tracked throughout the first part of the verse (as, say, in 'Baby's In Black').

The pre-chorus – the B section: 'yes, she loves *you'*

After repeating this hybrid Four-Chord Turnaround, the next eight-bar section then delivers another variation on 'I-vi-IV-V' – one that deviates by only one note from this standard blueprint.

The B section – the pre-chorus (0.26)

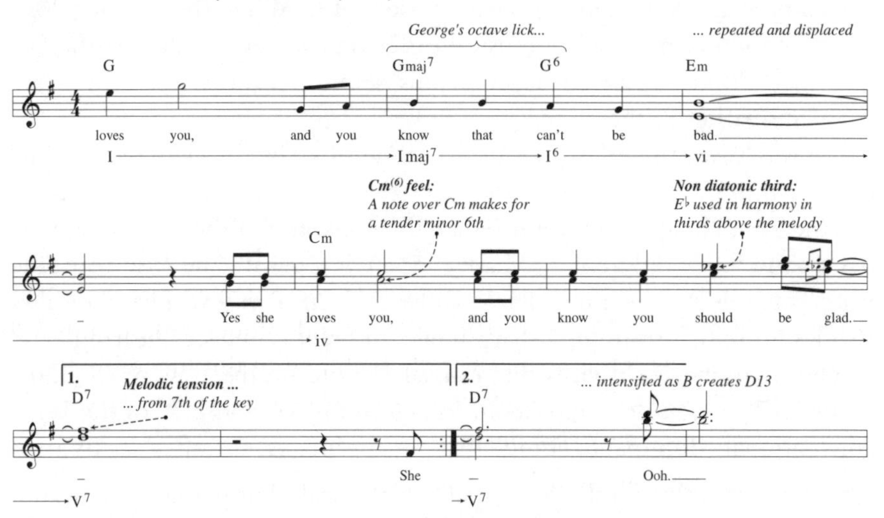

We start with a now strident drop to Em, made all the more poignant by the dark E note on 'bad', and harmonised by a jarring open fifth. All in appropriate contrast to the earlier mellow treatment of 'love'.

The plunge to Em is reinforced by the descending guitar line that we hear twice in the first four bars. Most obviously in the jangly lead descent at 0.30 (which will reappear at 1.33), but also in the preceding bar where implied Gmaj7 and G6 chords are just discernible as the two guitars develop a different rhythmic texture (first at 0.26). This is a reminder that the essential G-F♯-E motif is a recurring thread throughout the song – and isn't just confined to the vocal 'yeah, yeah, yeah' mantra.

Following this Em (at 0.32) is a C *minor* chord that, if pressed, this author would nominate as The Greatest Beatles Chord Change Ever. Of all the many novel touches that make 'She Loves You' so special, the lowering of the third degree on the subdominant at this point is arguably the most deeply emotionally effective of all.

That's not to say that this cycle I-vi-iv-V was in any way 'invented' or 'discovered' by The Beatles, or that it is particularly unique. It can be heard on several pre-Beatles songs in mainstream pop, most effectively in Santo & Johnny's delicate steel guitar instrumental, 'Sleepwalk'.[10]

It's a simple but very special progression that works every time. Indeed, The Beatles had already used the vi-iv switch themselves in 'Ask Me Why' back on *Please Please Me*. However, the effect here is especially striking given the context. We have already heard a C *major* chord containing an E *natural* note, as we would expect in the key of G. While the E♭ note alone creates contrast, the sense of musical order is positively trashed by the fact that this Cm is delivered a precarious semitone above the Bm heard moments earlier in the verse.[11]

It is this 'thwarting of expectations' – intensified by the clash of roots and tones within such a short space of time – that creates the magical effect that lifts the soul. The lyrics may just restate the message, but the messenger now has a completely different emphasis – don't you get it? She *loves* you! Add in the melody note – a mellow 6th above the Cm – and you have another Beatles hook that prompts a sharp intake of breath on every hearing.

The harmony vocal visits that crucial E♭ note on the way up to F♯, the melodic 7th which now appears in its rightful place as the 3rd of the D7, a conventional dominant chord that re-orientates us after a two-bar excursion that borrows iv from the parallel minor.

The 'she loves you' revelation is rammed home not only by the lyrics, harmony, melody and complementary guitar lick but also, far more subliminally, by the switch from a 1-bar to a 2-bar harmonic pattern – a

[10] The same powerful cycle can be found in many post-'She Loves You' hits, ranging from Roy Orbison's 'Pretty Woman' to Robbie Williams' 'Old Before I Die' (both songs use A-F♯m-Dm7-E7).

[11] MacDonald describes the 'violent push' to C minor, *Revolution In The Head*, p. 75; while Pollack emphasizes the false relations of Eb and E natural, 'Notes on … Series' no. 5, 2000. *The 'Official' rec.music.beatles Home Page*, www.recmusicbeatles.com.

slower rate of change that perhaps depicts the recipient of the song sitting down and taking it all in.

The 'pre-chorus' description (used out of habit and as a convention among many Beatles fans) is perhaps a misnomer as, at this point in the song, we are actually denied the chorus. We return to verse 2 with George's blues lick now heard over the closing D7.

The A and B sections are then repeated, happily delivering their self-contained interest a further time while subliminally making us crave the chorus all the more.

Notice that it is only on the repeat of the pre-chorus that we get that trademark Beatles 'ooh', here on a D7 supercharged by that held B harmony. The gesture was resisted at 0.37, but at 1.02 it heralds the chorus with a symbolic fanfare introducing another hearing of the awesome intro.

The C section – the chorus variation

In fact the intro is not simply the song's chorus brought to the top of the tune, as is often assumed. As with 'Help!' the intro is a unique section, and while certain elements reappear later we never hear it the same way again, either lyrically or musically.

Not content with the already extreme novelty of the intro (a sequence that would have made a fine enough chorus at this point), The Beatles now jettison it in mid-stream as the message is redelivered with its all-important punchline – it's not any old love, it's 'a love *like that*'.

Chorus at (1.04)

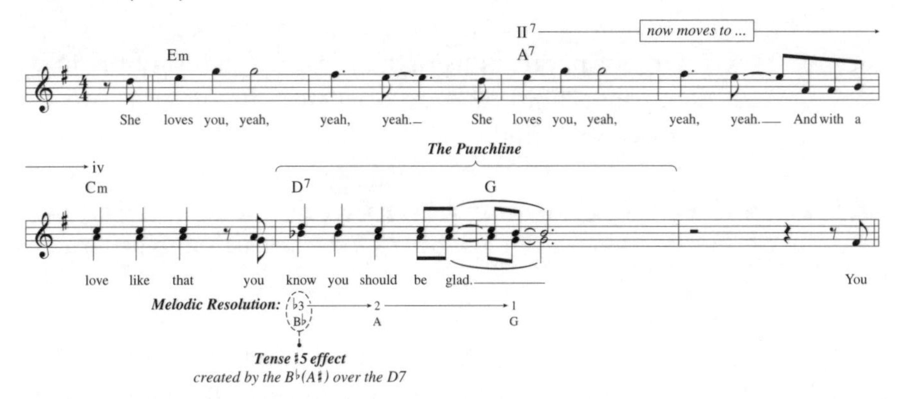

The Beatles confirm this lyrical change of emphasis by following A7 not with IV (as we found in the intro) but by the hallowed Cm, the iv heard in the pre-chorus. This shift is arguably even more outrageous as, in addition to the juxtaposition of E and E♭, the C♯ to C dichotomy now occurs *in consecutive chords*. Played in a continuous sequence the change would probably be too much, but by punctuating it with those pounding teenage heartbeat 'stops' at 1.10, the result is a musical and semantic climax.

This 'borrowed' iv then moves on to V, leading the song to a cadence on G where, at last, the listener can take a breather.

However, we can't leave this cadence without focusing on the extreme melodic subtlety of the B♭ pitch on the word 'know'. Play it slowly on an acoustic guitar in a darkened room to appreciate just how good it is.

A lesser songwriter would surely have constructed a melody that descended from the C (for a straight D7), or perhaps the B (for a D6). But the effective D7♯5 that The Beatles give us here provides an altered jazz tinge which reminds us that 'She Loves You' is most certainly not breezy, unchallenging pop.

We're still only 1.13 into the song – how much better can it get? Not much it would seem, given that we've now covered the mechanics of each of the A, B and C sections that make up the song. But still The Beatles haven't used up all their tricks . . .

The chorus turnaround cycle (1.53)

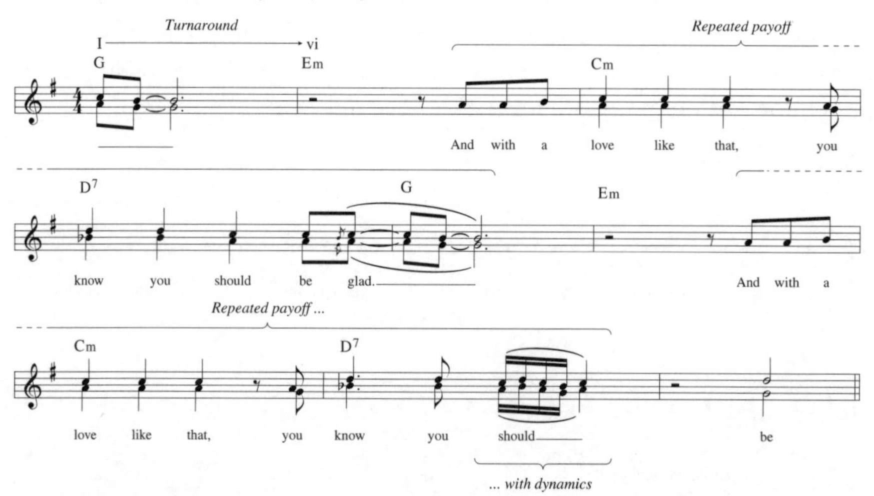

After bounding back through A-B-C, the second chorus features a 'round the block' tag effect, bouncing off the tonic to the vi. It's hardly disparaging to call this turnaround a 'trick' – for a start it featured on the very next single, 'I Want To Hold Your Hand'.

Cued by the dynamics of the stop on 'know' and the drawn out 'should', the repeated chorus line acts as a last tightening of the spring ahead of a tension-busting flourish as the intro harmony now reappears in its third and final form.

The C section – the coda variation: a final twist

The 'she loves you' motif is now sliced in half to leave us with just the 'yeah, yeah, yeahs', while the chord sequence is subtly displaced – the Em now follows the G, creating I-vi-IV-I.

George's descending line (previously heard on 'bad' in the pre-chorus) now takes the place of the first 'round' of vocals (at 2.07), now re-harmonised on G having been previously heard over Em.

But what happened to that pioneering A7? At 2.10 comes the twist that sends 'She Loves You' even further into the stratosphere. It seems that George wasn't going to let the novelty of the A7 chord go without a fight – the deeply dark sound we hear in this bar, for the only time in the song, is Harrison delivering a partial A7 shape – complete with a non-diatonic C♯ – over Em harmony in the bass and rhythm guitar.

The coda (2.06)

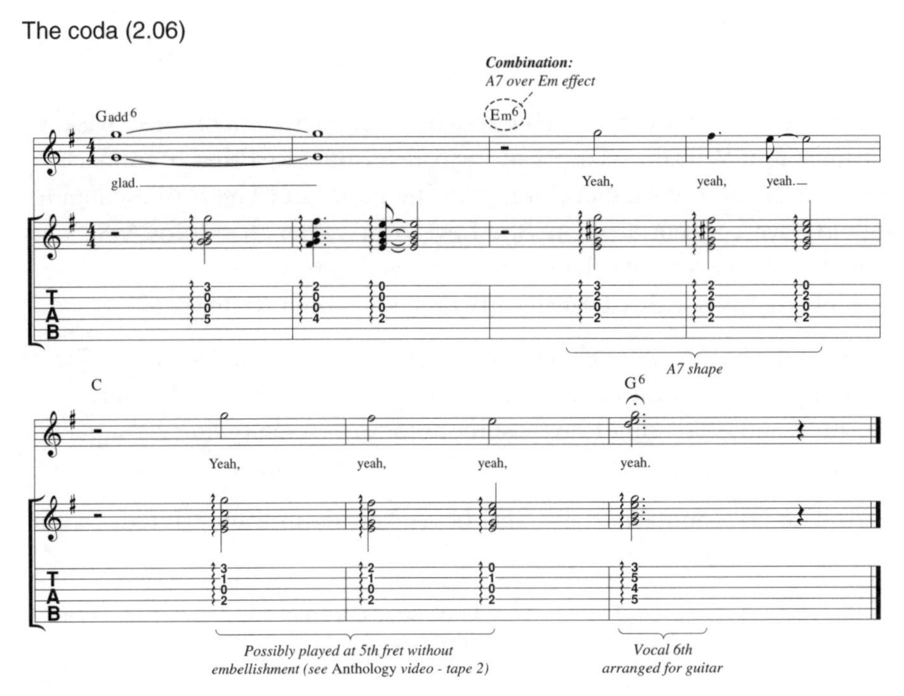

These final bars have long puzzled guitarists, and the presence of this C♯ is the secret to understanding the sudden 'spy flick' sound that surfaces for just a few beats. When added to John's straightforward Em chord, George's C♯ creates the chord of Em6, a distinctly 007-sounding sonority that derives from the E melodic minor scale, the master source of so many of those sixties spy movie themes.

This minor 6th now becomes the backdrop for further colour as the penultimate 'yeah, yeah, yeah' motif unfolds. The melodic F♯ now creates a 9th, resulting in an overall intense sonority of Em6/9, a chord that many jazzy and minor key pop songs use as a sophisticated super-dissonant ending chord.[12]

Compare the following harmonisation chart of this closing C section with the one for the intro to see how The Beatles create deft novelty through careful reworking of earlier themes.

'Yeah, Yeah, Yeah!' – reharmonisation of a single motif

Time	**Chord**	**Three-note motif** *(1st time guitar only)*		
		'Yeah!'	'Yeah!'	'Yeah!'
		G	F♯	E
2.07	G	8	7	6
2.10	Em^{6}	♭3	2 (9)	1
2.13	C	5	♯4	3
		Triad tones	**'colour'**	Triad tones

And so, finally, we reach *that* added sixth. As we mentioned back in Chapter 5, if William Mann had been determined to find a connection between the end of Mahler's 'Song Of The Earth' and The Beatles, then he should have concentrated on 'She Loves You' rather than 'Not A Second Time', as the two works share a climactic added 6th close.

And what was it that Benjamin Britten said about Mahler's 6th?

> 'It has the beauty of loneliness and of pain: of strength and freedom. The beauty of disappointment and never-satisfied love. The cruel beauty of nature, and everlasting beauty of monotony . . . serenity literally super-natural . . . that final chord is printed on the atmosphere.'[13]

And so its counterpart in 'She Loves You' is forever printed on the atmosphere of pop music.

[12] Brian Setzer's final Cm6/9 on The Stray Cats' 'Stray Cat Strut' is one distinctive example.

[13] Stephen E. Hefling, *Mahler; Das Lied Von Der Erde*, p. 116.

For all its hallowed status, in the spirit of Lennon's 'variations on a theme', let's explore some possible inspirations behind pop's greatest single.

McCartney readily admits to the influence of the 'third party' themes of 'Forget Him', a No. 13 UK hit for Bobby Rydell in the summer of '63.[14] And there is also some intriguing musical overlap, even if Rydell's orchestrated crooning is far removed from The Fabs euphoric combo attack.

As well as Paul's favourite iii chord in its (C major) verse, 'Forget Him' also features the unusual iv-V7 ploy – and even precedes it with a non-functioning II7: the D7 which, reinforced with a strong F♯, plunges to Fm (on 'care', at 0.28).[15]

Meanwhile, in addition to Santo & Johnny's I-vi-iv-V on 'Sleepwalk', cue up a handful of The Beatles' more familiar early live covers.

As we saw in Chapter 3, the verse of 'More Than I Can Say' (The Crickets/Bobby Vee) unfolds I-vi-iii, followed by a notable II7-IV-I cadence.

Then there's Gene Vincent's version of 'Summertime' that intriguingly features the Cm-D7 move as *both* Imperfect and Perfect cadences, complete with tell-tale rhythmic 'stops'.[16]

Compare, also, the deeply affecting drop to Em in 'She Loves You' (on 'bad') with the pivotal moment in The Everly Brothers 'Cathy's Clown' where, after a prolonged stay on G we plunge to Em ('I cry each *time*', at 0.25).

But as a final piece of indulgent speculation, let's dissect what must be the only piece of music on a Beatles record to have gone virtually unnoticed. But then that's because the 'impromptu' instrumental, 'Dear Wack!', track 22 on CD 1 of *Live At The BBC*, is just a frivolous piece of throwaway noodling. Or is it?[17]

'Dear Wack!' (0.10-0.25)

Bar	1	2	3	4	5	6	7	8
Chord	C	Cm^6	G^6	A^9	C	E^9 D^7	G E♭	E♭ G
Function	IV	iv	I	II	IV	VI V	I ♭VI	♭VI I

[14] Paul: 'There was a Bobby Rydell song out at the time and, as often happens, you think of one song when you write another', *The Beatles Anthology*, p. 96.

[15] Melodically, both verses open with a 1-2-3 walk ('For-get him'/'[you] think you lost'), while Everett brilliantly spots the repeated 8-7-6 descents in measures 17-18 of 'Forget Him', *The Beatles As Musicians: The Quarry Men Through Rubber Soul*, p.175.

[16] In the key of Gm, the 'hanging' Cm-D7 appears on 'and the livin is wooo hooh' (at 0.15); with the cadential iv-V-I on 'Hush now don't you cry' (at 0.27).

[17] 'Dear Wack!' was recorded at The Beeb on July 30th, 1963 (29 days after the recording of 'She Loves You'), and broadcast on 24th August – the day after 'She Loves You' hit the shops.

These 8 bars (which are repeated before Brian Matthew calls time) feature some of the most interesting harmony heard on *Live At The BBC* and include many of the same elements that created such novelty in 'She Loves You'. Six of the latter's seven basic chords are here but, equally striking, are their *qualities* and *root movement*. Not only do we find (in the same key of G) those breathtaking G added 6th and Cm6th chords, but also an example of a secondary dominant II chord shifting non-functionally to IV.

Meanwhile, if the absence of the Em chord seems a sticking point to our argument of songwriting themes and traditions, then read on.

... it must have been Moonglow

Far from being a meaningless jam made up by Harrison to show off his slick shapes, 'Dear Wack!' is actually 'Moonglow', a favourite early Beatles 'late night cabaret' cover from the Hamburg days.

It's a song that George himself would refer to regularly in interviews – right up to and including his *Anthology* memoirs.[18] As a jazz standard it's been covered by everyone from Nat King Cole to k. d. Lang. While it may normally be confined to the cocktail circuit, a closer look at its harmony and melody reveals some interesting points.

'Moonglow'

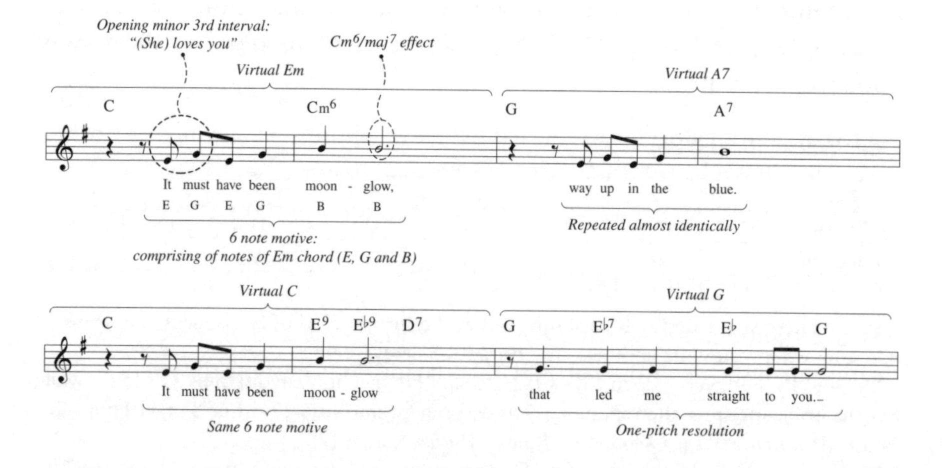

[18] *The Beatles Anthology*, pp. 44 and 49. Other references include Harrison's comments in 'The Long And Winding Road' by Vic Garbarini, *Guitar World*, February 1997, p. 31.

Both 'She Loves You' and 'Moonglow' draw their flavour from a repeated E-to-G interval that appears at the heart of a clearly defined opening six-note motif which is then repeated (virtually identically) three times, and reharmonised.

Analysis of the 'Moonglow' motif also demonstrates that the only missing chord from 'She Loves You' – the Em – is not really missing at all. With its E-G-B melody spelling out an E minor triad, the sound of E minor is very much present. In this way both songs are characterised by major/relative minor ambiguity without a formal modulation. Accordingly, one could suggest that an alternative harmony for 'Moonglow's' tune is indeed an opening E minor, which means we can cheekily distil the entire progression into the now familiar sequence: Em-A7-C-G. Try it for size.

The fact that 'Moonglow' was originally conceived with a closing added 6th chord – and was usually covered as such – is just a final point of detail.[19] How ironic that a song as seemingly superficial as 'She Loves You' achieves its effect through intricate harmonisation that can be compared to that of a jazz standard.

More importantly, it would appear to confirm that an awareness of the structures of certain sophisticated compositions (often tackled by The Beatles in their early live sets) was fundamental in helping them develop the harmonic awareness that ultimately marked them out as superior song-writers. As such, 'Moonglow' stands out as a pivotal piece in their musical development – a point that George Harrison effectively confirms:

> 'We were forced to learn to play *everything* to fill those eight-hour sets. Suddenly, we were even playing movie themes, like 'A Taste Of Honey' and 'Moonglow', learning new chords, jazz voicings, the whole bit. We learned a *lot* from doing that. Eventually, it all combined together to make something new and we found our voice as a band.'[20]

'She Loves You' – perfect pop

For all its outrageous novelty, 'She Loves You' has been described by expert Beatle analysts as 'not particularly daring' in certain respects.[21] The

[19] Check out the Nat King Cole version of 'Moonglow' to hear (in the key of E♭) an E♭6 chord at 1.21 (and a closing D♭6 at 2.51 following the modulation to D♭).

[20] Vic Garbarini, 'When We Was Fab', *Guitar World*, January 2001, p. 74.

[21] Pollack refers to the 'totally four-square' phrasing, regular 'harmonic rhythm' and 'static' key scheme; 'Notes on … Series' no. 5, 2000. *The 'Official' rec.music.beatles Home Page*, www.recmusicbeatles.com.

predictable phrase lengths and highly symmetrical eight-bar-structured sections seem to be the main gripe, with the lack of formal modulation being another issue for *connoisseurs* (arguably this represents a technical regression from 'From Me To You').

Paradoxically, one could argue this works in its favour. 'She Loves You' operates within a metrically predictable framework and a single formal key scheme (like most chart pop of the last half century) – the basic terms of reference to which listeners have always been so intuitively programmed. Yet it compensates with such novel single-key harmony that the absence of a modulation is not even noticed.

One possibility is that 'She Loves You' shuns a key shift because it is designed to operate entirely in the here and now. It does not need the shift in *time* that a modulation would conjure. OK, there's some past tense in the lyric (e.g., 'yesterday'), but we're not dwelling in the past. What matters is the delivery of the message in the present – and whatever might happen in the future once we've had time to digest it.

As Mellers first described so eloquently:

> 'It exists in the moment, without before or after...the timeless present-affirming modality is instinctive.'[22]

As such, the play between major and relative minor emerges as the embodiment of subtlety. As Everett describes, the Em chord in the song 'often assumes a primary position over that of the tonic, as a dark shadow engulfing the brighter major mode'.[23]

When it comes to pop perfection 'She Loves You' represents a high-water mark in The Beatles story. A peak that, in terms of purity of concept and delivery, they would never top. 'Yesterday' may have clocked up more air-plays, 'In My Life' and 'Strawberry Fields' may have enjoyed more street credibility, 'Here, There And Everywhere' may more be musically intricate, and 'Lucy In The Sky With Diamonds' and 'Because' might indeed be more semantically challenging, but 'She Loves You' is surely the quintessential single on The Planet Earth jukebox.

Never mind that it was penned in Newcastle, was recorded with the muddiest of lo-fi two-track technology; and has been desecrated down the

[22] *Twilight Of The Gods*, pp. 32–3.

[23] Everett, 'Voice Leading and Harmony as Expressive Devices in the Early Music of The Beatles: "She Loves You"'; *College Music Symposium*, 32, p. 27.

years by everyone from Peter Sellers and Pinky & Perky to Tottenham Hotspur F.C. and boy band, A1. It is still the benchmark for what the stereotypical chart hit *should* be. Pop maestro Pete Waterman pays the ultimate tribute to its innate commercialism when he says: 'Every morning I get up and try and write "She Loves You".'[24]

And so, as we reach the end of this rambling technical road, we are reminded of the ephemeral nature of mass appeal and the fact that no amount of analysis can quite capture the power of the perfect pop song.

As Paul McCartney says: 'We did some great stuff . . . but exact analysis was never our bag'.[25]

[24] In conversation with the author, March 2000. Tributes to 'She Loves You' have spanned *Rolling Stone*'s Dave Marsh, who refers to its 'definitive rock 'n' roll greatness' (Riley, *Tell Me Why*, p. 399), through to Butch Vig of Garbage who, 37 years on, praises its 'trashy garage-band energy' (*Rolling Stone*, Issue 863, 1st March 2001, p. 32). Mark Ellen describes it as 'the perfect synthesis of what made the Fabs great', 'A Good Yeah', 1000 Days Of Beatlemania, *MOJO*, Special Limited Edition (Winter 2002), p.60. Greil Marcus sums it up: 'were a Martian to land on earth and ask you the meaning of rock and roll....what would you play to explain?...You start, perhaps, with 'She Loves You'. "That", you say with pride, "is rock and roll!"'; *Stranded: Rock And Roll For A Desert Island*, p.252.

[25] McCartney interviewed by Tony Bacon, *Total Guitar*, Issue 14, January 1996, p.42.

APPENDIX 1

A Beginner's Guide to Music Theory

Essential Scales and Chords

This appendix is intended as a brief introduction to the musical and analytical tools that are used throughout this book. It is recommended that readers with little or no musical knowledge read this appendix first, before moving on to Chapter 1.

Wherever possible, musical notation has been avoided and information has been presented in the simplest, most practical form possible. In most cases, it is possible to understand the examples without being able to read music, although in certain chapters (particularly those on melody), readers may find it advantageous.

Readers with some understanding of music theory may also find what follows helpful, as it lays out in simple terms the framework of scales and chords that we will be using to identify the Songwriting Secrets of The Beatles.

The 12 Notes in Music

When, in the quote that begins this book, John Lennon says: 'there are only a few notes', he means that there are 12, to be precise.

These 12 notes form a complete musical 'alphabet', known as the *chromatic scale* – 12 successive steps that link any note to the same note, one octave higher. (Musicians give notes that are an octave apart the same name, because, although they differ in pitch, they 'sound' very similar to each other, due to certain physical similarities.[1])

[1] Doubling the frequency of a note (which is the same as halving its wavelength) will transpose it up an octave.

For example, on the piano keyboard, a chromatic scale can be created by playing all the keys, white *and* black, in ascending or descending order. On the guitar, you could play the same scale by starting from the open string and playing a note at every fret, up to the 12th fret.

These 12 steps are named after only seven different letters of the alphabet. We use *sharps* (denoted by ♯) and *flats* (denoted by ♭) to fill in the rest of the steps. Here is a chromatic scale starting on the note C:

The chromatic scale

Semitones		1	2	3	4	5	6	7	8	9	10	11	12
Chromatic notes	C	C♯	D	D♯	E	F	F♯	G	G♯	A	A♯	B	C
The 7 letters	1		2		3	4		5		6		7	

The musical distance between each of the steps in this scale is exactly the same, and is called a *semitone.*[2]

This 12-note chromatic scale is the ultimate source of all Western music, and is constantly referred to by musicians, rock stars, critics and journalists. As Ray Connolly says:

> 'From these notes come just about every tune any of us has ever heard, played in different sequences, it's true, with different rhythms. These notes are all a composer has to work with.'[3]

However, fortunately for the novice musician, *in practice* certain notes occur more frequently than others.[4]

This is because pop music is regarded as *tonal*, which means that its melodies and chords tend to gravitate towards a single pitch, known as a *tonic*, or *key centre*. Around that tonic, certain groups of pitches tend to be favoured.

[2] A sharp (♯) raises a note by a semitone, a flat (♭) lowers it by a semitone.

[3] *Plagiarism? You hum it and I'll make it pay*, by Ray Connolly, *Daily Mail*, December 17th 1998, p. 13.

[4] Pop songs that bring into play all of the available 12 notes in music typically tend to be relatively ambitious constructions that either move between keys, or shift between different modes, however briefly. Intricate McCartney compositions like 'Catswalk' (recorded by the Chris Barber Band in 1967) and 'Step Inside Love' are examples of highly sophisticated structures that are closer to jazz than mainstream pop and rock. The highlights of these two songs are analysed in Chapter 10 and 17, respectively.

This is the concept behind any scale, of which the most fundamental examples are the traditional major and minor scales. These subsets of the chromatic scale each consist of seven out of the possible 12 notes – but they have their own *unique interval structure* which defines their sound.

It is by building these scales and their associated chords that we can begin to understand the language of pop.

The major scale – 'Do Re Mi' and beyond

The major scale's origins date from at least AD 1040, when the music teacher and monk Guido d'Arezzo introduced a system of naming pitches to help singers learn new music: *ut*, *re*, *mi*, *fa*, *sol* and *la*. When *ut* became *do*, and *ti* was tacked on as a seventh pitch to bring us back to *do*, as Julie Andrews sang in *The Sound Of Music,* the hills would come alive …

The diatonic major scale – key of C

Here is the major scale, starting on the note C:

Interval		1		1	0.5		1		1		1	0.5	
Scale notes	C		D		E	F		G		A		B	C
Pitch number	1		2		3	4		5		6		7	8
Sol-fa notation	*do*		*re*		*mi*	*fa*		*sol*		*la*		*ti*	*do*

We can express this more formally in conventional notation, as follows:

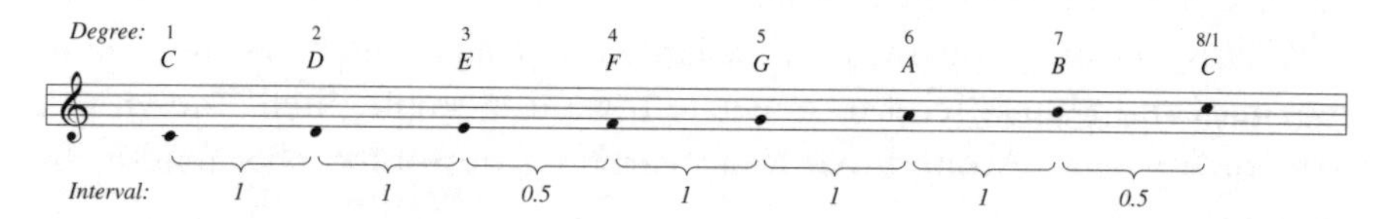

Comparing the C major scale to the C chromatic scale confirms that we have extracted seven notes. These are the seven plain alphabetical letters, which leave behind the five others (those with sharps or flats – suffixes known as *accidentals).*

This is particularly easy to appreciate on the piano, where from any C note, one can play seven consecutive white notes before reaching the next C which lies eight notes (or an *octave*) above the first. The black notes, which are not used in this scale, represent the fact that certain notes in the chromatic scale have been 'skipped'.

In the chromatic scale all the steps were an equal distance apart (a semitone). However, in the major scale the distance between successive notes is now a *whole tone*, *except* between the 3rd and 4th note (here E and F), and the 7th and the octave (here B and C), where the semitone interval is retained. On the diagram above, whole tones are marked as '1', and semitones as '0.5'.

For the purposes of this book the major scale is taken as the defining scale of popular music, and its interval structure will be used as a benchmark for everything else that follows.

So we define the major scale, very simply, with the formula: 1-2-3-4-5-6-7.

Voice leading: the 7-8 ascent and 5-4-3-2-1 descent

Play a C major scale on piano or guitar, and notice the way that the seventh note (sometimes called the *leading* note) has an air of tension as it waits impatiently to 'bring us back to *do*', just as Julie Andrews suggests. The positioning of this note a semitone below the tonic is a defining characteristic of the major scale.

The leading note helps to establish the *key centre* because it is awkward-sounding or *dissonant* – it 'wants' to move upwards to the *tonic* note of the scale. Its presence helps to propel a major scale melody, taking us from tension to resolution.

Think of 'God Save The Queen' (the national, rather than the Punk, anthem) – it is impossible to stop the tune on the penultimate note, our ears expect the B note to rise a semitone, thereby *leading* us into the C of 'Queen'.

'God Save The Queen'

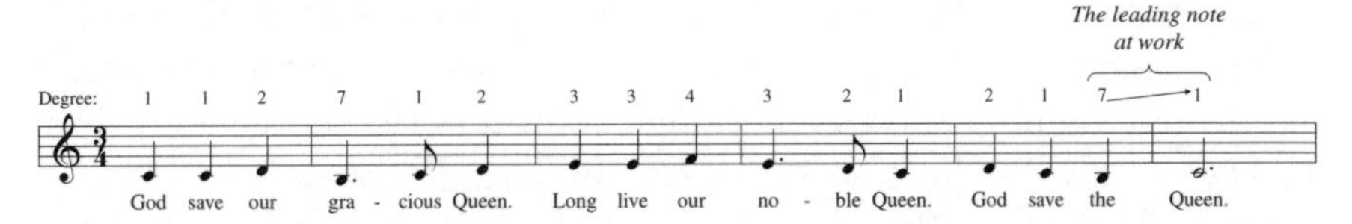

This simple example illustrates how a leading note is one important way in which a tune can achieve *resolution*; a sense of 'arrival' at the tonic of the key.

We can see this most basic of major scale truths in operation in dozens of Beatles songs. McCartney's 'I Will', from *The White Album*, is a particularly good example of a Beatles major scale melody as it uses all seven notes of the scale (which is why we instinctively regard this song as highly 'melodic').

In the example below, we've labelled the major scale pitches 1-2-3-4-5-6-7, and highlighted the leading note effect – which leads the tune to the tonic on three occasions.[5]

'I Will'

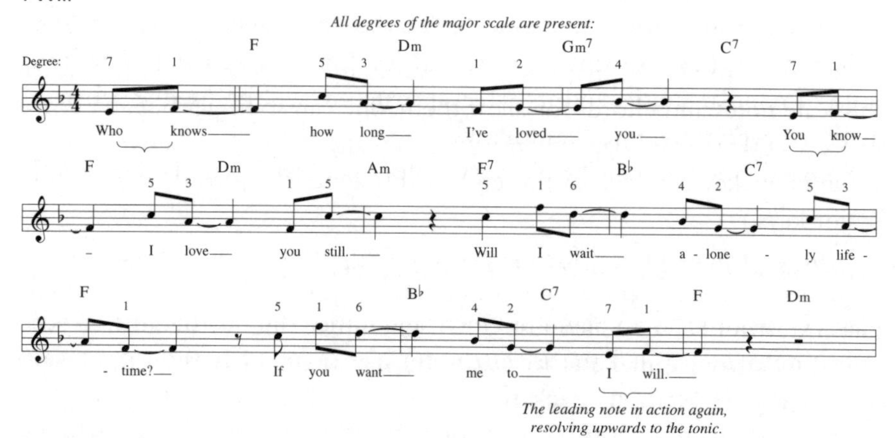

'I Will' also shows how so many melodies display a more fundamental type of voice-leading, where the scale degrees *descend* through 5-4-3-2-1. Look closely. Starting with the tense C note (on 'still'), Paul's tune visits each of the notes A, G♯ and F♯ before closing on the E tonic. Chapter 1 elaborates on how this 'structural' feature lends an intuitive sense of 'order' to so much tonal music.

Keys and the numerical reference points

While at first sight this numbering system appears to add an extra layer of complexity to our alphabetical notation system, in actual fact, it simplifies things greatly by being independent of the key of the song in question.

For example, in 'I Will' it allowed us instantly to identify the major scale and the leading note effect even though we had in fact moved away from the key of C, with which we were becoming familiar, *to the key of F.*

The major scale of F major retains the identical interval sequence as C major – this rigid formula of whole and half steps is maintained *whatever key we are in.* However, we now find a different overall collection of notes as one flattened note, B♭, is required to maintain the major scale formula when starting the scale on F.

[5] Sometimes the effect can be spotted easily as part of a longer 6-7-8 melodic climb, as in 'I Should Have Known Better' ('and I do', E-F♯-G), or 'The Long And Winding Road' where 'lead me to your door' does just that.

The diatonic major scale – key of F

Interval		1		1	0.5		1		1		1	0.5	
Scale notes	F		G		A	B♭		C		D		E	F
Pitch number	1		2		3	4		5		6		7	8
Sol-fa notation	*do*		*re*		*mi*	*fa*		*sol*		*la*		*ti*	*do*

There are in fact 12 major keys in music, and while it is useful to learn the scale notes and chords for all of them, one can soon get bogged down in a sea of sharps and flats when trying to make *comparisons* between songs in different keys. (Refer to the end of this appendix for a table of all 12 major keys.)

A numerical naming system provides an important tool when discussing sequences that exist in a range of different keys. In any key, we can simply talk in terms of '7-to-8' (or just '7-8') when referring to the leading note effect, whether we mean B-to-C (in the key of C), E-to-F (in the key of F), or C♯-to-D (in the key of D).

Building chords – the harmonised major scale

So far we have only been concerned with *individual notes*, such as we find in a melody. Yet while we can happily sing these 'tunes' on their own, melody is only part of the songwriting equation. We need *chords* to support the tune and embellish it with the *harmonic* colour that comes from sounding several notes at the same time.

Where do these chords come from?

They come from the very same source as the melody: the major scale. This time, however, rather than just sounding the notes of the scale individually in a sequence, we 'stack' them and play them at the same time.

This 'stacking' process – known as *harmonisation* – can be carried out for each of the seven major scale degrees. Thus we can create a family of chords for each major key.

Chords in all the main genres of Western music are built by a process called *harmonising in thirds*. For example, we could start to build a chord of C by stacking the *third* note of the scale, E, on top of the *tonic,* C.

So for each tone in the scale, we add the 'next-but-one' note in the scale sequence (which we view as the *third* in relation to the note we are building on). We don't need to worry about the notes of the scale 'running out' because if necessary we can just extend the scale into the next octave.

Here's what this first level of harmonisation looks like:

Harmonisation in Thirds

Stage 1: The root and third

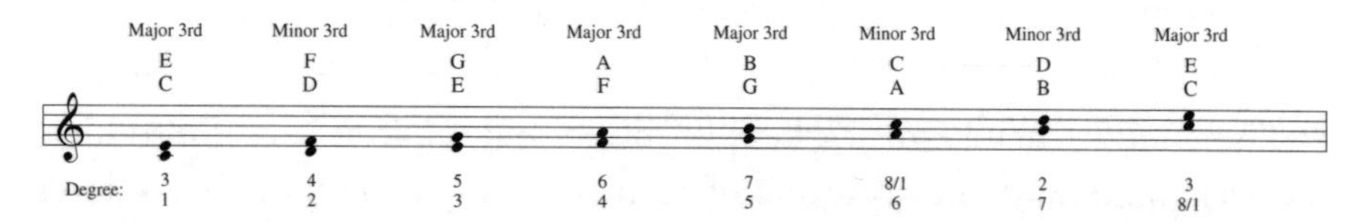

These two-note structures are not technically chords, but *doublestops* or *diads*. We need another note to give us the *triad* that is the minimum requirement for a true chord. We find it by taking the harmonisation process up another level. This time we take the next-but-one note *after the third*, to give us the *fifth* of the chord.

Stage 2: The root, third and fifth

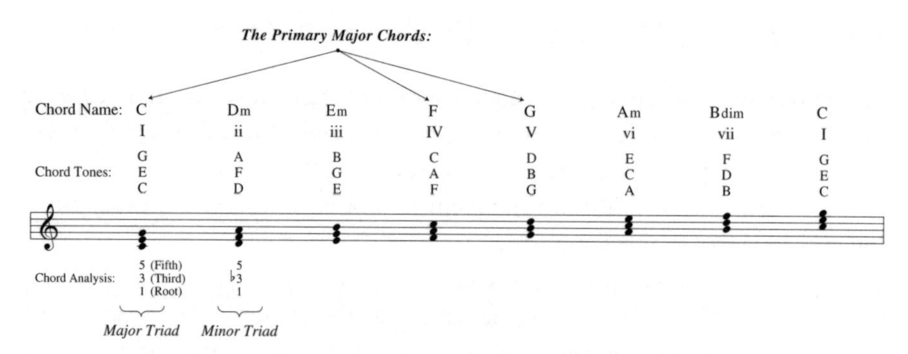

The combined scale and chord framework developed so far can be condensed into the following table.

Pitch number	1		2		3	4		5		6		7	8
Scale notes	C		D		E	F		G		A		B	C
Chords in C	C		Dm		Em	F		G		Am		Bdim	C
Chord formula	I		ii		iii	IV		V		vi		vii dim	I

The Roman Numeral System

Note that, as we have moved from single notes to chords, the *Arabic* numerals have become *Roman* (so the note '1' has become the chord 'I'). This is a convention that will be followed throughout this book: melodic analysis will always use Arabic numerals (e.g., 1 for tonic, 8 for octave), while harmonic analysis will always use Roman numerals.

This system is a fundamental language that is essential to understanding virtually every principle in this book.

Major and minor thirds – the vital distinction

Because the interval pattern of the major scale contains a mixture of tones and semitones, not all the thirds we used when harmonising the scale are the same in terms of their distance from the root. Check them on the guitar or the piano: the distance between the C root and its third (the E note) is different from that between D and *its* third, F.

It is this quirk of diatonic harmonisation that explains the presence of both major chords and minor chords in the family, each with their dramatically different sound.

Look at the bottom row of the table above – the 'm' suffix distinguishes *minor* chords from *major* ones on certain *predetermined* scale degrees.

This difference is reflected in the Roman numerals: our convention is that major chords are always shown in upper case, and minor chords in lower case. For example, the chord I is major, while the chord ii is minor.

Let's look at these two types of triad more closely.

Building the C major triad

The C major chord consists of the notes C, E and G. These notes are called the *root* (C), *major third* (E) and *perfect fifth* (G), respectively.

The *major third* is 4 semitones above the root, while the *perfect fifth* is 7 semitones about the root.

Because of this structure we refer to the chord as C major, or just plain C (which always assumes that the third is major), with a formula abbreviated as '1-3-5'.

The minor triad – D minor

For the chord built on the second note of the scale, we have D, F, A, which creates the D minor.

While the distance between the root and the fifth is the same as for a major chord, the distance from D to F is only *three* semitones. This interval is called a *minor* third, and a minor chord's formula is therefore given as 1-♭3-5, reflecting this flattened third.

Straightforward major and minor triads account for six of the seven chords in the harmonised scale. The exception is the chord built on the seventh degree, the leading note.

The special case of the diminished triad

Here we find a root and minor third joined by a fifth degree. However, this is no longer the perfect fifth of seven semitones which we find in both major and minor chords – this fifth is flattened by a semitone.

The resulting six-semitone interval between B and F is referred to as a *diminished fifth* or, since it is equivalent to three whole tones, a *tritone,* a term that will become synonymous with extreme dissonance.

The structure of this maverick chord is 1-♭3-♭5, and it is termed a *diminished triad*. Over the course of this book, it will emerge as the black sheep of the harmonised scale family, for while the '7' regularly appears as an individual pitch in melodies, or as a passing tone in basslines, the *whole* triad, vii dim, is extremely rare in pop music.

At this point it is useful to summarise all the terms that we have introduced to describe the major scale and the chords that result from its harmonisation:

Pitch number	**Name**	**Chord number**
1	Tonic or key-centre	I
2	Supertonic	ii
3	Mediant	iii
4	Subdominant	IV
5	Dominant	V
6	Submediant or relative minor	vi
7	Leading note	vii
8	Octave	I

Refer to the end of this appendix for a master chart of all 12 keys, listing all the major scale triads we will be encountering.

How the Roman Numeral System helps us to appreciate the music of The Beatles

This book aims to create a framework within which we can identify and appreciate musical *relationships* that occur in pop music, some simple and common, others rare. The Roman Numeral system allows us to do just that by creating a method of labelling chord progressions that is constant for every key.

For example, the constituents of the Three-Chord Trick can be defined as the I, IV, and V chords – the three primary (major) triads in *any* key. This is *always* the case even though different songs may feature the seemingly unrelated chord families of C, F and G (in the key of C); A, D and E (in the key A); or E, A and B (in the key of B). When musicians talk of 'one-four-five', this is what they mean.

The fact that the Roman Numeral system is *transferable* between keys is the single most important rationale for its use. It enables us to recognise the *function* of chords within a song and to recognise familiar sequences across a whole catalogue of songs, again, irrespective of which of the 12 keys they appear in.

The same system allows us to work 'backwards', and to transpose a progression quickly from one key to another, thereby allowing us to play songs in the most suitable key for our own individual purposes.

Here is an example of how to switch a sequence between keys, as we move 'I Will' from the key of F back to our 'default' key of C.

Transposing a chord progression

Original progression
in the key of F

	F	Dm	Gm^7	C^7	F	Dm	Am	F^7
Who	knows how	long I've	loved you.	You	know I	love you	still.	Will I wait

Major Scale Formula:	I	ii	iii	IV	V	vi	vii
Key of F:	F	Gm	Am	B$\flat$	C	Dm	Edim

Original progression
as a formula

	I	vi	ii^7	V^7	I	vi	iii	I^7
Who	knows how	long I've	loved you.	You	know I	love you	still.	Will I wait

Major Scale Formula:	I	ii	iii	IV	V	vi	vii
Key of C:	C	Dm	Em	F	G	Am	Bdim

The same progression
remapped to the key of C

	C	Am	Dm^7	G^7	C	Am	Em	C^7
Who	knows how	long I've	loved you.	You	know I	love you	still.	Will I wait

Adding 'sevenths' to the harmonised major scale triads

This extract of 'I Will' includes several chords known as 'sevenths'. These chords are created by a further application of 'harmonisation in thirds', adding a further note to the basic triad, a seventh away from the root.

Stage 3: The root, third, fifth and seventh

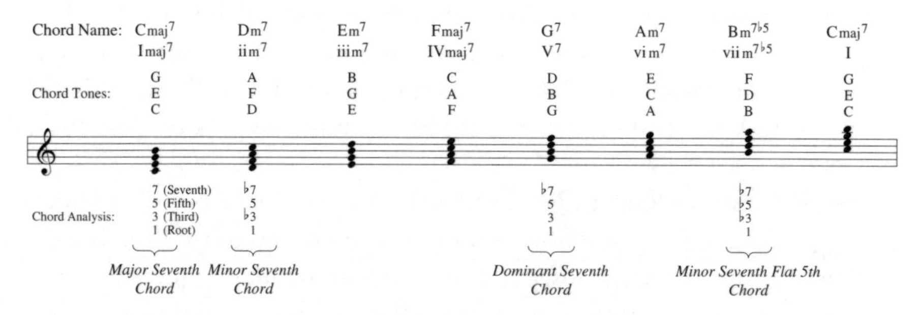

We can summarise the family of harmonised diatonic seventh chords, in the key of C, as follows:

Scale notes	C	D	E	F	G	A	B
Seventh chords in C	Cmaj^{7}	Dm^{7}	Em^{7}	Fmaj^{7}	G^{7}	Am^{7}	Bm$^{7\flat5}$
Chord formula	Imaj^{7}	ii^{7}	iii^{7}	IVmaj^{7}	V^{7}	vi^{7}	vii$^{7\flat5}$

Major and minor sevenths

Like the thirds in the triad, sevenths also appear in major and minor forms.

Those that are located 11 semitones above the root (a semitone below the octave) are known as *major* sevenths. They appear only on the major triads of I and IV – these chords are given the formula 1-3-5-7 (i.e., the C-E-G-B notes that comprise C major 7th).

These major sevenths contrast with those that are located ten semitones above the root. These *flattened* sevenths occur over three *different* types of triad:

1) The minor triads – giving rise to the *minor* seventh chord (1-♭3-5-♭7); e.g., Dm7: D-F-A-C.
2) The major triad on the V chord, creating what it is known as a *dominant seventh* chord: 1-3-5-♭7. This is essentially a minor seventh combined with a major triad.
3) The diminished triad on the vii, giving rise to the 'minor seventh flat five' chord whose formula is an even more dissonant: 1-♭3-♭5-♭7; the Bm7♭5 here contains the notes: B-D-F-A.

Once again the harmonised diatonic sevenths can be constructed in every key – refer to the end of this appendix for a full table.

While much folk and early rock 'n' roll can be played with simple triads, seventh chords form an essential part of more sophisticated pop music. The Beatles' exploitation of these sounds was essential to both their rich-textured sound and to the interesting voice-leading and resolution in many of their chord sequences.

Other 'extensions', 'additions' and 'alterations'

In theory, we can continue our harmonisation beyond the seventh to create even more exotic constructions such as 9th, 11th and 13th chords. However, *in practice*, these chords (which, as described, assume the presence of all the members) are relatively rare in pop. More common are those that leave out certain notes, due mainly to the practicalities of guitar voicings.

Meanwhile, in jazzy and 'rich pop' harmony we sometimes find even more exotic 'altered' chords that generate tension by *altering* the triad tones themselves – perhaps by sharpening, or flattening, the 5th of the chord, or perhaps by combining a dark *minor* 3rd against a *major* 3rd *in a single chord.*

All these extra chords – and many others ranging from 'suspensions' to triad 'inversions' – are introduced and appreciated systematically throughout this book. A summary of particularly interesting chords (together with their formulas and representative examples of 'Beatles usage') is included in Appendix 2.

The minor scale

A brief look at the construction of the diatonic natural minor scale, and its chord family will form a useful background at this stage, and later for reference purposes.

The distinctive, haunting chords of the minor tonality are again built by stacking thirds, but this time on the *natural minor scale* itself, a structure that contrasts notably from the major scale.

The easiest way to understand the natural minor scale is to introduce the concept of the *relative* minor.

Finding the interval structure – the relative connection

In every key there is a strong relationship between the I and vi chords whose triads share two notes in common. For example the chords of C and Am both contain the notes C and E.

The chord of Am is said to be the *relative minor* of C. Again, this 'relative' relationship holds true for the I and vi chords *in every key*. Em is the relative minor of G, Fm is the relative minor of A♭, Dm is the relative minor of F, and so on.

The relationship between C major and A minor

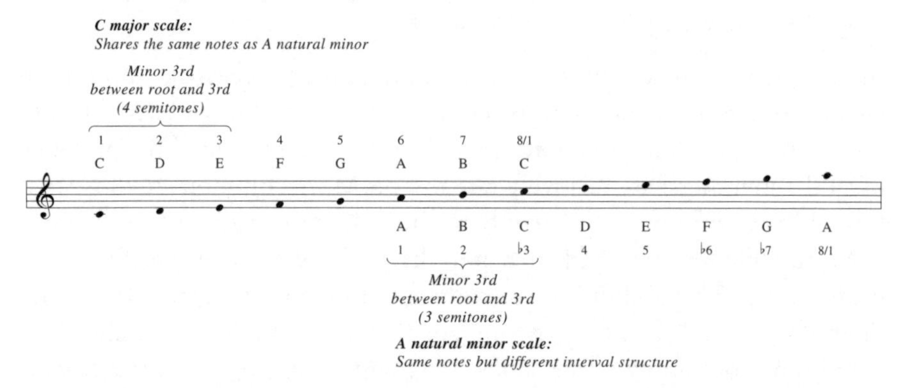

As we can see, the A natural minor *scale* contains *exactly* the same notes as the C major scale but, crucially, it now has A as the tonic, the starting and ending point of the scale. This means that the natural minor scale has a completely different *interval structure* from that of the major scale.

This is reflected in the scale formula: '1-2-♭3-4-5-♭6-♭7'.

We have nominated the major scale as the reference point against which all other scales will be measured – hence this formula defines certain alterations to the basic major pattern. In particular, the third, sixth and seventh degrees are flattened when compared to the positions of their counterparts in the major scale.

The Diatonic natural minor scale – A minor

Interval		1	0.5		1		1	0.5		1		1	
Scale notes	A		B	C		D		E	F		G		A
Pitch number	1		2	♭3		4		5	♭6		♭7		8

For an example of the flavour of this scale, listen to the following extract of the 'The Fool On The Hill' in which Paul McCartney moves to the key of D minor, and thoughtfully crafts a melody that uses each of the seven pitches in the D natural minor scale.

'The Fool On The Hill'

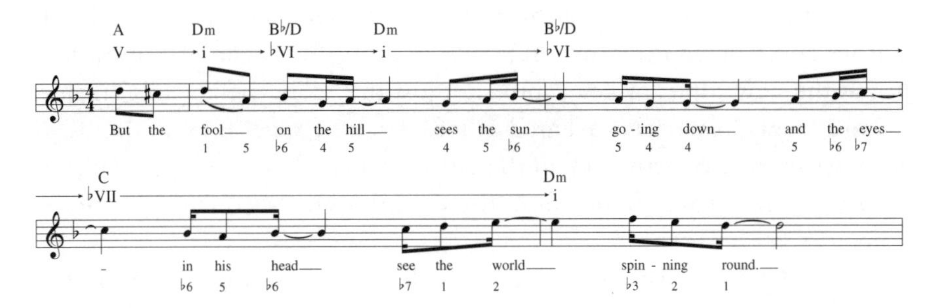

Most fundamentally, as with any minor *chord*, the minor scale has, as its third, a note that is a *minor* third away from the root. This, along with the other specific intervals, especially the ♭6, gives this collection of notes a distinctively darker, haunting and more challenging sound than the major scale.

The full set of 12 natural minor scales is summarised at the end of this appendix.

Harmonising the natural minor scale

To create the appropriate family of chords for our new scale, theory again instructs us to 'harmonise in thirds'. Thankfully, the relative relationship with the major scale means that we don't have to go through this laboriously all over again. If we simply renumber our family of major chords, starting on A, we can easily create a set of harmonised chords for A natural minor:

A natural minor – diatonic harmonised triads

Pitch number	1		2	♭3		4		5	♭6		♭7		8
Scale notes	A		B	C		D		E	F		G		A
Chords in Am	Am		Bdim	C		Dm		Em	F		G		Am
Chord formula	i		ii dim	♭III		iv		v	♭VI		♭VII		i

A natural minor – diatonic harmonised seventh chords

Scale notes	A	B	C	D	E	F	G
Seventh chords in Am	Am^{7}	Bm$^{7\flat5}$	Cmaj^{7}	Dm^{7}	Em^{7}	Fmaj^{7}	G^{7}
Chord formula	i^{7}	ii$^{7\flat5}$	♭IIImaj^{7}	iv^{7}	v^{7}	♭VImaj^{7}	♭VII^{7}

In the same way that the scale of A minor contained exactly the same notes as the scale of C major, this is exactly the same collection of chords that we constructed for C major. However, crucially, we are now regarding Am as the new tonic, or key centre, not just the 'vi' in the key of C major.

No longer do we have a Three-Chord Trick of *major* I, IV,V chords, as *minor* triads now occupy each of these slots. Meanwhile, the strange 'minor seventh flat five' has switched from the seventh to the second degree of the scale.

While the C major and A minor scales share the exact same notes, chords, and key signatures, their interval structure confirms that they should not be thought of as the same scale (as is sometimes implied). Nevertheless, the extent to which any song is in the key of C major or the key of A minor depends on the emphasis given to the various notes and chords.

The triads and seventh chords of all 12 harmonised natural minor scales are given at the end of this appendix.

We can round off this discussion by setting out the C natural minor scale. Compare this to our initial C *major* scale to confirm just how the interval structures of the two scales differ:

C natural minor

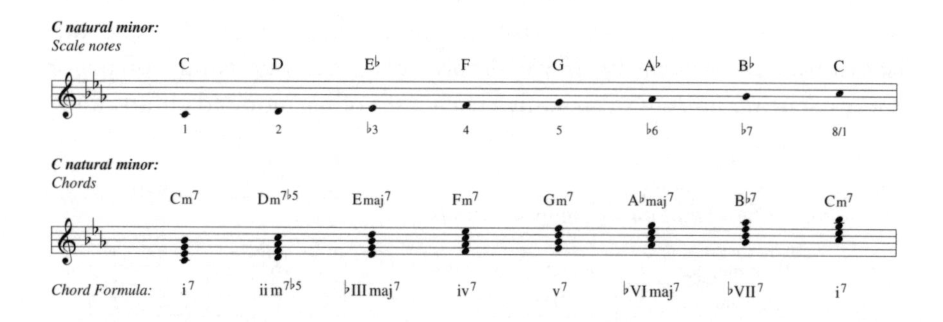

In summary, these major and minor scales and their associated chords are essential theoretical tools for this entire book.

They reappear throughout our discussions, with any deviation, or development, always presented as an incremental embellishment of these basic blueprints.

Keep this in mind and every theoretical discussion in this book should be fathomable.

Summary charts – major and minor notes and chords

MAJOR

The Major scale in the 12 keys in music

1	2	3	4	5	6	7	8
A	B	C♯	D	E	F♯	G♯	A
B♭	C	D	E♭	F	G	A	B♭
B	C♯	D♯	E	F♯	G♯	A♯	B
C	D	E	F	G	A	B	C
C♯	D♯	E♯	F♯	G♯	A♯	B♯	C♯
D	E	F♯	G	A	B	C♯	D
E♭	F	G	A♭	B♭	C	D	E♭
E	F♯	G♯	A	B	C♯	D♯	E
F	G	A	B♭	C	D	E	F
F♯	G♯	A♯	B	C♯	D♯	E♯	F♯
G	A	B	C	D	E	F♯	G
A♭	B♭	C	D♭	E♭	F	G	A♭

The harmonised major scale – diatonic triads

I	ii	iii	IV	V	vi	vii dim	I
A	Bm	C♯m	D	E	F♯m	G♯dim	A
B♭	Cm	Dm	E♭	F	Gm	Adim	B♭
B	C♯m	D♯m	E	F♯	G♯m	A♯dim	B
C	Dm	Em	F	G	Am	Bdim	C
C♯	D♯m	E♯m	F♯	G♯	A♯m	B♯dim	C♯
D	Em	F♯m	G	A	Bm	C♯dim	D
E♭	Fm	Gm	A♭	B♭	Cm	Ddim	E♭
E	F♯m	G♯m	A	B	C♯m	D♯dim	E
F	Gm	Am	B♭	C	Dm	Edim	F
F♯	G♯m	A♯m	B	C♯	D♯m	E♯dim	F♯
G	Am	Bm	C	D	Em	F♯dim	G
A♭	B♭m	Cm	D♭	E♭	Fm	Gdim	A♭

The harmonised major scale – diatonic seventh chords

Imaj^7	ii^7	iii^7	IVmaj^7	V^7	vi^7	vii$^{7♭5}$	Imaj^7
Amaj^7	Bm^7	C♯m^7	Dmaj^7	E^7	F♯m^7	G♯m$^{7♭5}$	Amaj^7
B♭maj^7	Cm^7	Dm^7	E♭maj^7	F^7	Gm^7	Am$^{7♭5}$	B♭maj^7
Bmaj^7	C♯m^7	D♯m^7	Emaj^7	F♯^{7}	G♯m^7	A♯m$^{7♭5}$	Bmaj^7
Cmaj^7	Dm^7	Em^7	Fmaj^7	G^7	Am^7	Bm$^{7♭5}$	Cmaj^7
C♯maj^7	D♯m^7	E♯m^7	F♯maj^7	G♯^{7}	A♯m^7	B♯m$^{7♭5}$	C♯maj^7
Dmaj^7	Em^7	F♯m^7	Gmaj^7	A^7	Bm^7	C♯m$^{7♭5}$	Dmaj^7
E♭maj^7	Fm^7	Gm^7	A♭maj^7	B♭^{7}	Cm^7	Dm$^{7♭5}$	E♭maj^7
Emaj^7	F♯m^7	G♯m^7	Amaj^7	B^7	C♯m^7	D♯m$^{7♭5}$	Emaj^7
Fmaj^7	Gm^7	Am^7	B♭maj^7	C^7	Dm^7	Em$^{7♭5}$	Fmaj^7
F♯maj^7	G♯m^7	A♯m^7	Bmaj^7	C♯^{7}	D♯m^7	E♯m$^{7♭5}$	F♯maj^7
Gmaj^7	Am^7	Bm^7	Cmaj^7	D^7	Em^7	F♯m$^{7♭5}$	Gmaj^7
A♭maj^7	B♭m^7	Cm^7	D♭maj^7	E♭^{7}	Fm^7	Gm$^{7♭5}$	A♭maj^7

Natural Minor

The natural minor scale in the 12 keys in music

1	2	♭3	4	5	♭6	♭7	8
A	B	C	D	E	F	G	A
A♯	B♯	C♯	D♯	E♯	F♯	G♯	A♯
B	C♯	D	E	F♯	G	A	B
C	D	E♭	F	G	A♭	B♭	C
C♯	D♯	E	F♯	G♯	A	B	C♯
D	E	F	G	A	B♭	C	D
D♯	E♯	F♯	G♯	A♯	B	C♯	D♯
E	F♯	G	A	B	C	D	E
F	G	A♭	B♭	C	D♭	E♭	F
F♯	G♯	A	B	C♯	D	E	F♯
G	A	B♭	C	D	E♭	F	G
G♯	A♯	B	C♯	D♯	E	F♯	G♯

The harmonised minor scale – diatonic triads

i	**ii dim**	**♭III**	**iv**	**v**	**♭VI**	**♭VII**	**i**
Am	Bdim	C	Dm	Em	F	G	Am
A♯m	B♯dim	C♯	D♯m	E♯m	F♯	G♯	A♯m
Bm	C♯dim	D	Em	F♯m	G	A	Bm
Cm	Ddim	E♭	Fm	Gm	A♭	B♭	Cm
C♯m	D♯dim	E	F♯m	G♯m	A	B	C♯m
Dm	Edim	F	Gm	Am	B♭	C	Dm
D♯m	E♯dim	F♯	G♯m	A♯m	B	C♯	D♯m
Em	F♯dim	G	Am	Bm	C	D	Em
Fm	Gdim	A♭	B♭m	Cm	D♭	E♭	Fm
F♯m	G♯dim	A	Bm	C♯m	D	E	F♯m
Gm	Adim	B♭	Cm	Dm	E♭	F	Gm
G♯m	A♯ dim	B	C♯m	D♯m	E	F♯	G♯m

The harmonised minor scale – diatonic seventh chords

i^7	**ii$^{7\flat5}$**	**♭IIImaj^7**	**iv^7**	**v^7**	**♭VImaj^7**	**♭VII^7**	**i^7**
Am^7	Bm$^{7\flat5}$	Cmaj^7	Dm^7	Em^7	Fmaj^7	G^7	Am^7
A♯m^7	B♯m$^{7\flat5}$	C♯maj^7	D♯m^7	E♯m^7	F♯maj^7	G♯^{7}	A♯m^7
Bm^7	C♯m$^{7\flat5}$	Dmaj^7	Em^7	F♯m^7	Gmaj^7	A^7	Bm^7
Cm^7	Dm$^{7\flat5}$	E♭maj^7	Fm^7	Gm^7	A♭maj^7	B♭^{7}	Cm^7
C♯m^7	D♯m$^{7\flat5}$	Emaj^7	F♯m^7	G♯m^7	Amaj^7	B^7	C♯m^7
Dm^7	Em$^{7\flat5}$	Fmaj^7	Gm^7	Am^7	B♭maj^7	C^7	Dm^7
D♯m^7	E♯m$^{7\flat5}$	F♯maj^7	G♯m^7	A♯m^7	Bmaj^7	C♯^{7}	D♯m^7
Em^7	F♯m$^{7\flat5}$	Gmaj^7	Am^7	Bm^7	Cmaj^7	D^7	Em^7
Fm^7	Gm$^{7\flat5}$	A♭maj^7	B♭m^7	Cm^7	D♭maj^7	E♭^{7}	Fm^7
F♯m^7	G♯m$^{7\flat5}$	Amaj^7	Bm^7	C♯m^7	Dmaj^7	E^7	F♯m^7
Gm^7	Am$^{7\flat5}$	B♭maj^7	Cm^7	Dm^7	E♭maj^7	F^7	Gm^7
G♯m^7	A♯m$^{7\flat5}$	Bmaj^7	C♯m^7	D♯m^7	Emaj^7	F♯^{7}	G♯m^7

APPENDIX 2

Beatles Chords in Practice

1. A guide to essential Beatles chords

This appendix lists the construction and sound of many of the chords that are found in The Beatles' catalogue. It is intended as a basic reference section, and all the important constructions are dealt with in the main text.

The formula in each case refers to the theoretical structure of the chord, and not necessarily to the precise content, or ordering, of the notes in the selected example – certain notes are often omitted in practice, due to the practicalities of guitar voicings, and because certain notes are less important than others when defining the essence of a chord. For example, the guitar voicing of the D7♯9 in 'Taxman' contains no 5th degree because the fingering of the 5th-string guitar voicing naturally omits the 5th degree. In some cases a partial construction will already be explicit from the 'add' suffix. For example, while a truly 'textbook' dominant 13th chord should contain 9th and 11th degrees, a dominant 7th add 13 (such as we find in 'Because') is defined by the presence of a 6th – deemed a 13th when added to a 'plain' dominant 7th chord.

Instrumental and vocal chords

In each case chords have been selected for their basic sound, either played by a single instrument or heard as a result of combined instruments.

The melody note from the vocal *may* reinforce the chord by sounding a note already within the instrumental cluster. For example, the 9th degree in the minor 9th chord of 'Julia' is heard in the melody *as well as* the guitar chord.

1) TRIADS

Name	Formula	Song	Chord	Lyric
Major	1-3-5	'Yellow Submarine'	G & D major	'*We* all live in a *Yellow* Submarine'
Minor	1-♭3-5	'All I've Got To Do'	C♯m	'Whenever *I*...'
Major Augmented	1-3-♯5	'It's Only Love'	D aug	'*My oh my*'
Minor Augmented	1-♭3-♯5	'Eleanor Rigby'	Em aug	'Where *do they all come* from?'
Diminished	1-♭3-♭5	'Because'	D dim	'Aah, *aah*' (0.28-0.29)

2) HYBRID TRIADS AND DIADS (no thirds)

Name	Formula	Song	Chord	Lyric
5	1-5	'Yesterday'	G^5	*Opening chord*[1]
Sus 2	1-2-5	'A Day In The Life'	Asus2	*Chord after* 'Who made the grade'
Sus 4	1-4-5	'We Can Work It Out'	Dsus4	'Try to see it *my* way'

3) SEVENTH CHORDS

Name	Formula	Song	Chord	Lyric
Major 7th	1-3-5-7	'It Won't Be Long'	E major^7	*Final chord*
Minor 7th	1-♭3-5-♭7	'Yesterday'	F♯m^7	'Yesterday, *love was*'
Dominant 7th	1-3-5-♭7	'Back In The USSR'	E^7	*Opening chord*
Diminished 7th	1-♭3-♭5-♭♭7	'Michelle'	B dim^7	'that go to-ge-ther well' (0.14)
Minor 7♭5	1-♭3-♭5-♭7	'Because'	D♯m$^{7♭5}$	'it turns me *on*' (0.37)
Minor (maj 7th)	1-♭3-5-7	'Cry Baby Cry'	Em(maj^7)	'The King of Mari*gold*'
Dominant 7 sus 4	1- 4-5-♭7	'I Don't Want To Spoil The Party'	D^7sus^4	*Opening chord* (0.03)

[1] Played as G5, but heard in F as McCartney is tuned a whole step down (as explained by Paul on *Anthology II*).

4) TRIADS WITH ADDED NOTES

In all these cases a note is added to a triad without a seventh extension.

Name	Formula	Song	Chord	Lyric
Major 6th	1-3-5-6	'All My Loving'	G^6	*Penultimate chord*
Minor 6th	1-♭3-5-6	'Real Love'	Am^6	'No need to be a-*lone*'
Major 6/9	1-3-5-6-9	'No Reply'	$C^{6/9}$	*Final chord* (2.10)
Major add 9	1-3-5-9	'Getting Better'	F add^9	*Opening chords*
Minor add 9	1-♭3-5-9	'Golden Slumbers'	Dm add^9	'Sleep pretty darling, do not cry...' (0.26)

5) EXTENDED CHORDS

In these chords a seventh is included, prior to further extensions to the 9th and/or the 13th (equivalent to the 6th).

Name	Formula	Song	Chord	Lyric
Major 9th	1-3-5-7-9	'Sun King'	D $major^9$	'Here *comes* the Sun King' (0.29)
Minor 9th	1-♭3-5-♭7-9	'Julia'	Am^9	'Julia, Ju-li-*a*' (0.20)
Dominant 9th	1-3-5-♭7-9	'This Boy'	D^9	Bridge lead-in (0.59)
Dominant 9 sus 4	1-4-5-♭7-9	'She's Leaving Home'	B^9sus^4	'Leaving the note' (0.23)
Dominant 7 add 13	1-3-5-♭7-13	'Because'	A^7add^{13}	'the world is *round*' (0.53)
Dominant 7 add 13	1-3-5-♭7-13	'September In The Rain'	G^7add^{13}	*Repeated intro chord*[2]
Minor 7 add 13	1-♭3-5- ♭7 -13	'Happiness Is A Warm Gun'	Am^7add^{13}	'She's not a *girl*'[3]
Minor 6 (major 7th)	1-♭3-5-7-13	'Dear Wack!' (a.k.a. 'Moonglow')	$Cm^6(maj^7)$	*Second chord* (0.12 and 0.29)

[2] Two versions of the dominant 7th add 13 have been included as an excuse to contrast a conventional inversion ('Because') with the cult guitar shape that opens 'September In The Rain' (see Chapter 12, page 443, footnote 13).

[3] This is basically an Am6 chord, but listen closely to Lennon's 'Donovan picking pattern', which features the G note (m7) as well.

6) ALTERED DOMINANT CHORDS

Alteration refers to the sharpening or flattening of the 5th and/or 9th degree.

Name	Formula	Song	Chord	Lyric
Dominant 7♯5	1-3-♯5-♭7	'The Sheik Of Araby'	A7♯5	'You'll *rule this world*'
Dominant 7♯9	1-3-5-♭7 -♯9	'Taxman'	D7♯9	'Let me tell you how it will be...'
Dominant 7♭9	1-3-5-♭7 -♭9	'I Want You (She's So Heavy)'	E7♭9	'It's driving me mad' (0.54)

TRIAD INVERSIONS

Here the first note in each formula (which corresponds to the bass note to the right of the '/' in each 'slash' chord) is heard as the lowest note in the chord. This defines the type of inversion – even if, in practice, the other notes of the chord are stacked in different orders above it.

Type	Formula	Song	Chord/Bass note	Lyric
Major 1st inversion	3-5-1	'Penny Lane'	A/C♯	'In my ears and *in my* eyes'
Major 2nd inversion	5-1-3	'I've Got A Feeling'	D/A	'I've got a *feeling*'
Major 3rd inversion	7-5-1-3	'A Day In The Life'	C/B	'About a *lucky man who*'
Minor 1st inversion	♭3-5-1	'Long Long Long'	Gm/B♭	'...long time...' (0.17)
Minor 2nd inversion	5-1-♭3	'Revolution' (single version)	C♯m/G♯	'*...but when you talk about des*-truction'
Minor 3rd inversion	♭7-5-1-♭3	'The Fool On The Hill'	Em/D	'A-*lone on the hill*'

2. Getting started

The following chart summarises the The Beatles' versatility when choosing an initial chord change. In each case, the tonic is heard as the first chord, followed by a change to one of the other major or minor chords of the chromatic scale.

The opening change

Scale step	Formula	Song	Lyric	Opening tonic	First change
2	ii	'Ticket To Ride'	'is going a-*way*'	A	Bm
	II	'Eight Days A Week'	'I need your *love, babe*'	D	E^7
♭3	♭III	'Magical Mystery Tour'	'Roll up, *roll up for the*'	E	G
3	iii	'A Day In The Life'	'I read the *news today*'	G	Bm
	III	'You're Going To Lose That Girl'	'If you don't take her *out tonight*'	E	$G\sharp^7$
4	iv	'That Means A Lot'	'Friends said that your *love won't mean a* lot'	E	Am
	IV	'Love Me Do'	'Love , love me *do*'	G	C
5	v	'She's Leaving Home'	'Wednesday *morning at* five o'clock'	E	Bm
	V	'I Want To Hold Your Hand'	'I'll tell you *something*'	G	D
♭6	♭VI	'It Won't Be Long'	'Every night, when *everybody has* gone'	E	C
6	vi	'This Boy'	'That boy...'	D	Bm
	VI	'Good Day Sunshine'	'I need to laugh, *and when the* sun is out'	A	$F\sharp^7$
♭7	♭VII	'I'll Be Back'	'If you *break my heart*'	Am	G^6
7	vii	'Yesterday'	'Yesterday, *love was*'	G	$F\sharp m^7$
	VII	'I'm So Tired'	'I'm so *tired*'	A	G♯

The Beatles did build chords on the dissonant slots of i, ♭II, ♭ii, ♭V, ♭v, ♭vi and ♭vii (as we discuss elsewhere in the book), though these chords are typically too awkward to use as an opening chord change.

3. Where do I go now?

Having finished the verse, or 'A' section, how do you find contrasting harmony? This is one area in which The Beatles' songwriting superiority asserted itself, and the following chart shows how they were able to start a new section on almost every one of the 12 'destinations' in the chromatic scale (again, with either a major or minor chord).

This list has been drawn up irrespective of whether or not the song goes on to assert a new tonality – the aim here is just to show the range of options open to songwriters.

With the exception of ♭II, ♭ii and ♭iii, each new 'section' is a bridge or middle eight.

Scale step	Formula	Song	Lyric	Previous tonic	New chord
1	i	'Michelle'	'I *love you, I love you*'	F	Fm
	I	'I Feel Fine'	'*I'm so* glad'	G	G
♭2	♭ii	'Cry Baby Cry'	'Let me take you back'	Em	Fm
	♭II	'Lucy In The Sky With Diamonds'	'*Cellophane* flowers'	A	B♭
2	ii	'Help!'	'Help me if you can'	A	Bm
	II	'Dr Robert'	'Well, well, well'	A	B
♭3	♭iii	'And I Love Her'	Guitar solo	E	Gm
	♭III	'Two Of Us'	'*You and I have* memories'	G	B♭
3	iii	'I'll Cry Instead'	'Don't want to *cry*'	G	Bm
	III	'You Can't Do That'	'Everybody's *green*'	G	B^7
4	iv	'Lady Madonna'	'Friday night arrives'	A	Dm^7
	IV	'Ticket To Ride'	'*I don't know why she's riding so high*'	A	D^7
♭5	♭V	'Catswalk'	Link to bridge	Gm	D♭
5	v	'From Me To You'	'I've got *arms*'	C	Gm
	V	'Love Me Do'	'Someone to love'	G	D
♭6	♭VI	'Come And Get It'	'Did I hear you say'	E	C
6	vi	'We Can Work It Out'	'Life is very short'	D	Bm
	VI	'Something'	'... You're asking me'	C	A
♭7	♭vii	'I'm Only Sleeping'	'*Keeping an eye on* the world'	Em	Dm
	♭VII	'Penny Lane'	'Penny *Lane is in my*'	B	A
7	vii	'Yesterday'	'*Why* she had to go'	G	F♯m^7

4. Methods of modulation – a summary of Beatles tools

The following chart is designed to capture the various mechanisms by which The Beatles switched keys, and to encourage an appreciation of the range of modulatory mechanisms they used to transport us so effortlessly to, and from, a range of brave new harmonic worlds.

In each case the last chord in the sequence is the new tonic, though sometimes the 'connecting' or 'preparatory' chord is highlighted to reflect the most prominent musical highlight. All formulas (some of which carry the author's own affectionate 'labels' to help distinguish them) are viewed in terms of the key of arrival. Hence the V-I move in 'Penny Lane' reflects entry into the chorus key of A.

Cadence	Formula	Model example	Transition	Chord change
'Sudden' Perfect	V-I	'Here, There And Everywhere'	'I want her everywhere'	F^{7}-B♭
'Standard' Perfect	(IV)-V-I	'Penny Lane'	'very strange'	(F♯)-E^{7}-A
'Extra' Perfect	ii-V-I	'From Me To You'	'I got arms'	Gm-C-F
'Borrowed' Perfect	iv-V-I	'I'm Only Sleeping'	'Keeping an eye'	Dm-E^{7}-Am
'Augmented 6th' Perfect	♭VI-V-i	'Catswalk'	Verse - bridge	D♭-C^{7}-Fm
Super Phrygian	♭II-V-I	'Do You Want To Know A Secret?'	'really care... listen'	F-B^{7}-E
Diatonic 'drop'	iii-ii-I	'Lucy In The Sky With Diamonds'	'... cellophane flowers'	Dm-Dm/C-B♭
Plagal	IV-i	'Girl'	'She's the kind of girl'	D^{7}-Am
Minor Plagal	iv-I	'The Continuing Story Of Bungalow Bill'	'... saxon mother's son'	Fm-C
Aeolian	♭VII-i	'Not A Second Time'	'Not a second time'	D^{7}-Em
	♭VII-I	'Something'	'... You're asking me'	G-A
Phrygian	♭II-I	'You're Going To Lose That Girl'	'What else can I do?'	F-E
Diminished sub for V^{7}	vii dim^{7}-I	'Because'	'Love is old, love is new'	D dim-F♯

APPENDIX 3

An Introduction to Harmonisation

A beginners' guide to how tunes 'work' over chords

If *harmony* can be defined as the structure, function and relationship of chords, then *melody* – the 'tune' – is a succession of notes, varying in pitch and length, with an organised, recognisable shape.[1]

However, what really matters is the musical effect created by the *merging of harmony and melody.* The *way* that the chords support a melody is known as *harmonisation*, a principle that describes this 'blend', arguably the essence of songwriting magic.

Even if we can never quite capture the intangible inspiration behind a classic song, there are nevertheless certain basic principles of harmonisation that underlie the process. They apply equally to songwriters making their first fumbling footsteps, and to music enthusiasts analysing and appreciating the wonders of The Beatles' back catalogue.

The choice of harmonisation determines the feel and character of a melody, whether it feels simple, or down to earth; or more sophisticated, challenging, poignant or ambiguous. These types of adjectives (which we often use to describe a tune) can usually be related directly to the harmonisation itself.

This 'Introduction to Harmonisation' uses just a handful of Beatles examples to illustrate how individual melodies are supported by the underlying chords.

[1] *The Oxford Dictionary Of Music.*

Basic reference points – triad and non-*triad tones*

The choice of pitch in relation to the prevailing chord is critical in this regard. If we stick to the diatonic major scale for now (leaving the other *chromatic* notes for later), we can distinguish between two basic categories:

1) Triad tones - the root, 3rd, and 5th that make up the basic chord itself. These are obvious choices that guarantee that a melody feels 'safe', 'grounded' and 'consonant'.
2) Other scale tones. These cover the 7^{ths} (already likely to be present in a V chord, i.e., a V7 chord), as well as the 9^{ths}, 6^{ths}, and 4^{ths}. These sounds bring varying degrees of tension to a melody, especially when emphasized on strong downbeats. They add colour to a tune by mixing their respective dissonance with the predictable consonance of the triad tones.

Nursery rhyme chants, for example – of which The Beatles had their own portfolio – tend to home in on triad tones, making the choruses of 'Yellow Submarine', 'All Together Now' and 'Lucy In The Sky With Diamonds' instantly sing-able by all on *karaoke* night. These same melodies wouldn't be singled out as some of the Beatles' finest – for the same reason. This is in stark contrast to the willowy lines of moving ballads like 'Yesterday' and the dark haunting phrases of 'Strawberry Fields' – they challenge the listener (and certainly the would-be singer) through the use of *non-triad* tones that sit, more exotically, 'outside' their underlying chords.

'Simple' melody – triad tone tunes and nursery rhymes

Let's start off simply. For those of us not blessed with tuneful inspiration, who may struggle to invent melodies, the first port-of-call should be the triad tones of the basic chords in a key. These are pitches already represented by the notes in the chord sequence itself, and they guarantee – by definition – that your melody will work.

Take 'All Together Now', which most would agree is one of the simplest of Beatles songs. This is for a number of reasons – certainly the lyrics aren't too taxing, the chords focus on a repeated alternation between I and V, and the structure of the melody is hardly intricate.

Watch how The Beatles repeat the major 3rd of the tonic four times, before rising a half-step for their next note as the chord changes.

'All Together Now' (verse)

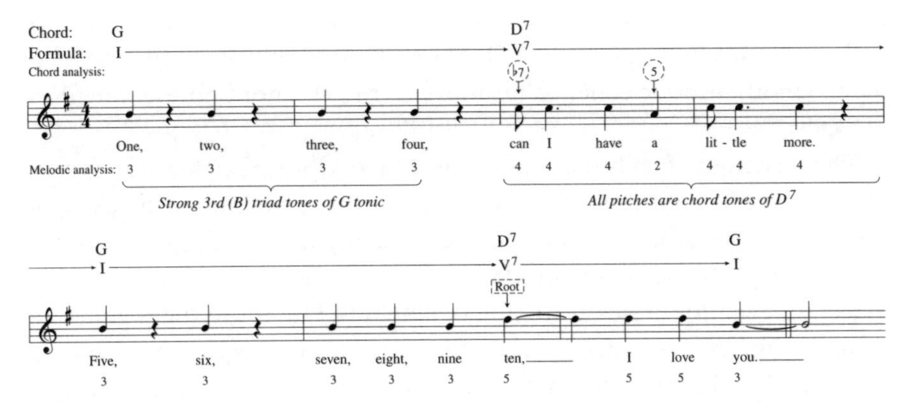

Harmonisation requires us to view notes in a melody both in terms of the parent major scale and *also* the prevailing chord. In terms of the parent major scale, the B to C melody moves from the 3rd to the 4th of the major scale of G ('3-4').

However, 'All Together Now' has a far more consonant feel because *in relation to the prevailing chord*, D7 at this point, the C note does not represent the 4th degree, but rather the ♭7th of the chord, thereby reinforcing the D7. The C is *contained within* the chord, which means that while it is not as predictably 'inside' as the root, 3rd or 5th, it is only one level removed.

The only other pitch in this extract of the melody is a D note reached at the climax of the phrase (appropriately on the 'ten' in the song's 1-10 count). Once again, this melody note is also a chord tone – this time it's the 'inside' root of the V chord. The phrase then resolves immediately at the start of the next bar as the song returns to the G chord, and the tune itself to the same major 3rd pitch that we started on.

Our next example, the chorus of 'Lucy In The Sky With Diamonds', is only slightly more complicated:

'Lucy In The Sky With Diamonds'

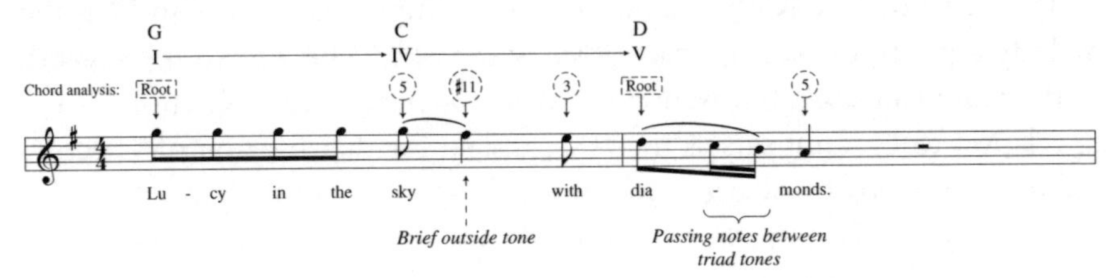

Again the melody starts out on a single, repeated triad tone on the tonic chord. This time it's a G note, the tonic of the home key, which is used for each of the words 'Lucy in the'. This same G note then becomes the 5th of the C (another inside tone), as we move to the IV chord on the downbeat of 'sky'.

The harmony finally completes its Three-Chord Trick cycle with a move to the V, book-ended by strong triad tones in relation to the new prevailing chord (the root of D for 'Dia-', falling to A, the 5th, for '-monds').

This preponderance of 'inside' tones over the primary major triads makes for clear footholds as we sing the melody. The chord tones guide the way, acting as reference points that create an important sense of predictability throughout. That's not to say that we are necessarily criticising these indisputably 'simple' melodies. They often achieve vital contrast with more sophisticated, tense melodies in other sections of a song ('Lucy In The Sky With Diamonds' being a prime example).

Beyond the basic chord tones – melodic dissonance

While triad tones are essential reference points in the construction and harmonisation of a tune, they aren't the only thing happening in most melodies. It is those additional notes that provide the secret to preventing a melody from sounding bland. Melodies do not, and should not, plot a straight path through the guts of the chord sequence. They *need* to tap into the dissonance represented, in varying degrees, by other tones beyond, or 'outside', the triad.

'All Together Now' was certainly an example of extreme simplicity in a Beatles melody but, even there, the ♭7th of the V chord was a humble attempt at generating tension. Meanwhile, both 'Lucy In The Sky With Diamonds' and 'Yellow Submarine' boast some 'extra' notes in their tunes that are not accounted for in terms of any of the prevailing chord tones.

'Lucy In The Sky With Diamonds', for example, introduces an F♯ as the melody dips, on the second part of the word 'sky'. This note is the seventh of the parent G scale, but remember that it is heard over a C chord – and in relation to C it appears as the ♯11th, and so for that fraction of a second the total implied chord is a more exotic C add ♯11. Similarly, the C and B notes that unfold on the word 'diamonds' are 'outside' the underlying triad – they are the ♭7th and 6th of the D chord.

Of course, songwriters and musicians don't think in these terms – they would just sing a melody instinctively over this type of Three-Chord Trick. Nevertheless, we can see that non-triad tones are important in making a melody 'work', even if in this context those notes are merely *linking* the strong chord tones. While they are essential to the character of the line, the non-triad tones are not *as* important as the essential triad tones, especially those that fall on the *strong downbeats*. The triad tones form the skeleton of the melody – indeed, a child or karaoke novice attempting to sing the tune for the first time might easily miss out the non-triad tones, and home in on those strong pitches.

We instinctively regard melody notes that fall on downbeats as more important than those on the upbeats, and this is an essential part of appreciating melodies and, equally, the nature of the chosen harmonisation.

Contrast the off-beat, 'non-chord' tones in 'Lucy In The Sky With Diamonds' with the second degree of the scale (the '2' or 9th) that emerges in the first bar of 'We Can Work It Out':

'We Can Work It Out'

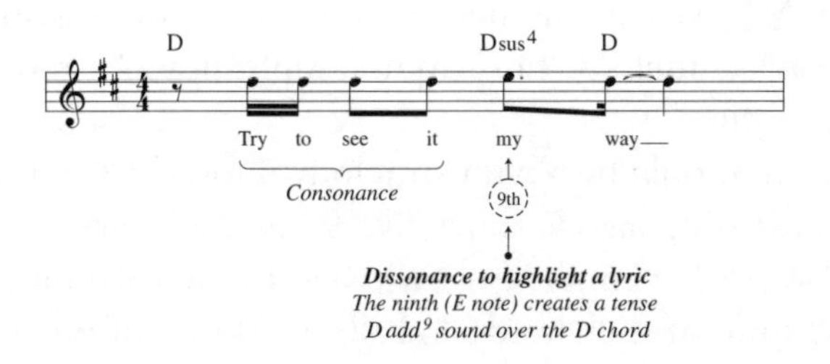

As with 'Lucy In The Sky With Diamonds' the melody starts out with a repeated tonic, this time for each of the first four words: 'Try to see it ...'. Again, this 'grounds' the tune and, again as in 'Lucy', we even return to the same pitch at the end of the phrase, on 'way'.

However, look at the status of the pitch on 'my'. It is stressed on the strong downbeat (beat 3 in the bar), and also enjoys greater time value than the earlier notes. This non-chord tone – brought in from the remaining tones up for grabs in the D major scale – is now fundamental to the melody.

It is far more than just a passing note between two triad tones, or a note that might have sounded as a voice slurs between notes that are spaced apart. To reach that E requires a conscious departure from our tonic base, moving assertively from 1 to 2 before returning home on 'way'.

This second degree of the major scale may not seem like a big deal – after all, 'Lucy' also featured the same note (A, in the key of G, which concludes the phrase on 'diamonds'). The difference, however, is in the way that the note is harmonised.

This scale degree is a perfect match for the V chord of the key where it appears as the 5th (in the key of D, E is the 5th of A). Play 'We Can Work It Out' with an I-V-I change in the first bar, moving to an A chord on the word 'my', and you'll hear the difference. The song still works - but, if anything, *too* well. For there is now a predictability to it that The Beatles' harmonisation avoids. By staying on D-rooted harmony *throughout* the first bar, they ensure that the melodic E note creates an 'add 9' effect above the prevailing chord. The result is a more interesting, challenging, sound.

Hence the *music* is as responsible as the lyrics for the way in which we hear the line – not just 'Try to see it my way,' but with specific emphasis: 'Try to see it MY way'. This demonstrates how, by 'leaning' on tones beyond the triad, a melody can acquire sophistication, moving beyond nursery rhyme status.

The conclusion should be obvious: melody is inseparable from harmony. If nominally interesting *melodic* tones, like 9^{ths} and 6^{ths}, become 'lost' as triad tones themselves, so the emphasis is switched to the harmony, directing us more to the texture of the chords and the workings of inner *voice-leading* within *a chord progression*. Subjects that, for this very reason, form so much of the analysis in this book.

Of course, the nature of harmony is that notes from the melody combine with notes in the underlying chord to determine the complete, *overall* sonority that the listener ultimately enjoys. So, whether you play a C major 7th with your guitar, or sing a B note over a C major triad, the resulting chord is the same: C major seventh, if *texturally* different.

Similarly, it is important to accept that there is no 'correct' strategy when it comes to harmonising a melody – it all depends on the effect you want.

A glimpse of chord substitution

Harmonisation is as much about the *choice* of chord underneath as it is about melody note on top. Let's now try to move away from the primary I, IV and V chords.

How can we do this? As an exercise let's see how The Beatles effectively turned the old English nursery rhyme, 'Three Blind Mice', into the famous refrain to 'All You Need Is Love'. This requires us to take our first step into the world of chord *substitution*, a principle that will emerge as one of the most important songwriting secrets of The Beatles.

Look first at 'Three Blind Mice', whose chords in their most primitive form follow the same I-V-I premise as 'All Together Now'. Again the song 'works' by using a three-note melody whose pitches correspond directly to the chord tones of the two primary triads in the progression. This time the line is '3-2-1', reflecting a phrase which starts on the major 3rd, descends a whole step to the second, and finally moves by another whole step to the tonic of the key, G major.

Here is the very simplest manifestation of the descending voice leading principle we introduced in Appendix 1. Notice how it creates a self-contained musical motif that intuitively leads us gently to the most satisfying 'close' of a tonic pitch over tonic I chord.

'Three Blind Mice'

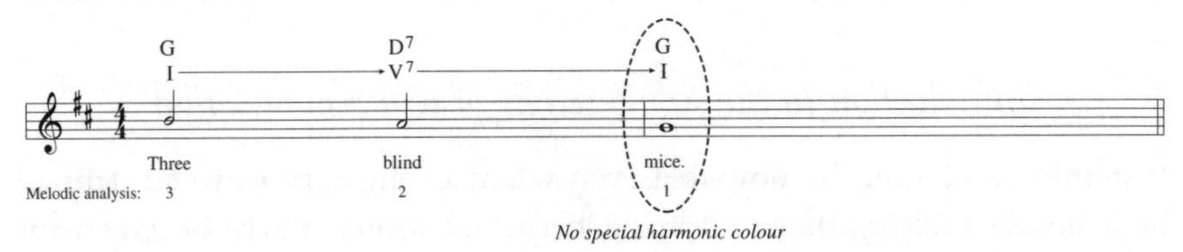

The Beatles used this same melodic descent in numerous songs throughout their catalogue, including for the 'Love, love, love' chant of 'All You Need Is Love'.[2] The following extract confirms that both feature exactly the same notes in relation to the key centre, with identical note values. There is, however, a vital difference in the harmonisation.[3]

[2] Having grasped the concept of 3-2-1, check out next how other Beatles tunes target the tonic from 'further back' in the scale. E.g. the 4-3-2-1 of 'Ob-La-Di, Ob-La-Da' (as 'li-fe goes on' drops to Bb, at 0.42); and the 5-4-3-2-1 of the 'All My Loving' refrain (ending with '... to you', on E at 0.22).

[3] We will ignore for the time being the metric quirk of a dropped beat in the second bar of 'All You Need Is Love', and the descending bass line.

'All You Need Is Love'

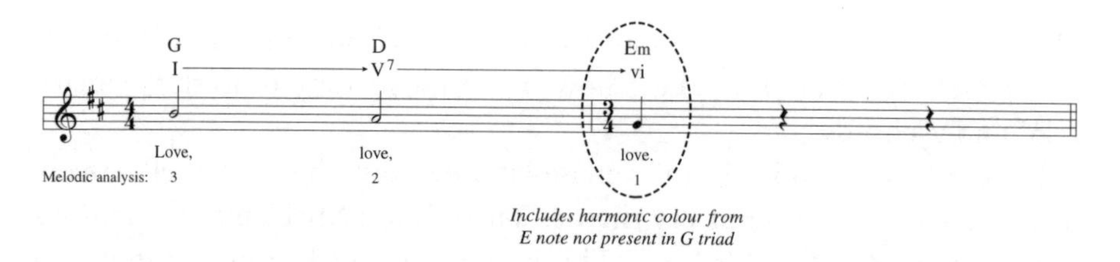

The fact that the final G note in 'All You Need Is Love' appears not as the root of the predictable G chord (as in 'Three Blind Mice') but rather as the ♭3rd of the E minor chord, subtly changes the context.

Why? Because this choice of harmonisation means that the listener is now introduced to the E note contained in the E minor chord. This is the sixth of the parent G major scale, and adds extra colour and tension that is lacking in the more primitive harmonisation of the nursery rhyme.

Substitution brings musical interest to a song simply by supporting the *same melody* note with a *different chord* from what we might have expected.

The melody may be the element of the song that you whistle in the street but, as this last exercise demonstrates, it does not fully explain why a song 'works'. It is with the help of this *'vi-for-I' substitution* that The Beatles' 'version' of this nursery rhyme takes on a new dimension.

Introduction to the subtle secrets of re-*harmonisation*

It should be obvious by now that even when a song appears to be defined by a simple melody, the underlying harmony should never be taken for granted. The chords of a song are not *necessarily* 'implied' by a tune, as novice musicians might assume. The same melody can be 'dressed-up' and take on a whole new identity purely by harmonising it in a different way.

The Beatles confirm that they understand this implicitly in those songs where they not only harmonise a melody – but *re-harmonise* it. This acknowledges that there is not necessarily one 'best' way to harmonise a melody line, and for any particular pitch in a given melody a songwriter can change the supporting chord.

Take a look at 'Yes It Is', a song perhaps most famous for its painstakingly constructed three-part harmony. However, here we have just extracted what is the arguably the strongest individual melody line:

'Yes It Is'

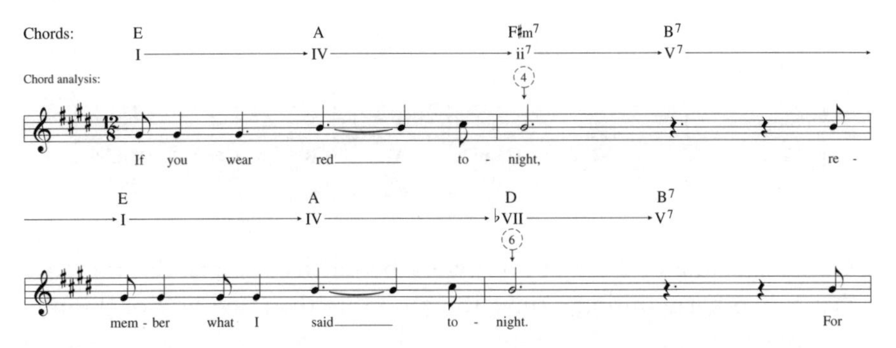

The extract opens with a two-bar phrase whose melodic pitches are repeated identically to form the first 4-bar section. Notice that the sound of the crucial second syllable of 'to-*night'* (which we hear at 0.15) is subtly different from the one we have already heard (first at 0.08). The Beatles have switched the chord under that B note. This B pitch is the familiar 5th of the parent scale of E major and, when sung over the F♯m7, it appears as a delicately haunting 4th above the minor chord. However, *second time around*, the same B is *re-harmonised* by a steelier D major, over which it is now heard as a more luscious 6th.

Play the song and listen carefully to the sound of the B note over these two chords. They are markedly different and yet combine over the course of the section to give great depth to the song. This type of re-harmonisation is a rarely appreciated Beatles songwriting secret, and one that can be seen in action in songs ranging from primal Beatlemania classics like 'I Want To Hold Your Hand', to more textured later masterpieces, such as 'Hello Goodbye'.

The harmonisation and reharmonisation of that B pitch on 'tonight' confirms that the melody *on its own* simply doesn't explain the way the song unfolds. The following table recognises that this one note could have been harmonised in a number of ways (each having a different effect on the listener) by using different chords from the parent diatonic scale – E major.

Harmonising the B note of 'tonight'

Diatonic options

Formula	I	ii	iii	IV	V	vi	vii
Chord	E	F♯m7	G♯m7	A	B	C♯m7	D♯m7♭5
B note is:	5th	4th	♭3rd	2nd	Root	7th	♯5th

Certainly some of these options work better than others. But the point is that, when harmonising a tune, there is more than one way of skinning a cat. Songwriters of differing sophistication, or those working in different musical genres, might well have harmonised the very same tune of 'Yes It Is' in a completely different way.

For instance, the harmonically challenged 'folkie' might have just returned to the E chord itself and conceived the B note as its 5th. Or we could have moved directly to the B chord – the V – where it naturally fits perfectly as the root. More jazz-conscious writers, meanwhile, might have developed elaborate textures with the C♯m7, or even G♯m7 chords (though the dissonant D♯m7♭5 would perhaps be a step too far).

Beyond the diatonic scale – an early taste of 'borrowing'

However, the D chord The Beatles actually chose is not a member of the cosy, diatonic harmonised scale of E major at all. It is brought in for added colour *from elsewhere in the chromatic spectrum*. As such it is an example of the musical principle of 'borrowing' a chord; another quintessential Beatle subject to which Chapter 7 is entirely devoted.

Consider that, in theory at least, a note can be harmonised by a chord built on *any* of the 12 notes in music. This means that there are five additional roots to be considered that are not already taken care of by our 7-note major scale. Sure enough, The Beatles' D chord in 'Yes It Is' is built on one of these:

Non-Diatonic options

Formula	♭II	♭III	♭V	♭VI	♭VII
Chord	F	G	B♭	C	D
B note is:	♭5th	3rd	♭2nd	7th	6th

Don't think for a minute that these more exotic options are not viable: for example, a rocker would happily harmonise that B with a G major chord, the C major 7th would be perfect for romantic sixties French film music, the F wouldn't escape the attention of the flamenco fan, while the B♭, ultra-dissonant to most ears, would nevertheless go down a treat with many 'Death Metal' outfits.

The Beatles used their awareness of such non-diatonic chords throughout their career. As we discuss in Chapter 7, this ♭VII fitted the bill as a variation to the harmony of 'Yes It Is', delivering a tougher rehearing as the rogue chord powers its way on to V.

If The Beatles' ♭VII in 'Yes It Is' seemed a bit of a luxury given that they already had a perfectly good choice of chord with that F♯m7, then there are many other situations where a particular rogue chord is an essential requirement to get a melody out of a tight spot.

'It's Only Love' is one such example. While it's only speculation, it seems likely that John conceived the melody first, given its resolutely descending path, clearly defined by a distinctive, chromatic semitone drop that can be clearly traced from the root of the parent key of C.

'It's Only Love'

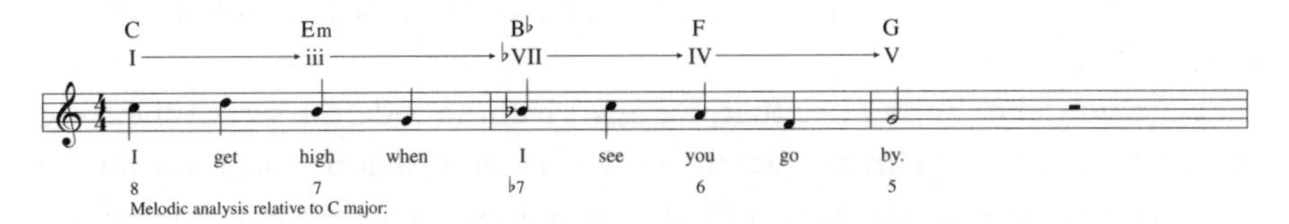

The tune's basic premise can be reduced to an effortless '8-7-♭7-6' that finally succumbs to a whole-step jump down to the '5'. The only problem for John Lennon is that the third note in the descent, B♭, is not in the C major scale – it is the ♭7th of C, whose diatonic major scale of course descends '8-7-6', with a whole step between the B and the A.

Moreover, the B♭ note is clearly an integral part of the melody, emerging on the strong first beat of the second bar, giving it far greater status than a passing or 'neighbour' tone. Yet the non-diatonic nature of the B♭ means that, by definition, Lennon has far fewer harmonisation options (than he had, say, in 'Yes It Is') because this ♭7th pitch is *already outside the scale* – thereby effectively ruling out all the diatonic triads in the key of C.

One solution might have been to turn the tonic chord into a bluesy C7, perhaps following a C major 7th – in this way John might have created a 'I-Imaj7-I7' progression, something that we find, for example, in George Harrison's 'Something'. Try playing 'It's Only Love' in this way to see that this progression certainly works. Apologies to John Lennon for this purely academic exercise!

'It's Only Love' – re-harmonised!

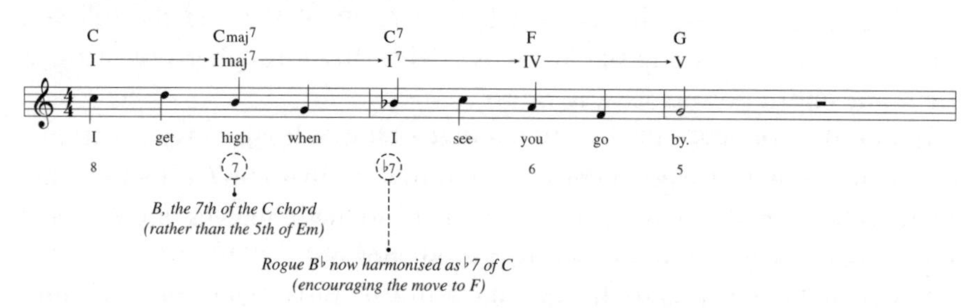

Whether Lennon actually tried this alternative harmonisation we'll never know, but we do know that that his finished song is defined by far greater *movement in the harmony*, with the B♭ note harmonised as the root of the ♭VII chord itself. The result is a busier progression which, it could be argued, better captures the sense of movement already implicit in the lyrical theme.

It is essential to appreciate that, for any given melody, the *feel* of the song hinges to an overwhelming extent on the harmonisation – and not just in a ballad context like 'Yes It Is' and 'It's Only Love', where the premium on a 'melodic feel' might appear to be paramount. The Beatles were constantly applying the subtlest of harmonisation principles to even the rockiest of songs.

Our final example looks at the inspired choice of ending chords at the close of 'A Hard Day's Night.'

Notice how the 'signature' melody, which opens every verse, is reheard at the end of the song – but not over the standard I-IV-I verse sequence with which we have become familiar. Now the same tune concludes over another rogue ♭VII, this time one that takes the place of the final tonic on which the song 'should' end. The repeated melodic D note, around which much of the song hinges, is again in evidence – but now it is re-harmonised. Previously it was heard as both the 5th of G, and the 9th of C, but we are finally left with it ringing in our ears as the 6th of F.

'A Hard Day's Night'

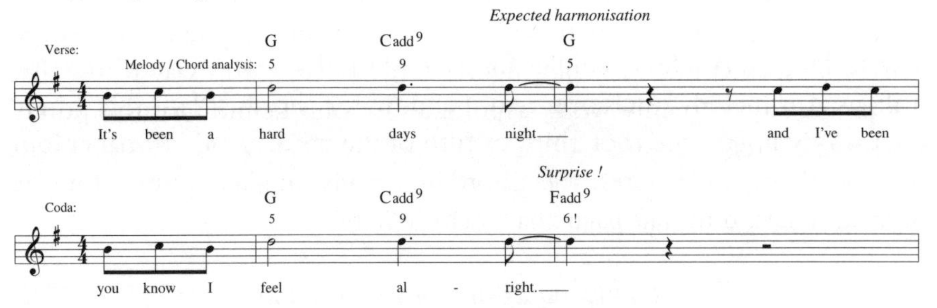

At a stroke, the aura of the entire song changes. It's as if the singer has finally been relieved of the burden which he has been gradually unloading over the course of the song. Beatles expert Wilfrid Mellers suggests that 'the coda crystallises the ambivalence between Home and World Outside,' adding that the repeated D notes which 'in the initial phrase spelt tedium ("work all day") … now suggest peace'.[4]

To a very great extent, it is the 'add 6' character of the final chord that helps to evoke this sense. But, more importantly, this effect is delivered not on the tonic, but on that unlikely finishing ♭VII chord (F), a whole step down from the tonic (in the key of G).

This introduction is intended above all to confirm the one essential principle of harmonisation – that, just as there is no single 'correct' melody implied by a given chord progression, so there is no predetermined harmonic path for a given melody.

Harmonisation is the process whereby different chords are 'juggled' to create different effects when supporting a melody note. It is a musical principle of which The Beatles were grandmasters. At every turn, their catalogue reminds us that keeping an open mind to the potential of the complete lexicon of chords, when supporting even the simplest of melodies, is one of the secrets of great songwriting.

Melody plus chord equals Harmonisation

The variety of overall sonorities that can be created by using different melody notes over instrumental chords is confirmed in the following tables.

[4] *Twilight Of The Gods: The Music Of The Beatles*, pp. 44-5. Mellers conducts his analysis in the key of C major (presumably with reference to early seventies sheet music), but his observations are equally applicable whatever the key.

triad + melody note = overall sonority

The tables give Beatles examples for each of the 12 notes in the chromatic scale used as melody notes over major and minor chords. Obviously where the melody note is the root, third or fifth of the triad, no additional colour is implied. In other cases, the chord is usually implied purely for the fleeting duration of that particular melody note.

Melody notes over a major triad

Degree	Song	Lyric	Melody	Chord	Total sonority
1	'Here, There And Everywhere'	'*Here...*'	G	G	G
♭2	'Strawberry Fields Forever'[5]	'*No*-thing is real'	G	F♯^{7}	F♯$^{7\flat 9}$
2	'I'm So Tired'	'I'm *so* tired'	B	A	A add^{9}
♯2/♭3	'The Word'	'Say the *word*'	F	D^{7}	D$^{7\sharp 9}$
Blue♭3	'Yer Blues'[6]	'Yes, I'm *lone*-ly'	G	E	E$^{7\sharp 9}$
3	'Penny Lane'	'Penny *Lane*'	D♯	B	B
4	'I Feel Fine'	'Baby's *good* to *me* you *know*'	C	G^{7}	G^{7} add^{11}
♯4	'A Day In The Life'	'I just *had* to laugh'	B	F	F add$^{\sharp 11}$
♭5	'Blue Jay Way'	'They'll be over soon they *said*'	G♭	C^{5}	C add$^{\flat 5}$
5	'A Hard Day's Night'	'A *hard* day's *night*'	D	G	G
♯5	'She Loves You'	'You *know you* should be glad'	A♯	D^{7}	D^{7}aug
6	'She Loves You'	'*Yeah!*' (0.10 & 2.16)	E	G	G^{6}
♭7	'I Wanna Be Your Man'	'I wanna *be* your lover, *ba*-by'	D	E^{7}	E^{7}
7	'Something'	'Something in the way she *moves*'	B	C	C maj^{7}

[5] Very rare dissonant effect but seek out a McCartney example in the bridge of 'Love Of The Loved' where C hangs above B7 on 'you *love* me' (0.43). And a Harrison example in 'I Me Mine' where the F note creates E7♭9: '*coming on strong*'.

[6] The blues context is worth distinguishing as the ♭3rd here is rarely a precise pitch. The bluesy effect is often the direct result of being slightly sharp, somewhere between ♭3rd and major 3rd.

Melody notes over a minor triad

Degree	Song	Lyric	Melody	Chord	Total sonority
1	'Things We Said Today'	'*You* say *you* will *love* me'	A	Am	Am
♭2	'Bungalow Bill'	Intro guitar figure	F	Em	Em add♭9
2	'And I Love Her'	'I give her *all* my love'	D♯	C♯m	C♯m add9
♭3	'Because'	'Be-*cause* the world'	E	C♯m	C♯m
4	'Help!'	'Help me if you can'	E	Bm	Bm add11
♭5	'Strawberry Fields Forever'	'going to Strawber-*ry* Fields'	B♭	Em	Em add♭5
Blue♭5	'I Want You'[7]	'I want *you*' (0.22)	E♭	Am	Am add♭5
5	'I Me Mine'	'*All* through the day'	E	Am	Am
♯5	'The Fool On The Hill'	'But the fool *on* the hill'	A♯	Dm	Dm aug
6	'She Loves You'	'Yes, she *loves you*'	A	Cm	Cm6
♭7	'Penny Lane'	'A portrait of the *Queen*'	A	Bm	Bm7
7	'Nowhere Man'	'Making all his *no*-where plans'	G♯	Am	Am (maj7)

A Guide To Intervals

Melodic Intervals

This section gives Beatles examples for each of the 12 ascending and descending intervals in music. This provides a useful way for readers to familiarise themselves with the unique sound of each interval, and also demonstrates the huge range of melodic ideas at work in The Beatles catalogue.

In each case the interval in question starts on the underlined lyric and moves to the lyric that is *italicised*. The scale tone numbers relate to the chord in question, which is the tonic I chord unless otherwise stated.

For example, 'Nowhere Man' illustrates an ascent of a perfect fourth as the A note on the first two lyrics ('he's a') rises five semitones to D, taking us to the tonic (here numbered as '8' to help depict the rise).

[7] Again, the blues context is important as the ♭5th is rarely a precise pitch. The bluesy effect of the tone is achieved by being either slightly flat (–) or slightly sharp (+); or, as famously here, wavering between sharp and flat.

Ascending intervals

Semitones	Interval name	Song	Lyric	Scale tones
+ 1	Minor second	'I Will'	'Who *knows*'	E-F (7-8)
+ 2	Major second	'Here, There And Everywhere'	'Here, *there*'	G-A (1-2)
+ 3	Minor third	'Happiness Is A Warm Gun'	'She's *not* a girl'	E-G (5-♭7)
+ 4	Major third	'Penny Lane'	'Pen(ny) *Lane*'	B -D♯ (1-3)
+ 5	Perfect fourth	'Nowhere Man'	'He's a *real*'	B-E (5-8)
+ 6	Augmented fourth	'Blue Jay Way'	'There's (a) *fog*'	C-G♭(1-♭5)
+ 7	Perfect fifth	'She Said She Said'	'She *said*'	A-E (1-5)
+ 8	Minor sixth	'Because'	'Be-*cause*'	G♯-E (5-♭3)
+ 9	Major sixth	'Got To Get You Into My Life'	'I *was alone*'	D-B (5-3)
+ 10	Minor seventh	'She Came In Through The Bathroom Window'	'She *came*'	A-G (1-♭7)
+ 11	Major seventh	'She's A Woman'	'She is-n't... *She's* a woman'	A-G♯(1-7)[8]
+ 12	Octave	'Tell Me What You See'	'If *you* let me'	D-D (5-5)

Descending intervals

Semitones	Interval name	Song	Lyric	Scale tones
- 1	Minor second	'Something'	'she *moves*'	C-B (8-7)
- 2	Major second	'Yesterday'	'Yes - *terday*'	G-F (2-1)
- 3	Minor third	'Hey Jude'	'Hey *Jude*'	C-A (5-3)
- 4	Major third	'I'll Get You'	'Oh *yeah*'	F♯-D (3-1)
- 5	Perfect fourth	'Dear Prudence'	'Dear Prud-*ence*'	D-A (8-5)
- 6	Augmented fourth	'Strawberry Fields Forever'	'Nothing is *real*'	A♯-E(3-♭7)
- 7	Perfect fifth	'Honey Pie'	'Ho-ney *Pie*'	D-G (5-1)
- 8	Minor sixth	'Misery'	'The world *is*	F-A (4-6)[9]
- 9	Major sixth			
- 10	Minor seventh	'A Hard Day's Night'	'Tight... *It's* been a hard day's'	A-B (9-3)
- 11	Major seventh			
- 12	Octave	'You've Got To Hide Your Love Away'	'Hey, *you've* got to hide'	G-G (5-5)

[8] This is not a great example as it relates to the transition between the last and first notes of two adjacent song sections rather than an obvious interval *within* a discrete phrase.

[9] This is an exception in that it relates to a IV chord (F major) that unusually starts the song, and not the tonic in the key of C.

Many alternative examples could have been chosen for the categories of major seconds, thirds, perfect fourths and fifths, as these are the most common intervals in pop. The wider intervals are less common, principally because they are harder to sing, while the augmented fourth and major seventh are particularly rare, due to their dissonance. The latter is a highly unusual interval most famous for its appearance in the jazz standard 'I Will Wait For You' ('If it takes forever'), as well as the suitably stratospheric 'Theme From *Star Wars*'.

This interval seems to have been too 'out there' for The Beatles to use as an opener, but, technically at least, they achieve this 11-semitone jump in 'She's A Woman' when going from the stable root note at the end of the verse to the ambitious major 7th that starts the bridge. If eagle-eyed readers can spot a better example (and a descending major sixth and seventh), the author would welcome suggestions.

Meanwhile, let's not forget those 'unison' Beatles intros that feature two prominent opening syllables *on the same note*, e.g., 'Michelle' ('<u>Mich</u>-*elle*', C-to-C, or '<u>5</u>-*5*', in the key of F), or, indeed, 'This Boy' ('<u>That</u> *boy*', <u>F♯</u>-*F♯*, or '<u>3</u>-*3*', in the key of D).

Of course, there's no reason to stop at the octave – we can keep on going right up. 'Eleanor Rigby' features a full 15-semitone jump when the line '<u>where</u> *do* they all belong' (E to the G in the *next* octave) is repeated (first at 0.42).

APPENDIX 4

An Introduction to Beatles Song Form

What is the perfect form for a pop song? While this question may never be answered satisfactorily, The Beatles' catalogue can certainly give us a clue as to some of the best blueprints for sequencing the main elements of a composition.

Creating a checklist of essential ingredients shouldn't be too difficult.

We can instantly accept that we need a *verse* – every song has one (think of 'Yellow Submarine' with its four-part story-line). Verses will need to be interspersed with a *chorus* – just like they are in 'Yellow Submarine' or, equally famously, 'Penny Lane'. Then we'll need a *bridge* (or 'middle eight') of new material, preferably in a new key, just as The Beatles first started crafting so effectively back on 'From Me To You'.

In addition to these essential structural elements we might expect to encounter some other important sections. These might include an *intro,* especially one with a 'theme motif' that can recur as a link at other key moments, adding a sense of thematic unity (e.g., the instantly hummable, six-note melody of 'In My Life'). We might also expect to find a *pre-chorus* section, which injects extra anticipatory momentum into songs like 'Got To Get You Into My Life', raising the heart rate ahead of the sing-along climax. There might even be time for a deft *instrumental* somewhere along the way, such as the guitar solo in 'Something'. Finally the song might be rounded off with a *coda*.

But can we cram all these elements into one song? In some cases, almost. We only need to go back to the most recent 'Beatles' single, 'Real Love', to find a song that includes almost all these elements. Admittedly there's no real coda here (just a chorus that is extended before fading out), and the bridge section of new material is heard only as an instrumental, but otherwise, the structure seems like a 'form formula' for a pop song.

'Real Love' – summary of structure

A/B/C	Section	Time	Bars	Harmonic activity
	Intro	0.01	4	Em
A	Verse 1	0.12	8	E major descent
A	Verse 2	0.34	8	E major descent
B	Pre-chorus	0.55	4	E-Am^6
	Chorus	1.06	8	I-vi-IV-V
	Link	1.17	4	Em
A	Verse 3	1.28	8	E major descent
B	Pre-chorus	1.52	4	E-Am^6
	Chorus	2.01	8	I-vi-IV-V
C	Bridge (instrumental)	2.12	8	F♯m-B shift
A	Verse 4	2.26	8	E major descent
B	Pre-chorus	2.47	4	E-Am^6
	Chorus	2.58	8	I-vi-IV-V
B	Chorus (repeat to fade)	3.20	8	I-vi-IV-V

We can view the essence of the song as consisting of 8-bar 'A' sections, representing the verses, and 12-bar 'B' sections, which combine the pre-chorus and chorus (A is always followed by B). The basic *unit of form* on which the song is founded is 'ABAB' with the once-heard bridge providing contrast as an 8-bar C section.

Meanwhile, the *ordering* of these sections beyond this unit, together with other subsidiary material (such as the intro/link) are best thought of as matters of arrangement, beyond the basic composition.

AABA or ABAB?

Such ABAB schemes are often thought of as quintessential in modern pop. Certainly many Beatles songs were structured in this way: 'Can't Buy Me Love', 'Every Little Thing', 'Drive My Car', 'Good Day Sunshine', 'Penny Lane', 'Hello Goodbye' and 'Come Together' are just some of the dozens that hinge on clearly defined verses and choruses; with others like 'Girl' and 'I'm Only Sleeping' supplementing this with a later 'C' bridge. Even seemingly experimental outings as 'Love You To' can still be seen to fit comfortably into an alternating ABAB scheme.

And yet this structure is by no means representative of The Beatles catalogue. At one extreme we can find the straight, repeated 'A' structures of primitive 12-bar blues songs like 'I'm Down', and other songs of varying harmonic complexity, from 'Rocky Racoon' to 'You Know My Name'. At the other extreme, there are the labyrinthine, multi-sectional constructions that started as early as 'Ask Me Why', and continued through to 'I Am The Walrus' and 'You Never Give Me Your Money'.

Fundamentally the form of many of The Beatles finest hits fails to follow ABAB for the simple, yet often overlooked reason, that they lack a chorus.

Think of 'I Should Have Known Better', 'Yesterday', 'Lady Madonna', 'Hey Jude' and 'Oh! Darling' and dozens of others whose title phrases appear as the very first words. None of these songs has a formal chorus (although one could argue that 'Hey Jude' creates one in the form of its sing-along extended coda).

Then there is the whole category of songs with 'through-composed verses', where the title 'payoff' line appears at the end of this A section. 'Misery', 'From Me To You', 'Yes It Is', 'And I Love Her', 'That Means A Lot', 'The Night Before' and 'You Won't See Me' are just a few that deliver their message in this way.

Still others make us wait for this lyrical hook perhaps until the end of the B section, which could be regarded as a proper formal refrain. 'Not A Second Time' and 'In My Life' spring to mind even if these refrain section could be just as easily described as bridges or 'middles'. Others, like 'P.S. I Love You' appear to take this refrain route, only to repeat the section immediately making us believe that it may in fact have been the verse! Similarly, a song like 'Nowhere Man' features a contrasting section that appears to be a bridge – yet we hear it three times in the song as if it were a chorus. Indeed, The Beatles' catalogue includes dozens of songs whose forms cannot be neatly pigeon-holed.

The most important principle that emerges is perhaps that the vast majority of songs can at least be distilled into two or three contrasting sections that each constitute a discrete songwriting idea – whatever their length and however we choose to label them.

More specifically, most songs can be seen in terms of an identifiable opening nucleus of ABAB or AABA.[1]

[1] For a statistical look at form choices in the early years of The Beatles, see Fitzgerald, 'Lennon-McCartney and the Early British Invasion 1964–66', *The Beatles, Popular Music and Society – A Thousand Voices*, edited by Ian Inglis, especially pp. 71–3.

While it is tempting to generalise that the former *tend* to capture the verse/chorus arrangement while the latter define the chorus-free songs, there are too many exceptions. Take 'Lady Madonna', an ABAB form where the nature of the B is more clearly a bridge than a chorus, while 'Penny Lane' has the AABA of a 'through composed verse' structure but clearly features two verses before a rousing B chorus – rather than a bridge.

The A and B tags get around this problem by reflecting the fact that while the A section will usually be a verse, the precise identity of the B section may vary between bridge, chorus or pre-chorus. Beyond this, a C (and occasionally a D) section may then be added; again this will *normally* be a middle eight, but it could be a chorus.

Viewing song structures in this way helps to simplify things considerably, while also drawing attention to the task of *arranging* the song: ordering and embellishing a structure beyond this 'core' scheme.

To illustrate this, the following charts attempt to distil some of The Beatles' greatest songs by grouping the 27 songs on the *1* compilation according to their basic structural components.[2]

This is intended as a guide to demonstrate the notion of digestible A, B and C 'units', and how these can be given a variety of descriptions (readers may well disagree with the author's choice of 'chorus/bridge/link and coda').

While all these songs follow similar patterns of form in their early stages, they ultimately all diverge to a greater or lesser extent from these rigid structures. What emerges is that when it comes to structuring a pop song, there are no rules, no superior blueprints or even 'suggested commercial guidelines' – whatever the A & R men tell us.

After all, the whole point of *1* is that every song reached the hallowed Number 1 spot in either the UK or the US charts – in most cases, both.

[2] Dedicated students may want to check out the main source for our analysis: 'The Concepts Of Form And Its Change In The Singles Of The Beatles', by Terhi Nurmesjärvi, reprinted in *Beatlestudies 1* [2000], University of Jyvaskyälä.

Beatles form: The 1 album in perspective

AABA form

'Love Me Do'

A/B/C	Section	Bars	Lyric
	Intro	8	*Harmonica solo*
A	Verse	13	'Love, love me do'
A	Verse	13	'Love, love me do'
B	Bridge	8	'Someone to hold'
A	Verse	13	'Love, love me do'
A	(Solo)	12	*Harmonica solo*
A	Verse	13	'Love, love me do'
	Coda	Fade	*Harmonica solo*

(and 'From Me To You', 'I Want To Hold Your Hand', 'A Hard Day's Night', 'I Feel Fine', 'Yesterday', 'Yellow Submarine', 'We Can Work It Out', 'Hey Jude', 'Something', 'Come Together' and 'The Long And Winding Road'.)

ABAB form

'Eight Days A Week'

A/B/C	Section	Bars	Lyric
	Intro	4	*Guitar riff*
A	Verse	8	'Ooh, I need your love, babe'
B	Chorus	8	'Hold me, love me'
A	Verse	8	'Love you every day'
B	Chorus	8	'Hold me, love me'
C	Bridge	8	'Eight days a week'
A	Verse	8	'Ooh, I need your love, babe'
B	Chorus	8	'Hold me, love me'
C	Bridge	8	'Eight days a week'
A	Verse	8	'Love you every day'
B	Chorus	8	'Hold me, love me'
	Coda	4 + 4	*Tag + intro figure*

(and 'Ticket To Ride', 'Help!', 'Day Tripper', 'Lady Madonna', 'Get Back', 'Let It Be' and 'The Ballad Of John And Yoko'.)

Chorus at start of song

'She Loves You'

A/B/C	Section	Bars	Lyric
C1	Chorus	8	'She loves you'
A	Verse	8	'You think you've lost your love'
B	Bridge	8	'She says she loves you'
A	Verse	8	'She said you hurt her so'
B	Bridge	8	'She says she loves you'
C2	Chorus	8	'She loves you'
A	Verse	8	'You know it's up to you'
B	Bridge	8	'She says she loves you'
C3	Chorus	15	*With turn around*
C4	Chorus	7	*Closing variation*

(and 'Can't Buy Me Love' and 'Eleanor Rigby'. Note – these C-section intros are different from other chorus openings where a B section is brought to the top (e.g. 'Paperback Writer'), and also from those featuring a dedicated, once-heard intro (e.g. 'Help!')).

Irregular bar counts

'Hello Goodbye'[3]

A/B/C	Section	Bars	Lyric
A	Verse	9	'You say yes, I say no'
B	Chorus	7	'Hello, hello'
A	Verse	9	'You say high, I say low'
B	Chorus	7	'Hello, hello'
A	Verse	9	*Solo*
B	Chorus	7	'Hello, hello'
A	Verse	9	'You say yes, I say no'
B	Chorus	6	'Hello, hello'
B	Chorus/end	7	'Hello, hello'
	Coda	Fade	'Hela, hela, helloa'

(and 'Love Me Do' and 'Yesterday'.)

[3] As we discuss in Chapter 14, irregular bar counts can be combined with irregular *beat* counts implying mixed metre. Here, for example, the ninth bar of the verse has only *two* rather than four beats: implying a bar of 2/4 (or *half* a bar in 4/4 time). Meanwhile, note the later six-bar chorus as it moves directly into the final chorus culminating in the descending bassline.

Abbey Road *side 2 – 'The Long One' in focus*

Side 2 of *Abbey Road* represents a self-contained challenge for musicians looking to test their understanding of the finer points of pop. It acts as a comprehensive showcase that brings together many of the principles discussed throughout this book.

The following chart is a summary of the main tonal schemes at play throughout side 2, and the musical devices used to effect the modulations – both *within* certain songs, as well as at the point of transition *between* them.

Track	Song	Time	Key	Modulation	Lyric
7	'Here Comes The Sun'	0.01	A	None	*Instrumental intro*
8	'Because'	0.01	C♯m	Direct	*Instrumental intro*
		1.31	F♯	D dim as vii dim^7 of IV	'Love is old'
		1.43	C♯m	G♯^{7}as V of i	'The sky is blue'
9	'You Never Give Me Your Money'	0.01	Am	D dim as vii dim^7 of i	*Instrumental intro*
		1.10	C	G as V of C	'Out of college'
		2.28	A	Diminished ascent	'One sweet dream'
10	'Sun King'	0.01	E	Direct	*Instrumental*
		0.59	C	Dm^7/G as ii/V of I	'Here comes'
		1.57	E	F♯m^7-B^6 as ii-V of I	'Quando paramucho'
11	'Mean Mr Mustard'	0.01	E	None	'Mean Mr Mustard'
12	'Polythene Pam'	0.01	E	None	'Well you should see'
13	'She Came In Through The Bathroom Window'	0.06	A	5-4-3-2-1 descent	'She came in through'
		0.47	C	ii-V-I starting on Dm	'Tuesday's on the'
		0.48	A	Direct	*Instrumental*
		1.51	C	ii-V-I starting on Dm	'Tuesday's on the'
		1.52	A	Direct	'Oh yeah'
14	'Golden Slumbers'	0.01	Am	Cycle of fifths start	'Once there was'
		0.21	C	Cycle of fifths target	'to get back home'
		1.02	Am	Cycle of fifths start	'Once there was'
		1.20	C	Cycle of fifths target	'to get back home'
15	'Carry That Weight'	0.01	C	Direct	'Boy, you're gonna'
		0.24	Am	Cycle of fifths reprise	*Instrumental*
		1.07	C	Direct	'Boy, you're gonna'
		1.30	A?	C-A ambiguity	
16	'The End'	0.07	A	IV-♯IV- I	*Ahead of drum roll*
		1.47	C	IV-iii-ii-vi-ii-V-I	'The love you make'
17	'Her Majesty'	0.01	D	Direct	'Her Majesty's a ...'

The medley is usually described as starting with 'You Never Give Me Your Money', although many Beatles experts have described both the musical and thematic connection of the two opening songs.[4] They are therefore included here - not least for the secret segue that connects 'Because' and 'You Never Give Me Your Money', as discussed in Chapter 11.

Putting 'Her Majesty' in her place

'Her Majesty' was famously cut from the original medley, where it sat between 'Mean Mr Mustard' and 'Polythene Pam'. However, a listen to bootlegs of the original running order reveals how its rogue D tonality, sandwiched between two songs in the key of E, was reached by a direct jump, and returned to the key of E by means of a Double Plagal sequence.

Track	Song	Time	Key	Modulation	Lyric
11	'Mean Mr Mustard'	0.01	E	Direct from 'Sun King'	'Mean Mr Mustard'
12	'Her Majesty'	0.01	D	Direct from B^7	'Her Majesty's a ...'
13	'Polythene Pam'	0.01	E	Double Plagal	'Well you should see'

[4] This swansong has been the subject of some of the finest analysis and description in Beatles culture. Each of the following analyses are highly recommended: Vic Garbarini, *Guitar World*, June 1999, p. 200; Riley, *Tell Me Why*, pp. 325–37; Everett, *The Beatles As Musicians*, pp. 256–71; Gauldin, 'Beethoven, *Tristan*, and The Beatles; *College Music Symposium*, 30, pp. 149–51.

APPENDIX 5

Science, Surprise and the 'Tingle' Factor

The word 'unexpected' crops up throughout this book perhaps because, as one musicologist explained when praising The Beatles, 'all great works seem to contain it.'[1]

Thirty years on, the nature of musical 'surprise' has become the subject of serious study as academics and scientists attempt to understand the intangible elements in music that have the power to move us.

It seems that the underlying physics of music ensures that, to a great extent, listeners register surprise in an almost objective way. This appendix provides a brief summary of some interesting findings with respect to classical music. It turns out that these conclusions can also be applied to the music of The Beatles, supporting much of this book's analytical approach.

Consider the following claim by musicologist John Sloboda:

> 'There are ten key musical features which tend to recur again and again at times of high emotionality. We can summarise them by saying that they all have something to do with the creating and violating of expectations.'[2]

Sloboda was reporting on a series of quasi-scientific experiments conducted at Keele University into how humans respond to music. A range of volunteers were played classical musical extracts that they had

[1] Ned Rorem, 'The music of The Beatles', *New York Review Of Books*, 18th January 1968 [reprinted in *The Lennon Companion*, 'Mind Games', p. 105].

[2] John Sloboda, 'Brain Waves To The Heart', *BBC Music Magazine*, November 1998, pp. 31–3.

never heard before and asked to choose emotional adjectives that best described the character of the piece. Amazingly, there was found to be close agreement across a broad spectrum of the population, including small children, on the location of the most emotionally intense moments.[3]

The studies concluded that emotion is integral to the way humans listen to and appreciate music – and is independent from any personal associations we may have (the 'they're playing our tune' syndrome). More specifically, there appears to be a common understanding about how we respond to even the subtlest of changes in harmony and melody.

Leading musicians, from Leonard Bernstein to George Martin, have long maintained that because tonal music derives its laws from the natural harmonic series, whose relationships are built into nature, humans are instinctively programmed to respond to certain musical principles from birth.[4] It seems that we subliminally acknowledge that certain manoeuvres in music instinctively 'work', creating an almost guaranteed effect on our emotions.

For this particular study, classical music was chosen partly because it was free of pop's 'baggage' of preconceptions relating to fashion, image, genre, instrumentation, and especially lyrics, which so often lead the listener to an emotional conclusion.

Nevertheless, a look at the list confirms that the same features occur across a whole spectrum of pop music. Indeed they all recur regularly throughout the music of The Beatles.

Here is the list, together with just one chosen Beatles example, and a chapter reference where the mechanics of the device are discussed in more detail with direct reference to that, and other, Beatles songs.

[3] The study even refers to the 'tingle factor', which can manifest itself in shivers down the spine, goose pimples or even tears. 'Different listeners report 'tingles' in the same places in a piece of music of music – and these responses tend to be consistent over time,' added Sloboda.

[4] Bernstein refers to the counterpart of The Harmonic Series that exists throughout nature – the vibrations and frequencies that mirror the fundamental principles of tonal music; *The Unanswered Question: Six Harvard Lectures*. See also George Martin's 3-part BBC *Rhythm Of Life* series.

A guide to the 'tingle' factor

1. Harmony descending through a circle of fifths to the tonic

A classic formula, involving varying lengths of 'journey' round the cycle, from the simple 'ii-V-I' through to 'vii-iii-vi-ii-V-I'.

Beatles example: 'Golden Slumbers' (verse). *See Chapter 3.*

2. Melodic appoggiaturas

Non-triad tones which *lean* on the harmony on strong beats, before resolving onto a strong chord tone on a weak beat.

Beatles example: 'Yesterday' (opening word). *See Chapter 14.*

3. Melodic or harmonic sequences

Repeating a melodic motif, or chord progression, identically at a different interval.

Beatles example: 'Bungalow Bill' (chorus). *See Chapter 14.*

4. Enharmonic change

A sudden change in harmony created by adding an unexpected (usually non-diatonic) chord to a note.

Beatles example: 'Only A Northern Song' (chorus). *See Chapter 15.*

5. Harmonic or melodic acceleration to a cadence

Increasing the rate of change of chords, or melody notes, ahead of a natural point of resolution.

Beatles examples [harmonic]: 'When I'm Sixty-Four' ('Will you still need me will you still feed me?'); [melodic]: 'A Hard Day's Night' ('But when I get home to you'). *See Chapters 7 and 15.*

6. Delay of the final cadence

Withholding of an expected resolution to a chord change – typically by diverting the dominant away from the tonic in favour of the relative minor, for a 'deceptive', or 'interrupted' cadence.

Beatles example: 'Do You Want To Know A Secret' (verse and coda). *See Chapter 5.*

7. New or unprepared harmony

A catch-all section that actually encompasses many of the other categories on the list. It is in this vast area that arguably The Beatles' greatest songwriting proficiency lies, emerging in all their finest songs. Our first reference is the legendary 'wave of her hand' chord change in 'Here, There And Everywhere' (verse). *See Chapter 3.*

8. Sudden dynamic or textural change

This category covers the subtleties of performance and arrangement.

Beatles example: 'A Day In The Life' (the transitions from orchestral mayhem to combo minimalism, e.g., at 2.15). *See Chapter 16.*[5]

9. Repeated syncopation

Definitions of syncopation vary widely and can be used to describe any unusual rhythm. Best appreciated as an unusual variation, or *subversion*, of the expected beat.

Beatles example: 'Happiness Is A Warm Gun' ('Mother Superior jumped the gun'). *See Chapter 14.*

10. Prominent event earlier than prepared for

This category covers various devices, from structural features such as bringing a chorus to the top ('She Loves You'; *Coda Chapter*); through to premature modulations (bar 2 of 'Yesterday'). *See Chapter 3.*

There is an essential principle that underlies all these categories, as Sloboda points out:

[5] While this book focuses essentially on the harmonic, melodic and rhythmic aspects of Beatles songwriting, performance and instrumentation are referred to periodically, and a model of their crucial role in the finished recording is presented in Chapter 16.

> 'Because tonal music is governed by common rules and conventions, we learn from early childhood onwards to expect certain musical events to follow one another. Composers play on our expectations by doing the unexpected . . . thus creating local rises and falls in tension, suspense, resolution and relaxation.'[6]

Of course the 'unexpected' can only exist in relation to the 'expected', and many Beatles songs *contrast* novel harmony with standard sequences so common that they are accepted as cliché. A full range of stock progressions, including diatonic 'walks' up and down a scale, Three-Chord Tricks, Four Chord Turnarounds, and Cycles Of Fifths, are not merely grudgingly found in 'great' pop songs, they are essential to them.

Far from shunning such clichés, The Beatles embraced them. Ultimately this book is an attempt to highlight the ways in which they managed to offset the familiar with ingenious deviations from convention.

[6] John Sloboda, 'Brain Waves To The Heart', *BBC Music Magazine*, November 1998, p. 32.

APPENDIX 6

A Summary of Early Beatles Influences

The eclectic nature of The Beatles' influences is confirmed both by the range of formally recorded covers heard on various official and unofficial Beatles albums, and, perhaps more revealingly, by the many songs that found their way into their live sets in those formative years.

This appendix lists a wide selection of those cover versions – with the exception of staple three-chord, I-IV-V rock 'n' roll songs, whose harmonic construction is not of particular interest. The remaining songs are an important source from which The Beatles became acquainted with some essential songwriting principles.

They demonstrate that The Beatles were directly exposed to – and surely influenced by – plenty of great songwriting in their formative years.

For each song, we list the performer whose version The Beatles used as the model for their cover, the musical technique or concept being used, and the chapter in this book in which that technique is discussed. Readers are encouraged to seek out the chord changes in question and study them in context.

The first part of the appendix focuses on cover versions that are available on commercial Beatles recordings; the second part lists other songs that The Beatles were known to have performed live (and which were not covered in part one); while the third part concentrates on songs that they are not known to have performed, but which have been mentioned specifically as being important or influential.

Part 1 – selected cover songs recorded by The Beatles

Please Please Me

'Anna (Go To Him)' Arthur Alexander (1962)
I-vi-I-vi relative minor vamp (D-Bm-D-Bm)
Chapter 3

'Baby It's You' The Shirelles (1961)
I-vi-I-vi relative minor vamp (G-Em-G-Em)
Chapter 3

'A Taste Of Honey' Lenny Welch (1962)
Chromatic minor descent (F♯m-F♯m(maj7)-F♯m7-B)
Chapter 9
Dorian IV chord
Chapter 8
Aeolian cadence (♭VII-i: E-F♯m)
Chapter 5

With The Beatles

'Till There Was You' Peggy Lee (1961)
Complete case study in Chapter 16

'Please Mr Postman' The Marvelettes (1961)
I-vi-IV-V Turnaround cycle (A-F♯m-D-E)
Chapter 3

'You've Really Got A Hold On Me' The Miracles (1962)
II7-V7-I cadence (B7-E7-A)
Chapter 4
9th appoggiaturas (strong B notes over A chords)
Chapter 15

'Devil In Her Heart' The Donays (1962)
IV-iv-I 'Minor Plagal' cadence (C-Cm-G)
Chapter 2

Beatles For Sale

'Mr Moonlight' Dr Feelgood and the Interns (1962)
I-VI7-ii-V7-I Cycle Of Fifths refrain (F♯-D♯7-G♯m-C♯ -F♯)
Chapter 4

'Honey Don't' Carl Perkins (1956)
I-♭VI-I 'flat submediant' (E-C-E)
Chapter 7

Help!

'Act Naturally' Buck Owens (1963)
II7-V7 Imperfect cadence at end-bridge (A7-D7)
Chapter 4

Anthology 1

'My Bonnie' Tony Sheridan and The Beatles (1961)
Chromatic descent to VI9 (A-F♯9)
Chapter 4

'Ain't She Sweet' Gene Vincent (1956)/Duffy Power (1959)
Extreme Cycle Of Fifths – all dominants (E-G♯7-C♯7-F♯7-B7-E)
Chapter 4
IV-iv-I 'Minor Plagal' cadence (A-Am-E)
Chapter 2

'Three Cool Cats' The Coasters (1959)
II7-V7-i (F♯7-B7-Em)
Aeolian rock descent: i-♭VII-♭VI-V (Em-D-C-B7)
Chapter 6

'Besame Mucho' The Coasters (1960)
Minor-to-Parallel major switch (Gm-G major)
Chapter 6

'The Sheik Of Araby' Joe Brown and the Bruvvers (1961)
Diminished substitution: I-I dim-ii-V (C-Cdim-Dm7-G9)
Chapter 11
Interrupted cadence – V-vi (G-Am)
Chapter 5

'How Do You Do It' (Mitch Murray composition)
I-vi-ii-V Doo Wop Cycle (G-Em-Am-D7)
ii-V-I-vi displaced Cycle (Am-D-G-Em)
Chapter 3

'Lend Me Your Comb' Carl Perkins (1957)
I-♭III-IV-V Rock run (E-G-A-B)
Chapter 7

'Shout' The Isley Brothers (1959)
I-vi-I-vi relative minor vamp (E-C♯m-E-C♯m)
Chapter 3

Live At The Star-Club, Hamburg[1]

'Where Have You Been All My Life' Arthur Alexander (1962)
I-vi-IV-V Turnaround cycle (F-Dm-B♭-C)
Chapter 3

'Falling In Love Again' Marlene Dietrich (1930)
Cycle Of Fifths, bridge from the III7 (G♯7-C♯m-F♯7-B7-E)
Chapter 4

'Hallelujah, I Love Her So' Eddie Cochran (1960)/Ray Charles (1956)
Ascent into the 5th of tonic: IV-♯IVdim-I (C-C♯dim-G/D)
Chapter 11

'I Wish I Could Shimmy Like My Sister Kate' The Olympics (1961)
Cycle Of Fifths (ambiguous rock cycle) (A-D-G-C)
Chapter 4

'Red Sails In The Sunset' Joe Turner (1959)/Emile Ford and the Checkmates (1960)
Diatonic/chromatic unfolding of tonic: I-ii-iii-biii [ii-V-I] (A-Bm7-C♯m7-Cm7[-Bm7-E7-A])
Chapter 3

'I Remember You' Frank Ifield (1962)
I-VII (B♭-A)
Chapter 4

[1] Source: *Last Night In Hamburg*, Rockcartoon Cat: RCAR 1025213.

IV-III-VI modulation to VI major (E♭-D-G)
Chapter 16
Deceptive cadences (B♭-Cm7-F7 to D♭-E♭m7-A♭7)
Chapter 12
Phrygian close: ♭II-I (C♭-B♭)

Live At The BBC

'Keep Your Hands Off My Baby' Little Eva (1963)
I-vi-IV-V Turnaround cycle (G-Em-C-D)
Chapter 3
V-I-V-I bridge (D7-G-D7-G)
Chapter 1

'Some Other Guy' Ritchie Barrett (1962)
♭VII-I 'rock' cadence (C-D)
Chapter 7

'Soldier Of Love' Arthur Alexander (1962)
vi-I Aeolian vamp (C♯m-E) and relative minor vamp: I-vi-I-vi
Chapters 3 and 6
Secondary dominant ascent III-IV (E-G♯7-A-B)
Chapter 4

'To Know Her Is To Love Her' The Teddy Bears (1958)
Outrageous middle eight (on the ♭III)
Chapter 16

'Dear Wack!' a.k.a. 'Moonglow
See discussion of 'She Loves You' in Coda Chapter

'The Honeymoon Song' Marino Marini and his Quartet (1959)
Mediant/relative minor alternation: iii-vi-iii-vi (C♯m-G♯m-C♯m-G♯m)
ii-V-I Perfect cadence (F♯m-B-E)
Chapter 3
Deceptive cadence: [V-IV-iii]-ii-vi (F♯m-C♯m)
Chapter 5

'Nothin' Shakin'' Eddie Fontaine (1958)
Imperfect cadence II7-V7 (B7-E7)
Chapter 4

'I Just Don't Understand' Ann-Margret [Olson] (1961)
i-iv-V7 minor key sequence (Em-Am-B7)
Chapter 6

'So How Come (No One Loves Me)' The Everly Brothers (1960)
Double Plagal Cadence: ♭VII-IV-I (F-C-G)
Chapter 8

'I Got To Find My Baby' Chuck Berry (1960)
Diatonic unfolding of tonic: I-ii-iii-♭iii [ii-V-I] (G-Am7-Bm7-B♭m7 [Am7-D7-G]) (1.41-1.45)
Chapter 3

'Don't Ever Change' The Crickets (1962)
Augmented ascent: I-Iaug-I6 (E-Eaug-E6), and bridge on IV
Augmented vi-I link (C♯m-Eaug-E)
Chapter 9
Secondary dominant: [V/vi] IV-III7-vi (A-G♯7-C♯m)
Chapter 4
Diatonic descent: V-IV-iii-ii-I (B-A-G♯m)
Chapter 1

The Complete Silver Beatles[2]

'Take Good Care Of My Baby' Bobby Vee (1961)
I-vi-IV-V Turnaround cycle (G-Em-C-D)
Chapter 3
Truck Driver's Modulation to ♭II via connecting V-I (key of G to key of A♭ via Eb7)
Chapter 10

The Beatles With Tony Sheridan[3]

'Why' Tony Sheridan
Mixolydian I-♭VII-I vamp (A-G-A)
Chapters 7 and 8
I-iii-ii-V7 melodic cycle (A-C♯m7-Bm7-E)
Chapter 3
IV-iv-I 'Minor Plagal' cadence (D-Dm [6th])
Chapter 2

[2] Source: Audiofidelity AFELP 1047, September 1982.
[3] Source: *The Early Tapes Of The Beatles* (The Beatles With Tony Sheridan/Tony Sheridan And The Beat Brothers), Spectrum Cat. 550 037-2.

I-♭VI-I coda embellishment (A-F-A)
Chapters 7 and 16

'Sweet Georgia Brown' [standard]
Extreme Cycle Of Fifths: all dominants (D7-G7-C7-F7)
Verse structure
Chapter 4

Part 2 – selected cover songs from early Beatles live sets

'Apache' The Shadows (1960)
Dorian I-IV-I (Am-D-Am)
Chapter 8
♭VII as pivot to relative major (F-G7-C)
Chapter 6

'Are You Lonesome Tonight' Elvis Presley (1961)
I-I7-IV bridge (C-C7-F)
Chapter 4

'Beautiful Dreamer' Slim Whitman (1954)
Truck Driver's Modulation to ♭II (switch from key of G to key of G♯)
Chapter 10

'Begin The Beguine' Pat Boone (1957)
ii-V-I modulation to ♭VII ([C]-Cm-F-B♭)
ii-V-I modulation to ♭VI (B♭m-E♭7-A♭)
Chapter 10

'Cathy's Clown' The Everly Brothers (1960)
Extended I-vi-IV-V to emphasize drop to vi (G-Em)
Chapter 3

'Crackin' Up' Bo Diddley (1959)
Added 6th and added 9th chords
Chapter 13

'Come Go With Me' The Del-Vikings (1957)
I-vi-ii-V Doo Wop sequence (A♭-Fm-B♭m-E♭7)
Chapter 3

'Darktown Strutters' Ball' Joe Brown and the Bruvvers (1960)
I-II pop/rock ascent (A-B)
Chapter 4
II-IV non-functioning secondary dominant (B-D)
Chapter 4

'Don't Let The Sun Catch You Crying' Ray Charles (1960)[4]
Diatonic ascent: I-ii-iii-IV-V (E-F♯m)
Chapter 3
Tritone substitute run ♭III-II-♭II-I (G-F♯-F-E)
Chapter 12
Rare VII7 to modulate to III, prior to VI-II-V-I return (D♯7-G♯ [C♯-F♯-B-E])
Chapter 10

'Everyday' Buddy Holly and the Crickets (1957)
Flat side Cycle Of Fifths: IV-♭VII-♭III-♭VI-[V] (A♭-D♭-G♭-C♭-B♭)
Chapter 7

'Good Golly Miss Molly' Little Richard (1958)
Metric embellishment (Bar of 2/4 inserted)
Chapter 14

'Harry Lime' [*The Third Man* theme] Anton Karas (1949)/Chet Atkins (1960)
Direct modulation to key of ♭VII (Key of G to key of F)
Chapter 10

'Hit The Road Jack' Ray Charles (1961)
Aeolian rock descent: i-♭VII-♭VI-V7 (A♭m-G♭-F♭-E♭7)
Chapter 6

'How High The Moon' Les Paul with Mary Ford (1951)
Restless tonal movement through ii-V-I jazz modulations
Chapter 17

'I Wonder If I Care As Much' The Everly Brothers (1960)
I-vi-I-vi vamp (A-F♯m-A-F♯m)
Chapter 3

'If You Gotta Make A Fool Of Somebody' James Ray (1961)
Unusual rhythm: 3/4 Waltz time
Chapter 14

[4] Based on bootleg of McCartney playing the song (in the key of E, though slightly sharp) at a 1990 soundcheck. Ray Charles original in key of F.

I-ii-♯ii-iii chromatic ascent to mediant (G-Am-A♯m-Bm)
iii-vi alternations (Bm7-Em7-Bm7)
Melodic Cycle Of Fifths runs: iii-vi-ii-V (Bm7-Em7-Am7-D7)
Chapter 3

'It's Now Or Never' Elvis Presley (1960)
Strong minor iv Plagal return to I (Am-E)
Chapter 3

'The Loco-motion' Little Eva (1962)
I-vi-I-vi vamp on both I and IV (E♭-Cm-E♭-Cm/A♭-Fm-A♭-Fm)
Chapter 3

'Love Me Tender' Elvis Presley (1956)
Secondary dominant showcase: I-II7 (D-E7), I-III7 (D-F♯7)
Chapter 4
IV-iv minor drop (G-Gm)
Chapter 3

'Love Of My Life' The Everly Brothers (1959)
I-vi-I-vi relative minor vamp (D-Bm)
Chapter 3
Slick modulation to II: IV-VI7-II (G-B7-E)
Chapter 10

'Mama Said' The Shirelles (1961)
I-vi-I-vi vamp (B-G♯m)
Slick 'sec dom' bridge: IV-iii-III7-vi-II7-V7 (E-D♯m-D♯7-G♯m-C♯7-F♯7)

'Maybe Baby' Buddy Holly and the Crickets (1958)
I-vi-I-vi relative minor vamp (A-F♯m-A-F♯m)
Chapter 3

'Moonglow' The McGuire Sisters (1956)
a.k.a. 'Dear Wack!' [see above]

'More Than I Can Say' Bobby Vee (1961)[5]
Deceptive mediant switch: I-vi-iii-[II7-V7-I] (D♭-B♭m-Fm)
Chapter 3 and Coda chapter

[5] The Crickets had recorded an earlier version in 1959, which Lewisohn suggests as an alternative influence.

'Over The Rainbow' Gene Vincent and his Blue Caps (1959)
Paul's 'formula': I-iii (F-Am)
Chapter 3
Minor Plagal IV-iv-I (B♭-B♭m-F)
Chapter 2
Chromatic major 7th close (G♭maj7–Fmaj7)
Rare I-VII^7-iii secondary dominant shift (F-E7-Am)
Chapter 4

'Peggy Sue' Buddy Holly (1957)
I-♭VI-I 'flat submediant' (A-F-A)
Chapter 7

'A Picture Of You' Joe Brown and the Bruvvers (1962)
Rock preparation of V7: I-♭VII-V7 (A-G-E7)
Chapter 7
Melodic bridge vamp: iii-ii-iii-ii (C♯m-Bm)
Chapter 3

'Raining In My Heart' Buddy Holly (1959)
Augmented ascent: I-Iaug-I6-I7 (G-G aug-G6-G7)
Chapter 9
ii-V-I modulation to the key of IV (Dm7-G-C)
Chapter 16

'Runaway' Del Shannon (1961)
Aeolian rock descent: i-♭VII-♭VI-V (Am-G-F-E7)
Parallel major bridge (A major from A minor)
Chapter 6

'Shakin' All Over' Johnny Kidd and the Pirates (1960)
Aeolian i-iv-v (Em-Am-Bm)
Chapter 6

'Sharing You' Bobby Vee (1962)
I-vi-IV-V turnaround cycle (E♭-Cm-A♭-B♭)
Chapter 3

'Stand By Me' Ben E. King (1961)
I-vi-IV-V turnaround cycle (A-F♯m-D-E)[6]
Chapter 3

[6] See John Lennon's cover, on the album *Rock 'n' Roll* (1975), also in the key of A.

'September In The Rain' Dinah Washington (1961)
Striking I-♭VI move (A♭-F♭)
Mellow ♭VII-V preparation: I-IV-♭VII-[ii]-V (A♭-D♭-G♭-[B♭m-E♭7])
Chapter 7
ii-V-I modulation to the key of IV (E♭m7-A♭-D♭)
Truck driver's modulation to ♭II via connecting V-I
Chapter 10

'September Song'[7] Johnnie Ray (1959)
I-[i]-♭VI-I opening verse move (C-[Cm6]-A♭-C)
Chapter 7
Diminished bridge harmony (Fm-Cdim-Fm)
Chapter 11
♭VII-I closing cadence (B♭7-C)
Chapter 7

'Summertime' Gene Vincent and his Blue Caps (1958)
iv-V Imperfect cadence (Cm-D7)
iv-V-i Perfect cadence (Cm-D7-Gm)
Coda chapter

'Up A Lazy River' Gene Vincent and his Blue Caps (1958)
Extended Cycle Of Fifths: all dominants (E7-A7-D7-G7)
Chapter 4
VI chord turnaround: II-V-I-VI (A7-D7-G7-E7)
Chapter 4

'True Love' Bing Crosby & Grace Kelly (1956)[8]
IV-i dim-I (A♭-E♭dim-E♭)
Chapter 11
Key switch: ii-V-I-VI in the key of ♭III [from iv] (A♭m-D♭7-G♭7-E♭7)
Chapter 10

'Walk Don't Run' The Ventures (1960)
Aeolian descent: i [and I]-♭VII-♭VI-V (Am/A-G-F-E7)
Chapter 6

'Will You Love Me Tomorrow?' The Shirelles (1961)
Secondary dominant III7-vi (E7-Am)
Chapter 4

[7] Apparently recorded in The Beatles' first Hamburg session (Autumn 1960), though no copy has surfaced; see Dowlding, *Beatlesongs*, p. 305.
[8] Elvis recorded a version in 1957 which Lewisohn suggests as an alternative influence.

IV-iii diatonic descent (F-Em)
Chapter 3
V7 'sus' 4-3 return to home key (G7sus4-G7-C)
Chapter 10

'Wooden Heart' Elvis Presley (1960)
I-ii-I diatonic move (E-F♯m7-E)
Chapter 3

'Your True Love' Carl Perkins (1957)
Cycle Of Fifths, bridge from the III7 (G♯7-C♯7- F♯7-B7-E)
Chapter 4

Part 3 – honorary mentions

As above, this list is purposely limited to songs with harmonic interest beyond I-IV-V. However, readers should check out some of The Beatles' other favourite Three-Chord Trick songs, such as Chuck Berry's 'Havana Moon' and 'Brown Eyed Handsome Man', Little Richard's 'Shake A Hand', and Wanda Jackson's 'Let's Have A Party'.

'All My Trials'[9] Joan Baez (1960)
I-v minor shift (D-Am)
Chapters 16 and 17

'Forget Him'[10] Bobby Rydell (1963)
Paul's 'formula': I-iii (C-Em)
Chapter 3
Non-functioning 'sec dom' II7-iv-V7 (D7-Fm-G7)
Chapter 4 and Coda Chapter

'Ghost Riders In The Sky'[11] Frankie Laine
Haunting i-♭VI-i vamps and cadence (Em-C-Em)
Chapter 6
Augmented ascent in minor (Em-Em aug-Em6)
Chapter 9

[9] Miles, *Many Years From Now*, p. 151.
[10] *The Beatles Anthology*, p. 96
[11] *The Beatles Anthology*, p. 36.

'I Really Love You'[12] The Stereos (1961)
Repeated ii-V-I (Bm-E9-A)
Chapter 3

'I'll Be Home'[13] Pat Boone (1960)
IV-iv-I-[VI7] minor Plagal shift (D♭-D♭m-A♭-[F7])
Chapter 2

'I'm Wishing'[14] *Snow White & The Seven Dwarfs* (1937)
Repeated ii-V-I (Bm7-E9-A)
Chapter 3
Deceptive ♭III-V move (C to E7)
Chapter 7

'Jezebel'[15] Frankie Laine (1951)
I-♭VII-I Mixolydian vamp (B♭-A♭-B♭)
Chapters 7 and 8
Phrygian rock run: [IV-♭III]-♭II-I ([E♭-D♭]-C♭-B♭)
Chapter 8
♭II-for-V7 tritone play: ♭VII-♭II-I (A♭-C♭-B♭)
Chapter 12

'Lonesome Town'[16] Ricky Nelson (1958)
I-III7-IV-V secondary dominant run (C-E7-F-G)
Chapter 4

'Moon River'[17] Danny Williams (1961)
Atmospheric Imaj7-♭VIImaj7 vamp (E♭maj7-D♭maj7)
Chapter 7
Slick shift to relative minor: vii7♭5-III7-vi (D♯m-G7-Cm)
Extreme Cycle Of Fifths: ♯iv7♭5-VII-iii-VI-ii-V (Am7♭5-D7-Gm-C7-Fm-B♭7-[E♭])
Chapter 3

[12] George Harrison refers to this song as another musical inspiration for 'Do You Want To Know A Secret?'.
[13] 'Paul McCartney's Rock & Roll Roots', *BBC Radio 2*, 25th December 1999.
[14] Miles, *Many Years From Now*, p. 95.
[15] *Anthology* video (Tape 1) includes a brief clip of 'Jezebel' (at the moment of the Phrygian rock run).
[16] One of Paul and Linda's early favourites, as explained by McCartney when covering the song on *Run Devil Run* and at the Linda McCartney Tribute concert at The Albert Hall.
[17] *The Beatles Anthology*, p. 198.

'One Fine Day'[18] The Chiffons (1963)
Slick I-V-vi-iv cycle (F♯-C♯7-D♯m-Bm)
Chapter 16
ii-V-I modulation to the key of IV (C♯m-F♯7-B)
Chapter 10

'Only The Lonely'[19] Roy Orbison (1960)
Opening I-ii-V7 (F-Gm-C7)
Chapter 3

'Pretty Woman'[20] Roy Orbison (1964)
I-vi-I-vi relative minor vamp (A-F♯m-A-F♯m)
Chapter 3
ii-V-I modulation to ♭III (Dm-G-C-[Am])
Chapter 16
Mellow I-vi-iv-V cycle (A-F♯m-Dm-E)
Coda Chapter

'Remember (Walkin' In The Sand)' The Shangri-las (1964)
Minor key cycle: i-♭VI-iv-V (Dm-B♭-Gm-A)
Chapter 16

'Smoke Gets In Your Eyes'[21] The Platters (1959)
Climactic III7-IV secondary dominant (G♯7-A)
Chapters 4 and 17
Ultra slick Dim for dom substitution (A♯dim [for D♯7] to G♯m7 [iii])
Chapter 11
Outrageous functional modulation to ♭VI (G[natural]-C[natural])
Chapter 10

'Unforgettable'[22] Nat King Cole
Tonal ambiguity: G-C key teasing
Chapter 17
Dissonant diminished opening change (G-Gdim/C♯)
Tritone root movement (A7-F)
Chapters 3 and 12

[18] Suggested as a pivotal Goffin and King composition by Turner, *A Hard Day's Write*, p. 13.
[19] *The Playboy Interviews*, p. 150.
[20] Miles, *Many Years From Now*, p. 151.
[21] See Paul's references to The Beatles' favourite Hamburg jukebox; 'Paul McCartney's Rock & Roll Roots', *BBC Radio 2*, 25th December 1959.
[22] *The Beatles Anthology*, p. 302.

APPENDIX 7

Song Index

This appendix is intended as a quick guide for the reader who comes across a song in the text and wishes to locate it quickly in their CD collection. It lists all original Beatles songs, as well as songs by other writers that were covered by The Beatles, together with the original British albums on which they appeared.

It does not include any compilation, or greatest hits albums (e.g., *1*, the *Red* and *Blue* albums, etc.).

Song	Album
12-Bar Original	*Anthology 2*
A Day In The Life	*Sgt. Pepper's Lonely Hearts Club Band*
	Anthology 2
A Hard Day's Night	*A Hard Day's Night*
	Live At The BBC
	Anthology 1
A Hard Day's Night (out-takes)	*Mythology (a.k.a. The John Barrett Tapes)*
A Shot Of Rhythm And Blues	*Live At The BBC*
A Taste Of Honey	*Please Please Me*
	Live At The BBC
Abbey Road medley (original sequence)	*Mythology (a.k.a. The John Barrett Tapes)*
Across The Universe	*Let It Be*
	Past Masters Vol. 2
	Anthology 2
Act Naturally	*Help!*
Ain't She Sweet	*Anthology 1*
	Anthology 3

All I've Got To Do	*With The Beatles*
All My Loving	*With The Beatles*
	Live At The BBC
	Anthology 1
All Things Must Pass	*Anthology 3*
All Together Now	*Yellow Submarine*
All You Need Is Love	*Yellow Submarine*
And I Love Her	*A Hard Day's Night*
	Anthology 1
And Your Bird Can Sing	*Revolver*
	Anthology 2
Anna (Go To Him)	*Please Please Me*
Another Girl	*Help!*
Any Time At All	*A Hard Day's Night*
Ask Me Why	*Please Please Me*
Baby's In Black	*Beatles For Sale*
Baby, It's You	*Please Please Me*
	Live At The BBC
Back In The U.S.S.R.	*The Beatles (The White Album)*
Bad Boy	*Past Masters Vol. 1*
Beautiful Dreamer	*BBC Radio 2; 2.1.63*
Because	*Abbey Road*
	Anthology 3
Being For The Benefit Of Mr Kite	*Sgt. Pepper's Lonely Hearts Club Band*
	Anthology 2
Besame Mucho	*Anthology 1*
Birthday	*The Beatles (The White Album)*
Blackbird	*The Beatles (The White Album)*
	Anthology 3
Blue Jay Way	*Magical Mystery Tour*
Blue Suede Shoes	*Anthology 3*
Boys	*Anthology 1*
	Please Please Me
Can't Buy Me Love	*A Hard Day's Night*
	Live At The BBC
	Anthology 1
Carol	*Live At The BBC*
Carry That Weight	*Abbey Road*
Catswalk	*Cavern rehearsal – 1962*
Cayenne	*Anthology 1*
Chains	*Please Please Me*
Clarabella	*Live At The BBC*
Come And Get It	*Anthology 3*

Get Back	*Let It Be*
	Past Masters Vol. 2
	Anthology 3
Getting Better	*Sgt. Pepper's Lonely Hearts Club Band*
Girl	*Rubber Soul*
Glad All Over	*Live At The BBC*
Glass Onion	*The Beatles (The White Album)*
	Anthology 3
Golden Slumbers	*Abbey Road*
Good Day Sunshine	*Revolver*
Good Morning, Good Morning	*Sgt. Pepper's Lonely Hearts Club Band*
	Anthology 2
Goodnight	*The Beatles (The White Album)*
	Anthology 3
Got To Get You Into My Life	*Revolver*
	Anthology 2
Hallelujah, I Love Her So	*Anthology 1*
	Live At The Star-Club, Hamburg
Happiness Is A Warm Gun	*The Beatles (The White Album)*
	Anthology 3
Hello Little Girl	*Anthology 1*
Hello Goodbye	*Anthology 2*
Help!	*Help!*
	Anthology 2
Helter Skelter	*The Beatles (The White Album)*
	Anthology 3
Her Majesty	*Abbey Road*
Here Comes The Sun	*Abbey Road*
Here, There And Everywhere	*Revolver*
Hey Bulldog	*Yellow Submarine*
Hey Jude	*Past Masters Vol. 2*
	Anthology 3
Hold Me Tight	*With The Beatles*
Honey Don't	*Beatles For Sale*
	Live At The BBC
Honey Pie	*The Beatles (The White Album)*
	Anthology 3
How Do You Do It	*Anthology 1*
I Am The Walrus	*Magical Mystery Tour*
	Anthology 2
I Call Your Name	*Past Masters Vol. 1*
I Don't Want To Spoil The Party	*Beatles For Sale*
I Feel Fine	*Past Masters Vol. 1*

I'm So Tired	*The Beatles (The White Album)*
	Anthology 3
I've Got A Feeling	*Let It Be*
	Anthology 3
I've Just Seen A Face	*Help!*
If I Fell	*A Hard Day's Night*
If I Needed Someone	*Rubber Soul*
If You've Got Trouble	*Anthology II*
In My Life	*Rubber Soul*
In Spite Of All The Danger	*Anthology 1*
It Won't Be Long	*With The Beatles*
It's All Too Much	*Yellow Submarine*
It's Only Love	*Help!*
	Anthology 2
Johnny B. Goode	*Live At The BBC*
Julia	*Anthology 3*
	The Beatles (The White Album)
Junk	*Anthology 3*
Kansas City	*Beatles For Sale*
	Anthology 1
Keep Your Hands Off My Baby	*Live At The BBC*
Komm, Gib Mir Deine Hand	*Past Masters Vol. 1*
Lady Madonna	*Past Masters Vol. 2*
	Anthology 2
Leave My Kitten Alone	*Anthology 1*
Lend Me Your Comb	*Anthology 1*
Let It Be	*Let It Be*
	Past Masters Vol. 2
	Anthology 3
Like Dreamers Do	*Anthology 1*
Little Child	*With The Beatles*
Lonesome Tears In My Eyes	*Live At The BBC*
Long Long Long	*The Beatles (The White Album)*
Long Tall Sally	*Past Masters Vol. 1*
	Live At The BBC
	Anthology 1
Los Paranoias	*Anthology 3*
Love Me Do	*Please Please Me*
	Past Masters Vol. 1
	Live At The BBC
	Anthology 1
Love Of The Loved	*Decca Audition 1.1.62*
Love You To	*Revolver*

One After 909	*Let It Be*
	Anthology 1
Only A Northern Song	*Yellow Submarine*
	Anthology 2
Ooh! My Soul	*Live At The BBC*
P.S. I Love You	*Please Please Me*
Paperback Writer	*Past Masters Vol. 2*
Penny Lane	*Anthology 2*
Piggies	*The Beatles (The White Album)*
	Anthology 3
Please Mr Postman	*With The Beatles*
Please Please Me	*Please Please Me*
	Anthology 1
Polythene Pam	*Abbey Road*
	Anthology 3
Rain	*Past Masters Vol. 2*
Real Love	*Anthology 2*
Red Sails In The Sunset	*Live At The Star-Club, Hamburg*
Revolution	*Past Masters Vol. 2*
Revolution 1	*The Beatles (The White Album)*
Revolution 9 (instrumental)	*The Beatles (The White Album)*
Rip It Up	*Anthology 3*
Rock And Roll Music	*Live At The BBC*
	Anthology 2
	Beatles For Sale
Rocky Raccoon	*The Beatles (The White Album)*
	Anthology 3
Roll Over Beethoven	*With The Beatles*
	Live At The BBC
	Anthology 1
Run For Your Life	*Rubber Soul*
Savoy Truffle	*The Beatles (The White Album)*
Searchin'	*Anthology 1*
September In The Rain	*Decca Audition 1.1.62*
Sexy Sadie	*The Beatles (The White Album)*
	Anthology 3
Sgt. Pepper's Lonely Hearts Club Band	*Sgt. Pepper's Lonely Hearts Club Band*
Sgt. Pepper's Lonely Hearts Club Band	*Sgt. Pepper's Lonely Hearts Club Band*
(Reprise)	*Anthology 2*
Shake, Rattle & Roll	*Anthology 3*
She Came In Through The Bathroom Window	*Abbey Road*
	Anthology 3

The Long And Winding Road	*Let It Be*
	Anthology 3
The Night Before	*Help!*
The Sheik Of Araby	*Anthology 1*
The Word	*Rubber Soul*
There's A Place	*Please Please Me*
Things We Said Today	*A Hard Day's Night*
	Live At The BBC
Think For Yourself	*Rubber Soul*
This Boy	*Past Masters Vol. 1*
	Anthology 1
Three Cool Cats	*Anthology 1*
Ticket To Ride	*Help!*
	Live At The BBC
	Anthology 2
Till There Was You	*With The Beatles*
	Live At The BBC
	Anthology 1
To Know Her Is To Love Her	*Live At The BBC*
Tomorrow Never Knows	*Revolver*
	Anthology 2
Too Much Monkey Business	*Live At The BBC*
Twist And Shout	*Please Please Me*
	Anthology 1
Two Of Us	*Let It Be*
	Anthology 3
Wait	*Rubber Soul*
We Can Work It Out	*Past Masters Vol. 2*
What Goes On	*Rubber Soul*
What You're Doing	*Beatles For Sale*
What's The New Mary Jane	*Anthology 3*
When I Get Home	*A Hard Day's Night*
When I'm Sixty Four	*Sgt. Pepper's Lonely Hearts Club Band*
Where Have You Been All My Life	*Live At The Star-Club, Hamburg*
While My Guitar Gently Weeps	*The Beatles (The White Album)*
	Anthology 3
Why (Can't You Love Me Again)	*The Beatles With Tony Sheridan*
Why Don't We Do It In The Road	*The Beatles (The White Album)*
	Anthology 3
Wild Honey Pie	*The Beatles (The White Album)*
With A Little Help From My Friends	*Sgt. Pepper's Lonely Hearts Club Band*
Within You, Without You	*Sgt. Pepper's Lonely Hearts Club Band*
	Anthology 2

FURTHER READING

The following selection of publications is both a bibliography and a highly recommended source for the reader intent on further musical challenges.

Alan W. Pollack's 'Notes on … Series', featuring theoretical analysis and performance observations on some 200 Beatles songs, represents a most practical and informative destination. Elsewhere on the Internet, Ger Tillekens' articles on chord substitution and semantic interpretation in Beatles music, along with Ian Hammond's labyrinthine streams of consciousness, are also yours for the price of a local phone call. Indeed, the absence of any discussion of 'Revolution 9' in this book is essentially down to the definitive treatment found at www.beathoven.com.

In old-fashioned print, Terence O'Grady's original 1975 dissertation is both rewarding and accurate. Meanwhile, both volumes of Walter Everett's *The Beatles As Musicians* are unquestionably the ultimate source for the advanced reader, containing a lifetime's feast of musical detail and, in particular, taking the technical and semantic analysis of Beatles voice leading to a level far beyond this modest introduction.

Advanced readers are also encouraged to sample the rarified atmosphere of the *Beatlestudies* project, co-ordinated by the Department of Music at the University of Jyväskylä, Finland. And if these intriguing submissions seem like the last word on the music of The Beatles, then Philip Tagg at the University Of Liverpool throws down the gauntlet with his forays at the cutting edge of semiotics, reminding us that our investigations into how The Fab Four communicate so effectively with their listeners have perhaps barely scratched the surface.

Bibliography

1. Beatles references – technical

Benitez, Vincent. 'Twentieth Century Musical Concepts And The Music of The Beatles', *The Journal Of The Georgia Association Of Music Theorists* (*GAMUT*), Vol. 9 (1999), pp. 91-3.

Buk, Askold. 'Magical Mystery Tour', *Guitar World*, Vol. 15, No. 2 (February 1994), p. 57.

Buk, Askold. 'White Light. White Heat. An Exhaustive Guitar Guide To *The White Album*', *Guitar World Acoustic*, No. 41 (2001), pp. 49–56.

Buk, Askold & Scapelliti, Christopher. 'Here Come Ol' Flat–Top: How To Play The Acoustic Songs Of John Lennon', *Guitar World Acoustic*, Issue 29 (1998).

Brown Jimmy. 'Unplugging – While My Guitar Gently Strums', *Guitar World Acoustic*, No. 41 (2001), p. 35.

Chappell, Jon. 'Performance Notes For "Strawberry Fields Forever"' [and intricate transcription by Jeff Jacobson], *Guitar For The Practising Musician*, Vol. 10, No. 7 (May 1993).

Collaros, Pandel. 'The Music Of The Beatles In Undergraduate Music Theory Instruction', advance draft from *Beatlestudies 3,* University of Jyväskylä, Finland, Department of Music, 2001.

Cooke, Deryck. 'The Lennon-McCartney songs', *The Listener* (1st February 1968). Reprinted in *The Lennon Companion* (Eds. Thomson and Gutman), p. 109.

Eerola, Tuomas. 'The Rise And Fall Of The Experimental Style Of The Beatles', *Beatlestudies 1 – Songwriting, Recording And Style Change*, University of Jyväskylä, Finland, Department of Music Research Reports 19, 1998.

Everett, Walter. 'Voice Leading And Harmony As Expressive Devices In The Early Music Of The Beatles: "She Loves You"', *College Music Symposium* [Journal Of The College Music Society], 32 (1992), pp. 19–35.

Everett, Walter. 'The Beatles As Composers: The Genesis Of *Abbey Road*, Side Two', *Concert Music, Rock And Jazz Since 1945*, Elizabeth West Marvin and Richard Herrman [Eds.], Rochester University Press, 1995.

Everett, Walter. *The Beatles As Musicians: Revolver Through The Anthology*, Oxford University Press, 1999.

Everett, Walter. 'Confessions From Blueberry Hell, Or, Pitch Can Be A Sticky Substance', Chapter 10, *Expression In Pop-Rock Music, A Collection Of Critical And Analytical Essays* [edited by Everett], Garland Publishing, 2000.

Everett, Walter. *The Beatles As Musicians: The Quarry Men Through Rubber Soul*, Oxford University Press, 2001.

Fitzgerald, Jon. 'Lennon-McCartney And The Early British Invasion, 1964–6', in *The Beatles, Popular Music And Society: A Thousand Voices*, edited by Ian Inglis, Macmillan Press, 2000.

Fujita, Tetsuya; Hagino, Yuji; Kubo, Hajime and Sato, Goro. *The Beatles Complete Scores*, Hal Leonard/Wise Publications, 1993.

Gauldin, Robert. 'Beethoven, *Tristan* and The Beatles', *College Music Symposium 32* (1992).

Gress, Jesse. *Sgt. Pepper's Lonely Hearts Club Band* (1992); *Revolver* (1993); *Abbey Road* (1993); *Rubber Soul* (1994); Authentic Transcriptions With Notes And Tablature, *Guitar Recorded Versions*, Hal Leonard.

Gress, Jesse. *The Beatles Guitar Techniques*, Wise Publications, 1994.

Gress, Jesse. '"The End" – An exclusive lesson on the three-way solo showdown from *Abbey Road*', *How To Play Guitar* [Miller Freeman], 'Solo Secrets' Issue, (1995).

Gress, Jesse. '"Oh! Darling" – Singing and Playing the *Abbey Road* classic', *Bass Player*, Vol. 11, No. 2 (February 2000), p. 53.

Hammond, Ian. 'Because' [parts 1-4]; 'The Chromatic Sub-Tonic' [parts 1 and 2]; 'The Lucy'; 'The Great Ham-Fisted Gretty Chord'; 'Across The Universe'; 'Old Sweet Songs' [among others] (1999–2002); www.beathoven.com.

Heinonen, Yrjö. 'Michelle, Ma Belle – Songwriting As Coping With Inner Conflicts', *Beatlestudies 1 – Songwriting, Recording and Style Change*, University of Jyväskylä, Finland, Department of Music Research Reports 19, 1998.

Heinonen, Yrjö. 'In Search of Lost Order – Archetypal Meanings In "Lucy In the Sky With Diamonds"', *Beatlestudies 2 – History, Identity, Authenticity,* University of Jyväskylä, Finland, Department of Music Research Reports 23, 2000.

Heinonen, Yrjö & Eerola, Tuomas. 'The Beatles and Their Times', *Beatlestudies 2 – History, Identity, Authenticity,* University of Jyväskylä, Finland, Department of Music Research Reports 23, 2000.

Hilborne, Phil. 'Phil Hilborne's A–Z Of Great Riffs – B: The Beatles', *Guitar Techniques*, Issue 2 (April 1994), pp. 54–60.

Johansson, KG. 'The Harmonic Language Of The Beatles', Luleå University Of Technology, School of Music In Piteå; STM-Online, Vol. 2 (1999).

Jones, Joff. *The Beatles Guitar Book*, Authentic Transcriptions With Notes And Tablature, *Guitar Recorded Versions*, Hal Leonard, 1990.

Ingham, Chris. 'The Quintessence of Beatleosity [Doctor Rock Dissects The Hits, No. 6]', *MOJO,* Issue 24 (November 1995), p. 35.

Koskimäki, Jouni & Heinonen, Yrjö. 'Variation As The Key Principle Of Arrangement In "Cry, Baby Cry"', *Beatlestudies 1 – Songwriting, Recording and Style*

Change, University of Jyväskylä, Finland, Department of Music Research Reports 19, 1998.

Koskimäki, Jouni. 'Happiness Is . . . A Good Transcription', *Beatlestudies 2 – History, Identity, Authenticity,* University of Jyväskylä, Finland, Department of Music Research Reports 23, 2000.

MacDonald, Ian. *Revolution In The Head: The Beatles' Records And The Sixties*, Fourth Estate, 1994.

Mann, William. 'What Songs The Beatles Sang', *The Times*, Friday 27th December 1963, p. 4.

Marten, Neville. 'Get On The White Track', Classic Album Techniques, The Beatles White Issue, *Guitarist*, Issue 178 (February 1999), pp. 162–6.

McCarthy, L.J.K. 'Slow Down! – How The Beatles Changed The Rhythmic Paradigm of Pop & Rock', advance draft from *Beatlestudies 3,* University of Jyväskylä, Finland, Department of Music, 2001.

Mellers, Wilfrid. *Twilight Of The Gods: The Music Of The Beatles*, Schirmer/ Macmillan, 1973.

Marshall, Wolf. *The Beatles Hits* (1997), *The Beatles Favorites* (1998), *The Beatles Bass* (1998), *Signature Licks Series*, Hal Leonard.

Martin, George. *Making Music: The Guide To Writing, Performing And Recording* [songwriting interview with Paul McCartney, p. 62], New York Quill, 1983.

Moore, Allan F. *The Beatles: Sgt Pepper's Lonely Hearts Club Band*, Cambridge Handbooks, Cambridge University Press, 1997.

Niemi, Seppo. 'Band On The Record – The Beatles' Recordings From The Historical And Technological Points Of View', *Beatlestudies 2 – History, Identity, Authenticity,* University of Jyväskylä, Finland, Department of Music Research Reports 23, 2000.

Newell, Roger. 'The Paul McCartney Interview', *Bassist*, February 2000, p. 21.

Noble, Douglas J. 'Georgie Boy – George Harrison retrospective', *The Guitar Magazine*, Vol. 2, No. 1 (May 1992), p. 34 [analysis p. 77].

Noble, Douglas J. 'George Harrison' [style analysis]. *The Guitar Magazine*, Vol. 12, No. 6 (December 2001), pp. 41–5.

Nurmesjärvi, Terhi. 'The Concept of Form And Its Change In The Singles Of The Beatles', *Beatlestudies 1 – Songwriting, Recording and Style Change*, University of Jyväskylä, Finland, Department of Music Research Reports 19, 1998.

Nurmesjärvi, Terhi. 'You Need Another Chorus', *Beatlestudies 2 – History, Identity, Authenticity,* University of Jyväskylä, Finland, Department of Music Research Reports 23, 2000.

O'Grady, Terence J. *The Beatles: A Musical Evolution,* Twayne, 1984.

O'Grady, Terence J. 'The Music of The Beatles from 1962 to *Sgt Pepper's Lonely Hearts Club Band*', PhD Dissertation, University Of Wisconsin-Madison, 1975.

Okun, Milton [Ed.]. *The Beatles Guitar,* Play It Like It Is, Cherry Lane, 1984.

Pedler, Dominic. 'The Beatles: The Top 10 Songwriting Tricks Of All Time', *Total Guitar,* Issue 60 (September 1999), pp. 28–42.

Pedler, Dominic. 'Here, There And Everywhere – The Greatest Beatles Song Of All Time?', *Total Guitar,* Issue 60 (September 1999), pp. 44–5.

Pedler, Dominic. 'The Songwriting Roots Of The Beatles', *Total Guitar,* Issue 90 (November 2001), pp. 32–45.

Pedler, Dominic. 'There Goes The Sun – The George Harrison Obituary', *Total Guitar,* Issue 93, February 2002, pp. 38–41.

Pollack, Alan W. 'Notes on ... Series', *The 'Official' rec.music.beatles Home Page,* http://www.recmusicbeatles.com (1989–2001).

Porter, Steven C. 'Rhythm And Harmony In The Music Of The Beatles', PhD Dissertation, The City University of New York, 1979.

Prown, Pete. '25 Classic Beatles Riffs', *Guitar,* Vol. 13, No. 2 (December 1995), p. 57.

Reising, Russell [Ed.]. *'Every Sound There Is': The Beatles'* Revolver *And The Transformation Of Rock And Roll,* Ashgate, 2002.

Rifkin, Joshua. 'On The Music Of The Beatles', in *The Lennon Companion* (Eds. Thomson and Gutman), p. 113.

Riley, Tim. *Tell Me Why: A Beatles Commentary,* First Vintage Books, 1989.

Rooksby, Rikky. *The Beatles Complete Chord Songbook,* Wise Publications, 1999.

Rorem, Ned. 'The Music Of The Beatles', *New York Review Of Books,* 18th January 1968. Reprinted in *The Lennon Companion* (Eds. Thomson and Gutman), p. 105.

Scott, Derek B. '(What's The Copy?) The Beatles And Oasis', advance draft from *Beatlestudies 3,* University of Jyväskylä, Finland, Department of Music, 2001.

Skinner, Tony. 'Novice Beatles Chords', *Total Guitar,* Issue 82 (April 2001), p. 96.

Tamm, Eric. 'Beyond Strawberry Fields: Lennon's Later Style', in *The Lennon Companion* (Eds. Thomson and Gutman), p. 211.

Thomson, Elizabeth & Gutman, David (Eds.). *The Lennon Companion,* Macmillan, 1987.

Tillekens, Ger. 'The Sound Of The Beatles' [a summary of his book, *Het Geluid van De Beatles,* Het Spinhuis (Amsterdam), 1998], www.icce.rug.nl/~soundscapes (May 1998).

Tillekens, Ger. 'Baroque and folk and ... John Lennon', www.icce.rug.nl/~soundscapes (September 1998).

Tillekens, Ger. 'A Beatles' Odyssey – Alan Pollack's Musicological Journey Through The Beatles' Songs', www.icce.rug.nl/~soundscapes (March 1999).

Tillekens, Ger. 'Words And Chords: The Semantic Shifts Of The Beatles Chords', www.icce.rug.nl/~soundscapes (June 2000).

Tucker, Tim. 'Secondary Dominants – "Your Mother Should Know"', *Total Guitar*, Issue 5 (April 1995), p. 76.

Valdez, Stephen. 'Vocal Harmony As A Structural Device In The Commercial Recordings Of The Beatles, 1962–1970', advance draft from *Beatlestudies 3,* University of Jyväskylä, Finland, Department of Music, 2001.

Villinger, Alexander. *Die Beatles Songs – Analysen Zur Harmonik Und Melodik*, Boscolo & Mohr, 1983.

Wagner, Naphtali. 'Tonal Oscillation In The Beatles' Songs', advance draft from *Beatlestudies 3,* University of Jyväskylä, Finland, Department of Music, 2001.

2. Beatles references – general

Bacon, Tony. 'The Paul McCartney Interview', *Total Guitar*, Issue 14 (January 1996), p. 40.

Badman, Keith. *The Beatles After The Break Up: 1970–2000,* Omnibus Press, 1999.

Badman, Keith. *The Beatles – Off The Record*, Omnibus Press, 2000.

Beatles, The. *The Beatles Anthology*, 8-part video documentary, Apple/EMI/ Picture Music International, 1996.

Beatles, The. *The Beatles Anthology*, Cassell & Co., 2000.

Beatlology Magazine. 'You Know My Name: The Jim Valence Interview', Vol. 2, No.1 (September/October 1999).

Bell, Max. 'B is For ... The Beatles' [*A Hard Day's Night* review], *Evening Standard* [*Hot Tickets*], (4–10th May 2001), p. 33.

Carr, Roy & Tyler, Tony. *The Beatles: An Illustrated Record*, Harmony Books, 1978.

Carter, Chris. 'The Quiet One Speaks [The George Harrison Interview]', *Record Collector*, No. 262 (June 2001), p. 88.

Castleman, Harry & Podrazik, Walter J. *The Beatles Again?*, Pierian Press, 1977.

Chrometalk Classic Interviews. *The Beatles As It Happened*, 4-CD box set, 2000.

Cunningham, Mark. 'All My Yesterdays', *The Guitar Magazine*, Vol. 3, Issue 7 (September 1993), p. 30.

Cunningham, Mark. 'The Beatles: [*Anthology 1* feature]', *Total Guitar*, Issue 14 (January 1996), p. 36.

Cunningham, Mark. 'All White Now', The Beatles White Issue, *Guitarist*, Issue 178 (February 1999), pp. 74–83.

Coleman, Ray. *McCartney – Yesterday And Today*, Boxtree, 1995.

Davies, Hunter. *The Beatles: The Authorised Biography*, Cassell & Co., 2001 [revised].

Delilah Films. *The Compleat Beatles*, 'rockumentary' narrated by Malcolm McDowell, 1982.

Di Perna, Alan. 'The Fifth Beatle', *Guitar World*, Vol. 18, No. 11 (November 1988), p. 44.

Doggett, Peter. 'The Beatles In Hamburg', *Record Collector*, No. 41 (January 1983), p. 4.

Doggett, Peter. *Abbey Road/Let It Be* [Classic Rock Albums], Schirmer, 1998.

Doggett, Peter. 'A Hard Day's Write' [*The Beatles Anthology* preview], *Record Collector*, No. 253 (September 2000), pp. 23–7.

Doney, Malcolm. *Lennon And McCartney*, Midas, 1981.

Dowlding, William J. *Beatlesongs*, Fireside, 1989.

Du Noyer, Paul. 'But Now They're *Really* Important', *Q*, Issue 111 (December 1995), p. 121.

Du Noyer, Paul. 'All He Needs Is Love, Up Close And Personal', *MOJO Collections*, Issue 2, spring 2001, pp. 43–5.

Ellen, Mark. 'Yesterday (Take 2)' [*Anthology 2* review], *MOJO,* Issue 29 (April 1996), p. 78.

Forte, Dan. 'The Jungle Music And Posh Skiffle Of George Harrison', *Guitar Player*, Issue 215, Vol. 21, No. 11 (November 1987), p. 83.

Garbarini, Vic. 'The Long And Winding Road', *Guitar World*, Vol. 17, No. 2 (February 1997), p. 28.

Garbarini, Vic. 'The Beatles – *Abbey Road*', *Guitar World*, Vol. 19, No. 6 (June 1999), p. 86.

Garbarini, Vic. '60 Minutes With . . . Paul McCartney: The Hour Of Music That Rocks My World', *Guitar World*, Vol. 20, No.1 (January 2000), p. 42.

Garbarini, Vic. 'When We Was Fab', *Guitar World*, Vol. 21, No. 1 (January 2001), p. 69.

Garbarini, Vic. 'The George Harrison Interview', *Total Guitar*, Issue 80 (February 2001), p. 30.

Giuliano, Geoffrey. *Two of Us: John Lennon & Paul McCartney, Behind the Myth*, Penguin Studio, 1999.

Graff, Gary. 'Yesterday and Today' [Paul McCartney Interview], *Guitar World*, Vol. 20, No.1 (January 2000), p. 38.

Grove Dictionary Of Music [2001 edition]. 'The Beatles (Works)'; 2, p. 23.

Grove Dictionary Of Music [2001 edition]. 'The British Isles: From Rock'n'Roll To Rock', Pop IV, 1 (i), p. 112.

Giuliano, Geoffrey & Devi, Vrnda. *Glass Onion – The Beatles In Their Own Words*, Da Capo, 1999.

Guitar For The Practicing Musician. 'Paul McCartney: Getting Better All The Time' [Excerpts from MTV interview], May 1993, p. 98.

Hammond, Ian. '"I was nervously waiting . . ." – An Interview With Alan W. Pollack', www.icce.rug.nl/~soundscapes (February 2000).

Harrison, George. *Yahoo!* online chat, 15th February 2001. See reference to transcript at www.allthingsmustpass.com.

Harry, Bill. *The Beatles Encyclopedia [Revised and Updated]*, Virgin Publishing, 1992.

Henderson, Dave. *The Beatles Uncovered*, The Black Book Company, 2000.

Hertsgaard, Mark. *A Day in the Life: The Music and Artistry of The Beatles*, Delacorte, 1995.

Ingham, Chris. 'Spirit of Ecstasy' [*Anthology 3* review], *MOJO*, Issue 36 (November 1996), p. 104.

Inglis, Ian. The Beatles, *Popular Music and Society – A Thousand Voices*, Macmillan Press, 2000.

Irvin, Jim. 'Little Sir Echo' [*Run Devil Run* review and Paul McCartney interview], *MOJO*, Issue 72 (November 1999), pp. 90–4.

Kozinn, Allan. *The Beatles*, Phaidon Press, 1995.

Laing, Dave. 'Notes For A Study Of The Beatles', Chapter 9 in *The Sound Of Our Time*, Quadrangle Books, 1969.

Leigh, Spencer. 'The George Martin Interview', *Stars In My Eyes – Personal Interviews With Top Music Stars*, pp. 93–101, Raven Books (Music), February 1980.

Lewisohn, Mark. *The Beatles Live!*, Henry Holt & Company, 1986.

Lewisohn, Mark. *The Complete Beatles Recording Sessions*, Hamlyn/EMI, 1988.

Lewisohn, Mark. *The Complete Beatles Chronicle*, Pyramid, 1992.

MacDonald, Ian. 'A Perfect Match' [The Lennon & McCartney songwriting partnership], *MOJO*, 1000 Days Of Beatlemania, The Early Years – April 1, 1962 to December 31, 1964, Special Limited Edition (Winter 2002), pp. 82–87.

MacLaughlan, D.L. 'Meet The Beatles Again', *Guitar,* Vol. 13, No. 2 (December 1995), p. 63.

Marten, Neville [*et al*]. 'Fab Gear: Beatle Tracks and Guitars', *Guitarist*, Live 2001, p. 78.

Martin, George (with Hornsby, Jeremy). *All You Need Is Ears*, St. Martin's Press, 1979.

Martin, George. *The Making Of Sgt Pepper*, BBC documentary (1992).

Martin, George (with Pearson, William). *Summer of Love: The Making Of Sgt. Pepper*, Pan Books, 1995.

McCartney, Paul. 'Paul McCartney's Rock & Roll Roots', *BBC Radio 2,* 25th December 1999.

Melody Maker. 'How To Write A Hit' [Lennon and McCartney interview], 1st February, 1964, p. 11.

Mendelson, John [*et al*]. 'Nine Ways Of Looking At The Beatles 1963–1973', *Stereo Review*, p. 61.

Miles, Barry. *The Beatles In Their Own Words*, Omnibus Press, 1978.

Miles, Barry. *Paul McCartney – Many Years From Now*, Secker & Warburg, 1997.

MOJO. 'The Beatles – 'They're Back!', Special Collectors Edition, Issue 24 (November 1995).

MOJO. 'John Lennon: [His Life, His Music, His People, His Legacy]', Special Edition (Winter 2000).

MOJO. 1000 Days That Shook The World, The Psychedelic Beatles – April 1, 1965 to December 26, 1967, Special Limited Edition (Winter 2001).

MOJO. 1000 Days Of Beatlemania, The Early Years – April 1, 1962 to December 31, 1964, Special Limited Edition (Winter 2002).

MOJO. 1000 Days Of Revolution, The Beatles' Final Years – Jan 1, 1968 to September 27, 1968, Special Limited Edition (Spring 2003).

Mulhern, Tom. 'The Paul McCartney Interview', *Guitar Player*, Issue 246, Vol. 24, No.7 (July 1990), p. 16.

Murray, Charles Shaar. 'Mont Blanc – Big, Beautiful, Tricky To Assimilate And White' [Review of *The White Album*, 30th anniversary limited edition], *MOJO*, Issue 62 (January 1999), p. 94.

Murray, Charles Shaar. 'The Numbers Racket – Does The Fabs' "Best Of" Add Up?' [Review of the *1* album], *MOJO*, Issue 85 (December 2000), p. 94.

Norman, Philip. *Shout! – The True Story Of The Beatles*, Penguin Books, 1993.

Mytkowicz, Bob. 'Fab Gear! – Guitars Of The Beatles', *Guitar Player*, Issue 215, Vol. 21, No. 11 (November 1987), p. 99.

Pedler, Dominic. 'John Lennon'; 'A Day In The Life'; 'Abbey Road': Beatles retrospectives in *Music Of The Millennium*, Special Edition, Future Publishing/Channel 4, 1999.

Pedler, Dominic. 'Move Of The Month – Chords That Sound Great Together: 1–17', *Total Guitar*, Issues 96-112 (May 2002–August 2003) [continuing series].

Q magazine. 'The Beatles – Band Of The Century', Collectors Limited Edition, November 1999.

Rolling Stone. 'The Beatles – Inside The Hit Factory: The Stories Behind The Making Of 27 Number 1 Songs', Issue 863 (March 2001), p. 30.

Rotondi, James and Obrecht Jas. 'The Genius of John Lennon', *Guitar Player*, Issue 297, Vol. 28, No. 9 (September 1994), p. 64.

Rowley, David. *Beatles For Sale: The Musical Secrets Of The Greatest Rock 'n' Roll Band Of All Time*, Mainstream, 2002.

Saki. 'Saki Reviews The Book Reviews', *The 'Official' rec.music.beatles Home Page*, www.recmusicbeatles.com.

Scapelliti, Christopher. 'Mother Nature's Songs', *Guitar World Acoustic*, No. 41 (2001), p. 42.

Sheff, David & Golson, G. Barry. *The Playboy Interviews With John Lennon And Yoko Ono*, Playboy Press, 1981.

Snow, Mat. 'We're A Damn Good Little Band' [The McCartney interview for *Anthology 3*], *MOJO*, Issue 35 (October 1996), p. 64.

Taylor, Derek. 'One More For The Road' [Paul, George And Ringo celebrate *Abbey Road* and reminisce . . .], *MOJO*, Issue 83 (October 2000), p. 67.

The Times. 'Seen But Hardly Heard' [Review of The Beatles' Christmas Show at the Astoria, Finsbury Park], Friday 27th December 1963, p. 4.

Turner, Steve. *A Hard Day's Write*, Carlton, 1999.

UNCUT magazine. 'The Beatles 50 Greatest Songs – All-Star Vote', Issue 50 (July 2001), pp. 28–64.

Ushanov, T.P. 'Not A Second Time – A Study In Rock Semiotics', www.icce.rug.nl/~soundscapes (1996).

Webb, Bernard. 'Mythology Of The Beatles – Secrets Of The John Barrett Tapes', *Record Collector*, No. 250 (June 2000), pp. 41–7.

Wells, David. 'Silence In Court! – The Sticky Story Of Musical Plagiarism', *Record Collector*, No. 284 (April 2003), pp. 83–89.

Wenner, Jann. *Lennon Remembers: The Rolling Stone Interviews*, Penguin, 1973.

3. Theory and other songwriting references

BBC Radio 1. 'Where's There's A Hit There's A Writ', presented by Simon Bates, 21st February 1989.

Bernstein. Leonard. *The Bernstein Lecture Series*. BBC archive.

Braheny, John. *The Craft And Business Of Song Writing*, Writer's Digest Books, 1995.

Chappell, Jon. 'The Return of The Songwriter', *Guitar*, Vol. 13, No. 7 (May 1996), p. 67.

Connolly, Ray. 'Plagiarism? You hum it and I'll make it pay', *Daily Mail*, 17th December 1998, p. 13.

Citron, Stephen. *Songwriting: A Complete Guide To The Craft*, Limelight Editions, 1995.

Denyer, Ralph. *The Guitar Handbook*, Pan, 1982.

Dunsby, Jonathan & Whittall, Arnold. 'Schenkerian Analysis', *Music Analysis: In Theory and Practice*, Faber Music, 1988.

Fischer, Peter. *Blues Guitar Rules*, AMA Verlag, 1995.

Gambale, Frank. *Modes: No More Mystery* [the video], DCI Music Productions, 1991.

Gress, Jesse. 'A Connoisseur's Guide To Harmony – Twelve Gourmet Recipes For Killer Chord Progressions', *Guitar Player*, Issue 345, Vol. 32, No. 9, p. 80.

Harp, David. *Music Theory Made Easy* [Second Revised Edition], Musical I Press, 1994.

Haunschild, Frank, *The New Harmony Book – A Musical Workbook For Classical, Rock, Pop And Jazz Music*, AMA Verlag, 1997.

Hefling, Stephen E. *Mahler – Das Lied Von Der Erde*, Cambridge Music Handbooks, Cambridge University Press, 2000.

Ingham, Chris. 'Doctor Rock Dissects The Hits', Nos. 1–16, *MOJO*, Issues 14–44 [occasional series] (January 1995–May 1997).

Jack, Adrian. 'The Harmonic Series', Nos. 1–12, *BBC Radio 3*, 27th December 1998–2nd January 1999.

Jones, Timothy. *Beethoven – The 'Moonlight' And Other Sonatas, Op. 27 and Op. 31*, Cambridge Music Handbooks, Cambridge University Press, 1999.

Kolb, Tom. Modal Mastery, Lesson Lab, *Guitar One*, June 2000, p. 31.

Latarski, Don. *The Progressive Guitarist – Practical Theory For Guitar: A Player's Guide To Essential Music Theory In Words, Music, Tablature And Sound*, CPP/Belwin Inc., 1993.

Leigh, Spencer. *Brother, Can You Spare A Rhyme? 100 Years Of Hit Songwriting*, Spencer Leigh Limited, 2000.

Lowe, Steve. 'Why Can't Rock Stars Be Original?', Q *magazine*, Issue 165 (June 2000), pp. 30–2.

Martin, George. *George Martin's Rhythm Of Life*, 3-part BBC TV series.

Marten, Neville [*et al*]. 'The Ten Greatest Guitars in The World Ever!', *Guitarist*, Issue 53 (December 2000), p. 70.

Middleton, Richard. *Studying Popular Music*, Open University Press, 1997.

MOJO. 'The 100 Greatest Singles of All Time', Issue 45 (August 1997), p. 42.

MOJO. 'The 100 Greatest Songs of All Time', Issue 81 [Songwriters Special] (August 2000), p. 49.

Moore, Allan F. 'Patterns of Harmony', *Popular Music*, 11/1 (1992), pp. 73–106.

Moore, Allan F. *Rock: The Primary Text*, Buckingham: Open University Press, 1993. Second Edition: Ashgate, 2001.

Moore, Allan F. 'The So-Called "Flattened Seventh" In Rock', *Popular Music* 14/2 (1995), pp. 185–201.

Morgen, Howard and Ferguson, Jim. 'All About Chord Progressions, Parts 1, 2 And 3', *Guitar Player*, Issues 223–5, Vol. 22, Nos. 7, 8 and 9 (July–September 1988).

Q magazine. 'The 100 Greatest British Albums Ever!', Issue 165 (June 2000), p. 59.

Randall, Judithe and Robin. 'Songwriting 101 – A Crash Course On Getting Started', *Guitar One*, August 1988, p. 29.

Reynolds, Fletcher M. '*Selle v. Gibb* And The Forensic Analysis Of Plagiarism', *College Music Symposium* 32 (1992), pp. 56–78.

Roland, Paul. *Teach Yourself Rock and Pop*, Hodder & Stoughton, 1999.

Rooksby, Rikky. *How To Write Songs On Guitar – A Guitar-Playing And Songwriting Course*, Outline Press, 2000.

Rotundi, James [*et al*]. 'The Song's The Thing' – Songwriting Special, *Guitar Player*, Issue 286, Vol. 27, No. 10 (October 1993), p. 26.

Satriani, Joe. 'Music Theory, Chords and Intervals', *Guitar World*, Vol. 18, No. 4 (April 1988), p. 98.

Sloboda, John. 'Music In Mind: Brain Waves to The Heart', *BBC Music Magazine*, Vol. 7, No.3 (November 1998), pp. 31–3.

Sokolow, Fred. *The Complete Jazz Guitar*, Almo, 1980.

Stewart, Dave. *Inside The Music: The Musician's Guide To Composition, Improvisation, And The Mechanics Of Music*, Miller Freeman, 1999.

Tagg, Philip. 'Analysing Popular Music Theory, Method and Practice', *Popular Music* 2 (1982), p. 39.

Tagg, Philip. 'Tritonal Crime And Music As Music – Paper Written In Honour Of Maestro Morricone' [assisted by Bob Clarida, New York], University Of Liverpool, November 1999.

Tagg, Philip. 'Tagg's Harmony Handout – Or "Definitions Of Terms To Do With Tonal Polyphony"', version 2, Liverpool, August 2000.

Tagg, Philip. 'Melody and Accompaniment', *Encyclopedia Of Popular Music Of The World*, www.tagg.org.

Tagg, Philip. 'Introductory notes to the Semiotics of Music', version 3.2, Liverpool, 2000, www.tagg.org.

Tagg, Philip. 'Musicology And The Semiotics Of Popular Music', in *Semiotica*, 66-1/3 Mouton de Gruyter (Amsterdam), 1987, pp. 279–98; [version at www.tagg.org].

Taylor, Eric. *The AB Guide To Music Theory, Part I and II*, The Associated Board of Royal Schools of Music, 1989/1991.

Tucker, Tim. Monthly Theory column, *Total Guitar*, Issues 1–17 (December 1994–April 1996).

Walser, Robert. *Running With The Devil: Power, Gender, And Madness In Heavy Metal Music*, Wesleyan University Press, 1993.

Webb, Jimmy. *Tunesmith: Inside The Art Of Songwriting*, Hyperion, 1998.

Wyatt, Keith & Schroeder, Carl. *Harmony & Theory – Musicians Institute Essential Concepts*, Hal Leonard, 1998.

INDEX

12/15(196114)